POSTCARDS FROM

Frommer's
California 2003

W9-BYQ-979

A surfer braves the waves at Huntington Beach, site of the U.S. Open of Surfing every August. See chapter 14. © Sunstar/Instock.

Few sights are more breathtaking than a view of San Francisco from the Golden Gate Bridge, which you can cross by foot. See chapter 4. © Jose Fuste Raga/The Stock Market.

This view from Alamo Square offers a fantastic juxtaposition of San Francisco architecture—sharp-edged Financial District skyscrapers behind a row of Victorian "Painted Ladies." See chapter 4. © Alan Kearney/Viesti Collection, Inc.

Learn about the wonderful world of winemaking in Napa Valley. See chapter 6.
© Catherine Karnow Photography.

Emerald Bay is one of Lake Tahoe's prettiest little inlets. See chapter 8.
© Robert Holmes Photography.

The Merced River is just one of many of the awe-inspiring treasures you'll find in Yosemite National Park. See chapter 9. © Christopher Talbot Frank Photography.

You can gape at the majestic sequoias, the world's largest trees, in Mariposa Grove at Yosemite National Park. See chapter 9. © Jose Fuste Raga/The Stock Market.

A view of Big Sur at dusk, one of the most romantic and relaxing places on earth.
See chapter 11. © David D. Keaton/The Stock Market.

Palm trees mix with skyscrapers in a view from the steps of the Central Library in downtown Los Angeles. See chapter 13. © *Richard Cummins Photography.*

Skateboarders, surfers, cyclists, and roller skaters are all in on the action at Venice Beach. See chapter 13. © *Stephen Wilkes/The Image Bank.*

Glorious or grotesque? Form your own opinions about the unique Joshua trees at Joshua Tree National Park, a popular place for climbing, biking, and hiking. See chapter 15.
© Photophile.

Spectacular sand dunes in the Mojave National Preserve are famous for "booming."
See chapter 15 for details. © *Christopher Talbot Frank Photography.*

A New Star-Rating System & Other Exciting News from Frommer's!

In our continuing effort to publish the savviest, most up-to-date, and most appealing travel guides available, we've added some great new features.

Frommer's guides now include a new **star-rating system.** Every hotel, restaurant, and attraction is rated from 0 to 3 stars to help you set priorities and organize your time.

We've also added **seven brand-new features** that point you to the great deals, in-the-know advice, and unique experiences that separate travelers from tourists. Throughout the guide, look for:

Finds	Special finds—those places only insiders know about
Fun Fact	Fun facts—details that make travelers more informed and their trips more fun
Kids	Best bets for kids—advice for the whole family
Moments	Special moments—those experiences that memories are made of
Overrated	Places or experiences not worth your time or money
Tips	Insider tips—some great ways to save time and money
Value	Great values—where to get the best deals

We've also added a **"What's New"** section in every guide—a timely crash course in what's hot and what's not in every destination we cover.

Here's what the critics say about Frommer's:

"Amazingly easy to use. Very portable, very complete."

—*Booklist*

"Detailed, accurate, and easy-to-read information for all price ranges."
—*Glamour Magazine*

"Hotel information is close to encyclopedic."
—*Des Moines Sunday Register*

"Frommer's Guides have a way of giving you a real feel for a place."
—*Knight Ridder Newspapers*

Other Great Guides for Your Trip:

Frommer's Irreverent Guide to Los Angeles
Frommer's Los Angeles
Frommer's Memorable Walks in San Francisco
Frommer's Portable Disneyland®
Frommer's San Diego
Frommer's San Francisco
Frommer's San Francisco with Kids

Frommer's®

California

2003

by Erika Lenkert, Matthew Richard Poole
& Stephanie Avnet Yates

Wiley Publishing, Inc.

Published by:

Wiley Publishing, Inc.

909 Third Ave.
New York, NY 10022

Copyright © 2003 Wiley Publishing, Inc., New York, New York. All rights
reserved. No part of this publication may be reproduced, stored in a retrieval system or transmitted in any form or by any means, electronic, mechanical, photo-
copying, recording, scanning or otherwise, except as permitted under Sections 107
or 108 of the 1976 United States Copyright Act, without either the prior written
permission of the Publisher, or authorization through payment of the appropriate
per-copy fee to the Copyright Clearance Center, 222 Rosewood Drive, Danvers,
MA 01923, (978) 750-8400, fax (978) 750-4744. Requests to the Publisher for
permission should be addressed to the Legal Department, Wiley Publishing, Inc.,
10475 Crosspoint Blvd., Indianapolis, IN 46256, (317) 572-3447, fax (317)
572-4447, E-Mail: permcoordinator@wiley.com.

Wiley and the Wiley Publishing logo are trademarks or registered trademarks of
Wiley Publishing, Inc. in the United States and other countries and may not be
used without written permission. Frommer's is a trademark or registered trademark
of Arthur Frommer. Used under license. All other trademarks are the property of
their respective owners. Wiley Publishing, Inc. is not associated with any product
or vendor mentioned in this book.

ISBN 0-7645-6695-4
ISSN 1044-2146

Editor: Myka Carroll
Production Editor: Bethany André
Cartographer: John Decamillis
Photo Editor: Richard Fox
Production by Wiley Indianapolis Composition Services

Front cover photo: Giant sequoias in Yosemite National Park
Back cover photo: The Giant Dipper Roller Coaster in Mission Bay, San Diego

For information on our other products and services or to obtain technical support,
please contact our Customer Care Department within the U.S. at 800-762-2974,
outside the U.S. at 317-572-3993 or fax 317-572-4002.

Wiley also publishes its books in a variety of electronic formats. Some content that
appears in print may not be available in electronic formats.

Manufactured in the United States of America

5   4   3   2

Contents

8 The Far North: Lake Tahoe, the Shasta Cascades & Lassen Volcanic National Park   240

by Matthew Richard Poole

9 The High Sierra: Yosemite, Mammoth Lakes & Sequoia/Kings Canyon   283

by Matthew Richard Poole

10 Sacramento, the Gold Country & the Central Valley   316

by Matthew Richard Poole

11 The Monterey Peninsula & the Big Sur Coast   350

by Matthew Richard Poole

12 The Central Coast   394

by Stephanie Avnet Yates

13 Los Angeles   444

by Matthew Richard Poole

14 Side Trips from Los Angeles   550

by Matthew Richard Poole

List of Maps

An Invitation to the Reader

In researching this book, we discovered many wonderful places—hotels, restaurants, shops, and more. We're sure you'll find others. Please tell us about them, so we can share the information with your fellow travelers in upcoming editions. If you were disappointed with a recommendation, we'd love to know that, too. Please write to:

Frommer's California 2003
Wiley Publishing, Inc. • 909 Third Ave. • New York, NY 10022

An Additional Note

Please be advised that travel information is subject to change at any time—and this is especially true of prices. We therefore suggest that you write or call ahead for confirmation when making your travel plans. The authors, editors, and publisher cannot be held responsible for the experiences of readers while traveling. Your safety is important to us, however, so we encourage you to stay alert and be aware of your surroundings. Keep a close eye on cameras, purses, and wallets, all favorite targets of thieves and pickpockets.

New! Frommer's Star Ratings & Icons

Every hotel, restaurant, and attraction listing in this guide has been ranked for quality, value, service, amenities, and special features using a star-rating scale. In country, state, and regional guides, we also rate towns and regions to help you narrow down your choices and budget your time accordingly. Hotels and restaurants in the Very Expensive and Expensive categories are rated on a scale of one (highly recommended) to three stars (exceptional). Those in the Moderate and Inexpensive categories rate from zero (recommended) to two stars (very highly recommended). Attractions, towns, and regions are rated according to the following scale: zero stars (recommended), one star (highly recommended), two stars (very highly recommended), and three stars (must-see).

In addition to the rating system, we also use seven icons to highlight insider information, useful tips, special bargains, hidden gems, memorable experiences, kid-friendly venues, places to avoid, and other useful information:

| Finds | Fun Fact | Kids | Moments | Overrated | Tips | Value |

The following abbreviations are used for credit cards:

AE	American Express	DISC	Discover	V	Visa
DC	Diners Club	MC	MasterCard		

FROMMERS.COM

Now that you have the guidebook to a great trip, visit our website at **www.frommers.com** for travel information on nearly 2,500 destinations. With features updated regularly, we give you instant access to the most current trip-planning information available. At Frommers.com, you'll also find the best prices on airfares, accommodations, and car rentals—and you can even book travel online through our travel booking partners. At Frommers.com, you'll also find the following:

- Online updates to our most popular guidebooks
- Vacation sweepstakes and contest giveaways
- Newsletter highlighting the hottest travel trends
- Online travel message boards with featured travel discussions

About the Authors

Native San Franciscan **Erika Lenkert** divides her time between Napa Valley and her hometown, where she seeks adventure, great food, and great accommodations. When she's not traveling, authoring her restaurant column in *San Francisco Magazine,* or writing articles for *Elite Traveler, Wine Country Living,* and *Four Seasons Magazine,* she's testing recipes for her new book on effortless and elegant entertaining to be published by McGraw Hill.

A native of Los Angeles and an avid traveler, antiques hound, and pop-history enthusiast, **Stephanie Avnet Yates** believes that California is best seen from behind the wheel of a little red convertible. In addition to contributing to travel websites and magazines, Stephanie writes and/or edits several regional guidebooks, and is the author of *Frommer's San Diego* and *Frommer's Wonderful Weekends from Los Angeles.* She confesses to a special fondness for San Diego, having once attended UCSD. Online, Stephanie can be reached directly at savvy_girl@hotmail.com.

Matthew Richard Poole, a native Northern Californian, has authored and contributed to more than two dozen travel guides to California, San Francisco, Las Vegas, Hawaii, and destinations abroad. Before becoming a full-time travel writer and photographer, Matthew worked as an English tutor in Prague, a ski instructor in the Swiss Alps, and a scuba instructor in Maui. Addicted to a life of freedom, he spends most of his time on the road doing research and avoiding commitments.

What's New in California

From San Francisco's freshly reno-vated hotels to San Diego's continually improving animal parks, there's no shortage of new experiences awaiting you in California. Here are the high-lights of what you can look forward to during your trip.

PLANNING YOUR TRIP If you're concerned about how changing air-port security measures will affect your flight plans, check out our special **"Air Travel Security Measures"** informa-tion. We've provided helpful tips to help you sail through the airport, as well as contact information for the most up-to-date regulations about what you can and cannot bring onboard your flight. See chapter 2 for complete details.

There's good news for outdoors types: You can now reserve online for both national and state park camp-sites, selecting exactly where and when you want to go—without "camping" on the phone on hold for a reserva-tionist! For national parks (including all Yosemite sites), log on to **http://reservations.nps.gov**. The state park system is handled at **www.reserve america.com**; just select "California" from their handy pull-down menu and choose from nearly 400 different campgrounds.

SAN FRANCISCO Where to Stay Most exciting on the hotel front is that rates are down from last year. You'll also get more for your money since hotels put some of their profits into recent renovations.

My favorite hotel, the **Four Seasons Hotel San Francisco,** 757 Market St., between Third and Fourth sts. (✆ **800/332-3442** or 415/633-3000), set new luxury standards for the city when it opened in late 2000. On the heels of a $10 million room renovation, **Campton Place Hotel,** 340 Stockton St. (✆ **800/235-4300** or 415/781-5555), completely overhauled their revered restaurant. The hip **Hotel Triton,** 342 Grant Ave. (✆ **800/433-6611** or 415/394-0500), gussied up their rooms and lobby. The **Handlery Union Square Hotel,** 351 Geary St. (✆ **800/843-4343** or 415/781-7800), may be in an old building, but after their renovations, it's a whole new— and worlds better—hotel. They've also added LA-based chain restaurant The Daily Grill, which for those in the know is a great place to get affordable American dining staples like pasta, burgers, and meatloaf.

The **Hilton San Francisco,** 333 O'Farrell St. (✆ **800/HILTONS** or 415/771-1400), is still too huge to be personal, but it's sitting prettier thanks to a renovation of 1,300 of their 1,900 rooms and the addition of a huge health club. The affordable **Andrews Hotel,** 624 Post St., between Jones and Taylor sts. (✆ **800/926-3739** or 415/563-6877), upped the comfort ante with new mattresses and carpet-ing in most rooms. **The Clarion Bed-ford Hotel,** 761 Post St. (✆ **800/252-7466** or 415/673-6040), is tak-ing a stab at trendiness with all-new and dramatically "retro" rooms.

Sweet and petit **King George Hotel,** 334 Mason St. (© **800/288-6005** or 415/781-5050), made their hotel even more enchanting with a new pub and business center. **The Savoy Hotel,** 580 Geary St. (© **800/227-4223** or 415/441-2700), lost its longtime resident restaurant Brasserie Savoy and is looking for a replacement. Previously stodgy **Shannon Court,** 550 Geary St. (© **800/228-8830** or 415/775-5000), is on its way to a renaissance since Joie de Vivre hotels bought the Spanish Revival structure and is remodeling. The Castro's best hotel, **The Parker Guest House,** 520 Church St. (© **888/520-7275** or 415/621-3222), has added a 10-room annex and hot tub.

Where to Dine Food is still the focus in the city surrounded on all sides by edible wonders from the land, sea, and vineyards. New additions include the fantastic **Isa,** 3324 Steiner St. (© **415/567-9588**), which serves outstanding French (yes, *French*) tapas. See chapter 4 for complete details.

THE WINE COUNTRY The high life is still going strong in Napa Valley, especially with Napa's new food museum **Copia: The American Center for Wine, Food & the Arts,** 500 First St., Napa (© **707/259-1600**), and the delicious and amazingly affordable new restaurant **ZuZu,** 829 Main St., Napa (© **707/224-8555**), which serves Spanish fare. See "Napa Valley" in chapter 6 for complete details.

THE NORTHERN COAST It's all about location, and the **Whale Watch Inn By the Sea,** 35100 Hwy. 1, Gualala (© **800/942-5342** or 707/884-3667), perched 90 feet above the water on 2 cliff-side acres, has one of the best on the northern coast. All of the very private guest rooms come with ocean views, decks, and fireplaces—a sure-fire combo for a night of steamy romance. There's even a private stairway that leads to a ½-mile-long beach with tidal pools.

In typical California fashion, the **Jenner Inn,** 10400 Calif. 1, Jenner (© **800/732-2377** or 707/865-2377), now offers its guests yoga classes several times weekly and has even added a small meditation cabin. See chapter 7 for details.

THE FAR NORTH South Lake Tahoe's $1 billion redevelopment plan—which will eventually include a 91,000-square-foot convention center, 1,000 additional hotel rooms, a theater complex, and "environmentally friendly" shopping areas—reached new heights with the completion of the **Heavenly Valley Ski Resort gondola** (© **775/586-7000**). The 2½-mile ride on state-of-the-art "cars" takes passengers from the Stateline casinos to a huge observation deck perched on the side of a mountain, 9,123 feet above sea level. The views, of course, are spectacular, not only of Lake Tahoe but also of Nevada's Carson Valley and the Desolation Wilderness to the west. See "Lake Tahoe" in chapter 8 for further details.

THE HIGH SIERRA Dan Braun and his team of Yosemite guides have recently taken over the **Evergreen Lodge,** 33160 Evergreen Rd. in Groveland (© **800/935-6343** or 209/379-2606), right on the border of Yosemite National Park. The result is a guaranteed good time when you book a few nights at one of the 18 cozy cabins scattered throughout a wooded grove of towering pines. Not only will Braun and company take you on guided hikes, river rafting, horseback riding, and mountain biking throughout Yosemite, they also host campfire stories, serve pitchers of beer at the classic old bar, keep the pool clean, and heat up the hot tubs nightly. It's the ideal Yosemite experience without the maddening crowds. See "Yosemite's Gateways" in chapter 9 for complete details.

SACRAMENTO, THE GOLD COUNTRY & THE CENTRAL VALLEY We've got a whole passel of new additions to this chapter, starting with two new top restaurants in Sacramento: the ever-so-stylish **Esquire Grill,** 1221 K St. (© **916/ 448-8900**), serving entrees such as spit-roasted pork chops with buttermilk onion rings and house-made applesauce; and **The Waterboy,** 20th Street and Capitol Avenue (© **916/ 498-9891**), where chef/owner Rick Mahan uses Niman Ranch naturally raised meats and local organic produce to create outstanding dishes.

Up in the Gold Country near Sutter Creek is the new **Sutter Gold Mine** tour company, off Hwy. 49 (© **888/818-7462**), which hosts the most entertaining and educational attraction in the Gold Country. Don a hard hat and delve deep into a modern gold mine filled with gold and gemstones that are embedded in the quartz of the Comet Vein. It's a thrill for kids and a must for heavy-machinery buffs.

There are a couple of Gold Country restaurants we've added as well. **Crusco's Ristorante,** 1240 S. Main St., Angels Camp (© **209/736-1440**), offers a classic Italian menu where every dish is made from scratch using generations of chef/owner Celeste Lusher's family recipes. Say hello to her daughter Sarah in the kitchen (she makes a mean penne rigate). For a more casual meal, head to **Firewood,** 420 Main St. (© **209/ 728-3248**), in the friendly town of Murphys. The open-air establishment specializes in fast, inexpensive, and delicious dishes such as Baja-style fish tacos, drippingly juicy burgers, and superb gourmet pizzas baked in a wood-burning oven. See chapter 10 for complete details.

THE MONTEREY PENINSULA & THE BIG SUR COAST True to its name, the **Babbling Brook Bed & Breakfast Inn,** 1025 Laurel St., Santa Cruz (© **800/866-1131** or 831/ 427-2456), has a series of verdant waterfalls cascading past your window, lulling you to sleep. Oozing with charm, the rooms in this popular inn are like little treehouses perched over and around a meandering brook running through an acre of gardens. If you're in search of a romantic B&B in Santa Cruz, this one's the best. See "Santa Cruz" in chapter 11 for details.

THE CENTRAL COAST Heading to **Hearst Castle**? First-timers should allow plenty of time on the "enchanted hill," since popular Tour One (the best introductory experience) now includes a showing of *Hearst Castle: Building the Dream* in the giant screen National Geographic Theatre at the visitor center. Make your reservations early—this tour always books up fast (© **800/ 444-4445**).

Speaking of advance reservations, garden lovers heading to Santa Barbara will want to reserve early to guarantee highly coveted spaces on **Ganna Walska Lotusland's** docent-guided tours (© **805/969-9990**). This spectacular Montecito estate combines whimsy and artistry, showcasing succulents, cacti, and tropicals. Rare specimens include the last living examples of some prehistoric varieties, plus vast, romantic pools of lotus flowers.

Santa Barbara also makes the news by welcoming the stylish **Hotel Oceana,** 202 W. Cabrillo Blvd. (© **800/965-9776** or 805/965-4577), to East Beach. This low-rise amalgam of four 1940s motels maintains its vintage architecture and charm while injecting contemporary comforts and a breezy, coastal style. With swimming pools, the beach, a mini-spa, and the original Sambo's coffee shop next door, Oceana is well suited for family vacations and romantic weekends alike. See chapter 12 for details.

LOS ANGELES Where to Stay It seems like wherever you turn, LA's hotels are upping the ante with stylish face-lifts and new personalities. At the **Century Plaza Hotel & Spa,** 2025 Ave. of the Stars, Century City (② **800/WESTIN-1** or 310/277-2000), the much-anticipated 35,000-square-foot **Spa Mystique**—the largest in LA—in now open for business. This gorgeous Asian-inspired pamper palace features 27 indoor treatment rooms, outdoor cabanas, and even a meditation garden. Book an appointment even if you're not staying at the hotel.

Where to Dine Here's something new: Peranakan cuisine. Pasadena's new **Nonya** restaurant, 61 N. Raymond St. (② **626/583-8398**), combines Chinese and Malaysian styles for a truly unique dining experience. The designer dining room is a must-see as well.

If you're young, pretty, hip, and hungry, head to **El Coyote,** 7312 Beverly Blvd. (② **323/939-2255**), where the rowdy bar scene is filled with slick showbiz player-types, rockers, and wannabe movie stars swilling cheap margaritas. Great fajita platters as well.

At **Crustacean,** 9646 Little Santa Monica Blvd. (② **310/205-8990**), a real Vietnamese princess runs the show at this see-and-be-seen Beverly Hills hot spot. If you love Dungeness crab and juicy prawns, you'll want what's in the An Family's Secret Kitchen.

After Dark The downtown arts triumvirate of the Dorothy Chandler Pavilion, the Ahmanson Theater, and the Mark Taper Forum—long referred to as the Music Center—has a new name: **The Performing Arts Center of Los Angeles County,** 135 N. Grand Ave. (② **213/972-7200**). It's a mouthful, but it reflects the diversity of these powerhouse venues, which will soon be joined by the **Walt Disney Concert Hall,** designed by Frank Gehry and currently under construction.

Across town, in the fast-improving Hollywood nightlife district, serious rock/pop aficionados are flocking to the new **Knitting Factory,** 7021 Hollywood Blvd. (② **323/463-0204**), which brings the wired-for-the-21st-century New York club into the heart of historic Hollywood. And West Hollywood's LunaPark is no more, but that club/restaurant's well-located multilevel space has been transformed into another West Coast branch of a New York hot spot, **Moomba,** 665 N. Robertson Blvd. (② **310/652-6364**). Boasting excellent food in a sophisticated party atmosphere, the club is also environmentally and socially conscious, a welcome trend indeed. See chapter 13 for complete details.

SIDE TRIPS FROM LOS ANGELES Hey, is that an island out there? Ditch smoggy LA for a day and head for the party on **Catalina Island.** An hour-long boat ride (or 15 min. by helicopter) from Long Beach lands you in little ol' Avalon, where the weekend summer scene is an orgy of shorts, tank tops, and an endless supply of tropical cocktails. Check out the new sections we've added on barhopping, diving, snorkeling, sea kayaking, and Catalina's Grand Casino Tour to discover the best of Catalina Island.

Other additions include: the **St. Regis Monarch Beach Resort & Spa,** 1 Monarch Beach Rd., Dana Point (② **800/325-3589** or 949/234-3200), the finest new luxury hotel I've ever reviewed; and the **Yard House** restaurant, 401 Shoreline Village Dr.,

Long Beach (© **562/628-0455**), featuring great food, one of the world's largest selections of draft beers, and sunny deck seating overlooking the marina. See chapter 14 for complete details.

THE SOUTHERN CALIFORNIA DESERT Native American gaming has been around in the desert for many years now, but recently the industry seems to have joined the major leagues, with a professionalism and polish that create a "virtual Vegas." Suddenly casinos aren't an afterthought but the main event—even Donald Trump has thrown his hat into the ring with **Trump 29 Casino,** 46-200 Harrison Place, Coachella (© **866/TRUMP-29**). Whether you go for true Vegas-style gaming, big-name entertainment, or the universally loved all-you-can-eat prime rib buffet, these glitzy newcomers are all the rage. See "The Palm Springs Desert Resorts" in chapter 15 for details.

SAN DIEGO & ENVIRONS No one visits San Diego without experiencing one of the city's fantastic animal parks, and each has some new residents to crow about. At Balboa Park's **San Diego Zoo,** 2920 Zoo Dr. (© **619/234-3153**), construction is underway to transform the outdated "monkey yard," one of the zoo's original enclosures, into the bio-climatically correct (and multi-species) Heart of the Zoo. By Memorial Day

2003, you'll see Borneo and Sumatran orangutans cavorting in their new home.

At the **San Diego Wild Animal Park,** 15500 San Pasqual Valley Rd., Escondido (© **760/747-8702**), they've been rescuing and breeding endangered California condors for years, and in 2001, for the first time, they allowed visitors a peek. The condors continue to be a huge success story, as visitors flock to see these eerily impressive birds along the mountain trails of **Condor Ridge,** a habitat created for some of California's critically endangered species; along with condors, you'll see thick-billed parrots, black-footed ferrets, hawks, owls, and bighorn sheep.

Meanwhile, a hilarious new animal show awaits at **SeaWorld,** 500 Sea World Dr., Mission Bay (© **619/226-3901**), which recently welcomed *Pets Rule!,* whose remarkable cast of trained cats, dogs, and other domestic animals were all adopted from local shelters and given a new life in the SeaWorld spotlight. In addition to illustrating how the same techniques used to train killer whales and seals can teach your household pet to have perfect comic timing, the show provides some insight into the behavioral world of our favorite companions. For details about all three parks, see "The Main Attractions: The Zoo, SeaWorld & the Wild Animal Park" in chapter 16.

1

The Best of California

by Erika Lenkert, Matthew Richard Poole & Stephanie Avnet Yates

In my early 20s, I took the requisite college student's pilgrimage to Europe, exploring its finer train stations and sleeping on the premier park benches from London to Istanbul. I was relatively anonymous—just another tanned and skinny, blond and blue-eyed American lugging around 60 pounds of backpack. That is, until I crossed over into the former Eastern Bloc.

The reaction was dramatic, almost palpable. Like Moses parting the sea, I would wander through the crowded streets of Prague and citizens would stop, stare, and sidestep as if a scarlet *A* was emblazoned across my chest. It wasn't until a man who spoke faltering English finally approached me that I discovered the reason for my newfound celebrity status.

"Eh, you. Where you from? No, no. Let me guess." He steps back, gives a cursory examination followed by pregnant pause. "Ah. I've got it! California! You're from California, no?" A gleam in his eyes as I tell him that, yes, he's quite correct. "Wonderful! Wonderful!" A dozen or so pilsners later with my loquacious new friend and it all becomes clear to me: To him, I truly am a celebrity—a rich, convertible-driving surfer who spends most his days lazing on the beach, fending off hordes of buxom blondes while I argue with my agent via my portable phone. The myth is complete. I *am* the Beach Boys. I *am Baywatch.* Status by association. The tentacles of Hollywood have done what no NATO pact could achieve—they've leapfrogged the staid issues of capitalism versus communism by offering a far more potent narcotic: the alluring mystique of sun-drenched California, of movie stars strolling down Sunset Boulevard, of beautiful women in tight shorts and bikini tops roller-skating along Venice Beach. In short, they've bought what we're selling.

Of course, the allure is understandable. It really is warm and sunny most days of the year, movie stars actually do abound in Los Angeles, and you can't swing a cat by its tail without hitting a rollerblading babe in Venice Beach. This part of the California mystique—however exaggerated it may be—truly does exist, and it's not hard to find.

But there's more—a lot more—to California that isn't scripted, sanitized, and squeezed through a cathode-ray tube to the world's millions of mesmerized masses. Beyond the glitter and glamour of Hollywood is an incredibly diverse state that, if it ever seceded from the Union, would be one of the most productive and powerful nations in the world. We've got it all: misty redwood forests, an incredibly verdant Central Valley teeming with agriculture, the mighty Sierra Nevada Mountain Range, eerily fascinating deserts, a host of world-renowned cities, and, of course, hundreds of miles of stunning coastline.

And despite the endemic crime, pollution, traffic, and bowel-shaking earthquakes for which California is famous, we're still the golden child of the United States, America's spoiled rich kid whom everyone else either loves or loathes.

(Neighboring Oregon, for example, sells lots of license-plate rims that proudly state, "I hate California.") But, truth be told, we really don't care what anyone thinks of us. Californians *know* they live in one of the most diverse and interesting places in the world, and we're proud of the state we call home.

Granted, there's no guarantee that you'll bump into Arnold Schwarzenegger or learn how to surf, but if you have a little time, a little money, and—most importantly—an adventurous spirit, then Erika, Stephanie, and I will help guide you through one of the most fulfilling vacations of your life. The three of us travel the world for a living, but we *choose* to live in California, simply because there's no other place on earth that has so much to offer.

—Matthew Richard Poole

1 The Best of Natural California

- **Point Reyes National Seashore:** This extraordinarily scenic stretch of coast and wetlands is one of the best bird-watching spots in California for shorebirds, songbirds, and waterfowl, as well as osprey and red-shouldered hawks. You might even catch a glimpse of a whale from the Point Reyes Lighthouse. See "Point Reyes National Seashore" in chapter 7.

- **Redwood National & State Parks:** Come see the world's largest and most majestic trees at this arboreal Eden. More than 300 bird species and 100 mammals can also be seen, many of them year-round. Howland Hill Road is a must-do. See "Redwood National & State Parks" in chapter 7.

- **Lake Tahoe:** One of the world's most magnificent bodies of fresh water, sparkling Lake Tahoe is famous for its pure, azure water and incredible volume. In fact, it's so deep that the water it contains—close to 40 trillion gallons—could cover the entire state of California to a depth of 14½ inches. See "Lake Tahoe" in chapter 8.

- **Mount Shasta:** One of the most spectacular sights in all of California is the mighty volcano Mount Shasta, a solitary tower of rock and snow rising thousands of feet above the valley floor. And if you're in good shape, it makes for an exhilarating climb as well. See "Mount Shasta & the Cascades" in chapter 8.

- **Yosemite National Park:** You're in for the ultimate treat at Yosemite. Nothing in the state—maybe even the world—compares to this vast wilderness playground and its miles of rivers, lakes, peaks, and valleys. With 3 out of 10 of the world's tallest waterfalls, the largest single granite monolith in the world, and some of the world's largest trees, Yosemite is one of the most fantastic natural places on the planet. You'll have a sweeping 180° view of it all from high atop Glacier Point, where a majestic High Sierra panorama unfolds at 3,200 feet. See "Yosemite National Park" in chapter 9.

- **Elkhorn Slough** (Moss Landing): It's as close as you might ever get to feeling like you're on a *National Geographic* adventure. Captain Gideon's 2-hour cruise takes you into the heart of the northern California shore's wildlife reserve, where you'll encounter dozens of otters and harbor seals and hundreds of bird species. See "Monterey" in chapter 11.

- **Big Sur:** Rock-strewn beaches, towering cliffs, and redwood forests combine to form what may be the world's most dramatic coastal panorama. Our favorite vantage point for taking it all in is Garrapata State Park, a 2,879-acre preserve that lords over 4 spectacular miles of coastline. See "The Big Sur Coast" in chapter 11.

- **Point Lobos State Reserve:** Take Calif. 1 about 4 miles south of Carmel to view harbor seals, sea lions, and sea otters at play. From December to May, gray whales pass by on their migration south. The area is filled with nature walks. See "The Big Sur Coast" in chapter 11.

- **Cachuma Lake:** Situated on mountainous and scenic Calif. 154, halfway between Solvang and Santa Barbara, is this stunning winter home to dozens of American bald eagles. Loons, white pelicans, and Canada geese are some of the other migratory birds that call this glassy lake home part of the year. See "The Central Coast Wine Country: Paso Robles & the Santa Ynez Valley" in chapter 12.

- **Channel Islands National Park:** This is California in its most natural state. Paddle a kayak into sea caves; camp among indigenous island fox and seabirds; and swim, snorkel, or scuba-dive tide pools and kelp forests teeming with wildlife. The channel waters are prime for whale-watching, and winter brings elephant-seal mating season, when you'll see them and their sea-lion cousins sunbathing on cove beaches. See "Channel Islands National Park" in chapter 12.

- **Joshua Tree National Park:** You'll find awesome rock formations, groves of flowering cacti and stately Joshua trees, ancient Native American petroglyphs, and shifting sand dunes in this desert wonderland—and a brilliant night sky, if you choose to camp here. See "Joshua Tree National Park" in chapter 15.

- **Death Valley National Park:** Its inhospitable climate makes it the state's most unlikely tourist attraction—but the same conditions that thwarted settlers create some of the most dramatic landscapes you'll ever see. Mesmerizing rock formations, ever-changing dry lake beds, and often stifling heat provide the setting for relics of hardy 19th-century borax miners and (fool-) hardy dwellers from the 1930s. See "Death Valley National Park" in chapter 15.

- **Torrey Pines State Reserve:** Poised on a majestic cliff overlooking the Pacific Ocean, this reserve is home to the rare Torrey pine. Exhibits on the local ecology are housed in the visitor center, and numerous hiking trails fan out throughout the park. See "Exploring the Area" in chapter 16.

- **Anza-Borrego Desert State Park:** The largest state park in the lower 48 states attracts the most visitors during the spring wildflower season, when a kaleidoscopic carpet blankets the desert floor. Others come year-round to hike the more than 100 miles of designated trails. See "Anza-Borrego Desert State Park" in chapter 16.

2 The Best Beaches

- **Drake's Beach:** This is a massive stretch of white sand at Point Reyes National Seashore, west of Inverness. Winds and choppy seas make it rough for swimmers, but sun worshippers can have their Marin County tan for the day. If the rangers say it's all right, beach driftwood can make a romantic campfire in the early evening. See

"Point Reyes National Seashore" in chapter 7.

- **Sonoma Coast State Beaches:** Stretching about 10 miles from Bodega Bay to Jenner, these beaches attract more than 300 species of birds. From December to September, look for osprey. Seal pups can be spotted from March to June, and the gray whale from December to April. See "Along the Sonoma Coast" in chapter 7.

- **Santa Cruz's Beaches:** Northern California's answer to SoCal's fun-in-the-sun beach scene, Santa Cruz has 29 miles of beaches that are varied enough to please all comers: surfers, swimmers, fishers, sailboarders, the sand-pail-and-shovel set, and the bikini and biceps crowd. For starters, just walk down the steps from the famous Santa Cruz Beach Boardwalk to the mile-long, white sand Main Beach, complete with summer lifeguards and golden oldie tunes drifting over the sand from the boardwalk's live concerts. See "Santa Cruz" in chapter 11.

- **Pfeiffer Beach:** This is one of Big Sur's best-kept secrets. It can be accessed via an unmarked paved road on the right-hand side of Calif. 1, 1 mile south of Pfeiffer State Park. There are no signs, so you'll have to do some sleuthing, but once you've parked behind the trail of cars on the side of the road and made it to the beach, you'll know why locals want to keep this spot all to themselves. See "The Big Sur Coast" in chapter 11.

- **Sand Dollar Beach:** The best Big Sur beach lies beyond Pacific Valley—ideal for swimming and surfing, with a panoramic view of Cone Peak, one of the coast's highest mountains. See "The Big Sur Coast" in chapter 11.

- **Santa Barbara's East Beach:** This wide swath of clean white sand hosts beach umbrellas, sand-castle builders, and spirited volleyball games. A grassy, parklike median keeps the happy beachgoers insulated from busy Cabrillo Boulevard. On Sundays, local artists display their wares beneath the elegant palm trees. See "Santa Barbara" in chapter 12.

- **La Jolla's Beaches:** Roughly translated, *La Jolla* means "the jewel," and the beaches of La Jolla's cliff-lined coast truly are gems. Each has a distinct personality: Surfers love Windansea's waves, and La Jolla Shores is popular for swimming and sunbathing. See "Beaches" in chapter 16.

- **Coronado Beach:** On the west side of Coronado extending to the Hotel del Coronado, this beautiful beach is uncrowded and great for watching the sunset. Marilyn Monroe romped in the surf here during the filming of *Some Like It Hot*. See "Beaches" in chapter 16.

3 The Best Golf Courses

- **Pebble Beach Golf Links:** The famous 17-Mile Drive is the site of 10 national championships and the winter telecast of the celebrity-laden AT&T Pebble Beach National Pro-Am. The raging nearby Pacific and a scenic backdrop of the Del Monte Forest justify astronomical greens fees. See "Pebble Beach & the 17-Mile Drive" in chapter 11.

- **Spyglass Hill** (Pebble Beach): Five holes border the ocean, and the rest extend deep within Del Monte Forest. The holes here have been called "long and unforgiving" by golf magazines. Its slope rating of 143 makes it one of the toughest courses in California. See "Pebble Beach & the 17-Mile Drive" in chapter 11.

- **Poppy Hills** (Pebble Beach): *Golf Digest* has called this Robert Trent Jones Jr.–designed course "one of the world's top 20 courses." Also used for AT&T festivities, it cuts right through the pines of Del Monte Forest. It's maintained in state-of-the-art condition and, unlike some of its competitors, is rarely overcrowded. See "Pebble Beach & the 17-Mile Drive" in chapter 11.

- **The Links at Spanish Bay** (Pebble Beach): The Links were also designed by Robert Trent Jones Jr., with a little help from Tom Watson and former USGA president Frank Tatum. Their aim was to simulate the experience of playing golf on true Scottish links. Holes 14 through 18—taking you to the sea and back again through high dunes—call for some trick shot making, but make the whole experience worthwhile. See "Pebble Beach & the 17-Mile Drive" in chapter 11.

- **Westin Mission Hills Resort, Pete Dye Course** (Rancho Mirage): Since 1987, when course architect Pete Dye sculpted this links-style, par-70 challenger, players have wrangled with the pot bunkers, hidden pin placements, and carries over water that are his classic trademarks. Rolling fairways and railroad ties also characterize Dye's 6,706-yard classic. The course takes full scenic advantage of the lavender hills all around. See "The Palm Springs Desert Resorts" in chapter 15.

- **PGA West TPC Stadium Course** (La Quinta): The par-3 17th hole has a picturesque island green where Lee Trevino made Skins Game history with a spectacular hole-in-one. The rest of Pete Dye's 7,261-yard design is flat with huge bunkers, lots of water, and severe mounding throughout. The PGA West is part of the La Quinta Resort & Club, where world-class golf, dining, spa, and discreetly elegant quarters come together. See "The Palm Springs Desert Resorts" in chapter 15.

- **Torrey Pines Golf Course** (La Jolla): Two gorgeous 18-hole championship courses overlook the ocean and provide players with plenty of challenge. In February, the Buick Invitational Tournament is held here; the rest of the year, these popular municipal courses are open to everybody See "Outdoor Pursuits" in chapter 16.

- **Coronado Municipal Golf Course** (San Diego): This 18-hole, par-72 municipal course overlooking Glorietta Bay is located to the left of the Coronado Bay Bridge. It's the first thing you see when you arrive in Coronado—a fabulous welcome for duffers. See "Outdoor Pursuits" in chapter 16.

4 The Best Californian Travel Experiences

- **Hot-Air Ballooning over Napa Valley:** It's all the rage, and for good reason: Northern California's temperate weather allows for ballooning year-round, and the valley is simply beautiful from up high. Flights are best right after sunrise, when the air is calm and cool. Hotels throughout the valley can arrange a trip aloft for you, or you can book one directly with **Bonaventura Balloon Company** (© **800/FLY-NAPA**) or **Adventures Aloft** (© **800/944-4408**). See "Hot-Air Ballooning over the Valley" in chapter 6.

- **Taking a Mud Bath in Calistoga:** In this town's famous volcanic-ash mud—mixed with mineral water—you can get buck naked and covered in gooey mud. At a dozen or so places you can immerse yourself in the mud, followed by a mineral-water shower and a whirlpool bath, and then a steam bath. It's perhaps the most relaxing experience in California. See "Find the New You—in a Calistoga Mud Bath" in chapter 6.

- **Rafting Scenic Northern California Rivers:** You can whitewater raft through thrilling cascades of raging Class IV water or float peacefully through tranquil vistas of blue skies, deep forests, and abundant wildlife. The fastest flows are in the spring, naturally. Depending on the river and the time of year, some trips are okay for children over age 6. See chapters 7 and 8.

- **A Train Ride through the Redwoods:** Where else on this planet would you get an opportunity to ride a historic steam train through a remote coastal redwood forest? The **Skunk Train** (☎ **800/77-SKUNK**) in Fort Bragg once lugged logs and now takes tourists on an all-day outing through a redwood forest, an 80-mile journey that crosses over 31 bridges and trestles and through two deep tunnels. They even offer a Sunset Dinner BBQ excursion. See "Fort Bragg" in chapter 7.

- **Exploring a Real Gold Mine:** Don your hardhat, "tag in," board the mine shuttle, and experience just what it's like to be a modern gold miner. The **Sutter Gold Mine** tour company (☎ **888/818-7462**) takes you deep into a real gold mine that's loaded with gemstones and gold deposits. You'll learn all about how gold mining works and even get an opportunity to sluice for some real gold and gemstones. See "A Modern Gold Mine Tour" in chapter 10.

- **Riding the Amtrak Rails Along the Southern California Coast:** Relive the golden age of train travel and see the natural beauty of California, avoiding the crowded highways at the same time. Spanish-style Union Station, a marble-floored Streamline Moderne masterpiece, is the Los Angeles hub. Trains run between LA and the romantic mission towns of San Juan Capistrano, San Diego, Santa Barbara, and San Luis Obispo. The scenery includes lush valleys, a windswept coastline, and the occasional urban stretch. Call **Amtrak** (☎ **800/USA-RAIL**) for information.

- **Skydiving over Southern California:** Enjoy a bird's-eye view of the Southland. Local schools offer instruction at all levels (including tandem jumps for first-timers). At the **California City Skydive Center** (☎ 800/2-JUMP-HI) in the Mojave Desert, you can soar through the same skies as the space shuttle, which lands at nearby Edwards Air Force Base. Other options include three world-renowned schools: **Skydiving Adventures** at Hemet-Ryan Airport (☎ 800/526-9682; www.skydivehemet.com), the **Perris Valley Skydiving School** (☎ 800/832-8818; www.skydiveperris.com), and **Jim Wallace Skydiving** (☎ 800/795-DIVE; www.jimwallace-skydiving.com) at Skylark Airport at Lake Elsinore.

- **Celebrity Spotting at LA Cemeteries:** Okay, so it's a rather morbid method for seeing Hollywood stars, but we absolutely guarantee you'll get within 6 feet of many famous (and very former) celebrities. Los Angeles cemeteries such as **Westwood Memorial Park** and **Hollywood Forever** are the resting places for Marilyn Monroe, Natalie Wood, Walter Matthau, Rudolph Valentino, Alfalfa, and Douglas Fairbanks *père et fils*. See "Stargazing, Part II: The Less-than-Lively Set" in chapter 13.

- **Watching a TV Sitcom Taping:** Alternately boring and fascinating (the old hurry-up-and-wait syndrome), being in the audience is your chance to wander the sound-stage, marvel at the cheesy three-wall sets that look so real on TV, and get an inside look at the bloopers that never make it to broadcast—and are often far more entertaining than the scripted dialogue. See "TV Tapings" in chapter 13.

- **Getting Up Close to the Desert's Gigantic Windmills:** Anyone who's driven through the desert near Palm Springs has marveled at these looming structures. Curiosity proved to be the mother of invention, and now visitors have a chance to see, touch, and learn about the surprisingly efficient power generators, why they're clustered here, and just what is the difference between wind *turbines* and wind *mills*. See "En Route to the Palm Springs Resorts" in chapter 15.

- **Climb into Sunny Jim Cave** (La Jolla): Get in touch with your inner pirate when you descend a precarious staircase through solid rock, emerging inside an enormous sea cave—rumored to have once been a landing for Prohibition-era bootleggers—on the La Jolla coast. Hand-carved nearly 100 years ago, the tunnel is safer than it feels (honest!), and offers a cool treat . . . though not for the faint-of-heart. See "Exploring the Area" in chapter 16.

5 The Best of Small-Town California

- **St. Helena:** A small town in the heart of the Napa Valley, St. Helena is known for its Main Street, which is lined with Victorian storefronts featuring intriguing wares. In a horse and buggy, Robert Louis Stevenson and his new bride, the cantankerous Fanny, made their way down this street. Come for the old-timey, tranquil mood and the wonderful food. See "Napa Valley" in chapter 6.

- **Mendocino:** An artists' colony with a New England flavor, Mendocino served as the backdrop for *Murder, She Wrote*. Perched on the cliff tops above the Pacific Ocean, it's filled with small art galleries, general stores, weathered wooden houses, and elbow-to-elbow tourists. See "Mendocino" in chapter 7.

- **Arcata:** If you're losing your faith in America, a few days spent at this Northern California coastal town will surely restore it. Arcata has it all: its own redwood forest and bird marsh, a charming town square, great family-owned restaurants, and even its own minor-league baseball team, which draws the whole town together for an afternoon of pure camaraderie. See "Eureka & Environs" in chapter 7.

- **Nevada City:** The whole town is a national historic landmark and the best place to understand gold-rush fever. Settled in 1849, it offers fine dining and shopping and a stock of multi-gabled Victorian frame houses of the Old West. Relics of the cannibalistic Donner Party are on display at the

1861 Firehouse No. 1. See "The Gold Country" in chapter 10.

- **Pacific Grove:** You can escape the Monterey crowds by heading just 2 miles west to Pacific Grove, which is known for its tranquil waterfront location and quiet, unspoiled air. Thousands of monarch butterflies flock here between October and March to make their winter home in Washington Park. See "Pacific Grove" in chapter 11.

- **Cambria:** Near Hearst Castle, Cambria benefits from a constant stream of visitors, who bring the right amount of sophistication to this picturesque coastal town. Moonstone Beach holds a string of seaside lodges; farther north are dozens of sunbathing elephant seals, while the village itself is filled with charming B&Bs, artists' studios and galleries, and friendly shops. See "San Simeon: Hearst Castle" in chapter 12.

- **Ojai:** When Hollywood needed a Shangri-La for the movie *Lost Horizon,* filmmakers drove north to idyllic Ojai Valley, an unspoiled hideaway of eucalyptus groves and small ranches warmly nestled among soft, green hills. Ojai is the amiable village at the valley's heart. It's a mecca for artists, free spirits, and weary city folk in need of a restful weekend in the country. See "The Ojai Valley" in chapter 12.

- **Ventura:** This charming mission town is filled with colorful Victorians. It's also home to a pleasantly eclectic old Main Street lined with thrift and antiques shops, used-record stores, friendly diners, and even old-time saloons operating beneath broken-down, second-story hotels. Don't miss the historic mission on its landscaped plaza, and the Deco-era Greek Revival San Buenaventura City Hall looming over the town, bedecked with smiling stone faces of the founding Franciscan friars. See "En Route to Los Angeles: Ventura" in chapter 12.

- **Julian:** This old mining town in the Cuyamaca Mountains near San Diego is well known today for its wildflower fields, the fall apple harvest, and tasty flavored breads from Dudley's Bakery. There's plenty of pioneer history here, too, including a local-history museum, a schoolhouse built around 1888, and mining demonstrations. A smattering of antiques shops, plenty of barbecue, and an old-fashioned soda fountain operating since 1886 round out the experience. See "Julian: Apples, Pies & a Slice of Small-Town California" in chapter 16.

6 The Best Family Vacation Experiences

- **San Francisco:** The City by the Bay is filled with unexpected pleasures for every member of the family. Ride the cable cars that "climb halfway to the stars" and visit the Exploratorium, the California Academy of Sciences (which includes the Steinhart Aquarium), the zoo, the ships at the National Maritime Museum, Golden Gate Park, Sony's Metreon

Entertainment Center, and much more. See chapter 4.

- **Lake Tahoe:** California's Disneyland of outdoor adventure, Lake Tahoe has loads of family-fun things to do. Skiing, snowboarding, hiking, tobogganing, swimming, fishing, boating, water-skiing, mountain biking—the list is nearly endless. See "Lake Tahoe" in chapter 8.

- **Yosemite National Park:** Camping or staying in a cabin in Yosemite is a premier family attraction in California. Sites are scattered over 17 different campgrounds, and the rugged beauty of the Sierra Nevada Mountains surrounds you. During the day, the family calendar is packed with hiking, bicycling, white-water rafting, and even mountaineering to rugged, snowy peaks. See "Yosemite National Park" in chapter 9.
- **Santa Cruz:** Surfing, sea kayaking, hiking, fishing, and great shopping, not to mention those fantastic beaches and the legendary amusement park on the boardwalk—this wonderfully funky bayside town has everything you need for the perfect family vacation. See "Santa Cruz" in chapter 11.
- **Monterey:** It's been called "Disneyland-by-the-Sea" due to its wealth of family-friendly activities, including those on Cannery Row and Fisherman's Wharf. Be sure to check out the state-of-the-art aquarium. See "Monterey" in chapter 11.
- **Big Bear Lake:** Families flock year-round to this lake in the San Bernardino Mountains, and not just for the skiing. Horseback riding, miniature golf, watersports, and the Alpine Slide (kind of a

snowless bobsled) are fun alternatives, and you can see and learn about native wildlife at the Moonridge Animal Park. The recently expanded village has a movie theater, arcade, and dozens of cutesy bear-themed businesses. The area's woodsy cabins are perfect for families. See "Big Bear Lake & Lake Arrowhead" in chapter 14.
- **Disneyland:** The "Happiest Place on Earth" is family entertainment at its best, further enhanced by its sister theme park, **California Adventure.** Whether you're wowed by Disney animation, thrilled by the roller-coaster rides, or interested in the history and hidden secrets of this pop-culture icon, you won't walk away disappointed. Be sure to get a Fast Pass to skip those long lines. See "The Disneyland Resort" in chapter 14.
- **San Diego Zoo, Wild Animal Park, & SeaWorld:** San Diego boasts three of the world's best animal attractions. At the zoo, animals live in creatively designed habitats such as Tiger River and Hippo Beach. At the Wild Animal Park, 3,000 animals roam freely over 2,200 acres. And SeaWorld, with its ever-changing animal shows and exhibits, is an aquatic wonderland. See "The Main Attractions: The Zoo, SeaWorld & the Wild Animal Park" in chapter 16.

7 The Best Architectural Landmarks

- **The Golden Gate Bridge** (San Francisco): More tomato red than golden, the city's famous bridge remains a stunning visual for the San Francisco skyline. It's also an excellent expanse to stroll, provided you dress appropriately. See p. 112.
- **The Civic Center** (San Francisco): The creation of designers

John Bakewell Jr., and Arthur Brown Jr., this is perhaps the most beautiful beaux-arts complex in America. See "Exploring the City" in chapter 4.
- **The Painted Ladies** (San Francisco): The so-called Painted Ladies are the city's famous, ornately decorated Victorian homes. Check out the brilliant

beauties around Alamo Square. Most of the extant 14,000 structures date from the second half of the 19th century. See "Exploring the City" in chapter 4.

- **The Carson House** (Eureka): This house is a splendidly flamboyant Victorian—and one of the state's most photographed Queen Anne–style structures. It was built in 1885 by the Newsom brothers for William Carson, the local timber baron. Today, it's the headquarters of a men's club. See "Eureka & Environs" in chapter 7.

- **California State Capitol** (Sacramento): Built in 1869 and completely renovated in 1976, the dazzling white capitol building has the original statuary (which was lost for a while) restored along its eaves; historical rooms furnished with antiques from the original offices; a strangely interesting collection of portraits of California governors (don't miss Jerry Brown); and a dome that from the inside looks like a Fabergé egg. It also has a few oddities such as gargoyles hidden in the ornate moldings. See p. 318.

- **Mission San Carlos Borromeo del Rio Carmelo** (Carmel): The second mission founded in California in 1770 by Father Junípero Serra (who is buried here) is perhaps the most beautiful. Its stone church and tower dome have been authentically restored, and a peaceful garden of California poppies adjoins the church. Sights include an early kitchen and the founding father's spartan sleeping quarters. See "Carmel-by-the-Sea" in chapter 11.

- **The Theme Building** (Los Angeles): The spacey *Jetsons*-style "Theme Building," which once loomed over underdeveloped LAX, still holds court in the center of the airport and unmistakably signals your arrival. Enjoy the view of arriving and departing jets from the building's observation deck or its groovy *Star Trek*–ish Encounter LAX restaurant and bar, whose eerie purple neon lights flood the surrounding area after dark. See "Exploring the City" in chapter 13.

- **Tail o' the Pup** (Los Angeles): One of the few remaining examples of 1950s representational architecture, locals adored this closet-sized, hot dog–shaped wiener dispensary so much that when it was threatened by the developer's bulldozer, they spoke out en masse to save it. Thank them by stopping by for a Baseball Special. See p. 511.

- **The Gamble House** (Pasadena): The Smithsonian Institution calls this Pasadena landmark, built in 1908, "one of the most important houses in the United States." Architects Charles and Henry Greene created a masterpiece of the Japanese-influenced Arts and Crafts movement. Tours are conducted of the spectacular interior, designed by the Greenes down to the last piece of teak furniture and coordinating Tiffany lamp, and executed with impeccable craftsmanship. After you're done, stroll the immediate neighborhood to view several more Greene-and-Greene creations. See p. 516.

- **Balboa Park** (San Diego): These Spanish-Mayan–style buildings were originally built as temporary structures for the Panama-California Exposition between 1915 and 1916. Set amidst the vast hilly terrain of one of the country's finest city parks, the ornately decorated and imposing facades have a special magic. Although some have been rebuilt over the years, many of the original buildings still remain, housing San Diego's finest museums. See "Exploring the Area" in chapter 16.

- **Hotel del Coronado** (Coronado): The "Hotel Del" stands in all its ornate Victorian red-tiled glory on some of the loveliest beach in Southern California. Built in 1888, it's one of the largest remaining wooden structures in the world. Even if you're not staying, stop by to take a detailed tour of the splendidly restored interiors, elegant grounds, and fascinating mini-museum of the hotel's spirited history. On your way to Coronado, you can't miss the soaring **Coronado Bay Bridge,** an architectural landmark in its own right. See p. 654.

8 The Best Museums

- **The Exploratorium** (San Francisco): The hands-on, interactive Exploratorium boasts 650 exhibits that help show how things work. You use all your senses and stretch them to a new dimension. Every exhibit is designed to be useful. See p. 118.
- **California State Railroad Museum** (Sacramento): Old Sacramento's biggest attraction, the 100,000-square-foot museum was once the terminus of the Transcontinental and Sacramento Valley railways. The largest museum of its type in the United States, it displays 21 locomotives and railroad cars, among other attractions. One sleeping car simulates travel, with all the swaying and flashing lights of lonely towns passed in the night. See p. 318.
- **J. Paul Getty Museum at the Getty Center** (Los Angeles): Since opening in 1997, the Getty has been deluged by visitors eager to see whether this ambitiously conceived (14 years and $1 billion in the making) complex fulfills its promise as the cultural cornerstone of LA. Besides boasting a permanent art collection and notable visiting exhibits, the center is a striking—and starkly futuristic—architectural landmark. From its picturesque vantage point, the Getty offers panoramic city and ocean views. See p. 504.

- **Autry Museum of Western Heritage** (Los Angeles): This one's a treat for both young and old. Relive California's historic cowboy past and see how the period has been depicted by Hollywood through the years, from Disney cartoon re-creations to founder Gene Autry's "singing cowboy" films to popular 1960s TV series. Highlights include a life-size woolly mammoth and a glimmering vault of ornate frontier firearms. See p. 517.
- **Petersen Automotive Museum** (Los Angeles): This museum is a natural for Los Angeles, a city whose personality is so entwined with the popularity of the car. Impeccably restored vintage autos are displayed in life-size dioramas accurate to the last period detail (including an authentic 1930s–era service station). Upstairs galleries house movie-star and motion-picture vehicles, car-related artwork, and visiting exhibits. See p. 518.
- **The Museums of Balboa Park** (San Diego): Located in a relaxed, verdant setting, these museums offer a unique variety of cultural experiences. Highlights include the Aerospace Historical Center, Museum of Man, Museum of Photographic Arts, Model Railroad Museum, Natural History Museum, and the lily pond and Botanical Building. Check

in at the House of Hospitality for a map and "Passport to Balboa Park," a low-cost pass to a combination of the museums. See "Exploring the Area" in chapter 16.

- **Museum of Contemporary Art (MCA) (San Diego):** MCA is actually one museum with two locations: one in La Jolla (p. 680), the other downtown (p. 678). Perched on a seaside cliff, the La Jolla branch wins praise for outstanding views, site-specific outdoor sculpture, and the recent restoration of the museum's facade, a 1916 Irving Gill–designed home originally built for benefactor Ellen Browning Scripps. The permanent collection is known internationally, and focuses primarily on work produced since 1950.

9 The Best Luxury Hotels & Resorts

- **Ritz-Carlton San Francisco** (© 800/241-3333): Two short blocks from the top of Nob Hill, San Francisco's Ritz is world-renowned among discerning travelers for its superfluously accommodating staff, luxurious amenities, and top-rated restaurant. Another bonus is the most lavish brunch in town, served on Sundays in the Terrace Room or on the patio amidst blooming rose bushes. See p. 87.

- **Auberge du Soleil** (Rutherford; © 707/963-1211): The "Inn of the Sun," a Relais & Châteaux member in a 33-acre olive grove, stands above the vineyards of Napa Valley. This French country–style inn is the Wine Country's best resort. Each of the spacious villas is named after a region of France and exudes an ambience of romantic exclusivity. See p. 177.

- **Meadowood Napa Valley** (St. Helena; © 800/458-8080): A retreat of charm and style, this 256-acre Wine Country estate was inspired by New England's grand cottages. With its plethora of sports facilities and stress-relieving treatments, it attracts such clients as megabuck novelist Danielle Steele. See p. 177.

- **The Estate by the Elderberries** (Oakhurst; © 559/683-6860): Close to Yosemite, the Château du Sureau and Erna's Elderberry House, established in 1984, evoke the best of Europe. Exquisite furnishings, individually decorated rooms, and a cuisine worthy of the stars make for a memorable lodging and dining experience at this gateway to the wilderness. See p. 286.

- **Casa Palmero Resort** (Pebble Beach; © 800/654-9300): A small, ultra-luxury resort on the first tee of the Pebble Beach Golf Course, Casa Palmero has just 24 cottages and suites, all very intimate and private. In addition, you have the splendors of Pebble Beach, its fabulous golf links, fine restaurants, and gorgeous scenery to amuse you. See p. 374.

- **Post Ranch Inn** (Big Sur; © 800/527-2200): The freestanding, architecturally sophisticated cabins—which virtually hang over the cliffs of Big Sur—combined with first-rate amenities, hiking trails, spectacular views, a top-notch restaurant, and a celestial outdoor heated pool make this one of the most exclusive—and romantic—resorts we've ever visited. See p. 387.

- **Ventana Inn and Spa** (Big Sur; © 800/628-6500): A luxurious wilderness resort on 243 mountainous, oceanfront acres, this place is chic, tranquil, and hip—the pioneer sylvan retreat at Big Sur is a magnet for celebrities. Accommodations in one- and two-story buildings—each "worthy of the wild"—blend in with the dramatic Big Sur coastline. The cuisine is first-rate. See p. 388.

- **Four Seasons Biltmore** (Santa Barbara; ☏ **800/332-3442**): Open since 1927, the Biltmore has palm-studded formal gardens and a prime beachfront location along "America's Riviera." Meander through the elegant Spanish-Moorish arcades and walkways, all accented by exquisite Mexican tile, and then play croquet on manicured lawns or relax at the Coral Casino Beach and Cabana Club. The rooms are the epitome of refined luxury, and the service couldn't be more friendly and accommodating. See p. 472.

- **Shutters on the Beach** (Santa Monica; ☏ **800/334-9000**) and **Casa del Mar** (Santa Monica; ☏ **800/898-6999**): If a luxurious oceanfront room at either of these hip hotels doesn't put a spring in your relationship, it's hard to imagine what will. Which one is best for you depends on your taste: Shutters is dressed up like a really rich friend's contemporary-chic beach house, while the glamorous Casa del Mar is an impeccably restored Deco-era delight. See p. 468 and p. 467.

- **The Inn on Mt. Ada** (Santa Catalina Island; ☏ **800/608-7669**): This former mansion of the wealthy Wrigley family is one of the most exclusive B&B experiences you'll ever have. With only six guest rooms, the hilltop inn's hefty rates include all your meals (and thoughtful snacks laid out

each afternoon), plus the use of a golf cart to putter around this auto-eschewing island paradise. You'll feel like an honored guest at a friend's Mediterranean villa. See p. 557.

- **Ritz-Carlton Laguna Niguel** (Dana Point; ☏ **800/241-3333**): This jewel in the Ritz-Carlton chain is well known for its warmth, charm, picture-perfect setting, and impeccable service. On dramatic cliffs overlooking 2 miles of prime beach, the Ritz is done in an easy yet elegant nautical-seashore decor, accented by well-chosen antiques and fine art. See p. 586.

- **La Quinta Resort & Club** (La Quinta; ☏ **800/854-1271**): This luxury resort, set in a grove of palms at the base of the rocky Santa Rosa Mountains, is surrounded by some of the desert's best golf courses. Single-story, Spanish-style cottages are surrounded by a gardenlike setting and 24 "private" swimming pools. The tranquil lounge and library in the unaltered original hacienda hearkens back to the early days of the resort, when Clark Gable, Greta Garbo, and other luminaries regularly escaped to the seclusion of La Quinta's casitas. See p. 613.

- **La Valencia Hotel** (La Jolla; ☏ **800/451-0772**): Meticulously preserved to look just as it has since opening in 1926, this elegant Spanish-Moorish grande dame is still the choice of celebrities and the centerpiece of La Jolla's charming clifftop "village." The hotel's rich history and lavish good taste are reflected everywhere, and the ocean views are stupendous. See p. 652.

10 The Best Affordable Small Hotels & Inns

- **The Laurel** (San Francisco; ℂ **800/552-8735** or 415/567-8467): Fashionable digs with Zen-like accouterments and ample amenities don't get any cheaper than they do at this posh Pacific Heights neighborhood motel; see p. 89. Runner-up is favorite standby **Hotel Bohème** (San Francisco; ℂ **415/433-9111**). The rooms may be small and lack extra amenities and parking, but they're the prettiest rooms in the heart of North Beach. Plus, you need only step outside your door to find some of the city's best cafes, restaurants, and nightlife. See p. 87.

- **St. Orres** (Gualala; ℂ **707/884-3303**): Designed in a Russian style—complete with two Kremlin-esque onion-domed towers—St. Orres offers secluded accommodations constructed from century-old timbers salvaged from a nearby mill. One of the most eye-catching inns on California's North Coast. See p. 210.

- **Albion River Inn** (Albion; ℂ **800/479-7944**): Easily one of the best rooms-with-a-view on the California coast, the Albion River Inn is dripping with romance. Perched on a cliff overlooking the rugged shoreline, most of the luxuriously appointed rooms have Jacuzzi tubs for two, elevated to window level. Add champagne and you're guaranteed to have a night you won't soon forget. See p. 217.

- **River Ranch Lodge** (Lake Tahoe; ℂ **800/535-9900**): Situated alongside the Truckee River, the River Ranch has long been one of our favorite affordable inns at Lake Tahoe. It has everything you'd want in a mountain lodge: rustic decor, a great bar and outdoor deck overlooking the river (a real party on sunny summer days), a restaurant serving wood-oven–roasted Montana elk loin and other hearty dishes, and a happening après-ski scene thanks to nearby Alpine Meadows and Squaw Valley ski resorts. See p. 258.

- **Olallieberry Inn** (Cambria; ℂ **888/927-3222**): Nestled in the charming town of Cambria, this 1873 Greek Revival house, furnished in a romantic floral-and-lace Victorian style, is a perfect base for exploring Hearst Castle. The gracious innkeepers have your comfort and convenience at heart, providing everything from directions to Moonstone Beach to restaurant recommendations—and a scrumptious breakfast in the morning, of course. See p. 400.

- **Cottage Inn by the Sea** (Pismo Beach; ℂ **888/440-8400**): Feeling more intimate than its 80 rooms would suggest, this affordable seaside hotel is perched above the crashing waves of Pismo Beach with rolling green ranchland as a backdrop. It's the antithesis of the chain motel conformity usually found at this price range, filled with thoughtful touches and better-than-average decor. A retro farmhouse-themed breakfast room is fully stocked each morning; the morning meal is complimentary. See p. 410.

- **Casa Malibu** (Malibu; ℂ **800/831-0858**): This beachfront motel will fool you from the front. Its cheesy 1970s entrance, right on noisy Pacific Coast Highway, belies the quiet, restful charm found within. Situated around the courtyard garden are 21 rooms, many with private decks above the Malibu sands. Rooftops and balconies are festooned with bougainvillea vines, creating an effect reminiscent of a Mexican seaside village. There's easy beach access, and one elegant suite that was Lana Turner's favorite. See p. 469.

• Los Angeles is home to two upstart hangouts, catering to an MTV generation with more style than bucks: **The Standard** (ⓒ 323/650-9090) is a Warhol-hued party place combining 1970s chic, '60s architecture, and jet-age modernity with touches like a barbershop/tattoo parlor in the lobby; see p. 475. Across town, **Avalon Hotel** (ⓒ 800/535-4715) exudes a postwar Hollywood glamour accented with midcentury modern furnishings and a sophisticated 1950s aura inspired by the hotel's classic lines; see p. 473. Both hotels offer

top-of-the-line luxury amenities—at ultra-reasonable rates.

• **Casa Cody** (Palm Springs; ⓒ 760/320-9346): You'll feel more like a house guest at this 1920s Spanish-style *casa* that's blessed with peaceful, blossoming grounds and two swimming pools. The Southwestern-style rooms are large and equipped for extended stays, and the hotel is just a couple of easy blocks from the heart of the action. See p. 611.

• **Gaslamp Plaza Suites** (San Diego; ⓒ 800/874-8770): This impeccably restored Victorian at the center of the vibrant Gaslamp Quarter still boasts the exquisite interiors (the finest wood, marble, etched glass) that must've cost a fortune in 1913. The hotel carries itself with an elegance and drama that belie its bargain rates; room appointments say "indulgence" rather than "economy," too. See p. 641.

11 The Best Places to Stay with the Kids

• **The Lost Whale Bed & Breakfast Inn** (Trinidad; ⓒ 800/677-7859): Parents will love the beautiful inn and the outdoor spa, and kids will love the enclosed play area and the menagerie of horses, goats, and other animals down the road. It has a private beach, and it's near interesting redwood parks. Best of all, no one has to cook because a fabulous breakfast is included. See p. 231.

• **KOA Kamping Kabins** (Point Arena; ⓒ 800/562-4188): Once you see the adorable little log cabins at this KOA campground, you can't help but admit that, rich or poor, this is one cool way to spend the weekend on the coast. Rustic is the key word here: mattresses, a heater, and a light bulb are the standard amenities. All you need

is some bedding (or sleeping bags), cooking and eating utensils, and a bag of charcoal for the barbecue out on the front porch. See p. 212.

• **Camping at Yosemite's Tuolumne Meadows** (ⓒ 800/436-7275): It's especially memorable in late spring, when the meadow is carpeted with wildflowers. At an elevation of 8,600 feet, this is the largest alpine meadow in the High Sierra and a gateway to the "high country." A large campground with a full-scale naturalist program is operated here by park authorities. True adventurers should backpack into the wilderness. See p. 297.

• **City Hotel** and **Fallon Hotel** (Columbia; ⓒ 800/532-1479): Some parents may roll their eyes a bit at this preserved gold-rush town that looks like a television setting, but it's really rather remarkable, with rides on a 100-year-old stagecoach, a working blacksmith shop, lots of relics from mining days to peruse, and Victorian hotels that are reasonably priced and dish up a great buffet breakfast. Cars are barred from the dusty main street so everybody wanders up and down gawking just like they used to. See p. 342.

- **Oceanfront Camping at Big Sur:** Kirk Creek Campground, about 3 miles north of Pacific Valley, offers camping with dramatic ocean views and access to the beach. But there are dozens more—take your pick. See p. 386.

- **Best Western Cavalier Oceanfront Resort** (San Simeon; © **800/826-8168**): Sooner or later, every family visits iconic Hearst Castle, combining a memorable tourist attraction with even more memorable coastal scenery. Maximize the location at this truly oceanfront hotel that's kid-, pet-, and wallet-friendly—plus it's a stone's throw away from Hearst Castle. You can gather for a sunset bonfire overlooking the sea, then step next door to a bevy of casual restaurants; after dinner, rent a PG movie for the in-room VCR. See p. 400.

- **Grey Squirrel Resort** (Big Bear Lake; © **800/381-5569**): Like a camp for kids and adults alike, this cluster of kitchen-equipped cottages near the lake and Big Bear's charming village offers economical lodgings for a single night or the entire season (winter or summer). Enjoy a heated, enclosed pool, fire pit, barbecues, volleyball and basketball courts— plus nearby skiing, boat rental, and plenty of other family recreation. See p. 565.

- **Disneyland Resort Hotels** (Anaheim; © **714/956-MICKEY**): The Holy Grail of Disney-goers has always been the "Official Hotel of the Magic Kingdom," including the original **Disneyland Hotel** (p. 576) and newcomers **Paradise Pier Hotel** (p. 576) and the **Grand Californian** (p. 576). An easy monorail or tram ride to the parks' main gate (the Grand Californian even opens directly into California Adventure) means you'll be able to return to your room anytime, whether to take a much-needed nap or to change your soaked shorts after a water ride. Because they're attractions unto themselves, these hotels are the very best choice for Disney-bound families with small children.

- **Marriott's Desert Springs Spa & Resort** (Palm Desert; © **800/331-3112**): In the spirit of Disneyesque resorts, this enormous oasis welcomes with a whimsical lobby "rain forest" that features tropical birds and gondolas ferrying guests to their rooms. Once settled, kids will find hours worth of fun at the many lagoonlike pools and play areas (supervised children's programs are always available), while grown-ups luxuriate on the golf course, tennis court, or in the 30,000-square-foot day spa. See p. 613.

- **Crystal Pier Hotel** (San Diego; © **800/748-5894**): Occupying a historic private pier that extends into the Pacific Ocean, this property affords guests the unusual experience of actually sleeping *over* the ocean in a darling cottage. Ideal for beach-loving families, who can enjoy the soothing sound of waves or head out for boardwalk action; beach gear is even available for rental. See p. 649.

12 The Best Restaurants

- **San Francisco's Finest:** We can't choose! It's practically sacrilege to even attempt to name the "top" San Francisco restaurant. But for a perfect combo of great food and atmosphere, we always count on **Boulevard** (© 415/543-6084; p. 96), **Restaurant Gary Danko** (© 415/749-2060; p. 101), **Zuni Café** (© 415/552-2522; p. 106) and **Kokkari** (© 415/981-0983; p. 98).

- **Chez Panisse** (Berkeley; © 510/ 548-5525): This is the culinary domain of Alice Waters, often called "the queen of California cuisine." Her food captivates the senses and the imagination. Although originally inspired by the Mediterranean, her kitchen has found its own style. Even Bill Clinton deserted the Big Mac for some Chez Panisse delights, such as grilled fish wrapped in fig leaves with red-wine sauce, and Seckel pears poached in red wine with burnt caramel. See p. 142.

- **Bistro Don Giovanni** (Napa; © 707/224-3300): *Shhh. . . .* Don't tell anyone, but in this Napa Valley dining room you can get an incredible meal without a reservation. Just drop in to the cheery, large restaurant, wait for a seat at the bar, and order off the fantastic Italian menu. It does the trick every time. See p. 183.

- **The French Laundry** (Yountville; © 707/944-2380): The best restaurant in the Wine Country also happens to be one of the top-ranked restaurants in the nation. Renowned chef and owner Thomas Keller, dubbed "Chef of the Nation" in 1997 by judges of the James Beard Award, offers a multicourse masterpiece that almost justifies the 6-month waiting list (though we offer some tips on how to skip the wait). See p. 182.

- **Restaurant 301** (Eureka; © 800/ 404-1390): Mark and Christi Carter are passionate about food and wine, which is why their hotel restaurant has long been considered the very best on the northern coast. Most of the herbs and many of the vegetables served are picked fresh from the hotel's organic gardens across the street. Indulge in their prix-fixe five-course dinner menu—artichoke, green lentil, and fennel salad; warm chèvre cake appetizer; tiger prawns with sesame, ginger, and soy—where each course is paired with a recommended wine by the glass (Mark is a Grand Award recipient from *Wine Spectator* magazine). See p. 228.

- **Erna's Elderberry House** (Oakhurst; © 559/683-6800): It's like a beacon shining across the culinary wasteland of the region around Yosemite. The six-course menu—which changes nightly— is an almost perfect blend of continental and Californian. The food is bountiful and as fully satisfying as the elegant European ambience. Fresh, fresh, fresh— and no natural flavor is cooked beyond recognition. Ingredients are deftly and skillfully handled to bring out their natural flavors. See p. 286.

- **bouchon santa barbara** (Santa Barbara; © 805/730-1160): With an always-intriguing seasonal menu derived from Santa Barbara County's Wine Country and abundant fresh ingredients, this intimate restaurant (whose name means "wine cork") lies hidden behind a grandiose shrubbery portal in the heart of downtown. The food and service are always impeccable, and an experienced staff stands ready to help coordinate by-the-glass (or even half-glass) wines for each course, should you desire. See p. 431.

- **The Ranch House** (Ojai; ℂ 805/646-2360): This charming restaurant has been placing its emphasis on using the freshest vegetables, fruits, and herbs since it opened its doors in 1965, long before it became a national craze. If you stroll through the lush herb garden before your meal, you might later recognize the freshly snipped sprigs that will aromatically transform your simple meat, fish, or game dish into a work of art. See p. 436.

- **Patina** (Los Angeles; ℂ 323/467-1108): The flagship restaurant of superchef Joachim Splichal, who also conceived the (slightly) more affordable Pinot eateries, Patina's menu consistently wows otherwise jaded Angelenos, who keep coming back to this beautifully comfortable Cal-French dining room. Meticulously chosen seasonal menus are always fine-tuned to perfection, featuring partridge, pheasant, or other game in winter, and spotlighting exotic vegetables and tropical fish in summer. See p. 494.

- **Röckenwagner** (Santa Monica; ℂ 310/399-6504): LA's gossipy tongues regularly wag about handsome chef Hans Röckenwagner, but he seems more concerned with maintaining the culinary perfection that propelled him from obscurity in funky Venice to this gallery-like space on Santa Monica's trendy Main Street. Although he trained in Europe, Röckenwagner co-opts ethnic dishes from around the world and elevates them to culinary works of multicultural art. Don't be surprised to find Scandinavian treats like spätzle, Knödel, and smoked salmon sharing space with Pacific Rim elements like mangoes, wasabi, and hoisin. See p. 485.

- **Azzura Point** (Coronado; ℂ 619/424-4000): With its plushly upholstered, gilded, and view-endowed setting, this stylishly contemporary hotel dining room wins continual raves from deep-pocketed San Diego foodies willing to cross the bay for inventive and artistic creations from Azzura Point's pedigreed chefs. For chic fine cuisine, it's definitely the best in town. See "Where to Dine" in chapter 16.

- **George's at the Cove/George's Ocean Terrace** (La Jolla; ℂ 858/454-4244): Tasty smoked chicken-broccoli–black-bean soup is an enduring dish; it's on the menu at the fancy downstairs dining room *and* the breezy upstairs cafe. The two also share an *aah*-inspiring ocean view and attentive service. The downstairs kitchen turns up the finesse factor for inventive and formal California cuisine, while the cafe offers crowd-pleasing versions. See p. 664.

13 The Best Culinary Experiences

- **A Dim Sum Lunch, San Francisco–Style:** Eating a dim sum lunch is like Christmas morning, only the continual stream of presents is edible, including the wrappers. Throughout the meal, waiters stop at your table and offer an exotic selection of appetizer-size Chinese dishes—from dumplings and pot stickers to salt-fried shrimp, shark-fin soup, and stuffed eggplant. No one this side of

China does dim sum as well as San Francisco. Our favorite place to indulge is **Ton Kiang** (© 415/ 387-8273). See p. 106.

- **Dungeness Crab at San Francisco's Fisherman's Wharf:** Crabs, which are best consumed as soon as possible after being cooked, emerge right from boiling pots onto your plate. You crack the shells and pick the delectable meat out. Gastronomes treasure even the edible organs (crab butter) inside the carapace. See "Exploring the City" in chapter 4.

- **Grazing at San Francisco's Farmers Market:** Head to San Francisco's Embarcadero on Tuesday or Saturday morning and join the locals as they feast on the freshest vegetables, fruits, and prepared foods from some of the city's beloved restaurants. See "Exploring the City" in chapter 4.

- **A San Francisco Burrito:** No matter where we go in California, we just can't find a burrito as luscious as those served throughout San Francisco. The tortilla-wrapped meal takes on a gourmet dimension here: flavored tortillas; fresh-grilled meats, fish, and vegetables; three types of beans; a symphony of salsas; guacamole; and sour cream all tidily tucked in the perfect to-go feast. See **Taquerias La Cumbre** on p. 108 in chapter 4.

- **A Decadent Meal in the Wine Country:** The Wine Country atmosphere sets a better stage for indulgent dining than anywhere else in the state. Add the best wines and some of the most talented chefs in the nation and you've got what we consider the ultimate dining experience. Deep-pocketed diners simply must reserve an evening at **The French Laundry** in St. Helena (© 707/ 944-2380)—if, that is, they can

get through to a reservationist; see p. 182. More moderately priced memories can be made at **Bistro Jeanty** (© 707/944-0103; p. 183) and **ZuZu** (© 707/224-8555; p. 186).

- **Gourmet Food Shopping in Napa Valley:** This is gourmet grocery shopping at its finest. New York's **Dean & DeLuca** (© 707/ 967-9980) opened its gastronomic warehouse in 1997 as a world's fair of foods, where everything is beautifully displayed and often painfully pricey. If you're into food, you've got to check this place out. Across the street is the **Oakville Grocery Co.** (© 707/ 944-8802), which has a small-town vibe and crowds liable to send any claustrophobe into a rage. You'll find shelves crammed with perfect picnic provisions. See "Gourmet Picnics, Napa-Style" in chapter 6.

- **Tomales Bay Oysters: Johnson's Oyster Farm** (© 415/669-1149) sells its farm-fresh oysters—by the dozen or the hundreds—for a fraction of the price you'd pay at a restaurant. Our modus operandi is to 1) buy a couple dozen, 2) head for an empty campsite along the bay, 3) fire up the barbecue pit (don't forget the charcoal), 4) split and 'cue the little guys, 5) slather them in Johnson's special sauce, and then 6) slurp 'em down—yum. See "Point Reyes National Seashore" in chapter 7.

- **Grand Central Market** (Los Angeles; © 213/624-2378): Fresh-produce stands, exotic spice and condiment vendors, butchers and fishmongers, and prepared-food counters create a noisy, fragrant, vaguely comforting atmosphere in this LA mainstay. The gem of the airy, cavernous complex is the fresh juice bar at the southwest corner.

A market fixture for many years, it dispenses dozens of varieties from an elaborate system of wall spigots (just like an old-fashioned soda fountain), deftly blending unlikely but heavenly combinations. See "Shopping" in chapter 13.

- **Enjoying a Gourmet Picnic at the Hollywood Bowl:** What better way to spend a typically warm LA evening than under the stars with a picnic basket, bottle of wine, and some naturally amplified entertainment? Home of the Los Angeles Philharmonic, the Bowl hosts visiting performers ranging from chamber music quartets to jazz greats to folk humorists. The imposing white Frank Lloyd Wright–designed band shell always elicits appreciative gasps from first-time Bowlgoers. See p. 542.

- **Sunday Champagne Brunch Aboard the _Queen Mary_** (Long Beach; © **562/435-3511** or 562/432-6964): This elegant ocean liner was the largest, finest vessel when she was built in 1934, and the grandeur of those Atlantic-crossing days remains. A sumptuous buffet-style feast, accompanied by a harp soloist and ice sculpture, is presented in the richly wood-furnished, first-class dining room. Walk off your overindulgence on the spectacular teak decks and through the Art Deco interiors. See p. 552.

- **A Date with the Coachella Valley:** Some 95% of the world's dates are farmed here in the desert. While the groves of date palms make evocative scenery, it's their savory fruit that draws visitors to the National Date Festival in Indio each February. Amid the Arabian Nights Parade and dusty camel races, you can feast on an exotic array of plump Medjool, amber Deglet Noor, caramel-like Halawy, and buttery Empress dates. The rest of the year, date farms and markets throughout the valley sell dates from the season's harvest, as well as date milkshakes, sticky-date coconut rolls, and more. See "Sweet Treat of the Desert: The Coachella Valley Date Gardens" in chapter 15.

- **San Diego County Farmers Markets:** The bountiful harvest of San Diego County is sold on various days at moveable markets throughout the area. Finds are fresh local fruits, vegetables, and flowers, as well as specialty items such as raw apple cider (in the fall), macadamia nuts, and rhubarb pies. See "Shopping" in chapter 16.

14 The Best of the Performing Arts & Special Events

- **The San Francisco Opera:** This world-class company performs at the War Memorial Opera House, which is modeled after the Opéra Garnier in Paris. The opera season opens with a gala in September and runs through December. This was the first municipal opera in the United States, and its brilliant productions and members have been acclaimed by critics throughout the world. See p. 132.

- **The American Conservatory Theater** (San Francisco): The A.C.T. is one of the nation's leading regional theaters, dating from 1967. It's been called the American equivalent of the British National Theatre, the Berliner Ensemble, and the Comédie Française in Paris. Both classical and experimental works are brilliantly performed. See p. 132.

- **World Championship Great Arcata to Ferndale Cross-Country Kinetic Sculpture Race** (Arcata; © **800/346-3482**): One of California's most bizarre outdoor events, the Kinetic Sculpture Race is a 3-day event held every Memorial Day weekend where wacky handmade people-powered vehicles trudge 38 miles over land, sand, mud, and water. This kooky competition draws more than 10,000 rowdy spectators. Pure madness. See "The Avenue of the Giants" in chapter 7.
- **The Monterey Jazz Festival** (© **800/307-3378**): When the third weekend of September rolls around, the Monterey Fairgrounds hosts this fabled classic, drawing jazz fans from around the world. The 3-day festival (which is usually sold out about a month in advance) is known for presenting the sweetest jazz west of the Mississippi. See "California Calendar of Events" in chapter 2.
- **The Hollywood Bowl** (Los Angeles): This iconic outdoor amphitheater is the summer home of the Los Angeles Philharmonic, a stage for visiting virtuosos—including the occasional pop star—and the setting for several splendid fireworks shows throughout the summer. Those lucky enough to obtain box seats can set their own private table. See p. 542.
- **The Viper Room** (Los Angeles): Head to this West Hollywood closet for a glimpse of LA's hippest scene. Owner Johnny Depp took this small but historic club space on the famous Sunset Strip and gave it an atmospheric Art Deco vibe. Visiting celebrities

and musicians can be found mingling and listening to live bands every night of the week. After midnight or so, don't be surprised if big-name recording artists take the stage for an impromptu jam. See p. 544.
- **Festival of Arts & Pageant of the Masters** (Laguna Beach): These events draw enormous crowds to the Orange County coast every July and August. Begun in 1932 by a handful of area painters, the festival has grown to showcase hundreds of artists. In the evening, crowds marvel at the Pageant of the Masters' *tableaux vivants,* in which costumed townsfolk pose convincingly inside a giant frame and depict famous works of art, accompanied by music and narration. See "The Orange Coast" in chapter 14.
- **The Globe Theatres** (San Diego): This Tony Award–winning theater, fashioned after Shakespeare's original stage, produced the revival of *Damn Yankees,* and has billed such notable performers as John Goodman, Marsha Mason, Cliff Robertson, Jon Voight, and Christopher Walken. See p. 686.
- **La Jolla Playhouse:** Winner of the 1993 Tony Award for Outstanding American Regional Theater, the LJ Playhouse stages six productions each year in its 400-seat Mandell Weiss Theater and 400-seat Mandell Weiss Forum on the campus of UCSD. Expect a fair share of nationally acclaimed directors and highly touted revivals, such as when Matthew Broderick starred in *How to Succeed in Business Without Really Trying* before it went on to Broadway accolades. See p. 687.

15 The Best Websites

- **California National Parks (www. nps.gov/parklists/ca.html):** California has preserved much of its glorious heritage in its parks. The state is home to about two dozen national parks, monuments, seashores, and recreation areas. The National Park Service's index includes detailed information on visiting, camping, getting around, and recommended activities.

- **CitySearch San Francisco (bay area.citysearch.com):** The substantial articles and listings cover all of the city's entertainment highlights. The events calendar links to goings-on throughout the Bay Area; the "Visitor" section includes tips on getting around.

- **San Francisco Chronicle (sfgate. com):** Find out the latest on restaurants, arts, and general local happenings at this information-packed site.

- **Oakland.com (www.oakland. com):** This site offers numerous links to attractions, shopping, and the arts around Oakland; in addition, its Dining section offers detailed descriptions and recommendations.

- **Ganna Walska Lotusland (www. lotusland.org):** Available spots for the intimate—and intriguing—tours of this extraordinary garden estate in the rich Santa Barbara hills can be nearly impossible for all but the most diligent advance planners to find. But you can take a detailed virtual tour online and learn all about this highly personal garden's unique benefactress, the rare and beautiful cacti and succulents she favored, and the modern gardening science that helps the many nearly extinct varieties thrive.

- *Los Angeles* **Magazine (www.la mag.com):** The online edition of *Los Angeles* magazine offers "The Guide," an oft-updated listing of LA's theater, music scene, museums, and more, as well as an excellent "Dining Out" guide listing hundreds of restaurants organized geographically. Very cool.

- **@LA (www.at-la.com):** This exceptional search engine (much-used by savvy locals) provides links to almost 60,000 sites in thousands of categories related to all of Southern California.

- **Disneyland Resort (www. disneyland.com):** Check out the resorts, dining facilities, travel package options, and activities and rides in the Magic Kingdom. Get specific hours and ride closures in advance by selecting the day of your visit; this site is guaranteed to rev up your enthusiasm level.

- **Palm Springs Desert Resorts Convention and Visitors Authority (www.palmsprings usa.com):** If it relates to the Coachella Valley resort cities, you'll find it on this website. Whether you need information on the latest desert recreation trends, answers to FAQs, or links to just about every other desert URL, it's all a mouse-click away. True desert rats can even sign up for their free monthly e-newsletter.

- **San Diego Zoo (www.sandiego zoo.com):** The zoo site is organized by exhibit, with descriptions and photos previewing all the resident critters. Details are provided on tours, plus directions and other logistical information.

2

Planning Your Trip to California

by Stephanie Avnet Yates

In the pages that follow, we've compiled everything you need to know to handle the practical details of planning your trip in advance—from making campsite reservations to finding great deals on the Internet, plus a calendar of events and much more.

1 Visitor Information & Money

VISITOR INFORMATION

For information on the state as a whole, contact the **California Office of Tourism,** 801 K St., Suite 1600, Sacramento, CA 95812 (✆ **800/GO-CALIF;** www.gocalif.ca.gov), and ask for a free information packet. In addition, almost every city and town in the state has a dedicated tourist bureau or chamber of commerce that will be happy to send you information on its particular parcel. These are listed under the appropriate headings in the geographically organized chapters that follow.

International travelers should also see chapter 3, "For International Visitors," for entry requirements and other pertinent information.

INFORMATION ON CALIFORNIA'S PARKS To find out more about California's national parks, contact the **Pacific West Region Information Center,** National Park Service, 1111 Jackson St., Suite 700, Oakland, CA 94607 (✆ **510/817-1300;** www.nps.gov). Reservations can be made at national park campsites by calling ✆ **800/365-CAMP** (800/436-PARK for Yosemite) or logging on to **http://reservations.nps.gov.**

For information on state parks, contact the **Department of Parks and Recreation,** P.O. Box 942896, Sacramento, CA 94296-0001 (✆ **800/777-0369;** http://cal-parks.ca.gov). Thousands of campsites are on the department's reservation system, and can be booked up to 8 weeks in advance by calling **Park-Net** at ✆ **800/444-PARK.** You can also get reservations information online at **www.reserveamerica.com.**

For information on fishing and hunting licenses, contact the **California Department of Fish and Game,** License and Revenue Branch, 3211 S St., Sacramento, CA 95816 (✆ **916/227-2245;** www.dfg.ca.gov).

MONEY

ATMs are linked to networks that most likely include your bank at home. **Cirrus** (✆ 800/424-7787; www.mastercard.com) and **Plus** (✆ 800/843-7587; www.visa.com) are the two most popular networks in the United States; call or check online for ATM locations in California. Be sure to find out your daily withdrawal limit before you depart. Keep in mind that many banks impose a fee every time a card is used at an ATM in a different bank. On top of this, the bank from which you withdraw cash may charge its own fee.

You can also get cash advances on your credit card at an ATM if you know your personal identification number (PIN). If you've forgotten yours, or didn't even know you had one, call the number on the back of your credit card and ask the bank to send it to you. It usually takes 5 to 7 business days, though some banks will provide the number over the phone if you tell them your mother's maiden name or pass some other security clearance. Keep in mind that credit-card companies try to protect themselves from theft by limiting the funds someone can withdraw away from home. It's therefore best to call your credit-card company before you leave and let them know where you're going and how much you plan to spend.

Almost every credit-card company has an emergency toll-free number to call if your card is stolen. Be sure to block charges against your account immediately and file a police report. Your credit-card company may be able to wire you a cash advance off your credit card immediately, and in many places, they can deliver an emergency credit card in a day or two. To report a lost or stolen card, contact **Visa** at ✆ 800/336-8472; **American Express,** ✆ 800/221-7282; **MasterCard,** ✆ 800/307-7309; **Discover,** ✆ 800/347-2683; or **Diners Club,** ✆ 800/234-6377.

2 When to Go

CLIMATE

California's climate is so varied that it's impossible to generalize about the state as a whole.

San Francisco's temperate marine climate means relatively mild weather year-round. In summer, temperatures rarely top 70°F (21°C; pack sweaters, even in Aug), and the city's famous fog rolls in most mornings and evenings. In winter, the mercury seldom falls below freezing, and snow is almost unheard of. Because of San Francisco's fog, summer rarely sees more than a few hot days in a row. Head a few miles inland, though, and it's likely to be clear and hot.

The Central Coast shares San Francisco's climate, although it gets warmer as you get farther south. Seasonal changes are less pronounced south of San Luis Obispo, where temperatures remain relatively stable year-round. The northern coast is rainier and foggier; winters tend to be mild but wet.

Summers are refreshingly cool around Lake Tahoe and in the Shasta Cascades—a perfect climate for hiking, camping, and other outdoor activities and a popular escape for residents of California's sweltering deserts and valleys who are looking to beat the heat. Skiers flock to this area for terrific snowfall from late November to early April.

Southern California—including Los Angeles and San Diego—is usually much warmer than the Bay Area, and it gets significantly more sun. This is the place to hit the beach. Even in winter, daytime thermometer readings regularly reach into the 60s°F (15°C–20°C) and warmer. Summers can be stifling inland, but Southern California's coastal communities are always comfortable. The area's limited rainfall is generally seen between January and mid-April, and is rarely intense enough to be more than a slight inconvenience. It's possible to sunbathe throughout the year, but only die-hard enthusiasts and wet-suited surfers venture into the ocean in winter. The water is warmest in summer and fall, but even then, the Pacific is too chilly for many.

The deserts, including Palm Springs and the desert national parks, are sizzling hot in summer; temperatures regularly top 100°F (38°C). Winter is the time to visit the desert resorts (and remember, it gets surprisingly cold at night in the desert).

San Francisco's Average Temperatures (°F)

	Jan	Feb	Mar	Apr	May	June	July	Aug	Sept	Oct	Nov	Dec
Avg. High	56	59	60	61	63	64	64	65	69	68	63	57
Avg. Low	46	48	49	49	51	53	53	54	56	55	52	47

Los Angeles's Average Temperatures (°F)

	Jan	Feb	Mar	Apr	May	June	July	Aug	Sept	Oct	Nov	Dec
Avg. High	65	66	67	69	72	75	81	81	81	77	73	69
Avg. Low	46	48	49	52	54	57	60	60	59	55	51	49

AVOIDING THE CROWDS

If you're planning a summertime visit, you're not alone. The period between Memorial Day and Labor Day is the height of the tourism season virtually everywhere in the state—except for desert areas like Palm Springs and Death Valley, where sizzling temperatures keep all but the hardiest bargain hunters away. California's pleasant summer weather (with relatively low humidity) has a lot to do with these numbers, but the season is also popular simply because that's when most people, especially families with kids, get to take that precious vacation time. So, naturally, prices are highest between May and September in much of the state, and can fall dramatically outside of that period—exceptions to this rule include the aforementioned deserts and winter ski resorts. *Insider tip:* What Californians know, however, is the best time to travel the state is autumn—roughly from late September to early December—when crowds drop off, "shoulder season" rates kick in, and winter rains are still months away. In fact, you might be lucky enough to enjoy the renewed warm days of "Indian summer" that often occur during the autumn season.

CALIFORNIA CALENDAR OF EVENTS

January

Tournament of Roses, Pasadena. A spectacular parade down Colorado Boulevard, with lavish floats, music, and extraordinary equestrian entries, followed by the Rose Bowl Game. Call © **626/449-4100** or visit www.tournamentofroses.com for details, or just stay home and watch it on TV (you'll have a better view). January 1.

Bob Hope Chrysler Classic, Palm Springs Desert Resorts. 2003 marks the 44th year of this weeklong PGA golf tournament, which raises money for charity and includes a celebrity-studded Pro-Am. For spectator information and tickets, call © **888/MR-BHOPE** or 760/346-8184. Mid- to late January.

AT&T Pebble Beach National Pro-Am, Pebble Beach. A PGA-sponsored tour where pros are teamed with celebrities to compete on three world-famous golf courses. Call © **800/541-9091** or 831/649-1533, or visit www.attpbgolf.com. Late January.

February

Chinese New Year Festival & Parade. The largest Chinese New Year festival in the United States is in San Francisco. The celebration includes a Golden Dragon parade with lion dancing, marching bands, a street fair, flower sales, and festive food. Call © **415/982-3000** or visit www.chineseparade.com for the 2003 schedule.

LA's celebration is colorful as well, with dragon dancers parading through the streets of downtown's Chinatown. Chinese opera and other events are scheduled. For this year's schedule, contact the Chinese Chamber of Commerce at ℂ **213/ 617-0396.**

National Date Festival, Indio. Crowds gather to celebrate the Coachella Valley desert's most beloved cash crop with appropriately themed events like camel and ostrich races, the Blessing of the Date Garden, and festive Arabian Nights pageants. Plenty of date-sampling booths are set up, along with rides, food vendors, and other county-fair trappings. Call ℂ **800/ 811-3247** or 760/863-8247, or visit www.datefest.org. Two weeks in February.

Mustard Festival, Napa Valley. Celebrating the blossom of yellow-petalled mustard flowers, which coat the valley during February and March, the event was originally conceived to drum up interest in visiting during this once-slow season. The festival has evolved into 6 weeks of events ranging from a kick-off gourmet gala at the CIA Greystone to a wine auction, golf benefit, recipe and photography competitions, and plenty of food and wine celebrations. For information and a schedule of events, call ℂ **707/259-9020** or 707/938-1133, or visit online at www. mustardfestival.com. February and March.

March

Return of the Swallows, San Juan Capistrano. Each St. Joseph's Day, visitors flock to this charming village for the arrival of the mission's loyal flock of swallows that will nest and remain until October. The celebration includes a parade, dances, and special programs. Call ℂ **949/ 248-2048** for details. March 19.

Santa Barbara International Film Festival. For 10 days each March, pretty Santa Barbara does its best impression of Cannes. There's a flurry of foreign and independent film premieres, personal appearances by noted actors and directors, and symposia on hot cinematic topics. For a rundown of events, call ℂ **805/963-0023;** www.sbfilm festival.org. Mid-March.

Kraft Nabisco Championship, Rancho Mirage. This 33-year-old LPGA golf tournament takes place near Palm Springs. After the celebrity Pro-Am early in the week, the best female pros get down to business. For further information, call ℂ **760/324-4546** or visit www.nabiscochampionship.com. Other special-interest events for women usually take place around the tournament, including the country's largest annual lesbian gathering. Last week of March.

Redwood Coast Dixieland Jazz Festival, Eureka. Three days of jazz featuring 12 of the best Dixieland groups, including a variety of jam sessions. Call ℂ **707/445-3378.** Late March.

April

San Francisco International Film Festival. One of the oldest film festivals in the United States, featuring more than 100 films and videos from more than 30 countries. Tickets are relatively inexpensive, and screenings are very accessible to the general public during 2 weeks mid-month. Call ℂ **415/931-FILM** or visit www.sffs.org.

Toyota Grand Prix, Long Beach. An exciting weekend of Indy-class auto racing and entertainment in and around downtown Long Beach, drawing world-class drivers from the United States and Europe. Contact the **Grand Prix Association** at ℂ **888/52-SPEED** or 562/981-2600, or www.longbeachgp.com. Mid-April.

Renaissance Pleasure Faire, San Bernardino. One of America's largest Renaissance festivals, this annual happening is set in Glen Helen Regional Park in LA's relatively remote countryside. Performers (and many attendees) dress in 16th-century costume and revel in this festive re-creation of a medieval English village. For ticket information, call ℂ **800/52-FAIRE** or log on to http://renaissance-faire.com. Weekends from late April to Memorial Day.

Ramona Pageant, Hemet. A unique outdoor play that portrays the lives of the Southern California Mission Indians. The play was adapted from Helen Hunt Jackson's 1884 novel *Ramona.* Call ℂ **909/658-3111** or visit www.ramona pageant.com for details. Late April to early May.

Del Mar National Horse Show. Horse-and-rider teams compete in national championships at the Del Mar Fairgrounds. Call ℂ **858/792-4288** or 858/755-1161 for more information. Late April to early May.

May

Cinco de Mayo. A weeklong celebration of one of Mexico's most jubilant holidays takes place throughout the city of Los Angeles near May 5. The fiesta's carnival-like atmosphere is created by large crowds, live music, dances, and food. The main festivities are held in El Pueblo de Los Angeles State Historic Park, downtown, with other events around the city. Call ℂ **213/485-6855** for information. There's also a Cinco de Mayo celebration in San Diego, featuring folkloric music, dance, food, and historical reenactments. It's held in Old Town. Call ℂ **619/296-3161** for more information.

Calaveras County Fair and Jumping Frog Jubilee, Angels Camp. The event is inspired by Mark Twain's story "The Celebrated Jumping Frog of Calaveras County." Entrants from all over the world arrive with their frog participants. There's also a children's parade, livestock competition, rodeo, carnival, and fireworks. Call ℂ **209/736-2561** or visit www.frog town.org. Third weekend in May.

Bay to Breakers Foot Race, San Francisco. One of the city's most popular annual events, it's really more fun than run. Thousands of entrants show up dressed—or undressed—in their best costumes for the approximately 7½-mile run. Call ℂ **415/777-7770** or log on to www.baytobreakers.com. Third Sunday of May.

Paso Robles Wine Festival. What began as a small, neighborly gathering has grown into the largest outdoor wine tasting in California. The 3-day event features winery open houses and tastings, a golf tournament, 5K run and 10K bike ride, and concerts, plus a carnival-like festival in downtown's City Park. For a schedule of events and fees, call ℂ **800/549-WINE** or visit www.pasowine.com. Third weekend in May.

Carnival, San Francisco. The Mission District's largest annual event is a 2-day series of festivities that culminates with a parade on Mission Street over Memorial Day weekend. More than half a million spectators line the route, and the samba musicians and dancers continue to play on 14th Street, near Harrison, at the end of the march. Call the **Mission Economic and Cultural Association** at ℂ **415/826-1401.** Memorial Day weekend.

June

Playboy Jazz Festival, Los Angeles. Bill Cosby is the traditional master of ceremonies, presiding over top artists at the Hollywood Bowl. Call ℂ **310/449-4070.** Mid-June.

Lesbian & Gay Freedom Day Parade. It's celebrated all over the state, but San Francisco's party draws up to half a million participants. The parade's start and finish have been moved around in recent years to accommodate road construction, but traditionally it begins and ends at Civic Center Plaza, where hundreds of food, art, and information booths are set up around several soundstages. Call ℂ **415/864-3733** for information. Usually the third or last weekend of June.

Ojai Music Festival. This 5-day event has been drawing world-class classical and jazz personalities to the open-air Libbey Bowl since 1947. Past events have featured Igor Stravinsky, Aaron Copland, and the Juilliard String Quartet. Seats (and local lodgings) fill up quickly; call ℂ **805/646-2094** for more information, or log on to www.ojai festival.org. First half of June.

Mariachi USA Festival, Los Angeles. A 2-day family-oriented celebration of Mexican culture and tradition at the Hollywood Bowl, where festival-goers pack their picnic baskets and enjoy music, ballet folklorico, and related performances by special guests. Call ℂ **323/848-7717.** Late June.

July

Mammoth Lakes Jazz Jubilee. A 4-day festival featuring 20 bands on 10 different stages, plus food, drink, and dancing—all under the pine trees and stars. Call ℂ **800/ 367-6572** or 760/934-2478. Second weekend in July.

Festival of Arts & Pageant of the Masters, Laguna Beach. A fantastic performance-art production in which live actors re-create famous old-masters paintings.

Other festivities include live music, crafts sales, art demonstrations and workshops, and the grass-roots Sawdust Festival across the street. Grounds admission is $3 to $5; pageant tickets range from $15 to $65. Call ℂ **800/487-FEST** or 949/494-1145, or check out www.foapom.com. July through August.

Gilroy Garlic Festival. A gourmet food fair with more than 85 booths serving garlicky food from almost every ethnic background, plus close to 100 arts, crafts, and entertainment booths. Call ℂ **831/842-1625** or visit www.gilroygarlic festival.com. Last full weekend in July.

Shakespeare at the Beach, Lake Tahoe. A bewitching experience of the Bard at Sand Harbor on the shore beneath the stars. Call ℂ **702/832-1606.** Three weeks in late July and August.

Beach Festival, Huntington Beach. Two straight weeks of fun in the sun, featuring two surfing competitions—the U.S. Open of Surfing *and* the world-class Pro of Surfing—plus several extreme sport events such as in-line skating, BMX biking, skateboarding, and more. Includes entertainment, food, tons of product booths and giveaways— and plenty of tanned, swimsuit-clad bodies of both sexes. For more information, call ℂ **714/969-3492** or log on to www.hbvisit.com. End of July.

August

Old Spanish Days Fiesta, Santa Barbara. The city's biggest annual event, this 5-day festival features a grand parade with horse-drawn carriages, music and dance performances, *mercados* (marketplaces), and a rodeo. Call ℂ **805/962-8101** or visit www.oldspanishdays-fiesta.org. Early August.

Nisei Week Japanese Festival, Los Angeles. This weeklong celebration of Japanese culture and heritage is held in Little Tokyo at the Japanese American Cultural and Community Center Plaza. Festivities include parades, food, music, arts, and crafts. Call © 213/687-7193. Mid-August.

California State Fair, Sacramento. At the California Exposition Grounds, a gala celebration with livestock, carnival food, exhibits, and entertainment on 10 different stages, plus thoroughbred racing and a 1-mile monorail for panoramic views over the scope of it all. Call © 916/263-FAIR or visit www.bigfun.org. Late August to early September.

September

Los Angeles County Fair. Horse racing, arts, agricultural displays, celebrity entertainment, and carnival rides are among the attractions of the largest county fair in the world, held at the Los Angeles County Fair and Exposition Center, in Pomona. Call © 909/623-3111 or visit www.fairplex.com for information. Throughout September.

Sausalito Art Festival. A juried exhibit of more than 180 artists. It's accompanied by music provided by Bay Area jazz, rock, and blues performers and international cuisine enhanced by wines from some 50 different Napa and Sonoma producers. Call © 415/332-3555 or log on to www.sausalitoartfestival.org for information. Labor Day weekend.

San Diego Street Scene. The historic Gaslamp Quarter is transformed by this 3-day extravaganza featuring food, dance, international character, and live music on 12 separate stages. Saturday is set aside as an all-ages day; attendees must be 21 or over the other 2 days. Call

© 619/557-0505 for more information. First weekend after Labor Day.

Monterey Jazz Festival. Features top names in traditional and modern jazz. One of the oldest annual jazz festivals in the world. Call © 800/307-3378 or 831/373-0244. Mid-September.

Danish Days, Solvang. Since 1936 this 3-day event has been celebrating old-world customs and pageantry with a parade, gymnastics exhibitions by local schoolchildren, demonstrations of traditional Danish arts and crafts, and plenty of *aebleskivers* (Danish fritters) and *medisterpolse* (Danish sausage). Call © 800/GO-SOLVANG for further information.

Watts Towers Day of the Drum Festival, Los Angeles. Celebrating the historic role of drums and drummers, this event features a variety of unique performances, from Afro-Cuban folkloricos to East Indian tabla players. Call © 213/ 847-4646. Late September.

October

Catalina Island Jazz Trax Festival. Great contemporary jazz artists travel to the island to play in the legendary Avalon Casino Ballroom. The festival is held over two consecutive 3-day weekends. Call © 888/330-5252 or visit www.jazztrax.com for advance ticket sales and a schedule of performers. Early October.

Sonoma County Harvest Fair, Sonoma County Fairgrounds. A 3-day celebration of the harvest with exhibitions, art shows, and annual judging of the local wines. Call © 707/545-4203. Dates vary.

The Half Moon Bay Art & Pumpkin Festival, Half Moon Bay. The festival features a Great Pumpkin Parade, pie-eating contests, a pumpkin-carving competition, arts and crafts, and all manner of squash cuisine. The highlight of the event is the Giant Pumpkin weigh-in contest, won recently by an 875-pound monster. Colorful to the extreme. For exact date and details, call the Pumpkin Hotline at ✆ 650/726-9652.

Western Regional Final Championship Rodeo, Lakeside. Top cowboys from 11 western states compete in seven rodeo events, including calf roping, barrel racing, bull riding, team roping, and steer wrestling. Held at the Lakeside Rodeo Grounds, Calif. 67 and Mapleview Avenue, Lakeside. Call ✆ 619/561-4331. Mid-October.

Halloween, San Francisco. The City by the Bay celebrates with a fantastical parade organized at Market and Castro, and a mixed gay-straight crowd revels in costumes of extraordinary imagination. October 31.

November

Doo Dah Parade, Pasadena. An outrageous spoof of the Rose Parade, featuring participants such as the Precision Briefcase Drill Team and a kazoo band. Call ✆ 626/440-7379. Sunday before Thanksgiving.

Hollywood Christmas Parade. This spectacular star-studded parade marches through the heart of Hollywood. For more information, call ✆ 323/469-2337. Sunday after Thanksgiving.

December

How the Grinch Stole Christmas, San Diego. In honor of the late Theodor Geisel ("Dr. Seuss," a

 Whale-Watching

Each winter, pods of California gray whales making their annual migration from their Alaskan feeding grounds to breeding lagoons at the southern tip of Baja pass close by California shores; if you've ever been lucky enough to spot one of these graceful behemoths, you'll understand why whale-watching is such an eagerly anticipated activity. From December to March, you can view this spectacular parade from land or sea. Recommended spots include **Point Reyes National Seashore** (✆ 415/669-1534), where a historic lighthouse offers whale- and elephant-seal–viewing; **Monterey Peninsula,** where January's WhaleFest (✆ 831/644-7588) celebrates these special mammals from the Monterey Aquarium down through Big Sur; **Point Vicente Lighthouse and Interpretive Center** (✆ 562/377-5370), on the windswept Palos Verdes Peninsula south of Los Angeles; and San Diego's **Cabrillo National Monument** (✆ 619/557-5450; www.nps.gov/cabr), which offers a glassed-in observatory and educational whale exhibits.

Boat excursions depart from a number of locations, including **Morro Bay** (Virg's Landing, ✆ 800/762-5263 or 805/772-1222), **Santa Barbara** (The Condor, ✆ 888/77-WHALE or 805/963-3564), **Ventura Harbor** (Island Packers, ✆ 805/642-1393; www.islandpackers.com), and **San Diego** (San Diego Harbor Excursions, ✆ 800/442-7847 or 619/234-4111). Also in San Diego, the **Natural History Museum** (✆ 619/232-3821, ext. 203; www.sdnhm.org) offers fascinating, naturalist-led, half-day whale-watching trips for passengers 12 and older.

former San Diego resident), the lobby of Loews Coronado Bay Resort is transformed into Whoville, where the Cat in the Hat assembles eager young audiences for regular readings of the beloved Christmas story. Punch and cookies are served at this free event, and carolers also perform following each reading. For more information, call ✆ **619/424-4000.** December 1 to December 24.

Christmas Boat Parade of Lights. Following longstanding tradition, sailors love to decorate their craft with colorful lights for the holidays. Several Southern California harbors hold nighttime parades to showcase these creations, which range from tiny dinghies draped with a single strand of lights to showy yachts with entire Nativity scenes twinkling on deck. Call the following for schedules and information: **Ventura Harbor** (✆ 805/382-3001), **Marina Del Rey** (Los Angeles; ✆ 310/821-0555), **Long Beach** (✆ 562/435-4093), **Huntington Harbour** (✆ 714/840-7542), or **Mission Bay** (San Diego; ✆ 619/488-0501).

New Year's Eve Torchlight Parade, Big Bear Lake. Watch dozens of nighttime skiers follow a serpentine path down Snow Summit's ski slopes bearing glowing torches—it's one of the state's loveliest traditions. Afterward, the party continues indoors with live bands and plenty to eat and drink. For more information on this 21-and-over event, call ✆ **909/866-5766** or visit www. snowsummit.com.

3 Insurance

TRAVEL INSURANCE AT A GLANCE

Check your existing insurance policies before you buy travel insurance to cover trip cancellation, lost luggage, or medical expenses. You're likely to have partial or complete coverage. But if you need some, ask your travel agent about a comprehensive package. The cost of travel insurance varies widely, depending on the cost and length of your trip, your age and overall health, and the type of trip you're taking. Insurance for extreme sports or adventure travel, for example, will cost more than coverage for a cruise. Some insurers provide packages for specialty vacations, such as skiing or backpacking. More dangerous activities may be excluded from basic policies. And keep in mind that in the aftermath of the World Trade Center attacks, a number of airlines, cruise lines, and tour operators are no longer covered by insurers. *The bottom line:* Always, always check the fine print before you sign on; more and more policies have built-in exclusions and restrictions that may leave you out in the cold if something does go awry.

For information, contact one of the following popular insurers:

- **Access America** (✆ 800/284-8300; www.accessamerica.com)
- **Travel Guard International** (✆ 800/826-1300; www.travel guard.com)
- **Travel Insured International** (✆ 800/243-3174; www.travel insured.com)
- **Travelex Insurance Services** (✆ 800/228-9792; www.travelex-insurance.com)

TRIP-CANCELLATION INSURANCE (TCI)

There are three major types of trip-cancellation insurance—one, in the event that you prepay a cruise or tour that gets cancelled, and you can't get your money back; a second when you or someone in your family gets sick or dies, and you can't travel (but beware that you may not be covered for a pre-existing condition); and a third, when bad weather makes travel impossible. Some insurers provide coverage for events like jury duty; natural disasters close to home, like floods or fire; even the loss of a job. A few have added provisions for cancellations due to terrorist activities. Always check the fine print before signing on, and don't buy trip-cancellation insurance from the tour operator that may be responsible for the cancellation; buy it only from a reputable travel insurance agency. Don't overbuy—you won't be reimbursed for more than the cost of your trip.

MEDICAL INSURANCE

If you worry about getting sick away from home, consider purchasing medical travel insurance and carry your ID card in your purse or wallet. In most cases, your existing health plan will provide the coverage you need—but check, particularly if you're insured by an HMO. Members of **Blue Cross/Blue Shield** can now use their cards at select hospitals in most major cities worldwide (✆ **800/810-BLUE** or www.bluecares.com for a list of hospitals).

If you suffer from a chronic illness, consult your doctor before your departure. For conditions like epilepsy, diabetes, or heart problems, wear a **MedicAlert Identification Tag** (✆ **800/825-3785;** www.medic alert.org), which will immediately alert doctors to your condition and give them access to your records through MedicAlert's 24-hour hot line.

Some credit cards (American Express and certain gold and platinum Visa and MasterCards, for example) offer automatic flight insurance against death or dismemberment in case of an airplane crash if you charged the cost of your ticket.

If you require additional insurance, try one of the following companies:

- **MEDEX International,** 9515 Dereeco Rd., Timonium, MD 21093-5375 (✆ 888/MEDEX-00 or 410/453-6300; fax 410/453-6301; www.medexassist.com)
- **Travel Assistance International,** 9200 Keystone Crossing, Suite 300, Indianapolis, IN 46240 (✆ **800/821-2828;** www.travel assistance.com; for general information on services, call the company's Worldwide Assistance Services, Inc., at ✆ **800/777-8710**).

LOST-LUGGAGE INSURANCE

On domestic flights, checked baggage is covered up to $2,500 per ticketed passenger. If you plan to check items more valuable than the standard liability, you may purchase "excess valuation" coverage from the airline, up to $5,000. Be sure to take any valuables or irreplaceable items with you in your carry-on luggage. If you file a lost-luggage claim, be prepared to answer detailed questions about the contents of your baggage, and be sure to file a claim immediately, as most airlines enforce a 21-day deadline. Before you leave home, compile an inventory of all packed items and a rough estimate of the total value to ensure you're properly compensated if your luggage is lost. You will only be reimbursed for what you lost, no more. Once you've filed a complaint, persist in securing your reimbursement; there are no laws governing the length of time it takes for a carrier to reimburse you. If you arrive at a destination without your bags, ask the airline to forward them to your hotel or to your next destination; they will usually comply. If your bag is delayed or lost, the airline may reimburse you for reasonable expenses, such as a toothbrush or a set of clothes, but the airline is under no legal obligation to do so.

Lost luggage may also be covered by your homeowner's or renter's policy. Many platinum and gold credit cards cover you as well. If you choose to purchase additional lost-luggage insurance, be sure not to buy more than you need. Buy in advance from the insurer or a trusted agent (prices will be much higher at the airport).

4 Tips for Travelers with Special Needs

TRAVELERS WITH DISABILITIES

California's spirit of tolerance and diversity has made it a welcoming place for travelers with disabilities. Strict construction codes make most public facilities and attractions extremely accessible (though some historic sites and older buildings simply can't accommodate drastic remodeling), and the state provides many services for those with disabilities.

A little advance planning is always useful. There are more resources out there than ever before. *A World of Options,* a 658-page book for travelers with disabilities, covers everything from biking trips to scuba outfitters. It costs $45 (less for members) and is available from **Mobility International USA,** P.O. Box 10767, Eugene, OR 97440 (℡ **541/343-1284,** voice and TTY; www.miusa.org). Annual membership for Mobility International is $35, which includes their quarterly newsletter, *Over the Rainbow.*

You can join **The Society for Accessible Travel & Hospitality** (SATH), 347 Fifth Ave., Suite 610, New York, NY 10016 (℡ **212/ 447-7284;** www.sath.org), for $45 annually, $30 for seniors and students, to gain access to a vast network of connections in the travel industry. The society provides information sheets on travel destinations and referrals to tour operators that specialize in travelers with disabilities. Its quarterly magazine, *Open World,* is full of good information and resources. A year's subscription is included with membership, or costs $18 ($35 outside the U.S.).

Access-Able Travel Source is a homegrown online tip sheet that offers a comprehensive online index of accessible hotels, restaurants, attractions, and disabled-service providers around the country; log on to www.access-able.com or call ℡ **303/ 232-2979.**

The U.S. National Park Service offers a **Golden Access Passport** that gives free lifetime entrance to U.S. national parks for persons who are blind or permanently disabled, regardless of age. You may pick up a Golden Access Passport at any NPS entrance-fee area by showing proof of medically determined disability and eligibility for receiving benefits under federal law. Besides free entry, the Golden Access Passport also offers a 50% discount on federal-use fees charged for such facilities as camping, swimming, parking, boat launching, and tours. For more information, click onto www.nps.gov/fees_passes.htm or call ℡ **888/GO-PARKS.**

Many of the major car-rental companies now offer hand-controlled cars for drivers with disabilities. **Avis** (℡ **800/230-4898;** www.avis.com) can provide such a vehicle at any of its locations in the United States with 48-hour advance notice; **Hertz** (℡ **800/ 654-3131;** www.hertz.com) requires between 24 and 72 hours of advance reservation at most of its locations. **Wheelchair Getaways** (℡ **800/642-2042;** www.wheelchair-getaways.com) rents specialized vans with wheelchair lifts and other features for those with disabilities in more than 100 cities across the United States.

GAY & LESBIAN TRAVELERS

The **International Gay & Lesbian Travel Association** (IGLTA) (℗ **800/448-8550** or 954/776-2626; www.iglta.org) links travelers with the appropriate gay-friendly service organizations or tour specialists. With around 1,200 members, it offers quarterly newsletters, marketing mailings, and a membership directory that's updated quarterly.

Out and About (℗ 800/929-2268 or 415/486-2591; www.outandabout.com) offers guidebooks and a monthly newsletter packed with good information on the global gay and lesbian scene. A year's subscription to the newsletter costs $49.

SENIOR TRAVEL

Nearly every attraction in California offers a senior discount; age requirements vary, and specific prices are discussed throughout this book. Public transportation and movie theaters also have reduced rates. Don't be shy about asking for discounts, but always carry some kind of identification, such as a driver's license, that shows your date of birth. Also, mention the fact that you're a senior when you first make your travel reservations. For example, both **Amtrak** (℗ **800/USA-RAIL;** www.amtrak.com) and **Greyhound** (℗ **800/229-9424;** www.greyhound.com) offer discounts to persons over 62.

Members of **AARP** (formerly known as the American Association of Retired Persons), 601 E St. NW, Washington, DC 20049 (℗ **800/424-3410** or 202/434-2277; www.aarp.org), get discounts on hotels, airfares, and car rentals. AARP offers members a wide range of benefits, including *Modern Maturity* magazine and a monthly newsletter. Anyone over 50 can join; membership is $10 per year.

The **U.S. National Park Service** offers a **Golden Age Passport** that gives seniors 62 years or older lifetime entrance to U.S. national parks for a one-time processing fee of $10, which must be purchased in person at any NPS facility that charges an entrance fee. Besides free entry, a Golden Age Passport also offers a 50% discount on federal-use fees charged for such facilities as camping, swimming, parking, boat launching, and tours. For more information, click onto www.nps.gov/fees_passes.htm or call ℗ **888/GO-PARKS.**

The Book of Deals is a collection of more than 1,000 senior discounts on airlines, lodging, tours, and attractions around the country; it's available for $9.95 by calling ℗ **800/460-6676.** *101 Tips for the Mature Traveler* is available from Grand Circle Travel (℗ **800/221-2610** or 617/350-7500; fax 617/346-6700). Other helpful books include *The 50+ Traveler's Guidebook* (St. Martin's Press), and *Unbelievably Good Deals and Great Adventures That You Absolutely Can't Get Unless You're Over 50* (Contemporary Publishing Co.).

FAMILY TRAVEL

Several books offer tips on traveling with kids. *Family Travel* (Lanier Publishing International) and *How to Take Great Trips with Your Kids* (The Harvard Common Press) are full of good general advice. *The Unofficial Guide to California with Kids* (Wiley, Inc.) is an excellent resource that covers the entire state. It rates and ranks attractions for each age group, lists dozens of family-friendly accommodations and restaurants, and suggests lots of beaches and activities that are fun for the whole clan.

Helpful websites include **Family Travel Network** (www.familytravelnetwork.com), which offers travel tips and reviews of family-friendly destinations, vacation deals, and thoughtful features; **Travel Internationally with Your Kids** (www.travelwithyourkids.com), a comprehensive site offering sound advice for traveling with children; and **The Busy Person's Guide to Traveling with Children** (http://wz.com/travel/TravelingWithChildren.

html), which offers a "45-second newsletter" in which experts weigh in on the best websites and resources for tips for traveling with children.

5 Getting There

BY PLANE

All major U.S. carriers serve the San Francisco, Sacramento, San Jose, Los Angeles, John Wayne (Orange County), and San Diego airports. They include **American** (© 800/433-7300; www.aa.com), **Continental** (© 800/525-0280; www.continental.com), **Delta** (© 800/221-1212; www.delta.com), **JetBlue** (© 800/538-2583; www.jetblue.com), **Northwest** (© 800/225-2525; www.nwa.com), **Southwest** (© 800/435-9792; www.southwest.com), **United** (© 800/241-6522; www.united.com), and **US Airways** (© 800/428-4322; www.usairways.com). The lowest round-trip fares to the West Coast from New York fluctuate between about $350 and $500; from Chicago, they range from $300 to $400. International travelers should also see "Getting to the U.S.," in chapter 3, for information on overseas flights into California. For details on air travel within California, see "Getting Around," later in this chapter.

FLYING FOR LESS: TIPS FOR GETTING THE BEST AIRFARE

Passengers who can book their tickets in advance, stay over Saturday night, or travel at off-peak hours will pay a fraction of the full fare. Airlines periodically lower prices on their most popular routes. Check your newspaper for advertised discounts or call the airlines directly and ask if any **promotional rates** or special fares are available. If your schedule is flexible, ask if you can secure a cheaper fare by staying an extra day or by flying midweek. (Many airlines won't volunteer this information.)

Consolidators—wholesalers who buy tickets in bulk at a discount—offer some of the best deals around. Their ads usually run in the Sunday travel section of your newspaper, and many have set up online reservations systems. There are lots of fly-by-night consolidators, though, and problems can range from disputing never-received tickets to finding you have no seat booked when you get to the airport. Play it safe by going with a reputable business; our favorite has always been **Cheap Tickets** (© 800/377-1000; www.cheaptickets.com). **Council Travel** (© 800/226-8624; www.counciltravel.com) and **STA Travel** (© 800/781-4040; www.statravel.com) cater especially to young travelers, but their bargain-basement prices are available to people of all ages. Other reliable consolidators include **TravelHUB** (© 888/AIR-FARE; www.travelhub.com), which represents nearly 1,000 travel agencies, many of whom offer consolidator and discount fares; **FlyCheap** (© 800/FLY-CHEAP; www.flycheap.com); or "rebators" such as **Travel Avenue** (© 800/333-3335; www.travelavenue.com) and the **Smart Traveller** (© 800/448-3338 in the U.S. or 305/448-3338), which rebate part of their commissions to you.

It's possible to get some great deals on airfares, hotels, and car rentals via **Internet travel agencies.** See "Planning Your Trip Online," below, for more information on resources on the Web.

BY CAR

If you're planning a road trip, it's a good idea to be a member of the **Automobile Association of America**

Air Travel Security Measures

In the wake of the terrorist attacks of September 11, 2001, the airline industry implemented sweeping security measures in airports. Expect a lengthier check-in process and occasional delays. Although regulations vary from airline to airline, you can expedite the process by taking the following steps:

- **Arrive early.** Arrive at the airport at least 90 minutes before your scheduled flight.
- **Be sure to carry plenty of documentation.** A government-issued photo ID (federal, state, or local) is now required. You may need to show this at various checkpoints. With an E-ticket, you may be required to have with you printed confirmation of purchase, and perhaps even the credit card with which you bought your ticket. This varies from airline to airline, so call ahead to make sure you have the proper documentation. And be sure that your ID is *up-to-date:* An expired driver's license, for example, may keep you from boarding the plane altogether.
- **Know what you can carry on—and what you can't.** Travelers in the United States are now limited to one carry-on bag, plus one personal bag (such as a purse or a briefcase). The Transportation Security Administration has been updating their regulations regarding prohibited carry-on items, which include corkscrews, pocketknives, and scissors; check their website at www.tsa.gov for the current list.
- **Prepare to be searched.** Expect spot-checks. Electronic items, such as a laptop or cellphone, should be readied for additional screening. Limit the metal items you wear on your person.
- **It's no joke.** When a check-in agent asks if someone other than you packed your bag, don't decide that this is the time to be funny. The agents will not hesitate to call security.
- **No ticket, no gate access.** Only ticketed passengers will be allowed beyond the screener checkpoints, except for those people with specific medical or parental needs.

(AAA). Members (only those who carry their cards with them) not only receive free roadside assistance, but also have access to a wealth of free travel information, including detailed maps. Also, many hotels and attractions throughout California offer discounts to AAA members—always inquire. Call © **800/922-8228** or visit www.aaa.com for membership information.

Here are some handy driving times if you're on one of those see-the-USA car trips. From Phoenix, it's about 6 hours to Los Angeles on I-10. Las Vegas is 265 miles northeast of Los Angeles (about a 4-hr. drive).

San Francisco is 227 miles southwest of Reno, Nevada, and 577 miles northwest of Las Vegas. It's a long day's drive 640 miles south from Portland, Oregon, on I-5. The drive between San Francisco and LA takes about 6 hours on I-5, closer to 8 hours on the more scenic U.S. 101.

BY TRAIN

Amtrak (© **800/USA-RAIL;** www. amtrak.com) connects California with about 500 American cities. The *Sunset Limited* is Amtrak's regularly scheduled transcontinental service, originating in Florida and making 52 stops along the way as it passes through Alabama, Mississippi, Louisiana, Texas, New Mexico, and Arizona before arriving in Los Angeles 2 days later. The train, which runs three times weekly, features reclining seats, a sightseeing car with large windows, and a full-service dining car. Round-trip coach fares begin at around $300; several varieties of sleeping compartments are also available for an extra charge.

Amtrak's *Coast Starlight* travels along the Pacific Coast between Seattle and Los Angeles. This stylish train (and wonderfully scenic route) has been steadily growing in popularity; for more information, see "Getting Around," later in this chapter.

PACKAGE TOURS

Independent fly and drive packages (no escorted tour groups, just a bulk rate on your airfare, hotel, and possibly rental car) are offered by **American Airlines Vacations** (© 800/321-2121; www.aavacations.com), **Continental Airlines Vacations** (© 800/301-3800; www.coolvacations. com), **Delta Vacations** (© 800/221-6666; www.deltavacations.com), **Southwest Airlines Vacations** (© 800/423-5683; www.swavacations.com), and **United Vacations** (© 888/854-3899; www.unitedvacations.com).

Liberty Travel (© 888/271-1584; www.libertytravel.com) is one of the oldest and biggest packagers; they offer great deals—with or without air—to the many popular California destinations, including San Diego and Disneyland. **Online Vacation Mall** (© 800/839-9851; www.online vacationmall.com) allows you to search for and book packages offered by a number of tour operators and airlines. The **United States Tour Operators Association's** website (www. ustoa.com) has a search engine that allows you to look for operators that offer packages to a specific destination. Other travel websites featuring packages include **Travelution** (© 800/903-1616; www.travelution. com) and **Site59** (www.site59.com). Travel packages are also listed in the travel section of your local Sunday newspaper.

Availability varies widely based upon season and demand, but it always pays to investigate what these major air carriers are offering to encourage you to fly with them. The packages are best suited to travelers who can be flexible in the following ways:

- Try not to be too picky about your hotel. That's not to say packages force you to stay in dumps, but you'll have a limited selection. The biggest hotel chains and resorts also offer package deals. If you already know where you want to stay, call the hotel itself and ask if it can offer land-air packages.

- If you can schedule your departure and arrival so you're not flying on the weekend, airfares will usually be at least $25 to $50 lower per person. And it goes without saying that the popular season, summer, is the most restrictive season, though package deals can still save you some money over booking separately.

- Engage the reservationist in conversation, mentioning all the activities you're considering for your visit. All of the companies have access to various goodies they can hitch to your package for far less than you'd pay separately. Examples include tickets to Universal Studios or Disneyland; passes for city tours, studio tours, and other excursions; tickets for theater events; car-rental upgrades; and more.

A Tale of Two States

It doesn't take a psychiatrist to figure out that California suffers from an acute case of bipolar schizophrenia. We Californians may, on the surface, appear to be one big *Happy Days* family, but in reality we've divided our state into separate factions worthy of Montague and Capulet. That is, you're either a Northern Californian or a Southern Californian, two opposing tribes that have little in common. In fact, which side you even choose to visit may reveal something about yourself.

All the California glamour, wealth, fame, fast cars, surf scenes, and buxom blondes you see on television are pure southern invention. If this is the California you're looking for, head due south—assuming you're not terribly interested in intellectual stimulation, you won't be disappointed. In fact, it's nearly impossible not to be immediately swept up by the energy and excitement that places like West Hollywood and Venice Beach exude. It's a narcotic effect, the allure of flashy wealth, gorgeous bodies, and celebrity status. Even watching it all as a bystander imparts a heady mixture of thrill and envy.

Northern California may be frightfully demure in comparison, but in the long run, its subdued charms and natural beauty prevail. Wealth is certainly in abundance, but rarely displayed. The few hard bodies that exist are usually swathed in loose jeans and shirts. The few celebrities who live here keep very low profiles, and are more likely to be on their ranches than Rodeo Drive. Ostentation in any form is looked down upon (of course, it's okay to own a BMW, as long as it's slightly dirty), and unlike Los Angeles, you can actually explore smog-free San Francisco on foot.

Ironically, it's the Northern Californians who think of themselves as superior for having prudently eschewed the trappings of wealth and status (LA-bashing is a popular pastime). Southern Californians, on the other hand, couldn't care less what the northerners think of them; it's all sour grapes as they bask poolside 300 sunny days of the year. In fact, most Southern Californians would be perfectly content as their own state were it not for one key factor: water. Northern California holds two-thirds of the state's watershed, and without the incredibly complex system of aqueducts, reservoirs, and dams that keep huge flows going southward, Southern California's 14 million citizens would be in a world of hurt.

Will Californians ever agree to a legally mutual breakup? The idea has been bandied about the state capital for years, but it consistently meets its Waterloo when it comes to water rights, always a hotly contested issue in California politics. But regardless of our polarized views and lifestyles, most Californians do agree on one thing: We're still the best damn dysfunctional state in America.

—*Matthew Richard Poole*

6 Planning Your Trip Online

Researching and booking your trip online can save time and money. Then again, it may not. It is simply not true that you always get the best deal online. Most booking engines do not include schedules and prices for budget airlines, and from time to time you'll get a better last-minute price by calling the airline directly, so it's best to call the airline to see if you can do better before booking online.

On the plus side, Internet users today can tap into the same travel-planning databases that were once accessible only to travel agents—and do it at the same speed. Sites such as **Frommers.com, Travelocity.com, Expedia.com,** and **Orbitz.com** allow consumers to comparison shop for airfares, access special bargains, book flights, and reserve hotel rooms and rental cars.

But don't fire your travel agent just yet. Although online booking sites offer tips and hard data to help you bargain-shop, they cannot endow you with the hard-earned experience that makes a seasoned, reliable travel agent an invaluable resource, even in the Internet age. And for consumers with a complex itinerary, a trusty travel agent is still the best way to arrange the most direct flights to and from the best airports.

Still, there's no denying the Internet's emergence as a powerful tool in researching and plotting travel time. The benefits of researching your trip online can be well worth the effort.

Last-minute specials, such as weekend deals or Internet-only fares, are offered by airlines to fill empty seats. Most of these are announced on Tuesday or Wednesday and must be purchased online. They are only valid for travel that weekend, but some can be booked weeks or months in advance. Sign up for weekly e-mail alerts at airline websites or check mega-sites that compile comprehensive lists of last-minute specials, such as **Smarter Living** (smarterliving. com) or **WebFlyer** (www.webflyer. com).

Some sites, such as Expedia.com, will send you **e-mail notification** when a cheap fare becomes available to your favorite destination. Some will also tell you when fares to a particular destination are lowest.

 Frommers.com: The Complete Travel Resource

For an excellent travel-planning resource, we highly recommend **Frommers.com** (www.frommers.com). We're a little biased, of course, but we guarantee that you'll find the travel tips, reviews, monthly vacation giveaways, and online-booking capabilities thoroughly indispensable. Among the special features are our popular **Message Boards,** where Frommer's readers post queries and share advice (sometimes even our authors show up to answer questions); **Frommers.com Newsletter,** for the latest travel bargains and inside travel secrets; and Frommer's **Destinations Section,** where you'll get expert travel tips, hotel and dining recommendations, and advice on the sights to see for more than 2,500 destinations around the globe. When your research is done, the **Online Reservation System** (http://www.frommers.com/book_a_trip/) takes you to Frommer's favorite sites for booking your vacation at affordable prices.

TRAVEL PLANNING & BOOKING SITES

Keep in mind that because several airlines are no longer willing to pay commissions on tickets sold by online travel agencies, these agencies may either add a $10 surcharge to your bill if you book on that carrier, or neglect to offer those carriers' schedules.

The list of sites below is selective, not comprehensive. Some sites will have evolved or disappeared by the time you read this.

- **Travelocity** (www.travelocity.com or http://.frommers.travelocity.com) and **Expedia** (www.expedia.com) are among the most popular sites, each offering an excellent range of options. Travelers search by destination, dates, and cost.
- **Orbitz** (www.orbitz.com) is a popular site launched by United, Delta, Northwest, American, and Continental airlines. You get, among other offerings, available fares from more than 450 airlines.
- **Qixo** (www.qixo.com) is another powerful search engine that allows you to search for flights and accommodations from some 20 airline and travel-planning sites (such as Travelocity) at once. Qixo sorts results by price.
- **Priceline** (www.priceline.com) lets you "name your price" for airline tickets, hotel rooms, and rental cars. For airline tickets, you can't say what time you want to fly—you have to accept any flight between 6am and 10pm on the dates you've selected, and you may have to make one or more stopovers. Tickets are nonrefundable, and no frequent-flyer miles are awarded.

SMART E-SHOPPING

The savvy traveler is armed with insider information. Here are a few tips to help you navigate the Internet successfully and safely:

- **Know when sales start.** Last-minute deals may vanish in minutes. If you have a favorite booking site or airline, find out when last-minute deals are released to the public. (For example, Southwest's specials are posted every Tues at 12:01am Central time.)
- **Shop around.** If you're looking for bargains, compare prices on different sites and airlines—and against a travel agent's best fare. Try a range of times and alternative airports before you make a purchase.
- **Stay secure.** Book only through secure sites (some airline sites are not secure). Look for a key icon (Netscape) or a padlock (Internet Explorer) at the bottom of your Web browser before you enter credit-card information or other personal data.
- **Avoid online auctions.** Sites that auction airline tickets and frequent-flier miles are the number-one perpetrators of Internet fraud, according to the National Consumers League.
- **Maintain a paper trail.** If you book an E-ticket, print out a confirmation, or write down your confirmation number, and keep it safe and accessible—or your trip could be a virtual one!

ONLINE TRAVELER'S TOOLBOX

Veteran travelers usually carry some essential items to make their trips easier. Following is a selection of online tools to bookmark and use.

- **Visa ATM Locator** (www.visa.com), for locations of Plus ATMs worldwide, or **MasterCard ATM Locator** (www.mastercard.com), for locations of Cirrus ATMs worldwide.

- **Intellicast** (www.intellicast.com) and **Weather.com** (www.weather.com). Gives weather forecasts for all 50 states and for cities around the world.
- **Mapquest** (www.mapquest.com). This best of the mapping sites lets you choose a specific address or destination, and in seconds it will return a map and detailed directions.
- **Cybercafes.com** (www.cybercafes.com) or **Internet Café Guide** (www.netcafeguide.com/map index.htm). Locate Internet cafes at hundreds of locations around the globe.

7 Getting Around

BY CAR

California's freeway signs frequently indicate direction by naming a town rather than a point on the compass. If you've never heard of Canoga Park, you might be in trouble—unless you have a map. The best state road guide is the comprehensive **Thomas Bros. *California Road Atlas,*** a 300-plus-page book of maps with schematics of towns and cities statewide. It costs about $25, a good investment if you plan to do a lot of exploring. Smaller, accordion-style maps are handy for the state as a whole or for individual cities and regions; you'll find a very useful one inserted in the back of this book.

If you're heading into the Sierra or Shasta-Cascades for a winter ski trip, top up on antifreeze and carry snow chains for your tires. (Chains are mandatory in certain areas.)

Sample Distances Between Key California Cities:

San Francisco	
87 miles SW of Sacramento	321 miles NW of Santa Barbara
115 miles NW of Monterey	379 miles NW of Los Angeles
278 miles SE of Eureka	548 miles NW of San Diego

Sacramento	
87 miles NE of San Francisco	383 miles N of Los Angeles
185 miles NE of Monterey	391 miles NE of Santa Barbara
304 miles SE of Eureka	484 miles NW of Palm Springs

Los Angeles	
96 miles SE of Santa Barbara	379 miles SE of San Francisco
103 miles W of Palm Springs	383 miles S of Sacramento
120 miles NW of San Diego	659 miles SE of Eureka
332 miles SE of Monterey	

DRIVING RULES California law requires both drivers and passengers to wear seat belts. Children under 4 years or 40 pounds must be secured in an approved child safety seat. Motorcyclists must wear helmets. Auto insurance is mandatory; the car's registration and proof of insurance must be carried in the car.

You can turn right at a red light, unless otherwise indicated—but be sure to come to a complete stop first. Pedestrians always have the right-of-way.

Many California freeways have designated carpool lanes, also known as high-occupancy vehicle (HOV) lanes or "diamond" lanes. Some require two passengers, others three. Most on-ramps are metered during even light congestion to regulate the flow of traffic onto the freeway; cars in HOV lanes can pass the signal without stopping. All other drivers are required to observe the stoplights—fines begin at around $271.

CAR-RENTAL AGENCIES California is one of the cheapest places in the United States to rent a car. The best-known firms, with locations throughout the state and at most major airports, include **Alamo** (© 800/462-5866; www.alamo.com), **Avis** (© 800/230-4898; www.avis.com), **Budget** (© 800/527-0700; https://rent.drivebudget.com), **Dollar** (© 800/800-3665; www.dollar.com), **Hertz** (© 800/654-3131; www.hertz.com), **National** (© 800/227-7368; www.nationalcar.com), and **Thrifty** (© 800/847-4389; www.thrifty.com).

Many rental agencies have begun offering a variety of essential or just helpful extras, such as cellphones, child seats, and specially equipped vehicles for travelers with disabilities. Ask about additional fees when you make your reservation.

DEMYSTIFYING RENTER'S INSURANCE Before you drive off in a rental car, be sure you're insured. Hasty assumptions about your personal auto insurance or a rental agency's additional coverage could end up costing you tens of thousands of dollars—even if you're involved in an accident that was clearly the fault of another driver.

If you already hold a **private auto insurance** policy, you are most likely covered in the United States for loss of or damage to a rental car, and liability in case of injury to any other party involved in an accident. Be sure to find out whether you're covered in the area you're visiting, whether your policy extends to all persons who will be

driving the rental car, how much liability is covered in case an outside party is injured in an accident, and whether the type of vehicle you are renting is included under your contract. (Rental trucks, sport-utility vehicles, and luxury vehicles or sports cars may not be covered.)

Most **major credit cards** provide some degree of coverage as well—provided they were used to pay for the rental. Terms vary widely, however, so be sure to call your credit-card company directly before you rent.

If you're **uninsured,** your credit card may provide primary coverage as long as you decline the rental agency's insurance. This means that the credit card may cover damage or theft of a rental car for the full cost of the vehicle. (In a few states, however, theft is not covered; ask specifically about state law where you will be renting and driving.) If you already have insurance, your credit card may provide secondary coverage—which basically covers your deductible.

Credit cards **will not cover liability,** or the cost of injury to an outside party and/or damage to an outside party's vehicle. If you do not hold an insurance policy, you may seriously want to consider purchasing additional liability insurance from your rental company. Be sure to check the terms, however: Some rental agencies only cover liability if the renter is not at fault.

The basic insurance coverage offered by most car-rental companies, known as the **Loss/Damage Waiver (LDW)** or **Collision Damage Waiver (CDW),** can cost as much as $20 per day. It usually covers the full value of the vehicle with no deductible if an outside party causes an accident or other damage to the rental car. Liability coverage varies according to the company policy and state law, but the minimum is usually at least $15,000.

If you are at fault in an accident, however, you will be covered for the full replacement value of the car but not for liability. In California, you can buy additional liability coverage for such cases. Most rental companies will require a police report in order to process any claims you file, but your private insurer will not be notified of the accident.

BY PLANE
In addition to the major carriers listed earlier in "Getting There," several smaller airlines provide service within the state, including **American**

Eagle (© 800/433-7300), **America West** (© 800/235-9292), **Southwest** (© 800/435-9792), **United Express** (© 800/241-6522), and **US Airways Express** (© 800/428-4322). The round-trip fare between Los Angeles and San Francisco ranges from $79 to $200. See the section titled "Orientation" in each city's chapter for further information.

BY TRAIN
Amtrak (© 800/USA-RAIL; www.amtrak.com) runs trains up and down the California coast, connecting San Diego, Los Angeles, and San Francisco,

---

 ### The *Coast Starlight:* All Aboard for Nostalgia

If you're traveling by rail along the California coast, or even as far north as Seattle, treat yourself to a ride aboard Amtrak's luxurious *Coast Starlight.* In an effort to recapture the glory days of 1940s Streamline luxury liners, Amtrak is pulling out all the stops on these double-decker Superliners, complete with a gourmet dining car, first-class and coach lounge cars, standard and deluxe sleeping compartments, and enough diversions (including feature-length films, live entertainment, games for kids and adults, and a full bar) to make the overnight, 2-day trip a pleasure. All sleeping-car fares include three meals daily, prepared fresh onboard with an emphasis on regional flavor, and wines from vintners in Washington, Oregon, and California, as well as seasonal specials from along the *Coast Starlight's* route.

While coach tickets are comparable to airplane fares, the surcharge for sleeping compartments adds considerably to the cost of the trip. All fares quoted are for one-way adult tickets. Children ages 2 to 15 travel for half-price, and seniors 62 and older receive a 15% discount. Coach fare buys assigned seating in surprisingly comfortable upper-level reclining chairs. Blankets and pillows are offered in the evening, and fold-up leg rests help make sleeping more comfortable than you might imagine. Between San Francisco and Los Angeles, one-way adult coach fare ranges from $54 to $77; between Seattle and LA, it's $102 to $170. Based on travel between Seattle and LA, a standard sleeping compartment for two adds $255, a deluxe with private bathroom is $525, and a family sleeper for two adults and two kids (no bathroom) is $485.

It's advisable to book several months ahead for peak periods (summer, weekends, and holidays). Since the splendid views depend on daylight, also consider carefully before traveling during the very short days of winter. For information and tickets, call **Amtrak** (© 800/USA-RAIL) or visit its special *Coast Starlight* website at **www.coast starlight.com.**

Tips Bicycling Tours

Combine an interest in biking with California's spectacular scenery by signing up for a weeklong or weekend tour with **Backroads,** 801 Cedar St., Berkeley, CA 94710 (© **800/GO-ACTIVE** or 510/527-1555; www.backroads. com). Focusing on coastal routes, wine country rides, and even a microbrew program, the tours vary in difficulty and comfort; some are camping trips, while others accommodate you in luxury B&Bs. Professional leaders accompany each group, while a support van trails with gear, baggage, and provisions. Tours include all meals and overnight accommodations, and range in price from $150 to $275 per day, per person.

---

and all points in between. There are multiple trains each day, and rates fluctuate according to season and special promotions. One-way fares for popular segments can range from $20 (Los Angeles–Santa Barbara) to $27 (Los Angeles–San Diego) to $58 (San Francisco–Los Angeles). Also see "The *Coast Starlight:* All Aboard for Nostalgia" on p. 48 for more information about train travel in California.

8 Recommended Reading

by Matthew Richard Poole

There's no shortage of reading material about the history and culture of California, one of the most romanticized places on earth. Almost from the beginning, novelists and poets were an essential part of California's cultural mosaic, and the works they've created offer a fascinating window into the lives and legends that have greatly influenced California's inception and fervid growth.

HISTORICAL PERSPECTIVES

Readers are spoiled for choices when it comes to fictionalized accounts of California's pioneers. Salinas native John Steinbeck, one of the state's best-known authors, paints a vivid portrayal of proletarian life in the early to mid-1900s. His *Grapes of Wrath* remains the classic account of itinerant farm laborers coming to California in the midst of the Great Depression. *Cannery Row* has forever made the Monterey waterfront famous, and *East of Eden* offers insight into the way of life in the Salinas Valley.

Famed humorist and storyteller Mark Twain penned vivid tales during California's gold-rush era, including one of his most popular works, "The Celebrated Jumping Frog of Calaveras County" (an annual Gold Country competition that still has legs). Other good gold-rush reads include Bret Harte's *The Luck of Roaring Camp*, a sentimental tale of hard-luck miners and their false toughness, and J. S. Holliday's *The World Rushed In*, one of the finest nonfiction accounts of the gold rush still in print.

San Francisco was also a popular setting for many early works, including Twain's *San Francisco*, a collection of articles that glorified "the liveliest, heartiest community on our continent." It was also the birthplace of Jack London, who wrote several short stories of his younger days as an oyster pirate on the San Francisco Bay, as well as *Martin Eden*, his semiautobiographical account of life along the Oakland shores.

A much-heralded anthology containing selections from writers representing all the varied cultures in California's diverse history, *The*

Literature of California: Writings from the Golden State, was recently published by the University of California Press.

Finally, for what some critics consider the best novel ever written about Hollywood, turn to Nathanael West's *The Day of the Locust*, a savage and satirical look at 1930s life on the fringes of the film industry.

MYSTERY & MAYHEM

For all you mystery buffs headed to California, two must-reads include Frank Norris's *McTeague: A Story of San Francisco*, a violent tale of love and greed set at the turn of the 20th century, and Dashiell Hammett's *The Maltese Falcon*, a steamy detective novel that captures the seedier side of San Francisco in the 1920s (you can even take a walking tour of Hammett's famous haunts). Another favorite is Raymond Chandler's *The Big Sleep*, in which private dick Philip Marlowe plies the seedier side of Los Angeles in the 1930s.

California has always been a hotbed for alternative—and, more often than not, controversial—literary styles. Joan Didion, in her novel *Slouching Toward Bethlehem*, and Hunter S. Thompson, in his columns for the *San Francisco Examiner* (brought together in the collection *Generation of Swine*), both used a "new journalistic" approach in their studies of San Francisco in the 1960s. Tom Wolfe's early work *The Electric Kool-Aid Acid Test* follows the Hell's Angels, the Grateful Dead, and Ken Kesey's Merry Pranksters as they ride through the hallucinogenic 1960s. Meanwhile, Beat writers Allen Ginsberg and Jack Kerouac were penning protests against political conservatism—and promoting their bohemian lifestyle—in the former's controversial poem "Howl" (daringly published by Lawrence Ferlinghetti, poet and owner of City Lights in San Francisco's North Beach district) and the latter's famous tale of American adventure, *On the Road*.

CONTEMPORARY FICTION

If you're interested in a contemporary look back at four generations in the life of an American family, you can do no better than Wallace Stegner's *Angle of Repose*. The winner of the Pulitzer Prize in 1971, this work chronicles the lives of pioneers on the western frontier. Among Stegner's many other works of fiction and nonfiction about the West is his novel *All the Little Live Things*, which explores the conflicts faced by retired literary agent Joe Allston; the book is set in the San Francisco Bay Area of the 1960s. *The Spectator Bird* (winner of the 1976 National Book Award) revisits Allston's character as he reflects on his life and his memories of a search for his roots.

SPECIAL-INTEREST READS

Geology buffs will want to pack a copy of *Assembling California*, John McPhee's fascinating observation of California's complex geological history. Most of this volume was previously published in the *New Yorker*. Mike Davis's *City of Quartz* and *Ecology of Fear* offer a critical perspective on the social and natural history of Los Angeles.

Outdoor enthusiasts have literally dozens of sporting books to choose from, but most comprehensive is Foghorn Press's excellent outdoor series—*California Camping, California Fishing, California Golf, California Beaches*, and *California Hiking*—available at every major bookstore in the state. Another recommended choice is *Frommer's Great Outdoor Guide to Northern California*.

FAST FACTS: California

Earthquakes In the rare event of an earthquake, you should know a few simple precautions that every California schoolchild is taught: If you're in a tall building, don't run outside; instead, move away from windows and toward the building's center. Crouch under a desk or table, or stand against a wall or under a doorway. If you're in bed, get under the bed or stand in a doorway, or crouch under a sturdy piece of furniture. When exiting the building, use stairwells, *not* elevators.

If you're in your car, pull over to the side of the road and stop, but wait until you're away from bridges or overpasses, as well as telephone or power poles and lines. Stay in your car.

If you're out walking, stay outside and away from trees, power lines, and the sides of buildings.

Emergencies To reach the police, ambulance service, or fire department, dial © **911.** No coins are needed at pay phones for 911 calls.

Liquor Laws Liquor and grocery stores, as well as some drugstores, can legally sell packaged alcoholic beverages between 6am and 2am. Most restaurants, nightclubs, and bars are licensed to serve alcoholic beverages during the same hours. The legal age for the purchase and consumption of alcoholic beverages is 21; proof of age is strictly enforced.

Taxes California's state sales tax is 7 5%. Some cities include an additional percentage, so the tax varies throughout the state. Hotel taxes are almost always higher than tariffs levied on goods and services.

Time California and the entire West Coast are in the Pacific time zone, 3 hours earlier than the East Coast.

3

For International Visitors

by Matthew Richard Poole

Whether it's your first visit or your 10th, a trip to the United States may require an additional degree of planning. This chapter will provide you with essential information, helpful tips, and advice for the more common problems that some visitors encounter.

1 Preparing for Your Trip

ENTRY REQUIREMENTS

Immigration laws are a hot issue in the United States these days, and the following requirements may have changed somewhat by the time you plan your trip. Check at any U.S. embassy or consulate for current information and requirements. You can also check the **U.S. State Department's** website at **www.state.gov**.

VISAS

The U.S. State Department has a **Visa Waiver Pilot Program** allowing citizens of certain countries to enter the United States without a visa for stays of up to 90 days. At press time these countries included Andorra, Australia, Austria, Belgium, Brunei, Denmark, Finland, France, Germany, Iceland, Ireland, Italy, Japan, Liechtenstein, Luxembourg, Monaco, the Netherlands, New Zealand, Norway, Portugal, San Marino, Singapore, Slovenia, Spain, Sweden, Switzerland, the United Kingdom, and Uruguay. Citizens of these countries need a valid passport, proof of financial solvency, and a round-trip air or cruise ticket in their possession upon arrival. If they first enter the United States, they may also visit Mexico, Canada, Bermuda, and/or the Caribbean islands and return to the United States without a

visa. Further information is available from any U.S. embassy or consulate. Canadian citizens may enter the United States without visas; they need only proof of residence.

Citizens of all other countries must have (1) a valid passport that expires at least 6 months later than the scheduled end of their visit to the United States, and (2) a visitor visa, which may be obtained with a nonrefundable US$45 application fee from any U.S. consulate.

OBTAINING A VISA To obtain a visa, the traveler must submit a completed application form (either in person or by mail) with a 1½-inch-square photo, and must demonstrate binding ties to a residence abroad. Usually you can get a visa at once or within 24 hours, but it may take longer during the summer rush from June to August. If you cannot go in person, contact the nearest U.S. embassy or consulate for directions on applying by mail. Your travel agent or airline office may also be able to provide you with visa applications and instructions. The U.S. consulate or embassy that issues your visa will determine whether you will be issued a multiple- or single-entry visa and any restrictions regarding the length of your stay.

British subjects can obtain up-to-date passport and visa information by calling the **U.S. Embassy Visa Information Line** (✆ **0891/200-290**) or the **London Passport Office** (✆ **0990/210-410** for recorded information) or they can find the visa information on London's American Embassy website (**www.usembassy.org.uk**).

Irish citizens can obtain up-to-date passport and visa information through the **Embassy of USA Dublin,** 42 Elgin Rd., Dublin 4, Ireland (✆ **353/1-668-8777**), or by checking the embassy's website at **www.usembassy.ie**.

Australian citizens can obtain up-to-date passport and visa information by calling the **U.S. Embassy Canberra,** Moonah Place, Yarralumla, ACT 2600 (✆ **02/6214-5600**), or check the visa page on the website (**www.usis-australia.gov**).

Citizens of **New Zealand** can obtain up-to-date passport and visa information by calling the **U.S. Embassy New Zealand** at ✆ **644/472-2068** or get the information directly from the website (**http://usembassy.org.nz**).

MEDICAL REQUIREMENTS

Unless you're arriving from an area known to be suffering from an epidemic (particularly cholera or yellow fever), inoculations or vaccinations are not required for entry into the United States. If you have a disease that requires treatment with narcotics or syringe-administered medications, carry a valid signed prescription from your physician to allay any suspicions that you may be smuggling narcotics (a serious offense that carries severe penalties in the U.S.). See "Insurance" below for information about health insurance for your trip.

For HIV-positive visitors, requirements for entering the United States are somewhat vague and change frequently. According to the publication *HIV and Immigrants: A Manual for AIDS Service Providers,* although INS doesn't require a medical exam for everyone trying to come into the United States, INS officials may keep out people who they suspect are HIV positive. INS may stop people because they look sick or because they are carrying AIDS/HIV medicine.

If an HIV-positive non-citizen applying for a nonimmigrant visa knows that HIV is a communicable disease of public health significance but checks "No" on the question about communicable diseases, INS may deny the visa because they think the applicant committed fraud. If a non-immigrant visa applicant checks "Yes," or if INS suspects the person is HIV positive, it will deny the visa unless the applicant asks for a special waiver for visitors. This waiver is for people visiting the United States for a short time, to attend a conference, for instance, to visit close relatives, or to receive medical treatment. It can be a confusing situation, so for up-to-the-minute information concerning HIV-positive travelers, contact the Center for Disease Control's **National Center for HIV** (✆ **404/332-4559;** www.hivatis.org) or the **Gay Men's Health**

Tips **Immigration Issues**

If you have questions about U.S. Immigration policies or laws, call the **Immigration and Naturalization Service's "Ask Immigration System"** at ✆ **800/375-5283** or visit the INS website at www.ins.usdoj.gov. Representatives are available Monday through Friday from 9am to 3pm; a 24-hour automated information option also addresses common questions.

Crisis (© **212/367-1000;** www.gmhc.org).

PASSPORT INFORMATION

Safeguard your passport in a secure place like a money belt. If you lose it, visit the nearest consulate of your native country as soon as possible for a replacement. You can download passport applications from the Internet sites listed below.

FOR RESIDENTS OF CANADA

You can pick up a passport application at one of 28 regional passport offices or most travel agencies. As of December 11, 2001, Canadian children must have their own passport. However, if you hold a valid Canadian passport issued before December 11, 2001, that bears the name of your child, the passport remains valid for you and your child until it expires. Passports cost C$85 for those 16 years and older (valid 5 years), C$35 for children 3 to 15 (valid 5 years), and C$20 for children under 3 (valid for 3 years). Applications, which must be accompanied by two identical passport-sized photographs and proof of Canadian citizenship, are available at travel agencies throughout Canada or from the central **Passport Office, Department of Foreign Affairs and International Trade,** Ottawa K1A 0G3 (© **800/567-6868;** www.dfait-maeci.gc.ca/passport). Processing takes 5 to 10 days if you apply in person, or about 3 weeks by mail.

FOR RESIDENTS OF THE U.K.

To pick up an application for a standard 10-year passport (5-year passport for children under 16), visit the nearest passport office, major post office, or travel agency. You can also contact the **United Kingdom Passport Service** at © **0870/571-0410** or visit their website at **www.ukpa.gov.uk.** Passports are £30 for adults and £16 for children under 16, with an additional £15 fee if you apply in person at a passport office. Processing takes about 2 weeks.

FOR RESIDENTS OF IRELAND

You can apply for a 10-year passport, costing 57€, at the main **Passport Office,** Setanta Centre, Molesworth Street, Dublin 2 (© **01/671-1633;** www.gov.ie/iveagh). You can also apply at 1A South Mall, Cork (© **021/272-525**), or over the counter at most main post offices. Travelers under 18 and over 65 must apply for a 3-year passport, which costs 12€.

FOR RESIDENTS OF AUSTRALIA

You can pick up an application from your local post office or any **Australian State Passport Office,** but you must schedule an interview at a passport office to present your application materials. Call the passport office information service at © **131-232** or visit the government website at **www.passports.gov.au** for complete details. Passports for adults cost A$136; A$68 for those under 18.

FOR RESIDENTS OF NEW ZEALAND

You can pick up a passport application at any New Zealand Passports Office or download it from their website. Contact the **Passports Office** at © **0800/225-050** in New Zealand or 04/474-8100, or log on to **www.passports.govt.nz.** Passports for adults are NZ$80; NZ$40 for children under 16.

CUSTOMS

WHAT YOU CAN BRING IN

Every visitor more than 21 years of age may bring in, free of duty, the following: (1) 1 liter of wine or hard liquor; (2) 200 cigarettes, 100 cigars (but not from Cuba), or 3 pounds of smoking tobacco; and (3) $100 worth of gifts. These exemptions are offered to travelers who spend at least 72 hours in the United States and who have not claimed them within the preceding 6 months. It is altogether forbidden to bring into the country foodstuffs

Tips Driver's Licenses

The United States recognizes most foreign driver's licenses. You might want to get an international driver's license if your home license is not written in English.

(particularly fruit, cooked meats, and canned goods) and plants (vegetables, seeds, tropical plants, and the like). Foreign tourists may bring in or take out up to $10,000 in U.S. or foreign currency with no formalities; larger sums must be declared to U.S. Customs on entering or leaving, which includes filing form CM 4790. For more specific information regarding U.S. Customs, call your nearest U.S. embassy or consulate, or the **U.S. Customs** office at ℂ **202/927-1770** or www.customs.ustreas.gov.

WHAT YOU CAN TAKE HOME U.K. citizens returning from a non-EC country have an allowance of 200 cigarettes; 50 cigars; 250 grams of smoking tobacco; 2 liters of still table wine; 1 liter of spirits or strong liqueurs (over 22% volume); 2 liters of fortified wine, sparkling wine or other liqueurs; 60 cubic centimeters (ml) perfume; 250 cubic centimeters (ml) of toilet water; and £145 worth of all other goods, including gifts and souvenirs. People under 17 cannot have the tobacco or alcohol allowance. For more information, call the **HM Customs & Excise** at ℂ **0845/010-9000**, or log on to www.hmce.gov.uk.

Canadian citizens who've been out of the country for over 48 hours may bring back C$200 worth of goods, and if you've been gone for 7 consecutive days or more, not counting your departure, the limit is C$750. The limit for alcohol is up to 1.5 liters of wine or 1.14 liters of liquor, or 24 12-ounce cans or bottles of beer; and up to 200 cigarettes, 50 cigars, or 200 grams of tobacco. You may not ship tobacco or alcohol, and you must be of legal age for your province to bring these items through Customs. For the helpful booklet *I Declare,* call the **Canada Customs and Review Agency** at ℂ **800/461-9999** in Canada or 204/983-3500, or visit its website at www.ccra-adrc.gc.ca.

The duty-free allowance in **Australia** is A$400 or, for those under 18, A$200. Citizens can bring in 250 cigarettes or 250 grams of loose tobacco, and 1,125 milliliters of alcohol. If you're returning with valuables you already own, such as foreign-made cameras, you should file form B263. A helpful brochure available from Australian consulates or Customs offices is *Know Before You Go.* For more information, call the **Australian Customs Service** at ℂ **1300/363-263,** or log on to www.customs.gov.au.

The duty-free allowance for **New Zealand** is NZ$700. Citizens over 17 can bring in 200 cigarettes, 50 cigars, or 250 grams of tobacco (or a mixture of all three if their combined weight doesn't exceed 250g); plus 4.5 liters of wine and beer, or 1.125 liters of liquor. New Zealand currency does not carry import or export restrictions. Fill out a certificate of export, listing the valuables you are taking out of the country; that way, you can bring them back without paying duty. Most questions are answered in a free pamphlet available at New Zealand consulates and Customs offices: *New Zealand Customs Guide for Travellers, Notice no. 4.* For more information, contact **New Zealand Customs,** The Customhouse, 17–21 Whitmore St., Box 2218, Wellington (ℂ **04/473-6099** or 0800/428-786; www.customs.govt.nz).

INSURANCE

Though lack of health insurance may prevent you from being admitted to a hospital in non-emergencies, don't worry about being left on a street corner to die: The American way is to fix you now and bill the living daylights out of you later.

Health insurance is not required of travelers, but it's highly recommended. Unlike many European countries, the United States does not usually offer free or low-cost medical care to its citizens or visitors. Doctors and hospitals are expensive, and in most cases will require advance payment or proof of coverage before they render their services. Policies can cover everything from the loss or theft of your baggage and trip cancellation to the guarantee of bail in case you're arrested. Good policies will also cover the costs of an accident, repatriation, or death. Packages such as **Europ Assistance's "Worldwide Healthcare Plan"** are sold by European automobile clubs and travel agencies at attractive rates. **Worldwide Assistance Services, Inc.** (℮ 800/821-2828; www.worldwideassistance.com) is the agent for Europ Assistance in the United States.

British travelers will notice that most big travel agents offer their own insurance, which they'll probably try to sell you when you book a holiday. Think before you sign. Britain's Consumers' Association recommends that you insist on seeing the policy and reading the fine print before buying travel insurance. **The Association of British Insurers** (℮ 020/7600-3333; www.abi.org.uk) gives advice by phone and publishes *Holiday Insurance,* a free guide to policy provisions and prices. You might also shop around for better deals: Try **Columbus Direct** (℮ 020/7375-0011; www.columbusdirect.net).

Canadians should check with their provincial health plan offices or call HealthCanada (℮ 613/957-2991) to find out the extent of their coverage and what documentation and receipts they must take home in case they are treated in the United States.

MONEY

CURRENCY   The U.S. monetary system is painfully simple: The most common bills (all ugly, all green) are the $1 (colloquially, a "buck"), $5, $10, and $20 denominations. There are also $2 bills (seldom encountered), $50 bills, and $100 bills (the last two are usually not welcome as payment for small purchases). Note that newly designed bills are now in circulation. Despite rumors to the contrary, the old-style bills are still legal tender.

There are six denominations of coins: 1¢ (1 cent, or a penny), 5¢ (5 cents, or a nickel), 10¢ (10 cents, or a dime), 25¢ (25 cents, or a quarter), 50¢ (50 cents, or a half dollar), and the $1 piece (the older, large silver dollar, the small Susan B. Anthony coin, and the newer Sacagawea coin).

Note: The "foreign-exchange bureaus" so common in Europe are rare even at airports in the United States, and nonexistent outside major cities. It's best not to change foreign money (or traveler's checks denominated in a currency other than U.S. dollars) at a small-town bank, or even a branch in a big city; in fact, leave any currency other than U.S. dollars at home—it may prove a greater nuisance to you than it's worth.

TRAVELER'S CHECKS   Though traveler's checks are widely accepted, make sure that they're denominated in U.S. dollars, as foreign-currency checks are often difficult to exchange. The three traveler's checks that are most widely recognized—and least likely to be denied—are **Visa, American Express,** and **Thomas Cook.** Be sure to record the numbers of the checks, and keep that information separately in case they get lost or stolen. Most California businesses are pretty good about taking traveler's checks, but you're better off cashing them in at a bank (in small amounts, of course) and paying in cash. *Note:* You'll need identification, such as a driver's license or passport, to change a traveler's check.

CREDIT CARDS & ATMS   Credit cards are the most widely used form of payment in the United States; the most commonly accepted cards are **Visa** (BarclayCard in Britain), **MasterCard** (EuroCard in Europe, Access in Britain, Chargex in Canada), **American Express, Diners Club,** and **Discover.** You must have a credit or charge card to rent a car. Occasionally a store or restaurant may not take credit cards—particularly in the rural areas—so be sure to ask in advance. Most businesses display a sticker near their entrances to let you know which cards they accept. (*Note:* Often businesses require a minimum purchase price, usually around $10, for use of a credit card.)

It is strongly recommended that you bring at least one major credit card. Hotels, car-rental companies, and airlines usually require a credit-card imprint as a deposit against expenses, and in an emergency a credit card can be priceless.

You'll find automated teller machines (ATMs) in just about every town in California, and on every block in the business districts of the big cities. Some ATMs will allow you to draw U.S. currency against your bank and credit cards. Check with your bank before leaving home, and remember that you will need your personal identification number (PIN) to do so. Most accept Visa, MasterCard, and American Express, as well as ATM cards from other U.S. banks. Expect to be charged up to $3 per transaction, however, if you're not using your own bank's ATM. *Tip:* One way around these fees is to ask for cash back at grocery stores that accept ATM cards and don't charge usage fees. Of course, you'll have to purchase something first. For more information on ATMs, see "Visitor Information & Money" in chapter 2.

MONEYGRAMS   If the proverbial poop hits the fan once you're in the United States, you can also have someone wire money to you very quickly via **Western Union.** Call ⟳ **800/325-6000** or visit www.westernunion.com for the office nearest you.

SAFETY

While tourist areas are generally safe, crime is still a problem, and U.S. urban areas tend to be less safe than those in Europe or Japan. Always stay alert. Ask your hotel front-desk staff or the city or area's tourist office if you're in doubt about which neighborhoods are safe.

Avoid deserted areas, especially at night, and don't go into public parks at night unless there's a concert or similar event that will attract a crowd. Avoid carrying valuables with you on the street, and don't display expensive cameras or electronic equipment. Hold on to your pocketbook, and place your billfold in an inside pocket. In theaters, restaurants, and other public places, keep your possessions in sight.

Remember also that hotels are open to the public, and in a large hotel, security may not be able to screen everyone entering. Always lock your room door—don't assume that inside your hotel you are automatically safe.

Driving safety is important, too. Ask your rental agency about personal safety, and ask for a traveler-safety brochure when you pick up your car. Ask for written directions to your destination or a map with the route clearly marked. (Many agencies offer the option of renting a cellular phone for the duration of your car rental; check with the rental agent when you pick up the car.) Try to arrive and depart during daylight hours.

Recently, more crime has involved cars and drivers. If you drive off a highway into a doubtful neighborhood, leave the area as quickly as possible. If you have an accident, even on the highway, stay in your car with the doors locked until you assess the situation or until the police arrive. If you're bumped from behind on the street or are involved in a minor accident with no injuries, and the situation appears to be suspicious, motion to the other driver to follow you. Never get out of your car in such situations. Go directly to the nearest police precinct, well-lit service station, or 24-hour store.

Always try to park in well-lit and well-traveled areas. Never leave any packages or valuables in sight. If someone attempts to rob you or steal your car, don't try to resist the thief or carjacker. Report the incident to the police department immediately by calling ✆ **911.** This is a free call, even from pay phones.

2 Getting to the U.S.

AIRLINES
In addition to the domestic U.S. airlines listed in chapter 2, many international carriers serve SFO, LAX, and other U.S. gateways. These include, among others: **Aer Lingus** (✆ 01/ 886-8888 in Dublin; www.aerlingus. ie), **Air Canada** (✆ 800/776-3000; www.aircanada.ca), **British Airways** (✆ 0845/773-3377 in the U.K.; www.british-airways.com), **Japan Airlines** (✆ 0354/89-1111 in Tokyo; www.jal.co.jp), **Qantas** (✆ 13-13-13 in Australia; www.qantas.com.au), and **Virgin Atlantic** (✆ 01293/ 747-747 in the U.K.; www.virgin-atlantic.com). British Airways and Virgin Atlantic offer direct flights to San Francisco and Los Angeles from London. **Air New Zealand** (✆ 73-7000 in New Zealand; www.airnew zealand.co.nz) also flies direct to California.

Overseas visitors can take advantage of the APEX (Advance Purchase Excursion) reductions offered by all major U.S. and European carriers. For additional money-saving airline advice, see "Getting There" in chapter 2.

IMMIGRATION & CUSTOMS CLEARANCE
Visitors arriving by air, no matter what the port of entry, should cultivate patience and resignation. Getting through immigration control may take as long as 3 hours, especially on summer weekends, so have this guidebook or something else to read handy. Add the time it takes to clear Customs, and you'll see that you should make a 2- to 3-hour allowance for delays when you plan your connections between international and domestic flights.

In contrast, for the traveler arriving by car or rail from Canada, the border-crossing formalities have been streamlined to the vanishing point. People traveling by air from Canada, Bermuda, and some places in the Caribbean can sometimes clear Customs and Immigration at the point of departure, which is much quicker.

3 Getting Around the U.S.

BY PLANE
Some major American carriers— including **Delta** and **Northwest**— offer travelers on their transatlantic or transpacific flights special low-price tickets on U.S. continental flights under the **Discover America** program (sometimes called **Visit USA,** depending on the airline). Offering one-way travel between U.S. destinations at

significantly reduced prices, this coupon-based airfare program is the best and easiest way to tour the United States at a low cost. You must purchase these discounted fare coupons abroad in conjunction with your international ticket. Ask your travel agent or the airline reservations agent about this program well in advance of your departure date—preferably when you buy your international ticket—since the regulations may affect your trip planning, and conditions can change without notice.

BY TRAIN

International visitors can buy a **USA Rail Pass,** good for 15 or 30 days of unlimited travel on **Amtrak** (© **800/ USA-RAIL;** www.amtrak.com). The pass is available through many foreign travel agents. Prices (in U.S. dollars) in 2002 for a 15-day pass were $295 off-peak, $440 peak; a 30-day pass was $385 off-peak, $550 peak. (With a foreign passport, you can also buy passes at some Amtrak offices in the U.S., including Los Angeles, San Francisco, Chicago, New York, Miami, Boston, and Washington, D.C.) Reservations are generally required and should be made for each part of your trip as early as possible.

BY BUS

Although bus travel is often the most economical form of public transit for short hops between U.S. cities, it can also be slow and uncomfortable— certainly not an option for everyone (particularly when Amtrak, which is far more luxurious, offers reasonable rates). **Greyhound/Trailways** (© **800/229-9424**), the sole nationwide bus line, offers an **International Ameripass** that must be purchased before coming to the United States, or by phone through the Greyhound International Office at the Port Authority Bus Terminal in New York City (© **212/971-0492**). The pass

can be obtained from foreign travel agents and costs less than the domestic version. 2003 passes cost as follows: 7 days, $204; 10 days, $254; 15 days, $314; 21 days, $364; 30 days, $424; 45 days, $464; or 60 days, $574. You can get more info on the pass at **www.greyhound.com**, or by calling © **402/330-8552.** In addition, special rates are available for seniors and students.

BY CAR

The most cost-effective, convenient, and comfortable way to travel around the United States—especially California—is by car. The interstate highway system connects cities and towns all over the country; in addition to these high-speed, limited-access roadways, there's an extensive network of federal, state, and local highways and roads. California has no toll roads, but it does charge a toll fee at many major bridges. Some of the national car-rental companies that have offices in California include **Alamo** (© 800/ 462-5866; www.alamo.com), **Avis** (© 800/230-4898; www.avis.com), **Budget** (© 800/527-0700; www.rent. drivebudget.com), **Dollar** (© 800/ 800-3665; www.dollar.com), **Hertz** (© 800/654-3131; www.hertz.com), **National** (© 800/227-7368; www. nationalcar.com), and **Thrifty** (© 800/ 847-4389; www.thrifty.com).

If you plan on renting a car in the United States, you probably won't need the services of an additional automobile organization. If you plan to buy or borrow a car, automobile-association membership is recommended. **AAA,** the **American Automobile Association** (© 800/922-8228 for Northern California and © 800/924-6141 for Southern California; www.aaa.com), is the country's largest auto club and supplies its members with maps, insurance, and, most important, emergency road service. The cost of joining runs from $66 for singles to

$93 for two members, but if you're a member of a foreign auto club with reciprocal arrangements, you can enjoy free AAA service in America.

For detailed information on car rentals see "Getting Around" in chapter 2.

 FAST FACTS: For the International Traveler

Business Hours Banks and offices are usually open weekdays from 9am to 5pm. Stores, especially in shopping complexes, tend to stay open until about 9pm on weekdays and 6pm on weekends.

Climate See "When to Go" in chapter 2.

Currency & Currency Exchange See "Entry Requirements" and "Money" under "Preparing for Your Trip," earlier in this chapter.

Drinking Laws The legal age for purchase and consumption of alcoholic beverages is 21. Proof of age is required and often requested at bars, nightclubs, and restaurants, so bring an ID when you go out. Supermarkets and convenience stores in California sell beer, wine, and liquor.

Do not carry open containers of alcohol in your car or any public area that isn't zoned for alcohol consumption. The police can, and probably will, fine you on the spot. And nothing will ruin your trip faster than getting a citation for DUI ("driving under the influence"), so don't even think about driving while intoxicated.

Electricity Like Canada, the United States uses 110 to 120 volts AC (60 cycles), compared to 220 to 240 volts AC (50 cycles) in most of Europe, Australia, and New Zealand. If your small appliances use 220 to 240 volts, you'll need a 110-volt transformer and a plug adapter with two flat parallel pins to operate them here. Converters that change 220-240 volts to 110-120 volts are difficult to find in the United States, so bring one with you.

Embassies & Consulates All embassies are in Washington, D.C. Some consulates are in major U.S. cities, and most nations have a mission to the United Nations in New York. If your country isn't listed below, call Washington, D.C., directory assistance (℃ 202/555-1212) for the number of your national embassy.

The embassy of **Australia** is at 1601 Massachusetts Ave. NW, Washington, DC 20036 (℃ 202/797-3000; www.austemb.org). The nearest consulate is at 2049 Century Park E., 19th Floor, Los Angeles, CA 90067 (℃ 310/229-4800).

The embassy of **Canada** is at 501 Pennsylvania Ave. NW, Washington, DC 20001 (℃ 202/682-1740; www.canadianembassy.org). The nearest consulate is at 300 S. Grand Ave., 10th Floor, Los Angeles, CA 90071 (℃ 213/346-2700).

The embassy of **Ireland** is at 2234 Massachusetts Ave. NW, Washington, DC 20008 (℃ 202/462-3939; www.irelandemb.org). The nearest consulate is at 44 Montgomery St., Suite 3830, San Francisco, CA 94104 (℃ 415/392-4214).

The embassy of **Japan** is at 2520 Massachusetts Ave. NW, Washington, DC 20008 (℃ **202/238-6700**; http://www.us.emb-japan.go.jp/). The nearest consulate is at 50 Fremont St., San Francisco, CA 94105 (℃ **415/777-3533**).

The embassy of **New Zealand** is at 37 Observatory Circle, Washington, DC 20008 (℃ **202/328-4800**; www.nzemb.org). The nearest consulate is at 12400 Wilshire Blvd., Suite 1150, Los Angeles, CA 90025 (℃ **310/207-1605**).

The embassy of the **United Kingdom** is at 3100 Massachusetts Ave. NW, Washington, DC 20008 (℃ **202/462-1340**; www.britainusa.com/consular/embassy). The nearest consulate is at 11766 Wilshire Blvd., Suite 400, Los Angeles, CA 90025 (℃ **310/481-0031**).

Emergencies Call ℃ **911** to report a fire, call the police, or get an ambulance anywhere in the United States. This is a toll-free call (no coins are required at public telephones). If that doesn't work, another useful way of reporting an emergency is to call the telephone company operator by dialing 0 (zero, not the letter *O*).

If you encounter traveler's problems, call the **Traveler's Aid Society** (℃ **310/646-2270**), a nationwide, nonprofit, social-service organization that helps travelers in difficult straits. Its services might include reuniting families separated while traveling, providing food and/or shelter to people stranded without cash, or even emotional counseling.

Gasoline (Petrol) Petrol is known as gasoline (or simply "gas") in the United States, and petrol stations are known as both gas stations and service stations. Gasoline costs about half as much as it does in Europe (about $1.45 per gallon at press time), and taxes are already included in the printed price. One U.S. gallon equals 3.8 liters or 0.85 Imperial gallons.

Holidays Banks, government offices, post offices, and many stores, restaurants, and museums are closed on the following legal national holidays: January 1 (New Year's Day), the third Monday in January (Martin Luther King Jr. Day), the third Monday in February (Presidents' Day, Washington's Birthday), the last Monday in May (Memorial Day), July 4th (Independence Day), the first Monday in September (Labor Day), the second Monday in October (Columbus Day), November 11 (Veterans Day/Armistice Day), the fourth Thursday in November (Thanksgiving Day), and December 25 (Christmas).

Legal Aid The foreign tourist will probably never become involved with the American legal system. If you are "pulled over" for a minor infraction (for example, of the highway code, such as speeding), never attempt to pay the fine directly to a police officer; this could be construed as attempted bribery, a much more serious crime. Pay fines by mail, or directly into the hands of the clerk of the court. If accused of a more serious offense, say and do nothing before consulting a lawyer. Everyone has the right to remain silent, whether he or she is suspected of a crime or actually arrested. Once arrested, a person can make one telephone call to a party of his or her choice. Call your embassy or consulate.

Mail If you aren't sure what your address will be in the United States, mail can be sent to you, in your name c/o General Delivery, at the main post office of the city or region where you expect to be. Call ℭ **800/ASK-USPS** (275-8777), or log on to **www.usps.com** for more information. The addressee must pick mail up in person and must produce proof of identity (driver's license or passport, for example). Most post offices will hold your mail for up to 1 month, and are open Monday through Friday from 8am to 5pm, and Saturday from 9am to 3pm.   Generally found at intersections, mailboxes are blue with an eagle logo and carry the inscription U.S. MAIL. Domestic postage rates are 23¢ for a postcard and 37¢ for a letter. International rates vary; visit a post office for precise postage information and stamps.

Medical Emergencies To call an ambulance, dial ℭ **911** from any phone—no coins are needed in pay phones.

Smoking Heavy smokers are in for a tough time in California. There is no smoking in public buildings, sports arenas, elevators, theaters, banks, lobbies, restaurants, offices, stores, bed-and-breakfasts, most small hotels, and bars. That's right—as of January 1, 1998, you can't even smoke in a bar in California. (The only exception is a bar where drinks are served solely by the owner.) You will find, however, a few neighborhood bars that turn the other cheek and pass you an ashtray.

Taxes In the United States there is no value-added tax (VAT) or other indirect tax at the national level. Sales tax is levied on goods and services by state and local governments, however, and is not included in the price tags you'll see on merchandise. This tax is not refundable. Sales tax in California is 8%. Hotel tax is charged on the room tariff only (which is not subject to sales tax) and is set by the city, ranging from 12% to 17% around Southern California.

Telephone & Fax The telephone system in the United States is run by private corporations, so rates, especially for long-distance service and operator-assisted calls, can vary widely. Generally, hotel surcharges on long-distance calls are astronomical, so you're usually better off charging the call to a telephone charge card or a credit card—or using a **public pay telephone,** which you'll find clearly marked in most public buildings and private establishments as well as on the street. Convenience stores and gas stations often have them. Many convenience groceries and other stores sell **prepaid calling cards** in denominations up to $50; these can be the least expensive way to call home. Many public phones at airports now accept American Express, MasterCard, and Visa credit cards. **Local calls** made from public pay phones cost either 25¢ or 35¢. Pay phones do not accept pennies, and few will take anything larger than a quarter.

Most long-distance and international calls can be dialed directly from any phone. For **direct overseas calls,** dial 011 (the international access code), then the country code (Australia, 61; Republic of Ireland, 353; New Zealand, 64; United Kingdom, 44), followed by the city code, then the local number. To place a call to Canada or the Caribbean, just dial 1, the area code, and the local number.

Calls to area codes **800, 888,** and **877** are toll-free. However, calls to numbers in area codes **700** and **900** (chat lines, bulletin boards, "dating" services, and so on) can be very expensive—usually a charge of 95¢ to $3 or more per minute, and they sometimes have minimum charges that can run as high as $15 or more.

For **reversed-charge or collect calls,** and for **person-to-person calls,** dial 0 (zero) followed by the area code and number you want; an operator comes on the line to assist you.

For **directory assistance** ("information"), dial ℂ **411.** 411 operators can also provide long-distance information; or you can dial 1, then the appropriate area code and **555-1212.**

Before calling from a hotel room, always ask the hotel phone operator if there are any telephone surcharges. They can sometimes be reduced by calling collect or by using a telephone charge card. Hotel charges, which can be exorbitant, can be avoided altogether by using a pay phone in the lobby.

Most hotels have **fax machines** available for guest use (be sure to ask about the charges), and many places even have in-room fax machines. A less expensive way to send and receive faxes is to visit **Mail Boxes Etc.,** a national chain of office service stores. You can search for convenient locations online at www.mbe.com.

Telephone Directory There are two kinds of telephone directories in the United States. The general directory is the so-called **White Pages,** which lists private and business subscribers in alphabetical order. The inside front cover lists the emergency number for police, fire, and ambulance, and other vital numbers (like the Coast Guard, poison-control center, crime-victims hot line, and so on). The first few pages are devoted to community-service numbers, including a guide to long-distance and international calling, complete with country codes and area codes.

The second directory, printed on yellow paper (hence its name, the **Yellow Pages**), lists local services, businesses, and industries by type of activity, with an index at the back. The listings cover not only such obvious items as automobile repairs by make of car and drugstores (pharmacies), often by geographical location, but also restaurants by type of cuisine and geographical location, bookstores by special subject or language, places of worship by religious denomination, and other information that the tourist might otherwise not readily find. The Yellow Pages also include city plans or detailed maps, often showing postal ZIP codes and public-transportation routes.

Time The continental United States is divided into **four time zones:** Eastern Standard Time (EST), Central Standard Time (CST), Mountain Standard Time (MST), and Pacific Standard Time (PST). When it is 9am in Los Angeles or San Francisco (PST), it is noon in New York (EST), 5pm in London (GMT), and 2am the next day in Sydney.

Daylight saving time is in effect from 1am on the first Sunday in April to 1am on the last Sunday in October, except in Arizona, Hawaii, part of Indiana, and Puerto Rico. Daylight saving time moves the clock 1 hour ahead of standard time.

For the correct time, call ℂ **POP-CORN** (767-2676) in any California area code.

Tipping Tipping is so ingrained in the American way of life that the annual income tax of tip-earning service personnel is based on how much they *should* have received in light of their employers' gross revenues. Accordingly, they may have to still pay tax on tips they never received.

Here are some rules to follow:

In hotels, tip **bellhops** at least $1 per bag ($3–$5 if you have a lot of luggage), and tip the **maid or chamber staff** $2 per day. Tip the **doorman** or **concierge** only if he or she has provided you with some specific service (for example, calling a cab for you or obtaining difficult-to-get theater tickets). Tip the **valet parking attendant** $2 every time you get your car.

In restaurants, bars, and nightclubs, tip **service staff** 15% to 20% of the check, tip **bartenders** 10% to 15%, tip **checkroom attendants** $1 per garment, and tip **valet-parking attendants** $2 per vehicle. Tip the **doorman** if he or she has provided you with some specific service (such as calling a cab). Tipping is not expected in cafeterias and fast-food restaurants, but is expected at buffet-style restaurants and steakhouses where servers may bring food you've ordered, clear your table, and refill your drinks.

Tip **cab drivers** 15% of the fare.

As for other service personnel, tip **skycaps** at airports at least $1 per bag ($2–$5 if you have a lot of luggage), and tip **hairdressers** and **barbers** 15% to 20%.

Tipping gas-station attendants or ushers at movies and theaters is not expected.

Toilets Restrooms are common in California shopping malls, museums, hotel lobbies, and department stores, but difficult to find on the street or in smaller shops. Restrooms in cafes and restaurants are for patrons only, but if you really need one, just order a coffee or ask to use the pay phone, usually conveniently placed beside the restrooms. Large hotels and fast-food restaurants are probably the best bet for clean facilities. If possible, avoid the toilets at parks and beaches, which tend to be dirty.

4

San Francisco

by Erika Lenkert

Consistently rated one of the top tourist destinations in the world, San Francisco abounds in multiple dimensions. Its famous, thrilling streets go up, and they go down; its multifarious citizens—and their adopted cultures, architectures, and cuisines—hail from San Antonio to Singapore; and its politics range from hyper-liberalism to an ever-encroaching wave of conservatism. Even something as mundane as fog takes on a new dimension as it creeps from the ocean and slowly envelops San Francisco in a resplendent blanket of mist.

From an outsider's perspective, San Francisco is still very much the city it's reputed to be. The restaurant scene is booming, boutiques abound, the Castro is the Castro, political correctness is hip, and all the goings-on in the unique neighborhoods take place against picture-perfect backdrops of famous bridges, bay vistas, cable cars, and colorful only-in-San-Francisco city life. But from an insider's view, the historic City by the Bay is striving to maintain its identity while embracing an evolution spawned by the rise and fall of high-tech and dot-commercialization and the effects of September 11 on our ever-important tourist industry and attitudes as a whole. The result? San Francisco is settling back into itself. Housing prices may not be "affordable," but they're headed in the right direction. Commercial and residential expansion has slowed. And the already-crowded city's growing pains that resulted from a 7.3% population expansion over 10 years are starting to wane since fortune seekers disappeared along with the promise of instant riches. Plainly put, the city's not as invincible or as high on itself these days.

But that's not all bad news. In fact, it's a good thing for you—especially since hotels and restaurants have lowered their prices in hopes of befriending the reluctant traveler, dining reservations are easier to come by, and traffic, though still prevalent, is less horrific. On top of that, you'll still encounter classic San Francisco: Feel the cool blast of salt air as you stroll across the Golden Gate, stuff yourself on dim sum, and walk along the beach, pierce your nose, see a play, rent a Harley—the list is endless. It's all happening in San Francisco, and everyone's invited.

1 Orientation

ARRIVING

BY PLANE

Two major airports serve the Bay Area: San Francisco International and Oakland International. All the major car-rental companies have desks at the airports; see "Getting Around" later in this chapter for details on car rentals.

SAN FRANCISCO INTERNATIONAL AIRPORT   San Francisco International Airport (© **650/877-0118;** www.flysfo.com), located 14 miles south of downtown directly on U.S. 101, is served by almost four dozen major scheduled carriers. Travel time to downtown during commuter rush hours is about 50 minutes; at other times it's about 20 to 25 minutes.

The airport offers a toll-free hot line available Monday through Friday from 7:30am to 5pm (PST) for information on ground transportation (© **800/736-2008**). The line is answered by a real person who will provide you with a run-down of all your options for getting into the city from the airport. Each of the three main terminals also has a desk where you can get the same information.

A cab from the airport to downtown will cost $28 to $32, plus tip. **SFO Airporter** buses (© **650/624-0500;** www.sfoairporter.com) depart from outside the lower-level baggage claim area to downtown San Francisco every 30 minutes from 6:15am to 9:15pm. They stop at several Union Square–area hotels, including the Grand Hyatt, San Francisco Hilton, San Francisco Marriott, Westin St. Francis, Parc Fifty-Five, Hyatt Regency, and Sheraton Palace. No reservations are needed. The cost is $12 each way; children under age 2 ride free.

Other private shuttle companies offer door-to-door airport service, in which you share a van with a few other passengers. **SuperShuttle** (© **415/558-8500;** www.supershuttle.com) will take you anywhere in the city, charging $17 to a residence or business, plus $8 for each additional person, and $50 to charter an entire van for up to seven passengers. Keep in mind that this shuttle demands they pick you up 2 hours before your flight, 3 hours during holidays.

The San Mateo County Transit system, **SamTrans** (© **800/660-4287** in Northern California, or 650/508-6200; www.samtrans.com), runs two buses between the airport and the Transbay Terminal at First and Mission streets. The no. 292 bus costs $2.20 and makes the trip in about 55 minutes. The KX bus costs $3 and takes only 35 minutes but permits only one carry-on bag. Both buses run daily. The no. 292 starts at 5:27am, and the KX starts at 6:03am. Both run frequently until 8pm, then hourly until about midnight.

OAKLAND INTERNATIONAL AIRPORT   Located about 5 miles south of downtown Oakland, at the Hagenberger Road exit off Calif. 17 (I-880), Oakland International Airport (© **510/577-4000;** www.oaklandairport.com) is used primarily by passengers with East Bay destinations. Many San Franciscans, however, prefer this less-crowded, accessible airport when flying during busy periods. Without traffic, a car or taxi ride to the airport is a quick 20 to 30 minutes; with traffic, give yourself at least an hour. It's also accessible by BART (see below for details), which is not influenced by traffic because it travels on its own tracks.

Again, taxis from the airport to downtown San Francisco are expensive, costing approximately $45, plus tip.

Bayporter Express (© **415/467-1800**) is a shuttle service that charges $23 for the first person, $10 for each additional person, to downtown San Francisco (it costs more to outer areas of town). Shuttles, usually located to the right of the airport exit, will take you to the city for around $20 per person. These are independently owned and prices vary, so ask and make any negotiations (sometimes possible) before you ride.

The cheapest way to downtown San Francisco (and easiest during traffic snarls) involves taking the shuttle bus from the airport to **BART** (Bay Area Rapid Transit; © **510/464-6000;** www.bart.gov). The **AirBART** shuttle bus runs about every 15 minutes Monday through Saturday from 6am to 11:30pm and Sunday from 8:30am to 11:30pm, stopping in front of Terminals 1 and 2 near the ground transportation signs. The cost is $2 for the 10-minute ride to BART's Coliseum terminal. BART fares vary, depending on your destination; the trip to downtown San Francisco costs $2.75 and takes 20 minutes once onboard. The entire excursion should take around 45 minutes.

BY CAR

San Francisco is accessible via several major highways: **U.S. 101** and **Calif. 1** from the north and south; and **I-80** and **I-580** from the northeast and east, respectively. If you drive from Los Angeles, you can either take the longer coastal route along Calif. 1/U.S. 101 (437 miles, or 11 hr.), or the inland route along I-5 to I-580 (389 miles, or 6½ hr.). From Mendocino, it's a little over 3 hours along Calif. 1, and about 3¼ hours along U.S. 101; and from Sacramento, it's 88 miles, or 1½ hours, along I-80.

BY TRAIN

San Francisco–bound **Amtrak** (☏ **800/USA-RAIL;** www.amtrak.com) trains leave from New York and cross the country via Chicago. The journey takes about 3½ days, and seats sell quickly. At this writing, the lowest round-trip fare costs anywhere from $429 from New York and from $359 from Chicago. These heavily restricted tickets are good for 45 to 180 days and allow up to three stops along the way, depending on your ticket.

Round-trip tickets from Los Angeles can be purchased for as little as $87. Trains actually arrive in Emeryville, just north of Oakland, and connect with regularly scheduled buses to San Francisco's Ferry Building and Caltrain station in downtown San Francisco.

Caltrain (☏ **800/660-4287** or 415/546-4461; www.caltrain.com) operates train services between San Francisco and the towns of the peninsula. The city depot is at 700 Fourth St., at Townsend Street.

VISITOR INFORMATION

The **San Francisco Visitor Information Center,** Hallidie Plaza, 900 Market St. (at Powell St.), Lower Level, San Francisco, CA 94102 (☏ **415/391-2000;** www.sfvisitor.org), is the best source for any kind of specialized information about the city. Even if you don't have a specific question, you may want to request their free *Visitors Planning Guide* and *San Francisco Visitors.*

CITY LAYOUT

San Francisco occupies the tip of a 32-mile-long peninsula between San Francisco Bay and the Pacific Ocean. Its land area measures about 46 square miles. Twin Peaks, in the geographic center of the city, is more than 900 feet high.

San Francisco may seem confusing at first, but it quickly becomes easy to negotiate. The city's downtown streets are arranged in a simple grid pattern, with the exception of Market Street and Columbus Avenue, which cut across the grid at right angles to each other. Hills appear to distort this pattern, however, and can be disorienting. But as you learn your way around, these same hills will become your landmarks and reference points.

MAIN ARTERIES & STREETS   **Market Street** is San Francisco's main thoroughfare. Most of the city's buses travel this route on their way to the Financial District from the outer neighborhoods to the west and south. The tall office buildings clustered downtown are at the northeast end of Market; 1 block beyond lie the Embarcadero and the Bay.

San Francisco at a Glance

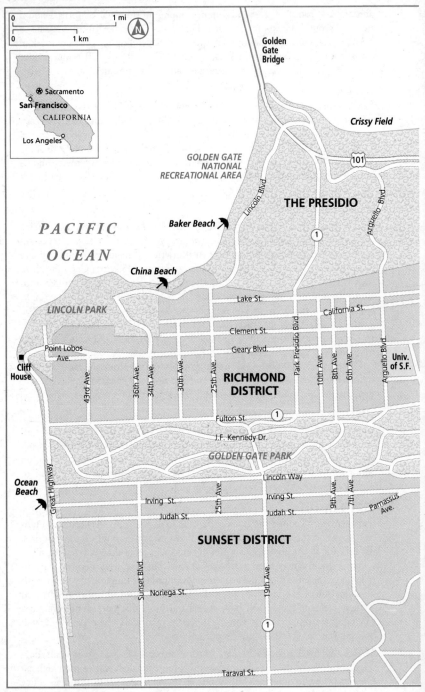

0 | 1 mi
0 | 1 km

Golden Gate Bridge

Crissy Field

CALIFORNIA

⊛ Sacramento
○ San Francisco
○ Los Angeles

GOLDEN GATE NATIONAL RECREATIONAL AREA

101

THE PRESIDIO

Lincoln Blvd

Arguello Blvd

Baker Beach

PACIFIC OCEAN

China Beach

LINCOLN PARK

Lake St.

California St.

Clement St.

Point Lobos Ave.

Geary Blvd.

Park Presidio Blvd.

Arguello Blvd.

Univ. of S.F.

Cliff House

43rd Ave.

36th Ave.

34th Ave.

30th Ave.

25th Ave.

RICHMOND DISTRICT

10th Ave.

8th Ave.

6th Ave.

Fulton St.

1

J.F. Kennedy Dr.

GOLDEN GATE PARK

Ocean Beach

Great Highway

Lincoln Way

Irving St.

25th Ave.

Irving St.

9th Ave.

7th Ave.

Parnassus Ave.

Judah St.

Judah St.

SUNSET DISTRICT

Sunset Blvd.

Noriega St.

19th Ave.

1

Taraval St.

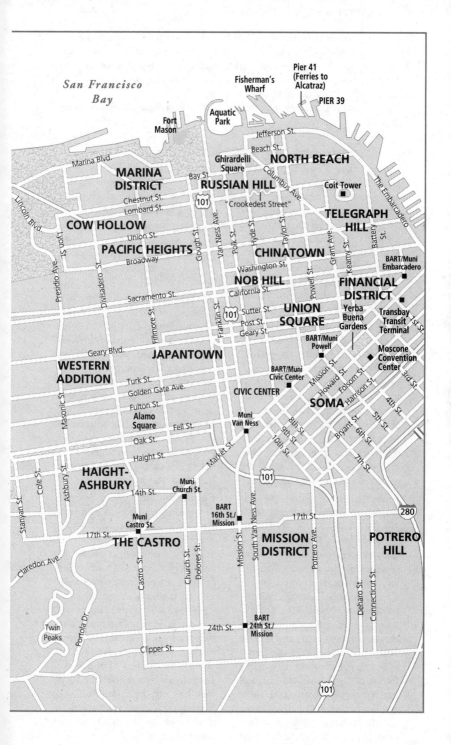

The **Embarcadero** curves along San Francisco Bay from south of the Bay Bridge to the northeast perimeter of the city and terminates at Fisherman's Wharf, the famous tourist-oriented pier. Aquatic Park, Fort Mason, and the Golden Gate National Recreation Area are located farther on around the bay, occupying the northernmost point of the peninsula.

From the eastern perimeter of Fort Mason, **Van Ness Avenue** runs due south, back to Market Street.

NEIGHBORHOODS IN BRIEF

Union Square Union Square is the commercial hub of the city. Most major hotels and department stores are crammed into the area surrounding the actual square (named for a series of violent pro-Union mass demonstrations staged here on the eve of the Civil War), with a plethora of upscale boutiques, restaurants, and galleries tucked between the larger buildings.

Nob Hill/Russian Hill Bounded by Bush, Larkin, Pacific, and Stockton streets, Nob Hill is the genteel, well-heeled district of the city, still occupied by the major power brokers and the neighborhood businesses they frequent. Russian Hill extends from Pacific to Bay and from Polk to Mason. It's marked by steep streets, lush gardens, and high-rises occupied by both the moneyed and the more bohemian.

SoMa No part of San Francisco has been more affected by recent development than South of Market (dubbed "SoMa"). The once desolate area grew to be the hub of dot-commercialization and $750,000 lofts, as well as urban entertainment à la Yerba Buena Gardens and the Museum of Modern Art. It is officially demarcated by the Embarcadero, Highway 101, and Market Street, with the greatest concentrations of interest around Yerba Buena Center, along Folsom and Harrison streets between Steuart and Sixth, and Brannan and Market. Along the waterfront are an array of restaurants and the new and absolutely fab Pacific Bell Park. Farther west, around Folsom between 7th and 11th streets, is where much of the city's nightclubbing occurs.

Financial District East of Union Square, this area bordered by the Embarcadero and Market, Third, Kearny, and Washington streets is the city's business district and stomping grounds for many major corporations. The pointy Trans-America Pyramid, at Montgomery and Clay streets, is one of the area's most conspicuous features. To its east stands the sprawling Embarcadero Center, an 8½-acre complex housing offices, shops, and restaurants. Farther east still is the World Trade Center, standing adjacent to the old Ferry Building, the city's pre-bridge transportation hub. Ferries to Sausalito and Larkspur still leave from this point.

Chinatown The official entrance to Chinatown is marked by a large red-and-green gate on Grant Avenue at Bush Street. Beyond lies a 24-block labyrinth, bordered by Broadway, Bush, Kearny, and Stockton streets, filled with restaurants, markets, temples, and shops—and, of course, a substantial percentage of San Francisco's Chinese residents. Chinatown is a great place for urban exploration all along Stockton, Grant, and Portsmouth Square, and the alleys that lead off them like Ross and Waverly. This area is jam-packed, so don't even think about driving around here.

North Beach The Italian quarter, which stretches from Montgomery and Jackson to Bay Street, is one of the best places in the city to grab some coffee, pull up a cafe chair, and do some serious people-watching. Nightlife is equally happening: Restaurants, bars, and clubs along Columbus and Grant avenues attract folks from all over the Bay Area to fight for a parking place and romp through the festive neighborhood. Down Columbus toward the Financial District are the remains of the city's Beat generation landmarks, including Lawrence Ferlinghetti's City Lights Bookstore and Vesuvio's Bar. Broadway—a short strip of sex joints—cuts through the heart of the district. Telegraph Hill looms over the east side of North Beach, topped by Coit Tower, one of San Francisco's best vantage points.

Fisherman's Wharf North Beach runs into Fisherman's Wharf, which was once the busy heart of the city's great harbor and waterfront industries. Today, it is a tacky-but-attractive tourist area with little if any authentic waterfront life, except for recreational boating and some friendly sea lions.

Marina District Created on landfill for the Panama-Pacific Exposition of 1915, the Marina boasts some of the best views of the Golden Gate, as well as plenty of grassy fields alongside San Francisco Bay (check out newly restored Crissy Fields). Streets are lined with elegant, Mediterranean-style homes and apartments, which are inhabited by the city's well-to-do singles and wealthy families. Here, too, are the Palace of Fine Arts, the Exploratorium, and Fort Mason Center. The main street is Chestnut between Franklin and Lyon, which is lined with shops, cafes, and boutiques. Because of its landfill foundation, the Marina was one of the city's hardest-hit districts in the 1989 quake.

Cow Hollow Located west of Van Ness Avenue, between Russian Hill and the Presidio, this flat area supported 30 dairy farms in 1861. Today, Cow Hollow is largely residential and occupied by the city's young and yuppie. Its two primary commercial thoroughfares are Lombard Street, known for its many relatively inexpensive motels; and Union Street, a flourishing shopping sector filled with restaurants, pubs, cafes, and shops.

Pacific Heights The ultra-elite, such as the Gettys and Danielle Steel—and those lucky enough to buy before the real-estate boom—reside in the mansions and homes that make up Pacific Heights. When the rich meander out of their fortresses, they wander down to Union Street, a long stretch of boutiques, restaurants, cafes, and bars.

Japantown Bounded by Octavia, Fillmore, California, and Geary streets, Japantown shelters only a small percentage of the city's Japanese population, but it's still a cultural experience (albeit rather anticlimactic) to explore these few square blocks and the shops and restaurants within them.

Civic Center Although millions of dollars have been expended on brick sidewalks, ornate lampposts, and elaborate street plantings, the southwestern section of Market Street remains downright dilapidated. The Civic Center, at the "bottom" of Market Street, is an exception. This large complex of buildings includes the domed City Hall, the Opera House, Davies Symphony Hall, and the city's main library. The landscaped plaza connecting the buildings is the staging area for San Francisco's demonstrations for or against just about everything.

Haight-Ashbury Part trendy, part nostalgic, part funky, the Haight, as it's most commonly known, was the soul of the psychedelic and free-loving 1960s and the center of the counterculture movement. Today, the neighborhood straddling upper Haight Street on the eastern border of Golden Gate Park is more gentrified, but the commercial area still harbors all walks of life. Leftover aging hippies mingle outside Ben & Jerry's ice-cream shop with grungy, begging street kids, nondescript marijuana dealers, and people with Day-Glo hair. But you don't need to be a freak or wear tie-dye to enjoy the Haight: The food, shops, and bars cover all tastes. From Haight Street, walk south on Cole Street for a more peaceful and quaint neighborhood experience.

Richmond & Sunset Districts San Francisco's suburbs of sorts, these are the city's largest and most populous districts, consisting mainly of homes, small shops, and neighborhood restaurants. Though both districts border Golden Gate Park and Ocean Beach, only a small percentage of tourists venture into "The Avenues," as this area is referred to by locals.

The Castro One of the liveliest streets in town, Castro is practically synonymous with San Francisco's gay community. Located at the very end of Market Street, between 17th and 18th streets, the Castro supports dozens of shops, restaurants, and bars catering to the gay community. Open-minded straight people are welcome, too.

Mission District This is another area greatly affected by the city's new wealth. The Mexican and Latin American populations, along with their cuisine, traditions, and art, still make the Mission District a vibrant area to visit. Some parts of the neighborhood are still poor and sprinkled with the homeless, gangs, and drug addicts, but more and more young urbanites are infiltrating, moving into the "reasonably" priced rentals (reasonable is a relative term) and forging the endless oh-so-hot restaurants and bars that stretch from 16th Street and Valencia to 25th and Mission streets. Less adventurous tourists still duck into Mission Dolores, cruise by a few of the 200-plus amazing murals, and head back downtown. Don't be afraid to visit this area, but do use caution at night.

2 Getting Around

BY PUBLIC TRANSPORTATION

The San Francisco Municipal Railway, better known as **Muni** (© 415/673-6864), operates the city's cable cars, buses, and Metro streetcars. Together, these three public transportation services crisscross the entire city, making San Francisco fully accessible to everyone. Buses and Metro streetcars cost $1 for adults, 35¢ for children ages 5 to 17, and 35¢ for seniors over 65. Cable cars cost $3 ($1 for seniors 9pm–midnight and 6–7am). Needless to say, they're packed primarily with tourists. Exact change is required on all vehicles except cable cars.

For detailed route information, phone Muni or consult the bus map at the front of the Yellow Pages. If you plan on making extensive use of public transportation, you may want to invest in a comprehensive route map ($2), sold at the San Francisco Visitor Information Center (see "Visitor Information" in the "Orientation" section, earlier in this chapter) and in many downtown retail outlets.

Muni **discount passes,** called "Passports," entitle holders to unlimited rides on buses, Metro streetcars, and cable cars. A Passport costs $6 for 1 day, and $10 or $15 for 3 or 7 consecutive days. Muni's "City Pass," which costs $33 for adults, $26 for seniors 65 and older, and $24 for kids 5 to 17, entitles you to unlimited rides for 7 days, plus admission at the California Academy of Sciences, Museum of Modern Art, Exploratorium, and Blue & Gold Fleet Bay Cruise. You can buy a Passport or City Pass at the San Francisco Visitor Information Center, the Holiday Inn Civic Center, and the TIX Bay Area booth at Union Square. But for the Blue & Gold Fleet tour to be included, you must purchase tickets through them by calling Blue & Gold Fleet at ✆ **415/705-5555.** A $2.25 fee applies to this service.

BY CABLE CAR   San Francisco's cable cars may not be the most practical means of transport, but these rolling historic landmarks sure are a fun ride. There are only three lines in the city, and they're all concentrated in the downtown area. The most scenic, and exciting, is the **Powell-Hyde line,** which follows a zigzag route from the corner of Powell and Market streets, over both Nob Hill and Russian Hill, to a turntable at gaslit Victorian Square in front of Aquatic Park. The **Powell-Mason line** starts at the same intersection and climbs over Nob Hill before descending to Bay Street, just 3 blocks from Fisherman's Wharf. The least scenic is the **California Street line,** which begins at the foot of Market Street and runs a straight course through Chinatown and over Nob Hill to Van Ness Avenue. All riders must exit at the last stop and wait in line for the return trip. The cable car system operates daily from approximately 6:30am to 12:30am.

BY BUS   Buses reach almost every corner of San Francisco and travel over the bridges to Marin County and Oakland. All are numbered and display their destinations on the front. Stops are designated by signs, curb markings, and yellow bands on adjacent utility poles, and most bus shelters exhibit Muni's transportation map and schedule. Many buses travel along Market Street or pass near Union Square and run daily from about 6am to midnight, after which there is infrequent all-night "Owl" service. If you can help it, for safety and convenience, avoid taking buses late at night.

Popular tourist routes are nos. 5, 7, and 71, all of which run to Golden Gate Park; 41 and 45, which travel along Union Street; and 30, which runs between Union Square and Ghirardelli Square.

BY METRO STREETCAR   Five of Muni's six Metro streetcar lines, designated J, K, L, M, and N, run underground downtown and on the street in the outer neighborhoods. The sleek railcars make the same stops as BART (see below) along Market Street, including Embarcadero Station (in the Financial District), Montgomery and Powell streets (both near Union Sq.), and the Civic Center (near City Hall). Past the Civic Center, the routes branch off in different directions: The J line will take you to Mission Dolores; the K, L, and M lines to Castro Street; and the N line parallels Golden Gate Park and now extends all the way to the Embarcadero. Metros run about every 15 minutes, more frequently during rush hours. Service is offered Monday through Friday from 5am to 12:30am, on Saturday from 6am to 12:20am, and on Sunday from 8am to 12:20am. The L and N lines operate all day and all night.

The most recent streetcar additions are not newcomers at all, but San Francisco's beloved 1930s streetcars. The beautiful, rejuvenated multicolored cars on the F Market line now run along the Embarcadero from Fisherman's Wharf to Market Street, and then to the Castro and back. It's a quick and charming way to get up- and downtown without any hassle.

BY BART BART, an acronym for **Bay Area Rapid Transit** (© 650/992-2278), is a futuristic-looking, high-speed rail network that connects San Francisco with the East Bay—Oakland, Richmond, Concord, and Fremont. Four stations are located along Market Street (see "By Metro Streetcar," above). Fares range from $1.10 to $4.30, depending on how far you go. Tickets are dispensed from machines in the stations and are magnetically encoded with a dollar amount. Computerized exits automatically deduct the correct fare. Children 4 and under ride free. Trains run every 15 to 20 minutes, Monday through Friday from 4am to midnight, Saturday from 6am to midnight, and Sunday from 8am to midnight.

A $2.5 billion, 33-mile BART extension, currently under construction, includes a southern line that is planned to extend all the way to San Francisco International Airport. It will open, presumably, around the beginning of 2005, but we're not holding our breath.

BY TAXI

If you're downtown during rush hours or leaving from a major hotel, it won't be hard to hail a cab—just look for the lighted sign on the roof that indicates if one is available. Otherwise, it's a good idea to call one of the following companies to arrange a ride: **Veteran's Cab** (© 415/552-1300), **Luxor Cabs** (© 415/282-4141), or **Yellow Cab** (© 415/626-2345). Rates are approximately $2.50 for the first mile and $1.80 for each mile thereafter.

BY CAR

In this crowded and compact city, a car can be your worst nightmare. You're likely to end up stuck in traffic with lots of aggressive and frustrated drivers (especially downtown), pay upward of $30 a day in parking, and spend a good portion of your vacation looking for a parking space. But if you want to venture outside of the city, driving is the best way to go.

RENTALS The major car-rental companies operating in the city include **Alamo** (© 800/462-5866), **Avis** (© 800/230-4898), **Budget** (© 800/527-0700), **Dollar** (© 800/800-3665), **Hertz** (© 800/654-3131), **National** (© 800/227-7368), and **Thrifty** (© 800/847-4389).

PARKING If you want to have a relaxing vacation here, don't even attempt to find street parking downtown or in Nob Hill, North Beach, or Chinatown; by Fisherman's Wharf; or on Telegraph Hill. Park in a garage or take a cab or a bus. If you do find street parking, pay attention to street signs that will explain when you can park and for how long. Be especially careful not to park in zones that are tow areas during rush hours.

When parking on a hill, apply the hand brake, put the car in gear, and *curb your wheels*—toward the curb when facing downhill, away from the curb when facing uphill. Curbing your wheels will not only prevent a possible "runaway," but also keep you from getting a ticket—an expensive fine that is aggressively enforced.

 FAST FACTS: San Francisco

American Express For travel arrangements, traveler's checks, currency exchange, and other member services, American Express has an office 455 Market St. at First Street (© 415/536-2600), open Monday through Friday from 8:30am to 5:30pm and Saturday from 9am to 2pm. To report lost or stolen traveler's checks, call ℂ **800/221-7282.** For American Express Global Assist, call ℂ **800/554-2639.**

Dentist In the event of a dental emergency, see your hotel concierge or contact the **San Francisco Dental Office,** 131 Steuart St. (ℂ **415/777-5115**), between Mission and Howard streets, which offers emergency service and comprehensive dental care Monday, Tuesday, and Friday from 8am to 4:30pm, Wednesday and Thursday from 10:30am to 6:30pm.

Doctor **Saint Francis Memorial Hospital,** 900 Hyde St., between Bush and Pine streets on Nob Hill (ℂ **415/353-6000**), provides 24-hour emergency-care service. The hospital also operates a physician-referral service (ℂ **800/333-1355**).

Drugstores See "Pharmacies," below.

Emergencies Dial ℂ **911** for the police, an ambulance, or the fire department.

Pharmacies There are **Walgreens** drugstores all over town, including one at 135 Powell St. (ℂ **415/391-4433**). The store is open Monday through Friday from 8am to midnight, Saturday from 8am to midnight, and Sunday from 9am to 10pm, but the pharmacy has more limited hours: Monday through Friday from 8am to 9pm, Saturday from 9am to 5pm, and closed Sunday. The branch on Divisadero Street at Lombard (ℂ **415/931-6415**) has a 24-hour pharmacy. The pharmacy at **Merrill's,** 805 Market St. (ℂ **415/431-5466**), is open Monday through Friday from 8:30am to 6:30pm and Saturday from 9:30am to 5:30pm, while the rest of the drugstore is open Monday through Friday from 7am to 9pm, Saturday from 9am to 7pm, and Sunday from 9:30am to 6pm.

Police For emergencies, dial ℂ **911** from any phone; no coins are needed. For other matters, call ℂ **415/553-0123.**

Post Office There are dozens of post offices located all around the city. The closest office to Union Square is inside Macy's department store, 170 O'Farrell St. (ℂ **800/275-8777**).

Safety Few locals would recommend walking alone late at night in certain areas, particularly the Tenderloin, between Union Square and the Civic Center. Compared with similar areas in other cities, however, even this section of San Francisco is relatively tranquil. Other areas where you should be particularly alert are the Mission District, around 16th and Mission streets; the lower Fillmore area, around lower Haight Street; and the SoMa area south of Market Street.

Taxes An 8.5% sales tax is added at the register for all goods and services purchased in San Francisco. The city hotel tax is a whopping 14%. There is no airport tax.

Transit Information Call **Muni** at ℂ **415/673-6864** Monday through Friday between 7am and 5pm and Saturday and Sunday between 9am and 5pm. At other times, recorded information is available.

Useful Telephone Numbers **Tourist information** (ℂ 415/283-0176); **highway conditions** (ℂ 800/427-7623); **Moviefone** (ℂ 415/777-FILM).

Weather Call ℂ **831/656-1725** to find out when the next fog bank is rolling in.

3 Where to Stay

San Francisco is an extensive—and expensive—hotel town, especially considering its relatively small size. I can't cover them all in this guide, so if you'd like a larger selection, check out *Frommer's San Francisco 2003*, which has dozens of other options.

Most of the hotels listed below are within easy walking distance of Union Square, and accessible via cable car. Union Square is near the city's major shops, the Financial District, and all transportation. Prices listed below do not include state and city taxes, which total 14%.

The price categories below reflect the prices of double rooms during the high season, which runs approximately April through September. (In reality, rates vary greatly these days since tourism has been down since Sept 11, 2001.) So remember: These are rack (or published) rates; you can almost always get a better deal if you inquire about packages, weekend discounts, corporate rates, and family plans.

Bed-and-Breakfast Inns Online (www.bbonline.com/ca) offers a small selection of accommodations in San Francisco. **San Francisco Reservations,** 360 22nd St., Suite 300, Oakland, CA 94612 (© **800/677-1500** or 510/628-4450; www.hotelres.com), arranges reservations at more than 300 of San Francisco's hotels and often offers discounted rates.

In addition to the hotels listed below, I also recommend those represented by the reasonably priced and fashionable **Joie de Vivre** hotel chain (© **800/SF-TRIPS;** www.sftrips.com) and **Personality Hotels** (© **800/553-1900;** www. personalityhotels.com), which spiffs up older buildings in central locales. Pricier options include those from the **Kimpton Group,** such as the **Juliana Hotel** (© **800/328-3880**) and the new **Hotel Serrano** (© **415/885-2500**), the latter of which opened in mid-1999; and the stately **Donatello** (© **800/227-3184**). The **Hilton San Francisco** (© **800/HILTONS**) and **San Francisco Marriott** (© **800/228-9290**) both have impersonal convention-hotel ambience, but are conveniently located downtown and have enough rooms to sleep thousands.

UNION SQUARE
VERY EXPENSIVE

Campton Place Hotel ★★★   With a $10 million room renovation completed at the end of 2000, this already fabulous luxury boutique hotel offers some of the best accommodations in town—not to mention the most expensive. Along with gutting the rooms and replacing the furnishings with limestone, pear wood, and more Italian-modern and Asian-influenced decor, management changed the rooms' layout for the better. By eliminating 17 of the once-cramped rooms, they made the new 110 units more spacious. Two executive suites and one luxury suite push the haute envelope to even more luxurious heights. Discriminating returning guests will still find superlative service, extra-large beds, exquisite bathrooms, bathrobes, top-notch toiletries, slippers, and every necessity and whim that's made Campton Place a favored temporary address. Revered chef Laurent Manrique delights diners at the excellent Campton Place Restaurant, which as this book goes to press is undergoing its own face-lift.

340 Stockton St. (between Post and Sutter sts.), San Francisco, CA 94108. © **800/235-4300** or 415/781-5555. Fax 415/955-5536. www.camptonplace.com. 110 units. $345–$475 double; $550–$2,000 suite. American breakfast $19. AE, DC, MC, V. Valet parking $32. Cable car: Powell-Hyde and Powell-Mason lines (1 block W). Bus: 2, 3, 4, 30, or 45. **Amenities:** Restaurant; access to nearby health club; concierge; courtesy car; secretarial services; 24-hr. room service; in-room massage; babysitting; laundry service; same-day dry cleaning. *In room:* A/C, TV w/pay movies, fax, dataport, minibar, hair dryer, iron, safe.

Prescott Hotel 🏨🏨 It may be small, but boutique Prescott has some big things going for it. The staff treats you like royalty, rooms are attractively unfrilly and masculine, the location (just a block from Union Sq.) is perfect, and limited room service is provided by one of the most popular restaurants in the city, Postrio. Dark tones of green, plum, and burgundy blend well with the cherry-wood furnishings in each of the soundproof rooms; the view, alas, isn't so pleasant. The very small bathrooms contain terry robes and hair dryers, but only the suites have Jacuzzi bathtubs. Concierge-level guests are pampered with free continental breakfast, evening cocktails, and even head and shoulder massages.

545 Post St. (between Mason and Taylor sts.), San Francisco, CA 94102. ✆ 800/283-7322 or 415/563-0303. Fax 415/563-6831. www.kimptongroup.com. 164 units. $270–$325 double; $300 concierge-level double (including breakfast and evening cocktail reception); from $365 suite. AE, DC, DISC, MC, V. Valet parking $35. Cable car: Powell-Hyde and Powell-Mason lines (1 block E). Bus: 2, 3, 4, 30, 38, or 45. **Amenities:** Restaurant/bar; small exercise room; concierge; limited courtesy car; limited room service. In room: TV w/pay movies, minibar, hair dryer, iron, safe.

Westin St. Francis 🏨🏨 *Kids* Although the St. Francis is too massive to offer the personal service you get at the smaller deluxe hotels on Nob Hill, few other hotels in San Francisco can match its majestic aura. It sounds corny, but the St. Francis is so intertwined with the city's past that it truly is San Francisco: Stroll through the vast, ornate lobby and you can feel 100 years of history oozing from its hand-carved redwood paneling. The hotel did a massive $50 million renovation in 1996 and threw in another $60 million in 1999, replacing the carpeting, furniture, and bedding in every main-building guest room, gussying up the lobby, and restoring the facade. Today the rooms in the Tower, which was built in the 1970s and renovated in 2001, evoke a contemporary design in the vein of W Hotel style. The historic main building accentuates its history with traditional, more elegant ambience, high ceilings, and crown molding. Even if you stay elsewhere, it's worth a visit if only to partake of high tea at the Compass Rose, one of San Francisco's most enduring and enjoyable traditions.

The Westin Kids Club program means that when families check in, the kids receive age-specific gifts.

335 Powell St. (between Geary and Post sts.), San Francisco, CA 94102. ✆ 800/WESTIN-1 or 415/397-7000. Fax 415/774-0124. www.westin.com. 1,195 units. Main building: $199–$499 double; Tower (Grand View): $219–$549 double; from $550 suite. Extra person $30. Continental breakfast $15–$18. AE, DC, DISC, MC, V. Valet parking $39. Cable car: Powell-Hyde and Powell-Mason lines (direct stop). Bus: 2, 3, 4, 30, 38, 45, or 76. Pets under 35 lb. accepted with $30 fee. **Amenities:** 2 restaurants; bar; elaborate health club and spa; concierge; car-rental desk; business center; 24-hr. room service. In room: A/C, TV, dataport, minibar, fridge, hair dryer.

EXPENSIVE

Handlery Union Square Hotel 🏨 A mere half-block from Union Square, the Handlery was already a good deal before the 1906 building and its more modern annex underwent a complete overhaul in 2002. Now you'll find every amenity you could possibly need, plus lots of extras, in the extremely tasteful and modern (although sedate and a little dark) rooms. Literally everything's new here: mattresses, alarm radios, voice mail, refrigerators, light fixtures, paint, carpets, and furnishings. Perks include adjoining decent LA-based chain restaurant The Daily Grill, outdoor heated pool, and club-level options (in the newer building) that include larger rooms, a complimentary morning newspaper, turndown service, bathroom scale, robes, two phones, and adjoining doors that make them great choices for families. Downsides? Not a lot of direct light, no grand feeling in the lobby, and lots of trekking if you want to go to and from the adjoining buildings that make up the hotel.

San Francisco Accommodations

The Abigail Howard Johnson Hotel **36**
The Andrews Hotel **20**
Beck's Motor Lodge **1**
Campton Place Hotel **30**
The Clarion Bedford Hotel **21**
The Commodore Hotel **19**
Edward II Inn & Suites **5**
The Fairmont Hotel & Tower **16**
The Four Seasons San Francisco **32**
The Golden Gate Hotel **18**
Handlery Union Square Hotel **27**
The Harbor Court **35**
Hotel Bijou **24**
The Hotel Bohème **13**
Hotel Del Sol **7**
Hotel Diva **26**
The Hotel Majestic **3**
Hotel Triton **31**
The Huntington Hotel **17**
King George Hotel **25**
The Laurel **4**
The Mandarin Oriental **14**
The Marina Inn **8**
The Mark Hopkins Intercontinental **16**
The Palace Hotel **34**
The Parker Guest House **2**
The Phoenix Hotel **37**
Prescott Hotel **27**
The Queen Anne Hotel **3**
The Ritz-Carlton **15**
The San Remo Hotel **12**
The Savoy Hotel **22**
Shannon Court **20**
Sheraton Fisherman's Wharf Hotel **10**
Sir Francis Drake **29**
The Tuscan Inn **11**
Union Street Inn **6**
W San Francisco Hotel **33**
The Warwick Regis **23**
Westin St. Francis **28**
The Wharf Inn **9**

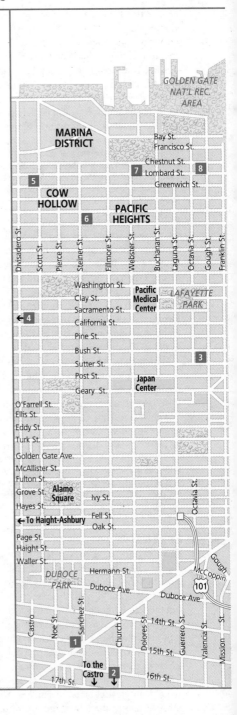

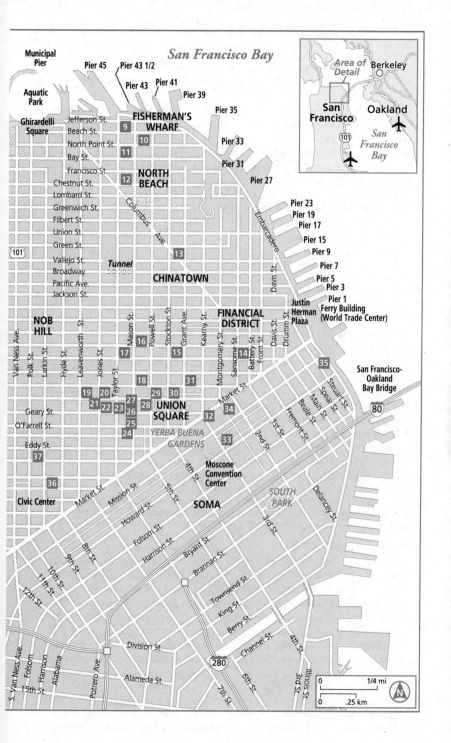

San Francisco Bay

Municipal Pier

Pier 45   Pier 43 1/2

Aquatic Park   Pier 43   Pier 41

Ghirardelli Square   Pier 39

Jefferson St.   FISHERMAN'S WHARF   Pier 35

Beach St.   9

North Point St.   10   Pier 33

Bay St.   11   Pier 31

Francisco St.   Pier 27

Chestnut St.   12   NORTH BEACH

Lombard St.

Greenwich St.   Pier 23

Filbert St.   Pier 19

Union St.   Pier 17

Green St.   Pier 15

101   Pier 9

Vallejo St.   13   Pier 7

Broadway   Tunnel   Pier 5

Pacific Ave.   CHINATOWN   Pier 3

Jackson St.   Pier 1

NOB HILL   FINANCIAL DISTRICT   Justin Herman Plaza   Ferry Building (World Trade Center)

16

17   35

18   San Francisco-Oakland Bay Bridge

19   20   29   30   31   80

21   22   23   27   28   UNION SQUARE

Geary St.   26   32   34

O'Farrell St.   25

24   YERBA BUENA GARDENS   33

Eddy St.

37   Moscone Convention Center

36   SOUTH PARK

Civic Center   Market St.   Mission St.   SOMA

Howard St.

Folsom St.

Harrison St.   Bryant St.

Brannan St.

Townsend St.

King St.

Berry St.

Division St.   Channel St.

280   Alameda St.

Area of Detail   Berkeley

San Francisco   Oakland

101   San Francisco Bay

0   1/4 mi

0   .25 km

N

79

351 Geary St. (between Mason and Powell sts.), San Francisco, CA 94102. ✆ **800/843-4343** or 415/781-7800. Fax 415/781-0269. www.handlery.com. 377 units. $195 double; club section from $289 double; from $260 suite. Extra person $10. AE, DC, DISC, MC, V. Parking $28. Cable car: Powell-Hyde and Powell-Mason lines (direct stop). Bus: 2, 3, 4, 30, 38, or 45. **Amenities:** Restaurant; heated outdoor pool; access to nearby health club ($10 per day); sauna; barber shop; limited room service; babysitting; same-day laundry. *In room:* A/C, TV w/Nintendo and pay movies, dataport, fridge, hair dryer, iron, safe.

Hotel Diva ⭐   The Diva is the prima donna of San Francisco's affordable modern hotels. A profusion of curvaceous glass, marble, and steel marks the Euro-tech lobby; the minimalist rooms, spotless and neat, are softened with utterly fashionable "Italian modern" furnishings of monochromatic colors, silver, and wood. Personally, I find the hotel a little on the cold side (figuratively speaking). But toys and services abound, including VCRs (with a discreet video vending machine), Nintendo, and breakfast delivered to your room. *Insider tip:* Reserve one of the rooms ending in "09," which have extra-large bathrooms with vanity mirrors and makeup tables. The downside: views that make you want to keep the chic curtains closed.

440 Geary St. (between Mason and Taylor sts.), San Francisco, CA 94102. ✆ **800/553-1900** or 415/885-0200. Fax 415/346-6613. www.hoteldiva.com. 111 units. $189 double; $229 junior suite; $550 suite. Rates include continental breakfast. AE, DC, DISC, MC, V. Valet parking $27. Cable car: Powell-Mason line. Bus: 38 or 38L. **Amenities:** Exercise room; concierge; secretarial services; limited room service from nearby California Pizza Kitchen; laundry service; dry cleaning. *In room:* A/C, TV/VCR, CD player, fax, dataport, minibar, hair dryer, iron, safe.

Hotel Triton ⭐⭐   Described as chic, retro-futuristic, and even neo-baroque, the Triton begs attention, from the Dalí-esque lobby and designer suites à la Jerry Garcia, Santana, and Wyland (the ocean artist) to the New York hip clientele lounging in the funky lobby. Two dozen environmentally sensitive "Eco-Rooms"—with biodegradable soaps, filtered water and air, and all-natural linens—were also installed to please the tree-hugger in all of us. Good news: All the rooms were completely redone in 2001 and 2002 and the hotel serves coffee each morning and wine, beer, and tarot readings every evening (included in the room rate) in the lobby. Adjoining Café de la Presse, a European-style newsstand and outdoor cafe, serves breakfast, lunch, and dinner.

342 Grant Ave. (at Bush St.), San Francisco, CA 94108. ✆ **800/433-6611** or 415/394-0500. Fax 415/394-0555. www.hotel-tritonsf.com. 140 units. $119–$239 double; $299 suite. AE, DC, DISC, MC, V. Parking $30. Cable car: Powell-Hyde and Powell-Mason lines (2 blocks W). Pets accepted with $50 fee. **Amenities:** Cafe; exercise room; business center; room service 7am–11pm; same-day laundry service and dry cleaning. *In room:* A/C, TV w/pay movies, fax, dataport, minibar, hair dryer, coffeemaker, iron.

Sir Francis Drake ⭐⭐   The Sir Francis Drake, which has undergone millions in renovations over the past 10 years, is a hotel for people who are willing to trade a chipped bathroom tile or oddly matched furniture for the opportunity to vacation in pseudo-grand fashion. Allow Tom Sweeny, the ebullient (and legendary) Beefeater doorman, to handle your bags as you enter the elegant, captivating lobby. Sip cocktails or swing dance to a live orchestra at the superchic retro Starlight Room while overlooking the city. Dine at Scala's Bistro, one of the hottest restaurants downtown, and get comfortable in a room amidst the historic hotel's 21 floors, or dine at Scala's, one of downtown's best Italian restaurants. In short, live like the king or queen of Union Square without all the pomp, circumstance, and credit-card bills.

450 Powell St. (at Sutter St.), San Francisco, CA 94102. ✆ **800/227-5480** or 415/392-7755. Fax 415/391-8719. www.sirfrancisdrake.com. 417 units. $219–$259 double; $500–$700 suite. AE, DC, DISC, MC, V. Valet parking $32. Cable car: Powell-Hyde and Powell-Mason lines (direct stop). Bus: 2, 3, 4, 45, or 76. **Amenities:**

(*Kids* **Family-Friendly Hotels**

Westin St. Francis (p. 77)   All children under 12 are given a Kids Club hat on arrival, and special sports bottles and complimentary refills in the restaurants. Kids ages 3 to 7 also get fun stuff like dinosaur soaps and sponges, and coloring books.

The Wharf Inn (p. 88)   No whining about when you'll get there 'cause you're already there—right smack dab in the middle of the wharf. Plus, parking is free, and there's no charge for packing along an extra monster.

2 restaurants; bar; exercise room; concierge; limited room service; same-day laundry and dry cleaning. *In room:* A/C, TV w/pay movies, dataport, minibar, hair dryer, iron on request.

MODERATE

A few worthy hotel companies operate many properties throughout the city. **Holiday Inn** (✆ 800/465-4329; www.basshotels.com/holiday-inn) has several strategic locations.

The Andrews Hotel ✰   For the location and price, the Andrews is a safe bet for an enjoyable stay. Two blocks west of Union Square, the Andrews was a Turkish bath before its conversion in 1981. As is typical in Euro-style hotels, the rooms are small but well maintained and comfortable, with nice touches like white lace curtains and fresh flowers. Upgrades in 2002 included new mattresses and carpets (in most rooms); the staff is now moving on to the bathrooms, which tend to be tiny.

624 Post St. (between Jones and Taylor sts.), San Francisco, CA 94109. ✆ 800/926-3739 or 415/563-6877. Fax 415/928-6919. www.andrewshotel.com. 48 units (some with shower only). $105–$125 double; $145–$155 superior rooms. Rates include continental breakfast and evening wine. AE, DC, MC, V. Valet parking $20. Cable car: Powell-Hyde and Powell-Mason lines (3 blocks E). Bus: 2, 3, 4, 30, 38, or 45. **Amenities:** Restaurant; access to nearby health club; concierge; room service 5:30–10pm; babysitting; nearby coin-op laundry and laundry service; dry cleaning. *In room:* TV/VCR w/pay movies and video library, dataport, fridge in suites only, coffeemaker and hair dryer on request, iron.

The Clarion Bedford Hotel ✰✰ *(Value)*   This 17-story favorite located 3 blocks from Union Square has taken a seriously sharp turn with its new "hip and retro look," introduced in 2002. Personally, I'm not a fan of the all-lavender lobby or the Jonathan Adler–like masculine color scheme of blue and brown that makes up the renovated rooms (only half of all the rooms; the remaining 50%, destined for the same design fate, maintains flowery, lighter decor). But if cheap-chic is your gig, you'll be thrilled with this package, which includes a large spotless room with a new mattress, a writing desk, armchair, and a well-stocked honor bar with plenty of munchies; service from an enthusiastic, attentive, and professional staff; and complimentary wine hour, *USA Today*, and limo service to Union Square. Although closets are big, bathrooms are small. Most rooms are sunny and bright, with priceless views of the city (the higher the floor, the better the view).

The hotel's bistro, Café 44, which is virtually in the lobby, has a small, beautiful mahogany bar opposite the registration desk.

761 Post St. (between Leavenworth and Jones sts.), San Francisco, CA 94109. ✆ 800/252-7466 or 415/673-6040. Fax 415/563-6739. www.hotelbedford.com. 144 units. $159–$199 double; from $209 suite. Kids

under 17 and pets stay free. Continental breakfast $8.50. AE, DC, DISC, MC, V. Valet parking $25. Cable car: Powell-Hyde and Powell-Mason lines (4 blocks E). Bus: 2, 3, 4, or 27. Pets under 25 lb. accepted with $50 deposit. **Amenities:** Restaurant/bar; secretarial services; room service (breakfast only); laundry service; dry cleaning. *In room:* TV w/pay movies and Nintendo, dataport, minibar, coffeemaker, hair dryer, iron.

The Commodore Hotel ★★

If you're looking to pump a little fun and fantasy into your vacation, this low-budget trendy spot is the place. The "Neo-Deco" rooms, all of which were upgraded in 2001, feature bright colors, whimsical furnishings, pretty artwork, and recently refurbished bathrooms. One unrenovated room is generic motel style and has twin beds with hard mattresses and a small bathroom. Stealing the show is the Red Room, a swank and dim bar and lounge that's ruby red through and through. Adjoining is the stylish Titanic Café, a cute little diner serving buckwheat griddlecakes, Vietnamese tofu sandwiches, and salads.

825 Sutter St. (at Jones St.), San Francisco, CA 94109. ℂ **800/338-6848** or 415/923-6800. Fax 415/923-6804. www.thecommodorehotel.com. 110 units. $125–$169 double. AE, DC, DISC, MC, V. Parking $22. Bus: 2, 3, 4, 27, or 76. **Amenities:** Diner; bar; access to nearby health club ($15 per day); concierge; tour and car-rental desk. *In room:* TV w/pay movies, dataport, coffeemaker, hair dryer, iron.

The Fitzgerald ★

The Fitzgerald's guest accommodations may be outfitted with newish furniture and sweet striped wallpaper, and accented with bright bedspreads and patterned carpet, but some of the rooms are really small. (One that I saw had a dresser less than a foot from the bed.) Of course, at $80 per night there's no room for complaining. But do ask for a larger room. If you can live without a sizable closet, you'll find that the price, breakfast (home-baked breads, scones, muffins, juice, tea, and coffee), and cleanliness of this hotel make it a good value. Take heed: The view of the Golden Gate that's printed on the brochure is not actually visible from the hotel.

620 Post St. (between Jones and Taylor sts.), San Francisco, CA 94109. ℂ **800/334-6835** or 415/775-8100. Fax 415/775-1278. www.fitzgeraldhotel.com. 39 units. $79–$189 double. Extra person $10. Rates include continental breakfast. Lower rates in winter. AE, DC, DISC, MC, V. Self-parking $20. Cable car: Powell-Hyde and Powell-Mason lines. Bus: 2, 3, 4, or 27. **Amenities:** Access to a nearby indoor pool and exercise room; concierge; in-room massage; dry cleaning. *In room:* TV, dataport, hair dryer.

King George Hotel ★★ (Value)

Built in 1914 for the Panama-Pacific Exhibition, this utterly delightful hotel has fared well over the years, continuing to draw a mostly European clientele. The location—surrounded by cable-car lines, the Theater District, Union Square, and dozens of restaurants—is superb, and the rooms are surprisingly quiet for such a busy area. Though the very clean rooms can be small, a complete room renovation in 1999 made the most of the space with new mattresses, desks, and a handsome study-like ambience. A big hit since it started a few years back is the hotel's English afternoon tea, served in the Windsor Tea Room Thursday through Sunday from 3 to 6:30pm.

334 Mason St. (between Geary and O'Farrell sts.), San Francisco, CA 94102. ℂ **800/288-6005** or 415/781-5050. Fax 415/835-5991. www.kinggeorge.com. 152 units. $155 double; $240 suite. Breakfast $6.50–$8. Special-value packages available seasonally. AE, DC, DISC, MC, V. Self-parking $18, valet parking $20. Cable car: Powell-Hyde and Powell-Mason lines (1 block W). Bus: 2, 3, 4, 30, 38, or 45. **Amenities:** Access to health club ½ block away; concierge; secretarial services; 24-hr. room service; same-day laundry service and dry cleaning. *In room:* TV w/pay movies and Nintendo, dataport, hair dryer, iron, safe.

The Savoy Hotel ★★ (Value)

The European-style Savoy is one of my favorite moderately priced downtown hotels (the Warwick Regis is my other top pick; see below). With a nice cozy French provincial apartment-like feel to each room, old well-cleaned bathrooms with original tile, 18th-century period furnishings, fluffy featherbeds, and goose-down pillows, it's easy to relax here. Not all rooms are alike—they can be small, but each has beautiful patterned draperies, triple sheets, full-length mirrors, and two-line telephones. Guests also enjoy free overnight shoeshines and late-afternoon cookies, sherry, and tea. The restaurant that was here closed and the hotel is currently in search of a new occupant.

580 Geary St. (between Taylor and Jones sts.), San Francisco, CA 94102. ℂ 800/227-4223 or 415/441-2700. Fax 415/441-0124. www.thesavoyhotel.com. 83 units. $149–$189 double; from $205 suite. Rates include late-afternoon cookies, sherry, and tea. Ask about package, government, senior, and corporate rates. AE, DC, DISC, MC, V. Parking $18. Bus: 2, 3, 4, 27, or 38. **Amenities:** Concierge; laundry service; dry cleaning. *In room:* TV, dataport, hair dryer, iron.

Shannon Court *Value*   In previous years I've skipped including this 1929 Spanish Revival hotel because it was just too dismal. But no longer! Local hip hoteliers Joie de Vivre wisely got their hands on this place and are revamping its 173 large, bright guest rooms. There's no fixing the dark and gloomy hallways, but once inside your abode, you'll find plenty to cheer about, like new furnishings (call to confirm their 2002 renovations are complete), firm mattresses, double-paned windows that open, quiet surroundings, all-around cleanliness, voice mail, lots and lots of elbow room, and corporate floors (14th and 15th floors) with irons, coffeemakers, and robes. Bathrooms are old but clean, and most have tubs. Feel like splurging? Go for one of the five penthouse-level suites, which have sweet terraces with a New York vibe. Another bonus: Until the word gets out, the prices are bound to be a serious bargain. *Tip:* Rooms above the ninth floor have good, but not great, southern views of the city.

550 Geary St. (between Jones and Taylor sts.), San Francisco, CA 94102 ℂ 800/228-8830 or 415/775-5000. www.jdvhospitality.com. 173 units. $169–$229 double. Rates include morning and afternoon coffee, tea, and cookies. AE, DC, DISC, MC, V. Valet parking $25. Bus: 2, 3, 4, 27, or 38. **Amenities:** Restaurant; concierge; laundry service; dry cleaning. *In room:* TV w/pay movies and Nintendo, fridge, hair dryer.

The Warwick Regis *Value*   Louis XVI might have been a rotten monarch, but he certainly had taste. Fashioned in the style of pre-Revolutionary France, the Warwick is awash with pristine French and English antiques, Italian marble, chandeliers, four-poster beds, hand-carved headboards, and the like. The result is an expensive-looking hotel that, for all its pleasantries and perks, is surprisingly affordable when compared to its Union Square contemporaries. Rooms can be on the small side, but they're some of the city's most charming. Bathrooms are charming but small. Honeymooners should splurge on the fireplace rooms with canopy beds—ooh la la! Adjoining the lobby is La Scene Café, a beautiful place to start your day with a latte and end it with a nightcap.

490 Geary St. (between Mason and Taylor sts.), San Francisco, CA 94102. ℂ 800/827-3447 or 415/928-7900. Fax 415/441-8788. www.warwickregis.com. 80 units. $159–$219 double; $189–$289 suite. AE, DC, DISC, MC, V. Parking $28. Cable car: Powell-Hyde and Powell-Mason lines. Bus: 2, 3, 4, 27, or 38. **Amenities:** Restaurant; access to nearby health club ($10 per day); concierge; business center; secretarial services; 24-hr. room service; babysitting; laundry service; dry cleaning. *In room:* TV, dataport, minibar, hair dryer, iron, safe.

INEXPENSIVE

The Golden Gate Hotel   Among San Francisco's small hotels occupying historic buildings are some real gems, and the Golden Gate Hotel is one of them. It's 2 blocks north of Union Square and 2 blocks down (literally) from the crest of Nob Hill, with cable car stops at the corner for easy access to Fisherman's Wharf and Chinatown. (The city's theaters and best restaurants are also within walking distance.) But the best thing about the Golden Gate Hotel is that it's a family-run establishment: John and Renate Kenaston are hospitable innkeepers who take obvious pleasure in making their guests comfortable. Each individually decorated room has handsome antique furnishings (plenty of wicker) from the early 1900s, quilted bedspreads, and fresh flowers. (Request a room with a claw-foot tub if you enjoy a good, hot soak.) Complimentary afternoon tea is served daily from 4 to 7pm, and guests are welcome to use the house fax and computer free of charge.

775 Bush St. (between Powell and Mason sts.), San Francisco, CA 94108. C 800/835-1118 or 415/392-3702. Fax 415/392-6202. www.goldengatehotel.com. 23 units, 14 with bathroom. $85 double without bathroom; $130 double with bathroom. Rates include continental breakfast and afternoon tea. AE, DC, MC, V. Self-parking $15. Cable car: Powell-Hyde and Powell-Mason lines (1 block E). Bus: 2, 4, 30, 38, or 45. Powell & Market BART. **Amenities:** Access to health club 1 block away; activities desk; laundry service and dry cleaning next door. *In room:* TV, dataport, hair dryer and iron upon request.

Hotel Bijou ✮ *Value*   Three words sum up this hotel: clean, colorful, and cheap. Although it's on the periphery of the gritty Tenderloin (just 3 blocks off Union Sq.), this 1911 hotel is cheery, bright, and perfect for the budget traveler who wants a little style with their savings. The hotel's age is disguised with lively decor, a Deco theater theme, and a heck of a lot of vibrant paint. Off the small lobby is a "theater" where guests can watch San Francisco–based movies nightly (cute old-fashioned theater seating in front of a basic TV showing videos). Upstairs, rooms named after locally made films are small but clean and colorful (think buttercup, burgundy, and purple), and have all the basics from clock radios, dressers, and small desks to tiny bathrooms (one of which is so small you have to close the door to access the toilet). Alas, some mattresses could be firmer and there's one small and slow elevator.

111 Mason St., San Francisco, CA 94102. C 800/771-1022 or 415/771-1200. www.sftrips.com. 65 units. $95–$139 double. Rates include coffee and tea in the lobby and continental breakfast. AE, DC, DISC, MC, V. Valet parking $21. Bus: All Market St. buses. Metro: Powell St. station. **Amenities:** Concierge; limited room service; same-day dry cleaning and laundry service. *In room:* TV, dataport, hair dryer, iron.

SOMA
VERY EXPENSIVE

The Four Seasons Hotel San Francisco ✮✮✮   A perfect combination of elegance and modern luxury, Four Seasons does everything right. Take the elevators up to the lobby and you're instantly surrounded by calm, cool, and collected hotel perfection and a sexy cocktail lounge that's sure to be your second home. Not too trendy, not too traditional, rooms are just right, with custom-made mattresses and pillows that guarantee the all-time best night's sleep, beautiful works of art, and huge luxury marble bathrooms with deep tubs and Bulgari toiletries. Many of the oversize rooms (starting at 460 sq. ft. and including 46 suites) overlook Yerba Buena Gardens. Adding to the perks are free access to the building's huge Sports Club L.A., round-the-clock business services, a 2-block walk to Union Square and the Moscone Convention Center, and a vibe that combines sophistication and hipness.

757 Market St. (between 3rd and 4th sts.), San Francisco, CA 94103. C 800/332-3442 or 415/633-3000. Fax 415/633-3009. www.fourseasons.com. 277 units. $469–$600 double; $800 executive suite. AE, DC, DISC, MC, V. Parking $35. Bus: All Market St. buses. Metro: Powell St. **Amenities:** Restaurant; bar; spa; huge fitness center; 24-hr. multilingual concierge; high-tech business center; secretarial services; salon; 24-hr. room service; in-room massage; overnight dry cleaning and laundry service. *In room:* A/C, TV w/pay movies, fax, minibar, hair dryer, safe.

The Harbor Court ✮✮   When the Embarcadero Freeway was torn down after the Big One in 1989, one of the major benefactors was this hotel, whose backyard view went from a wall of cement to a dazzling view of the Bay Bridge (a bay-view room costs extra). Located just off the Embarcadero at the edge of the Financial District, this former YMCA books a lot of corporate travelers, but anyone who prefers stylish, high-quality accommodations—half-canopy beds, large armoires, writing desks, soundproof windows—and a lively scene will be very content here.

165 Steuart St. (between Mission and Howard sts.), San Francisco, CA 94105. © **800/346-0555** or 415/882-1300. Fax 415/882-1313. www.harborcourthotel.com. 131 units. $165–$399 double. Continental breakfast $12. AE, DC, MC, V. Parking $28. Muni Metro: Embarcadero. Bus: 14, 32, or 80X. Pets accepted. **Amenities:** Access to adjoining health club and large, heated indoor pool; courtesy car; room service (breakfast only); same-day laundry service and dry cleaning. *In room:* A/C, TV, fax, dataport, minibar, hair dryer, iron, safe.

W San Francisco Hotel ★★★ Starwood Hotels & Resorts' 31-story, 423-room property adjacent to the San Francisco Museum of Modern Art is the most hip hotel in town (at least until Ian Schrager unveils his newly renovated Clift Hotel). Sophisticated, sleek, and stylish, its octagonal, three-story glass entrance and lobby give way to a great lounge and two bars. The interior has a residential feel in the guest rooms, and a hip, urban style throughout. All guest rooms offer a "luxury" bed with goose-down comforters and pillows, an oversize dark wood desk, and upholstered chaise lounge, plus louvered blinds opening to usually great city views. Rooms also feature a compact media wall complete with Sony CD and video cassette players with an extensive CD library, 27-inch color TV, plus Internet service via an infrared keyboard and portable two-line phones. Bathrooms are supersleek and stocked with Aveda products.

181 3rd St. (between Mission and Howard sts.), San Francisco, CA 94103. © **800/877-WHOTEL** or 415/777-5300. Fax 415/817-7800. www.whotels.com. 423 units. From $469 double; from $1,800 suite. AE, DC, DISC, MC, V. Valet parking $38. Muni Metro: J, K, L, or M to Montgomery. Bus: 15, 30, or 45. **Amenities:** Restaurant; 2 bars; heated atrium pool and whirlpool; fitness center; concierge; business center; secretarial services; limited room service; same-day laundry and dry cleaning. *In room:* A/C, TV/VCR w/pay movies and Internet access, fax, dataport, minibar, coffeemaker, hair dryer, iron, safe.

FINANCIAL DISTRICT
VERY EXPENSIVE

The Mandarin Oriental ★★★ *Finds* The common areas here are a bit cold and impersonal, but the rooms are superfluously appointed and the views divine, making this a top choice for luxury travelers. The large rooms are located between the 38th and 48th floors of a high-rise, which affords them extraordinary views. Not all units have tub-side views (get one that does and you'll never forget it!), but all have well-stocked marble bathrooms that include such luxuries as terry- and cotton-cloth robes, makeup mirrors, and silk slippers. The less opulent rooms are done in a kind of reserved contemporary decor with Asian accents. Don't miss out on the Asian teatime, complete with a bento box of uncommonly delicious goodies.

222 Sansome St. (between Pine and California sts.), San Francisco, CA 94104. © **800/622-0404** or 415/276-9888. Fax 415/433-0289. www.mandarinoriental.com. 158 units. $515–$540 double; $675–$725 signature rooms; from $1,400 suite. Continental breakfast $21, American breakfast $32. AE, DC, DISC, MC, V. Valet parking $34. Muni Metro: J, K, L, or M to Montgomery. Bus: All Market St. buses. **Amenities:** Restaurant; bar; fitness center; concierge; car-rental desk; business center; 24-hr. room service; in-room massage; laundry service; same-day dry cleaning. *In room:* A/C, TV w/pay movies, CD player, fax, dataport, minibar, hair dryer, iron, safe.

The Palace Hotel ★ Every time you walk through these doors, you'll be reminded how incredibly majestic old luxury really is. The original 1875 Palace was rebuilt after the 1906 quake; the most spectacular attribute is still the old regal lobby and the Garden Court, a San Francisco landmark that has been restored to its original heart-stopping grandeur. Regrettably, the rooms have that standardized, chain-hotel appearance.

2 New Montgomery St. (at Market St.), San Francisco, CA 94105. ℭ 800/325-3535 or 415/512-1111. Fax 415/543-0671. www.sfpalace.com. 551 units. $300–$560 double; from $550 suite. Extra person $40. Continental breakfast $16, deluxe continental $18. Children under 18 sharing existing bedding stay free in parents' room. Weekend rates and packages available. AE, DC, DISC, MC, V. Parking $30. Muni Metro: All Market St. trams. Bus: All Market St. buses. **Amenities:** 4 restaurants; health club with a skylight-covered heated lap pool; whirlpool; sauna; concierge; business center; 24-hr. room service; laundry and dry cleaning. In room: A/C, TV w/pay movies, dataport, minibar, hair dryer, iron, safe.

NOB HILL
VERY EXPENSIVE

The Fairmont Hotel & Tower 🏮🏮   The granddaddy of Nob Hill's ritzy hotels, the Fairmont wins top honors for the most awe-inspiring lobby in San Francisco. Even if you're not staying here, it's worth a trip to gape at its massive marble columns, vaulted ceilings, velvet chairs, gilded mirrors, and spectacular wraparound staircase. In previous years the rooms fell short, but thanks to an $85 million renovation completed in 2001, the glamour carries to guest rooms where everything is brand spanking new and in good taste. In addition to the expected luxuries, you'll find goose-down pillows, electric shoe buffers, large walk-in closets, and multi-line phones with voice mail. Whatever you do, make a point of getting to the Tonga Room, a fantastically kitsch, Disneyland-like tropical bar and restaurant where happy hour hops and rain falls every 20 minutes.

950 Mason St. (at California St.), San Francisco, CA 94108. ℭ 800/527-4727 or 415/772-5000. Fax 415/772-5013. www.fairmont.com. 600 units. Main building $289–$409 double, from $500 suite; Tower $269–$359 double, from $800 suite. Extra person $30. Continental breakfast $14. AE, DC, DISC, MC, V. Parking $32. Cable car: California St. line (direct stop). **Amenities:** 2 restaurants; bar; health club ($15 daily); concierge; tour desk; car-rental desk; business center; shopping arcade; salon; 24-hr. room service; massage; babysitting; same-day laundry service and dry cleaning. In room: A/C, TV w/pay movies and PlayStation, fax, dataport, kitchenette in some units, minibar, coffeemaker, hair dryer, iron, safe.

The Huntington Hotel 🏮🏮🏮   The stately Huntington has long been a favorite retreat for Hollywood stars and political VIPs who desire privacy and security. Family-owned since 1924—a real rarity among large hotels—this place eschews pomp and circumstance; absolute privacy and unobtrusive service are its mainstays. Though the elaborate 19th-century–style lobby is rather petite, the apartment-like guest rooms are quite large and feature Brunschwig and Fils fabrics, French antiques, and city views.

1075 California St. (between Mason and Taylor sts.), San Francisco, CA 94108. ℭ 800/227-4683 or 415/474-5400. Fax 415/474-6227. www.huntingtonhotel.com. 140 units. $310–$445 double; $485–$1,110 suite. Continental breakfast $13. Special packages available. AE, DC, DISC, MC, V. Valet parking $20. Cable car: California St. line (direct stop). Bus: 1. **Amenities:** Restaurant; lounge; indoor heated pool (for ages 16 and up); health club and new spa; steam room; sauna; concierge; massage; babysitting; same-day laundry service and dry cleaning. In room: A/C, TV w/pay movies, fax, dataport, kitchenette in some units, minibar, fridge in some units, hair dryer, iron, safe.

The Mark Hopkins Intercontinental 🏮🏮   Built in 1926 on the spot where railroad millionaire Mark Hopkins's turreted mansion once stood, the 19-story Mark Hopkins is one of the city's most classy historic luxury hotels. A complete room renovation in 2000 resulted in exceedingly comfortable neoclassical rooms with all the fancy amenities you'd expect from a world-class hotel, including custom furniture, plush fabrics, sumptuous bathrooms, and extraordinary city views. Luxury suites, added in early 2001, are twice the size of most San Francisco apartments and cost close to a month's rent per night. The Top of the Mark, a fantastic bar and lounge, where Pacific-bound servicemen went to toast their good-bye to the States during World War II, underwent a $1.5 million renovation. Now, dancing to live jazz or swing is done in spruced up, old-fashioned style. (Romantics, this place is for you.)

1 Nob Hill (at California and Mason sts.), San Francisco, CA 94108. ☎ 800/327-0200 or 415/392-3434. Fax 415/421-3302. www.markhopkins.net. 390 units. $380–$500 double; from $610 suite; from $3,000 luxury suite. Continental breakfast $14, breakfast buffet $21. AE, DC, DISC, MC, V. Valet parking $40. Cable car: California St. line (direct stop). Bus: 1. **Amenities:** 2 restaurants; 2 bars; exercise room; concierge; car-rental desk; business center; secretarial services; 24-hr. room service; massage; babysitting; laundry service and dry cleaning; concierge-level floors. *In room:* A/C, TV w/pay movies, VCR in suites only, dataport, minibar, coffeemaker, hair dryer, iron, safe.

The Ritz-Carlton ★★★   Ranked among the top hotels in the world (as well as the top hotel in the city) by readers of *Condé Nast Traveler*, the Ritz-Carlton has been the benchmark of San Francisco luxury hotels since it opened in 1991. A Nob Hill landmark, it's outfitted with the finest furnishings, fabrics, and artwork, and the rooms offer every possible amenity and service, from Italian-marble bathrooms with double sinks to plush terry robes. The more expensive rooms offer good views of the city. Club rooms have a dedicated concierge, separate elevator-key access, and complimentary buffet meals throughout the day.

600 Stockton St. (between Pine and California sts.), San Francisco, CA 94108. ☎ 800/241-3333 or 415/296-7465. Fax 415/986-1268. www.ritzcarlton.com. 336 units. $475–$575 double; $595–$695 club-level double; from $700 suite. Buffet breakfast $18; Sun brunch $55. Weekend discounts and packages available. AE, DC, DISC, MC, V. Parking $45. Cable car: Powell-Hyde and Powell-Mason lines (direct stop). **Amenities:** 2 restaurants; bar; indoor heated pool; outstanding health club; Jacuzzi; sauna; concierge; courtesy car; business center; secretarial services; 24-hr. room service; in-room massage and manicure; babysitting; same-day laundry service and dry cleaning. *In room:* A/C, TV w/pay movies, dataport, minibar, hair dryer, iron, safe.

NORTH BEACH
MODERATE
The Hotel Bohème ★★ *(Finds*   North Beach romance awaits you at the Bohème. Although located in the center of North Beach, this recently renovated hotel's style and demeanor are more reminiscent of a prestigious home in upscale Nob Hill. The decor evokes the Beat generation, which flourished here in the 1950s; rooms are small but hopelessly romantic, with gauze-draped canopies and walls artistically accented with lavender, sage green, black, and pumpkin. The staff is ultra-hospitable, and bonuses include free sherry in the lobby each afternoon. Take note: While the bathrooms are sweet, they're also absolutely tiny (no tubs). *Tip:* Request a room off the street side; they're quieter.

444 Columbus Ave. (between Vallejo and Green sts.), San Francisco, CA 94133. ☎ 415/433-9111. Fax 415/362-6292. www.hotelboheme.com. 16 units (all with shower only). $164–$184 double. Rates include afternoon sherry. AE, DISC, DC, MC, V. Parking $28 at nearby public garage. Cable car: Powell-Mason line. Bus: 12, 15, 30, 41, 45, or 83. **Amenities:** Concierge. *In room:* TV, dataport, hair dryer.

INEXPENSIVE
The San Remo Hotel ★★ *(Value*   Located in a quiet North Beach neighborhood and within walking distance of Fisherman's Wharf, this small European-style pensione is one of the best budget hotels in San Francisco. The rooms are small and bathrooms are shared, but all is forgiven when it comes time to pay the bill. Rooms are decorated in a cozy country style with brass and iron beds, armoires, and wicker furnishings; most have ceiling fans. The shared bathrooms, each immaculately clean, feature claw-foot tubs and brass pull-chain toilets with

oak tanks and brass fixtures. If the penthouse is available, book it: You won't find a more romantic place to stay in San Francisco for so little money. (It's got its own bathroom, TV, fridge, and patio.)

2237 Mason St. (at Chestnut St.), San Francisco, CA 94133. ℂ 800/352-REMO or 415/776-8688. Fax 415/776-2811. www.sanremohotel.com. 62 units, 61 with shared bathroom. $55–$95 double; $155 penthouse suite. AE, DC, MC, V. Self-parking $10–$14. Cable car: Powell-Mason line. Bus: 10, 15, 30, or 47. Metro: F. **Amenities:** Access to nearby health club; massage; coin-op laundry. *In room:* Ceiling fan.

FISHERMAN'S WHARF
EXPENSIVE
Sheraton Fisherman's Wharf Hotel ⚓ Built in the mid-1970s, this modern, four-story hotel offers the reliable comforts of a Sheraton in San Francisco's most popular tourist area. In other words, the clean, modern rooms, which were completely renovated in 1995, are comfortable and well equipped but nothing unique to the city. The Corporate Floor caters exclusively to business travelers.

2500 Mason St. (between Beach and North Point sts.), San Francisco, CA 94133. ℂ 800/325-3535 or 415/362-5500. Fax 415/956-5275. www.sheratonatthewharf.com. 525 units. $165–$380 double; from $550–$1,000 suite. Extra person $20. Continental breakfast $17. AE, DC, DISC, MC, V. Valet parking $30. Cable car: Powell-Mason line (1 block E, 2 blocks S). Bus: 10 or 49. Metro: F. **Amenities:** Restaurant; bar; outdoor heated pool; exercise room; concierge; business center; salon; car-rental desk; room service (6am–midnight); laundry service; dry cleaning. *In room:* A/C, TV, fax in club-level rooms, dataport, coffeemaker, hair dryer.

The Tuscan Inn ⚓⚓ The Tuscan is the best hotel at Fisherman's Wharf. Like an island of respectability in a sea of touristy schlock, it offers a level of style and comfort far beyond its neighbors. Splurge on parking—cheaper than the wharf's outrageously priced garages—and then make your way toward the plush lobby warmed by a grand fireplace. Even the rooms, each equipped with writing desks and armchairs, are a cut above competing neighborhood hotels. The only caveat is the lack of views—a small price to pay for a good hotel in a great location. The adjoining Cafe Pescatore, which is open for breakfast, lunch, and dinner, serves standard Italian fare in an airy setting.

425 North Point St. (at Mason St.), San Francisco, CA 94133. ℂ 800/648-4626 or 415/561-1100. Fax 415/561-1199. www.tuscaninn.com. 221 units. $189–$269 double; $279–$339 suite. Rates include coffee, tea, and evening fireside wine reception. AE, DC, DISC, MC, V. Parking $22. Cable car: Powell-Mason line. Bus: 15, 32, or 42. Pets accepted with $50 fee. **Amenities:** Access to nearby gym; concierge; courtesy car; secretarial services; room service 7am–9:30pm; same-day laundry and dry cleaning. *In room:* A/C, TV w/pay movies, dataport, minibar, hair dryer, iron.

MODERATE
The Wharf Inn ⚓⚓ *Kids* My top choice for good-value lodging at Fisherman's Wharf, The Wharf Inn boasts newly refurbished rooms, done in handsome tones of forest green, burgundy, and pale yellow, that come with all the standard amenities, including complimentary coffee and tea. Its main attribute, however, is its location—right smack dab in the middle of the wharf, 2 blocks away from PIER 39 and the cable-car turnaround, and within walking distance of the Embarcadero and North Beach. The inn is ideal for car-bound families, as parking is free (that saves $25 a day right off the bat) and there's no charge for packing along an extra person.

2601 Mason St. (at Beach St.), San Francisco, CA 94133. ℂ 800/548-9918 or 415/673-7411. Fax 415/776-2181. www.wharfinn.com. 51 units. $99–$199 double; $270–$399 penthouse. AE, DC, DISC, MC, V. Free parking. Cable car: Powell-Mason line. Bus: 15, 32, or 42. Metro: F. **Amenities:** Access to nearby health club ($10 per day); concierge; tour desk; car-rental desk. *In room:* TV, dataport, coffeemaker and hair dryer on request.

COW HOLLOW/PACIFIC HEIGHTS
EXPENSIVE

Union Street Inn 🏨🏨   This two-story Edwardian may front the perpetually busy (and chichi) Union Street, but it's quiet as a church on the inside. All individually decorated rooms are comfortably furnished, and most come with canopied or brass beds with down comforters, fresh flowers, bay windows (beg for one with a view of the garden), and private bathrooms (a few even have Jacuzzi tubs). An extended continental breakfast is served in the parlor, in your room, or on an outdoor terrace overlooking a lovely English garden. The ultimate honeymoon retreat is the private carriage house behind the inn, but any room at this warm, friendly place is guaranteed to please.

2229 Union St. (between Fillmore and Steiner sts.), San Francisco, CA 94123. ✆ **415/346-0424.** Fax 415/922-8046. www.unionstreetinn.com. 5 units, 1 cottage. $159–$239 double; $269 cottage. Rates include breakfast, hors d'oeuvres, and evening beverages. AE, MC, V. Parking $15. Bus: 22, 28, 41, 45, or 47. *In room:* TV.

MODERATE

Hotel Del Sol 🏨🏨 *Value*   Two-level Hotel del Sol's sunshine theme attracts a youngish clientele to its hip motel, located 2 blocks off busy (and bland) Lombard Street. With a centerpiece courtyard and pool and the Miami Beach–style use of vibrant color—as in the yellow, red, orange, and blue exterior—the atmosphere at the del Sol is unexpectedly festive. Fair-weather fun doesn't stop at the front door of the 54 spacious rooms, which boast equally colorful (read: loud) interior decor and unexpected extras like a CD player and tips to the town's happenings and shopping meccas.

3100 Webster St. (at Greenwich St.), San Francisco, CA 94123.✆ **800/738-7477** or 415/921-5520. Fax 415/931-4137. www.thehoteldelsol.com. 57 units, including 10 1-bedroom suites. $119–$165 double; $160–$235 suite. Rates include continental breakfast. AE, DC, DISC, MC, V. Bus: 22, 28, 41, 43, 45, or 76. **Amenities:** Heated outdoor pool; sauna; dry cleaning. *In room:* TV/VCR w/pay movies, CD player, dataport, kitchenette in some units, iron.

The Laurel 🏨🏨 *Value*   If you don't mind being out of the downtown area, this motel is one of the most tranquil, lovely, and affordable places to rest your head. Tucked just beyond the southernmost tip of the Presidio and its winding roads shaded by eucalyptus, the outside isn't impressive. But inside it's très chic and modern, with Zen-like influences. Some rooms have excellent city views and all have CD players, VCRs, and spiffy bathrooms. But wait! There's more: concierge services, complimentary continental breakfast, 24-hour coffee and tea service, pet-friendly rooms, and topping it off, free parking and a hip bar/lounge called G.

444 Presidio Ave. (at Masonic Ave.), San Francisco, CA 94115. ✆ **800/552-8735** or 415/567-8467. Fax 415/928-1866. www.thelaurelinn.com. 49 units. $150–$175 double. Rates include continental breakfast, afternoon lemonade and cookies. AE, DC, DISC, MC, V. Free parking. Muni Metro: 1, 3, 4, or 43. Pets accepted. **Amenities:** Adjoining bar; concierge; coin-op laundry. *In room:* TV/VCR, dataport, kitchenette in some rooms, hair dryer, iron.

INEXPENSIVE

Edward II Inn & Suites 🏨🏨   This three-story, self-styled "English Country" inn has a room for almost anyone's budget, ranging from pensione rooms with shared bathrooms to luxuriously appointed suites and cottages with living rooms, kitchens, and whirlpool tubs. Originally built to house guests who attended the 1915 Pan-Pacific Exposition, it's now run by innkeepers Denise and Bob Holland, who have done a fantastic job maintaining its worldly charm.

Regardless of their rate, all rooms are spotlessly clean and comfortably appointed with cozy antique furnishings and plenty of fresh flowers. The only caveat is that its Lombard Street location is usually congested with traffic, but nearby Chestnut and Union streets offer some of the best shopping and dining in the city. The price includes continental breakfast, and there's an adjoining pub.

3155 Scott St. (at Lombard St.), San Francisco, CA 94123. © 800/473-2846 or 415/922-3000. Fax 415/931-5784. www.edwardii.com. 32 units, 21 with private bathroom. $83–$88 double with shared bathroom; $115 double with private bathroom; $185–$235 suite or cottage. Extra person $25. Rates include continental breakfast and evening sherry. AE, MC, V. Self-parking $12 across the street. Bus: 28, 43, or 76. **Amenities:** Pub (open Thurs–Sat). *In room:* TV, hair dryer and iron available on request.

The Marina Inn ★★ *Value* How this 1924 four-story Victorian offers so much for so little is mystifying. Each guest room looks as though it's been culled from a country-furnishings catalog, complete with rustic pinewood furniture, a four-poster bed with a silk-soft comforter, and pretty wallpaper. There are even high-class touches that many expensive hotels don't include: new remote-control TVs discreetly hidden in pine cabinetry, full bathtubs with showers, and nightly turndown service with chocolates on your pillow. Add to that complimentary continental breakfast, afternoon sherry, friendly service, and an armada of nearby shops and restaurants, and there you have it: My number-one choice for Best Overall Value. *Note:* Be sure to request one of the quieter rooms away from busy Lombard Street.

3110 Octavia St. (at Lombard St.), San Francisco, CA 94123. © 800/274-1420 or 415/928-1000. Fax 415/928-5909. www.marinainn.com. 40 units. Nov–Feb $65–$105 double; Mar–May $75–$125 double; June–Oct $85–$135 double. Rates include continental breakfast and afternoon sherry. AE, DC, MC, V. Bus: 28, 30, 43, or 76. *In room:* TV, hair dryer and iron on request.

JAPANTOWN & ENVIRONS
EXPENSIVE
The Hotel Majestic ★★ The Majestic, built in 1902, meets every professional need while retaining a seriously opulent ambience of a luxurious old-world boutique hotel. The lobby alone will sweep you into another era with its tapestries, brocades, Corinthian columns, and intricate, lavish detail. Rooms are furnished with French and English antiques, the centerpiece of each being a large four-poster canopy bed; you'll also find mirrored armoires and antique reproductions. All drapes, fabrics, carpet, and bedspreads were replaced in 1997, half the bathrooms and guest rooms underwent a $2 million renovation in 1999, and new paint and wallpaper were added in 2002. Extras include a well-lit full-size desk and bathrobes; some rooms also have fireplaces and easy access to a fantastic and intimate bar and elegant California-Asian restaurant, Perlot.

1500 Sutter St. (between Octavia and Gough sts.), San Francisco, CA 94109. © 800/869-8966 or 415/441-1100. Fax 415/673-7331. www.thehotelmajestic.com. 58 units. $175–$285 double; from $350 suite. Continental breakfast $8.50. Rates include complimentary coffee in lobby 6:30–9am and wine and appetizers 4–6pm. Group, government, corporate, and relocation rates available. AE, DC, DISC, MC, V. Valet parking $23. Bus: 2, 4, 42, 47, or 49. **Amenities:** Restaurant; bar; access to nearby health club ($10 per day); concierge; 24-hr. room service; in-room massage; babysitting; same-day dry cleaning and laundry service. *In room:* TV, dataport, fridge in some units, hair dryer, iron.

MODERATE
The Queen Anne Hotel ★★ This majestic 1890 Victorian is a charming boutique hotel that remains true to its heritage and emulates San Francisco's golden days. The lavish "grand salon" greets you with English oak paneling and antiques; rooms follow suit with antique armoires, marble-top dressers, and

other period pieces. Some have corner turret bay windows that look out onto tree-lined streets, plus separate parlor areas and wet bars; others have cozy reading nooks and fireplaces. All rooms have phones in the bathroom, computer hookups, and fridges. You can relax in the parlor, with its impressive floor-to-ceiling fireplace, or in the hotel library. Amenities include room service, concierge, and complimentary afternoon tea and sherry. There's also access to an off-premises health club with a lap pool.

1590 Sutter St. (between Gough and Octavia sts.), San Francisco, CA 94109. 📞 800/227-3970 or 415/441-2828. Fax 415/775-5212. www.queenanne.com. 48 units. $139–$199 double; $199–$350 suite. Extra person $10. Rates include continental breakfast, afternoon tea and sherry, and morning newspaper. AE, DC, DISC, MC, V. Parking $14. Bus: 2, 3, or 4. **Amenities:** Access to nearby health club; 24-hr. concierge; business center; same-day dry cleaning. *In room:* TV, dataport, hair dryer, iron, safe.

CIVIC CENTER
MODERATE

The Phoenix Hotel 🐸🐸 Situated on the fringes of the less-than-pleasant Tenderloin District, this retro 1950s-style choice is a gathering place for visiting rockers, writers, and filmmakers who crave a dose of Southern California on their trips to San Francisco. The focal point of the pastel-painted Palm Springs–style hotel is a heated, paisley-muraled pool set in a modern-sculpture garden. The rooms, while far from plush, are comfortably outfitted with bamboo furnishings and original local art. In addition to the usual amenities, the inn's own closed-circuit channel shows films exclusively made in or about San Francisco. Services include on-site massage and—woo hoo!—free parking. Backflip, a groovy and dim cocktail lounge, is a great place to hang.

601 Eddy St. (at Larkin St.), San Francisco, CA 94109. 📞 800/248-9466 or 415/776-1380. Fax 415/885-3109. www.sftrips.com. 44 units. $165–$205 double; $175–$195 suite. Rates include continental breakfast. AE, DC, MC, V. Free parking. Bus: 19, 31, 38, 42, or 47. **Amenities:** Bar; heated outdoor pool; concierge; tour desk; limited room service; in-room massage; same-day laundry and dry cleaning. *In room:* TV, dataport, hair dryer and iron available on request.

INEXPENSIVE

The Abigail Howard Johnson Hotel 🐸🐸 *Value* Although it doesn't get much press, the Abigail is one of the better value-priced hotels in the city; what it lacks in luxury it more than makes up for in charm. The rooms, while on the small side, are clean, cute, and comfortably furnished with cozy antiques and down comforters. Morning coffee and pastries greet you in the beautiful faux-marble lobby, while lunch and dinner are served in the chichi organic vegan restaurant, Millennium.

246 McAllister St. (between Hyde and Larkin sts.), San Francisco, CA 94102. 📞 800/446-4656 or 415/626-6500. Fax 415/626-6580. www.abigailhotel.com. 61 units. $88–$159 standard double; $99–$169 deluxe double; $300 suite. Extra person $10. Rates include continental breakfast. AE, DC, DISC, MC, V. Valet parking $20. Muni Metro: All Market St. trams. Bus: All Market St. buses. **Amenities:** Restaurant; bar; concierge; same-day dry cleaning. *In room:* TV, dataport, fridge upon request, hair dryer, iron.

THE CASTRO
MODERATE

The Parker Guest House 🐸🐸 This is the best B&B option in the Castro, and one of the best in the entire city. The gay-friendly, 5,000-square-foot, beautifully restored Edwardian home is a few blocks from the heart of Castro's action. The bright, cheery urban compound boasts period antiques, and spacious guest rooms are wonderfully appointed with smart, patterned furnishings, voice mail, robes, and a spotless private bathroom (plus amenities) en suite or across the hall. A fire burns nightly in the cozy living room, and guests are welcome to make themselves at home in the wood-paneled common library (with fireplace and piano), sunny breakfast room overlooking the garden, formal dining room, and spacious garden with fountains and a steam room. As this book goes to press, the owners of The Parker House are in the process of completing renovation on an adjoining sister property and a new hot tub.

520 Church St. (between 17th and 18th sts.), San Francisco, CA 94114. © **888/520-7275** or 415/621-3222. Fax 415/621-4139. www.parkerguesthouse.com. 20 units. $100–$180 double; $200 junior suite. Rates include extended continental breakfast and evening wine and cheese. AE, DISC, MC, V. Self-parking $15. Muni Metro: J Church. Bus: 22 or 33. **Amenities:** Access to nearby health club; steam room; concierge. *In room:* TV, dataport, iron, hair dryer.

INEXPENSIVE

Beck's Motor Lodge ✲   A run-of-the-mill motel swathed in vibrant color, here the ultra-tidy rooms are standard but contemporary with motel furnishings, a sun deck overlooking upper Market Street's action, and free parking. Unless you're into B&Bs, this is really your only choice in the area—fortunately, it's very well maintained.

2222 Market St. (at 15th St.), San Francisco, CA 94114. © **800/227-4360** in the U.S. except Calif., or 415/621-8212 (from Calif., call collect to make reservations). Fax 415/241-0435. 58 units. $119–$145 double. AE, DC, DISC, MC, V. Free parking. Bus: 8 or 37. Metro: F. **Amenities:** Coin-operated washing machines. *In room:* TV, dataport, fridge, coffeemaker.

4 Where to Dine

San Francisco's dining scene is one of the best in the world. Since space is limited, I had to make tough choices, but the end result is a cross section of San Francisco's best restaurants in every price range. For a greater selection of reviews, see *Frommer's San Francisco 2003.*

Note: If you want a table at a top restaurant, make your reservation weeks in advance—perhaps through **www.opentable.com**, which gives real-time reservations to many Bay Area establishments.

UNION SQUARE
EXPENSIVE

Masa's ✲✲✲ FRENCH   One of the city's veteran contenders for best French restaurant underwent major changes in early 2001, including a new chef and updated interior. Executive Chef Ron Siegel deftly designs three-, six-, and nine-course tasting menus within an almost startlingly trendy (think hip hotelier Ian Schrager) room. Fortunately, beyond the small, minimalist bar and illuminated white curtains, one thing has remained the same: a dedication to culinary excellence. Anticipate delicate seared scallops elevated both literally and figuratively by microgreens and a dab of decadent *uni* (sea urchin) and savory skate balanced atop a short rib ravioli bathed in a mushroom jus. Desserts are too precious and are better to look at than they are to eat. But the candy cart, which is wheeled by so you can select lollipops, chocolates, and mini-cookies, almost makes up for it.

In the Hotel Vintage Court, 648 Bush St. (at Stockton St.). © **415/989-7154.** Reservations required; accepted up to 3 months in advance. Fixed-price dinner $65–$109. AE, DC, DISC, MC, V. Tues–Sat 5:30–9:30pm. Closed 1st 2 weeks in Jan, 1st week in July. Valet parking $9. Cable car: Powell-Mason and Powell-Hyde lines. Bus: 2, 3, 4, 30, or 45.

MODERATE

Kuleto's ✲✲ ITALIAN   It's not a destination restaurant, but if you're downtown and hungry, Kuleto's is a great place to feast. Skip the wait for a table, muscle a seat at the antipasto bar, and fill up on appetizers, which are often better than the entrees. For a main course, try penne pasta drenched in tangy lamb-sausage marinara sauce, clam linguine (generously overloaded with fresh clams), or any of the fresh-fish specials grilled over hardwoods. If you don't arrive by 6pm, expect to wait—this place fills up fast.

In the Villa Florence Hotel, 221 Powell St. (between Geary and O'Farrell sts.). © 415/397-7720. Reservations recommended. Breakfast $5–$10; main courses $10–$20. AE, DC, MC, V. Mon–Fri 7–10:30am, Sat–Sun 8–10:30am; daily 11:30am–11pm. Cable car: Powell-Mason and Powell-Hyde lines. Muni Metro: Powell. Bus: 2, 3, 4, or 38.

Le Colonial ★★ *Finds* VIETNAMESE   Sexy, French-Vietnamese plantation environs and delicious—albeit pricey—Vietnamese food make this an excellent choice for an all-around fun experience. One of my favorite reasons to enter the long dining room and beautiful front patio is the sea bass. Wrapped in banana leaf with glass noodles, ginger, scallions, and cilantro, the buttery fish is genuine bliss. Then again, the vibrant flavors of tender wok-seared beef tenderloin with watercress onion salad are outstanding as well. I can't say enough about the upstairs lounge, where romance reigns, with cozy couches, seductive surroundings (and, often, live jazz), and a kicked-back cocktail crowd of swank professionals.

20 Cosmo Place (off Taylor St., between Post and Sutter sts). © 415/931-3600. Reservations recommended. Main courses $16–$33. AE, DC, DISC, MC, V. Sun 5–10pm, Mon–Wed 5:30–10pm, Thurs–Sat 5:30–11pm. Valet parking $5 1st hr., $2 each additional half-hr. Bus: 2, 3, 4, or 27.

Scala's Bistro ★★ FRENCH/ITALIAN   This polished Italian dining room with high ceilings and big booths is one of the better restaurants in Union Square. The Parisian-bistro/old-world atmosphere has just the right balance of elegance and informality, which means it's perfectly okay to have some fun here (and apparently most people do). Expect a fantastic array of Italian and French dishes that are priced surprisingly low. Start with the Earth and Surf calamari appetizer or grilled portobello mushrooms. Generous portions of the moist, rich duck-leg confit will satisfy hungry appetites, but if you can only order one thing, make it Scala's signature dish: the seared salmon. Finish with the creamy Bostini cream pie, a dreamy combo of vanilla custard and orange chiffon cake with a warm chocolate glaze.

In the Sir Francis Drake hotel, 432 Powell St. (at Sutter St.). © 415/395-8555. Reservations recommended. Breakfast $7–$10; lunch and dinner main courses $12–$24. AE, DC, DISC, MC, V. Mon–Fri 7am–midnight, Sat–Sun 8am–midnight. Cable car: Powell-Hyde line. Bus: 2, 3, 4, 30, 45, or 76.

INEXPENSIVE

Café Claude ★★ FRENCH   For a little bit of Paris off Powell Street, try Café Claude, a crowded and lively restaurant tucked into a narrow lane near Union Square. With prices topping out at about $12 for main courses such as *poussin rôti* (roast Cornish hen with potatoes and aioli), French shepherd's pie, or *poisson du jour* (fish of the day), Café Claude is a good value. There is live jazz Thursday and Friday from 8 to 11pm and Saturday from 7 to 10pm. Outdoor seating is available when the weather permits.

7 Claude Lane (off Sutter St.). © 415/392-3515. www.cafeclaude.com. Reservations recommended. Main courses $10–$13. AE, DC, DISC, MC, V. Mon 11:30am–2:30pm, Tues–Wed and Sat 11:30am–10pm, Thurs–Fri 11:30am–10:30pm. Cable car: Powell-Mason and Powell-Hyde lines.

Sanraku Japanese Restaurant ★ *Value* JAPANESE/SUSHI   A perfect combination of great Japanese dishes and sushi at bargain prices makes this bright

San Francisco Dining

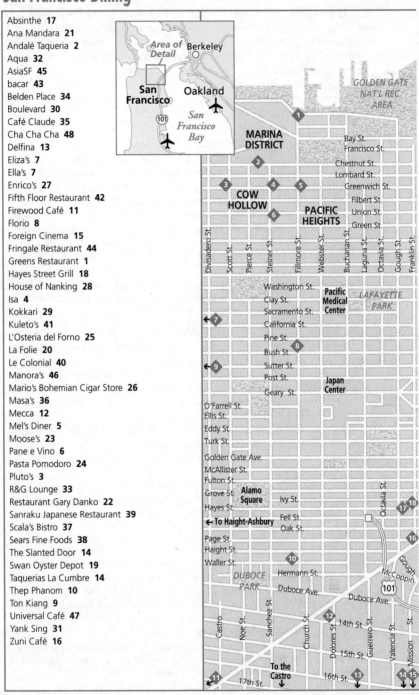

San Francisco Bay

Haight-Ashbury

Municipal Pier

Pier 45
Pier 43 1/2
Pier 43
Pier 41
Pier 39
Pier 35
Pier 33
Pier 31
Pier 27

Aquatic Park

Jefferson St.
Beach St.
North Point St.
Bay St.
Francisco St.
Chestnut St.
Lombard St.
Greenwich St.
Filbert St.
Union St.
Green St.
Vallejo St.
Broadway
Pacific Ave.
Jackson St.
Washington St.
Clay St.
Sacramento St.
Geary St.
O'Farrell St.
Eddy St.

FISHERMAN'S WHARF

Ghirardelli Square

NORTH BEACH

Columbus Ave.

Tunnel

CHINATOWN

NOB HILL

Van Ness Ave.
Polk St.
Larkin St.
Hyde St.
Leavenworth
Jones St.
Taylor St.
Mason St.
Powell St.
Stockton St.
Grant Ave.
Kearny St.
Montgomery St.
Sansome St.
Battery St.
Front St.
Davis St.
Drumm St.

FINANCIAL DISTRICT

Justin Herman Plaza

Ferry Building (World Trade Center)

Pier 23
Pier 19
Pier 17
Pier 15
Pier 9
Pier 7
Pier 5
Pier 3
Pier 1

Embarcadero

San Francisco-Oakland Bay Bridge

UNION SQUARE

YERBA BUENA GARDENS

Moscone Convention Center

SOMA

Market St.
Mission St.
Howard St.
Folsom St.
Harrison St.
Bryant St.
Brannan St.
Townsend St.
King St.
Berry St.
Channel St.
Division St.
Alameda St.

Civic Center

2nd St.
3rd St.
4th St.
5th St.
6th St.
7th St.
8th St.
9th St.
10th St.
11th St.
12th St.
15th St.

Steuart St.
Main St.
Beale St.
Spear St.
Fremont St.
1st St.
Delancey St.

SOUTH PARK

S. Van Ness Ave.
Folsom
Harrison
Alabama
Potrero Ave.

Illinois St.
3rd St.
4th St.

Haight-Ashbury

Conservatory Dr.
McLaren Lodge
John F. Kennedy Dr.
GOLDEN GATE PARK
Kezar
Pavilion
Kezar Stadium

Fulton St.
Grove St.
Hayes St.
Fell St.
PANHANDLE
Oak St.
Page St.
Haight St.
Waller St.
Frederick St.
Carl St.
Parnassus Ave.

Conservatory Dr.
Cole St.
Ashbury St.
Shrader St.
Stanyan St.
Belvedere St.
Clayton
Downey
Beulah St.
Cole St.
Masonic Ave.
Delmar St.

95

and busy restaurant one of my downtown favorites. A box lunch might include a California roll, soup, seaweed salad, deep-fried salmon roll, and beef with noodles with steamed rice, all at a digestible $7.75. The main menu, which is always available, features truly irresistible sesame chicken with teriyaki sauce and rice, tempura, a vast selection of rolls, and delicious combination plates that mix sushi, sashimi, and teriyaki. Dinner does brisk business, too, but magically there always seems to be an available table.

704 Sutter St. (at Taylor St.). ✆ 415/771-0803. www.sanraku.com. Main courses $5.50–$15 lunch, $12–$19 dinner. AE, DISC, MC, V. Mon–Fri 11am–3pm and 3:30–10pm; Sat–Sun 4–10pm. Cable car: Powell-Mason line. Bus: 2, 3, 4, 27, or 38.

Sears Fine Foods ★★ *Kids* AMERICAN   Sears is not just another pink-tabled diner run by motherly matrons—it's an institution, famous for its crispy, dark-brown waffles, light sourdough French toast, and silver-dollar–size Swedish pancakes served in funky old-fashioned surroundings. As the story goes, Ben Sears, a retired clown, founded the diner in 1938. His Swedish wife, Hilbur, was responsible for the legendary pancakes, which are still whipped up according to her family's secret recipe. Sears also offers a "healthy-heart menu," classic lunch fare, and big slices of pie for dessert.

439 Powell St. (between Post and Sutter sts.). ✆ 415/986-1160. Reservations accepted for parties of 6 or more. Breakfast $3–$8; salads and soups $3–$8; main courses $6–$10. No credit cards. Thurs–Mon 6:30am–2:30pm. Cable car: Powell-Mason and Powell-Hyde lines. Bus: 2, 3, 4, or 38.

SOMA
EXPENSIVE

bacar ★★ AMERICAN BRASSERIE   No other dining room makes wine as integral to the meal as popular new bacar. Up to 250 eclectic, fashionable diners pack into the warehouse-restaurant's three distinct areas—the casual (loud) downstairs salon, the bustling bar and loud mezzanine, or the more quiet upstairs, which looks down on the mezzanine's action—for chef Arnold Eric Wong's "American Brasserie" (i.e., French Bistro with a California twist) cuisine. During a recent visit, a creamy salt cod and crab brandade wowed the table, and zesty roasted mussels with chile and garlic begged for us to soak up the sauce with accompanying grilled bread. Just as much fun is the wine selection, which gives you 1,000 choices. Around 100 come by the glass, 2-ounce pour, or 250- or 500-milliliter decanter, and Wine Director Debbie Zachareas is almost always available to introduce you to new and exciting options. Vibrant in both energy and design, bacar is definitely the hot spot right now, so don't be surprised if even with a reservation you have to wait for a table.

448 Brannan St. (at 3rd St.). ✆ 415/904-4100. www.bacarsf.com. Reservations recommended. Main courses $8.50–$14 lunch, $12–$29 dinner. AE, MC, V. Sun 5:30–11pm; Mon–Fri 11:30am–2:30pm; Mon–Thurs 5:30–midnight; Fri–Sat 5:30pm–1am. Valet parking (Mon–Sat dinner only) $9. Bus: 15, 30, 45, 76, or 81.

Boulevard ★★★ *Finds* AMERICAN   Master restaurant designer Pat Kuleto and chef Nancy Oaks are behind one of my—and the city's—all-time favorites. What's the winning combination? The dramatic Belle Epoque interior combined with Oaks's well-sculpted, mouthwatering dishes. Starters alone could make a perfect meal, especially if you indulge in the sweetbreads wrapped in prosciutto on watercress and Lola Rose lettuce with garlic croutons and a whole-grain mustard vinaigrette; Sonoma foie gras with elderberry syrup, toast, and Bosc pear salad; or Maine sea scallops on garlic-mashed-potato croustade with truffle and portobello-mushroom relish. The nine or so main courses are equally creative and might include pan-roasted miso-glazed sea bass with asparagus salad, Japanese rice, and shiitake-mushroom broth, or spit-roasted cider-cured pork loin with sweet-potato–swirled mashed potatoes and sautéed baby red chard. Vegetarian items, such as wild-mushroom risotto with fresh chanterelles and Parmesan, are also offered. Three levels of formality—bar, open kitchen, and main dining room—keep things from getting too snobby.

1 Mission St. (between Embarcadero and Steuart sts.). ℂ 415/543-6084. Reservations recommended. Main courses $14–$25 lunch, $24–$30 dinner. AE, DC, DISC, MC, V. Mon–Fri 11:30am–2pm; Sun–Wed 5:30–10pm; Thurs–Sat 5:30–10:30pm. Valet parking $10. Bus: 15, 30, 32, or 45.

Fifth Floor Restaurant ★★★ MODERN FRENCH   Chef Laurent Gras's arrival here at the end of 2001 was the best thing that's happened to San Francisco dining in a long time. Hailing from Restaurant Alain Ducasse and Waldorf Astoria's Peacock Alley, Gras's cuisine is as luxurious as the decor of rich colors and fabrics, red leather and velvet banquettes, Frette linens, zebra-striped carpeting, and a club-like atmosphere. Here nearly everything is original and incredibly well executed. You'd be a fool to pass on the avocado dome hiding a mound of crabmeat brought to life with jalapeño, and basil. "Lobster cappuccino" is a genius combination of lobster broth emulsified with chestnuts, prawns, and sautéed lobster. Main courses like veal tournedos caramelized with sweetbread, black pepper jus, and braised potato, or slow-baked lamb with truffle, pistachio, and olives with steamed cabbage are also precisely prepared. Whatever you do, don't skip the butterscotch pudding, which defies description, and do follow the lead of sommelier Raj Parr, who's famous for an outstanding wine list that's big on little wineries and specialties from Burgundy.

In the Hotel Palomar, 12 4th St. (at Market St.). ℂ 415/348-1555. Reservations recommended. Main courses $33–$39; tasting menu $85. AE, DC, DISC, MC, V. Mon–Thurs 5:30–10pm; Fri–Sat 5:30–11pm. Valet parking $10. Bus: All Market St. buses.

MODERATE

Fringale Restaurant ★★ *Value* FRENCH   Still one of San Francisco's better restaurants for the money a decade after opening, Fringale—colloquial French for "sudden urge to eat"—has enjoyed a waiting list since the day chef and co-owner Gerald Hirigoyen opened this small bistro. Within the small and airy dining environment, guests begin their meals with steamed mussels with fried garlic vinaigrette, or roasted quail with apple risotto and foie gras. Among the 10 courses on the seasonally changing menu, you might find rack of lamb with potato gratin or pork tenderloin confit with cabbage and onion and apple marmalade. Desserts are worth savoring, too, particularly the Gateau Basque (which has won me many culinary friends since I began preparing it myself, with the help of Hirigoyen's cookbook). The mostly French waiters provide charming service, and prices are surprisingly reasonable for such high-quality cuisine.

570 4th St. (between Brannan and Bryant sts.). ℂ 415/543-0573. Reservations recommended. Main courses $9–$20 lunch, $9.50–$23 dinner. AE, MC, V. Mon–Fri 11:30am–3pm; Mon–Sat 5:30–10:30pm. Bus: 30 or 45.

Yank Sing ★★ CHINESE/DIM SUM   Loosely translated as "a delight of the heart," Yank Sing does great dim sum. Like most good dim sum meals, at Yank Sing you get to choose the small dishes from a cart that's continually wheeled around the dining room. Confident, experienced servers take the nervousness out of novices—they're good at guessing your gastric threshold. Most dim sum dishes are dumplings, filled with tasty concoctions of pork, beef, fish, or vegetables. Spareribs, stuffed crab claws, scallion pancakes, pork buns, and other palate-pleasers complete the menu.

101 Spear St. (at Mission St. at Rincon Center). ℂ 415/957-9300. Dim sum $2.80–$4.50 for 2 to 4 pieces. AE, DC, MC, V. Mon–Fri 11am–3pm, Sat–Sun 11am–4pm. Free validated parking in Rincon Center Garage on weekends. Cable car: California St. line. Bus: 1 or 42.

INEXPENSIVE

AsiaSF ⋆ CALIFORNIA/ASIAN   At AsiaSF you'll be entertained by Asian men—dressed as women—who lip-sync show tunes as they dish out an excellent grilled shrimp and herb salad, Asian-influenced hamburgers, pot stickers, duck quesadillas, and chicken sate. Fortunately, the food and the atmosphere are as colorful as the staff, which means a night here is more than a meal—it's a very happening event.

201 9th St. (at Howard St.). ℂ 415/255-8889. www.asiasf.com. Reservations recommended. Main courses $9–$19. AE, DC, DISC, MC, V ($25 minimum). Mon–Wed 6–10pm, Thurs–Sun 5–10pm. Bus: 9, 12, or 47. Metro: Civic Center stop on underground Muni and BART.

Manora's ⋆ THAI   Ever-bustling Manora's cranks out dependable Thai to an eclectic mix of local diners. It's perpetually packed (unless you come early), so you'll be seated sardine-like at one of the cramped but well-appointed tables. During the dinner rush, the noise level can make conversation among larger parties almost impossible, but the food is so good, you'll probably prefer to turn toward your plate and stuff your face. Start with tangy soup or chicken satay. Follow with any of the wonderful dinner dishes—which should be shared—and a side of rice. There are endless options, including a vast array of vegetarian plates. *Tip:* Come before 7pm or after 9pm if you don't want a loud, rushed meal.

1600 Folsom St. (at 12th St.). ℂ 415/861-6224. Reservations recommended for 4 or more. Main courses $7–$12. MC, V. Mon–Fri 11:30am–2:30pm; Mon–Sat 5:30–10:30pm; Sun 5–10pm. Bus: 9, 12, or 47.

FINANCIAL DISTRICT
EXPENSIVE

Aqua ⋆⋆⋆ SEAFOOD   Without question, Aqua remains San Francisco's finest seafood restaurant. Heralded chef Michael Mina dazzles his customers with a bewildering juxtaposition of earth and sea in his seasonally changing menus. The ahi tartare, for example, is mixed table-side with pears, pine nuts, quail egg, and mint—it's truly divine and one of the best I've ever had. The roasted spot prawn with crab stuffing, citrus hollandaise, and hot and sour vinaigrette is deliciously creative, the miso-marinated Chilean sea bass and grilled medaillons of ahi tuna and foie gras in pinot sauce are other show stoppers. Desserts are equally impressive, particularly the Aqua soufflé of the day. My only complaint: The dining room is rather stark and noisy.

252 California St. (near Battery). ℂ 415/956-9662. Reservations required. Main courses $29–$39; 5-course tasting menu $85 or $125; vegetarian tasting menu $55. AE, DC, MC, V. Mon–Fri 11:30am–2pm; Mon–Sat 5:30–10:30pm. Bus: All Market St. buses.

MODERATE

Kokkari ⋆⋆⋆ (Value) GREEK   It figures that it would take a French chef to make Greek food fabulous, and executive chef Jean Alberti, the mastermind behind the moussaka, does exactly that. In truth, there are few restaurants I continually like as much as Kokkari ("Ko-*car*-ee"). The love affair begins with the setting: a beautifully rustic living-room–like dining area with a commanding fireplace and oversize furnishings, and ends with Alberti's traditional Aegean dishes. Hearty eaters should opt for the to-die-for moussaka (eggplant, lamb, potato, and béchamel). Another boon: quail stuffed with winter greens served on oven-roasted leeks, orzo, and wild rice *pilafi*. Don't leave without sinking your fork into an order of *Kalithopita*, the most velvety chocolate cake you'll ever eat.

Dining with the Sun on Your Face at Belden Place

San Francisco has always been woefully lacking in the alfresco dining department. One exception, however, is Belden Place, an adorable little brick alley in the heart of the Financial District that is closed to everything but foot traffic. When the weather is agreeable, the restaurants that line the alley break out the big umbrellas, tables, and chairs à la Boulevard St-Michel and voilà—a bit of Paris just off Pine Street.

A handful of adorable cafes line Belden Place and offer a wide variety of cuisine. There's **Cafe Bastille,** 22 Belden Place (✆ **415/986-5673**), your classic French bistro and fun speakeasy basement serving excellent crepes, mussels, and French onion soup along with live jazz on weekends; **Cafe Tiramisu,** 28 Belden Place (✆ **415/421-7044**), a stylish Italian hot spot serving addictive risottos and gnocchi; and **Plouf,** 40 Belden Place (✆ **415/986-6491**), which specializes in big bowls of mussels slathered in a choice of seven sauces as well as fresh seafood. **B44,** 44 Belden Place (**415/986-6287**), serves up a side order of Spain alongside its revered paella and other seriously zesty Spanish dishes.

Conversely, come at night for a Euro-speakeasy vibe with your dinner.

200 Jackson St. (at Front St.). ✆ **415/981-0983**. www.kokkari.com. Reservations recommended. Main courses $15–$21 lunch, $17–$33 dinner. AE, DC, DISC, MC, V. Mon–Fri 11:30am–2:30pm, bar menu 2:30–5:30pm; Mon–Thurs 5:30–10pm; Fri 5:30–11pm; Sat 5–11pm. Valet parking (dinner only) $8. Bus: 12, 15, 41, or 83.

CHINATOWN
INEXPENSIVE

House of Nanking ✿ CHINESE   To its legion of fans, the wait at this dive—sometimes up to an hour—is worth what's on the plate. When the line is reasonable, I drop by for a plate of pot stickers and chef-owner Peter Fang's signature shrimp-and-green-onion pancake, served with peanut sauce. You can select from a good number of pork, rice, beef, seafood, chicken, or vegetable dishes, but I suggest you trust the waiter when he recommends a special, or simply point to what looks good on someone else's table. Even with an expansion that doubled the space, seating is tight, so prepare to be bumped around a bit and don't expect good service—it's all part of the Nanking experience.

919 Kearny St. (at Columbus Ave.). ✆ **415/421-1429**. Reservations not accepted. Main courses $6–$12. MC, V. Mon–Fri 11am–10pm, Sat noon–10pm, Sun 4–10pm. Bus: 9, 12, 15, or 30.

R&G Lounge ✿✿ CHINESE   If you want a sure thing in Chinatown, go directly to two-story R&G Lounge. During lunch, both newly redecorated floors are packed with hungry neighborhood workers who go straight to the $5 rice-plate specials. But even then you can order from the dinner menu, which features legendary (and very greasy and rich) deep-fried salt-and-pepper crab. Personal favorites include R&G Special Beef, which melts in your mouth and explodes with the tangy flavor of the accompanying sauce or savory seafood in a clay pot, delicious classic roast duck, and the adzuki-bean-pudding finale.

631 Kearny St. (at Clay St.). ✆ **415/982-7877**. Reservations recommended. Main courses $7–$25. AE, DC, DISC, MC, V. Mon–Thurs 11am–9:30pm, Fri 11am–10pm, Sat 11:30am–10:30pm, Sun 11:30am–9:30pm.

Parking is validated across the street at Portsmouth Sq. garage or Holiday Inn after 5pm. Bus: 1, 9AX, 9BX, 12, or 15.

RUSSIAN HILL
INEXPENSIVE

Swan Oyster Depot ★★ *Finds* SEAFOOD   Swan Oyster Depot is a unique San Francisco dining experience you shouldn't miss. Opened in 1912, this tiny hole-in-the-wall boasts only 20 or so seats, jammed cheek-by-jowl along a long marble bar. Most patrons come for a quick cup of chowder or a plate of oysters on the half shell that arrive chilling on crushed ice. The menu is limited to fresh crab, shrimp, oyster, clam cocktails, Maine lobster, and Boston-style clam chowder, all of which are exceedingly fresh. *Note:* Don't let the lunchtime line dissuade you—it moves fast.

1517 Polk St. (between California and Sacramento sts.). © **415/673-1101.** Reservations not accepted. Seafood cocktails $7–$15; clams and oysters on the half shell $7–$7.25 per half dozen. No credit cards. Mon–Sat 8am–5:30pm. Bus: 27.

NORTH BEACH
MODERATE

Enrico's ★ MEDITERRANEAN   Enrico's is the most fun sidewalk restaurant and supper club destination on this North Beach strip. Families might want to skip this one, but anyone with an appreciation for live jazz (played nightly), late-night noshing, and people-watching from the outdoor patio would be quite content spending an alfresco evening under the heat lamps. (However, the best view of the band is from inside.) Chewy brick-oven pizza, a handful of pastas, zesty tapas, and thick steaks are hot items on the menu, which changes monthly.

504 Broadway (at Kearny St.). © **415/982-6223.** www.enricossidewalkcafe.com. Reservations recommended. Main courses $7–$12 lunch, $11–$23 dinner. AE, MC, V. Sun–Thurs 11:30am–11pm, Fri–Sat 11:30am–midnight; bar daily 11:30am–1:30am or earlier depending on patronage. Valet parking (dinner only) $10. Bus: 12, 15, 30, or 83.

Moose's ★★ *Value* MEDITERRANEAN/CALIFORNIA   A big blue neon moose marks your arrival to North Beach's most schmoozy restaurant, where Nob Hill socialites and local politicians come to dine and be seen. But convivial Moose's is not just an image. The food on recent visits has been very, very good. Appetizers include a truly good Caesar salad and a perfect Dungeness crab cake with apple salad and Meyer lemon aïoli. Main courses (especially meats) tend to be lovingly prepared. Try the cast-iron roasted halibut; wood-oven-roasted game hen with leek smashed potatoes, baby carrots, and wild-mushroom jus; or red-wine–braised lamb shank with creamy polenta, mustard greens, and orange-mint gremolata. Other reasons to love Moose's: They make a darned good hamburger, have a casual bar and live jazz nightly, and serve Sunday brunch.

1652 Stockton St. (between Filbert and Union sts.). © **800/28-MOOSE** or 415/989-7800. www.mooses.com. Reservations recommended. Main courses $13–$26. AE, DC, MC, V. Mon–Wed 4–11pm, Thurs 11:30am–11pm, Fri–Sat 11:30am–midnight (bar menu 2:30–5:30pm), Sun 10am–11pm (bar menu 2:30–5pm). Valet parking $6 lunch, $9 dinner for 3 hr. Bus: 15, 30, 41, or 45.

INEXPENSIVE

L'Osteria del Forno ★★ ITALIAN   L'Osteria del Forno might be only slightly larger than a walk-in closet, but it's one of the top three authentic Italian restaurants in North Beach. Peer in the window facing Columbus Avenue, and you'll probably see two Italian women with their hair up, sweating from the heat of the brick-lined oven, which cranks out the best focaccia (and focaccia sandwiches) in the city. There's no pomp or circumstance: Locals come here strictly to eat. The menu features a variety of superb pizzas, salads, soups, and fresh pastas, plus a good selection of daily specials (pray for the roast pork braised in milk), which includes a roast of the day, pasta, and ravioli. Small baskets of warm focaccia keep you going until the arrival of the entrees, which should always be accompanied by a glass of Italian red. Good news for folks on the go: You can get pizza by the slice.

519 Columbus Ave. (between Green and Union sts.). © 415/982-1124. Reservations not accepted. Sandwiches $5.50–$6.50; pizzas $10–$17; main courses $6–$11. No credit cards. Sun–Mon and Wed–Thurs 11:30am–10pm, Fri–Sat 11:30am–10:30pm. Bus: 15 or 41.

Mario's Bohemian Cigar Store ★ *Finds* ITALIAN Across the street from Washington Square is one of North Beach's most popular neighborhood hangouts. The century-old bar—small, well worn, and perpetually busy—is best known for its focaccia sandwiches, including meatball and eggplant. Wash it all down with an excellent cappuccino or a house Campari as you watch the tourists stroll by. And no, they do not sell cigars.

566 Columbus Ave. (at Union St.). © 415/362-0536. Sandwiches $6.75–$7.25. No credit cards. Daily 10am–10pm. Closed Dec 24–Jan 1. Bus: 15, 30, 41, or 45.

Pasta Pomodoro ★★ *Kids* *Value* ITALIAN If you're looking for a good, cheap meal in North Beach—or anywhere else in town, for that matter—this San Francisco chain can't be beat. There's usually a 20-minute wait for a table, but after you're seated, you'll be surprised at how promptly you're served. Every dish is fresh and sizable, and best of all, they cost a third of what you'll pay elsewhere. Winners include the spaghetti *frutti di mare* made with calamari, mussels, scallops, tomato, garlic and wine, or *cavatappi pollo* with roast chicken, sun-dried tomatoes, cream, mushrooms, and Parmesan—both are under $7.

655 Union St. (at Columbus Ave.). © 415/399-0300. Reservations not accepted. Main courses $6–$11. MC, V. Sun–Thurs 11am–11pm, Fri–Sat 11am–midnight. Cable car: Powell-Mason line. Bus: 15, 30, 41, or 45. There are 12 other locations, including 2027 Chestnut St., at Fillmore St. (© 415/474-3400); 2304 Market St., at 16th St. (© 415/558-8123); 3611 California St. (© 415/831-0900); and 816 Irving St., between 9th and 10th sts. (© 415/566-0900).

FISHERMAN'S WHARF
EXPENSIVE

Restaurant Gary Danko ★★★ *Finds* MODERN CLASSIC Gary Danko, who received the James Beard Foundation award for best chef in California and made San Francisco's Ritz-Carlton Dining Room the top dining destination during his reign from 1991 to 1996, still tops the charts after his 1999 opening. Within the romantic yet unfussy wood, split-dining room thoughtfulness is woven into the experience with the intricacy of a master embroiderer. The three- to five-course price-fixed menu is freestyle, so whether you want a sampling of appetizers or a flight of meat courses, you need only ask. Top picks? Glazed oysters, which were as creamy as the light accompanying sauce graced with leeks and intricately carved "zucchini pearls"; seared foie gras with peaches, caramelized onions, and verjus sauce; and adventurous Moroccan spiced squab with chermoula and orange-cumin carrots. Diners at the small bar have the option of ordering a la carte and everyone has access to the stellar, but expensive, wine list. If after dinner you have the will to pass on the glorious cheese cart or caramel almond peaches with buttermilk ice cream prepared tableside, a plate of petit fours reminds you that Gary Danko is one sweet and memorable meal.

800 North Point St. (at Hyde St.). © **415/749-2060.** www.garydanko.com. Reservations required. 3- to 5-course fixed-price menu $55–$74. AE, DC, MC, V. Sun–Wed 5:30–9:30pm, Thurs–Sat 5:30–10pm. Closed Thanksgiving, Dec 25 and 31, July 4. Valet parking $10. Cable car: Hyde. Bus: 42.

MODERATE

Ana Mandara *★★ Kids* VIETNAMESE   Don Johnson is part owner but the real star is the Vietnamese food in an outstandingly beautiful setting. Amid a shuttered room with mood lighting, palm trees, and Vietnamese-inspired decor, diners (mostly tourists) splurge on crisp spring rolls; Dungeness crab with zesty lemon sauce; buttery Chilean sea bass, lovingly wrapped and steamed in banana leaf with shiitake mushrooms and miso sauce; a sculptural "lobster tower" with rice, avocado, and daikon sprouts; and wok-charred tournedos of beef tenderloin with sweet onions and peppercress.

891 Beach St. (at Polk St.). © **415/771-6800.** Reservations recommended. Main courses $18–$28. www.anamandara.com. AE, DISC, MC, V. Mon–Fri 11:30am–2pm; Sun–Thurs 5:30–10pm, Fri–Sat 5:30–10:30pm. Valet parking $8. Bus: 19, 30, 32, or 42.

MARINA DISTRICT, COW HOLLOW & PACIFIC HEIGHTS
EXPENSIVE

La Folie *★★ Finds* FRENCH   My mother and I call this unintimidating, cozy, relaxed French restaurant "the house of foie gras" because on our first visit, virtually every dish overflowed with the ultra-rich delicacy. But in truth, while foie gras is still celebrated, there's more to chef Roland Passot's fantastic menu: melt-in-your-mouth starters such as the roast quail and—drum roll please—foie gras with salad, wild mushrooms, and roasted garlic, and very generous main courses such as rôti of quail and squab stuffed with wild mushrooms and wrapped in crispy potato strings, or roast venison with vegetables, quince, and huckleberry sauce. The country-French decor is tasteful but not too serious, with whimsical chandeliers and a cloudy sky painted overhead. Finish off with any of the delectable desserts and when you're done, you're sure to loosen your belt a few notches.

2316 Polk St. (between Green and Union sts.). © **415/776-5577.** Reservations recommended. Main courses $32–$45; 4-course tasting menu $75; 5-course chef's tasting menu $85; vegetarian tasting menu $55. AE, DC, DISC, MC, V. Mon–Sat 5:30–10pm. Bus: 19, 41, 45, 47, 49, or 76.

MODERATE

Ella's *★★ Kids* AMERICAN/BREAKFAST   Although this homey American restaurant serves (quiet) dinners on weeknights, it's well known throughout town as the undisputed king of breakfasts. Unfortunately, its acclaim means you're likely to wait up to an hour on weekends. But midweek and in the wee hours of morning, it's possible to slide into a counter or table seat in the colorful split dining room and lose yourself in outstanding and obscenely generous servings of chicken hash, crisped to perfection and served with eggs any way you like them, with fluffy buttermilk biscuits. Pancakes, omelets, and the short list of other breakfast essentials are equally revered. Service can be slow, but at least the busboys are quick to fill coffee cups. Come lunchtime and the far more mellow dinner, solid entrees like salads or grilled salmon with mashed potatoes remind you what's great about good old American cooking.

500 Presidio Ave. (at California St.). © **415/441-5669.** Reservations are accepted for breakfast for parties of 8 or more and are always accepted for lunch and dinner. Main courses $3.75–$8.25 breakfast, $11–$17 dinner. AE, MC, V. Mon–Fri 7am–9pm, Sat–Sun 8:30am–2pm. Bus: 1, 5, or 43.

Florio *★★* FRENCH/ITALIAN BISTRO   When I'm in the mood for a good meal without hoopla, I head directly to bistro-like Florio. It's not only because the staff is friendly, or because if it's booked, I can always eat at the bar, or even because the place is small enough that I don't feel like I'm being rushed in and out as quickly as possible. The real reason is because I'm addicted to the shrimp and white-bean salad, steak frites, and virtually every other little comfort dish that makes its way to the table. The wines by the glass (and by the bottle) always disappoint, but I don't care. I pull up a chair, make myself at home, and enjoy casual and cozy surroundings and consistently satisfying food. I suggest you do the same.

1915 Fillmore St. (between Pine and Bush sts.). ℂ 415/775-4300. Most main courses $18–$20. AE, MC, V. Sun–Thurs 5:30–10pm, Fri–Sat 5:30–11pm. Bus: 3, 22, 41, or 45.

Greens Restaurant ★★ *Finds* VEGETARIAN Knowledgeable locals swear by Greens, where executive chef Annie Somerville (author of *Fields of Greens*) cooks with the seasons, using produce from Green Gulch Farm and other local organic farms. Located in an old warehouse, with enormous windows overlooking the bridge and the bay, the restaurant is both a pioneer and a legend. A weeknight dinner might start with such appetizers as mushroom faro soup with asiago cheese and tarragon or grilled portobello and endive salad. Entrees run the gamut from pizza with wilted escarole, red onions, lemon, asiago, and Parmesan to Vietnamese yellow curry or risotto with black trumpet mushrooms, leeks, savory spinach, white truffle oil, Parmesan Reggiano, and thyme. A special four-course dinner is served on Saturday. Adjacent to the restaurant, Greens To Go bakery sells homemade breads, sandwiches, soups, salads, and pastries.

Building A, Fort Mason Center (enter Fort Mason opposite the Safeway at Buchanan and Marina sts.). ℂ 415/771-6222. Reservations recommended. Main courses $9.50–$12 lunch, $15–$20 dinner; fixed-priced dinner $48; brunch $8–$12. DISC, MC, V. Tues–Fri 11:30am–2pm, Sat 11:30am–2:30pm, Sun 10am–2pm; Mon–Fri 5:30–9:30pm, Sat 5:30–9pm. Greens To Go Mon–Fri 8am–9:30pm, Sat 8am–4:30pm, Sun 9am–3:30pm. Free parking. Bus: 28 or 30.

Isa ★★ FRENCH TAPAS Luke Sung has captured my and many locals' hearts by creating the kind of menu that foodies dream of: a smattering of small dishes that allow you to try numerous items in one sitting. It's a good thing the menu, considered "French tapas," offers snack sizes at affordable prices. After all, it's a lot to ask a diner to choose between sweetbreads and mushroom ragout, seared foie gras with caramelized apples, potato-wrapped sea bass in brown butter, and rack of lamb. But here a table for two could choose all of them and one or two more and not need to be rolled out the door afterward. Adding to the allure is the warm boutique dining environment—60 seats scattered amidst a very small dining room in the front and a tented, heated patio out back that sets the mood with a warm yellow glow. Cocktailers, drink elsewhere: Isa serves beer and wine only.

3324 Steiner St. (between Lombard and Chestnut sts.). ℂ 415/567-9588. Reservations recommended. Main courses $9–$16. AE, MC, V. Tues–Thurs 5:30–10pm, Fri–Sat 5:30–10:30pm. Bus: 22, 28, 30, 30X, 43, or 76.

Pane e Vino ★★ *Kids* ITALIAN The authentic Italian food is consistently excellent (try not to fill up on the outstanding breads), the prices reasonable, and the mostly Italian-accented staff always smooth and efficient under pressure. The two small dining rooms—separated by an open kitchen from which heavenly aromas emanate—offer only limited seating, so expect a wait even if you have reservations. The wide selection of appetizers includes a fine carpaccio and the hugely popular chilled artichoke stuffed with bread and tomatoes and served with vinaigrette. A favorite, the antipasti of mixed grilled vegetables always spurs a fork fight. A similarly broad selection of pastas is available, including a flavorful *pennette alla boscaiola* with porcini mushrooms and pancetta in a tomato cream sauce. Other specialties include a chicken breast marinated in lime juice and herbs. Top dessert picks are any of the Italian ice creams, the crème caramel, and the creamy tiramisu.

3011 Steiner St. (at Union St.). ℂ 415/346-2111. Reservations recommended. Main courses $8.50–$20. AE, MC, V. Mon–Thurs 11:30am–3pm and 5–10pm, Fri–Sat 11:30am–10pm, Sun 5–10pm. Valet parking (Mon–Sat evenings only) $8. Bus: 41 or 45.

INEXPENSIVE

Andalé Taqueria ✷✷ *(Kids)* *(Value)* MEXICAN   Andalé (Spanish for "hurry up") offers incredible high-end fast food for the health-conscious and the just plain hungry in an attractive and casual setting. Lard, preservatives, or canned items are eschewed for salad dressings made with double virgin olive oil; whole vegetarian beans (not refried); skinless chicken; salsas and *aguas frescas* (fruit drinks) made from fresh fruits and veggies; and mesquite-grilled meats. Add the location (on a sunny shopping stretch), sophisticated decor, full bar, and check-me-out patio seating (complete with corner fireplace), and it's no wonder the good-looking, fitness-fanatic Marina District considers this place home. Cafeteria-style service keeps prices low.

2150 Chestnut St. (between Steiner and Pierce sts.). ℂ 415/749-0506. Reservations not accepted. Most dishes $5.25–$9.50. AE, MC, V. Mon–Thurs and Sun 11am–10pm, Fri–Sat 11am–10:30pm. Bus: 22, 28, 30, 30X, 43, 76, or 82X.

Eliza's ✷✷ *(Kids)* *(Value)* CHINESE   Despite the humorous train-wreck-like design of modern architecture, glass art, and color, this perennially packed neighborhood haunt serves some of the freshest, best-tasting Chinese in town. Unlike most comparable options, here the atmosphere (albeit unintentionally funky) and presentation parallel the food. The fantastically fresh soups, salads, seafood, pork, chicken, duck, and such specials as spicy eggplant are outstanding and served on beautiful Italian plates. (Get the sea bass with black-bean sauce and go straight to heaven!) I often come at midday and order the wonderful Kung Pao chicken lunch special: a mixture of tender chicken, peanuts, chile peppers, subtly hot sauce, and perfectly crunchy vegetables. It's 1 of 21 main-course choices that come with rice and soup for around $5. The place is also jumping at night, so prepare to stand in line.

2877 California St. (at Broderick St.). ℂ 415/621-4819. Reservations not accepted. Main courses $4.50–$5.15 lunch, $5.25–$9 dinner. MC, V ($10 minimum). Mon–Fri 11am–3pm and 5–9:45pm, Sat 11am–9:45pm, Sun noon–9:45pm. Bus: 6, 7, 21, 66, or 71.

Mel's Diner ✷✷ *(Kids)* AMERICAN   Sure, it's contrived, touristy, and nowhere near healthy, but when you get that urge for a chocolate shake and banana cream pie at the stroke of midnight—or when you want to entertain the kids—no other place in the city comes through like Mel's Diner. Modeled after a classic 1950s diner, right down to the nickel jukebox at each table, Mel's harks back to the halcyon days when cholesterol and fried foods didn't jab your guilty conscience with every greasy, wonderful bite. Too bad the prices don't reflect the '50s; a burger with fries and a Coke runs about $8.

There's another Mel's at 3355 Geary St., at Stanyan Street (ℂ **415/387-2244**); it's open Thursday through Saturday from 6am to 3am.

2165 Lombard St. (at Fillmore St.). ℂ **415/921-3039.** Main courses $4–$5.50 breakfast, $6–$8 lunch, $8–$12 dinner. No credit cards. Sun–Wed 6am–2am, Thurs 6am–3am, Fri–Sat 24 hr. Bus: 22, 30, or 43.

Pluto's ✦ *Value* CALIFORNIA Pluto's combines assembly-line efficiency with high quality. The result is cheap, fresh fare ranging from humongous salads with a dozen choices of toppings to oven-roasted poultry and grilled meats (the flank steak is great), sandwiches, and a wide array of sides like crispy garlic potato rings, seasonal veggies, and barbecued chicken wings. Drinks include cappuccino, tea, sodas, bottled brews, and Napa wines, and desserts are home-made. The ordering system can be bewildering to newcomers: Grab a checklist and hand it to the food servers, who will check off your order and relay it to the cashier. Seating is limited during the rush, but the turnover is fairly fast. A second location is at 627 Irving St., at Seventh Avenue (© **415/753-8867**).

3258 Scott St. (at Chestnut St.). © **415/7-PLUTOS.** Reservations not accepted. Main courses $3.50–$5.75. MC, V. Mon–Fri 11am–10pm, Sat–Sun 9:30am–10pm. Bus: 28, 30, or 76.

CIVIC CENTER
MODERATE

Absinthe ✦✦ *Value* SOUTHERN FRENCH This Hayes Valley hot spot is a sexy, fun, *and* reasonably priced restaurant preferred by everyone from the the-atergoing crowd to the young and chic. Decor is scrumptious brasserie and the fare is tasty—from the specialty cocktails, and good wine list to the slew of seafood starters, including oysters and cold seafood platters. Appetizers range from classic (Caesar salad, French onion soup) to modern luxe (perhaps grilled asparagus with black-truffled mayonnaise, or lamb's lettuce with pickled beets and walnuts). Main courses are equally satisfying, with the likes of coq au vin to an excellent burger.

398 Hayes St. (at Gough St.). © **415/551-1590.** www.absinthe.com. Reservations recommended. Brunch $6–$12; most main courses $8.50–$18 lunch, $14–$28 dinner. AE, DC, DISC, MC, V. Tues–Fri 11:30am–mid-night, Sat 10:30am–midnight, Sun 10:30am–10:30pm. Valet parking (Tues–Sat) $8. Bus: 21.

Hayes Street Grill ✦✦ SEAFOOD For well over a decade this small, no-nonsense seafood restaurant (owned and operated by revered food writer and chef Patricia Unterman) has maintained a solid reputation among San Fran-cisco's picky epicureans for its impeccably fresh and straightforwardly prepared fish. Choices ranging from Hawaiian swordfish to Puget Sound salmon—cooked to perfection, naturally—are matched with your sauce of choice (Szechuan peanut, tomatillo salsa, or shallot butter) and a side of their signature french fries. Fancier seafood specials are available, too, such as paella with clams, mussels, scallops, calamari, chorizo, and saffron rice, as well as an impressive selection of garden-fresh salads and local grilled meats. Finish with the out-standing crème brûlée.

320 Hayes St. (near Franklin St.). © **415/863-5545.** Reservations recommended. Main courses $8.75–$19 lunch, $12–$20 dinner. AE, DC, DISC, MC, V. Mon–Fri 11:30am–2pm; Mon–Thurs 5–9:30pm, Fri 5–10:30pm, Sat 5:30–10:30pm, Sun 5–8:30pm. Bus: 19, 31, or 38.

Zuni Café ✦✦✦ *Finds* MEDITERRANEAN Delicious, trendsetting Zuni Café is, and probably always will be, a local favorite. Its expanse of windows and prime lower Castro location guarantee good people-watching, but even better is the action within: attractive 30- and 40-somethings crowding in for the flavors of chef Judy Rodgers's incredibly satisfying Mediterranean-influenced menu. For the full effect, stand at the bustling, copper-topped bar, and order a glass of wine and a few oysters from the oyster menu. (A dozen or so varieties are on hand at all times.) Then take a seat amidst the exposed-brick, two-level maze of little dining rooms. Although the changing menu always includes meat (such as New

York steak with Belgian endive gratin) and fish (grilled or braised in the kitchen's brick oven), the proven winners are Rodgers's brick-oven–roasted chicken for two with Tuscan-style bread salad, the polenta with mascarpone, and the hamburger on grilled rosemary focaccia bread (a strong contender for the city's best burger).

1658 Market St. (at Franklin St.). © **415/552-2522.** Reservations recommended. Main courses $10–$19 lunch, $15–$26 dinner. AE, MC, V. Tues–Sat 11:30am–midnight, Sun 11am–11pm. Valet parking $7. Muni Metro: All Market St. lines. Bus: 6, 7, 71, or 75.

HAIGHT-ASHBURY
INEXPENSIVE

Cha Cha Cha ★★ *Value* CARIBBEAN   Put your name on the mile-long list, crowd into the minuscule bar, and drink sangria while you wait. When you finally get seated (generally at least an hr. later), you'll dine in a loud—and I mean *loud*—dining room with Santería altars, banana trees, and plastic tropical tablecloths. Do as I do and order from the tapas menu, sharing such dishes as some of the city's best fried calamari, fried new potatoes, Cajun shrimp, and mussels in saffron broth, all of which are accompanied by rich, luscious sauces. This is the kind of place where you can take friends in a partying mood, let your hair down, and make an evening of it. If you want the flavor without the festivities, come during lunch.

A second, larger location is open in the Mission at 2327 Mission St., between 19th and 20th streets (© **415/648-0504**).

1801 Haight St. (at Shrader St.). © **415/386-7670.** Reservations not accepted. Tapas $4.50–$8.75; main courses $9–$15. MC, V. Daily 11am–4pm; Sun–Thurs 5–11pm, Fri–Sat 5–11:30pm. Muni Metro: N. Bus: 6, 7, 66, 71, or 73.

Thep Phanom ★★ THAI   By successfully incorporating flavors from India, China, Burma, Malaysia, and more recently the West, Thep Phanom has risen through the ranks to become one of the best Thai restaurants in San Francisco. (The line out the front door proves it's no secret.) Start with the signature dish, *ped swan*—boneless duck in a light honey sauce served on a bed of spinach. *Larb ped* (minced duck salad), velvety basil-spiked seafood curry served on banana leaves, and spicy *yum plamuk* (calamari salad) are also recommended. The Haight location attracts an eclectic crowd; the atmosphere is informal, and the decor quite tasteful.

400 Waller St. (at Fillmore St.). © **415/431-2526.** Reservations recommended. Main courses $7–$14. AE, DC, DISC, MC, V. Daily 5:30–10:30pm. Bus: 6, 7, 22, 66, or 71.

RICHMOND & SUNSET DISTRICTS
INEXPENSIVE

Ton Kiang ★★ *Kids* *Finds* CHINESE/DIM SUM   Ton Kiang is the number-one place in the city to do dim sum. Wait in line (which is out the door anytime between 11am and 1:30pm), get a table on the first or second floor, and say yes to dozens of delicacies, which are brought to the table for your approval. From stuffed crab claws, roast Peking duck, and a gazillion dumpling selections (including scallop and vegetable, shrimp, and beef) to the delicious and hard-to-find *doa miu* (snow pea sprouts flash-sautéed with garlic and peanut oil), shark-fin soup, and a mesmerizing mango pudding, every tray of morsels coming from the kitchen is an absolute delight. Though it's hard to get past the dim sum, which is served all day every day, the full menu of Hakka cuisine is worth investigation as well. This is definitely one of my favorite places to do lunch, and it happens to have an unusually friendly staff.

5821 Geary Blvd. (between 22nd and 23rd aves.). ℂ **415/387-8273.** Reservations accepted for parties of 8 or more. Dim sum $2–$5.50. AE, MC, V. Mon–Sat 10:30am–10pm, Sun 9am–10pm. Bus: 38.

THE CASTRO
MODERATE

Mecca ★★ *Finds* AMERICAN   In 1996, Mecca entered the scene in a decadent swirl of chocolate-brown velvet, stainless steel, cement, and brown Naugahyde, unveiling the kind of industrial-chic supper club that makes you want to order a martini just so you'll match the ambience. A night here promises a live DJ spinning hot grooves (or live entertainment on Mon), and a fine American meal served at tables tucked into several dining nooks. Menu options include such classic starters as Osetra caviar, oysters on the half shell, and Caesar salad. Main courses include sake-and-miso–glazed black cod, cilantro lemon chicken, and grilled prime rib steak. The food is very good, but it's that only-in–San Francisco vibe that makes this place the smokin' hot spot in the Castro.

2029 Market St. (by 14th and Church sts.). ℂ **415/621-7000.** www.sfmecca.com. Reservations recommended. Main courses $16–$32. AE, DC, MC, V. Mon–Thurs 5–11pm, Fri–Sat 5pm–midnight, Sun 4–10pm; bar remains open later. Valet parking $8. Muni Metro: F, K, L, or M. Bus: 8, 22, 24, or 37.

INEXPENSIVE

Firewood Café ★★ *Value* ITALIAN/AMERICAN   One of the sharpest rooms in the neighborhood, the colorful Firewood put its money in the essentials and eliminated extra overhead. There are no waiters or waitresses; everyone orders at the counter and then relaxes at the single family-style table, one of the small tables facing the huge street-side windows, or in the cheery back dining room. Fresh salads come with a choice of three "fixins" ranging from caramelized onions to spiced walnuts, and three gourmet dressing options. Pastas might include three tortellini selections, such as roasted chicken and mortadella. There are gourmet pizzas, calamari with lemon-garlic aioli, and an herb-roasted half or whole chicken with roasted new potatoes. Wines are reasonably priced and yummy desserts top off at $2.95.

4248 18th St. (at Diamond St.). ℂ **415/252-0999.** Reservations not accepted. Main courses $6.25–$9. MC, V. Daily 11am–11pm. Muni Metro: F, K, L, or M. Bus: 8, 33, 35, or 37.

MISSION DISTRICT
MODERATE

Foreign Cinema ★★ CALIFORNIA   This place is so chic that it's hard to believe it's a San Francisco restaurant. An indoor seat is a lovely place to watch San Francisco's most fashionable; outdoors (heated, partially covered, but still chilly), the enormous foreign film showing on the side of an adjoining building steals the show. In 2001 husband and wife team John Clark and Gayle Pirie stepped into the kitchen and are now creating a Mediterranean menu. Snackers find solace in oysters, a devilish brandade gratin, and the cheese selections. Heartier eaters can opt for roasted half chicken with golden chanterelle and red mustard green risotto or grilled Meyer Ranch natural tri-tip with Tuscan-style beans and rosemary-fried peppercorn sauce. The food's fine, but truth be told, I'd come here even if the food sucked. It's just that cool.

2534 Mission St. (between 21st and 22nd sts.). ℂ **415/648-7600.** www.foreigncinema.com. Reservations recommended. Main courses $14–$20. AE, MC, V. Sun–Wed 6–10pm, Thurs–Sat 6–11pm. Valet parking $8. Bus: 14, 14L, or 49.

The Slanted Door ★★ *Finds* VIETNAMESE   This place is so popular that Mick Jagger and President Clinton each made stopovers last time they hit town. Why? Despite the sometimes can't-be-bothered staff, the colorful industrial-chic warehouse serves incredibly fresh and flavorful Vietnamese food. Pull up a modern, color-washed chair and order anything from clay-pot catfish or amazing green-papaya salad to steamed chicken with black-bean sauce, long beans with shrimp, or vegetarian noodles sautéed with mushrooms, lily buds, tofu, bamboo, and shiitake mushrooms. *Note:* The restaurant is expanding their Valencia Street location and has relocated to a temporary space at 100 Brannan St. (same phone number), so confirm where they're located and their open hours when you make a reservation.

584 Valencia St. (at 17th St.). ℂ **415/861-8032.** Reservations recommended. Main courses $8.50–$16 lunch, $9–$27 dinner. MC, V. Mon–Sun 11:30am–3pm; Sun–Thurs 5:30–10pm, Fri–Sat 5:30–10:30pm. Valet parking (dinner only) $7. Bus: 22, 26, 33, 49, or 53. BART: 16th St. Station.

Universal Café ★★ *Finds* AMERICAN/FRENCH   Not only does the intimate, rather cramped place look good—suave and stylish, with thick floor-to-ceiling windows and a row of tables running the length of the restaurant and paralleling the bar and open kitchen—it also attracts a nightly gaggle of locals. They come for phenomenal focaccia sandwiches (such as moist and memorable salmon), huge leafy salads, and inventive thin-crust pizzas at lunch. Superb dinner dishes include braised duck leg on a bed of creamy polenta; sea bass served with risotto, spinach, and caramelized onions; and hearty pot roast with lumpy mashed potatoes and fresh veggies. Granted, it's on the way to nowhere, but if you want an authentic small-restaurant charming San Francisco experience, this is as good as it gets.

2814 19th St. (at Bryant St.). ℂ **415/821-4608.** Reservations recommended for dinner. Main courses $6–$8 breakfast (full on weekends, continental on weekdays), $7–$15 lunch, $11–$24 dinner. AE, MC, V. Tues–Fri 11:30am–2:30pm; Sat–Sun 9am–2:30pm; Tues–Thurs 6–10pm; Fri–Sat 6–11pm; Sun 5:30–10pm. Bus: 27.

INEXPENSIVE

Delfina ★★ *Finds* SEASONAL ITALIAN   Delfina eschews bells, whistles, bigtime design, and fancy preparations for something that used to be utterly San Francisco: straightforward simplicity and a small-business feel. Unpretentious atmosphere, unreasonably reasonable prices, and chef and co-owner Craig Stoll's ultra-fresh seasonal Italian cuisine mean you're in for a price-painless and delicious experience from the minute you're seated by Craig's wife, Ann Spencer, to the time you receive your surprisingly low (by local standards) bill. Winter might welcome slow-roasted pork shoulder or gnocchi with squash and chestnuts, while spring indulgence could include sand dabs with frisee, fingerling potatoes and lemon-caper butter or lamb with polenta and sweet peas. Trust me: Order the buttermilk *panna cotta*. The only downside: It's impossible to find parking—literally—and there's no valet.

3621 18th St. (between Dolores and Guerrero sts.). ℂ **415/552-4055.** www.delfinasf.com. Reservations required. Main courses $9–$18. MC, V. Sun–Thurs 5:30–10pm, Fri–Sat 5:30–11pm. Bus: 26 or 33. Metro: J.

Taquerias La Cumbre ★★ MEXICAN   While most restaurants gussy up their gastronomic goods with million-dollar decor and glamorous gimmicks, La Cumbre's celebrity is the burrito. Craftily constructed with fresh pork, steak, chicken, or vegetables, plus cheese, beans, rice, salsa, and maybe a dash of guacamole or sour cream, there is hardly a better ultra-cheap meal. That it's served in a cafeteria-like brick-lined room with overly shellacked tables and chairs is all the better: There's no mistaking the attraction here.

515 Valencia St. (between 16th and 17th sts.). ℂ **415/863-8205.** Reservations not accepted. Tacos and burritos $3.50–$6.50; dinner plates $5–$7. DISC, MC, V. Mon–Sat 11am–10pm, Sun noon–9pm. BART: Mission. Bus: 14, 22, 33, 49, or 53.

5 The Top Attractions

MAJOR SAN FRANCISCO SIGHTS

Alcatraz Island ★★★   Visible from Fisherman's Wharf, Alcatraz Island (aka "The Rock") has seen a checkered history. It was discovered in 1775 by Juan Manuel Ayala, who named it after the many pelicans that nested on the island. From the 1850s to 1933, when the army vacated the island, it served as a military post protecting the bay shoreline. In 1934 the buildings of the military outpost were converted into a maximum-security prison. Given the sheer cliffs, treacherous tides and currents, and frigid temperatures of the waters, it was believed to be a totally escape-proof prison. Among the famous gangsters who were penned in cell blocks A through D were Al Capone; Robert Stroud, the so-called Birdman of Alcatraz (because he was an expert in ornithological diseases); Machine Gun Kelly; and Alvin Karpis. It cost a fortune to keep them imprisoned here because all supplies, including water, had to be shipped in. In 1963, after an apparent escape in which no bodies were recovered, the government closed the prison, and in 1972 it became part of the Golden Gate National Recreation Area. The wildlife that was driven away during the military and prison years has begun to return—the black-crested night heron and other seabirds are nesting here again—and a new trail has been built that passes through the island's nature areas. Tours, including an audio tour of the prison block and a slide show, are given by the park's rangers, who entertain their guests with interesting anecdotes.

It's a popular excursion and space is limited, so purchase tickets as far in advance as possible. The tour is operated by **Blue & Gold Fleet** (© **415/705-5555;** www.blueandgoldfleet.com) and can be charged to American Express, MasterCard, or Visa ($2.25 per ticket service charge on phone orders). You can also buy tickets in advance from the Blue & Gold ticket office on Pier 41.

Wear comfortable shoes and take a heavy sweater or windbreaker—even when the sun's out, it's cold. The National Park Service also notes that there are a lot of steps to climb on the tour.

Pier 41, near Fisherman's Wharf. © 415/773-1188 (info only). Admission (includes ferry trip and audio tour) $13 adults with headset, $9.25 without; $12 seniors 62 and older with headset, $7.50 without; $8 children 5–11 with headset, $6 without; free for children under 5. Winter daily 9:30am–2:15pm; summer daily 9:15am–4:15pm. Advance purchase advised; evening tours are available; call for information. Ferries depart at 15 and 45 min. after the hr. Arrive at least 20 min. before sailing time.

Cable Cars ★★★   Designated official historic landmarks by the National Park Service in 1964, the city's beloved cable cars clank across the hills like mobile museum pieces. Each weighs about 6 tons and is hauled along by a steel cable, enclosed under the street in a center rail. They move at a constant 9½ miles per hour—never more, never less. This may strike you as slow, but it doesn't feel that way when you're cresting an almost perpendicular hill and looking down at what seems like a bobsled dive straight into the ocean. But in spite of the thrills, they're perfectly safe.

The Powell-Hyde and Powell-Mason lines begin at Powell and Market sts.; the California St. line begins at the foot of Market St. © 415/673-6864. www.sfcablecar.com. Fare $3.

Coit Tower ★★   In a city known for its panoramic views and vantage points, Coit Tower is "The Peak." If it's a clear day, it's wonderful to get here by walking up the Filbert Steps (thereby avoiding a traffic nightmare), and then taking in the panoramic views of the city and bay at the base of the tower. (In fact, I'd

Major San Francisco Sights

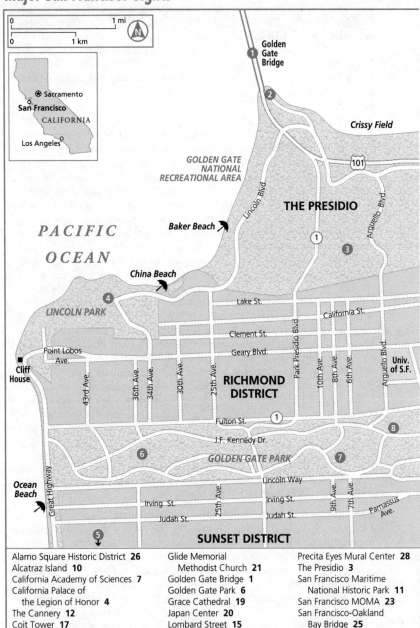

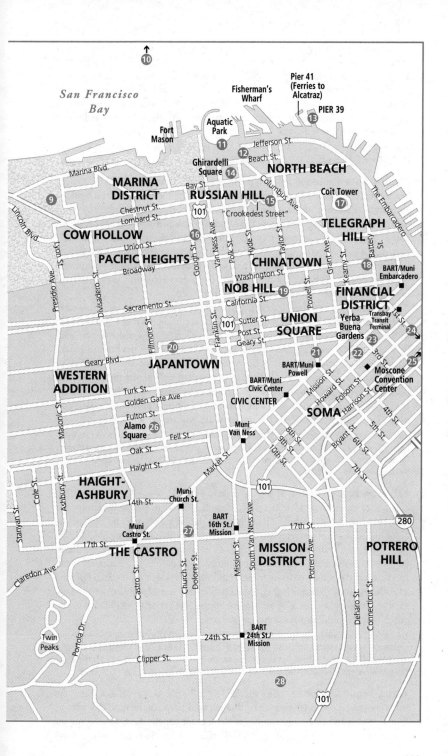

San Francisco
Bay

Pier 41
(Ferries to
Alcatraz)

Fisherman's
Wharf

PIER 39

13

Aquatic
Park

Fort
Mason

11

Jefferson St.

12

Beach St.

Ghirardelli
Square

14

NORTH BEACH

Marina Blvd.

MARINA
DISTRICT

Bay St.

RUSSIAN HILL

Columbus Ave.

Coit Tower

17

9

Chestnut St.

15

Lombard St.

101

"Crookedest Street"

The Embarcadero

TELEGRAPH
HILL

COW HOLLOW

16

Union St.

PACIFIC HEIGHTS

Broadway

CHINATOWN

18

BART/Muni
Embarcadero

Washington St.

NOB HILL

19

FINANCIAL
DISTRICT

Sacramento St.

California St.

UNION
SQUARE

Yerba
Buena
Gardens

Transbay
Transit
Terminal

24

101

Sutter St.

23

Post St.

22

Geary St.

25

Geary Blvd.

20

JAPANTOWN

21

BART/Muni
Powell

Moscone
Convention
Center

WESTERN
ADDITION

Turk St.

Mission St.

Howard St.

Golden Gate Ave.

BART/Muni
Civic Center

Folsom St.

Harrison St.

Fulton St.

CIVIC CENTER

SOMA

Alamo
Square

26

Fell St.

Oak St.

Muni
Van Ness

8th St.

Bryant St.

Haight St.

9th St.

10th St.

7th St.

HAIGHT-
ASHBURY

Market St.

Muni
Church St.

101

280

14th St.

27

17th St.

BART
16th St./
Mission

Muni
Castro St.

17th St.

THE CASTRO

MISSION
DISTRICT

POTRERO
HILL

Claredon Ave.

BART
24th St./
Mission

24th St.

Twin
Peaks

Clipper St.

28

101

recommend not paying the admission and going to the top; the view is just as good from the parking area and you can see the murals for free.) Completed in 1933, the tower is the legacy of Lillie Hitchcock Coit, a wealthy eccentric who left San Francisco a $125,000 bequest. Inside the base of the tower are the impressive WPA murals titled *Life in California, 1934,* which were completed during the New Deal by more than 25 artists, many of whom had studied under master muralist Diego Rivera.

Atop Telegraph Hill. (℃ **415/362-0808.** Admission (to the top of the tower) $3.75 adults, $2.50 seniors, $1.50 children 6–12; free for children under 6. Daily 10am–6pm. Bus: 39.

Golden Gate Bridge 🌟🌟🌟
With its gracefully swung single span, spidery bracing cables, and sky-high twin towers, the bridge looks more like a work of abstract art than one of the greatest practical engineering feats of the 20th century. Construction began in May 1937 and was completed at the then-colossal cost of $35 million. Contrary to pessimistic predictions, the bridge neither collapsed in a gale or earthquake nor proved to be a white elephant. A symbol of hope when the country was afflicted with widespread unemployment, the Golden Gate single-handedly changed the Bay Area's economic life, encouraging the development of areas north of San Francisco.

The mile-long steel link (longer if you factor in the approach), which reaches a height of 746 feet above the water, is an awesome bridge to cross. You can park in the lot at the foot of the bridge on the city side, and then make the crossing by foot. Back in your car, continue to Marin's Vista Point, at the bridge's northern end. Look back and you'll be rewarded with one of the most famous cityscape views in the world. Millions of pedestrians walk across the bridge each year. You can walk out onto the span from either end. Note that it's usually windy and cold, and the bridge vibrates. Still, walking even a short way is one of the best ways to experience the immense scale of the structure.

Hwy. 101 N. www.goldengatebridge.org. $3 toll collected when driving S. Bridge-bound Golden Gate Transit buses ((℃ **415/923-2000**) depart every 30 to 60 min. during the day for Marin County, starting from the Transbay Terminal (Mission and First sts.) and stopping at Market and 7th sts., at the Civic Center, and along Van Ness Ave. and Lombard St.

San Francisco Museum of Modern Art (MOMA) 🌟
MOMA's collection consists of more than 15,000 works, including close to 5,000 paintings and sculptures by artists such as Henri Matisse, Jackson Pollock, and Willem de Kooning. Other artists represented include Diego Rivera, Georgia O'Keeffe, Paul Klee, the Fauvists, and exceptional holdings of Richard Diebenkorn. MOMA was also one of the first to recognize photography as a major art form; its extensive collection includes more than 9,000 photographs by such notables as Ansel Adams, Alfred Stieglitz, Edward Weston, and Henri Cartier-Bresson. Phone for current details of upcoming special events and whatever you do, check out the fabulous MuseumStore and cafe.

151 3rd St. (2 blocks S of Market St., across from Yerba Buena Gardens). (℃ **415/357-4000.** www.sfmoma. org. Admission $10 adults, $7 seniors, $6 students over 12 with ID, free for children 12 and under. Half-price for all Thurs 6–8:45pm; free to all 1st Tues of each month. Thurs 11am–8:45pm, Fri–Tues 11am–5:45pm. Closed Wed and major holidays. Muni Metro: J, K, L, or M to Montgomery Station. Bus: 15, 30, or 45.

Yerba Buena Center for the Arts & Yerba Buena Gardens 🌟🌟 *Kids*
An urban interactive wonderland, Yerba Buena could keep you busy all day with its 5-acre garden and cafes, and consists of the **Center for the Arts,** which presents music, theater, dance, and visual arts; **Galleries and Arts Forum,** which features

three galleries and a space designed specially for dance; **Zeum** (© **415/777-2800;** www.zeum.org), a part of the children's addition that includes a cafe, interactive cultural center, ice-skating rink, fabulous 1906 historic carousel, and interactive play and learning garden; Sony's futuristic retail and entertainment mecca **Metreon Entertainment Center** (© **415/537-3400**), a 350,000-square-foot complex housing movie theaters, an **IMAX** theater, small restaurants, interactive attractions (including a restaurant and attraction that features Maurice Sendak's *Where the Wild Things Are*), and shops; a virtual bowling alley; and a child-care center.

701 Mission St. © 415/978-ARTS (box office). www.yerbabuenaarts.org. Admission $6 adults, $3 seniors and students. Free to all 1st Thurs of each month 5–8pm. Tues–Wed and Fri–Sun 11am–6pm, Thurs 11am–8pm. Muni Metro: Powell or Montgomery. Bus: 30, 45, or 9X.

GOLDEN GATE PARK ★★★

Everybody loves Golden Gate Park: people, dogs, birds, frogs, turtles, bison, trees, bushes, and flowers. Literally everything feels unified here in San Francisco's enormous arboreal front yard, conveniently located between Fulton Street and Lincoln Way with the main entrance at Fell and Stanyan streets.

Totaling 1,017 acres, Golden Gate Park is a truly magical place. Spend one sunny day stretched out on the grass along JFK Drive, have a good read in Shakespeare Garden, or stroll around Stow Lake and you, too, will understand the allure. It's an interactive botanical symphony—and everyone is invited to play in the orchestra.

The park is made up of hundreds of gardens and attractions linked by wooded paths and paved roads. While many sites worth seeing are clearly visible, the park has infinite hidden treasures, so make your first stop the **McLaren Lodge and Park Headquarters** (© **415/831-2700**) if you want detailed information on the park.

Of the dozens of special gardens in the park, most recognized are the Rhododendron Dell, the Rose Garden, the Strybing Arboretum (see below), and, at the western edge of the park, a springtime array of thousands of tulips and daffodils around the Dutch windmill. An incredible, lower-key attraction is AIDS Memorial Grove, a peaceful place for reflection near the northeastern side of the park.

In addition to the highlights discussed below, the park contains several recreational facilities: tennis courts; baseball, soccer, and polo fields; a golf course; riding stables; and fly-casting pools. Bus: 16AX, BX, 5, 6, 7, 66, or 71.

MUSEUMS INSIDE THE PARK

California Academy of Sciences (Kids)   Clustered around the Music Concourse in Golden Gate Park are three outstanding world-class museums and exhibitions that are guaranteed to entertain every member of the family.

The **Steinhart Aquarium** is the most diverse aquarium in the world, housing some 14,000 specimens, including amphibians, reptiles, marine mammals, penguins, and much more. Youngsters will love the California tide pool and a hands-on area where they can touch starfish and sea urchins. The living coral reef is the largest display of its kind in the country. In the Fish Roundabout, visitors are surrounded by fast-swimming schools of fish kept in a 100,000-gallon tank.

The **Morrison Planetarium** presents daily seasonal and ongoing light shows. Sky shows offer guided tours through the universe projected onto a 65-foot domed ceiling. Approximately four major exhibits, with titles such as "Stargazer's Guide to the Galaxy" and "The Living Universe" are presented each year. Call for general information, show schedules, prices, and sky-watching tips (© 415/750-7141).

The **Natural History Museum** includes several halls displaying classic dioramas of fauna in their habitats. The "Wild California" exhibition includes a 14,000-gallon aquarium and seabird rookery, life-size battling elephant seals, and two larger-than-life views of microscopic life forms. In Wattis Hall, visitors can walk through an exhibit of nearly 1,500 different skulls exploring the tremendous range of scientific information that scientists discover from their studies. Hohfeld Hall allows visitors to experience a simulation of two of San Francisco's biggest earthquakes, determine what their weight would be on other planets, see a real moon rock, and learn about the rotation of the planet at a replica of Foucault's pendulum (the real one is in Paris).

On the Music Concourse of Golden Gate Park. © 415/750-7145 for recorded information. http://www.cal academy.org/. Admission (aquarium, Natural History Museum, and Planetarium) $8.50 adults, $5.50 seniors 65 and over and students 12–17, $2 children 4–11, free for children under 4. Free to all 1st Wed of each month. Planetarium shows $2.50 adults, $1.25 seniors 65 and over and children under 18. Summer (Memorial Day to Labor Day) daily 9am–6pm; rest of year daily 10am–5pm; 1st Wed of each month 10am–9pm year-round. Muni Metro: N to Golden Gate Park. Bus: 5, 44, or 71.

OTHER PARK HIGHLIGHTS

BEACH CHALET   First listed on the National Register of Historic places in 1981, the Spanish-Colonial Beach Chalet, 1000 Great Hwy., at the west end of Golden Gate Park near Fulton Street (© **415/386-8439**), was designed by the architect Willis Polk in 1925. Built with a 200-seat restaurant upstairs and a public lounge and changing rooms on the first floor, it was a popular stopover for generations of beachgoers. In the late 1930s, the federal government's Works Progress Administration (WPA) commissioned Lucien Labaudt (who also painted Coit Tower's frescoes) to create incredible frescoes, mosaics, and wood carvings of San Francisco life. After decades of use, the chalet grew old and worn, forcing its closure in 1981; but in December 1996, the historic Beach Chalet reopened its doors, and through the original mosaics and new literature and displays, it continues to celebrate the city's heritage. The upstairs restaurant is far too modern to wax historical, but it's a great place to stop for a house-made brew and a glimpse of the expansive Pacific.

CONSERVATORY OF FLOWERS (1878)   This striking assemblage of glass and iron, modeled on the famous glass house at Kew Gardens in London, usually exhibits a rotating display of plants and shrubs. Unfortunately, it's closed to visitors until further notice, but the exterior architecture and surrounding gardens alone are worth a look.

JAPANESE TEA GARDEN (1894)   Developed for the 1894 Midwinter Exposition, this garden would be a quiet place with cherry trees, shrubs, and bonsai crisscrossed by winding paths and high-arched bridges crossing over pools of water—were it not for the hordes of tourists and screaming children who can all but destroy any semblance of peace. Come early to enjoy the focal points and places for contemplation, including the massive bronze Buddha that was cast in Japan in 1790 and donated by the Gump family, the Shinto wooden pagoda, and the Wishing Bridge, which reflected in the water looks as though it completes a circle. The garden is open daily November through February from 8:30am to 5pm (teahouse 10am–4:30pm), March through October from 8:30am to 6pm (teahouse 10am–5:30pm). For information on admissions, call © **415/752-4227**. For the teahouse, call © **415/752-1171**.

Golden Gate Park

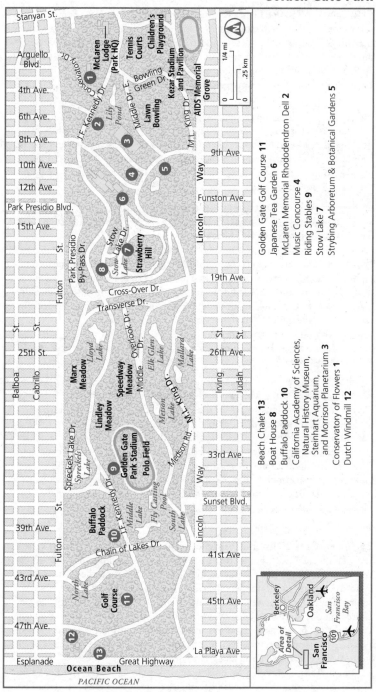

Stanyan St.
Arguello Blvd.
4th Ave.
6th Ave.
8th Ave.
10th Ave.
12th Ave.
Park Presidio Blvd.
15th Ave.
Balboa St.
Cabrillo St.
25th St.
39th Ave.
43rd Ave.
47th Ave.
Esplanade

Conservatory Dr.
McLaren Lodge (Park HQ)
Tennis Courts
Children's Playground
J.F. Kennedy Dr.
Bowling Green Dr.
Middle Dr. E.
Kezar Stadium and Pavilion
Lily Pond
Lawn Bowling
M.L. King Dr.
AIDS Memorial Grove
9th Ave.
Funston Ave.
Lincoln Way
Stow Lake Dr.
Strawberry Hill
Stow Lake
Park Presidio By-Pass Dr.
Fulton St.
19th Ave.
Cross-Over Dr.
Transverse Dr.
Lloyd Lake
Marx Meadow
Speedway Meadow
Overlook Dr.
Middle Dr.
Elk Glen Lake
Mallard Lake
Metson Lake
M.L. King Dr.
Medson Rd.
26th Ave.
Irving St.
Judah St.
33rd Ave.
Lindley Meadow
Spreckels Lake Dr.
Spreckels Lake
Golden Gate Park Stadium Polo Field
Fly Casting Pool
J.F. Kennedy Dr.
Buffalo Paddock
Middle Lake
South Lake
Chain of Lakes Dr.
Sunset Blvd.
Lincoln Way
41st Ave.
North Lake
Golf Course
45th Ave.
La Playa Ave.
Great Highway
Ocean Beach
PACIFIC OCEAN

1/4 mi
.25 km

Golden Gate Golf Course **11**
Japanese Tea Garden **6**
McLaren Memorial Rhododendron Dell **2**
Music Concourse **4**
Riding Stables **9**
Stow Lake **7**
Strybing Arboretum & Botanical Gardens **5**

Beach Chalet **13**
Boat House **8**
Buffalo Paddock **10**
California Academy of Sciences, Natural History Museum, Steinhart Aquarium, and Morrison Planetarium **3**
Conservatory of Flowers **1**
Dutch Windmill **12**

Berkeley
Oakland
San Francisco Bay
Area of Detail
San Francisco
101

115

STRYBING ARBORETUM & BOTANICAL GARDENS Some 6,000 plant species grow here, among them rare species, very ancient plants in a special "primitive garden," and a grove of California redwoods. Open Monday through Friday from 8am to 4:30pm, and Saturday and Sunday from 10am to 5pm. For more information, call © **415/753-7090.**

STOW LAKE & STRAWBERRY HILL ✦ *Kids* Rent a paddleboat, rowboat, or motorboat here and cruise around the circular lake as painters create still lifes and joggers pass along the grassy shoreline. Ducks waddle around waiting to be fed, and turtles bathe on rocks and logs. Strawberry Hill, the 430-foot-high artificial island that lies at the center of Stow Lake, is a perfect picnic spot and boasts a bird's-eye view of San Francisco and the bay. It also has a waterfall and peace pagoda. To reach the boathouse, call © **415/752-0347.** Boat rentals are available daily from 9am to 4pm.

6 Exploring the City

SPECIAL POINTS OF INTEREST

Mission Dolores ✦ This is the oldest structure in the city, built on order of Franciscan Father Junípero Serra by Father Francisco Palou. It was constructed of 36,000 sunbaked bricks and dedicated in June 1776 at the northern terminus of El Camino Real, the Spanish road from Mexico to California. It's a moving place to visit, with its cool, serene buildings with thick adobe walls and especially the cemetery and gardens where the early settlers are buried.

16th St. (at Dolores St.). © 415/621-8203. Donations appreciated. May–Oct daily 9am–4:30pm; Nov–Apr daily 9am–4pm; Good Friday 9am–noon. Closed Thanksgiving, Dec 25. Muni Metro: J. Bus: 14, 26, or 33 to the corner of Church and 16th sts.

Lombard Street Known (erroneously) as the "crookedest street in the world," the whimsically winding block of Lombard Street between Hyde and Leavenworth streets puts smiles on the faces of thousands of visitors each year. The elevation is so steep that the road has to snake back and forth to make a descent possible. This short stretch is one-way, downhill, and fun to drive. Take the curves slowly and in low gear, and expect a wait during the weekend. Save your film for the bottom, where, if you're lucky, you can find a parking space and take a few snapshots of the silly spectacle. You can also take staircases (without curves) up or down on either side of the street.

Between Hyde and Leavenworth sts.

ARCHITECTURAL HIGHLIGHTS

The **Alamo Square Historic District** contains many of the city's 14,000 Victorian "**Painted Ladies,**" homes that have been restored and ornately painted by residents. The small area—bordered by Divisadero Street on the west, Golden Gate Avenue on the north, Webster Street on the east, and Fell Street on the south, about 10 blocks west of the Civic Center—has one of the city's largest concentrations of these. One of the most famous views of San Francisco, which you'll see on postcards and posters all around the city, depicts sharp-edged Financial District skyscrapers behind a row of Victorians. This view can be seen from Alamo Square at Fulton and Steiner streets.

Built in 1881 to a design by Brown and Bakewell, **City Hall** and the **Civic Center** are part of a "City Beautiful" complex done in the beaux-arts style. The dome rises to a height of 308 feet on the exterior and is ornamented with oculi and topped by a lantern. The interior rotunda soars 112 feet and is finished in

America Online Keyword: Travel

Booked seat 6A, open return.

Rented red 4-wheel drive.

Reserved cabin, no running water.

Discovered space.

With over 700 airlines, 50,000 hotels, 50 rental car companies and 5,000 cruise and vacation packages, you can create the perfect getaway for you. Choose the car, the room, even the ground you walk on.

Travelocity.com
A Sabre Company
Go Virtually Anywhere.

Travelocity,® Travelocity.com® and the Travelocity skyline logo are trademarks and/or servicemarks of Travelocity.com L.P., and Sabre® is a trademark of an affiliate of Sabre Inc. © 2002 Travelocity.com L.P. All rights reserved.

© 2002 Yahoo! Inc.

Book your air, hotel, and transportation all in one place.

Hotel or hostel? Cruise or canoe? Car? Plane? Camel? Wherever you're going, visit Yahoo! Travel and get total control over your arrangements. Even choose your seat assignment. So. One hump or two? travel.yahoo.com

powered by
COMPAQ

YAHOO!
Travel

Do You
YAHOO!?

oak, marble, and limestone with a monumental marble staircase leading to the second floor; City Hall is worth seeing as it just underwent a total renovation and retrofitting.

The **Flood Mansion,** 1000 California St., at Mason Street, was built between 1885 and 1886 for James Clair Flood, who, thanks to the Comstock Lode, rose from being a bartender to being one of the city's wealthiest men. The house cost $1.5 million (the fence alone carried a price tag of $30,000!). It was designed by Augustus Laver and modified by Willis Polk after the earthquake to accommodate the Pacific Union Club.

The **Octagon House,** 2645 Gough St., at Union Street (© **415/441-7512**), is an eight-sided, cupola-topped house dating from 1861. Its features are extraordinary, especially the circular staircase and ceiling medallion. Inside, you'll find furniture, silverware, and American pewter from the colonial and Federal periods. There are also some historic documents, including signatures of 54 of the 56 signers of the Declaration of Independence. Even if you're not able to visit during open hours, this strange structure is worth a look. It's open February through December on the second Sunday and second and fourth Thursdays of each month from noon to 3pm; closed January and holidays.

The **Palace of Fine Arts,** on Baker between Jefferson and Bay streets, is the only building to survive from the Pan-Pacific Exhibition of 1915. Constructed by Bernard Maybeck, it was rebuilt in concrete using molds taken from the original in the 1950s. It now houses the Exploratorium (p. 118).

The **TransAmerica Pyramid,** 600 Montgomery St., between Clay and Washington streets, is the tallest structure in San Francisco's skyline—48 stories tall and capped by a 212-foot spire.

Although the **San Francisco–Oakland Bay Bridge** is visually less appealing than the Golden Gate Bridge, it is in many ways more spectacular. Opened in 1936, before the Golden Gate, it's 8¼ miles long, one of the world's longest steel bridges. It's not a single bridge at all, but actually a dovetailed series of spans joined in midbay—at Yerba Buena Island—by one of the world's largest (in diameter) tunnels. To the west of Yerba Buena, the bridge is really two separate suspension bridges, joined at a central anchorage. East of the island is a 1,400-foot cantilever span, followed by a succession of truss bridges.

A CHURCH

Glide Memorial United Methodist Church ✦ *Moments*   There would be nothing special about this plain, Tenderloin-area church if it weren't for its exhilarating pastor, Cecil Williams. Williams's enthusiastic and uplifting preaching and singing with the homeless and poor people of the neighborhood crosses all socioeconomic boundaries and has attracted nationwide fame. Go for an uplifting experience.

330 Ellis St. (W of Union Sq.). © **415/771-6300.** Services Sun at 9 and 11am. Muni Metro: Powell. Bus: 37.

MUSEUMS

Also see "The Top Attractions," earlier in this chapter.

California Palace of the Legion of Honor ✦✦   Designed as a memorial to California's World War I casualties, the neoclassical structure is an exact replica of the Legion of Honor Palace in Paris, right down to the inscription HONNEUR ET PATRIE above the portal. Reopened after a 2-year, $29-million renovation and seismic upgrading project that was stalled by the discovery of almost 300 coffins, the museum's collection contains paintings, sculpture, and decorative arts from Europe, as well as international tapestries, prints, and drawings. The chronological display of more than 800 years of European art includes a fine collection of Rodin sculpture.

In Lincoln Park (34th Ave. and Clement St.). ℭ **415/750-3600** or 415/863-3330 (recorded information). www.thinker.org. Admission $8 adults, $6 seniors 65 and over, $5 youths 12–17, free for children under 12. Fees may be higher for special exhibitions. Free to all 2nd Tues of each month. Tues–Sun 9:30am–5pm. Bus: 18 or 38.

The Exploratorium ★ *Kids* This fun, hands-on science fair contains more than 650 permanent exhibits that explore everything from color theory to Einstein's theory of relativity. Optics is demonstrated in booths where you can see a bust of a statue in three dimensions—but when you try to touch it, you discover it isn't there! The same surreal experience occurs with an image of yourself: When you stretch your hand forward, a hand comes out to touch you, and the hands pass in midair. Every exhibit is designed to be used. You can whisper into a concave reflector and have a friend hear you 60 feet away, or you can design your own animated abstract art—using sound.

3601 Lyon St., in the Palace of Fine Arts (at Marina Blvd.). ℭ **415/563-7337** or 415/561-0360 (recorded information). www.exploratorium.edu. Admission $10 adults, $7.50 seniors and college students with ID, $6 visitors w/disabilities and children 5–17, free for children 4 and under. Free to all 1st Wed of each month. AE, MC, V. Summer (Memorial Day to Labor Day) and holidays, Mon–Tues and Thurs–Sun 10am–6pm; Wed 10am–9pm. Rest of the year Tues and Thurs–Sun 10am–5pm; Wed 10am–9pm. Closed Thanksgiving, Dec 25. Free parking. Bus: 30 from Stockton St. to the Marina stop.

San Francisco Maritime National Historical Park *Kids* Shaped like an Art Deco ship and located near Fisherman's Wharf, the National Maritime Museum is filled with sailing, whaling, and fishing lore. Exhibits include intricate model craft, scrimshaw, and a collection of shipwreck photographs and historic marine scenes, including an 1851 snapshot of hundreds of abandoned ships, deserted en masse by crews dashing off to participate in the gold rush. The museum's walls are lined with finely carved, painted wooden figureheads from old windjammers.

Two blocks east, at Aquatic Park's Hyde Street Pier, are several historic ships that are open to the public. The *Balclutha,* one of the last surviving square-riggers, was built in Glasgow, Scotland, in 1886 and was used to carry grain from California around Cape Horn at a near-record speed of 300 miles a day; it rounded the treacherous Cape 17 times in its career. Visitors are invited to spin the wheel, squint at the compass, and imagine they're weathering a mighty storm. Kids can climb into the bunking quarters, visit the "slop chest" (galley to you, matey), and read the sea chanteys (clean ones only) that decorate the walls.

The 1890 *Eureka* still carries a cargo of nostalgia for San Franciscans. It was the last of 50 paddle-wheeled ferries that regularly plied the bay; it made its final trip in 1957. Restored to its original splendor, the side-wheeler is loaded with deck cargo, including antique cars and trucks.

At the pier's small-boat shop, visitors can follow the restoration progress of historic boats from the museum's collection. It's behind the maritime bookstore on your right as you approach the ships.

At the foot of Polk St. (near Fisherman's Wharf). ℭ **415/556-3002.** www.maritime.org. Museum free; ships $6 adults, $2 seniors over 62 and youths 12–17, free for children under 12; a family ticket for 2 adults and up to 4 children is $13. Museum daily 10am–5pm. Ships on Hyde St. Pier May 15–Sept 15 daily 9:30am–5:30pm; Sept 16–May 14 daily 9:30am–5pm. Closed Jan 1, Thanksgiving, Dec 25. Cable car: Powell-Hyde St. line to the last stop. Bus: 19, 30, 32, 42, or 47.

NEIGHBORHOODS WORTH SEEKING OUT

For self-guided walking tours of San Francisco's neighborhoods, pick up a copy of *Frommer's Memorable Walks in San Francisco.*

THE CASTRO   Castro Street around Market and 18th streets is the center of the city's gay community, which is catered to by the many stores, restaurants, bars, and other institutions here. Among the landmarks are Harvey Milk Plaza, the Quilt Project, and the Castro Theatre, a 1920s movie palace.

CHINATOWN   California Street to Broadway and Kearny to Stockton Street are the boundaries of today's Chinatown. San Francisco is home to the second-largest community of Chinese in the United States, but the majority of them do not live and work in these 24 blocks, although they do return to shop and dine here on weekends.

The gateway at Grant and Bush marks the entry to Chinatown. Walk up Grant, which has become the tourist face of Chinatown, to California Street and Old St. Mary's.

The heart of Chinatown is at **Portsmouth Square,** where you'll find Chinese-American locals playing board games (often gambling) or just sitting quietly. This square was the center of early San Francisco and the spot where the American flag was first raised on July 9, 1846. From the square, Washington Street leads up to Waverly Place, where you can see three temples.

Explore the area at your leisure, or see "Organized Tours," later in this chapter, if you'd like to join a special-interest walking tour.

FISHERMAN'S WHARF & THE NORTHERN WATERFRONT   Few cities in America are as adept at wholesaling their historical sites as San Francisco, which has converted Fisherman's Wharf into one of the most popular tourist destinations in the world. Unless you come really early in the morning, you won't find any traces of the traditional waterfront life that once existed here; the only serious fishing going on is for tourist dollars. A small fleet of fewer than 30 boats still operates from here, but basically Fisherman's Wharf has been converted into one long shopping mall stretching from Ghirardelli Square at the west end to PIER 39 at the east. Some people love it, others can't get far enough away from it, but most agree that Fisherman's Wharf, for better or for worse, has to be seen at least once in a lifetime.

Ghirardelli Square, at 900 North Point, between Polk and Larkin streets (© 415/775-5500), is best known as the former chocolate-and-spice factory of Domingo Ghirardelli. The factory has been converted into a 10-level mall containing more than 50 stores and 11 dining establishments. Scheduled street performers play regularly in the West Plaza. The stores generally stay open until 8 or 9pm in the summer and 6 or 7pm in the winter.

⟨Finds Amazing Graze at the Farmers Market

There's no better way to enjoy a bright San Francisco morning than strolling and snacking through this **gourmet street market** ★★. Every Saturday from 8:30am to 1:30pm, Northern California fruit, vegetable, bread, and dairy vendors join local restaurateurs in selling fresh, delicious edibles along the Embarcadero at Green Street (about a 15-min. walk from Fisherman's Wharf). You can also pick up locally made vinegars and oils, which make wonderful gifts. There's another market on Tuesday at Justin Herman Plaza (Market St. and Embarcadero) from 10:30am to 2:30pm. For more information, call © **415/353-5650;** to get there, take bus no. 2, 7, 8, 9, 14, 21, 31, 32, 66, or 71.

The Cannery, at 2801 Leavenworth St. (© **415/771-3112;** www.thecannery. com), was built in 1894 as a fruit-canning plant and converted in the 1960s into a mall containing more than 50 shops and several restaurants and galleries. Vendors' stalls and sidewalk cafes are set up in the courtyard amid a grove of century-old olive trees, and on summer weekends, street performers are out in force entertaining tourists.

PIER 39, on the waterfront at Embarcadero and Beach Street (© **415/981-8030**), is a 4½-acre waterfront complex, a few blocks east of Fisherman's Wharf. Ostensibly a re-creation of an early-20-century street scene, it features walkways of aged and weathered wood salvaged from demolished piers. But don't expect a slice of old-time maritime life. This is the busiest mall of the group, with more than 100 touristy stores. In addition, there are 20 or so restaurants and snack outlets, some with good views of the bay.

In recent years some 600 California **sea lions** have taken up residence on the adjacent floating docks. They sun themselves and honk and bellow playfully. The latest major addition to Fisherman's Wharf is **Aquarium of the Bay,** a $38-million, 707,000-gallon marine attraction filled with sharks, stingrays, and more, all witnessed via a moving footpath that transports visitors through clear acrylic tunnels.

The shops are open daily from 10:30am to 8:30pm. Cable car: Powell-Mason line to Bay Street.

THE MISSION DISTRICT   Once inhabited almost entirely by Irish immigrants, the Mission is now the center of the city's Latino community and the city's dot-commercialization, an oblong area stretching roughly from 14th to 30th streets between Potrero Avenue in the east and Dolores on the west. Some of the city's finest Victorians still stand in the outer areas, though many seem strangely out of place in the mostly lower-income neighborhoods. The heart of the community lies along 24th Street between Van Ness and Potrero, where dozens of excellent ethnic restaurants, bakeries, bars, and specialty stores attract a hip crowd from all over the city. Strolling through the Mission District at night should be done cautiously on the outskirts, but it's quite safe during the day and highly recommended.

For even better insight into the community, go to the **Precita Eyes Mural Arts Center,** 2981 24th St., between Harrison and Alabama streets (© **415/285-2287**), and take one of the 2-hour tours conducted on Saturday and Sunday at 11am and 1:30pm, which cost $10 for adults, $8 for students with ID, $5 for seniors, and $2 for under-18s. You'll see 85 murals in an 8-block walk. Every year it also holds a Mural Awareness Month (usually in May) when tours are given daily. Most tours leave from 2981 24th St.; call ahead to confirm.

At 16th and Dolores is the **Mission San Francisco de Assisi** (better known as **Mission Dolores;** see p. 116), which is the city's oldest surviving building and the district's namesake.

NOB HILL   When the cable car was invented in 1873, this hill became the most exclusive residential area in the city. The Big Four and the Comstock Bonanza kings built their mansions here, but the structures were all destroyed by the 1906 earthquake and fire. Only the Flood Mansion, which serves today as the Pacific Union Club, and the Fairmont (which was under construction when the earthquake struck) were spared. The area is now home to some of the city's most upscale hotels, as well as Grace Cathedral, which stands on the

Crocker Mansion site. Stroll around and enjoy the views, and perhaps pay a visit to Huntington Park.

NORTH BEACH   In the late 1800s, an enormous influx of Italian immigrants into North Beach firmly established this aromatic area as San Francisco's "Little Italy." Today, dozens of Italian restaurants and coffeehouses continue to flourish in what is still the center of the city's Italian community. Walk down Columbus Avenue any given morning and you're bound to be bombarded with the wonderful aromas of roasting coffee and savory pasta sauces. Though there are some interesting shops and bookstores in the area, it's the eclectic little cafes, delis, bakeries, and coffee shops that give North Beach its Italian-bohemian character.

For a proper perspective of North Beach, sign up for **Javawalk** with coffeenut Elaine Sosa (p. 122).

PARKS, GARDENS & ZOOS

In addition to **Golden Gate Park** and **Golden Gate National Recreation Area** and the **Presidio** (see section 8, below), San Francisco boasts more than 2,000 additional acres of parkland, most of which are perfect for picnicking.

Lincoln Park, at Clement Street and 34th Avenue, a personal favorite, occupies 270 acres on the northwestern side of the city and contains the California Palace of the Legion of Honor (see "Museums," earlier in this chapter) and a scenic 18-hole municipal golf course. But the most dramatic features of the park are the 200-foot cliffs that overlook the Golden Gate Bridge and San Francisco Bay. Take bus no. 38 from Union Square to 33rd and Geary streets, and then transfer to bus no. 18 into the park.

San Francisco Zoo & Children's Zoo   Located between the Pacific Ocean and Lake Merced, in the southwest corner of the city, the San Francisco Zoo houses more than 1,000 inhabitants, which are contained in landscaped enclosures guarded by concealed moats. The Primate Discovery Center is particularly noteworthy for its many rare and endangered species. Expansive outdoor atriums, sprawling meadows, and a midnight world for exotic nocturnal primates house such species as the ruffed-tailed lemur, black-and-white colobus monkeys, patas monkeys, and emperor tamarins, pint-size primates distinguished by their long, majestic mustaches.

Other highlights include Koala Crossing, housing kangaroos, emus, and walleroos; Gorilla World, one of the world's largest exhibits of these gentle giants; and Penguin Island, home to a large breeding colony of Magellanic penguins. The Feline Conservation Center is a wooded sanctuary and breeding facility for the zoo's endangered snow leopards, Persian leopards, and other jungle cats. And the Lion House is home to rare Sumatran and Siberian tigers, a rare white Bengal tiger, and the African lions (you can watch them being fed at 2pm Tues–Sun).

At the Children's Zoo, adjacent to the main park, the barnyard is alive with domestic animals such as sheep, goats, ponies, and a llama. Also of interest is the Insect Zoo, which showcases a multitude of insect species, including the hissing cockroach and walking sticks.

Sloat Blvd. and 47th Ave. and Great Hwy. ✆ **415/753-7080.** www.sfzoo.org. Admission to main zoo and children's zoo $10 adults, $7 seniors and youths 12–17, $4 children 3–11, free for children under 3 accompanied by an adult. Free to all 1st Wed of each month, except $2 fee for children's zoo. Carousel $2. Main zoo daily 10am–5pm. Children's Zoo daily 10am–5pm. Muni Metro: L from downtown Market St. to the end of the line.

7 Organized Tours

ORIENTATION TOURS
THE 49-MILE SCENIC DRIVE

The self-guided, 49-mile drive is one easy way to orient yourself and to grasp the beauty of San Francisco and its extraordinary location. Beginning in the city, it follows a rough circle around the bay and passes virtually all the best-known sights, from Chinatown and the Golden Gate Bridge to Ocean Beach, Seal Rocks, Golden Gate Park, and Twin Peaks. Originally designed for the benefit of visitors to San Francisco's 1939 and 1940 Golden Gate International Exposition, the route is marked with blue-and-white seagull signs. Although it makes an excellent half-day tour, this mini-excursion can easily take longer if you decide, for example, to stop to walk across the Golden Gate Bridge or to have tea in Golden Gate Park's Japanese Tea Garden.

The San Francisco Visitor Information Center, at Powell and Market streets, distributes free route maps. Since a few of the Scenic Drive marker signs are missing, the map will come in handy. Try to avoid the downtown area during the weekday rush hours from 7 to 9am and 4 to 6pm.

BOAT TOURS

One of the best ways to look at San Francisco is from a boat bobbing on the bay. The **Blue & Gold Fleet** tours the bay year-round in a sleek, 400-passenger sightseeing boat, complete with food and beverage facilities. The fully narrated, 1¼-hour cruise passes beneath the Golden Gate and Bay bridges, and comes within yards of Alcatraz Island. Frequent daily departures from Pier 41 begin at 10am in summer and 11am in winter. Tickets cost $18 for adults, $14 for kids 12 to 17 and seniors over 62, $10 for kids 5 to 11; children under 5 sail free. For recorded information, call 📞 **415/773-1188;** for tickets, which cost an additional $2.25 each when ordered via phone, call 📞 **415/705-5555** or visit www.blueandgoldfleet.com.

The **Red & White Fleet** also offers daily bay cruises, which depart from Pier 43½ and travel under the Golden Gate Bridge and past the Marin Headlands, Sausalito, Tiburon, Angel Island, and Alcatraz. Prices are $18 for adults, $14 for seniors over 60 and kids 12 to 18, $10 for children 5 to 11, and free for children under 5. Call 📞 **415/447-0597** for information, or check out their website at www.redandwhite.com.

SPECIAL-INTEREST WALKING TOURS

AN INSIDER'S TOUR OF CHINATOWN   Founded by author, TV personality, cooking instructor, and restaurant critic Shirley Fong-Torres, **Wok Wiz Chinatown Walking Tours** (📞 **415/981-8989;** www.wokwiz.com) takes you into nooks and crannies not usually seen by tourists. Each guide is intimately acquainted with all of Chinatown's back ways, alleys, and small businesses, as well as the area's history, folklore, culture, and food. The 2½-hour tours are conducted daily from 10am to 1:30pm and include a dim sum (Chinese) lunch. Groups are generally held to a maximum of 12, and reservations are essential. Prices (including lunch) are $40 for adults, $35 for seniors 60 and older, and $35 for children under 12. Additional tours are offered and prices are less when lunch is excluded.

NORTH BEACH CAFE SOIREE   Self-described "coffeehouse lizard" Elaine Sosa leads **Javawalk,** a 2-hour walking tour. Aside from visiting cafes, Javawalk also serves up a good share of historical and architectural trivia. Sosa keeps the tour interactive and fun, and it's obvious that she knows a wealth of tales and trivia about the history of coffee and its North Beach roots. Tours are given Tuesday through Saturday at 10am. The price is $20 for adults and $10 for kids 12 and under. For information and reservations, call © **415/673-9255.**

THE VICTORIAN LEGACY   Jay Gifford, founder of **Victorian Homes Historical Walking Tour** (© 415/252-9485) and San Francisco resident for 2 decades, portrays his enthusiasm and love of San Francisco throughout this highly entertaining 2½-hour tour. Set at a very leisurely place, it incorporates a wealth of interesting knowledge about San Francisco's Victorian architecture, as well as the city's storied history—particularly the periods just before and after the great earthquake and fire of 1906. You'll stroll through the neighborhoods of Japantown, the Western Addition (where you can take a break to cruise the trendy shops on Fillmore St.), and onward to Pacific Heights and Cow Hollow. In the process you'll see more than 200 meticulously restored Victorians, including the one where *Mrs. Doubtfire* was filmed. Jay's guests often find they are the only ones on the quiet neighborhood streets, where tour buses are forbidden. The tour ends with a trolley ride back to Union Square, passing though North Beach and Chinatown. Tours, which start at Union Square at 11am, are offered daily year-round and cost $20 per person. Reservations are required. You can preview the tour at **www.victorianwalk.com.**

8 Golden Gate National Recreation Area & the Presidio

GOLDEN GATE NATIONAL RECREATION AREA

No urban shoreline is as stunning as San Francisco's. Golden Gate National Recreation Area, which wraps around the northern and western edges of the city and is run by the National Park Service, lets visitors fully enjoy it. Along this shoreline are several landmarks, and from its edge visitors have views of the bay and the ocean. Muni provides transportation to most sites, including Aquatic Park, the Cliff House, and Ocean Beach. For more information, see "Outdoor Pursuits," below, or contact the **National Park Service** (© 415/556-0560).

Here's a brief rundown of the major features of the recreation area, starting at the northern section and moving westward around the coastline:

Aquatic Park, adjacent to the Hyde Street Pier, is a small swimming beach, although it's not that appealing and the water's ridiculously cold.

Fort Mason Center occupies an area from Bay Street to the shoreline and consists of several buildings and piers, which were used during World War II. Today, they're occupied by a variety of museums, theaters, and organizations, as well as by **Greens Restaurant** (p. 103), which affords views of the Golden Gate Bridge. For information on Fort Mason Center events, call © **415/441-5706.**

Farther west along the bay at the northern end of Fillmore, **Marina Green** is a favorite spot for flying kites or watching the sailboats on the bay. Next stop along the bay is the St. Francis Yacht Club. From here begins the 3½-mile paved **Golden Gate Promenade,** a favorite biking and hiking path that defines the outer limits of the Presidio (see below) and leads to the fantastic and recently reestablished marshland preserve **Crissy Fields,** which is the city's latest favorite playground, complete with sandy beach, lots of native birds, and jogging paths.

Fort Point (© 415/556-1693), a National Historic Site sitting directly under the Golden Gate Bridge, was built in 1853 to protect the narrow entrance to the harbor. You might recognize it from Alfred Hitchcock's *Vertigo;* the master of

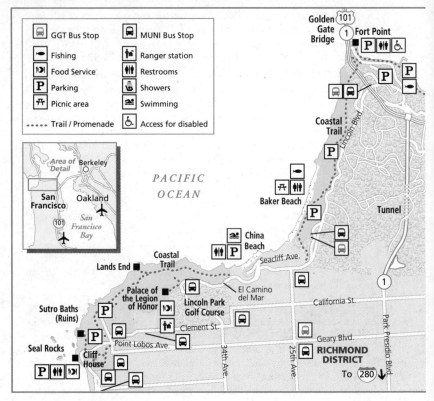

suspense filmed some of the most important scenes here. During the Civil War, the brick Fort Point was manned by 140 men and 90 pieces of artillery to prevent a Confederate takeover of California. Rangers in Civil War regalia lead regular tours and sometimes fire the old cannons.

Lincoln Boulevard sweeps around the western edge of the bay to two of the most popular beaches in San Francisco. **Baker Beach,** a small and beautiful strand just outside the Golden Gate where the waves roll ashore, is a fine spot for sunbathing, walking, or fishing—it's packed on sunny days. Because of the cold water and the roaring currents that pour out of the bay twice a day, swimming is not advised here for any but the most confident. (You'll also see some nude sunbathers here.) Here you can pick up the **Coastal Trail,** which leads through the Presidio (see below). A short distance from Baker, **China Beach** is a small cove where swimming is permitted. Changing rooms, showers, a sun deck, and restrooms are available.

A little farther around the coast appears **Land's End,** looking out to Pyramid Rock. Both a lower and an upper trail provide hiking opportunities amid windswept cypress and pines on the cliffs above the Pacific.

Still farther along the coast lie **Point Lobos,** the **Sutro Baths,** and the **Cliff House.** The latter has been serving refreshments to visitors since 1863 and is slated to undergo renovation in the coming year. Here you can view the **Seal Rocks,** home to a colony of sea lions and many marine birds. The **visitor center**

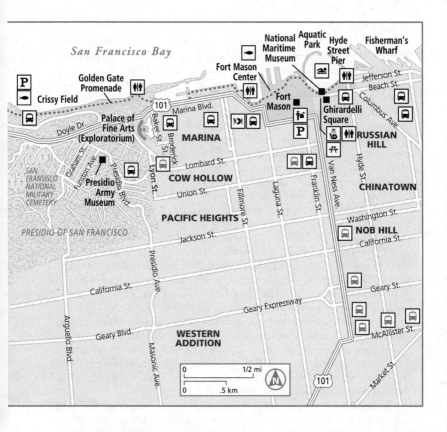

here (© 415/556-8642) is open daily from 10am to 5pm. Kids and adults will enjoy the **Musée Mécanique** (© 415/386-1170), an authentic old-fashioned arcade with 150 coin-operated amusements, which may or may not remain depending on whether locals put enough pressure on powers that be during renovations. Only traces of the Sutro Baths remain today northeast of the Cliff House. This swimming facility was a major summer attraction that could accommodate 24,000 people, but it burned down in 1966. A little farther inland at the western end of California Street is **Lincoln Park,** which contains a golf course and the Palace of the Legion of Honor.

From the Cliff House, the Esplanade continues south along the 4-mile-long **Ocean Beach,** which is not suitable for swimming. At the southern end of Ocean Beach is another area of the park around **Fort Funston** where there's an easy loop trail across the cliffs (for information, call the ranger station at © 415/239-2366). Here, too, you can watch the hang gliders taking advantage of the high cliffs and strong winds.

Farther south along I-280, **Sweeney Ridge,** which can only be reached by car, affords sweeping views of the coastline from the many trails that crisscross these 1,000 acres of land. It was from here that the expedition led by Don Gaspar de Portolá first saw San Francisco Bay in 1769. It's located in Pacifica and can be reached via Sneath Lane off Calif. 35 (Skyline Blvd.) in San Bruno.

THE PRESIDIO

In October 1994, the Presidio was transferred from the U.S. Army to the National Park Service and became one of a handful of urban national parks that combines historical, architectural, and natural elements into one giant arboreal expanse—not to mention a previously private golf course and a home for George Lucas's production company.

The 1,480-acre area incorporates a variety of terrain—coastal scrub, dunes, and prairie grasslands that shelter many rare plants and more than 150 species of birds, some of which nest here. There are also more than 350 historic buildings, a national cemetery, and a variety of terrain and natural habitats. The National Park Service offers a number of walking and biking tours around the Presidio; reservations are required.

Walkers and joggers will enjoy the forests of the Presidio. It was once a bleak field of wind-blasted rock, sand, and grass, but in a strangely humanitarian gesture, 60,000 trees were planted in the 1880s to make the place more livable for the troops. Today, on the 2-mile **Ecology Loop Trail,** walkers can see more than 30 different species of those trees, including redwood, spruce, cypress, and acacias. Hikers can follow the 2½-mile **Coastal Trail** from Fort Point along this part of the coastline all the way to Land's End. It follows the bluff top from Baker Beach to the southern base of the Golden Gate Bridge.

Crissy Field is a former airfield that in recent years has become known as one of the see-and-be-seen proving grounds of California's windsurfing culture. Between March and October, hundreds come to try their hand. The beach here provides easy water access and plenty of room to rig up, but is not recommended for the inexperienced. This is also a popular place for joggers en route from the Marina District to Fort Point and back. At the west end of Crissy Field is a pier that can be used for fishing and crabbing.

The Presidio is currently undergoing major changes so that it may pay for its upkeep. For schedules, maps, and general information about ongoing developments at the Presidio, the best source is the **Golden Gate National Recreation Area Headquarters** at Fort Mason, Building 102, San Francisco, CA 94123 (© **415/556-0560**). For additional information, call the **Visitor Information Center** at © **415/561-4323.** Take the no. 28, 76, or 82X bus.

9 Outdoor Pursuits

The prime places to enjoy all kinds of recreational activities in San Francisco have already been described earlier in this chapter. See "The Top Attractions," earlier in this chapter, for a complete description of Golden Gate Park, and section 8 for complete details on Golden Gate National Recreation Area and the Presidio.

BEACHES There are only two beaches in San Francisco that are safe for swimming: **Aquatic Park,** which is a ridiculously small patch of sand adjacent to the Hyde Park Pier, and **China Beach,** a small cove on the western edge of the South Bay. But dip in at your own risk—there are no lifeguards on duty, and the water is painfully cold.

Baker Beach, a small, beautiful strand just outside the Golden Gate, isn't the best place for swimming due to strong currents, but it's great for sunning, walking, picnicking, or fishing. It's wonderful to sit here on a sunny day and take in the view of the bridge. You'll climb down a very long flight of stairs from the street to reach the beach.

Ocean Beach, at the end of Golden Gate Park, on the westernmost side of the city, is San Francisco's largest beach (4 miles long). Just offshore, at the northern end of the beach in front of the Cliff House, are the jagged Seal Rocks, which are inhabited by various shorebirds and a large colony of barking sea lions. Bring binoculars for a close-up view. Ocean Beach is for strolling or sunning, but don't swim here—tides are tricky, and each year bathers and surfers drown in the rough waters.

BICYCLING   Two city-designated bike routes are maintained by the Recreation and Parks Department. One winds for 7½ miles through Golden Gate Park to Lake Merced; the other traverses the city, starting in the south, and follows a route over the Golden Gate Bridge. A bike map is available from the San Francisco Visitor Information Center and from bicycle shops all around town.

A massive new seawall, constructed to buffer Ocean Beach from storm-driven waves, doubles as a public walk and bikeway along 5 waterfront blocks of the Great Highway between Noriega and Santiago streets. It's an easy ride from the Cliff House or Golden Gate Park.

There's also great biking in the Presidio. From here, you can venture across the Golden Gate Bridge and into the Marin hills.

Avenue Cyclery at 756 Stanyan St., at Page Street (© 415/668-8016), rents bikes for $5 per hour or $25 per day and is open daily April through September from 10am to 7pm and October through March from 10am to 6pm.

CITY STAIR-CLIMBING   You don't need a StairMaster in San Francisco. The **Filbert Street Steps,** 377 of them running between Sansome Street and Telegraph Hill, scale the eastern face of Telegraph Hill, from Sansome and Filbert past charming 19th-century cottages and lush gardens. Napier Lane, a narrow wooden plank walkway, leads to Montgomery Street. Turn right and follow the path to the end of the cul-de-sac, where another stairway continues to Telegraph's panoramic summit.

The **Lyon Street Steps,** between Green Street and Broadway, comprise another historic stairway street, containing four steep sets of stairs totaling 288 steps. Begin at Green Street and climb all the way up, past manicured hedges and flower gardens, to an iron gate that opens into the Presidio. A block east, on Baker Street, another set of 369 steps descends to Green Street.

GOLF   Golden Gate Park Course, 47th Avenue and Fulton Street (© 415/751-8987), is a nine-hole, par-27 course over 1,357 yards. All holes are par 3, tightly set, and well trapped with small greens. Greens fees are very reasonable: $10 per person Monday through Friday and $13 Saturday and Sunday. The course is open daily from 6am to dusk.

Lincoln Park Golf Course, 34th Avenue and Clement Street (© 415/221-9911), San Francisco's prettiest municipal course, has terrific views and fairways lined with Monterey cypress trees. Its 18 holes encompass 5,081 yards, for a par 68. Greens fees are $23 per person Monday through Friday and $27 Saturday and Sunday. The course is open daily from 6:30am to dusk.

Presidio Golf Course (© 415/561-4664), one of the city's finest, charges $44 Monday through Friday, $77 Saturday and Sunday; carts are included and rates decrease later in the day.

SKATING   Although people skate in Golden Gate Park all week long, Sunday is best, when John F. Kennedy Drive, between Kezar Drive and Transverse Road, is closed to cars. A smooth "skate pad" is located on your right, just past the Conservatory. **Skates on Haight,** 1818 Haight St. (© 415/752-8376), is the best place to rent either in-line or conventional skates and is located only a block from the park. Protective wrist guards and kneepads are included free. The cost is $6 per hour for in-line or "conventionals," $24 for all-day use. A major credit card and ID deposit are required.

10 Shopping

Store hours vary, but are generally Monday through Saturday from 10am to 6pm and Sunday from noon to 5pm. Most department stores stay open later, as do shops around Fisherman's Wharf.

Sales tax in San Francisco is 8.5%. If you live out of state and buy an expensive item, consider having the store ship it home for you. You'll have to pay for its transport, but will escape paying the sales tax.

UNION SQUARE & ENVIRONS   San Francisco's most congested and popular shopping mecca is centered around Union Square. Most of the big department stores and many high-end specialty shops are in this area. Be sure to venture to Grant Avenue, Post and Sutter streets, and Maiden Lane.

If you're into art, pick up *The San Francisco Gallery Guide,* a comprehensive, bimonthly publication listing the city's current shows (most of which are downtown). It's available free by mail; send a self-addressed stamped envelope to San Francisco Bay Area Gallery Guide, 1369 Fulton St., San Francisco, CA 94117 (© **415/921-1600**). You can also pick one up at the San Francisco Visitor Information Center at 900 Market St. (at Powell St.).

One of my favorite galleries is the **Catharine Clark Gallery,** on the second floor at 49 Geary St., between Kearny and Grant streets (© **415/399-1439**). It exhibits up-and-coming contemporary artists, mainly from California, and nurtures beginning collectors by offering an unusual interest-free purchasing plan.

Of the area's specialty stores, century-old **Gump's,** 135 Post St., between Kearny Street and Grant Avenue (© **415/982-1616**), is a must-visit. A virtual treasure trove of household items and gifts, it offers a collection of Asian antiquities, contemporary art glass, exquisite jade and pearl jewelry, and more.

Music aficionados will choose to get lost in **Virgin Megastore,** Market Street at Stockton (© **415/397-4525**), with thousands of CDs (including an impressive collection of imports), videos, laser discs, and a multimedia department. Its literary equivalent is nearby **Borders Books & Music,** 400 Post St., at Powell (© **415/399-1633**), which has thousands of titles and a cafe.

While the department stores have plenty of clothes, real fashion fiends will want to check out the boutiques. For men, **Cable Car Clothiers,** 246 Sutter St., between Grant Avenue and Kearny Street (© **415/397-4740**), is a popular stop for traditional attire, such as three-button suits with natural shoulders, Aquascutum coats, McGeorge sweaters, and Atkinson ties. The most fashionable-modern-rather-than-corporate man heads to **MAC,** 5 Claude Lane, off Sutter Street between Grant Avenue and Kearny Street (© **415/837-0615**), where imported tailored suits come in designs by London's Paul Smith, Belgium's SO, Italy's Alberto Biani, and New York's John Bartlett. (Their women's store is located at 1543 Grant Ave., between Filbert and Union sts.; © **415/837-1604.**)

Wilkes Bashford, 375 Sutter St., at Stockton Street (© **415/986-4380**), is one of the most expensive and well-known clothing stores in the city, offering fashions for both sexes. It stocks only the finest clothes (which can often be seen on Mayor Willie Brown), including men's Kiton and Brioni suits (at $2,500 and up, they're considered some of the most expensive suits in the world).

For what I consider the best in women's fashions, check out **Métier,** 355 Sutter St., between Grant and Stockton streets (© **415/989-5395**). Its inventory of European ready-to-wear lines is expensive, but in the best taste; featured designers include Italian designer Anna Molinari, Alberto Biani, and Los Angeles designer Katayone Adeli, as well as a distinguished collection of antique-style, high-end jewelry from LA's Kathie Waterman and ultra-popular custom-designed poetry jewelry by Jeanine Payer.

CHINATOWN   When you pass under the gate to Chinatown on Grant Avenue, say good-bye to the world of fashion and hello to a swarm of cheap tourist shops selling everything from linen and jade to plastic toys and $2 slippers. The real gems are tucked on side streets or in small, one-person shops selling Chinese herbs, original art, and jewelry. Grant Avenue is the area's main thoroughfare, and side streets between Bush Street and Columbus Avenue are full of restaurants, markets, and eclectic shops. Walking is best, since traffic through this area is slow at best and parking is next to impossible. Most of the stores in Chinatown are open daily from 10am to 10pm. The area is serviced by bus lines 9X, 15, 30, 41, and 45.

Of the endless array of trinket shops scattered through the compact neighborhood, two worth noting are **Eastwind Books & Arts,** 1435 Stockton St., at Columbus Avenue (© **415/772-5877** Chinese department, 415/772-5899 English department; info@eastwindsf.com), which carries an incredible selection of Chinese books, stationery, and stamps, as well as Asian-American and English books covering everything from health and cooking to martial arts and medicine. At the mystical **Ten Ren Tea Company,** 949 Grant Ave., between Washington and Jackson streets (© **415/362-0656**), you can enjoy a steaming cup of roselle tea, made of black tea and hibiscus, while you browse the selection of almost 50 traditional and herbal teas and related paraphernalia.

SOMA   Though this area isn't suitable for strolling, you'll find almost all the discount shopping in warehouse spaces south of Market. You can pick up a discount-shopping guide at most major hotels. Many buses pass through this area, including routes 9, 12, 14, 15, 19, 26, 27, 30, 42, 45, and 76.

An all-time favorite is the **SFMOMA MuseumStore,** 151 Third St., 2 blocks south of Market Street, across from Yerba Buena Gardens (© **415/357-4035**). Its array of artistic cards, books, jewelry, housewares, knickknacks, and creative tokens of San Francisco makes this one of the locals' favorite shops. It also offers far more tasteful mementos than most Fisherman's Wharf options.

Fashionable bargain hunters head to **Jeremys,** 2 South Park, at Second Street between Bryant and Brannan streets (© **415/882-4929**), where top designer fashions from shoes to suits come at rock-bottom prices. For the more adventurous thrift shopper, there's the **North Face** discount outlet, 1325 Howard St., between 9th and 10th streets (© **415/626-6444**). The sporting, camping, and hiking equipment is still expensive, but the skiwear, boots, sweaters, and goods such as tents, packs, and sleeping bags are far less expensive than if you buy them at a retail shop.

Another worthy stop is the **Wine Club San Francisco,** 953 Harrison St., between Fifth and Sixth streets (© **415/512-9086**), which offers bargain prices on more than 1,200 domestic and foreign wines. Bottles cost from $4 to $1,100.

HAYES VALLEY   It may not be the prettiest area in town, but while most neighborhoods cater to more conservative or trendy shoppers, lower Hayes Street, between Octavia and Gough, celebrates anything vintage, artistic, or downright funky. Though still in its developmental stage, it's definitely the most interesting new shopping area in town, with furniture and glass stores, thrift shops, trendy shoe stores, and men's and women's clothiers. There are also lots of great antiques shops south on Octavia and on nearby Market Street. Bus lines include nos. 16AX, 16BX, and 21.

If you have a fetish for foot fashions, you must check out **Bulo,** 437A Hayes St., at Gough Street (℃ **415/864-3244**), which carries nothing but imported Italian men's and women's shoes that run the gamut from casual to dressy, reserved to wildly funky. Shop for the sale items unless you're ready to drop around $200 per pair.

THE CASTRO   You could easily spend all day wandering through the house-wares and men's-clothing shops of the Castro. Buses serving this area include nos. 8, 24, 33, 35, and 37.

Citizen Clothing, 536 Castro St., between 18th and 19th streets (℃ **415/ 558-9429**), is a popular shop for stylish casual clothing.

Our favorite chocolate shop, **Joseph Schmidt Confections,** 3489 16th St., at Sanchez Street (℃ **415/861-8682**), adds a whole new dimension to designer chocolate. Here the sinful sweets take the shape of exquisite sculptural master-pieces that are so beautiful, you'll be hesitant to bite the head off your adorable chocolate panda bear. Prices are also remarkably reasonable.

UNION STREET   Union Street, from Fillmore to Van Ness, caters to the upper-middle-class crowd. It's a great place to stroll; to window-shop the plethora of boutiques, cafes, and restaurants; and to watch the beautiful people parade by. Bus lines include nos. 22, 41, 42, and 45.

Among the dozens of fashion and home boutiques is **Three Bags Full,** 2181 Union St., at Fillmore (℃ **415/567-5753**), where expensive, handmade, and one-of-a-kind knitwear is both playful and extravagant.

CHESTNUT STREET   Parallel to and a few blocks north of Union Street, Chestnut is a younger Union Street, with endless shopping and dining choices, and the ever-tanned, superfit population of postgraduate singles who hang around cafes and scope each other out. The area is serviced by bus lines 22, 28, 30, 41, 42, 43, and 76.

FISHERMAN'S WHARF & ENVIRONS   The tourist-oriented malls— Ghirardelli Square, PIER 39, the Cannery, and the Anchorage—run along Jefferson Street and include hundreds of shops, restaurants, and attractions.

Locals tend to avoid this part of town, but do venture to **Cost Plus Imports,** 2552 Taylor St., between North Point and Bay streets (℃ **415/928-6200**), a vast warehouse crammed to the rafters with Chinese baskets, Indian camel bells, Malaysian batik scarves, and innumerable other items from Algeria to Zanzibar. There's also a decent wine section. Adjoining is a **Barnes & Noble** "superstore," at 2550 Taylor, between Bay and North Point (℃ **415/292-6762**).

FILLMORE STREET   Some of the best shopping in town is packed into 5 blocks of Fillmore Street in Pacific Heights. From Jackson to Sutter streets, Fill-more is the perfect place to grab a bite and peruse the high-priced boutiques, crafts shops, and incredible housewares stores. It's serviced by bus lines 1, 2, 3, 4, 12, 22, and 24.

One of my absolute favorite housewares shops is **Zinc Details,** 1905 Fill-more St., between Bush and Pine streets (℃ **415/776-2100**), which has an amazing collection of locally handcrafted glass vases, pendant lights, ceramics, and furniture. Each piece is a true work of art created specifically for the store (except vintage items).

HAIGHT STREET Green hair, spiked hair, no hair, or mohair—even the hippies look conservative next to Haight Street's dramatic fashion freaks. The shopping in the 6 blocks of upper Haight Street, between Central Avenue and Stanyan Street, reflects its clientele and offers everything from incense and European and American street styles to furniture and vintage and übertrendy clothing. Bus lines 7, 66, 71, and 73 run down Haight Street. The Muni Metro N line stops at Waller Street and at Cole Street.

Less wearable, but equally collectable are the oldies-but-goodies at **Recycled Records,** 1377 Haight St., between Central and Masonic streets (© **415/626-4075**). Easily one of the best used-record stores in the city, this loud shop has a good selection of promotional CDs and cases of used classic rock LPs. Sheet music, tour programs, and old *TV Guides* are also sold.

NORTH BEACH Along with a great cup of coffee, Grant and Columbus avenues cater to their hip clientele with a small but worthy selection of boutiques and specialty shops.

You can pick up a great gift for yourself or anyone else at **Biordi Art Imports,** 412 Columbus Ave., at Vallejo Street (© **415/392-8096**). Its Italian Majolica pottery is both exquisite and unique.

For a dose of local color, join the brooding literary types who browse **City Lights Booksellers & Publishers,** 261 Columbus Ave., at Broadway (© **415/362-8193**), the famous bookstore owned by renowned Beat-generation poet Lawrence Ferlinghetti. The shelves here are stocked with a comprehensive collection of art, poetry, and political paperbacks, as well as more mainstream books.

Fun mementos are for sale at **Quantity Postcards,** 1441 Grant St., at Green Street (© **415/986-8866**), where you'll find the perfect postcard for literally everyone you know, as well as some depictions of old San Francisco and movie stars, plus Day-Glo posters featuring concert-poster artist Frank Kozik.

11 San Francisco After Dark

For up-to-date nightlife information, turn to the *San Francisco Weekly* and the *San Francisco Bay Guardian,* both of which contain comprehensive current listings. They're available free at bars and restaurants, and from street-corner boxes all around the city. *Where,* a free tourist monthly, also has information on programs and performance times; it's available in most of the city's finer hotels. The Sunday edition of the *San Francisco Examiner* and *Chronicle* also features a "Datebook" section, printed on pink paper, with information and listings on the week's upcoming events.

GETTING TICKETS Half-price tickets to theater, dance, and music performances are available from **Tix Bay Area** (© **415/433-7827**) on the day of the show only; tickets for Sunday and Monday events, if available, are sold on Saturday. Tix also sells advance, full-price tickets for most performance halls, sporting events, concerts, and clubs. A service charge, ranging from $1 to $3, is levied on each ticket. Only cash or traveler's checks are accepted for half-price tickets; Visa and MasterCard are accepted for full-price tickets. Tix is located inside the Union Square Garage (on Geary St. at Powell St.). It's open Tuesday through Thursday from 11am to 6pm, Friday and Saturday from 11am to 7pm.

Tickets to most theater and dance events can also be obtained through **City Box Office,** 180 Redwood St., Suite 100, between Golden Gate and McAllister streets off Van Ness Avenue (✆ **415/392-4400;** www.cityboxoffice.com). MasterCard and Visa are accepted.

Tickets.com (✆ **415/478-2277** or 510/762-2277; www.tickets.com) sells computer-generated tickets to concerts, sporting events, plays, and special events, and it imposes a hefty service charge. Call for the local office nearest you.

For information on local theater, check out **www.bayareatheatre.org**.

THE PERFORMING ARTS

American Conservatory Theater (A.C.T.)   A.C.T. made its debut in 1967 and quickly established itself as the city's premier resident theater group. The troupe is so venerated that A.C.T. has been compared to the superb British National Theatre, the Berliner Ensemble, and the Comédie Française. The A.C.T. season runs September through July and features both classical and experimental works. Performing at the Geary Theater, 415 Geary St. (at Mason St.). ✆ 415/749-2ACT. www.act-sfbay.org. Tickets $15–$61.

The Magic Theatre   The highly acclaimed Magic Theatre continues to be a major West Coast company dedicated to presenting the works of new playwrights; over the years it has nurtured the talents of such luminaries as Sam Shepard and Jon Robin Baitz. Shepard's Pulitzer Prize–winning play *Buried Child* premiered here. A more recent production included Matthew Wells' *Schrodinger's Girlfriend*. The season usually runs September through July; performances are offered Wednesday through Sunday. Performing at Building D, Fort Mason Center, Marina Blvd. (at Buchanan St.). ✆ 415/441-8822. www.magictheatre.org. Tickets $10–$37. Discounts for students and seniors.

Philharmonia Baroque Orchestra   Acclaimed by the *New York Times* as "the country's leading early music orchestra," Philharmonia Baroque performs in San Francisco and all around the Bay Area. The season lasts September through April. Performing in Herbst Theater, 401 Van Ness Ave. ✆ 415/392-4400 (box office) or 415/252-1288 (administrative offices). www.philharmonia.org. Tickets $30–$50.

San Francisco Ballet   Founded in 1933, the San Francisco Ballet is the oldest professional ballet company in the United States and regarded as one of the country's finest, performing an eclectic repertoire of full-length, neoclassical, and contemporary ballets. Even the *New York Times* proclaimed, "The San Francisco Ballet under Helgi Tomasson's leadership is one of the spectacular success stories of the arts in America." The 2003 season runs February through June. All performances are accompanied by the San Francisco Ballet Orchestra. War Memorial Opera House, 301 Van Ness Ave. (at Grove St.). ✆ 415/865-2000 for tickets and information. Tickets $10–$110.

San Francisco Opera   The San Francisco Opera was the first municipal opera in the United States, and is one of the city's cultural icons. All productions have English supertitles. The season starts in September and lasts just 14 weeks. Performances are held most evenings, except Monday, with matinees on Sundays. Tickets go on sale as early as June, and the best seats quickly sell out. Unless Pavarotti or Domingo is in town, some less-coveted seats are usually available until curtain time. War Memorial Opera House, 301 Van Ness Ave. (at Grove St.). ✆ 415/864-3330 (box office). www.sfopera.com. Tickets $23–$165.

> ### *Tips* Teatro ZinZanni
>
> Hungry for dinner and a damned good time? It ain't cheap, but Teatro ZinZanni is a delightfully rollicking ride of food, whimsy, drama, and song within a stunningly elegant 1926 tent on the Embarcadero. Part musical theater and part comedy show, the 3½-hour show includes a surprisingly decent four-course meal served by dozens of performers who weave the audience and astounding physical acts (think Cirque du Soleil) into their wacky and playful world. Shows are held Wednesday through Sunday and tickets are $99 to $125 including dinner. The tent is located at Pier 29 on the Embarcadero at Battery Street. Call ✆ **415/438-2660** or visit www.teatrozinzanni.org for more details.

San Francisco Symphony   Founded in 1911, the internationally respected San Francisco Symphony has long been an important part of this city's cultural life under such legendary conductors as Pierre Monteux and Seiji Ozawa. In 1995, Michael Tilson Thomas took over from Herbert Blomstedt and has already led the orchestra to new heights, crafting an exciting repertoire of classical and modern music. The season runs September through June; tickets are very hard to come by, but there's usually someone outside the hall trying to sell their tickets the night of the show. Summer symphony activities include a Composer Festival and a Summer Pops series. Performing at Davies Symphony Hall, 201 Van Ness Ave. (at Grove St.). ✆ **415/864-6000** (box office). www.sfsymphony.org. Tickets $12–$73.

COMEDY & CABARET

Beach Blanket Babylon *(Finds)*   Now a San Francisco tradition, *Beach Blanket Babylon* is best known for its outrageous costumes and oversize headdresses. It's been playing almost 22 years now, and still almost every performance sells out. It's wise to write for tickets at least 3 weeks in advance, or obtain them through Tix (✆ **415/433-7827**). At Club Fugazi, Beach Blanket Babylon Blvd., 678 Green St. (between Powell St. and Columbus Ave.). ✆ **415/421-4222.** Tickets $20–$55.

Cobb's Comedy Club   Located in the Cannery at Fisherman's Wharf, Cobb's features such national headliners as George Wallace, Emo Philips, and Jake Johannsen. There's comedy every night, including a 15-comedian All-Pro Monday showcase (a 3-hr. marathon). Cobb's is open to those 18 and over, and occasionally to kids ages 16 and 17 if they're accompanied by a parent or legal guardian (call ahead first). The Cannery, 2801 Leavenworth St. (at Beach St.). ✆ **415/928-4320.** Cover Mon–Wed $10, Thurs, and Sun $10–$13, Fri–Sat $13–$15. 2-beverage minimum nightly. Validated parking at Anchorage Shopping Center Garage.

THE CLUB & MUSIC SCENE
ROCK & BLUES CLUBS

Biscuits & Blues   With a crisp, blow-your-eardrums-out sound system, a New Orleans–speakeasy (albeit commercial) appeal, and a nightly lineup of live entertainment, there's no better place to muse the blues than at this basement-cum-nightclub. 401 Mason (at Geary St.). ✆ **415/292-2583.** Cover (during performances) $5–$15.

Blue Bar   If you're passing by North Beach, you should drop in to this cozy-chic, live jazz and blues venue with cushy couches and laid-back atmosphere.

The restaurant's full menu is available here—a plus for late-night eaters and a bummer for those who come exclusively for the music. Below the Black Cat Cafe, 501 Broadway (at Kearny St.). ☎ 415/981-2233. Cover $5 Wed–Sun.

The Fillmore *Finds* Reopened after years of neglect, The Fillmore, made famous by promoter Bill Graham in the 1960s, is once again attracting big names. Check the local listings in magazines, or call the theater for information on upcoming events. 1805 Geary Blvd. (at Fillmore St.). ☎ 415/346-6000. www.thefillmore. com. Tickets $9–$25.

Lou's Pier 47 Club There are few locals in the place, but Lou's happens to be a good old-fashioned casual spot where you can let your hair down with Cajun seafood (downstairs), other tourists, and live jazz, blues, rock, and country bands (upstairs). Major happy-hour specials (Mon–Fri 4–7pm) and a vacation attitude make the place one of the more sloppy happy spots near the Wharf. There's no cover for the first band, which plays nightly from 4 to 8pm, but it will cost you for the second, which comes on at 9pm. 300 Jefferson St. (at Jones St.). ☎ 415/771-5687. Cover $5–$10.

Slim's Co-owned by musician Boz Scaggs, who sometimes takes the stage under the name "Presidio Slim," this glitzy restaurant and bar seats 300, serves California cuisine, and specializes in excellent American music—homegrown rock, jazz, blues, and alternative—almost nightly. 333 11th St. (at Folsom St.). ☎ 415/522-0333. www.slims-sf.com. Cover free–$20. 2-drink minimum when seated at a table.

JAZZ & LATIN CLUBS

Cafe du Nord *Finds* Although it's been around since 1907, this basement-cum-supper-club has finally been recognized as a respectable jazz venue. With a younger generation now appreciating the music, the place is often packed, from the 40-foot mahogany bar to the back room with a pool table. Du Nord is even putting out its own compilation CDs now, which are definitely worth purchasing. 2170 Market St. (at Sanchez St.). ☎ 415/861-5016.

Jazz at Pearl's This is one of the best venues for jazz in the city. Ribs and chicken are served with the sounds, too, with prices ranging from $4 to $12. The live jams last until 2am nightly. 256 Columbus Ave. (at Broadway). ☎ 415/291-8255. 2-drink minimum.

DANCE CLUBS

Club Ten 15 Get decked out and plan for a late-nighter if you're headed to this enormous party warehouse. Three levels and dance floors offer a variety of venues, complete with a 20- and 30-something gyrating mass that lives for the DJs' pounding house, disco, and acid-jazz music. Each night is a different club that attracts its own crowd, ranging from yuppie to hip-hop. 1015 Folsom St. (at Sixth St.). ☎ 415/431-1200. Cover $5–$15.

Nickie's Bar-be-cue Don't show up here for dinner—the only hot thing you'll find is the small, crowded dance floor. But don't let that stop you from checking it out. Nickie's is a sure thing. Every time I come here, the old-school disco hits are in full force, casually dressed happy dancers lose all inhibitions, and the crowd is mixed with all types of friendly San Franciscans. This place is perpetually hot, so dress accordingly and don't expect a full bar—it's beer and wine only. 460 Haight St. (between Fillmore and Webster sts.). ☎ 415/621-6508. www. nickies.com. Cover $3–$5.

Paradise Lounge   Labyrinthine Paradise features three dance floors simultaneously vibrating to different beats. Smaller, auxiliary spaces include a pool room with half a dozen tables. Poetry readings are also given. 1501 Folsom St. (at 11th St.). ✆ 415/861-6906. Cover $3–$15.

SUPPER CLUBS

If you can eat dinner, listen to live music, and dance (or at least wiggle in your chair) in the same room, it's a supper club—that's my criteria.

Harry Denton's Starlight Room   Come dressed to the nines or in casual attire to this old-fashioned cocktail-lounge-turned-nightclub, where tourists and locals sip drinks at sunset and boogie down to live swing and big-band tunes after dark. The room is classic 1930s San Francisco, with red-velvet banquettes, chandeliers, and fabulous views. But what really attracts flocks of all ages is a night of Harry Denton–style fun, which usually includes plenty of drinking and unrestrained dancing. At the Sir Francis Drake Hotel, 450 Powell St., 21st floor. ✆ 415/395-8595. Cover $5 Wed–Thurs after 7pm, $10 Fri–Sat after 8pm.

Julie's Supper Club   Julie's is a longtime standby for cocktails and late dining. Divided into two rooms, the vibe is very 1950s cartoon, with a space-aged *Jetsons* appeal. Good-looking singles prowl, cocktails in hand, as live music plays by the front door. The food is hit-or-miss, but the atmosphere is definitely a casual and playful winner with a little interesting history: This building is one location where the Symbionese Liberation Army held Patty Hearst hostage back in the 1970s. Menu items range from $9 to $20. 1123 Folsom St. (at Seventh St.). ✆ 415/861-0707. $5 cover on weekends.

RETRO CLUBS

Club Deluxe   Before the recent 1940s trend hit the city, Deluxe and its fedora-wearing clientele had been celebrating the bygone era for years. And fortunately, even with all the retro-hype, the vibe here hasn't changed. Expect an eclectic mix of throwbacks and generic San Franciscans in the intimate, smoky bar and adjoining lounge, and live jazz or blues most nights. Although many regulars dress the part, there's no attitude here—so come as you like. 1511 Haight St. (at Ashbury St.). ✆ 415/552-6949. Cover $2–$10.

THE BAR SCENE

Finding your idea of a comfortable bar has a lot to do with picking a neighborhood filled with your kind of people and investigating that area. There are hundreds of bars throughout San Francisco, and although many are obscurely located and can't be classified by their neighborhood, the following is a general description of what you'll find and where:

- **Chestnut and Union Street** bars attract a post-collegiate crowd.
- Young alternatives frequent **Mission District** haunts.
- **Upper Haight** caters to eclectic neighborhood cocktailers.
- **Lower Haight** is skate- and snowboarder grungy.
- Tourists mix with theatergoers and thirsty businesspeople in **downtown** pubs.
- **North Beach** serves all types.
- **Castro** caters to gay locals and tourists.
- **South of Market** (SoMa) offers an eclectic mix.

Backflip Adjoining the rock 'n' roll Phoenix Hotel, this shimmering aqua-blue cocktail lounge—designed to induce the illusion that you're carousing in the deep end—serves "cocktail fare" to mostly young, fashionable types, so please don't order a Cosmopolitan. 601 Eddy St. (at Larkin St.). *C* **415/771-FLIP.**

The Bubble Lounge Toasting the town is a nightly event at this relatively new champagne bar. With 300 champagnes (and around 30 by the glass), brick walls, couches, velvet curtains, and a pool table within its two levels, there's plenty of pop in this fizzy lounge. 714 Montgomery St. (at Columbus Ave.). *C* **415/434-4204.**

The Red Room At one time the hottest cocktail lounge in town (though it's cooled off a bit), this ultra-modern, Big Apple–style bar and lounge reflects no other spectrum but ruby red. Really, you gotta see this one. 825 Sutter St. (at Jones St.). *C* **415/346-7666.**

Spec's Its incognito locale on Saroyan Place, a tiny alley at 250 Columbus Ave., makes Spec's less of a walk-in bar and more of a lively locals' hangout. Its funky decor—maritime flags that hang from the ceiling, exposed brick walls lined with posters, photos, and various oddities—gives it character that intrigues every visitor. A "museum," displayed under glass, contains memorabilia and items brought back by seamen who drop in between sails, and the clientele is funky enough to keep you preoccupied while you drink a beer. 12 Saroyan Place (off Columbus Ave.). *C* **415/421-4112.**

Tosca *(Finds* Open daily from 5pm to 2am, Tosca is a low-key and large popular watering hole for local politicos, writers, media types, incognito visiting celebrities such as Johnny Depp or Nicolas Cage, and similar cognoscenti of unassuming classics. Equipped with dim lights, red leather booths, high ceilings, and the requisite vintage jukebox spilling out Italian arias, it's everything you'd expect an old North Beach legend to be. 242 Columbus Ave. (between Broadway and Pacific Ave.). *C* **415/986-9651.**

Vesuvio Situated along Jack Kerouac Alley across from the famed City Lights Bookstore, this renowned literary beatnik hangout isn't just riding its historic coattails. Popular with neighborhood writers, artists, songsters, and wannabes, Vesuvio is crowded with self-proclaimed philosophers, along with everyone else ranging from longshoremen and cab drivers to businesspeople. 255 Columbus Ave. (at Broadway). *C* **415/362-3370.**

BREWPUBS

Gordon Biersch Brewery Restaurant Popular with the young Republican crowd (loose ties and tight skirts predominate), this modern, two-tiered brewery and restaurant attracts a more upscale clientele than your typical beer garden. The food—beer-braised lamb shank, baby-back ribs, lemon roasted half chicken—is pretty good, but it's the gourmet lagers and ales that account for the line out the door. *One caveat:* When the lower-level bar fills up, you practically have to shout to be heard. 2 Harrison St. (on the Embarcadero). *C* **415/243-8246.**

San Francisco Brewing Company The bar is one of the city's few remaining old saloons, aglow with stained-glass windows, tile floors, skylights, a mahogany bar, and a massive overhead fan running the full length of the bar—a bizarre contraption crafted from brass and palm fronds. Menu items range from $3.70 (curiously, for *edamame,* or soybeans) to $20 for a full rack of baby-back ribs with all the fixings. The happy-hour special, a dollar per 10-ounce microbrew beer (or $1.75 a pint), runs daily from 4 to 6pm and midnight to 1am. 155 Columbus Ave. (at Pacific St.). ✆ 415/434-3344. www.sfbrewing.com.

Thirsty Bear Brewing Company   Seven superb, handcrafted varieties of brew, ranging from a fruit-flavored Strawberry Ale to a steak-in-a-cup stout, are always on tap at this stylish high-ceilinged brick edifice. Excellent Spanish food, too. Pool tables and dartboards are upstairs, and live music (jazz, flamenco, blues, alternative, and classical) can be heard most nights. 661 Howard St. (1 block E of the Moscone Center). ✆ 415/974-0905.

COCKTAILS WITH A VIEW

In addition to these options, see p. 135 for a full review of **Harry Denton's Starlight Room.**

The Carnelian Room   On the 52nd floor of the Bank of America building, the Carnelian Room offers uninterrupted views of the city. From a window-front table, you feel as if you can reach out, pluck up the TransAmerica Pyramid, and stir your martini with it. *Note:* The restaurant has the most extensive wine list in the city—1,275 selections to be exact. 555 California St., in the Bank of America Building (between Kearny and Montgomery sts.). ✆ 415/433-7500. Jacket and tie required for men.

Cityscape   When you sit under the glass roof and sip a drink here, it feels as though you're out under the stars and enjoying views of the bay. There's nightly dancing to a DJ's picks from 10pm. The mirrored columns and floor-to-ceiling draperies help create an elegant and romantic ambience. Atop Hilton Tower I, 333 O'Farrell St. (at Mason St.), 46th floor. ✆ 415/923-5002.

Equinox   The sales "hook" of the Hyatt's rooftop Equinox is a revolving floor that gives each table a 360° panoramic view of the city every 45 minutes. In addition to cocktails, dinner is served daily. In the Hyatt Regency Hotel, 5 Embarcadero Center. ✆ 415/788-1234.

Top of the Mark *Finds*   This is one of the most famous cocktail lounges in the world. During World War II, it was considered de rigueur for Pacific-bound servicemen to toast their good-byes to the States here. The spectacular glass-walled room features an unparalleled view. Live entertainment is offered at 8:30pm nightly, when there's a $6 to $10 cover. Drink prices range from $6 to $8. In the Mark Hopkins Intercontinental, 1 Nob Hill (between California and Mason sts.). ✆ 415/616-6916.

GAY AND LESBIAN BARS & CLUBS

The Café   When this place first got jumping, it was the only predominantly lesbian dance club on Saturday nights in the city. But once the guys found out how much fun the girls were having, they joined the party. Today it's still a very happening mixed gay and lesbian scene with two bars; a steamy, free-spirited dance floor; and a small patio. 2367 Market St. (at Castro St.). ✆ 415/861-3846.

The EndUp   It's a different nightclub every night of the week, but regardless of who's throwing the party, the place is always jumping with the DJs blasting tunes. There are two pool tables, a flaming fireplace, an outdoor patio, and a mob of gyrating souls on the dance floor. Some nights are straight, so call for gay nights. 401 Sixth St. (at Harrison St.). ✆ 415/357-0827.

The Stud   The Stud has been around for over 30 years, is one of the most successful gay establishments in town, and is mellow enough for straights as well as gays. The interior has an antiques-shop look and a miniature train circling over the bar and dance floor. Music here is a balanced mix of old and new, and nights vary from cabaret and oldies to disco. Call in advance for the evening's venue. Drink prices range from $1.25 to $5.75. 399 Ninth St. (at Harrison St.). ℂ **415/863-6623.** Cover $2–$6 Fri–Sat.

Twin Peaks Tavern   Right at the intersection of Castro, 17th, and Market streets is one of the Castro's most famous gay hangouts, which caters to an older crowd and is considered the first gay bar in America. Because of its relatively small size and desirable location, the place becomes fairly crowded and convivial by 8pm, earlier than many neighboring bars. 401 Castro St. (at 17th and Market sts.). ℂ **415/864-9470.**

5

The San Francisco Bay Area

by Erika Lenkert

Without question, the Bay City is captivating. But don't let it ensnare you to the point of ignoring its environs, which contain a multitude of natural spectacles like Mount Tamalpais and Muir Woods; scenic communities like Tiburon, Sausalito, and Half Moon Bay; and cities like gritty Oakland and its youth-oriented next-door neighbor, Berkeley. A little farther north stretch the valleys of Napa and Sonoma, the finest wine region in the nation (see chapter 6, "The Wine Country"). And to the south lie high-tech Silicon Valley and San Jose, Northern California's largest city.

1 Berkeley

10 miles NE of San Francisco

Until the 1990s, the University of California at Berkeley and its first-rate academic standards, 17 Nobel Prize winners, and protests that led to the most well known student riots in U.S. history were the primary reasons that Berkeley is something more than a quaint, sleepy town east of the big city. But the race to find affordable Bay Area housing has made the East Bay portal even more of a hub. Today, there's still hippie idealism in the air, but the radicals have aged; the 1960s are largely present in tie-dye and paraphernalia shops (which are joined by national chains along Telegraph Ave.). Meanwhile, communities and upscale restaurants and shops continue to flourish. All in all, it's an entertaining town with all types of people, a beautiful campus, vast parks, and some incredible restaurants.

ESSENTIALS
GETTING THERE The Berkeley **BART** (Bay Area Rapid Transit) station is 2 blocks from the university. The fare from San Francisco is less than $3. For information, call BART at ⓒ **510/793-2278** or log on to www.bart.gov.

If you're coming **by car** from San Francisco, take I-80 east to the University Avenue exit. Count on walking some distance, as you won't find a parking spot near the university.

VISITOR INFORMATION The **Berkeley Convention & Visitors Bureau,** 2015 Center St., Berkeley, CA 94703 (ⓒ **800/847-4823** or 510/549-7040; www.berkeleycvb.com), can answer your questions and even find accommodations for you. Call the **Visitor Hotline** (ⓒ **510/549-8710**) for information on events and happenings in Berkeley.

EXPLORING THE UNIVERSITY & ENVIRONS
Hanging out is the preferred Berkeley pastime, and the best place to do it is on **Telegraph Avenue,** the street that leads to the campus's southern entrance. Most of the action lies between Bancroft Way and Ashby Avenue, where

coffeehouses, restaurants, shops, great book and record stores, and crafts booths swarm with life.

Pretend you're local: Plant yourself at a cafe, sip a latte, and ponder something intellectual while you survey the town's unique population bustling by. Bibliophiles must stop at **Cody's Books,** 2454 Telegraph Ave. (© **510/845-7852;** www.codysbooks.com), to peruse its gargantuan selection of titles, independent-press books, and magazines. If used and antiquarian books are your thing, stop by **Moe's Books,** 2476 Telegraph Ave. (© **510/849-2087;** www.moesbooks. com). With four floors of new, used, and out-of-print books, you're unlikely to leave empty-handed.

UC Berkeley itself is worth a stroll as well. It's a beautiful old campus with plenty of woodsy paths, architecturally noteworthy buildings, and 32,000 students scurrying to and from classes. Among the architectural highlights of the campus are a number of buildings by Bernard Maybeck, Bakewell and Brown, and John Galen Howard. Contact the **Visitor Information Center,** 101 University Hall, 2200 University Ave., at Oxford Street (© **510/642-5215;** www. berkeley.edu/visitors), to join a free, regularly scheduled campus tour (Mon–Sat at 10am and 1pm and Sun at 1pm; no tours offered from mid-Dec to mid-Jan), or stop by the office and pick up a self-guided walking-tour brochure. If you're interested in notable off-campus buildings, contact the **Berkeley Convention and Visitors Bureau** (© **510/549-7040;** www.berkeleycvb.com) for an architectural walking-tour brochure.

You'll find the university's southern entrance at the northern end of Telegraph Avenue, at Bancroft Way. Walk through the main entrance into **Sproul Plaza.** Here, when school is in session, you'll encounter the gamut of Berkeley's inhabitants as well as the **Student Union,** complete with a bookstore, cafes, and an information desk on the second floor, where you can pick up a free map of Berkeley along with the local student newspaper (also found in dispensers throughout campus). You might be lucky enough to stumble upon some impromptu musicians or a heated—and sometimes absurd—debate. There's always something going on, so stretch out on the grass for a few minutes and take in the Berkeley vibe.

For viewing more traditional art forms, there are some noteworthy museums here, too. The **Lawrence Hall of Science,** Centennial Drive near Grizzly Peak (© **510/642-5132**), offering hands-on science exploration, is open from 10am to 5pm daily and is a wonderful place to watch the sunset. Admission is $8 for adults; $6 for seniors, students, and children ages 7 to 18; $4 for children 3 to 6; free for kids under 3. The **UC Berkeley Art Museum,** 2626 Bancroft Way (© **510/642-0808;** www.bampfa.berkeley.edu), is open Wednesday through Sunday from 11am to 7pm. Admission is $6 for adults; $4 for seniors, students, and children ages 12 to 17; and free for kids under 12 and UC students. This museum includes a substantial collection of Hans Hofmann paintings, a sculpture garden, and the **Pacific Film Archive,** main entrance at 2625 Durant Ave. (© **510/642-1124**).

OFF-CAMPUS ATTRACTIONS

PARKS   Unbeknownst to many travelers, Berkeley has some of the most extensive and beautiful parks around. If you enjoy hiking, getting a breath of California air, and sniffing a few roses, or just want to wear out the kids, jump in your car and make your way to **Tilden Park** (© **510/843-2137**), where you'll find plenty of flora and fauna, hiking trails, an old steam train and merry-go-round, a farm and nature area for kids, and a chilly tree-encircled lake. On the

The San Francisco Bay Area

0 ... 5 mi
0 ... 5 km

Sacramento
San Francisco
CALIFORNIA
Los Angeles

● **Sonoma**

● **Napa**

29 121
121 221

12 121

12
121

29

12

To Sacramento ↗

12

Napa County Airport

Marine World Pkwy.

116

Sears Point

Arnold Dr.

37

● **Vallejo**

Marin County Airport

Novato

37

101

780

San Pablo Bay

Marinwood

Martinez

4

Fairfax

San Rafael

Pinole

San Pablo

80

San Anselmo

Larkspur

San Rafael–Richmond Bridge

Richmond

580

● El Cerrito

MT. TAMALPAIS STATE PARK

Corte Madera

San Quentin

Stinson Beach

Mill Valley

MUIR WOODS NATIONAL MONUMENT

131 ○ Tiburon

Albany

80

Berkeley

See Berkeley map

580

Muir Beach

Marin City

Sausalito

Emeryville

● **Piedmont**

1

101

Golden Gate Bridge

Point Bonita

101

San Francisco–Oakland Bay Bridge

80

Oakland

580

13

GOLDEN GATE NATIONAL RECREATION AREA

SAN FRANCISCO

See Oakland map

61

880

580

1

280

● **Alameda**

San Leandro

PACIFIC OCEAN

280

Daly City

Oakland International Airport

61

35

San Lorenzo

101

San Francisco Bay

Pacifica

South San Francisco

1

35

380

San Francisco International Airport

San Mateo Bridge

92

Rockaway Beach

San Bruno

To Half Moon Bay ↓

⌒Finds Sweet Sensations at Berkeley's Chocolate Factory

If you haven't had chocolate nibs, you haven't lived—at least that's what chocoholics are likely to discover upon visiting Scharffen Berger Chocolate Maker (ⓒ 510/981-4050; www.scharffenberger.com), California's runaway-success chocolatier that opened its factory and retail shop doors in Berkeley in mid-2001. Within the brick building, visitors can not only taste the "nibs" or crunchy roasted and shelled cocoa beans, but also see how the famous chocolate company uses vintage European equipment during regularly scheduled tours (call for details). And let's not forget there are plenty of tasty products, from candy bars to cocoa powder and chocolate sauce, available in the retail shop. The factory is located at 914 Heinz Ave.; from I-80 East, take the Ashby Avenue exit, turn left on Seventh Street and right on Heinz.

---

way, stop at the colorful terraced **Rose Garden,** located in north Berkeley on Euclid Avenue between Bay View and Eunice Street.

Another worthy nature excursion is the **University of California Botanical Garden,** in Strawberry Canyon on Centennial Drive (ⓒ 510/643-2755; www.mip.berkeley.edu/garden), which features a vast collection of plant life ranging from cacti to redwoods.

SHOPPING   If you're itching to exercise your credit cards, head to one of two places. **College Avenue** from Dwight all the way down to the Oakland border is crammed with eclectic boutiques, antiques shops, and restaurants. The other option is **Fourth Street** in west Berkeley, just 2 blocks north of the University Avenue exit off I-80, where you can grab a cup of java, read the paper at a patio table, and then hit the **Crate & Barrel Outlet,** 1785 Fourth St., between Hearst and Virginia (ⓒ 510/528-5500), where prices are 30% to 70% off retail, or any of the small, wonderful stores crammed with imported and locally made housewares. Nearby is **REI,** the Bay Area's favorite outdoor outfitter, at 1338 San Pablo Ave., near Gilman Street (ⓒ 510/527-4140).

WHERE TO STAY

Unfortunately, even a little research will prove that Berkeley's not remotely close to a good hotel town. Most accommodations are extremely basic motels and funky B&Bs. The one exception is **The Claremont Resort & Spa,** 41 Tunnel Rd., Berkeley (ⓒ 800/551-7266 or 510/843-3000; www.claremontresort.com), a grand Victorian hotel with upgrades that include modern rooms, a fancy spa and gym, a hip bar, and grandiose surroundings. Prices range from $260 to $400, double occupancy. Another option is to contact **Berkeley & Oakland Bed and Breakfast Network** (ⓒ 510/547-6380; www.bbonline.com/ca/berkeley-oakland), which books visitors into private homes and apartments in the East Bay area.

WHERE TO DINE
EXPENSIVE

Chez Panisse ⭐⭐⭐ CALIFORNIA   California cuisine is greatly a product of Alice Waters's genius, and for that reason her dining room is a must-stop on any foodie's itinerary. Read the menus posted outside and you'll understand why. Most of the produce and meat comes from local farms and is organically

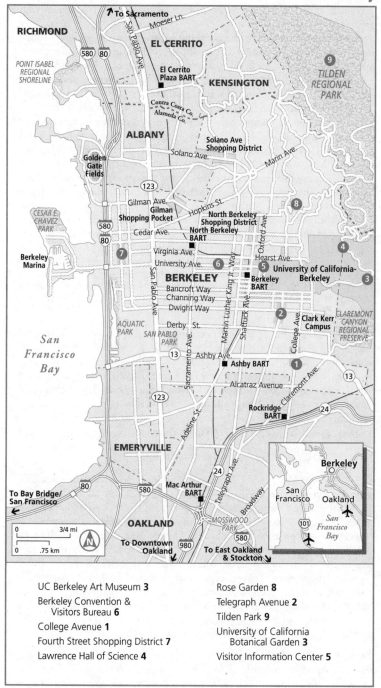

Berkeley

RICHMOND

POINT ISABEL
REGIONAL
SHORELINE

↑ To Sacramento

Moeser Ln.

EL CERRITO

KENSINGTON

El Cerrito
Plaza BART

TILDEN
REGIONAL
PARK

Contra Costa Co.
Alameda Co.

ALBANY

Solano Ave.

Solano Ave
Shopping District

Marin Ave.

Golden
Gate
Fields

CESAR E.
CHAVEZ
PARK

Gilman Ave.

Gilman
Shopping Pocket

Hopkins St.

North Berkeley
Shopping District

North Berkeley
BART

Cedar Ave.

Berkeley
Marina

Virginia Ave.

University Ave.

Oxford Ave.

Hearst Ave.

University of California-
Berkeley

BERKELEY

Bancroft Way

Channing Way

Dwight Way

Derby St.

Berkeley
BART

CLAREMONT
CANYON
REGIONAL
PRESERVE

AQUATIC
PARK

SAN PABLO
PARK

San
Francisco
Bay

San Pablo Ave.

Sacramento Ave.

Martin Luther King Jr. Way

Shattuck Ave.

College Ave.

Clark Kerr
Campus

Ashby Ave.

Ashby BART

Alcatraz Avenue

Claremont Ave.

Adeline St.

Rockridge
BART

EMERYVILLE

To Bay Bridge/
San Francisco
←

Mac Arthur
BART

Telegraph Ave.

Broadway

OAKLAND

MOSSWOOD
PARK

To Downtown
Oakland

To East Oakland
& Stockton ↘

0   3/4 mi
0   .75 km

Berkeley

San
Francisco

Oakland

San
Francisco
Bay

UC Berkeley Art Museum **3**

Berkeley Convention &
  Visitors Bureau **6**

College Avenue **1**

Fourth Street Shopping District **7**

Lawrence Hall of Science **4**

Rose Garden **8**

Telegraph Avenue **2**

Tilden Park **9**

University of California
  Botanical Garden **3**

Visitor Information Center **5**

produced, and after all these years, Alice still attends to her restaurant with great integrity and innovation.

Alice's creations are served in a delightful redwood-and-stucco cottage with a brick terrace filled with flowering potted plants. There are two separate dining areas—the upstairs cafe and the downstairs restaurant, both offering Mediterranean-inspired cuisine, all of which is guided by the freshest seasonal and organic ingredients. In the woodsy and casual upstairs cafe, you'll pass a tempting display of pastries and fruit, and large bouquets of fresh flowers, which adorn an oak bar. At lunch or dinner, a delicately smoked gravlax or a roasted-eggplant soup with pesto, followed by lamb ragout garnished with apricots, onions, and spices served with couscous, might be featured. The cozy downstairs restaurant, strewn with blossoming floral bouquets, is an appropriately warm environment to indulge in the fixed-price, four-course gourmet dinner, which is served Tuesday through Thursday. Friday and Saturday, it's four courses plus an aperitif, and Monday is bargain night with a three-course dinner for $39.

The menu, which changes daily, is posted outside the restaurant each Saturday for the following week. Meals are complemented by an excellent wine list.

1517 Shattuck Ave. (between Cedar and Vine). (510/548-5525; cafe reservations 415/548-5049. Fax 510/548-0140. www.chezpanisse.com. Reservations required. Restaurant fixed-price menu $45–$75; cafe main courses $15–$25. AE, DC, DISC, MC, V. Restaurant seatings Mon–Sat 6–6:30pm and 8:30–9:30pm. Cafe Mon–Thurs 11:30am–3pm and 5–10:30pm, Fri–Sat 11:30am–3:30pm and 5–11:30pm. From I-80 N, take the University Ave. exit and turn left onto Shattuck Ave. BART: Berkeley.

MODERATE

Cafe Rouge BISTRO   After cooking at San Francisco's renowned Zuni Cafe for 10 years, chef and owner Marsha McBride launched her own restaurant, a sort of Zuni East. She brought former staff members and some of the restaurant's flavor with her, and now her sparse, loft-like dining room serves salads, rotisserie chicken with oil and thyme, grilled lamb chops, steaks, and homemade sausages. East Bay carnivores are especially happy with the burger; like Zuni's, it's top-notch.

1782 4th St. (between Delaware and Hearst). (510/525-1440. Reservations recommended. Main courses $9.50–$24. AE, MC, V. Daily 11:30am–3pm; Tues–Sat 3–5pm (interim menu); Tues–Thurs 5:30–9:30pm; Fri–Sat 5:30–10:30pm; Sun 5–9pm.

O Chamé JAPANESE   Spare and plain in its decor, with ochre-colored walls marked with etched patterns, this spot has a meditative air to complement the traditional and experimental Japanese-inspired cuisine coveted by lovers of "clean," light food. The menu, which changes daily, offers meal-in-a-bowl dishes ($9–$13) that allow a choice of soba or udon noodles in a clear soup with a variety of toppings—from shrimp and wakame seaweed to beef with burdock root and carrot; appetizers and salads, which include a flavorful melding of grilled shiitake mushrooms and sweet peppers and portobello mushrooms, watercress, and green-onion pancakes; a sashimi of the day; and specials that range from $10 to $18 and always include a delicious roasted salmon.

1830 4th St. (near Hearst). (510/841-8783. Reservations recommended Fri–Sat. Main courses $9–$19. AE, DC, MC, V. Mon–Sat 11:30am–3pm; Mon–Thurs 5:30–9pm, Fri–Sat 5:30–9:30pm.

Rivoli *Finds* CALIFORNIA   One of the favored dinner destinations in the East Bay, Rivoli offers top-notch food at amazingly reasonable prices. The owners have done the most with an otherwise uninteresting space by creating a warm, intimate dining room, which overlooks a sweet little garden with visiting raccoons and possums, and is preceded by a wine bar near the entrance. Aside from a few house favorites, the menu changes entirely every 3 weeks to serve whatever's freshest and in season; the wine list follows suit with around a dozen by-the-glass options hand-picked to match the food. Most dishes shine, such as chicken cooked with prosciutto di Parma, potato and scallion soufflé, Marsala jus, snap peas, and baby carrots; artichoke lasagna with ricotta, mint salsa, and tomato sauce; and braised lamb shank with green garlic risotto, sautéed spinach, and oven-dried tomatoes. Finish the evening with an assortment of cheeses or a warm chocolate truffle torte with hazelnut ice cream, orange crème anglaise, and chocolate sauce.

1539 Solano Ave. Ⓒ 510/526-2542. www.rivolirestaurant.com. Reservations recommended. Main courses $14–$17. AE, DISC, MC, V. Mon–Thurs 5:30–9:30pm, Fri 5:30–10pm, Sat 5–10pm, Sun 5–9pm.

INEXPENSIVE

Cambodiana's ⚜ CAMBODIAN   For those who relish the spicy cuisine of Cambodia, this is quite a find. The decor is as colorful as the fare—brilliant blue, yellow, and green walls with Breuer-style chairs. Especially tasty choices include curry (chicken, beef, and so on), and Naga dishes with a sauce of tamarind, turmeric, lemon grass, shrimp paste, coconut-milk galanga, shallot, lemon leaf, sugar, and green chile. This sauce may smother salmon, prawns, chicken, or steak. Another tempting dish is chicken *chaktomuk,* prepared with pineapple, red peppers, and zucchini in soy and oyster sauce. There are plenty of vegetarian and low-cal options, too.

2156 University Ave. (between Shattuck and Oxford). Ⓒ 510/843-4630. Reservations recommended. Main courses $6.50–$15. AE, DC, MC, V. Tues–Fri 11:30am–9pm, Sat–Sun 5–9:30pm.

2 Oakland

10 miles E of San Francisco

Although it's less than a dozen miles from San Francisco, the city of Oakland is worlds apart from its sister city across the bay. Originally little more than a cluster of ranches and farms, Oakland's size and stature exploded practically overnight as the last mile of transcontinental railroad track was laid down. Major shipping ports soon followed, and to this day Oakland has retained its hold as one of the busiest industrial ports on the West Coast.

The price for all this economic success, however, has been Oakland's lowbrow reputation as a predominantly working-class city, forever in the shadow of San Francisco's chic spotlight. However, with progressive Mayor Jerry Brown at the helm and housing prices and weather far more inviting than they are in San Francisco, "Oaktown" is in a renaissance, and its future continues to look brighter and brighter with plenty of pleasant surprises for those who venture this way. Rent a sailboat on Lake Merritt, stroll along the waterfront, explore the fantastic Oakland Museum—they're all great reasons to hop the bay and spend a fog-free day exploring one of California's largest and most ethnically diverse cities.

ESSENTIALS

GETTING THERE   Bay Area Rapid Transit (BART) makes the trip from San Francisco to Oakland through one of the longest underwater transit tunnels in the world. Fares range from $1 to $4, depending on your station of origin; children 4 and under ride free. BART trains operate Monday through Friday from 4am to midnight, Saturday from 6am to midnight, and Sunday from 8am to midnight. Exit at the 12th Street station for downtown Oakland.

By car from San Francisco, take I-80 across the San Francisco–Oakland Bay Bridge and follow the signs to downtown Oakland. Exit at Grand Avenue South for the Lake Merritt area.

VISITOR INFORMATION   A calendar of events and a free copy of the 60-page *Destination Oakland* guide are available online or by mail from the **Oakland Convention and Visitors Bureau,** 475 14th St., Suite 120, Oakland, CA 94612 (© **510/839-9000;** www.oaklandcvb.com). The city also sponsors free guided tours, including African-American Heritage and neighborhood tours; call © **510/238-3234** for details.

CITY LAYOUT   Downtown Oakland is bordered by Grand Avenue on the north, I-980 on the west, Inner Harbor on the south, and Lake Merritt on the east. Between these landmarks are three BART stations (12th St., 19th St., and Lake Merritt), City Hall, the Oakland Museum, Jack London Square, and several other sights.

WHAT TO SEE & DO

Lake Merritt is Oakland's primary tourist attraction, along with Jack London Square (see below). Three and a half miles in circumference, the tidal lagoon was bridged and dammed in the 1860s and is now a wildlife refuge that's home to flocks of migrating ducks, herons, and geese. It's surrounded on three sides by the 122-acre **Lakeside Park,** a popular place to picnic, feed the ducks, and escape the fog. At the **Municipal Boathouse** (© **510/444-3807**), in Lakeside Park along the north shore, you can rent sailboats, rowboats, pedal boats, and canoes for $6 to $12 per hour. Another option is to take an hour-long gondola ride with **Gondola Servizio** (**510/663-6603;** www.gondolaservizio.com). Experienced gondoliers will serenade you as you glide across the lake; the cost is $45 or $75 for two depending on the time.

Another site worth visiting is Oakland's **Paramount Theatre,** 2025 Broadway (© **510/893-2300;** www.paramounttheatre.com), an outstanding example of Art Deco architecture and decor. Built in 1931 and authentically restored in 1973, it now functions as the city's main performing-arts center featuring incredible talent like Nina Simone and Alicia Keys. Guided tours of the 3,000-seat theater are given the first and third Saturdays of each month, excluding holidays. No reservations are necessary; just show up at 10am at the box-office entrance on 21st Street at Broadway. Cameras are allowed, and admission is $1.

If you take pleasure from strolling sailboat-filled wharves or are a die-hard fan of Jack London, you might actually enjoy a visit to **Jack London Square** (© **510/814-6000;** www.jacklondonsquare.com). Oakland's only patent tourist area, this low-key version of San Francisco's Fisherman's Wharf shamelessly plays up the fact that Jack London spent most of his youth along this waterfront. The square fronts the harbor, housing a tourist-tacky complex of boutiques and eateries that are about as far away from the "call of the wild" as you can get. Most are open Monday through Saturday from 10am to 7pm (some restaurants stay open later). One of the best options is live jazz at **Yoshi's World Class Jazz House & Japanese Restaurant** (，510 Embarcadero W. (© **510/238-9200;** www.yoshis.com), which also serves decent sushi in its adjoining restaurant. In the center of the square is a small reconstructed version of the Yukon cabin in which Jack London lived while prospecting in the Klondike during the gold rush of 1897.

In the middle of Jack London Square, you'll find a more authentic memorial, **Heinold's First and Last Chance Saloon** (© **510/839-6761**)—a funky,

Oakland

To 580
Bay Bridge/San Francisco

Grand Ave.

23rd St.

W. Grand Ave.

21st St.

Children's Fairyland

LAKESIDE PARK

22nd St.

21st St.

20th St.

Harrison St.

Municipal Boathouse (Rentals)

Greyhound Bus Depot

20th St.

Williams St.

19th St.

19th St. BART

SNOW PARK

Lakeside Dr.

19th St.

Lake Merritt

Brush St.

Castro St.

18th St.

17th St.

16th St.

18th St.

17th St.

Broadway

Franklin St.

Webster St.

Harrison St.

Alice St.

Jackson St.

Madison St.

Oak St.

17th St.

Camron–Stanford House

The Rotunda

15th St.

City Hall

14th St.

City Center

Preservation Park

13th St.

12th St.

12th St./City Center BART

15th St.

14th St.

13th St.

Post Office

12th St.

Oakland Museum of California

Martin Luther King Jr. Way

11th St.

10th St.

Oakland Convention Center

CHINATOWN

11th St.

LINCOLN SQUARE

10th St.

9th St.

Brush St.

Castro St.

OLD OAKLAND

9th St.

8th St.

7th St.

Asian Cultural Center

MADISON PARK

9th St.

8th St.

7th St.

Lake Merritt BART

Laney College

To Bay Bridge/ San Francisco

880

JEFFERSON SQUARE

6th St.

CHINESE GARDEN

6th St.

Fallon St.

880

To Oakland International Airport

5th St.

4th St.

5th St.

4th St.

Jefferson St.

3rd St.

Clay St.

Washington St.

Broadway

Franklin St.

Webster St.

Harrison St.

Alice St.

Jackson St.

Madison St.

Oak St.

3rd St.

2nd St.

Victory Ct.

Embarcadero

Embarcadero

ESTUARY PARK

Jack London Square

Alameda/ Oakland Ferry Terminal

Water Taxi

Webster St. Tube

Posey Tube

■ BART Station
i Information

Ferry to Alameda & San Francisco

0 ——— 1/4 Mi
0 ——— 0.25 Km

Berkeley
Area of Detail

San Francisco

Oakland

San Francisco Bay

101

ACCOMMODATIONS ■

Clarion Suites Lake Merritt
Hotel **6**

DINING ◆

Citron **1**
Oliveto Cafe
& Restaurant **2**
Yoshi's World Class Jazz
House and Japanese
Restaurant **8**

ATTRACTIONS ●

Jack London Square **9**
Lake Merritt **5**
Lakeside Park **4**
Oakland Museum of
California **7**
Paramount Theatre **3**

friendly little bar and historic landmark that's actually worth a visit. This is where London did some of his writing and most of his drinking; the corner table he used has remained exactly as it was nearly a century ago. Also in the square are the mast and nameplate from the **USS *Oakland,*** a ship that saw extensive action in the Pacific during World War II.

The square is located at Broadway and Embarcadero. Take I-880 to Broadway, turn south, and go to the end. Via BART, get off at the 12th Street station, then walk south along Broadway (about half a mile) or take bus no. 51a to the foot of Broadway.

Oakland Museum of California 🛆   Located 2 blocks south of Lake Merritt, this museum includes just about everything you'd want to know about the state and its people, history, culture, geology, art, environment, and ecology. Inside a low-swept, modern building set among sweeping gardens and terraces, it's actually three museums in one: exhibitions of works by California artists from Bierstadt to Diebenkorn; collections of artifacts from California's history, from Pomo Indian basketry to Country Joe McDonald's guitar; and re-creations of California habitats from the coast to the mountains. The museum holds major shows of California artists and exhibitions dedicated to major California movements. There are 45-minute guided tours leaving the gallery information desks on request or by appointment. There is also a fine cafe, a **gallery** (© **510/834-2296**) selling works by California artists, and a book and gift shop. The cafe is open Wednesday through Saturday from 10am to 4pm and Sunday from noon to 4pm.

1000 Oak St. (at 10th St.) © **888/625-6873,** or 510/238-2200 for recorded information. www.museumca. org. Admission $6 adults, $4 students and seniors, free for children under 6. Free to all 2nd Sun of each month. Wed–Fri 10:30am–4:30pm, Sat–Sun 1:30–4:30pm; open until 9pm the 1st Thurs of the month. Closed Jan 1, July 4th, Thanksgiving, Dec 25. From I-880 N, take the Oak St. exit; the museum is 5 blocks E. Or take I-580 to I-980 and exit at the Jackson St. ramp. BART: Lake Merritt station; walk 1 block N.

WHERE TO STAY

Two fine midrange hotel options in Oaktown are the **Waterfront Plaza Hotel,** 10 Washington St., Jack London Square (© **800/729-3638** or 510/836-3800; info@waterfrontplaza.com), and the **Oakland Marriott City Center,** 1001 Broadway (© **510/451-4000;** fax 510/835-3466). Most major motel chains also have locations (and budget prices) around town and near the airport.

Clarion Suites Lake Merritt Hotel 🛆🛆   Six-floor Lake Merritt Hotel is so delightfully charming in its Art Deco glory, it's impossible not to love the place. The completely renovated rooms and suites are cheery; many rooms overlook Lake Merritt, which is across the street. The decor is fresh with bright colors, fun lampshades, Deco-style armoires, new bathrooms (but old tile), and lots of homey touches and amenities. The suites are full-blown apartments. Completing the cozy picture are the comfy and swank sitting area—all dark with high ceiling and grand piano—and the beautiful restaurant, Madison's, which offers astounding lakefront views from huge picture windows.

1800 Madison St. (at 17th St.), Oakland, CA 94612. © **800/933-4683** or 510/832-2300. Fax 510/832-7150. www.clarioninn.com. 52 units. $179–$289 double. AE, DC, MC, V. Valet parking $14. **Amenities:** Restaurant; complimentary passes to nearby health club; concierge; shuttle service; room service; same-day dry cleaning. *In room:* TV, dataport, kitchenette in suites, fridge, coffeemaker, hair dryer, iron, safe.

WHERE TO DINE

Citron 🛆🛆 FRENCH/MEDITERRANEAN   This petite, adorable French bistro was an instant smash when it first opened in 1992, and it continues to draw raves for its small yet enticingly eclectic menu. Chef Chris Rossi draws the flavors of France, Italy, and Spain together with fresh California produce for Chez Panisse-like results. Although the menu changes every few weeks, dishes range from Sonoma rack of lamb, which is grilled then baked with an aïoli-breadcrumb crust and served atop grilled ratatouille Provençal with waffle-cut potato chips or Spicy Bayou seafood stew brimming with fried oysters, shrimp, snapper, and bell pepper and tomato sauce. The fresh salads and Citron "40 clove" chicken are also superb.

5484 College Ave. (off the NE end of Broadway between Taft and Lawton sts.). © 510/653-5484. Reservations recommended. Main courses $18–$28; 5-course fixed-price menu (Sun–Fri only) $26–$32. AE, DC, DISC, MC, V. Mon–Thurs 5:30–9:30pm, Fri 5:30–10pm, Sat 5–10pm, Sun 5–9pm.

Oliveto Cafe & Restaurant ★★ ITALIAN   It's been years since Paul Bertolli, former chef at the world-renowned Chez Panisse restaurant, jumped ship to open one of the top Italian restaurants in the Bay Area (certainly the best in Oakland). But time hasn't changed this restaurant's popularity. During the week it's a madhouse at lunchtime, when BART commuters pile in for the wood-fired pizzas and tapas served at the restaurant's lower-level cafe. The upstairs restaurant—suavely bedecked with neo-Florentine decor and a partial open kitchen—is slightly more civil, packed nightly with fans of Bertolli's house-made pastas, sausages, and prosciutto. A noteworthy addition include a wood-burning oven, and flame-broiled rotisserie from which an assortment of pricey grills, braises, and roasts anchor the daily changing menu. But it's the reasonably priced pastas, pizzettas, and awesome salads that offer the most bang for your buck. *Tip:* There's free parking in the lot at the rear of the Market Hall building.

Rockridge Market Hall, 5655 College Ave. (off the NE end of Broadway at Shafter/Keith St., across from the Rockridge BART station). © 510/547-5356. Reservations recommended for restaurant. Main courses $9–$15 lunch, $16–$30 dinner. AE, DC, MC, V. Mon–Fri 11:30am–2pm; Mon–Wed 5:30–9pm, Thurs–Sat 5:30–10pm, Sun 5–9pm.

3 Sausalito

5 miles N of San Francisco

Just off the northern end of the Golden Gate Bridge is the eclectic little town of Sausalito, a slightly bohemian, nonchalant, and studiedly quaint adjunct to San Francisco. With approximately 8,000 residents, Sausalito feels rather like St. Tropez on the French Riviera—minus the starlets and the European aristocracy. It has its quota of paper millionaires, but they rub their permanently suntanned shoulders with a good number of hard-up artists, struggling authors, shipyard workers, and fishers. Next to the swank restaurants, plush bars, and antiques shops and galleries, you'll see hamburger joints, beer parlors, and secondhand bookstores.

Above all, Sausalito has scenery and sunshine, for once you cross the Golden Gate Bridge, you're out of the San Francisco fog patch and under blue California sky (I hope). Almost all the tourist action, which is basically limited to window-shopping and eating, takes place at sea level on Bridgeway.

ESSENTIALS

GETTING THERE   The **Golden Gate Ferry Service** fleet, Ferry Building (© **415/923-2000**), operates between the San Francisco Ferry Building, at the foot of Market Street, and downtown Sausalito. Service is frequent, departing at reasonable intervals every day of the year except New Year's Day, Thanksgiving Day, and Christmas Day. Phone for an exact schedule. The ride takes a half-hour, and one-way fares to Sausalito are $5.60 for adults, $2.45 on weekdays and $4.20 on weekends for kids 6 to 12, $2.80 for seniors and passengers with disabilities, and free for children under 6. Family rates are available on weekends.

Ferries of the **Blue & Gold Fleet** (© **415/705-5555;** www.blueandgoldfleet.com) leave from Pier 41 (Fisherman's Wharf) and cost $12 round-trip; half price for kids 5 to 11. Boats run on a seasonal schedule; phone or check out the website for departure information.

By car from San Francisco, take U.S. 101 north, then the first right after the Golden Gate Bridge (Alexander exit). Alexander becomes Bridgeway in Sausalito.

EXPLORING THE TOWN

Sausalito is a mecca for shoppers seeking handmade, original, and offbeat clothes and footwear, as well as arts and crafts. The town's best shops are found in the alleys, malls, and second-floor boutiques reached by steep, narrow staircases on and off **Bridgeway,** Sausalito's main touring strip, which runs along the water. Those in the know make a quick detour to **Caledonia Street,** which runs parallel to and 1 block inland from Bridgeway. Not only is it less congested, but there's also a far better selection of cafes and shops.

Bay Model Visitors Center *Kids*   The U.S. Army Corps of Engineers uses this high-tech, 1½-acre model of San Francisco's bay and delta to resolve problems and observe the impact changes in water flow will have. The model reproduces (in scale) the rise and fall of tides, the flows and currents of water, and the mixing of fresh water and saltwater, and indicates trends in sediment movement. There's a 10-minute film and a tour, but the most interesting time to visit is when it's in use, so call ahead.

2100 Bridgeway. © 415/332-3871. www.spn.usace.army.mil/bmvc. Free admission. Summer (Memorial Day to Labor Day) Tues–Fri 9am–4pm, Sat–Sun and holidays 10am–5pm; rest of year Tues–Sat 9am–4pm.

WHERE TO STAY

Casa Madrona ★★   Sooner or later most visitors to Sausalito look up and wonder at the ornate mansion on the hill. It's part of Casa Madrona, a hideaway by the bay built in 1885 by a wealthy lumber baron. Successive renovations and extensions have added a rambling, New England–style building to the hillside below the main house. Now a certified historic landmark, the hotel offers rooms, suites, and cottages, which are accessed by steep, gorgeously landscaped pathways. The 16 newest units are each uniquely decorated by different local designers. The "1,000 Cranes" is Asian in theme, with lots of ash wood and lacquer. "Artist's Loft" is reminiscent of a rustic Parisian artist's studio complete with easel and paints. "Summer House" is decked out in white wicker. Other rooms in the mansion are decorated in a variety of styles; some have Jacuzzis, and others have fireplaces. The newest rooms overlook the water with panoramic views of the San Francisco skyline and bay. As of press time, 31 new rooms and a full-service spa have been added.

801 Bridgeway, Sausalito, CA 94965. © 800/567-9524 or 415/332-0502. Fax 415/332-2537. www.casa madrona.com. 34 units. $188–$275 double; $340 Madrona Villa suite. Rates include breakfast (served 7:30–9:30am). 3-night minimum anytime from Apr–Sept. AE, MC, V. Valet parking $12. Ferry: Walk across the street from the landing. From U.S. 101 N, take the 1st right after the Golden Gate Bridge (Alexander exit); Alexander becomes Bridgeway. **Amenities:** Restaurant; Jacuzzi; concierge; room service (breakfast and dinner); babysitting; laundry service; dry cleaning. *In room:* TV/VCR, dataport, minibar, coffeemaker, hair dryer.

The Inn Above Tide ★★   Perched directly over the bay atop well-grounded pilings, this former luxury apartment complex underwent a $4-million transformation into one of Sausalito's finest accommodations. It's the view that clinches it: Every room comes with an unparalleled panorama of the San Francisco Bay, including a postcard-quality vista of the city glimmering in the distance. Should you manage to tear yourself away from your private deck (I was tempted to drag my mattress outside), you'll find that 22 of the sumptuously appointed rooms sport a romantic little fireplace; some have a vast sunken tub with Jacuzzi jets, remote-control air-conditioning, and wondrously comfortable queen- or king-size beds. Soothing shades of pale green and blue highlight the decor, which blends in well with the bayscape outside. Be sure to request that your breakfast and newspaper be delivered to your deck, and then cancel your early appointments: On sunny mornings, nobody checks out early.

30 El Portal (next to the Sausalito Ferry Landing), Sausalito, CA 94965. ✆ 800/893-8433 or 415/332-9535. Fax 415/332-6714. www.innabovetide.com. 30 units. $235–$600 double. Rates include continental breakfast and evening wine and cheese. AE, DC, MC, V. Valet parking $12. **Amenities:** Limited concierge; in-room massage; same-day laundry service and dry cleaning. *In room:* A/C, TV, dataport, minibar, fridge, hair dryer.

WHERE TO DINE

Guernica ★ FRENCH/BASQUE   Established in 1976, Guernica is one of those funky old kinds of restaurants that you'd probably pass up for something more chic and modern down the street if you didn't know better. What? You don't know about Guernica's legendary Paella Valenciana? Well, now you do, so be sure to call ahead and order it in advance, and bring a partner 'cause it's served for two but will feed three. Begin with an appetizer of artichoke hearts or escargots. Other main courses range from pork loin "New Orleans style" to a hearty Rack of Lamb Guernica. Rich desserts include such in-season specialties as strawberry tart, peach Melba, and Basque-style rice pudding.

2009 Bridgeway. ✆ 415/332-1512. Reservations recommended. Main courses $12–$22. AE, MC, V. Tues–Sun 5–10pm. From U.S. 101 N, take the 1st right after the Golden Gate Bridge (Alexander exit); Alexander becomes Bridgeway in Sausalito.

Sushi Ran ★★ SUSHI/JAPANESE   San Franciscans often cross the bridge just to cram into the bar, window seats, and more roomy back dining area of this top-quality sushi favorite for standard rolls (yellowtail, unagi, maguro, and the like) and specialty rolls (crab, avocado, and beyond). You'll also find a slew of creative dishes such as generously sized and unbelievably moist and buttery miso-glazed sea bass (a must-have), oysters on the half shell with ponzu sauce and tobiko, and a Hawaiian-style ahi poke salad with seaweed dressing that's authentic enough to make you want to hula. Pay the extra $5 or so for fresh wasabi, select from the fine sake and wine list, and don't miss dessert—especially if it's green-tea bread pudding, which tastes way better than it sounds.

107 Caledonia St. ✆ 415/332-3620. www.sushiran.com. Reservations recommended. Sushi $5–$14; main courses $8.50–$16. AE, DC, MC, V. Mon–Fri 11:45am–2:30pm and 5:30–11pm, Sat 5:30–11pm, Sun 5–10:30pm. From U.S. 101 N, take the 1st right after the Golden Gate Bridge (Alexander exit); Alexander becomes Bridgeway in Sausalito. At Johnson St. turn left, then right onto Caledonia.

4 Angel Island & Tiburon

8 miles N of San Francisco

A federal and state wildlife refuge, **Angel Island** is the largest of the San Francisco Bay's three islets (the others being Alcatraz and Yerba Buena). The island has been, at various times, a prison, a quarantine station for immigrants, a missile base, and even a favorite site for duels. Nowadays, though, most of the people who visit here are content with picnicking on the large green lawn that fronts the docking area. Loaded with the appropriate recreational supplies, they claim a barbecue, plop their fannies down on the lush green grass, and while away an afternoon free of televisions and traffic. Hiking, mountain biking, and guided tram tours are also popular activities.

Tiburon, situated on a peninsula of the same name, looks like a cross between a fishing village and a Hollywood western set—imagine San Francisco reduced to toy dimensions. This seacoast town rambles over a series of green hills and ends up at a spindly, multicolored pier on the waterfront, like a Fisherman's Wharf in miniature. But in reality, it's an extremely plush patch of yacht-club suburbia, as you'll see by both the marine craft and the homes of their owners. **Main Street** is lined with ramshackle, color-splashed old frame houses that shelter chic boutiques, souvenir stores, antiques shops, and art galleries. Other roads are narrow, winding, and hilly, leading up to dramatically situated homes. The view of San Francisco's skyline and the islands in the bay is a good enough reason to pay the precious price to live here.

ESSENTIALS
GETTING THERE   Ferries of the **Blue & Gold Fleet** (© **415/705-5555;** www.blueandgoldfleet.com) leave from Pier 41 (Fisherman's Wharf) and travel to both Angel Island and Tiburon. Boats run on a seasonal schedule; phone for departure information. The round-trip fare is $11 to Angel Island or Tiburon, half price for kids ages 5 to 11, and free for kids under 5. Catch the **Tiburon–Angel Island Ferry** (© **415/435-2131**) to Angel Island from the dock located at Tiburon Boulevard and Main Street. The 15-minute round-trip, which only runs on weekends, costs $5.50 for adults, $4.50 for children 5 to 11, $1 for bikes. One child under 5 rides free with each paying adult.

By car from San Francisco, take U.S. 101 to the Tiburon/Highway 131 exit, then follow Tiburon Boulevard all the way into downtown, a 40-minute drive from San Francisco.

ANGEL ISLAND
Passengers disembark from the ferry at **Ayala Cove,** a small marina abutting a huge lawn area equipped with tables, benches, barbecue pits, and restrooms. Also at Ayala Cove are a small store, gift shop, cafe (with surprisingly good grub), and an overpriced mountain-bike rental shop (helmets included).

Among the 12 miles of Angel Island's hiking and mountain-bike trails is the **Perimeter Road,** a partly paved path that circles the island and winds its way past disused troop barracks, former gun emplacements, and other military buildings; several turnoffs lead up to the top of Mount Livermore, 776 feet above the bay.

Sometimes referred to as the "Ellis Island of the West," from 1910 to 1940 Angel Island was used as a holding area for Chinese immigrants awaiting their citizenship papers. You can still see some faded Chinese characters on the walls of the barracks where the immigrants were held. During the warmer months, you can camp at a limited number of sites; reservations are required and can be obtained by calling © **800/444-7275.**

Also offered at Angel Island are guided **sea-kayak tours.** The all-day trips, which include a catered lunch, combine the thrill of paddling stable one-, two-, or three-person kayaks with an informative, naturalist-led tour that encircles the island (conditions permitting). All equipment is provided, kids are welcome, and no experience is necessary. Rates run about $100 per person; a shorter trip takes 2½ hours and costs $75 per person. For more information, call **Sea Trek** (© **415/332-8494**).

The most recent tour addition is the 1-hour **Angel Island Tram Tour** (© **925/426-3058;** www.angelisland.com), which costs $12 for adults, $11 for seniors, and $7.50 for children ages 6 to 12; children under 6 ride free. For recorded information on **Angel Island State Park,** call © **415/435-1915.**

TIBURON

The main thing to do in Tiburon is stroll along the waterfront, pop in to the stores, and spend an easy $50 on drinks and appetizers before heading back to the city. For a taste of the Wine Country, stop in at **Windsor Vineyards,** 72 Main St. (© **800/214-9463** or 415/435-3113), which has a Victorian tasting room dating back to 1888. Thirty-five choices are available for a free tasting. Wine accessories and gifts—glasses, cork pullers, gourmet sauces, posters, and maps—are also for sale. Carry-packs (which hold six bottles) are available; ask about personalized labels for your own selections. The shop is open Sunday through Thursday from 10am to 6pm, Friday and Saturday until 7pm.

WHERE TO DINE

Guaymas MEXICAN   Guaymas offers authentic Mexican regional cuisine and a spectacular panoramic view of San Francisco and the bay. In good weather, the two outdoor patios are almost always packed with diners soaking in the sun. Inside, colorful Mexican artwork aids the festive scene. Should you feel chilled, to the rear of the dining room is a beehive-shaped adobe fireplace.

Guaymas is named after a fishing village on Mexico's Sea of Cortez, and both the town and the restaurant are famous for their *camarones* (giant shrimp). In addition, the restaurant features ceviche, handmade tamales, and charcoal-grilled beef, seafood, and fowl. Save room for dessert, especially the outrageously scrumptious fritter with "drunken" bananas and ice cream. In addition to a good selection of California wines, the restaurant offers an exceptional variety of tequilas, Mexican beers, and mineral waters flavored with flowers, grains, and fruits.

5 Main St. © **415/435-6300.** Reservations recommended. Main courses $12–$29. AE, DC, DISC, MC, V. Mon–Thurs 11:30am–10pm, Fri–Sat 11:30am–11pm, Sun 10:30am–10pm. Ferry: Walk about 10 paces from the landing. From U.S. 101, exit at Tiburon/Hwy. 131; follow Tiburon Blvd. 5 miles and turn right onto Main St. Restaurant is behind the bakery.

Sam's Anchor Café ★ (Finds) SEAFOOD   Summer Sundays are liveliest in Tiburon, when weekend boaters tie up at the docks of waterside restaurants like this one. Sam's is the kind of place where you and your cronies can take off your shoes and have a fun, relaxed time eating burgers and drinking margaritas outside on the pier. The fare is typical—sandwiches, salads, and seafood such as deep-fried oysters—but the quality and selection is inconsequential: Beers, burgers, and a designated driver are all you really need.

27 Main St. © **415/435-4527.** www.samscafe.com. Main courses $9–$13 brunch, $9–$21 lunch, $9–$24 dinner. AE, DC, DISC, MC, V. Mon–Thurs 11am–10pm, Fri 11am–10:30pm, Sat 10am–10:30pm, Sun 9:30am–10pm. Ferry: Walk from the landing. From U.S. 101, exit at Tiburon/Hwy. 131, follow Tiburon Blvd. 4 miles, and turn right onto Main St.

5 Muir Woods & Mount Tamalpais

12 miles N of the Golden Gate Bridge

While the rest of Marin County's redwood forests were being devoured to feed the building spree in San Francisco around the turn of the 20th century, the trees of Muir Woods, in a remote ravine on the flanks of Mount Tamalpais, escaped destruction in favor of easier pickings.

MUIR WOODS

Although the magnificent California redwoods have been successfully transplanted to five continents, their homeland is a 500-mile strip along the mountainous coast of southwestern Oregon and Northern California. The coast redwood, or *Sequoia sempervirens,* is the tallest tree in the immediate region, and the largest-known specimen (located in the Redwood National Forest) towers 368 feet. It has an even larger relative, the *Sequoiadendron giganteum* of the California Sierra Nevada, but the coastal variety is stunning enough. Soaring toward the sky like a wooden cathedral, seeing it is an experience you won't soon forget.

Granted, Muir Woods is tiny compared to the Redwood National Forest farther north, but you can still get a pretty good idea of what it must have been like when these redwood giants dominated the entire coastal region. What is truly amazing is that they exist a mere 6 miles (as the crow flies) from San Francisco; close enough, unfortunately, that tour buses arrive in droves on the weekends. You can, however, avoid the masses by hiking up the **Ocean View Trail** and returning via the **Fern Creek Trail**—a moderate hike that shows off the woods' best sides and leaves the tour-bus crowd behind.

To reach Muir Woods from San Francisco, cross the Golden Gate Bridge heading north on U.S. 101, take the Stinson Beach/Calif. 1 exit heading west, and follow the signs (and the traffic). The park is open daily from 8am to sunset; the entrance fee is $3 per person 17 years or older. There's a small gift shop, educational displays, and docent-led tours that you're welcome to stand in on. For more information, call the **Muir Woods information line** (② **415/388-2595**).

If you don't have a car, you can book a bus trip with the **Red & White Fleet,** which takes you straight to Muir Woods via the Golden Gate Bridge, and on the way back makes a short stop in Sausalito. The 3½-hour tours run several times daily and cost $33 for adults, $16 for children ages 5 through 11, and are free for kids under 5. Call for more information and specific departure times (② **877/855-5506** or 415/447-0597).

MOUNT TAMALPAIS

The birthplace of mountain biking, Mount Tam—as the locals call it—is the Bay Area's favorite outdoor playground and the most dominant mountain in the region. Most every local has his or her secret trail and scenic overlook, as well as an opinion on the dilemma between mountain bikers and hikers (a touchy subject around here). The main trails—mostly fire roads—see a lot of foot and bicycle traffic on the weekends, particularly on clear, sunny days when you can see a hundred miles in all directions, from the foothills of the Sierra to the western horizon. It's a great place to escape from the city for a leisurely hike and to soak in the breathtaking views of the bay.

To get to Mount Tamalpais **by car,** cross the Golden Gate Bridge heading north on U.S. 101 and take the Stinson Beach/Calif. 1 exit. Follow the shoreline highway about 2½ miles and turn onto the Panoramic Highway heading west. After about 5½ miles, turn onto Pantoll Road and continue for about a mile to Ridgecrest Boulevard. Ridgecrest winds to a parking lot below East Peak. From here, it's a 15-minute hike up to the top.

6 Half Moon Bay

28 miles SW of San Francisco

A mere 45-minute drive from the teeming streets of San Francisco is a heavenly little seaside hamlet called Half Moon Bay, one of the finest—and friendliest—small towns on the California coast. While other coastal communities like Bolinas take strides to make tourists unwelcome, Half Moon Bay residents are disarmingly amicable, bestowing greetings on anyone and everyone who stops for a visit.

Only in the last decade has Half Moon Bay begun to capitalize on its golden beaches, mild climate, and close proximity to San Francisco, so you won't find the ultra-touristy machinations that result in gaudy theme parks and time-share condos. What you will find, however, is a peaceful, unfettered slice of textbook California: pristine beaches, redwood forests, nature preserves, rustic fishing harbors, horse ranches, organic farms, and a host of superb inns and restaurants—everything you need for the perfect weekend getaway.

Note: Temperatures rarely venture into the 70s (20s Celsius) in Half Moon Bay, so be sure to pack for cool (and often wet) weather.

ESSENTIALS

GETTING THERE   There's no public transportation from San Francisco to Half Moon Bay. There are two ways to get here by car: the fast way and the scenic way. To save time, take Calif. 92 west from either I-280 or U.S. 101 out of San Francisco, which will take you over a small mountain range and drop you directly into Half Moon Bay. A better—and far prettier—route is via Calif. 1, which technically starts at the south end of the Golden Gate Bridge and veers southwest to the shoreline a few miles south of Daly City. Both routes to Half Moon Bay are clearly marked with numerous signs, so don't worry about getting lost.

Downtown Half Moon Bay, however, is easy to miss since it's not on Calif. 1, but a few hundred yards inland. Head 2 blocks up Calif. 92 from the Calif. 1 intersection, then turn south at the Shell gas station onto Main Street until you cross a small bridge. For more information, call the **Half Moon Bay Coastside Chamber of Commerce** (© 650/726-8380; www.halfmoonbaychamber.org).

EXPLORING HALF MOON BAY & ENVIRONS

The best things to do in Half Moon Bay are the same things the locals do. For example, there's a wonderful **paved beach trail** that winds 3 miles from Half Moon Bay to picturesque Pillar Point Harbor, where you can watch the trawlers unload their daily catch. Walking, biking, jogging, and skating are all kosher, and be sure to keep a lookout for dolphins and whales. Bicycles can be rented from the **Bicyclery,** 101A and 101B Main St. (© 650/726-6000), in downtown Half Moon Bay. Prices range from $8 to $12 an hour to $25 to $30 per day.

Half Moon Bay is also known for its organically grown produce, and the best place to stock up on fruits and vegetables is the **Andreotti Family Farm,** 329 Kelly Ave., off Calif. 1 (© 650/726-9461), a charming old-fashioned outfit that's been in business since 1926. Every Friday, Saturday, and Sunday, a member of the Andreotti family slides open the door to their weathered old barn at 10am sharp to reveal a cornucopia of strawberries, artichokes, cucumbers, and more. Head toward the beach and you'll see the barn on your right-hand side. It's open until 6pm year-round.

BEACHES & PRESERVES   The 4-mile arc of golden-colored sand that rings Half Moon Bay is broken up into three state-run beaches—Dunes, Venice, and Francis—all part of **Half Moon Bay State Beach.** There's a $5-per-vehicle entrance fee for all three beaches. Though surfing is allowed, swimming isn't a good idea unless you happen to be cold-blooded.

A few miles farther north on Calif. 1 is the **Fitzgerald Marine Reserve,** one of the most diverse tidal basins on the West Coast, as well as one of the safest, thanks to a wave-buffering rock terrace 50 yards from the beach. Call ℂ **650/ 728-3584** before coming to find out when it's low tide (all the sea creatures are hidden at high tide) and to get information on the docent-led tour schedules (usually offered on Sat). Rubber-soled shoes are recommended. It's located at the west end of California Avenue off Calif. 1 in Moss Beach.

Sixteen miles south of Half Moon Bay on Calif. 1 (at the turnoff to Pescadero) is the **Pescadero Marsh Natural Preserve,** one of the few remaining natural marshes left on the central California coast. Part of the Pacific flyway, it's a resting stop for nearly 200 bird species, including great blue herons that nest in the northern row of eucalyptus trees. Passing through the marsh is the mile-long **Sequoia Audubon Trail,** accessible from the parking lot at Pescadero State Beach on Calif. 1 (the trail starts below the Pescadero Creek Bridge). Docent-led tours take place every Saturday at 10:30am and every Sunday at 1pm, weather permitting.

Starting in December and continuing through March, the **Año Nuevo State Reserve** is home to one of California's most amazing animal attractions: the hallowed breeding grounds of the northern elephant seal. Every winter, people reserve tickets months in advance for a chance to witness a fearsome clash between the 2½-ton bulls over mating privileges among the harems of females. Reservations are required for the 2½-hour naturalist-led tours (held rain or shine Dec 15–Mar 31). For tickets and tour information, call ℂ **800/444-4445.** Even if it's not mating season, you can still see the elephant seals lolling around the shore almost year-round, particularly between April and August when they come ashore to molt.

OUTDOOR PURSUITS   One of the most popular activities in town is horseback riding along the beach. **Sea Horse Ranch** (aka Friendly Acres Horse Ranch), on Calif. 1 a mile north of Half Moon Bay (ℂ **650/726-2362** or 650/ 726-8550), offers guided and unguided rides along the beach or on well-worn trails for about $40. Hours are daily from 8am to 6pm.

For golfers, there's **Half Moon Bay Golf Links,** 2000 Fairway Dr., at the south end of Half Moon Bay next to the Half Moon Bay Lodge (ℂ **650/726-6384**). Designed by Arnold Palmer, the ocean-side 18-hole course has been rated among the top 100 courses in the country, as well as the best in the Bay Area. Greens fees range from $133 to $154. Reserve your tee time as far in advance as possible.

SHOPPING   Main Street is a shopper's paradise. Dozens of small stores and boutiques line the ¼-mile strip, selling everything from feed and tack to custom furniture and camping gear. From north to south, must-see stops include the **Buffalo Shirt Company,** 315 Main St. (ℂ **650/726-3194**), which carries a fine selection of casual wear, Indian rugs, and outdoor gear; **Cartwheels,** 330 Main St. (ℂ **650/726-6060**), a nifty store specializing in rustic wood furniture, rugs, and toys; and **Half Moon Bay Feed & Fuel,** 331 Main St. (© **650/726-4814**), a great place to pick up a treat for your pet.

Cunha's Country Store, 448 Main St. (© **650/726-4071**), the town's beloved grocery and general store, is a mandatory stop for regular visitors from the Bay Area. And, of course, what would Half Moon Bay be without a good bookstore like **Coastside Books,** 432 Main St. (© **650/726-5889**), which also carries a fair selection of children's books and postcards. End your shopping spree with a stop at **Cottage Industries,** 621 Main St. (© **650/712-8078**), to marvel at the high-quality handcrafted furniture.

WHERE TO STAY

Beach House Inn ★   While the facade has a rather unimaginative Cape Cod look, the rooms at this three-story hotel are surprisingly well designed and decorated with modern prints, stylish furnishings, soothing yellow tones, and spectacular views of the bay and harbor. Every room comes fully loaded with a wood-burning fireplace, king-size bed and sleeper sofa, large bathroom, stereo with CD player, private patio or deck access, two color TVs and a VCR, *four* telephones with dataports and voice mail, and a kitchenette with microwave and fridge. Opt for one of the corner rooms, which offer a more expansive view for the same price.

4100 N. Cabrillo Hwy. (Hwy. 1), Half Moon Bay, CA 94019. © **800/315-9366** or 650/712-0220. Fax 650/712-0693. www.beach-house.com. 54 units. $199–$350 double. Rates include continental breakfast and Fri–Sat evening wine tasting. AE, DC, DISC, MC, V. From Half Moon Bay, go 3 miles N on Hwy. 1. **Amenities:** Heated outdoor pool; exercise room; oceanview whirlpool; concierge; room service (lunch and dinner); in-room massage; same-day laundry and dry cleaning. *In room:* TV/VCR, CD player, minibar, dataport, kitchenette, fridge, coffeemaker, hair dryer.

Cypress Inn on Miramar Beach ★★   A favorite place to stay in Half Moon Bay, the Cypress Inn is blissfully free of Victorian charm (nary a lace curtain in *this* joint). Instead you have a modern, artistically designed and decorated building infused with colorful native folk art and rustic furniture made of pine and heavy wicker. Each room has a billowy feather bed, private balcony, gas fireplace, private bathroom, and unobstructed oceanview. Adjacent to the inn are four Beach House rooms equipped with built-in stereo systems and hidden TVs, though they lack the Santa-Fe-meets-California effect that I adore in the main house. The ace in the hole is, however, that it's the only B&B perched right on the beach. This property is now under the corporate umbrella of Inns by the Sea.

407 Mirada Rd., Half Moon Bay, CA 94019. © **800/83-BEACH** or 650/726-6002. Fax 650/712-0380. www.innatdepothill.com. 12 units. $215–$365 double. Rates include breakfast; tea, wine, and hors d'oeuvres; and after-dinner treats. AE, DISC, MC, V. From the junction of Highways 92 and 1, go 3 miles N, then turn W and follow Medio to the end; hotel is at Medio and Mirada. **Amenities:** Room service (breakfast only). *In room:* TV, coffeemakers in some rooms, hair dryer, iron/ironing board on request.

Seal Cove Inn ★★   Before Karen Herbert and her husband, Rick, opened this top-notch B&B, she was the writer and publisher of Karen Brown's Country Inns Series, so you can bet she knows what it takes to create and run a superior bed-and-breakfast. The result is a stately, sophisticated B&B that harmoniously blends California, New England, and European influences in a spectacular setting. All rooms have wood-burning fireplaces, country antiques, original watercolors, grandfather clocks, hidden televisions with VCRs, and refrigerators stocked with free beverages. They overlook distant cypress trees and a colorful half-acre wildflower garden dotted with birdhouses. You'll find coffee and a newspaper outside your door in the morning, brandy and sherry by the living-room fireplace in the evening, and chocolates beside your turned-down bed at night. The ocean is just a short walk away.

221 Cypress Ave., Half Moon Bay, CA 94038. © 650/728-4114. Fax 650/728-4116. www.sealcoveinn.com. 10 units. $200–$300 double. Rates include breakfast, wine, and sherry. AE, DISC, MC, V. The inn is 6 miles N of Half Moon Bay off Hwy. 1; follow signs to Moss Beach Distillery. **Amenities:** Concierge. *In room:* TV/VCR, fax, minibar, fridge, hair dryer.

WHERE TO DINE

Pasta Moon ✿✿ ITALIAN   When visitors ask, "Where is the best place to eat around here?" the inevitable answer is Pasta Moon, a handsome nouveau Italian restaurant in downtown Half Moon Bay. It specializes in making everything from scratch and using only the freshest ingredients. Pasta dishes, which are always freshly made and perfectly cooked, earn the highest recommendations. They include house-made linguine with diver sea scallops, anchovies, garlic, chile flakes, and olive oil; and penne with spicy lamb sausage in Swiss chard tomato sauce and fresh ricotta cheese. For dessert, try the wonderful tiramisu, with its layers of Marsala-and-espresso–soaked ladyfingers and creamy mascarpone.

315 Main St., Half Moon Bay. © 650/726-5125. Reservations recommended. Main courses $9–$13 brunch, $15–$25 dinner. AE, DISC, MC, V. Mon–Fri 11:30am–2:30pm, Sat noon–3pm, Sun brunch 11am–2:30pm; Sun–Thurs 5:30–9:30pm; Fri–Sat 5:30–10pm.

7 San Jose

45 miles SE of San Francisco

Some may mourn the San Jose of yesterday, a sleepy small town of orchards, crops, and cattle, but those days are long gone. Founded in 1717 and previously dwelling in the shadows of San Francisco, San Jose is now Northern California's largest city. With surveys that declare it one of the safest and sunniest cities in the country and rank it the fifth most popular place to live in America, San Jose is a force to be reckoned with. Today, the prosperity of Silicon Valley has transformed what was once an agricultural backwater into a thriving city of restaurants, shops, a state-of-the-art light-rail system, a sports arena (go Sharks!), and a reputable art scene.

ESSENTIALS

GETTING THERE   BART (© 510/465-2278; www.bart.gov) travels from San Francisco to Fremont in 1¼ hours; you can take a bus from there. **Caltrain** (© 800/660-4287 or 408/271-4980; www.caltrain.com) operates frequently from San Francisco and takes about 1 hour and 25 minutes.

VISITOR INFORMATION   For information, contact the **San Jose Convention & Visitors Bureau,** located in the San Jose McEvery Convention Center, 150 W. San Carlos St., San Jose, CA 95113 (© **408/977-0900;** www.sanjose. org).

GETTING AROUND   Light Rail (© **408/321-2300**) is your best option for getting around. A ticket is good for 2 hours and stops include Paramount's Great America, the Convention Center, and downtown museums. Fares are $1.25 for adults, 70¢ for children ages 5 to 17, 40¢ for seniors and travelers with disabilities, and children age 4 and under ride for free. Or you can use the historic trolleys, which operate in a loop around downtown (in summer only). Tickets can be purchased at Light Rail stations.

MUSEUMS WORTH SEEKING OUT

Children's Discovery Museum *(Kids)*   Here the kids will find more than 150 interactive exhibits, as well as shows and workshops, which explore science, humanities, arts, and technology. ZoomZone consists of science and art activities designed by kids for kids; Bubbalogna, an exhibit that explores the whimsical and scientifically intriguing world of bubbles, draws rave reviews. Smaller kids enjoy dressing up in costumes and playing on the fire truck.

180 Woz Way. © 408/298-5437. www.cdm.org. Admission $7 adults, $6 seniors, $7 children 1–17. Tues–Sat 10am–5pm, Sun noon–5pm.

Rosicrucian Egyptian Museum & Planetarium   The Rosicrucian is associated with an educational organization that traces its origins back to the ancient Egyptians, who strongly believed in the afterlife and reincarnation. On display are human and animal mummies, funerary boats, and canopic jars, as well as jewelry, pottery, and bronze tools. There's also a replica of a noble Egyptian's tomb. *Note:* At press time, the Planetarium was closed for earthquake renovation; call for more information.

1342 Naglee Ave. © 408/947-3636. www.rosicrucian.org. Museum admission $9 adults, $7 seniors, $5 children 5–10, free for children under 5. Planetarium admission $4 adults, $3 children; call for showtimes. Tues–Fri 10am–5pm, Sat–Sun 11am–6pm. Closed major holidays.

San Jose Historical Museum   Twenty-six original and replica buildings on 25 acres in Kelley Park have been restored to represent life in 1880s San Jose. The usual cast of characters is here—the doctor, the printer, the postmaster—with an occasional local surprise, such as the 1888 Chinese temple and the original Stevens fruit barn.

1650 Senter Rd. © 408/287-2290. Admission $6 adults, $5 seniors, $4 children 6–17, free Tues–Fri and for children under 6. Tues–Sun noon–5pm.

San Jose Museum of Art *(star)*   This contemporary art museum features revolving exhibitions, post-1980 works as well as older contemporary art from its permanent collection. The renovated Historic Wing now includes a cafe, bookstore, and education center. Public tours of exhibitions are offered every day at 12:30 and 2:30pm. On the second Saturday of each month at 12:30pm, the public gallery tour is signed for deaf and hearing-impaired visitors. Groups are asked to call and make reservations at least 1 week in advance.

110 S. Market St. © 408/294-2787 or 408/271-6840. www.sjmusart.org. Free admission. Tues–Thurs and Sat–Sun 11am–5pm, Fri 11am–10pm except in Dec when it closes at 5pm. Closed major holidays.

Tech Museum of Innovation *(star)* *(Kids)*   Now housed in a 132,000-square-foot facility, the Tech Museum allows visitors to grapple with the latest in modern technology. You can create your own virtual roller-coaster ride, survive an earthquake on a giant shake table, operate an underwater ROV (remotely operated vehicle) à la *Titanic,* and play with tons of other cool high-tech stuff. There's also an IMAX Dome Theater, Jet Pack simulator, and Virtual Bobsled ride, the same used to train Olympic competitors.

201 S. Market St., downtown at the corner of Park and Market sts. © 408/294-TECH. www.thetech.org. Admission $9 adults, $8 seniors 65 and over, $7 children 3–12, free for children under 3; additional fee for IMAX shows. Daily 10am–5pm.

THEME PARK THRILLS

Paramount's Great America, Great America Parkway (off U.S. 101), Santa Clara (© **408/988-1776;** www.pgathrills.com), provides 100 acres of family

The Winchester Mystery House: A Monument to One Woman's Paranoia

Begun in 1884, the **Winchester Mystery House,** 525 S. Winchester Blvd., at the intersection of I-280 and Highway 17, San Jose (© **408/247-2101, www.winchestermysteryhouse.com**), is the legacy of Sarah L. Winchester, widow of the son of the famous rifle magnate. After the deaths of her husband and baby daughter, Mrs. Winchester consulted with a seer, who proclaimed that the family had been targeted by the evil spirits of those killed with Winchester repeaters, who would only be appeased by perpetual construction on the Winchester mansion. Convinced that she'd live as long as the building continued, the widow used much of her $20-million inheritance to finance the construction, which went on 24 hours a day, 7 days a week, 365 days a year, for 38 years. (Ricki Lake would love to have her as a guest.)

As you can probably guess, this is no ordinary home. With 160 rooms, it sprawls across a half-dozen acres. And it's full of disturbing features: a staircase leading nowhere, a Tiffany window with a spider's web design, and doors that open onto blank walls. There are 13 bathrooms, 13 windows and doors in the old sewing room, 13 palms lining the main driveway, 13 hooks in the séance room, and chandeliers with 13 lights. Such schemes were designed to confound the spirits that seemed to plague the heiress.

Tours of the house and grounds are $17 for adults, $14 for seniors age 65 and over, $11 for children 6 to 12, and free for kids under 6; a behind-the-scenes tour is also offered for guests over 12. Tours leave about every 20 to 30 minutes and last around 65 minutes. The house is open daily from 9am to 8pm in the summer; winter hours vary, so call ahead.

entertainment. A pretty cool place to lose your lunch, the park includes such favorites as the *Top Gun* suspended jet coaster, the *Seventh Portal,* a 3-D motion-simulator adventure, a 3-acre Nickelodeon Center for children, "Drop Zone" (the world's tallest free-fall ride), the Xtreme Skyflyer, which combines skydiving with hang gliding, and the new Pyscho Mouse roller coaster and go-carts. Be sure to check for concerts and special events. Admission is $44 for adults and children ages 7 to 17, $38 for seniors age 60 and over, and $34 for children 3 to 6. Parking is $10 per vehicle. Seasonal hours and open days vary, but it's open daily June through August. Call for more information and note the schedule is subject to change due to weather, so be sure to call ahead. From San Francisco, take U.S. 101 south for about 45 miles to the Great America Parkway exit.

WHERE TO STAY

Fairmont   Ideally situated near the Convention Center and the Center of Performing Arts, this hotel is in a landmark building. A popular spot to have afternoon tea or cocktails, the lobby attracts many who are just passing through. The hotel places an emphasis on comfort: The guest rooms offer many modern features such as fax and high-speed modem lines, while other amenities include 24-hour room service and a rooftop pool surrounded by tropical foliage. The most high-end of the hotel's three restaurants is The Grill, which serves steakhouse cuisine. There's also a Chinese restaurant and a coffee shop that's nicely accented with a massive marble soda fountain.

170 S. Market St., San Jose, CA 95113. ✆ **800/527-4727** or 408/998-1900. Fax 408/287-1648. 541 units. $180–$400 double; $359–$1,800 suite. AE, DC, DISC, MC, V. **Amenities:** 3 restaurants; bar; heated outdoor pool; health club; spa; sauna; concierge; car-rental desk; business center; secretarial services; 24-hr. room service; in-room massage; same-day laundry service and dry cleaning. *In room:* A/C, TV w/pay movies, VCR and fax in suites, dataport, minibar, hair dryer, iron.

WHERE TO DINE

Emile's ✿✿ CONTEMPORARY EUROPEAN   The kitchen uses the Bay Area's bounty of local produce to create exceptional contemporary cuisine at Emile's, a San Jose institution for fine dining since 1973. Mirrors, recessed lighting, and large, bold floral arrangements create an elegant atmosphere. To start, try seared Sonoma foie gras on caramelized brioche with huckleberry-port reduction, baby arugula, and blood-orange vinaigrette. Follow with veal tenderloin medallions and white gulf prawns, sautéed with shallots and green peppercorns, wild-mushroom risotto and a light cream sauce, or perhaps New Zealand lamb rack served with a rosemary lamb jus reduction. For dessert, go with the warm chocolate truffle cake with raspberry sorbet.

545 S. 2nd St. ✆ **408/289-1960**. www.emiles.com. Reservations recommended. Main courses $25–$34; 8-course menu $75 without wine and $100 with wine. AE, DC, DISC, MC, V. Tues–Sat 6–10pm.

Paolo's ✿ NORTHERN ITALIAN   Paolo's attracts a business crowd at lunchtime and a rather cultured crowd in the evening. The cuisine is refined northern Italian, with innovative flourishes. Among the appetizers, for instance, is the tuna carpaccio with capers, olives, anchovy, sage, basil, and basil oil. The main dishes might include sea scallops baked in foil with romaine lettuce, black truffle, herbs, and pancetta or veal saltimbocca (veal stuffed with sage, fontina, Vald'osta cheese and covered with Marsala wine sauce and forest mushrooms). Desserts also stretch beyond the typical Italian favorites to include a chocolate torte with orange-caramel sauce, or *semifreddo* of cookies and cream with vanilla bean gelato and shaved Italian chocolate. An extensive wine list features more than 600 selections.

333 W. San Carlos St. ✆ **408/294-2558**. Reservations recommended. Main courses $13–$28. AE, DC, DISC, MC, V. Mon–Fri 11am–2:30pm; Mon–Sat 5:30–10pm.

6

The Wine Country

by Erika Lenkert

California's Napa and Sonoma valleys are two of the most famous winegrowing regions in the world, and two of my favorite places to visit in the state. The workaday valleys that are a way of life for thousands of vintners are also the ultimate retreat for wine lovers and romantics. Hundreds of wineries are nestled among the vines, and most are open to visitors. But even if you don't want to wine-taste, the fresh country air, beautiful rolling countryside, and world-class restaurants and spas are reasons enough to come. If you can, plan on spending more than a day here; you'll need a couple of days just to get to know one of the valleys. No matter how long you stay, you'll probably never get enough of the Wine Country's romantic, indulgent atmosphere.

While Napa and Sonoma are close to each other (about a half-hour drive apart), each is attraction-packed enough that your best bet is to focus on just one of the valleys, especially if your time is limited. I recommend that you read about each below, then decide which one is right for you—unless, of course, you're lucky enough to have time to explore both.

1 Napa Valley

The most obvious distinction between the two valleys is size—Napa Valley dwarfs Sonoma Valley both in population, number of wineries, and sheer volume of tourism (and in summertime, serious traffic). Napa is definitely the more commercial of the two, with dozens more wineries, spas (some at far cheaper rates), and a far superior selection of fine restaurants, hotels, and quintessential Wine Country activities like hot-air ballooning, all of which are set amidst rolling, mustard flower-covered hills and vast stretches of vineyards. And if your goal is to really learn about the wonderful world of winemaking, world-class wineries such as Sterling and Robert Mondavi offer the most interesting and edifying wine tours in North America, if not the world. The combined attractions make Napa the place to come for the ultimate Wine Country experience.

Napa Valley is relatively condensed. It's just 25 miles long, which means you can venture from one end to the other in around half an hour (traffic permitting). Conveniently, most of the large wineries—as well as most of the hotels, shops, and restaurants—are located along a single road, Calif. 29, which starts at the mouth of the Napa River, near the north end of San Francisco Bay, and continues north to Calistoga and the top of the growing region. Every Napa Valley town and winery can be reached from this main thoroughfare.

ESSENTIALS
GETTING THERE From San Francisco, cross the Golden Gate Bridge and continue north on U.S. 101. Turn east on Calif. 37 (toward Vallejo), then north on Calif. 29, the main road through Napa Valley.

The Wine Country

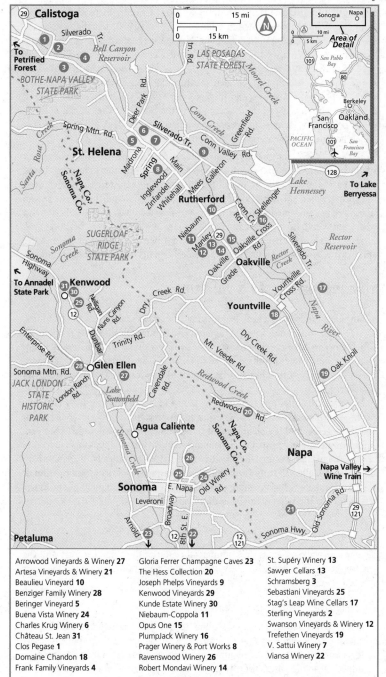

Arrowood Vineyards & Winery **27**
Artesa Vineyards & Winery **21**
Beaulieu Vineyard **10**
Benziger Family Winery **28**
Beringer Vineyard **5**
Buena Vista Winery **24**
Charles Krug Winery **6**
Château St. Jean **31**
Clos Pegase **1**
Domaine Chandon **18**
Frank Family Vineyards **4**

Gloria Ferrer Champagne Caves **23**
The Hess Collection **20**
Joseph Phelps Vineyards **9**
Kenwood Vineyards **29**
Kunde Estate Winery **30**
Niebaum-Coppola **11**
Opus One **15**
PlumpJack Winery **16**
Prager Winery & Port Works **8**
Ravenswood Winery **26**
Robert Mondavi Winery **14**

St. Supéry Winery **13**
Sawyer Cellars **13**
Schramsberg **3**
Sebastiani Vineyards **25**
Stag's Leap Wine Cellars **17**
Sterling Vineyards **2**
Swanson Vineyards & Winery **12**
Trefethen Vineyards **19**
V. Sattui Winery **7**
Viansa Winery **22**

VISITOR INFORMATION You can get Wine Country maps and brochures from the **Wine Institute** at 425 Market St., Suite 1000, San Francisco, CA 94105 (© **415/512-0151**). Once in Napa Valley, stop first at the **Napa Conference & Visitors Bureau,** 1310 Town Center Mall, Napa, CA 94559 (© **707/226-7459**), and pick up the slick *Napa Valley Guide,* or call in advance to order its $10 package, which includes the guide plus a bunch of brochures, a map, *Four Perfect Days in the Wine Country Itinerary,* and hot-air balloon discount coupons. If you don't want to pay the bucks for the official publications, point your browser to **www.napavalley.com**, the NVCVB's official site, which has much of the same information for free.

WHEN TO GO The beauty of the valley is striking any time of the year, but it's most memorable in September and October when the grapes are being pressed and the wineries are in full production. Another great time to come is the spring, when the mustard flowers are in full bloom and the tourist season hasn't yet begun; you'll find less traffic and fewer crowds at the wineries and restaurants, and better deals on hotel rooms. While winter is beautiful and promises the best budget rates, the vines are dormant and rain is likely, so bring appropriate shoes and an umbrella. Summer? Say hello to hot weather and lots of traffic.

TOURING THE VALLEY & WINERIES

The Napa Valley has more than 280 wineries, each offering distinct wines, atmosphere, and experience—so touring the valley takes a little planning. Decide what you're most interested in and chart your path from there. Ask locals which vintners have the type of experience you're looking for. Whatever you do, plan to visit no more than four or five wineries in 1 day. Above all, take it slowly. The Wine Country should never be rushed; like a great glass of wine, it should be savored.

Most wineries offer tours daily from 10am to 4:30pm. Tours usually chart the process of winemaking from the grafting and harvesting of the vines to the pressing of the grapes and the blending and aging of the wines in oak casks. They vary in length, detail, and formality, depending on the winery. Most tours are free.

The towns and wineries below are organized geographically, from south to north along Calif. 29, from Napa village to Calistoga. I've included a handful of my favorites below; for a complete list of wineries, be sure to pick up one of the free guides to the valley (see "Essentials," above).

NAPA

55 miles N of San Francisco

The city of Napa serves as the commercial center of the Wine Country and the gateway to Napa Valley. Most visitors whiz right past it on their way to the heart

---

Tips **Reservations at Wineries**

Plenty of wineries' doors are open to everyone between 10am and 4:30pm. Most wineries that require reservations to visit do so because of local permitting laws. A few limit guests to create a more intimate experience. In many cases, they'll be just as happy to see you if you arrive unannounced, but it's always best to call ahead if you have your heart set on visiting a winery that requests that you make reservations.

The Ins & Outs of Shipping Wine Home

Perhaps the only thing more complex than that $800 case of cabernet you just purchased are the rules and regulations regarding shipping it home. Due to absurd and forever fluctuating "reciprocity laws"—which were supposedly created to protect the business of the country's wine distributors—wine shipping is limited by state regulations that vary in each of the 50 states. Shipping rules also vary from winery to winery. Hence, depending on which state you live in, sending even a single bottle of wine can be a truly Kafkaesque experience.

To avoid major hassles, do your homework before you buy. Talk to wineries, shipping companies, and the companies below about whether they can ship. Be skeptical of any winery that tells you it can ship to non-reciprocal states—if they run into problems, you'll never get your wine. Find out if you can order the wine on the Internet through a wine e-commerce site. If you have to find a shipping company yourself, keep in mind that it's technically illegal to box your own wine and send it to a non-reciprocal state; the shippers could lose their license, and you could lose your wine. However, if you do get stuck shipping illegally (not that I'm recommending you do that), you might want to disguise your box and head to a post office, UPS, or other shipping company outside of the Wine Country area; it's far less obvious that you're shipping wine from, say, Vallejo or San Francisco than from Napa Valley.

Mail Boxes Etc., 3212 Jefferson St. in the Grape Yard Shopping Center, Napa (© **707/259-1398**), claims to pack and ship anything anywhere. Rates for a case of wine to Los Angeles were quoted at approximately $25 for ground shipping and $67 to New York.

The staff at **St. Helena Mailing Center,** 1241 Adams St., at Highway 29, St. Helena (© **707/963-2686**), tells us that they will pack and ship anywhere in the United States. Rates are around $21 per case for ground delivery to Los Angeles, $66 to New York. While those who live in reciprocal states insure their package for up to $100, the Mailing Center does not insure packages shipped to non-reciprocal states. However, it's no big deal; each bottle is packed in Styrofoam and should make it home without a problem.

In Sonoma, the **Wine Exchange of Sonoma,** 452 First St. E., between East Napa and East Spain streets (© **707/938-1794**), will ship your wine, but you must buy an equal amount of the same wine at the store (which they assured us would be in stock, and probably at a better rate). Another branch of **Mail Boxes Etc.,** 19229 Sonoma Hwy., at Verano Street (© **707/935-3438**), claims they will ship your wine to any state.

of the valley, but if you do veer off the highway, you'll be surprised to discover a small but burgeoning community of 72,585 residents and some of the most affordable accommodations in the area. It is also in the process of gentrification, thanks to (relatively) affordable housing, a charming old-fashioned downtown, and new restaurants and attractions like Copia: The American Center for Wine,

Food & the Arts. Heading north on either Highway 29 or the Silverado Trail leads you to Napa's wineries and the more quintessential Wine Country atmosphere of vineyards and wide-open country views.

The biggest new attraction in Napa Valley, **Copia: The American Center for Wine, Food & the Arts** ⚘, 500 First St. (© **707/259-1600**), opened at the end of 2001 with a mission to explore how wine and food influence our culture. This $50 million multifaceted facility, chaired by Robert Mondavi, tackles the topic in myriad ways, including visual arts à la rotating exhibits, vegetable and herb gardens, culinary demonstrations, wine classes, concerts, and opportunities to dine and drink on the premises. Day passes include entrance into the building and gardens, exhibitions, tours, and free 30-minute introductory classes. More advanced food, wine, garden, and art classes cost extra. A cafe offers gourmet picnic items, while the adjoining restaurant, Julia's Kitchen, named after Chef Child, is a more formal French-California affair; do make reservations for the restaurant as it's bound to be busy. Admission is $13 for adults, $10 for students and seniors 65 and over, and $7.50 for children ages 6 to 12. The center is open Thursday through Monday from 10am to 5pm in the fall and winter; and Monday, Tuesday, and Thursday from 10am to 5pm, Friday through Sunday from 10am to 9pm in the spring and summer.

Anyone with an appreciation for art absolutely must visit the **di Rosa Preserve,** which through a private tour explores the collection and 53-acre grounds of Rene and Veronica di Rosa, who have been collecting contemporary American art for more than 40 years. Their world-renowned collection features over 1,500 works in all media by more than 600 Greater Bay Area artists. Their treasures are displayed practically everywhere, from along the shores of their 30-acre lake to each nook and cranny of their century-old winery-turned-residence, adjoining building, two additional galleries, and gardens. It's located at 5200 Sonoma Hwy. (Calif. 121/12). Visits are by appointment only, when a maximum of 25 guests are guided through the preserve. Each tour lasts 2 to 2½ hours and costs $12 per person. Call © **707/226-5991** for reservations.

Antiques hounds should plan to spend at least an hour at **Red Hen's** co-op collection of antiques. You'll find everything from baseball cards to living-room sets, and prices are remarkably affordable. You can't miss this enormous red-barn–style building at 5091 St. Helena Hwy., on Calif. 29 at Oak Knoll Avenue West (© **707/257-0822**). It's open daily from 10am to 5:30pm.

South of downtown Napa, 1⅓ miles east of Calif. 29 on Calif. 12, is the **Chardonnay Golf Club** (© **707/257-8950**), a challenging 36-hole land-links golf complex with first-class service. There are three nines of similar challenge, all starting at the clubhouse so that you can play the 18 of your choice. You pay just one fee, which makes you a member for the day. Privileges include the use of a golf cart, the practice range (including a bucket of balls), and services usually found only at a private club. Starting times can be reserved up to 2 weeks in advance. Greens fees (including mandatory cart and practice balls) are $70 Monday through Friday, $90 weekends and holidays; at 2pm, fees go down to $45 and $60, respectively, and at 4pm they drop to $35. Limited space is available to play the private course, which goes for $125 per person.

Artesa Vineyards & Winery _Finds_ Views, modern architecture, seclusion, and region-specific pinot-noir flights are the reasons this is one of my favorite stops. Arrive on a day when the wind is blowing less than 10 mph and the fountains are captivating; they automatically shut off with higher winds. Inside the cescue-grass covered winery is a very tasteful gift shop, a room outlining history and details on the Carneros region, and a long bar where $2 tastes or $6 flights include everything from chardonnays and pinot noirs to sauvignon blanc, cabernet sauvignon, zinfandel, and sparkling wine. Sorry, but their permits don't allow for picnicking. To find the winery, turn north on Dealy Lane from Old Sonoma Road off Highway 12/121 and turn right on Henry Road.

1345 Henry Rd., Napa. ℂ **707/224-1668**. www.artesawinery.com. Daily 10am–5pm; tours daily at 11am and 2pm.

The Hess Collection ★★ *Finds*   No place in the valley brings together art and wine better than this combination winery and art gallery on the side of Mount Veeder. Swiss art collector Donald Hess acquired the old Christian Brothers Winery in 1978; along with producing wine, he also funded a huge restoration and expansion project to honor wine and the fine arts. The result is a working winery interspersed with gloriously lit rooms that exhibit his truly stunning art collection; the free self-guided tour takes you through these galleries as it introduces you to the winemaking process.

For a $3 tasting fee, you can sample the winery's current cabernet and chardonnay as well as one other featured wine. If you want to take some with you, by-the-bottle prices start at $9.95 for the second-label Hess select brand, while most other selections range from $15 to $35. The only downside: Staff can be stuffy.

4411 Redwood Rd., Napa. ℂ **707/255-1144**. www.hesscollection.com. Daily 10am–4pm. Closed 1st week of Jan. From Hwy. 29 N, exit at Redwood Rd. W and follow Redwood Rd. for 6½ miles.

Trefethen Vineyards   Listed on the National Register of Historic Places, the vineyard's main building was constructed in 1886 and remains Napa's only wooden, gravity-powered winery. The bucolic brick courtyard is surrounded by oak and cork trees, and free wine samples are distributed in the brick-floored, wood-beamed tasting room. Although Trefethen is one of the valley's oldest wineries, it did not produce its first chardonnay until 1973—but thank goodness it did. Its whites and reds are both award winners and a pleasure to the palate.

1160 Oak Knoll Ave. (E of Hwy. 29), Napa. ℂ **707/255-7700**. www.trefethen.com. Daily 10am–4:30pm. Tours by appointment only.

Stag's Leap Wine Cellars   Founded in 1972, Stag's Leap shocked the oenological world in 1976 when its 1973 cabernet won first place over French wines in a Parisian blind tasting. For $5 per person, you can be the judge of the winery's current releases, or you can fork over another fiver for one of Stag's Leap's best-known wines, Cabernet Sauvignon Cask 23 (when available). The 1-hour tour runs through everything from the vineyard to production facilities, tasting, and their new caves.

5766 Silverado Trail, Napa. ℂ **707/944-2020**. www.cask23.com. Daily 10am–4:30pm. Tours by appointment only. From Hwy. 29, go E on Trancas St. or Oak Knoll Ave., then N to the cellars.

YOUNTVILLE
70 miles N of San Francisco

The town of Yountville was founded by the first white American to settle in the valley, George Calvert Yount. While it lacks the small-town charm of neighboring St. Helena and Calistoga—primarily because it has no rambunctious main street—it does serve as a good base for exploring the valley, and it's home to a handful of excellent wineries, inns, boutiques, and a small stretch of fab restaurants, including world-renowned The French Laundry.

Riding the Napa Valley Wine Train

You don't have to worry about drinking and driving if you tour the Wine Country aboard the **Napa Valley Wine Train,** a rolling restaurant that makes a leisurely 3-hour journey through the vineyards of Napa, Yountville, Oakville, Rutherford, and St. Helena. You'll love riding in the vintage-style cars, each finished with polished mahogany paneling and etched-glass partitions.

During the trip, optional gourmet meals are served complete with all the finery—damask linen, bone china, silver flatware, and etched crystal. The fixed menus consist of three to five courses. In addition to the dining rooms, the train pulls a Wine Tasting Car, a Deli Car, and four 50-passenger lounges. One trip offers an optional stop in Yountville and at the Grgich Winery in Rutherford for a tour of the barreling, bottling, and winemaking process, followed by a tasting.

The train departs from the **McKinstry Street Depot,** 1275 McKinstry St. (near 1st St. and Soscol Ave.), Napa (✆ **800/427-4124** or 707/253-2111; www.winetrain.com). Train fare and travel packages range from $35 for a daytime ride without a meal to $99 for a multi-course gourmet wine dinner. Departures are Monday through Friday at 11:30am, and Saturday, Sunday, and holidays at 9am (brunch), 12:30pm, and 6:30pm. (The schedule is reduced Jan–Feb.) *Tip:* Sit on the west side for the best views. Fair warning: Photos are taken before you board (to be sold to you later), so if you want this moment captured on film, be prepared.

Domaine Chandon ★★ *(Finds)* Founded in 1973 by French champagne house Moët et Chandon, the valley's most renowned sparkling winery raises to the grand occasion with truly elegant grounds and atmosphere. Here quintessentially manicured gardens showcase locally made sculpture, guests linger—their glasses fizzing with bubbly—under the patio's umbrella shade, and in the restaurant diners indulge in a formal French-inspired meal. If you can pull yourself away from the Salon's bubbly (sold in tastings for $8–$12 and served with complimentary bread and spread), the comprehensive tour of the facilities is interesting, very informative, and friendly. There's a shop, a small gallery housing artifacts from Moët et Chandon that depict the history of champagnes, and revolving art exhibits (available for purchase), which in 2001 included watercolor works of French artist Guy Buffet. *Note:* The restaurant tends to require reservations.

1 California Dr. (at Hwy. 29), Yountville. ✆ **707/944-2280.** www.chandon.com. Jan–Mar Wed–Sun 10am–6pm; Apr–Dec daily 10am–6pm. Free tours every hr. on the hr. 11am–5pm.

OAKVILLE
68 miles N of San Francisco

Driving farther north on the St. Helena Highway (Calif. 29) brings you to the Oakville Cross Road and the famous picnic-fare favorite **Oakville Grocery Co.** (see "Gourmet Picnics, Napa-Style" on p. 187).

PlumpJack Winery If most wineries are like a traditional and refined Brooks Brothers suit, PlumpJack stands out as the Todd Oldham of wine tasting: chic, colorful, a little wild, and popular with a young and old crowd. Like the franchise's PlumpJack restaurant and wine shop in San Francisco and its resort in Tahoe, this playfully medieval winery is a welcome diversion from the same old, same old. But with Getty bucks behind what was once Villa Mt. Eden winery, the budget covers far more than just atmosphere: There's some serious winemaking going on here, too. For $5 you can sample the cabernet, sangiovese, and chardonnay—each an impressive product from a winery that's only been open to the public since mid-1997. The few vintages for sale currently range from $28 to $50. There are no tours or picnic spots, but this refreshingly stylized and friendly facility will make you want to hang out for a while nonetheless.

620 Oakville Cross Rd. (just W of the Silverado Trail), Oakville. © 707/945-1220. www.plumpjack.com. Daily 10am–4pm.

Robert Mondavi Winery ⭐ *Finds*   At Mondavi's magnificent mission-style facility, almost every variable in the winemaking process is controlled by computer (fascinating to watch!). After the tour, you can taste the results in selected current wines, free of charge, but anyone really interested in learning more about wine should explore their extensive array of more in-depth tours and tastings offered for a fee and by appointment. You can also taste without taking the tour, but it will cost you: The Rose Garden (an outdoor tasting area open in summer) offers an etched Reidel glass and three wines for $10; tastings in the ToKalon Room go from $3 for a 3-ounce taste to $30 for a rare library wine.

 Hot-Air Ballooning over the Valley

Admit it—floating across lush green pastures in a hot-air balloon is something you've always dreamed of doing. Well, here's your chance, because believe it or not, Napa Valley is the busiest hot-air balloon "flight corridor" in the *world*. Northern California's temperate weather allows for ballooning year-round, and on summer weekends in the valley, it's a rare day when you don't see at least one of the colorful airships floating above the vineyards.

Trips usually depart early in the morning, when the air is cooler and the balloons have better lift. (**Note:** When weather conditions aren't optimal, balloon companies often launch flights from locations up to an hour's drive outside of the valley. You won't know until the morning of the flight, but you should be able to cancel on the spot if you desire.) Flight paths vary with the direction and speed of the changing breezes, so "chase" crews on the ground must follow the balloons to their undetermined destinations. Most flights last about an hour and end with a traditional champagne celebration and breakfast. Reservations are required and should be made far in advance. Prices run close to $200 per person for the basic package, which includes shuttle service from your hotel. Wedding, wine tasting, picnic, and lodging packages are also available. For more information or reservations, call Napa's **Bonaventura Balloon Company** (© 800/FLY-NAPA) or **Adventures Aloft** (© 800/944-4408 or 707/944-4408; www.nvaloft. com), Napa Valley's oldest hot-air-balloon company.

Fridays feature an "Art of Wine and Food" program, which includes a slide presentation on wine history, a tour, and a three-course luncheon with wine pairing; the cost is around $65, and you must reserve in advance. The Vineyard Room usually features an art show; in summer, the winery also hosts some great outdoor jazz concerts. Call to learn about upcoming events.

7801 St. Helena Hwy. (Hwy. 29), Oakville. ⓒ **800/MONDAVI** or 707/226-1395. www.robertmondavi winery.com. May–Oct daily 9:30am–5:30pm; Nov–Apr daily 9:30am–4:30pm. Reservations recommended for guided tour; book a week ahead, especially for weekend tours.

Opus One   A visit to Opus One is a very serious and stately affair. Robert Mondavi and Baroness Phillipe de Rothschild are to thank for this winery, which caters to one ultra-premium wine offered here for a whopping $25 per 4-ounce taste (and a painful $140 per bottle). Architecture buffs in particular will appreciate the tour, which takes in both the impressive Greco-Roman-meets-20th-century building and the no-holds-barred ultra-high-tech production and aging facilities.

Wine lovers happily fork over the cash for a taste: It's likely to be one of the most memorable reds you'll ever sample. Grab your glass and head to the redwood rooftop deck to enjoy the view—definitely the most kicked-back spot in the whole place!

7900 St. Helena Hwy. (Hwy. 29), Oakville. ⓒ **707/944-9442**. www.opusonewinery.com. Daily 10:30am–3:30pm. Tours by appointment only; in high season, book a month in advance.

RUTHERFORD
3 miles N of Oakville

If you so much as blink after Oakville, you're likely to overlook Rutherford, the next small town that borders on St. Helena. Rutherford has its share of spectacular wineries, but you won't see most of them while driving along Calif. 29.

Swanson Vineyards & Winery ⭐ _Finds_   The valley's most posh and unique wine tasting is yours with a reservation and $25 fee at Swanson. Here the shtick is more like a private party, which they call a "_Sa_-lon." You and up to seven other guests sit at a centerpiece round table in a vibrant coral parlor adorned with huge paintings, sea shells, and a fireplace, and take in the uncommonly refined yet whimsical atmosphere. The table's set more for a dinner party than a tasting, with Reidel stemware, slivers of a fine cheese or two, crackers, and one superb chocolate Alexis ganache-filled bonbon, which you will be glad to know can be purchased on the premises. Over the course of the hour or more snack-and-sip event, a winery host will pour four wines and discuss the history and fine points of each. You're likely to be in store for a bright pinot grigio, old vine syrah, and hearty Alexis, their signature cab-syrah blend. But just as important to the experience is the everyday conversation and making of new friends, which almost invariably occurs since the experience puts everyone in such a festive mood. Definitely a must-do for those who don't mind spending the money.

1271 Manley Lane, Rutherford. ⓒ **707/967-3500**. www.swansonvineyards.com. Appointments available Tues–Sun 10am–5pm.

Sawyer Cellars _Finds_   The most attractive thing about Sawyer, aside from its clean and tasty wines, is its ability to embody a dedication to extremely high quality and maintain humble, accommodating attitude. Step one foot into the simple restored 1920s barn to see what I mean. Whatever you ask, the tasting-room host will answer. Whatever your request, they do their best to accommodate. Want to picnic on the back patio overlooking the vineyards? Be their guest.

Like to participate in crush? Come on over and get your hands dirty. Reserve their charming wine library for a private luncheon? Pay a minimal fee and make yourself at home. Here you can tour the property on a little tram or learn more about winemaker Brad Warner, who spent 30 years at Mondavi before embarking on this exclusive endeavor. Or simply drop in and spend $5 to taste delicious estate-made wines: sauvignon blanc, merlot, cabernet sauvignon, and Meritage ($18–$38 for current releases), which some argue are worth twice the price. With only 3,500 cases total production and a friendly attitude, this is a rare treat.

8350 St. Helena Hwy. (Hwy. 29), Rutherford. © 707/963-1980. www.sawyercellars.com. Mon and Wed–Sat 10am–5pm, Sun and Tues by appointment. Tours by appointment only.

St. Supéry Winery The outside may look like a modern corporate office building, but inside you'll find a functional and welcoming winery that encourages first-time wine tasters to learn more about oenology. On the self-guided tour, you can wander through the demonstration vineyard and learn about growing techniques. Inside, kids gravitate toward "SmellaVision," an interactive display that teaches you how to identify different wine ingredients. Adjoining is the Atkinson House, which chronicles more than 100 years of winemaking history. For $5, you'll get lifetime tasting privileges, and though they probably won't be pouring their ever-popular Moscato dessert wine, the sauvignon blanc, chardonnay, and cab flow freely. Prices range from $15 for a bottle of 1999 sauvignon blanc to a pricey $85 for the 1997 reserve cab, but the average bottle sells for just a little more than $20. In the tasting room, a large barn-like space, the hospitable hosts pour a $5 or $10 sampling; both include a keepsake wineglass.

8300 St. Helena Hwy. (Hwy. 29), Rutherford. © 800/588-0298 or 707/963-5221. www.stsupery.com. Daily 10am–4:30pm. Tours by appointment only.

Niebaum-Coppola ★ *Finds* Hollywood meets Napa Valley at Francis Ford Coppola's historic winery (pronounced *Nee*-bomb *Coh*-pa-la), previously Inglenook Vineyards. Coppola bought and restored the beautiful 1880s ivy-draped stone winery and surrounding property to its historic dimensions, gilding it with the glitz and glamour you'd expect from Tinseltown in the process. On display are Academy Awards and memorabilia from his movies.

In spite of all the Hollywood hullabaloo, wine is not forgotten. Available for tasting are a Rubicon (a blend of 3 grapes, aged for more than 5 years), cabernet franc, merlot, chardonnay, zinfandel, and others, all made from organically grown grapes and ranging from around $12 to more than $80. There's also a wide variety of expensive and affordable gift items. The steep $7.50-per-person tasting fee might make you wonder whether a movie is included in the price—it's not, but you'll at least get to keep the souvenir glass. And at $20 a pop for the château and garden tour, you've gotta wonder whether you're *funding* his next film. But the grounds are indeed spectacular, and the 1½-hour journey includes a private tasting and glass.

Regardless, do visit the grounds—they're absolutely stunning, it costs nothing to stroll, and you're welcome to picnic at any of the designated garden sites.

1991 St. Helena Hwy. (Hwy. 29), Rutherford. © 707/968-1100. www.niebaum-coppola.com. Daily 10am–5pm (until 6pm Memorial Day to Labor Day). Tours daily at 10:30am and 2:30pm.

Beaulieu Vineyard Bordeaux native Georges de Latour founded the third-oldest continuously operating winery in Napa Valley in 1900—and, with the help of legendary oenologist André Tchelistcheff, produced world-class, award-winning wines that have been served by every president of the United States since Franklin D. Roosevelt. The brick-and-redwood tasting room isn't much to look at, but with Beaulieu's (pronounced *Bowl*-you) stellar reputation, they have no need to impress visually. They do, however, offer tastings for $5 as well as a variety of bottles for under $20. The Private Reserve Tasting Room offers a flight of reserve wines to taste for $25—but if you want to take a bottle to go, it may cost as much as $130. A free tour explains the winemaking process and the vineyard's history.

1960 St. Helena Hwy. (Hwy. 29), Rutherford. © 707/967-5230. www.bvwine.com. Daily 10am–5pm. Tours daily 11am–4pm.

ST. HELENA
73 miles N of San Francisco

This quiet, attractive little town, located 17 miles north of Napa on Calif. 29, is home to a slew of beautiful old homes as well as first-rate restaurants and accommodations. The former Seventh Day Adventist village manages to maintain a pseudo Old West feel while simultaneously catering to upscale shoppers with deep pockets—hence **Vanderbilt and Company,** 1429 Main St., between Adams and Pine streets (© 707/963-1010), purveyor of gorgeous cookware and fine housewares; it's open daily from 9:30am to 5:30pm.

Shopaholics won't be able to avoid at least one sharp turn off Calif. 29 for a stop at the **St. Helena Premium Outlets,** located 2 miles north of downtown St. Helena (© 707/963-7282), whose stores include Donna Karan, Coach, Movado, London Fog, and more; open daily from 10am to 6pm.

One last favorite stop: **Napa Valley Olive Oil Manufacturing Company,** 835 Charter Oak Rd. (© 707/963-4173), at the end of the road behind Tra Vigne restaurant. This tiny market presses and bottles its own oils and sells them at a fraction of the price you'll pay elsewhere. They also have an extensive selection of Italian cooking ingredients, imported snacks, and excellent deals on exotic mushrooms.

If you'd like to go **bicycling,** the quieter northern end of the valley is an ideal place to rent a bike and ride the Silverado Trail. **St. Helena Cyclery,** 1156 Main St. (© 707/963-7736), rents bikes for $7 per hour or $25 a day, including rear rack and picnic bag.

V. Sattui Winery *Kids*   At this combination winery and enormous gourmet deli (pronounced Vee Sa-*too*-ee), you can fill up on wine, paté, and cheese samples without ever reaching for your pocketbook. The gourmet store stocks more than 200 cheeses, sandwich meats, breads, exotic salads, and delicious desserts, such as a white chocolate cheesecake.

Meanwhile, the long wine bar in the back offers everything from chardonnay, sauvignon blanc, Riesling, cabernet, and zinfandel to a tasty Madeira and a muscat dessert wine. Their wines aren't distributed, so if you taste something you simply must have, buy it. (If you buy a case, ask to talk with a manager, who'll give you access to the less crowded, more exclusive private tasting room.) Wine prices start around $9, with many in the $13 range; reserves top out at around $75. V. Sattui's expansive, lively, and grassy picnic facilities make this a favorite for families. ***Note:*** To use the facilities, food and wine must be purchased here.

1111 White Lane (at Hwy. 29), St. Helena. © 707/963-7774. www.vsattui.com. Winter daily 9am–5pm; summer daily 9am–6pm.

Joseph Phelps Vineyards *★*   Visitors interested in intimate, comprehensive tours and a knockout tasting should schedule a tour at this stellar winery. The winery was founded in 1973 and has since become a major player in both the region and the worldwide wine market. Phelps himself is attributed with a long list of valley firsts, including launching the syrah varietal in the valley and extending the 1970s Berkeley food revolution (led by Alice Waters) up to the Wine Country via his store, the Oakville Grocery Co. (see "Gourmet Picnics, Napa-Style" on p. 187). The tour and tasting are only available via reservation, and the location—a quick and unmarked turn off the Silverado Trail in Spring Valley—is impossible to find unless you're looking for it.

Those in the know come to this modern, state-of-the-art winery and find an air of seriousness that hangs heavier than harvest grapes. Fortunately, the mood lightens as the well-educated tour guide explains the details of what you're tasting while pouring samples of five to six wines, which may include Riesling, sauvignon blanc, Gewürztraminer, syrah, merlot, zin, and cab. Unfortunately, some wines are so popular that they sell out quickly; come late in the season and you may not be able to taste or buy them. The three excellently located picnic tables, on the terrace overlooking the valley, are available by reservation.

Taplin Rd. (off the Silverado Trail), P.O. Box 1031, St. Helena. **©** **800/707-5789.** www.jpvwines.com. Mon–Sat 9am–5pm; Sun 9am–4pm. Tours and tastings by appointment only; tastings $5 per person, $10 per person for reserve tastings.

Prager Winery & Port Works If you want a real down-home, off-the-beaten-track experience, Prager's can't be beat. Turn the corner from Sutter Home and roll into the small gravel parking lot. Pull open the creaky old wooden door, pass the oak barrels, and you'll quickly come upon the clapboard tasting room. Most days, your host will be Jim Prager himself, who's a sort of modern-day Santa Claus in both looks and demeanor, but you won't have to sit on his lap for your wish to come true. Just fork over $5 (refundable with purchase) and he'll pour you samples of his delicious $25 Sweet Claire dessert wine, a late-harvest Johannisberg Riesling, the recently released 10-year-old port (which costs $45 per bottle and has won various awards), and a few other yummy selections. Also available is "Prager Chocolate Drizzle," a chocolate liqueur that tops ice creams and other desserts.

1281 Lewelling Lane (just W of Hwy. 29, behind Sutter Home), St. Helena. **©** **800/969-PORT** or 707/963-7678. www.pragerport.com. Daily 10:30am–4:30pm.

Beringer Vineyards Follow the line of cars just north of St. Helena's business district to Beringer Vineyards, where everyone stops at the remarkable Rhine House to taste wine and view the hand-dug tunnels carved out of the mountainside. Founded in 1876 by brothers Jacob and Frederick, this is the oldest continuously operating winery in the Napa Valley—it was open even during Prohibition, when Beringer kept afloat by making "sacramental" wines. While their white zinfandel is still the winery's most popular nationwide seller, their reserve chardonnay is regularly high-ranked among top California wines. Three-dollar tastings of current vintages are soon to be conducted in new facilities, but for now are held in the gift shop, where there's also a large selection of bottles for less than $20. Reserve wines are available on the second floor of the Rhine House for a fee of $2 to $10 per taste.

2000 Main St. (Hwy. 29), St. Helena. **©** **707/963-7115.** www.beringervineyards.com. Off-season daily 9:30am–5pm (last tour 4pm, last tasting 4:30pm); summer 9:30am–6pm (last tour 5pm, last tasting 5:30pm). $5 45-min. tours every 30 min. (free for anyone under 21 and accompanied by an adult).

Charles Krug Winery Founded in 1861, Krug was the first winery built in the valley and is today owned by the family of Peter Mondavi (yes, Robert is his brother). It's worth paying your respects here with a $3 tour, which takes just under an hour and encompasses a walk through the historical redwood Italianate wine cellar, built in 1874, as well as the vineyards, where you'll learn more about grapes and varietals. The tour ends with a tasting in the retail center. But you don't have to tour to taste: Just stop by and fork over $3 to sip current releases, $5 to sample reserves; you'll also get a souvenir glass. On the grounds are picnic facilities with umbrella-shaded tables overlooking vineyards or the historic wine cellar. At press time, tours were not being given due to renovations, so call to confirm before arriving for a tour.

2800 St. Helena Hwy. (just N of the tunnel of trees at the northern end of St. Helena), St. Helena. (C) 707/963-5057. www.charleskrug.com. Daily 10:30am–5pm. Tours daily at 11:30am, 1:30, and 3:30pm.

CALISTOGA
81 miles N of San Francisco

The last tourist town in Napa Valley was named by Sam Brannan, entrepreneur extraordinaire and California's first millionaire. After making a bundle supplying miners during the gold rush, he went on to take advantage of the natural geothermal springs at the north end of the Napa Valley by building a hotel and spa here in 1859. Flubbing up a speech in which he compared this natural California wonder to New York State's Saratoga Springs resort, he serendipitously coined the name "Calistoga," and it stuck. Today, this small, simple resort town with 5,190-plus residents and an old-time main street (no building along the 6-block stretch is more than two stories high) is popular with city folk who come here to unwind. Calistoga is a great place to relax and indulge in mineral waters, mud baths, Jacuzzis, massages, and, of course, wine. The vibe is more casual—and a little groovier—than you'll find in neighboring towns to the south.

   Old Faithful Geyser of California, 1299 Tubbs Lane ((C) 707/942-6463), is one of only three "old faithful" geysers in the world. It's been blowing off steam at regular intervals for as long as anyone can remember. The 350°F (176°C) water spews out to a height of about 60 feet every 40 minutes, day and night (varying with natural influences such as barometric pressure, the moon, tides, and tectonic stresses). The performance lasts about a minute, and you can watch the show as many times as you wish. Bring along a picnic lunch to munch on between spews. An exhibit hall, gift shop, and snack bar are open every day. Admission is $6 for adults, $5 for seniors, $2 for children ages 6 to 12, and free for children under 6. Open daily from 9am to 6pm (to 5pm in winter). To get here, follow the signs from downtown Calistoga; it's between Calif. 29 and Calif. 128.

   You won't see thousands of trees turned into stone, but you'll still find many interesting petrified specimens at the **Petrified Forest,** 4100 Petrified Forest Rd. ((C) 707/942-6667). Volcanic ash blanketed this area after the eruption of Mount St. Helena three million years ago. As a result, you'll find redwoods that have turned to rock through the slow infiltration of silicas and other minerals, as well as petrified seashells, clams, and marine life, indicating that water covered this area even before the redwood forest. Admission is $5 for adults, $4 for seniors and youths 12 to 17, $2 for children 5 to 11, and free for children under 4. Open daily from 10am to 5:30pm (to 4:30pm in winter). Heading north from Calistoga on Calif. 128, turn left onto Petrified Forest Road, just past Lincoln Street.

   Cycling enthusiasts can rent bikes from **Getaway Adventures BHK** (Biking, Hiking, and Kayaking), 1117 Lincoln Ave. ((C) 800/499-BIKE or 707/

763-3040; www.getawayadventures.com). Full-day tours cost $105 and include lunch and a visit to four or five wineries; downhill cruises (about half the price) are available for people who hate to pedal. Bike rental without a tour costs $9 an hour, $20 per half day, or $28 per day.

If you like horses and venturing through cool, misty forests, then $40 will seem like a bargain for a 1½-hour ride with a friendly tour guide from **Napa Valley Trail Rides** (✆ **707/996-8566;** www.napasonomatrailrides.com). After you've been saddled and schooled in the basics of horse handling at the stable, you'll be led on a leisurely stroll (with the occasional trot thrown in for excitement) through beautiful Bothe–Napa Valley State Park, located off Calif. 29 near Calistoga. Also offered are a Western Barbecue Ride, Sunset Ride, Full-Moon Ride, and Gourmet Boxed Lunch Ride & Winery Tour.

Frank Family Vineyards ⭐ *Finds* "Wine dudes" Bob, Dennis, and Rich will do practically anything to maintain their rightfully self-proclaimed reputation as the "friendliest winery in the valley." The name may have changed from Kornell Champagne Cellars to Frank-Rombauer to Frank Family, but the vibe's remained constant; it's all about down-home, friendly fun. No muss, no fuss, no intimidation factor. At Frank Family, you're part of their family—no joke. They'll greet you like a long lost relative and serve you all the bubbly you want (four to six varieties: Brut, blanc de blanc, blanc de noir, and extra-dry reserve, ranging from $20–$70 a bottle). Still-wine lovers can slip into the equally casual back room to sample chardonnay and a very well received cabernet sauvignon. Be sure to embark on the tour of the oldest champagne cellar in the region and ask about Marie Antoinette's relationship with glassware. Behind the tasting room is a choice picnic area, situated under the oaks and overlooking the vineyards.

1091 Larkmead Lane (just off the Silverado Trail), Calistoga. ✆ **707/942-0859.** Daily 10am–5pm. Tours by appointment only.

Schramsberg *Finds* This 200-acre champagne estate, a landmark once frequented by Robert Louis Stevenson, has a wonderful old-world feel and is one of my all-time favorite places to explore. Schramsberg is the label that presidents serve when toasting dignitaries from around the globe, and there's plenty of historic memorabilia in the front room to prove it. But the real mystique begins when you enter the champagne caves, which wind 2½ miles (the longest in North America, they say) and were partly hand-carved by Chinese laborers in the 1800s. The caves have an authentic Tom Sawyer ambience, complete with dangling cobwebs and seemingly endless passageways; you can't help but feel you're on an adventure. The comprehensive, unintimidating tour ends in a charming tasting room, where you'll sit around a big table and sample several surprisingly varied selections of bubbly. Tasting prices are a bit dear at $10 per person, but it's money well spent. Note, however, that tastings are only offered to those who take the free tour, and you must reserve a spot in advance. The only bummer: They're not stellar at returning phone calls if you leave a message on the machine, and it's even worse with e-mail responses.

1400 Schramsberg Rd. (off Hwy. 29), Calistoga. ✆ **707/942-2414.** www.schramsberg.com. Daily 10am–4pm. Tours and tastings by appointment only.

Sterling Vineyards *Kids* No, you don't need climbing shoes to reach this dazzling white Mediterranean-style winery, perched 300 feet up on a rocky knoll. Just hand over $6 and you'll arrive via aerial tram, which offers unparalleled bucolic views along the way. If you've been here before, even before embarking you'll notice major changes due to a complete renovation in 2001.

Once you're back on land, follow the self-guided tour (the most comprehensive in the entire Wine Country) of the winemaking process. The winery produces more than 200,000 cases per year. If you're not into taking the tram or you have kids in tow, visit anyway; there's an elevator that can take you to the tasting room, and kids get a goodie bag and a hearty welcome (a rarity at wineries). Samples at the panoramic tasting room are included in the tram fare. Expect to pay anywhere from $14 to $100 for a souvenir bottle ($20 is the average).

1111 Dunaweal Lane (off Hwy. 29, just S of Calistoga), Calistoga. ℂ **707/942-3344**. www.sterling vineyards.com. Daily 10:30am–4:30pm.

Clos Pegase *Finds*   Renowned architect Michael Graves designed this incredible oasis, which integrates art, 20,000 square feet of aging caves, and a luxurious hilltop private home on its 450 acres. Viewing the art here is as much the point as tasting the wines, which cost $2.50 to $5 per three premium wines. Bottles cost from $13 for the 2000 Vin Gris Merlot to as much as $75 for the 1997 Hommage Artist Series Reserve, an extremely limited blend of the winery's finest lots of cabernet sauvignon and merlot. The grounds at Clos Pegase (pronounced *Clo* Pay-*goss*) feature an impressive sculpture garden as well as scenic picnic spots.

1060 Dunaweal Lane (off Hwy. 29 or the Silverado Trail), Calistoga. ℂ **707/942-4981**. www. clospegase.com. Daily 10:30am–5pm. Tours daily at 11am and 2pm.

WHERE TO STAY
Accommodations here run the gamut—from motels and B&Bs to world-class luxury retreats—and all are easily accessible from the main highway. While I recommend shacking up in the more romantically pastoral areas such as St. Helena, there's no question you're going to find better deals in the towns of Napa or laid-back Calistoga.

Keep in mind that during the high season—between June and November—most hotels charge peak rates and sell out completely on weekends; many have a 2-night minimum. If you need help organizing your Wine Country vacation,

Find the New You—in a Calistoga Mud Bath

The one thing you should do while you're in Calistoga is what people have been doing here for the last 150 years: Take a mud bath. The natural baths are composed of local volcanic ash, imported peat, and naturally boiling mineral hot-springs water, all mulled together to produce a thick mud that simmers at a temperature of about 104°F (40°C). Follow your soak in the mud with a warm mineral-water shower, a whirlpool bath, a visit to the steam room, and a relaxing blanket-wrap. The outcome: a rejuvenated, revitalized, squeaky-clean new you.

Indulge yourself at any of these Calistoga spas: **Dr. Wilkinson's Hot Springs,** 1507 Lincoln Ave. (ℂ 707/942-4102); **Golden Haven Hot Springs Spa,** 1713 Lake St. (ℂ 707/942-6793); **Calistoga Spa Hot Springs,** 1006 Washington St. (ℂ 707/942-6269); **Calistoga Village Inn & Spa,** 1880 Lincoln Ave. (ℂ 707/942-0991); **Indian Springs Resort,** 1712 Lincoln Ave. (ℂ 707/942-4913); **Nance's Hot Springs,** 1614 Lincoln Ave. (ℂ 707/942-6211); or **Roman Spa Motel,** 1300 Washington St. (ℂ 707/942-4441).

> ## *Tips* Reliable Chains
>
> Wherever tourist dollars are to be had, you're sure to find big hotels with familiar names catering to independent vacationers, business travelers, and groups. **Embassy Suites**, 1075 California Blvd., Napa, CA 94559 (© **800/ 362-2779** or 707/253-9540; www.embassysuites.com), offers 205 of its usual two-room suites. Each has a kitchenette, coffeemaker, modem capability, and two TVs; there are indoor and outdoor pools and a restaurant. Rates range from $190 to $280 and include cooked-to-order breakfast. The 191-room **Napa Valley Marriott**, 3425 Solano Ave., Napa, CA 94558 (© **800/ 228-9290** or 707/253-7433; www.marriott.com), has lighted tennis courts, an exercise room, a heated outdoor pool and spa, and two restaurants; rates range from $154 to $320.

contact one of the following companies: **Accommodation Referral Bed & Breakfast Exchange** (© **800/240-8466,** 800/499-8466 in California, or 707/965-3400), which also represents hotels and inns; **Bed & Breakfast Inns of Napa Valley** (© **707/944-4444**), an association of B&Bs that provides inn descriptions and makes reservations; or **Napa Valley Reservations Unlimited** (© **800/251-NAPA** or 707/252-1985), which is also a source for everything from hot-air balloon and glider rides to wine-tasting tours by limousine.

VERY EXPENSIVE

Auberge du Soleil ★★★ This spectacular Relais & Châteaux property, set high above the Napa Valley in a 33-acre olive grove, is quiet, indulgent, and luxuriously romantic. The Mediterranean-style rooms are large enough to get lost in—and you might want to once you discover all the amenities. The bathtub alone—an enormous hot tub with a skylight overhead—will entice you to grab a glass of complimentary California red and settle in for a while. A wood-burning fireplace is surrounded by oversize, cushy furniture—the ideal place to relax and listen to CDs (the stereo comes with a few selections, and there's also a VCR). Fresh flowers, original art, terra-cotta floors, and natural-wood and leather furnishings whisk you out of the Wine Country and into the Southwest. Each sun-washed private deck has views of the valley that are nothing less than spectacular. Those with money to burn should opt for the $2,200-per-night cottage suite; the 1,800-square-foot hideaway's got two fireplaces, two full bathrooms, a den, and a patio Jacuzzi. Now *that's* living. All guests have access to a celestial swimming pool, new exercise room, and the most fabulous spa in the Wine Country, which opened in 2001. Only guests can use the spa, but if you want to get all the romantic grandeur of Auberge, have lunch on the patio at the wonderful restaurant overlooking the valley.

180 Rutherford Hill Rd., Rutherford, CA 94573. © 800/348-5406 or 707/963-1211. Fax 707/963-8764. www.aubergedusoleil.com. 50 units. $350–$600 double. AE, DC, DISC, MC, V. From Hwy. 29 in Rutherford, turn right on Calif. 128 and go 3 miles to the Silverado Trail, turn left and head N about 200 yd. to Rutherford Hill Rd., turn right. **Amenities:** Restaurant; 3 outdoor pools ranging from hot to cold; 3 tennis courts; health club and full-service spa; sauna; steam; bike rental; concierge; secretarial services; salon; 24-hr. room service; massage; same-day laundry service and dry cleaning. *In room:* A/C, TV/VCR w/pay movies, CD player, dataport, kitchenette, minibar, fridge, coffeemaker, hair dryer, iron.

Meadowood Napa Valley ★★★ *Finds* Less reclusive than Auberge du Soleil, Meadowood is the summer camp for wealthy grown-ups. The resort, tucked away on 250 acres of pristine mountainside amidst a forest of madrone and oak trees, is quiet and exclusive enough to make you forget that busy wineries are just 10 minutes away. Rooms, furnished with American country classics, have beamed ceilings, private patios, stone fireplaces, and wilderness views; many are individual suite-lodges that are so far removed from the common areas that you must drive to get to them (lazier folks can opt for more centrally located accommodations). You can spend your days playing golf, tennis, or croquet; lounging around the pools or spa; or hiking the surrounding areas. Those who actually want to leave the property to do some wine tasting can check in with John Thoreen, the hotel's wine tutor, whose sole purpose is to help guests better understand and enjoy Napa Valley wines.

900 Meadowood Lane, St. Helena, CA 94574. ⓒ **800/458-8080** or 707/963-3646. Fax 707/963-3532. www.meadowood.com. 85 units. $360–$590 double; 1-bedroom suite from $580; 2-bedroom from $910; 3-bedroom from $1,265; 4-bedroom from $1,620. Ask about promotional offers and off-season rates. 2-night minimum stay on weekends. AE, DISC, DC, MC, V. **Amenities:** 2 restaurants; 2 large, heated outdoor pools; golf course; 7 tennis courts; 2 croquet lawns; health club and full-service spa; Jacuzzi; sauna; concierge; secretarial services; room service; same-day laundry service and dry cleaning. *In room:* A/C, TV, dataport, minibar, kitchenette in some rooms, coffeemaker, hair dryer, iron.

Napa River Inn ★★ It's not a contender compared to Meadowood and Auberge, but downtown Napa's newest and most luxurious hotel is also a lot cheaper and manages an old-world boutique feel through most of its three buildings housing 66 rooms. The main building, part of the newly renovated Napa Mill and Hatt Market, is an 1884 historic landmark. Each of the fantastically appointed rooms is exceedingly romantic with burgundy-colored walls, original brick, wood furnishings, plush fabrics, and seats in front of the gas fireplace. A gilded claw-foot tub beckons in the luxury bathroom. The newest addition is a brand-new building with bright and airy accommodations overlooking the Napa River. Less luxurious, but equally well-appointed are the nautical-themed mustard-and-brown (yuck!) colored rooms that also overlook the riverfront, but have less daylight. Extra perks abound and include complimentary vouchers to a full breakfast and evening cocktails at one of the adjoining restaurants. A small but excellent spa is located in the hotel's parking lot.

500 Main St., Napa, CA 94599. ⓒ **877/251-8500** or 707/251-8500. Fax 707/251-8504. www.napariverinn.com. 66 units. $149–$300 double. Rates include vouchers to a full breakfast and evening cocktails at 1 of the adjoining restaurants. AE, DC, DISC, MC, V. **Amenities:** Restaurant; concierge; business services; same-day laundry service and dry cleaning. *In room:* A/C, TV, CD player, dataport, coffeemaker, hair dryer, iron, safe.

Napa Valley Lodge ★★ (Finds) Many frequent visitors compare this contemporary hotel to the town's popular Vintage Inn, noting that it's even more personable and accommodating. The lodge is just off Calif. 29, though they do a good job of disguising it. The newly upgraded guest rooms are large, ultraclean, and better appointed than many in the area. Many have vaulted ceilings and 33 have fireplaces. All come with a king- or queen-size bed, wicker furnishings, robes, and either a private balcony or a patio, and all the bathrooms include a vanity area and nice tile work. The cheapest rooms are at ground level; these are smaller and get less sunlight than those on the second floor. Extras include afternoon tea and cookies in the lobby, Friday-evening wine tasting in the library, and a full champagne breakfast—with all this, it's no wonder AAA gave the Napa Valley Lodge the four-diamond award for excellence. Ask about winter discounts—they can be as much as 30%.

2230 Madison St., Yountville, CA 94599. ⓒ **800/368-2468** or 707/944-2468. Fax 707/944-9362. www.woodsidehotels.com. 55 units. $282–$585 double. Rates include champagne breakfast buffet, afternoon tea and cookies, and Fri-evening wine tasting. AE, DC, DISC, MC, V. **Amenities:** Heated outdoor pool; hot tub; redwood sauna; small exercise room; concierge. *In room:* A/C, TV w/pay movies, dataport, mini-bar, coffeemaker, hair dryer, iron.

MODERATE

Cedar Gables Inn ★★ *Finds* Innkeepers Margaret and Craig Snasdell have developed quite a following with their cozy, romantic B&B in Old Town Napa. The Victorian was built in 1892, and rooms reflect the era with rich tapestries and stunning gilded antiques. Five rooms have fireplaces; five have whirlpool tubs; and all feature queen-size brass, wooden, or iron beds. Guests meet each evening in front of the roaring fireplace in the family room for complimentary wine and cheese. At other times, it's a perfect place to cuddle up and watch the large-screen TV.

486 Coombs St., Napa, CA 94559. ✆ **800/309-7969** or 707/224-7969. Fax 707/224-4838. www. cedargablesinn.com. 9 units. $169–$279 double; winter $129–$249 double. Rates include full breakfast and port. AE, DISC, MC, V. From Hwy. 29 N, exit onto 1st St. and follow signs to downtown; turn right onto Coombs St.; the house is at the corner of Oak St. *In room:* A/C, TV, dataport, hair dryer, iron.

Cottage Grove Inn ★★ Standing in two parallel rows at the end of the main strip in Calistoga are the perfect couples' retreats—cottages that, although located on a residential street, seem well removed from the action once you've stepped across the threshold. Each compact guesthouse comes complete with a wood-burning fireplace, homey furnishings (perfect for curling up in front of the fire), cozy quilts, and an enormous bathroom with a skylight and a deep, two-person Jacuzzi tub, plus such niceties as gourmet coffee, stereo with CD player, VCR (a video library is on-site), wet bar, and fridge. Smokers beware—it's not allowed inside, but you can puff all you want on the small front porch. Several major spas are within walking distance. This is my top pick if you want to do the Calistoga spa scene in comfort and style. One cabin is accessible for travelers with disabilities.

1711 Lincoln Ave., Calistoga, CA 94515. ✆ **800/799-2284** or 707/942-8400. Fax 707/942-2653. www. cottagegrove.com. 16 cottages. $235–$295 double. Rates include continental breakfast and evening wine and cheese. AE, DC, DISC, MC, V. *In room:* A/C, TV/VCR, CD player, dataport, fridge, coffeemaker, hair dryer.

Maison Fleurie ★★ Maison Fleurie is one of the prettiest hotels in the Wine Country, a trio of beautiful 1873 brick-and-fieldstone buildings overlaid with ivy. Seven rooms are located in the main house—a charming Provençal replica complete with thick brick walls, terra-cotta tile, and paned windows—while the remaining rooms are split between the old bakery building and the carriage house. All have private bathrooms, and some feature private balconies, patios, sitting areas, Jacuzzis, and fireplaces. Breakfast is served in the quaint little dining room; afterward, you're welcome to wander the landscaped grounds, use the pool or outdoor spa, or snack on afternoon hors d'oeuvres. It's truly impossible not to enjoy your stay at Maison Fleurie.

6529 Yount St. (between Washington St. and Yountville Cross Rd.), Yountville, CA 94599. ✆ **800/788-0369** or 707/944-2056. Fax 707/944-9342. www.foursisters.com. 13 units. $110–$260 double. Rates include full breakfast and afternoon hors d'oeuvres. AE, DC, MC, V. **Amenities:** Heated outdoor pool; Jacuzzi; free bikes. *In room:* A/C, TV, dataport, hair dryer, iron.

Rancho Caymus Inn ★ This Spanish-style hacienda, with two floors open-ing onto wisteria-covered balconies, was the creation of sculptor Mary Tilden Morton (of Morton Salt). Morton wanted each room in the hacienda to be a work of art, so she hired the most skilled craftspeople of her day. She designed the adobe fireplaces herself, and wandered through Mexico and South America purchasing artifacts for the property.

Guest rooms are situated around a whimsical garden courtyard with an enormous outdoor fireplace. The mix-and-match interior decor is on the funky side, with overly varnished dark-wood furnishings and braided rugs. The inn is cozy, however, and rooms are decent-size, split-level suites with queen beds. Other amenities include wet bars, sofa beds in the sitting areas, and small private patios. Most of the suites have fireplaces, and five have kitchenettes and whirlpool tubs. A complimentary continental breakfast, which includes fresh fruit, granola, orange juice, and breads, is served in the inn's dining room.

Since chef Ken Frank's La Toque opened here, this funky inn has also become a dining destination (see "Where to Dine," below, for complete details).

1140 Rutherford Rd. (P.O. Box 78), Rutherford, CA 94573. ☎ **800/845-1777** or 707/963-1777. Fax 707/963-5387. www.ranchocaymus.com. 26 suites. $155–$255 double; from $285 master suite; $385 2-bedroom suite. Rates include continental breakfast. AE, DC, MC, V. From Hwy. 29 N, turn right onto Rutherford Rd./Calif. 128 E.; the hotel is on your left. **Amenities:** Restaurant. *In room:* A/C, TV, dataport, kitchenette in some rooms, minibar, fridge in some rooms, hair dryer, iron.

Wine Country Inn ★★   Just off the highway behind Freemark Abbey Vineyard, this attractive wood-and-stone inn, complete with a French-style mansard roof and turret, overlooks a pastoral landscape of Napa Valley vineyards. The individually decorated rooms are outfitted with iron or brass beds, antique furnishings, and handmade quilts; most have fireplaces and private terraces overlooking the valley, while others have private hot tubs. One of the inn's best features, besides the absence of TVs, is the outdoor pool (heated year-round), which is attractively landscaped into the hillside.

Another favorite is the selection of suites, which come with stereos, plenty of space, and lots of privacy. Wine and appetizers are served nightly, along with a big dash of hotel-staff hospitality in the inviting living room. A full buffet breakfast is served there, too. *Note:* Half the bathrooms have showers only. Ongoing renovations ensure updated rooms, and five new luxury cottages will be open by spring 2003.

1152 Lodi Lane, St. Helena, CA 94574. ☎ **707/963-7077.** Fax 707/963-9018. www.wine-country-inn.com. 24 units (12 with shower only). $130–$345 double. Rates include breakfast and appetizers. MC, V. **Amenities:** Heated outdoor pool; Jacuzzi; concierge. *In room:* A/C, stereo, hair dryer.

INEXPENSIVE

Along with the listings below, I also recommend **Napa Valley Railway Inn,** 6503 Washington St., adjacent to the Vintage 1870 shopping complex, Yountville (☎ **707/944-2000**), which rents private railway cars converted into adorable hotel rooms; and **Dr. Wilkinson's Hot Springs,** 1507 Lincoln Ave. (☎ **707/942-4102**), which recently underwent a major renovation.

Calistoga Spa Hot Springs ★ *Kids*   Very few hotels in the Wine Country welcome children, which is why I strongly recommend the Calistoga Spa Hot Springs for families. Even if you don't have kids in tow, it's still a great bargain, offering unpretentious yet clean and comfortable rooms with kitchenettes, as well as a plethora of spa facilities, including exercise rooms, four naturally heated outdoor mineral pools, aerobic facilities, volcanic-ash mud baths, mineral baths, steam baths, blanket wraps, massage sessions, and more. All of Calistoga's best shops and restaurants are within easy walking distance, and you can even whip up your own grub at the barbecues set up near the large pool and patio area.

1006 Washington St. (at Gerrard St.), Calistoga, CA 94515. ℂ **707/942-6269.** www.calistogaspa.com. 57 units, 1 family unit. Winter $90 double, $110 family unit; summer $110 double, $130 family unit. MC, V. **Amenities:** 3 heated outdoor pools; kids' wading pool; exercise room; spa. *In room:* A/C, TV, kitchenette, fridge, coffeemaker, hair dryer on request, iron.

Chablis Inn ⋆

There's no way around it. If you want to sleep cheaply in a town where the average room goes for upwards of $200 per night in high season, you're going to have to motel it. But look on the bright side: Since your room is likely to be little more than a crash pad after a day of eating and drinking, a clean bed and a remote control are all you'll really need. But Chablis offers much more than that: Some of the super-clean motel-style rooms boast kitchenettes and/or whirlpool tubs. Guests have access to an outdoor heated pool and Jacuzzi. Friendly owner Ken Patel is on hand most of the time and is constantly upgrading his tidy highway-side hostelry.

3360 Solano Ave., Napa, CA 94558. ℂ **707/257-1944.** Fax 707/226-6862. www.chablisinn.com. 34 units. Apr to mid-Nov $80–$150 double; mid-Nov to Mar $70–$120 double. Rates include continental breakfast. AE, DC, DISC, MC, V. **Amenities:** Heated outdoor pool; Jacuzzi. *In room:* A/C, TV, dataport in some rooms, kitchenette in some rooms, fridge, coffeemaker, hair dryer.

El Bonita Motel ⋆ *Kids*

This 1930s Art Deco motel was built a bit too close to Calif. 29 for comfort, but the 2½ acres of beautifully landscaped gardens behind the place (away from the road) help even the score. The rooms, while small, are spotlessly clean and decorated with new furnishings; some have kitchens or whirlpool bathtubs. Families, attracted to the larger bungalows with kitchenettes, often regard El Bonita as one of the best values in Napa Valley— especially considering the heated outdoor pool, Jacuzzi, and spa facility.

195 Main St. (at El Bonita Ave.), St. Helena, CA 94574. ℂ **800/541-3284** or 707/963-3216. Fax 707/963-8838. www.elbonita.com. 41 units. $89–$259 double. Rates include continental breakfast. AE, DC, DISC, MC, V. **Amenities:** Heated outdoor pool; spa; Jacuzzi. *In room:* A/C, TV, fridge, coffeemaker, microwave, hair dryer, iron.

White Sulphur Springs Retreat & Spa ⋆⋆ *Value*

If your idea of the ultimate vacation is a cozy cabin set among 330 acres of creeks, waterfalls, hot springs, hiking trails, and redwood, madrone, and fir trees, paradise is a short winding drive away from downtown St. Helena. Established in 1852, Sulphur Springs claims to be the oldest resort in California. Guests stay at the inn or in small and large creek-side cabins, which were recently renovated. Each is decorated with simple but homey furnishings; some have fireplaces or wood-burning stoves, and/or kitchenettes. From here you can venture off on a hike; take a dip in the natural hot sulphur spring; lounge by the pool; sit under a tree and watch for deer, foxes, raccoons, spotted owls, or woodpeckers; or schedule a day of massage, aromatherapy, and other treatments in the spa. ***Note:*** No RVs are allowed without advance notice, and no pets or smoking are allowed.

3100 White Sulphur Springs Rd., St. Helena, CA 94574. ℂ **800/593-8873** in CA or 707/963-8588. Fax 707/963-2890. www.whitesulphursprings.com. 36 units, including 14 with shared bathroom and 9 cottages. Carriage House (shared bathroom) $90–$110 double; Inn $115–$155 double; Creekside Cottages $155–$245. Rates include continental breakfast. Extra person $30. Off-season and midweek discounts available. 2-night minimum stay on weekends Apr–Oct and all holidays. MC, V. **Amenities:** Heated outdoor pool; full-service spa. *In room:* A/C, TV, hair dryer on request.

Wine Valley Lodge ⋆ *Value*

Dollar for dollar, the Wine Valley Lodge offers the most for the least in all of the Wine Country. Located at the south end of town in a quiet residential neighborhood, the mission-style motel is extremely well kept and accessible, just a short drive from Calif. 29 and the wineries to the north. Soft pastels dominate the color scheme, featured prominently in the matching quilted bedspreads, furniture, and objets d'art. The clincher on the whole deal is a fetching little oasis in the center courtyard, consisting of a sun deck, barbecue, and pool flanked by a cadre of odd teacup-shaped hedges.

200 S. Coombs St. (between 1st and Imola sts.), Napa, CA 94559. ℂ **800/696-7911** or 707/224-7911. www.winevalleylodge.com. 54 units. $69–$119 double; $120–$165 deluxe. AE, DC, DISC, MC, V. **Amenities:** Heated outdoor pool. *In room:* A/C, TV.

WHERE TO DINE

To best enjoy Napa's restaurant scene, keep one thing in mind: *reserve*—especially for seats in a more renowned room.

EXPENSIVE

Auberge du Soleil ★★ *(Finds* CONTINENTAL/CALIFORNIA   There is no better restaurant view than that at Auberge du Soleil. Perched on a hillside overlooking the valley, alfresco dining rises to an entirely new level here, particularly on warm summer afternoons at sunset. In fact, I recommend coming during the day (request terrace seating) to dine above the vines. The kitchen turns out beautifully prepared seasonal dishes such as sautéed sweetbreads, venison loin with butternut squash, stuffed squab, and roasted saddle of lamb—nothing mind-blowing, but certainly good.

180 Rutherford Hill Rd., Rutherford. ℂ **707/963-1211.** Reservations recommended. Main courses $17–$20 lunch, $25–$30 dinner. AE, DISC, MC, V. Daily 7–11am, 11:30am–2:30pm, and 6–9:30pm.

The French Laundry ★★★ CLASSIC AMERICAN/FRENCH   It's almost futile to include this restaurant, since the likelihood of securing a reservation—or getting through on the reservation line for that matter—is about as likely as driving Highway 29 without passing a winery. But, several years after renowned chef and owner Thomas Keller bought the place and caught the attention of epicureans worldwide (including the judges of the James Beard Awards, who dubbed him 1997's "Chef of the Nation"), the discreet restaurant is still one of the hottest dinner tickets *in the world.* So, at least you can read about it. *Tip:* If you can't get a reservation, try walking in—on occasion folks don't make their reservation and tables open up—especially during lunch on rainy days.

Here the atmosphere is as serious as the diners who quietly swoon over the ongoing parade of precious bite-size delights delivered to the table. Technically, the prix-fixe menu offers a choice of five or nine courses (including a vegetarian menu), but after a slew of cameo appearances from the kitchen, everyone starts to lose count. Signature dishes include Keller's "tongue in cheek" (a marinated and braised round of sliced lamb tongue and tender beef cheeks) and "macaroni and cheese" (sweet butter-poached Maine lobster with creamy lobster broth and orzo with mascarpone cheese). Portions are small, but only because Keller wants his guests to taste as many different things as possible—nobody leaves hungry. The excellent staff is well acquainted with the wide selection of regional wines; the house charges a $50 corkage fee if you choose to bring your own bottle. On warm summer nights, request a table in the flower-filled garden. But keep in mind, the French Laundry experience focuses on food in such a way that it is most appreciated by serious foodies who revel in 4-hour meals and unparalleled culinary artistry.

6640 Washington St. (at Creek St.), Yountville. ℂ **707/944-2380.** Reservations required. Vegetarian menu $80; 5-course menu $105; chef's 9-course tasting menu $120. AE, MC, V. Fri–Sun 11am–1pm; daily 5:30–9:30pm.

La Toque ★★★ FRENCH-INSPIRED   Don't come here without an appetite or a nice outfit. Renowned Ken Frank left Los Angeles's Fenix at the Argyle Hotel to open one of the Wine Country's most formal dining rooms—and once you sit down to the five-course extravaganza, you can't refrain from gobbling up all the delicious—and generous—creations that come your way. Each table at the elegant restaurant adjoining Rancho Caymus Inn is well spaced, making plenty of room to showcase Frank's memorable and innovative French-inspired cuisine. The menu might feature an incredible Indian spice–rubbed foie gras with Madras carrot purée (one of the best I've had); melt-in-your-mouth yellowfin tuna with braised daikon, red wine, and sautéed pea sprouts; knock-out Maine lobster with creamy orzo and lobster cabernet sauce; and, should you find room and the extra few bucks for the cheese course, delicious selections served with walnut bread. For an additional $32 per person, my party drank splendid and well-paired wines with each course. Alas, I did not have room for desserts of chocolate *panna cotta* with vanilla Anglaise and toasted pineapple fritter with vanilla bean ice cream—but I couldn't help but eat it anyway.

1140 Rutherford Cross Rd., Rutherford. ℂ 707/963-9770. www.latoque.com. Reservations recommended. Fixed-price menu $72. AE, MC, V. Wed–Sun 5:30–10pm.

MODERATE

All Seasons Café ★★ CALIFORNIA   Wine Country devotees often wend their way to the All Seasons Café in downtown Calistoga because of its extensive wine list and knowledgeable staff. The trick here is to buy a bottle of wine from the cafe's wine shop, then bring it to your table; the cafe adds a corkage fee of around $10 instead of doubling the price of the bottle (as they do at most restaurants). The diverse menu ranges from pizzas and pastas to such main courses as braised lamb shank osso buco in an orange, Madeira, and tomato sauce. Anything with the house-smoked salmon or spiced sausages is also a safe bet. Chef John Coss saves his guests from any major faux pas by matching wines to his dishes on the menu, so you know what's just right for smoked salmon and Crescenza cheese pizza.

1400 Lincoln Ave. (at Washington St.), Calistoga. ℂ 707/942-9111. Reservations recommended on weekends. Main courses $7.50–$13 lunch, $10–$19 dinner. MC, V. Mon–Tues and Thurs–Fri 11am–3pm; daily 5:30–9pm. Wine shop Thurs–Tues 11am–7pm.

Bistro Don Giovanni ★★ *Value* REGIONAL ITALIAN   Donna and Giovanni Scala—who also run Scala's Bistro in San Francisco—own this bright, bustling, and cheery Italian restaurant, which also happens to be one of my favorite restaurants in Napa Valley. The menu features pastas, risottos, pizzas (baked in a wood-burning oven), and a half dozen other main courses. Every time I grab a menu, I can't get past the beet and haricots verte salad and pasta with duck Bolognese. On the rare occasion that I do, I am equally smitten with outstanding thin-crust pizzas fresh from the wood-burning oven, seared salmon filet perched atop a tower of buttermilk mashed potatoes, and steak frites. Alfresco dining on the patio is available—and highly recommended on a warm, sunny day.

4110 St. Helena Hwy. (Hwy. 29, just N of Salvador Ave.), Napa. ℂ 707/224-3300. Reservations recommended. Main courses $12–$24. AE, DC, DISC, MC, V. Sun–Thurs 11:30am–10pm; Fri–Sat 11:30am–11pm.

Bistro Jeanty ★★ FRENCH BISTRO   This casual, warm bistro with muted buttercup walls and two dining rooms divided by the bar is the brainchild of chef Phillipe Jeanty, who a few years back left his highly reputed 18-year post at Domaine Chandon to open one of the hottest (and most moderately priced) new restaurants in town. Jeanty was previously known for formal French cooking, but his charming and cheery bistro offers far more laid-back but equally worship-worthy fare. Outstanding classic French bistro fare comes in the form of an all-day menu, which includes his legendary tomato soup in a puff pastry, foie gras paté, steak tartare, and house-smoked trout with potato slices basking in a light olive oil and vinegar bath; daube de boeuf simmered in red wine and served with mashed potatoes, fresh peas, and baby carrots; and cassoulet with white beans, fennel sausage, pork, and duck leg. I'll return frequently for the decadent fall-off-the-bone coq au vin with an earthy, smoky red wine sauce and delicate deep-fried smelt special, which came in a wax-paper cone accompanied by a seasoned mayo dipping sauce. I, like most San Franciscans, consider this place a must-stop on the Wine Country itinerary.

6510 Washington St., Yountville. ℭ 707/944-0103. www.bistrojeanty.com. Reservations recommended. Appetizers $4.50–$7.50; most main courses $14–$19. MC, V. Daily 11:30am–10:30pm. Closed Thanksgiving and Dec 25.

Bouchon ★★ FRENCH BISTRO   Perhaps to appease the crowds who never get a reservation at The French Laundry, Thomas Keller teamed up with his brother Joseph to open a far more casual French brasserie called Bouchon. You'll have to call in advance for an opportunity to sample the French fare, which is served in a dining room designed by Adam Tihany (who also conceptualized New York's Le Cirque 2000). Along with a raw bar, expect steak frite, mussels marinieres, grilled cheese sandwiches, and other heavenly French classics at far more down-to-earth prices. My all-time favorites: the bibb lettuce salad (seriously, trust me on this), french fries (perhaps the best in the valley), and roasted chicken bathing in wild mushroom ragout. An added bonus (especially for restless residents) is the late hours.

6534 Washington St. (at Humbolt), Yountville. ℭ 707/944-8037. Reservations recommended. Main courses $12–$17. AE, DC, MC, V. Daily 11:30am–2pm and 5:30–10:45pm.

Catahoula ★ AMERICAN/SOUTHERN   The domain of chef Jan Birnbaum, formerly of New York's Quilted Giraffe and San Francisco's Campton Place, this restaurant is the current favorite in town. And for good reason: It's the only place in Napa where you can get a decent rooster gumbo. You'd have to travel all over Louisiana to find another pan-fried jalapeño-pecan catfish like this one. Catahoula is funky and fun, and the food that comes out of the wood-burning oven—like the roast duck with chile-cilantro potatoes or the whole roasted fish with lemon broth, orzo, and escarole—is exciting (and usually spicy). Start with the spicy gumbo ya ya with andouille sausage, and finish with what may be a first for many non-Southerners—buttermilk ice cream.

1457 Lincoln Ave. (between Washington and Fairway sts.), Calistoga. ℭ 707/942-2275. Reservations recommended. Main courses $11–$22. DISC, MC, V. Sat–Sun 10am–3:30pm; daily 5:30–10:30pm.

Tra Vigne Restaurant ★★★ ITALIAN   Tra Vigne's combination of good ultra-fresh food, high-energy atmosphere, gorgeous patio seating, all-day service, and "reasonable" prices makes this restaurant a long-standing favorite among visitors and locals alike. Whether guests are in the Tuscany-evoking courtyard (heated on cold nights) or in the center of the bustling scene, they're usually thrilled just to have a seat. Though the wonderful bread served with house-made flavored olive oils is tempting, save room for their rich and robust California dishes, such as standbys like short ribs; frito misto; irresistible oven-roasted polenta with cheese, mushrooms, and balsamic reduction; and outstanding whole roasted fish. Equally tempting are the fresh pastas—such as spaghettini with cuttlefish Bolognese and spring onions—and delicious desserts.

The adjoining Cantinetta offers a small selection of sandwiches, pizzas, and lighter meals, and an exciting new wine program, which features 100 by-the-glass selections.

1050 Charter Oak Ave., St. Helena. ℂ **707/963-4444**. Reservations recommended. Main courses $13–$22. DC, DISC, MC, V. Daily 11:30am–10pm.

Wappo Bar & Bistro ✿✿ GLOBAL   One of the best alfresco dining experiences in the Wine Country is under Wappo's honeysuckle and vine covered arbor, but you'll also be comfortable inside this small bistro at one of the well-spaced, well-polished tables. The menu offers a wide range of choices, from Chilean sea bass with mint chutney to roast rabbit with oven tomato *tagliarini* (long paper-thin pasta). Desserts of choice are the black-bottom coconut cream pie and the strawberry rhubarb pie.

1226B Washington St. (off Lincoln Ave.), Calistoga. ℂ **707/942-4712**. Main courses $14–$20. AE, MC, V. Wed–Mon 11:30am–2:30pm and 6–9:30pm.

Wine Spectator Greystone Restaurant ✿ CALIFORNIA   This place offers a combination visual and culinary feast that's unparalleled in the area, if not the state. The room itself is an enormous stone-walled former winery, but the festive decor and heavenly aromas warm the space up. Cooking islands—complete with scurrying chefs, steaming pots, and rotating chicken—provide edible entertainment. The "tastings" (appetizer) menu features fresh ingredient-inspired dishes, including a perfect calamari sautéed with smoked paprika, garlic, and rosemary; a fine seafood and white bean salad; and an unimpressive mushroom piroshki with caramelized onions. Portions are small but affordable; pastas and salads are a bit heftier. Main courses, such as a crispy fried lamb shank with cranberry beans, cherry tomatoes, and spinach, are well portioned, but I recommend you opt for a barrage of appetizers for your table to share. You should also order the "Flights of Fancy," where for around $20 you can sample three 3-ounce pours of local wines such as white Rhônes, pinot, or zinfandel. While the food is serious, the atmosphere is playful—casual enough that you'll feel comfortable in jeans or shorts.

At the Culinary Institute of America at Greystone, 2555 Main St., St. Helena. ℂ **707/967-1010**. Reservations recommended. Tastings $5–$8; main courses $14–$24. AE, DC, MC, V. Daily 11:30am–10pm.

INEXPENSIVE

The Cantinetta ✿✿ WINE BAR/ITALIAN DELI   Regardless of where I dine while in the valley, I always make a point of stopping at the Cantinetta for an espresso and a snack. Part cafe, part shop, and part wine bar, it's a casual place with a few tables and a counter. The focaccias (I've never had better in my life!), pasta salads, and pastries are outstanding, and there's also a selection of cookies and other wonderful treats, flavored oils (free tastings), wines, and an array of gourmet items, many of which were created here. You can also get great picnic grub to go, but it'd be sinful not to sample at least a few wines from their 100-plus bottle list.

At Tra Vigne Restaurant, 1050 Charter Oak Ave., St. Helena. ℂ **707/963-8888**. Main courses $4–$7. DC, DISC, MC, V. Daily 11:30am–6pm.

Smokehouse Café ✿✿ *Kids*   There are some darned good spareribs and house-smoked meats coming from this little kitchen in Calistoga. But that doesn't mean you shouldn't start with the Sacramento delta crawfish cakes and husk-roasted Cheyenne corn, then move on to the slow pig sandwich, a half slab of ribs, or homemade sausages—all of which take up to a week to prepare (not while you wait, luckily). The clincher is the fluffy all-you-can-eat cornbread dipped in pure cane syrup, which comes with every full-plate dinner. Kids are especially catered to—a rarity in these parts—and patio dining is available in summer.

1458 Lincoln Ave., Calistoga. © **707/942-6060.** Main courses $8–$21. MC, V. Daily 8:30am–9pm (Jan–Feb closed for dinner Tues–Wed).

Taylor's Refresher ⭐ DINER   It isn't every day that a roadside burger shack gets a huge spread in *Food & Wine* magazine, but then again, Taylor's Refresher isn't your average fast-food stop. At this completely outdoor diner built in 1949, you order at the counter, settle at a picnic table in the front facing Highway 29 or the relatively more pastoral back, and wait for your name to be called. When it is, you'll receive an excellent burger on a surprisingly soft but sturdy bun, fries, creamy shakes, and even their own company-made ding-dongs. Those who are less carnivorous can opt for an ahi tuna burger.

933 Main St., St. Helena. © **707/963-3486.** Main courses $2.50–$9.65. AE, MC, V. Daily 11am–8pm.

ZuZu ⭐⭐ TAPAS   The most exciting restaurant opening of 2002 wasn't a big fancy dining room, but rather this tiny downtown spot serving delicious affordable small plates of Spanish fare ($2–$11!). A local place to the core, here no reservations are taken and residents crowd into the cramped wine bar until they can be seated either downstairs or up. The environment is comfortable and warm, and the food is seriously good. Chef Charles Weber presides over the tiny kitchen cranking out sizzling skillets of fantastic paella, fresh and clean corn soup, addictive sizzling prawns with requisite bread-dipping sauce, light and delicate sea scallop ceviche salad, and Moroccan barbecued lamb chops with a sweet and spicy sauce guaranteed to make you swoon. Desserts aren't as fab, but who cares?

829 Main St., Napa. © **707/224-8555.** Reservations not accepted. Tapas $2–$10. AE, MC, V. Mon–Thurs 11:30am–10:30pm, Fri 11:30am–midnight, Sat 4pm–midnight, Sun 4–10:30pm.

2 Sonoma Valley

Sonoma is often thought of as the "other" Wine Country, forever in the shadow of Napa Valley. Truth is, it's a very different experience. Sonoma still manages to maintain a backcountry ambience thanks to its much lower density of wineries, restaurants, and hotels; because it's far less traveled than its neighbor to the east, it offers a more genuine "escape from it all" experience. Small, family-owned wineries are its mainstay, just like in the old days of winemaking, when everyone started with the intention of going broke and loved every minute of it. Unlike the rigidly structured tours at many of Napa Valley's corporate-owned wineries, tastings and tours on the Sonoma side of the Mayacamas Mountains are usually free and low-key, and come with plenty of friendly banter between the winemakers and their guests.

ESSENTIALS
GETTING THERE   From San Francisco, cross the Golden Gate Bridge and stay on U.S. 101 north. Exit at Calif. 37; after 10 miles, turn north onto Calif. 121. After another 10 miles, turn north onto Calif. 12 (Broadway), which will take you directly into the town of Sonoma.

VISITOR INFORMATION   While you're in Sonoma, stop by the **Sonoma Valley Visitors Bureau,** 453 First St. E. (© **707/996-1090;**

Gourmet Picnics, Napa-Style

You could easily plan your whole trip around restaurant reservations. But put together one of the world's best gourmet picnics, and the valley's your oyster.

One of the finest gourmet food stores in the Wine Country, if not all of California, is the **Oakville Grocery Co.,** 7856 St. Helena Hwy., at Oakville Cross Road (© **707/944-8802**). Here you can put together the provisions for a memorable picnic—or, if you give them at least 24 hours' notice, the staff can prepare a picnic basket for you. The store, with its small-town vibe and claustrophobia-inducing crowds, is crammed with the best breads and the choicest selection of cheeses in the northern Bay Area, as well as patés, cold cuts, crackers, top-quality olive oils, fresh foie gras, smoked Norwegian salmon, fresh caviar (Beluga, Sevruga, Osetra), and, of course, an exceptional selection of California wines. The Grocery Co. is open daily from 9am to 6pm; it also has an espresso bar tucked in the corner (open daily 7am–3pm), offering breakfast and lunch items, house-baked pastries, and 15 wines available by the glass or for tasting.

Another of my favorite places to fill a picnic basket is New York City's version of a swank European marketplace, **Dean & Deluca,** 607 S. Main St. (Calif. 29), north of Zinfandel Lane and south of Sulphur Springs Road in St. Helena (© **707/967-9980**). The ultimate gourmet grocery store is more like a world's fair of foods, where everything is beautifully displayed and often painfully pricey. But even if you choose not to buy, this place is definitely worth a browse. Check out the 200 domestic and imported cheeses; shelves of tapenades, pastas, oils, hand-packed dried herbs and spices, chocolates, sauces, and cookware; an espresso bar; one hell of a bakery section; and more. The wine shop boasts a 1,200-label collection. Hours are Monday through Saturday from 10am to 7pm (the espresso bar is open 8am–7pm), and Sunday from 10am to 6pm.

My favorite stop, **Palisades Market,** 1506 Lincoln Ave., Calistoga (© **707/942-9549**), is a much more intimate affair and serves the best sandwiches I've ever had (our side of Italy). You can also drop in for wine, juice, soda, cheese, tamales, green salads, lasagna, soup, picnic items, and every kind of treat you can think of, but under no circumstances skip the sandwiches. Hours are Sunday through Wednesday from 7:30am to 6pm and Thursday through Saturday from 7:30am to 7pm.

www.sonomavalley.com). It's open daily from 9am to 7pm in summer and from 9am to 5pm in winter. An additional **Visitors Bureau** is located a few miles south of the square at 25200 Arnold Dr. (Calif. 121), at the entrance to Viansa Winery (© **707/996-5793**); it's open daily from 9am to 4pm, from 9am to 5pm in summer.

If you prefer some advance information, you can contact the Sonoma Valley Visitors Bureau to order the $2 *Sonoma Valley Visitors Guide,* which lists most every lodging, winery, and restaurant in the valley.

WHEN TO GO See "When to Go" in the Napa section, earlier in this chapter.

TOURING THE VALLEY & WINERIES

Sonoma Valley is currently home to about 35 wineries (including California's first winery, Buena Vista, founded in 1857) and 13,000 acres of vineyards, which produce roughly 25 types of wines totaling more than five million cases a year.

The towns and wineries covered below are organized geographically from south to north, starting at the intersection of Calif. 37 and Calif. 121 in the Carneros District and ending in Kenwood. The wineries here tend to be a little more spread out than they are in Napa, but they're easy to find. Still, it's best to decide which wineries you're most interested in and devise a touring strategy before you set out so you don't find yourself doing a lot of backtracking.

I've reviewed my favorite Sonoma Valley wineries here—more than enough to keep you busy tasting wine for a long weekend. For a complete list of local wineries, pick up one of the free guides to the valley available at the Sonoma Valley Visitors Bureau (see "Visitor Information," above).

THE CARNEROS DISTRICT

As you approach the Wine Country from the south, you must first pass through the Carneros District, a cool, windswept region that borders the San Pablo Bay and marks the entrance to both Napa and Sonoma valleys. Until the latter part of the 20th century, this mixture of marsh, sloughs, and rolling hills was mainly used as sheep pasture (*carneros* means sheep in Spanish). After experimental plantings yielded slow-growing yet high-quality grapes—particularly chardonnay and pinot noir—several Napa and Sonoma wineries expanded their plantings here, eventually establishing the Carneros District as an American Viticultural Appellation.

Viansa Winery and Italian Marketplace ℱ This sprawling Tuscany-style villa is perched atop a knoll overlooking the entire lower valley. Viansa is the brainchild of Sam and Vicki Sebastiani, who left the family dynasty to create their own temple to food and wine (*Viansa* being a contraction of Vicki and Sam). While Sam, a third-generation winemaker, runs the winery, Vicki manages the marketplace, a large room crammed with a cornucopia of high-quality preserves, mustards, olive oils, pastas, salads, breads, desserts, Italian tableware, cookbooks, and wine-related gifts.

The winery, which does an extensive mail-order business through its Tuscany Club (worth joining if you love getting mail and good wine), has quickly established a favorable reputation for its cabernet, sauvignon blanc, and chardonnay, blended from premium Napa and Sonoma grapes. Sam is also experimenting with Italian grape varieties such as muscat canelli, sangiovese, and nebbiolo, most of which are sold exclusively at the winery. Five-dollar tastings are poured at the east end of the marketplace, and the self-guided tour includes a trip through the underground barrel-aging cellar adorned with colorful hand-painted murals.

25200 Arnold Dr. (Calif. 121), Sonoma. ☎ 800/995-4740 or 707/935-4700. www.viansa.com. Daily 10am–5pm; summer 9am–5:30pm. Daily self-guided tours.

Gloria Ferrer Champagne Caves (Finds When you have it up to here with chardonnays and pinots, it's time to pay a visit to Gloria Ferrer, the grande dame of the Wine Country's sparkling-wine producers. Who's Gloria, you ask? She's the wife of José Ferrer, whose family has been making sparkling wine for the past 5 centuries and whose company, Freixenet, is the largest producer of sparkling wine in the world. Glimmering like Oz high atop a gently sloping hill, the estate overlooks the verdant Carneros District; on a sunny day, enjoying a glass of brut while soaking in the magnificent views is a must.

If you're unfamiliar with the term *méthode champenoise,* be sure to take the free 30-minute tour of the fermenting tanks, bottling line, and caves brimming with racks of yeast-laden bottles. Afterwards, retire to the elegant tasting room for a flute of brut or cuvée ($3.50–$6 a glass, $16 and up per bottle), find an empty chair on the veranda, and say, "Ahhh. *This* is the life." There are picnic tables, but it's usually too windy up here for comfort, and you have to purchase a bottle of their sparkling wine to reserve a table.

23555 Carneros Hwy. (Calif. 121), Sonoma. (C) **707/996-7256**. www.gloriaferrer.com. Daily 10am–5:30pm. Tours daily 11am–4pm.

SONOMA

At the northern boundary of the Carneros District along Calif. 12 is the center-piece of Sonoma Valley, the midsize town of Sonoma, which owes much of its appeal to Mexican general Mariano Guadalupe Vallejo. It was Vallejo who fash-ioned this pleasant, slow-paced community after a typical Mexican village— right down to its central plaza, Sonoma's geographical and commercial center. The plaza sits at the top of a T formed by Broadway (Calif. 12) and Napa Street. Most of the surrounding streets form a grid pattern around this axis, making Sonoma easy to negotiate. The plaza's Bear Flag Monument marks the spot where the crude Bear Flag was raised in 1846, signaling the end of Mexican rule; the symbol was later adopted by the state of California and placed on its flag. The 8-acre park at the center of the plaza, complete with two ponds populated with ducks and geese, is perfect for an afternoon siesta in the cool shade.

The best way to see the town of Sonoma is to follow the **Sonoma Walking Tour** map, provided by the Sonoma League for Historic Preservation. Tour high-lights include General Vallejo's 1852 Victorian-style home; the Sonoma Barracks, erected in 1836 to house Mexican army troops; and the Blue Wing Inn, an 1840 hostelry built to accommodate travelers—including John Fremont, Kit Carson, and Ulysses S. Grant—and new settlers while they erected homes in Sonoma. You can purchase the $2.75 map at the Mission (see below).

The **Mission San Francisco Solano de Sonoma,** on Sonoma Plaza at the corner of First Street East and Spain Street ((C) **707/938-9560**), was founded in 1823. It was the northernmost, and last, mission built in California. It was also the only one established on the northern coast by the Mexican rulers, who wished to protect their territory from expansionist Russian fur traders. It's now part of Sonoma State Historic Park. Admission is $1 for adults, free for children ages 12 and under. It's open daily from 10am to 5pm except Thanksgiving, Christmas, and New Year's Day.

Sebastiani Vineyards Winery What started in 1904, when Samuele Sebas-tiani began producing his first wines, has, in three successive generations, now grown into a small empire and Sonoma County's largest winery, producing some *six million* cases a year. After a few years of seismic retrofitting, the original 1904 winery is now open to the public with more extensive educational tours, an 80-foot S-shaped tasting bar, and lots of shopping opportunities in the gift shop. In the contemporary tasting room's mini-museum area you can see the winery's original early-20th-century crusher and press, as well as the world's largest collection of oak-barrel carvings, crafted by local artist Earle Brown. If it's merely wine that interests you, you can sample an extensive selection of wines free. Bottle prices are reasonable, ranging from $15 to $75. A picnic area is adjacent to the cellars, though a far more scenic spot is located across the parking lot in Sebastiani's Cherryblock Vineyards.

389 4th St. E., Sonoma. ⓒ **800/888-5532** or 707/938-5532. www.sebastiani.com. Daily 10am–5pm. Call for tour schedules.

Buena Vista Winery   The patriarch of California wineries was founded in 1857 by Count Agoston Haraszthy, the Hungarian émigré who is universally regarded as the father of California's wine industry. A close friend of General Vallejo, Haraszthy returned from Europe in 1861 with 100,000 of the finest vine cuttings, which he made available to all winegrowers. Although Buena Vista's winemaking now takes place at an ultra-modern facility in the Carneros District, the winery still maintains a complimentary tasting room inside the restored 1862 Press House—a beautiful stone-crafted room brimming with wines, wine-related gifts, and accessories (as well as a small art gallery along the inner balcony).

Tastings are free for most wines, $3 for the really good stuff. There's also a self-guided tour that you can follow any time during operating hours; a "Historical Presentation," offered daily at 2pm, details the life and times of the count.

18000 Old Winery Rd. (off E. Napa St., slightly NE of downtown), Sonoma. ⓒ **800/926-1266** or 707/938-1266. www.buenavistawinery.com. Daily 10am–5pm. Self-guided tours only.

Ravenswood Winery   Compared to old heavies like Sebastiani and Buena Vista, Ravenswood is a relative newcomer to the Sonoma wine scene, but it has quickly established itself as the sine qua non of zinfandel. In fact, Ravenswood is the first winery in the United States to focus primarily on zins, which make up about three-quarters of its 500,000-case production; it also produces merlot, cabernet sauvignon, and a small amount of chardonnay.

The winery is smartly designed—recessed into the Sonoma hillside to protect its treasures from the simmering summers. Tours follow the winemaking process from grape to glass, and include a visit into the aromatic oak-barrel-aging rooms. A gourmet "Barbecue Overlooking the Vineyards" is held each weekend (11am–4:30pm, from Memorial Day to the end of Sept; call for details and reservations), though you're welcome to enjoy your own picnic at any of their tables. Tastings are free and generous.

18701 Gehricke Rd. (off Lovall Valley Rd.), Sonoma. ⓒ **800/NO-WIMPY** or 707/938-1960. www.ravenswood-wine.com. Daily 10am–4:30pm. Tours by reservation only.

GLEN ELLEN

About 7 miles north of Sonoma on Calif. 12 is the town of Glen Ellen, which, though just a fraction of the size of Sonoma, is home to several of the valley's finest wineries, restaurants, and inns. Aside from the addition of a few new restaurants, this charming Wine Country town hasn't changed much since the days when Jack London settled on his Beauty Ranch, about a mile west. If you haven't yet decided where you want to set up camp during your visit to the Wine Country, I highly recommend this lovable little town.

Hikers, horseback riders, and picnickers will enjoy **Jack London State Historic Park,** 2400 London Ranch Rd., off Arnold Drive (ⓒ **707/938-5216**). Within its 800 acres, which were once home to the renowned writer, you'll find 9 miles of trails, the remains of London's burned-down dream house, preserved structures, a museum, and plenty of ideal picnic spots. The park is open daily from

10am to 7pm in summer, from 10am to 5pm in winter; the museum is open year-round from 10am to 5pm. Admission is $3 per car or $2 per seniors' car.

Arrowood Vineyards & Winery This utterly picturesque winery is perched on a gently rising hillside lined with perfectly manicured vineyards. Tastings take place in the Hospitality House, the newer of Arrowood's two stately gray-and-white buildings fashioned after New England farmhouses, complete with wrap-around porches. Arrowood's focus is on making world-class wine with minimal intervention, and his results are impressive. Mind you, excellence doesn't come cheaply: Prices start at $29 for a 1999 chardonnay and quickly climb to $85 for their reserve cabernet. Tastings are $5.

14347 Sonoma Hwy. (Calif. 12), Glen Ellen. ℂ **707/938-5170.** www.arrowoodvineyards.com. Daily 10am–4:30pm. Tours by appointment only, daily at 10:30am and 2:30pm.

Benziger Family Winery *(Finds* A visit here confirms that you are indeed visiting a "family" winery; at any given time, three generations of Benzigers (pronounced *Ben*-zigger) may be running around tending to chores, and you're instantly made to feel as if you're part of the clan. The pastoral, user-friendly property features an exceptional self-guided tour, gardens, an art gallery, and a spacious tasting room manned by an amiable staff. The $5, 40-minute tram tour, pulled by a beefy tractor, is both informative and fun as it winds through the estate vineyards before making a champagne-tasting pit stop on a scenic bluff. *Tip:* Tram tickets—a hot item in the summer—are available on a first-come, first-served basis, so either arrive early or stop by in the morning to pick up afternoon tickets.

Tastings of the standard-release wines are free. The winery offers several scenic picnic spots.

1883 London Ranch Rd. (off Arnold Dr., on the way to Jack London State Historic Park), Glen Ellen. ℂ **800/989-8890** or 707/935-3000. www.benziger.com. Tasting room daily 10am–5pm. $5 tram tours daily (weather permitting) at 11:30am, 12:30, 2, and 3:30pm.

KENWOOD

A few miles north of Glen Ellen along Calif. 12 is the tiny town of Kenwood, the northernmost outpost of the Sonoma Valley. The town itself consists of little more than a few restaurants, wineries, and modest homes recessed into the wooded hillsides.

Kunde Estate Winery Expect a friendly, unintimidating welcome at this scenic winery, run by four generations of the Kundes since 1904. One of the largest grape suppliers in the area, the Kunde family (pronounced *Kun*-dee) converted 800 acres of their 2,000-acre ranch to growing ultra-premium quality grapes, which they provide to about 30 Sonoma and Napa wineries. Hence, all their wines are "estate" (made from grapes grown on their own property). The free new-release tastings are offered in a spiffy 17,000-square-foot winemaking facility. Private tours are available by appointment, but the picnic tables and man-made pond can be spontaneously enjoyed.

10155 Sonoma Hwy., Kenwood. ℂ **707/833-5501.** www.kunde.com. Tastings daily 10:30am–4pm. Cave tours Fri–Sun approximately every half-hr. from 11am–4pm.

Kenwood Vineyards Kenwood's history dates back to 1906, when the Pagani brothers made their living selling wine straight from the barrel and into the jug. In 1970, the Lee family bought the place and converted the aging winery into a modern, high-production facility concealed in the original barn-like buildings. Since then, Kenwood's wines have earned a solid reputation for consistent quality with each of their varietals: cabernet sauvignon, chardonnay, zinfandel, pinot noir, merlot, and their most popular wine, sauvignon blanc—a crisp, light wine with hints of melon.

Though the winery looks rather modest in size, its output is staggering: nearly 500,000 cases of ultra-premium wines fermented in steel tanks and French and American oak barrels. Popular with wine collectors is winemaker Michael Lee's Artist Series cabernet sauvignon, a limited production from the winery's best vineyards featuring labels with original artwork by renowned artists. The tasting room, housed in one of the old barns, offers free tastings of most varieties, as well as gift items for sale.

9592 Sonoma Hwy. (Calif. 12), Kenwood. ⓒ **707/833-5891**. www.kenwoodvineyards.com. Daily 10am–4:30pm. Tours at 11:30am and 2:30pm daily.

Château St. Jean *(Finds)*   Château St. Jean is notable for its exceptionally beautiful buildings, landscaped grounds, and gourmet market-like tasting room. Among California wineries, it's a pioneer in vineyard designation—the procedure of making wine from, and naming it for, a single vineyard. A private drive takes you to what was once a 250-acre country retreat built in 1920; a well-manicured lawn overlooking the meticulously maintained vineyards is now a picnic area, complete with a fountain and picnic tables. There's a self-guided tour with detailed and photographic descriptions of the winemaking process. When you're done, be sure to walk to the top of the faux medieval tower for a magnificent view of the valley.

Back in the elegant tasting room—split into three areas to better handle the traffic—you can sample Château St. Jean's wide array of wines. They range from chardonnays and cabernet sauvignon to fumé blanc, merlot, Johannisburg Riesling, and Gewürztraminer. Tastings are $5 per person.

8555 Sonoma Hwy. (Calif. 12), Kenwood. ⓒ **800/543-7572** or 707/833-4134. www.chateaustjean.com. Tasting daily 10am–6pm. At the foot of Sugarloaf Ridge, just N of Kenwood and E of Hwy. 12.

WHERE TO STAY

If you're having trouble finding a vacancy, try calling the **Sonoma Valley Visitors Bureau** at ⓒ **707/996-1090.** They'll try to refer you to a lodging that has a room to spare, but they won't make reservations for you. Another option is calling the **Bed and Breakfast Association of Sonoma Valley** (ⓒ **800/969-4667**), which will refer you to a member B&B and make reservations for you as well.

VERY EXPENSIVE

Gaige House Inn ★★★ *(Finds)*   The Gaige House is the best B&B I've ever stayed in. The inn's owners, Ken Burnet, Jr., and Greg Nemrow, turned what was already a fine bed-and-breakfast into the finest in the Wine Country, and they've done it by offering a level of service, amenities, and decor normally associated with outrageously expensive resorts (and without the snobbery). Breakfast and afternoon appetizers are made with herbs from the inn's garden and prepared by a chef who was featured at the James Beard House in 2001. Firm mattresses are graced with wondrously silk-soft linens and premium down comforters, and even the furniture and artwork are of museum quality. Behind the inn is a 1½-acre oasis with perfectly manicured lawns, a 40-foot-long swimming pool, and a creek-side hammock shaded by a majestic Heritage oak. All rooms, each artistically designed in a plantation theme with Asian and Indonesian influences, have private bathrooms and king- or queen-size beds; two rooms have Jacuzzi tubs, and several have fireplaces. On sunny days, breakfast is served at individual tables on the large terrace. Evenings are best spent in the reading parlor sipping premium wines.

13540 Arnold Dr., Glen Ellen, CA 95442. ℂ **800/935-0237** or 707/935-0237. Fax 707/935-6411. www.gaige.com. 15 units. Summer $250–$375 double, $375–$575 suite; winter $150–$325 double, $325–$550 suite. Rates include full breakfast and evening wines. AE, DC, DISC, MC, V. **Amenities:** Large heated pool; Jacuzzi; in-room massage. *In room:* A/C, TV, fax, dataport, hair dryer, iron, safe.

Kenwood Inn & Spa ★★   Inspired by the villas of Tuscany, the honey-colored Italian-style buildings, flower-filled flagstone courtyard, and pastoral views of vineyard-covered hills are enough to make any northern Italian home-sick. Every spacious room here is lavishly and exquisitely decorated with imported tapestries, velvets, and antiques; each has a fireplace, balcony (unless you're on the ground floor), feather bed, and down comforter—but no phone or TV, so you can relax. A minor caveat is road noise, which you're unlikely to hear from your room, but can be slightly heard over the tranquil piped-in music around the courtyard and pool.

An impressive two-course gourmet breakfast is served poolside or in the Mediterranean-style dining room; my meal consisted of a poached egg accompanied by light, flavorful potatoes, red bell peppers, and other roasted vegetables, all artfully arranged, followed by a delicious homemade scone with fresh berries and a small lemon tart.

10400 Sonoma Hwy., Kenwood, CA 95452. ℂ **800/353-6966** or 707/833-1293. Fax 707/833-1247. www.kenwoodinn.com. 12 units. Apr–Oct $295–$475 double; Nov–Mar $265–$425 double. Rates include gourmet breakfast and bottle of wine. 2-night minimum on weekends Apr–Oct. AE, MC, V. **Amenities:** Heated outdoor pool; full-service spa; concierge. *In room:* CD player, hair dryer, iron, no phone.

Sonoma Mission Inn, Spa & Country Club ★★★   Set on 12 meticulously groomed acres, the Wine Country's most extensive super-spa, the Sonoma Mission Inn, consists of a massive three-story replica of a Spanish mission (well, aside from the pink paint job) built in 1927, an array of satellite wings housing numerous super-luxury suites, and, of course, the world-class spa facilities, which include pools filled with naturally heated artesian mineral water. It's a popular retreat for the wealthy and the well known, so don't be surprised if you see Barbra Streisand or Harrison Ford strolling around in skivvies. Big changes have occurred since the resort changed ownership a few years ago, including 70 new guest rooms and suites, a $20-million spa facility (you won't even recognize the old one), and the acquisition of the Sonoma Golf Club.

The modern rooms are furnished with plantation-style shutters, ceiling fans, down comforters, and such extra amenities as bathroom scales and oversize bath towels. The Wine Country rooms feature king-size beds, desks, refrigerators, and huge limestone and marble bathrooms; some offer wood-burning fireplaces, and many have balconies. The older, slightly smaller Historic Inn rooms are sweetly appointed with homey furnishings, and most have queen-size beds. For the ultimate in luxury, however, the opulently appointed Mission Suites are the way to go.

18140 Sonoma Hwy. (Calif. 12), P.O. Box 1447, Sonoma, CA 94576. ℂ **800/862-4945** or 707/938-9000. Fax 707/935-1205. www.sonomamissioninn.com. 230 units. $299–$1,200 double. AE, DC, MC, V. From central Sonoma, drive 3 miles N on Hwy. 12 and turn left on Boyes Blvd. **Amenities:** 2 restaurants; 2 large, heated outdoor pools; golf course; tennis courts; health club and spa; Jacuzzi; sauna; bike rental; concierge; business center; salon; room service 6am–11pm; babysitting; same-day laundry service and dry cleaning. *In room:* A/C, TV, dataport, minibar, hair dryer, iron, safe.

MODERATE

Beltane Ranch ⋆ *Finds*   The word "Ranch" conjures up an image of a big ol' two-story house in the middle of hundreds of rolling acres; the kind of place where you laze away the day in a hammock watching the grass grow or pitching horseshoes in the garden. Well, friend, you can have all that and more at the Beltane Ranch, a century-old, buttercup-yellow manor that's been everything from a bunkhouse to a brothel to a turkey farm. You simply can't help but feel your tensions ease away as you kick your feet up on the shady wraparound porch overlooking the vineyards, sipping a cool, fruity chardonnay. Each room is uniquely decorated with American and European antiques; all have private bathrooms, sitting areas, and separate entrances. A big country breakfast is served in the garden on the porch overlooking the vineyards. For exercise, you can play tennis on the private court or hike the trails meandering through the 1,600-acre estate. *Tip:* Request one of the upstairs rooms, which has the best views.

11775 Sonoma Hwy. (Hwy. 12), Glen Ellen, CA 95442. ⓒ **707/996-6501**. www.beltaneranch.com. 5 units, 1 cottage. $130–$180 double; $220 cottage. Rates include full breakfast. No credit cards; personal checks accepted. **Amenities:** Tennis court. *In room:* No phone.

El Dorado Hotel ⋆⋆   This place may look like a 19th-century Wild West relic from the outside, but inside it's all 20th-century deluxe. Each modern, handsomely appointed guest room—designed by the same folks who put together the ultra-exclusive Auberge du Soleil (p. 177) resort in Rutherford—has French windows and tiny terraces; some offer lovely views of the plaza, while others overlook the hotel's private courtyard and heated lap pool. All rooms (except those for guests with disabilities) are on the second floor, and have private bathrooms with plush towels. The two rooms on the ground floor are off the private courtyard, and each has a partially enclosed patio. Breakfast, served either inside or out in the courtyard, includes coffee, fruits, and freshly baked breads and pastries. Within the hotel is Piatti, an uneven restaurant serving regional Italian cuisine.

405 1st St. W., Sonoma, CA 95476. ⓒ **800/289-3031** or 707/996-3030. Fax 707/996-3148. www.hotel eldorado.com. 27 units. Summer $220–$265 double; winter $195–$235 double. Rates include continental breakfast and bottle of wine. AE, MC, V. **Amenities:** Restaurant; heated outdoor pool; access to nearby health club; bike rental; concierge; room service 11:30am–10pm; laundry service; dry cleaning. *In room:* A/C, TV, dataport, hair dryer.

Glenelly Inn ⋆⋆   This former 1916 railroad inn is positively drenched in serenity. Located well off the main highway on an oak-studded hillside, the inn comes with everything you would expect from a country retreat—long verandas with comfy wicker chairs and views of the verdant Sonoma hillsides; a hearty country breakfast served beside a large cobblestone fireplace; and bright, immaculate rooms with private entrances, authentic antiques, old-fashioned claw-foot tubs, Scandinavian down comforters, firm mattresses, and ceiling fans. The simmering hot tub is ensconced within a grapevine- and rose-covered arbor.

5131 Warm Springs Rd. (off Arnold Dr.), Glen Ellen, CA 95442. ⓒ **707/996-6720**. Fax 707/996-5227. www.glenelly.com. 8 units. $135–$190 double. Rates include full breakfast. MC, V. *In room:* No phone.

INEXPENSIVE

Sonoma Hotel ⋆⋆   This cute little historic hotel on Sonoma's tree-lined town plaza places an emphasis on 19th-century elegance and comfort. Built in 1880 by German immigrant Henry Weyl, each of its attractive guest rooms is decorated in early California style with French country furnishings, antique beds, and period decorations. In a bow to modern luxuries, recent additions include private bathrooms in each of the rooms, as well as cable TVs, phones with dataports, and (this is crucial) air-conditioning. Perks include fresh coffee and pastries in the morning and complimentary wine and cheese in the evening. Also within the hotel is "the girl & the fig" (see below), a popular restaurant serving California-French cuisine.

110 W. Spain St., Sonoma, CA 95476. © 800/468-6016 or 707/996-2996. Fax 707/996-7014. www.sonoma hotel.com. 16 units. Summer $110–$245 double. Winter Sun–Thurs $95–$170 double; Fri–Sat $115–$195 double. Rates include continental breakfast and evening wine and cheese. AE, DC, MC, V. *In room:* A/C, TV, dataport.

Victorian Garden Inn ⊛ Proprietor Donna Lewis runs what is easily the cutest B&B in Sonoma Valley. A small picket fence and wall of trees enclose an adorable Victorian garden brimming with bowers of violets, roses, camellias, and peonies, all shaded under flowering fruit trees. Four guest rooms—three in the century-old water tower and one in the main house, an 1870s Greek Revival farmhouse—are in keeping with the Victorian theme: white wicker furniture, floral prints, padded armchairs, and claw-foot tubs. The most popular rooms are in the Top o' the Tower, which has its own entrance and view overlooking the garden, and the Woodcutter's Cottage, which has its own entrance and garden view, plus a sofa and armchairs set in front of the fireplace. A breakfast of croissants, muffins, gourmet coffee, and fruit picked from the garden is served at the dining table, in the garden, or in your room; evening wine and sherry are served in the parlor. Leisure time can be spent in the pool or along the shaded wraparound porch.

316 E. Napa St., Sonoma, CA 95476. © 800/543-5339 or 707/996-5339. Fax 707/996-1689. www. victoriangardeninn.com. 4 units. $125–$240 double. Rates include continental breakfast. AE, DC, MC, V. **Amenities:** Outdoor pool; business center; concierge; room service 8am–5pm; laundry service; dry cleaning. *In room:* A/C.

WHERE TO DINE

Though Sonoma Valley has far fewer visitors than Napa Valley, its restaurants are often equally as crowded, so be sure to make reservations in advance.

EXPENSIVE

Depot Hotel–Cucina Rustica Restaurant ⊛ NORTHERN ITALIAN Michael Ghilarducci has been the chef and owner here for the past 14 years, which means he's either independently wealthy or a darn good cook. Fortunately, it's the latter. Located a block north of the plaza in a handsome, historic 1870 stone building, the Depot Hotel offers pleasant outdoor dining in an Italian garden complete with a reflection pool and cascading Roman fountain. The menu is unwaveringly Italian, filled with a plethora of classic dishes such as spaghetti Bolognese and veal alla parmigiana. Start with the bounteous antipasto misto and end the feast with a dish of Michael's handmade Italian ice cream and fresh-fruit sorbets.

241 1st St. W. (off Spain St.), Sonoma. © 707/938-2980. www.depothotel.com. Reservations recommended. Main courses $12–$22. AE, DISC, MC, V. Wed–Fri 11:30am–5pm; Wed–Sun 5–9pm.

the girl & the fig ⊛⊛ COUNTRY FRENCH Already well established in its new downtown Sonoma digs (it used to be in Glen Ellen), this is the new home for Sondra Bernstein's (the girl) beloved and cozy restaurant. Here the cuisine is nouveau country with French nuances, and yes, figs are sure to be on the menu in one form or another. The wonderful winter fig salad contains arugula, pecans, dried figs, Laura Chenel goat cheese, and fig-and-port vinaigrette. Chef John Toulze uses garden-fresh produce and local meats, poultry, and fish whenever possible, in dishes such as pork tenderloin with a potato-leek pancake and roasted beets, and sea scallops with lobster-scented risotto. For dessert, try the warm pear galette topped with gingered crème fraîche, a glass of Quady Essensia Orange Muscat, and a sliver of raclette from the cheese cart. Sondra knows her wines, and will be happy to choose the best accompaniment to your meal.

110 W. Spain St., Sonoma ℂ **707/938-3634.** www.thegirlandthefig.com. Reservations recommended. Main courses $12–$19. AE, MC, V. Daily 11:30am–11pm.

Glen Ellen Inn Restaurant 🍴 CALIFORNIA Christian and Karen Bertrand run this popular Glen Ellen restaurant. The dining room is so quaint and cozy that you feel as if you're dining in their home, but that's exactly the place's charm. Garden seating is the favored choice on sunny days, but the covered, heated patio is always welcoming. First courses from Christian's open kitchen might include a wild-mushroom-and-sausage "purse" served in a brandy cream sauce, and warm goat-cheese croquettes. Main courses change with the seasons, but might range from linguine with artichoke hearts and feta to stellar late-harvest ravioli stuffed with pumpkin, walnuts, and sun-dried cranberries on a bed of butternut squash. Other favorites include the marinated pork tenderloin on smoked mozzarella polenta, topped with roasted pepper onion compote; and the utterly tender Nebraska corn-fed filet mignon in a foie gras–brandy reduction sauce. The wine list offers numerous Sonoma selections, as well as more than a dozen wines by the glass. *Tip:* There's a small parking lot behind the restaurant.

13670 Arnold Dr., Glen Ellen. ℂ **707/996-6409.** www.glenelleninn.com. Reservations recommended. Main courses $12–$22. AE, MC, V. Daily 5:30–9:30pm. Closed Mon–Thurs last week in Jan.

Kenwood Restaurant & Bar 🍴🍴 CALIFORNIA/CONTINENTAL This is what California Wine Country dining should be (but what it often, disappointingly, is not). From the terrace of the Kenwood Restaurant, diners enjoy a view of the vineyards set against Sugarloaf Ridge as they imbibe Sonoma's finest at umbrella-covered tables. On nippy days you can retreat inside to the Sonoma-style roadhouse, with its shiny wood floors, pine ceiling, vibrant artwork, and cushioned rattan chairs set at white cloth-covered tables. Chef Max Schacher serves first-rate cuisine, perfectly balanced between tradition and innovation, and complemented by a reasonably priced wine list. Great starters are the Dungeness crab cake with herb mayonnaise; the super-fresh sashimi with ginger, soy, and wasabi; and the wonderful Caesar salad. Main-dish choices might include poached salmon in a creamy caper sauce, prawns with saffron Pernod sauce, or braised Sonoma rabbit with grilled polenta. But the Kenwood doesn't take itself too seriously: Sandwiches and burgers also are available.

9900 Sonoma Hwy., Kenwood. ℂ **707/833-6326.** Reservations recommended. Main courses $13–$26. MC, V. Tues–Sun 11:30am–9pm.

Meritage 🍴🍴 SOUTHERN FRENCH/NORTHERN ITALIAN Learning from the previous occupants' mistakes—that Sonoma ain't New York City and shouldn't treat its customers that way—chef-owner Carlo Cavallo eliminated the big-city attitude and prices at his new restaurant without diminishing style, service, and quality. The former executive chef for Giorgio Armani, Cavallo combines the best of southern French and northern Italian cuisines (hence "Meritage," after a blend made with traditional Bordeaux varieties), giving

Gourmet Picnics, Sonoma-Style

Sure, Sonoma has plenty of restaurants, but when the weather's warm, there's no better way to have lunch in the Wine Country than by toting a picnic basket to your favorite winery and basking under the sweet Sonoma sunshine. Even Sonoma's central plaza, with its many picnic tables, is a good spot to set up a gourmet spread.

But first you need grub, so head to the venerable **Sonoma Cheese Factory,** on the plaza at 2 Spain St. (② 707/996-1000), to stock up for an alfresco fete. The factory offers award-winning house-made cheeses and an extraordinary variety of imported meats and cheeses; a few are set out for tasting every day. Also available are caviar, gourmet salads, paté, and homemade Sonoma Jack cheese. Pick up some good, inexpensive sandwiches, such as fire-roasted pork loin or New York steak. While you're there, you can watch a narrated slide show about the cheese-making process. The factory is open daily from 8:30am to 5:30pm.

Sonomans yet another reason to eat out. The menu, which changes twice daily, is a good read: handmade roasted pumpkin tortellini in Parmesan cheese sauce; napoleon of escargot in champagne and wild-thyme sauce; organic greens, strawberries, corn, and French feta salad; and wild-boar chops in white truffle sauce with mashed potatoes. Shellfish fans can't help but love the oyster raw bar and options of live crab and lobster. A lovely garden patio is prime positioning for sunny breakfasts and lunches and summer dinners. Such edible enticement—combined with reasonable prices, excellent service, a stellar wine list, cozy booth seating, a handsome dining room, and Carlo's practiced charm—make Meritage a trustworthy option.

522 Broadway, Sonoma. ② 707/938-9430. www.sonomameritage.com. Reservations recommended. Main courses $13–$30. AE, MC, V. Mon 11:30am–3pm, Wed–Sun 8am–9pm.

MODERATE

Cafe La Haye ★★ ECLECTIC   Well-prepared, wholesome food, an experienced wait staff, friendly owners, soothing atmosphere, and reasonable prices—including a modestly priced wine list—make La Haye a favorite. Within the small split-level dining room pleasantly decorated with hardwood floors, an exposed-beam ceiling, and revolving contemporary artwork, the vibe is small-business. The straightforward, seasonally inspired cuisine, which chefs bring forth from the tiny open kitchen, is delicious and wonderfully well priced. Although the menu is small, it offers just enough options. Expect a risotto special; pasta such as fresh tagliarini with butternut squash, prosciutto, sage, and garlic cream; and pan-roasted chicken breast, perhaps with goat cheese-herb stuffing, caramelized shallot jus, and fennel mashed potatoes. Meat eaters are sure to be pleased with filet of beef seared with black pepper-lavender sauce served with Gorgonzola-potato gratin, and no one can resist the creative salads. Sunday brunch includes a handful of creative breakfast and lunch dishes.

140 E. Napa St., Sonoma. ② 707/935-5994. Reservations recommended. Main courses $12–$20. MC, V. Tues–Sat 5:30–9pm, Sun brunch 9:30am–2pm.

Della Santina's ★★ ITALIAN Those of you who just can't take another expensive, chichi California meal should follow the locals to this friendly, traditional Italian restaurant. Every classic Tuscan dish I tried was refreshingly authentic and well flavored—without overbearing sauces or one *hint* of California pretentiousness. Start with traditional antipasti, especially the sliced mozzarella and tomatoes or the delicious white beans. The nine pasta dishes are, again, wonderfully authentic (gnocchi lovers, rejoice!). The spit-roasted meat dishes are a local favorite (though I found them a bit overcooked), and for those who can't choose among chicken, pork, turkey, rabbit, or duck, there's a selection that offers a choice of three. Don't worry about breaking your bank on a bottle of wine, as most of the savory choices here go for under $25.

133 E. Napa St. (just E of the square), Sonoma. ℂ **707/935-0576.** Reservations recommended. Main courses $9–$15. AE, DISC, MC, V. Daily 11:30am–3pm and 5pm–9:30pm.

INEXPENSIVE

Café Citti NORTHERN ITALIAN If you're this far north into the Wine Country, then you're probably doing some serious wine tasting. If that's the case, then you don't want to spend half the day at a fancy, high-priced restaurant. What you need is Café Citti (pronounced *Cheat*-ee), a roadside do-it-yourself Italian trattoria that is both good and cheap. You order from the huge menu board displayed above the open kitchen. Afterwards you grab a table (the ones on the patio, shaded by umbrellas, are the best on warm afternoons), and a server will bring your meal. It's all hearty, home-cooked Italian. Standout dishes are the green-bean salad, tangy Caesar salad, focaccia sandwiches, and roasted rotisserie chicken stuffed with rosemary and garlic. The freshly made pastas come with a variety of sauces; try the zesty marinara. Wine is available by the bottle, and the espresso is plenty strong. Everything on the menu board is available to go, which makes Café Citti an excellent resource for picnic supplies.

9049 Sonoma Hwy., Kenwood. ℂ **707/833-2690.** Main courses $10–$16. MC, V. Daily 11am–3:30pm; Sun–Thurs 5:30–8:30pm, Fri–Sat 5–9pm.

Cucina Viansa ★★ ITALIAN DELI Cucina Viansa is the sexiest thing going in downtown Sonoma, a suave deli and wine bar owned by Sam and Vicki Sebastiani, who also run Viansa Winery (p. 188). It's a visual masterpiece, with shiny black-and-white checkered flooring, long counters of Italian marble, track lighting, and a center deli and wine bar where a crew of young men slice meats, pour wines, and scoop gelato. Start by sampling the preserves and jams near the entrance, then wander the aisle and choose among the armada of cured meats, cheese, fruit, pastas, salads, and breads lining the deli. Popular choices are the hefty sandwiches on herbed focaccia bread or the herb-marinated rotisserie chickens served by the half with your choice of pasta or salad. Roasted turkey, duck, pork, lamb, and rabbit also are available. Opposite the deli is the wine bar, featuring all of Viansa's current wine releases for both tasting and purchase, as well as a small selection of microbrewed beers on tap. On your way out, stop at the gelateria and treat yourself to some intense Italian ice cream.

400 1st St. E., Sonoma. ℂ **707/935-5656.** Deli items $5–$9. AE, DISC, MC, V. Sun–Thurs 10am–6pm, Fri–Sat 10am–11pm.

7

The Northern Coast

by Matthew Richard Poole

Heading north from San Francisco, you'll come upon a California that hardly resembles the southern part of the state. It's an entirely different landscape, in climate as well as flora and fauna. You can forget about California's fabled surfing-and-bikini scene this far north; instead, you'll find miles and miles of rugged coastline with broad beaches and tiny bays harboring dramatic rock formations—from chimney stacks to bridges and blowholes—carved by the ocean waves.

You may think you've arrived in Alaska when you hit the beaches of Northern California. Take a dip in the sea and you'll soon agree with the locals: When it comes to swimming, the Arctic waters along the northern coast are best left to the sea lions. But that doesn't mean you can't enjoy the beaches, whether by strolling along the water or taking in the panoramic views of towering cliffs and seascapes. And unlike their southern counterparts, the beaches along the northern coast are not likely to be crowded, even in summer.

The best time to visit is in the spring or fall. In spring, the headlands are carpeted with wildflowers—golden poppy, iris, and sea foam—and in fall, the sun shines clear and bright. Summers are typically cool and windy, with the ubiquitous fog burning off by the afternoon.

The most scenic way to reach Stinson Beach, Gualala, Mendocino, and points north is to drive along the coast via Calif. 1. The larger freeway, U.S. 101, runs inland through Healdsburg and Cloverdale and is much faster, but doesn't provide the spectacular views of coastal cliffs and windswept beaches you will see on Calif. 1. A good compromise if you're headed to, say, Mendocino, is to take U.S. 101 to Cloverdale, then cut over on Calif. 128 to the coast.

Oh, and one last thing: Dress warmly.

1 Point Reyes National Seashore ★★★

35 miles NW of San Francisco

The national seashore system was created to protect rural and undeveloped stretches of the coast from the pressures brought on by soaring real-estate values and increasing population. Nowhere is the success of the system more evident than at Point Reyes. Residents of the surrounding towns—**Inverness, Point Reyes Station,** and **Olema**—have steadfastly resisted runaway development. You won't find any strip malls or fast-food joints here—just laid-back coastal towns with cafes and country inns where gentle living prevails.

The park, a 71,000-acre hammer-shaped peninsula jutting 10 miles into the Pacific and backed by Tomales Bay, is loaded with wildlife, ranging from tule elk, birds, and bobcats to gray whales, sea lions, and great white sharks. Aside from its beautiful scenery, it also boasts historical treasures that offer a window into California's coastal past, including lighthouses, dairies and ranches, the site of Sir Francis Drake's 1579 landing, plus a complete replica of a coastal Miwok Indian village.

Though the peninsula's people and wildlife live in harmony above the ground, the situation beneath the soil is much more volatile. The infamous San Andreas Fault separates Point Reyes—the northernmost landmass on the Pacific Plate—from the rest of California, which rests on the North American Plate. Point Reyes is making its way toward Alaska at a rate of about 2 inches per year, but there have been times when it has moved much faster. In 1906, Point Reyes jumped north almost 20 feet in an instant, leveling San Francisco and jolting the rest of the state. The half-mile **Earthquake Trail,** near the Bear Valley Visitor Center, illustrates this geological drama with a loop through an area torn by the slipping fault. Shattered fences, rifts in the ground, and a barn knocked off its foundation by the quake illustrate how alive the earth is here. If that doesn't convince you, a seismograph in the visitor center will.

ESSENTIALS
GETTING THERE   Point Reyes is only 35 miles northwest of San Francisco, but it takes at least 90 minutes to reach by car (it's all the small towns, not the topography, that slow you down). The easiest route is via Sir Francis Drake Boulevard from U.S. 101 south of San Rafael; it takes its sweet time getting to Point Reyes, but does so without any detours. For a much longer but more scenic route, take the Stinson Beach/Calif. 1 exit off U.S. 101 just south of Sausalito and follow Calif. 1 north.

VISITOR INFORMATION   As soon as you arrive at Point Reyes, stop at the **Bear Valley Visitor Center** (*©* 415/464-5100; www.nps.gov/pore) on Bear Valley Road (look for the small sign posted just north of Olema on Calif. 1) and pick up a free Point Reyes trail map. The rangers here are extremely friendly and helpful, and can answer any questions you have about the National Seashore. Be sure to check out the great natural history and cultural displays as well. It's open Monday through Friday from 9am to 5pm, Saturday and Sunday from 8am to 5pm.

FEES & PERMITS   Entrance to the park is free. Camping is $10 per site per night, and permits are required; reservations can be made up to 3 months in advance by calling *©* 415/663-8054 Monday through Friday from 9am to 2pm.

WHAT TO SEE & DO
When heading out to any part of the Point Reyes coast, expect to spend the day surrounded by nature at its finest. The park encompasses several surf-pounded beaches, bird estuaries, open swaths of land with roaming elk, and the Point Reyes lighthouse—a favorite among visitors who are awestruck by the spectacular views of the coast. But bear in mind that, as beautiful as the wilderness can be, it's also untamable. Waters in these areas are not only bone chilling and home to a vast array of sea life, including sharks, but are also unpredictable and dangerous. There are no lifeguards on duty, and waves and riptides strongly discourage swimming. Pets are not permitted on any of the area's trails.

By far the most popular—and crowded—attraction at Point Reyes National Seashore is the venerable **Point Reyes Lighthouse** *(¥)*, located at the westernmost tip of Point Reyes. Even if you plan to forego the 308 steps down to the lighthouse, it's still worth the visit to marvel at the dramatic scenery, which includes thousands of common murres and prides of sea lions that bask on the rocks far below (binoculars come in handy). The lighthouse visitor center

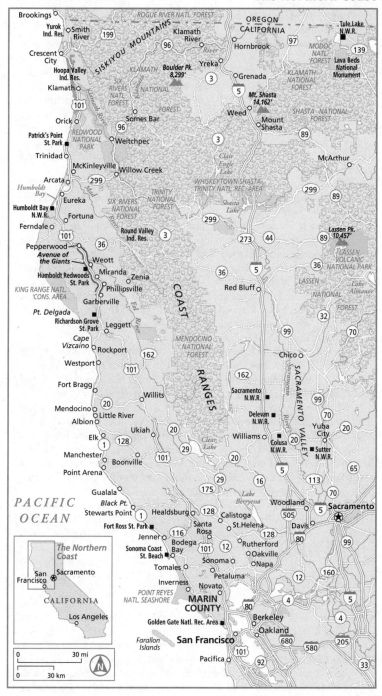

(☏ 415/669-1534) is open Thursday through Monday from 10am to 4:30pm, weather permitting.

The lighthouse is also the top spot on the California coast to observe **gray whales** as they make their southward and northward migration along the coast from January to April. The annual round-trip is 10,000 miles—one of the longest mammal migrations known. The whales head south in December and January, and return north in March. *Tip:* If you plan to drive out to the lighthouse to whale-watch, arrive early as parking is limited. If possible, come on a weekday. On a weekend or holiday from December to April (weather permitting), it's wise to park at the Drake's Beach Visitor Center and take the shuttle bus to the lighthouse, which costs $3.50 for adults and is free for kids age 12 and under. Dress warmly—it's often quite cold and windy—and bring binoculars.

Whale-watching is far from the only activity offered at the Point Reyes National Seashore. Rangers conduct many different tours on weekends: You can walk along the **Bear Valley Trail,** spotting the wildlife at the ocean's edge; see the waterfowl at **Fivebrooks Pond;** explore tide pools; view some of North America's most beautiful ducks in the wetlands of **Limantour;** hike to the promontory overlooking **Chimney Rock** to see the sea lions, elephant seals, harbor seals, and seabirds; or take a self-guided walk along the **San Andreas Fault** to observe the site of the epicenter of the 1906 earthquake and learn about the regional geology. And this is just a sampling. Since tours vary seasonally, you can either call the **Bear Valley Visitor Center** (☏ 415/464-5100) or request a copy of *Park Paper,* which includes a schedule of activities and other useful information. Many of the tours are suitable for travelers with disabilities.

North and South **Point Reyes Beaches** face the Pacific and withstand the full brunt of ocean tides and winds—so much so that the water is far too rough for even wading. Until a few years ago, entering the water was actually illegal, but persistent surfers went to court for their right to shred the mighty waves. Today, the park service strongly advises against taking on the tides, so play it safe and stroll the coastline. Along the southern coast, the waters of **Drake's Beach** can be as tranquil and serene as Point Reyes's are turbulent. Locals come here to sun and picnic; occasionally a hearty soul ventures into the cold waters of Drake's Bay. But keep in mind that storms generally come inland from the south and almost always hit Drake's before moving north or south. A powerful weather front can turn wispy waves into torrential tides.

Some of the park's best—and least crowded—highlights can only be approached on foot, such as **Alamere Falls** , a freshwater stream that cascades down a 40-foot bluff onto Wildcat Beach, or **Tomales Point Trail** , which passes through the Tule Elk Reserve, a protected haven for roaming herds of tule elk that once numbered in the thousands. Hiking most of the trails usually ends up being an all-day outing, however, so it's best to split a 2-day trip within Point Reyes National Seashore into a "by car" day and a "by foot" day.

If you're into bird-watching, you definitely want to visit the **Point Reyes Bird Observatory** (☏ 415/868-1221; www.prbo.org), one of the few full-time ornithological research stations in the United States, located at the southeast end of the park on Mesa Road. This is where ornithologists keep an eye on more than 400 feathered species. Admission to the visitor center and nature trail is free, and visitors are welcome to observe the tricky process of catching and banding the birds. It's open daily from 15 minutes after sunrise until sunset. Banding hours vary seasonally; call ☏ 415/868-0655 for exact times.

Point Reyes National Seashore & Bodega Bay

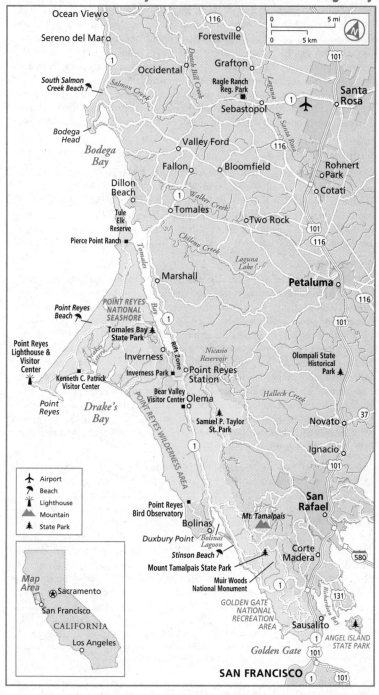

Ocean View

Sereno del Mar

116

Forestville

South Salmon
Creek Beach

Occidental

Grafton

5 mi

0   5 km

101

1

Salmon Creek

Dutch Bill Creek

Ragle Ranch
Reg. Park

Sebastopol

1

Santa
Rosa

Bodega
Head

Bodega
Bay

Valley Ford

Laguna de Santa Rosa

116

Fallon

Bloomfield

Rohnert
Park

Dillon
Beach

Tule
Elk
Reserve

1

Walker Creek

Tomales

Cotati

Pierce Point Ranch

Chileno Creek

Two Rock

101

116

Tomales Bay

Marshall

Laguna
Lake

Petaluma

116

Point Reyes
Beach

POINT REYES
NATIONAL
SEASHORE

1

Drakes Estero

Rift Zone

101

Tomales Bay
State Park

Inverness

Nicasio
Reservoir

Olompali State
Historical
Park

Point Reyes
Lighthouse &
Visitor
Center

Kenneth C. Patrick
Visitor Center

Inverness Park

Point Reyes
Station

Halleck Creek

Point
Reyes

Drake's
Bay

Bear Valley
Visitor Center

Olema

Novato

37

POINT REYES WILDERNESS AREA

Samuel P. Taylor
St. Park

Ignacio

1

101

San
Rafael

Point Reyes
Bird Observatory

Bolinas

Mt. Tamalpais

Duxbury Point

Bolinas
Lagoon

Corte
Madera

580

Airport

Beach

Lighthouse

Mountain

State Park

Stinson Beach

Mount Tamalpais State Park

Muir Woods
National Monument

1

Richardson Bay

131

Map
Area

Sacramento

San Francisco

CALIFORNIA

Los Angeles

GOLDEN GATE
NATIONAL
RECREATION
AREA

Golden Gate

SAN FRANCISCO

Sausalito

1

ANGEL ISLAND
STATE PARK

101

1

101

One of my favorite things to do in Point Reyes is paddle through placid **Tomales Bay,** a haven for migrating birds and marine mammals. Kayak trips, including sunset outings, full-moon paddles, and day trips, are organized by **Tomales Bay Sea Kayaking Center** (© 415/663-1743; www.tamalsaka.com). Instruction, clinics, and boat delivery are available, and all ages and levels are welcome. Prices start at $60 per person for tours. Half-day rentals begin at $35 for one, $50 for two. Don't worry, the kayaks are very stable, and there are no waves to contend with. The launching point is located on Calif. 1 at the Marshall Boatworks in Marshall, 8 miles north of Point Reyes Station. It's open daily from 9am to 6pm.

WHERE TO STAY

If you're having trouble finding a vacancy, **Inns of Marin** (© 800/887-2880 or 415/663-2000) and **West Marin Network** (© 415/663-9543) are two reputable services that will help you find accommodations, ranging from one-room cottages to inns and complete vacation homes. Keep in mind that many places here have a 2-night minimum, although in slow season they may make an exception. They'll also refer you to restaurants, hiking, and attractions in the area.

EXPENSIVE

Blackthorne Inn ⭐⭐ This elaborate redwood home with its octagonal widow's walk, spiral staircase, turrets, and multiple decks looks more like a super deluxe treehouse than a B&B. My favorite—and the most expensive—unit is the Eagle's Nest, an octagonal room enclosed by glass and topped with a private sun deck with a catwalk leading to the private bathroom. The largest room is the Forest View, a two-room suite complete with deck, which has a private entrance and a sitting area facing the woods; it's furnished with white wicker and natural rattan, and decorated with floral fabrics and modern lithographs. All have private bathrooms. The main sitting room in the house features a large stone fireplace, skylight, wet bar, and stained-glass windows, and is surrounded by a huge deck.

266 Vallejo Ave. (off Sir Francis Drake Blvd., S of Inverness), Inverness Park, P.O. Box 712, Inverness, CA 94937. © 415/663-8621. Fax 415/663-8635. www.blackthorneinn.com. 4 units. $225–$325 double. Rates include buffet breakfast. MC, V. **Amenities:** Nearby golf course; Jacuzzi. *In room:* Coffeemaker.

Manka's Inverness Lodge ⭐⭐ If there were ever a reason to pack your bags and leave San Francisco for a day or two, this is it. A former hunting-and-fishing lodge, Manka's Inverness Lodge looks like something out of a Hans Christian Andersen fairy tale, right down to the tree-limb bedsteads and cooks roasting venison sausage in front of the hearth. It's all terribly romantic in a Jack London sort of way, and tastefully done as well. The lodge consists of an excellent restaurant on the first floor (see "Where to Dine," below), four rooms upstairs (room nos. 1 and 2 come with large private decks), four rooms in the Redwood Annex, and two spacious one-bedroom cabins located behind the lodge. For the ultimate romantic splurge, inquire about these secluded cabins: Fishing and Manka's, or at the water's edge, the Boathouse and Chicken Ranch.

30 Calendar Way (on Argyle St. off Sir Francis Drake Blvd., 1½ blocks N of downtown Inverness), P.O. Box 1110, Inverness, CA 94937. © 800/58-LODGE or 415/669-1034. Fax 415/669-1598. www.mankas.com. 12 units. $185–$465. MC, V. **Amenities:** Restaurant; bike rental; limited room service; in-room massage. *In room:* TV in some units, kitchenette, fridge, coffeemaker, hair dryer, no phone.

MODERATE

An English Oak Bed and Breakfast ⭐ This venerable two-story farmhouse has survived everything from a major earthquake to a recent forest fire, which is lucky for you because you'll be hard-pressed to find a better B&B for the price in Point Reyes. Loaded with charm, right down to the profusion of flowers and vines outside and comfy chairs fronting a toasty-warm wood-burning stove inside, it's in a great location, too, with two good restaurants within walking distance and the entire National Seashore at your doorstep. One of the units is a private cottage with TV, a fully equipped kitchen, and two futon couches in the living area, suitable for children.

88 Bear Valley Rd., Olema, CA 94950. ✆ 415/663-1777. www.anenglishoak.com. 4 units. $95–$160 double. Rates include breakfast. MC, V. *In room:* Coffeemaker in some units, hair dryer, iron.

Point Reyes Country Inn & Stables ⚐ Are you and your horse dreaming of a country getaway? Then book a room at Point Reyes Country Inn & Stables, a ranch-style home on 4 acres that offers pastoral accommodations for two- and four-legged guests (horses only), plus access to plenty of hiking and riding trails. Each of the six B&B rooms has a private bathroom and either a balcony or a garden. The innkeepers have also added two studios (with kitchens) above the stables, plus they rent out two cottages on Tomales Bay equipped with decks, stocked kitchens, fireplaces, and a shared dock.

12050 Calif. 1 (P.O. Box 501), Point Reyes Station, CA 94956. ✆ 415/663-9696. Fax 415/663-8888. www.ptreyescountryinn.com. 10 units. $95–$115 studio; $110–$170 double; $190–$200 cottage. $10–$15 per horse. Rates include breakfast in the B&B rooms, breakfast provisions in the cottages. MC, V. **Amenities:** Nearby golf course. *In room:* No phone.

INEXPENSIVE

Point Reyes Hostel ⭐*Value* Located deep within Point Reyes National Seashore, this beautiful old ranch-style complex has 44 dormitory-style accommodations, including one room that's reserved for families (though at least one child must be 5 years old or younger). There are also two common rooms, each warmed by wood-burning stoves on chilly nights, as well as a fully equipped kitchen, barbecue (BYO charcoal), and patio. If you don't mind sharing your sleeping quarters with strangers, this is a deal that can't be beat. Reservations (and earplugs) are strongly recommended.

P.O. Box 247 (off Limantour Rd.), Point Reyes Station, CA 94956. ✆ 415/663-8811. www.norcalhostels.org. 44 bunks; 1 private unit for parent(s) with child age 5 or under. $14 per adult, $7 per child under 17 with parents. 5 nights out of 30 maximum stay. MC, V. Reception hours 7:30–10am and 4:30–9:30pm daily.

WHERE TO DINE

The Gray Whale ⭐*Value* ITALIAN For more than a decade, The Gray Whale has been a popular pit stop for Bay Areans heading to the lighthouse at Point Reyes. Why so popular? First off, it's cheap: Sandwiches—such as the roasted eggplant with pesto and mozzarella—are under $7, as are most of the salads and pastas. Second, it's pretty good: Personal favorites are the specialty pizzas, such as the Californian (artichoke hearts, fresh basil, and tomatoes) and the Vegetarian (baked eggplant, roasted onions and romas, broccoli, and piles of freshly grated Parmesan cheese). Veteran hikers and mountain bikers stop by for an espresso booster, sipped on the small patio overlooking the block-long town of Inverness.

12781 Sir Francis Drake Blvd., Inverness. ✆ 415/669-1244. Main courses $5–$10. MC, V. Daily 11am–8pm.

Manka's Inverness Lodge ⭐⭐ CALIFORNIA/WILD GAME Manka's reputation is built in large part on its restaurant, which dominates the bottom floor of the lodge. The restaurant dinners are prix fixe, and the specialty of the house is fire-grilled wild game, although if you call ahead you may be able to arrange something tamer. The seasonal menu features such things as pheasant with a Madeira jus, mashed potatoes, and a wild huckleberry jam; black buck antelope chops with sweet-corn salsa; or everybody's favorite, pan-seared elk tenderloin. The restaurant's boast is that the majority of the fish, fruits, and vegetables it serves are grown and raised or caught within 15 minutes of its kitchen. The wine cellar features more than 150 selections.

On Argyle St. (off Sir Francis Drake Blvd., 1½ blocks N of downtown Inverness), Inverness. © **800/58-LODGE** or 415/669-1034. www.mankas.com. Reservations recommended. Prix-fixe menu Thurs, Fri, Sun $48 per person; Sat $68 per person; Mon $32 per person. MC, V. Thurs–Mon 6–9pm (spring hours may vary—call ahead).

Station House Café ⭑ AMERICAN This friendly, low-key establishment has been a local favorite for more than 2 decades, thanks to its open kitchen, outdoor garden dining area (key on sunny days), and live music on weekends. Breakfast dishes range from a hangtown fry with local Johnson's oysters and bacon to eggs served with creamed spinach to mashed-potato pancakes. Lunch and dinner specials might include fettuccine with fresh local mussels steamed in a white-wine-and-butter sauce, or two-cheese polenta served with fresh spinach sauté and grilled garlic-buttered tomato—all made from local produce, seafood, and organically raised Niman-Schell Farms beef. Fresh salmon is also always on the menu. The cafe has an extensive list of California wines, plus local and imported beers.

Main St., Point Reyes Station. © **415/663-1515.** www.stationhousecafe.com. Reservations recommended. Breakfast $4.50–$8; main courses $9–$22. DISC, MC, V. Sun–Thurs 8am–9pm, Fri–Sat 8am–10pm. Closed Wed in winter.

Taqueria La Quinta (Value MEXICAN Fresh, fast, good, and cheap: What more could you ask for in a restaurant? Taqueria La Quinta has been one of my favorite lunch stops in downtown Point Reyes for years and years. A huge selection of Mexican-American standards are posted above the counter. My favorite is chile verde in a spicy tomatillo sauce with a side of handmade corn tortillas. Those in the know inquire about the seafood specials. Since it's all self-serve, you can skip the tip, but watch out for the salsa—that sucker's hot.

11285 Calif. 1 (at 3rd and Main sts.), Point Reyes Station. © **415/663-8868.** Main courses $5–$9. No credit cards. Wed–Mon 11:30am–7:30pm.

2 Along the Sonoma Coast

BODEGA BAY

Beyond the tip of the Point Reyes peninsula, the road curves around toward the coastal village of Bodega Bay, which supports a fishing fleet of around 300 boats. It's a good place to stop for lunch or a stroll around town. Despite the droves of tourists who arrive on summer weekends, Bodega Bay is still a mostly working-class fishing town—the sort of place where most people start their day before dawn mending nets, rigging fishing poles, and talking shop. There are several interesting shops and galleries, though the best show in town—especially for kids—is at **Tides Wharf,** where the fishing boats come in to unload their daily catch, which is promptly gutted and packed in ice.

Bodega Head State Park ⭑ is a great vantage point for whale-watching during the annual migration season from January to April. At **Doran Beach,** there's a large bird sanctuary (willets, curlews, godwits, and more), and the **U.C. Davis Bodega Marine Laboratory** (© **707/875-2211**) next door conducts guided tours of its lab projects on Friday afternoons between 2 and 4pm. (Suggested donation is $2.)

The **Bodega Harbour Golf Links**, at 21301 Heron Dr. (© **707/875-3538;** www.bodegaharbourgolf.com), offers a panoramic ocean-side setting. It's an 18-hole Scottish-style course designed by Robert Trent Jones Jr. A warm-up center and practice facility is free of charge to registered golfers. Rates range from $60 with cart Monday through Thursday, $70 on Friday, and $90 on weekends. If golfing isn't your thing, you can go horseback riding through some spectacular coastal scenery by contacting **Chanslor Horse Stables** (© **707/875-3333;** www.chanslor.com), which also has pony rides for the kids. It's open daily from 9am to 5pm.

One of the bay's major events is the **Fisherman's Festival** in April. Local fishing boats, decorated with ribbons and banners, sail out for a Blessing of the Fleet, while up to 25,000 landlubbers enjoy music, a lamb-and-oyster barbecue, and an arts-and-crafts fair. For more information about this festival and other goings-on in Bodega Bay, call or stop in at the **Bodega Bay Area Visitors Center,** 850 Calif. 1, Bodega Bay, CA 94923 (© **707/875-3866;** www.bodega bay.com). Open daily, it has lots of brochures about the town and the surrounding area, including maps of the Sonoma Coast State Beaches and the best local fishing spots.

A few miles inland on Calif. 1 (toward Petaluma) is the tiny town of **Bodega** (pop. 100), famous as the setting of Alfred Hitchcock's *The Birds,* which was filmed here in 1961. Fans will want to visit the Potter School House and St. Teresa's Church.

WHERE TO STAY

Bodega Bay Lodge and Spa ★★   Located near Doran Beach State Park, this is the best hotel in Bodega Bay. Each of the newly remodeled rooms has plush furnishings, a fireplace, and a private balcony with sweeping views of the bay and bird-filled marshes. If you can afford the elbow room, opt for one of the luxury suites. Guests have complimentary access to a fitness center and sauna, as well as to a beautiful fieldstone spa and heated pool perched above the bay and surrounded by flower gardens. The lodge's Duck Club Restaurant also enjoys a reputation as Bodega Bay's finest. Large picture windows take advantage of the bay view, a sublimely romantic setting for Sonoma County cuisine such as roasted Petaluma duck and fresh fish caught by the Bodega fleet.

103 Calif. 1, Bodega Bay, CA 94923. © **800/368-2468** or 707/875-3525. Fax 707/875-2428. www. bodegabaylodge.com. 84 units. Sun–Thurs $210–$240 double, $400 suite; Fri–Sat $235–$285 double, $450 suite. 2-night minimum on weekends. AE, DC, DISC, MC, V. **Amenities:** Restaurant; heated outdoor pool with ocean view; nearby golf course; full service spa and fitness center; concierge; room service; in-room massage; babysitting; coin-op laundry. *In room:* A/C, TV w/pay movies, fax, dataport, minibar, fridge, coffeemaker, hair dryer, iron, safe.

Inn at the Tides ★   The larger of Bodega Bay's two upscale lodgings, the other being Bodega Bay Lodge, the Inn at the Tides consists of a cluster of condo-like wood complexes perched on the side of a gently sloping hill. The selling point here is the view; each unit is staggered just enough to guarantee a view of the bay across the highway. The rooms are tastefully modern and the inn's amenities are first-rate, such as the strikingly attractive indoor-outdoor pool. The Bay View Restaurant is open Wednesday through Sunday for dinner only, offering ocean views, a well-prepared albeit traditional choice of entrees, and a romantic, somewhat formal ambience. Be sure to check their website for special package deals.

800 Coast Hwy. 1 (P.O. Box 640), Bodega Bay, CA 94923. ℂ **800/541-7788** or 707/875-2751. Fax 707/875-3285. www.innatthetides.com. 86 units. Summer Sun–Thurs $169–$249, Fri–Sat $199–$284. Winter rates drop about 20%. Rates include continental breakfast. Golf packages available. AE, DC, DISC, MC, V. **Amenities:** Restaurant; partially outdoor heated pool; nearby golf course; exercise room; Jacuzzi; Finnish sauna; room service; in-room massage; babysitting (with advance notice); self-service laundry. *In room:* TV w/pay movies, minibar, coffeemaker, hair dryer, iron.

WHERE TO DINE

In addition to the following choices, see "Where to Stay," above, for hotel restaurants.

Lucas Wharf Deli 🌟 *Value* DELI   I always stop here whenever I pass through Bodega Bay. Most visitors don't even give it a glance as they head into the adjacent restaurant, but that's because they don't know about the big bowls of fresh, tangy crab cioppino doled out, in season, for only $5.25 a pint—a third of the restaurant price. It's a fabulously messy affair, best devoured at the nearby picnic tables. Great fish and chips are available year-round. The deli is also open for breakfast.

595 Calif. 1, Bodega Bay. ℂ **707/875-3562.** Deli items $4–$10. MC, V. Sun–Thurs 9am–6pm, Fri–Sat 9am–7pm.

Tides Wharf Restaurant SEAFOOD/PASTA   In summer, as many as 1,000 diners a day pass through the Tides Wharf. Back in the early 1960s, it served as one of the settings for Hitchcock's *The Birds*, but don't expect the weatherbeaten, board-and-batten luncheonette you saw in the movie—a $6 million renovation gentrified, enlarged, and redecorated the place beyond recognition. The best tables offer views overlooking the ocean, and the bill of fare is what you might expect at a seaside eatery: oysters on the half shell, clam chowder, and all the fish that the owners (who send their own fishing boat out into the Pacific every day) can dredge up from the cold blue waters offshore. Prime rib, pasta, and poultry dishes are available as well. Adjacent to the restaurant are a fishprocessing plant, snack bar, and gift shop.

835 Calif. 1. ℂ **707/875-3652.** http://www.innatthetides.com/tideswharf.html. Main courses $14–$37. AE, DISC, MC, V. Mon–Fri 7:30am–9pm, Sat–Sun 7am–9:30pm.

THE SONOMA COAST STATE BEACHES, JENNER & FORT ROSS STATE HISTORIC PARK 🌟🌟

Along 13 winding and utterly picturesque miles of Calif. 1—from Bodega Bay to Goat Rock Beach in Jenner—stretch the Sonoma Coast State Beaches. These beaches are ideal for walking, tide-pooling, abalone picking, fishing, and birdwatching for such species as great blue heron, cormorant, osprey, and pelican. Each beach is clearly marked from the road, and numerous pullouts are provided for parking. Even if you don't stop at any of the beaches, the drive alone is spectacular.

At **Jenner,** the Russian River empties into the ocean. **Penny Island,** in the river's estuary, is home to otters and many species of birds; a colony of harbor seals lives out on the ocean rocks. **Goat Rock Beach** is a popular breeding ground for the seals; pupping season begins in March and lasts until June.

From Jenner, an 11-mile drive along some very dramatic coastline will bring you to **Fort Ross State Historic Park** (ℂ **707/847-3286;** www.parks. sonoma.net/fortross.html), a reconstruction of the fort that was established here in 1812 by the Russians as a base for seal and otter hunting (it was abandoned in 1842). At the visitor center, you can view the silver samovars and elaborate table services that the Russians used. The fenced compound contains several buildings, including the first Russian Orthodox church ever built on the North American continent outside Alaska. A short history lesson about the fort is offered at 11:30am, 1:30pm, and 3:30pm between Memorial Day and Labor Day, and at noon and 2pm the rest of the year. Call ahead to be sure. The park also offers beach trails and picnic grounds on more than 1,000 acres. Admission to the park is $2 per car per day.

North from Fort Ross, the road continues to **Salt Point State Park** (C 707/ 847-3221). This 3,500-acre expanse contains 30 campsites, 14 miles of hiking trails, dozens of tide pools, a pygmy forest, and old Pomo village sites. Your best bet is to pull off the highway any place that catches your eye and start exploring on foot. At the north end of the park, head inland on Kruse Ranch Road to the 317-acre **Kruse Rhododendron Reserve** (C 707/847-3221), a forested grove of wild pink and purple flowers where the *Rhododendron californicum* grow up to a height of 18 feet under the redwood-and-fir canopy. Admission to the park is $2 per car per day.

WHERE TO STAY

Jenner Inn ⟨★⟩   The worst-kept secret on the northern coast is Jenner Inn, a hodgepodge of individually designed and decorated houses and cottages scattered along the coast and inland along the Russian River. Couples from the Bay Area who want to stay along the coast for a night, but dread the long drive to Mendocino, usually wend their way here for an easy weekend getaway. Most of the houses are subdivided into suites, while second honeymooners vie for the ultra-private oceanfront cottages. Wicker furniture, wood paneling, and private bathrooms and entrances are standard, though each lodging has its own distinct personality: Some have kitchens, while others have fireplaces, porches, or private decks. Naturally, the private cottages overlooking the Pacific are the priciest, but for about $130, most people are content with one of the small suites. The inn now offers yoga classes several times weekly and has added a small meditation cabin. A complimentary full breakfast is served in the main lodge. In addition to the bed-and-breakfast accommodations, the inn rents out vacation homes located along the river, within Jenner Canyon, or overlooking the ocean.

10400 Calif. 1 (P.O. Box 69), Jenner, CA 95450. C 800/732-2377 or 707/865-2377. Fax 707/865-0829. www.jennerinn.com. 20 units (plus several vacation homes). $95–$375 double. Rates include full breakfast. AE, MC, V. *In room:* Kitchen in some units, fridge, coffeemaker, hair dryer, iron, phones in cottages only.

WHERE TO DINE

River's End INTERNATIONAL   Outwardly unpretentious yet deceptively urbane, this small seaside restaurant offers an artfully rustic setting, with big windows overlooking the coast (seals and sea lions might happen to be cavorting offshore). The menu, which changes monthly, is wonderfully eclectic, offering everything from coconut shrimp, pheasant breast, racklets of elk, seafood, and steaks. Local Sonoma products—game, lamb, poultry, vegetables—are used whenever possible, including Sonoma microbrews and wines. After dinner, take the remainder of your wine to the outside deck and enjoy the sunset.

Calif. 1, Jenner. C 707/865-2484. Reservations recommended. Main courses $13–$28. MC, V. Summer Thurs–Mon 11:30am–9pm; winter (Nov–Apr) Fri–Sun noon–9pm.

Sizzling Tandoor ⟨Value⟩ INDIAN   Something of a nonsequitur along a rather desolate stretch of Calif. 1 between Bodega Bay and Jenner, the Sizzling Tandoor serves huge, inexpensive plates of classic Indian cuisine. The lonely location, though peculiar, is superb: Perched high atop a windswept hill, the restaurant boasts an exquisite view of the Russian River far below. The large array of curries and kabobs are accompanied by soup, vegetables, pulao rice, and the best naan (Indian bread) I've ever had. Even if you're not hungry, order some naan to go—it makes the perfect road snack.

9960 Calif. 1 (at the S end of the Russian River Bridge), Jenner. © **707/865-0625**. Main courses $9–$14. AE, DISC, MC, V. Mon–Thurs 11:30am–9pm, Fri–Sun 11:30am–9:30pm.

GUALALA & POINT ARENA

Back on Calif. 1 heading north, you'll pass through Sea Ranch, a series of condominium beach developments, before you reach the small coastal community of Gualala (pronounced Wah-*la*-la). Back in the old days, Gualala was an industrious, vivacious logging town. A few real-life suspender-wearing lumberjacks still end their day at the Gualala Hotel's saloon, but for the most part this coastal town's main role is providing gas, groceries, and hardware for area residents. Just outside of town are several excellent parks, hiking trails, and about 10 or so public beaches that are ideal for sunbathing.

The **Gualala River,** adjacent to the town of the same name, is suitable for canoeing, rafting, and kayaking, because all powerboats and jet skis are forbidden. Along its banks you're likely to see osprey, herons, egrets, and ducks; steelhead, salmon, and river otters make their home in the waters. Canoes and kayaks can be rented in Gualala for 2 hours, a half day, or a full day from **Adventure Rents** (© **888/881-4386** or 707/884-4386; www.adventurerents. com), in downtown Gualala on Calif. 1, north of the Chevron. Prices range from $25 for a few hours on a river canoe to $80 for a full day on an ocean kayak.

Point Arena lies a few miles north of Gualala. Most folks stop here for the view at the **Point Arena Lighthouse** ★ (© **707/882-2777;** www.mcn. org/1/palight), which was built in 1870 after 10 ships ran aground here on a single night during a storm. A $4-per-person fee ($1 for children under 12) covers parking, entrance to the lighthouse museum, and a surprisingly interesting tour of the six-story, 145-step lighthouse. It's open daily from 10am to 4:30pm (11am–3:30pm Oct–Mar); the half-hour tours are given every 20 minutes.

WHERE TO STAY

St. Orres ★★ An extraordinary Russian-style building—complete with two onion-domed towers—St. Orres lies 1½ miles north of Gualala. The complex was built in 1972 with century-old timbers salvaged from a nearby mill. It offers secluded cottage-style accommodations on 42 acres, as well as eight rooms in the main building (these rooms are handcrafted and share three bathrooms decorated in brilliant colors). Other units are very private. Some have wet bars, sitting areas with Franklin stoves, and French doors leading to decks with a distant ocean view. Seven cottages border St. Orres Creek and have exclusive use of a spa facility that includes a hot tub, sauna, and sun deck. The most luxurious is Pine Haven, with two bedrooms, two redwood decks, two bathrooms, a tiled breakfast area, a beach-stone fireplace, and a wet bar. The Black Chanterelle is as exotic as it sounds, with domes, a sauna and Jacuzzi, a fireplace, and an ocean view. Full breakfast is delivered to the cottages. The hotel's restaurant, open for dinner only, is located in a dramatic setting below one of the main building's onion domes. Light filters through stained-glass windows onto strands of ivy that cascade down from the upper balcony. The menu is inspired by Pacific Northwest cuisine and includes wild boar, pheasant, venison, quail, and rack of lamb.

36601 Calif. 1, P.O. Box 523, Gualala, CA 95445. © **707/884-3303.** Fax 707/884-1840. www.saintorres.com. 8 units (sharing 3 bathrooms), 13 cottages. $80–$95 double; cottage $110–$235 double. Rates include full breakfast. MC, V. **Amenities:** Restaurant; bar; nearby golf course; Jacuzzi; sauna; bike rental; in-room massage; babysitting. *In room:* Kitchenette in some units, fridge, coffeemaker, hair dryer, iron.

Whale Watch Inn By the Sea ⭐   This inn has one of the best vantage points along the northern coast to contemplate spectacular ocean vistas. Perched 90 feet above the water in five contemporary buildings on 2 cliff-side acres, the Whale Watch's very private guest rooms all have ocean views, decks, and fireplaces. Room styles range from traditional bed-and-breakfast to French Provincial to contemporary casual, so check out the pictures on the website before you make your reservation. For a closer encounter with nature, a private stairway leads to a half-mile long beach with tidal pools. If you and your friends want to form your own pod, the Whale Watch building has a large common room with a circular fireplace, floor-to-ceiling windows, and a wraparound deck for prime—what else?—whale-watching.

35100 Hwy. 1, Gualala, CA 95445. ✆ **800/942-5342** or 707/884-3667. Fax 707/884-3667. www.whale-watch.com. 18 units. $180–$300 double. Rates include full breakfast delivered to room at prearranged time. AE, MC, V. **Amenities:** Nearby golf course. *In room:* Hair dryer, phone upon request; kitchen, fridge, and coffeemaker in some units.

WHERE TO DINE

The Food Company (*Value*) DELI   If the St. Orres restaurant (see above) is out of your price range, you'll be happy to know that you can have an equally romantic lunch or dinner just down the road for a fraction of the price. Place your order at the deli counter, grab a bottle of wine from the rack, then head to the adjacent garden and plop your collective fannies at one of the picnic tables. The menu offers a dizzying array of specials from around the globe—corn tamales, Greek moussaka, lamb curry, quiche Lorraine, pasta puttanesca—as well as fresh-baked breads, pastries, and sandwiches. Better yet, order it all to go and head for the beach.

38411 Calif. 1 (at Robinsons Reef Rd.), Gualala. ✆ **707/884-1800.** Most items $7–$12. MC, V. Daily 8–10:30am; Sun–Thurs 11am–7pm, Fri–Sat 11am–8pm (closing hr. flexible).

Pangaea ⭐⭐ (*Finds*) ECLECTIC   Northern-coast locals have been raving about this place since the day it opened. Everything that comes out of the kitchen is wondrously fresh, inventive, and organically grown and/or raised. For starters, order the house-made rabbit terrine served with cornichons (crisp, tart pickles made from tiny gherkin cucumbers), mustard, mixed greens, and grilled bread, followed by the Thai-style crab cakes flavored with ginger scallions and served with a Thai green-curry coconut sauce. And how's this for a salad: Oz Farm lettuces with shaved fennel, Pecorino Toscana, spiced pecans, and a citrus vinaigrette. Entrees range from Moroccan braised lamb shanks with broccoli rabe and baby artichokes to rare seared ahi atop baby basmati with Thai red curry, baby bok choy, and fennel/cucumber slaw. Desserts—warm bittersweet chocolate cake served with vanilla ice cream and caramel sauce, crème brûlée with fresh blackberries—are equally impressive, as is the hip decor.

250 Main St., Point Arena. ✆ **707/882-3001.** www.pangaeacafe.com. Reservations recommended. Main courses $17–$26. MC, V. Wed–Sun 6–9pm.

NORTH FROM POINT ARENA

Driving north from Point Arena, you'll pass Elk (a good place to stop for lunch), Manchester, Albion, and Little River on your way to Mendocino.

WHERE TO STAY

Greenwood Pier Inn ✦   Perched on the edge of a dramatic bluff, the Greenwood Pier Inn is an eclectic, New Age kind of place. It's the unique domain of Kendrick Petty, who owns and operates this quartet of cafe, country store, garden shop, and accommodations. Kendrick is an artist and passionate gardener whose collages, tiles, and marble work can be seen in the interiors of several of the buildings in the complex and also outside in the gardens. Of the accommodations, which are in various buildings in addition to the main inn, the Cliffhouse is my top choice: a seaside redwood cabin complete with a fireplace, a large deck, and an upper-level bathtub with ocean views. All the rooms have private decks, fireplaces or wood burners, and lie within 100 feet of the cliff edge. A beautiful new building, called The Tower, has three levels: a two-person Jacuzzi at the bottom, an incredible deck overlooking the ocean on the second level, and, up a library ladder, there's a full-size bed facing an ocean view. A continental breakfast is delivered to your room; breakfast, lunch and dinner—roast pork loin, grilled rack of lamb, grilled Chilean sea bass—are served daily in the cafe.

5928 Calif. 1 (P.O. Box 336), Elk, CA 95432. ℂ 707/877-9997. Fax 707/877-3439. www.greenwood pierinn.com. 12 units. $130–$300 double. Rates include continental breakfast. AE, MC, V. Pets accepted in some units for $15 per night. **Amenities:** Restaurant; nearby golf course; oceanview Jacuzzi; in-room massage. *In room:* Fridge, coffeemaker, hair dryer in some units, no phone.

Harbor House Inn ✦✦   While the Greenwood Pier Inn is New Age, the darkly beautiful, redwood-sided, two-story Harbor House is very traditional. It was built in 1916 by the president of the Goodyear Redwood Lumber Co. as a hideaway for corporate executives. This is not a hotel, but an upscale inn offering 3 acres of gardens, access to a private beach, and views overlooking the Pacific. None of the units has a TV or phone, and that's how guests here like it. Five of the rooms in the main building have their own fireplaces, many are furnished with antiques originally purchased by the lumber executives, and all have private bathrooms. The four cottages tend to be small but have fireplaces and private decks. Set dinners, included in the rates, change nightly and feature California and Pacific Northwest cuisines, making use of local herbs, freshly baked breads, and vegetables from the inn's own gardens.

5600 S. Calif. 1 (P.O. Box 369), Elk, CA 95432. ℂ 800/720-7474 or 707/877-3203. Fax 707/877-3452. www.theharborhouseinn.com. 10 units. $235–$425 double (winter rates are considerably less). Extra person $100. Rates include full breakfast and 4-course dinner. AE, MC, V. **Amenities:** Restaurant; nearby golf course; in-room massage. *In room:* A/C, coffeemaker, hair dryer, iron in cottages, and no phone.

KOA Kamping Kabins *Kids*   "What? You expect me to stay at a Kampgrounds of America?!" You bet. Once you see these neat little log "kabins," you can't help but admit that, rich or poor, this is one great way to spend a weekend on the coast. The cabins have one or two bedrooms with log-frame double beds or bunk beds for the kids and sleep four to six people, respectively. Rustic is the key word here: Mattresses, a heater, and a light bulb are your standard amenities. Beyond that, you're on your own, but basically all you need is some bedding or a sleeping bag, cooking and eating utensils, and a bag of charcoal for the barbecue in front of the cabin. Enjoy your meal at the picnic table or on the front porch in the log porch swing. If this is all a little too spartan for you, opt for one of the fully furnished "kottages," both decked out with private bathrooms, fireplaces, comfy beds, and other creature comforts. Hot showers, bathrooms, laundry facilities, a small store, and a swimming pool are a short walk away, as is Manchester Beach. It's kid heaven.

On Kinney Rd. (off Calif. 1, 5 miles N of Point Arena). ✆ **800/562-4188** or 707/882-2375. Fax 707/882-3104. www.manchesterbeachkoa.com. 24 cabins, 2 cottages. $48–$62 cabin (up to 6 people); $128–$138 cottage (up to 4 people). AE, DISC, MC, V. **Amenities:** Heated outdoor pool (seasonal); spa; children's center and playground; coin-op laundry. *In room:* TV and kitchenette in cottages, no phone.

WHERE TO DINE

Ledford House ⭐ NEW AMERICAN   If James Beard were alive today, he'd feel right at home at this innovative but simply decorated restaurant overlooking the pounding surf of the Pacific from a bluff above. The kitchen offers self-styled "New American cuisine," experimenting with the bounty of the Golden State to fashion rich combinations and harmonious flavors. One part of the menu is reserved primarily for the pastas and hearty stews suitable to this far-northern setting, such as their award-winning Antoine's cassoulet, a jumble of pork, lamb, garlic sausage, and duck confit slowly cooked with white beans. Although the menu changes seasonally, for a taste of California, try the salmon primavera with lemon-caper butter, or the crisp-roasted duckling with wild-huckleberry sauce. Evenings bring live jazz in the cocktail lounge.

3000 N. Calif. 1, Albion. ✆ **707/937-0282.** www.ledfordhouse.com. Reservations recommended. Main courses $22–$26. AE, MC, V. Wed–Sun 5–9pm.

3 Mendocino ⭐⭐⭐

166 miles N of San Francisco

Mendocino is, to my mind, *the* premier destination on California's northern coast. Despite (or because of) its relative isolation, it emerged as one of Northern California's major centers for the arts in the 1950s. It's easy to see why artists were—and still are—attracted to this idyllic community, a cluster of New England–style sea captains' homes and small stores set on headlands overlooking the ocean.

At the height of the logging boom, Mendocino became an important and active port. Its population was about 3,500, and eight hotels were built, along with 17 saloons and more than a dozen bordellos. Today, it has only about 1,000 residents, most of whom reside on the north end of town. On summer weekends, the population seems more like 10,000, as hordes of tourists drive up from the Bay Area—but despite the crowds, Mendocino still manages to retain its small-town charm.

ESSENTIALS

GETTING THERE   The fastest route from San Francisco is via U.S. 101 north to Cloverdale. Then take Calif. 128 west to Calif. 1, then go north along the coast. It's about a 4-hour drive. (You could also take U.S. 101 all the way to Ukiah or Willits, and cut over to the west from there.) The most scenic route from the Bay Area, if you have the time and your stomach doesn't mind the twists and turns, is to take Calif. 1 north along the coast the entire way; it's at least a 5- to 6-hour drive.

VISITOR INFORMATION   You can stock up on lots of free brochures and maps at the **Fort Bragg/Mendocino Coast Chamber of Commerce,** 332 N. Main St. (P.O. Box 1141), Fort Bragg, CA 95437 (✆ **800/726-2780** or 707/961-6300; www.mendocinocoast.com). Pick up a copy of the center's monthly magazine, *Arts and Entertainment,* which lists upcoming events throughout Mendocino. It's available at numerous stores and cafes, including the Mendocino Bakery, Gallery Bookshop, and Mendocino Art Center.

EXPLORING THE TOWN

Stroll through town, enjoy the architecture, and browse through the dozens of galleries and shops. My favorites include the **Highlight Gallery,** 45052 Main St. (© **707/937-3132**), for its handmade furniture, pottery, and other craft work; and the **Gallery Bookshop & Bookwinkle's Children's Books,** at Main and Kasten streets (© **707/937-2665;** www.gallerybooks.com), one of the best independent bookstores in Northern California, with a wonderful selection of books for children and adults. Another popular stop is **Mendocino Jams & Preserves,** 440 Main St. (© **800/708-1196** or 707/937-1037), which offers free tastings of its natural, locally made gourmet wares on little bread chips.

After exploring the town, walk out on the headlands that wrap around the town and constitute **Mendocino Headlands State Park** ✦. (The visitor center for the park is in the Ford House on Main St.; © **707/937-5397.**) Three miles of trails wind through the park, giving visitors panoramic views of sea arches and hidden grottoes. If you're here at the right time of year, the area will be blanketed with wildflowers; when I last stopped by, I could pick fresh blackberries beside the trails. The headlands are home to many unique species of birds, including black oystercatchers. Behind the Mendocino Presbyterian Church on Main Street is a trail leading to stairs that take you down to the beach, a small but picturesque stretch of sand where driftwood formations have washed ashore.

On the south side of town, **Big River Beach** is accessible from Calif. 1; it's good for picnicking, walking, and sunbathing.

In town, stop by the **Mendocino Art Center,** 45200 Little Lake St. (© **707/937-5818;** www.mendocinoartcenter.org), the town's unofficial cultural headquarters. It's also known for its gardens, three galleries, and shops that display and sell local fine arts and crafts. Admission is free; open daily from 10am to 5pm.

For a special treat, go to **Sweetwater Spa & Inn,** 955 Ukiah St. (© **800/300-4140** or 707/937-4140; www.sweetwaterspa.com), which offers group and private saunas and hot-tub soaks by the hour. Additional services include Swedish or deep-tissue massages. Reservations are recommended. Private tub prices are $10 per person per half-hour, $13 per person per hour. Group tub prices are $8.50 per person with no time limit. Special discounts are available on Wednesdays. The spa is open Monday through Thursday from 1 to 10pm, Friday and Sunday from noon to 10pm, and Saturdays and holidays from noon to 11pm.

OUTDOOR PURSUITS

Explore the Big River by renting a canoe, kayak, or outrigger from **Catch a Canoe & Bicycles Too** (© **707/937-0273;** www.stanfordinn.com), open daily from 9am to sunset and located on the grounds of the Stanford Inn by the Sea (see "Where to Stay," below). If you're lucky, you'll see some osprey, blue herons, harbor seals, deer, and wood ducks. These same folks will also rent you a mountain bike (of much better quality than your usual bike rental), so you can head up Calif. 1 and explore the nearby state parks on two wheels.

Horseback riding (both English and western) on the beach and into the redwoods is offered by **Ricochet Ridge Ranch,** 24201 N. Calif. 1, Fort Bragg (© **888/873-5777** or 707/964-PONY; www.horse-vacation.com). Prices range from $40 for a 2-hour beach ride to $200 for an all-day beach and redwoods trail ride.

In addition to Mendocino Headlands State Park (see "Exploring the Town," above), there are several other state parks near Mendocino; all are within an easy drive or bike ride and make for a good day's outing. Information on all the parks' features, including maps of each one, is found in a brochure called *Mendocino Coast State Parks,* available from the visitor center in Fort Bragg. These areas include **Manchester State Park,** located where the San Andreas Fault sweeps to the sea; **Jughandle State Reserve;** and **Van Damme State Park** ✿, with a sheltered, easily accessible beach.

My favorite of these parks, located directly on Calif. 1 just north of Mendocino, is **Russian Gulch State Park** ✿✿. It's one of the region's most spectacular parks, where roaring waves crash against the cliffs that protect the park's California coastal redwoods. The most popular attraction is the **Punch Bowl,** a collapsed sea cave that forms a tunnel through which waves crash, creating throaty echoes. Inland, there's a scenic paved bike path, and visitors can also hike along miles of trails, including a gentle, well-marked 3-mile **Waterfall Loop** that winds past tall redwoods and damp green foliage to a 36-foot-high waterfall. Admission is $2 and camping is $12 per night. Call ✆ **800/444-7275** for reservations; for general state park information, call ✆ **707/937-5804** or visit www.cal-parks.ca.gov.

Fort Bragg is just a short distance up the coast; deep-sea fishing charters are available from its harbor.

WHERE TO STAY
EXPENSIVE
Stanford Inn by the Sea ✿✿   Just south of Mendocino, this rustic but ever-so-sumptuous lodge occupies 11 acres of land abutting the Big River. The grounds are captivating, with tiers of elaborate gardens, a pond for ducks and geese, and fenced pastures containing horses, curious llamas, and old gnarled apple trees. The solarium-style indoor hot tub and pool surrounded by tropical plants is gorgeous. The luxuriously furnished rooms come with special touches such as thick robes, down comforters, fresh flowers, and works by local artists. All have fireplaces or stoves and private decks from which you can gaze on the Pacific. Second honeymooners should inquire about the romantic River Cottage; families will want the big ol' renovated barn. Pets are welcome here and receive the royal treatment. The inn also has a small massage studio, individual and group yoga lessons, and the only totally vegetarian restaurant on the Mendocino coast, which has become a big hit with both guests and locals.

N. Calif. 1 and Comptche Ukiah Rd. (P.O. Box 487), Mendocino, CA 95460. ✆ **800/331-8884** or 707/937-5615. Fax 707/937-0305. www.stanfordinn.com. 33 units. $235–$295 double; $310–$720 suite. Rates include breakfast. AE, DC, DISC, MC, V. Pets accepted with $25 fee. **Amenities:** Vegetarian restaurant; nearby golf course; solarium-style pool, spa, and sauna; exercise room; kayak and canoe rental; complimentary bikes; concierge; courtesy car; business center; secretarial services; evening room service; in-room massage. *In room:* TV/VCR w/pay movies, dataport, kitchenette and minibar in some units, fridge, coffeemaker, hair dryer, iron.

MODERATE
Agate Cove Inn ✿✿   Good luck trying to find an accommodation with a more beautiful coastal setting than Agate Cove Inn's. Words can barely convey the almost surreal splendor of the view from the inn's front lawn, a sweeping, unfettered vista of the sea and its surging waves crashing onto the dramatic bluffs. Situate yourself on one of the Adirondack chairs with a good book, and you'll never want to leave. The inn consists of a main house trimmed in blue and white, surrounded by a bevy of single and duplex cottages. All but 1 of the 10 spacious units have views of the ocean, king- or queen-size beds, down

comforters, fireplaces, and private decks. In the morning, a fantastic country breakfast is served in the main house's enclosed porch (yes, with the same ocean view).

11201 N. Lansing St. (P.O. Box 1150), Mendocino, CA 95460. © **800/527-3111** or 707/937-0551. Fax 707/937-0550. www.agatecove.com. 10 units. $119–$269 double. Rates include full breakfast. AE, MC, V. **Amenities:** Nearby golf course; concierge; activities desk; in-room massage. *In room:* TV/VCR w/complimentary videos, CD player, iron, hair dryer, no phone.

Joshua Grindle Inn ★★ When it was built in 1879, this stately Victorian was one of the most substantial and impressive houses in Mendocino, owned by the town's wealthiest banker. Now the oldest B&B in Mendocino, it features redwood siding, a wraparound porch, and large emerald lawns. From its prettily planted gardens, there's a view across the village to the distant bay. There are five rooms in the main house, two in the cottage, and three in the water tower. All have well-lit, comfortably arranged sitting areas; some offer fireplaces, three have deep-soak tubs, and three have whirlpool tubs. Each is individually decorated: The library, for example, has a New England feel with its four-poster pine bed, floor-to-ceiling bookcase, and 19th-century tiles around the fireplace depicting Aesop's fables. Sherry, sweets, and tea are served in the parlor in front of the fireplace; breakfast is offered in the dining room. In addition to the inn, the proprietors also have a beautiful two-bedroom, two-bathroom oceanview rental home with floor-to-ceiling windows, a large kitchen, and a wood-burning fireplace. It's located a few minutes north of Mendocino, and rates range from $245 to $375, depending on occupancy.

44800 Little Lake Rd. (P.O. Box 647), Mendocino, CA 95460. © **800/GRINDLE** or 707/937-4143. www. joshgrin.com. 10 units. June–Oct $130–$245 double; Nov–May Mon–Thurs $115–$195 double, Fri–Sun $130–$245 double. Rates include full breakfast, afternoon tea, and wine. MC, V. **Amenities:** Nearby golf course; concierge. *In room:* TV/DVD in some units, hair dryer, no phone.

MacCallum House ★★ A historic 1882 gingerbread Victorian mansion, MacCallum House is one of Mendocino's top accommodations. Originally owned by local matriarch Daisy MacCallum, the house still bears the imprint of this daughter of the town's richest lumber baron. It remained in the family until 1974, when it was turned into a B&B. Now owned by resident proprietors Melanie and Joe Redding, the home has been preserved with all of its original furnishings and contents—right down to Daisy's Christmas cards and books of pressed flowers. Boasting the occasional Tiffany lamp or authentic Persian carpet, each uniquely decorated guest room is exquisitely furnished with many original pieces—a Franklin stove, a handmade quilt, a cushioned rocking chair, or a child's cradle. All have private bathrooms, many equipped with claw-foot or spa tubs for two. The luxurious barn suite, complete with a stone fireplace, can accommodate up to six adults. The popular dinner restaurant on the premises serves California cuisine.

45020 Albion St. (P.O. Box 206), Mendocino, CA 95460. © **800/609-0492** or 707/937-0289. Fax 707/964-2243. www.maccallumhouse.com. 19 units. $120–$195 double. Extra person $15. AE, MC, V. **Amenities:** Restaurant; cafe; bar; concierge. *In room:* Fridge and coffeemaker in some units.

Mendocino Hotel & Garden Suites ★ Right in the heart of town, this 1878 hotel evokes California's gold-rush days. Beveled-glass doors open into a Victorian-style lobby and parlor where you might expect to see Mae West. The hotel's decor combines antiques and reproductions, like the oak reception desk from a demolished Kansas bank. Remington paintings, stained-glass lamps, and Persian carpets contribute to the Wild West aura. Guest rooms feature hand-painted French porcelain sinks with floral designs, quaint wallpaper, old-fashioned beds and armoires, and photographs and memorabilia of historic Mendocino. About half the rooms are located in four handsome small buildings behind the main house. Many of the deluxe rooms have fireplaces, as well as modern bathrooms and good views. Suites have an additional parlor, as well as a fireplace or balcony.

45080 Main St. (P.O. Box 587), Mendocino, CA 95460. © **800/548-0513** or 707/937-0511. Fax 707/937-0513. www.mendocinohotel.com. 51 units, 37 with private bathroom. $95 double with shared bathroom, $120–$215 double with private bathroom; $275 suite. Extra person $20. AE, MC, V. **Amenities:** 2 restaurants; 2 bars; nearby golf course; access to nearby health club ($5); room service. *In room:* TV, hair dryer.

INEXPENSIVE

Mendocino Village Inn & Spa ⭐ This historic Victorian Inn is just across the street from the headlands, overlooking the ocean and the Big River beach. A garden of flowers, plants, and frog ponds fronts the large blue-and-white guesthouse, which was built in 1882 by a local doctor and later occupied by famed local artist Emmy Lou Packard. Each pretty room is individually decorated, and many have fireplaces and Jacuzzi tubs. The Queen Anne Room features a four-poster canopy bed and other Victorian furnishings, and the sentimental Madge's Room is named for a child who etched her name in the window glass almost a century ago (you can still see it). Except for two attic units, all have private bathrooms, and four rooms have private outside entrances. Complimentary beverages are served in the evening, and all guests have spa privileges at the nearby Sweetwater Spa.

44860 Main St. (P.O. Box 626), Mendocino, CA 95460. © **800/882-7029** or 707/937-0246. www.mendocinoinn.com. 12 units, 10 with private bathroom. $85–$95 double with shared bathroom; $125–$195 double with private bathroom; $165 Water Tower suite. Winter midweek discounts. Rates include full breakfast and evening refreshments. MC, V. **Amenities:** Spa privileges and massage discount at adjacent Sweetwater Spa.

IN NEARBY ALBION & LITTLE RIVER

Albion River Inn and Restaurant ⭐⭐ A quarter-mile north of Albion (or 6 miles south of Mendocino), this modern, beautiful inn overlooks the mouth of the Albion River from a bluff some 90 feet above the Pacific. The view is, of course, spectacular. A plaintive harbor horn in the area adds to the seaside atmosphere. (If you are a light sleeper, earplugs are provided). The rooms are attractively decorated in a contemporary style with comfortable furnishings; all have ocean views, and most have decks. You'll find wingbacks placed in front of the fireplaces, down comforters on the queen and king-size beds, well-lit desks, binoculars for wildlife viewing, and bathrobes. *Insider tip:* If you really want to impress your sweetie, reserve one of the rooms with a spa tub for two, which has a large picture window offering dazzling views of the coast. The cuisine at the inn's respected restaurant changes daily, featuring fresh local produce whenever possible, but the view from the tables remains the same: stellar. The award-winning wine list is also impressive. Evenings, soft piano music adds to the romantic atmosphere.

3790 N. Calif. 1 (P.O. Box 100), Albion, CA 95410. © **800/479-7944** or 707/937-1919. Fax 707/937-2604. www.albionriverinn.com. 20 units. $200–$250 double; $290–$310 spa suite. Rates include full breakfast. AE, DC, DISC, MC, V. **Amenities:** Restaurant. *In room:* CD player, fridge, coffeemaker, hair dryer, iron.

Glendeven ⭐⭐ Named 1 of the 12 best inns in America by *Country Inns* magazine, this 1867 farmhouse has been converted into a place of exceptional style and comfort. Accommodations are spread across 2½ acres that encompass the main house, the Carriage House Suite, and an addition known as Stevenscroft. Each room is individually decorated with a well-balanced mixture of antiques and contemporary pieces, and original art. Most have ocean views, fireplaces, and porches. Etta's Suite in the Farmhouse includes an antique walnut bed, while the Eastlin and Carriage House suites are furnished with king-size feather beds. The four rooms in the Stevenscroft annex are also spacious and beautifully furnished. A vacation rental house, La Bella Vista, has two bedrooms, two bathrooms, a kitchen, Jacuzzi, and its namesake beautiful view of the ocean and surrounding gardens. Adjacent to the inn are the numerous fern-lined canyon trails to the ocean and beaches of Van Damme State Park.

8205 N. Hwy. 1, Little River, CA 95456. ℂ 800/822-4536 or 707/937-0083. Fax 707/937-6108. www. glendeven.com. 10 units. Weekend and summer rates $135–$225. Ask about off-season midweek specials. Rates include full breakfast. AE, DISC, MC, V. **Amenities:** In-room massage (with notice). *In room:* Hair dryer, no phone.

Heritage House ★★   Famous as the site of the romantic movie *Same Time, Next Year,* most of the rooms at this traditional country-club–style property have great views of the ocean and rugged coastline. Thirty-seven seafront acres of lush gardens house a variety of accommodations ranging from the merely attractive to frankly lush. Only three guest rooms are located in the ivy-covered New England–style main building; the other accommodations are in cottages grouped two to four under one common roof. Rooms are individually decorated with original antiques and locally made furnishings, with every kind of amenity, including bathrobes, umbrellas, wine splits, and newspaper delivery. Most have wood-burning fireplaces or stoves, private decks, sitting areas, and ocean views; several suites have wet bars and Jacuzzis. Wooded trails wind along the dramatic coastline, offering spectacular scenery. The reliable Heritage House dining room is in a magnificent setting overlooking the ocean, features a seasonal menu, and has a highly touted wine cellar.

5200 N. Calif. 1, Little River, CA 95456. ℂ 800/235-5885 or 707/937-5885. Fax 707/937-0318. www. heritagehouseinn.com. 66 units. Summer $150–$500 double; winter $150–$425 double. Extra person $20. AE, MC, V. **Amenities:** Restaurant; concierge; tour and activities desk; in-room massage. *In room:* Fax, dataport, fridge, coffeemaker, hair dryer, iron, no phone.

WHERE TO DINE
EXPENSIVE

Café Beaujolais ★★★ AMERICAN/FRENCH   This is one of Mendocino's—if not Northern California's—top dining choices. The venerable French country–style tavern is set in a early 1900s house; rose-colored carnival-glass chandeliers add a burnish to the oak floors and the heavy oak tables adorned with flowers. On warm summer nights, request a table at the enclosed deck overlooking the "designer" gardens.

Though Café Beaujolais started out as a breakfast-and-lunch place, it's strictly a dinner house now. (Yes, their famed weekend brunch has been discontinued.) The menu changes weekly and usually lists about five main courses, such as wild-sturgeon filet pan-roasted with truffle emulsion sauce, roast free-range duck with wild-huckleberry sauce, or broiled Wildwood Ranch pork loin chop with yam purée. *Note:* The restaurant usually closes for a winter vacation for most of December.

961 Ukiah St. ℂ 707/937-5614. Fax 707/937-3656. www.cafebeaujolais.com. Reservations recommended. Main courses $21–$28. AE, DISC, MC, V. Daily 5:45–9pm.

The 955 Ukiah Street Restaurant ★★ CALIFORNIA/FRENCH   Shortly after this building's construction in the 1960s, the region's most famous painter,

Emmy Lou Packard, commandeered its premises as an art studio for the creation of a series of giant murals. Today, it's a large but surprisingly cozy restaurant, accented with massive railway ties and vaulted ceilings. Ask for a window table overlooking the gardens. The cuisine is creative and reasonably priced, a worthy alternative to the perpetually booked Café Beaujolais next door. It's hard to pick a favorite dish from the menu, although the phyllo-wrapped red snapper with pesto and lime has a zesty tang, while the crispy duck with ginger, apples, and a Calvados sauce would earn enthusiastic friends in Normandy.

955 Ukiah St. © 707/937-1955. www.955restaurant.com. Reservations recommended. Main courses $12–$26. MC, V. Wed–Sun 6–10pm.

MODERATE

Bay View Café ⋆ AMERICAN   This reasonably priced cafe is one of the most popular in town. From the second-floor dining area of the cafe, there's a sweeping view of the Pacific and faraway headlands; to reach it, climb a flight of stairs running up the outside of the town's antique water tower, then detour sideways. Surrounded by dozens of ferns suspended from the ceiling, you'll find a menu with Southwestern selections (the marinated chicken breast is very popular), a good array of sandwiches (my favorite is the hot crabmeat with avocado slices), fish and chips, and the fresh catch of the day. Breakfast ranges from the basic bacon 'n' eggs to eggs Florentine and honey-wheat pancakes.

45040 Main St. © 707/937-4197. Reservations not accepted. Main courses $6–$15. No credit cards. Summer daily 8am–9pm; winter Mon–Thurs 8am–3pm, Fri–Sun 8am–9pm.

The Moosse Café ⋆ CALIFORNIA BISTRO   This petite cafe set in a New England–style home is another one of the most popular restaurants in Mendocino. In 1995, the place was gutted and redone, resulting in an attractive, modern interior. The menu, which changes seasonally, boasts many local items such as organic herbs and vegetables, as in the outstanding Caesar salad. I also enjoyed the roast chicken with garlic mashed potatoes and the swordfish special, which came with a pile of fresh vegetables. Other popular entrees are the mixed seafood cakes served over basmati rice with a roasted red pepper rémoulade, and the lavender-smoked double-thick pork chop served with roasted yam and apple purée. Service is friendly; my only complaint is that the tables are a bit too close together, especially if it's crowded.

390 Kasten St. (at Albion St.). © 707/937-4323. Reservations recommended for dinner. Main courses $13–$19. MC, V. Daily 11:30am–3:30pm; Sun–Thurs 5:30–9pm, Fri–Sat and holidays 5:30–10pm.

INEXPENSIVE

You'd be surprised what $5 will get you for lunch if you know where to go. **Tote Fete Bakery** (© 707/937-3140) has a wonderful little carryout booth at the corner of Albion and Lansing streets. I like the foil-wrapped barbecue chicken sandwiches, but the pizza, focaccia bread, and twice-baked potatoes are also good choices. Dine at the stand-up counter, or opt for a picnic at the headlands down the street.

Regardless of preference—beef, chicken, turkey, or veggie—burger lovers won't be let down at **Mendo Burgers** (© 707/937-1111), arguably the best burger joint on the northern coast. A side of thick, fresh-cut fries is mandatory, as is a pile of napkins. Hidden behind the Mendocino Bakery and Café at 10483 Lansing St., it's a little hard to find, but well worth searching out.

In the back of the **Little River Market** (© 707/937-5133), located directly across from the Little River Inn on Calif. 1, is a trio of small tables overlooking the beautiful Mendocino coastline. Order a tamale, sandwich, or whatever else is on the menu at the tiny deli inside the market, or buy a loaf of legendary Café Beaujolais bread sold at the front counter and your favorite spread.

4 Fort Bragg

10 miles N of Mendocino; 176 miles N of San Francisco

As Mendocino coast's commercial center—hence the site of most of the area's fast-food restaurants and supermarkets—Fort Bragg is far more down to earth than Mendocino. Inexpensive motels and cheap eats used to be its only attractions, but over the past few years, gentrification has quickly spread throughout the town as the logging and fishing industries have continued to decline. With no room left to open new shops in Mendocino, many gallery, boutique, and restaurant owners have moved up the road. The result is a huge increase in Fort Bragg's tourist trade, particularly during the annual Whale Festival in March and Paul Bunyan Days over Labor Day weekend.

To explore the town properly, get a free walking-tour map from the **Fort Bragg/Mendocino Coast Chamber of Commerce,** 332 N. Main St. (P.O. Box 1141), Fort Bragg, CA 95437 (© **800/726-2780** or 707/961-6300; www. mendocinocoast.com). The friendly staff can answer any questions about Mendocino, Fort Bragg, and the surrounding region.

SHOPPING & EXPLORING THE AREA

The town doesn't boast as many well-coiffed stores and galleries as its dainty cousin to the south, but it does have some worthwhile shopping spots. **Antiques shops** line Franklin Street between Laurel and Redwood (aka "Antiques Row"), and several boutiques are housed within the newly refurbished **Union Lumber Company Store,** an impressive edifice built almost entirely with handcrafted redwoods (on the corner of Main and Redwood sts.).

For the Shell of It, 344 N. Main St. (© **707/961-0461**), stocks handmade jewelry, chimes, and collectibles made of shells or designed around a nautical theme, as well as rocks, gems, minerals, and fossils. The **Hot Pepper Jelly Company,** 330 N. Main St. (© **707/961-1899**), is famous for its assortment of Mendocino food products—dozens of varieties of pepper jelly, plus local mustards, syrups, and biscotti along with hand-painted porcelain bowls, unusual baskets, and more. The **Mendocino Chocolate Company,** 542 N. Main St. (© **707/964-8800**), makes and sells homemade chocolates and truffles, which it ships all over the world. Painters, jewelers, sculptors, weavers, potters, woodworkers, and other local artists display their works at **Northcoast Artists,** 362 N. Main St. (© **707/964-8266**). At **Windsong,** 324 N. Main St. (© **707/ 964-2050**), predominantly a nice used-book store, you'll also find a clutter of colorful kites, cards, candles, and other gifts.

Fort Bragg is also the home of the **Mendocino Coast Botanical Gardens,** 18220 N. Calif. 1 (© **707/964-4352;** www.gardenbythesea.org), about 7 miles north of Mendocino. This clifftop public garden, set among the pines along the rugged coast, nurtures rhododendrons, fuchsias, azaleas, and a multitude of flowering shrubs. The area contains bridges, streams, canyons, dells, picnic areas, and trails for easy walking. Admission is $6 for adults, $5 for seniors ages 60 and over, $3 for children 13 to 17, $1 for children 6 to 12, and free for children 5 and under. (Children under 18 must be accompanied by an adult.) Open March through October daily from 9am to 5pm, November through February daily from 9am to 4pm.

From Fort Bragg, the **Skunk Train** ☆ (© **800/77-SKUNK** or 707/964-6371; www.skunktrain.com) gives riders a fine tour of the area's redwoods. Locals have always said of the logging trains, "You can smell 'em before you can see 'em," which explains the nickname. The trains, which can be boarded at the Fort Bragg Depot at the foot of Laurel Avenue in Fort Bragg (2 blocks from the Grey Whale Inn), travel 40 miles inland along the Redwood Highway (U.S. 101) to Willits. It's a scenic route through the redwood forest, crossing 31 bridges and trestles and cutting through two deep tunnels. The round-trip takes about 8 hours, allowing plenty of time for lunch in Willits before you return on the afternoon train. The trains run full-day trips daily from Memorial Day weekend to the last weekend in October, but call for exact times, as schedules vary. Half-day trips are offered daily from March 1 to the end of November. During the summer months, it's a good idea to make advance reservations. Tickets cost $39 for a full-day trip, from $29 to $39 for a half-day trip, depending whether you ride the steam engine, diesel, or motor car; children ages 3 to 16 board for $22 full day, $16 to $18 half day. Serious train buffs can ride in the locomotive cab with the engineer for $100. Family packages are also available.

Also worth checking out is the **North Coast Brewing Company,** 455 N. Main St. (© **707/964-2739;** www.northcoastbrewing.com), which offers free tours of the brewery Monday through Friday at 1pm. Across the street is the Brewing Company's pub, open for lunch and dinner (see "Where to Dine," below).

OUTDOOR PURSUITS

Fort Bragg is the county's sport-fishing center. Just south of town, **Noyo Fishing Center,** 32440 N. Harbor, Noyo (© **707/964-3000;** www.fortbragg fishing.com), is a good place to buy tackle and the best source of information on local fishing boats. Lots of party boats leave from the town's harbor, as do whale-watching tours.

Lost Coast Kayaking, located in Van Damme State Park (© **707/937-2434**), offers kayak tours of the coastline's numerous sea caves. All the necessary equipment is provided; all you need to bring is a bathing suit and about $45 for the 2-hour tour (closed during the winter).

Three miles north of Fort Bragg, off Calif. 1, lies **MacKerricher State Park** (© **707/937-5804**), a popular place for biking, hiking, and horseback riding. This enormous 1,700-acre park has 142 campsites and 8 miles of shoreline. For a true biking or hiking venture, travel the 8-mile-long "Haul Road," an old logging road (partly washed out, but safe) that provides fine ocean vistas all the way to Ten Mile River. Harbor seals make their home at the park's Laguna Point Seal Watching Station.

WHERE TO STAY

Beachcomber Motel *Value*   If the room rates in Mendocino have you reconsidering a visit to the coast, the Beachcomber Motel may be just what you're looking for. Granted, the rather plain guest rooms lack the fancy antique and lace accouterments you'll find at most B&Bs in the area, but they are definitely spacious, comfortable, and equipped with the basic necessities. None of this really matters, though, since you'll be spending most of your time on the huge back deck that overlooks the cool blue Pacific and gorgeous sunsets. Better yet, directly across from the motel are MacKerricher State Park's miles of beaches and dunes. If you really want to save a bundle, get a room with a kitchenette, stock up on groceries, and make use of the large barbecue area. Low-end rates are for a standard room with no ocean view and the top rate is for the deluxe suite with king bed, Jacuzzi, fireplace, and ocean view. Three units here are wheelchair accessible.

1111 N. Main St., Fort Bragg, CA 95437. ℂ **800/400-7873** or 707/964-2402. Fax 707/964-8925. www.thebeachcombermotel.com. 75 units. $59–$250 double. Rates include continental breakfast. AE, DC, DISC, MC, V. Pets accepted with $10 fee. **Amenities:** Exercise room. *In room:* TV/VCR, dataport, fridge, coffeemaker, kitchenette in suites.

Colombi Motel *(Value)*   Considering a room here costs about a quarter of the average room rate in Mendocino, the Colombi Motel is what we travel writers call a real score. For only 50 bones, you get a lot for your money at this humble little motel just off Fort Bragg's main strip: It's clean and neat, has all the essentials (including kitchens in some rooms), and you even get your own covered carport. Families will want to reserve one of the two-bedroom units that sleep up to six. Across the street is a laundromat, a small cafe serving good Mexican food, and the Colombi Market, which is where the motel's guests check in and where you can get free ice and coffee.

600 E. Oak St., Fort Bragg, CA 95437. ℂ **707/964-5773** or 707/964-8015. Fax 707/964-5627. 22 units. Winter $35–$85 double; summer $40–$95 double. MC, V. *In room:* TV, kitchen in some units, fridge.

Grey Whale Inn *(★)*   Located in downtown Fort Bragg and a short walk from the beach, this stately B&B was originally built as a hospital in 1915, hence the wide hallways and large guest rooms. The handsome redwood building is now a well-run, relaxed inn, furnished with antiques, handmade quilts, and plenty of local art. Each room is unique: Two have ocean views, four have fireplaces, one has a whirlpool tub, three have private decks, and one offers a shower with wheelchair access. The buffet breakfast, served in the newly remodeled Breakfast Room, includes a hot entree, homemade bread or coffee cake, and fresh fruit.

615 N. Main St., Fort Bragg, CA 95437. ℂ **800/382-7244** or 707/964-0640. Fax 707/964-4408. www.greywhaleinn.com. 14 units. $130–$230 double. Discounted winter rates available midweek Nov–Mar. Rates include buffet breakfast. AE, MC, V. **Amenities:** Access to nearby health club; game room; in-room massage. *In room:* TV, some units w/VCR, kitchenette, fridge hair dryer, and iron.

WHERE TO DINE

North Coast Brewing Company *(★)* AMERICAN   Since it opened in 1988, this homey brewpub has been the most happening place in town, especially during happy hour, when the bar and dark-wood tables are occupied by boisterous locals. The brewery's proudest achievement, however, was being ranked "one of the ten best breweries in the world" in 1998 by the Beverage Testing Institute. The building that houses the pub is a dignified, century-old redwood structure, which in previous lives has functioned as a mortuary, an annex to the local Presbyterian church, an art studio, and administration offices for the College of the Redwoods. Nine different types of beer are available (to go, even) year-round, in addition to seasonal brews. Standard fare such as burgers and barbecued chicken sandwiches are supplemented by more substantial dishes, ranging from wild-mushroom ravioli to Cuban hanger steak and genuine Carolina barbecue pork served with corn cakes and slaw. After your meal, browse the retail shop or take a free tour of the brewery (see "Shopping & Exploring the Area," above).

444 N. Main St. ℂ **707/964-3400.** www.northcoastbrewing.com. Reservations accepted for large parties only. Main courses $7–$22. DISC, MC, V. Daily 11:30am–11pm.

The Restaurant *(Kids)* PACIFIC NORTHWEST/CALIFORNIA   One of the oldest family-run restaurants on the coast, this small, unpretentious Fort Bragg landmark is known for its good dinners and Sunday brunches. The eclectic menu offers dishes from just about every corner of the planet: New York strip steak, a Provençal-style seafood stew, and a few lighter, less expensive options such as the Asian Noodle Bowl filled with bay shrimp and fresh vegetables. My favorite is the super fresh blackened local rockfish. There are also a few vegetarian specialties, including grilled polenta with melted mozzarella and sautéed mushrooms, topped with tomato-herb sauce and Parmesan cheese. A nicely priced kids' menu is available as well. The comfortable booth section is the best place to sit if you want to keep an eye on the entertainment—courtesy of ebullient chef Jim Larsen—in the kitchen.

418 N. Main St. ℂ 707/964-9800. www.therestaurantfortbragg.com. Reservations recommended. Dinner $13–$22; Sun brunch $5–$10. MC, V. Thurs–Tues 5–9pm; Sun brunch 10am–1pm.

Viraporn's Thai Café THAI   Born in northern Thailand, Viraporn Lobell attended cooking school and apprenticed in restaurants in her homeland before coming to the United States. After working at Mendocino's premier restaurant, Café Beaujolais, she opened her own restaurant in Fort Bragg, giving local Thai-food fans good reason to cheer. Viraporn works wonders with Thai mainstays such as pad Thai, lemon grass soup, spring rolls, and satays, all of which have a pleasant balance of the five traditional Thai flavors of tart, bitter, hot, sweet, and salty. Viraporn also whips up some wonderful curry dishes, best washed down with a cool, super sweet Thai iced tea.

500 S. Main St. (across from PayLess drugstore off Calif. 1) ℂ 707/964-7931. Main courses $3.95–$9.95. No credit cards. Wed–Mon 11:30am–2:30pm and 5–9pm.

5 The Avenue of the Giants ★★

From Fort Bragg, Calif. 1 continues north along the shoreline for about 30 miles before turning inland to Leggett and the Redwood Highway (U.S. 101), which runs north to Garberville. Six miles beyond Garberville, the **Avenue of the Giants** (Calif. 254) begins around Phillipsville. The Avenue of the Giants is one of the most spectacular scenic routes in the West, cutting along the Eel River through the 51,000-acre Humboldt Redwoods State Park. It roughly parallels U.S. 101, and there are about a half-dozen interchanges between the two roads

 A Feast in the Forest

As if riding through a towering redwood forest on an antique train wasn't cool enough, the folks running the Skunk Train (see "Shopping & Exploring the Area," above) in Fort Bragg have added a new **Sunset Dinner BBQ** excursion. For about $50 per adult and $28 for kids, y'all get to ride in a 1925 or 1935 vintage motorcar to the century-old Northspur Station at the base of the Noyo River Canyon—a secluded, forested glen accessible only by train. Passengers are then greeted with huge baskets and trays of homemade bread, barbecued chicken and ribs, baked beans, garden salads, and a "surprise" dessert. Trains depart from both Fort Bragg and Willits every Saturday evening between May 25 and August 31 and every Wednesday evening between June 19 and August 28. For more information call ℂ 800/77-SKUNK or visit their website at www.skunktrain.com.

if you don't want to drive the whole thing. The Avenue ends just south of Scotia; from here, it's only about 10 miles to the turnoff to Ferndale, about 5 miles west of U.S. 101.

For more information or a detailed map of the area, go to the **Humboldt Redwoods State Park Visitor Center** in Weott (© **707/946-2263;** www. humboldtredwoods.org), in the center of the Avenue of the Giants.

TOURING THE AVENUE

Thirty-three miles long, the Avenue of the Giants was left intact for sightseers when the freeway was built. The giants, of course, are the majestic coast redwoods *(Sequoia sempervirens);* more than 50,000 acres of them makes up the most outstanding display in the redwood belt. Their rough-bark columns climb 100 feet or more without a branch and soar to a total height of more than 340 feet. With their immunity to insects and fire-resistant bark, they have survived for thousands of years. The oldest dated coast redwood is more than 2,200 years old.

Sadly, the route has several tacky attractions that attempt to turn the trees into some kind of freak show. My suggestion is to skip these and appreciate the trees by taking advantage of the trails and the campgrounds off the beaten path. As you drive along, you'll see numerous parking areas with short loop trails leading into the forest. From south to north, the first of these "attractions" is the **Chimney Tree,** where J. R. R. Tolkien's Hobbit is rumored to reside. This living, hollow redwood is more than 1,500 years old. Nearby are a gift shop and a burger place. Then there's the **One-Log House,** a small apartment-like house built inside a log. At Myers Flat midway along the Avenue, you can also drive your car through a living redwood at the **Shrine Drive-Thru Tree.**

A few miles north of Weott is **Founders Grove,** named in honor of those who established the Save the Redwoods League in 1918. Farther north, close to the end of the Avenue, stands the 950-year-old **Immortal Tree,** just north of Redcrest. Near Pepperwood at the end of the Avenue, the **Drury Trail** and the **Percy French Trail** are two good short hikes. The park itself is also good for mountain biking. Ask the rangers for details. For more information, contact Humboldt Redwoods State Park (© **707/946-2409;** www.humboldtredwoods.org).

The state park has three **campgrounds** with 248 campsites: Hidden Springs, half a mile south of Myers Flat; Burlington, 2 miles south of Weott, near park headquarters; and Albee Creek State Campground, 5 miles west of U.S. 101 on the Mattole Road north of Weott. Reservations are advised in the summer months; you can make then online via **ReserveAmerica** at www.reserveamerica. com or call © **800/444-7275.** Remaining sites are on a first-come, first-served basis. You'll also come across picnic and swimming facilities, motels, resorts, restaurants, and numerous rest and parking areas.

WHERE TO STAY & DINE NEAR THE SOUTHERN ENTRANCE

Benbow Inn ☆☆   This elegant National Historic Landmark, overlooking the Eel River and surrounded by marvelous gardens, has housed such notable persons as Eleanor Roosevelt, Herbert Hoover, and Charles Laughton. Constructed in 1926 in a mock Tudor style, it's named after the well-to-do family who built it. Guests enter through a grand hall and into the sumptuous lobby with its huge fireplace surrounded by cushy sofas, grandfather clocks, Oriental carpets, and cherrywood wainscoting. Rooms vary in size and amenities, though all are tastefully decorated with period antiques; the deluxe units have fireplaces, Jacuzzis, private entrances, and patios. The Honeymoon Cottage is the most popular accommodation, with its vaulted ceilings, canopy bed, wood-burning fireplace, and private patio overlooking the river. A comfortable annex with elegant woodwork was added in the 1980s. Beautiful Benbow Lake State Park is right out the front door. Complimentary afternoon tea and scones are served in the lobby at 3pm, hors d'oeuvres in the lounge at 5pm, and port wine at 9pm—all very proper, of course. The dramatic high-ceilinged dining room opens onto a spacious terrace and offers internationally inspired main courses.

445 Lake Benbow Dr., Garberville, CA 95542. ⓒ 800/355-3301 or 707/923-2124. Fax 707/923-2122. www.benbowinn.com. 55 units. $130–$275 double; $350 cottage. AE, DISC, MC, V. **Amenities:** Restaurant; bar; nearby golf course; complimentary bikes; guided day hikes; courtesy car; babysitting (with advance notice). *In room:* A/C, coffeemaker, hair dryer, iron; some units with TV/VCR, minibar, fridge.

FERNDALE ⓖ

The village of Ferndale, beyond the Avenue of the Giants and west of U.S. 101, has been declared a historic landmark because of its many Victorian homes and storefronts (which include a smithy and a saddlery). About 5 miles inland from the coast and close to the redwood belt, Ferndale is one of the best-preserved Victorian hamlets in Northern California. Despite its unbearably cute shops, it is nonetheless a vital part of the northern coastal tourist circuit.

What's less readily known about this small town is that it has a number of artists in residence and is home to one of California's oddest happenings, the **World Championship Great Arcata to Ferndale Cross-Country Kinetic Sculpture Race,** a bizarre 3-day event held every Memorial Day weekend. The race, which draws more than 10,000 spectators, is run 38 miles over land, sand, mud, and water in whimsically designed, handmade, people-powered vehicles that have to be seen to be believed—dragons, Christmas trees, flying saucers, pyramids to mention but a few. Awards range from Best Art to Best Engineering to Best Bribe and as the Grand Prizes are worth about $15, inspired madness is the only incentive. Stop in at the museum at 780 Main St. if you want to see a few past race entries, although they're poor, pale facsimiles of the contrivances in glorious action.

WHERE TO STAY

Gingerbread Mansion ⓖⓖ This peach-and-yellow structure with stained glass and other fine architectural details is one of Ferndale's most frequently photographed Victorians. Built in 1899 as the home of a local doctor and his family and now run by Ken Torbert, it's beautifully furnished with antiques. Some of the large guest rooms have two old-fashioned claw-foot tubs for bubble baths for two, and others offer fireplaces. My favorite room is the attic-level Empire Suite, a lavish spare-no-expense blowout with Ionic columns, massage-jet shower, two fireplaces, and a king-size bed draped with Royal Sateen fabric. The new ultra-luxurious Veneto Room is also very impressive. Bathrobes and thick, extra-large towels are provided. Beds are turned down for the night, and you'll find hand-dipped chocolates on the nightstand. When you rise, there's morning coffee or tea outside your door, enough to sustain you until your breakfast of fruit, cheese, muffins, breads, cakes, and a baked egg dish. Afternoon tea with sandwiches, pastries, and fresh fruit are also served.

400 Berding St. (P.O. Box 40), Ferndale, CA 95536. ⓒ 800/952-4136 or 707/786-4000. Fax 707/786-4381. www.gingerbread-mansion.com. 11 units. $150–$210 double; $170–$385 suite. Extra person $40. Rates include full breakfast and afternoon tea. AE, MC, V. **Amenities:** Concierge; activities desk. *In room:* Hair dryer, no phone.

WHERE TO DINE

Curley's Grill ⊛ CALIFORNIA GRILL   This bright and lively restaurant specializes in California-inspired grilled foods, but don't think for a moment that the menu is limited to steaks, prime rib, and barbecued baby-back ribs. Owner Curley Tait also grills up such items as portobello mushroom towers, pork loin with caramelized onion sauce, polenta with a sausage-tomato sauce, crab cakes, and some of the freshest seafood and vegetables on the California coast. Curley has added homemade breads and desserts to the menu as well. Curley's also offers an interesting selection of California wines, and has a Victorian-style full bar area.

400 Ocean St., inside the Victorian Inn. ℂ **707/786-9696.** Main courses $9–$18. DISC, MC, V. Daily 11:30am–9pm; breakfast Sat–Sun 8–11am.

6 Eureka & Environs ⊛

296 miles N of San Francisco

EUREKA

On first glance, Eureka (pop. 27,000) doesn't look very appealing: Fast-food restaurants, cheap motels, and shopping malls predominate on the main thoroughfare. But if you turn west off U.S. 101 anywhere between A and M streets, you'll discover **Old Town Eureka** along the waterfront, which is worth exploring. It has a large number of Victorian buildings, a museum, and some good-quality stores and restaurants.

The city's newest development is a waterfront boardwalk between C and F streets, adjacent to the Old Town historic district. The boardwalk opens a section of the waterfront that was previously closed to the public, offering sweeping views of the harbor and bay.

For more visitor information, contact or visit the **Eureka/Humboldt County Convention and Visitors Bureau,** 1034 Second St., Eureka, CA 95501 (ℂ **800/346-3482** or 707/443-5097; www.redwoodvisitor.org), or the **Eureka Chamber of Commerce,** 2112 Broadway, Eureka, CA 95501 (ℂ **800/356-6381** or 707/442-3738; www.eurekachamber.com).

WHAT TO SEE & DO

The **Clarke Memorial Museum,** 240 E St. (ℂ **707/443-1947**), has a fine collection of Native American baskets and other historic artifacts. The other popular attraction is the extraordinary architectural gem, the **Carson House** ⊛, built from 1884 to 1886 for lumber baron William Carson. A three-story conglomeration of ornamentation, its design is a mélange of styles—Queen Anne, Italianate, Stick, and Eastlake. It took 100 men more than 2 years to build. Today it's a private club, so you can only marvel at the exterior of this 18-room mansion—said to be the most photographed Victorian home in the United States—from the sidewalk. Across the street stands the **"Pink Lady,"** designed for William Carson as a wedding present for his son. Both testify to the wealth that was once made in Eureka's lumber trade. As early as 1856, there were already seven sawmills producing two million board feet of lumber every month. A meticulously restored building in Old Town now houses the **Morris Graves Museum of Art,** 636 F St., Eureka (ℂ **707/442-0278;** www.thepalette.com), with four galleries showcasing local artists as well as traveling exhibitions.

Humboldt Bay, where the town stands, was discovered by white settlers in 1850. In 1853, Fort Humboldt was established to protect settlers from local

Native American communities. Ulysses S. Grant was stationed here for 5 months until he resigned after serious disputes with his commanding officer about his drinking. The fort was abandoned in 1870. Today, the fort offers a self-guided trail past a series of logging exhibits, plus a reconstructed surgeon's quarters and a restored fort hospital, used today as a museum housing Native American artifacts and military and pioneer paraphernalia. **Fort Humboldt State Historic Park** is located at 3431 Fort Ave. (© **707/445-6567**). Admission is free; it's open daily from 8am to 5pm.

OUTDOOR PURSUITS

Humboldt Bay supplies a large portion of California's fish, and Eureka has a fishing fleet of about 200 boats. To get a better view (and perspective) of the bay and surrounding waters, you can board skipper Leroy Zerlang's *Madaket*—said to be the oldest passenger-carrying vessel in operation in the United States—for a 75-minute **Humboldt Bay Harbor Cruise,** departing from the foot of L Street in downtown Eureka. Tickets are $11 per person, free for children ages 4 and under. Call © **707/445-1910** for a recorded departure schedule.

For more active water recreation, kayaks, canoes, and sailboats can be rented from **Hum Boats,** on F Street (© **707/443-5157;** www.humboats.com), which also provides tours and lessons.

Humboldt County is also suitable for biking because it's relatively uncongested. Bikes can be rented from **Pro Sport Center,** 508 Myrtle Ave. (© **707/443-6328**). Fishing, diving, biking, and hiking information are also available here.

Humboldt Bay is an important stopover point along the Pacific Flyway and is the winter home for thousands of migratory birds. South of town, the **Humboldt Bay National Wildlife Refuge** ⚐, 1020 Ranch Rd., Loleta (© **707/733-5406**), provides an opportunity to see many of the 200 or so species that live in the marshes and willow groves—including Pacific black brant, western sandpiper, northern harrier, great blue heron, and green-winged teal. The egret rookery on the bay, best viewed from Woodley Island Marina across the bay en route to Samoa, is spectacular. Peak viewing for most species of water birds and raptors is between September and March. The refuge's entrance is off U.S. 101 north at the Hookton Road exit. Cross the overpass and turn right onto Ranch Road.

WHERE TO STAY

Abigail's Elegant Victorian Mansion Bed & Breakfast ⚐   For anyone interested in Victorian history and design, this is a special experience; those who just want comfort, service, a true gourmet breakfast, and a beautiful garden will also find this lodging ideal. The 1888 house, a National Historic Landmark, is the labor of love of owners Doug and Lily Vieyra, who have combed the country for the fabrics and designs that now provide the most authentic Victorian atmosphere I have ever encountered in the United States. The wallpapers are extraordinary— brilliant blues, golds, jades, and reds in intricate patterns that feature peacocks and mythological figures. Doug pays attention to every detail, from the butler who greets you in morning dress to the silent movies and period music on the phonograph. Each unit is individually furnished: The Van Gogh room contains the Belgian bedroom suite of Lily's mother. The Lily Langtry room, named after the actress and king's mistress who stayed here when she performed locally, features a four-poster bed and Langtry memorabilia. Guests can play croquet on the manicured lawn, where ice-cream sodas and lemonade are served in the afternoon.

1406 C St. (at 14th St.), Eureka, CA 95501. ℂ **707/444-3144.** Fax 707/442-3295. www.eureka-california.com. 4 units. $95–$215 double. Additional person $40–$50. Rates include breakfast. MC, V. **Amenities:** Sauna; complimentary bikes; Swedish massage; laundry service. *In room:* A/C.

Hotel Carter, Carter House, Bell Cottage, & Carter Cottage ★★★   At

the north end of Eureka's Old Town is the original building that launched Carter's renowned hostelry empire: the Carter House. Copied from a famous 1884 San Francisco Victorian, it was constructed by Mark Carter as a family home in 1982. Soon afterwards, Mark and his wife, Christi Carter, began taking guests, and before long they built a stately hotel across the street, the Hotel Carter. Later, the pretty Victorian Bell Cottage was acquired, and most recently the ultra-luxurious Carter Cottage.

The 23 rooms in the large, full-service Hotel Carter have modern furnishings and pine four-posters. The suites have such luxury appointments as fireplaces and Jacuzzis, and distant views of the waterfront can be seen from the tubs. There are seven rooms in the original Carter House, which is furnished with antiques, Oriental rugs, and modern artwork. The Bell Cottage's rooms are also individually decorated in grand Victorian fashion. If you really want to splurge, however, reserve the Carter Cottage, a small home that's been converted into one of the most luxurious lodgings in Northern California, a mini-mansion replete with a chef's kitchen, two fireplaces, a grand bathroom with a whirlpool tub for two, a private deck, and even a wine cellar. On the ground level of the Hotel Carter is one of Eureka's finest restaurants, Restaurant 301 (see "Where to Dine," below).

301 L St., Eureka, CA 95501. ℂ **800/404-1390** or 707/444-8062. Fax 707/444-8067. www.carterhouse.com. 32 units. $125–$187 double; $297–$326 suite; $497 Carter Cottage. Packages available. AE, DC, DISC, MC, V. From U.S. 101 N, turn left onto L St. and go to Third St. **Amenities:** Restaurant; nearby golf course; activities desk; wine shop; in-room massage; babysitting; laundry service. *In room:* A/C, TV/VCR w/pay movies, kitchen in some units, hair dryer, iron.

WHERE TO DINE

Ramone's Bakery & Cafe (Value) BAKERY   Ramone's combines a bakery on one side with a small dining room on the other. The baked items are extraordinary—try any one of the croissants, Danish, or muffins, and you won't be disappointed. The bakery offers a few lunch specials to choose from among the breads and pastries, such as soups, salads, sandwiches, and more. At any time of the day, it's a great place to stop in for a light, inexpensive meal and cup of coffee. There's a second bakery location at 2223 Harrison St., in Eureka, as well as one in Arcata at 747 13th St., at Wildberries Marketplace.

209 E St. (in Old Town). ℂ **707/445-2923.** www.ramonesbakery.com. Main courses $4–$6. No credit cards. Mon–Sat 7am–6pm, Sun 7am–4pm.

Restaurant 301 ★★★ CALIFORNIA   The large, light, and airy dining room adjacent to the hotel's lobby has tall windows looking out on the waterfront. It's the best restaurant in the area, with most of the herbs and many of the vegetables picked fresh from the hotel's organic gardens across the street. At dinner, diners may order either a la carte or off the Discovery Menu, a highly recommended prix-fixe five-course dinner menu that pairs each course with suggested wines by the glass. A typical dinner may begin with an artichoke, green lentil, and fennel salad, followed by a warm chèvre cake appetizer, then on to a grilled duck breast served with a seasonal fruit and zinfandel sauce. The cuisine also displays Asian accents, as in the chicken with spicy peanut sauce and the tiger prawns with sesame, ginger, and soy. If you're an oyster lover, start with a few Humboldt Bay oysters roasted with barbecue sauce. There's an excellent and extensive wine list (a Grand Award recipient from *Wine Spectator* magazine), courtesy of the 301 Wine Shop within the hotel, and a new wine bar.

In the Hotel Carter, 301 L St. ✆ **800/404-1390** or 707/444-8062. Reservations required. Main courses $18–$26. AE, DC, DISC, MC, V. Breakfast daily 7:30–10am; dinner daily 6–9pm.

Samoa Cookhouse ✦ *Finds* AMERICAN   During the lumber industry's heyday, cookhouses (like this one dating from 1885) were common, serving as community centers. Here the mill men and longshoremen at the Hammond Lumber Company came to chow down on three hot meals before, during, and after their 12-hour workday. The food is still hearty—though not necessarily healthy by today's waist-conscious standards—and served family-style at long tables covered with red-checkered cloths. Nobody leaves hungry. The price includes soup, salad, fresh-baked bread, the main course, and dessert (usually pie). The lunch-and-dinner menu still features a different dish each day—roast beef, fried or barbecued chicken, ham, or pork chops. Breakfast typically includes eggs, potatoes, sausage, bacon, pancakes, and all the orange juice and coffee you can drink. Adjacent to the dining room is a small museum featuring memorabilia from the lumbering era. This is the last cookhouse in the West, so bring the kids before it vanishes into history.

Cookhouse Rd., Samoa. ✆ **707/442-1659.** www.humboldtdining.com/cookhouse. Reservations accepted for large groups only. Main courses $7.45–$12. AE, DISC, MC, V. Mon–Sat 7am–3:30pm and 5–10pm, Sun 7am–10pm (closes 1 hr. earlier in winter). From U.S. 101, take Samoa Bridge to the end and turn left on Samoa Rd., then take the 1st left.

ARCATA ✦

From Eureka it's only 7 miles to Arcata, one of my favorite towns on the northern coast. Sort of a cross between Mayberry and Berkeley, it has an undeniable small-town flavor—right down to the bucolic town square—yet it possesses that intellectual and environmentally conscious esprit de corps so characteristic of university towns (Arcata is the home of Humboldt State University).

There are loads of family-type things to do here. On Wednesday, Friday, and Saturday evenings between June and July, Arcata's semipro baseball team, the **Humboldt Crabs,** partake in America's favorite pastime at Arcata Ballpark, at Ninth and F streets. Also worth a stop: the kid-friendly **Humboldt State University Natural History Museum,** 1315 G St. (✆ 707/826-4479), which is open Tuesday through Saturday from 10am to 5pm; **Tin Can Mailman,** at 10th and H streets (✆ 707/822-1307), a wonderful used-book store with more than 130,000 titles; **Redwood Park** (east end of 11th St.), which has an outstanding playground for kids and miles of forested hiking trails; and the **Humboldt Brewing Company,** 10th and I streets (✆ 707/826-BREW), creators of the heavenly Red Nectar Ale (call for tour information).

A few miles north of Willow Creek lies the Hoopa Indian Reservation. In the Hoopa Shopping Center, the **Hoopa Tribal Museum** (✆ 530/625-4110) archives the culture and history of the native people of Northern California, including their ceremonial regalia, basketry, canoes, and tools. Guided tours of Hoopa Valley's historic sites, including the traditional village of Takimildiñ, are available through the museum by appointment. Hours are Monday through Friday from 8am to noon and 1 to 5pm year-round, and in summer on Saturday from 10am to noon and 1 to 4pm.

OUTDOOR PURSUITS

The **Arcata Marsh and Wildlife Sanctuary** ✦, at the foot of South I Street (② 707/826-2359), is a thought-provoking excursion. The 154-acre sanctuary—which doubles as Arcata's integrated wetland wastewater treatment plant—is a stopover for marsh wrens, egrets, and other waterfowl, including the rare Arctic loon. Each Saturday at 8:30am and 2pm there are free 1-hour guided tours starting at the cul-de-sac at the foot of South I Street. The town populace is very proud of its environmentally pleasing wastewater solution, boasting that "Arcata Residents Flush with Pride."

Heading east from Arcata, Calif. 299 leads to the Trinity River in the heart of **Six Rivers National Forest.** Willow Creek and Somes Bar are the prime recreational centers for the area. Here visitors can sign up for canoeing, rafting, and kayaking trips with such outfitters as **Aurora River Adventures,** in Willow Creek (② **800/562-8475** or 530/629-3843; www.rafting4fun.com), which offers some offbeat, educationally oriented excursions that are great for kids, as well as gnarly Class V trips for the more daring. They also rent equipment for self-guided adventures.

WHERE TO STAY

Hotel Arcata *Value*   This is the town's most prominent hotel, and many guests are parents visiting their offspring at Humboldt State University. Located at the northeast corner of the town plaza, the Hotel Arcata consists of a handsome early 1900s brick facade and an equally appealing lobby (the staff is quite friendly as well). The individually decorated rooms range from small singles starting at a modest $66, and twice that amount for a large Executive Suite that overlooks the plaza. The mini-suites are the quietest, and a bargain at $88. On the premises, under different management, is a Japanese restaurant called Tomo. If you can't afford the more sumptuous Lady Anne B&B (see below), this is definitely the next best choice.

708 9th St., Arcata, CA 95521. ② 800/344-1221 or 707/826-0217. Fax 707/826-1737. www.hotelarcata. com. 32 units. $66–$110 double; $116–$138 executive suite. Rates include continental breakfast. AE, DC, DISC, MC, V. Pets accepted with $5-a-day fee and $50 deposit. **Amenities:** Restaurant; free passes to nearby indoor pool and health club; salon; executive suites. *In room:* TV, dataport, coffeemaker.

The Lady Anne ✦   Easily Arcata's finest lodging, this Queen Anne–style bed-and-breakfast is kept in top-notch condition by innkeepers Sharon Ferrett and Sam Pennisi, who also served a term as Arcata's mayor. The large, cozy guest rooms are individually decorated with period antiques, lace curtains, Oriental rugs, and English stained glass. For second honeymooners, there's the Lady Sarah Angela Room with its four-poster bed and pleasant bay view. Breakfast is served in the grand dining room, warmed on winter mornings by a toasty fire. On summer afternoons, you can lounge on the veranda with a book or play a game of croquet on the front lawn. Several good dining options are only a few blocks away at Arcata Plaza.

902 14th St., Arcata, CA 95521. ② **707/822-2797.** www.humboldt1.com/~ladyanne. 5 units. $100–$120 double. Rates include breakfast. MC, V. *In room:* Hair dryer, iron, no phone.

WHERE TO DINE

Abruzzi ITALIAN   The best way to review your dining options in Arcata is to stroll downtown to Jacoby's Storehouse, a converted mid-19th-century brick warehouse located at the southwest corner of the town plaza, and ponder the menus posted outside the Abruzzi and Plaza Grill (see below). Abruzzi is generally acknowledged as the best Italian restaurant in town. Replete with dark woods and dim lighting, it has all the makings for a romantic dinner. Specialties include range-fed veal picatta and sea scallops with langostinos tossed with cheese tortellini. Well-seasoned filet steaks are available as well. The standout dessert is the chocolate paradiso, a dense chocolate cake set in a pool of champagne mousseline. All meals begin with a basket of warm bread sticks, focaccia, and a baguette that you can smell all the way down the street.

Jacoby's Storehouse (at the corner of 8th and H sts.). © **707/826-2345**. Reservations recommended. Main courses $9–$22. AE, DISC, MC, V. Daily 5:30–9pm.

Folie Douce _ʕ_ BISTRO   Humboldt Hip meets Cuisine Chic at Folie Douce, the most energized and inventive restaurant in town. Designer wood-oven-fired pizza is its mainstay, such as the grilled duck sausage fennel, chèvre, and sun-dried tomato pizza, or the spicy shrimp with fontina, mozzarella, and scallions combo. But the appetizers and entrees are equally intriguing. The highlight of your vacation may well be the artichoke-heart cheesecake appetizer, followed by a plate of grilled wild-rice polenta in a light cream sauce. Other heartier menu items range from a fat filet mignon to roast duck. The restaurant has a serious wine list. This small, festive off-street eatery is extremely popular, so be sure to make reservations.

1551 G St. (between 15th and 16th sts.). © **707/822-1042**. www.holyfolie.com. Reservations recommended. Main courses $9–$27. AE, DISC, MC, V. Tues–Thurs 5:30–9pm, Fri–Sat 5:30–10pm.

Plaza Grill _(Kids_ AMERICAN   If the prices at Abruzzi are a bit more than you care to spend, consider the Plaza Grill, located directly above Abruzzi. Despite efforts to make it more upscale, it can't seem to shake its image as a college-student burger joint, but a nice one. The menu is more substantial than you'd think, with a choice of salads, sandwiches, burgers, fish platters, chicken specialties, steaks, and all kinds of coffee drinks. There's a very reasonably priced children's menu.

Jacoby's Storehouse (at the corner of 8th and H sts.). © **707/826-0860**. Main courses $7–$17. AE, DISC, MC, V. Sun–Thurs 5–8:30pm, Fri 5–11pm, Sat 5–10:30pm.

TRINIDAD & PATRICK'S POINT STATE PARK _ʕ_

Back on U.S. 101 north of Arcata, you'll come to **Trinidad,** a tiny coastal fishing village of some 400 people. One of the smallest incorporated cities in California, it occupies a peninsula 25 miles north of Eureka. If you're not into fishing, there's little to do in town except poke around at the handful of shops, walk along the busy pier, and wish you owned a house here.

Five miles north of Trinidad takes you to the 640-acre **Patrick's Point State Park** _ʕ_, 4150 Patrick's Point Dr. (© **707/677-3570**), which has one of the finest ocean access points in the north at sandy **Agate Beach.** It's suitable for driftwood picking, rockhounding, and camping on a sheltered bluff. The park contains a re-creation of a Sumeg Village, which is actively used by the Yurok people and neighboring tribes. A self-guided tour takes you to replicas of family homes and sweat houses.

WHERE TO STAY

The Lost Whale Inn Bed & Breakfast Inn _ʕʕ (Kids_   This modern version of a blue-and-gray Cape Cod–style house is set on 4 acres of seafront land studded with firs, alders, spruces, and redwoods. Its owners welcome children (there's a playground and pygmy-goat farm on the premises) and adults (there's also a Jacuzzi with a view of the sea), and they claim that it's the only hotel in the state of California with its own private beach with tide pools and sea lions.

Afternoon tea and an artfully prepared and presented breakfast are included in the rates. The decor is eclectic, with lots of paintings, plus an outdoor deck facing the surf. Part of the grounds is devoted to a kitchen garden with fresh herbs and vegetables. Families should inquire about the three furnished homes—including a wonderful farmhouse—that the innkeepers also rent out. A recent addition is a rebuilt beach trail with stairs and handrails.

3452 Patrick's Point Dr., Trinidad, CA 95570. ℂ 800/677-7859 or 707/677-3425. Fax 707/677-0284. www.lostwhaleinn.com. 8 units. Summer $170–$200 double; winter $140–$170 double. Rates include country breakfast and afternoon tea. AE, DISC, MC, V. **Amenities:** Oceanview Jacuzzi; children's playground and playhouse; game room; business center. *In room:* No phone.

Trinidad Bay Bed & Breakfast ⚜ Set 175 feet above the ocean, all rooms at this picturesque Cape Cod–style home have sweeping views of Trinidad Bay. On a clear day, you can see up to 65 miles of the rugged coastline. Your hosts are Corlene and Don Blue (Cordon Blue to their friends), two innkeepers who have created what many visitors think is the most charming inn around. Rare for an older B&B, all the rooms have private bathrooms. Decor throughout is an eclectic mix of New England–style antiques and a collection of antique clocks. If it's available, opt for the Mauve Fireplace Suite, with its wraparound window, large wood-burning fireplace, king-size bed, and private entrance.

560 Edwards St. (P.O. Box 849), Trinidad, CA 95570-0849. ℂ 707/677-0840. Fax 707/677-9245. www.trinidadbaybnb.com. 4 units. Summer $150–$180 double; winter $135–$165 double. Rates include breakfast. MC, V. Closed Dec–Jan. *In room:* Fridge, coffeemaker, hair dryer, iron, no phone.

Trinidad Inn *Value* There's a bevy of inexpensive motels in these parts, but the Trinidad Inn is the best of the lot. It's located 2 miles north of Trinidad on a serene stretch of road ensconced by a towering cadre of aromatic redwoods. Both the motel's exterior—trimmed in pretty shades of white and blue—and guest rooms are impeccably maintained. Each room is unique: Some are family units that hold up to four persons, while others offer a comfortable queen bed, and private bathroom for as little as $70 per night (access to the adjoining kitchen is an extra $10). A good room for couples is number 10, an adorable little cottage complete with a full kitchen, living room, private bathroom, bedroom, and small patio. Each morning fresh coffee, tea, and homemade raspberry scones and muffins are served under the gazebo in the flower-filled garden. Guests are free to use the picnic table and barbecue, or wander through the adjacent forest to the beaches a short stroll away.

1170 Patrick's Point Dr., Trinidad, CA 95570. ℂ 707/677-3349. www.trinidadinn.com. 10 units. $70–$130 double. Rates include continental breakfast. AE, DC, DISC, MC, V. From U.S. 101, take the Trinidad exit and head 2 miles N on Patrick's Point Dr. Pets accepted with $10 fee and $20 deposit. *In room:* TV, no phone.

WHERE TO DINE

Larrupin Café ★★ AMERICAN Located on a quiet country road 2 miles north of Trinidad, this highly popular and beautifully decorated restaurant sports an eclectic blend of Indonesian and African artifacts mingled with colorful urns full of exotic flowers and romantic candlelit tables. The recently added new patio with a reflecting pool and bamboo fencing is a real charmer as well. Dinner starts with an appetizer board stocked with gravlax, paté, dark pumpernickel, apple slices, and sauce, followed by a red- and green-leaf salad tossed with a Gorgonzola vinaigrette. Many menu items are barbecued over mesquite fires, such as a hefty cut of halibut that's basted with lemon butter and served with mustard-flavored dill sauce, and the fantastic pork ribs served with a side of sweet and spicy barbecue sauce. Another recommended dish is the barbecued Cornish game hen served with an orange-and-brandy glaze. For appetizers, the barbecued oysters are divine, especially in winter, when the fireplace casts a much welcomed warmth. Heaven is a slice of pecan-chocolate pie topped with hot buttered rum sauce, or the sinfully good triple-layer chocolate cake layered with caramel and whipped cream.

1658 Patrick's Point Dr. (C) **707/677-0230.** Reservations recommended. Main courses $15–$22. No credit cards. Thurs–Mon 10am–2pm (coffee and light dishes only) and 5–9pm.

The Seascape Restaurant *Finds* CALIFORNIA   Established in the 1940s, this is an endearingly unpretentious cross between a cafe and a diner, with three dining rooms, great ocean views, overworked but cheerful waitresses, and a nostalgic aura. Folks pop in for coffee or snacks from early morning until after sundown, but by far the biggest seller here is the Trinidad Bay Platter ($18). Heaped with halibut, scallops, and shrimp, and accompanied by salad and rice pilaf, it's even more popular than the prawn brochette, which draws a close second. How fresh is the fish? As the menu states, "Availability of seafood depends on Season, Weather conditions, Regulations and Luck." Halibut, rock cod, sole, and other local catches can be prepared in six different styles, including charbroiled and sautéed in garlic, onions, and mushrooms. For you laterisers, breakfast is served until 4pm.

Beside the pier at the foot of Bay St. (C) **707/677-3762.** Full dinners $9.50–$22. DISC, MC, V. Daily 7am–9pm.

ORICK

From Trinidad, it's about another 15 miles to Orick. You can't miss it: Just look for the dozens of burl stands alongside the road. Carved with chisels and chain saws, these former redwood logs have been transformed into just about every creature you can imagine—perhaps a gift for your mother-in-law?

At the south end of Orick is the town's saving grace, the sleek **Redwood National Park Information Center** (☆ ((C) **707/464-6101,** ext. 5265). If you plan to spend any amount of time exploring the park, stop here first and pick up a free map; the displays of fauna and wildlife aren't too bad, either. It's open daily from 9am to 5pm.

The first of the parks that make up Redwood National Park, Prairie Creek, is 6 miles north of Orick. About 14 miles farther on is the mouth of the **Klamath River,** famous for its salmon, trout, and steelhead. Tours aboard a jet boat take visitors upriver from the estuary to view bear, deer, elk, osprey, hawks, otters, and more along the riverbanks. Rates for the 30-mile scenic trip (offered May 1–Oct 30) are $20 for adults, $10 for children ages 4 to 11, and free for kids under 4. For more information and reservations, contact **Klamath River Jet Boat Tours,** Klamath ((C) **800/887-JETS** or 707/482-7775).

A more serene alternative to exploring the Klamath is taking a ranger-led **kayak tour.** Offered only during the summer months (and only if they have enough money in their budget), the trip costs about $50 and includes all the requisite kayak gear. For more information, call the Redwood National Park Information Center at the phone number listed above.

From Klamath, it's another 20 miles to Crescent City, gateway to the other parks that make up Redwood National Park.

7 Crescent City

79 miles N of Eureka; 375 miles N of San Francisco

Crescent City itself has little to offer, but it makes a good base for exploring Redwood National Park and the Smith River, one of the great recreational rivers of the West. The **Battery Point Lighthouse,** at the foot of A Street (© **707/ 464-3089**), which is accessible on foot only at low tide, houses a museum with exhibits on the coast's history. Tours of the lighthouse ($2 for adults, 50¢ for children) are offered Wednesday through Sunday from 10am to 4pm, tides permitting, April through September.

Another draw is the **Smith River National Recreation Area** ⚛, east of Jedediah Smith State Park and part of Six Rivers National Forest. The Area Headquarters is at 10600 U.S. 199, Gasquet (© **707/457-3131;** www. delnorte.org/srnra.html), which is reached via U.S. 199 from Crescent City (about a 30-min. drive). Maps of the forest can be obtained here, at the Supervisor's Office in Eureka, or at either of the Redwood National Park centers in Orick and Crescent City.

The 300,000-plus acres of wilderness offer camping at five modest-size campgrounds (all with fewer than 50 sites) along the Smith River. Sixteen trails attract hikers from across the country. The easiest short trail is the **McClendon Ford,** which is 2 miles long and drops from 1,000 to 800 feet in elevation to the south fork of the river. Other activities include mountain biking, white-water rafting, kayaking, and fishing for salmon and trout.

For information, contact the **Crescent City–Del Norte County Chamber of Commerce,** 1001 Front St., Crescent City, CA 95531 (© **800/343-8300** or 707/464-3174; www.northerncalifornia.net).

WHERE TO STAY

Crescent Beach Motel *(Value)*   Crescent City doesn't have any fancy hotels or bed-and-breakfasts, but it does have lots of modestly priced motels, the best of which is the Crescent Beach Motel. Near the highway, about a mile south of town, this single-story structure is the only local motel set directly on the beach. The freshly remodeled and refurbished rooms are clean and simple. Four of the units face the highway; try to get one of the others, all of which have sliding-glass doors to decks and a small lawn area overlooking the bay. One of the city's most popular restaurants, the Beachcomber (see "Where to Dine," below), is located next door.

1455 Redwood Hwy. S. (U.S. 101), Crescent City, CA 95531. © **707/464-5436.** www.crescent beachmotel.com. 27 units. Summer $73–$85 double; winter $50–$59 double. AE, DISC, MC, V. *In room:* TV, no phone.

Curly Redwood Lodge *(Value)*   This is a blast from the past, the kind of place where you might have stayed as a kid during one of those cross-country vacations in the family station wagon. It was built in 1957 on grasslands across from the town's harbor, and is completely trimmed with lumber from a single ancient redwood. Although they're not full of the latest high-tech gadgets, the bedrooms are among the largest and best soundproofed in town, and certainly the most evocative of a bygone, more innocent age. In winter, about a third of the rooms (the ones upstairs) are locked and sealed. Overall, the aura is more akin to Oregon than anything you might imagine in California.

701 Redwood Hwy. S. (U.S. 101), Crescent City, CA 95531. © **707/464-2137.** Fax 707/464-1655. www.curlyredwoodlodge.com. 36 units. Summer $60–$86 double; winter $39–$68 double. Winter rates include breakfast. AE, DC, MC, V. *In room:* TV.

WHERE TO DINE

Beachcomber SEAFOOD   The decor is as predictably nautical as the name implies: rough-cut planking and a scattering of driftwood, fishnets, and buoys dangling above a dimly lit space. The restaurant lies beside the beach, 2 miles south of Crescent City's center. The cuisine is a joy to fish lovers who prefer not to mask the flavor of their seafood with complicated sauces. Most of the dishes are grilled over madrone-wood barbecue pits, a technique perfected since this place was established in 1975. Pacific salmon, halibut, lingcod, shark, sturgeon, Pacific snapper, oysters, and steamer clams are house specialties that have visitors lining up, especially on Friday and Saturday nights.

1400 U.S. 101. ℂ 707/464-2205. Reservations recommended. Main courses $6–$15. MC, V. Thurs–Tues 5–9pm. Closed Dec–Jan and part of Feb.

Harbor View Grotto Restaurant & Lounge SEAFOOD/STEAKS   This restaurant has been specializing in fresh seafood at market prices since 1961. It has distant views of the ocean and harbor from the dining room and lounge. The "light eaters" menu includes a choice of a cup of white chowder (made fresh daily) or salad, a main course, and vegetables; heartier appetites can choose from among three different cuts of prime rib. Menu items include fresh, locally caught fish like Pacific snapper and salmon. Crab or shrimp Louis, as well as crabmeat or shrimp sandwiches, are popular in season.

150 Starfish Way. ℂ 707/464-3815. Reservations recommended. Main courses $4–$9 lunch, $6–$20 dinner. DISC, MC, V. Daily 11:30am–9pm, later in the summer months.

8 Redwood National & State Parks ★★

40 miles N of Eureka; 336 miles N of San Francisco

It's impossible to explain the feeling you get in the old-growth forests of Redwood National and State Parks without resorting to Alice-in-Wonderland comparisons. Like a tropical rain forest, the redwood forest is a multistoried affair, the tall trees being only the top layer. Everything seems big, misty, and primeval—flowering bushes cover the ground, 10-foot-tall ferns line the creeks, and the smells are rich and musty. It's so *Jurassic Park* that you can't help but half expect to turn the corner and see a dinosaur.

When Archibald Menzies first noted the botanical existence of the coast redwood in 1794, more than two million acres of redwood forest carpeted California and Oregon. By 1965, heavy logging had reduced that to 300,000 acres, and it was obvious something had to be done if any redwoods were to survive. The state created several parks around individual groves in the 1920s, and in 1968, the federal government created Redwood National Park. In May 1994, the National Park Service and the California Department of Parks and Recreation signed an agreement to manage these four redwood parks cooperatively, hence the Redwood National *and* State Parks.

Although logging of old-growth redwoods in the region is still a major bone of contention among the government, private landowners, and environmentalists, it's an auspicious sign that contention even exists, a sign that perhaps we have all learned to see the forest *and* the trees for what they are—the undisputed monarchs of all living things, a thriving link to the age of dinosaurs, and a humble reminder that the age of mankind is but a hiccup in time to the venerable *Sequoia sempervirens.*

ESSENTIALS

GETTING THERE   The southern gateway to the Redwood National and State Parks is the town of Orick, which you can identify by the dozens of burl stands alongside the road. U.S. 101 runs right through the middle of town. The northern gateway to the park is Crescent City, your best bet for a cheap motel, gas, fast food, and outdoor supplies.

VISITOR INFORMATION   In Orick you'll find the **Redwood Information Center,** P.O. Box 7, Orick, CA 95555 (© 707/464-6101, ext. 5265), one of California's rare examples of well-placed tax dollars (though some may dispute this because it's located near a floodplain and within a tsunami zone). Stop here and pick up a free map; it's open daily from 9am to 5pm. If you missed the Orick center, don't worry: About 10 miles farther north on U.S. 101 is the **Prairie Creek Visitor Center** (© 707/464-6101, ext. 5300), which carries all the same maps and information. It's open daily from 9am to 5pm in summer, daily from 10am to 4pm (sometimes later) in winter.

Before touring the park, pick up a free guide at the **Redwood National and State Parks Headquarters and Information Center,** 1111 Second St. (at K St.), Crescent City, CA 95531 (© 707/464-6101, ext. 5064). It's open daily from 9am to 5pm.

If you happen to be arriving via U.S. 199 from Oregon, the rangers manning the **Hiouchi Information Station** (© 707/464-6101, ext. 5067) and **Jedediah Smith Visitor Center** (© 707/464-6101, ext. 5113) can also supply you with the necessary maps and advice. Both are open daily in summer from 9am to 5pm, and in winter when staffing is available.

For more information about the Redwood National and State Parks, visit their website at **www.nps.gov/redw**.

FEES & PERMITS   Admission to the national park is free, but to enter any of the three state parks (which contain the best redwood groves), you'll have to pay a $2 day-use fee, which is good at all three. The camping fee is $12 for drive-in sites. (Reservations are highly recommended in summer.) Walk-in sites are free, though a permit is required.

RANGER PROGRAMS   The park service runs interpretive programs—from trees to tide pools, legends to landforms—at the Hiouchi, Crescent Beach, and Redwood information centers during summer months, as well as year-round at the park headquarters in Crescent City. State rangers lead campfire programs and numerous other activities throughout the year as well. Call the **Parks Information** service for both the national and state parks (© 707/464-6101, ext. 5265) to get information on current schedules and events.

EXPLORING THE PARKS BY CAR

If you're approaching the park from the south, be sure to take the detour along U.S. 101 called the **Newton B. Drury Scenic Parkway** ✰, which passes through dazzling groves of redwoods and elk-filled meadows before leading back onto the highway 8 miles later. Another spectacular route is the **Coastal Drive** ✰, which winds through stands of redwoods and offers grand views of the Pacific.

The most amazing car-friendly trail in all the Redwood National and State Parks is the hidden, well-maintained gravel **Howland Hill Road** ✰✰ that winds for about 12 miles through Jedediah Smith Redwoods State Park. It's an unforgettable journey through an unbelievably spectacular old-growth redwood forest—considered by many to be one of the most beautiful areas in the world.

Redwood National & State Parks

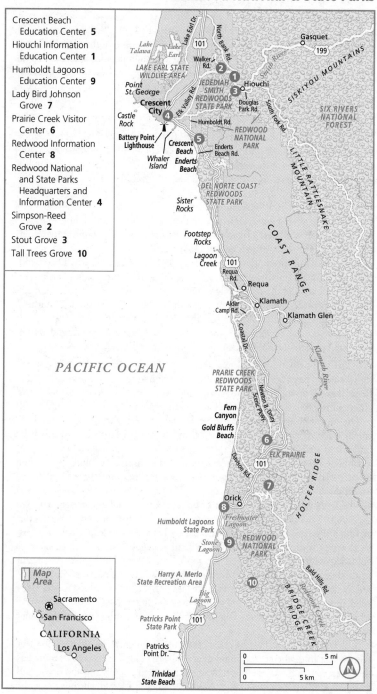

Crescent Beach
Education Center **5**

Hiouchi Information
Education Center **1**

Humboldt Lagoons
Education Center **9**

Lady Bird Johnson
Grove **7**

Prairie Creek Visitor
Center **6**

Redwood Information
Center **8**

Redwood National
and State Parks
Headquarters and
Information Center **4**

Simpson-Reed
Grove **2**

Stout Grove **3**

Tall Trees Grove **10**

Lake Earl Dr.

North Bank Rd.

101

Gasquet

199

*Lake
Talawa*

*Lake
Earl*

Walker
Rd.

LAKE EARL STATE
WILDLIFE AREA

*Point
St. George*

JEDEDIAH
SMITH
REDWOODS
STATE PARK

Hiouchi

Smith River

SISKIYOU MOUNTAINS

**Crescent
City**

Elk Valley Rd.

Douglas
Park Rd.

South Fork Rd.

SIX RIVERS
NATIONAL
FOREST

*Castle
Rock*

Humboldt Rd.

REDWOOD
NATIONAL
PARK

LITTLE RATTLESNAKE MOUNTAIN

Battery Point
Lighthouse

**Crescent
Beach**

Enderts
Beach Rd.

*Whaler
Island*

**Enderts
Beach**

DEL NORTE COAST
REDWOODS
STATE PARK

COAST RANGE

*Sister
Rocks*

*Footstep
Rocks*

*Lagoon
Creek*

101

Requa
Rd.

Requa

Klamath

Klamath River

Alder
Camp Rd.

Klamath Glen

Coastal Dr.

PACIFIC OCEAN

PRARIE CREEK
REDWOODS
STATE PARK

Newton B. Drury Scenic Pkwy.

**Fern
Canyon**

**Gold Bluffs
Beach**

ELK PRAIRIE

101

Davison Rd.

HOLTER RIDGE

Orick

Humboldt Lagoons
State Park

*Freshwater
Lagoon*

REDWOOD
NATIONAL
PARK

Bald Hills Rd.

*Stone
Lagoon*

Harry A. Merlo
State Recreation Area

*Big
Lagoon*

BRIDGE CREEK RIDGE

Redwood Creek

Patricks Point
State Park

101

Patricks
Point Dr.

*Trinidad
State Beach*

Map
Area

Sacramento

San Francisco

CALIFORNIA

Los Angeles

0   5 mi

0   5 km

N

To get here from U.S. 101, keep an eye out for the 76 gas station at the south end of Crescent City; just before the station, turn right on Elk Valley Road, and follow it to Howland Hill Road, which will be on your right. After driving through the park, you'll end up at U.S. 199 near the town of Hiouchi, and from here it's a short jaunt west to get back to U.S. 101. Plan at least 2 to 3 hours for the 45-mile round-trip, or all day if you want to do some hiking or mountain biking in the park. This drive is not recommended for trailers and motor homes.

SPORTS & OUTDOOR PURSUITS

BEACHES, WHALE-WATCHING & BIRD-WATCHING   The park's beaches vary from long white-sand strands to cobblestone pocket coves. The water temperature is in the high 40s to low 50s (low 10s Celsius) year-round; it's often rough out there, so swimmers and surfers should be prepared for adverse conditions.

Crescent Beach is a long sandy beach just 2 miles south of Crescent City that's popular with beachcombers, surf fishermen, and surfers. Just south of Crescent Beach is **Endert's Beach,** a protected spot with a hike-in campground and tide pools at the southern end of the beach.

High coastal overlooks (like Klamath overlook and Crescent Beach overlook) make great whale-watching outposts during the southern migration in December and January and the return migration in March and April. The northern sea cliffs also provide valuable nesting sites for marine birds like auklets, puffins, murres, and cormorants. Birders will thrill at the park's freshwater lagoons as well. These coastal lagoons are some of the most pristine shorebird and water-fowl habitats left, and are chock-full of hundreds of different species.

HIKING   The park's official map and guide, available at any of the information centers, provides a fairly good layout of hiking trails within the park. Regardless of how short or long your hike may be, dress warmly and bring plenty of water and sunscreen. Pets are prohibited on all of the park's trails.

The most popular walk is the short, heavily traveled **Fern Canyon Trail** 🏵, which leads to an unbelievably lush grotto of lady, deer, chain, sword, five-finger, and maidenhair ferns clinging to 50-foot-high vertical walls divided by a babbling brook. It's only about a 1½-mile walk from Gold Bluffs Beach, but be prepared to scramble across the creek several times on your way via small footbridges.

The **Lady Bird Johnson Grove Loop** 🏵 is an easy, 1-hour self-guided tour that loops 1 mile around a glorious lush grove of mature redwoods. It's the site at which the national park was dedicated by Lady Bird Johnson in 1968. Also an easy trek is the **Yurok Loop Nature Trail** at Lagoon Creek. The 1-mile self-guided trail gradually climbs to the top of rugged sea bluff (with wonderful panoramic views of the Pacific) before looping back to the parking lot. If some-one's willing to act as shuttle driver, have him or her meet you at the Requa Trail-head and take the 4-mile coastal trail to the mouth of the Klamath. And for the whiner in your group, there's **Big Tree Trail,** a quarter-mile paved trail leading to a really big tree.

Tall Trees Trail leads to the one of the world's tallest trees—perhaps 365 feet tall, 14 feet in diameter, and more than 600 years old. This was once touted as the tallest tree in the world, but new candidates keep popping up and this proud giant has also lost a couple of feet. Now, who knows? It's still worth it to see the contender. You'll have to go to the Redwood Information Center near Orick (see "Essentials" above) to obtain a free map and permit to drive to the trailhead of

Tall Trees Grove. Only 50 permits are issued per day on a first-come, first-served basis because of a small parking area. After driving to the trail head, you have to walk a steep 1⅓ miles down into the grove. The trail is 3¼ miles round-trip.

WILDLIFE VIEWING   One of the most striking aspects of Prairie Creek Redwood State Park is its 200- to 300-strong herd of **Roosevelt elk** ⚲, usually found in the appropriately named Elk Prairie in the southern end of the park. These gigantic beasts can weigh 1,000 pounds, and the bulls carry huge antlers from spring to fall. Elk are also sometimes found at Gold Bluffs Beach—it's an incredible rush to suddenly come upon them out of the fog or after a turn in the trail. Nearly a hundred **black bears** also call the park home but are seldom seen. Unlike those at Yosemite and Yellowstone, these bears are still afraid of people. Keep them that way by giving them a wide berth, observing food-storage etiquette while camping, and disposing of garbage properly.

WHERE TO STAY

Five small campgrounds are located in the national park proper. Four of the walk-in (more like backpack-in) camps—Little Bald Hills, Nickel Creek, Flint Ridge, and Butler Creek—are free, and only one (the Redwood Creek Gravel Bar) requires a permit from the visitor center in advance.

Most car campsites are in the **Prairie Creek** and **Jedediah Smith state parks,** which lie entirely inside the national park. Prairie Creek contains two campgrounds, at Elk Prairie and Gold Bluffs Beach. Sites are $12 per night and can be reserved by calling the ReserveAmerica reservations system (✆ **800/444-7275;** www.reserveamerica.com). It helps if you know what campground and if possible which site you would like.

If the camping areas above are all filled, try the **Mill Creek Campground,** in Del Norte Coast Redwoods State Park (part of RNSP), located 7 miles south of Crescent City on U.S. 101, which has 145 tent or RV sites. The walk-in tent sites are actually quite nice, situated amidst the forest. Fees are $12 per night. The ReserveAmerica system (see above) handles reservations for this campground as well.

A number of bed-and-breakfasts and funky roadside motels are available in the surrounding communities of Crescent City, Orick, and Klamath. The **Crescent City/Del Norte Chamber of Commerce** (✆ **800/343-8300**) can probably steer you toward the proper match.

Redwood National Park AYH Hostel (*Value*)   The only lodging actually within the park, this settler's homestead was remodeled in 1987 to accommodate 30 guests dormitory-style (that is, bunks and shared bathrooms). The location of this hostel is perfect, a mere 100 yards from the beach, and surrounded by hiking trails leading along the Redwood Coast (the staff leads nature walks and is well versed in local history). A couple's room is available for an additional $10, with advance notice, and the hostel even takes reservations by credit card (strongly recommended in the summer). The nightly rate includes use of the showers, common room with VCR and videos, redwood deck, help-yourself common kitchen, laundry room, dining room, pellet stove, and bicycle storage.

14480 U.S. 101 (at U.S. 101 and Wilson Creek Rd., across from False Klamath Cove), Klamath, CA 95548. ✆ **800/909-4776,** ext. 74, or 707/482-8265. Fax 707/482-4665. www.norcalhostels.org. 28 bunks, 1 couple's room. $14–$16. DISC, MC, V.

8

The Far North: Lake Tahoe, the Shasta Cascades & Lassen Volcanic National Park

by Matthew Richard Poole

Dominated by the eternally snow-capped Mount Shasta—visible for 100 miles around on a clear day—California's upper northern territory is among the least-toured sections of the state. Often referred to as "the Far North," this vast region stretches from the rice fields north of Sacramento all the way to the Oregon border. In fact, the area is so immense that the state of Ohio would fit comfortably within its borders.

The Far North is a virtual outdoor playground for the adventurous traveler, offering myriad inexpensive recreational activities such as hiking, climbing, skiing, white-water rafting, and mountain biking. Other attractions, both artificial and natural, range from the amazing Shasta Dam to Lava Beds National Monument, which has dozens of caves to explore, and Lassen Volcanic National Park, a towering laboratory of volcanic phenomena.

Directly south of the Cascade Range is one of the most popular recreational regions in the Golden State: Lake Tahoe. Situated at 6,225 feet above sea level in the Sierra Nevada Mountains, it straddles the border between Nevada and California. Although the lake has been marred by overdevelopment—particularly along the casino-riddled southern shore—the western and eastern coastlines still provide quiet havens for hiking and cycling. The surrounding mountains offer some of the best skiing in the United States at more than a dozen resorts.

1 Lake Tahoe ★★★

107 miles E of Sacramento; 192 miles E of San Francisco; 45 miles SW of Reno, NV

Lake Tahoe is one of our great national treasures. It's not only stunningly beautiful, but the air is crisp and clear, and the sun shines 80% of the time. In summer, you can enjoy boating and watersports, sandy beaches, bicycling, golf, tennis, hiking, camping, ballooning, horseback riding, rock climbing, bungee jumping, parasailing, skating—the array of possibilities is endless. In winter, with an average snowfall of 409 inches, Lake Tahoe is one of the nation's premier ski destinations, offering 15 downhill resorts and 10 cross-country ski centers. There's also snowboarding, ice-skating, snowshoeing, snowmobiling, sleigh riding, sledding, and snow play. Year-round activities include fishing, Vegas-style gambling, and big-name entertainment in the casinos.

Then there is the lake. It's disputable whether Lake Tahoe is the most beautiful lake in the world, but it's hard to imagine any spot as captivating. When Mark Twain first saw it, he declared it "the fairest picture the whole earth

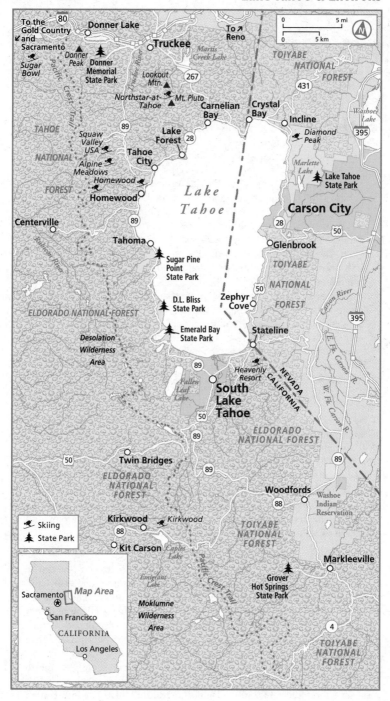

A Tale of Two Shores

Before you visit Tahoe for the first time, it's important to know that there's a huge difference between the North and the South Shores. Don't let the "City" in North Shore's "Tahoe City" fool you: The entire town can be driven through in a couple of minutes, whereas South Lake Tahoe is brimming with high-rise casinos, motels, and mini-malls. Where you choose to stay is important because driving from one end of the lake to the other takes an hour or more in the summer and can be downright treacherous in the winter.

So which side is for you? If you're here for gambling or entertainment, stay south: The selection of casinos is better and there's more action. If it's the great outdoors you're after, or simply a relaxing retreat, head north. The scenic North Shore offers a better selection of quality resorts and vacation rentals, while the bustling South Shore shoots for quantity, offering more lodging options, often at better rates. The woodsy West Shore has the most camping spots, while the East Shore has been protected from development and has no commercial activity.

Wherever you stay, you'll find no shortage of water and mountain sports activities. The lake is crowded during the summer and ski seasons, so plan far ahead. It's much easier to get reservations for the spring and fall, and the rates are significantly lower. There are also numerous vacation homes and condominiums available to rent; call the visitor-center bureaus or visit the websites listed below under "Visitor Information" for a list of rental agents.

affords." Famed for its crystal-clear water (a white dinner plate at the depth of 75 ft. would be clearly visible from the surface) and its size, 22 miles long and 12 miles wide, it is the largest alpine lake in North America. Its average depth is 989 feet with the deepest point being 1,645 feet, containing enough water to cover the entire state of California to a depth of 14½ inches. Surrounded by the majestic peaks of the Sierra Nevadas, its waters seem to soak up the colors of the sky and the mountains, creating a kaleidoscope of sparkling blues, greens, and purples. It's a sight that will lure you back year after year.

ESSENTIALS

GETTING THERE   It's a 4-hour drive from San Francisco; take I-80 east to Sacramento, then U.S. 50 to the South Shore, or I-80 east to Calif. 89 or Calif. 267 to the North Shore. Be prepared for snow in the winter. During heavy storms, you won't be permitted to pass the CHP (California Highway Patrol) checkpoints without four-wheel-drive or chains. From Los Angeles, it's a grueling 9-hour drive; take I-5 through the Central Valley to Sacramento, and then follow the directions above.

Reno-Tahoe International Airport (45 min. to North Shore, 90 min. to South Shore) offers regularly scheduled service by 10 major airlines, including **American** (© 800/433-7300), **Delta** (© 800/221-1212), and **United** (© 800/241-6522). Rent a car or take a shuttle up to the lake: **No Stress Express** (© 888/4-SHUTTLE; www.nostressexpress.com) serves the North and West Shores; **Tahoe Casino Express** (© **800/446-6128;** www.tahoe casinoexpress.com) serves the South Shore (1-day advance reservations recommended). To get to the lake, take U.S. 395 South to either Route 431 for the North Shore or U.S. 50 for the South Shore. While all of the roads leading to the lake are scenic, the panoramic views as you descend into the Lake Tahoe Basin from Route 431 are spectacular. Pull into the overlook and enjoy the moment.

Amtrak (© **800/USA-RAIL;** www.amtrak.com) stops in Truckee, 10 miles north of the lake. Public transportation (TART or Truce Trolley) is available from the train depot, or you can take a taxi to the North Shore. **Greyhound Bus Lines** (© **800/229-9424;** www.greyhound.com) serves both Truckee and South Lake Tahoe with daily arrivals from San Francisco and Sacramento.

VISITOR INFORMATION   If you are in Tahoe City, stop by the **Visitor Service Center,** 245 North Lake Blvd. (© **888/434-1262** or 530/583-3494; www.tahoefun.org). In Incline Village, go to the **Incline Village/Crystal Bay Visitors Center,** 969 Tahoe Blvd. (© **800/468-2463** or 775/832-1606; www.gotahoe.com). In South Lake Tahoe, go to the **Lake Tahoe Visitors Authority,** 1156 Ski Run Blvd. (© **800/288-2463** or 530/544-5050; www. virtualtahoe.com), or to the **South Lake Tahoe Chamber of Commerce,** 3066 Lake Tahoe Blvd. (© **530/541-5255;** www.tahoeinfo.com). Countless other websites are chock-full of information about Lake Tahoe, including www. skilaketahoe.com, www.laketahoeconcierge.com, and www.tahoevacationguide. com.

WHAT TO SEE & DO
SKIING & SNOWBOARDING
With the largest concentration of ski resorts in North America, Lake Tahoe offers California's best skiing. The ski season typically lasts from November to May and frequently extends into the summer. Lift tickets last winter ranged from $35 to $60 per day for adults and from free to $29 for children, with special rates for teens and seniors. Ticket prices go up every year, but bargains are available, particularly during midweek. Many resorts, hotels, and motels offer special ski packages. Contact the visitor centers or visit the websites listed in "Visitor Information," above, to look for these great values. The ski resorts all offer instruction for adults and children, equipment rental, special-terrain courses for snowboarding, and restaurants. Most have free shuttles.

Alpine Meadows ★★★ *Kids*   In addition to its 12 lifts, this world-class resort has recently installed a beginner surface lift designed especially for children, novice skiers, and snowboarders. With more than 100 runs over 2,000 acres, Alpine has something for everyone: unique kids' programs and a family ski zone, as well as its "wild side," for the double black diamond crowd. You can get a great bargain through its Bed and Board package, which provides lift tickets and lodging (© **800/949-3296**). Alpine also offers ski and snowboard instruction for all ages, excellent snowboarding-terrain parks, snowshoe rentals, snow play areas, and special events like the funky Wayne Wong World Hot Dog Skiing Championship.

2600 Alpine Meadows Rd., Tahoe City, CA 96145. © **800/441-4423** or 530/583-4232. www.skialpine.com.

Diamond Peak ★ *Kids* *Value*   This smaller and less expensive resort has spectacular lake views and prides itself on being a premier destination for families. Whether your child chooses to ski or snowboard, there will be some something available, including a snow play program for the younger ones who aren't quite ready to learn to ski yet. Kids love the snowboard park and sledding area. Located in the heart of the quiet, upscale community of Incline Village, this is a great choice for a low-key, less crowded, and beautiful skiing adventure. The Diamond Peak Cross Country and Snowshoe Center (same telephone number), just east of Incline Village on NV Route 431, is absolutely gorgeous and even allows dogs to share in the fun in the afternoon.

1210 Ski Way, Incline Village, NV 89451. ✆ **775/832-1177** or 775/831-3249. www.diamondpeak.com.

Heavenly Resort ★★ *Kids* This hugely popular resort has 4,800 skiable acres, 27 lifts (including a 50-passenger aerial tram), 82 runs, and the highest elevation (10,000 ft.) of any resort at the lake. Skiers of all levels will find something here to challenge them. One hundred percent of the mountain is available to snowboarders, along with a snowboard park and specially constructed terrain features. Heavenly offers day care for infants through 6 years, child care and ski combinations for ages 3 to 5, and full-day programs for older kids. It's the only ski resort on the South Shore. With the nearby arcades, recreation centers, bowling alleys, and movie theaters, this is a good choice if you have teenagers or if you want to visit the big casinos. The latest addition to the resort is the $20-million Heavenly Gondola, featuring state-of-the-art cars holding up to eight people that can take you from the South Shore downtown area up to an observation deck at 9,200 feet on Heavenly Mountain—a 2½-mile journey.

P.O. Box 2180 (on Ski Run Blvd.), Stateline, NV 89449. ✆ **775/586-7000**. www.skiheavenly.com.

Homewood Mountain Resort ★ *Kids* *Value* Homewood is one of my favorite small ski areas, a homey little resort with 1,260 acres, 56 runs, 8 lifts, and spectacular lake views. It's a good family resort with child care for ages 2 to 6 and ski schools for ages 4 to 12. Lift tickets were only $38 last winter, and children under 10 skied free when accompanied by an adult.

5145 W. Lake Blvd., Homewood, CA 96141 (6 miles S of Tahoe City and 19 miles N of S. Lake Tahoe on Calif. 89). ✆ **530/525-2992**. www.skihomewood.com.

Kirkwood ★★★ *Kids* Kirkwood's only drawback is that it's 30 miles south of South Lake Tahoe; otherwise, it's one of the top ski areas in Tahoe, with lots of snow and excellent spring skiing. It has 2,300 skiable acres, 12 lifts, and 65 trails. Many programs are offered for the children, including child care for the younger ones (ages 2–6). The Cross Country Ski Center (✆ **209/258-7248**) is one of the best around, offering lessons for all ages, and spectacular scenery. Kirkwood is also ideal for summertime hiking, horseback riding, mountain biking, and rock climbing. With ample lodging (✆ **800/967-7500**) and dining options, this is a wonderful year-round vacation destination. There's a free shuttle service to South Lake Tahoe.

Off Hwy. 88 at Carson Pass, P.O. Box 1, Kirkwood, CA 95646. ✆ **209/258-6000**. www.kirkwood.com.

Northstar-at-Tahoe ★★ *Kids* With 63 runs covering 2,400 acres on two mountains, Northstar is consistently rated among the top Far West resorts. Its sophisticated series of lifts, including an express gondola, insure speedy access to the slopes and short lift lines. Whatever age or experience level, you will find something here. Guided snowcat tours test the skills of expert skiers and snowboarders on 200 acres of ungroomed, out-of-boundary terrain. The Learning Center offers coaching in skiing, snowboarding, cross-country, and the new snow toys. Child care (ages 2–6) is provided, as well as instruction for the younger set, including the new "magic carpet" lift and special "Paw" courses. It's hard to imagine more ways to have fun in the snow than you will find at North-star—skiing, snowboarding, cross-country, telemarking, dog-sled tours, sleigh rides, tubing, snowmobile tours, and an amazing evening adventure park called Polaris Park. Check out the snow toys such as the snowscoot, the skifox, the snowbike, and the amazing Zorb, a 9½-foot plastic ball that carries a harnessed-in thrill seeker on an exciting 30- to 40-second ride down a special course. See p. 344 for a full review of Northstar-at-Tahoe Resort.

P.O. Box 129, Truckee, CA 96160 (6 miles N of Kings Beach). ☎ 800/466-6784 or 530/562-1010. www.north starattahoe.com.

Squaw Valley USA ★★★ *Kids*   Site of the 1960 Olympic Winter Games, Squaw is one of the world's finest year-round resorts. Skiing is spread across six peaks with one of the most advanced lift systems in the world providing access to over 4,000 acres of skiable terrain—70% geared toward beginners and inter-mediates and 30% for the advanced, expert, and/or insane. Children's World offers child care (reservations required; call ☎ **530/581-7280** between 1 and 4pm) and snow school. For nonskiers and skiers alike, High Camp, at the top of the cable car, has the Olympic Ice Pavilion (year-round ice-skating), a swim-ming lagoon and spa (spring and summer), snow tubing, snowboarding school, bungee jumping, restaurants, and bars. Squaw also has an arcade, cinema, climbing wall, and Central Park (a snowboarder's dream). The Cross-Country Ski Center (☎ 530/583-6300) has 400 beautiful acres of groomed trails. For those who can't get enough of a good thing, Squaw offers free night skiing with the purchase of a full-day lift ticket. Children ages 12 and under ski for only $5. See p. 257 for a full review of The Resort at Squaw Creek.

Olympic Valley, CA 96146 (6 miles N of Tahoe City). ☎ 800/545-4350 or 530/583-6985. www.squaw.com.

Sugar Bowl ★★ *Kids*   If you are driving from the Bay Area or Sacramento on I-80 and don't want to drive all the way to Tahoe, Sugar Bowl is an excellent place to ski. This medium-size resort (13 lifts, 1,500 skiable acres) offers child care, ski school, snowboard parks, and lodging at the foot of the mountains. It was a popular hideaway for the Hollywood jet set of the 1940s and '50s.

P.O. Box 5, Norden, CA 95724 (3 miles E of the Soda Springs/Norden exit of I-80). ☎ 530/426-9000. www.sugarbowl.com.

MORE WINTER FUN

CROSS-COUNTRY SKIING   In addition to the major resorts, here are some excellent choices: **Royal Gorge Cross-Country Ski Resort** ★★★, Soda Springs, near Sugar Bowl (☎ **800/500-3871** or 800/666-3871; www.royal gorge.com), has 90 trails, including 28 novice trails and four ski lifts, and is one of the largest and best cross-country resorts anywhere. **Tahoe Cross Country Ski Area** ★, 925 Country Club Dr., Tahoe City (☎ **530/583-5475;** www.tahoexc.org), is a small (14 trails), full-service ski center run by a nonprofit community group and is easy and convenient to North Shore visitors. **Spooner Lake Cross Country Ski Area** ★, near the intersection of Highway 28 and U.S. 50 on the East Shore (☎ **888/858-8844;** www.spoonerlake.com), is a quiet, full-service ski center off the beaten path, but it offers some of the most scenic skiing at the lake.

ICE-SKATING   Accessible only by a scenic tram ride (included in the admis-sion fee of $20 for adults, $10 for children), **Squaw Valley's High Camp** ★★ (☎ **530/583-6985**) has one of the world's most beautiful and unusual ice rinks. It's open daily from 11am to 9pm (11am–4pm Apr 14–June 22).

SNOWMOBILING   Snowmobile rental and tours are available at several locations in the Lake Tahoe Area. Call ahead for reservations and directions. The **Zephyr Cove Snowmobile Center,** 760 U.S. 50, about 4 miles northeast of the casinos (℃ 775/588-3833), offers several tours daily for all experience levels. The cost for a standard 2-hour tour is about $90 for a single rider, $125 for two. **Snowmobiling Unlimited** (℃ 530/583-7192; www.snowmobiling unlimited.com) offers 2-hour backcountry tours from Brockway Summit, about 3 miles north of Kings Beach on Calif. 267; prices are $90 for one, $120 for two. **TC Snomos,** 205 River Rd., Tahoe City (℃ 530/581-3906), starts its tours right in Tahoe City, and charges $75 for one and $100 for two.

SNOW PLAY   For snow play other than at the big resorts, try the **North Tahoe Regional Park,** at the top of National Avenue off Highway 28, Tahoe Vista (℃ 530/546-5043). This ultimate snow play hill has a $5 fee that includes a choice of sled, tube, or saucer. **Taylor Creek Snow Park,** off Calif. 89 in South Lake Tahoe (℃ 530/573-2674), is run by the U.S. Forest Service. Bring your own equipment for sledding and tubing. For information about all the California Sno Park locations, call the **Sno Park Hotline** at ℃ 916/324-1222.

SUMMER ACTIVITIES
BALLOONING   See the lake and mountains from 8,000 to 10,000 feet above with **Lake Tahoe Balloons** (℃ 800/872-9294; www.bigmoo.com/laketahoe balloons) in South Lake Tahoe. A 1-hour tour and brunch costs about $175 per person.

BEACHES   Here are a few popular spots around the lake. All have sandy beaches, picnic areas, and restrooms; many have playgrounds. Remember that this is an alpine lake so the water is very cold.

> **Baldwin Beach:** Calif. 89, 4 miles north of South Lake Tahoe
> **Commons Beach Park:** Downtown Tahoe City, free movie (Fri at dusk)
> **Connolly Beach:** U.S. 50 at Timber Cove Lodge; boat launches
> **D. L. Bliss State Park:** South of Meeks Bay on Calif. 89; camping, trails
> **El Dorado Beach:** Between Rufus Allen and Lakeview in South Lake Tahoe
> **Kings Beach State Recreation Center:** Hwy. 28 in Kings Beach
> **Pope Beach:** Calif. 89, 2 miles north of South Lake Tahoe
> **Sand Harbor:** 4 miles south of Incline Village on Hwy. 28; lifeguards
> **Sugar Pine Point:** Calif. 89, just south of Tahoma; camping, trails, pier
> **Zephyr Cove Beach:** U.S. 50 at Zephyr Cove

BICYCLING   There are many miles of paved bicycle paths around the lake. Incline Village has a scenic, easy 2½-mile path along Lakeshore Boulevard. This is a safe choice for younger children. In Tahoe City you can follow the path in three directions. The one that follows Truckee River is a relaxing, beautiful ride. On the South Shore, the Pope-Baldwin bike path runs parallel to Calif. 89 through Camp Richardson and the Tallac Historic Site. Nearby in South Lake Tahoe, a paved pathway runs from El Dorado Beach along the lake, paralleling U.S. 50. The Tahoe City trails are my personal favorites, especially the Truckee River section. You can rent a bicycle from any of the shops listed below.

Mountain biking is big at Lake Tahoe. For serious mountain bikers, there is a dizzying choice of trails. At both **Northstar-at-Tahoe Resort** (℃ 530/562-1010; p. 344) and **Squaw Valley USA** (℃ 530/583-6985; p. 245), you can take the cable car (Squaw) or chairlift (Northstar) up with your bike and ride the trails all the way down. For other trails, check with one of the bicycle-rental shops for maps and information. In North Tahoe, try **The Back Country,** 255 N. Lake Blvd., Tahoe City (© 530/581-5861); **Olympic Bike Shop,** 620 N. Lake Blvd., Tahoe City (© 530/581-2500); **Tahoe Bike & Ski,** 8499 N. Lake Blvd., Kings Beach (© 530/546-7437); or **Porter's Sports Shop,** 885 Tahoe Blvd., Incline Village (© 775/831-3500). In South Tahoe, try **Anderson's Bike Rental,** 645 Emerald Bay Rd. (© 530/541-0500), or **Lakeview Sports,** 3131 Hwy. 50 at El Dorado Beach (© 530/544-0183).

Another great choice is **Cyclepaths Mountain Bike Adventures,** 1785 W. Lake Blvd. in Tahoe Park, a few miles south of Tahoe City (© **800/780-BIKE;** www.cyclepaths.com), where you can arrange a guided off-road tour. Whether you're into hard-core downhill single track or easy-going scenic outings, the expert guides will provide you with all the necessary equipment, food, and transportation. They offer day tours ($29 and up), weekenders ($199), and 3- and 5-day adventure camps (rates vary).

BOATING, WATERSPORTS & PARASAILING   Nothing beats actually getting out on the water. Take a guided tour, go off on your own, or just paddle around. Here are a few reliable choices: **Zephyr Cove Marina** (© **775/ 588-3833;** www.tahoedixie2.com) is the lake's largest marina. It's the home of the paddle-wheeler M.S. *Dixie II* and the catamaran *Woodwind II.* Here you can parasail (© 775/588-3530), charter sport-fishing trips (© 775/586-9338), or take guided tours. You can also rent motorized boats, pontoon boats, pedal boats, kayaks, canoes, water-ski equipment, and jet skis. **Tahoe City Marina** (© **530/583-1039**), 700 N. Lake Blvd., Tahoe City, rents motorized boats, sailboats, and fishing boats. Sailboat cruises are available. This is also the location for **Lake Tahoe Parasailing** (© **530/583-7245**).

Lighthouse Water Sports, 950 N. Lake Blvd., Tahoe (© **530/583-7245**), rents jet skis, paddleboats, and canoes. **Tahoe Paddle and Oar,** North Lake Beach Center, 7860 N. Lake Blvd., Kings Beach (© **530/531-3029**), is a good place to rent kayaks, canoes, pedal boats, and windsurfing equipment. Paddling around on a calm day in the clear waters of Crystal Bay is great fun. **Action Water Sports** has two locations: 3411 Lake Tahoe Blvd. at Timber Cove Marina, South Lake Tahoe (© **530/544-2942**); and across from the Hyatt in Incline Village (© **775/831-4386**). You can rent boats, kayaks, jet skis, paddleboats, and other water toys here; parasailing and guided tours are also available. **Camp Richardson Marina,** 1900 Jameson Beach Rd., off Calif. 89 on the South Shore (© **530/542-6570**), located on a long sandy beach, rents power- and ski boats, jet skis, kayaks, and paddleboats. It also offers fishing charters, ski school, cruises on the *Woodwind I* sailboat, and guided raft and kayak tours to Emerald Bay. **SunSports,** 3564 Lake Tahoe Blvd., South Lake Tahoe (© **530/ 541-6000**), provides rentals, tours, and lessons for kayaking, rafting, sailing, and scuba diving.

CAMPING   If you have an appetite for the great outdoors, here are a few of the many good campgrounds at Tahoe:

D. L. Bliss State Park, on the western shore (© **530/525-7277**), has 168 campsites, fine beaches, and hiking trails.

Sugar Pine Point State Park, also on the western shore (© **530/525-7982**), offers 175 campsites, a picnic area, a beach, a nature center, and cross-country skiing, and is open year-round.

Campground by the Lake, 1150 Rufus Allen Blvd., South Lake Tahoe (© **530/542-6059**), features 170 campsites, a boat ramp, a gym, and a history museum.

Zephyr Cove RV Park and Campground, located at Zephyr Cove Resort on U.S. 50 (© 775/588-6644), has a beach, a marina, and complete facilities.

FISHING The cold, clear waters of Lake Tahoe are home to kokanee salmon and rainbow, brown, and Mackinaw trout. With lots of hiding places in the deep water, fishing here is a challenge, and many anglers opt to use a guide or charter boat. There are dozens of charter companies offering daily excursions. Rates run about $65 for a half day to $95 for a whole day (bait, tackle, fish cleaning, and food included). On the North Shore, try **Mickey's Big Mack Charters** at the Sierra Boat Company in Carnelian Bay (© 530/546-4444; www.mickeysbig mack.com); or **Reel Deal Sportfishing,** Tahoe City (© 530/581-0924). On the South Shore, try **Avid Fisherman,** Zephyr Cove (© 775/588-7675); **Blue Ribbon Fishing Charters,** Tahoe Keys Marina (© 530/541-8801); or **Tahoe Sportfishing,** 900 Ski Run Blvd. (© 800/696-7797 or 530/541-5448).

FITNESS CENTERS & SPAS Soak your tired body at the end of the day at the **North Tahoe Beach Center,** 7860 N. Lake Blvd., Kings Beach (© 530/546-2566). Besides a full line of exercise equipment, the center boasts a huge 26-foot spa, saunas, weight gym, TV, Ping-Pong, fireplace, lockers, and showers, all for $7 for adults and $3 for children. The **Incline Recreation Center,** 980 Incline Way, Incline Village (© 775/832-1310), is a gorgeous facility with a heated indoor Olympic-size swimming pool, aerobics, basketball gym, cardiovascular fitness room, lounge, fireplace, and on-site child care. The fee is $11 for adults and $6 for children.

GOLF With its world-class golf courses, mild summer weather, and magnificent scenery, Lake Tahoe is a golfer's paradise. All of the following courses are very busy in the summer so call far in advance for tee times. For more information about Tahoe-area golf courses, log on to **www.tahoesbest.com/Golf**.

Starting at the north end of the lake, there are four highly rated courses: **Incline Village Championship Course,** 955 Fairway Blvd., and the smaller **Incline Village Mountain (Executive) Course,** 690 Wilson Way (© 775/832-1144 for both); **Northstar-at-Tahoe Resort** (© 530/562-2490; p. 344); and **The Resort at Squaw Creek** (© 800/327-3353; p. 257).

In the south, there's **Edgewood,** U.S. 50 at Lake Parkway, Stateline, NV (© 775/588-3566), home of the Celebrity Golf Championship; and **Lake Tahoe Golf Course,** 2500 Emerald Bay Rd., South Lake Tahoe, CA (© 530/577-0788). In addition, there are some good nine-hole municipal courses: **Old Brockway Golf Course,** 7900 N. Lake Blvd., Kings Beach (© 530/546-9909); **Tahoe City Golf Course,** 251 N. Lake Blvd., Tahoe City (© 530/583-1516); and **Bijou Municipal Golf Course,** 3436 Fairway Ave., South Lake Tahoe (© 530/542-6097).

HIKING The mountains surrounding Lake Tahoe are crisscrossed with hiking trails graded for all levels of experience. Before setting out, you may wish to contact the local visitor centers or sporting goods shops for a map and more in-depth information on particular trails, or hire a guide. Try **Tahoe Trips & Trails** (© 530/583-4506; www.tahoetrips.com) for short and long guided hikes. Everything is provided: food, drinks, transportation, and great information about the lake. Going on your own? Some of the most popular short hikes in the area are:

Eagle Falls/Eagle Lake: This moderately easy trail is well marked and begins at Eagle Picnic Area, directly across Calif. 89 from Emerald Bay. It's only about ⅓ of a mile to the steel footbridge overlooking the falls and 2 miles round-trip

(1½–2 hr.) to Eagle Lake. Be sure to sign in at the self-registration station at the trail head.

Emerald Bay/Vikingsholm: The trail starts at the parking area on the north side of Emerald Bay, on Highway 89. It's a wide, well-maintained trail, but fairly steep, about 2½ miles round-trip. At the bottom of the trail is a picnic area, as well as world-famous Vikingsholm, a replica of a Scandinavian castle.

Nevada Shoreline: Begin at the paved parking lot on the west side of Highway 28, 3 miles south of Sand Harbor. The trail drops to the beach and follows the shoreline, passing Chimney Beach, Secret Harbor, and Whale Beach. The trail eventually connects to a service road that can be followed back up to the parking area. It's an easy 4-mile hike, with a vertical climb of only 300 feet.

Shirley Lake: This trail leads to Shirley Lake, then down to Shirley Canyon. Take the tram at Squaw Valley up to High Camp and hike down, or vice-versa. The trail begins at the end of Squaw Creek Road, next to the cable-car building. It's a 4-mile hike, easy to moderate in difficulty, with some steep sections.

HORSEBACK RIDING   Most stables offer a variety of guided trail rides and lessons for individuals, families, and groups. Choose the one that appeals to your sense of adventure: 1- to 2-hour trail rides; breakfast, lunch, or dinner rides; half-day, full-day, overnight, and extended pack trips. Expect to pay $20 to $25 for a 1-hour ride, $6 for a half-hour pony ride. Saddle up and savor the scenery. Try **Alpine Meadows Stables,** Alpine Meadows Road, Tahoe City (© 530/583-3905); **Northstar Stables,** Highway 267, 6 miles north of Kings Beach (© 530/562-2480); **Squaw Valley Stables,** 1525 Squaw Valley Rd., north of Tahoe City (© 530/583-7433); **Camp Richardson Corral,** Calif. 89, South Lake Tahoe (© 530/541-3113); or **Zephyr Cove Stables,** Zephyr Cove Resort, U.S. 50 at Zephyr Cove (© 775/588-5664).

IN-LINE SKATING   Although there are many trails around the lake, the best one for blading is the well-paved bicycle- and pedestrian-only path that hugs the Truckee River between Tahoe City and Squaw Valley. Skates and protective gear can be rented for $12 per half day, $18 per full day, from the nearby **Squaw Valley Sport Shop,** 170 N. Lake Blvd., Tahoe City (© **530/583-6278**).

RIVER RAFTING   For a swift but gentle ride down the Truckee River (the lake's only outlet), try **Truckee River Raft Rental,** 185 River Rd., Tahoe City (© **530/583-0123**). Only available in the summer, the rates are $25 for adults and $20 for children (5 years and up).

TENNIS   The mild summer weather at Lake Tahoe is perfect for great tennis. If you want to sharpen your skills, **Northstar-at-Tahoe Resort** (© **530/562-0321;** p. 344) offers several excellent tennis packages for its guests only. **Squaw Creek** (© **530/581-6694;** p. 257) tennis courts are open to the public for $12 an hour. **Kirkwood** (p. 244), **Caesars Tahoe** (p. 253), and **Harveys Casino Resort** (p. 254) all feature tennis courts for a fee.

Budget-minded players looking for good local courts should visit Tahoe Lake School on Grove Street in Tahoe City, or Tahoe Regional Park, at the end of National Avenue in Tahoe Vista. South Tahoe Intermediate School on Lyons Avenue has eight lighted courts and charges a manageable $3 per hour. South Tahoe High School, 1735 Lake Tahoe Blvd., has free courts.

LAKE CRUISES

If you can possibly fit a cruise into your vacation plans, you won't regret it. It's one of the best ways to see the lake.

M.S. *Dixie II,* Zephyr Cove Marina, 4 miles north of the casinos on U.S. 50 (© 775/882-0786; www.tahoedixie2.com), is a 570-passenger vessel with bars, a dance floor, and a full dining room. Emerald Bay scenic cruises cost $24 for adults, $7 for children. They also have champagne-brunch and breakfast cruises ($27), dinner cruises ($39), and sunset dinner-dance cruises ($49).

Hornblower's *Tahoe Queen* (© 800/238-2463 or 530/541-3364; www.hornblower.com), departing from the Marina Village at Ski Run Boulevard in South Lake Tahoe, is an authentic paddle-wheeler with a capacity of 500. It offers Emerald Bay sightseeing tours ($22 adults, $11 children) and dinner/dance cruises ($40), as well as full-service charters. Live music, buffet breakfast, dinner, and appetizers are all available onboard. The **Hornblower Ski Shuttle** ($87, including lift ticket, food, and ground transportation) is the world's only known water-borne ski shuttle. On the way to Squaw Valley, enjoy a breakfast buffet, and on the way home, experience a fun-filled après-ski party. This ski shuttle allows skiers staying on the South Shore an opportunity to ski one of the finest resorts on the North Shore without the hassle of driving. Buses pick up passengers from their hotels in the morning and drop them off at night.

The ***Tahoe Gal*** (© 800/218-2464 or 530/583-0141; www.tahoegal.com), departing from the Lighthouse Marina (behind Safeway) in Tahoe City, is the only cruise boat on the North Shore. Cruises include Scenic Shoreline ($19 adults, $8 children), Emerald Bay ($24 adults, $12 children), Happy Hour (4:30–6pm; $20 for two adults, $7 children), and Sunset Dinner ($20 adults and $10 children). Note that all prices are for the cruise only; food and beverages are an additional charge.

Woodwind Sailing Cruises (© 888/867-6394; www.sailwoodwind.com) specializes in daily sightseeing cruises ($24 adults, $22 seniors, $10 children 3–12), sunset champagne cruises ($28), weddings, and charters. The Woodwind fleet includes the original ***Woodwind I,*** a 30-passenger Searunner trimaran sailing to Emerald Bay from Camp Richardson Marina in South Lake Tahoe, and the new ***Woodwind II,*** a 50-passenger Searunner catamaran sailing from Zephyr Cove Marina.

A DRIVE AROUND THE LAKE

Overwhelmed by all of the choices? Get in your car and take a leisurely drive around the lake. It's only a 72-mile trip, but you should plan on taking several hours, even in the best of weather. In the worst of weather, don't try it! Parts of the road, if not closed, can be icy and dangerous. On a mild day though, it will be a memorable experience. If your car sports a tape deck, consider buying *Drive Around the Lake,* a drive-along audio cassette that contains facts, legends, places of interest, and just about everything else you could possible want to know about the lake. It's available at numerous gift shops or at the **South Lake Tahoe Chamber of Commerce,** 3066 Lake Tahoe Blvd. (© 530/541-5255; www.tahoeinfo.com), which is closed on Sundays.

We'll start at the California-Nevada border in South Lake Tahoe and loop around the western shore on Calif. 89 to Tahoe City and beyond. U.S. 50, which runs along the south shore, is an ugly, overdeveloped strip that obliterates any view of the lake. Keep heading west, and you will soon be free of this unattractive stretch.

First stop is the **Tallac Historic Site,** site of the former Tallac Resort and a cluster of rustic 100-year-old mansions that provide a fascinating glimpse into Tahoe's past. In its heyday, the resort included two large hotels, a casino, and numerous outbuildings. Throughout the summer here the Valhalla Festival of

Arts and Music (© **888/632-5859** or 530/541-4975; www.valhalla-tallac.com) showcases jazz, bluegrass, rock, mariachi, and classical music. Summer highlights include June's Valhalla Renaissance Festival, July's Native American Fine Arts Festival, and August's Great Gatsby Festival.

From here the highway winds northward along the shore until you reach **Cascade Lake** on the left and **Emerald Bay** ★★ on the right. The Emerald Bay Lookout is a spectacular picture-taking spot. Emerald Bay's deep green water is the site of the only island in Lake Tahoe, Fannette Island. The small structure atop the island is the teahouse, built by Ms. Lora Knight, who also constructed **Vikingsholm** ★ (© **530/541-3030;** www.vikingsholm.com), a 38-room Scandinavian Castle built in 1929, located at the head of Emerald Bay. Tours ($3) of this unique structure are available from mid-June to Labor Day every half-hour from 10am to 4pm. Even if you don't want to take the tour, it's a pleasant walk from the parking area down to the beach and the mansion's grounds. Just remember that you have to walk back up. Across the highway, there's another parking area. From here, it's a short, steep ¼-mile hike to a footbridge above **Eagle Falls.** Then it's about a mile farther up to **Eagle Lake.**

Continuing on, it's only about 2 miles to **D. L. Bliss State Park** (© **530/ 525-7982**), where you'll find one of the lake's best beaches. It gets crowded in the summer, so arrive early to get a parking place. The park also contains 168 campsites and several trails, including one along the shoreline.

In about 7 miles you will reach **Sugar Pine State Park** (© **530/525-7232**), the largest (2,000 acres) of the lake's parks and also the only one that has year-round camping. In summer, you can visit the beaches in the park plus a nature center and miles of trails; in winter, there's cross-country skiing on well-maintained trails.

Continuing on through the small town of **Homewood** (site of the ski resort), **Sunnyside,** on the right, is a pleasant place to stop for a lakeside lunch. Or, if you feel like taking a stroll, drive on to Tahoe City where there is a beautiful paved path along the Truckee River. Check out the big trout at **Fanny Bridge** ★ first. If you would like to see **Squaw Valley** and **Alpine Meadows,** take a left at Calif. 89. A ride on the Squaw Valley cable car (© **530/583-6985**) will reward you with incredible vistas from 2,000 feet above the valley floor. It operates year-round and costs $17 for adults, $14 for seniors, and $5 for children under 13. Back on Calif. 28, as you leave **Tahoe City,** you will pass a string of interesting, small malls at 700 through 850 North Lake Blvd. If you enjoy just wandering around, this is a good area to stop and eat, watch the activity at the **Tahoe City Marina** (parasailing, cruises on the *Tahoe Gal,* and boat rental), or visit the interesting shops.

Continuing around the lake on Calif. 28, you'll reach Carnelian Bay, Tahoe Vista, and Kings Beach before crossing the state line into Nevada. **Kings Beach State Recreation Area** ★ (© **530/546-7248**) is a long, wide beach and picnic area. It is jammed in the summer with sunbathers and swimmers. As you approach **Crystal Bay,** you will immediately know you have crossed the state line by the string of small casinos that suddenly appear. The **Cal-Neva Resort, Spa & Casino** (p. 258) on the right was once owned by Frank Sinatra and has a very colorful, celebrity-filled history. The state line goes right through the lodge, and gambling is allowed only on the Nevada side. This is worth stopping to see.

Your journey next takes you to woodsy Incline Village, arguably the most beautiful community on the lake. Take a right on Lakeshore Boulevard to view the elegant estates. Lunch or dinner time? The magnificent **Lone Eagle Grille**

Moments Gondola to Heaven

If you want a preview of what it's like to be in heaven, take a ride on the new Heavenly Valley Ski Resort gondola. At a cost of a mere $20 million, the gondola consists of state-of-the-art "cars" that whisk you from South Shore's downtown area up the mountain to Heavenly Resort's 14,000-square-foot observation deck. Each car holds up to eight people. The 2½-mile ride rises to an elevation of 9,123 feet, offering passengers shore-to-shore views of Lake Tahoe, Carson Valley to the east, and Desolation Wilderness to the west (all best seen at sunset).

The gondola is located a half-block west of Stateline, an easy walk from the downtown hotels. It's open year-round Monday through Friday from 10am to sunset, and Saturday and Sunday from 9am to sunset. Tickets are $20 for adults, $12 for children ages 6 to 12, and free for kids 5 and under.

(p. 261), at Lakeshore and Country Club Drive, offers panoramic lake views as well as good food.

Remember Hoss and Little Joe? The **Ponderosa Ranch** (© 775/831-0691; www.ponderosaranch.com) off Highway 28 at the east end of Incline Village, home to television's *Bonanza,* features the Cartwright Ranch House, an entire Old West town complete with working blacksmiths, a saloon, a hay wagon breakfast, a shootin' gallery, and even live gunfights. It's open daily from April to October from 9:30am to 6pm; admission is $9.50 for adults, $4.50 for children ages 5 to 11, and free for children under 5.

The East Shore of the lake is largely undeveloped and very scenic. Drive about 4 miles south of Incline Village to **Sand Harbor** ★ (© 775/831-0494), one of the lake's best-loved beaches, and home to the very popular **Lake Tahoe Shakespeare Festival** (© 800/747-4697; www.tahoebard.com) every mid-July through August. In addition to turquoise blue water dotted with big boulders and a wide sandy beach, you'll find nature trails, picnic areas, and boating.

Going south you will come to an outcropping called **Cave Rock** where the highway passes through 25 yards of solid stone. Farther along is **Zephyr Cove Resort and Marina,** home to the M.S. *Dixie II* and a beehive of watersports activity. You'll then return to Stateline and South Lake Tahoe, your original starting point.

WHERE TO STAY
SOUTH SHORE & SOUTH LAKE TAHOE
Expensive

Black Bear Inn ★★   Situated within a wooded acre near Heavenly Ski Resort, this neo-rustic lodge offers luxury accommodations in a tranquil setting and convenient location. The great room, with its beamed ceilings, grand piano, country antiques, large rock fireplace, and complimentary evening hors d'oeuvres, offers a relaxing environment after a long day of outdoor activities. Or better yet, soak your tired body in the sheltered Jacuzzi. Breakfast—included in the room rate—is an event in itself, offering fresh-baked muffins, eggs Benedict, omelets, and other hearty fare. Each of the spacious guest rooms has a king-size bed, private bathroom, and gas fireplace. For additional privacy, request one of the three cabins located behind the inn.

1202 Ski Run Blvd., South Lake Tahoe, CA 96150. ℂ 877/232-7466 or 530/544-4451. www.tahoeblack bear.com. 5 lodge rooms, 3 cabins. $205–$245 lodge rooms; $265–$475 cabins. Rates include full breakfast. MC, V. **Amenities:** Nearby golf course; Jacuzzi. *In room:* A/C, TV/VCR, dataport, hair dryer; kitchenette, fridge, and coffeemaker in cabins.

Caesars Tahoe   This 16-story hotel, built in the early 1980s, has the same glitter, glitz, and campy references to Roman mythology that Caesars Palace in Las Vegas has perfected for decades. The guest rooms, many of which offer beautiful views of the lake, are furnished with contemporary hardwood pieces and equipped with extra-large tubs (Roman-style, of course). There's also a variety of suites, ranging from dignified executive-style to lavishly appointed themed suites (kinky, baby). Highlights include a full casino with sports booking, the Circus Maximus showroom featuring top-name entertainment, and a lagoon-style indoor pool, plus indoor and outdoor wedding chapels. If you feel like gettin' jiggy with it, Nero 2000 has live music and the biggest dance floor around. Planet Hollywood, chock-full of Hollywood memorabilia, is another favorite hangout. You can even indulge yourself with a cruise around the lake on the *Odyssey,* Caesars' own luxury yacht.

55 U.S. 50 (P.O. Box 5800), Lake Tahoe, NV 89449. ℂ 800/648-3353 or 775/588-3515. www.caesars.com/ tahoe. 440 units. $79–$300 double; $370–$950 suite. Packages available. AE, DC, MC, V. **Amenities:** 6 restaurants; 4 lounges; indoor pool; 3 outdoor tennis courts; health club; spa; Jacuzzi; sauna; ski rental; bike rental; video arcade; activities desk; car-rental desk; business center; shopping arcade; salon; 24-hr. room service; in-room massage; babysitting; dry cleaning; executive-level rooms. *In room:* A/C, TV, dataport, kitchenette and minibar in suites, fridge upon request, hair dryer, iron, safe.

Embassy Suites Resort ⊀ (Kids)   Perched on the edge of the state line and just steps away from Heavenly's new gondola, this is the only major non-casino hotel on Tahoe's south shore, earning its keep by luring the upscale gambling crowd and the convention business with its uncommonly large suites. A nine-story chateau-style hotel, the roofline is pierced with a double layer of dormers; equally impressive is the massive inner atrium filled with plants. The one- and two-bedroom suites all have a separate living room with sofa bed, armchair, a well-lit dining/work table, a microwave, and a wet bar. Complimentary cooked-to-order breakfasts are served in a garden atrium. For wining and dining, try Zachary's, Pasquale's wood-fired pizzas, or Turtles sports bar, which opens onto an outdoor deck and turns into a disco later in the evening. In the summer, all guests have access to a private beach, and family skiers fill up the place in winter, partly because kids 18 and under stay free.

4130 Lake Tahoe Blvd., South Lake Tahoe, CA 96150. ℂ 800/362-2779 or 530/544-5400. Fax 530/544-4900. www.embassy-suites.com. 400 suites. $149–$359 double. Rates include full breakfast and evening cocktail reception. Special packages available. Children 18 and under stay free in parents' room. AE, DC, DISC, MC, V. **Amenities:** Restaurant; pizzeria; sports bar; indoor pool; outdoor sun deck; health club; spa; Jacuzzi; dry sauna; watersports equipment rental; concierge; car-rental desk; limited room service; in-room massage; babysitting; same-day dry cleaning; executive-level rooms. *In room:* A/C, TV/VCR, dataport, minibar, fridge, coffeemaker, hair dryer, iron.

Harrah's Casino Hotel ⊀ (Kids)   Understatement is not a word that comes to mind when you visit Harrah's, Tahoe's most highly rated hotel and casino, and its complete remodeling has made what was already luxurious and glitzy even more so. Harrah's takes great pride in its special blend of luxury, beauty, unparalleled guest service, and casino entertainment. The large rooms have two bathrooms, each with its own TV and telephone so you won't miss anything while bathing, and those thick, fluffy, white towels Sinatra always demanded. Most have bay windows overlooking the lake or the mountains. With families in mind, the casino has an enormous fun center with the latest in video and arcade games, virtual reality, and an indoor "playscape" for young children. Weddings and parties can be arranged aboard the private yacht, the *Tahoe Star*. The legendary South Shore Room features showbiz stars, and, in case you've forgotten what you're there for, the casino is a gambler's dream.

P.O. Box 8, Stateline, NV 89449. (C) **800/427-7247** or 775/586-6607. Fax 775/586-6601. www.harrahs tahoe.com. 525 units. $109–$229 double; $229–$399 suite. Packages available. AE, DC, DISC, MC, V. **Amenities:** 3 restaurants; cafe; deli; coffeehouse; indoor pool; full-service health club and spa; family fun center; game room; shopping arcade; salon; 24-hr. room service; in-room massage; same-day dry cleaning. *In room:* A/C, TV/VCR, coffeemaker, hair dryer, iron, safe.

Harveys Casino Resort, Lake Tahoe *Kids*   With its two massive towers and 740 rooms, Harveys is the largest (and possibly the ugliest) hotel in Tahoe. It features an 88,000-square-foot casino, eight restaurants (including a Hard Rock Cafe), and a cabaret with some of the most glittering, bespangled entertainment in town. More than a hotel, Harveys is like a city unto itself. There's a children's day camp, beauty and barber shops, and even a wedding chapel should you get the urge. Heck, you never have to see the real world again. Try to get a room between the 15th and 19th floors in the Lake Tower, where every unit has a view of both Lake Tahoe and the surrounding Sierra.

U.S. 50 at Stateline Ave. (P.O. Box 128), Stateline, NV 89449. (C) **800/HARVEYS** or 775/588-2411. Fax 775/588-6643. 740 units. $89–$299 double; $299–$699 suite. AE, DC, DISC, MC, V. **Amenities:** 8 restaurants; 10 bars; outdoor heated pool; nearby golf course; health club; spa; Jacuzzi; sauna; watersports equipment rental; children's day camp; video arcade; concierge; car-rental desk; business center; shopping arcade; salon; 24-hr. room service; in-room massage; laundry service; same-day dry cleaning. *In room:* A/C, TV w/pay movies, dataport, minibar, coffeemaker, hair dryer, iron, safe.

Tahoe Seasons Resort   Big, modern, and loaded with luxuries, the Tahoe Seasons lies in a relatively uncongested residential neighborhood at the base of the Heavenly Valley Ski Resort, 2 miles from Tahoe's casinos. Every unit here is a spacious, attractive suite, sleeping up to four in the smaller one and six in the larger one. Most have gas fireplaces, and all have huge whirlpool spas complete with shoji screens (just in case you plan on losing your shirt in more ways than one). Skiing isn't the only activity around here: Play a round of tennis on the roof or hop aboard the free casino shuttles.

3901 Saddle Rd., off Ski Run Blvd. (P.O. Box 5656), South Lake Tahoe, CA 96157. (C) **800/540-4874** or 530/541-6700. Fax 530/541-7342. www.tahoeseasons.com. 160 suites. Summer $170–$240 double; winter $180–$250 double; spring and fall $122–$200 double. Seasonal packages available. AE, MC, V. **Amenities:** Restaurant; pub; outdoor heated pool; nearby golf course; 2 rooftop tennis courts; complimentary use of health club at Harveys Resort; game room; concierge; tour and activities desk; courtesy car; room service; in-room massage; same-day dry cleaning. *In room:* A/C, TV/VCR, dataport, fridge, coffeemaker, hair dryer on request, iron.

Moderate

Best Western Station House Inn *Value*   Ensconced amid towering pines trees but just 3 blocks from the casinos, the Best Western Station House Inn was built in the late 1970s and is one of the few hotels in town that still has its own private "gated" beach on the lake. Okay, so it's not a particularly exciting hotel (the decor is corporate dull), but the location is ideal, the large swimming pool and hot tub are a huge bonus, and it even has its own *Wine Spectator* award-winning restaurant, LewMarNel's. The complimentary cooked-to-order breakfast and free shuttle service make staying here a particularly good value.

901 Park Ave., South Lake Tahoe, CA 96150. (C) **800/822-5953** or 530/542-1101. Fax 530/542-1714. www.stationhouseinn.com. 100 units. $98–$138 double; $135–$165 suite; $200–$300 cabin. Rates include

full breakfast. Packages available. AE, DC, DISC, MC, V. **Amenities:** Restaurant; heated outdoor pool; Jacuzzi; babysitting. *In room:* A/C, TV, coffeemaker, hair dryer.

Camp Richardson Resort ★★ *Kids*

If you are planning a family vacation, a reunion, or just a weekend getaway, Camp Richardson has it all (really, I love this place). Located on a long sandy beach on the southwest shore, this rustic, woodsy resort offers a wide array of activities as well as several lodging and dining choices. Its two restaurants offer lakeside dining, but there are also more-informal dining options, plus a general store, a candy store, and an ice-cream parlor. The sports center rents all the seasonal equipment you'll need. You can ski right along the shore here, or try scaling the rock-climbing wall. The full-service marina rents power- and ski boats, jet skis, kayaks, and paddleboats, and also offers guided tours, cruises, and chartered fishing trips. There's even a stable for horseback riding. Lodging options include a hotel, cabins, a beachside inn, a marina duplex, tent campgrounds, and an RV park. The children will fall into bed exhausted at night with all of the available organized activities. Cabins are only rented by the week in the summer and fill up quickly, so plan early. *Tip:* Be sure to check their website for seasonal money-saving packages.

Jameson Beach Rd. (P.O. Box 9028), South Lake Tahoe, CA, 96158. ℂ **800/544-1801** or 530/541-1801. Fax 530/541-1802. www.camprichardson.com. $65–$175 hotel; $90–170 cabins per day, $565–$1,625 per week in summer. Camping or RV hookup $17–$26 per day. **Amenities:** 2 restaurants; deli; cafe; marina; Jacuzzi; sports center with bike, snowshoe, and ski rental; children's program; tour and activities desk. *In room:* Coffeemaker. Inn has TV; duplex has TV, kitchen; cabin has kitchen. Hotel and cabin units have no phone.

Horizon Casino Resort *Value*

This massive resort hotel stands next to the even larger Harveys, and though it's not as well known as the other casinos, it charges less for basically the same facilities. The lobby is a cheesy sea of white marble and mirrors, and the standard rooms are decorated in typical bland yet inoffensive style (the suites, however, are far racier). The upper floors of the two towers naturally open onto the best views of mountains and the lake. Besides the 42,000-square-foot gaming room, the resort has a multiplex movie theater, cabaret, lounge, nightclub, the largest outdoor pool in Tahoe, and restaurants ranging from buffet to gourmet.

U.S. 50 (P.O. Box C), Lake Tahoe, NV 89449. ℂ **800/648-3322** or 775/588-6211. Fax 775/588-0349. www.horizoncasino.com. 539 units. Summer $119–$169 double; winter $99–$169 double; $250–$500 suite. Children 11 and under stay free in parents' room. Packages available. AE, DISC, DC, MC, V. **Amenities:** 3 restaurants; large heated outdoor pool; nearby golf course; health club; 3 Jacuzzis; bike and ski rental; video arcade; concierge; car-rental desk; business center; shopping arcade; salon; 24-hr. room service; in-room massage; babysitting; laundry service; same-day dry cleaning; executive-level rooms. *In room:* A/C, TV w/pay movies, dataport, minibar, fridge, coffeemaker, hair dryer, and iron in suites.

Lakeland Village Beach & Mountain Resort ★ *Kids*

This condominium resort is a good choice for families. Clustered on 19 lightly forested acres of prime shoreline property, the half residential condo/half holiday resort complex was built in the 1970s. The layout is a complicated labyrinth of redwood buildings that blend into the surrounding landscape. The only drawback is the proximity to traffic headed into Lake Tahoe, although some units are quieter than those in the main lodge, which lies adjacent to the road. The units, ranging from studios to four-bedroom lakeside apartments, are streamlined California architecture, and many have upstairs sleeping lofts. All rooms come with fully equipped kitchens and fireplaces. Perks include a large private beach opening directly onto the lake, access to a boat dock, and free shuttle service to Heavenly and the casinos.

3535 Lake Tahoe Blvd., South Lake Tahoe, CA 96150. 𝄞 **800/822-5969** or 530/544-1685. Fax 530/541-6278. www.lakeland-village.com. 212 condo units. $88–$290 double; $135–$975 for a 1–4 bedroom town house. Children stay free in parents' room. AE, DISC, MC, V. **Amenities:** 2 heated outdoor pools; nearby golf course; 2 outdoor tennis courts; 2 Jacuzzis; sauna; children's play area and wading pool; seasonal concierge; room service; laundry service; same-day dry cleaning. *In room:* TV/VCR, dataport, kitchen, fridge, coffeemaker, hair dryer, iron.

Inexpensive

Viking Motor Lodge *(Value)* You get a lot for your money here: agreeable accommodations, access to a private beach, and an easy walk to the casinos and the Heavenly gondola. Nothing fancy, but the rooms are clean and pleasant, and have all the standard conveniences. If you're traveling with kids, you may want one of the units with a kitchen. Be sure to inquire about the ski and golf packages.

4083 Cedar Ave., South Lake Tahoe, CA 96150. 𝄞 **800/288-4083** or 530/541-5155. Fax 530/541-5643. www.tahoeviking.com. 76 units. $49–$110 double. Children 11 and under stay free in parents' room. Rates include continental breakfast. Packages available. AE, DC, DISC, MC, V. **Amenities:** Outdoor heated pool; nearby golf course; Jacuzzi. *In room:* TV/VCR, dataport, fridge on request, coffeemaker, kitchen in 14 units, hair dryer, iron.

NORTH SHORE/TAHOE CITY
Expensive

Hyatt Regency Lake Tahoe ⚡ *(Kids)* If you like to gamble but hate gauche, glitzy casinos, you'll like the Hyatt in Incline Village. Located amid towering pines and mountains on the lake's pristine northeast shore, it's far, far classier and quieter than the casino hotels you'll find along Stateline. The resort's private beach, loaded with water toys—catamaran cruises, boat rentals, jet skis, parasailing—is available only to guests. The adjoining Lakeside Cottages are a wee bit o' heaven for families or honeymooners who want beachfront access and large, comfortable rooms with unobstructed panoramas of the lake. A bonus for families is the popular Camp Hyatt, which lets kids ages 3 to 12 get a break from their parents for the day. In addition to its other restaurants, the Lone Eagle Grille (p. 261) is one of the most beautiful restaurants on the lake. Be sure to take a walk (or a run) down Lakeshore Boulevard to see the magnificent estates fronting the lake. Scheduled to open in July 2003 is a 15,000-square-foot spa facility with a multi-tiered swimming pool and an entire 150-room wing of "Spa Terrace" guest rooms.

Country Club at Lakeshore, 111 Country Club Dr., Incline Village, NV 89451. 𝄞 **888/899-5019** or 775/832-1234. Fax 775/831-7508. www.laketahoehyatt.com. 405 units, 24 cottages. $160–$330 double; $405–$1,385 cottages. Packages available. AE, DC, DISC, MC, V. **Amenities:** 4 restaurants; 4 lounges; nearby golf course; watersports equipment rental; bike rental; children's program; video arcade; concierge; tour and activities desk; car-rental desk; business center; room service; in-room massage; laundry service; same-day dry cleaning; executive-level rooms. *In room:* A/C, TV w/pay movies, dataport, minibar, fridge, coffeemaker, hair dryer, iron, safe.

Northstar-at-Tahoe Resort ⚡⚡⚡ *(Kids)* The folks at Northstar continue to come up with even more ways to have fun year-round—the list of activities is mind-boggling. Priding itself on being the ultimate, self-contained, family destination, there is something here for everyone. The Northstar Village and Lodge are surrounded by a honeycomb of fully equipped redwood condos and vacation homes, all nestled among the pines. Lodging options range from a hotel room in the lodge to a five-bedroom house, with every size in between. Summer activities include golf, swimming, tennis, mountain biking, hiking, fly-fishing, rock climbing, rope courses, and horseback riding. See "Skiing & Snowboarding," earlier in this chapter, for winter activities.

Off Hwy. 267, Box 129, Northstar-at-Tahoe, CA 96160. (C) **800/466-6784** or 530/562-1010. Fax 530/562-2215. www.skinorthstar.com. 262 units. $195–$325 double in lodge; $178–$989 condos, homes. Packages available. AE, DISC, MC, V. **Amenities:** Restaurant; cafe; deli; bar; outdoor heated pool; heated lap pool year-round; children's pool; golf course; 10 tennis courts; health club; 3 outdoor Jacuzzis; sauna; bike rental; children and teen center; game room/video arcade; tour and activities desk; business center; babysitting; laundry facilities. *In room:* TV/VCR, coffeemaker, kitchen in condos, hair dryer, iron.

PlumpJack Squaw Valley Inn ★★★

Part ski chalet, part boutique hotel, PlumpJack Squaw Valley Inn is easily Tahoe's most refined and elegant hotel and restaurant. Granted, it lacks the fancy toys offered by its competitor across the valley, The Resort at Squaw Creek (see below), but the PlumpJack is unquestionably more genteel, a tribute to the melding of artistry and hostelry. The entire hotel is draped in muted, earthy tones; swirling sconces and sculpted metal accents are candy for the eyes, while the rest of your body parts are soothingly enveloped in thick hooded robes, terry-cloth slippers, and down comforters atop expensive mattresses. Each room has mountain views for your pampered body to contemplate. The inn's equally fine restaurant, PlumpJack Café, is reviewed on p. 262.

1920 Squaw Valley Rd. (P.O. Box 2407), Olympic Valley, CA 96146. (C) **800/323-7666** or 530/583-1576. Fax 530/583-1734. www.plumpjack.com. 61 units. Summer $145–$370; winter $175–$545. Rates include continental breakfast. AE, DISC, MC, V. **Amenities:** Restaurant; bar; heated outdoor pool (seasonal); nearby golf course; 2 Jacuzzis; bike rental; concierge; room service; in-room massage; laundry service; same-day dry cleaning; executive-level rooms. *In room:* TV w/pay movies, dataport, minibar, fridge, coffeemaker in suites, hair dryer; 1 unit available with kitchenette.

The Resort at Squaw Creek ★★★ (Kids)

The most deluxe resort on the lake is the $130-million Resort at Squaw Creek. You can't beat the resort's ski-in/ski-out access to Squaw Valley skiing—in fact, a chairlift lands just outside the door. Don't ski? Don't worry. There are lots of other sports facilities to keep active travelers happy, including 20 miles of groomed cross-country skiing trails (marked for hiking and biking in the summer), sleigh and dog-sled rides, an ice-skating rink, and, in summer, a world-class golf course and an equestrian center with riding stables. Particularly good for families, trained counselors lead a "Mountain Buddies" program for kids ages 4 to 13, offering different activities every day. While the standard guest rooms are not particularly spacious, they're well equipped with attractive furnishings, original artwork, and even windows with beautiful views that open to let in the mountain air. Suites come in all different sizes and configurations. The latest improvement is a $3 million expansion of their spa facilities.

400 Squaw Creek Rd., Olympic Valley, CA 96146. (C) **800/403-4434** or 530/583-6300. Fax 530/581-6632. www.squawcreek.com. 403 units. $250–$395 double; $450–$1,900 suite. Packages available. AE, DC, DISC, MC, V. Valet parking $15; free self-parking. **Amenities:** 4 restaurants; deli; 4 bars; 3 pools (1 heated); golf course; 2 outdoor tennis courts; health club; region's largest spa; indoor and outdoor Jacuzzis; dry saunas; bike rental; children's program; video arcade; concierge; activities desk; courtesy car; business center; secretarial services; shopping arcade; salon; room service; in-room massage; babysitting; laundry service; same-day dry cleaning. *In room:* A/C, TV w/pay movies, dataport, minibar, coffeemaker, kitchen in some units, hair dryer, iron.

The Shore House ★★

This romantic little bed-and-breakfast inn, right on the lake, is a real charmer. Each individually decorated room has its own entrance, handmade log furniture, knotty-pine walls, a gas-log fireplace, and a blissfully comfortable feather bed. Guests have access to a private beach and landscaped lawn that overlook the lake, as well as an in-house spa. Boat owners can even make use of its six buoys and private dock. Planning on tying the knot? No problem: The charming hosts can help—Marty's a minister of the Universal

Life Church, and Barb can provide the marriage license. They even have a pretty area for small, romantic weddings, and a honeymoon cottage with a two-person spa tub.

7170 N. Lake Blvd. (P.O. Box 499), Tahoe Vista, CA 96148. ℂ 800/207-5160 or 530/546-7270. Fax 530/546-7130. www.shorehouselaketahoe.com. 8 units, 1 cottage. $160–$240 double; $225–$285 cottage. Rates include full breakfast. DISC, MC, V. **Amenities:** Jacuzzi; massage. *In room:* A/C, fridge, hair dryer, no phone.

Moderate

Cal-Neva Resort, Spa & Casino ⋆
You might guess from its name that the state line literally runs right through this hotel, but you could never imagine its colorful, sometimes scandalous history. Ownership has been passed around by names like "Pretty Boy," "Babyface," and Sinatra, who built the famed Celebrity Room where many big names sang for their supper. It's here that Marilyn Monroe is alleged to have had her rendezvous with John F. Kennedy (you can even see the secret tunnel). Respectability, however, has laid claim to the Cal-Neva, and it is now a popular (and reputable) lakeside resort. Almost all of the rooms in the lodge have lake views and are quite elegantly decorated. Besides the casino (on the Nevada side of the hotel, of course), the Cal-Neva offers the full array of sport and spa options, a complete wedding-planning service, and two wedding chapels. Even if you don't stay here, stop by and take a look.

2 Stateline Rd. (Box 368), Crystal Bay, NV 89402-0368. ℂ 800/225-6382 or 775/832-4000. Fax 775/831-9007. www.calnevaresort.com. 188 units, 9 chalets, 3 bungalows. $79–$189 double; $179–$269 suite, chalet, or bungalow. Packages available. AE, DC, DISC, MC, V. **Amenities:** Lake-view restaurant; heated outdoor pool; nearby golf course; 2 outdoor tennis courts; full-service European health spa; Jacuzzi; large video arcade; concierge; business center; salon; room service. *In room:* A/C, TV, fax, dataport, coffeemaker, hair dryer, iron.

Meeks Bay Resort ⋆
Located 10 miles south of Tahoe City, rustic Meeks Bay Resort is one of the oldest hostelries on the lake and something of a historical landmark. Opened as a public campground in 1920, its sweeping lakefront location boasts one of the finest beaches on the lake. During the next 50 years, the resort grew to include cabins and other improvements, and attracted many celebrities from Southern California. Acquired by the U.S. Forest Service in 1974, the property is open during summers only. Most rentals are on a weekly basis and consist of motel lodging or modest wood cabins perched near the lake. Facilities include a full marina with boat rentals, a campground with RV access ($20 a night, 4-night minimum), a beachfront snack bar, a playground, and a visitor center with a cultural display, coffee bar, and retail store. The Kehlet House, set on a rock that juts out into the lake, is the resort's prime accommodation. Owned at one time by William Hewlett, co-founder of the Hewlett-Packard Corporation, and later the summer residence of billionaire Gordon Getty, it has seven bedrooms, three bathrooms, a large kitchen, a living room, and water on three sides. The entire house is rented by the week, sleeps a dozen, and costs $3,850. Make all reservations here early.

P.O. Box 787, Tahoma, CA 96142 ℂ 877/326-3357 or 530/525-6946. Fax 530/525-4028. www.meeksbay resort.com. 21 units, 28 campsites. $85–$195 double per night; $770–$1,650 per week. AE, MC, V. Open May–Nov only. **Amenities:** Watersports equipment rental. *In room:* Kitchen in log cabins.

River Ranch Lodge & Restaurant ⋆⋆
The River Ranch Lodge has long been one of my favorite places to stay in Lake Tahoe. Situated alongside the Truckee River, the lodge is mere minutes away from Alpine Meadows and Squaw Valley ski resorts, and a short drive (or ride along the bike path) into Tahoe City. The best rooms in this rustic lodge have balconies that overlook the

river. All have a handsome mountain-home decor, lodgepole pine furniture, and down comforters. Room nos. 9 and 10, the farthest from the road, are my top choices. In summer, guests relax under umbrellas on the huge patio overlooking the river, working down burgers and beer while watching the rafters float by. During the ski season, the River Ranch's spectacular circular cocktail lounge and dining area, which cantilevers over the river, is a popular après-ski hangout. Also a big hit is the handsome River Ranch Lodge Restaurant, which serves fresh seafood, thick steaks, rack of lamb, and more exotic meats such as wood-oven roasted Montana elk loin with a dried-cherry/port sauce.

On Calif. 89, at Alpine Meadows Rd. (P.O. Box 197), Tahoe City, CA 96145. ℂ 800/535-9900 or 530/583-4264. Fax 530/583-7237. www.riverranchlodge.com. 19 units. $100–$160 double. Rates include continental breakfast. Packages available. AE, MC, V. **Amenities:** Restaurant; bar; golf course nearby; concierge. *In room:* TV, dataport, iron.

Sunnyside Lodge ⭐⭐ Built as a private home in 1908, this hotel and restaurant is one of the few grand old lodges still left on the lake. Located 2 miles south of Tahoe City, it looks very much like a giant wood cabin, complete with dormers, steep pitched roofs, and natural-wood siding; rustic looking but fairly sophisticated. Stretching across the building, a large deck fronts a tiny marina and gravel beach. The Lakefront rooms are the most desirable and go for about $15 more than the others—well worth the added expense. Five units have rock fireplaces. Most of the lodge's ground floor is dominated by the popular Sunnyside Restaurant (p. 263).

1850 W. Lake Blvd. (P.O. Box 5969), Tahoe City, CA 96145. ℂ 800/822-2754 or 530/583-7200. Fax 530/583-2551. www.sunnysideresort.com. 23 units. $100–$250 double. Rates include continental breakfast. Packages available. AE, MC, V. **Amenities:** Restaurant; bar; nearby golf course; watersports equipment rental; room service. *In room:* TV/VCR, fridge in some units, hair dryer, iron.

Tahoma Meadows Bed & Breakfast ⭐ *Kids* Nothing glitzy about this historic bed-and-breakfast, just some cute little red cabins nestled on a gentle forest slope. Many have claw-foot tubs, and all have down comforters, ceiling fans, gas fireplaces, and lots of rustic charm. The largest cabin, Treehouse, sleeps six and is ideal for families. In the main lodge upstairs is the highly recommended Stoneyridge Cafe serving breakfast, lunch, and dinner. Nearby activities include skiing at Ski Homewood (including shuttle service) and sunbathing at the lakeshore just across the street.

6821 W. Lake Blvd. (P.O. Box 810), Homewood, CA 96141. ℂ 800/355-1596 or 530/525-1553. www.tahomameadows.com. 14 units. $95–$295 double. Rates include full breakfast. AE, DISC, MC, V. Pets accepted in some units with $25 fee. 8½ miles from Tahoe City. **Amenities:** Cafe; nearby golf course. *In room:* TV/VCR, kitchen in some units, no phone.

Inexpensive

Ferrari's Crown Resort *Value* If you are looking for convenient, lakefront accommodations at a reasonable price, this family-operated motel is a great choice. The Ferrari family has proudly offered a warm family atmosphere to its guests since 1957. Family suites are completely equipped with kitchenettes and gas fireplaces, and can sleep up to seven. Nothing fancy here, but this place is well run, the rooms are very inviting, and you can't beat the location. Plan a trip during the off-season to take advantage of their great bargain rates.

8200 N. Lake Blvd. (P.O. Box 845), Kings Beach, CA 96143. ℂ 800/645-2260 or 530/546-3388. Fax 530/546-3851. www.tahoecrown.com. 45 units. $45–$95 double; $70–$210 2-bedroom suites or lakefront rooms. Packages available. AE, DISC, MC, V. **Amenities:** Heated outdoor pool (seasonal); nearby golf course; free passes to nearby health club; Jacuzzi. *In room:* A/C, TV; stocked kitchenette, fridge, coffeemaker, hair dryer, and iron in some units.

Lake of the Sky Motor Inn *Value*   This remodeled 1960s-style A-frame motel in the heart of Tahoe City offers clean, quiet, inexpensive accommodations in a central location—only steps away from shops and restaurants and a main stop for the ski shuttles. Just the basics here—TV, phone, bathroom—so plan on spending most of your time outdoors. Some rooms have lake views, and there's an attractively landscaped picnic-and-barbecue area.

955 N. Lake Blvd. (P.O. Box 227), Tahoe City, CA 96145. (C) **530/583-3305.** Fax 530/583-7621. 23 units. $59–$129 double. Children 11 and under stay free in parents' room. Rates include continental breakfast. AE, DC, DISC, MC, V. **Amenities:** Heated outdoor pool (seasonal); nearby golf course. *In room:* TV, dataport, fridge in some units.

WHERE TO DINE
SOUTH SHORE & SOUTH LAKE TAHOE
Expensive

Evan's American Gourmet Café ★★★ AMERICAN/CONTINENTAL
After a dinner at Evan's, you'll feel you've had not just a good meal but a great dining experience. The restaurant's impeccable service, award-winning wine list, and unyielding attention to detail serve as a perfect backdrop for the creative culinary artistry of Chef Aaron Maffit. The philosophy here is to use only the finest, freshest ingredients and not overwhelm them with heavy sauces or over-stylized culinary technique. The cuisine is an original blend of styles from around the world, with each dish being an artistic creation. For appetizers, typical choices are sautéed Dungeness crab cakes on roasted red pepper purée with crème fraîche or foie gras on crispy spice bread with port and apple cider fumet. Entrees might include breast and confit leg of duck with roast onion and savory bread pudding and hazelnut sauce, or roast Cevena venison with balsamic roast cherries, fresh tarragon, and lacquered root vegetables. If you have room, the desserts are luscious as well as beautiful. Seats are limited in this cozy little restaurant so be sure to call ahead for reservations.

536 Emerald Bay Rd., South Lake Tahoe. (C) **530/542-1990.** www.evanstahoe.com. Reservations required (must confirm by 4pm). Main courses $18–$25. DISC, MC, V. Daily 5:30–9:30pm.

Fresh Ketch ★★ SEAFOOD   Ensconced in a small marina at the foot of Tahoe Keys Boulevard, Fresh Ketch has long been regarded as South Lake's premier seafood restaurant. Try to get a window table so you can watch the marina activities. For starters, I always order half a dozen oysters and the seared ahi tuna with ponzu and wasabi dipping sauces. Then it's on to the sautéed sea bass encrusted with pistachio, herbs, and garlic, or the big ol' Alaskan king crab, steamed in the shell and served with the requisite drawn butter. There's also a modest selection of meat and poultry dishes, including a great surf-and-turf of petite mignon and lobster. For dessert, the calorie fest continues with a big slice of Kimo's Hula Pie. Prices are a bit steep, but you can always join the locals at the bar and order from the extensive bar menu, which offers everything from blackened mahimahi to fresh fish tacos and fish and chips, all for under $10. There's also live music Friday and Saturday evenings.

2433 Venice Dr. (C) **530/541-5683.** Reservations recommended. Main courses $17–$24, market price for crab and lobster. AE, DC, DISC, MC, V. Daily 11:30am–10pm (bar open until midnight).

Moderate

Cantina Bar & Grill ★ MEXICAN   The Cantina Bar & Grill is a favorite local hangout and serves the best Mexican food in South Lake. With friendly service, three sports televisions, and 30 kinds of beer, joviality reigns. The menu is well priced and extensive, offering Cal-Mex specialties such as tacos, burritos, and enchiladas along with a half-dozen Southwestern dishes such as smoked chicken polenta and grilled pork chops with jalapeño mashed potatoes. The steak fajitas get a thumbs-up, as do the barbecued baby-back ribs. To demonstrate their sense of whimsy and eclectic ethnic appeal, they offer an Oriental chicken salad, a Southwestern Reuben sandwich, a French dip, and a stir-fry wrap as well as a few vegetarian selections.

765 Emerald Bay Rd. (C) **530/544-1233**. www.cantinatahoe.com. Main courses $8–$15. MC, V. Daily 11:30am–10:30pm (bar open until midnight).

Scusa! ✶ ITALIAN   This is one of the local's favorite Italian restaurants. The decor is nothing to write home about, but the fresh pasta and other Italian dishes are satisfying and reasonably priced. The menu might include offerings such as smoked chicken ravioli, stuffed eggplant, and baked penne pasta with smoked mozzarella, prosciutto, and baked garlic cloves.

1142 Ski Run Blvd. (C) **530/542-0100**. Main courses $9–$18. AE, DISC, MC, V. Daily 5:30–10pm.

Inexpensive

Sprouts Natural Foods Café ✶✶ *Value* HEALTH FOOD/JUICES   Sprouts owner Tyler Cannon has filled a much-needed niche in South Lake, serving wholesome food that looks good, tastes good, and *is* good. Most everything is made in-house, including the soups, smoothies, and fresh-squeezed juices. Menu items range from rice bowls to sandwiches (try the Real Tahoe Turkey), huge burritos, coffee drinks, muffins, fresh-fruit smoothies, and a marvelous mayo-free tuna sandwich made with yogurt and packed with fresh veggies. Order from the counter, then scramble for a vacant seat (outdoor tables are coveted). This is also an excellent place to pack a picnic lunch.

3123 Harrison Ave. (at U.S. 50 and Alameda St., next to Lakeview Sports). (C) **530/541-6969**. Meals $4.50–$6.75. No credit cards. Daily 8am–10pm.

Yellow Sub *Value* SANDWICHES   When it comes to picnic supplies, there's stiff competition in South Lake Tahoe: three sandwich shops on this single block alone. Still, my favorite is Yellow Sub, voted best deli sandwich shop by readers of the *Tahoe Daily Tribune* for 6 years straight. It offers a whopping 21 versions of overstuffed subs—made in 6-inch and 12-inch varieties—as well as several kinds of wraps. The shop is hidden in a small shopping center across from the El Dorado Campground.

983 Tallac Ave. (at U.S. 50). (C) **530/541-8808**. Sandwiches and wraps $3.20–$7.15. No credit cards. Daily 10:30am–10pm.

NORTH SHORE/TAHOE CITY
Expensive

Lone Eagle Grille ✶✶✶ AMERICAN   If you want to see the most beautiful restaurant in all of Tahoe, don't miss the Lone Eagle Grille, right on the lake in Incline Village. Superlatives are inadequate to describe this architectural gem. It captures the charm of a grand "Old Tahoe" lodge with its massive stone fireplaces and towering open beamed ceilings while offering stunning lake views through its expansive windows. For lunch you can choose from an extensive selection of soups, salads, pastas, pizzas, specialty sandwiches, and a few main dishes. The French onion soup and the spit-roasted chicken are particularly good. In addition to the highly recommended items from the specialty grille, the dinner menu might include chile-lime sea bass, ginger-roasted duck, or stuffed

Sonoma chicken breast. The dry-aged, mesquite-grilled Black Angus steaks are particularly good. Great pride is taken in the wine list, and the service is attentive and friendly.

111 Country Club Dr. (across from the Hyatt), Incline Village, NV. ℂ 775/832-3250. Reservations recommended. Lunch $9–$14; dinner $19–$40; brunch $25, includes champagne. AE, DC, DISC, MC, V. Daily 11:30am–2:30pm and 6–10pm; Sun brunch 10:30am–2:30pm.

PlumpJack Café ★★★ MODERN AMERICAN   Squaw Valley's investors have spent oodles of money trying to turn the ski resort into a world-class destination, and one major step in the right direction is the sleek and sexy Plump-Jack Café. Although dinner prices have dropped slightly (guests balked at the original outrageous rates), none of PlumpJack's high standards have diminished. Expect impeccable service regardless of your attire (this is, after all, a ski resort), and heady menu choices ranging from risotto with shiitake mushrooms and fava beans to roasted rabbit atop a golden potato purée, plus a fabulous dish of braised oxtail paired with horseradish mashed potatoes and carrots. Those already familiar with PlumpJack in San Francisco know that the reasonably priced wine list is among the nation's best.

In the PlumpJack Squaw Valley Inn, 1920 Squaw Valley Rd., Squaw Valley. ℂ 530/583-1576. www.plump jack.com. Reservations recommended. Main courses $17–$20. AE, MC, V. Daily 7am–10pm, 11:30am–2:30pm, and 5:30–10pm.

Sunsets on the Lake ★★ NORTHERN ITALIAN/CALIFORNIA   The only tough choice here is deciding which is better—the panoramic view of the lake or the spectacular cuisine. A rustic, romantic ambience is created by a large fireplace, white-clothed tables, and—of course—a gorgeous lake view. Recommended dishes include the fantastic braised lamb shank, a hefty hunk of tender lamb perfectly complemented by shiitake mushrooms, caramelized vegetables, and garlic mashed potatoes. If the duck is among the specials, order it: Each tender slice explodes with flavor. When the snow melts, the heated outdoor deck and "Island Bar" are open for dining and drinks. They even provide blankets for an especially cozy sunset cocktail hour.

7360 N. Lake Blvd. (at North Tahoe Marina), Tahoe Vista. ℂ 530/546-3640. Reservations recommended. Main courses $18–$24. AE, DC, DISC, MC, V. Winter daily 5–10pm; June 25–Sept 7 daily 11:30am–midnight.

Wolfdale's ★★ CALIFORNIA/JAPANESE   Wolfdale's has long been one of Tahoe's finest restaurants. The innovative chefs know how to put a personal spin on regional ingredients, fusing flavors and textures of the East and the West. Although the menu changes frequently, a "cuisine unique" experience—as they're fond of calling it—might begin with tea-smoked duck with peanut noodles and mango chutney or sashimi with ginger and wasabi. The spinach salad tossed with smoked local trout, olives, and grated eggs is particularly memorable. Main courses are equally inventive, such as grilled game hen with Thai dipping sauce, or Alaskan halibut and sea scallops wrapped in Swiss chard with leek sauce.

640 N. Lake Blvd., Tahoe City. ℂ 530/583-5700. Reservations recommended. Main courses $18–$24. DISC, MC, V. Wed–Mon 6–10pm (open daily July–Aug).

Moderate

Café 333 ★★ ECLECTIC AMERICAN   The cuisine at this chic little cafe has been described as contemporary French country style with a San Francisco flair. Whatever you call it, the food is outstanding. If you're tired of the same old breakfasts, you'll love your choices here. Try the Breakfast Strata ("Bread Pudding" baked with prosciutto, spinach, tomato, basil, mascarpone, Parmesan, and cream), the chicken hash, or the caramelized-apple French toast. Gourmet coffees, baked goods, and creative omelets also grace the menu. For lunch you can't go wrong with any of their tasty salads, sandwiches, or pastas. The dinner menu might include grilled vegetable risotto or salmon with fresh herbed gnocchi and Gorgonzola sauce. The desserts are made in-house and include such tempters as crème brûlée, caramel chocolate pecan pie, and berry shortcake. They need more room to accommodate their enthusiastic guests, but the ambience is so cheerful that somehow you don't mind sometimes rubbing elbows.

333 Village Blvd., Incline Village. (C) 775/832-7333. Breakfast $7–$9; lunch $8–$12; dinner $15–$24. MC, V. Daily 7:30am–3pm and 5:30–9pm.

Gar Woods Grill & Pier ⊛ AMERICAN   Named after the builder of those beautiful mahogany race boats that used to grace the lake in the 1930s and 1940s, Gar Woods attempts to capture the nostalgia and atmosphere of that old wooden boat era. Whether folks are watching Monday-night football or drinking a famous "Wet Woody," it seems like there is always something festive going on in the bar. And on a sunny day, it's great fun to sit out on the lakeside deck to enjoy the good food and good cheer. The menu is wide-ranging, covering everything from a shrimp and lobster bisque to a pepper and garlic turkey burger with curly fries. Appetizers go from beer-battered coconut prawns to sashimi. Dinner entrees include nothing out of the ordinary, but the preparation is good and the service is friendly. Try the sumptuous Sunday brunch—it's more food than you could ever imagine for $26.

5000 N. Lake Blvd., Carnelian Bay. (C) 800/BY-TAHOE or 530/546-3366. www.garwoods.com. Lunch $9–$14; dinner $14–$27; brunch $26. AE, DISC, MC, V. Mon–Sat 11:30am–10pm, Sun 10:30am–10pm.

Sunnyside Restaurant ⊛ SEAFOOD/AMERICAN   In summer, when the sun is shining, there's no more highly coveted table in Tahoe than one on Sunnyside's lakeside veranda. Guests can also dine in the lodge's more traditional dining room with its 1930s aura. Nothing out of the ordinary here: The lunch menu has fresh pastas, burgers, chicken, and fish sandwiches, together with a variety of soups and salads. Dinners are fancier, with such main courses as Australian lobster tail, lamb chops with roasted-garlic chutney butter, and fresh salmon oven-baked on a cedar plank.

At the Sunnyside Lodge, 1850 W. Lake Blvd., Tahoe City. (C) 800/822-2754 or 530/583-7200. www. sunnysideresort.com. Main courses $14–$24. AE, DISC, MC, V. Oct–June daily 4–9:30pm; July–Sept Sun–Thurs 11am–9:30pm, Fri–Sat 11am–10pm; year-round Sun brunch 9:30am–2pm.

Inexpensive

Bridgetender Tavern and Grill (Value) PUB GRUB   Although it's located in one of the most popular tourist areas in North Lake, the Bridgetender is a locals' hangout through and through. Still, they're surprisingly tolerant of out-of-towners, who come for the cheap grub and huge selection of draft beers. The tavern is built around a trio of ponderosa pines that blend with the decor so well you hardly notice them. Big burly burgers, salads, pork ribs, and such round out the menu, and the daily beer specials—posted on the wall in Day-Glo colors—are definitely worth going over. In summer, dine outside among the pines.

30 W. Lake Blvd. (at Fanny Bridge), Tahoe City. (C) 530/583-3342. Burgers, salads, and ribs $5–$8. MC, V. Daily 11am–2am.

Fire Sign Café ⊛ (Value) AMERICAN   Choosing a place to have breakfast in North Tahoe is a no-brainer. Since the late 1970s, the Fire Sign Café has been the locals' choice—which explains the lines out the door on weekends. Just about everything is made from scratch, such as the delicious coffee cake that accompanies the big plates of bacon and eggs or blackberry-buckwheat pancakes. Even the salmon for chef and owner Bob Young's legendary salmon omelet is smoked in-house. Lunch—burgers, salads, sandwiches, burritos, and more—is also quite popular, particularly when the outdoor patio is open.

1785 W. Lake Blvd., Tahoe City. (C) **530/583-0871**. Breakfast and lunch $4–$9. MC, V. Daily 7am–3pm.

Izzy's Burger Spa *Value* BURGERS   It's just a simple, wooden A-frame building containing a small short-order grill, but Izzy's Burger Spa flips an unusually hefty and tasty burger and an equally enticing grilled chicken-breast sandwich. On a sunny day, the best seats are at the picnic tables set out front.

100 W. Lake Blvd. (at Fanny Bridge), Tahoe City. (C) **530/583-4111**. Burgers $4–$7. No credit cards. Daily 11am–7pm.

TAHOE AFTER DARK

Tahoe is not particularly known for its nightlife, although there's always something going on in the showrooms of the major casino hotels on the South Shore. Call **Harrah's** ((C) 775/588-6611), **Harveys** ((C) 775/588-2411), **Caesars** ((C) 775/588-3515), and the **Horizon** ((C) 775/588-6211) for current show schedules and prices. Most cocktail shows cost $15 to $40. On the North Shore, there's usually live music nightly in **Bullwhackers Pub,** at the Resort at Squaw Creek ((C) 530/583-6300; p. 257). The **Pierce Street Annex,** 850 North Lake Blvd. ((C) 530/583-5800), behind the Safeway in Tahoe City, has pool tables, shuffleboard, and DJ dancing every night. It's one of the livelier places around. If it's just a casual cocktail you're after, my favorite spot is the cozy fireside lounge at **River Ranch Lodge,** which cantilevers over a turbulent stretch of the Truckee River, on Calif. 89 at the entrance to Alpine Meadows ((C) **530/583-4264**).

2 Mount Shasta & the Cascades ★★

274 miles N of San Francisco

Chances are, your first glimpse of Mount Shasta's majestic, snowcapped peak will result in a twang of awe. A dormant volcano with a 17-mile-diameter base, it stands in virtual isolation 14,162 feet above the sea. When John Muir first saw Shasta from 50 miles away in 1874, he wrote: "[I] was alone and weary. Yet my blood turned to wine, and I have not been weary since." He went on to describe it as "the pole star of the landscape," which indeed it is.

Keep in mind, however, that dining and lodging in these parts lean more toward sustenance than indulgence: It's the fresh air, not fresh fish, that lures visitors this far north. You can leave the dinner jacket at home—all that's really required when visiting the Far North are a pair of broken-in hiking boots, binoculars (the bald eagle is a common sight in these parts), some warm clothing, and an adventurous spirit.

ESSENTIALS

GETTING THERE   From San Francisco, take I-80 to I-505 to I-5 to Redding. From the coast, pick up Calif. 299 east a few miles north of Arcata to Redding.

Redding Municipal Airport, 6751 Woodrum Circle ((C) 530/224-4399), is serviced by **United Express** ((C) 800/241-6522) and **Horizon Air** ((C) 800/547-9308). **Amtrak** ((C) 800/USA-RAIL) stops in Dunsmuir and Redding.

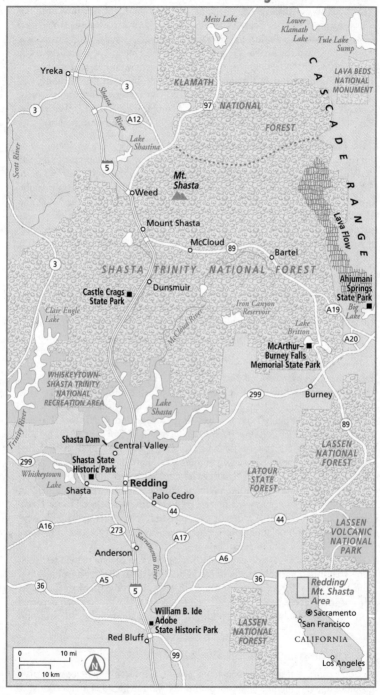

Meiss Lake

Lower Klamath Lake

Tule Lake Sump

LAVA BEDS NATIONAL MONUMENT

Yreka

KLAMATH

3

97

NATIONAL

FOREST

A12

Lake Shastina

Mt. Shasta

Weed

Mount Shasta

McCloud

89

Bartel

SHASTA TRINITY NATIONAL FOREST

Dunsmuir

Castle Crags State Park

Iron Canyon Reservoir

Ahjumani Springs State Park

A19

Big Lake

Clair Engle Lake

Lake Britton

A20

McArthur– Burney Falls Memorial State Park

WHISKEYTOWN- SHASTA TRINITY NATIONAL RECREATION AREA

Lake Shasta

299

Burney

89

Shasta Dam

Central Valley

Shasta State Historic Park

Whiskeytown Lake

Shasta

Redding

Palo Cedro

44

LATOUR STATE FOREST

LASSEN NATIONAL FOREST

299

A16

273

44

44

LASSEN VOLCANIC NATIONAL PARK

Anderson

A17

A6

36

36

A5

5

William B. Ide Adobe State Historic Park

LASSEN NATIONAL FOREST

Redding/ Mt. Shasta Area

Sacramento

San Francisco

CALIFORNIA

Red Bluff

99

Los Angeles

0   10 mi

0   10 km

N

VISITOR INFORMATION   Regional information can be obtained from the following organizations: **Shasta Cascade Wonderland Association,** 1699 Calif. 273, Anderson, CA 96007 (© 800/474-2782 or 530/365-7500; www.shasta cascade.org); **Mount Shasta Visitors Bureau,** 300 Pine St., Mount Shasta, CA 96067 (© 800/926-4865 or 530/926-4865; www.mtshastachamber.com); **Redding Convention & Visitors Bureau,** 777 Auditorium Dr., Redding, CA 96001 (© 800/874-7562 or 530/225-4100; www.visitredding.org); **Trinity County Chamber of Commerce,** 210 N. Main St., P.O. Box 517, Weaverville, CA 96093 (© 800/487-4648 or 530/623-6101; www.trinitycounty.com).

THE REPUBLIC OF CALIFORNIA

En route to Mount Shasta from the south, you may want to stop near Red Bluff at **William B. Ide Adobe State Historic Park,** 21659 Adobe Rd. (© **530/ 529-8599**), for a picnic along the Sacramento River and a visit to an adobe home dating back to 1852. The 4-acre park commemorates William B. Ide, the Republic of California's first and only president. The Republic of California was proclaimed on June 14, 1846, following the Bear Flag Rebellion and lasted only 3 weeks. In summer, the park is open from 8am to sunset, the house from noon to 4pm; call ahead in winter. Parking costs $3 per vehicle.

REDDING

The major town and gateway to the region is Redding, the hub of the panoramic Shasta-Cascade region, lying at the top of the Sacramento Valley. From here, you can either turn westward into the wilderness forest of Trinity and the Klamath Mountains, or north and east into the Cascades and Shasta Trinity National Forest.

In Redding, with its fast-food joints, gas stations, and cheap motels, summer heat generally hovers around 100°F (38°C). A city of some 80,000, Redding is the transportation hub of the upper reaches of Northern California. It has little of interest; it's mainly useful as a base for exploring the natural wonders nearby. Information is available from the **Redding Convention & Visitors Bureau,** 777 Auditorium Dr., Redding, CA 96001 (© **800/874-7562** or 530/225-4100; www.visitredding.org), west of I-5 on Calif. 299. It's open Monday through Friday from 8am to 5pm. Ahead and northeast, Mount Shasta rises to a height of more than 14,000 feet. From Redding, I-5 cuts north over the Pit River Bridge, crossing Lake Shasta and leading eventually to the mount itself. Before striking north, however, you may want to explore **Lake Shasta** and see **Shasta Dam.** Another option is to take a detour west of Redding to Weaverville, Whiskeytown–Shasta Trinity National Recreation Area, and Trinity Lake (see "Whiskeytown National Recreation Area," below).

About 3 miles west, stop at the old mining town of **Shasta,** which has been converted into a state historic park (© **530/243-8194**). Shasta was founded on gold and was the "Queen City" of the northern mines in the Klamath Range. Its life was short, and it expired in 1872 when the Central Pacific Railroad bypassed it in favor of Redding. Today, the business district is a ghost town, complete with

---

Tips **Shasta Vs. Mount Shasta**

Don't confuse the old mining town, Shasta, located a few miles west of Redding, with the much larger community, Mount Shasta, a major tourist destination located on Interstate 5 near the base of Mount Shasta.

a restored general store and a Masonic hall. The **1861 courthouse** has been converted into a museum where you can view the jail and a gallows out back, as well as a remarkable collection of California art assembled by Mae Helen Bacon Boggs. The collection includes works by Maynard Dixon, Grace Hudson, and many others. It's open Wednesday through Sunday from 10am to 5pm. Admission is $2 for adults, $1 for children ages 6 to 12.

Continue along Calif. 299 west to Calif. 3 north, which will take you to Weaverville and then to the west side of the lake and Trinity Center.

WHERE TO STAY

In addition to Tiffany House (see below), Redding has a **Doubletree Motor Inn** (© 800/222-8733 or 530/221-8700) and a **La Quinta Inn** (© 800/NU-ROOMS** or 530/221-8200). Both are fine choices.

Tiffany House Bed and Breakfast Inn   Despite the fact that this two-story gray-and-white house wasn't built until 1939, everyone in town refers to it as a Victorian. A sweeping view of the Lassen Mountain Range is visible from every guest room and cottage, as well as from the oversize deck, which seems to float above the garden in back. There's also a Music Room with piano and a Victorian Parlor with fireplace, games, and puzzles. Each guest room is appointed with a queen-size bed and antique furnishings, and all have private bathrooms and soft robes. Top choice is the secluded Lavinia's Cottage, which has a 7-foot spa tub, sitting area, and magnificent laurel-wreath iron bed.

1510 Barbara Rd., Redding, CA 96003. © **530/244-3225.** www.sylvia.com/tiffany.htm. 4 units. $90–$110 double; $140 cottage. Rates include full breakfast. AE, DISC, MC, V. **Amenities:** Outdoor pool; nearby golf courses; Jacuzzi; game room. *In room:* A/C, hair dryer, no phone.

WHERE TO DINE

Jack's Grill ✸ STEAKHOUSE   This building was originally constructed in 1835 as a secondhand-clothing store. The second floor served as a brothel in the late 1930s, and an entrepreneur named Jack Young set up the main floor as a steak house (his establishment serviced all of a body's needs, you might say). Today, it's a local favorite. Waiting for a table over drinks in the bar is part of the fun. Good old-fashioned red meat is supplemented by a couple of seafood dishes, such as deep-fried jumbo prawns and ocean scallops. It's a very fetching spot, with good, honest tavern food and a jovial crowd. Be prepared to wait on weekends.

1743 California St. © **530/241-9705.** www.jacksgrillredding.com. Reservations not accepted. Main courses $9.15–$22. AE, DISC, MC, V. Mon–Sat 4–11pm.

WEAVERVILLE

Weaverville was a gold-mining town in the 1850s, and part of the history of the place is captured at the **Jake Jackson Memorial Museum–Trinity County Historical Park,** 508 Main St. (© **530/623-5211**). The collection of memorabilia, from firearms to household items, is interesting for what it reveals about the residents of the town—Native Americans, miners, pioneers, and especially the Chinese. In the gold-rush era, the town was half Chinese, with a Chinatown of about 2,500 residents. Admission is free, but a donation of $1 is suggested.

Across the parking lot, you can view the oldest continuously used Taoist temple in California at the **Joss House State Historic Park** (© **530/623-5284**). This well-preserved temple was built by immigrant Chinese miners in 1874. Admission is $2 for adults, free for children ages 16 and under.

WHERE TO DINE

LaGrange Café ★★ *(Finds)* CREATIVE TRADITIONAL CUISINE
Weaverville isn't exactly a star in the culinary firmament, but there is one bright
spot, far and away the best food in town. Heck, it would be considered really
good in Redding, Sacramento, or Tahoe. Recently relocated from its original
home down the street, the restaurant now has digs worthy of its cuisine. It's
in Weaverville's historic district; two adjoining buildings were combined and
stripped down to the original old brick walls to make a spacious, attractive
dining area with a sit-down bar. Chef and owner Sharon Heryford's menu
includes the local favorite—chicken enchiladas with marinated tri-tip—plus seasonal items such as the local rabbit, braised with mushrooms, fresh herbs, and
white wine. The tender Duane's Chicken served with wheat pilaf is also popular.
The interesting menu includes other things like buffalo steaks, venison bratwurst,
and wild-boar sausages. Heryford's buffalo ragout won third place in a national
contest. The 135-plus selections on the wine list make it one of the strongest in
Northern California. Desserts, like a sinfully rich banana cream pie and that
quintessential comfort food, bread pudding, are all made on the premises.

226 Main St. (C) **530/623-5325**. Main courses $10–$25. AE, DISC, MC, V. Mon–Thurs 11am–9pm, Fri–Sun
11am–10pm.

THE TRINITY ALPS

West of Weaverville stretch the Trinity Alps, with Thompson Peak rising to more
than 9,000 feet. The second-largest wilderness area in the state lies between the
Trinity and Salmon rivers and contains more than 55 lakes and streams. Its
alpine scenery makes it popular with hikers and backpackers. You can access the
Pacific Crest Trail west of Mount Shasta at Parks Creek, South Fork Road, or
Whalen Road, and also from Castle Crags State Park. For trail and other information, contact the forest service at Weaverville ((C) **530/623-2121**).

The Fifth Season, 300 N. Mount Shasta Blvd. ((C) **530/926-3606;** www.the
fifthseason.com), offers mountaineering and backpack rentals and will provide
trail maps and other information concerning Shasta's outdoor activities.

Living Waters Recreation ((C) **800/994-RAFT** or 530/926-5446; www.
livingwatersrec.com) offers half-day to 2-day rafting trips on the Upper Sacramento, Klamath, Trinity, and Salmon rivers. **Trinity River Rafting Company,**
on Calif. 299W in Big Flat ((C) **800/30-RIVER** or 530/623-3033), also operates local white-water trips.

For additional outfitters and information, contact the **Trinity County
Chamber of Commerce,** 210 N. Main St. (P.O. Box 517), Weaverville, CA
96093 ((C) **800/487-4648** or 530/623-6101; www.trinitycounty.com).

WHISKEYTOWN NATIONAL RECREATION AREA

In adjacent Shasta County, Whiskeytown National Recreation Area is on the
eastern shore of Trinity Lake, a quiet and relatively uncrowded lake with 157
miles of shoreline. When this reservoir was created, it was officially named Clair
Engle, after the politician who created it. But locals insist on calling it Trinity
after the name of the river that used to rush through the region past the towns
of Minersville, Stringtown, and an earlier Whiskeytown. All of these were
destroyed when the river was dammed. They now lie submerged under the lake's
glassy surface.

Both Trinity Lake and the Whiskeytown National Recreation Area are in the
Shasta Trinity National Forest, 1.3 million acres of wilderness with 1,269 miles

of hiking trails. For information on trails, contact **Shasta Trinity National Forest** (© 530/244-2978; www.r5.fs.fed.us/shastatrinity).

LAKE SHASTA

Heading north on I-5 from Redding, travel about 12 miles and take the Shasta Dam Boulevard exit to the **Shasta Dam and Power Plant** (© 530/275-4463; www.shastalake.com/shastadam), which has an overflow spillway that is three times higher than Niagara Falls. The huge dam—3,460 feet long, 602 feet high, and 883 feet thick at its base—holds back the waters of the Sacramento, Pit, and McCloud rivers. A dramatic sight indeed, it is a vital component of the Central Valley water project. At the visitor center is a series of photographs and displays covering the dam's construction period. You can either walk or drive over the dam, but far more interesting are the **free 1-hour tours** given daily from 9am to 5pm on the hour in the summer, and at 10am, noon, and 2pm Labor Day to Memorial Day. The guided tour takes you deep within the dam's many chilly corridors (not a good place for claustrophobes) and below the spillway. It's an entertaining way to beat the summer heat. *Note:* Tours may be cancelled due to security reasons; call ahead.

Lake Shasta has 370 miles of shoreline and attracts anglers (bass, trout, and king salmon), water-skiers, and other boating enthusiasts—two million, in fact, in summer. The best way to enjoy the lake is aboard a houseboat; they can be rented from several companies, including **Antlers Resort & Marina,** P.O. Box 140, Antlers Rd., Lakehead, CA 96051 (© 800/238-3924 or 530/238-2553; www.shastalakevacations.com); and **Packers Bay Marina,** 16814 Packers Bay Rd., Lakehead, CA 96051 (© 800/331-3137 or 530/275-5570; www.packers bay.com). There is a 1-week minimum during the summer, and a 3- to 4-day minimum during the off-season.

While you're here, you can visit **Lake Shasta Caverns** (© 800/795-CAVE or 530/238-2341; www.lakeshastacaverns.com). These caves contain 20-foot-high stalactite and stalagmite formations—60-foot-wide curtains of them in the great Cathedral Room. To see the caves, drive about 15 miles north of Redding on I-5 to the O'Brien/Shasta Caverns exit. A ferry will take you across the lake and a short bus ride will follow to the cave entrance for a 2-hour-long tour. Admission is $17 for adults, $9 for children ages 4 to 12, and free for kids under 4. The caverns are open daily from 9am to 3pm year-round.

For information about the Lake Shasta region, contact the **Redding Convention & Visitors Bureau,** 777 Auditorium Dr., Redding, CA 96001 (© 800/874-7562 or 530/225-4100; www.visitredding.org), west of I-5 on Calif. 299. It's open Monday through Friday from 8am to 5pm.

MOUNT SHASTA ✦✦✦

A volcanic mountain with eight glaciers, **Mount Shasta** is a towering peak of legend and lore. It stands alone, always snowcapped, unshadowed by other mountains—visible from 125 miles away. Although it's been dormant since 1786, eruptions cannot be ruled out, and indeed, hot sulfur springs bubble at the summit. The springs saved John Muir on his third ascent of the mountain in 1875. Caught in a severe snowstorm, he and his partner took turns submersing themselves in the hot mud to survive.

Many New Agers are convinced that Mount Shasta is the center of an incredible energy vortex. These devotees flock to the foot of the mountain. In 1987, the foothills were host to the worldwide Harmonic Convergence, calling for a planetary union and a new phase of universal harmony. Yoga, massage, meditation, and metaphysics are all the rage here. These New Agers seem to coexist harmoniously with those whose metaphysical leanings begin and end with Dolly Parton song lyrics.

Those who don't want to climb can drive up to about 7,900 feet. From the town of Mount Shasta, drive 14 miles up the Everitt Memorial Highway to the end of the road near Panther Meadow. At the **Everitt Vista Turnout**, you'll be able to stop and see the Sacramento River Canyon, the Eddy Mountains to the west, and glimpses of Mount Lassen to the south. You can also take the short hike through the forests to a lava outcrop overlooking the McCloud area.

Continue on to **Bunny Flat**, a major access point for climbing in summer and also for cross-country skiing and sledding in winter. The highway ends at the Old Ski Bowl Vista, providing panoramic views of Mount Lassen, Castle Crags, and the Trinity Mountains.

While in Mount Shasta, visit the **Fish Hatchery** at 3 N. Old State Rd. (© **530/926-2215**), which was built in 1888. Here you can observe rainbow and brown trout being hatched to stock rivers and streams statewide—millions are born here annually. You can feed them via coin-operated food dispensers, and observe the spawning process on certain Tuesdays during the fall and winter. Admission is free; hours are daily from 8am to sunset. Adjacent to the hatchery is the **Sisson Museum** (© **530/926-5508**), which displays a smattering of local-history exhibits. It's open daily year-round, from 10am to 4pm in summer, from 1 to 4pm in winter; admission is free.

OUTDOOR PURSUITS

GOLF & TENNIS   Golfers should head for the 27-hole Robert Trent Jones Jr. golf course at **Lake Shastina Golf Resort,** 5925 Country Club Dr., Weed (© **800/358-4653** or 530/938-3201; www.lakeshastina.com), or the 18-hole course at **Mount Shasta Resort,** 1000 Siskiyou Lake Blvd., Mount Shasta (© **800/958-3363** or 530/926-3030; www.mountshastaresort.com). The Mount Shasta resort also has tennis courts.

MOUNTAIN CLIMBING   Mount Shasta attracts thousands of hikers from around the world each year, from timid first-timers to serious mountaineers who search for the most difficult paths up. The hike isn't technically difficult, but it's a demanding ascent that takes about 8 hours of continuous exertion, particularly when the snow softens up. (*Tip:* Start early, while the snow is still firm.) Before setting out, hikers must secure a permit by signing in at the trail head or at the **Mount Shasta Ranger District** office, which also gives out plenty of good advice for amateur climbers. The office is at 204 W. Alma St., off North Mount Shasta Boulevard in Mount Shasta (© **530/926-4511**). Be sure to wear good hiking shoes and carry crampons and an ice ax, a first-aid kit, a quart of water per person, and a flashlight in case it takes longer than anticipated. Sunblock is an absolute necessity. All the requisite equipment can be rented at **The Fifth Season,** 300 N. Mount Shasta Blvd. (© **530/926-3606;** www.thefifthseason. com). (By the way, for those mere mortals who just want to hike and don't feel compelled to summit, there are lots of low elevation trails.)

Weather can be extremely unpredictable, and every year hikers die on this dormant volcano, usually from making stupid mistakes. For **weather and climbing conditions,** call © **530/926-5555** for recorded information. Traditionally, climbers make the ascent from the Sierra Lodge at Horse Camp, which can be reached from the town of Mount Shasta via Alma Street and the Everitt Memorial Highway or from Bunny Flat.

For more information as well as supervised trips, contact **Shasta Mountain Guides,** 1938 Hill Rd. (© **530/926-3117;** www.shastaguides.com). This outfitter offers a 2-day climb that follows the traditional John Muir route and costs $285. It also offers a glacier climb and rock climbing in Castle Crags State Park, backpacking trips, plus cross-country and telemark skiing. You can take its basic rock-climbing course for $85, mountaineering course for $85, or one of its 3-day ski and snowboard descents for $385.

Also nearby is **Castle Crags State Park** (© **530/235-2684**), a 4,300-acre park with 64 campsites and 28 miles of hiking trails. Here, granite crags that were formed 225 million years ago tower more than 6,500 feet above the Sacramento River. The park is filled with dogwood, oak, cedar, and pine as well as tiger lilies, azaleas, and orchids in summer. You can walk the 1-mile Indian Creek nature trail or take the easy 1-mile Root Creek Trail. The entrance fee is $5 per vehicle per day. Castle Crags is off I-5, about 50 miles north of Redding.

OTHER WARM-WEATHER ACTIVITIES   Mount Shasta offers some excellent **mountain biking.** In the summer, ride the chairlifts to the top of Mount Shasta Ski Park and bike down the trails. An all-day chairlift pass is $15 (© **530/926-8610;** www.skipark.com). Another good source for renting mountain bikes and getting trail information is **Shasta Cycling** (© **530/ 938-3002).**

For fishing information or guided trips, call **Jack Trout Flyfishing Guide** (© **530/926-4540**). Two other recommended sources are **Mount Shasta Fly Fishing** (© **530/926-6648**) and **Hart's Guide Service** (© **530/926-2431**).

SKIING   In winter, visitors can ski at **Mount Shasta Board & Ski Park,** 104 Siskiyou Ave., Mount Shasta (© **800/SKI-SHASTA** or 530/926-8610; www.ski park.com), which has 31 runs with 80% snowmaking, three triple chairlifts, and a surface lift. Lift tickets are $33 on weekends, $29 during the week. There's also a Nordic ski center with 16 miles of groomed trails, as well as a Terrain Park that's geared toward snowboarders. The Learning Center offers instruction for adults and children. In summer, you can ride the chairlifts to scenic views, mountain-bike down the trails (an all-day pass costs $15), or practice on the two-story climbing wall. Access to the park is 10 miles east of Mount Shasta (the town) on Calif. 89.

WATERSPORTS   The source of the headwaters of the Sacramento River accumulates in **Lake Siskiyou,** a popular spot for boating, swimming, and fishing—and a great vantage point for photographs of Mount Shasta and its reflection. Water-skiing and jet-skiing are not allowed, but windsurfing is, and boat rentals are offered at **Lake Siskiyou Camp Resort,** 4239 W. A. Barr Rd., Mount Shasta (© **888/926-2618** or 530/926-2618; www.lakesis.com).

WHERE TO STAY

Best Western Tree House   Just off the main highway, this motor inn is one of the best places to stay in the town of Mount Shasta, and it keeps its prices low. The lobby and refurbished rooms, some with decks and fridges, are pleasant enough, plus there's a huge indoor pool, usually deserted, making this a family favorite. Downhill and cross-country ski areas are 10 miles away.

111 Morgan Way (at I-5 and Lake St.), Mount Shasta, CA 96067. © **800/780-7234** or 530/926-3101. Fax 530/926-3542. www.bestwestern.com. 95 units. $82–$125 double. AE, DC, DISC, MC, V. **Amenities:** Restaurant; bar; indoor pool; nearby golf course; exercise room; Jacuzzi; video arcade; business center; secretarial services. *In room:* A/C, TV, fridge, coffeemaker, hair dryer, iron.

McCloud Guest House ⭐   Off Calif. 89, west of McCloud, and set among the oak and pine trees of Mount Shasta's lower slopes, this graceful old home has a wraparound veranda and dormer windows, and overlooks beautifully groomed grounds. Built in 1907 as a residence for the president of the McCloud River Lumber Company, the handsome house was nicely restored in 1984 and changed ownership in 1999. Upstairs, there's a large comfortable parlor with an antique billiards table from the Hearst Collection. Off the parlor are five individually decorated rooms with white iron beds. Three of the rooms have claw-foot tubs; the other two have showers only. The innkeepers take great pride in the creative gourmet breakfasts served in the leaded- and stained-glassed dining room. In addition to a whipped fruit drink, fresh fruit, and homemade pastries, the menu might include a California soufflé or Belgian waffles. As for nearby recreation, they offer a Ski & Stay package, excellent fly-fishing, and two nearby golf courses.

606 W. Colombero Dr. (P.O. Box 1510), McCloud, CA 96057. ⓒ **877/964-3160** or 530/964-3160. Fax 530/964-3202. www.mccloudguesthouse.com. 5 units (2 with shower only). $95–$130 double. Rates include full breakfast. AE, DISC, MC, V. **Amenities:** Nearby golf course; sauna; massage upon request. *In room:* Iron, no phone.

Mount Shasta Ranch B&B ⭐   Mount Shasta Ranch was conceived and built in 1923 by one of the country's most famous horse trainers and racing tycoons, H. D. ("Curley") Brown, as the centerpiece of a private retreat and thorough-bred-horse ranch. Despite the encroachment of nearby buildings, the main house and its annex are still available as a cozy B&B with touches of nostalgia, the occasional antique, and spectacular views of Mount Shasta. Four bedrooms (the ones with private bathrooms) are in the main house; the remaining five share two bathrooms in the carriage house. It's a 3-minute trek to the shores of nearby Lake Siskiyou (15 min. to the ski slopes), or you could stay here to enjoy the Jacuzzi, Ping-Pong tables, pool table, darts, and horseshoes.

1008 W. A. Barr Rd., Mount Shasta, CA 96067. ⓒ **530/926-3870.** Fax 530/926-6882. www.stayinshasta. com. 10 units, 5 with private bathroom; 1 cottage. $60–$80 double with shared bathroom, $110 double with private bathroom; $115 cottage for 2. Rates include country breakfast (except cottage). AE, DISC, MC, V. Take Central Mount Shasta exit off I-5 to W. A. Barr Rd. Pets accepted with $10 fee. **Amenities:** Nearby golf course; game room. *In room:* A/C, TV, kitchen in 2 units, no phone.

Railroad Park Resort *(Kids)*   Lying a quarter of a mile from the Sacramento River, this is an offbeat place that kids will enjoy. It's located at the foot of Castle Crags and contains a campground and RV park, four rustic cabins, and the Caboose Motel. Railroad cabooses have been converted into rooms, leaving their pipes, ladders, and lofts in place. Located around the fenced-in kidney-shaped pool, they're furnished with modern brass beds, table and chairs, and dressers. The restaurant and lounge are also in vintage railroad cars.

100 Railroad Park Rd., Dunsmuir, CA 96025. ⓒ **530/235-4440.** Fax 530/235-4470. www.rrpark.com. 27 units. $75–$100 double. $10 less off-season. Extra person $10. AE, DISC, MC, V. Take Railroad Park exit off I-5, 1 mile S of Dunsmuir. Pets accepted with $10 fee. **Amenities:** Restaurant; lounge; outdoor pool; Jacuzzi; game room; coin-op laundry. *In room:* A/C, TV, fridge, coffeemaker; minibar and microwave in some units.

Stewart Mineral Springs Resort *(Finds)*   Stewart Mineral Springs is one of the most unusual health spas in California, loaded with lore and legends. It lies above cold-water springs that Native Americans valued for their healing powers. Don't expect anything approaching a European spa or big-city luxury here. Everything is deliberately rustic, with as few intrusions from the urban world as possible. Designed in a somewhat haphazard compound of about a dozen build-ings, 4 miles west of the town of Weed, it occupies a 37-acre site of sloping, forested land accented with ponds, gazebos, and decorative bridges and is riddled with hiking and nature trails, freshwater streams, and a swimming hole.

Activities revolve around hiking, nature-watching, and taking the healing waters of the legendary springs. The bathhouse is the curative headquarters of the resort and contains 13 private rooms where water from the springs is heated and run into tubs for soaking. A staff member will describe the rituals for you: A 20-minute soak is followed by a visit to a nearby sauna and an immersion in the chilly waters of Parks Creek, just outside the bathhouse. Other feel-good options include massages ($30 per half-hr. session). On Saturdays, medicine man Walking Eagle guides guests on a spiritual journey within the Native American Purification Sweat Lodge. Heck, they even have a juice bar. If you opt for treatment and R&R here, you won't be alone. Despite its rusticity, the place has been discovered by young Hollywood, including many soap actors, San Francisco 49ers football players, and local newscasters.

4617 Stewart Springs Rd., Weed, CA 96094. ✆ 530/938-2222. Fax 530/938-4283. www.stewartmineral springs.com. 6 tepees (for up to 4 persons), 4 motel rooms, 6 apt units, 5 cabins with kitchens, and a large A-frame house (suitable for 10 persons). $24 double tepee; $45–$79 double in motel, apts, and cabins; $325 for house. $5 for each extra person. DISC, MC, V. Leashed pets accepted with $3-per-day fee. **Amenities:** Restaurant (closed in winter); spa; sauna; massage. *In room:* Kitchen and coffeemaker in cabins and some units, no phone.

WHERE TO DINE

The Bagel Cafe and Bakery *Value* AMERICAN   This is the hands-down winner for a low-cost meal in Mount Shasta. Packed daily with locals, the lively little cafe serves the best coffee in the region, as well as wonderful pizza by the slice, soups, salads, sandwiches, and desserts; and you can "build a bagel" sandwich. If you're planning on spending the day in the great outdoors, stop here first for a large coffee and sandwich to go.

315 N. Mount Shasta Blvd., Mount Shasta ✆ 530/926-1414. Sandwiches and salads $5–$7. No credit cards. Daily 7am–4pm.

Café Maddalena ★★★ *Finds* SARDINIAN/MEDITERRANEAN COUNTRY COOKING   Owner and chef Maddalena Serra, who hails from Sardinia, has created a wonderful restaurant in the refurbished old railroad quarter of Dunsmuir. The smells wafting from this small place will literally draw you in. Maddalena cooks in full sight of the happy, satisfied (and stuffed) customers, preparing dishes like pasta Marco—fresh fettuccine with shrimp, tomatoes, cream, and herbs all wrapped in flaky dough and baked in a pizza oven. Everything is made fresh daily, including the breads and desserts. Try the deceptively simple yet utterly scrumptious *panna cotta,* a cream flan with lemon, vanilla, and caramelized sugar. A memorable and special place.

5801 Sacramento Ave., Dunsmuir. ✆ 530/235-2725. Reservations strongly recommended. Main courses $10–$19. MC, V. Thurs–Sun 5–10pm. Closed mid-Dec to mid-May.

Lily's ✿ AMERICAN   Set in a white-clapboard, early 1900s house in a residential neighborhood south of the town center, this friendly little restaurant has a front porch, a picket fence, a back garden, and dining in two rooms inside and two patios out. It's popular for breakfast, when chunky breads, omelets, and polenta fritters start the morning off right. Lunch and dinner dishes—tamale pie, chicken curry, scampi al roma, and Kung Pao shrimp salad—span the globe. Popular dishes are the enchiladas *suizas* stuffed with shrimp, crab, and fresh spinach, and Chicken Rosie, a tender breast of chicken simmered with raspberries, hazelnut liqueur, and cream.

1013 S. Mount Shasta Blvd., Mount Shasta. ℂ 530/926-3372. www.lilysrestaurant.com. Reservations recommended. Breakfast $7–$11; lunch $8–$12; dinner $14–$23. AE, DISC, MC, V. Mon–Fri 7am–9pm, Sat–Sun 7am–9:30pm.

MCARTHUR–BURNEY FALLS MEMORIAL STATE PARK ✦

On its way to Lassen Volcanic National Park (see below) from Mount Shasta, Calif. 89 east loops back south to **McArthur–Burney Falls Memorial State Park** (ℂ 530/335-2777). One of the most spectacular features of this 910-acre park is **Burney Falls** ✦✦, an absolutely gorgeous waterfall that cascades over a 129-foot cliff. Theodore Roosevelt once called the falls "the eighth wonder of the world." Giant springs lying a few hundred yards upstream feed the falls and keep them flowing—100 million gallons every day—even during California's legendary dry spells.

The half-mile **Headwater Trail** will take you to a good vantage point above the falls. If you're lucky, you can observe the black swifts that nest in the mossy crevices behind the cascade. Other birds to look for include barn and great horned owls, the belted kingfisher, the common flicker, and even the Oregon junco. The year-round park also has 5 miles of nature trails, 128 campsites, picnicking grounds, and good fishing for bass, crappie, brown trout, rainbow trout, and brook trout. For **camping reservations,** call ℂ 800/444-PARK (7275).

From here, Lassen Volcanic National Park lies about 40 miles south.

3 Lassen Volcanic National Park ✦

45 miles E of Redding; 255 miles NE of San Francisco

Stashed away in the far northeastern corner of California, Lassen Volcanic National Park is a remarkable reminder that North America is still forming, and that the ground below is alive with the forces of creation and, sometimes, destruction. Lassen Peak is the southernmost peak in a chain of volcanoes (including Mount Saint Helens) that stretches all the way from British Columbia.

Although it's dormant, 10,457-foot **Lassen Peak** is still very much alive. It last awakened in May 1914, beginning a cycle of eruptions that spit lava, steam, and ash until 1921. The eruption climaxed in 1915 when Lassen blew its top, sending a mushroom cloud of ash 7 miles high that was seen from hundreds of miles away. The peak itself has been dormant for nearly ¾ of a century now, but the area still boils with a ferocious intensity: Hot springs, fumaroles, geysers, and mud pots are all indicators that Lassen hasn't had its last word. Monitoring of geothermal features in the park shows that they are getting hotter, not cooler, and some scientists take this as a sign that the next big eruption in the Cascades is likely to happen here.

Until then, the park gives visitors an interesting chance to watch a landscape recover from the massive destruction brought on by an eruption. To the north of Lassen Peak is the aptly named **Devastated Area,** a huge swath of volcanic destruction steadily repopulating with conifer forests. Forest botanists have revised their earlier theories that forests must be preceded by herbaceous growth after watching the Devastated Area immediately revegetate with a diverse mix of eight different conifer species, four more than were present before the blast.

The 108,000-acre park is a place of great beauty. The flora and fauna here are an interesting mix of species from the Cascade Range, which stretches north from Lassen, and species from the Sierra Nevada Range, which stretches south. The resulting blend accounts for an enormous diversity of plants: 715 distinct species have been identified in the park. Although it is snowbound in winter,

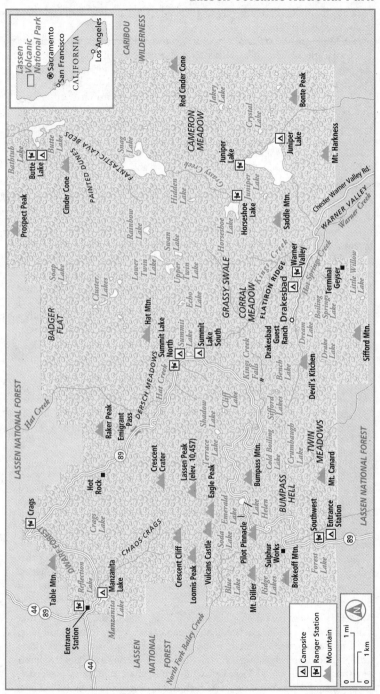

Lassen Volcanic National Park
CALIFORNIA
⊛ Sacramento
◉ San Francisco
◦ Los Angeles

Legend:
△ Campsite
🏠 Ranger Station
▲ Mountain

0 — 1 mi
0 — 1 km

Lassen is an important summer feeding ground for transient herds of mule deer and numerous black bears.

In addition to the volcano and all its geothermal features, Lassen Volcanic National Park includes miles of hiking trails, 50 beautiful alpine lakes, large meadows, cinder cones, lush forests, cross-country skiing, and great backcountry camping. In fact, three-quarters of the park is designated wilderness.

And crowds? Forget it. Lassen is one of the least-visited national parks in the lower 48 states, so crowd control isn't as big a consideration here as in other places. Unless you're here on the Fourth of July or Labor Day weekend, you won't encounter anything that could rightly be called a crowd. Even then, you can escape the hordes simply by skipping the popular sites like Bumpass Hell or the Sulphur Works and heading a few miles down any of the backcountry trails.

ESSENTIALS

GETTING THERE   One of the reasons Lassen Volcanic National Park is one of the least visited national parks is its remote location. The most foolproof route here is to take Calif. 44 east from Redding, which leads directly to the northern gateway to the park. A shortcut if you're coming from the south along I-5 is Calif. 36 in Red Bluff, which leads to the park's southern gateway. If you're arriving from the east via I-80, take the U.S. 395 turnoff at Reno and head to Susanville. Depending on which end of the park you're shooting for, take either Calif. 44 (to the northwest entrance) or Calif. 36 (to the southwest entrance) from Susanville. The $10-per-car entrance fee, valid for a week, comes with a copy of the *Lassen Park Guide,* a handy little newsletter listing activities, hikes, and points of interest. Camping fees range from $8 to $14.

Only one major road, Calif. 89 (aka the Park Rd.), crosses the park in a 39-mile half-circle with entrances and visitor centers at either end.

Most visitors enter the park at the southwest entrance station, drive through the park, and leave through the northwest entrance, or vice versa. Two other entrances lead to remote portions of the park. Warner Valley is reached from the south on the road from Chester. The Butte Lake entrance is reached by a cut-off road from Calif. 44 between Calif. 89 and Susanville.

VISITOR INFORMATION   **Ranger stations** are clustered near each entrance and provide the full spectrum of interpretive displays, ranger-led walks, informational leaflets, and emergency help. The largest **visitor center** is located just inside the northwest entrance station at the Loomis Museum. The park information number for all requests is ☎ **530/595-4444,** or you can visit www.nps.gov/lavo or write Lassen Volcanic National Park, P.O. Box 100, Mineral, CA 96063-0100.

Because of the dangers posed by the park's thermal features, rangers ask that you remain on trails at all times. Fires are allowed in campgrounds only; please make sure they're dead before leaving them. Mountain bikes are prohibited on all trails.

WEATHER   Lassen Volcanic National Park is in one of the coldest places in California. Winter begins in late October and doesn't release its grip until June. Even in the summer, you should plan for possible rain and snow. Temperatures at night can drop below freezing at any time. Winter, however, shows a different and beautiful side of Lassen that more people are starting to appreciate. Since most of the park is over a mile high and the highest point is 10,457 feet, snow accumulates in incredible quantities. Don't be surprised to find snow banks lining the Park Road into July.

EXPLORING THE PARK

The highlight of Lassen is, of course, the volcano and all of its offshoots: boiling springs, fumaroles, mud pots, and more. You can see many of the most interesting sites in a day, making it possible to visit Lassen as a short detour from I-5 or US 395 on the way to or from Oregon. Available at park visitor centers, the *Road Guide to Lassen Park* is a great traveling companion that will explain a lot of the features you'll see as you traverse the park.

Bumpass Hell ✿, a 1½-mile walk off the Park Road in the southern part of the park, is the largest single geothermal site in the park—16 acres of bubbling mud pots cloaked in a stench of rotten-egg-smelling sulfur. The hike leads you through a quiet and peaceful meadow of wildflowers and chirping birds before arriving at the geothermal site. The name comes from an early Lassen traveler, Bumpass, who lost a leg after he took a shortcut through the area while hunting and plunged into a boiling pool. Stay on the wooden catwalks that safely guide visitors past the pyrite pools, steam vents, and noisy fumaroles, and you won't suffer Bumpass's fate.

Sulphur Works ✿ is another stinky, steamy example of Lassen's residual heat. Two miles from the southwest park exit, the ground roars with seething gases escaping from the ground.

Boiling Springs Lake and **Devil's Kitchen** are two of the more remote geothermal sites; they're located in the Warner Valley section of the park, which can be reached by hiking from the main road or entering the park through Warner Valley Road from the small town of Chester.

OUTDOOR PURSUITS

In addition to the activities below, free naturalist programs are offered daily in the summer, highlighting everything from flora and fauna to geologic history and volcanic processes. For more information, call the **park headquarters** at ✆ **530/595-4444.**

CANOEING & KAYAKING Paddlers can take canoes, rowboats, and kayaks on any of the park lakes except Reflection, Emerald, Helen, and Boiling Springs. Motors, including electric motors, are strictly prohibited on all park waters. Park lakes are full of trout, and fishing is popular. You must have a current California fishing license, which you can obtain in Red Bluff at **Lassen Ranch and Home Store,** 22660 Antelope Rd. (✆ **530/527-6960**).

CROSS-COUNTRY SKIING The park road usually closes due to snow in November, and most years it doesn't open until June, so cross-country skiers have their run of the park. Snowmobiles were once allowed but are now forbidden. Marked trails of all skill levels leave from Manzanita Lake at the north end of the park and Lassen Chalet at the south. Most visitors come to the southwest entrance, where the ski chalet offers lessons, rental gear, and a warm place to stay. Popular trips are the beginners' trails to Lake Helen or Summit Lake. More advanced skiers can make the trek into Bumpass Hell, a steaming valley of sulfuric mud pots and fumaroles.

You can also ski the popular 30-mile course of the Park Road in an overnight trek, but doing this involves a long car shuttle. For safety reasons, the park requires all skiers to register at the ranger stations before heading into the backcountry, whether for an overnight or just the day. For more information contact the **park headquarters** at ✆ **530/595-4444.**

HIKING Most Lassen visitors drive through in a day or two, see the geothermal hot spots, and move on. That leaves 150 miles of trails and expanses of backcountry to the few who take the time to get off-road. The *Lassen Trails* booklet available at the visitor centers gives good descriptions of some of the most popular hikes and backpacking destinations. Anyone spending the night in the backcountry must have a wilderness permit issued at the ranger stations. And don't forget to bring plenty of water, sunscreen, and warm clothing.

The most popular hike in the park is the **Lassen Peak Trail** ⚡, a 2½-mile climb from the Park Road to the top of the peak. The trail may sound short, but it's steep and generally covered with snow until late summer. At an elevation of 10,457 feet, though, you'll get a view of the surrounding wilderness that's worth every step of the way. On clear days, you can see south all the way to Sutter Buttes near Yuba City and north into the Cascades. The round-trip takes about 4 to 5 hours.

Running a close second in popularity is **Bumpass Hell Trail.** This 1½-mile walk off the Park Road in the southern part of the park deposits you right in the middle of the largest single geothermal site in the park. (See "Exploring the Park," above.)

The **Cinder Cone Trail,** located in the northeast corner of the park, is another worthy hike, best reached from Butte Lake Campground at the far northeast corner of the park. If 4 miles seems too short, you can extend the hike (and shorten the drive) by walking in about 8 miles from Summit Lake on the Park Road. Now dormant, Cinder Cone is generally accepted as the source of mysterious flashing lights that were seen by early settlers to the area in the 1850s. Black and charred-looking, Cinder Cone is bare of any sort of life and surrounded by dunes of multihued volcanic ash.

SNOWSHOEING From January to March, park naturalists give free 2-hour eco-adventure snowshoe hikes across Lassen's snowpacked hills. The tours take place on Saturdays at 1:30pm at the Lassen Chalet, located at the park's southwestern entrance. You must be at least 8 years old, be warmly dressed, and be wearing boots. Snowshoes are provided free of charge on a first-come, first-served basis, although a $1 donation is requested for upkeep. For more details, call park headquarters (© **530/595-4444,** ext. 5133).

CAMPING

Car campers have their choice of seven park campgrounds with a total of 375 sites, more than enough to handle the trickle of visitors who come to Lassen every summer. In fact, so few people camp in Lassen that there is no reservations system except for at the **Lost Creek Group Campground,** and stays are granted a generous 14-day limit. Sites do fill up on weekends, so your best bet is to get to the park early on Friday to secure a place to stay. If the park is packed, there are 43 campgrounds in surrounding Lassen National Forest, so you're bound to find a site somewhere.

By far the most "civilized" campground in the park is at **Manzanita Lake,** where you can find hot showers, electrical hookups, flush toilets, and a camper store. When Manzanita fills up, rangers open the **Crags Campground** overflow camp, about 5 miles away and much more basic. Further within the park along Calif. 89 is **Summit Lake Campgrounds,** located on the north and south ends of Summit Lake. It's a pretty spot, often frequented by deer, and it's a launching point for some excellent day hikes.

On the southern end of the park, you'll find **Southwest Campground,** a walk-in camp directly adjacent to the Lassen Chalet parking lot.

The two remote entrances to Lassen and Warner Valley have their own primitive campgrounds with pit toilets and no water, but the price is right—free.

Backcountry camping is allowed almost everywhere, and traffic is light. Ask about closed areas when you get your wilderness permit, which are issued at the ranger stations and required for anyone spending the night in the backcountry.

WHERE TO STAY
INSIDE THE PARK

Drakesbad Guest Ranch ★★★ *(Finds)*   The only lodge operating within Lassen Park is Drakesbad Guest Ranch, hidden in a high mountain valley inside the park and surrounded by meadows, lakes, and streams. It's famous for its rustic cabins, lodge, and steaming thermal swimming pool (where they offer massage service), fed by a natural hot spring and open 24 hours a day. Drakesbad is as deluxe as a place with some electricity and no phones can be, with handmade quilts on every bed and kerosene lamps to read by. Full meal service is available—and it's very good. Since the lodge is extremely popular and only open from June to mid-October, reservations are booked as far as 2 years in advance (although May or June are good times to call to take advantage of cancellations).

c/o California Guest Services, 2150 N. Main St., no. 5, Red Bluff, CA 96080. © **530/529-1512.** Fax 530/529-4511. www.drakesbad.com. 19 units. $115–$140 per person, double occupancy. Rates include meals. DISC, MC, V. **Amenities:** Restaurant; hot-spring fed pool; children's center. *In room:* No phone.

NEAR THE PARK

The Bidwell House ★★   In 1901, General John Bidwell, a California senator who made three unsuccessful bids for the U.S. presidency, built a country retreat and summer home for his beloved young wife, Annie. After her death, when Chester had developed into a prosperous logging hamlet, the building, with its farmhouse-style design and spacious veranda, was converted into the headquarters for a local ranch. Today, the house sits at the extreme eastern end of Chester, adjacent to a rolling meadow. The lake is visible across the road, and inside, Ian and Kim James maintain one of the most charming B&Bs in the region. Seven of the rooms have Jacuzzi tubs, and three offer wood-burning stoves. Breakfast is presented with fanfare and many gourmet touches, including home-baked breads and scrumptious omelets.

1 Main St. (P.O. Box 1790), Chester, CA 96020. © **530/258-3338.** www.bidwellhouse.com. 14 units, 12 with private bathroom. $75–$150 double; $165 for cabin (sleeps 6). Rates include full breakfast. MC, V. **Amenities:** Nearby golf course. *In room:* TV.

Lassen Mineral Lodge *(Kids)*   A mere 9 miles south of Lassen Volcanic National Park's southern entrance, the Lassen Mineral Lodge offers 20 motel-style accommodations in a forested setting. In summer, the lodge is almost always bustling with guests and customers who venture into the gift shop, ski shop, general store, and full-service restaurant and bar. This is probably the best lodging option for families in the Lassen area.

On Hwy. 36E (P.O. Box 160), Mineral, CA 96063. © **530/595-4422.** Fax 530/595-4452. www.mineral lodge.com. 20 units. $65–$85 double. AE, DISC, MC, V. **Amenities:** Restaurant and saloon; coin-op laundry. *In room:* Kitchens in some units, no phone.

Mill Creek Resort *(Kids)*   Set deep within the forest next to ol' Mill Creek, the Mill Creek Resort is that rustic mountain retreat you've always dreamed of while slaving away in the office. A homey country general store and coffee shop serve as the resort's center, a good place to stock up on food while exploring Lassen

Volcanic National Park. Nine housekeeping cabins, available on a daily or weekly basis, are clean, cute, and outfitted with vintage 1930s and 1940s furniture, including kitchens (a good thing, since restaurants are scarce in this region). Pets are welcome, too.

1 Calif. 172 (3 miles S of Calif. 36), Mill Creek, CA 96061. © **888/595-4449** or 530/595-4449. www. millcreekresort.net. 9 units. $75–$100 per cabin. No credit cards. Pets accepted. **Amenities:** Bike rental; coin-op laundry (open May–Oct.). *In room:* Kitchen, coffeemaker, no phone.

WHERE TO DINE
INSIDE THE PARK
The only restaurant within Lassen Volcanic National Park (besides the Drakesbad Guest Ranch; see above) is the **Summer Chalet Café** (© **530/595-3376**), which serves inexpensive, basic breakfasts, as well as sandwiches and burgers for lunch. Located at the park's south entrance, it's open daily from 8am to 6pm (grill closes at 4pm, however) from mid-May to mid-October, weather permitting.

NEAR THE PARK
When you're this far into the wilderness, the question isn't *which* restaurant to choose, but *if* there is a restaurant to choose. If bacon and eggs, sandwiches, steaks, chicken, burgers, pizza, and salads aren't part of your diet, you're in big trouble unless you packed your own grub.

Deciding where you're going to eat near Lassen Volcanic National Park depends mostly on which side you're on, north or south. Near the north entrance to the park in the town of Old Station is **Uncle Runt's Place** (© **530/335-7215**), which serves your standard steaks, chicken, burgers, and sandwiches for lunch and dinner. At the south entrance to the park, the closest restaurant is the **Lassen Mineral Lodge** (see "Where to Stay," above) in the town of Mineral, which serves the usual uninspired American fare.

The best approach, however, is to stay at a B&B or lodge that offers meals to its guests—such as the **Bidwell House** or **Drakesbad Guest Ranch**—or at least provides a kitchen to cook your own meals, such as the **Mill Creek Resort** (see above). Food and camping supplies are available at the **Manzanita Lake Camper Store** (© **530/335-7557**; open mid-May to mid-Oct) located at the north entrance to the park, or **Lassen Mineral Lodge,** on Calif. 36 in Mineral, at the southern end of the park (© **530/595-4422**). They also sell or rent just about every outdoor toy you'd ever want to play with in Lassen Park, including cross-country and alpine ski equipment.

4 Lava Beds National Monument

324 miles NE of San Francisco; 50 miles NE of Mount Shasta

Lava Beds takes a while to grow on you. It's a seemingly desolate place with high plateaus, cinder cones, and rolling hills covered with lava cinders, sagebrush, and twisted junipers. Miles of land just like it cover most of this corner of California. So why, asks the first-time visitor, is this a national monument? The answer lies underground.

The earth here is like Swiss cheese, so porous in places that it actually makes a hollow sound. When lava pours from a shield volcano, it doesn't cool all at once; the outer edges cool first and the core keeps flowing, forming underground tunnels like a giant pipeline system.

More than 330 lava-tube caves lace the earth at Lava Beds—caves that are open to the public to explore on their own or with park rangers. Whereas most caves lend themselves to a fear of getting lost with their huge chambers, multiple entrances, and bizarre topography, these are simple, relatively easy-to-follow tunnels with little room to go wrong. Once inside, you'll feel that this would be a great place for a game of hide-and-seek.

ESSENTIALS
GETTING THERE   The best access to the park it from Highway 139, 4 miles south of Tulelake.

VISITOR INFORMATION   Call the **Lava Beds National Monument** headquarters (© **530/667-2282;** www.nps.gov/labe) for information on ranger-led hikes, cave trips, and campfire programs. The visitor center is located at the southern end of the park.

ENTRY FEES   The entry fee is $5 per vehicle for 7 days, and camping costs $10 a day.

WHEN TO GO   Park elevations range from 4,000 to 5,700 feet, and this part of California can get cold any time of year. Summer is the best time to visit, with average temperatures in the 70s°F (20s°C); winter temperatures plunge down to about 40°F (4°C) in the day and as low as 20°F (-7°C) by night. Summer is also the best time to participate in ranger-led hikes, cave trips, and campfire programs.

EXPLORING THE PARK
A hike to **Schonchin Butte** (¾ mile each way) will give you a good perspective on the wildly stark beauty of the monument and nearby Tule Lake Valley. Wildlife lovers should keep their eyes peeled for terrestrial animals like mule deer, coyote, marmots, and squirrels, while watching overhead for bald eagles, 24 species of hawks, and enormous flocks of ducks and geese headed to the Klamath Basin, one of the largest waterfowl wintering grounds in the Lower 48. Sometimes the sky goes dark with ducks and geese during the peak migrations.

The caves at **Lava Beds** are open to the public with very little restriction or hassle. All you need to see most of them are a good flashlight or headlamp, sturdy walking shoes, and a sense of adventure. Many of the caves are entered by ladders or stairs, others still, by holes in the side of a hill. Once inside, walk far enough to round a corner, and then shut off your light—a chilling experience, to say the least.

One-way **Cave Loop Road,** just southwest of the visitor center, is where you'll find many of the best cave hikes. About 15 lava tubes have been marked and made accessible. Two are ice caves, where the air temperature remains below freezing year-round and ice crystals form on the walls. If exploring on your own gives you the creeps, check out **Mushpot Cave.** Almost adjacent to the visitor center, this cave has been outfitted with lights and a smooth walkway; you'll have plenty of company.

Hardened spelunkers will find enough remote and relatively unexplored caves in the monument to keep themselves busy. Many caves require specialized climbing gear.

Above ground, several trails crisscross the monument. The longest of these, the **Lyons Trail** (8¼ miles one-way), spans the wildest part of the monument, where you are likely to see plenty of animals. The **Whitney Butte Trail** (3 miles one-way) leads from Merill Cave along the shoulder of 5,000-foot Whitney Butte to the edge of the Callahan Lava Flow and monument boundary.

PICNICKING, CAMPING & ACCOMMODATIONS

The 43-unit **Indian Well Campground** near the visitor center has spaces for tents and small RVs year-round, with water available only during the summer. The rest of the year, you'll have to carry water from the nearby visitor center.

Two **picnic grounds,** Fleener Chimneys and Captain Jacks Stronghold, have tables but no water; open fires are prohibited.

There are no hotels or lodges in the monument, but numerous services are available in nearby Tulelake and Klamath Falls. For more information, call or write **Lava Beds National Monument,** P.O. Box 867, Tulelake, CA 96134 (© **530/667-2282**).

The High Sierra: Yosemite, Mammoth Lakes & Sequoia/Kings Canyon

by Matthew Richard Poole

The national parks of California's Sierra are meccas for travelers from around the globe. The big attraction is Yosemite, of course, but the entire region is packed with natural wonders and adventures.

It was in Yosemite that naturalist John Muir found "the most songful streams in the world . . . the noblest forests, the loftiest granite domes, the deepest ice-sculpted canyons." Even today, few visitors would disagree with Muir's early impressions as they explore this land of towering cliffs, alpine lakes, river beaches, and dazzling fields of snow in winter. Yosemite Valley, lush with waterfalls and dramatic peaks reaching toward the sky, is the most central and accessible part of the park, stretching for some 7 miles from Wawona Tunnel in the west to Curry Village in the east. If you visit during spring or early fall, you'll encounter fewer problems with crowds and have more opportunities to

see the park's splendor the way it was meant to be seen.

Across the heart of the Sierra Nevada, in east-central California, Sequoia and Kings Canyon National Parks comprise a vast, mountainous region that stretches some 1,300 square miles, taking in the giant sequoias for which they're fabled. This is a land of alpine lakes, granite peaks, and deep canyons. At 14,495 feet, Mount Whitney is the highest point in the lower 48 states.

Another big attraction in the area is Mammoth Lakes, one of the major playgrounds of California, where you can enjoy dozens of recreational activities in a setting of lakes, streams, waterfalls, and rugged meadows. Glaciers in unrecorded times carved out much of this panoramic region.

Because of the vast popularity of the parks, facilities can be strained at peak visiting times. Always make your reservations in advance if possible (and that definitely includes camping).

1 Yosemite's Gateways

The good news: Towns on each gateway's periphery are virtually built around the tourism industry. They offer plenty of places to stay and eat and have natural wonders of their own. The bad news: If you stay here, reaching any point within the park requires at least a half-hour drive (usually closer to an hr.), which is especially frustrating during high season, when motor homes and overall congestion cause traffic to move at a snail's pace. A new, controversial park plan is being debated that would cut the number of day-use parking places in the park from 1,600 to 550, encourage bus and shuttle usage, reduce lodging rooms from 1,260 to 981, restore 180 acres to their natural state, and eliminate a 3¼-mile section of road to be replaced with a foot-and-bike trail.

In the meantime, there's no shortage of options to encourage you to help the park by leaving your car at your lodging or a parking area and entering on convenient, inexpensive buses (and then moving around the valley floor on free, readily available shuttles). The **Yosemite Area Regional Transit System** (YARTS) (© 877/989-2787; www.yarts.com) provides round-trip transit service from communities within Mariposa, Merced, and Mono counties to Yosemite. The Merced route along Highway 140 operates year-round, although the winter schedule is limited. Fares for riding YARTS vary, but generally range from $7 to $15 round-trip for adults, including entrance to the park, with discounts for children and seniors. Summer routes originate at Coulterville, Mammoth Lake and Lee Vining, and Wawona. For information on the Highway 120 east service (Mammoth Lakes to Yosemite Valley) call © **800/427-7623,** from May until it snows (typically Sept or Oct).

Should you need to reserve accommodations outside the park, choose based on which gate offers you easiest access. Our selections below are grouped by the three most popular entrances: The west entrances are Big Oak Flat (via Calif. 120), which is 88 miles east of Manteca and accommodates traffic from San Francisco, and Arch Rock (via Calif. 140), which is 75 miles northeast of Merced and is the easiest route from central California. The South Entrance is Wawona (via Calif. 41), which is 64 miles north of Fresno and the passage leading from Southern California.

BIG OAK FLAT ENTRANCE

The Big Oak Flat entrance is 150 miles east of San Francisco and 130 miles southeast of Sacramento. Among the string of small communities along the way is **Groveland** (24 miles from the park's entrance), a throwback to gold-mining days, complete with rednecks, the oldest saloon in the state, and at least some semblance of a real town. It'll take around an hour to reach the park entrance from Groveland, but at least there's some extracurricular activity if you're planning to stay in the area awhile. Big Oak Flat has a few hotels as well, but no town. Call the visitor information number below for details.

GETTING THERE If you're driving from San Francisco, take I-580 (which turns into I-205) to Manteca, then Calif. 120 east.

VISITOR INFORMATION Contact the **Highway 120 Chamber of Commerce** (© **800/449-9120;** www.groveland.org) for an exhaustive list of hotels, motels, cabins, RV parks, and campsites in the area.

WHERE TO STAY & DINE

Besides the places mentioned below, there are not a lot of great dining options. Ask anyone in town, and they'll point you to more offerings.

Evergreen Lodge ★★ *(Kids)* If you are looking for *the* classic Yosemite experience, you'll want to book a cabin at the Evergreen Lodge. This idyllic hideaway—located 40 minutes east of Groveland right next to Yosemite—has it all: quaint cabins in the woods, a beautiful old bar, excellent food, and even guided day and overnight trips. The 18 recently renovated cabins, scattered throughout a wooded grove of towering pines, come with private bathrooms, rocking chairs on your front porch, and cozy quilted beds. On warm nights, you can enjoy a pitcher of beer and a game of Ping-Pong on the outdoor patio, or sit around the campfire telling stories and roasting marshmallows. There are endless hiking and biking trails and, in summer, access to tennis courts, a pool (major family fun), and horseback riding right next door at neighboring Camp Mather. Dan "Burly Boy" Braun, an Evergreen owner and one of the leading Yosemite experts, is in charge of the outdoor programs and just might be your guide. In 2004, the Evergreen plans to stay open year-round, add new cabins, a new campfire/ amphitheater area, spacious hot tubs, and a recreation center complete with library, lectures, and meeting facilities.

33160 Evergreen Rd. (at Calif. 120), Groveland, CA 95321. ℭ 800/935-6343 or 209/379-2606. Fax 209/ 379-2607. www.evergreenlodge.com. 18 units. Apr–Oct $79–$89 double, $94–$109 cabin (with 1 queen and 2 single beds), $109–$124 2-bedroom cottage. Rates include continental breakfast. AE, DISC, MC, V. Closed in winter (until 2004). From San Francisco, take I-580 E. (which turns into I-205) to Manteca; take Calif. 120 E. through Groveland; turn left at Hetch Hetchy/Evergreen Rd. **Amenities:** Restaurant; bar; deli; heated outdoor pool and tennis courts at neighboring Camp Mather for day-use fee (summer only). *In room:* TV.

The Groveland Hotel ⭐   Constructed around 1850, this adorable historic hotel complements the surroundings of the Wild West–like town. Rooms are sweetly appointed with antiques as well as modern amenities, and the suite has a spa tub and fireplace. The staff is both friendly and accommodating. The most expensive, fanciest, and best restaurant in town is on the premises, and the super-cool Iron Door Saloon (the other place to eat well) is across the street. Smoking is not permitted in this hotel.

18767 Main St. (P.O. Box 289), Groveland, CA 95321. ℭ 800/273-3314 or 209/962-4000. Fax 209/962-6674. www.groveland.com. 17 units. $145–$165 double; $210 suite. Rates include extended continental breakfast. AE, DC, DISC, MC, V. Pets accepted. **Amenities:** Restaurant; nearby golf course; small game room; concierge; business center; secretarial service; limited room service; babysitting; laundry service. *In room:* A/C, TV/VCR in some units, dataport, minibar, coffeemaker, hair dryer, iron.

ARCH ROCK ENTRANCE

This is the most heavily used entrance to the park, offering easy access to the valley.

GETTING THERE   Arch Rock is 75 miles northeast of Merced. If you're driving from central California, take I-5 to Calif. 99 to Merced, then Calif. 140 east through El Portal.

   Greyhound (ℭ 800/229-9424; www.greyhound.com) and **Amtrak** (ℭ 800/USA-RAIL; www.amtrak.com) have routes to Fresno from many cities. **VIA Adventures** (ℭ 800/VIA-LINE or 209/384-1315; www.via-adventures. com) offers service from Merced Amtrak Passenger Station to Yosemite Valley Visitor Center and Yosemite Lodge. Coaches, which can be wheelchair lift equipped with advance notice, provide several round-trips daily between Merced and Yosemite.

WHERE TO STAY

Yosemite View Lodge   Once you've come this far, you're practically at the gate, so it's literally shocking to drive onto this gargantuan compound amidst the otherwise awesome natural surroundings. But the crowds need to stay somewhere, and this mega-motel under perpetual construction is scheduled to eventually offer around 500 rooms. The motel-style units include fridges, microwaves, and HBO; some offer kitchenettes, river views, balconies, and fireplaces. The indoor pool is very popular with kids. There's also a general store. The restaurant provides okay food, but it would be pricey for a family. If this place is booked, they also represent other properties in the vicinity, although they're not nearly as close to the entrance. Call ahead for information or check out the helpful website which also provides weather and road conditions.

11136 Hwy. 140 (P.O. Box D), El Portal, CA 95318. (C) **888/742-4371** or 209/379-2681. Fax 209/379-2704. www.yosemite-motels.com. 279 units. Apr–Oct $125–$155 double; Nov–Mar $82–$155 double. 2-night minimum during holidays. MC, V. Pets accepted with $5-per-night fee. **Amenities:** Restaurant; pizza parlor; lounge; indoor and outdoor heated pools; 4 Jacuzzis; tour and activities desk. *In room:* A/C, TV, fridge, kitchenette in some units.

SOUTH ENTRANCE

The South Entrance is 332 miles north of Los Angeles, 190 miles east of San Francisco, 59 miles north of Fresno, and 33 miles south of Yosemite Valley. Fish Camp and Oakhurst are the closest towns to the South Entrance at Wawona. This entrance to the valley leads through the Wawona Tunnel to the **Tunnel View** where you must stop to admire the panorama. If you've never been to Yosemite before, we promise this is the view you will never, ever forget.

GETTING THERE   If you're driving from Los Angeles, take I-5 to Calif. 99 north, then Calif. 41 north. Fresno-Yosemite International Airport, in nearby Fresno, is 93 miles south of Yosemite Village. The airport is served by Alaska Airlines, America West, American, Continental, Delta, Horizon, and United; all major car companies are represented at the airport. From the airport, take Calif. 41 north to the South Entrance.

VISITOR INFORMATION   Ask the **Yosemite Sierra Visitors Bureau,** 40637 Calif. 41, Oakhurst, CA 93644 (C) **559/683-4636;** www.yosemite-sierra.org), for a helpful brochure on the area, and be sure to check out its excellent online guide.

WHERE TO STAY & DINE

If you can't afford to eat at the opulent Erna's Elderberry House in Oakhurst (see below), try the pleasant **Three Sisters Café,** 39993 Hwy. 41 (C) **559/642-2253),** for breakfast, lunch, or dinner. For more dining and lodging options, contact the Visitors Bureau, above.

The Estate by the Elderberries ★★★   Its kudos say it all: five diamonds, five stars, and hailed by *Zagat* as one of the top three small hotels in the United States. This is the ultimate in luxurious lodging, decadent dining, and exclusivity, and it's only a 20-minute drive from the South Entrance to Yosemite along Calif. 41. The house—"built to look old"—dates only from 1991 and is set back off the road on the crest of a hill. From the renowned restaurant, a pathway leads through fragrant gardens to the house, which resembles a French château, complete with turret and terra-cotta tile roof.

The interior is exquisitely furnished with fine antiques, rugs, and fabrics. Each individually decorated room has a wood-burning fireplace and a wrought-iron balcony. Beds are covered in the finest Italian linens and down comforters; some rooms have whirlpool tubs. This is where Hollywood's elite often head for their escapes. Celebrities fleeing Los Angeles will be especially fond of the $2,800-per-night Villa Sureau ($2,500 without the butler), a two-bedroom, two-bathroom luxury villa with a library, full kitchen, and 24-hour butler service. The restaurant on the premises, **Erna's Elderberry House** (C) **559/683-6800),** is famous in its own right, offering impeccable food, ambience, and service. The six-course prix-fixe menu ($75) changes daily.

48688 Victoria Lane (P.O. Box 577), Oakhurst, CA 93644. (C) **559/683-6860.** Fax 559/683-0800. www. chateaudusureau.com. 10 units. $375–$550 double. Rates include full European breakfast. Extra person $75.

Moments White-Water Rafting on the Tuolumne

One of the most depressing facts about Yosemite tourism is that few folks do more than get out of their car, take a brief walk around the valley floor, "ooh" and "ah," snap some photos, and go back to their hotel. But if you really want to experience the wonders of the outdoors, contact **Ahwahnee Whitewater**, P.O. Box 1161, Columbia, CA 95310 (*©* **800/359-9790** or 209/533-1401; www.ahwahnee.com). Its rafting trips offer one of the best ways to truly interact with nature—especially if you're not the type to throw on a backpack and hoof it. The 1- to 3-day trips are ideal for white-water rebels in the spring (when the melting snow makes the ride most exciting) and for families later in the season. Although the trip doesn't go through the park, it's still an all-wilderness adventure—except they make the arrangements, provide and cook the food (gourmet by camping standards), steer the rafts, and practically hand you an experience you'll never forget. All you need to do is reserve well in advance, and if you're going on an overnight trip (highly recommended!), bring a tent, sleeping bag, and a few other camping accouterments—and get ready for a great time.

AE, DISC, MC, V. **Amenities:** Restaurant; bar; outdoor pool; nearby golf course; spa services; concierge; activities desk; 24-hr. room service; in-room massage; laundry service; same-day dry cleaning. *In room:* A/C, TV/VCR on request, CD player, hair dryer.

Hound's Tooth Inn ⟨★⟩   This bed-and-breakfast is in a great location for visitors to Yosemite as it's only 12 miles from the southern entrance. It has comfortable, pretty rooms (some with spas or fireplaces), and is decorated in a Victorian style with a mix of reproductions and antiques, wallpaper, lace valances, and original art. Our favorite rooms are the Hound's Tooth, with a king bed, fireplace, and view of the Sierra; and the Victorian Tower, with a romantic decor complete with white sheer netting, rattan chairs, and a spa. Kids are welcome by prior arrangement.

42071 Hwy. 41, Oakhurst, CA 93644. *©* **888/642-6610** or 559/642-6600. Fax 559/658-2946. www.hounds toothinn.com. 12 units, 1 cottage. $95–$175 double; $225 cottage. Extra person $20. Rates include full breakfast. AE, DC, DISC, MC, V. *In room:* A/C, TV/VCR, hair dryer, iron; kitchenette, minibar, fridge, and coffeemaker in some units.

The Narrow Gauge Inn   If you want to stay in a place that celebrates the mountain atmosphere, book a room at this very friendly inn, just 4 miles south of the park entrance. All of the super-clean motel-style units have a rustic cabin feel, complete with A-frame ceilings, little balconies or decks, antiques, quilts, and lace curtains; some have wood-paneled walls. The higher the price of the room, the cuter it gets. (Room nos. 16 through 26 are the best and most secluded; they look directly into forest.) There are hiking trails on the property, as well as a wonderfully old-fashioned, lodge-style restaurant and buffalo bar—serving "Old California Rancho Cuisine"—that's open daily (though seasonally) from 5:30 to 9pm.

48571 Calif. 41, Fish Camp, CA 93623. *©* **888/644-9050** or 559/683-7720. Fax 559/683-2139. www.narrow gaugeinn.com. 26 units. Apr–Oct $129–229 double; Nov–Mar $79–99 double. Extra person $10. Children under 6 stay free in parents' room. Rates include continental breakfast. DISC, MC, V. Pets accepted with $25 fee. **Amenities:** Restaurant (seasonal); bar; outdoor heated pool (seasonal); Jacuzzi (seasonal). *In room:* TV, dataport, coffeemaker.

Tenaya Lodge *(★★)* *(Kids)*   Tenaya Lodge is the best resort outside the southern entrance to Yosemite; it's particularly idyllic for families. Camp Tenaya for Kids has nature hikes, arts and crafts, games, and music 7 days a week Memorial Day to Labor Day and on Friday and Saturday evenings. The three- and four-story complex, which is run by the Marriott chain, is set on a 35-acre tract of forested land a few miles outside the national park. Inside, the decor is a cross between an Adirondack hunting lodge and a Southwestern pueblo, with a lobby dominated by a massive river-rock fireplace rising three stories. The ultramodern rooms definitely do the trick with nice furnishings and roomy, well-appointed bathrooms.

1122 Calif. 41, Fish Camp, CA 93623. (© **800/635-5807** or 559/683-6555. Fax 559/683-8684. www.tenaya lodge.com. 244 units. Winter from $149 double; summer from $249 double. Buffet breakfast $15 per person. Children 17 and under stay free in parents' room. AE, DC, DISC, MC, V. **Amenities:** 2 restaurants; deli; indoor and outdoor pools; 2 nearby golf courses; exercise room; full-service spa; indoor and outdoor Jacuzzis; bike rental; children's program; game room; video arcade; activities desk; business center; secretarial services; room service; massage; babysitting; laundry service; dry cleaning. *In room:* A/C, TV w/pay movies, dataport, minibar, fridge on request, coffeemaker, hair dryer, iron, safe.

2 Yosemite National Park *(★★★)*

Yosemite is a place of record-setting statistics: the highest waterfall in North America and 3 of the world's 10 tallest waterfalls (Upper Yosemite Fall, Ribbon Fall, and Sentinel Falls); the tallest and largest single granite monolith in the world (El Capitan); the most recognizable mountain (Half Dome); one of the world's largest trees (the Grizzly Giant in the Mariposa Grove); and literally thousands of rare plant and animal species. But trying to explain its majesty is impossible: This is a place you simply must experience firsthand.

What sets the valley apart is its incredible geology. The Sierra Nevada was formed between 10 million and 80 million years ago, when a tremendous geological uplift pushed layers of granite lying under the ocean up into an impressive mountain range. Cracks and rifts in the rock gave erosion a start at carving canyons and valleys. Then, during the last ice age, at least three glaciers flowed through the valley, shearing vertical faces of stone and hauling away the rubble. The last glacier retreated 10,000 to 15,000 years ago, but left its legacy in the incredible number and size of the waterfalls pouring into the valley from hanging side canyons. From the 4,000-foot-high valley floor, the 8,000-foot tops of El Capitan, Half Dome, and Glacier Point look like the top of the world, but they're small in comparison to the highest mountains in the park, some of which reach over 13,000 feet. The 7-square-mile valley is really a huge bathtub drain for the combined runoff of hundreds of square miles of snow-covered peaks (which explains why the valley flooded during the great storm of 1997).

High-country creeks flush with snowmelt catapult over the abyss left by the glaciers and form an outrageous variety of falls, from tiny ribbons that never reach the ground to the torrents of Nevada and Vernal falls. Combined with the shadows and lighting of the deep valley, the effect of all this falling water is mesmerizing. All that vertical stone gets put to use by hundreds who flock to the park for some of the finest climbing anywhere.

The valley is also home to beautiful meadows and the Merced River. When the last glacier retreated, its debris dammed the Merced and formed a lake.

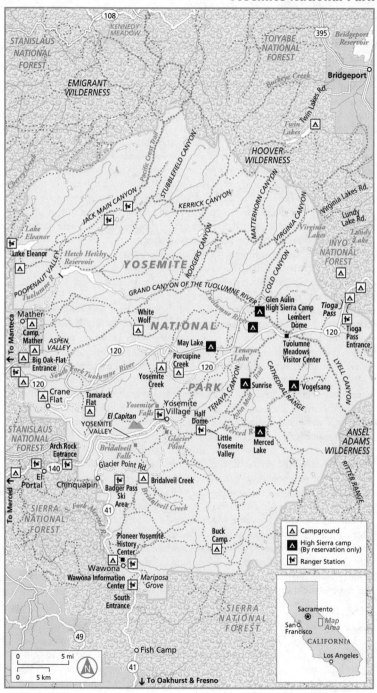

Legend:
- △ Campground
- ▲ High Sierra camp (By reservation only)
- 🏠 Ranger Station

Eventually, sediment from the river filled the lake and created the rich and level valley floor we see today. Tiny Mirror Lake was created later by rockfall that dammed up Tenaya Creek; the addition of a man-made dam in 1890 made it more of a lake than a pond. Rafters and inner-tubers enjoy the slow-moving Merced during the heat of summer.

Deer and **coyote** frequent the valley, often causing vehicular mayhem as one heavy-footed tourist slams on brakes to whip out the Handi-cam while another rubbernecker, also mesmerized, drives right into him. Metal crunches, tempers flare, and the deer daintily hops away.

Bears, too, are at home in the valley. Grizzlies are gone from the park now, but black bears are plentiful—and hungry for your food. Bears will rip into cars that have even the smallest treats inside, including things you think are safe inside your car's trunk. Each year as many as 500 bear-eats-car incidents occur, and several bears have had to be killed when they became too aggressive and destructive. If that doesn't deter you, you should know there is a fine of up to $5,000 for feeding park animals and your car can be impounded. There are food storage lockers throughout the park—please use them.

Right in the middle of the valley's thickest urban cluster is the **Yosemite Valley Visitor Center** (© 209/372-0200; www.nps.gov/yose), with exhibits that will teach you about glacial geology, history, and the park's flora and fauna. Check out the **Yosemite Museum** next door for insight into what life in the park was once like. Excellent exhibits highlight the Miwok and Paiute cultures that thrived here. The **Ansel Adams Gallery** (© 209/372-4413; www.adams gallery.com) displays the famous photographer's prints as well as other artists' works. You'll also find much history and memorabilia from the career of nature writer John Muir, one of the founders of the conservation movement.

While it's easy to let the tremendous beauty of the valley monopolize your attention, remember that 95% of Yosemite is wilderness. Of the four million visitors who come to the park each year, very few ever venture more than a mile from their cars. That leaves most of Yosemite's 750,000 acres open for anyone adventurous enough to hike a few miles. Even though the valley is a hands-down winner for dramatic freak-of-nature displays, the high country offers a more subtle kind of beauty: glacial lakes, roaring rivers, and miles of granite spires and domes. In the park's southwest corner, the Mariposa Grove is a striking forest of rare sequoias, the world's largest trees, as well as several meadows and the rushing south fork of the Merced River.

Tenaya Lake and Tuolumne Meadows are two of the most popular high-country destinations, as well as starting points for many great trails to the backcountry. Since this area of the park is under snow November through June, summer is really more like spring. From snowmelt to the first snowfall, the high country explodes with wildflowers and long-dormant wildlife trying to make the most of the short season.

ESSENTIALS

ENTRY POINTS   There are four main entrances to the park. Most valley visitors enter through the **Arch Rock Entrance** on Calif. 140. The best entrance for Wawona is the **South Entrance** on Calif. 41 from Oakhurst. If you're going to the high country, you'll save a lot of time by coming in through the **Big Oak Flat Entrance,** which puts you straight onto Tioga Road without forcing you to deal with the congested valley. The **Tioga Pass Entrance** is open only in summer and is only really relevant if you're coming from the east side of the Sierra (in which case it's your only choice). A fifth, little-used entrance is the **Hetch Hetchy Entrance** in the euphonious Poopenaut Valley, on a dead-end road.

FEES It costs $20 per car per week to enter the park or $10 per person per week. Annual Yosemite Passes are a steal at only $40. Wilderness permits are free, but reserving them requires a $5 fee per person. If you are 62 or older and you haven't purchased a lifetime Golden Age Passport for $10, what are you waiting for? You can apply for this passport here (or at any other national park or national forest), and you must show reasonable proof of age.

GAS There are no gas stations in Yosemite Valley, so be sure and fill up at a gas station before entering the park.

VISITOR CENTERS & INFORMATION There's a central, 24-hour recorded information line for the park (ⓒ **209/372-0200;** www.nps.gov/yose). All visitor-related service lines, including hotels and information, can be accessed by touch-tone phone at ⓒ **209/372-1000,** or at www.yosemitepark. com.

By far, the biggest visitor center is the **Valley Visitor Center** (ⓒ **209/372-0200).** The **Wawona Information Station** (ⓒ **209/375-9501)** gives general park information (closed in winter). For interesting biological and geological displays about the High Sierra, as well as trail advice, the **Tuolumne Meadows Visitor Center** (ⓒ **209/372-0263)** is great (closed in winter). All can provide you with maps, plus more newspapers, books, and photocopied leaflets than you'll ever read.

REGULATIONS Rangers in the Yosemite Valley spend more time being cops than being rangers. They even have their own jail, so don't do anything here you wouldn't do in your hometown. Despite the pressure, park regulations are pretty simple: Wilderness permits are required for all overnight backpacking trips; fishing licenses are required; utilize proper food-storage methods in bear country; don't collect firewood in the valley; no off-road bicycle riding; dogs are allowed in the park but must be leashed and are forbidden from trails; and *don't feed the animals.*

SEASONS Winter is our favorite time to visit the valley. It isn't crowded as it is in summer, and a dusting of snow provides a stark contrast to all that granite. To see the waterfalls at their best, come in spring when snowmelt is at its peak. Fall can be cool, but it's beautiful and much less crowded than summer. Sunshine seekers will love summer—if they can tolerate the crowds.

The high country is under about 20 feet of snow November through May, so unless you're snow camping, summer is pretty much the only season to pitch a tent. Even in summer, thundershowers are a frequent occurrence, sometimes with a magnificent lightning show. Mosquitoes can be a plague during the peak of summer, but the situation improves after the first freeze.

RANGER PROGRAMS Even though they're overworked just trying to keep the peace, Yosemite's wonderful rangers also take time to lead a number of educational and interpretive programs ranging from backcountry hikes to fireside talks to snow-country survival clinics. Call the main park information number with specific requests for the season and park area you'll be visiting. Also a great service are the free painting, drawing, and photography classes offered spring to fall at the Art Activity Center next to the Yosemite Museum Gallery in the valley.

AVOIDING THE CROWDS Unfortunately, popularity isn't always the greatest thing for wild places. Over the last 20 years, Yosemite Valley has set records for the worst crowding, noise, crime, and traffic in any California national park.

The park covers more than 1,000 square miles, but most visitors flock to the floor of Yosemite Valley, the 1-mile-wide, 7-mile-long glacial scouring that tore a deep and steep valley from the solid granite of the Sierra Nevada. It becomes a total zoo between Memorial Day and Labor Day. Cars line up bumper to bumper on almost any busy weekend. In 1995, Yosemite's superintendent closed the entrances to the park 11 times between Memorial Day and mid-August when the number of visitors reached the park's quota; she turned away 10,000 vehicles.

Our best advice is to try to come before Memorial Day or after Labor Day. If you must go in summer, do your part to help out. It's not so much the numbers of people that are ruining the valley, but their insistence on driving from attraction to attraction within the valley. Once you're here, park your car, then bike, hike, or ride the shuttle buses. You can rent bicycles at **Curry Village** (© 209/ 372-8319) and **Yosemite Lodge** (© 209/372-1208) in summer. It may take longer to get from point A to point B, but you're in one of the most gorgeous places on earth—so why hurry?

EXPLORING THE PARK
THE VALLEY

First-time visitors are often completely dumbstruck as they enter the valley from the west. The first two things you'll see are the delicate and beautiful **Bridalveil Fall** ✦✦ and the immense face of **El Capitan** ✦✦, a stunning and anything-but-delicate 3,593-foot-tall solid-granite rock. A short trail leads to the base of Bridalveil, which at 620 feet tall is only a medium-size fall by park standards, but one of the prettiest.

This is a perfect chance to get those knee-jerk tourist impulses under control early: Resist the temptation to rush around bagging sights like they're feathers for your cap. Instead, take your time and look around. One of the best things about the valley is that many of its most famous features are visible from all over. Instead of rushing to the base of every waterfall or famous rock face and getting a crick in your neck from staring straight up, go to the visitor center and spend a half-hour learning something about the features of the valley. Buy the excellent *Map and Guide to Yosemite Valley* for $2.50; it describes many hikes and short nature walks. Then go take a look. Walking and biking are the best ways to get around. To cover longer distances, the park shuttles run frequently around the east end of the valley.

If you absolutely must see it all and want to have someone tell you what you're seeing, the **Valley Floor Tour** is a 2-hour narrated bus or open-air tram tour (depending on the season) that provides an introduction to the valley's natural history, geology, and human culture. Fees are $21 for adults, $16 for kids ages 5 to 12, and kids under 5 tour for free, although they may have to sit on a parent's lap. Purchase tickets at valley hotels or call © 209/372-1240 for advance reservations.

Three-quarters of a mile from the visitor center is **The Ahwahnee Hotel** (p. 298). Unlike the rest of the hotel accommodations in the park, the Ahwahnee actually lives up to its surroundings. The native granite-and-timber lodge was built in 1927 and reflects an era when grand hotels were, well, grand. Fireplaces bigger than most Manhattan studio apartments warm the immense common rooms. Parlors and halls are filled with antique Native American rugs.

Don't worry about what you're wearing unless you're going to dinner—this is Yosemite, after all.

The best single view in the valley is from **Sentinel Bridge** ⚜ over the Merced River. At sunset, Half Dome's face functions as a projection screen for all the sinking sun's hues from yellow to pink to dark purple, and the river reflects it all. Ansel Adams took one of his most famous photographs from this very spot.

The **Nature Center at Happy Isles** ⚜ has great hands-on nature exhibits for kids, plus a wheelchair-accessible path along the banks of the Merced River.

VALLEY WALKS & HIKES   Yosemite Falls is within a short stroll of the visitor center. You can actually see it better elsewhere in the valley, but it's really impressive to stand at the base of all that falling water. The wind, noise, and blowing spray generated when millions of gallons catapult 2,425 feet through space onto the rocks below are sometimes so overwhelming you can barely stand on the bridge.

If you want more, the **Upper Yosemite Fall Trail** ⚜ zigzags 3½ miles from Sunnyside Campground to the top of Upper Yosemite Fall. This trail gives you an inkling of the weird, vertically oriented world climbers enter when they head up Yosemite's sheer walls. As you climb this narrow switchback trail, the valley floor drops away until people below look like ants, but the top doesn't appear any closer. It's a little unnerving at first, but braving it promises indescribable rewards. Plan on spending all day on this 7-mile round-trip trail because of the incredibly steep climb.

A mile-long trail leads from the Valley Stables (take the shuttle; no car parking) to **Mirror Lake** ⚜. The already tiny lake is gradually becoming a meadow as it fills with silt, but the reflections of the valley walls and sky on its surface remain one of the park's most unforgettable sights.

Also accessible from the Valley Stables or nearby Happy Isles is the best valley hike of all—the **John Muir Trail** ⚜⚜ to Vernal and Nevada falls. It follows the Sierra crest 200 miles south to Mount Whitney, but you only need go 1½ miles round-trip to get a great view of 317-foot Vernal Fall. Add another 1½ miles and 1,000 vertical feet for the climb to the top of Vernal Fall on the **Mist Trail** ⚜, where you'll get wet as you climb directly alongside the falls. On top of Vernal and before the base of Nevada Fall is a beautiful little valley and deep pool. For a truly outrageous view of the valley and one heck of a workout, continue on up the Mist Trail to the top of Nevada Fall. From 2,000 feet above Happy Isles where you began, it's a dizzying view straight down the face of the fall. To the east is an interesting profile perspective of Half Dome. Return either by the Mist Trail or the slightly easier John Muir Trail for a 7-mile round-trip hike.

Half Dome ⚜⚜⚜ may look insurmountable to anyone but an expert rock climber, yet thousands every year take the strenuous-but-popular cable route up the backside. It's almost 17 miles round-trip and a 4,900-foot elevation gain from Happy Isle on the John Muir Trail. Many do it in a day, starting at first light and rushing home to beat nightfall. A more relaxed strategy is to camp in the backpacking campground in Little Yosemite Valley just past Nevada Fall. From here, the summit is within easy striking distance of the base of Half Dome. If you plan to spend the night, you need a Wilderness Pass (see "Camping," below). You must climb up a very steep granite face using steel cables installed by the park service. In summer, boards are installed as crossbeams, but they're still far apart. Wear shoes with lots of traction and bring your own leather gloves for the cables (your hands will thank you). If there's any chance of a thunderstorm, the trail is closed—that cable turns into a lighting rod. The view from the top is an unbeatable vista of the high country, Tenaya Canyon, Glacier Point, and the awe-inspiring abyss of the valley below. When you shuffle up to the overhanging lip for a look down the face, be extremely careful not to kick rocks or anything else onto the climbers below, who are earning this view the hard way.

THE SOUTHWEST CORNER

This corner of the park is densely forested and gently sculpted in comparison to the stark granite that makes up so much of Yosemite. Coming from the valley, Calif. 41 takes you to **Tunnel View** ⋆⋆⋆, site of a famous Ansel Adams photograph, and the best scenic outlook of the valley accessible by car. Virtually the whole valley is laid out below: Half Dome and Yosemite Falls straight ahead in the distance, Bridalveil to the right, and El Capitan to the left.

A few miles past the tunnel, Glacier Point Road turns off to the east. Closed in winter, this winding road leads to a picnic area at **Glacier Point** ⋆⋆, site of another fabulous view of the valley, this time 3,000 feet below. Schedule at least an hour to drive here from the valley and an hour or two to absorb the view. This is a good place to study the glacial scouring of the valley below; the Glacier Point perspective makes it easy to picture the valley filled with sheets of ice.

Some 30 miles south of the valley on Calif. 41 are the **Wawona Hotel** (p. 298) and the **Pioneer Yosemite History Center.** The Wawona was built in 1879 and is the oldest hotel in the park. Its Victorian architecture evokes a time when travelers spent several days in horse-drawn wagons to get here. The Pioneer Center is a collection of early homesteading log buildings across the river from the Wawona.

One of the primary reasons Yosemite was first set aside as a park was the **Mariposa Grove** ⋆ of giant sequoias. (Many good trails lead through the grove.) These huge trees have personalities that match their gargantuan size. Single limbs on the biggest tree in the grove, the Grizzly Giant, are 10 feet thick. The tree itself is 209 feet tall, 32 feet in diameter, and more than 2,700 years old. Totally out of proportion with the size of the trees are the tiny cones of the sequoia. Smaller than a baseball and tightly closed, the cones won't release their cargo of seeds until opened by fire.

THE HIGH COUNTRY ⋆⋆⋆

The high country of Yosemite is stunning. Dome after dome of beautifully crystalline granite reflects the sunlight above deep-green meadows and icy-cold rivers.

Tioga Pass is the gateway to the high country. At times, it clings to the side of steep rock faces; in other places, it weaves through canyon bottoms. Several good campgrounds make it a pleasing overnight alternative to fighting summertime crowds in the valley, although use is increasing here, too. **Tenaya Lake** ⋆ is a popular windsurfing, fishing, canoeing, sailing, and swimming spot. The water is very chilly. Many good hikes lead into the high country from here, and the granite domes surrounding the lake are popular with climbers. Fishing here varies greatly from year to year.

Near the top of Tioga Pass is beautiful **Tuolumne Meadows** ⋆⋆. This enormous meadow covering several square miles is bordered by the Tuolumne River on one side and spectacular granite peaks on the other. The meadow is cut by many stream channels full of trout, and herds of mule deer are almost always present. The **Tuolumne Meadows Lodge** and store are a welcome counterpoint to the overdeveloped valley. In winter, the canvas roofs are removed and the buildings fill with snow. You can buy last-minute backpacking supplies here, and there's a basic burgers-and-fries cafe.

TUOLUMNE MEADOWS HIKES & WALKS   So many hikes lead from here into the backcountry that it's impossible to do them justice. A good trail passes an icy-cold spring and traverses several meadows.

On the far bank of the Tuolumne from the meadow, a trail leads downriver, eventually passing through the grand canyon of the Tuolumne and exiting at Hetch Hetchy. Shorter hikes will take you downriver past rapids and cascades.

An interesting geological quirk is the **Soda Springs** on the far side of Tuolumne Meadow from the road. This bubbling spring gushes carbonated water from a hole in the ground; a small log cabin marks its site.

For a great selection of Yosemite high-country hikes and backpacking trips, consult some of the specialized guidebooks to the area. Two of the best are published by Wilderness Press: *Tuolumne Meadows,* a hiking guide by Jeffrey B. Shaffer and Thomas Winnett; and *Yosemite National Park,* by Thomas Winnett and Jason Winnett.

SPORTS & OUTDOOR PURSUITS

BICYCLING   With 10 miles of bike paths in addition to the valley roads, biking is the perfect way to go. You can rent them at the **Yosemite Lodge** (*©* 209/ 372-1208) or **Curry Village** (*©* 209/372-8319) for $5.25 per hour or $20 per day. You can also rent bike trailers for little kids; $11 an hour or $33 a day. All trails in the park are closed to mountain bikes.

FISHING   The Merced River from Happy Isles downstream to the Pohono Bridge is catch-and-release only for native rainbow trout, and barbless hooks are required. Brown-trout limits are five fish per day and 10 in possession. Trout season begins on the last Saturday in April and continues through November 15. A California license is required and must be displayed by everyone 16 years old and over. **Licenses** are obtainable in the park at the Yosemite Village Sport Shop (*©* 209/372-1286).

HORSEBACK RIDING   Three stables offer scenic day rides and multi-day pack excursions in the park. **Yosemite Valley Stables** (*©* 209/372-8348) is open spring through fall. The other two—**Wawona** (*©* 209/375-6502) and **Tuolumne Stables** (*©* 209/372-8427)—operate only in summer. Day rides run from $40 to $80, depending on length. Multi-day backcountry trips cost roughly $100 per day and must be booked almost a year in advance. The park wranglers can also be hired to make resupply drops at any of the backcountry High Sierra Camps if you want to arrange for a food drop while on an extended trip. Log on to www.yosemiteparktours.com (click on "Summer Activities") for more information.

ICE-SKATING   In winter, the **Curry Village Ice Rink** (*©* 209/372-8341) is a lot of fun. It's outdoors and melts quickly when the weather warms up. Rates are $6.50 for adults and $5 for children. Skate rentals are available for $3.25.

ROCK CLIMBING   Much of the most important technical advancement in rock climbing came out of the highly competitive Yosemite Valley climbing scene of the 1970s and 1980s. Though other places have taken some of the limelight, Yosemite is still one of the most desirable climbing destinations in the world.

The **Yosemite Mountaineering School** (℄ **209/372-8344** or 209/372-8444; www.yosemitemountaineering.com) runs classes for beginners through advanced climbers. Considered one of the best climbing schools in the world, it offers private lessons for $170 per person per day, $90 for two people per day, $70 for three or more people per day, that will teach you basic body moves and rappelling, and will take you on a single-pitch climb. Classes run from early spring to early October in the valley, and during summer in Tuolumne Meadows.

SKIING & SNOWSHOEING   Opened in 1935, **Badger Pass** (℄ **209/372-8430;** www.yosemitepark.com/html/badgerpass.html) is the oldest operating ski area in California. It's nice for families. Four chairs and one rope tow cover a compact mountain of beginner and intermediate runs. At $31 for adults and $16 for children, it's a great place to learn how to ski or snowboard. There are naturalist-led winter children's programs and even babysitting.

Yosemite is also a popular destination for cross-country skiers and snowshoers. Both the Badger Pass ski school and the mountaineering school run trips and lessons for all abilities, ranging from basic technique to trans-Sierra crossings. There are two ski huts available on guided cross-country tours, including the spiffy **Glacier Point Hut** with its massive stone fireplace, beamed ceilings, and bunk beds; for information, call ℄ **209/372-8444.** Then there's the **Ostrander Hut** (℄ **209/372-0740**) with 25 bunks, and you have to pack in your own supplies. If you're on your own, Crane Flat is a good place to go, as is the groomed track up to Glacier Point, a 20-mile round-trip self-guided tour.

CAMPING
Campgrounds in Yosemite can be reserved up to 5 months in advance through the **National Park Reservation Service** (℄ **800/436-7275;** http://reservations. nps.gov). During the busy season, all valley campsites sell out within hours of becoming available on the service.

Backpacking into the wilderness and camping is always the least crowded option and takes less planning than reserving a campground. If you plan to backpack and camp in the wilderness, you must get a free **Wilderness Pass** (and still pay the park entrance fee). At least 40% of each trail head quota is allocated up to 24 hours in advance; the rest is available by mail. Write to the Wilderness Center, P.O. Box 545, Yosemite, CA 95389, and specify the dates and trail heads of entry and exit, principal destination, number of people, and any accompanying animals; include a $5 per person advance-registration fee. You may also secure a pass by calling ℄ **209/372-0740.**

VALLEY CAMPGROUNDS
Until January 1997, the park had five car campgrounds that were always full except in the dead of winter. Now the park has half the number of campsites available, and getting a reservation on short notice takes a minor miracle. (Yosemite Valley lost almost half of its 900 camping spaces in a freak winter storm that washed several campsites downstream and buried hundreds more beneath a foot of silt.)

The 2½ campgrounds that remain—**North Pines, Upper Pines,** and half of **Lower Pines**—charge $18 per night. All have drinking water, flush toilets, pay phones, fire pits, and a heavy ranger presence. Showers are available for a small fee at Curry Village. Upper Pines, North Pines, and Lower Pines allow small RVs (less than 40 ft. long). If you're expecting a real nature experience, skip camping in the valley unless you like doing so with 4,000 strangers.

Camp 4 (previously named Sunnyside campground) is a year-round, walk-in campground in the valley and fills up with climbers since it's only $5 per night. Hard-core climbers used to live here for months at a time, but the park service has cracked down on that. It still has a much more bohemian atmosphere than any of the other campgrounds.

CAMPGROUNDS ELSEWHERE IN THE PARK

Outside the valley, things start looking up for campers. Two car campgrounds near the South Entrance of the park, **Wawona** and **Bridalveil Creek,** offer a total of 210 sites with all the amenities. Wawona is open year-round, and reservations are required May through September; otherwise, it's first-come, first-served. Family sites at Wawona are $18 per night, and group sites, which hold up to 30 people, are $40 per night. Because it sits well above snow line at more than 7,000 feet, Bridalveil is open in summer only. Its rates are $12 per night for first-come, first-served sites, and $40 for group sites.

Crane Flat, Hodgdon Meadow, and Tamarack Flat are all in the western corner of the park near the Big Oak Flat Entrance. **Crane Flat** is the nearest to the valley, about a half-hour drive, with 166 sites, water, flush toilets, and fire pits. Its rates are $18 per night, and it's open June through September. **Hodgdon Meadow** is directly adjacent to the Big Oak Flat Entrance at 4,800 feet elevation. It's open year-round, charges $18 per night, and requires reservations May through September through the National Park Reservation Service. Facilities include flush toilets, running water, a ranger station, and pay phones. It's one of the least crowded low-elevation car campgrounds, but there's not a lot to do here. **Tamarack Flat** is a waterless, 52-site campground with pit toilets. Open June through October, it's a bargain at $8 per night.

Tuolumne Meadows, White Wolf, Yosemite Creek, and Porcupine Flat are all above 8,000 feet and open in summer only. **Tuolumne Meadows** ⭐ is the largest campground in the park, with more than 300 spaces, but it absorbs the crowd well and has all the amenities, including campfire programs and slide shows in the outdoor amphitheater. You will, however, feel sardine-packed between hundreds of other visitors. Half of the sites are reserved in advance; the rest are set aside on a first-come, first-served basis. Rates are $15 per night.

White Wolf, west of Tuolumne Meadows, is the other full-service campground in the high country, with 87 sites available for $18 per night for family sites, $40 for group sites. It offers a drier climate than the meadow and doesn't fill up as quickly. Sites are available on a first-come, first-served basis.

Two primitive camps, **Porcupine Flat** and **Yosemite Creek,** are the last to fill up in the park. Both have pit toilets but no running water, and charge $8 per night on a first-come, first-served basis.

Tips Securing Accommodations

All hotel reservations can be made exactly 366 days in advance. Call **Yosemite Concessions Services** at ℂ **559/252-4848** in the morning 366 days before your intended arrival for the best chance of securing your reservation. If you don't plan far in advance, it's good to call anyway—cancellations may leave new openings. Online reservations may be booked through **www.yosemitepark.com**. Keep in mind that reservations held without deposit must be confirmed on the scheduled day of arrival by 4pm. Otherwise, you'll lose your reservation.

WHERE TO STAY IN THE PARK

Yosemite Concessions Services, 5410 E. Home Ave., Fresno, CA 93727 (© 559/252-4848), operates all accommodations within the park and accepts all major credit cards. The reservations office is open Monday through Friday from 7am to 6pm, Saturday and Sunday from 8am to 5pm (PST). For more lodging options and information or to make an online reservation request, visit its website at **www.yosemitepark.com.**

An intriguing option bridging the gap between backpacking and staying in a hotel is Yosemite's five backcountry **High Sierra Camps** (© 559/253-5674). The five camps—Glen Aulin, May Lake, Sunrise, Merced Lake, and Vogelsang—make for good individual destinations. Or you can link several together, because they're arranged in a loose loop about a 10-mile hike from one another. Guests bunk dormitory-style in canvas tents; each camp has bathrooms and showers. Unguided stays cost $94 per night, per person; guided trips start at $375 for 4 nights (rates include breakfast and dinner). Due to the enormous popularity of these camps, reservations are booked by lottery. Applications are accepted from October 15 to November 30. The lottery is then held in December and the winning applicants are notified by the end of March.

The Ahwahnee Hotel ⭐⭐⭐ A National Historic Landmark noted for its striking architecture, the grand Ahwahnee is one of the most romantic and beautiful hotels in California. With its great lounge, grand gourmet dining room, outstanding views, and high-digit prices, it's a special-occasion sort of affair. Try to reserve one of the more spacious cottages, which cost the same as rooms in the main hotel. For the price you're paying, the hotel's guest rooms, although pleasant in warm woods and Indian motif fabrics, may seem simple to the point of austerity. On the other hand, when you can look out your window and see Half Dome, Yosemite Falls, or Glacier Point, why bother with fripperies?

© 559/252-4848. Fax 559/456-0542. www.yosemitepark.com. 99 units, 24 cottages. $366–$665 double. Children 12 and under stay free in parents' room. Extra person $21. AE, DC, DISC, MC, V. Pets not accepted, but there is a small kennel at the park stables. **Amenities:** Restaurant and lounge; heated outdoor pool; nearby golf course; 2 tennis courts; Jacuzzi; concierge; tour desk; room service; babysitting (need 2 weeks advance notice; child must be potty-trained and at least 2 years old). *In room:* A/C (ceiling fan in cottages), TV, fridge in cottages, coffeemaker, hair dryer, iron.

Curry Village (Kids) Accommodations at Curry Village, which celebrates its 104th birthday in 2003, range from a few motel-type rooms or heated wood cabins with private bathrooms to canvas tent cabins with central bathrooms. Ironically, the older wood cabins are the nicest. The tent cabins have wood floors and canvas walls. Without a real wall to stop noise, they lack any sort of privacy, but they're fun in that summer-camp sort of way. You'll have to sustain yourself with fast food from the village concessions, as no cooking is allowed in the rooms.

© 559/252-4848. Fax 559/456-0542. www.yosemitepark.com. 628 units. $54–$112 double. Children 12 and under stay free in parents' room. Extra person $8–$10, tent cabins $4. AE, DC, DISC, MC, V. **Amenities:** Buffet-style dining from spring to fall; fast-food court; heated outdoor pool; nearby golf course; bike rental; tour/activities desk. *In room:* No phone.

Wawona Hotel ⭐ If the Ahwahnee doesn't fit your plans or your pocketbook, the Wawona is the next best thing. Also a National Historic Landmark, the Wawona is a romantic throwback to another century. However, old-world charm has its ups and downs. Private bathrooms were not a big hit in the 19th century, rooms were small to hold in heat, there were no TVs or telephones, and walls were thin—and all of the above still applies today. Still, the Wawona is less commercial than other accommodations on the valley floor.

© 559/252-4848. www.yosemitepark.com. 104 units (52 with private bathroom). $101 double without private bathroom; $161 double with private bathroom. Children 12 and under stay free in parents' room. Extra person $17. AE, DC, DISC, MC, V. **Amenities:** Restaurant; outdoor pool; golf course; tennis court. *In room:* Iron, no phone.

Yosemite Lodge The next step down in valley accommodations, Yosemite Lodge is not actually a lodge but a large, more modern complex with two types of accommodations. The larger "Lodge" rooms with outdoor balconies have striking views of Yosemite Falls. Indeed the largest bonus—and curse—is that every room's front yard is the valley floor, which means you're near glorious larger-than-life natural attractions and equally gargantuan crowds.

© 559/252-4848. www.yosemitepark.com. 245 units. $112–$136 double. Children 12 and under stay free in parents' room. Extra person $10–$12. AE, DC, DISC, MC, V. **Amenities:** 2 restaurants; bar; food court; heated outdoor pool; nearby golf course; bike rental; tour/activities desk; babysitting.

3 Mammoth Lakes ★★

40 miles E of Yosemite; 319 miles E of San Francisco; 325 miles NE of Los Angeles

High in the Sierra, just southeast of Yosemite, Mammoth Lakes is surrounded by glacier-carved, pine-covered peaks that soar up from flower-filled meadows. It's an alpine region of sweeping beauty and one of California's favorite playgrounds for hiking, biking, horseback riding, skiing, and more. It's also home to one of the top-rated ski resorts in the world. At an elevation of 11,053 feet, Mammoth Mountain is higher than either Squaw or Heavenly so the snow stays firm longer in the year for spring skiing. You won't find the long lift lines that you find at Tahoe, either—there's more mountain and fewer people.

ESSENTIALS

GETTING THERE It's a 6-hour drive from San Francisco via Calif. 120 over the Tioga Pass in Yosemite (closed in winter); 5 hours north of Los Angeles via Calif. 14 and U.S. 395; and 3 hours south of Reno, Nevada, via U.S. 395. In winter, Mammoth is accessible via U.S. 395 from the north or the south.

Mammoth Air Charter (© 760/934-4279) offers charter flights to the area. It services Mammoth Lakes Airport on U.S. 395. The closest international airport is Reno-Tahoe Airport (© 775/328-6400). See "Lake Tahoe" in chapter 8 for airlines that service the Reno-Tahoe Airport.

VISITOR INFORMATION Contact the **Mammoth Lakes Visitors Bureau,** Calif. 203 (P.O. Box 48), Mammoth Lakes, CA 93546 (© **888/466-2666** or 760/934-2712; www.visitmammoth.com).

OUTDOOR PURSUITS

Mammoth Lakes is at the heart of several wilderness areas and is cut through by the San Joaquin and Owens rivers. Mammoth Mountain overlooks the Ansel Adams Wilderness Area to the west and the John Muir Wilderness Area to the southeast, and beyond to the Inyo National Forest and the Sierra National Forest.

The **Mammoth Mountain Ski Area** ★★ (© **888/462-6668** or 760/934-2571; www.mammothmountain.com) is the central focus for both summer and winter activities. Visitors can ride the lifts to see panoramic vistas; those who want an active adventure have a world of options. If you do hit the slopes in winter, you may want to use the free **Mammoth Area Shuttle** (MAS; www. mammothweb.com/shuttlemap) or **Mammoth Sierra Express** taxi service (© 760/934-TAXI) for transportation to and from town and the ski area. The shuttle makes convenient stops throughout town and eliminates the long wait you may encounter if you take your own car.

The park's recently renovated, state-of-the-art **Panorama Gondola** provides great viewing every day, winter or summer, weather permitting. Tickets are $17 for adults, $13 for seniors, $9 for children ages 7 to 12; kids under 7 ride free. The gondola carries eight passengers and stops midway up the mountain and at the summit with dazzling 360° views. In summer, you can use the gondola to gain access to the myriad hiking and biking trails on the mountain.

In addition to the activities described below, golf can be enjoyed at **Snowcreek Golf Course,** Old Mammoth Road (© 760/934-6633). Adventurers can also go hot-air ballooning with the **Mammoth Ballooning Co.** (© 760/934-7188).

HIKING   Trails abound in the Mammoth Lakes Basin area. They include the half-mile-long **Panorama Dome Trail,** which is just past the turnoff to Twin Lakes on Lake Mary Road, leading to the top of a plateau that provides a view of the Owens Valley and Lakes Basin. Another trail of interest is the 5-mile **Duck Lake Trail,** starting at the end of the Coldwater Creek parking lot with switchbacks across Duck Pass past several lakes to Duck Lake. The head of the **Inyo Craters Trail** is reached via a gravel road, off the Mammoth Scenic Loop Road. This trail takes you to the edge of these craters and a sign that explains how they were created.

For additional trail information and maps, contact the **Mammoth Ranger Station** (© 760/924-5500). For equipment and maps, go to **Footloose Sports Center,** at the corner of Canyon and Minaret (© 760/934-2400; www. footloosesports.com), which also rents in-line skates and mountain bikes.

HORSEPACKING TRIPS   The region is also an equestrian's paradise, and numerous outfitters offer pack trips. Among them are **Red's Meadows Pack Station,** Red's Meadows, past Minaret Vista (© 800/292-7758 or 760/934-2345); **Mammoth Lakes Pack Outfit,** Lake Mary Road, past Twin Lakes (© 760/934-2434), which offers 1- to 6-day riding trips and semiannual horse drives, plus other wilderness workshops; and **McGee Creek Pack Station,** McGee Creek Road, Crowley Lake (© 760/935-4324).

KAYAKING   Kayaks are available at Crowley Lake from **Caldera Kayaks** (© 760/935-4942; www.calderakayak.com), starting at $30 a day. This outfitter also offers tours on Crowley and Mono lakes and provides instruction as well.

MOUNTAIN BIKING   In summer, the mountain becomes one huge bike park and climbing playground. The bike park is famous for its **Kamikaze Downhill Trail,** an obstacle arena and slalom course where riders can test their balance and skill. Of course, there are also lots of trails for gentler folk who just want to commune with nature and get a little exercise. Bike shuttles will haul you and your bike to the lower mountain trails if you want to skip the uphill part, or the gondola will take you to the summit and you get down any way you can. There's also an area designed for kids. The park operates daily from 9am to 6pm, during summer months. A 1-day pass with unlimited access to the gondola, bike shuttle, and trail system is $28 for adults, $14 for kids ages 12 and under. There's a variety of rent-and-ride packages available; for more information, call © 800/MAMMOTH or visit www.mammothmountain.com.

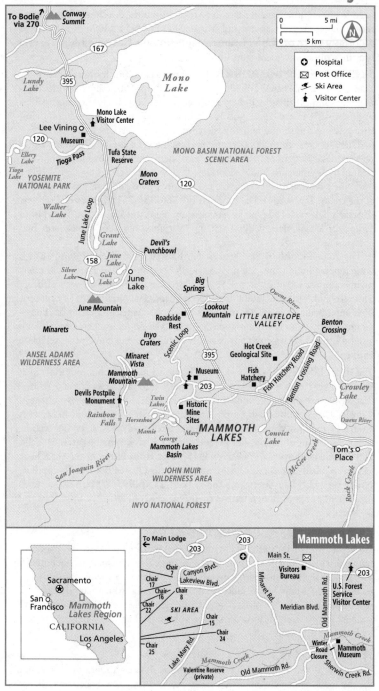

In town, mountain bikes can also be rented from the **Footloose Sports Center,** at the corner of Canyon and Minaret (℃ **760/934-2400;** www.footloose sports.com). The **NORBA National Mountain Bike Championships** are held here in summer.

SKIING & SNOWBOARDING   In winter, Mammoth Mountain has more than 3,500 skiable acres, a 3,100-foot vertical drop, 150 trails (32 with snow-making), and 30 lifts, including seven high-speed quads. The terrain is 30% beginner, 40% intermediate, and 30% advanced. It's known for power sun, ideal spring skiing conditions, and anywhere from 8 to 12 feet of snow.

There's a cross-country ski center at **Tamarack Lodge** (℃ **760/934-2442;** www.tamaracklodge.com), and for non-skiers there's snowmobiling, dog-sledding, snowshoeing, and sleigh rides.

If you're renting equipment, you'll save money if you do it in town instead of at the resort. Try **Sandy's Ski & Sports** (℃ **760/934-7518**), on Calif. 203 next to Schat's Bakery, for all types of winter equipment; and **Wave Rave Snowboard Shop,** on Main Street (Calif. 203; ℃ **760/934-2471**), for snowboards and accessories.

The **June Mountain Ski Area** ⚐ (℃ **888/JUNEMTN** or 760/648-7733; www.junemountain.com), 20 minutes north of Mammoth, is smaller and offers many summer activities. It has 500 skiable acres, a 2,590-foot vertical drop, 35 trails, and 8 lifts, including high-speed quads. The terrain is 35% beginner, 45% intermediate, and 20% advanced. It's at the center of a chain of lakes—Grant, Silver, Gull, and June—which can be viewed on a scenic driving loop around Calif. 158. It's especially beautiful in the fall when the aspens are ablaze with gold.

TROUT FISHING   Mammoth Lakes Basin sits in a canyon a couple of miles west of town. Here are the lakes—Mary, Mamie, Horseshoe, George, and Twin—that have made the region known for excellent trout fishing. Southeast of town, Crowley Lake is also famous for trout fishing, as are the San Joaquin and Owens Rivers. In addition, there are plenty of other lakes in which to spin your reel.

For fishing information and guides, contact **Rick's Sport Center,** at Calif. 203 and Center Street (℃ **760/934-3416**); **The Trout Fitter,** in the Shell Mart Center at Main Street and Old Mammoth Road (℃ **760/924-3676**); or **Kittredge Sports,** Main Street and Forest Trail (℃ **760/934-7566**), which rents equipment, supplies guides, teaches fly-fishing, and offers backcountry trips and packages.

EXPLORING THE SURROUNDING AREA

Bodie ⚐, one of the most authentic ghost towns in the West, lies about an hour's drive north of Mammoth, past the Tioga Pass entrance to Yosemite. In 1870, more than 10,000 people lived in Bodie; today, it's an eerie shell. En route to Bodie, you'll pass **Mono Lake** ⚐, near Lee Vining, which has startling tufa towers arising from its surface—limestone deposits formed by underground springs. It's a major bird-watching area—about 300 species nest or stop here during their migrations.

WHERE TO STAY

If you stay at the resort, you'll be steps from the lifts each morning. If you opt for the town, you're closer to the restaurants and nightlife. Regardless, they're within a 5-minute drive from each other, so whatever you choose, you're never too far from the action.

Tips **Winter Driving in the Sierra**

Winter driving in the Sierra Nevada Range can be dangerous. While the most hazardous roads are often closed, others are negotiable by vehicles with four-wheel-drive or with tire chains. Be prepared for sudden blizzards, and protect yourself by taking these important pre-trip precautions:

- Check road conditions before setting out by calling ✆ **800/427-7623.**
- Let the rental-car company you rent through know you're planning to drive in snow, and ask whether the antifreeze is prepared for cold climates.
- Make sure your heater and defroster work.
- Always carry chains. If there's a blizzard, the police will not allow vehicles without chains on certain highways. If you don't know how to put them on, you'll have to pay about $40 to have someone "chain up" your car at the side of the road.
- Recommended items include an ice scraper, a small shovel, sand or burlap for traction if you get stuck, warm blankets, and an extra car key (it's surprisingly common for motorists to lock their keys in the car while chaining up).
- Don't think winter ends in March. At the end of last April, snow was up to 7 feet high on the sides of the roads leading to the valley, and cold temperatures made more snowfall a very real possibility.

There are more than 700 campsites available in the area. These sites open on varying dates in June, depending on the weather. The largest campgrounds are at Twin Lakes and Cold Water (both in the Mammoth Lakes Basin), Convict Lake, and Red's Meadow. For additional information, call the **Mammoth Ranger Station** (✆ **760/924-5500**).

Holiday Inn ✯ This faux alpine lodge is Mammoth's newest hotel. A woodsy exterior with a river-rock base gives the three-story hotel a rustic appeal, while the interior boasts a more contemporary atmosphere. The generically decorated guest rooms contain all the comfort and amenities you could want, and come in variety of configurations, including a King/Kid suite with bunk beds. The suites offer a little extra room and Jacuzzi tubs. A spacious honeymoon suite caters to those who want romance in the great outdoors.

3236 Main St. (behind the Chevron station), Mammoth Lakes, CA 93546. ✆ **800/HOLIDAY** or 760/924-1234. Fax 760/934-3626. www.mammothholidayinn.com. 72 units. $129–$349 double and suite. Packages available. AE, DC, DISC, MC, V. **Amenities:** Cafe; bar; indoor heated pool; nearby golf course; exercise room; Jacuzzi; room service; coin-op laundry. *In room:* A/C, TV (VCR in some units), dataport, fridge, coffeemaker, kitchenette in some units, hair dryer, iron.

Mammoth Mountain Inn ✯ *Kids* Located opposite the ski lodge at the base of the ski resort, the inn started out in 1954 as only one building, but was expanded a decade later into a larger, glossier complex. Though it was remodeled in the early 1990s, it still retains the rustic charm you'd expect from a mountain resort. Rooms, which were recently upgraded with new carpets and furnishings, are well equipped and pleasantly furnished, but not exactly inspired. Families love this place for its day-care activities, cribs ($10 one-time charge), playground, box lunches and picnic tables, and game room. There's also an array of sports facilities, including bicycles, fishing or hiking guides, downhill or cross-country skiing, sleighing, horseback riding, and hay-wagon rides. Extras include free airport transportation and occasional entertainment.

Minaret Rd. (P.O. Box 353), Mammoth Lakes, CA 93546. ℂ **800/228-4947** or 760/934-2581. Fax 760/934-0701. www.mammothmountain.com. 173 units, 40 condos (some suitable for up to 13 people). Winter $125–$225 double; from $220–$535 condo. Summer $99–$150 double; from $150 condo. Ski and mountain-biking packages available. AE, MC, V. **Amenities:** Restaurant; bar; heated outdoor pool; nearby golf course; 2 indoor and 1 outdoor whirlpool spas; mountain-bike rental; day-care center; game room; video arcade; concierge; 24-hr. room service; babysitting; coin-op laundry; executive-level rooms. *In room:* TV (VCR in 1- and 2-bedroom units), dataport, coffeemaker, kitchen in some units, hair dryer, iron.

Motel 6 *(Value* The rooms may be small, but accommodations here are the nicest around in this price range. Although quarters are a bit more cramped than some other options, factor in the pool, vending machines, and free coffee in the lobby, and you've got all you really need to set up camp.

3372 Main St. (P.O. Box 1260), Mammoth Lakes, CA 93546. ℂ **800/4-MOTEL6** or 760/934-6660. Fax 760/934-6989. www.motel6.com. 151 units. Winter $50–$60 double; summer from $55 double. Extra person $6. AARP discounts. AE, DC, DISC, MC, V. Pets accepted (1 pet per room). **Amenities:** Heated outdoor pool (summer only); coin-op laundry. *In room:* A/C, TV, dataport.

Sherwin Villas *(Value* Just outside the center of town on Old Mammoth Road is this cluster of woodsy condos, perfect for larger families or groups of friends traveling together. Here you'll find one- to four-bedroom units, each with a fully stocked kitchen, fireplace, linens, and access to a free ski shuttle that will take you to the slopes (a 5-min. drive away). Considering how many people you can pack into these apartments—and that if you stay 4 weekday nights, the 5th night is free—it's a good deal. When making reservations, make sure you specify exactly what you're looking for; each condo is independently owned and varies dramatically in both decor and quality (you can see a few photos of each condo on their website).

362 Old Mammoth Rd. (P.O. Box 2249), Mammoth Lakes, CA 93546. ℂ **800/228-5291** or 760/934-4773. www.sherwinvillas.com. 70 condos. 1-bedroom unit for up to 4 people $100–$120 winter, from $95 summer; 2-bedroom loft for up to 6 people $140–$190 winter, from $115 summer; 3-bedroom unit for up to 8 people $155–$220 winter, from $135 summer; 4-bedroom unit for up to 10 people $195–$260 winter, from $155 summer. Extra person $10. MC, V. **Amenities:** Outdoor pool; tennis courts; 2 Jacuzzis; Finnish sauna; game room. *In room:* TV, kitchen, phone on request.

Sierra Lodge *(Value* In the heart of the resort town near the ski shuttle, this two-story inn offers clean, modern surroundings, rock-built fireplaces in the public areas, and a sincere effort to please its guests. Rooms are large and equipped with a kitchenette and utensils, but are unfortunately decorated in upscale-motel style. Still, everything is spotless and rooms have small patios or balconies. The newly added two-bedroom suite—equipped with two queen beds and a full-size pull-out sofa—is ideal for groups or families. Facilities include a fireside room for relaxing. Continental breakfast is the only meal served, but many restaurants are nearby.

3540 Main St. (Calif. 203; P.O. Box 9228), Mammoth Lakes, CA 93546. ℂ **800/356-5711** or 760/934-8881. Fax 760/934-7231. www.sierralodge.com. 36 units. $85–$159 double. Rates include continental breakfast. AE, DISC, MC, V. Pets accepted for $10 per night with $100 deposit. **Amenities:** Nearby golf course; outdoor Jacuzzi. *In room:* TV, dataport, kitchenette, fridge, hair dryer.

Tamarack Lodge & Resort   The lodge and cabin accommodations at this rustic lakeside retreat are nothing fancy, but that's exactly what's kept guests coming here since the 1920s. Folks relax in front of the fire in the sitting room or hang out in their rooms, which are intentionally rustic with knotty-pine walls and modern furnishings. The cabins, which can accommodate two to nine people, are dotted around the property and offer a variety of configurations, from studios with wood-burning stove and shower to two-bedroom/two-bathroom accommodations with fireplace. In the main lodge, there are rooms both with private bathrooms and with shared bathrooms. The lodge has a very popular cross-country ski center with more than 25 miles of trails and skating lanes, ski rentals, and a ski school. Boat and canoe rentals are also available. The dining room, overlooking Twin Lakes, offers California and Continental fare.

Twin Lakes Rd., off Lake Mary Rd. (P.O. Box 69), Mammoth Lakes, CA 93546. ℂ **800/MAMMOTH** or 760/ 934-2442. Fax 760/934-2281. www.tamaracklodge.com. 11 units, 6 with private bathroom; 27 cabins. $84–$230 double; $120–$350 cabin. AE, MC, V. **Amenities:** Restaurant; nearby golf course. *In room:* Fax, fridge, coffeemaker, kitchen in cabins, iron.

WHERE TO DINE

Nevados ★★ EUROPEAN/CALIFORNIA   What makes this restaurant a favorite with the locals? Well, owner/host Tim Dawson is on hand nightly to ensure that their every need is met, the innovative cuisine is fresh and home-made, and the tasty bread is house-baked. The clincher, though, is the fixed-price meal, which consists of a first course such as scallop-crab cakes, duck confit salad, or tuna sashimi; a main course featuring the likes of rosemary rack of lamb or grilled New York steak; and dessert (love that warm-pear-and-almond tart). Throw in the casual-but-sweet ambience (white tablecloths, candles, and French country murals) and the extensive selection of wines, single-malt scotches, and single-batch bourbons, and it's no wonder this is the hangout for ski instructors and race coaches.

Main St. (at Minaret Rd.). ℂ **760/934-4466.** Reservations recommended. Main courses $15–$25; fixed-price meal $33. AE, DC, DISC, MC, V. Daily 5:30–9:30pm.

The Restaurant at Convict Lake ★★ CONTINENTAL/FRENCH   After years of remaining a local secret, this place was awarded four-star status by ACCOMMODATIONS. With only 20 others in the state enjoying similar recognition, you can bet you'd better make reservations. The rustic-but-elegant dining room's ambience—surrounded by mountains amidst tiny wood cabins and a lake—makes for one heck of a special backdrop for this romantic dining diversion 5 miles south of the town of Mammoth Lakes. Within the woodsy, plank-sided cabin with a copper-hooded, freestanding fireplace and windows overlooking a forest of aspen, you can try such classic dishes as duck breast with Grand Marnier and sun-dried-cherry sauce, garnished with candied-orange zest. In season, the venison, pan-seared with kalamata olives, toasted cumin, and oven-dried tomatoes and served with a fine herb glaze, is worth the trip here.

Convict Lake Rd. ℂ **760/934-3803.** Reservations recommended. Main courses $14–$28. AE, MC, V. Summer daily 11am–2pm; year-round daily 5:30–9:30pm.

Shogun ★ JAPANESE   Sushi and tempura in an alpine setting may seem out of context, but this authentic Japanese restaurant, located on the second floor of a strip mall, consistently packs in both tourists and locals. Diners at the eight-seat sushi bar sup on sashimi, hand rolls, and a variety of sushi creations. Delicate tempura, sweet and tangy teriyaki dishes, and grilled yakitori skewers are offered individually or as combination dinners. Those with hearty appetites can order the Boat Dinner, which includes beef and chicken teriyaki, tempura, tonkatsu, sashimi or salmon, and dessert for $18 per person (minimum two people). Sake, beer, and cocktails are also available.

Old Mammoth Rd. (in the Sierra Center Mall). © 760/934-3970. Reservations recommended. Main courses $8.95–$18. AE, DC, DISC, MC, V. Mon–Sun 5–9:30pm.

Skadi ★★ ECLECTIC   The mini-mall where this restaurant is located (half a mile south of Mammoth Lake's center) may not be the home of the Viking goddess of skiing and hunting whose name this restaurant bears, but she wouldn't have cared once she saw the view—it encompasses most of the mountains for miles around. This universal favorite is perfect for an après-ski cocktail at the 14-seat bar, a snack from the substantial selection of appetizers and desserts, or a full-blown dinner on the town.

The decor has a big-city postmodern aura that's a welcome change after all that local alpine rusticity. Main courses are self-proclaimed "Alpine cuisine" and include such dishes as smoked trout Napoleon or grilled venison with lingonberries and a game sauce. Finish the evening with crème brûlée or the frozen macadamia-nut parfait.

587 Old Mammoth Rd. (in the Sherwin Plaza III shopping mall). © **760/934-3902.** Reservations recommended. Main courses $14–$22. AE, MC, V. Thurs–Sun 5:30–10pm.

Whiskey Creek AMERICAN   If you favor surf-and-turf fare combined with alpine atmosphere, you've found your dining spot. The building's wraparound windows encompass a view of the snow-clad mountains, and the menu is known for its beef, baby-back ribs, tequila shrimp, and lemon-garlic chicken. Although the dining room may offer a peaceful experience, the upstairs brewpub is a whole different world. The upstairs Mammoth Brewing Company and its live music (every night from 9pm until at least 1am) make this place the number one spot to mingle, slam suds, and get happy. (Think very crowded, post-collegiate frat party.) The cover ranges from free to $5.

24 Lake Mary Rd. (at Minaret Rd.). © **760/934-2555.** Reservations recommended. Main courses $12–$22. AE, DC, DISC, MC, V. Daily 5–10pm (summer 5:30pm); bar stays open until 2am.

4 Devils Postpile National Monument ★

10 miles W of Mammoth; 50 miles E of Yosemite's eastern boundary

Just a few miles outside the town of Mammoth Lakes, Devils Postpile National Monument is home to one of nature's most curious geological spectacles. Formed when molten lava cracked as it cooled, the 60-foot-high, blue-gray basalt columns that form the postpile look more like some sort of enormous eerie pipe organ or a jumble of string cheese than anything you'd expect to see made from stone. The mostly six-sided columns formed underground and were exposed when glaciers scoured this valley in the last ice age, some 10,000 years ago. Similar examples of columnar basalt are found in Ireland and Scotland.

Because of its high elevation (7,900 ft.) and heavy snowfall, the monument is open only from summer until early fall. The weather in summer is usually clear and warm, but afternoon thundershowers can soak the unprepared. Nights are still cold, so bring good tents and sleeping bags if you'll be camping. The Mammoth Lakes region is famous for its beautiful lakes—but unfortunately all that water also means lots of mosquitoes. Plan for them.

GETTING THERE

From late June to early September, cars are prohibited in the monument between 7:30am and 5:30pm because of the small roads' inability to handle the traffic. Visitors must take a shuttle bus to and from locations in the monument. While it takes some planning, the resulting peace and quiet are well worth the trouble and make you wonder why the park service hasn't implemented similar programs at Yosemite Valley and other traffic hot spots.

VISITOR INFORMATION   For information before you go, call © 760/934-2289 during open season, or © 760/872-4881 from November to May. You'll also find plenty of info at www.nps.gov/depo/depomain.htm.

HIKING

There's more to Devils Postpile than a bunch of rocks, no matter how impressive they might be. Located on the banks of the San Joaquin River in the heart of a landscape of granite peaks and crystalline mountain lakes, the 800-acre park is a gateway to a hiker's paradise. Short paths lead from here to the top of the postpile and to **Soda Springs,** a spring of cold carbonated water.

A longer hike (about 1¼ miles) from the separate Rainbow Falls Trailhead will take you to spectacular **Rainbow Falls** ⚘, where the entire middle fork of the San Joaquin plunges 101 feet from a lava cliff. From the trail, a stairway and short trail lead to the base of the falls and swimming holes below.

The **John Muir Trail,** which connects Yosemite National Park with Kings Canyon and Sequoia National Parks, and the **Pacific Crest Trail** both run through here. Named after the famous conservationist and author who is largely credited with saving Yosemite and popularizing the Sierra Nevada as a place worth preserving, the 211-mile John Muir Trail traverses some of the most rugged and remote parts of the Sierra. There are two accesses to it in Devils Postpile, one via the ranger station, the other from the Rainbow Falls Trailhead. From here, you can hike as far as your feet will take you north or south. *Note:* Mountain bikes are not permitted on trails.

CAMPING

While most visitors stay in or around Mammoth Lakes, the monument does maintain a 21-site campground with piped water, flush toilets, fire pits, and picnic tables on a first-come, first-served basis. Rates are $8 per night. Bears are common in the park, so take proper food-storage measures. Leashed pets are permitted on trails and in camp. Call the **National Park Service** (© 760/934-2289 or 760/872-4881 Nov–May; www.nps.gov/depo/depomain.htm) for details. There are several other U.S. Forest Service campgrounds nearby, including **Red's Meadow** and **Upper Soda Springs.**

5 En Route to Sequoia & Kings Canyon

Though **Visalia** is the official "gateway" and the city closest to Sequoia and Kings Canyon National Parks, it's still 40 minutes to the park entrance. Much closer to the entrance is the small town of **Three Rivers,** which until recently had little more than a few mediocre restaurants, coffee shops, and motels to offer visitors. That's changing with the opening of the **Shoshone Inn,** which has added 60 more hotel rooms in Visalia in addition to its two restaurants.

ESSENTIALS

GETTING THERE   If you're driving from San Francisco, take I-580 east to I-5 south to Calif. 198 east. The trip takes about 5 hours.

Amtrak (© **800/USA-RAIL;** www.amtrak.com) stops at nearby Hanford, and there's a shuttle from there to Visalia.

VISITOR INFORMATION   Contact the **Visalia Chamber of Commerce,** 720 W. Mineral King Rd, Visalia, CA 93291 (© **559/734-5486;** www.visalia chamber.org).

WHERE TO STAY

In Three Rivers try the **Holiday Inn Express,** 40820 Sierra Dr. (Calif. 198), Three Rivers, CA 93271 (© **800/HOLIDAY** or 559/561-9000), which has an outpost here. For other options, contact **The Reservation Centre** (© **559/561-0410;** www.rescentre.com).

Ben Maddox House ⚑   Set on a residential street of Victorian homes, 4 blocks from the town's main street, the Ben Maddox House is an impressive sight. Its triangular gable is punctuated with a round window and two extremely tall palm trees looming over the front yard. The house, built in 1876, is constructed of redwood, and its rooms retain their original dark-oak trim and white-oak floors. The six guest rooms contain 18th- and 19th-century furnishings, and the two front rooms have French doors leading to two small porch sitting areas. A full made-to-order breakfast is part of the treat.

601 N. Encina St., Visalia, CA 93291. © 800/401-9800 or 559/739-0721. Fax 559/625-0420. www.ben maddoxhouse.com. 6 units. $75–$90 single; $90–$110 double. Rates include breakfast. AE, DISC, MC, V. **Amenities:** Outdoor pool; nearby golf course. *In room:* A/C, TV w/free movies, dataport, fridge, hair dryer, iron.

Radisson Hotel   Seven blocks from the town center, the eight-story Radisson is the largest hotel in Visalia and a family favorite for those en route to Sequoia and Kings Canyon National Parks. Some of the attractively furnished rooms open onto balconies. This is not the most glamorous Radisson in California, but it's serviceable in every way. The restaurant serves breakfast, lunch, and dinner, with last seating at 10pm. The local bar provides entertainment on Friday and Saturday nights.

300 S. Court St., Visalia, CA 93291. © 800/333-3333 or 559/636-1111. Fax 559/636-8224. www.radisson. com/visaliaca. 201 units. $125–$150 double; $239–$469 suite. Extra person $15. Cribs provided free. AE, DC, MC, V. **Amenities:** Restaurant; bar; large pool; complete fitness center; Jacuzzi; bike rental; room service (until 2am); executive-level rooms. *In room:* A/C, TV/VCR w/pay movies, dataport, coffeemaker, iron.

WHERE TO DINE

The Vintage Press ⚑⚑ AMERICAN/CONTINENTAL   This has long been the best restaurant within a surrounding 100-mile radius, a culinary stopover of widely acknowledged merit in the gastronomic wasteland between Los Angeles and San Francisco. The design is reminiscent of a fin de siècle gin mill in gold-rush San Francisco, with a bar imported from that city manufactured by the Brunswick Company (of bowling-alley fame), lots of antiques bought at local auctions, and glittering panels of leaded glass and mirrors. The place is big enough (250 seats) to feed a boatload of gold-rush hopefuls and has a bustling bar and lounge where a pianist presents live music Thursday through Saturday from 5:30 to 9pm.

The menu is supplemented by daily specials—a zesty rack of lamb roasted in a cabernet sauce with rosemary and pistachios, for example. The regular menu offers about a dozen meat and fish dishes, with steaks as well as such choices as red snapper with lemon, almonds, and capers, or pork tenderloin with Dijon mustard, red chile, and honey. To start, I recommend farm-raised fresh oysters on the half shell or the wild mushrooms with cognac in puff pastry.

216 N. Willis St. ℂ **559/733-3033.** Reservations recommended. Main courses $13–$30. AE, DC, MC, V. Mon–Thurs 11:30am–2pm and 6–10:30pm, Fri–Sat 11:30am–2pm and 6–11pm, Sun 10am–2pm and 5–9pm.

6 Sequoia & Kings Canyon National Parks ★★

30 miles E of Visalia

Only 200 road miles separate Yosemite from Sequoia and Kings Canyon National Parks, but they're worlds apart. While the National Park Service has taken every opportunity to modernize, accessorize, and urbanize Yosemite, resulting in a frenetic tourist scene much like the cities so many of us strive to escape, at Sequoia and Kings Canyon, they've treated the wilderness beauty of the parks with respect and care. Only one road, the Generals Highway, loops through the area, and no road traverses the Sierra here. The park service recommends that vehicles over 22 feet long avoid the steep and windy stretch between Potwisha Campground and the Giant Forest in Sequoia National Park. Generally speaking, the park is much less accessible by car than most, but spectacular for those willing to head out on foot.

The Sierra Nevada tilts upward as it runs south. **Mount Whitney,** at 14,494 feet (the highest point in the lower 48 states), is just one of many high peaks in Sequoia and Kings Canyon. The **Pacific Crest Trail** also reaches its highest point here, crossing north to south through both parks. In addition to rocky, snow-covered peaks, Sequoia and Kings Canyon are home to the largest groves of giant sequoias in the Sierra Nevada, as well as the headwaters of the Kern, Kaweah, and Kings rivers. A few small, high-country lakes are home to some of

---

Tips **National Parks vs. National Forests: What You Don't Know Can Cost You**

Sierra, Inyo, and Sequoia national forests surround Kings Canyon and Sequoia national parks. What's the difference between a national park and a national forest? National parks are intended to strictly preserve natural and historic features, in addition to providing areas of easy-on-the-land recreation. National forests, on the other hand, operate under a multiple-use concept, sometimes including the harvesting of commodities such as lumber and minerals. National parks and national forests have different rules, and if you plan to travel in the area for a while you should know them. The same activity that's legal in a forest can earn you a fine in a park.

Parks forbid hunting; forests usually allow it. Dogs can be taken on forest trails, but not in parks. You can only camp in numbered sites in designated areas in parks; in the forest it's either campgrounds or, unless posted otherwise, near roadsides. You can ride your bike on a forest trail; in parks you must stay on the roads and helmets are required for persons 18 and younger. To protect the ecosystem in parks, you can't disturb anything—plants, pine cones, or rocks. In the forest, collecting a few things for personal use is permitted.

For more information, contact the **National Park Service** at ℂ **559/565-3341,** or the **Forest Service** at ℂ **559/784-1500.**

the only remaining pure-strain golden trout. Bears, deer, and numerous smaller animals and birds depend on the parks' miles of wild habitat for year-round breeding and feeding grounds.

Technically two separate parks, Sequoia and Kings Canyon are contiguous and managed jointly from the park headquarters at Ash Mountain, just past the entrance on Calif. 198 east of Visalia.

ESSENTIALS

Most visitors make a loop through the parks by entering at Grant Grove and leaving through Ash Mountain, or vice versa.

VISITOR INFORMATION The **Lodgepole** and **Grant Grove** visitor centers are the largest, with a full selection of park information and displays about the history, biology, and geology of this incredible place. Some time spent here will pay off by letting you decide which parts of the parks you most want to concentrate on. For visitor information before you go, log on to www.nps.gov/seki, www.sequoia-kingscanyon.com, or www.visitsequoia.com, or call © **559/565-3341.**

Park rangers offer hikes, campfire talks, and slide shows at several campgrounds and visitor centers during the summer.

FEES & PERMITS A $10-per-car fee is good for 7 days' entry at any park entrance. An annual pass costs $20; the Golden Age pass offers lifetime access for seniors 62 and over for $10; and blind or permanently disabled visitors get free entry with the Golden Access pass.

Wilderness permits are required for overnight backpacking trips in the parks. You can reserve the $10 permits in advance by writing the Wilderness Office, Superintendent, Sequoia and Kings Canyon National Parks, HCR 89 Box 60, Three Rivers, CA 93271 (© **559/565-3708**). You must reserve permits for climbing Mount Whitney via the Inyo National Forest. Reservations can be made by filling out an application form, preferably downloaded and printed from the park website (www.r5.fs.fed.us/inyo), and sending it to the Wilderness Reservations Office, Inyo National Forest, 873 N. Main, Bishop, CA 93514. At this writing, there is an experimental phone reservation system in progress. Reservations by phone will be accepted from 1 to 5pm Monday through Friday at © **760/873-2483.** Applications for the Mount Whitney trail are $15 a person.

REGULATIONS Mountain bikes and dogs are forbidden on all park trails (dogs are only permitted in developed areas, but must be leashed). The park service allows firewood gathering at campgrounds, although supplies can be scarce. Removing wood from living or standing trees is forbidden.

THE SEASONS In the high altitudes, where most Sequoia and Kings Canyon visitors are headed, the summers are short and the winters cold. Snow in July and August, although rare, is not unheard of. At mid-elevations, where the sequoias grow, spring can come as early as April and as late as June. Afternoon showers are occasional. In winter, only the main roads into the parks are usually open; the climate can range from bitter cold to pleasant and can change

---

⌐Tips **Fill 'er Up**

Note that there are no gas stations in the parks, so be sure to fill up your gas tank before you enter.

Sequoia & Kings Canyon National Parks

Map legend:
- △ Campground
- ⛨ Ranger Station

Inset (top right):
- Kings Canyon Nat'l Park, Bishop, Big Pine
- Independence
- Fresno
- Sequoia Nat'l Park
- Lone Pine
- Visalia, Three Rivers
- Highways: 41, 395, 180, 99, 245, 198, 190

California inset:
- Sacramento
- San Francisco
- Map Area
- CALIFORNIA
- Los Angeles

Main map labels:

- JOHN MUIR WILDERNESS
- Desolation Lake
- McClure Meadow
- Lake Sabrina
- South Lake
- INYO NATIONAL FOREST
- South Fork San Joaquin River
- LE CONTE DIVIDE
- Wanda Lake
- Martha Lake
- Le Conte Canyon
- Glacier Lodge
- JOHN MUIR WILDERNESS AREA
- Wishon Reservoir
- SIERRA NATIONAL FOREST
- John Muir & Pacific Crest Trail
- SIMPSON MEADOW
- Middle Fork Kings River
- Kings River
- MONARCH WILDERNESS AREA
- KINGS CANYON NATIONAL PARK
- KINGS CANYON
- Rae Lakes
- 180
- Hume Lake
- Grant Grove Visitor Center
- Big Stump Entrance
- Cedar Grove Village
- Road's End
- PARADISE VALLEY
- ←To Fresno
- Redwood Mountain Grove
- KINGS CANYON NATIONAL PARK
- JENNIE LAKES WILDERNESS AREA
- Generals Hwy
- Stony Creek
- Dorst
- Crystal Cave (Open Summer Only)
- 198
- Lodgepole Visitor Center
- Giant Forest Village
- General Sherman Tree
- Roaring River
- Charlotte Lake
- DEADMAN CANYON
- CLOUD CANYON
- KERN-KINGS DIVIDE
- Tyndall Creek
- Potwisha
- 198
- Middle Fork Kaweah R.
- Bearpaw Meadow
- GREAT WESTERN DIVIDE
- Ash Mtn.
- Buckeye Flat
- Ash Mountain Park Headquarters
- ←To Visalia
- Three Rivers
- SEQUOIA NATIONAL PARK
- Atwell Mill
- Silver City
- Mineral King
- Little Five Lakes
- Mt. Whitney
- Crabtree
- KERN CANYON
- Kern River
- Pacific Crest Trail
- Rock Creek
- Lookout Point
- Hockett Meadow
- GREAT WESTERN DIVIDE
- South Fork
- Kern Canyon
- INYO NATIONAL FOREST
- SEQUOIA NATIONAL FOREST

Scale: 5 mi / 5 km

minute by minute. The Generals Highway between Sequoia and Kings Canyon closes for plowing during and after snowstorms. Be ready for anything if you head into the backcountry on skis. In summer, poison oak and rattlesnakes are common in lower elevations, and mosquitoes are plentiful in all wet areas.

AVOIDING THE CROWDS   To escape the crowds and see less-used areas of the parks, enter on one of the dead-end roads to Mineral King or Cedar Grove (both open only in summer), or South Fork. The lack of through traffic makes these parts of the parks incredibly peaceful even at full capacity, and they're gateways to some of the best hiking.

EXPLORING THE PARKS

There are some 75 groves of giant sequoias in the parks, but the easiest places to see the trees are **Grant Grove** , in Kings Canyon near the park entrance on Calif. 180 from Fresno, or **Giant Forest** , a huge grove of trees containing 40 miles of footpaths, located 16 miles from the entrance to Sequoia National Park on Calif. 198. Saving the sequoias was one of the reasons Sequoia National Park was created in 1890 at the request of San Joaquin Valley residents, making it the second-oldest national park in the United States.

The 2-mile **Congress Trail** loop in Giant Forest starts at the base of the **General Sherman Tree** , the largest living thing in the world. Single branches of this monster are more than 7 feet thick. Each year, it grows enough wood to make a 60-foot-tall tree of normal dimensions. Other trees in the grove are nearly as large, and many of the peaceful-looking trees have also been saddled with strangely militaristic and political monikers like General Lee and Lincoln. Longer trails lead to remote reaches of the grove and nearby meadows.

Unlike the coast redwoods, which reproduce by sprouting or by seeds, giant sequoias only reproduce by seed. Adult sequoias rarely die of diseases and are protected from most fire by thick bark. The huge trees have surprisingly shallow roots, and most die from toppling when their roots are damaged for some reason and can no longer support them. These groves, like the ones in Yosemite, were explored by conservationist and nature writer John Muir, who named the Giant Forest.

Besides the sequoia groves, Sequoia and Kings Canyon are home to the most pristine wilderness in the Sierra Nevada. At **Road's End** on the Kings Canyon Highway (open from late May to early Nov), you can stand by the banks of the Kings River and stare up at granite walls rising thousands of feet above the river, the deepest canyon in the United States.

Near Giant Forest Village, **Moro Rock** is a 6,725-foot-tall granite dome formed by exfoliation of layers of the rock. A ¼-mile trail scales the dome for a spectacular view of the adjacent Canyon of the Middle Fork of the Kaweah. The trail gains 300 feet in 400 yards, so be ready for a climb.

Crystal Cave is located 15 miles from the Calif. 198 park entrance and an additional 7 miles to cave parking. Here you can take a 50-minute tour of Crystal's beautiful marble interior. The tour is $8 for adults, $6 for seniors, $4 for children ages 6 to 12, and free for kids 6 and under. Tickets are not sold at the cave and must be purchased at the Lodgepole or Foothills visitor centers at least 1½ hours in advance. Be sure to wear sturdy shoes and bring a jacket. For information, call © 559/565-3759 or log on to www.sequoiahistory.org. The cave is open mid-May to late September daily from 11 am to 4pm.

Boyden Cavern, on Calif. 180 in neighboring Sequoia National Forest, is a large cave where you can take a 45-minute tour to see stalactites and stalagmites.

A fee is charged; call ✆ **209/736-2708** for details or check the website at www.caverntours.com. The cave is open April through October daily from 10am to 5pm.

HIKING THE PARKS

Hiking and backpacking are what these parks are really all about. Some 700 miles of trails connect canyons, lakes, and high alpine meadows and snowfields.

When traveling overnight inside the parks' boundaries, overnight and/or day-use permits are required. If you want to do serious overnight backpacking, see "Fees & Permits" under "Essentials," above.

Some of the park's most impressive hikes start in the **Mineral King** section in the southern end of Sequoia. Beginning at 7,800 feet, trails lead onward and upward to destinations like Sawtooth Pass, Crystal Lake, and the old White Chief Trail to the now-defunct White Chief Mine. Once an unsuccessful silver-mining town in the 1870s, Mineral King was the center of a pitched battle in the late 1970s when developers sought to build a huge ski resort here. They were defeated when Congress added Mineral King to Sequoia National Park, and the wilderness remains unspoiled.

The **John Muir Trail,** which begins in Yosemite Valley, ends at Mount Whitney. For many miles it coincides with the **Pacific Crest Trail** as it skirts the highest peaks in the park. This is the most difficult part of the Pacific Crest, remaining above 10,000 feet most of the time and crossing 12,000-foot-tall passes.

Other hikers like to explore the northern part of Kings Canyon from **Cedar Grove** and **Road's End.** The **Paradise Valley Trail,** leading to beautiful Mist Falls, is a fairly easy day trip by park standards. The **Copper Creek Trail** immediately rises into the high wilderness around Granite Pass at 10,673 feet, one of the most strenuous day hikes in the parks.

If the altitude and steepness are too much for you at these trail heads, try some of the longer hikes in **Giant Forest** or **Grant Grove.** These forests are woven with interlocking loops that allow you to take as short or as long a hike as you want. The 6-mile **Trail of the Sequoias** in Giant Forest will take you to the grove's far-eastern end, where you'll find some of the finest trees. In Grant Grove, a 100-foot walk through the hollow trunk of the **Fallen Monarch** makes a fascinating side trip. The tree has been used for shelter for more than 100 years and is tall enough inside that you can walk through without bending over.

Perhaps the most traversed trail to the park is the **Whitney Portal Trail.** It runs from east of Sequoia near Lone Pine, through Inyo National Forest, to Sequoia's boundary, the summit of Mount Whitney. Though it's a straightforward walk to the summit and it's possible to bag it in a very long day hike, you'd better be in really good shape before attempting it. Almost half the people who attempt Whitney, including those who camp partway up, don't reach the summit. Weather, altitude, and fatigue can conspire to stop even the most prepared party. For more information, you can contact the **Mount Whitney Ranger Station** at ✆ **760/876-6200.** For wilderness permits, see "Essentials: Fees & Permits" at the beginning of this section.

The official park map and guide has good road maps for the parks, but for serious hiking you'll want to check out *Sierra South: 100 Back-Country Trips,* by Thomas Winnett and Jason Winnett (Wilderness Press). Another good guide is *Kings Canyon Country,* a hiking handbook by Ginny and Lew Clark. The Grant Grove, Lodgepole, Cedar Grove, Foothills, and Mineral King visitor centers all sell a complete selection of maps and guidebooks to the parks. Books and maps are also available by mail through the **Sequoia Natural History Association** (© 559/565-3759; www.sequoiahistory.org).

OTHER OUTDOOR PURSUITS

FISHING   Trout fishing in the lower altitudes is fairly limited; most fishing takes place along the banks of the Kings and Kaweah rivers. A few high-country lakes are refuges for trout and are not stocked with hatchery fish. Before venturing into the high country, inquire at a ranger station about the area you'll be visiting to find out about closures or specific regulations. A California fishing license is required for everyone over 16 years old. Tackle and licenses are available at several park stores.

RAFTING & KAYAKING   Only fairly recently have professional outfitters begun taking experienced rafters and kayakers down the Class IV and V Kaweah and Upper Kings Rivers outside the parks. Check **The Reservation Center** website at **www.sequoiapark.com** for a good list of companies running trips. Rafting and kayaking here are only for the very adventurous.

SKIING & SNOWSHOEING   **Wolverton,** 2 miles north of the General Sherman tree, has a snow-play and cross-country ski area. You can rent skis and snowshoes at the Lodgepole Market. In the **Giant Forest** and **Grant Grove** areas, there are about 50 miles of marked cross-country trails. Rangers offer naturalist talks and snowshoe walks some weekends. Rental equipment (including snowshoes) and lessons are available at the Grant Grove Market. For more information on cross-country skiing, sledding, or snowshoeing at Grant Grove, call © **559/335-5500;** for Wolverton, call © **559/565-3435.** Kids can sled and play in the snow-play areas near Wolverton and at Big Stump, Columbine, and Azalea in Grant Grove.

The Sequoia Natural History Association operates the **Pear Lake Ski Hut** for snowshoers and cross-country skiers, which can accommodate up to 10 people. Use of the facility is by lottery. For further information, call © **559/565-3759.**

CAMPING

There are 13 campgrounds in the parks, offering the most convenient and economical accommodations here, although none have hookups. Only two accept reservations: **Lodgepole Campground** and **Dorst Campground** in Sequoia (© **800/365-2267**). Both are close to Giant Forest. Lodgepole is within a short stroll of a restaurant, market, showers, laundry, and visitor center. With more than 200 sites each, they tend to be the noisiest campgrounds in Sequoia. Lodgepole charges $14 per night and Dorst charges $16 per night. Other campgrounds are first-come, first-served, and often fill up on weekends. Three campgrounds—Azalea, Lodgepole, and Potwisha—are open year-round. The rest are open from snowmelt through September. Call © **559/565-3341** for camping information. Even in summer, campers should prepare for rain and cold temperatures. Bring a good tent and warm sleeping bags. Also note that due to bears, proper food storage is required.

Smaller and more peaceful are **South Fork, Potwisha, Buckeye Flat, Atwell Mill,** and **Cold Springs.** Atwell Mill and Cold Springs have pit toilets and cost $8 per night. Potwisha and Buckeye Flat, with flush toilets and sinks, charge $14. South Fork, with pit toilets and no drinking water, charges $8.

Campers in the remote Cedar Grove area of Kings Canyon National Park in the Kings River gorge can choose from **Moraine, Sentinel, Sheep Creek,** and

Canyon View, which also has a group camp. All four have flush toilets and are convenient to some of the parks' best hiking. Sites cost $14. The small **Cedar Grove Village** offers a restaurant, motel, showers, and store. Sites cost $14.

Three campgrounds in the Grant Grove area will put you near the sequoias without the noise and crowds of Giant Forest Village. All three—**Sunset, Azalea,** and **Crystal Springs**—have flush toilets and phones. The area has an RV disposal site, a visitor center, and showers nearby. The charge is $14 per site.

WHERE TO STAY IN THE PARKS

Lodging in the parks ranges from rustic cabins with no bathrooms or heat to brand-new rooms with all the modern comforts (well, maybe not all—hot tubs aren't mentioned anywhere). New structures are increasing both the numbers of rooms available and the general comfort level. There are a dizzying array of types of rooms and cabins with prices that change seasonally. Your best bet is to check online for the location and accommodation that best suits your needs, and then call for the current price. **Lodging** in Kings Canyon is operated by the park concessionaire, Kings Canyon Park Services Co., P.O. Box 909, Kings Canyon National Park, CA 93633 (© **559/335-5500** for information and reservations; www.sequoia-kingscanyon.com).

Cedar Grove Lodge on the Kings River in the eastern section of Kings Canyon in Cedar Grove Village has 18 motel-style rooms and is open from early May to early October. Each room has two queen-size beds and a private bathroom. Grant Grove Village, on Calif. 180, 30 miles northwest of Giant Forest, offers a variety of cabins with private or shared bathrooms and tent cabins. The newest lodge in Kings Canyon is named after John Muir, and has 30 rooms, each with two queen beds and a private bathroom. The lodge features an extensive collection of Muir's writings, and paintings and photographs of his journeys decorate the walls.

Sequoia National Park is in the process of eliminating the old lodgings at Giant Forest and replacing them with new facilities. The attractive **Wuksachi Village & Lodge** ⓐ, 64740 Wuksachi Way in Lodgepole (© **888/252-5757** or 559/565-0340; www.visitsequoia.com), is Sequoia's most recent addition. It's open year-round, offering 102 rooms within the park from $86 to $123 off-season, and from $150 to $219 during peak season (Apr 1–Nov 30). Each room in the cedar-and-stone, mountain-themed lodge has two queens or a king and a sofa bed. Children under 12 can stay free in their parents' room. The Wuksachi Lodge dining room serves surprisingly good lunches and dinners, including a thoughtful kids' menu. The lodge offers winter ski promotions such as cross-country skis or snowshoes for two adults as part of the room rates. Unfortunately, you have to leave your (four-legged) furry friends at home.

10

Sacramento, the Gold Country & the Central Valley

by Matthew Richard Poole

On the morning of January 24, 1848, a carpenter named James Marshall was working on John Sutter's mill in Coloma when he made an exciting discovery: He stumbled upon a gold nugget on the south fork of the American River. Despite Sutter's wishes to keep the find a secret, word leaked out—a word that would change the fate of California almost overnight: *Gold!*

The news spread like wildfire, and a frenzy seized the nation: The gold rush was on. Within 3 years, the population of the state grew from a meager 15,000 to more than 265,000. Most of these newcomers were single men under the age of 40, and not far behind were the thousands of merchants, bankers, and women who made their fortunes catering to the miners, most of whom went bust in their search for instant wealth.

Sacramento grew quickly as a supply town at the base of the surrounding goldfields. The Gold Country boom lasted less than a decade; the gold supply was quickly exhausted, and many towns shrank or disappeared. Sacramento, however, continued to grow as the fertile Central Valley south of it exploited another source of wealth, becoming the vegetable and fruit garden of the nation.

A trip along Calif. 49 from the northern mines to the southern mines will give visitors a sense of what life might have been like on the rough mining frontier. Many of the small towns along this route seem frozen in time, right down to Main Street with its raised wooden sidewalks, double-porched buildings, ornate saloons, and Victorian storefronts. Each town tells a similar story of sudden wealth and explosive growth, yet each has also left behind its own unique imprint. Any fan of movie westerns will recognize the setting—hundreds, perhaps even thousands, of films have been shot in these parts.

At the base of the Gold Country's rolling hills is the sprawling and decidedly flat Central Valley. Some 240 miles long and 50 miles wide, it's California's agricultural breadbasket, the source of much of the bounty that is shipped across the nation and overseas. Much of the history of California has revolved around the struggle for control of the water used to irrigate the valley and make this inland desert bloom. Despite the scarcity of water (it receives less than 10 in. of rainfall per year), a breathtaking panorama of orange and pistachio groves, grapevines, and strawberry fields stretches uninterrupted for miles.

1 Sacramento 🌟

90 miles E of San Francisco; 383 miles N of Los Angeles

Sacramento, with a metropolitan population of nearly 1.7 million, is one of the state's fastest growing areas. In addition to being the state capital, it is a thriving shipping and processing center for the fruit, vegetables, rice, wheat, and dairy goods that are produced in the fertile Central Valley. In the past decade, it's also become an area of high-tech spillover from Silicon Valley, and more recently, a suburb for Bay Area workers seeking affordable homes. The quantity and quality of emerging downtown restaurants—such as the new Esquire Grill and The Waterboy—have greatly improved as well. This prosperous and politically charged city has broad, tree-shaded streets lined with some impressive Victorians and well-crafted bungalows. At its heart sits the capitol building—Sacramento's most visible attraction—in a large, perfectly kept park replete with flower gardens, memorial statuary, and curious squirrels.

Sacramento is far from a tourist town, but it does have its share of touristy activities. Visitors and locals alike enjoy spending the day walking through Old Sacramento, floating down the American River, or biking the shady paths along the Sacramento and American rivers. Locals fondly refer to their water-bordered town as "River City." And did we mention that in summer the weather is seriously hot? So much so that San Franciscans drive to Sacramento just to thaw out.

ESSENTIALS

GETTING THERE   If you're driving from San Francisco, Sacramento is located about 90 miles east on I-80. From Los Angeles, take I-5 through the Central Valley directly into Sacramento. From North Lake Tahoe, get on I-80 west, and from South Lake Tahoe take U.S. 50.

Sacramento International Airport (© 916/929-5411), 12 miles northwest of downtown Sacramento, is served by about a dozen airlines, including American, Alaska Airlines, America West, Continental, Delta, Northwest, Southwest, and United. **Taxi and Shuttle Service** (© 916/362-5525) will get you from the airport to downtown; it charges a flat rate of $15 to the capital, a bargain compared to the $25 a conventional taxi would cost.

Amtrak (© 800/USA-RAIL; www.amtrak.com) trains serve Sacramento daily. The Greyhound terminal is at 7th and L streets.

VISITOR INFORMATION   The **Sacramento Convention and Visitors Bureau,** 1303 J St., Sacramento, CA 95814 (© 916/264-7777; www.sacramentocvb.org), provides plenty of helpful information for travelers. It's open Monday through Friday from 8am to 5pm. Once in the city, you can also stop by the **Old Sacramento Visitor Center,** 1101 Second St. (© 916/442-7644), in Old Sacramento; it's usually open daily from 10am to 5pm. The city's major daily paper is the *Sacramento Bee* (www.sacbee.com).

ORIENTATION   Suburbia sprawls around Sacramento, but its downtown area is relatively compact. Getting around the city is made easy by a grid-like pattern of streets that are designated by numbers or letters. The capitol building, on 10th Street between N and L streets, is the key landmark. From the front of the capitol, M Street—which is at this point called Capitol Mall—runs 10 straight blocks to Old Sacramento, the oldest section of the city.

Kids Where the Wild Things Are

The best place to take little kids to let them tear around on a sunny afternoon in Sacramento is **Fairytale Town,** at William Land Park, Land Park Drive and Sutterville Road (© **916/264-5233**). Although the slides and other climbing toys are pretty basic and showing their age, little ones seem to think it's the best place in the world. After you've explored every nook and cranny, cross the street to the **Sacramento Zoo** (© **916/264-5885**), buy a big spool of cotton candy, and see the animals. Adjacent to Fairytale Town, there's also the small but pleasant **Funderland** amusement park (© **916/456-0115**) with inexpensive, kid-size rides, open all week in summer months and on spring and fall weekends when the weather is nice.

WHAT TO SEE & DO

In town, you'll want to stroll around **Old Sacramento** ☆, 4 square blocks at the foot of the downtown area that have become a major tourist attraction. These blocks contain more than 100 restored buildings (California's largest restoration project), including restaurants and shops. Although the area has cobblestone streets, wooden sidewalks, and authentic gold rush–era architecture, the high concentration of T-shirt shops and other gimmicky stores has turned it into a sort of historical amusement park. Nonetheless, there are interesting things to see here, such as where the Pony Express ended and the transcontinental railroad—and the Republican Party—began. The **California State Railroad Museum** (see below) is the dream of railroad buffs, and the **Sacramento Jazz Festival,** mostly Dixieland, is famous for attracting over 100 bands that congregate here from around the world for 4 days of madness over the Memorial Day weekend. While you're meandering, stop at the **Discovery Museum** ☆ at 101 I St. (© **916/264-7057;** www.thediscovery.org), which houses hands-on exhibits of California's history, highlighting the valley's agricultural gold rush as well as the real one in 1849. It's open Tuesday through Sunday from 10am to 5pm. Admission is $5 for adults, $4 for seniors over 60, $4 for kids ages 13 to 17, $3 for kids 6 to 12, and free for kids under 6.

THE MAIN ATTRACTIONS

California State Capitol ☆☆☆ Closely resembling a scale model of the U.S. Capitol in Washington, D.C., the beautiful, domed California state capitol was built in 1869 and massively renovated in 1976. Sacramento's most distinctive landmark, the capitol has been the stage of many important political dramas in California history. The 1-hour guided tours provide insight into both the building's architecture and the workings of the government it houses. *Note:* Security has gotten much tighter since the September 11, 2001, terrorist attacks, so be prepared to show some identification.

10th St. (between N and L sts.). © 916/324-0333. Free admission. Daily 9am–5pm. Tours offered every hr. on the hr. until 4pm. Closed Thanksgiving, Dec 25, and Jan 1.

California State Railroad Museum ☆☆☆ *Kids* Well worth visiting, this museum is the highlight of Old Sacramento. You won't miss much if you bypass the memorabilia displays and head straight for the museum's 105 shiny locomotives and rail cars, beautiful antiques that are true works of art. Afterward, you

Downtown Sacramento

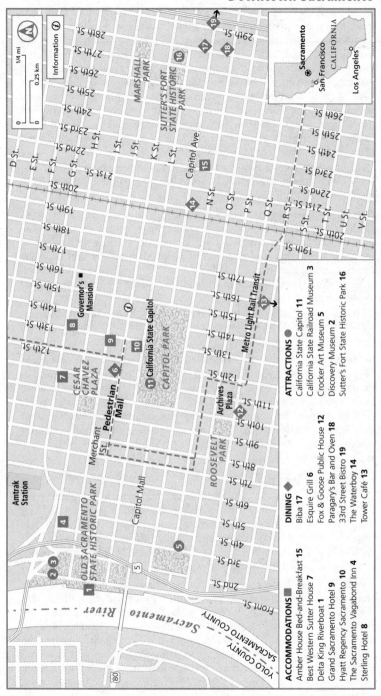

CALIFORNIA

Sacramento ✻
San Francisco
Los Angeles ○

ACCOMMODATIONS ■
Amber House Bed-and-Breakfast **15**
Best Western Sutter House **7**
Delta King Riverboat **1**
Grand Sacramento Hotel **9**
Hyatt Regency Sacramento **10**
The Sacramento Vagabond Inn **4**
Sterling Hotel **8**

DINING ◆
Biba **17**
Esquire Grill **6**
Fox & Goose Public House **12**
Paragary's Bar and Oven **18**
33rd Street Bistro **19**
The Waterboy **14**
Tower Café **13**

ATTRACTIONS ●
California State Capitol **11**
California State Railroad Museum **3**
Crocker Art Museum **5**
Discovery Museum **2**
Sutter's Fort State Historic Park **16**

319

can watch a 20-minute film on the history of the Western railroads that's quite good, then peruse related exhibits that tell the amazing story of the building of the transcontinental railroad. This museum is not just for train buffs: Over half a million people visit each year, and even the hordes of schoolchildren that typically mob this place shouldn't dissuade you from visiting one of the largest and best railroad museums in the country. Allow about 2 hours to see it all.

From April to September, on weekends and holidays from 11am to 5pm, **steam locomotive rides** carry passengers 6 miles along the Sacramento River. Trains depart on the hour from the Central Pacific Freight Depot in Old Sacramento, at K and Front streets. Fares are $6 for adults and children ages 13 and older, $3 for children 6 to 12, free for children under 6.

125 I St. (at 2nd St.). ℭ **916/445-6645.** Fax 916/327-5655. www.californiastaterailroadmuseum.org. Admission $3 adults 17 and older, free for children 16 and under. Daily 10am–5pm. Closed Thanksgiving, Dec 25, and Jan 1.

Crocker Art Museum ✦   This museum houses an outstanding collection of California art, as well as temporary exhibits from around the world. The museum itself is an imposing century-old Italianate building, with an ornate interior of carved and inlaid woods. The Crocker Mansion Wing, the museum's most recent addition, is modeled after the Crocker family home and contains works by Northern California artists from 1945 to the present. Plan to spend about an hour here.

216 O St. (at 3rd St.). ℭ **916/264-5423.** www.crockerartmuseum.org. Admission $6 adults, $4 seniors 65 and over, $3 students with ID, free for children 6 and under. Free for all every Sun 10am–1pm. Tues–Wed and Fri–Sun 10am–5pm, Thurs 10am–9pm. Closed major holidays.

Sutter's Fort State Historic Park ✦   John Sutter established this outpost in 1839, and the park, restored to its 1846 appearance, aims to recapture the pioneering spirit of 19th-century California. The usual exhibits are on hand—a blacksmith's forge, cooperage, bakery, and jail—and a self-guided audio tour is available. Historic demonstrations and live reenactments in costume are staged daily Memorial Day to Labor Day, when admissions are bumped to $3 for adults and $1 for children ages 6 to 16.

2701 L St. ℭ **916/445-4422.** Admission $1 adults, free for children 16 and under. Daily 10am–5pm.

OUTDOOR PURSUITS

BICYCLING   One good thing about a town that's as flat as a tortilla: It's perfect for exploring on a bike. One of the best places to ride is through Old Sacramento and along the 22-mile American River Parkway, which runs right through it. If you didn't bring your own wheels, the friendly guys at **City Bicycle Works,** 2419 K St., at 24th Street (ℭ **916/447-2453**), will rent you one for about $15 a day and point you in the right direction.

RIVER RAFTING   Sacramento lies nestled at the confluence of the American and Sacramento rivers, and rafting on the clear blue water of the American is immensely popular, especially on warm weekends. Several Sacramento-area outfitters rent rafts for 4 to 15 persons, along with life jackets and paddles for about $10 to $15 per person. Their shuttles drop you and your entourage upstream and meet you 3 to 4 hours later at a predetermined point downstream. A recommended outfitter is **American River Raft Rentals,** 11257 S. Bridge St. (at Sunrise Ave.), Rancho Cordova (ℭ **888/338-RAFT** or 916/635-6400; www.raftrentals.com).

WHERE TO STAY
EXPENSIVE

Amber House Bed-and-Breakfast ⭐⭐ Just 8 blocks from the capitol on a quiet neighborhood street, Amber House offers lovely, individually decorated rooms possessing all the amenities you could wish for. Named for famous artists, musicians, and writers, accommodations are located in adjacent historic houses: the Poet's Refuge, a well-crafted 1905 home with five rooms, and the Artist's Retreat, a Mediterranean-style house built in 1913. A third house—an old colonial-revival home called the Musician's Manor—is across the street, and its Mozart Room is the B&B's best, containing a four-poster queen bed, a heart-shaped Jacuzzi, a private patio, and three bay windows overlooking the tree-shaded street. A beautiful living room and library are available for guests' use. A fourth large, turreted home is currently being remodeled with the same atten-tion to total creature comfort as the other properties. It will be called The Library, featuring room decor with French, English, Southern plantation, and safari themes named after authors Christy, Hemingway, Fitzgerald, and Twain. (You match them up.) A full breakfast is served at the time and location you request—either in your room, in the large dining room, or outside on the veranda. Coffee and a newspaper are brought to your door early every morning, as are freshly baked cookies and wine or champagne every evening.

1315 22nd St., Sacramento, CA 95816. ℰ **800/755-6526** or 916/444-8085. Fax 916/552-6529. www.amber house.com. 18 units. $149–$319 double. Rates include breakfast. AE, DC, DISC, MC, V. **Amenities:** Compli-mentary bike use; concierge; in-room massage; laundry service; same-day dry cleaning. *In room:* A/C, TV/VCR, dataport, hair dryer, iron.

Grand Sacramento Hotel ⭐ This convention hotel opened in May 2001 with words of high praise for its high-tech amenities, a million-dollar public art collection, and the preservation of a beloved landmark. The hotel's 504 rooms are in a shiny, 26-story building adjoining a three-story building that was origi-nally Sacramento's public market from 1920 to the 1960s. This historic struc-ture, designed by Julia Morgan, architect for Hearst Castle, was a favorite gathering place for three generations of Sacramentans. Now housing the lobby, bar, and two restaurants, the site is once again a downtown focal point for resi-dents and travelers alike. The accommodations are convention-type hotel rooms—a mite anonymous, but not unpleasant.

1230 J St., Sacramento, CA 95814. ℰ **800/325-3535** or 916/447-1700. Fax 916/477-1701. www.sheraton. com. 504 units. $119–$275 double; from $350 suite. AE, DC, DISC, MC, V. Self-parking $10; valet parking $15. **Amenities:** 2 restaurants; bar; heated outdoor pool; health club; concierge; car-rental desk; business center; full-service salon; room service; in-room massage; babysitting; laundry service; same-day dry cleaning; club-level rooms. *In room:* A/C, TV w/pay movies, dataport, minibar, coffeemaker, hair dryer, iron.

Hyatt Regency Sacramento ⭐⭐ Sacramento's top hotel stands right in the heart of downtown, directly across from the California state capitol and adjacent to the convention center. It's the high-status address for visiting politicos and is popular with conventioneers as well, as its facilities and services are unmatched in the city. While the rooms themselves are not terribly distinctive, they conform to a high standard and come with all the amenities you expect from Hyatt. The best are the corner units with views facing the state capitol.

1209 L St., Sacramento, CA 95814. ℰ **800/233-1234** or 916/443-1234. Fax 916/321-3799. www. sacramento.hyatt.com. 503 units. $220–$260 double; from $375 suite. AE, DC, DISC, MC, V. Self-parking $12; valet parking $18. **Amenities:** 2 restaurants; bar; heated outdoor pool; nearby golf course; health club; Jacuzzi; concierge; car-rental desk; business center; full-service salon; room service; in-room massage; babysit-ting; laundry service; same-day dry cleaning; executive-level rooms. *In room:* A/C, TV w/pay movies, dataport, minibar, fridge upon request, coffeemaker, hair dryer, iron.

MODERATE

Best Western Sutter House (Value) You would never know from the plain, motel-like exterior that this is one of the best values in Sacramento. Rooms here are as up-to-date as any offered by upscale hotels such as the Hilton or the Hyatt, including well-coordinated furnishings and lots of amenities. There's a pool in the courtyard, and complimentary coffee and pastries are served each morning in the lobby. All of the rooms in Sutter House are nonsmoking.

1100 H St., Sacramento, CA 95814. ⓒ 800/830-1314 or 916/441-1314. Fax 916/441-5961. www.thesutter house.com. 98 units. $85–$160 double. Rates include continental breakfast. AE, DC, DISC, MC, V. **Amenities:** Solar-heated outdoor pool; access to fitness center; room service; same-day dry cleaning; executive-level rooms. *In room:* A/C, TV, fax, dataport, fridge, coffeemaker, hair dryer, iron.

Delta King Riverboat 🤾 The *Delta King* carried passengers between San Francisco and Sacramento in the 1930s. Permanently moored in Sacramento since 1984, the riverboat is now a somewhat gimmicky but nonetheless charming hotel. Staying here can be quite a novelty, but the staterooms in a boat are ultra-cozy and may bother landlubbers, especially if you're planning to spend a lot of time in your room. All units are nearly identical and have private bathrooms and low ceilings. The captain's quarters, a particularly pricey suite, is a unique, mahogany-paneled stateroom, complete with an observation platform and private deck.

The Pilothouse Restaurant is popular for local office parties. When the weather is nice, there's dining on outside decks with views of colorful Old Sacramento. Live entertainment is presented below decks in two shipboard venues on Friday and Saturday nights. In the Mark Twain Lounge, "Suspect's Murder Mystery Dinner Theatre," an interactive whodunit, challenges the audience to reveal the true murderer, played by period actors. It's $35 per person to attend, but that includes dinner, tax, and gratuity. Drinks, of course, are extra. Or for $14 a person you can see a local production of a Broadway play in the 75-seat Delta King Theatre.

1000 Front St., Old Sacramento, CA 95814. ⓒ 800/825-5464 or 916/444-5464. www.deltaking.com. 44 units. Sun–Thurs $119–$139 double, $400 captain's quarters; Fri–Sat $169 double, $400 captain's quarters. Riverside rooms are $15 extra. Rates include continental breakfast. AE, DC, DISC, MC, V. **Amenities:** Restaurant; lounge; laundry service; same-day dry cleaning. *In room:* A/C, TV, dataport, hair dryer, iron.

Sterling Hotel 🤾🤾 Set in the heart of Sacramento, 3 blocks from the capitol, this inn occupies a white-fronted Victorian mansion originally built in the 1890s and heavily renovated in 1995. The Sterling has all the charm of a small, well-managed, sophisticated inn, with a carefully tended flowering yard, tasteful decor, designer furnishings, Italian marble, and a Jacuzzi in every room. The Chanterelle, which serves well-prepared California regional cuisine in a dignified setting, is known as one of Sacramento's better restaurants.

1300 H St., Sacramento, CA 95814. ⓒ 800/365-7660 or 916/448-1300. Fax 916/448-8066. www.sterling hotel.com. 17 units. Sun–Thurs $179–$199 double; $325 suite. Fri–Sat $199–$249 double; $325 suite. Rates include continental breakfast. AE, DC, MC, V. **Amenities:** Restaurant; Jacuzzi; room service. *In room:* A/C, TV w/pay movies, dataport, fridge in most units, hair dryer, iron.

INEXPENSIVE

The Sacramento Vagabond Inn (Value) A reliable choice within walking distance of the state capitol, the Vagabond Inn has a host of free features, including local phone calls, weekday newspapers, and continental breakfast. Bedrooms are clean and comfortable, but not exceptional—it's the economical rates and the convenient location that make it worth your while. There's an adjoining 24-hour Denny's restaurant as well.

909 3rd St., Sacramento, CA 95814. ℂ 800/522-1555 or 916/446-1481. Fax 916/448-0364. 108 units. $85 double. Extra person $10. Children 18 and under stay free in parents' room. Rates include continental breakfast. AE, DC, DISC, MC, V. **Amenities:** Restaurant; heated pool; nearby golf course; laundry service; same-day dry cleaning. *In room:* A/C, TV, coffeemaker, fridge in some units, hair dryer, iron.

WHERE TO DINE
EXPENSIVE

Biba ★★★ ITALIAN   Locals flock to this sleek neo–Art Deco restaurant to sample the classical Italian cuisine of Bologna-born owner Biba Caggiano, who recently published her ninth cookbook. Although the menu changes seasonally, you can expect to find about 10 pastas and an equal number of main courses. There might be a delicate pappardelle with a fresh-seafood sauce, or a more pungent spaghetti alla Siciliana, which combines eggplant, tomatoes, capers, garlic, and anchovies. For a main course, the classic osso buco Milanese served with a soft, creamy polenta is excellent, but save room for the double-chocolate trifle made with dark and white chocolate, Grand Marnier–soaked pound cake, and raspberry purée.

2801 Capitol Ave. ℂ **916/455-2422.** www.biba-restaurant.com. Main courses $18–$28. AE, DC, MC, V. Mon–Fri 11:30am–2:30pm; Mon–Thurs 5:30–9:30pm, Fri–Sat 5:30–10:30pm.

MODERATE

Esquire Grill ★ AMERICAN GRILL   Right next door to Sacramento's convention center and short walks from the capitol building and the Hyatt Regency, the Esquire Grill was a hit from the minute it opened its handsome doors. The Michael Guthrie architectural group designed the restaurant using rich woods and warm colors. Sacramento has been struggling for years to revive its moribund downtown area and this urbane place is one giant step toward creating the revitalized metropolitan scene the city planners are hoping for. The bar is always lively with well-dressed folks supping martinis and Cosmopolitans, and the restaurant's food is classic American grill. Dinner specialties vary but might include a mixed fry of calamari, fennel, and onions; iron skillet-roasted New York steak; or spit-roasted pork chops with buttermilk onion rings and house-made applesauce. Some folks come just for the onion rings.

1221 K St. ℂ **916/448-8900.** Main courses $15–$46 ($46 is the price of porterhouse steak for 2). AE, DC, DISC, MC, V. Mon–Fri 11am–2:30pm; Sun–Thurs 4:30–10:30pm, Fri–Sat 4:30–11:30pm. Limited menu Mon–Fri 2:30–4:30pm.

Paragary's Bar and Oven ★★ MEDITERRANEAN   Occupying two distinct dining rooms just across the street from Twenty Eight, Paragary's is widely considered the best moderately priced restaurant in Sacramento's downtown area. During good weather, the best seats are outside amid the gorgeous fountains and plantings of the courtyard; other seating options include the formal fireplace room and the brightly lit cafe. The same menu is served no matter where you sit, with some of the best dishes coming from the kitchen's wood-burning pizza oven. But this is more than a gourmet pizza parlor, as evidenced by the grilled rib-eye steak with mashed potatoes, portobello mushrooms, and grilled leeks, or the hand-cut rosemary noodles with seared chicken, pancetta, artichokes, leeks, and garlic.

1401 28th St. ℂ **916/457-5737.** Main courses $12–$20. AE, DC, DISC, MC, V. Mon–Thurs 11:30am–11pm, Fri 11:30am–midnight, Sat 4:30pm–midnight, Sun 4:30–10pm.

33rd Street Bistro ★ BISTRO   Seattle transplants Fred Haynes (chef) and his brother Matt (manager) have taken an old brick building and transformed it into a bistro that's been a raging success since the day it opened. And it's popular for all the right reasons—the food is good (and priced right), the staff is friendly and helpful, and the ambience is warm and cheerful. Selections include a variety of Italian grilled sandwiches and house favorites such as wood-roasted vegetables with sun-dried tomatoes and goat-cheese crostini, Uncle Bum's jerk ribs with Jamaican barbecue sauce and key-lime crème fraîche, and wood-roasted pork loin with ancho-chile butter and linguisa risotto.

3301 Folsom Blvd. (at 33rd St.). ✆ 916/455-2282. Main courses $8–$19. AE, MC, V. Sun–Thurs 8am–10pm, Fri and Sat 8am–11pm.

The Waterboy ✿✿ COUNTRY FRENCH/CALIFORNIA   Until fairly recently, Sacramento had a slim list of really good restaurants, but now it has achieved hard-to-choose-where-to-go status. Right up at the top with the best on everybody's list is The Waterboy. It's got everything going for it: an appealing, airy, but unpretentious atmosphere, friendly and knowledgeable servers, and, best of all, outstanding food cooked perfectly. Chef/owner Rick Mahan uses Niman Ranch naturally raised meats and local organic produce, and he offers a particularly fine selection of wines. Main courses change with the seasons but include dishes such as saffron risotto, cassoulet, grilled duck breast, or pan-roasted pork chops.

20th St. and Capitol Ave. ✆ 916/498-9891. Main courses $14–$20. AE, DC, DISC, MC, V. Tues–Fri 11:30am–2:20pm; Sun and Tues–Thurs 5–9pm, Fri–Sat 5–10pm.

INEXPENSIVE

Fox & Goose Public House ✿✿ 𝘝𝘢𝘭𝘶𝘦 ENGLISH PUB   The Fox is your classic British pub, right down to the dartboard, giant picture of the queen, and numerous varieties of beers from across the pond. The soups at lunch are excellent, and the specials often include bangers and mash, Welsh rarebit, and Cornish pasties. The burnt cream dessert is famous. Either arrive early for lunch or be prepared for a wait, as locals love this place (no reservations taken and they won't even seat you until all the members of your party have arrived). Equally popular breakfasts include kippers, grilled tomatoes, and crumpets, as well as the ubiquitous waffles, omelets, and French toast. There's live entertainment by local bands 6 nights a week, as well as pub grub like fish and chips and hamburgers Monday through Friday from 5:30 to 9:30pm.

1001 R St. (at 10th St.). ✆ 916/443-8825. Reservations not accepted. Main courses $4–$7. AE, MC, V. Mon–Fri 7am–2pm, Sat–Sun 8am–1pm. Bar stays open until midnight Mon–Thurs, until 2am Fri–Sat.

Tower Café INTERNATIONAL   The Tower Café gets its name from the building in which it's located: a grand old 1939 movie house with a tall Art Deco spire. The restaurant occupies the same space in which a small mom-and-pop music store once stood. This former resident, Tower Records, has since grown

---

⌠Tips **Nightlife in Sacratomato**

If you're in need of some nocturnal entertainment in Sacramento, do what the locals do: Pick up a free copy of the *Sacramento News & Review* (SN&R). You'll find it in red boxes or racks at most major entertainment venues and shopping malls, as well as bookstores, coffee shops, music stores, and convenience stores throughout the downtown area. You can also peruse online at **www.newsreview.com/sacto**.

into America's second-largest record retailer. While it's unlikely that Tower Café will share the phenomenal success of its predecessor, it's popular with locals. The multicultural decor—kind of Art Deco meets *National Geographic*—is a feast for the eyes. Dishes reflect a variety of international flavors, from the Jamaican jerk chicken to Shanghai chow mein. Usually the food is good, especially the desserts, but once in awhile you get something that makes you wonder what's going on in the kitchen. On warm days, it seems as if everyone in the city is lunching here on the large outdoor deck (in fact, past patrons have included serious foodie Bill Clinton), so people-watching can be a real treat. The movie house typically shows good foreign films, and Tower Records is just across the street. These are all great places to round out a lazy River City afternoon.

1518 Broadway. ℂ 916/441-0222. Main courses $8–$14. AE, MC, V. Sun–Thurs 8am–10pm, Fri and Sat 8am–10:30pm, with dessert and drinks only until 11:30pm.

2 The Gold Country ★★

Cutting a serpentine swath for nearly 350 miles along aptly numbered Calif. 49, the Gold Country stretches from Sierra City to the foothills of Yosemite. Much of this rugged region still retains its '49er ambience: Mining sites, horse ranches, and Wild West saloons are common sights in these parts. Along with its numerous ghost towns and gold rush–era architecture, it's enough to make Gene Autry or Roy Rogers feel right at home.

The town of Placerville, 44 miles east of Sacramento at the intersection of U.S. 50 and Calif. 49, is in the approximate center of the Gold Country. To the north are the classic old mining towns of Grass Valley and Nevada City, while in the central and southern Gold Country are such well-preserved towns as Amador City, Sutter Creek, Columbia, and Jamestown, to name just a few.

In fact, the Gold Country is so immense that it would take weeks to thoroughly explore. But rather than provide an exhaustive list of each and every town, I have instead narrowed my coverage to include three of my favorite regions, each of which can be thoroughly explored in just 2 or 3 days: the utterly charismatic side-by-side towns of Nevada City and Grass Valley to the north; the well-preserved gold-rush communities of Amador City, Sutter Creek, and Jackson in the central Gold Country; and at the southern end of the Gold Country, the wonderfully authentic neighboring mining towns of Angels Camp, Murphys, Columbia, Sonora, and Jamestown.

Any of these three regions will provide an excellent base for exploring and experiencing the Gold Country, whether you're intent on panning for gold, exploring old mines and caverns, or rafting the area's many white-water rivers. In fact, the Gold Country is one of the most underrated and least congested tourist destinations in California, a winning combination of Old West ambience, adorable (and affordable) bed-and-breakfasts, and outdoor adventures galore.

THE NORTHERN GOLD COUNTRY: NEVADA CITY & GRASS VALLEY

Lying about 60 miles northeast of Sacramento, Nevada City and Grass Valley are far and away the top tourist destinations of the northern Gold Country.

These two historic towns were at the center of the hard-rock mining fields of Northern California. Grass Valley, in fact, was California's richest mining town, producing more than a billion dollars worth of gold. Both are attractive, although I usually spend most of my time traipsing through smaller Nevada City. Its wealth of Victorian homes and storefronts makes it one of the most appealing small towns in California, particularly in the fall when the maple trees are ablaze with color. (In fact, its entire downtown has been designated a National Historic Landmark.)

It's easy to get here. If you're driving from San Francisco, take I-80 to the Calif. 49 turnoff in Auburn and follow the signs heading north. For information about the area, contact the **Grass Valley & Nevada County Chamber of Commerce,** 248 Mill St., Grass Valley, CA 95945 (© **800/655-4667** in CA or 530/273-4667; www.gvncchamber.org), or the **Nevada City Chamber of Commerce,** 132 Main St., Nevada City, CA 95959 (© **800/655-NJOY** or 530/265-2692; www.nevadacitychamber.com).

NEVADA CITY ★★

Rumors of miners pulling a pound of gold a day out of Deer Creek brought thousands of fortune seekers to the area in 1849. Within a year, Nevada City was a boisterous town of 10,000, the third largest city in California. In its heyday, everyone who was anyone visited this rollicking Western outpost with its busy red-light district. Mark Twain lectured here in 1866, telling the audience about his trips to the Sandwich Islands (Hawaii). Former president Herbert Hoover also lived and worked here as a gold miner.

Pick up a walking-tour map at the **Chamber of Commerce,** 132 Main St., and stroll the streets lined with impressive Victorian buildings, including the **Firehouse Number 1 Museum,** 214 Main St. (© **530/265-5468**), complete with bell tower, gingerbread decoration, a small museum that displays mementos from the Donner Party, a Maidu Indian basket collection, and an altar from a temple originally located in the Chinese section of Grass Valley. Admission is free. It's open in summer daily from 11am to 4pm; from November 1 to May 1 hours are Thursday through Sunday from 11:30am to 4pm. The **National Hotel** (built between 1854–56) is here (I always stop in at the handsome gold rush–era bar for a spicy Bloody Mary), as is the **Nevada Theatre** (1865), one of the oldest theaters in the nation still operating as such. Today it's home to the Foothill Theatre Company.

If you want to see the source of much of the city's wealth, visit **Malakoff Diggins State Historic Park** ★, 23579 N. Bloomfield Rd. (© **530/265-2740**), 28 miles northeast of Nevada City. Once the world's largest hydraulic gold mine, it's an awesome (some might say disturbing) spectacle of hydraulic mining—nearly half a mountain has been washed away by powerful jets of water, leaving behind a 600-foot-deep canyon of exposed rock. In the 1870s, North Bloomfield, then located in the middle of this park, had a population of 1,500. Some of the buildings have been reconstructed and refurnished to show what life was like then. The 3,000-acre park also offers several hiking trails, swimming at Blair Lake, and 30 campsites that can be reserved through **ReserveAmerica** (© **800/444-7275;** www.reserveamerica.com). The museum is open daily in summer from 10am to 5pm, in winter on weekends only from 10am to 4pm. To reach the park, take Calif. 49 toward Downieville for 11 miles. Turn right onto Tyler-Foote Crossing Road for 17 miles. The name will change to Curzon Grade and then to Backbone. Turn right onto Derbec Road and into the park. The fee is $2 per car.

Another 6 miles up Calif. 49 from the Malakoff Diggins turnoff will bring you to Pleasant Valley Road, the exit that will take you (in about 7 miles) to one of the most impressive **covered bridges** in the country. Built in 1862, it's 225 feet long and was crossed by many a stagecoach (in autumn, it makes for a spectacular photo opportunity).

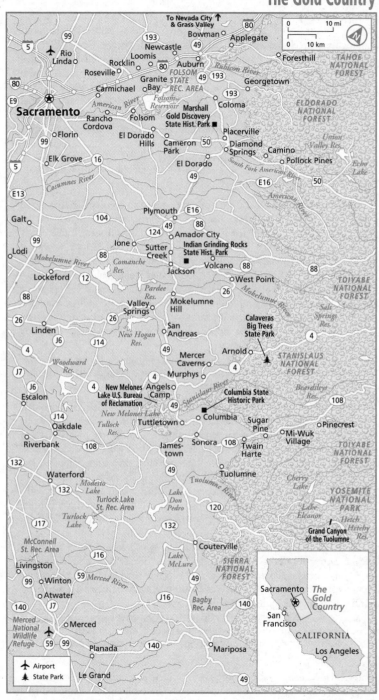

To Nevada City & Grass Valley

Bowman

Applegate

Newcastle

Foresthill

TAHOE NATIONAL FOREST

Rio Linda

Loomis

Rocklin

Auburn

Roseville

Granite Bay

Georgetown

FOLSOM STATE REC. AREA

Rubicon River

Carmichael

ELDORADO NATIONAL FOREST

American River

Folsom Reservoir

Coloma

E9

Sacramento

Rancho Cordova

Folsom

Marshall Gold Discovery State Hist. Park

Placerville

Union Valley Res.

Florin

El Dorado Hills

Cameron Park

Diamond Springs

Camino

Pollock Pines

Echo Lake

Elk Grove

El Dorado

South Fork American River

E16

50

Cosumnes River

American River

Galt

Plymouth

E16

Lodi

Amador City

88

Ione

124

Sutter Creek

Indian Grinding Rocks State Hist. Park

Mokelumne River

Comanche Res.

Jackson

Volcano

88

TOIYABE NATIONAL FOREST

Lockeford

Pardee Res.

West Point

Mokelumne River

Valley Springs

Mokelumne Hill

Salt Springs Res.

Linden

New Hogan Res.

San Andreas

Calaveras Big Trees State Park

Woodward Res.

Mercer Caverns

Arnold

STANISLAUS NATIONAL FOREST

Murphys

Beardsley Res.

Escalon

New Melones Lake U.S. Bureau of Reclamation

Angels Camp

Columbia State Historic Park

108

Oakdale

Tullock Res.

New Melones Lake

Stanislaus River

Columbia

Sugar Pine

Mi-Wuk Village

Pinecrest

Riverbank

Tuttletown

James-town

Sonora

Twain Harte

TOIYABE NATIONAL FOREST

Waterford

Modesto Lake

Tuolumne

Cherry Lake

Turlock Lake St. Rec. Area

Lake Don Pedro

YOSEMITE NATIONAL PARK

Turlock Lake

Tuolumne River

Lake Eleanor

Hetch Hetchy Res.

McConnell St. Rec. Area

Grand Canyon of the Tuolumne

Livingston

Lake McLure

Couterville

SIERRA NATIONAL FOREST

Winton

Merced River

Atwater

Bagby Rec. Area

Merced National Wildlife Refuge

Merced

Mariposa

Planada

Le Grand

✈ Airport
★ State Park

Sacramento

The Gold Country

San Francisco

CALIFORNIA

Los Angeles

Where to Stay

Deer Creek Inn Bed & Breakfast ⭐   An 1860 three-floor Victorian overlooking Deer Creek and within walking distance of downtown Nevada City, this inn feels like a warm home-away-from-home. The individually decorated rooms, most with private verandas facing the creek or town, are furnished with assorted antiques and four-poster or canopy beds with down comforters. Most bathrooms have claw-foot tubs. A full breakfast is served either out on the deck or in the formal dining room. Guests are invited to try a little panning of their own, fish, play croquet, or simply relax and enjoy the lawn and landscaped rose gardens along the creek.

116 Nevada St., Nevada City, CA 95959. © **800/655-0363** or 530/265-0363. Fax 530/265-0980. www.deer creekinn.com. 5 units. $110–$175 double. Rates include breakfast. AE, MC, V. **Amenities:** Nearby golf course; bike rental. *In room:* A/C, phone on request.

Emma Nevada House ⭐⭐   One of the finest—and prettiest—B&Bs in the Gold Country, Emma Nevada House is a picture-perfect Victorian that was the childhood home of 19th-century opera star Emma Nevada. You'll like everything about Emma Nevada: the quiet location, sun-drenched decks, wraparound porch, understated decor, and particularly breakfast, which is served in the beautiful hexagonal Sun Room. The guest rooms range from small and intimate to large and luxurious; all have private bathrooms and queen-size beds. Top choice for honeymooners is the Empress's Chamber, with its large wall of windows, soothing ivory and burgundy tones, and—of course—the Jacuzzi tub for two. You'll also like the fact that the shops and restaurants of Nevada City's Historic District are only a short walk away.

528 E. Broad St., Nevada City, CA 95959. © **800/916-EMMA** or 530/265-4416. Fax 530/265-4416. www. emmanevadahouse.com. 6 units. $115–$180 double. Rates include breakfast. AE, MC, V. **Amenities:** Concierge. *In room:* A/C, hair dryer, iron, phone on request.

National Hotel   You can't miss this classic three-story Victorian, the oldest hotel in continuous operation west of the Rocky Mountains, and it shows its age. Some folks feel this makes it more historic and authentic; others may opt for more upscale and restored lodgings. It's located near what was once the center of the town's red-light district. The lobby is full of mementos from that era, hence the grandfather clock and early square piano. The suites are replete with gold rush–era antiques and large, cozy beds. Most rooms have private bathrooms, and some come with canopy beds and romantic loveseats. A definite bonus during typically sweltering summers is the swimming pool filled with cool mountain water.

The hotel's Victorian dining room and bar, which serves traditional items such as prime rib, steaks, lobster tail, and homemade desserts, also has a gold-rush atmosphere; tables, for example, are lit with coal oil lamps. The hotel provides live entertainment on Friday and Saturday nights. There's also a popular Sunday brunch, one of the best in the county.

211 Broad St., Nevada City, CA 95959. © **530/265-4551.** Fax 530/265-2445. www.national-hotel.com. 42 units, 30 with private bathroom. $80–$100 double without bathroom; $100–$120 double with bathroom; $120–$130 suite with bathroom. AE, MC, V. **Amenities:** Restaurant; bar; outdoor pool; business center; room service. *In room:* A/C, TV, dataport.

Red Castle Inn Historic Lodgings ⭐   This elegant, comfortable hillside inn occupies a four-story Gothic Revival brick house built in 1860, situated in a secluded spot with a panoramic view of the town. The house retains its original woodwork, plaster moldings, ceiling medallions, and much of the handmade glass. It lacks modern intrusions like TVs and phones. Guests enjoy bountiful five-course buffet breakfasts and relax on the verandas that encircle the first two floors of the house and overlook the rose gardens. My favorite rooms are the Garden Room, with a canopy bed and French doors leading into the gardens, and the three-room garret suite tucked under the eaves, furnished with sleigh beds and featuring Gothic arched windows.

109 Prospect St., Nevada City, CA 95959. (C) **800/761-4766** or 530/265-5135. www.historic-lodgings.com. 7 units. $110–$165 double. Rates include breakfast. MC, V. *In room:* A/C, no phone.

Where to Dine

Citronée ★★ REGIONAL AMERICAN/INTERNATIONAL   After being underserved with serious restaurants for some years, Nevada City has taken a leap forward with two new, notable temples to fine cuisine—Citronée and New Moon (see below). It took a review by the *New York Times* to get California food mavens to turn their appetites from Napa and San Francisco to Citronée and the Gold Country. And owner/chef Robert Perez's restaurant is indeed worth exploring. For example, at lunch the barbecued brisket sandwich topped with white cheddar cheese on chipotle focaccia served with cayenne-dusted waffle potato chips is a must. The evening menu ranges from oven-roasted Maui onion stuffed with sautéed wild mushrooms on a bed of creamy polenta with a thyme lavender honey sauce, to the highly acclaimed rare seared ahi tuna with a crust of black and white sesame seeds served with a soy chile vinaigrette and wasabi crème fraîche. And if that isn't enough, ask for the menu gastronomique, a five-course surprise menu specially chosen each night. *Wine Spectator* magazine recently awarded Citronée its award of excellence for their selection of over 140 wines.

320 Broad St. (C) **530/265-5697**. Reservations recommended. Main courses $13–$25. AE, MC, V. Mon–Thurs 5:30–9:30 or 10:30pm, Fri–Sat 5–10pm.

Country Rose Café ★ COUNTRY FRENCH   The flowery country-French atmosphere of this popular Nevada City restaurant belies a serious (and seriously priced) menu put together by owner and chef Michael Johns. Dinner selections, written on a huge board that's lugged over to your table soon after you've been seated, are mostly French with a dash of Italian, Mexican, and American dishes. Skip the typical pastas and head straight for John's specialty—fresh fish prepared in a myriad of classic styles such as filet of sole dore, swordfish oskar, and sea bass with garlic-basil sauce. Other regular menu items include filet mignon, lobster, rack of lamb, and roast game hen, all served with soup or salad. Both lunch and dinner are served on the pretty walled-in patio in the summer, so be sure to request alfresco seating when making a reservation.

300 Commercial St. (C) **530/265-6252**. Reservations recommended. Main courses $14–$31. AE, DC, MC, V. Daily 11am–2:30pm; Sun–Thurs 5–9pm; Fri–Sat 5–10pm; Sun brunch 11am–2:30pm.

New Moon Café ★★ AMERICAN/INTERNATIONAL   After a 5-year hiatus, Nevada City's favorite chef, Peter Selaya, is back in the kitchen with a new restaurant and a menu of imaginatively prepared items that feature free-range and antibiotic-free meats and poultry, house-baked breads, house-made fresh pastas using organic flours and grains, and local organic vegetables when available— which is regularly in this hotbed of natural foodstuffs. So not only is the food healthy, it tastes great. Dinner entrees include the likes of a lean Niman Ranch top sirloin cap grilled with a roast garlic zinfandel and rosemary sauce, or fresh line-caught, wild salmon pan-seared with julienne vegetables and a beurre blanc verjus. The raviolis with different stuffings are made fresh daily, as are the house-made desserts. Fresh strawberry Napoleons recently tasted were beyond delicious.

Nevada City's balmy climate makes the front deck a great place to dine and people-watch.

203 York St. ✆ 530/265-6399. Reservations recommended. Main courses $15–$21. DC, MC, V. Tues–Fri 11:30am–2pm; Tues–Sun 5–8pm (or later).

GRASS VALLEY ✦

In contrast to Nevada City's "tourist town" image, Grass Valley is the commercial and retail center of the region. The **Empire Mine State Historic Park** ✦, 10791 E. Empire St., Grass Valley (✆ **530/273-8522**), the largest and richest gold mine in California, is just outside of town. This mine, which once had 367 miles of underground shafts, produced an estimated 5.8 million ounces of gold between 1850 and 1956, when it closed. Here you can look down the shaft of the mine, walk around the mine yard, and stroll through the gardens of the mine owner. From March to November, tours are given daily, and a mining movie is shown. You can also enjoy picnicking, cycling, mountain biking, or hiking in the 784-acre park. It's open year-round except for Thanksgiving, Christmas, and New Year's Day. Admission to the park, tour, and museum costs $1 for adults and children, and dogs are free.

In town, visitors can pick up a walking-tour map at the **Chamber of Commerce,** 248 Mill St. (✆ **530/273-4667;** www.gvncchamber.org), and explore the historic downtown area along Mill and Main streets. There are also a few museums that California-history and gold-mining buffs will want to visit: the **Grass Valley Museum,** 410 S. Church St., adjacent to St. Joseph's Cultural Center (✆ **530/273-5509**); the **North Star Mining Museum,** at the south end of Mill Street at Allison Ranch Road (✆ **530/273-4255;** open May–Oct); and the **Video History Museum,** in the center of Memorial Park off Calif. 174 (✆ **530/ 274-1126;** open May–Oct), which houses a collection of old films of the region from the 1920s.

Grass Valley was, for a time, the home of **Lola Montez,** singer, dancer, and paramour of the rich and famous. A fully restored home that she bought and occupied in 1853 can be viewed at 248 Mill St., now the site of Grass Valley's Chamber of Commerce. **Lotta Crabtree,** Montez's famous protégé, lived down the street at 238 Mill St., now an apartment house. Also pop into the **Holbrooke Hotel,** 212 Main St., to see the signature of Mark Twain, who stayed here, as did five U.S. presidents. The saloon has been in continuous use since 1852, and it's the place to meet the locals and have a tall cold one.

The surrounding region offers many recreational opportunities on its rivers and lakes and in the Tahoe National Forest. You can enjoy fishing, swimming, and boating at **Scotts Flat Lake** near Nevada City (east on Calif. 20) and at **Rollins Lake** on Calif. 174, between Grass Valley and Colfax. White-water rafting is available on several rivers. **Tributary Whitewater Tours,** 20480 Woodbury Dr., Grass Valley, CA 95949 (✆ **800/672-3846** or 530/346-6812; www. whitewatertours.com), offers ½- to 3-day trips March through October. The region is also ideal for mountain biking. The chambers of commerce publish a trail guide, but there's nowhere to rent a bike in either Nevada City or Grass Valley, so bring your own wheels. For regional hiking information, contact **Tahoe National Forest Headquarters,** at Coyote Street and Calif. 49 in Nevada City (✆ **530/265-4531;** www.r5.fs.fed.us/tahoe).

Where to Stay

Holbrooke Hotel ✦   This Victorian-era white-clapboard building was a rollicking saloon during the gold-rush days, and then evolved into a place for exhausted miners to "rack out." The oldest and most historic hotel in town, it has hosted a number of legendary figures since opening its doors: Ulysses Grant, Mark Twain, Benjamin Harrison, and Grover Cleveland, among others. Seventeen of the rooms lie within the main building. The remainder are in an adjacent annex, a house occupied long ago by the hotel's owner. Each guest room is decorated with an eclectic collection of gold rush–era furniture and antiques. All have cable TVs tucked away in armoires, and most bathrooms have claw-foot tubs. If you can, reserve one of the larger Veranda rooms that face Main Street and have access to the balconies; it's well worth the few extra dollars.

212 W. Main St., Grass Valley, CA 95945. ℭ **800/933-7077** or 530/273-1353. Fax 530/273-0434. www. holbrooke.com. 28 units. $58–$115 double; $100–$155 suite. Rates include breakfast. AE, DC, DISC, MC, V. **Amenities:** Restaurant; saloon; business center; salon. *In room:* A/C, TV.

Where to Dine

Arletta's at the Holbrooke AMERICAN   This elegant hotel dining room is the most formal place in town—an ironic twist, given its past life as a gold-rush saloon and a flophouse for drunken miners. In its way, it's the most authentic and nostalgic restaurant in a town filled with worthy hardworking competitors. Items on the ever-changing menu range from braised pork loin with red chile applesauce to grilled breast of chicken stuffed with boursin cheese, pine nuts, and roasted red peppers. Lunch prices are lower, ranging from $6.95 for a BLT with apple-wood smoked bacon to $8.95 for a tasty spinach pasta with portobello mushrooms, roasted garlic, red peppers, julienne vegetables, herbs, Parmesan cheese, and rock shrimp.

212 W. Main St. (in the Holbrooke Hotel). ℭ **530/273-1353.** www.holbrooke.com. Reservations recommended Fri–Sat nights. Main courses $13–$25. AE, DC, DISC, MC, V. Mon–Sat 11:30am–2pm and 5:30–9pm, Sun 10am–2pm and 5–8:30pm.

Tofanelli's (*Value* INTERNATIONAL   If a diet of meat and potatoes isn't your cup of tea, head to Tofanelli's, which specializes in good—and good for you—entrees for brunch, lunch, and dinner. You'll like the setting, a bright, cheery trio of dining areas (atrium, outdoor patio, and dining room) separated by exposed brick walls and decorated with beautiful prints and paintings. Specials on the menu, such as Gorgonzola ravioli topped with garlic cream sauce, or pad Thai noodles with fresh ginger and marinated beef, change weekly, but you can always rely on Tofanelli classics like Linda's famous vegetarian lasagna and the popular veggie burger. And yes, they serve good ol' New York steak, too. Don't you dare depart without a slice of Katherine's chocolate cake.

302 W. Main St. (across from the Holbrooke Hotel). ℭ **530/272-1468.** Main courses $7–$15. AE, MC, V. Mon–Fri 7am–8:30pm; Sat brunch 8:30am–3pm, dinner 5–9pm; Sun brunch 8:30am–3pm, dinner 5–8:30pm.

THE CENTRAL GOLD COUNTRY: AMADOR CITY, SUTTER CREEK & JACKSON

Though Placerville is technically the center of the Gold Country, it's the small trio of towns a few miles to the south—Amador City, Sutter Creek, and Jackson—that are far and away the most appealing destination in this beautiful region of rolling hills, dotted with solitary oaks and granite outcroppings. When the mining boom went bust, most of the towns were abandoned; nowadays, most of these restored gold-rush towns rely solely on tourism (hence the rapid conversion of many Victorian homes into B&Bs), though a few mines have reopened recently and are reportedly making a profit.

One of the advantages of staying in this area, 55 miles southeast of Sacramento, is that both the northern and southern regions of the Gold Country are

Poor but Proud

Three miles south of Placerville is the funky little town of El Dorado, whose claim to fame is gold of another kind—Galliano liqueur. Legend has it that, long ago, one of the town's locals became the proud new owner of a gold-colored Cadillac. To celebrate his new purchase, he went to the town saloon, Poor Red's, and asked the bartender to whip him up a commemorative drink, preferably something to match the color of his Caddy. Grabbing the only golden-hued elixir he could find, the bartender proceeded to mix a little of this with a jigger of that and presto! The Golden Cadillac cocktail was born. Word got around quickly about how great the drink was, and soon people from all over the *world* were literally lining up out the door for a glass of Poor Red's finest.

What? You don't believe me? Right then, go see for yourself. At the end of the bar in a glass showcase is a plaque—sent directly from the Galliano company in Italy—that honors Poor Red's as the largest user of Galliano liqueur in North America. And while you're there, you might as well try their barbecued chicken, ham, steak, and pork ribs—all of which are served big and priced small. **Poor Red's,** 6221 Pleasant Valley Rd., in downtown El Dorado (© **530/622-2901**), is open for lunch Monday through Friday and daily for dinner.

only a few hours' drive away (via very winding roads, however). If you're intent on seeing as much of the Gold Country as possible in a few days' time, any one of these three towns will suffice as a good home base.

To reach Amador City, Sutter Creek, or Jackson from Placerville, head south along Calif. 49 past Plymouth and Drytown. If you're coming straight here from Sacramento, take U.S. 50 to Placerville and head south on Calif. 49; Calif. 16 from Sacramento is another option, but only slightly faster. For more information about any of these towns, contact the **Amador County Chamber of Commerce,** 125 Peek St., Jackson (© **209/223-0350;** www.amadorcountychamber. com).

AMADOR CITY ✿
Once a bustling mining town, Amador City is now devoted mostly to dredging up tourist dollars. Although Amador City sounds large and impressive, it is in fact so tiny that it holds the title as the smallest incorporated city in California. Local merchants have made the most of a refurbished block-long boardwalk, converting the historic false-fronted buildings into a gallery of sorts; the stores sell everything from early 1900s antiques and folk art to handcrafted furniture, gold-rush memorabilia, rare books, and Native American crafts. Parking can be difficult, however, especially in summer.

Where to Stay & Dine
Imperial Hotel ✿ Proprietors Bruce Sherrill and Dale Martin did a brilliant job restoring this stately century-old brick hotel and restaurant, located at the foot of Main Street overlooking Amador City. The individually decorated rooms—all with private bathrooms—are furnished with brass, iron, or pine

beds and numerous antiques; two come with private balconies. My favorite room features hand-painted, whimsical furnishings by local artist John Johannsen. The Imperial Hotel restaurant, serving Mediterranean/California cuisine, has a sterling reputation, and hotel guests can take advantage of room service when it's open from 5 to 9pm. The restaurant is worth a detour, even if you aren't staying here.

Main St. (Calif. 49), P.O. Box 195, Amador City, CA 95601-0195. (C) **800/242-5594** or 209/267-9172. Fax 209/267-9249. www.imperialamador.com. 6 units. $85–$115 double. Rates include breakfast. AE, DISC, MC, V. **Amenities:** Restaurant; bar; room service; in-room massage. *In room:* A/C, hair dryer, no phone.

SUTTER CREEK

The self-proclaimed "nicest little town in the Mother Lode," Sutter Creek was named after sawmill owner John Sutter, employer of James Marshall (the first white man to discover gold in California). Railroad baron Leland Stanford made

 A Modern Gold Mine Tour

One of the most entertaining and educational attractions in the Gold Country is the Sutter Gold Mine Tours hour-long excursion into the bowels of a modern hard-rock gold mine. With an emphasis on authenticity, the tour starts with a ride on a mining shuttle to the mine, where you'll have to "tag in" and go through the safety training room, just as if you were one of the modern miners. Wearing your hardhat, you'll then proceed deep into the mine, learning about geology and the history of mining technology while marveling at the gemstones and real gold deposits embedded in the quartz of the Comet Vein (you'll even learn to spot the difference between real gold and "fool's gold").

After the tour, be sure to buy a bag of mining ore—about $5 per bag—head over to the wood sluice, grab one of the gold pans or sluice boxes, and pan for real gold. Each bag is guaranteed to hold either gold or gemstones (emeralds, amethysts, topaz, and many more birthstones), and there's always an assistant on hand to show you how it's done. The kids get a real kick out of this. Other diversions include the Company Store gift shop filled with a huge assortment of inexpensive semiprecious gems and minerals, and a small movie theater that offers a 1-hour documentary about the gold rush and a half-hour movie about modern gold mining (a heavy-machinery flick that kids will love). And if you're truly a gold-mine enthusiast, there's also a 3- to 4-hour "Deep Mine Experience" that really goes deep into the mine, but it's by reservation only.

The **Sutter Gold Mine** ((C) **888/818-7462;** www.suttergold.com) is open daily year-round from 9am to 5pm in the summer and 10am to 4pm October through May. The 1-hour Family Tour is $15 for adults and children ages 14 and older, $13 for AAA members and seniors 55 and older, and $10 for kids 4 to 13; kids under 4 are not allowed on the tour. The Family Tours take place on the hour and reservations are not necessary. The mine is located on Highway 49, about ½ mile south of Amador City, just north of Sutter Creek.

his fortune at Sutter Creek's Lincoln Mine, and then invested his millions to both build the transcontinental railroad and fund his successful campaign to become governor of California.

The town is a real charmer, lined with beautiful 19th-century buildings in pristine condition, including **Downs Mansion,** the former home of the foreman at Stanford's mine (now a private residence on Spanish St., across from the Immaculate Conception Church), and the landmark **Knight's Foundry,** 81 Eureka St., off Main Street, the last water-powered foundry and machine shop in the nation. There are also numerous shops and galleries along Main Street, though finding a free parking space can be a real challenge on summer weekends.

Where to Stay & Dine

The Foxes 🦊🦊 This 1857 clapboard house run by Annie and Bob Elliott is Sutter Creek's most elegant hostelry. The seven rooms are all uniquely decorated, each with a queen-size bed and down comforters. Five rooms, including the Garden Room and the Fox Den, have gas-burning fireplaces. The Fox Den also has a little library of its own, while the Anniversary room features a 9-foot-tall Renaissance Revival bed and a separate sitting room. All have private bathrooms. Breakfast, cooked to order and delivered on silver service along with the morning paper, can be served in your room or in the gazebo in the flower-filled garden.

77 Main St. (P.O. Box 159), Sutter Creek, CA 95685. © **800/987-3344** or 209/267-5882. Fax 209/267-0712. www.foxesinn.com. 7 units. $140–$215 double. Rates include breakfast. AE, DISC, MC, V. *In room:* A/C, TV/VCR, fridge, hair dryer, no phone.

Grey Gables Inn 🦊 The Grey Gables Inn is a postcard-perfect replica of a Victorian manor made all the more English by Roger and Sue Garlick, two amicable British expatriates who relish being innkeepers. The two-story B&B is surrounded by terraces of colorful gardens and embellished with fountains and vine-covered arbors. "A touch of the English countryside," says Sue. Each of the plushly carpeted guest rooms is named after a British poet; the Byron Room, for example, features hues of deep green and burgundy, dark-wood furnishings, and a Renaissance Revival bed. All rooms have queen or king beds, gas-log fireplaces, large armoires, and private bathrooms (a few with claw-foot tubs). Breakfast, delivered on fine English bone china, is served either in the formal dining room adjacent to the Victorian parlor or in your room. The only flaw in an otherwise perfect B&B is the bit-too-close proximity to heavily traveled Calif. 49, but once inside, you'll hardly notice. The shops and restaurants of Sutter Creek are within walking distance.

161 Hanford St., Sutter Creek, CA 95685. © **800/473-9422** or 209/267-1039. Fax 209/267-0998. www.grey gables.com. 8 units. $110–$200 double. AE, DC, DISC, MC, V. *In room:* A/C, hair dryer, no phone.

Zinfandels 🦊🦊 CALIFORNIA Greg West's Zinfandels has received nothing but kudos since it first opened in July 1996. Greg, a 6-year veteran of Greens Restaurant (p. 103), makes and bakes just about everything in-house, including the breads and pastries. Though the emphasis is on low-fat vegetarian fare such as butternut-squash risotto with pancetta, leeks, crimini mushrooms, and spinach, West also offers a trio of fresh fish, chicken, and beef dishes ranging from cannelloni filled with lamb sausage, chard, and smoked mozzarella to Petrale sole with a citrus-ginger beurre blanc. The menu changes monthly to take advantage of seasonal produce from local farms, and even the wines—paired with each dish—are provided by local wineries such as Sobon and Karly. An appealing alternative to a full sit-down dinner is the wine-tasting/appetizer/dessert room downstairs.

Coloma: Where the Gold Rush Began

Located on Calif. 49 between Auburn and Placerville, the town of Coloma ⭐ is so small, placid, and unpretentious that it's hard to imagine the significant role it played in the rapid development of California and the West. For it was here that James Marshall, working on John Sutter's mill, first discovered that there was gold aplenty in the foothills of California. Over the next 50 years, 125 *million* ounces of gold were taken from the Sierra foothills, an amount worth a staggering $50 billion today.

Although Marshall and Sutter tried to keep the discovery secret, word soon leaked out. Sam Brannan, who ran a general store at Fort Sutter, secured some gold samples himself—as well as significant amounts of choice Coloma real estate—and then headed for San Francisco, where he ran through the streets shouting, "Gold! Gold! Gold! From the American River!" San Francisco rapidly emptied as men rushed off to seek their fortunes at the mines (and make Sam Brannan's as well).

Coloma was quickly mined out, but its boom brought 10,000 people to the settlement and lasted long enough for residents to build a schoolhouse, a gunsmith, a general store, and a tiny, tin-roofed post office. The miners also planted oak and mimosa trees that shade the street during hot summers. About 70% of this quiet, pretty town lies in the **Marshall Gold Discovery State Historic Park** (© **530/622-3470**; www.coloma.com/gold), which preserves the spot where James Wilson Marshall discovered gold along the banks of the south fork of the American River.

Farther up Main Street is a huge replica of the mill Marshall was building when he made his discovery. The largest building in town, the mill is powered by electricity during the summer. Other attractions in the park include the **Gold Discovery Museum,** which relates the story of the gold rush, and a number of Chinese stores, all that remain of the once sizable local Chinese community. The park also has three picnic areas, four trails, recreational gold panning, and a number of buildings and exhibits relating the way of life that prevailed here in the 19th century. Admission is $5 per vehicle; hours are daily from 10am to 5pm, except on major holidays.

Folks also come here for white-water thrills on the American River. (Coloma is a popular launching point.) **White Water Connection,** in Coloma (© **530/622-6446**; www.whitewaterconnection.com), offers ½- to 2-day trips down the frothy forks of the American River. It's great fun and one of the Gold Country's best outdoor attractions.

51 Hanford St. © 209/267-5008. Reservations recommended. Main courses $17–$25. AE, DISC, MC, V. Thurs 5:30–9:30pm; Fri–Sun 11:30am–2:30pm and 5:30–9:30pm.

JACKSON ⭐

Jackson, the county seat of Amador County, is far livelier than its neighboring towns to the north. (It was the last place in California to outlaw prostitution.)

Be sure to take time to stroll through the center of town, browsing in the stores and admiring the Victorian architecture. Although the Kennedy and Argonaut mines ultimately produced more than $140 million in gold, Jackson initially earned its place in the gold rush as a supply center. That history is apparent in the town's wide Main Street, lined by tall buildings adorned with intricate iron railings.

Make no mistake: This is not a ghost town, but rather a modern mini-city that has worked to preserve its pre-Victorian influence. At the southern end of the street is the famous **National Hotel,** 2 Water St., at Main Street (*C* **209/ 223-0500;** www.national-hotel.com), one of California's oldest continuously operating hotels since it opened its doors in 1862. Will Rogers, John Wayne, Leland Stanford, and many other celebrities and big-time politicos of the 19th century stayed here. Today, the hotel's **Louisiana House Bar**—a cool, dark establishment where weary travelers can rest while a honky-tonk pianist beats out ragtime tunes and classic oldies—does a brisk business (alas, the guest rooms aren't nearly as enjoyable).

The **Amador County Museum,** a huge brick building at 225 Church St. (*C* **209/223-6386**), is where Will Rogers filmed *Boys Will Be Boys* in 1920. Today, the former home of Armistead Calvin Brown and his 11 children is filled with mining memorabilia and information on two local mines, the Kennedy and the Argonaut, that were among the deepest and richest in the nation. Within the museum is a working large-scale model of the Kennedy. The museum is open Wednesday through Sunday from 10am to 4pm; admission is by a contribution of any amount. Tours of the museum cost $2 and are offered Saturday and Sunday on the hour from 11am to 3pm.

If you would rather see the real thing, head to the **Kennedy Tailing Wheels Park,** site of the famous Kennedy and Argonaut mines, the deepest in the Mother Lode. The mines have been closed for decades, but the huge tailing wheels and head frames, used to convey mine debris over the hills to a settling pond, remain. To reach the park, take Main Street to Jackson Gate Road, just north of Jackson (no phone).

A few miles south of Jackson on Calif. 49 is one of the most evocative mining towns of the region: **Mokelumne Hill** ⚘. The town basically consists of one street overlooking a valley with a few old buildings, and somehow its sad, abandoned air has the mark of authenticity. At one time, the hill was dotted with tents and wood-and-tar paper shacks, and the town housed a population of 15,000, including an old French quarter and a Chinatown. But now many of its former residents are merely memorialized in the town's Protestant, Jewish, and Catholic cemeteries.

Where to Stay & Dine

Court Street Inn ⚘   Two blocks from Main Street, this Victorian beauty— listed on the National Register of Historic Places—was built circa 1870 and is brimming with elegant details such as eyelash shutters, embossed ceilings, and a marble fireplace. My favorite room is Burgundy Court, with its oak-mantled fireplace and handsome four-poster king-size bed. Romantics will like the Bordeaux Court's private sitting room and sleigh bed, or the separate and secluded Chablis Court with its own private terrace, skylight, and corner fireplace. The guest rooms are very nicely decorated; all have down bedding and gas or electric fireplaces, and some have whirlpool or claw-foot tubs. The separate two-story/two-bedroom Indian House cottage can accommodate up to four guests. There's a porch where guests can relax outside, and an outdoor Jacuzzi that's ideal for

A Visit to Volcano

About a dozen miles east of Jackson on Calif. 88 is the enchantingly decrepit town of Volcano ⍟, one of the most authentic ghost towns in the central Sierra. The town got its name in 1848, after miners mistook the origins of the enormous craggy boulders that lie in the center of town. The dark rock and blind window frames of a few backless, ivy-covered buildings give the town's main thoroughfare a haunted look. Sprinkled between boarded-up buildings, about 100 residents do business in the same sagging storefronts that a population of 8,000 frequented nearly 150 years ago.

One thing you'll notice about Volcano is the overwhelming silence of its streets. But the tiny, now-quiet burg has a rich history: Not only was this boomtown once home to 17 hotels, courts of quick justice, and the state's first lending library and astronomical observatory, but Volcano gold also supported the Union during the Civil War. Residents even smuggled a huge cannon to the front line in a hearse (it was never used). The story goes that had the enthusiastic blues actually fired it, it was so overcharged that "Old Abe" would have exploded. The cannon sits in the town center today, under a rusting weather vane.

Looming over the small buildings is the stately **St. George Hotel** ⍟ (*C* **209/296-4458;** www.stgeorgehotel.com), a three-story, balconied building that testifies to the $90 million in gold mined in and around the town. Its ivy-covered brick and shuttered windows will remind you of colonial New England. In 1998 new owners took over the run-down 20-room hotel and have totally turned it around. The restaurant serves brunch on Sunday, and dinner Thursday through Sunday. Even if you're not hungry, stop in for a libation at the classic old bar, the Whiskey Flat Saloon.

In summer, the **Volcano Theatre Company** performs at the town's outdoor amphitheater, hidden behind stone facades on Main Street, a block north of the St. George Hotel. It's a wonderful Gold Country experience. For information on upcoming performances, call *C* **209/296-2525.** And in early spring, hundreds of people come from all around to picnic amid the nearly half-million daffodils in bloom on **Daffodil Hill,** a 4-acre ranch 3 miles north of Volcano (follow the sign on Ram's Horn Grade).

stargazing. A full homemade breakfast (served outside on the terrace on sunny days) and complimentary evening refreshments are included in the room rate.

215 Court St., Jackson, CA 95642. *C* **800/200-0416** or 209/223-0416. Fax 209/223-5429. www.courtstreet inn.com. 6 units, 1 cottage. $115–$155 double; $175–$225 cottage. Rates include breakfast. AE, DISC, MC, V. **Amenities:** Jacuzzi. *In room:* A/C, TV on request, iron, no phone.

Mel and Faye's Diner *Value* AMERICAN   How can anybody not love a classic old roadside diner? In business since 1956, Mel and Faye have been cranking out the best diner food in the Gold Country for so long that it's okay to not feel guilty for salivating over the thought of a sloppy double Moo Burger smothered with onions and special sauce and washed down with a large chocolate shake.

And could you please add a large side of fries with that? And how much is a slice of pie? It's a time-honored Jackson tradition, so forget about your diet.

205 Calif. 49 (at Main St.). © 209/223-0853. Menu items $4–$8. DISC, MC, V. Daily 4:45am–10pm.

Upstairs Restaurant & Streetside Bistro ℱ INTERNATIONAL   This adorable little restaurant offers a limited menu that changes weekly, but you might stumble on some true culinary gems, such as pasta puttanesca with tomato-basil fettuccine and fresh Roma tomatoes, or julienned duck served with a blackberry-ginger sauce. Layne McCollum, a graduate of California's Culinary Academy, is known as the town's finest and most sophisticated chef, with a reputation for imaginative and innovative cuisine. Crisp white linens, bowls of fresh flowers, and background music provide a romantic backdrop to the restaurant's 12 candlelit tables. Lunch—quiche, soups, salads, and gourmet sandwiches such as smoked pork loin with red chile pesto on chipotle—is served until about 2:30pm in the bright, cheery Streetside Bistro, which is tastefully outfitted with wrought-iron furniture, tile flooring, and colorful oil paintings.

164 Main St. © 209/223-3342. Reservations recommended. Main courses $16–$30. AE, DISC, MC, V. Wed–Fri 11:30am–2:30pm, Sat–Sun 11:30am–3:30pm; Wed–Sun 5:30–9pm.

THE SOUTHERN GOLD COUNTRY: ANGELS CAMP, MURPHYS, COLUMBIA, SONORA & JAMESTOWN

No other region in the Gold Country offers more to see and do than these towns in the south, 86 miles southeast of Sacramento. From exploring enormous caverns to riding in the stagecoach and panning for real gold, the neighboring towns of Angels Camp, Murphys, Columbia, Sonora, and Jamestown offer a cornucopia of gold rush–related sites, museums, and activities. It's a great place to bring the family (kids love roaming around the dusty car-free streets of Columbia), and the region offers some of the best lodgings and restaurants in the Gold Country. In short, if you're the Type-A sort who needs to stay active, the southern Gold Country is for you.

To reach any of these towns from Sacramento, head south on Calif. 99 to Stockton, then take Calif. 4 east directly into Angels Camp. (From here, it's a short, scenic drive to all the other towns.) For a much longer but more scenic route, take U.S. 50 east to Placerville and head south on Calif. 49, which also takes you directly to Angels Camp.

ANGELS CAMP ℱ

You've probably heard of Angels Camp, the town that inspired Mark Twain to pen "The Celebrated Jumping Frog of Calaveras County." This pretty, peaceful Gold Country community is built on hills that are honeycombed with mine tunnels. In the 1880s and 1890s, five mines were located along Main Street—Sultana, Angel's, Lightner, Utica, and Stickle—and the town echoed with noise as more than 200 stamps crushed the ore. Between 1886 and 1910, the five mines generated close to $20 million.

But a far-more lasting legacy than the town's gold production is the **Jumping Frog Jubilee,** started in 1928 to mark the paving of the town's streets. To this day, the ribbiting competition takes place every third weekend in May. The record, 21 feet, 5¾ inches, was jumped in 1986 by "Rosie the Ribbiter," beating the old world record by 4½ inches. Livestock exhibitions, pageants, cook-offs, arm-wrestling tournaments, live music, carnival rides, a rodeo, and plenty of beer and wine keep the thousands of spectators entertained between jump-offs. (You can even rent a frog if you forgot to pack one.) For more information

and entry forms ($5 per frog), call the Jumping Frog Jubilee headquarters at
© **209/736-2561.**

Where to Stay

Cooper House Bed & Breakfast Inn ⭐ Once the home and office of a
prominent community physician, Dr. George P. Cooper, the Cooper House is
now Angels Camp's only B&B. This small Arts and Crafts home is mercifully
positioned well away from the hustle and bustle of the town's Main Street.
Owner and innkeeper Kathy Reese maintains three units, all with private bathrooms. The Zinfandel Suite has its own private entrance and deck, and the
Chardonnay Suite has a king-size bed, antique claw-foot bathtub, and a private
deck. The third bedroom, the Cabernet Suite, is midsize, with a queen bed,
adjoining sunroom, and splendid garden view.

1184 Church St. (P.O. Box 1388), Angels Camp, CA 95222. © **800/225-3764**, ext. 326, or 209/736-2145. 3
units. $125 double. Rate includes breakfast. MC, V. *In room:* A/C.

Where to Dine

Camps ⭐ FUSION Located on the edge of a sprawling golf resort on the
western fringes of Angels Camp is Camps, the culinary feather in the cap of
Greenhorn Creek, one of Northern California's newest destination retreats. The
restaurant's architects have successfully integrated the building into its natural
surroundings by constructing the outer walls with locally mined rhyolite and
painting it in natural earth tones. The interior is furnished with leather armchairs, wicker, and antique woods. The best seats in the house are on the spacious veranda overlooking the golf course, the perfect setting for executive chef
Robert Smith's fusion cuisine, a culinary composition that pairs local produce
with European, Asian, and Caribbean influences. Though the menu changes
seasonally, a typical dish may be macadamia-crusted halibut with a mandarin
orange beurre blanc. The house salad with American field greens, toasted pistachios, julienned red onions, and a raspberry vinaigrette is marvelous, as is the
duck à la orange served with a traditional brigade sauce and wild rice.

676 McCauley Ranch Rd. (½ mile W of Calif. 4/Calif. 49 junction off Angel Oaks Dr.). © **209/736-8181.**
www.greenhorncreek.com. Reservations recommended. Main courses $15–$24. AE, MC, V. Tues–Sat
11:30am–3pm; Wed–Sun 5:30–9pm; Sun brunch 11am–3pm.

Crusco's Ristorante ⭐ ITALIAN The sign at the entrance says it all: "Relax
and enjoy. This is not fast food." The point being that the overall dining experience is as important as the cuisine at Cursco's, a family-run restaurant headed
by Celeste Lusher, the amiable chef/owner who oversees the kitchen along with
her daughter Sarah while her husband and son-in-law cater to their customers.
Located in the heart of old-town Angels Camp, the restaurant's decor is an
attractive balance of 19th-century gold-rush architecture—exposed wood
beams, 1½-foot-thick stone walls, dark wood furnishings—and old-world
Mediterranean objets d'art such as faux columns and bas-relief sculptures. It's an
apropos setting for Lusher's classic Italian menu, made from scratch using generations of family recipes. Each meal begins with warm house-made focaccia
served with olive oil and balsamic vinegar, then come the tough choices: grilled
tenderloin of lamb with rosemary and garlic, the creamy polenta, or the hugely
popular penne rigate. For lunch, Celeste recommends the New York steak sandwich on fresh focaccia. Sampling a few of the house-made desserts is highly
advised as well.

1240 S. Main St. © **209/736-1440.** Reservations recommended. Main courses $14–$20. DISC, MC, V.
Thurs–Mon 11:30am–3pm and 5–9pm (possibly closed in spring—call ahead).

MURPHYS ⚲

From Angels Camp, a 20-minute drive east along Calif. 4 takes you to Murphys, one of our favorite Gold Country towns. Legend has it Murphys started as a former trading post set up by brothers Dan and John Murphy in cooperation with local Indians (John married the chief's daughter). These days, its peaceful community is made up of gingerbread Victorians shaded by tall locust trees bordering narrow streets. Be sure to take a stroll down Main Street, stopping in **Grounds** (p. 341) for a bite to eat and perhaps a cool draft of Murphys Red—direct from **Murphys Brewing Company**—at the rustic saloon within Murphys Historic Hotel and Lodge at 457 Main St.

While you're here, you might also want to check out **Ironstone Vineyards,** 1894 Six Mile Rd., 1 mile south of downtown Murphys (© 209/728-1251), a veritable wine theme park built by the Kautz family. It boasts an enormous tasting room, jewelry shop, museum housing the largest crystalline gold piece in existence, gallery, amphitheater, music room, caverns, park and gardens, and even a culinary center. It's open daily from 10am to 6pm.

Also in the vicinity—just off Calif. 4, 1 mile north of Murphys off Sheep Ranch Road—are the **Mercer Caverns** (© 209/728-2101). These caverns, discovered in 1885 by Walter Mercer, contain a variety of geological formations—crystalline stalactites and stalagmites—in a series of descending chambers. Tours of the well-lit caverns take nearly an hour. From Memorial Day to September, hours are Sunday through Thursday from 9am to 6pm, Friday and Saturday from 9am to 8pm; from October to late May, Sunday through Thursday from 10am to 4:30pm, Friday and Saturday from 10am to 6pm. Admission is $9 for adults, $5 for children ages 5 to 12, and free for children under 5.

Fifteen miles east of Murphys up Calif. 4 is **Calaveras Big Trees State Park** ⚲ (© 209/795-2334), where you can witness giant sequoias that are among the biggest and oldest living things on earth. It's a popular summer retreat that offers camping, swimming, hiking, and fishing along the Stanislaus River. It's open daily; admission is $2 per car for day use.

Where to Stay

Dunbar House, 1880 ⚲⚲   This pretty Italianate home, built in 1880 for the bride of a local businessman, is one of the finest B&Bs in the Gold Country. The inviting front porch, which overlooks the exquisite gardens, is decorated with wicker furniture and hanging baskets of ivy. Inside, the emphasis is on comfort and elegance. The recently redecorated rooms are furnished with quality antiques and equipped with every possible amenity. Beds have lace-trimmed linens and down comforters, and each room has a wood-burning stove and fridge stocked with mineral water and a complimentary bottle of wine. My favorite room, the Cedar, is a fabulous two-room suite with a private sun porch, whirlpool tub, and complimentary champagne. I also like the Sugar Pine suite, with its private balcony in the trees. Lemonade and cookies are offered in the afternoon, appetizers and wine in the early evening. Breakfast is served in your room, the dining room, or the garden.

271 Jones St., Murphys, CA 95247. © **800/692-6006** or 209/728-2897. Fax 209/728-1451. www.dunbar house.com. 5 units. $175–$225 double. Rates include breakfast and afternoon appetizers. AE, MC, V. *In room:* A/C, TV/VCR, hair dryer, iron.

Where to Dine

Firewood AMERICAN   Local restaurateur River Klass has recently opened this order-at-the-counter cafe just down the street from his Grounds restaurant (see below). The open-air establishment specializes in fast, inexpensive, and darn good dishes such as Baja-style fish tacos, drippingly juicy "not healthy" burgers, baby-back ribs with house-made barbecue sauce, and superb gourmet pizzas baked in a wood-burning oven (the prosciutto and arugula, shrimp and feta, and sausage and pepperoni versions are all big hits). Good micro-beer and local wine selections are available as well. *Note:* River might change the name of the restaurant due to legal reasons, but everything else will remain the same.

420 Main St. ℂ **209/728-3248.** Reservations not accepted. Main courses $5–$10. MC, V. Wed–Fri 11am–8pm, Sat–Sun 11am–9pm.

Grounds ✿ ECLECTIC   When River Klass moved here from the East Coast to open his own place, Murphys' restaurant-challenged residents heaved a collective sigh of relief. Its nickname is the "Rude Boy Cafe," after Klass's acerbic wit, but you'll find only happy smiles and friendly service from the energetic staff. The majority of Grounds's business is with the locals, who have become addicted to the potato pancakes that come with every made-to-order omelet. For lunch, try the sausage sandwich on house-baked bread or the grilled eggplant sandwich stuffed with smoked mozzarella and fresh basil. Although the menus change twice a week, typical dinner choices include fettuccine topped with sautéed shrimp, halibut, and mussels in a garlic cream sauce; grilled halibut served with rock shrimp and spinach dumplings; and a big, fat Angus rib-eye served with fresh grilled vegetables and garlic mashed potatoes. The wine list is equally impressive (and reasonably priced). The long, narrow dining rooms are bright and airy with pinewood furnishings, wood floors, and an open kitchen. On sunny days, request a table on the back patio.

402 Main St. ℂ **209/728-8663.** Reservations recommended. Main courses $7.50–$16. AE, DISC, MC, V. Mon–Tues 7am–4pm, Wed–Sat 7am–9pm, Sun 8am–9pm.

COLUMBIA

Though a little hokey and contrived, **Columbia State Historic Park** ✪✪ (ℂ **209/532-4301** for the museum and tours) is the best-maintained gold-rush town in the Mother Lode (as well as one of the most popular, so expect crowds in the summer). At one point, this boisterous mining town was the state's second largest city (and only two votes shy of becoming the state capital over Sacramento). When gold mining no longer panned out in the late 1850s, most of the town's 15,000 residents departed, leaving much of the mining equipment and buildings in place. In 1945, the entire town was turned into a Historic Park.

As a result, Columbia has been preserved and functions much as it did in the 1850s, with stagecoach rides, Western-style Victorian hotels and saloons, a newspaper office, a working blacksmith's forge, a Wells Fargo express office, and numerous other relics of California's early mining days. Cars are banned from its dusty streets, giving the shady town an authentic and noncommercial feel. Merchants still do business behind some storefronts, as horse, stagecoach, and pedestrian traffic wanders by.

If Columbia's heat and dust get to you, pull up a stool at the **Jack Douglass Saloon** on Main Street (no phone), open daily from 10am to 5pm. Inside the swinging doors of the classic Western bar, you can sample homemade sarsaparilla and wild cherry, drinks the saloon has been serving since 1857. The storefront's large shuttered windows open onto a dusty main street, so put up your boots, relax awhile, and watch the stagecoach go by.

Historical tours of the park depart from the Main Museum daily at 11am and 1:30pm. The 45-minute, $2 stroll takes you down Main Street and into dusty old structures that are off-limits to the general public.

Where to Stay & Dine

City Hotel ★ *Kids*   Established in 1856, the historic City Hotel was fully restored in 1975 by the State of California, the nonprofit City Hotel Corporation, and Columbia College, and is now run as a sort of on-the-job training center for hospitality-management students (hence the eager-to-please staff). It's a big, beautiful building, complete with a stately parlor furnished with Victorian sofas, antiques, and Oriental rugs. The largest guest rooms have two balconies overlooking Main Street; the units off the parlor are also spacious. The hallway rooms are smaller but still nicely furnished with Renaissance Revival beds and antiques. Each room has a sink and toilet, but the shower rooms are separate. A large buffet breakfast is served in the dining room. The hotel also runs a fine-dining restaurant serving classic Continental cuisine (roast rack of lamb, grilled salmon, and smoked duck breast) Tuesday through Sunday, as well as the What Cheer saloon. Noise from the saloon, though perhaps not as loud as when the customers packed pistols, does travel upstairs, so if you're a light sleeper, bring earplugs.

Main St. (P.O. Box 1870), Columbia State Park, CA 95310. ✆ **800/532-1479** or 209/532-1479. Fax 209/532-7027. www.cityhotel.com. 10 units (all with shared shower rooms). $105–$125 double. Rates include breakfast. DISC, MC, V. **Amenities:** Restaurant (open Tues–Sun); saloon; nearby golf course. *In room:* A/C, no phone.

Fallon Hotel ★ *Kids*   Opened in 1857, this hotel has been restored and decorated to evoke the 1890s. The classic two-story building retains many of its original antiques and furniture. The largest rooms are those along the front upper balcony. Only one unit has a full bathroom; the rest have a private sink and toilet, and showers are down the hall. Rooms are furnished with high-backed Victorian beds, marble-topped dressers, rockers, and similar oak pieces. A full breakfast is served in the downstairs parlor.

Washington St. (P.O. Box 1870), Columbia State Park, CA 95310. ✆ **800/532-1479** or 209/532-1470. Fax 209/532-7027. www.cityhotel.com. 14 units, 13 with shared bathroom. $60–$125 double. Rates include breakfast. DISC, MC, V. **Amenities:** Ice-cream parlor; nearby golf course. *In room:* A/C, no phone.

SONORA

Located a few miles south of Columbia, Sonora is the largest town in the southern Gold Country. (You'll know you've arrived when traffic starts to crawl.) Back in the gold-rush days, Sonora and Columbia were the two richest towns in the Mother Lode. Dozens of stores and small cafes line the main thoroughfare. If you can find a parking space, it's worth your while to spend an hour or two checking out the sites, including the 19th-century **St. James Episcopal Church,** at the top of Washington Street, and the **Tuolumne County Museum and History Center,** 158 W. Bradford Ave. (✆ **209/532-1317**), located in the 1857 County Jail. Admission is free, and it's open daily year-round: Sunday through Friday from 10am to 4pm, Saturday from 10am to 3:30pm.

Where to Dine

Diamondback Grill *Value* AMERICAN   For more than a decade, this modest little family-owned diner has whipped up the Gold Country's best burger: the Diamondback—a grilled-to-order half-pounder that comes with all the works, including fries. There are about a dozen other burgers to choose from, as well as gourmet sandwiches (go for the grilled eggplant with fresh tomato and mozzarella), house-made soups and pecan pies, a zesty black-bean-and-steak chili, and great specials listed daily on the board. There's also a good selection of beer and wine by the glass.

110 S. Washington St. ✆ 209/532-6661. Main courses $5–$10. No credit cards. Mon–Sat 11am–9pm; Sun 11am–5pm.

Fun Fact **How to Pan for Gold**

Find a gold pan, ideally a 12- to 15-inch steel pan. Place the pan over an oven burner, or better yet, in a campfire. This will darken the pan, making it easier to see any flakes of placer gold (many gold pans come already blackened). Find some gravel, sand, or dirt in a stream that looks promising or feels lucky. Scoop dirt into the pan until it's nearly full, then place it under water and keep it there while you break up the clumps of mud and clay and toss out any stones. Then grasp the pan with both hands. Holding it level, rotate it in swirling motions. This will cause the heavier gold to loosen and settle to the bottom of the pan. Drain off the dirty water and loose stuff. Keep doing this until gold and heavier minerals called "black sand" are left in the pan. Carefully inspect the black sand for nuggets or speck traces of gold. Who knows? You just might get lucky.

If this all seems too much to try on your own, you can sign up for a gold-panning lesson with Jamestown's **Gold Prospecting Adventures** (© **209/984-4653**; www.goldprospecting.com). The hour-long instruction costs about $15, and yes, you get to keep any gold you might find.

La Torre's North Beach Café ⊀ ITALIAN   Chef and owner Terry La Torre has turned this former auto-parts store into one of the most popular restaurants in Sonora. A longtime local and progeny of San Francisco restaurateurs, the well-rounded, mustachioed La Torre can usually be found draped in chef's whites, barking orders to his amiable staff. The place is almost always abuzz with customers who come to eat La Torre's cooking and to bask in his infectious banter. The menu is predominantly Italian, including a dozen or so pastas, fresh fish, veal, chicken, and steaks. The combination of fair prices, good food, and classic La Torre histrionics makes North Beach Café worth searching out.

14317 Mono Way/Calif. 108 (from central Sonora, go 3 miles E on Calif. 108). © **209/536-1852.** Main courses $7.50–$14. AE, MC, V. Daily 11am–9pm.

JAMESTOWN ⊀

About 4 miles southwest of Sonora on Calif. 49 is Jamestown, a 4-block-long town of old-fashioned storefronts and two rustic turn-of-the-20th-century hotels. Yes, there's gold in these parts, too, as the marker commemorating the discovery of a 75-pound nugget will attest (panning nearby Woods Creek is a popular pastime among both locals and tourists). If Jamestown looks eerily familiar to you, that's probably because you've seen it in the movies or on television. It's one of Hollywood's favorite Western movie sets; scenes from such films as *Butch Cassidy and the Sundance Kid* were shot here.

Jamestown's most popular attraction is the **Railtown 1897 State Historic Park** ⊀, a train buff's paradise featuring three original Sierra steam locomotives. These great machines were used in many a movie and television show, including *High Noon, Little House on the Prairie, Bonanza,* and *My Little Chickadee.* The trains at the roundhouse are on display daily year-round. Call for information on weekend rides and guided tours. The Depot Store and Museum are open daily from 9:30am to 4:30pm. The park is located near the center of town, on Fifth Avenue at Reservoir Road (☎ **209/984-3953;** www.csrmf.org/railtown).

Where to Stay & Dine

1859 Historic National Hotel & Restaurant ✮ Located in the center of town, this two-story classic Western hotel has been operating since 1859, making it one of the 10 oldest continuously operating hotels in the state. The saloon has its original 19th-century redwood bar, and you can imagine what it must have been like when miners traded gold dust for drinks. The rooms above are outfitted with numerous period antiques, as well as oak furnishings and brass beds. A recent addition is an authentic "Soaking Room," a private room equipped with a sort of 1800s claw-foot Jacuzzi for two (when cowboys longed for a good, hot soak). All units have private bathrooms. The restaurant on the main floor serves Continental cuisine with a California influence, such as brandy-apple pork, ruby trout amandine, and blackened prime rib with sautéed prawns.

77 Main St. (P.O. Box 502), Jamestown, CA 95327. ☎ **800/894-3446** or 209/984-3446. Fax 209/984-5620. www.national-hotel.com. 9 units. $90–$130 double. Rates include buffet breakfast. AE, DC, DISC, MC, V. Pets accepted with $10-per-night fee. **Amenities:** Restaurant; saloon; nearby golf course; concierge; tour/activities desk; business center; secretarial services; room service; in-room massage. *In room:* A/C, TV, dataport, coffeemaker, hair dryer.

Jamestown Hotel & Restaurant ✮ The most worked-over building in town, the Jamestown was originally built in 1858; it burned down and was rebuilt twice before 1915. To achieve the old-fashioned, brick-fronted Victorian look it sports today, a lot of stucco and Spanish-revival paraphernalia had to be removed. New innkeepers/owners Annette and Norbert Mede continue to make improvements to the venerable hotel, restoring much of its original appeal. Most of the lower floor is devoted to the front office, bar, and newly renovated restaurant run by Norbert, who also wears a chef's hat. The second floor contains a cadre of cozy bedrooms outfitted with antiques acquired along both coasts of North America. All of the spacious rooms are loaded with nostalgic charm; a few have sitting rooms and TVs with VCRs, and all have private bathrooms (some with claw-foot tubs). The most popular has its own balcony. The street-level rooms are the most luxurious, outfitted with whirlpool tubs, private patios, and individual heat and air-conditioning controls.

18153 Main St. (P.O. Box 539), Jamestown, CA 95327. ☎ **800/205-4901** or 209/984-3902. Fax 209/984-4149. www.jamestownhotel.com. 11 units. $105–$195 double. Rates include full breakfast. AE, DC, DISC, MC, V. **Amenities:** Restaurant; bar; activities desk; business center. *In room:* A/C, TV/VCR in some units, hair dryer, iron.

3 The Central Valley & Sierra National Forest

The Central Valley (also known as the San Joaquin Valley) is about as far as you can get from California's glamorous movie-stars-in-stretch-limos image. This hot, flat strip of farms, dairies, fast-food joints, cheap motels, and truck stops stretches for some 225 miles from Bakersfield to Redding. The 18,000-square-mile valley is central to the economy of the Golden State, in part because of its cultivated and irrigated fields, orchards, pastures, and vineyards.

The major traffic arteries through the valley are Calif. 99 and I-5. Calif. 99 links the agricultural communities, while I-5 provides access routes to the roadside attractions in the valley. Rivers cutting through the valley offer fishing, boating, house-boating on the delta, and white-water rafting on the rapids. And once you get off the freeways, the valley's spectacular landscapes provide unrivaled natural beauty. Many visitors drive through in spring just to view the orchards in bloom.

The Central Valley also stands on the doorstep of some of America's greatest attractions, the most well known being Yosemite National Park. See chapter 9 for coverage of two Central Valley towns, Merced and Visalia, which are good gateways to Yosemite, Sequoia, and Kings Canyon, respectively.

Fresno, although not much in itself, is on the doorstep of the Sierra National Forest and nearby natural attractions like the Millerton Lake State Recreation Area.

FRESNO

The running joke in California is that Fresno is the "gateway to Bakersfield." For most visitors, Fresno, located 185 miles southeast of San Francisco, is just a place to pass through en route to the state parks; it can, however, be a good place to stop for food and lodging, and it makes a good base for exploring the Sierra National Forest (see below).

Founded in 1874 in the geographic center of the state, Fresno lies in the heart of the Central Valley and has experienced incredible growth in recent years. Like most growing cities, it has been plagued by an increase in crime, drugs, and urban sprawl.

As the seat of Fresno County, the city handles more than $3 billion annually in agricultural production. It also contains Sun Maid, the world's largest dried-fruit packing plant, and Guild, one of the country's largest wineries.

If you have any reason at all to be in Fresno, try to visit between late February and late March so you can drive the **Fresno County Blossom Trail** 𝄞. This 62-mile, self-guided tour takes in the beauty of California's agrarian bounty at its peak. The trail courses through fruit orchards in full bloom and citrus groves with lovely orange blossoms and a heady natural perfume. The **Fresno Convention and Visitors Bureau,** 847 M St., third floor, in Fresno (© **800/788-0836** or 559/233-0836; www.fresnocvb.org), supplies full details, including a map.

WHERE TO STAY

San Joaquin 𝄞   Set on the northern edge of Fresno, this full-service hotel was conceived as an apartment complex in the 1970s. Around 1985, a lobby was added, the floor plans were adjusted, and the place was reconfigured as an all-suite hotel. Suites range from junior one-bedroom suites to three-bedroom suites with kitchens, and each is outfitted in a slightly different style, with light, contemporary colors and furniture. Room service is available from an independently managed restaurant down the street.

1309 W. Shaw Ave., Fresno, CA 93711. © **800/775-1309** or 559/225-1309. Fax 559/225-6021. www.sj hotel.com. 68 suites. $99–$205 suite. Rates include continental breakfast. AE, DC, DISC, MC, V. **Amenities:** Outdoor pool; Jacuzzi; business center; room service; laundry service. *In room:* A/C, TV/VCR, dataport, kitchen, fridge, coffeemaker, hair dryer, iron.

WHERE TO DINE

Veni, Vidi, Vici 𝄞 CALIFORNIA   The most innovative and creative restaurant in Fresno occupies a prominent position about 6 miles south of the commercial center, in a funky neighborhood known as the Tower District. The place's rustic exterior strikes an interesting contrast to the polished and artful interior on the other side of the 15-foot doors, where the decor is accented with exposed brick walls, hanging mirrors, and chandeliers fashioned from twisted wire and metal leaves.

The menu changes often but might include roasted loin of pork with Chinese black beans and citrus-flavored glaze, served with grilled portobello mushrooms, sun-dried tomatoes, risotto, and red-pepper coulis; or a wild-mushroom lasagna with preserved tomato sauce. There are also fresh-fish specials nightly. This is the only restaurant in Fresno that makes its own ice cream (the flavor of the day when we arrived was Technicolor lime sorbet). Have a scoop or two with the restaurant's perennial dessert favorite: bittersweet chocolate cake.

1116 N. Fulton St. ✆ 559/266-5510. Reservations recommended. Main courses $19–$26. AE, DC, DISC, MC, V. Tues–Sun 5–10pm (late-night menu Fri–Sat 10pm–midnight).

SIERRA NATIONAL FOREST ☆☆

Leaving Fresno's taco joints, used-car lots, and tract houses behind, an hour's drive and 45 miles northeast gets you to the Sierra National Forest, a land of lakes and coniferous forests lying between Yosemite, Sequoia, and Kings Canyon national parks. The entire eastern portion of the park is still unspoiled wilderness protected by the government. Development—some of it, unfortunately, beside the bigger lakes and reservoirs—is confined to the western side.

The 1.3-million-acre forest contains 528,000 acres of wilderness. The Sierra's five wilderness areas include Ansel Adams, Dinkey Lakes, John Muir, Kaiser, and Monarch (see below). The forest offers plenty of opportunities for fishing, swimming, sailing, boating, camping, water-skiing, white-water rafting, kayaking, and horseback riding, all regulated by certain guidelines. Downhill and cross-country skiing, as well as hunting, are also available, depending on the season. Backpackers looking to retreat to the wilderness will find solace here, as the park is traversed by some 1,100 miles of forest hiking trails.

ESSENTIALS

GETTING THERE   After visiting the ranger station at Oakhurst, take Calif. 41 to Calif. 49, the major road into the northern part of the national forest. This is more convenient for visitors approaching the park from Northern California. Calif. 168 via Clovis is the primary route from Fresno if you're headed for Shaver Lake. There is no approach road from the eastern Sierra, only from the west.

VISITOR INFORMATION & PERMITS   To learn about hiking, camping, or other activities, or to obtain the fire and wilderness permits needed for back-country jaunts, visit one of the ranger stations in the park's western section. These include **Mariposa and Minarets Ranger Station,** 57003 North Fork (✆ **559/877-2218**); and the **Pineridge Ranger Station,** 29688 Auberry Rd., Prather (✆ **559/855-5360**).

SUPPLIES   Shaver Lake is one place where you can stock up on goods and supplies if you're going into the wilderness, but stores in Fresno carry much of the same stuff at lower prices. Cheaper supplies are also available in the town of Clovis outside Fresno (which you must pass through en route to the forest), especially at the **Peacock Market,** at Tollhouse Road (3rd St.) and Sunnyside Avenue (✆ **559/299-6627**).

WEATHER   In the lower elevations, summer temperatures can frequently reach 100°F (38°C), but in the higher elevations, more comfortable temperatures in the 70s and 80s (20s Celsius) are the norm.

THE MAJOR WILDERNESS & RECREATION AREAS

ANSEL ADAMS WILDERNESS   Divided between the Sierra and Inyo national forests, this wilderness area covers 228,500 acres. Elevations range from

3,500 to 13,157 feet. The frost-free period extends from mid-July to August, the best time for a visit to the park's upper altitudes.

Ansel Adams is dotted with scenic alpine vistas, including steep-walled gorges and barren granite peaks. There are several small glaciers in the north and some fairly large lakes on the eastern slope of the precipitous Ritter Range. This vast wilderness has excellent stream and lake fishing, especially for rainbow, golden, and brook trout, and offers challenging mountain climbing on the Minarets Range. The wilderness is accessed by the Tioga Pass Road in the north, U.S. 395 and Reds Meadow Road in the east, the Minarets Highway in the west, and Calif. 168 to High Sierra in the south.

DINKEY LAKES WILDERNESS   The 30,000-acre Dinkey Lakes area was created in 1984 and occupies the western slope of the Sierra Nevada, southeast of Huntington Lake and just northwest of Courtright Reservoir. Most of the timbered, rolling terrain here is 8,000 feet above sea level, reaching its highest point (10,619 ft.) at Three Sisters Peak. Sixteen lakes are clustered in the west-central region. You can reach the area on Kaiser Pass Road (north), Red/Coyote Jeep Road (west), Rock Creek Road (southwest), or Courtright Reservoir (southeast), generally from mid-June to late October.

JOHN MUIR WILDERNESS   Occupying 584,000 acres in the Sierra and Inyo national forests, John Muir Wilderness—named after the naturalist—extends southeast from Mammoth Lakes along the crest of the Sierra Nevada for 30 miles before forking around the boundary of Kings Canyon National Park to Crown Valley and Mount Whitney. Elevations range from 4,000 to 14,496 feet at Mount Whitney, with many of the area's peaks surpassing 12,000 feet. The wilderness can be accessed from numerous points west of U.S. 395 between Mammoth Lake and Independence.

Split by deep canyons, the wilderness is also a land of meadows (especially beautiful when wildflowers bloom), lakes, and streams. The south and middle forks of the San Joaquin River, the north fork of Kings River, and many creeks draining into Owens Valley originate in the John Muir Wilderness. Mountain hemlock, red and white fir, and white-bark and western pine dot the park's landscape. Temperatures vary wildly throughout any 24-hour period: Summer temperatures range from 25°F to 85°F (-4°C–29°C), and the only really frost-free period is between mid-July and August. The higher elevations are marked by barren expanses of granite splashed with many glacially carved lakes.

KAISER WILDERNESS   Immediately north of Huntington Lake and some 70 miles northeast of Fresno, Kaiser is a 22,700-acre forest tract commanding a view of the central Sierra Nevada. It was named after Kaiser Ridge, which divides the area into two different regions. Four trail heads provide easy access to the wilderness, but the northern half is much more open than the forested southern half; the primary point of entry is the Sample Meadow Campground. All other lakes are approached cross-country. Winter storms begin to blow in late October, and the grounds are generally snow-covered until early June.

MONARCH WILDERNESS   Monarch is located at the southern end of the John Muir Wilderness, on the western border of Sequoia and Kings Canyon National Parks, approximately 65 miles east of Fresno via Calif. 180. The area extends across 45,000 acres in the Sierra and Sequoia national forests. The Sierra National Forest portion of the region—about 21,000 acres—is very rugged and hard to traverse. Steep slopes climb from the middle and main forks of Kings

River, with elevations increasing from 2,400 to more than 10,000 feet. Rock outcroppings are found throughout Monarch, and most of the lower elevations are mainly chaparral covered with pine stands near the tops of the higher peaks. Monarch is located at the southern end of the John Muir Wilderness, on the western border of Sequoia and Kings Canyon National Parks, approximately 65 miles east of Fresno via Calif. 180.

HUNTINGTON LAKE RECREATION AREA   At 7,000 feet, this area is a 2-hour drive east of Fresno via Calif. 168. The lake is one of the reservoirs in the Big Creek Hydroelectric System and has 14 miles of shoreline. It's a popular recreational area, offering camping, hiking, picnicking, sailing, swimming, windsurfing, fishing, and horseback riding—or you can just appreciate the beauty. The main summer season stretches from Memorial Day to Labor Day. There are seven campgrounds and four picnic areas in the Huntington Lake Basin, plus numerous hiking and riding trails.

NEIDER GROVE OF GIANT SEQUOIAS ⚸   This 1,540-acre tract in the Sierra National Forest contains 101 mature giant sequoias in the center of the Sequoia Range, south of Yosemite National Park. A visitor center stands near the Neider Grove Campground, with historical relics and displays, including two restored log cabins. The Bull Buck Tree—at one time thought to be the largest in the world—is 246 feet high and has a circumference at ground level of 99 feet. There's a mile-long, self-guided walk along the "Shadow of the Giants" National Recreational Trail in the southwest corner of the grove.

OUTDOOR PURSUITS

CAMPING   The Sierra National Forest seems like one vast campsite. Options range from unembellished, primitive wilderness camps to developed and often crowded campgrounds with snack bars, flush toilets, bathhouses, and hookups for RVs. For information and reservations, call the **National Recreation Reservation Service** toll-free at ✆ **877/444-6777,** or visit its website at www.reserve usa.com.

The major campgrounds are the Shaver Lake area; the Huntington Lake area (which has seven family campgrounds open from the end of June to Labor Day that must be reserved in advance); the Florence and Edison Lake area (first-come, first-served); the Dinkey Creek area (family and group camping); the Wishon and Courtright area (four campgrounds; first-come, first-served); the Pine Flat Reservoir (in the Sierra foothills, with two first-come, first-served campgrounds); and Upper Kings River, east of Pine Flat Reservoir (family campgrounds; first-come, first-served).

FISHING   The many streams of the Sierra are home to rainbow, golden, brown, and brook trout. The best freshwater angling is in the Pineridge and Kings River Rangers District. At the lower elevations, Shaver Lake, Bass Lake, and Pine Flat Reservoirs are known for their black-bass fishing. Questions about fishing in the national forest can be directed to the **California Department of Fish and Game,** 1234 E. Shaw Ave., Fresno, CA 93710 (✆ **559/243-4005**).

SKIING   Lying 65 miles northeast of Fresno on Calif. 168 in the Sierra National Forest, the **Sierra Summit Ski Area** offers mildly challenging alpine skiing, as well as marked trails for cross-country skiing and snowmobiling. The resort area has two triple and three double chairlifts, plus four surface lifts and 30 runs, the longest of which extends for 2¼ miles. There's a vertical drop-off at 1,600 feet. Other facilities include a lodge, snack bar, cafeteria, restaurant, and bar, all open daily from mid-November until mid-April. For resort information or a ski report, call ℭ **559/893-3311.**

The **Pineridge Ranger Station** (ℭ **559/855-5360**) also maintains several marked cross-country trails along Calif. 168, ranging from a 1-mile tour for beginners to a 6-mile trail for more advanced skiers.

WHITE-WATER RAFTING   The Upper Kings River, east of Pine Flat Reservoir, offers a 10-mile rafting run through Garnet Dike to Kirch Flat Campground. Rafting season is from late April to mid-July, with the highest waters in late May and early June. To get there, take Belmont Avenue in Fresno east (toward Pine Flat Reservoir) for about 63 miles. For more information about guided rafting trips on the Kings River, call **Kings River Expeditions** (ℭ **559/ 233-4881;** www.kingsriver.com).

11

The Monterey Peninsula & the Big Sur Coast

by Matthew Richard Poole

The Monterey Peninsula and the Big Sur coast comprise one of the world's most spectacular shorelines, skirted with cypress trees, rugged shores, and crescent-shaped bays. Monterey reels in visitors with its world-class aquarium and array of outdoor activities. Pacific Grove is so peaceful and quaint that the butterflies choose it as their yearly mating ground. Pebble Beach attracts the world's golfing elite, and although packed with tourists who come for the beaches, shops, and restaurants, tiny Carmel-by-the-Sea somehow remains romantic and sweet. Big Sur's dramatic and majestic coast, backed by pristine redwood forests and rolling hills, is one of the most breathtaking and tranquil environments on earth. And if you're traveling on Calif. 1 (which you should be), the magnificent coastline will guide you all the way through the region.

This chapter begins with Santa Cruz, located at the northwestern end of Monterey Bay. It's one of my favorite coastal destinations and home of the famous Santa Cruz Beach Boardwalk. Across Monterey Bay at the northern tip of the Monterey Peninsula are the seaside communities of Monterey and Pacific Grove, while Pebble Beach and Carmel-by-the-Sea hug the peninsula's south coast along Carmel Bay. Between the north and south coasts, which are only about 5 miles apart, are numerous golf courses, some of the state's most stunning homes and hotels, and the 17-Mile Drive, one of the most scenic coastal roads in the world.

Inland lies Carmel Valley, with its elegant inns and resorts, golf courses, and guaranteed sunshine, even when the coast is socked in with fog. Farther down the coast along Calif. 1 is Big Sur, a stunning 90-mile stretch of coast south of the Monterey Peninsula and west of the Santa Lucia Mountains.

1 Santa Cruz ★★

77 miles SE of San Francisco

For a small bayside city, Santa Cruz has a lot to offer. The main show, of course, is the Beach Boardwalk, the West Coast's only seaside amusement park, which attracts millions of visitors each year. But past the arcades and cotton candy is a surprisingly diverse and energetic city that has a little something for everyone. Shopping, hiking, mountain biking, sailing, fishing, kayaking, surfing, wine tasting, golfing, whale-watching—the list of things to do here is almost endless, making Santa Cruz one of the premier family destinations on the California coast.

ESSENTIALS

GETTING THERE   Santa Cruz is 77 miles southeast of San Francisco. The most scenic route to Santa Cruz is along Calif. 1 from San Francisco, which, aside from the "you fall, you die" stretch called Devil's Slide, allows you to cruise at a steady 50 mph along the coast. Faster but far less romantic is Calif. 17, which is accessed near San Jose from I-280, I-880, or U.S. 101, and literally ends at the foot of the boardwalk. The exception to this rule is on weekend mornings, when Calif. 17 tends to logjam with Bay Area beachgoers while Calif. 1 remains relatively uncrowded.

VISITOR INFORMATION   For information, contact the **Santa Cruz County Conference and Visitors Council,** 1211 Ocean St., Santa Cruz, CA 95060 (© **800/833-3494** or 831/425-1234; www.santacruzca.org), open Monday through Saturday from 9am to 5pm, Sunday from 10am to 4pm.

SPECIAL EVENTS   Special events include Shakespeare Santa Cruz in July and August (© **831/459-2121**), and Cabrillo Music Festival in August (© **831/426-6966**).

WHAT TO SEE & DO
BEACHES, HIKING, FISHING & MORE IN SANTA CRUZ
One of the few good ol'-fashioned amusement parks left in the world, the **Santa Cruz Beach Boardwalk** 👍👍 (© **831/426-7433**) draws more than three million visitors a year to its 30 rides and multitudes of arcades, shops, and restaurants. The park has two national landmarks—a 1924 wooden Giant Dipper roller coaster and a 1911 carousel complete with hand-carved wooden horses and a 342-pipe organ band. It's open daily in the summer (from Memorial Day weekend to Labor Day) and on weekends and holidays throughout the spring and fall, from 11am (noon sometimes in winter). Admission to the boardwalk is free, but an all-day "unlimited rides" pass will set you back $24. Check the boardwalk calendar (© **831/423-5590;** www.beachboardwalk.com) for special discounts, concerts and events, and up-to-date info on hours, which can often vary.

Here, too, is **Neptune's Kingdom,** 400 Beach St. (© **831/426-7433**), an enormous indoor family recreation center whose main feature is a two-story miniature golf course. Also on Beach Street is the **Municipal Wharf** (© **831/420-6025**), lined with shops and restaurants—a beachfront strip that is serenaded by the sea lions below. You can also crab and fish from here. Most shops are open daily from 7am to 9pm, the wharf daily from 5am to 2am. **Stagnaro's** (© **831/427-2334;** www.stagnaros.com) operates fishing and whale-watching trips from the wharf year-round, as well as hour-long narrated bay cruises for a mere $8 for adults, $5 for kids.

Farther down on West Cliff Drive, you'll come to a favorite surfing spot, **Steamer Lane,** where you can watch pro surfers shredding the waves. If you want to find out more about this local sport that's been practiced here for more than 100 years, go to the **Santa Cruz Surfing Museum,** at the memorial lighthouse (© **831/420-6289**), open Wednesday through Monday from noon to 4pm. Antique surfboards, videos, photographs, and other memorabilia depict the history and evolution of surfing around the world.

Continue along West Cliff and you'll eventually reach **Natural Bridges State** Beach, 2531 W. Cliff Dr. (© **831/423-4609;** www.scparkfriends.org/natbrdges), a large sandy beach with nearby tide pools and hiking trails. It's also home to a large colony of monarch butterflies that cluster and mate in the nearby eucalyptus grove.

Other Santa Cruz beaches worth noting are **Bonny Doon,** at Bonny Doon Road and Calif. 1, an uncrowded sandy beach and a major surfing spot accessible by a steep walkway; **Pleasure Point Beach,** East Cliff Drive at Pleasure Point Drive; and **Twin Lakes State Beach,** which is ideal for sunning and also provides access to Schwann Lagoon, a bird sanctuary.

In addition to hosting many cultural and sporting events, the University of California at Santa Cruz also features the **Seymour Marine Discovery Center** at the Long Marine Laboratory, 100 Shaffer Rd., at the northwest end of Delaware Avenue (© **831/459-3800**), where you can observe the activities of marine scientists and the species kept in tide-pool touch tanks and aquariums. Visitors get to learn firsthand how marine scientific research plays in the conservation of the world's oceans. Hours are Tuesday through Saturday from 10am to 5pm, and Sunday from noon to 5pm; admission is $5 for adults, $3 children ages 6 to 16, and free for kids under 6 (free admission for the 1st Tues of each month).

The **Santa Cruz Harbor,** 135 Fifth Ave. (© **831/475-6161;** www.santacruz harbor.org), is the place to head for boat rentals, open boat fishing (cod, shark, and salmon), and whale-watching trips. Operators include **Santa Cruz Sport-fishing Inc.** (© **831/426-4690;** www.santacruzsportfishing.com) and **Sham-rock Charters,** 2210 E. Cliff Dr. (© **831/476-2648**). Even if you're not into fishing, it's worth a walk down the harbor to browse through the numerous shops and restaurants.

Bikes—mountain, kids', tandem, hybrid—are available by the hour, day, or week from various bike-rental shops in convenient locations around the city. For a list of shops, call the **Santa Cruz Visitors Council** at © **800/833-3494,** or check the website at www.santacruzca.org. Figure on paying $25 a day, which includes helmets, locks, and packs.

There are several public golf courses, the best being the **Pasatiempo Golf Club,** at 18 Clubhouse Rd. (© **831/459-9155;** www.pasatiempo.com), which is rated among the top 100 courses in the United States. Greens fees are $135 Monday through Friday, $150 Saturday and Sunday.

Sea kayaking is also an option. Outfitters include **Kayak Connection,** 413 Lake Ave. No. 4 (© **831/479-1121;** www.kayakconnection.com), and **Venture Quest Kayaking** (© **831/427-2267;** www.kayaksantacruz.com), which rent single, double, and triple kayaks at Building No. 2 on the wharf and at 125 Beach St. across from the wharf. Classes, wildlife tours, and moonlight paddles are also available.

Surfing equipment can be rented at the **Cowell's Beach 'n' Bikini Surf Shop,** 109 Beach St. (© **831/427-2355**), and also from the **Club Ed Surf School** (© **800/287-SURF** or 831/459-6664; www.club-ed.com), on Cowell Beach in front of the West Coast Santa Cruz Hotel (formerly the Dream Inn). Both companies offer surf lessons: Club Ed's rates are $80 for a 2-hour group session, $80 for private lessons (equipment included), and $950 for a 7-day surf camp; Cowell's costs $70 for a 2-hour group lesson and includes the use of a board and wet suit.

IN NEARBY CAPITOLA & APTOS

South along the coast lies the small, attractive community of **Capitola** ✛ at the mouth of the Soquel Creek, which is a spawning ground for steelhead and salmon. You can fish without a license from the **Capitola Wharf,** 1400 Wharf Rd., or you can rent a fishing boat from **Capitola Boat and Bait** (© **831/462-2208;** www.santacruzboatrentals.net).

Capitola Beach fronts the bustling Esplanade. Surf-fishing and clamming are popular pastimes at Capitola's **New Brighton State Beach,** 1500 State Park Dr. (© **831/464-6330**), where camping is also allowed. Another popular Capitola activity is **antiquing** among the many stores along Soquel Drive between 41st and Capitola avenues.

Still farther south around the bay is **Aptos** ★, home to the 10,000-acre **Forest of Nisene Marks State Park** (© **831/763-7063**), which has hiking trails that wind through redwoods and past abandoned mining camps. Mountain bikers and leashed dogs are also welcome. This was the infamous epicenter of the 1989 earthquake. It's located at the end of Aptos Creek Road off Soquel Drive and is open year-round from sunrise to sunset.

In the redwood-forested mountains behind Santa Cruz, there are quite a few **wineries,** although visitors may not be familiar with the labels because the output is small and consumed locally. Most wineries are clustered around Boulder Creek and Felton or around Capitola. All offer tours by appointment; some feature regular tastings, including the **Bargetto Winery,** 3535 N. Main, Soquel (© **800/422-7438** or 831/475-2258; www.bargetto.com), which has a courtyard wine-tasting area overlooking the creek. For additional information, contact the **Santa Cruz Mountains Winegrowers' Association** (© **831/479-WINE;** www.scmwa.com).

WHERE TO STAY
IN SANTA CRUZ

Two **Travelodges** (© **800/578-7878;** www.travelodge.com), two **Best Westerns** (© **800/528-1234;** www.bestwestern.com), two **Super 8s** (© **800/800-8000;** www.super8.com), and an **Econo Lodge** (© **800/553-2666;** www.hotelchoice.com) provide moderate- and budget-priced accommodations in addition to the more inspiring choices below.

Babbling Brook Bed & Breakfast Inn ★★   With charm to spare, the rooms in this popular inn are like little treehouses perched over and around a meandering brook running through an acre of gardens, pines, and redwoods. Although it's located on a busy urban street, what you hear from your room is running water cascading over waterfalls and a large picturesque waterwheel. The romantic guest rooms are decorated in tasteful, simple style with lots of windows, skylights, open beam ceilings, balconies, and decks, and most have gas fireplaces. The inn is within a mile of the beach and the boardwalk and a short walk to the attractions of downtown Santa Cruz, a great place to browse and have dinner.

1025 Laurel St., Santa Cruz, CA 95060. © **800/866-1131** or 831/427-2456. Fax 831/427-2457. www.babblingbrookinn.com. 13 units. $165–250 double. Rates include full country-breakfast buffet. AE, DISC, MC, V. **Amenities:** Nearby golf. *In room:* TV (VCR in some units).

Casa Blanca Inn   Across from the wharf in a heavily trafficked area, this motel along the waterfront was once the Mediterranean-style Cerf Mansion, dating from 1918. Other motel-style accommodations have grown up around the main building. Originally the home of a federal judge, it offers individually decorated bedrooms, some with brass beds and velvet draperies. Some units contain fireplaces and terraces, and all are equipped with microwaves. Most of the rooms have views of the water. Casa Blanca Restaurant (p. 355) serves California-Continental cuisine in a romantic oceanview setting.

101 Main St. (at the corner of Beach St.), Santa Cruz, CA 95060. © **800/644-1570** or 831/423-1570. Fax 831/423-0235. www.casablanca-santacruz.com. 39 units. High season (summer) $96–$300 double; low

season $78–$295 double. AE, DC, DISC, MC, V. **Amenities:** Restaurant; bar; nearby golf course; room service; laundry service. *In room:* TV, dataport, minibar, fridge, coffeemaker, kitchen in some units, hair dryer, iron, safe.

Darling House ⚘ This stately Spanish-style house, designed in 1910 by William Weeks (architect of Santa Cruz's Coconut Grove), has a panoramic view of the Pacific Ocean and is situated in a quiet residential area within walking distance of the boardwalk and lighthouse. The gardens are fragrant with citrus and orchids, and contain some stately palms as well. From the tiled front veranda, guests enter an elegant interior, the focal point of which is the dining room handcrafted from tiger oak. The house boasts fine architectural features throughout, such as beveled glass, antiques, and handsome fireplaces. Each of the eight rooms is individually decorated; although all have sinks, only two come with private bathrooms. The Pacific Ocean room, decorated like a sea captain's quarters, features a fireplace, telescope, and one of the finest ocean views in Santa Cruz. Breakfast includes oven-fresh breads and pastries, fruit, and homemade granola made with walnuts from the Darling's own farm.

314 W. Cliff Dr., Santa Cruz, CA 95060. ⓒ 831/458-1958. www.darlinghouse.com. 8 units, 2 with bathroom. $95 double without bathroom; $260 double with bathroom. Rates include breakfast. AE, DISC, MC, V. **Amenities:** Concierge.

Edgewater Beach Motel If the other three inns listed here are booked, consider the Edgewater Beach Motel. It looks like a time capsule from the 1960s, which, oddly enough, makes it all the more appealing (how they kept the furnishings in such prime condition is a mystery). The motel offers a range of accommodations, from family suites with kitchens to rooms with fireplaces; most have microwaves. The Edgewater also sports a nice pool, sun deck, and barbecue area, but the real bonus is the location—the Santa Cruz Beach Boardwalk is only a block away. *Tip:* Inquire about the Edgewater's off-season mini-vacation packages, which can save you a bundle on room rates. Smoking is not permitted in any of the rooms.

525 2nd St., Santa Cruz, CA 95060. ⓒ 888/809-6767 or 831/423-0440. www.edgewaterbeachmotel.com. 17 units. Winter $85–$219 double; summer $139–$299 double. AE, DC, DISC, MC, V. **Amenities:** Outdoor heated pool. *In room:* TV/VCR, fridge, coffeemaker, fully equipped kitchen in suites.

IN NEARBY CAPITOLA

The Inn at Depot Hill ⚘⚘⚘ Located a few blocks from the bay front, this converted railroad station has been beautifully designed and decorated with great attention to detail, thanks to innkeeper extraordinaire Suzanne Lankes. Sporting fine fabrics and linens, all rooms and suites have wood-burning fireplaces, stereos, bathrobes, two-person showers, and full bathrooms. Most have private patios with private Jacuzzis (guests in the other rooms share a common Jacuzzi, and sign up for times). Perhaps you'll check into the Portofino Room, patterned after an Italian villa right down to the frescoes and stone cherub, or the Stratford-on-Avon, a replica of an English cottage.

The evening wine and hors d'oeuvres and the breakfast are of similar prime quality, and can be enjoyed either in your room or out back in the garden courtyard on wrought-iron tables shaded by market umbrellas.

250 Monterey Ave. (near Park Ave.), Capitola, CA 95010. ⓒ 800/572-2632 or 831/462-3376. Fax 831/462-3697. www.innatdepothill.com. 12 units. $235–$355 double. Rates include breakfast, afternoon tea or wine, hors d'oeuvres, and after-dinner dessert. AE, DC, DISC, MC, V. **Amenities:** Jacuzzi; room service. *In room:* A/C, TV/VCR, fax, dataport, hair dryer.

WHERE TO DINE
IN SANTA CRUZ

Café El Palomar MEXICAN If both O'Mei and Bittersweet Bistro (see below) are out of your price range, then head to the Santa Cruz Harbor and seat yourself at one of the seven tables at Café El Palomar. An offshoot of the far fancier El Palomar restaurant in the Pacific Garden Mall, the cafe serves Mexican food—chimichangas, burritos, tacos, chorizo, and more—for lunch and dinner, and standard American cafe fare for breakfast. For the money, it's *mucho bueno* grub.

2222 E. Cliff Dr. (at the Santa Cruz Harbor). ✆ 831/462-4248. Main courses $4–$6. AE, DISC, MC, V. Daily 7am–7pm (7am–5pm winter).

Casa Blanca Restaurant ✾ CALIFORNIA/CONTINENTAL The candlelit dining room at the Casa Blanca Inn was obviously built for romance, right down to the stellar views of the shimmering bay. The menu offers your classic fancy fare such as rack of lamb, grilled salmon, and sautéed chicken breast, but most folks come here primarily for the ambience. For a fiery start, try the fire-roasted Anaheim chiles stuffed with herbed chèvre and served with tomatillo salsa. Among the 10 or so main courses, I'd recommend any of the fresh-seafood dishes, perhaps the red snapper sautéed with capers, scallions, and lime sauce. The award-winning book-length wine list is excellent.

101 Main St. (at Beach St.). ✆ 831/426-9063. Reservations recommended. Main courses $15–$29. AE, DC, DISC, MC, V. Daily 5–9:30pm.

O'Mei ✾✾ PROVINCIAL SZECHUAN O'Mei's (pronounced Oh-*may*) mini-mall location may not be very inviting, but the fantastic food served here more than makes up for it. The menu features some unusual specialties such as Chengdu-bean-curd sea bass in a spicy *dou-ban* sauce (a rich, velvety wine-chile sauce), apricot-almond chicken, and lichee pi-pa bean-curd balls, along with more familiar dishes like chicken with cashews or beef with asparagus. Dinner starts with a dim sum–style tray of exotic vegetarian offerings such as sesame-cilantro-eggplant salad or pan-roasted peppers with feta cheese. A recommended dish is the sliced rock cod in black-bean and sweet-pepper sauce, followed by a scoop of black-sesame ice cream.

2316 Mission St. (where Calif. 1 turns into Mission St.). ✆ 831/425-8458. Reservations recommended. Main courses $9.25–$19. AE, MC, V. Mon–Fri 11:30am–2pm; Sun–Thurs 5–9pm, Fri–Sat 5–10pm.

IN NEARBY CAPITOLA & APTOS

Bittersweet Bistro ✾✾ CALIFORNIA What started out as a tiny operation within a small strip development has grown into one of the most popular restaurants in the Santa Cruz region. The relocation to bigger digs in Rio Del Mar hasn't tarnished chef and owner Thomas Vinolus's reputation for serving exceptional cuisine. The menu offers a wide array of carefully crafted dishes, ranging from pizzas from the wood-fired oven to grilled lamb porterhouse in a sun-dried–cranberry demi-glace. Fresh fish is Vinolus's forte, however, such as the Monterey Bay halibut, baked in parchment over fresh vegetables, or the roasted Chelis River wild sturgeon finished with an exotic mushroom sauce. Co-proprietor and wine director Elizabeth Vinolus has put together an exceptional wine list and often hosts winemaker dinners. "Bistro Hour" is from 3 to 6pm every afternoon, featuring half-price specials on gourmet pizzettas and special pricing on all wines by the glass, beer, and spirits.

787 Rio Del Mar Blvd., Aptos (about 10 miles SE of Santa Cruz on Calif. 1). ℭ **831/662-9799.** www.bitter
sweetbistro.com. Reservations recommended. Main courses $18–$24. AE, MC, V. Daily "bistro" lunch 3–6pm;
dinner 5:30–10pm; Sun brunch 10am–2pm.

Shadowbrook ℛ AMERICAN/CONTINENTAL Shadowbrook, one of
Capitola's most venerable and romantic restaurants, occupies a serene setting
above Soquel Creek. To reach the restaurant, diners either have to take the cable-
driven "hillavator" down or walk the long, steep bank of steps beside a running
waterfall. At the bottom is a log cabin built in the 1920s, which has been
enlarged and now contains a series of dining rooms on different levels: the
wood-paneled Wine Cellar, the airy Garden Room, the Fireplace Room, and the
creek-side Greenhouse.

The menu doesn't hold many surprises, featuring thick-cut prime rib and
steaks along with seafood such as scampi and grilled trout, plus pasta dishes
including shellfish linguine and porcini ravioli. Prawn cocktail, deep-fried artichoke hearts, and baked brie are among the appetizers. Standout desserts are the
mud pie and chocolate torte with raspberry sauce. If you don't have the time,
appetite, or budget for a big sit-down dinner, grab a seat in the lounge and nosh
on appetizers and light entrees prepared in the restaurant's wood-fired oven.

1750 Wharf Rd., Capitola. ℭ **831/475-1511.** Fax 831/475-7664. www.shadowbrook-capitola.com. Reservations recommended. Main courses $13–$24. AE, DC, DISC, MC, V. Mon–Fri 11:30am–9:30pm, Sat
4:30–10:30pm, Sun 10am–2:30pm and 4:30–9pm.

A SIDE TRIP TO MISSION SAN JUAN BAUTISTA

On U.S. 101, **San Juan Bautista** ℛ is a charming mission town that works hard
to honor its pioneer heritage by retaining the flavor of a 19th-century village.
The mission complex is perched in a picturesque farming valley, surrounded by
the restored buildings of the original city plaza.

From U.S. 101, take Calif. 156 east (south) to the center of town to the mission itself, which was founded in 1797. Here you'll see the largest church in the
mission chain and the only one in continuous service since its founding. The
padres here inspired many Native Americans to convert, creating one of the
largest congregations in all of California. The small museum contains many
musical instruments and transcriptions, evidence of the mission's musical
focus—it once boasted a formidable Native American boys' choir. Mission San
Juan Bautista is open daily year-round from 9:30am to 4:45pm. Suggested
donation is $1 per person. For further information, call ℭ **831/623-4528** or
check www.oldmission-sjb.org.

East of the church, perched at the edge of an abrupt drop created by the
movement of the San Andreas Fault, is a marker pointing out the path of the old
El Camino Real. Accompanying the marker are seismographic measuring
equipment and an earthquake science exhibit.

In addition to the mission, there's much to see on the restored city plaza. Be
sure to visit the **San Juan Bautista State Historic Park.** The park is comprised
of not only the old Plaza Hotel with its classic frontier barroom and furnished
rooms, but also the Plaza Hall, its adjoining stables and blacksmith shop, and
the Castro House, where the Breen family lived after traveling here with the ill-
fated Donner Party in 1846. Allow 1½ to 2 hours to see the entire plaza. Admission to the park buildings is $2 for adults, $1 for children ages 6 to 12 (separate
from your charge to the mission). Hours are daily from 10am to 4:30pm. For
further information (including event schedules), call ℭ **831/623-4881.**

2 Monterey ⊛⊛

45 miles S of Santa Cruz; 116 miles S of San Francisco; 335 miles N of Los Angeles

Originally settled in 1770, Monterey was one of the West Coast's first European settlements, and the capital of California under the Spanish, Mexican, and American flags. California's state constitution was drafted here in 1849, paving the way for admission to the Union a year later. In fact, many buildings from the early colonial era still stand. A major whaling center in the 1800s, Monterey eventually became the sardine capital of the Western Hemisphere when the first packing plant was built in 1900. By 1913, the boats were bringing in 25 tons of sardines a night to the 18 canneries. The gritty lives of the mostly working-class residents were forever captured by local hero John Steinbeck in his 1945 novel *Cannery Row.*

After the sardines disappeared, Monterey was forced to fish for tourist dollars instead; hence, an array of boutiques, knickknack stores, and theme restaurants now reside in converted sardine factories along the bay. Granted, plenty of history and heritage remains along Cannery Row, but you'll have to weed through the tourist schlock to find them. Its saving grace is the world-class aquarium and beautiful Monterey Bay, where sea lions and otters still frolic in abundance.

As you distance yourself from the Row, however, you'll soon discover that Monterey is a pleasant seaside community, replete with magnificent vistas, historic architecture, stately Victorians, and a number of quality lodgings and restaurants. More important, Monterey is only a short drive from Pacific Grove, Carmel, Pebble Beach, and Big Sur, and the lodgings here are far less expensive, which makes it a great place to set up base while exploring the Monterey coast.

ESSENTIALS

GETTING THERE   The region's most convenient runway, at the **Monterey Peninsula Airport** (© **831/648-7000**), is 3 miles east of Monterey on Calif. 68. American Eagle, Northwest, United, and US Airways offer daily flights in and out of Monterey.

Many area hotels offer free airport shuttle service. If you take a taxi, it will cost about $10 to $15 to get to a peninsula hotel. Several national car-rental companies have airport locations, including **Dollar** (© **800/800-3665;** www.dollar. com) and **Hertz** (© **800/654-3131;** www.hertz.com).

VISITOR INFORMATION   The **Monterey Peninsula Visitors and Convention Bureau** (© **888/221-1010** or 831/649-1770; www.monterey.com) has two visitor centers: one located in the lobby of the Maritime Museum at Custom House Plaza near Fisherman's Wharf, and the other at Lake El Estero on Camino El Estero. Both locations, open daily, offer an array of good maps, as well as free pamphlets and publications, including an excellent visitors' guide and the magazine *Coast Weekly.*

GETTING AROUND   The **Waterfront Area Visitor Express** (WAVE) shuttle operates each year from Memorial Day weekend to Labor Day and takes passengers to and from the aquarium and other waterfront attractions. The free shuttle departs from the downtown parking garages at Tyler Street and Del Monte Avenue every 10 to 12 minutes and operates all day between 9am and 6pm. Other WAVE stops include many hotels and motels in Monterey and Pacific Grove, which eliminates the stress of parking in crowded downtown. For further information, call **Monterey Salinas Transit** at © **831/899-2555.**

The Monterey Peninsula

Point Pinos

⑨

Sunset Dr

Asilomar Blvd

Asilomar State
Beach

*Spanish
Bay*

Spanish Bay
Golf Course
and Resort

⑩

Point Joe

17-Mile Dr.

17-Mile Dr.

⑪

Sloat Rd.

**DEL MONTE
PARK**

*Bird
Rock*

Bird Rock

Lopez Rd.

*Forest
Lake*

*Seal
Rock*

Spyglass Hill
Golf Course

Poppy Hills
Golf Course

Spyglass Hill

⑬

Forest Lake

⑫

*Cypress
Point*

Cypress Point
Golf Course

Clubhouse

Sunridge Rd.

Clubhouse

17-Mile Dr.

**PEBBLE
BEACH**

Alvarado Dr.

Lone Cypress
Tree

*Sunset
Point*

*Midway
Point*

Clubhouse

The Lodge
at Pebble Beach

*Stillwater
Cove*

⑭

Pebble Beach
Golf Links

Pescadero
Rocks

*Arrowhead
Point*

*Pescadero
Point*

⑮

*Carmel
Bay*

⑰

**San
Francisco**

Sacramento
✪

CALIFORNIA

*Monterey
Peninsula*

Los Angeles

*PACIFIC
OCEAN*

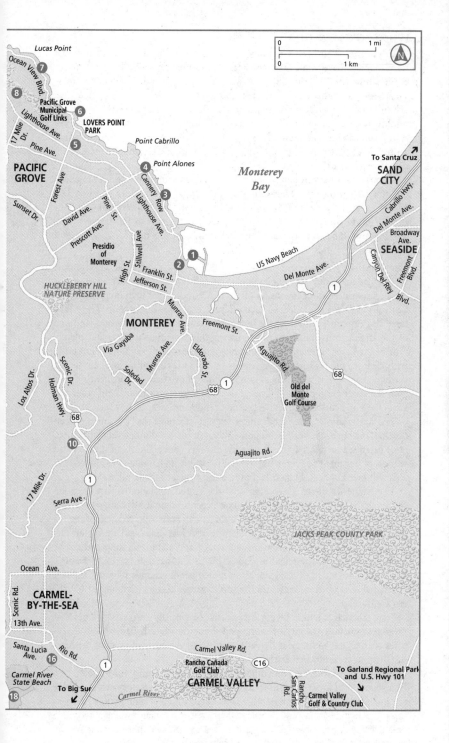

Lucas Point

Ocean View Blvd. **7**

8

Pacific Grove
Municipal
Golf Links **6**

17 Mile Dr.

Lighthouse Ave.

**LOVERS POINT
PARK**

Pine Ave.

5

Point Cabrillo

**PACIFIC
GROVE**

Forest Ave.

Sunset Dr.

David Ave.

Prescott Ave.

Pine St.

Cannery Row

4

Point Alones

3

Lighthouse Ave.

*Monterey
Bay*

To Santa Cruz ↗

**SAND
CITY**

Cabrillo Hwy.

Del Monte Ave.

Broadway
Ave.

SEASIDE

Canyon Del Rey

Freemont Blvd.

Blvd.

Presidio
of
Monterey

Stillwell Ave.

High St.

Franklin St.

2

1

US Navy Beach

Del Monte Ave.

1

*HUCKLEBERRY HILL
NATURE PRESERVE*

Jefferson St.

MONTEREY

Munras Ave.

Freemont St.

Via Gayuba

Munras Ave.

Eldorado St.

Soledad
Dr.

68

1

Aguajito Rd.

Old del
Monte
Golf Course

68

Los Altos Dr.

Scenic Dr.

Holman Hwy.

68

10

1

Aguajito Rd.

17 Mile Dr.

Serra Ave.

JACKS PEAK COUNTY PARK

Ocean   Ave.

Scenic Rd.

**CARMEL-
BY-THE-SEA**

13th Ave.

Santa Lucia
Ave.

16

Río Rd.

1

Carmel River
State Beach

18

To Big Sur ↙

Carmel Valley Rd.

Rancho Cañada
Golf Club

C16

CARMEL VALLEY

Rancho
San Carlos
Rd.

To Garland Regional Park
and U.S. Hwy 101

Carmel Valley
Golf & Country Club

Carmel River

0   1 mi
0   1 km

359

WHAT TO SEE & DO

The **National Steinbeck Center** 🏵 is not in town, but if you're a fan, you'll want to make the 20-mile drive northeast from Monterey on Calif. 68 to 1 Main St. in Salinas (© **831/796-3833;** www.steinbeck.org). An $11-million, 37,000-square-foot museum opened in mid-1998, offering walk-through interactive exhibits, a changing exhibition gallery, an orientation theater presenting a 10-minute video on Steinbeck's life, educational programs, a gift shop, and a cafe. Admission is $9.95 for adults, $7.95 for seniors over 62, $6.95 for children ages 13 to 17, $5.95 for children 6 to 12, and free for children under 6. Hours are daily from 10am to 5pm.

If you're traipsing through Monterey on a Tuesday afternoon, be sure to check out the **Old Monterey Marketplace** on Alvarado Street, from Pearl to Del Monte streets (© **831/655-8070;** www.oldmonterey.org), open from 4 to 8pm (until 7pm in winter). More than 100 vendors participate in this farmers market, bringing food, music, crafts, and entertainment together for an afternoon of flavorful festivities.

Monterey Bay Aquarium 🏵🏵🏵 *Kids*   The site of one of the world's most spectacular aquariums was not chosen at random. It sits on the border of one of the largest underwater canyons on earth (wider and deeper than even the Grand Canyon) and is surrounded by incredibly diverse local marine life. The Monterey Bay Aquarium is one of the best exhibit aquariums in the world, and one of the largest, too—home to more than 350,000 marine animals and plants. One of the living museum's main exhibits is a three-story, 335,000-gallon tank, with clear acrylic walls that give visitors an unmatched look at local sea life. A towering kelp forest, which rises from the floor of this oceanic zoo, gently waves with the water as hundreds of leopard sharks, sardines, anchovies, and other fish swim back and forth in an endless game of hide-and-seek.

The outstanding Outer Bay exhibit features creatures that inhabit the open ocean. This tank—holding a million gallons of water—houses yellowfin tuna, large green sea turtles, barracuda, sharks, the very cool giant ocean sunfish, and schools of bonito. The Outer Bay's jellyfish exhibit is guaranteed to amaze, and kids will love Flippers, Flukes, and Fun, a learning area for families.

The Mysteries of the Deep exhibit is the largest collection of live deep-sea species in the world—many of which have never been on display anywhere. The 7,000-square-foot exhibit highlights the underwater life collected from waters as deep as 3,300 feet, including such creatures as spider crabs, ratfish, filetail catsharks, predatory tunicates, mushroom corals, and California king crabs. The Splash Zone exhibit (designed for families with kids up to 9 years old) features daily programs and live exhibits of black-footed penguins, invertebrates, and fish whose habitats are coral reefs and the cooler waters and rocky shores of Northern California.

New this year is Jellies: Living Art, a series of specially designed galleries that explore the delicate beauty of exotic and domestic jellyfish (truly bizarre creatures such as the spectacular flower hat jelly and the blue jelly) along with art installations by renowned artists.

Additional exhibits re-create other undersea habitats found in Monterey Bay. Everyone falls in love with the sea otters playing in their two-story exhibit. There are also coastal streams, tidal pools, a sand beach, and a petting pool, where you can touch living bat rays and handle sea stars. Visitors can also watch a live video link that regularly transmits from a deep-sea research submarine maneuvering thousands of feet below the surface of Monterey Bay.

Tip: You can avoid lines at the gate by calling ℂ **800/756-3737** (or 831/648-4888 outside Calif.) and ordering tickets in advance.

886 Cannery Row. ℂ **800/756-3737** or 831/648-4888. Fax 831/648-4810. www.montereybayaquarium.org. Admission $18 adults, $15 students and seniors 65 and over, $7.95 visitors with disabilities and children 3–12, free for children under 3. AE, MC, V. Daily 10am–6pm.

Fisherman's Wharf Just like San Francisco's Fisherman's Wharf, this wooden pier is jam-packed with crafts and gift shops, boating and fishing operations, fish markets, and seafood restaurants—all trawling for tourist dollars. But Monterey's wharf does have redeeming qualities: The natural surroundings are so beautiful that if you cast your view toward the bobbing boats and surfacing sea lions, you might not even notice the hordes of tourists around you. Grab some clam chowder in a sourdough-bread bowl and find a seaside perch along the pier. Or, when the wind picks up, find a bay-front seat at one of the seafood restaurants (see "Where to Dine," later in this section).

If the seaside sights have got you itching to set sail, boats depart regularly from Fisherman's Wharf and will lead you on a number of ocean adventures. See "Outdoor Pursuits," below, for details on some of the offerings.

99 Pacific St. ℂ 831/649-6544.

Cannery Row *Overrated* Once the center for an industrial sardine-packing operation immortalized by John Steinbeck as "a poem, a stink, a grating noise, a quality of light, a tone, a habit, a nostalgia, a dream," this area today is better described as a strip congested with wandering tourists, tacky gift shops, over-priced seafood restaurants, and an overall parking nightmare. What changed it so dramatically? The silver sardines suddenly disappeared from Monterey's waters in 1948 as a result of overfishing, changing currents, and pollution. Fishermen left, canneries closed, and the Row fell into disrepair. But curious tourists continued to visit Steinbeck's fabled area, and where there are tourists, there are capitalists.

After visiting Cannery Row in the 1960s, Steinbeck wrote, "The beaches are clean where they once festered with fish guts and flies. The canneries that once put up a sickening stench are gone, their places filled with restaurants, antique shops, and the like. They fish for tourists now, not pilchards, and that species they are not likely to wipe out." And I couldn't put it any better.

Between David and Drake aves. ℂ 831/373-1902.

FOLLOWING THE PATH OF HISTORY

The dozen or so historic buildings clustered around Fisherman's Wharf and the adjacent town collectively comprise the "Path of History," a tour that examines 1800s architecture and lifestyle. Many of the buildings are a part of the **Monterey State Historic Park** ⚘, 20 Custom House Plaza (ℂ **831/649-7118**). Highlights include the **Custom House,** which was constructed around 1827 and is the oldest government building in California, and the **Maritime Museum of Monterey,** 5 Custom House Plaza (ℂ **831/372-2608**), which showcases ship models and other collections that relate the area's seafaring history, including a two-story-high, 10,000-pound Fresnel lens, used for nearly 80 years at the Point Sur lighthouse. Admission is $5 for adults, $2.50 for seniors and children ages 13 to 18, and free for children 12 and under; it's open Tuesday through Sunday from 11am to 5pm.

You can go the self-guided route by picking up a free tour booklet at the Monterey Peninsula Visitors and Convention Bureau (see above), the Cooper-Molera

Adobe (at the corner of Polk and Munras sts.), and various other locations. You may also opt to take the guided tour, which departs several times daily. The price is $5 for adults, $3 for youths ages 13 to 18, $2 for children 6 to 12, and free for children under 6. Call ℭ 831/649-7118 for exact schedule information, or visit the **State Park Visitor Center** at Stanton Center, 5 Custom House Plaza. A free film on the history of Monterey is shown here every 20 minutes.

MONTEREY WINE COUNTRY

The congestion and price of Napa and Sonoma vineyards and the increasingly lucrative and romantic occupation of winemaking have forced industry newcomers to plant their grapes elsewhere. Fortunately, much of the California coast offers perfect growing conditions. Nowadays, if you visit any area between Monterey and Santa Barbara, there's easy access to new appellations and a variety of boutique vintners making respectable wines. Stop by **A Taste of Monterey,** 700 Cannery Row (ℭ **831/646-5446;** www.tastemonterey.com), daily between 11am and 6pm to learn about and taste locally produced wines in front of huge bay-front windows. This is also the place to get a map and winery touring information.

OUTDOOR PURSUITS

Along with excellent scuba diving, the waters off Monterey are teeming with game fish. Among the public fishing boats are **Chris' Fishing Trips,** 48 Fisherman's Wharf (ℭ **831/375-5951;** www.chrissfishing.com), which offers large party boats. Cod and salmon are the main catches, with separate boats leaving daily. Another good choice is **Sam's Fishing Fleet,** 84 Fisherman's Wharf (ℭ **800/427-2675** or 831/372-0577; www.samsfishingfleet.com), which offers fishing excursions for cod, salmon, and whatever else is running, as well as whale-watching tours. Call or visit their websites for a complete price list and departure schedule. Check-in is 45 minutes prior to departure, and equipment rental costs a bit extra.

Several outfitters rent kayaks for a spin around the bay. Contact **Monterey Bay Kayaks,** 693 Del Monte Ave. (ℭ **800/649-5357** or 831/373-5357; www.montereykayaks.com), on Del Monte Beach north of Fisherman's Wharf, which offers instruction as well as natural-history tours that introduce visitors to the Monterey Bay National Marine Sanctuary and nearby Elkhorn Slough, one of the last remaining estuaries in California (see "The Otters, Seals & Birds of the Elkhorn Slough" on p. 363). Prices start at $55 for the tours, from $30 for rentals.

For bikes and in-line skates, as well as kayak tours and rentals, contact **Adventures by the Sea,** 299 Cannery Row (ℭ **831/372-1807;** www.adventuresbythe sea.com). Bikes cost $6 per hour or $24 per day; kayaks are $30 per person, or $50 for a 2½-hour tour; and skates are $12 for 2 hours, $24 for a day. Adventures by the Sea also has another location at 201 Alvarado Mall (ℭ **831/648-7235**), at the Doubletree Hotel.

Experienced scuba divers wishing to go out on an excursion can contact **Monterey Bay Dive Center,** 225 Cannery Row (ℭ **800/60-SCUBA** or 831/656-0454; www.mbdc.to), which arranges personal dives with a dive master and has scheduled weekend dives. **Aquarius Dive Shop,** 2040 Del Monte Ave. (ℭ **831/375-1933;** www.aquariusdivers.com), also has regularly scheduled trips and dive masters. Certification cards are required.

North of Monterey at Marina State Beach, you can learn to **hang-glide** during a 3-hour course that includes a minimum of five flights with **Western Hang**

(Kids The Otters, Seals & Birds of the Elkhorn Slough

One of my favorite stops along the coast is Moss Landing, which is 25 minutes north of Monterey on Calif. 1. Along the virtually one-street town are a few adorable down-home restaurants and antiques shops. But what really attracts me is Captain Yohn Gideon's **Elkhorn Slough Safari.** For $26 for adults or $19 for children 3 to 14, friendly Cap'n Gideon loads guests onto a 27-foot pontoon boat (safe for old and young) and embarks on a 2-hour tour of the wondrous Elkhorn Slough Wildlife Reserve, which, by the way, is like jumping into a *National Geographic* special. It's not uncommon to see a "raft" of up to 50 otters feet-up and sunning themselves, an abundance of lounging harbor seals, and hundreds of species of waterfowl and migratory shorebirds. An onboard naturalist answers questions, Cap'n Gideon educates on the surroundings, and binoculars are available. For reservations, schedules, and information, call ℭ **831/633-5555** or check out www.elkhornslough.com.

Gliders, Calif. 1 at Reservation Road, Marina (ℭ **831/384-2622;** www.western hanggliders.org). The cost is $98. Tandem flights, paragliding, and ultralights are available, too.

Need to keep the kids busy, or feeling playful yourself? The **Dennis the Menace Playground** ℛ at Camino El Estero and Del Monte Avenue, near Lake Estero (ℭ **831/646-3860**), is an old-fashioned playground created by Pacific Grove resident and cartoonist Hank Ketcham. It has bridges to cross, tunnels to climb through, and an authentic Southern Pacific Railroad engine teeming with wannabe conductors. There's also a hot dog and burger stand, and a big lake where you can rent paddleboats or feed the ducks. The park is open daily from 10am to sunset.

WHERE TO STAY

It seems there are only three types of choices for accommodations in Monterey: lace-and-flowers B&Bs, large corporate hotels with only a slight beachy feel (if even that), or run-of-the-mill motel digs. Consider which area you'd like to be in—beach, Cannery Row, wharf, secluded, central, and so forth—as well as how much you want to spend, then check out the options below or contact these two reservations services: **Resort 2 Me** (ℭ **800/757-5646;** www.resort2me.com), a local reservations service that offers free recommendations of Monterey Bay–area hotels in all price ranges; and **Monterey Land and See** (ℭ **877/ MONTEREY**), which represents numerous lodging facilities in Monterey, Carmel, and Pacific Grove.

EXPENSIVE

In addition to the choices below, there are two chain hotels conveniently located near Fisherman's Wharf: The **Monterey Marriott,** 350 Calle Principal, at Del Monte Blvd. (ℭ **800/228-9290** or 831/649-4234; www.marriott.com), offers some rooms with bay views, an outdoor pool, health club, Jacuzzi, and saunas. There's also the **Doubletree Hotel at Fisherman's Wharf,** 2 Portola Plaza (ℭ **800/222-8733** or 831/649-4511; www.doubletree.com). Less centrally located, but great for families and golfers, is the enormous **Hyatt Regency Monterey** resort, 1 Old Golf Course Rd. (ℭ **800/233-1234** or 831/372-1234; www.hyatt.com). It adjoins the Del Monte Golf Course and has three pools, two

Jacuzzis, a gym, tennis courts, and two restaurants. All three hotels are popular with business travelers and conventioneers.

Hotel Pacific ★★   Although it's not even remotely waterfront (it's close to the wharf and across the street from the Monterey Conference Center), this is my favorite upscale choice in Monterey. Beyond the elegant Spanish-Mediterranean architecture of the common areas, each unit is situated in 1 of 16 buildings clustered around courtyards and compact gardens complete with spas and fountains. The cozy Southwestern-style junior suites have fluffy down comforters atop four-poster feather beds (for the full effect, request a canopied bed), rustically stylish decor, terra cotta–tiled floors, and fireplaces surrounded by cushy couches and seats. Add to that two TVs, three phones, and gourmet coffee and tea—all of which make this a place where you'll want to hibernate awhile. Tiny closets are one of the few downsides.

300 Pacific St., Monterey, CA 93940. (C) **800/554-5542** or 831/373-5700. Fax 831/373-6921. www.hotel pacific.com. 105 suites. $229–$409 suite for 2. Rates include continental breakfast and afternoon tea. AE, DC, DISC, MC, V. **Amenities:** Nearby golf course; 2 Jacuzzis; room service; in-room massage; laundry service; same-day dry cleaning. *In room:* TV/VCR, dataport, minibar, coffeemaker, hair dryer, iron.

Monterey Plaza Hotel and Spa ★★   One of the most formal hotels in town, the Monterey Plaza is comprised of three buildings—two on the water and one across the street—that are connected by a second-story enclosed "skywalk." The public areas are elegantly decorated with imported marble, Brazilian teak, and attractive artwork. The stately bedrooms are more upscale-corporate than most around town and have double or king beds, decor reminiscent of 19th-century Biedermeier, and Italian marble bathrooms. Many units have balconies overlooking the water (sea otters included in the view). The least desirable rooms are across the street from the ocean. Extras include terry robes and an attentive and professional staff.

400 Cannery Row, Monterey, CA 93940. (C) **800/334-3999** in CA, 800/631-1339 outside of CA, or 831/646-1700. Fax 831/646-5937. www.woodsidehotels.com. 290 units. $185–$505 double; $510–$2,500 suite. Children 17 and under stay free in parents' room. Packages available. AE, DC, DISC, MC, V. Parking $14 per day. From Calif. 1, take the Soledad Dr. exit and follow the signs to Cannery Row. **Amenities:** 2 restaurants; nearby golf course; fully equipped fitness center; full-service European-style spa; Jacuzzi; dry sauna; concierge; tour desk; business center; secretarial services; shopping arcade; 24-hr. room service; in-room massage; laundry service; same-day dry cleaning; executive-level rooms. *In room:* TV w/pay movies, dataport, fully stocked minibar, fridge, coffeemaker, hair dryer, iron.

Old Monterey Inn ★★   Proprietors Ann and Gene Swett did a masterful job of converting their comfortable three-story family home into a vine-covered Tudor-style country inn. Although it's away from the surf, it's a perfect choice for romantics, with rose gardens, a bubbling brook, and brick-and-flagstone walkways shaded by a panoply of oaks. All but one guest room enjoy peaceful garden views and cozy beds with goose-down comforters and pillows. Most units also have feather beds and wood-burning fireplaces, and two open onto private patios. The guest rooms are all charmingly furnished and unique in character; two of my favorites are the Library and the Serengeti Room. Special touches are evident throughout, including fresh fruit, flowers, and candies, sachets by the pillow, and books and magazines. The private cottage out back has an English country look and comes with a double Jacuzzi, linen-and-lace draped king-size bed, wood-burning fireplace, sitting area, and private patio.

Breakfast, prepared by Gene, is also stellar, consisting of perhaps orange French toast, soufflé, or Belgian waffles. It's served in your room, the dining room, or the rose garden. The Swetts will also provide picnic blankets and towels for the beach.

At 5pm, guests retire to the living room for wine and hors d'oeuvres in front of a blazing fire.

500 Martin St. (off Pacific Ave.), Monterey, CA 93940. ℂ 800/350-2344 or 831/375-8284. Fax 831/375-6730. www.oldmontereyinn.com. 9 units, 1 cottage. $240–$390 double; from $450 cottage. Rates include full breakfast and evening wine and hors d'oeuvres. MC, V. Free parking. From Calif. 1, take the Soledad Dr. exit and turn right onto Pacific Ave., then left onto Martin St. **Amenities:** Nearby golf course; passes to nearby health club; Jacuzzi; concierge; tour desk; in-room massage. *In room:* TV/VCR, dataport, hair dryer, iron.

Spindrift Inn 🍷   Down in the middle of honky-tonk Cannery Row, but right along a narrow stretch of beach, this four-story hotel is an island of Continental style in a sea of commercialism. It's elegant and well maintained, and the rooms are sweetly decorated with feather beds (a few with canopies), hardwood floors, wood-burning fireplaces, and either cushioned window seats or private balconies. The luxurious bathrooms are adorned with marble and brass fixtures. Extras include terry robes and two phones. The ocean views are definitely worth the additional cost, although the place is still painfully expensive for what it offers—unless, of course, you get a deal.

652 Cannery Row, Monterey, CA 93940. ℂ 800/841-1879 or 831/646-8900. Fax 831/646-5342. www.spindriftinn.com. 42 units. $199–$329 double with Cannery Row view; $329–$459 double with ocean view. Rates include continental breakfast delivered to your room and afternoon wine and cheese. AE, DC, DISC, MC, V. Parking $14. **Amenities:** 2 restaurants; bar; nearby golf course; room service; in-room massage; same-day dry cleaning. *In room:* TV/VCR, fully stocked minibar, hair dryer.

MODERATE

Munras Avenue and northern Fremont Avenue are lined with moderate and inexpensive family-style motels, some independently owned and some chains. They're not as central as the downtown options, and atmosphere is seriously lacking on Fremont Avenue, but if transportation's not an issue, you can save a bundle by staying in one of these areas. If the selections below are full, try calling **Best Western** (ℂ **800/528-1234**) for several other options. There's also the **Cypress Gardens Inn,** 1150 Munras Ave. (ℂ **831/373-2761**), with a pool, Jacuzzi, free movie channels, and continental breakfast; dogs are welcome.

Fireside Lodge   Location is the primary advantage of this hotel near Fisherman's Wharf and downtown. The room furnishings are relatively standard but make an attempt at coziness with wicker chairs set around the gas-heated brick fireplace. Families on a budget will appreciate the kitchen facilities, plus the continental breakfast served daily in the hotel's lobby will ease the food bill, too.

1131 10th St., Monterey, CA 93940. ℂ 800/722-2624 in CA or 831/373-4172. Fax 831/655-5640. www.montereyfireside.com. 24 units. $69–$225 double. Rates include continental breakfast. AE, DC, DISC, MC, V. Pets accepted with $10 (under 20 lb.) or $20 (over 20 lb.) fee. **Amenities:** Nearby golf course; Jacuzzi. *In room:* TV, dataport, kitchenette, fridge.

The Jabberwock Bed & Breakfast 🍷   One of the better B&Bs in the area, the Jabberwock (named after a poem in Lewis Carroll's *Through the Looking Glass*) is 4 short blocks from Cannery Row. Although centrally located, the property is tranquil, and its half-acre garden with waterfalls offers a welcome respite from the downtown crowds. The seven rooms are individually furnished, some more elegantly than others; all have goose-down comforters and pillows, and three are romantically outfitted with Jacuzzi tubs for two, fireplaces, and king beds. The Toves Room has a huge walnut Victorian bed, the Borogrove has a fireplace and a view of Monterey Bay, the Mimsey has a fine ocean view from its window seat, and the Wabe has an Austrian carved bed. A full breakfast is served in the dining room or in your own room. Evening hors d'oeuvres are offered on the veranda, and a Vorpal rabbit tucks each guest in with cookies and milk.

598 Laine St., Monterey, CA 93940. © **888/428-7253** or 831/372-4777. Fax 831/655-2946. www. jabberwockinn.com. 7 units, 5 with bathroom. $115 double without private bathroom; $155–$265 double with private bathroom. Rates include full breakfast, afternoon aperitifs, and bedtime cookies. MC, V. **Amenities:** Nearby golf course; Jacuzzi; concierge; activities desk; in-room massage. *In room:* Hair dryer, no phone.

INEXPENSIVE

Opt for a motel to get the best rates in this town. Some reliable options are **Motel 6** (© 800/4-MOTEL6), **Super 8** (© 800/800-8000), and **Best Western** (© 800/528-1234).

Cypress Tree Inn *(Value)* Although it's not centrally located (2 miles from downtown), if you're on a budget and have transportation, you won't be sorry if you stay here. The staff is friendly, the large rooms are spotless, and all but one has a combination tub and shower. Nine rooms even have Jacuzzis. There are no designer soaps or other in-room treats (other than the taffy left by the maid), but the hostelry does have a handy coin-op laundry. RV spaces are also available.

2227 N. Fremont St., Monterey, CA 93940. © **800/446-8303** or 831/372-7586. Fax 831/372-2940. www. cypresstreeinn.com. 55 units. $52–$129 double. Rates include continental breakfast. AE, DC, DISC, MC, V. **Amenities:** Nearby golf course; Jacuzzi; sauna; coin-op laundry. *In room:* TV, dataport, fridge, kitchen or kitchenette in some units, hair dryer, iron.

WHERE TO DINE

Bubba Gump Shrimp Co. Restaurant & Market *(Overrated)* AMERICAN Culinary cognoscenti will flee in disgust at the sight of this tourist haven, but the fact is, lots of folks love this place. It could be the location—near the aquarium and offering a million-dollar unobstructed bay-front view—or the old boatyard decor that attracts visitors in droves. But it's more likely the entertainment value: Gump's (as in *Forrest Gump*) is packed with movie gimmicks and memorabilia. The food, unfortunately, is far less exciting. As the roll of paper towels at each table suggests, you're guaranteed a go with grease, which is likely to arrive in the form of fried and buttered-up seafood. The "Bucket of Boat Trash," for example, is shrimp and lobster tails cooked and served in a bucket with a side of fries and coleslaw. There are also pork chops, a veggie dish, salads, and burgers. The "market" referred to in the moniker is a gift shop packed with T-shirts, caps, and, of course, boxes of chocolate.

720 Cannery Row (at Prescott). © **831/373-1884.** Fax 831/373-1139. www.bubbagump.com. Main courses $7.95–$25. AE, DC, DISC, MC, V. Sun–Thurs 11am–10pm, Fri–Sat 11am–11pm.

Cafe Fina *(★)* ITALIAN/SEAFOOD While other pier-side restaurants lure tourists with little more than an outstanding view, Cafe Fina's mesquite-grilled meats, well-prepared fresh fish, brick-oven pizzas, and an array of delicious salads and pastas give even locals a reason to head to the wharf. Combine the food with a million-dollar vista and a casual atmosphere, and Cafe Fina ranks hands down as the best choice on the pier.

47 Fisherman's Wharf. © **831/372-5200.** Fax 831/3725209. www.cafefina.com. Reservations recommended. Main courses $14–$19. AE, DC, DISC, MC, V. Mon–Fri 11:30am–2:30pm, Sat–Sun 11:30am–3pm; daily 5–9:30pm.

John Pisto's Whaling Station Prime Steaks & Seafood AMERICAN/ STEAKHOUSE If you insist on eating on Cannery Row, come to this touristy restaurant known for its New York, porterhouse, and other steaks grilled over oak and mesquite. A 30-year tradition guarantees you an artichoke vinaigrette appetizer before your main course, which ranges from pasta and chicken to jumbo live Maine lobsters and live local abalone.

763 Wave St. (between Prescott and Irving aves.). ℂ **831/373-3778.** Fax 831/373-2460. www.pisto.com. Reservations recommended on weekends. Main courses start at $22. AE, DC, DISC, MC, V. Daily 5–10pm. From Calif. 1, take the Soledad Dr. exit and follow the signs toward Cannery Row; turn left on Wave St. 1 block before Cannery Row. Free valet parking on weekends.

Montrio ★★ AMERICAN BISTRO   Big-city sophistication meets old Monterey here. The enormous dining room is definitely the sharpest in town, mixing chic style with a playful canopied vineyard of modern light fixtures, clouds hanging from the ceiling, and the buzz of well-dressed diners. You can watch chefs scurry around in the open kitchen, but you're more likely to keep your eyes on the tasty dishes, such as the crispy Dungeness crab cakes with spicy rémoulade; succulent grilled pork chops with apple, pear, and currant compote; or an oven-roasted portobello mushroom with polenta and ragout of vegetables. Finish the evening with passion-fruit gratin with wild-berry coulis.

414 Calle Principal (at Franklin). ℂ **831/648-8880.** www.montrio.com. Reservations recommended. Main courses $12–$25. AE, DISC, MC, V. Sun–Thurs 5–10pm, Fri–Sat 5–11pm.

Stokes Restaurant and Bar ★★ CALIFORNIA/MEDITERRANEAN This historic adobe and board-and-batten house, built in 1833 for the town doctor, has been converted into one of Monterey's finest restaurants. It's quite the handsome establishment, consisting of a bar and several large dining rooms, all outfitted with terra-cotta floors, bleached-wood plank ceilings, and Southwestern-style wood chairs and tables. It's the perfect rustic-yet-contemporary showcase for chef Brandon Miller's carefully crafted California-Mediterranean fare: butternut-squash soup with apple cider and maple crème fraîche; cassoulet of duck confit and homemade currant sausage with chestnut beans; and lavender-infused pork chops served with savory bread pudding and pear chutney. Everything from Miller's new wood-burning oven—chicken, fish, pizza, clams—is highly recommended as well. Desserts are equally dreamy, and the wine list is excellent.

500 Hartnell St. (at Madison St). ℂ **831/373-1110.** Fax 831/373-1202. www.stokesadobe.com. Reservations recommended. Main courses $12–$23. AE, DC, DISC, MC, V. Mon–Thurs 11:30am–10pm, Fri–Sat 11:30am–10:30pm, Sun 4–10pm.

Tarpy's Roadhouse ★★ AMERICAN   Always a mandatory stop when I'm passing through Monterey is this lively Southwestern-style restaurant located a few miles east of downtown (and definitely worth the detour). The very handsome dining room has stylish yet soothingly rustic decor. On sunny afternoons, patrons relax under market umbrellas on the huge outdoor patio, sipping margaritas and munching on Tarpy's legendary Caesar salad. Come nightfall, the place fills quickly with tourists and locals who pile in for the hefty plate of bourbon-molasses pork chops or Dijon-crusted lamb loin. There's also a modest selection of fresh fish, shellfish, and vegetable dishes, but it's the good ol' meat 'n' potato mainstays that sell the best. (The thick, juicy meatloaf with garlic mashers and fresh veggies is a bargain at $13.)

2999 Monterey-Salinas Hwy. (at Calif. 68 and Canyon del Rey near the Monterey Airport). ℂ **831/647-1444.** Fax 831/647-1103. www.tarpys.com. Reservations recommended for dinner. Most main courses $14–$30. AE, DISC, MC, V. Daily 11:30am–10pm.

Wharfside Restaurant & Lounge SEAFOOD   While the fresh seafood is okay, the real attraction is the Wharfside's casual upstairs dining room, which offers a nautical decor and a great view from the end of Fisherman's Wharf (there's also downstairs and upper-deck outdoor seating). Choose from six different varieties of ravioli (made on the premises), such specialties as a combination bouillabaisse, and any of the house-made desserts. Daily specials usually include fresh seasonal fish, beef, and pasta. Clam chowder, sandwiches (including hot crab), and pizzas are on the regular menu.

60 Fisherman's Wharf, Monterey. © 831/375-3956. Fax 831/375-2967. Reservations recommended. Main courses $11–$20. AE, DC, DISC, MC, V. Daily 11am–10pm. Closed Dec 1–10.

3 Pacific Grove 🖈🖈

42 miles S of Santa Cruz; 113 miles S of San Francisco; 338 miles N of Los Angeles

Some compare 2½-square-mile Pacific Grove—the locals call it "P.G."—to Carmel as it was 20 years ago. Although tourists wind their way through here on oceanfront trails and dining excursions, the town remains quaint and peaceful— amazing considering that Monterey is a stone's throw away (a quarter of the Monterey Bay Aquarium is actually in Pacific Grove). While neighboring Monterey is comparatively congested and cosmopolitan, Pacific Grove is a community sprinkled with historic homes, blooming flowers, and the kind of tranquillity that inspires butterflies to flutter about and deer to meander fearlessly across the road in search of another garden to graze.

ESSENTIALS

VISITOR INFORMATION   Although the town is small, there is the **Pacific Grove Chamber of Commerce,** at the corner of Forest and Central avenues (© **800/656-6650** or 831/373-3304; www.pacificgrove.org).

ORIENTATION   Lighthouse Avenue is the Grove's principal thoroughfare, running from Monterey to the lighthouse at the very point of the peninsula. Lighthouse Avenue is bisected by Forest Avenue, which runs from Calif. 1 (where it's called Holman Hwy., or Calif. 68) to Lover's Point, an extension of land that sticks out into the bay in the middle of Pacific Grove.

WHAT TO SEE & DO

Pacific Grove is a town to be strolled, so park the car, put on your walking shoes, and make an afternoon of it. Meander around George Washington Park and along the waterfront around the point.

The **Point Pinos Lighthouse** 🖈, at the tip of the peninsula on Ocean View Boulevard (© **831/648-5716**), is the oldest working lighthouse on the West Coast. Its 50,000-candlepower beacon has illuminated the rocky shores since February 1, 1855, when Pacific Grove was little more than a pine forest. The museum and grounds are open, free to visitors, Thursday through Sunday from 1 to 4pm.

Marine Gardens Park 🖈, a stretch of shoreline along Ocean View Boulevard on Monterey Bay and the Pacific, is renowned not only for its ocean views and colorful flowers, but also for its fascinating tide-pool seaweed beds. Walk out to **Lover's Point** (named after Lovers of Jesus, not groping teenagers) and watch the sea otters playing in the kelp beds and cracking open an occasional abalone for lunch.

An excellent shorter alternative, or complement, to the 17-Mile Drive (see section 4, later in this chapter) is the scenic drive or bike ride along Pacific Grove's **Ocean View Boulevard** 🖈. This coastal stretch starts near Monterey's Cannery Row and follows the Pacific around to the lighthouse point. Here it turns into

Sunset Drive, which runs along secluded **Asilomar State Beach** ⚜ (© 831/ 648-3130). Park on Sunset and explore the trails, dunes, and tide pools of this sandy stretch of shore. You might find purple shore crabs, green anemone, sea bats, starfish, and limpets, as well as all kinds of kelp and algae. The 11 buildings of the conference center established here by the YWCA in 1913 are historic landmarks that were designed by noted architect Julia Morgan. If you follow this route during winter, a furious sea rages and crashes against the rocks.

To learn more about the marine and other natural life of the region, stop in at the **Pacific Grove Museum of Natural History,** 165 Forest Ave. (© 831/ 648-5716; www.pgmuseum.org). It has displays on monarch butterflies and their migration, stuffed examples of the local birds and mammals, and temporary exhibits and special events. Admission is free; hours are Tuesday through Sunday from 10am to 5pm.

Pacific Grove is widely known as "Butterfly Town, USA," a reference to the thousands of **monarch butterflies** that migrate here from November to February, traveling from as far away as Alaska. Many settle in the Monarch Grove sanctuary, a eucalyptus stand on Grove Acre Avenue off Lighthouse Avenue. George Washington Park, at Pine Avenue and Alder Street, is also famous for its "butterfly trees." To reach these sites, the butterflies may travel as far as 2,000 miles, covering 100 miles a day at an altitude of 10,000 feet. Collectors beware: The town imposes strict fines for molesting butterflies.

Just as Ocean View Boulevard serves as an alternative to the 17-Mile Drive, the **Pacific Grove Municipal Golf Course,** 77 Asilomar Ave. (© 831/648-5777), serves as a reasonably priced alternative to the high-priced courses at Pebble Beach. The back nine holes of this 5,500-yard, par-70 course overlook the sea and offer the added challenge of coping with the winds. Views are panoramic, and the fairways and greens are better maintained than most semi-private courses. There's a restaurant, pro shop, and driving range. Eighteen holes start at $32 Monday through Thursday and $38 Friday through Sunday and holidays; twilight rates are available. Optional carts cost $26.

The **American Tin Cannery Factory Premium Outlets,** 125 Ocean View Blvd., around the corner from the Monterey Bay Aquarium (© 831/372-1442; www.premiumoutlets.com), is a huge converted warehouse housing 40 factory-outlet shops. Labels represented here include Bass Shoes, Reebok, Nine West, OshKosh B'Gosh, Samsonite, Maidenform, and Izod. It's open Monday through Saturday from 10am to 7pm, Sunday from 10am to 6pm.

WHERE TO STAY

If you're having trouble finding a vacancy, try calling **Resort 2 Me** (© 800/757-5646; www.resort2me.com), a local reservations service that offers free recommendations of Monterey Bay–area hotels in all price ranges.

EXPENSIVE

Martine Inn ⚜⚜ One glance at the lavish Victorian interior and the incredible bay views and you'll know why this Mediterranean-style inn is one of the best B&Bs in the area. Enjoy the vista via binoculars that the management leaves out for guests, or stroll the bay-front promenade. You'll have to pay more if you want a fireplace and ocean view, though every room is a winner. Request a room with a bathtub if it matters to you; some have only a shower. The inn also maintains an adjacent Victorian cottage, which has been converted into a luxury suite. A full breakfast is served at lace-covered tables in the large front room; hors d'oeuvres are served in the evening. Guests also have access to two additional sitting quarters: a small room downstairs overlooking the ocean and a larger room with shelves of books.

255 Ocean View Blvd., Pacific Grove, CA 93950. © **800/852-5588** or 831/373-3388. Fax 831/373-3896. www.martineinn.com. 24 units. $170–$300 double. Rates include full breakfast and evening hors d'oeuvres. AE, DISC, MC, V. **Amenities:** Nearby golf course; Jacuzzi; game room; concierge; tour desk; room service; in-room massage; babysitting. *In room:* Fridge, hair dryer.

Seven Gables Inn ★★★   This is one of the most opulent B&Bs I've ever seen. Named after the seven gables that cap the hotel, the compound of Victorian buildings was constructed in 1886 by the Chase family (as in Chase Manhattan Bank). Outside is the coast road overlooking the sea; inside is a valuable collection of mostly European antiques. Everything here is luxurious and gilded, including the oceanview rooms, which are scattered among the main house, cottages (including a two-bedroom option), and the guesthouse. The accommodations are linked by verdant gardens filled with roses and marble sculpture. If the hotel's booked, ask about the Grand View Inn, a slightly less ornate but comparable B&B next door that's run by the same owners.

555 Ocean View Blvd., Pacific Grove, CA 93950. © **831/372-4341.** www.pginns.com. 14 units. $175–$385 double. Rates include breakfast and afternoon tea. 2-night minimum on weekends. MC, V. **Amenities:** Nearby golf course. *In room:* Hair dryer, fridge in some units, kitchenette in 1 unit, no phone.

MODERATE

Centrella Inn ★   A couple of blocks from the waterfront and from Lover's Point Beach, the two-story Centrella is an old turreted Victorian that was built as a boardinghouse in 1889. Today, the rooms are decorated in Victorian style, but they're somewhat plain—iron beds, side table, floor lamp, and armoire—although the bathrooms do have claw-foot tubs. In the back, connected to the house by brick walkways, are several private cottages and suites with fireplaces, and separate bedrooms and bathrooms. Two have private decks; the others offer decks facing the rose garden and patio, which is set with umbrella tables and chairs.

612 Central Ave., Pacific Grove, CA 93950. © **800/233-3372** or 831/372-3372. Fax 831/372-2036. www. centrellainn.com. 26 units. $119–$249 double; $189–$300 suites and cottages. Rates include buffet breakfast and evening hors d'oeuvres. AE, DISC, MC, V. **Amenities:** Nearby golf course. *In room:* TV in cottages, iron, fridge, hair dryer.

Gosby House ★   Originally a boardinghouse for Methodist ministers, this Victorian was built in 1888, 3 blocks from the bay. It's still one of the most charming Victorians in town, with individually decorated rooms, floral-print wallpapers, lacy pillows, and antique furnishings. Twelve guest rooms have fireplaces, and all come with the inn's trademark teddy bears. Especially noteworthy are the two Carriage House rooms, which come with TV/VCR, a fridge and coffeemaker, fireplace, balcony, and extra-large bathroom with spa tub. The house has a separate dining room and parlor, where guests gather for breakfast and complimentary wine and hors d'oeuvres in the afternoon. Other amenities include complimentary newspaper, twice-daily maid service, and bicycles.

643 Lighthouse Ave., Pacific Grove, CA 93950. © **800/527-8828** or 831/375-1287. Fax 831/655-9621. www. foursisters.com. 22 units, 20 with bathroom. $115 double without bathroom; $95–$170 double with bathroom. Rates include full breakfast and afternoon wine and hors d'oeuvres. AE, DC, MC, V. From Calif. 1, take Calif. 68 to Pacific Grove, where it turns into Forest Ave.; continue on Forest to Lighthouse Ave., turn left, and go 3 blocks. **Amenities:** Nearby golf course; complimentary bike use. *In room:* Hair dryer.

Green Gables Inn ★★   This beautiful 1888 Queen Anne–style mansion, which is decorated like an English country inn, forgoes opulence (and in some cases private bathrooms) to allow for reasonable rates and less formal accommodations. The rooms are divided between the main building and the carriage houses behind it. The Carriage House rooms, which are better for families, have large private bathrooms with Jacuzzi tubs. All accommodations are individually decorated with period furnishings, including some antiques and an occasional poster bed. Most rooms in the original home have ocean views and share two immaculate bathrooms. There's an antique carousel horse in the comfortable parlor, where complimentary wine, tea, and hors d'oeuvres are served each afternoon.

301 Ocean View Blvd., Pacific Grove, CA 93950. © **800/722-1774** or 831/375-2095. Fax 831/375-5437. www.foursisters.com. 11 units, 7 with bathroom. $120–$155 double without bathroom; $170–$200 double with bathroom; $200–$260 suite. Rates include full breakfast and afternoon wine and hors d'oeuvres. AE, MC, V. From Calif. 1, take the Pacific Grove exit (Calif. 68) and continue to the Pacific Ocean; turn right on Ocean View Blvd. and drive ½ mile to 5th St. **Amenities:** Complimentary bike use. *In room:* Iron.

Pacific Grove Inn Five blocks from the beach, this renovated 1904 Queen Anne–style mansion is one of the town's bevy of painted ladies. Despite heavy Victorian embellishments, the accommodations feel light and airy. Rooms come with queen- or king-size beds, and fireplaces. Afternoon tea is served in the parlor.

581 Pine Ave., Pacific Grove, CA 93950. © **800/732-2825** or 831/375-2825. Fax 831/375-0752. www.pacific grove-inn.com. 16 units. $99–$239 double; $119–$279 suite. Rates include buffet breakfast and afternoon tea. AE, DC, DISC, MC, V. From Calif. 1, take the Pacific Grove exit (Calif. 68) to the corner of Pine and Forest aves. **Amenities:** Nearby golf course. *In room:* TV/VCR, fridge, safe.

INEXPENSIVE
The Wilkies Inn (*Value*) This motel consistently charges less than the other hotels in town, gets an A+ for service, and is located on a tree-lined street with a resident deer who often drops by for breakfast (but please don't feed him). The motel boasts well-kept furnishings and carpets, and stylish bedspreads. All the squeaky-clean rooms come with free HBO and local calls; some have partial ocean views. Putting up with occasionally noisy plumbing and thin walls might be worth the money saved.

1038 Lighthouse Ave., Pacific Grove, CA 93950. © **866/372-5960** or 831/372-5960. Fax 831/655-1681. 24 units. $49–$210 double. Extra person $10. 2-night minimum on weekends. Rates include continental breakfast. Packages available. AE, DISC, MC, V. **Amenities:** Nearby golf course. *In room:* TV/VCR, dataport, coffeemaker, hair dryer, iron.

WHERE TO DINE
EXPENSIVE
Fandango (★★) MEDITERRANEAN Provincial Mediterranean specialties from Spain to Greece to North Africa spice up the menu with such offerings as seafood paella with North African couscous (the recipe has been in the owner's family for almost 200 years), cassoulet maison, cannelloni niçoise, and a Greek-style lamb shank. You'll feel transported straight to Europe in one of the five upstairs and downstairs dining rooms, cozied by roaring fires, wood tables, and antiqued walls. There's an award-winning international wine list with 450 options and a dessert menu that includes a Grand Marnier soufflé with fresh raspberry purée sauce and profiteroles. In winter, ask to be seated in the fireplace dining room, and in summer, request the terrace room—but whenever you come, expect everything here to be lively and colorful, from the regional decor to the owner himself.

223 17th St. © **831/372-3456.** Fax 831/372-2673. www.fandangorestaurant.com. Reservations recommended. Main courses $11–$24. AE, DC, DISC, MC, V. Mon–Sat 11am–3pm, Sun 10am–2:30pm; daily

5–9:30pm. From Calif. 1, take the Pacific Grove exit (Calif. 68), turn left on Lighthouse Ave., and continue a block to 17th St.

Joe Rombi's ☆ ITALIAN   In an area where most restaurants pack 'em in, Joe Rombi's offers a refreshingly intimate dining room with dimmed lights and enormous French antique posters. The food here is very fresh (lasagnas and pastas are made that day). Once seated at 1 of the 11 tables, you'll immediately be served a basket of fresh house-made focaccia to munch on while you peruse the limited menu of appetizers, soups, salads, pastas, and four main courses (some of which come with soup and salad). Go with the fish of the day—I had a halibut dish that any upscale San Francisco restaurant would be proud to serve.

208 17th St. (at Lighthouse Ave.). (℃ **831/373-2416.** Fax 831/373-2106. www.joerombis.com. Reservations recommended. Main courses $12–$21. AE, MC, V. Wed–Sun 5–10pm.

The Old Bath House ☆ CONTINENTAL   Romance is in the air at this restored Victorian restaurant, perched on the edge of the earth overlooking Lover's Point. It may be pricey and frequented by tourists, but dinner here is a stately affair with knockout bay views, superb service, and competently prepared cuisine. A popular starter is the grilled prawns and wild-boar sausage appetizer. Main courses range from oak-grilled filet mignon to scallops on lemon risotto. The signature dish is the duck merlot, served with a dried cherry-merlot reduction and risotto. End your decadent dinner with a plate of hot pecan ice-cream fritters.

620 Ocean View Blvd. (℃ **831/375-5195.** Fax 831/375-5379. www.oldbathhouse.com. Reservations required. Main courses $20–$30. AE, DC, DISC, MC, V. Mon–Fri 5–11pm, Sat–Sun 4–11pm.

MODERATE

The Fishwife at Asilomar Beach ☆ *Kids* SEAFOOD   The Fishwife is the ideal dining spot for anyone looking for a casual, affordable, and quality meal. The restaurant dates from the 1830s, when a sailor's wife started a small food market that became famous for its Boston clam chowder. Today, locals still return for the savory soup as well as some of the finest seafood in Pacific Grove. Two best-sellers at dinner are calamari steak sautéed with shallots, garlic, tomatoes, and white wine; and prawns Belize, served sizzling with red onions, tomatoes, fresh Serrano chiles, jicama, lime juice, and cashews. Steak and pasta dishes are also available, and all main courses come with vegetables, bread, black beans, and rice or potatoes. Kids get their own color-in menu, which has smaller portions for less than $6.

1996½ Sunset Dr. (at Asilomar Beach). (℃ **831/375-7107.** www.fishwife.com. Main courses $8.95–$15. AE, DISC, MC, V. Mon–Sat 11am–10pm, Sun 10am–10pm. From Calif. 1, take the Pacific Grove exit (Calif. 68) and stay left until it becomes Sunset Dr.; the restaurant will be on your left about 1 mile ahead, as you approach Asilomar Beach.

Peppers Mexicali Café ☆ MEXICAN/LATIN AMERICAN   Peppers is a casual, festive place serving good food at reasonable prices. The inviting dining room has wooden floors and tables, pepper art visible from every vantage point, and a perpetual crowd of diners who come to suck up beers and savor spicy specialties such as well-balanced seafood tacos and fajitas or house-made tamales and chiles rellenos. Other fire-starters include the snapper Yucatán, which is cooked with chiles, citrus cilantro, and tomatoes; and grilled prawns with lime-cilantro dressing. More than a dozen daily specials are offered as well, such as Mexican seafood paella and grilled mahimahi tacos. Add a substantial selection of cervezas, an addicting compilation of chips and salsa, and a friendly staff, and your taste buds are bound to bellow "Olé!"

170 Forest Ave. ℭ **831/373-6892**. Fax 831/373-5467. Reservations recommended. Main courses $7–$15. AE, DC, DISC, MC, V. Mon and Wed–Thurs 11:30am–10pm, Fri–Sat 11:30am–10:30pm, Sun 4–10pm.

INEXPENSIVE

First Awakenings 🌟 *Value* AMERICAN   What was once a dank canning factory is now a bright, huge, open restaurant offering one of the cheapest and healthiest breakfasts in the area. Eye-openers include eight varieties of omelets; granola with nuts, fruit, and yogurt; walnut and wheat pancakes; "gourmet" pancakes; and raisin French toast. At lunch, there's a fine choice of salads and a slew of sandwiches ranging from albacore to zucchini. On sunny days, take advantage of the outdoor patio tables.

In the American Tin Cannery, 125 Ocean View Blvd. ℭ **831/372-1125**. Reservations not accepted. Breakfast $3–$7; lunch $5–$7. AE, DISC, MC, V. Daily 7am–2:30pm. From Calif. 1, take the Pacific Grove exit (Calif. 68) and turn right onto Lighthouse Ave.; after a mile, turn left onto Eardley Ave., and take it to the corner of Ocean View.

4 Pebble Beach & the 17-Mile Drive 🌟🌟🌟

Pebble Beach is a world unto itself. Polo shirts, golf shoes, and big bankrolls are standard here, and if you have to ask how costly accommodations and greens fees are, you definitely can't afford them. In this elite golfers' paradise, endless grassy fairways are interrupted only by a few luxury resorts and cliffs where the ocean meets the land. In winter, it's also the site of the AT&T Pebble Beach National Pro-Am, a celebrity tournament originally launched in 1937 by crooner Bing Crosby.

THE 17-MILE DRIVE 🌟🌟

The beautiful 17-Mile Drive demands a leisurely afternoon. Pack a picnic, fork over $8 to enter the drive, and prepare to see some of the most exclusive coastal real estate in California.

The drive can be entered from any of five gates: two from Pacific Grove to the north, one from Carmel to the south, or two from Monterey to the east. The most convenient entrance from Calif. 1 is just off the main road at the Holman Highway exit. You may beat traffic by entering at the Carmel Gate and doing the tour backwards.

Admission to the drive includes an informative map that lists 26 points of interest along the way. Aside from homes of the ultra-rich, highlights include **Seal and Bird Rocks,** where you can see countless gulls, cormorants, and other offshore birds as well as seals and sea lions; and **Cypress Point Lookout,** which affords a 20-mile view all the way to the Big Sur Lighthouse on a clear day. Also visible is the famous **Lone Cypress** tree, inspiration to so many artists and photographers, which you can admire from afar but to which you can no longer walk. The drive also traverses the **Del Monte Forest,** thick with tame black-tailed deer and often described as some "billionaire's private game preserve."

One of the best ways to see 17-Mile Drive is by bike, but the ride toward Carmel is all downhill, so unless you're in great shape, arrange for a ride back. For further information, call the Pebble Beach Resort at ℭ **831/624-3811** or visit www.pebblebeach.com/17miledrive.html.

GREAT GOLF COURSES

Locals tell me it's almost impossible to get a tee time unless you're staying at the golf resort. If you're one of the lucky few, you can choose from several famous courses along the 17-Mile Drive.

PEBBLE BEACH GOLF LINKS ✦✦✦   The most famous course is Pebble Beach Golf Links (© **800/654-9300**) at The Lodge at Pebble Beach (p. 375). It's home in winter to the AT&T Pebble Beach National Pro-Am, a celebrity-laden tournament televised around the world. Jack Nicklaus has claimed, "If I could play only one course for the rest of my life, this would be it." He should know; he won both the 1961 U.S. Amateur and the 1972 U.S. Open here. Indeed, 10 national championships have been decided here. Herbert Warren Wind, dean of 20th-century golf writers, said, "There is no finer seaside golf course in creation"—and that includes the legendary Old Course at St. Andrews in Scotland. Built in 1919, this 18-hole course is 6,799 yards and par 72. It's precariously perched over a rugged ocean. Greens fees are a staggering $350 plus cart fee.

SPYGLASS HILL GOLF COURSE ✦✦   Also frequented by celebrities is this course at Stevenson Drive and Spyglass Hill Road (© **800/654-9300**). Its slope rating of 143 means that it's one of the toughest courses in California. It's a justifiably famous links: 6,859 yards and par 72 with five oceanfront holes. The rest reach deep into the Del Monte Forest. Greens fees are $260 plus cart. Reservations for non-guests should be made a month in advance. There's an excellent Grill Room on the grounds.

POPPY HILLS ✦✦   This 18-hole, 6,219-yard course on 17-Mile Drive (© **831/625-2035**) was named one of the world's top 20 by *Golf Digest.* It was designed by Robert Trent Jones Jr. in 1986. One golf pro said the course is "long and tough on short hitters." Greens fees are $125 Monday through Thursday and $150 Friday through Sunday, plus $30 for the cart rental. You can make reservations 30 days in advance.

THE LINKS AT SPANISH BAY ✦✦   Lying on the north end of 17-Mile Drive at the Pebble Beach Resort and Inn at Spanish Bay (© **800/654-9300**), this is the most easily booked course. Serious golfers say it's the most challenging of the Pebble Beach links. Robert Trent Jones Jr., Tom Watson, and Frank Tatum (former USGA president) designed it to duplicate a Scottish links course. Its fescue grasses and natural fairways lead to rolls and unexpected bounces for your ball. Greens fees are $215. Cart rental is an additional $25. Reservations can be made 60 days in advance.

DEL MONTE GOLF COURSE ✦   At 1300 Sylvan Rd. (© **831/373-2700**) lies the oldest course west of the Mississippi, charging some of the most "reasonable" greens fees: $95 per player, plus a cart rental of $20. The course, often cited in magazines for its "grace and charm," is relatively short—only 6,339 yards. This seldom-advertised course, which is located at the Hyatt east of Monterey, is part of the Pebble Beach complex, but is not along the 17-Mile Drive.

WHERE TO STAY & DINE

Casa Palmero Resort ✦✦✦   The Casa Palmero is a small, ultra-luxury resort on the first tee of the Pebble Beach Golf Links. The two-story villa is the newest firmament in the dazzling sister properties, which include the Inn at Spanish Bay and The Lodge at Pebble Beach. The more intimate and private of the three, Casa Palmero is fashioned as an old-world European villa with cool stucco walls, window boxes dripping bougainvillea, every modern creature comfort, and a staff to anticipate your every wish. It has 24 cottages and suites with varying amenities that include French doors opening onto private garden spas, oversize window-box sofas, wood-burning fireplaces, and oversize soaking tubs that open to the main room. "Convivial" areas, places where you can hang out with your friends, include a trellised patio, library, billiards parlor, living room, private dining room, executive boardroom and small conference room, intimate courtyards with fountains, and lavish outdoor pool pavilion.

1518 Cypress Dr. (on 17-Mile Dr.), Pebble Beach, CA 93953. © 800/654-9300 or 831/622-6650. Fax 831/622-6655. www.pebblebeach.com. 24 units. $625–$1,950 cottage or suite. $20 gratuity added. Rates include continental breakfast and evening hors d'oeuvres and cocktails. AE, MC, V. From Calif. 1 S, turn W onto Calif. 68 and S onto 17-Mile Dr., and follow the coastal road to the hotel. **Amenities:** 3 restaurants; outdoor heated pool; golf course; 12 tennis courts; health club; full-service spa; Jacuzzi; sauna; bike rental; concierge; 24-hr. room service; in-room massage; babysitting; laundry service; same-day dry cleaning; executive-level rooms. *In room:* TV/VCR w/pay movies, dataport, minibar, fridge, coffeemaker, hair dryer, iron, safe.

The Inn at Spanish Bay ★★★ Surrounded by the renowned Links at Spanish Bay golf course, the Inn at Spanish Bay is a plush three- and four-story low-rise, set on 236 manicured acres 10 miles north of The Lodge at Pebble Beach. Approximately half the rooms face the ocean and are more expensive than their counterparts, which overlook the forest. Each unit contains about 600 square feet of floor space and has a private fireplace and either an outdoor deck or a patio. The bathrooms are finished in Italian marble; the custom-made furnishings include four-poster beds with down comforters. My favorite time here is dusk, when a bagpiper strolls the terrace with a skirling tribute to Scotland.

2700 17-Mile Dr., Pebble Beach, CA 93953. © 800/654-9300 or 831/647-7500. Fax 831/644-7960. www.pebblebeach.com. 270 units. $450–$650 double; $1,750–$2,165 2-bedroom suite. $20 gratuity added. AE, DC, MC, V. From Calif. 1 S, turn W onto Calif. 68 and S onto 17-Mile Dr.; the hotel is on your right, just past the toll plaza. **Amenities:** 3 restaurants; bar/lounge; heated outdoor pool; golf course; 8 outdoor tennis courts (2 night-lit); health club; full-service spa; Jacuzzi; sauna; bike rental; concierge; tour desk; business center; shopping arcade; 24-hr. room service; in-room massage; babysitting; laundry service; same-day dry cleaning; executive-level rooms. *In room:* TV/VCR w/pay movies, dataport, minibar, fridge, coffeemaker, hair dryer, iron, safe in most units.

The Lodge at Pebble Beach ★★ For the combined cost of greens fees and a room here, you could easily create a professional putting green in your own backyard—and still have some money left over. But if you're a dedicated hacker, you've got to play here at least once. Look on the bright side—at least you can expect ultra-plush rooms equipped with every conceivable amenity, including wood-burning fireplaces. Most are in two-story cottage clusters, with anywhere from 8 to 12 units in each. Those opening onto the ocean carry the highest price tags.

1700 17-Mile Dr., Pebble Beach, CA 93953. © 800/654-9300 or 831/624-3811. Fax 831/625-8598. www.pebblebeach.com. 161 units. $500–$800 double; from $1,350 suite. $15 gratuity added. AE, MC, V. From Calif. 1 S, turn W on Calif. 68, turn S onto 17-Mile Dr., and follow the coastal road to the hotel. **Amenities:** 4 restaurants; bar/lounge; heated outdoor pool; golf course; 12 tennis courts; health club; full-service spa; Jacuzzi; sauna; bike rental; concierge; business center; shopping arcade; 24-hr. room service; in-room massage; babysitting; laundry service; same-day dry cleaning. *In room:* TV/VCR w/pay movies, dataport, minibar, fridge, coffeemaker, hair dryer, iron, safe in most units.

5 Carmel-by-the-Sea ★★

5 miles S of Monterey; 121 miles S of San Francisco; 33 miles N of Big Sur

If you visited the town officially known as Carmel-by-the-Sea dozens of years ago, you're likely to be of the school that criticizes its present-day overcommercialization. Carmel began as an artists' colony that attracted such luminaries as Robinson Jeffers, Sinclair Lewis, Robert Louis Stevenson, Ansel Adams, William Rose Benet, and Mary Austin. It was a nonconformist enclave where residents resisted assigned street numbers and lighting (they carried lanterns, which they considered more romantic).

Today, Carmel may not be the bohemian artists' village of seasoned travelers' memories, but it's still an adorable (albeit touristy) town that knows how to celebrate its surroundings. Vibrant wildflower gardens flourish along each residential street, gnarled cypress trees reach up from white sandy beaches, and at the end of each day, tourists magically disappear and the town—for a split second—feels undiscovered.

It's still intimate enough that there's no need for street numbers. Carmel's inns, restaurants, boutiques, and art galleries all identify their locations only by cross streets. A few hints such as Saks Fifth Avenue, convertible roadsters cruising through town, intolerable traffic, and lofty B&B rates indicate you're not in Kansas anymore, but rather a well-preserved upscale tourist haven.

If you're interested in saving a few dollars, I recommend staying in Pacific Grove. It's only a few miles away, has better rates, and you can easily day-trip into crowded Carmel.

ESSENTIALS

The **Carmel Business Association,** P.O. Box 4444, Carmel, CA 93921 (© **831/624-2522;** www.carmelcalifornia.org), is located on San Carlos between Fifth and Sixth streets. It distributes local maps, brochures, and publications. Pick up a copy of the *Guide to Carmel* and a schedule of local events. Hours are Monday through Friday from 9am to 5pm. On weekends, an information booth is set up from 11am to 3pm at Carmel Plaza, on Ocean Avenue between Junipero and San Carlos streets.

WHAT TO SEE & DO

A wonderful stretch of white sand backed by cypress trees, **Carmel Beach City Park** ☆☆ is a wee bit o' heaven on earth (though the jammed parking lot can feel more like a visit to a car rally). There's plenty of room for families, surfers, and dogs with their owners (yes, pooches are allowed to run off-leash here). If the parking lot is full, there are some spaces on Ocean Avenue, but take heed: They're generally good for 90-minute parking only, and you will get a ticket if you park for the day.

Farther south around the promontory, **Carmel River State Beach** ☆ is a less crowded option, with white sand and dunes, plus a bird sanctuary where brown pelicans, black oystercatchers, cormorants, gulls, curlews, godwits, and sanderlings make their home.

The **Mission San Carlos Borromeo del Rio Carmelo** ☆☆, on Basilica Rio Road at Lasuen Drive, off Calif. 1 (© **831/624-3600;** www.carmelmission.org), is the burial ground of Father Junípero Serra and the second-oldest of the 21 Spanish missions he established. Founded in 1771 on a scenic site overlooking the Carmel River, it remains one of the largest and most interesting of California's missions. The stone church, with its gracefully curving walls and Moorish bell tower, was begun in 1793. Its walls are covered with a lime plaster made of burnt seashells. The old mission kitchen, the first library in California, the high altar, and the flower gardens are all worth visiting. More than 3,000 Native Americans are buried in the adjacent cemetery; their graves are decorated with seashells. The mission is open June through August, Monday through Saturday from 9:30am to 7:30pm, Sunday from 10:30am to 7:30pm; in other months, Monday through Saturday from 9:30am to 4:30pm, Sunday from 10:30am to 4:30pm. A $2 donation is requested.

One of Carmel's prettiest homes and gardens is **Tor House** ⚘, 26304 Ocean View Ave. (© **831/624-1813;** www.torhouse.org), built by California poet Robinson Jeffers. Situated on Carmel Point, the house dates from 1918 and includes a 40-foot tower containing stones from around the world, which are embedded in the walls (there's even one from the Great Wall of China). Inside, an old porthole is reputed to have come from the ship on which Napoleon escaped from Elba in 1815. No photography is allowed. Admission is by guided tour only, and reservations are requested. It's $7 for adults, $4 for college students, and $2 for high-school students (no children under 12). Open on Friday and Saturday from 10am to 3pm.

If the tourists aren't lying on the beach in Carmel, then they're probably **shopping**—the *sine qua non* of Carmel activities. You'll be surprised at the number of shops packed into this small town—more than 500 boutiques offering unique fashions, baskets, housewares, imported goods, and a veritable cornucopia of art galleries. Most of the commercial action is packed along the small stretch of Ocean Avenue between Junipero and San Antonio avenues.

If you want to tour the **galleries,** pick up a copy of the *Carmel Gallery Guide* from the Carmel Business Association (see "Essentials," above).

Serious shoppers should also head south a few miles to the **Crossroads Shopping Center** (from Calif. 1 south, take the Rio Rd. exit west for 1 block and turn right onto Crossroads Blvd.). As far as malls go, this is a great one, with oodles of shopping and a few good restaurants.

WHERE TO STAY

If you're traveling with pets, your best bet is **The Cypress Inn,** Lincoln and Seventh (P.O. Box Y), Carmel-by-the-Sea, CA 93921 (© **800/443-7443** or 831/624-3871; www.cypress-inn.com), which is a moderately priced option run by owner and actress Doris Day.

EXPENSIVE

Carriage House Inn ⚘⚘   The luxurious atmosphere and superfluous pampering make this one of my top picks in the "downtown" area. Each room comes with a wood-burning fireplace and king-size bed with down comforter. Most of the second-floor rooms have sunken tubs and vaulted beam ceilings; first-floor rooms have single whirlpool tubs. Not only is breakfast delivered to guests' rooms, but there's also wine and hors d'oeuvres served in the afternoon and cappuccino, wine, and cheese in the evening. Plus, while almost all choices in the area are frill-and-lace, the Carriage House is a more mature, formal, yet cozy environment.

Junipero St., between 7th and 8th aves. (P.O. Box 1900), Carmel, CA 93921. © **800/433-4732** or 831/625-2585. Fax 831/624-0974. www.ibts-carriagehouse.com. 13 units. $229–$375 double; $279–$415 suite. Rates include continental breakfast and afternoon wine and hors d'oeuvres. AE, DISC, MC, V. Free parking. From Calif. 1, exit onto Ocean Ave. and turn left onto Junipero St. **Amenities:** Nearby golf course; concierge. *In room:* TV/VCR, minibar, coffeemaker, fridge, hair dryer, iron, safe.

Highlands Inn, Park Hyatt Carmel ⚘⚘   Four miles south of Carmel on a 12-acre cliff overlooking Point Lobos, this one- and two-story inn has attracted everyone from celebrities—Madonna, Sammy Hagar, Walt Disney, Marlon Brando—to honeymooners and business executives. It's rustic yet luxurious, with wildflowers gracing its pathways, plenty of character, and a rather exclusive atmosphere. The old-style main lounge dates from 1916 and has panoramic coastal vistas. The guest rooms are distributed throughout a cluster of buildings terraced into the hillside; a complete interior renovation in 2002 included new carpets, furniture, bathrooms, patio furniture, and slate tile in the bathroom and kitchen. Most units have decks or balconies and wood-burning fireplaces. The suites come with Jacuzzi tubs and fully equipped kitchens; four rooms have showers only.

120 Highlands Dr., Carmel, CA 93923. ℂ **800/682-4811** or 831/620-1234. Fax 831/626-8105. www. highlands-inn.com. 142 units. $205 double; $260–$695 spa suite; $485–$1,025 2-bedroom, full oceanview spa suite. AE, DC, DISC, MC, V. **Amenities:** 2 restaurants; lounge; outdoor heated pool; nearby golf course; exercise room; 3 outdoor Jacuzzis; complimentary bike use; concierge; tour/activities desk; business center; secretarial services; room service; in-room massage; babysitting; laundry service; same-day dry cleaning. *In room:* TV w/pay movies, VCR on request, CD player, fridge, coffeemaker, kitchen in suites, hair dryer, iron, safe.

La Playa ⭐ Only 2 blocks from the beach and yet within walking distance of town, the four-story La Playa is a romantic, Mediterranean-style villa built in 1904. Norwegian artist Christopher Jorgensen ordered its construction for his bride, an heiress of the Ghirardelli chocolate dynasty. The stylish lobby sets the elegant tone with its terra-cotta floors, Oriental rugs, and white marble fireplace. In the courtyard, walkways lead through beautifully landscaped grounds that surround a heated pool. Compared to the splendor of the lobby and grounds, the standard guest rooms are a bit of a disappointment. The walls are thin and the furnishings perfunctory. The luxury cottages are an improvement—all have kitchens, wet bars, garden patios, and limited room service, and most have wood-burning fireplaces—but yes, they're expensive.

Camino Real and 8th Ave. (P.O. Box 900), Carmel, CA 93921. ℂ **800/582-8900** or 831/624-6476. Fax 831/ 624-7966. www.laplayahotel.com. 80 units. $160–$315 double; $315–$625 suite or cottage. Complimentary valet parking. AE, DC, MC, V. **Amenities:** Restaurant; bar; outdoor heated pool; nearby golf course; bike rental; concierge; business center; room service; babysitting; same-day dry cleaning. *In room:* TV, fridge, hair dryer, iron.

Mission Ranch ⭐⭐ If you want to stay a bit off the beaten track, consider this converted 1850s dairy farm, which was purchased and restored by Clint Eastwood to preserve the vista of the nearby wetlands stretching out to the bay. The ranch's accommodations are spaciously scattered amid different structures, both old and new, and surrounded by wetlands and grazing sheep. Guest rooms range from "regulars" in the main barn (which are less desirable) to meadow-view units, each with a vista across the fields to the bay. As befits a ranch, rooms are decorated in a provincial style, with carved wooden beds bedecked with handmade quilts. Most are equipped with whirlpool baths, fireplaces, and decks or patios. The Martin Family farmhouse contains six units, all arranged around a central parlor, while the Bunkhouse (the oldest structure on the property) contains separate living and dining areas, bedrooms, and a fridge. Even if you're not staying here, call for a table at The Restaurant at Mission Ranch (p. 380).

26270 Dolores St., Carmel, CA 93923. ℂ **800/538-8221** or 831/624-6436. Fax 831/626-4163. 31 units. $100–$280 double. Rates include continental breakfast. AE, MC, V. **Amenities:** Restaurant; 6 tennis courts; exercise room; babysitting; laundry service; dry cleaning. *In room:* TV, dataport, fridge in some units, coffeemaker, hair dryer, iron.

MODERATE

Carmel Sands Lodge ⭐ The Sands is a motor lodge, but it's decorated better than most and is located on a quiet street in Carmel. The modern rooms have pretty bedspreads and updated furnishings; some have fireplaces and wet bars. There's a small pool, but it's practically in the center courtyard parking lot. Several restaurants are nearby. I like the quiet location here better than that of the comparable Carmel Village Inn (see below).

San Carlos and 5th (P.O. Box 951), Carmel, CA 93921. ℂ **800/252-1255** or 831/624-1255. Fax 831/624-2576. www.carmelsandslodge.com. 38 units. July–Oct $98–$169 double; Nov–June $79–$149 double. AE, DC, DISC, MC, V. From Ocean Ave., take a right onto San Carlos and go 2 blocks. **Amenities:** Restaurant; heated pool (seasonal); nearby golf course. *In room:* TV; minibar, fridge, coffeemaker and hair dryer in some units.

Carmel Village Inn   Well run and centrally located, the Village Inn is basically a motor lodge. The rooms, arranged around a courtyard and parking lot lined with potted geraniums, are outfitted with bland but functional decor. Breakfast, accompanied by the morning newspaper, is served in the downstairs lounge.

Ocean Ave. and Junipero St. (P.O. Box 5275), Carmel, CA 93921. ℂ **800/346-3864** or 831/624-3864. Fax 831/626-6763. www.carmelvillageinn.com. 48 units. $69–$190 double; $89–$380 triple or quad; from $108 suite. Rates include continental breakfast. AE, MC, V. From Calif. 1, exit onto Ocean Ave. and continue straight to Junipero St. **Amenities:** Babysitting. *In room:* Fax, fridge, kitchenette.

Cobblestone Inn ⊛   The Cobblestone may not be Victorian like other properties owned by the Four Sisters Inns, but it's just as flowery, well kept, and cute, with hand-stenciled wall decorations, fireplaces, and a trademark abundance of teddy bears. The first floor is completely constructed of stones taken from the Carmel River (hence the inn's name), and the rooms encircle a slate courtyard; some look out onto the brick patio where breakfast is occasionally served. The guest rooms vary in size; some can be small, and only the Honeymoon suite comes with a bathtub and VCR, but the largest units include a wet bar, sofa, and separate bedroom. Guests have the use of a comfortable living room with large stone fireplace. Extras include daily maid and turndown service and morning newspaper.

Junipero St. (between 7th and 8th aves., 1½ blocks from Ocean Ave.; P.O. Box 3185), Carmel, CA 93921. ℂ **800/833-8836** or 831/625-5222. Fax 831/625-0478. www.foursisters.com. 24 units. $125–$200 double; from $250 suite. Rates include full breakfast and afternoon wine and hors d'oeuvres. AE, DC, MC, V. **Amenities:** Complimentary bike use. *In room:* TV, dataport, fridge, hair dryer.

Normandy Inn ⊛   Three blocks from the beach, this French Provincial–style hotel is like something out of a storybook, especially with the array of colorful flowers that brighten up the property. Some of the guest rooms are showing their age a little, but they're well appointed with French country decor, feather beds, and down comforters. Some have fireplaces and/or kitchenettes. The tiny heated pool is banked by a sweet flower garden.

The three large family-style units are an especially good deal and accommodate up to eight; each one has three bedrooms, two bathrooms, a fully equipped kitchen, a dining room, a living room with a fireplace, and a back porch. Be sure to reserve far in advance, especially in summer.

Ocean Ave., between Monte Verde and Casanova sts. (P.O. Box 1706), Carmel, CA 93921. ℂ **800/343-3825** or 831/624-3825. Fax 831/624-4614. www.normandyinncarmel.com. 48 units. $99–$279 double; $169–$500 suites and cottages. Rates include continental breakfast. Extra person $10. AE, DC, MC, V. From Calif. 1, exit onto Ocean Ave. and continue straight for 5 blocks past Junipero St. **Amenities:** Outdoor pool (seasonal); nearby golf course. *In room:* TV, coffeemaker, kitchenette in some units, hair dryer, iron.

Sandpiper Inn by the Sea ⊛   A garden of flowers welcomes visitors to this quiet, relaxing, midscale Carmel standby that's been in business for more than 60 years. The inn's rooms, from which you can hear the surf, offer a range of well-kept accommodations. The highest priced are corner rooms with four-poster beds and plenty of windows framing the ocean view. All are decorated with handsome country antiques and fresh flowers that are changed daily; three have fireplaces. Carmel's fabled white-sand beaches are a mere 100 yards away.

2408 Bay View Ave., Carmel, CA 93923. ℭ **800/633-6433** or 831/624-6433. Fax 831/624-5964. www. sandpiper-inn.com. 17 units. $110–$285 double. Rates include extended continental breakfast and afternoon sherry/tea. AE, DISC, MC, V. **Amenities:** Nearby golf course; concierge; tour desk. *In room:* No phone.

WHERE TO DINE
EXPENSIVE

Anton & Michel ⭐ CONTINENTAL   This elegant restaurant, just across from Carmel Plaza, serves traditional French cuisine in one of the most formal rooms in town. During the day, it's best to dine fountain-side on the patio or encased in the glass-wrapped terrace. The view is equally alluring in the evening, when the courtyard is lit and the fountain's water sparkles with reflections. Decorated with French chandelier lamps and original oil paintings, the main dining room is a formal affair—but, as in most restaurants in town, patrons' attire need not match it. Appetizers include crab cakes with cilantro-pesto aïoli or delicate ravioli filled with ricotta cheese and spinach. Specialties include rack of lamb with an herb-Dijon mustard au jus and more eclectic items such as a chicken breast Jerusalem, sautéed with olive oil, white wine, cream, and artichoke hearts. The award-winning wine list is impressive.

At Court of the Fountain, Mission St. (between Ocean and 7th aves.). ℭ **831/624-2406.** www.carmelsbest. com. Reservations recommended. Main courses $17–$33. AE, DC, DISC, MC, V. Daily 11:30am–3pm and 5:30–9:30pm.

Casanova ⭐ NORTHERN ITALIAN/COUNTRY FRENCH   It's the engaging European ambience that has drawn both locals and tourists to Casanova for over a quarter of a century. The building, which once belonged to Charlie Chaplin's cook, is divided into three Belgian chalet–style dining rooms that serve as the perfect setting for leaning over a bottle of red wine and creating vacation memories. More festive folk step back to the old world–style covered patio where it's bustling and crowded. Because all dinner entrees include antipasto and a choice of appetizers (such as baked stuffed eggplant with rice, herbs, cheese, and tomatoes), prices here are not a bad deal (at least in overpriced Carmel). The menu features typical Mediterranean cuisine: paella, homemade pastas, meats, and fish. Casanova also boasts a *Wine Spectator*'s award–winning wine cellar featuring more than 1,600 French, California, German, and Italian wines.

5th Ave. (between San Carlos and Mission sts.). ℭ **831/625-0501.** www.casanovarestaurant.com. Reservations recommended. 3-course dinner $22–$43. MC, V. Mon–Sat 11:30am–3pm, Sun 10am–3pm; Sun–Thurs 5–10pm, Fri–Sat 5–10:30pm. From Calif. 1, take the Ocean Ave. exit and turn right on Mission, then left onto 5th Ave.

The Restaurant at Mission Ranch ⭐⭐ AMERICAN   Clint Eastwood bought this rustic out-of-the-way property in 1986 and restored the ranch-style building to its original integrity, and although the chance of seeing him brings in some folks, it's the views, quality food, and merry atmosphere that really make the place special. The wooden building is encased with large windows that accentuate the wonderful view of the marshlands, grazing sheep, and bay beyond. Warm days make patio dining the prime choice, but the key time to come is at sunset, when the sky is transforming and happy hour is in full swing (you'll find some of the cheapest drinks around, and Clint often stops by when he's in town). As you'd expect from the ranch motif, meat is king here: Burgers are freshly ground on-site, and prime rib with twice-baked potato and vegetables is the favored dish. There are, of course, wonderful seafood, chicken, and vegetarian options as well; and all dinners include soup or salad. Entertainment is provided at the piano bar, where locals and tourists have been known to croon their favorites. The Sunday buffet brunch with live jazz piano is also hugely popular; be sure to reserve a table.

At Mission Ranch, 26270 Dolores St. © **831/625-9040.** Fax 831/625-5502. Reservations recommended. Most main courses $17–$29. DC, MC, V. Sat 11am–2:30pm, Sun 9:30am–1:30pm; daily 4:30–9:30pm; bar stays open until midnight.

MODERATE

Flying Fish Grill ⭐ PACIFIC RIM/SEAFOOD   I always feel more confident when a restaurant's kitchen is actually run by its owner—and a dinner experience here will confirm that chef/proprietor Kenny Fukumoto is in the house. Dark, romantic, and Asian-influenced, the dining room has an intimate atmosphere with redwood booths (built by Kenny) and fish hanging (flying?) from the ceiling. The cuisine features fresh seafood with exquisite Japanese accents. Start with sushi, tempura, or any of the other exotic and tantalizing taste teasers. Then prepare your tongue for seriously sensational main courses. House favorites include a savory rare peppered ahi, blackened and served with mustard-and-sesame-soy vinaigrette and angel-hair pasta; and a pan-fried almond sea bass with whipped potatoes, Chinese cabbage, and rock shrimp stir-fry.

In Carmel Plaza, Mission St. (between Ocean and 7th aves.). © **831/625-1962.** Reservations recommended. Main courses $15–$24. AE, DISC, MC, V. Wed–Mon 5–10pm.

Grasing's Coastal Cuisine ⭐ CALIFORNIA   When chef Kurt Grasing and renowned Bay Area restaurateur Narsai David teamed together to open Grasing's Coastal Cuisine, the result was one of Carmel's best new restaurants. The bright, split-room dining area is simple yet stylish, with buttercup yellow walls, beaded lamps, and colorful artwork. Grasing's menu also reflects a stylish simplicity; ultra-fresh ingredients gleaned from California's coast and central valley regions are displayed in a modest fashion that belie an intense combination of textures and flavors. The warm Napa Salad, for example, appears ordinary enough, but "when I took it off the menu," says Grasing, "I still made 30 a night." Two other dishes that have generated such interest are the lobster risotto made with pearl pasta (rather than arborio rice, for a smoother texture) and the Bronzed Salmon served in a garlic cream sauce. Even the bread, which comes fresh from Gail's Bakery in Aptos, is fantastic. When the sun's out, request a table at the dog-friendly patio, and be sure to inquire about the very reasonable prix-fixe meal.

6th St. (at Mission St.). © **831/624-6562.** Reservations recommended. Main courses $17–$26. AE, MC, V. Daily 11am–4pm and 5–10pm.

Il Fornaio ⭐ ITALIAN   I don't care if it is a chain—Il Fornaio is still one of my favorite restaurants because I know I'm guaranteed a well-prepared mocha and thick chocolate-dipped biscotti at every outpost. There's also a great selection of salads (go with the simple house salad with shaved Parmesan, croutons, and a tangy light dressing), pastas, pizzas, and rotisserie chicken, duck, and rabbit fresh from the brick oven. The house-made breads and seeded breadsticks alone are reasons enough to come. I must admit that I was disappointed with the tasty-but-measly lasagna, so skip it and start with the seared swordfish antipasto with roast pepper and Dijon mustard, or decadent grilled polenta with sautéed wild mushrooms, provolone, and Italian truffle oil. Move on to a gourmet pizza or pasta. The large airy dining room and sunny terrace offer charming and diverse atmosphere. The Panetteria, a retail bakery, is the perfect place to pick up a gourmet picnic or have a breakfast snack.

Ocean Ave. (at Monte Verde). © **831/622-5100,** or 831/622-5115 for the bakery. Main courses $9.95–$25. AE, DC, MC, V. Daily 11:30am–11pm; Sat–Sun brunch 8am–2pm.

La Bohème ★ FRENCH COUNTRY   Like a set from Disney's "It's a Small World," La Bohème mimics a French street with cartoony asymmetrical shingled house facades and a painted blue sky overhead. Thankfully, the similarity stops with the decor, and there are no dolls singing anywhere—in French or English. Dinner here is utterly romantic French cuisine, served at cramped tables set with floral-print cloths in bright colors, hand-painted dinnerware, and vibrant bouquets. Dinner is a three-course, fixed-price feast consisting of a large salad, a tureen of soup, and a main dish (perhaps roast breast of duckling with green peppercorn sauce or filet mignon with cognac-cream sauce). Vegetarian specials are also available nightly. Homemade desserts and fresh coffee are sold separately, and are usually worth the extra expense.

Dolores St. and 7th Ave. ⓒ 831/624-7500. www.laboheme.com. Reservations not accepted. Prix-fixe 3-course dinner $24. MC, V. Daily 5:30–10pm. From Calif. 1, exit onto Ocean Ave. and turn left onto Dolores St.

Rio Grill ★★ AMERICAN   Both the food and the festive atmosphere (a cartoon mural of famous locals such as Clint Eastwood and the late Bing Crosby, plus playful sculpture, cactus, and other vibrant art) have kept this place popular for the past several years. The whimsical nature of the modern Santa Fe–style dining room belies the kitchen's serious preparations, which include homemade soups; a rich quesadilla with almonds, cheeses, and smoked-tomato salsa; barbecued baby-back ribs from a wood-burning oven; and fresh fish from an open oak grill. The restaurant's good selection of wines includes some rare California vintages and covers a broad price range.

Crossroads Shopping Center, 101 Crossroads Blvd. ⓒ 831/625-5436. www.riogrill.com. Reservations recommended. Main courses $8–$25. AE, DISC, MC, V. Sun–Thurs 11:30am–10pm, Fri–Sat 11:30am–11pm. From Calif. 1, take the Rio Rd. exit W for 1 block and turn right onto Crossroads Blvd.

INEXPENSIVE

Caffè Napoli ★ *Value* ITALIAN   The decor here is so quintessentially Italiana, with flags, gingham tablecloths, garlic, and baskets overhead, that I expected a flour-coated pot-bellied Padrino Napoli to emerge from the kitchen, embrace me wholeheartedly, and exclaim "Mangia! Mangia!" as he slapped down a bowl overflowing with sauce-drenched pasta. Of course, there is no Padrino here, and I received no welcoming hug, but I did indulge in the fine Italian fare that keeps locals coming back for more.

Ocean Ave. (between Dolores and Lincoln). ⓒ 831/625-4033. Reservations recommended. Main courses $10–$20. MC, V. Daily 11:30am–9pm.

6 Carmel Valley

3 miles SE of Carmel-by-the-Sea

Inland from Carmel stretches Carmel Valley, where wealthy folks retreat beyond the reach of the coastal fog and mist. It's a scenic and perpetually sunny valley of rolling hills dotted with manicured golf courses and many a tony pony ranch.

Hike the trails in **Garland Regional Park,** 8 miles east of Carmel on Carmel Valley Road (dogs are welcome off-leash). The sun really bakes you out here, so bring lots of water. You could also sign up for a trail ride or riding lesson at **The Holman Ranch,** 60 Holman Rd. (ⓒ **831/659-6054;** www.theholmanranch. com), 12 miles east of Calif. 1.

Golf is offered at several resorts and courses in the valley, notably at **Quail Lodge,** 8205 Valley Green Dr. (ⓒ **800/538-9516** or 831/620-8858; www.quail lodge.com), and **Rancho Cañada Golf Club,** Carmel Valley Road (ⓒ **800/ 536-9459** or 831/624-0111; www.ranchocanada.com).

While you're in the valley, taste the wines at the **Château Julien Winery,** 8940 Carmel Valley Rd. (© **831/624-2600;** www.chateaujulien.com), which is open Monday through Friday from 8am to 5pm, Saturday and Sunday from 11am to 5pm. Tours are available by reservation.

WHERE TO STAY

Quail Lodge Resort and Golf Club ★★   Lying in the foothills of the Santa Lucia Range, Quail Lodge has received Mobil's five-star ratings for more than 20 years. Its pastoral setting encompasses more than 850 acres of sparkling lakes, secluded woodlands, rolling meadows, an 18-hole championship golf course, and a new full-service spa. The guest rooms are in two-story balconied wings, with terraces overlooking the pool or 1 of the 10 man-made lakes, or in cottages holding five units each. Executive villas are the most expensive and luxurious accommodations.

The guest rooms are decorated in earth tones jazzed up with striped and checkered patterns. Higher-priced accommodations, on the upper floors, have cathedral ceilings. Every room has a separate dressing area and French doors opening to an ample balcony; some have fireplaces and wet bars. All units have coffeemakers, supplied with freshly ground beans; a fresh-fruit plate is delivered to each room daily as well. Afternoon tea is served in the lobby from 3 to 5pm.

8205 Valley Greens Dr., Carmel, CA 93923. © **888/828-8787** or 831/624-2888. Fax 831/624-3726. www. quaillodge.com. 97 units. Apr–Nov $270–390 double; $435–685 suite. Extra person $35. Call for winter specials. Packages available. AE, DC, DISC, MC, V. From Calif. 1 N, past the Carmel exits (after which the highway narrows to 2 lanes), turn E on Carmel Valley Rd. and continue 3.5 miles to Valley Greens Dr. Pets accepted with $100 fee per stay; $25 fee per extra pet. Pet amenities and doggie treats included. **Amenities:** 3 restaurants; 2 bars; 2 outdoor pools (1 heated); golf course; 4 tennis courts; exercise room; full spa services; Jacuzzi; bike rental; concierge; business center; room service; in-room massage; babysitting; laundry service; same-day dry cleaning; executive-level rooms. *In room:* TV w/pay movies, dataport, minibar, coffeemaker, hair dryer.

7 The Big Sur Coast ★★★

3 miles S of Carmel-by-the-Sea; 123 miles S of San Francisco; 87 miles N of Hearst Castle

Big Sur is more than a drive along one of the most dramatic coastlines on earth or a peaceful repose amid a forest of towering California redwoods. It's a stretch of vast wilderness so overwhelmingly beautiful—especially when the fog glows in the moonlight—that it enchants all who walk its majestic paths. It's also home to a particular breed of nature lover who prefers a rustic lifestyle to the rest of California's offerings. When the 1997 and 1998 El Niño storms caused landslides and major road damage, cutting the area off from civilization for months, reports from Big Sur were unusual: Some residents fled, vowing never to return; others loved it even though their incomes were temporarily all but eliminated. The remaining residents rejoiced in the temporary solitude; Post Ranch, the area's ultimate luxury resort, shared the impromptu intimacy with deep-pocketed guests by flying them in via helicopter (for an extra fee, of course). Such is the price paid for living amid the untamable California wilderness. The reopened roads are packed again, and driving through the region is painfully slow; rubberneckers admiring the view and nervous Nellies fearing the cliffs can't help but drive with their foot on the brakes.

Although there is an actual Big Sur Village approximately 25 miles south of Carmel, "Big Sur" refers to the entire 90-mile stretch of coastline between Carmel and San Simeon, blessed on one side by the majestic Santa Lucia Range and on the other by the rocky Pacific coastline. It's one of the most romantic and relaxing places on earth, and if you need respite from the rat race, I can recommend no better place to find it (although Yosemite, if you hike past the crowds, is equally rejuvenating). There's little more to do than explore the mountains and beaches, or just perch yourself atop the cliffs and take in the California sea air—but spend a few days here and you'll find that you need nothing else.

ESSENTIALS

VISITOR INFORMATION   Contact the **Big Sur Chamber of Commerce** (② 831/667-2100; www.bigsurcalifornia.org) for specialized information on places and events in Big Sur.

ORIENTATION   Most of this stretch is state park, and Calif. 1 runs its entire length, hugging the ocean the whole way. Restaurants, hotels, and sights are easy to spot—most are situated directly on the highway—but without major towns as reference points, their addresses can be obscure. For the purposes of orientation, I'll use the River Inn as a mileage guide. Located 29 miles south of Monterey on Calif. 1, the inn is generally considered to mark the northern end of Big Sur.

EXPLORING THE BIG SUR COAST

Big Sur offers visitors a profusion of tranquillity and natural beauty—ideal for hiking, picnicking, camping, fishing, and beachcombing.

The first settlers arrived here only a century ago, and the present highway was built in 1937, making the area accessible by car. (Electricity arrived only in the 1950s, and it's still not available in the remote inland mountains.) Big Sur's mysterious, misty beauty has inspired several modern spiritual movements (the Esalen Institute was the birthplace of the human potential movement). Even the tourist bureau bills the area as a place in which "to slow down . . . to meditate . . . to catch up with your soul." Take the board's advice and take your time—nothing better lies ahead.

The region affords a bounty of wilderness adventure opportunities. The inland **Ventana Wilderness,** which is maintained by the U.S. Forest Service, contains 167,323 acres straddling the Santa Lucia Mountains and is characterized by steep-sided ridges separated by V-shaped valleys. The streams that cascade through the area are marked by waterfalls, deep pools, and thermal springs. The wilderness offers 237 miles of hiking trails that lead to 55 designated trail camps—a backpacker's paradise. One of the easiest trails to access is the **Pine Ridge Trail** at Big Sur station (② 831/667-2315).

From Carmel, the first stop along Calif. 1 is **Point Lobos State Reserve** ★★ (② 831/624-4909; www.pt-lobos.parks.state.ca.us), 3 miles south of Carmel. Sea lions, harbor seals, sea otters, and thousands of seabirds reside in this 1,276-acre reserve. Between December and May, you can also spot migrating California gray whales just offshore. Trails follow the shoreline and lead to hidden coves. Note that parking is limited; on weekends especially, you need to arrive early to secure a place.

From here, cross the Soberanes Creek, passing **Garrapata State Park** (② 831/624-4909), a 2,879-acre preserve with 4 miles of coastline. It's unmarked and undeveloped, though the trails are maintained. To explore them, you'll need to park at one of the turnouts on Calif. 1 near Soberanes Point and hike in.

Ten miles south of Carmel, you'll arrive at North Abalone Cove. From here, Palo Colorado Road leads back into the wilderness to the first of the Forest Service camping areas at **Bottchers Gap** ($12 to camp, $5 to park overnight; ② 805/434-9199).

The Big Sur Coast

To Bixby Bridge, Garrapata State Park, & Point Lobos

Point Sur Lighthouse

POINT SUR STATE HISTORIC PARK

Point Sur

False Sur

California Sea Otter Game Refuge

VENTANA WILDERNESS

South Fork

Santa

Little Sur River

Lucia

ANDREW MOLERA STATE PARK

Gate

Gate

Camp Parking

Gate

Gate

Adams Hill

LOS PADRES

Range

Molera Point

Gate

Gate

Big Sur

NATIONAL FOREST

Big Sur River

PACIFIC OCEAN

Cooper Point

Park Headquarters

Pfeiffer Falls

PFEIFFER BIG SUR STATE PARK

Sawmill Flat

Weyland

Pfeiffer Beach

Pfeiffer Point

South Park Entrance

To Julia Pfeiffer Burns State Park

Wreck Beach

California Sea Otter Game Refuge

San Francisco

Sacramento

CALIFORNIA

Map Area

Los Angeles

PACIFIC OCEAN

0   1 mi
0   1 km

Continuing south, about 13 miles from of Carmel, you'll cross the **Bixby Bridge** and see the **Point Sur Lighthouse** off in the distance. The Bixby Bridge, one of the world's highest single-span concrete bridges, towers nearly 270 feet above Bixby Creek Canyon, and offers gorgeous canyon and ocean views from several observation alcoves at regular intervals along the bridge. The lighthouse, which sits 361 feet above the surf on a volcanic rock promontory, was built in 1889, when only a horse trail provided access to this part of the world. Tours, which take 2 to 3 hours and involve a steep half-mile hike each way, are scheduled on most weekends. For information, call © **831/625-4419** or log on to **www.lighthouse-pointsur-ca.org**. Admission is $5 for adults, $3 for youths ages 13 to 18, $2 for children 5 to 12, and free for kids under 5.

About 3 miles south of the lighthouse is **Andrew Molera State Park** (© **831/667-2315**), the largest state park on the Big Sur coast at 4,800 acres. It's much less crowded than Pfeiffer–Big Sur (see below). Miles of trails meander through meadows and along beaches and bluffs. Hikers and cyclists use the primitive trail camp about a third of a mile from the parking area. The 2½-mile-long beach, which is sheltered from the wind by a bluff, is accessible via a mile-long path flanked in spring by wildflowers, and offers excellent tide-pooling. You can walk the entire length of the beach at low tide; otherwise take the bluff trail above the beach. There are trails through the park for horseback riders of all levels of experience. **Molera Big Sur Trail Rides** (© **800/942-5486** or 831/625-5486; www.molerahorsebacktours.com) offers coastal trail rides daily from April to December, or until the rains come. Cost of rides vary but start at about $25 for a 1-hour ride along the beach. The park also has campgrounds.

Back on Calif. 1, you'll soon reach the village of Big Sur, where commercial services are available.

About 26 miles south of Carmel, you'll come to **Big Sur Station** (© 831/667-2315), where you can pick up maps and other information about the region. It's located a quarter mile past the entrance to **Pfeiffer–Big Sur State Park** ★ (© 831/667-2315), an 810-acre park that offers 218 camping sites along the Big Sur River (call © 800/444-7275 for camping reservations), picnicking, fishing, and hiking. It's a scenic park of redwoods, conifers, oaks, and open meadows. For this reason, it gets very crowded. The Big Sur Lodge in the park has cabins with fireplaces and other facilities (see p. 387 and the "Camping in Big Sur" box, below). Admission to the park is $5 per car, and it's open daily from dawn to dusk.

Just over a mile south of the entrance to Pfeiffer–Big Sur State Park is the turnoff to Sycamore Canyon Road (unmarked), which will take you 2 winding miles down to beautiful **Pfeiffer Beach** ★, a great place to soak in the sun on the wide expanse of golden sand. It's open for day-use only, there's no fee, and it's the only beach accessible by car (but not motor homes).

Back on Calif. 1, the road travels 11 miles past Sea Lion Cove to Julia Pfeiffer Burns State Park. High above the ocean is the famous **Nepenthe** restaurant (p. 391), the retreat bought by Orson Welles for Rita Hayworth in 1944. A few miles farther south is the **Coast Gallery** (© 831/667-2301), the premier local art gallery, which displays lithographs of works by Henry Miller. The gallery's casual Coast Cafe offers simple serve-yourself lunches of soup, sandwiches, baked goods, and coffee drinks. Miller fans will also want to stop at the **Henry Miller Memorial Library** (© 831/667-2574; www.henrymiller.org) on Calif. 1, 30 miles south of Carmel and a quarter mile south of Nepenthe restaurant. The library displays and sells books and artwork by Miller and houses a permanent collection of first editions. It also serves as a community art center, hosting concerts, poetry readings, and art exhibitions (check for upcoming events on the website). The rear gallery room is a video-viewing space where films about Henry Miller can be seen. There's a sculpture garden, plus tables on the adjacent lawn where visitors can rest and enjoy the surroundings. Admission is free; hours are Wednesday through Monday from 11am to 6pm.

Julia Pfeiffer Burns State Park ★★ (© 831/667-2315) encompasses some of Big Sur's most spectacular coastline. To get a closer look, take the trail from the parking area at McWay Canyon, which leads under the highway to a bluff overlooking an 80-foot-high McWay Waterfall dropping directly into the ocean. It's less crowded here than at Pfeiffer–Big Sur, and there are miles of trails to explore in the 3,580-acre park. Scuba divers can apply for permits to explore the 1,680-acre underwater reserve.

From here, the road skirts the Ventana Wilderness, passing Anderson and Marble Peaks and the Esalen Institute, before crossing the Big Creek Bridge to Lucia and several campgrounds farther south. **Kirk Creek Campground** ★, about 3 miles north of Pacific Valley, offers camping with ocean views and beach access. Beyond Pacific Valley, the **Sand Dollar Beach** ★ picnic area is a good place to stop and enjoy the coastal view and take a stroll. A half-mile trail leads down to the sheltered beach, from which there's a fine view of Cone Peak, one of the coast's highest mountains. Two miles south of Sand Dollar is **Jade Cove,** a popular spot for rockhounds. From here, it's about another 27 miles past the Piedras Blancas Light Station to San Simeon.

WHERE TO STAY

Only a handful of Big Sur's accommodations offer the kind of pampering and luxury you'd expect in a fine urban hotel; even direct-dial phones and TVs (often considered gauche in these parts) are rare. Big Sur hotels are especially busy in summer, when advance reservations are required. There are more accommodations than those listed here, so if you're having trouble securing a room or a site, contact the chamber of commerce (listed in the "Essentials" section earlier in this chapter) for other options.

Big Sur Lodge (*Kids*)   A family-friendly place, the Big Sur Lodge—sheltered by towering redwoods, sycamores, and broad-leafed maples—is situated in the enormous state park. The rustic motel-style cabins are huge, with high peaked cedar- and redwood-beamed ceilings. They're clean and heated, and have private bathrooms and reserved parking spaces. Some have fireplaces. All offer porches or decks with views of the redwoods or the Santa Lucia Range.

An advantage to staying here is that you're entitled to free use of all the facilities of the park, including hiking, barbecue pits, and picnic areas. In addition, the lodge has its own grocery store and laundry facilities.

In Pfeiffer–Big Sur State Park, Calif. 1 (P.O. Box 190), Big Sur, CA 93920. (*C*) **800/424-4787** or 831/667-3100. Fax 831/667-3110. www.bigsurlodge.com. 61 cottages. $89–$149 cottage for 2; $119–$219 cottage with kitchen or fireplace; $139–$239 cabin with kitchen and fireplace. Rates include park entrance fees. AE, MC, V. From Carmel, take Calif. 1 S 26 miles. **Amenities:** Restaurant; heated outdoor pool (seasonal); coin-op laundry. *In room:* Coffeemaker, kitchen in some units, no phone.

Deetjen's Big Sur Inn (*✦*)   Man, is this place cute. In the 1930s, before Calif. 1 was built, this homestead was an overnight stopping place on the coastal wagon road. It was begun by Norwegian homesteader Helmuth Deetjen, who over the years built several units constructed from hand-hewn logs and lumber. Folks either love or hate the accommodations, which are set in a redwood canyon. They're rustic, cozy, and adorable with their old-fashioned furnishings and down-home feel. But those who want extensive creature comforts should go elsewhere. Single-wall construction means that the rooms are far from soundproof, so children under 12 are allowed only if families reserve both rooms of a two-room building. There's no insulation, so prepare to crank up the fire or wood-burning stove. *Tip:* The cabins near the river offer the most privacy.

The restaurant (p. 391) is a local favorite and consists of four intimate, English country inn–style rooms lit by candlelight.

Calif. 1, Big Sur, CA 93920. (*C*) **831/667-2377.** www.deetjens.com. 20 units, 15 with bathroom. $75–$180 double with shared bathroom; $110–$195 double with private bathroom. MC, V. **Amenities:** Restaurant. *In room:* No phone.

Post Ranch Inn (*✦✦✦*)   This is one of my very favorite places to stay on the planet. Perched on 98 acres of pristine seaside ridges 1,200 feet above the Pacific, this romantic resort opened in 1992 and was instantly declared one of the world's finest retreats. What's the big deal? The Post Ranch doesn't attempt to beat its stunning natural surroundings, but rather to join them. The wood-and-glass guest cottages are built around existing trees—some are elevated on stilts to avoid damaging native redwood root structures—and the ultra-private Ocean and Coast cottages are so close to the edge of the earth, you get the impression that you've joined the clouds (imagine that from your private spa tub). Other

Camping in Big Sur

Big Sur is one of the most spectacular places in the state for camping. One of the most glorious settings can be found at **Pfeiffer–Big Sur State Park,** on Calif. 1, 26 miles south of Carmel (© **831/667-2315**). The 810-acre state park offers hundreds of secluded, woodsy sites on hundreds of acres of redwood forest. Hiking trails, streams, and the river are steps away from your sleeping bag, and the most modern amenities are the 25¢ showers (for 3 min.). Water faucets are located between sites, and each spot has its own picnic table and fire pit. There are, however, no RV hookups or electricity. Riverfront sites are most coveted, but others promise more seclusion among the shaded hillsides of the park. Campfire programs and nature walks are also offered. At the entrance are a store, gift shop, restaurant, and cafe. There's a total of 218 sites (fees are $12 for regular sites, $26 for group sites); call © **800/444-7275** or log on to www.reserveamerica.com for camping reservations. Senior discounts are available, and dogs are permitted ($1 per night extra).

The entrance to the **Ventana Campground,** on Calif. 1, 28 miles south of Carmel and 4¼ miles south of the River Inn (© **831/667-2712**; www.ventanabigsur.com), is adjacent to the entrance to the resort of the same name, but the comparison stops there. This is pure rusticity. The 75 campsites, on 40 acres of a redwood canyon, are set along a hillside and spaced well apart for privacy. Each is shaded by towering trees and has a picnic table and fire ring, but offers no electricity, RV hookups, or river access. There are, however, three bathhouses with hot showers (25¢ fee), which are conveniently located. To reserve a space, call and charge on a credit card (MasterCard or Visa) one night's deposit. Or you

cottages face the woodlands and are equally impressive in design. Each room contains a fireplace, terrace, massage table, and wet bar filled with complimentary goodies. The bathrooms, fashioned out of slate and granite, feature spa tubs. Also on the premises are the best Jacuzzi I've ever encountered (it's on a cliff and seems to join the sky), a mediocre pool, and sun decks. The only drawback is that the vibe can be stuffy, which is due more to the clientele than the staff (my Subaru was sneered upon). The Sierra Mar restaurant is open to guests only for continental breakfast, and to the public nightly for dinner. It, too, has floor-to-ceiling views of the ocean.

Calif. 1 (P.O. Box 219), Big Sur, CA 93920. © **800/527-2200** or 831/667-2200. Fax 831/667-2824. www.postranchinn.com. 30 units. $485–$935 double. Rates include continental breakfast. AE, MC, V. **Amenities:** Restaurant; bar/lounge; outdoor heated pool; exercise room; spa services; cliff-side Jacuzzi; game room; concierge; activities desk; room service; in-room massage. *In room:* A/C, CD player, minibar, coffeemaker, hair dryer, iron, safe.

Ventana Inn and Spa ☆☆☆   Luxuriously rustic and utterly romantic, Ventana has been a wildly popular wilderness outpost for more than 20 years, and with good reason. Located on 243 mountainous oceanfront acres, Ventana has an elegance that's atypical of the region, and has continually attracted famous guests such as Barbra Streisand, Goldie Hawn, and Francis Ford Coppola since its opening in 1975.

can mail a check for the deposit along with the dates you'd like to stay and a stamped, self-addressed envelope at least 2 weeks in advance (earlier during peak months). Rates are $25 for a site for two with one vehicle; $35 per night weekends. An additional person is $4 extra, and it'll cost you $5 to bring Fido. Rates include entrance fee for your car. Open April through October.

Big Sur Campground and Cabins is on Calif. 1, 26 miles south of Carmel (½ mile south of the River Inn; © **831/667-2322**). The sites are cramped, so the feel is more like a camping village than an intimate retreat. However, it's very well maintained and perfect for families, who love the playground, river swimming, and inner-tube rentals. Each campsite has its own wood-burning fire pit, picnic table, and fresh-water faucet within 25 feet of the pitching area. There are also RV water and electric hookups available. Facilities include bathhouses with hot showers, laundry facilities, an aged volleyball/basketball court, and a grocery store. There are 81 tent sites (30 RV-ready with electricity and water hookup), plus 13 cabins (all with shower). The all-wood cabins are absolutely adorable, with stylish country furnishings, wood-burning ovens, patios, and full kitchens. Rates are $26 for a tent site for two or an RV hookup (plus $3 extra for electricity and water), $48 for a tent cabin (bed, but no heat or plumbing), or $93 to $187 for a cabin for two. Rates include entrance for your car. MasterCard and Visa are accepted. Pets cost $4 for campsites and $12 for tent cabins; pets are not allowed in the other cabins. Open year-round.

The accommodations, in 12 one- and two-story natural-wood buildings along winding wildflower-flanked paths, blend in with the magical Big Sur countryside. The extensive grounds are dotted with hammocks and hand-carved benches, which are strategically located under shady trees and at vista points. The guest rooms are divinely decorated in warm, cozy luxury, with private terraces or balconies overlooking the ocean or forest. Most rooms offer wood-burning fireplaces, and some have Jacuzzis and high cathedral ceilings. A small fitness center offers the basics—but you'll be more inspired to hike the grounds, where you'll not only find plenty of pastoral respite, but also a pool, a rustic library, and clothing-optional tanning decks and spa tubs. This, along with Post Ranch, is one of the best retreats in the region, if not the state. But I can't say which is better. I prefer the rooms at Post Ranch, but the laid-back energy and the extensive grounds at Ventana. Families take heed: Children are permitted but not exactly embraced. Ventana's restaurant, Cielo (p. 390), is an incredibly romantic and first-rate dining experience.

Calif. 1, Big Sur, CA 93920. © **800/628-6500** or 831/667-2331. Fax 831/667-2287. www.ventanainn.com. 62 units. $340–$975 double; from $575 suite. Rates include continental breakfast and afternoon wine and cheese. AE, DC, DISC, MC, V. **Amenities:** Restaurant; 2 heated outdoor pools; exercise room; full spa with 2 Japanese hot baths; sauna; concierge; room service; in-room massage; laundry service; executive-level rooms. *In room:* A/C, TV/VCR, minibar, fridge, coffeemaker, hair dryer, iron, safe.

WHERE TO DINE

In addition to the following choices, you should try the **Big Sur Bakery and Restaurant** on Calif. 1, just past the post office and a mile south of Pfeiffer–Big Sur State Park (© **831/667-0520**). It offers friendly service and healthy fare, ranging from wood-fired pizzas and portobello mushroom burgers at lunch to salmon, tuna, and chicken selections at dinner. All the pastries are freshly baked on the premises, along with hearth-baked breads. It's open Tuesday through Sunday from 8am to 10pm; they close early on Monday.

Big Sur River Inn CALIFORNIA/AMERICAN   Popular with everyone from families to bikers, the River Inn is an unpretentious, rustic, down-home restaurant that's got something for all tastes. Trying to seat a small army? No problem. Want to watch sports on TV at a local bar? Pull up a stool. Looking to snag a few rays from a deck right beside the Big Sur River? Break out the suntan lotion. In winter, the wooden dining room is the prime spot; on summer days, some folks grab their patio chairs and cocktails and hang out literally midstream. Along with the local color, attractions include a full bar and good ol' American breakfasts (steak and eggs, omelets, pancakes, and so on, plus espresso, with most dishes for around $6), lunches (an array of salads, sandwiches, and baby-back ribs, or fish and chips), and dinners (fresh catch, pastas, burgers, or ribs).

On Calif. 1, 2 miles N of Pfeiffer–Big Sur State Park. © 831/667-2700. Fax 831/667-2743. www.bigsurriver inn.com. Main courses $8.75–$15 lunch; $8.95–$28 dinner. AE, DC, MC, V. Daily 8am–10pm; 8am–9pm in winter.

Café Kevah SOUTHWEST/CALIFORNIA   Located one level below Nepenthe (see below), Café Kevah offers the same celestial view at a fraction of the price, a more casual environment, and—depending on your taste—better food. Seating is entirely outdoors—a downside when the biting fog rolls in, but perfect on a clear day. You can order breakfast (served all day) or lunch from the small shack of a kitchen, then grab an umbrella-shaded table, and enjoy the feast for your eyes and taste buds. Fare here is more eclectic than Nepenthe's, with such choices as homemade granola, pastries, baby greens with broiled salmon and papaya, chicken brochettes, omelets, and new-potato hash. It ain't cheap, but innovative cuisine, the view, and a surprisingly decent mocha make it a worthwhile stopover. Don't forget to bring a coat.

On Calif. 1, 28 miles S of Carmel (5 miles S of the River Inn). © 831/667-2344. Appetizers $6.25–$12; main courses $11–$18. AE, MC, V. Daily 9am–4pm; closes when it rains.

Cielo Restaurant ★★ CALIFORNIA   Like the resort, Ventana's restaurant is woodsy but extravagant, and is an excellent place to dine alfresco at lunch or for a romantic dinner. The airy cedar interior is divided into two spaces: the lounge, where a wooden bar and cocktail tables look onto a roaring fire and through picturesque windows; and the dining room, which overlooks the mountains and/or the ocean. But in summer it's the outdoor patio, with its views of the ocean expanse and 50 miles of Big Sur coast, that's the coveted lunch spot. Unlike some costly restaurants in the area, a meal here is as gratifying as the surroundings. Lunch offers sandwiches, burgers, and an array of gourmet salads, as well as main courses such as grilled Atlantic salmon; dinner includes stellar starters like a perfectly dressed Caesar salad and a well-balanced chanterelle mushroom risotto, and main courses such as seared ahi tuna or roasted duck breast with hazelnut risotto and sun-dried cherry sauce.

At Ventana Inn and Spa, Calif. 1, Big Sur. ✆ 831/667-4242. Fax 831/667-2287. www.ventanainn.com. Reservations recommended for dinner. Main courses $11–$17 lunch; $23–$32 dinner. AE, DC, DISC, MC, V. Daily noon–3:30pm and 6–9pm.

Deetjen's Big Sur Inn Restaurant ⋆ AMERICAN With the feel of an English farmhouse, this cozy, country setting is the perfect venue for the delicious comfort food and friendly service that you'll find here. Mornings start off with a jump after a cup of the delicious and strong coffee, and breakfast offers all the basics: omelets, eggs Benedict, pancakes, and granola, most of which come piled high with breakfast potatoes. Dinner is highly regarded by locals, and might include lamb au jus and twice-baked potatoes; grilled chicken with mushrooms and a garlic Marsala sauce; and roast duckling with brandy, peppercorn, and molasses sauce.

On Calif. 1. ✆ 831/667-2378. www.deetjens.com. Reservations recommended. Main courses $4.25–$12 breakfast, $15–$33 dinner. MC, V. Daily 8am–noon and 6–9pm.

Nepenthe AMERICAN Stop by Nepenthe for two reasons: The views are outrageous, and the atmosphere rocks. Sitting 808 feet above sea level along the cliffs overlooking the ocean, Nepenthe is naturally celestial—especially when fog lingers above the water below. On a warm day, join the crowds on the terrace. On colder days, go the indoor route: The redwood-and-adobe structure offers a warmer and equally magical view, and with its big wood-burning fireplace, redwood ceilings, and large bay-front windows, the atmosphere is something you can't find anywhere else.

Unfortunately, that's not been my experience with the fare. I would scoff at a $11 burger (without fries!), $16 swordfish sandwich, and a $4 draft Budweiser anywhere else—but I'd cough up the cash all over again for an afternoon here. (Think of it as nominal admission to dine at heights only angels usually enjoy.) Lunch is adequate and basic: burgers, sandwiches, and salads. Dinner main courses include steak, broiled chicken, and fresh fish prepared any number of ways, though I suggest you come only for lunch and spend big dinner bucks elsewhere.

Calif. 1, 28 miles S of Carmel (5 miles S of the River Inn). ✆ 831/667-2345. Fax 831/667-2394. www. nepenthebigsur.com. Reservations accepted only for parties of 5 or more. Main courses $9–$25. AE, MC, V. Daily 11:30am–10pm.

8 Pinnacles National Monument ⋆

58 miles SE of Monterey

Once a little-known outpost of the national park system, the 24,000-acre Pinnacles National Monument has become one of the most popular weekend climbing destinations in central California over the past decade. The mild winter climate and plentiful routes make this a perfect off-season training ground for climbers. It's also a popular haven for campers, hikers, and nature lovers. One of the most unique chaparral ecosystems in the world supports a large community of plant and animal life here, including one of California's largest breeding populations of raptors.

The Pinnacles themselves—hundreds of towering crags, spires, and hoodoos—are seemingly out of place in the voluptuously rolling hills of the coast range. And they are, in fact, out of place, part of the eroded remains of a volcano formed 23 million years ago 195 miles south in the middle of the Mojave Desert. It was carried here by the movement of the San Andreas Fault, which runs just east of the park. (The other half of the volcano remains in the Mojave.)

You could spend days here without getting bored, but it's possible to cover the most interesting features in a weekend. With a single hike, you can go from the lush oak woodland around the Bear Gulch Visitor Center to the dry and desolate crags of the high peaks, then back down through a half-mile-long cave complete with underground waterfalls.

ESSENTIALS

GETTING THERE   Two entrances lead to the park. The **West Entrance** from Soledad and U.S. 101 is a dry, dusty, winding single-lane road (not suitable for trailers) with the best drive-up view of the park. It doesn't connect with the east side.

The alternative route is via the **East Entrance.** Unless you're coming from nearby, take the longer drive on Calif. 25 to enter through the east. Because most of the peaks of the Pinnacles face east and the watershed drains east, most of the interesting hikes and geologic features are on this side. No road crosses the park.

FEES   Park entrance fees, which are good for 7 days, are $2 per person or $5 per car.

VISITOR CENTER   The first place you should go upon entering the park from the east is the **Bear Gulch Visitor Center** (© **831/389-4485**), open daily from 9am to 5pm. This small center is rich with exhibits on the park's history, wildlife, and geology, and also has a great selection of nature handbooks and climbing guides for the Pinnacles. Climbers should check with rangers about closures and other information before heading out: Many routes are closed during hawk- and falcon-nesting season, and rangers like to know how many climbers are in the park.

Adjacent to the visitor center, the Bear Gulch picnic ground is a great place to fuel up before setting out on a hike or, if you're not planning to leave your car, one of the best places to gaze up at dramatic spires of the high peaks (the ultimate spot is from the west side).

For more information, log on to the park's website at **www.nps.gov/pinn**.

REGULATIONS & WARNINGS   Beware of poison oak, particularly in Bear Gulch. Rattlesnakes are common throughout the park but rarely seen. Bikes and dogs are prohibited on all trails, and no backcountry camping is allowed anywhere in the park.

Hiking through this variety of landscapes demands versatility. Come prepared with a good pair of hiking shoes, snacks, lots of water, and a flashlight.

Daytime temperatures often exceed 100°F (38°C) in summer, so the best time of year to visit is spring, when the wildflowers are blooming, or in the fall. Crowds are common during spring weekends.

HIKING & EXPLORING THE PARK

To see most of the park in a single, moderately strenuous morning, take the **Condor Gulch Trail** from the visitor center. As you climb quickly out of the parking area, the Pinnacles's wind-sculpted spires seem to grow taller. In less than 2 miles, you're among them, and Condor Gulch intersects with the **High Peaks Trail.** The view from the top spans miles: the Salinas Valley to your west, the Pinnacles below, and miles of coast to the east. After traversing the high peaks (including stretches of footholds carved in steep rock faces) for about a mile, the trail drops back toward the visitor center via a valley filled with eerie-looking hoodoos.

In another 1½ miles, you'll reach the reservoir marking the top of **Bear Gulch Cave,** which closes occasionally; in 1998, it closed due both to storm damage and to accommodate migrating Townsend bats, who in the past several years have come here to have their babies. It's usually open, but if you want to explore, you'll need your flashlight and you might get wet; still, this ½-mile-long talus cave is a thrill. From the end of the cave, you're just a short walk (through the most popular climbing area of the park) away from the visitor center. It's also possible to hike just Bear Gulch and the cave, then return via the **Moses Spring Trail.** It's about 2 miles round-trip, but you'll miss the view from the top.

If you're coming from the West Entrance, the **Juniper Canyon Trail** is a short (1¼ miles), but very steep, blast to the top of the high peaks. You'll definitely earn the view. Otherwise, try the short **Balconies Trail** to the monument's other talus cave, **Balconies Cave.** Flashlights are required here, too.

CAMPING

The park's campground on the west side was demolished by El Niño storms in 1997 and 1998 and is not scheduled for repair. Now the only campground is the privately run **Pinnacles Campground, Inc.,** on the east side (© **831/389-4462;** www.pinncamp.com), which charges $7 per person. It's just outside the park (off Calif. 25, 32 miles south of Hollister), with lots of privacy and space between sites, plus showers, a store, and a large swimming pool. It's close enough so you can hike into the park from the campground, though it will add a few miles to your outing. Though private campgrounds are often overdeveloped, the management here saw the benefits of leaving the surroundings natural. Dogs are not recommended, but you can bring them if you're willing to pay a $10 leash deposit. *Note:* No other animals are allowed at Pinnacles.

12

The Central Coast

by Stephanie Avnet Yates

California's Central Coast—a spectacular amalgam of beaches, lakes, and mountains—is the state's most diverse region. The narrow strip of coast that runs for more than 100 miles from San Simeon to Ventura spans several climate zones and is home to an eclectic mix of students, middle-class workers, retirees, farmers, computer techies, and fishermen. The ride along Calif. 1, which follows the ocean cliffs, is almost always packed with rental cars, RVs, and bicycles. Traffic may give your brakes a workout, but it also allows you to take longer looks at one of the most spectacular vistas in the world.

Whether you're driving up from Los Angeles or down from San Francisco, Calif. 1 is the most scenic and leisurely route. (U.S. 101 gets you there faster but is less picturesque.) Most bicyclists pedal from north to south, the direction of the prevailing winds. Those in cars may prefer to drive south to north so they can get a better look at the coastline as it unfolds toward the west. No matter which direction you drive, break out the camera—you're about to experience unparalleled beauty, California-style.

1 San Simeon: Hearst Castle

205 miles S of San Francisco (via Calif. 1); 254 miles NW of Los Angeles

Few places on earth compare to **Hearst Castle.** The 165-room estate of publishing magnate William Randolph Hearst, situated high above the coastal village of San Simeon atop a hill he called La Cuesta Encantada ("the Enchanted Hill"), is an ego trip par excellence. One of the last great estates of America's Gilded Age, it's an astounding, completely over-the-top monument to wealth—and to the power that money brings.

Hearst Castle is a sprawling compound of structures, constructed over 28 years in a Mediterranean Revival architectural style, set in undeniably magical surroundings. The focal point of the estate is the you-have-to-see-it-to-believe-it **Casa Grande,** a 100-plus-room mansion brimming with priceless art and antiques. Hearst acquired most of his vast European collection via New York auction houses, where he bought entire rooms (including walls, ceilings, and floors) and shipped them here. The result is an old-world castle done in a priceless mix-and-match style. You'll see fantastic 400-year-old Spanish and Italian ceilings, enormous 500-year-old fireplace mantels, 16th-century Florentine bedsteads, Renaissance paintings, Flemish tapestries, and innumerable other treasures.

Three opulent "guesthouses" also contain magnificent works of art. A lavish private movie theater was used to screen first-run films twice nightly—once for employees, and again for the guests and host.

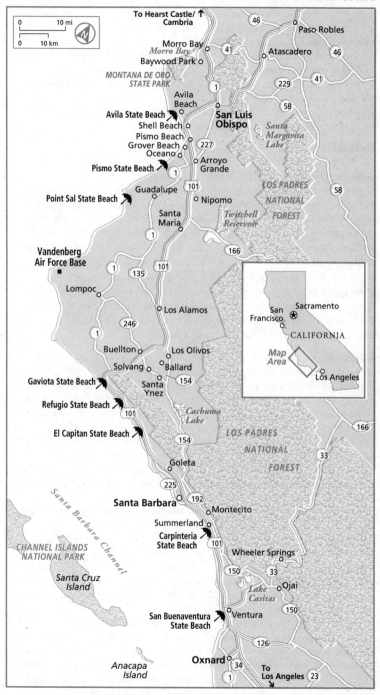

The Central Coast

0   10 mi
0   10 km

To Hearst Castle/ ↑
Cambria

Paso Robles

Morro Bay
Morro Bay
Baywood Park

Atascadero

*MONTANA DE ORO
STATE PARK*

Avila
Beach

Avila State Beach

**San Luis
Obispo**

*Santa
Margarita
Lake*

Shell Beach
Pismo Beach
Grover Beach
Oceano

Arroyo
Grande

**LOS PADRES
NATIONAL
FOREST**

Pismo State Beach

Guadalupe

Nipomo

Point Sal State Beach

Santa
Maria

*Twitchell
Reservoir*

**Vandenberg
Air Force Base**

Lompoc

Los Alamos

Buellton
Solvang
Santa
Ynez

Los Olivos
Ballard

*Cachuma
Lake*

Gaviota State Beach

Refugio State Beach

El Capitan State Beach

**LOS PADRES

NATIONAL

FOREST**

Goleta

Santa Barbara Channel

Santa Barbara

Montecito

Summerland
Carpinteria
State Beach

Wheeler Springs

*CHANNEL ISLANDS
NATIONAL PARK*

*Santa Cruz
Island*

*Lake
Casitas*

Ojai

San Buenaventura
State Beach

Ventura

*Anacapa
Island*

Oxnard

To
Los Angeles

Sacramento
San
Francisco

CALIFORNIA

*Map
Area*

Los Angeles

395

And then there are the swimming pools. The Roman-inspired indoor pool has intricate mosaic work, Carrara-marble replicas of Greek gods and goddesses, and alabaster globe lamps that create the illusion of moonlight. The breathtaking outdoor Greco-Roman Neptune pool, flanked by marble colonnades that frame the distant sea, is one of the mansion's most memorable features.

In 1957, in exchange for a massive tax write-off, the Hearst Corporation donated the estate to the state of California (while retaining ownership of approximately 80,000 acres). The California Department of Parks and Recreation now administers it as a State Historic Monument.

ESSENTIALS

GETTING THERE   Hearst Castle is located directly on Calif. 1, about 42 miles north of San Luis Obispo and 94 miles south of Monterey. From San Francisco or Monterey, take U.S. 101 south to Paso Robles, then Calif. 46 west to Calif. 1, and Calif. 1 north to the castle. From Los Angeles, take U.S. 101 north to San Luis Obispo, then Calif. 1 north to the castle. Park in the visitor center parking lot; a bus will take you up the hill to the estate. The movie theater and visitor center adjoin the parking lot and are easily accessible without heading up to the actual estate.

VISITOR INFORMATION   To get information about Hearst Castle, call © 805/927-2020 or log on to **www.hearstcastle.org**. For more information on nearby Cambria (see below), check out **www.cambria-online.com** or stop into the **Cambria Chamber of Commerce's** visitor center at 767 Main St., in the west village (**805/927-3624;** www.cambriachamber.org).

TOURING THE ESTATE

Hearst Castle can be visited only by guided tours, which are conducted daily beginning at 8:20am, except on New Year's Day, Thanksgiving, and Christmas. Two to six tours leave every hour, depending on the season. Allow 2 hours between starting times if you plan on taking more than one tour. Reservations are recommended and can be made up to 8 weeks in advance. Tickets can be purchased by phone through **California Reservations** (© **800/444-4445**). Daytime tours are $10 for adults, $5 for children ages 6 to 12, and free for children under 6. Evening tours are $20 for adults, $10 for children 6 to 12, and free for children under 6. Four distinct daytime tours are offered on a daily basis, each lasting almost 2 hours.

Tour 1 is usually recommended for first-time visitors and is the first to get booked up. In addition to the swimming pools, this tour visits several rooms on the ground floor of the main house (known as Casa Grande), including Hearst's private theater, where you'll see some home movies taken during the castle's heyday. You'll get to see the sculptures and flowers in the gardens and the formal esplanade, as well as the largest guesthouse, Casa del Sol. This tour now includes a viewing of the film *Hearst Castle: Building the Dream* (see below), but costs $4 more ($2 for kids) than the other three tours.

Tour 2 focuses on Casa Grande's upper floors, including Hearst's opulent library, private suite of rooms, and lots of fabulous bathrooms. Ongoing efforts are made to lend a lived-in look to the house; examples are the lifelike food displayed in the kitchen and pantry, and vintage sewing equipment in Marion Davies's suite. Although Tour 1 is commonly recommended for first-timers, Tour 2 is a perfectly fine choice if you're only planning to take one tour, particularly if your interest lies more in the home's private areas.

Tour 3 delves into the complex construction and subsequent alterations of Hearst Castle. You'll visit Casa del Monte, a guesthouse unaltered from its original design, then head to the North Wing of Casa Grande, the last portion of the property to be completed, to see the contrast in styles. A short video, which uses film and photographs from the 1920s and 1930s to go behind the scenes of the construction process, is shown. Tour 3 is especially fascinating for architecture buffs and detail hounds, but it shouldn't be the first and only tour you take if you've never visited the castle before.

Tour 4 is dedicated to the estate's gardens, terraces, and walkways, and is only offered from April to October. You'll also tour the Casa del Mar guesthouse, the wine cellar of Casa Grande, and the colorful dressing rooms at the Neptune Pool. Like Tour 3, this one is best taken after you've seen some of the more essential areas of the estate.

Evening tours are held most Friday and Saturday nights during spring and fall. These last about 30 minutes longer than the daytime tours, and visit highlights of the main house, the largest and most elaborate guesthouse, and the estate's pools and gardens, which are illuminated by hundreds of restored light fixtures. The pools in particular are most breathtaking when seen this way. The entire living-history experience is enhanced by docents dressed in period costume assuming a variety of roles.

Tip: Because these are walking tours, be sure to wear comfortable shoes—you'll be walking about a half mile per tour, which includes between 150 and 400 steps to climb or descend. (Wheelchair tours are available by calling ℂ **805/927-2020** at least 10 days in advance.)

The latest addition to the estate is the giant-screen **Hearst Castle National Geographic Theater,** which you can visit regardless of whether you take a tour. Films include *Hearst Castle: Building the Dream,* among others. For current information, call ℂ **805/927-6811** or visit their website at www.ngtheater.com. The Hearst film shows hourly at half past the hour, and tickets cost $7.50 for adults and $5.50 for children 12 and under.

WHAT TO SEE & DO IN NEARBY CAMBRIA

After driving for close to an hour without passing anything but lush green hills and nature at its most glorious (especially from Calif. 46 off U.S. 101), it's a remarkably quaint surprise to roll into the adorable coastal mini-town of Cambria, just south of San Simeon. Cambria, known as an artists' colony, is so charming that the town itself is reason enough to make the drive. With little more than 3 blocks worth of shops, restaurants, and a handful of B&Bs, Cambria is the perfect place to escape the everyday, enjoy the endless expanses of pristine coastal terrain, and meander through little shops selling local artwork and antiques.

Gray whales pass through the area from late December to early February, and for the past few years, hundreds of elephant seals have made the shore just north of the Hearst Castle entrance their year-round playground—much to the delight of locals and nature enthusiasts. Keep your distance from these mammoth mammals: They're a protected species and can be dangerous if molested. There is a parking lot, and docents are usually on hand to answer questions. The beaches and coves are also wonderful places for humans to frolic as well.

SHOPPING

Shopping is a major pastime in the village. Boutique owners are hyper-savvy about keeping their merchandise current—and priced just a hair lower than LA

(Fun Fact   **Weekends at the Ranch: William Randolph Hearst & the Legacy of Hearst Castle**

The lavish palace that William Randolph Hearst always referred to simply as "the ranch" took root in 1919. William Randolph ("W.R." to his friends) had inherited 275,000 acres from his father, mining baron George Hearst, and was well on his way to building a formidable media empire. He often escaped to a spot known as "Camp Hill" on his newly acquired lands in the Santa Lucia Mountains above the village of San Simeon, the site of boyhood family outings. Complaining that "I get tired of going up there and camping in tents," Hearst hired architect Julia Morgan to design the retreat that would become one of the most famous private homes in the world.

An art collector with indiscriminate taste and inexhaustible funds, Hearst overwhelmed Morgan with interiors and furnishings from the ancestral collections of Europe. Each week, railroad cars carrying fragments of Roman temples, lavish doors and carved ceilings from Italian monasteries, Flemish tapestries, hastily rolled paintings by the old masters, ancient Persian rugs, and antique French furniture arrived—5 tons at a time—in San Simeon. *Citizen Kane,* which depicts a Hearst-like mogul with a similarly excessive estate called Xanadu, has a memorable scene of hoarded priceless treasures warehoused in dusty piles, stretching as far as the eye can see. Like Kane, Hearst, once described as a man with an "edifice complex," purchased so much that only a fraction of what he bought was ever installed in the estate.

In 1925, Hearst separated from his wife and began to spend time in Los Angeles overseeing his movie company, Cosmopolitan Pictures. His principal starlet, Marion Davies, became W.R.'s constant companion and hostess at Hearst Castle; this would be her main role for the rest of his life. The ranch soon became a playground for the Hollywood crowd as well as dignitaries like Winston Churchill and playwright George Bernard Shaw, who is said to have wryly remarked of the estate, "This is the way God would have done it if He had the money."

or San Francisco. This close-knit community has always attracted artists and artisans of the highest quality. For the finest handcrafted glass artworks, from affordable jewelry to investment-scale sculpture, head to **Seekers Collection & Gallery,** 4090 Burton Dr. (© **805/927-4352;** www.seekersglass.com). Nearby, at **Moonstones Gallery,** 4070 Burton Dr. (© **805/927-3447**), you'll find a selection of works ranging from woven crafts to jewelry and an exceptional collection of woodcarvings and other crafts. If a visit to the nearby Paso Robles wine country has inspired you, **Fermentations,** 4056 Burton Dr. (© **805/927-7141**), has wines, wine accessories, and gifts, plus wine country gourmet goodies open for tasting. Women who appreciate casual style and ease of care mustn't miss **Leslie Mark,** 4070 Burton Dr. (© **805/927-1434;** www.lesliemark.com), and her deceptively simple line of versatile cotton and rayon separates. Across the street, **Heart's Ease,** 4101 Burton Dr. (© **800/266-4372** or 805/927-5224), is located inside a quaint historic cottage and is packed with

Despite its opulence, Hearst promoted "the ranch" as a casual weekend home. He regularly laid the massive refectory table in the dining room with paper napkins and bottled ketchup and pickles to evoke a rustic camp-like atmosphere. In Hearst's beautiful library, his priceless collection of ancient Greek pottery—one of the greatest collections of its kind in the world—is arranged casually among the rare volumes, like knickknacks.

The Hollywood crowd would take Hearst's private railway car from Los Angeles to San Luis Obispo, where a fleet of limousines waited to transport them to San Simeon. Those who didn't come by train were treated to a flight on Hearst's private plane from the Burbank airport (MGM head Irving Thalberg and his wife, Norma Shearer, preferred this mode of transportation). Hearst, an avid aviator, had a sizable landing strip built; Charles Lindbergh used it when he flew up for a visit in the summer of 1928.

Oh, if the walls could talk. Atop one of the castle's looming towers are the hexagonal Celestial Suites. One was a favorite of Clark Gable and Carole Lombard, who would be startled out of their romantic slumber by the clamor of 18 carillon bells directly overhead. David Niven, a frequent guest, was one of the unknown number who defied Hearst's edict against liquor in private rooms: Niven was called upon more than once to explain the several "empties" under the bed (which Cardinal Richelieu once owned and slept in) in his customary suite.

W. R. Hearst and Marion Davies hosted frequent costume parties at the ranch, which were as intricately planned as a movie production. The most legendary, the Circus Party, was held to celebrate W.R.'s 75th birthday on April 29, 1938. Much of Hollywood attended to honor the tycoon, including grande dame Bette Davis—dressed as a bearded lady.

an abundance of garden delights, apothecary herbs, and custom-blended potpourris.

WHERE TO STAY

Cambria's popularity in summertime and on holiday weekends makes advance planning a necessity. If my favorites below are full, try one of these recommended alternatives: **Captain's Cove Inn,** 6454 Moonstone Beach Dr. (© **800/ 781-COVE** or 805/927-8581), is a small beachfront B&B whose motel-style exterior belies the array of creature comforts cheerily provided by the family owners; or **Cambria Pines Lodge,** 2905 Burton Dr. (© **800/445-6868** or 805/ 927-4200; www.cambriapineslodge.com), a summer-camp, lodge-style compound with terrific family facilities nestled in the pines just a few blocks from the center of town. The **Ragged Point Inn,** 19019 Hwy. 1 (© **805/927-4502;** fax 805/927-8862), is located 15 miles north of Hearst Castle, and offers sweeping ocean views from every room.

Best Western Cavalier Oceanfront Resort ⭐ *Kids*   Of the dozen or so budget and midrange motels clustered along Highway 1 near Hearst Castle, this surprisingly nice chain is the only one that's actually oceanfront. Sprawled across a gentle slope, the hotel invites guests to huddle around cliffside bonfires each evening. Every room—whether you choose a basic double or opt for extras such as a fireplace, ocean view, wet bar, or oceanfront terrace—features an array of amenities (tape rentals for the VCR are conveniently next door). The Cavalier is top-notch in its class, and a terrific choice for Castle-bound families.

9415 Hearst Dr. (Calif. 1), San Simeon, CA 93452. 📞 **800/826-8168** or 805/927-4688. Fax 805/927-6472. www.cavalierresort.com. 90 units. $89–$209 double. AE, DC, DISC, MC, V. Pets accepted. **Amenities:** Restaurant; 2 outdoor heated pools; Jacuzzi; exercise room; concierge; room service 7am–9pm; coin-op laundry. *In room:* TV/VCR, dataport, minibar, coffeemaker, hair dryer, iron.

FogCatcher Inn ⭐ *Value*   You'll spot the FogCatcher by its faux English architecture (though a contemporary hotel), that fits right in with the mish-mash of styles on funky Moonstone Beach. The U-shaped building is situated so many rooms have unencumbered views of the crashing waves across the street; some gaze oceanward over a sea of parked cars, and others are hopelessly landlocked—be sure to inquire when reserving.

Though rates vary wildly according to view, each room interior sports identical amenities and comforts. Immaculately maintained and furnished in a comfy cottage style with oversize pine furniture, each room is made cozier by a gas fireplace and also boasts a microwave oven. Unlike many comparably priced Moonstone Beach lodgings, the FogCatcher has a heated swimming pool and Jacuzzi. Stop by the breakfast room in the morning for basic coffee, juice, and muffins to start the day.

6400 Moonstone Beach Dr., Cambria, CA 93428. 📞 **800/425-4121** or 805/927-1400. www.fogcatcher inn.com. Fax 805/927-0204. 60 units. $159–$309 double. Rates include continental breakfast. Substantial midweek and off-season discounts available. AE, DISC, MC, V. Pets accepted in select rooms with $25 fee. **Amenities:** Outdoor heated pool; Jacuzzi. *In room:* TV, minibar, fridge, coffeemaker, hair dryer, iron.

J. Patrick House ⭐   Hidden in a pine-filled residential neighborhood overlooking Cambria's village, this picture-perfect B&B is cozy, elegant, and welcoming. The main house is an authentic two-story log cabin, where each afternoon innkeepers Ann and John host wine and hors d'oeuvres next to the living-room fireplace, and each morning serve breakfast by windows overlooking a hummingbird-filled garden. Most guest rooms are in the adjacent carriage house and feature wood-burning fireplaces, feather duvets, bedtime milk and cookies, and country elements like knotty pine, bent-twig furniture, calico prints, and hand-stitched quilts. Amenities like phone, fax, and guest fridge are available in the common area.

2990 Burton Dr., Cambria, CA 93428. 📞 **800/341-5258** or 805/927-3812. Fax 805/927-6759. www.jpatrick house.com. 8 units. $145–$200 double. Rates include full breakfast, afternoon wine/hors d'oeuvres, and evening milk and cookies. Seasonal discounts and packages available. DISC, MC, V. *In room:* Hair dryer, iron available upon request, no phone.

Olallieberry Inn ⭐⭐   This 1873 Greek Revival house is my favorite B&B in the area. The grounds are perfectly manicured but bloom whimsically. In the afternoon the aromas of baked brie and homemade bread (served during the wine hour) waft through the main house, and the staff does everything imaginable to make your stay special. They also have a passion for cooking and gardening, but the decor doesn't fall by the wayside: A countrified berry motif reigns, and the guest rooms are lovingly and individually appointed. Each has its own private bathroom, although some are across or down the hall. Rooms in a newer adjoining building overlook a creek; they're remarkably charming and have a fireplace and private deck. The delicious full breakfast—accompanied by olallieberry jam, of course—is gourmet all the way. Amenities like phone, fax, and guest fridge are available in the common area.

2476 Main St., Cambria, CA 93428. ☎ **888/927-3222** or 805/927-3222. Fax 805/927-0202. www. olallieberry.com. 9 units. $110–$180 double; $195–$210 cottage suite. Rates include full breakfast and evening wine and hors d'oeuvres. AE, MC, V. **Amenities:** Massage. *In room:* Hair dryer, iron available upon request, no phone.

WHERE TO DINE

Tiny Cambria boasts an unusual concentration of superb restaurants. (The town's eateries repeatedly dominate Zagat's mere two pages of Central Coast listings.) In addition to the restaurants listed below, consider **Bistro Sole,** 1980 Main St. (☎ **805/927-0887**), a quaint and cozy bungalow with a sophisticated decor and eclectic California cuisine; **Moonstone Beach Bar & Grill,** 6550 Moonstone Beach Dr. (☎ **805/927-3859**), whose incredible view must be what accounts for prices on the expensive side for this tasty but casual restaurant— stick to breakfast or lunch; or local institution **Linn's Main Binn,** 2277 Main St. (☎ **805/927-0371**), a casual all-day diner featuring hearty homemade pot-pies, fresh-from-the-farm salads, breakfast treats, and Linn's famous fruit pies.

Robin's ✷ ECLECTIC   Robin's is a restaurant with something for everyone, from exotic dishes from Mexico, Thailand, India, and beyond to more straight-forward preparations like a tasty salad, a juicy steak, and an array of vegetarian dishes. Offerings include a salmon bisque appetizer; porcini ravioli with roasted-pepper-cream sauce, fresh spinach, basil, and Parmesan; and other flavorful combinations such as tandoori prawns with basmati brown rice, fruit chutney, and chapati. Don't miss dessert—try the espresso-soaked cake with mascarpone mousse and shaved chocolate or vanilla-custard bread pudding.

4095 Burton Dr., Cambria. ☎ **805/927-5007.** www.robinsrestaurant.com. Reservations recommended. Main courses $8–$13 lunch, $11–$17 dinner. MC, V. Daily 11am–9pm (open late in summer).

Sea Chest Oyster Bar ✷ SEAFOOD   Feeling like a dozen other seaside old-salt hangouts, the strangely familiar Sea Chest is a must for seafood lovers. Sporting a crusty nautical kitsch and warm, welcoming atmosphere, this gray clapboard cottage even has a game-filled lounge complete with cribbage, checkers, and chess to keep you amused during the inevitable wait for a table. Oysters are the main attraction: on the half shell, oyster stew, oysters Casino, oysters Rockefeller, or "devils on horseback" (with wine, garlic, and bacon). The menu is also filled with very fresh seafood from local and worldwide waters: steamed New Zealand green-lipped mussels, clams in several preparations, halibut, salmon, lobster, scampi, plus whatever looked good off the boats that morning. There's a respectable list of microbrewed and imported beers, along with a selection of Central Coast wines. *Note:* If you don't enjoy seafood, stay away—there's not even a token steak on this menu!

6216 Moonstone Beach Dr. ☎ **805/927-4514.** Reservations not accepted. Main courses $11–$22. No credit cards. Wed–Mon 5:30–9pm (open Tues May–Sept only).

Sow's Ear Café ✷✷ AMERICAN   This tiny old cottage at the center of the village has been transformed into a warm, romantic hideaway. The best tables are in the fireside front room, lit just enough to highlight its rustic wood-and-brick decor. Pigs appear everywhere, in oil paintings, small ceramic or cast-iron models, and the woodcut sow logo. Though the menu features plenty of contemporary California cuisine, the most popular dishes are American country favorites given a contemporary lift; these include a warmly satisfying chicken-fried steak with gravy, chicken and dumplings, and zesty baby pork ribs. Other standouts are parchment-wrapped salmon, and pork loin glazed with chunky olallieberry chutney. Every meal begins with the restaurant's signature marbled bread baked in terra-cotta flowerpots, and the wine list is among the area's best.

Early birds (5–6pm nightly) choose from six dinners from $11 to $13.

2248 Main St. ⊘ **805/927-4865.** Reservations recommended. Main courses $14–$22. AE, DISC, MC, V. Daily 5–9:30pm.

2 Morro Bay

124 miles S of Monterey; 235 miles S of San Francisco (via Calif. 1); 220 miles N of LA

Morro Bay is separated from the ocean by a long peninsula of towering sand dunes. It's best known for dramatic **Morro Rock,** an enormous egg-shaped monolith that juts out of the water just offshore. Across from the rock, a monstrous oceanfront electrical plant mars the visual appeal of the otherwise pristine bay, which is filled with birds, sea mammals, and calm water offering plenty of recreational activities.

Other than gawking at the amazing "Gibraltar of the Pacific," there's not all that much to see in the town itself. Motels, shops, and restaurants line the waterfront Embarcadero and adjacent blocks, but the town's best feature is its natural surroundings: The beaches and wildlife sanctuaries can be quite peaceful and wondrous.

ESSENTIALS

Morro Bay is located along U.S. 101 (itself only 4 lanes on this stretch). The **Morro Bay Chamber of Commerce,** 880 Main St., Morro Bay, CA 93442 (⊘ **800/231-0592** or 805/772-4467; www.morrobay.com), offers armfuls of area information. It's open Monday through Friday from 8:30am to 5pm and Saturday from 10am to 3pm.

EXPLORING THE AREA

Most visitors come to Morro Bay to ogle **Morro Rock,** the much-photographed Central Coast icon that anchors the mouth of the waterway. This ancient towering landmark, whose name comes from the Spanish word for a Moorish turban, is a volcanic remnant inhabited by the endangered peregrine falcon and other migratory birds.

BEACHES   Popular **Atascadero State Beach,** just north of Morro Rock, has gentle waves and lovely views. Restrooms, showers, and dressing rooms are available. Just north of Atascadero is **Morro Strand State Beach,** a long, sandy stretch with normally gentle surf. Restrooms and picnic tables are available here. Morro Strand has its own campgrounds; for information, call ⊘ **805/772-2560,** or reserve a spot through **Park-Net** (⊘ **800/444-7275;** www.reserve america.com).

STATE PARKS   Cabrillo Peak, located in the lovely **Morro Bay State Park** (⊘ **805/772-7434**), makes for a terrific day hike and offers fantastic 360° views from its summit. There's a faint zigzagging trail, but the best way to reach the top is by bushwhacking straight up the gentle slope—a hike that takes about 2 hours round-trip. To reach the trail head, take Calif. 1 south and turn left at the

Morro Bay State Park/Montana de Oro State Park exit. Follow South Bay Boulevard for ¾ of a mile, then take the left fork another half a mile to the Cabrillo Peak dirt parking lot, located on your left. The park also offers camping and a decent public **golf course** called Morro Bay, which charges $28 to $35 for greens fees (© **805/782-8060**).

South of Morro Bay in Los Osos is **Montana de Oro State Park** ("Mountain of Gold"), fondly known as "petite Big Sur" because of its stony cliffs and rugged terrain. There's great swimming at Spooner's Cove and lots of easy hiking trails here, including some that lead to spectacular coastal vistas or hidden forest streams. The Hazard Reef Trail will take you up on the Morro Bay Sandspit dunes. The park's campground is in the trees, across from the beach. For information, call the park rangers (© **805/528-0513**), or reserve a spot through **Park-Net** (© **800/444-7275;** www.reserveamerica.com).

ON THE WATER   You can venture out on a kayak tour with **Kayaks of Morro Bay** (© **800/925-2925** or 805/772-1119), which is located on the Embarcadero at Pacific Street. If you've always yearned for sailing lessons, call ahead to the **Sailing Center of Morro Bay** (© **805/772-6446**). It's next to Morro Bay Yacht Club and offers everything from 1-day intro classes to weeklong series and scheduled sunset sails.

IN TOWN   The Embarcadero is also home to the **Giant Chessboard,** whose 3-foot-tall redwood pieces were inspired by open-air boards in Germany. Nearby is the **Morro Bay Aquarium,** 595 Embarcadero (© **805/772-7647**), a modest operation notable for the injured or abandoned sea otters, seals, and sea lions it rescues and rehabilitates. During their stay, all the animals learn to perform tricks for a morsel of fishy food (50¢ per bag).

WHERE TO STAY

Baywood Bed & Breakfast Inn *Finds*   Located south of Morro Bay in Baywood Park, facing out onto Morro's "back bay," this two-story gray inn is a converted 1970s garden-style office building with spacious B&B suites, each furnished in a distinctive (over-the-top) theme and Grandma-style flair. Every room has a private entrance, gas fireplace, and microwave (plus a fridge stocked with complimentary sodas and snacks); all but a few have bay views. Included in your stay is a full breakfast each morning and a late-afternoon wine-and-cheese reception highlighted by a room tour. If you're looking for solitude, Baywood Park fits the bill. There are a couple of decent restaurants on the block, and pretty Montana de Oro is close by.

1370 2nd St. (2½ blocks S of Santa Ysabel Ave.), Baywood Park, CA 93042. © **805/528-8888.** Fax 805/528-8887. www.baywoodinn.com. 18 units. $90–$130 double; $130–$300 suite. Extra person $15. Rates include full breakfast and afternoon wine and cheese. MC, V. *In room:* TV/VCR, kitchenette, minibar, fridge, coffeemaker, hair dryer.

The Inn at Morro Bay   Despite a sleek brochure that hints at snooty glamour, this comfortable and affordable resort is smart enough to let its splendid natural surroundings be the focus of attention. Situated directly on the water, the inn's two-story Cape Cod–style buildings have contemporary interiors amid a quiet garden setting. The inn has quietly been enhancing itself with a spa ambience; new features include an on-site massage center and private balcony Jacuzzis for some guest quarters. Rates vary wildly according to view, with the best rooms enjoying unobstructed views of Morro Rock plus convenient access to a bay-front sun deck; those in back face the swimming pool, gardens, and eucalyptus-forested golf course at Morro Bay State Park (see above). The hotel has a romantic bay-side lounge and California/Mediterranean restaurant.

60 State Park Rd., Morro Bay, CA 93442. ℂ **800/321-9566** or 805/772-5651. Fax 805/772-4779. www.innat morrobay.com. 98 units. $99–$299 double. Midweek and seasonal discounts available. AE, DISC, MC, V. Take Main St. S, past park entrance. **Amenities:** Restaurant; lounge; outdoor heated pool; full-service spa; nearby golf and water recreation; complimentary bikes; room service 7am–10pm; massage; babysitting. *In room:* TV, dataport, fridge, coffeemaker, hair dryer, iron.

WHERE TO DINE

Hofbrau *Value* GERMAN/AMERICAN When you're hungry in Morro Bay and want something other than fish and chips, Hofbrau is the place. Although they do serve the standard wharf-side fare, the star here is the roast beef French Dip (their strategically placed carving station ensures its popularity). Those in the know order the mini-sandwich, which is a dollar less and just an inch shorter. As the name would suggest, they have a nice selection of beers as well as a kids' menu with six choices at $3.50, making this a great value for families.

901 Embarcadero. ℂ **805/772-2411.** Reservations not accepted. Most items $4.25–$8.75. AE, DISC, MC, V. Daily 11am–9pm.

Windows on the Water ⚑ CALIFORNIA If you're looking for a special meal in town, you'll find Morro Bay's best at this respected restaurant that takes full advantage of prime waterfront views with its airy, high-ceilinged, multilevel space. But chef Gerard Robert's cuisine—a California/French/Mediterranean hybrid incorporating local fresh seafood and produce—is the main attraction. On a given evening, the menu might include seared halibut in a Dijon crust off-set by sweet-tangy orange marmalade and tequila sauce, shellfish braised in champagne and tossed with house-made fettuccine, or pheasant breast enveloped in prosciutto and brie atop a Riesling reduction sauce. The wine list is composed of the choicest Central Coast vintages and select French bottles. The Sunday brunch is a rich prix-fixe indulgence if you're celebrating.

699 Embarcadero (in Marina Sq.). ℂ **805/772-0677.** www.windowsonthewater.net. Reservations recommended. Main courses $17–$27; brunch $23 ($13 for kids). AE, DC, DISC, MC, V. Tues–Sun 5–10pm; Sun 11am–2pm.

3 San Luis Obispo

38 miles S of Cambria; 226 miles S of San Francisco; 198 miles N of LA

Because the actual town of San Luis Obispo is not visible from U.S. 101, even many Californians don't know that it's more than another fast food-and-gasoline stopover on the highway. But its "secret" location is part of what helps this relaxed yet vital college town keep its charm and character intact.

San Luis Obispo (SLO to locals) is neatly tucked into the mountains about halfway between San Francisco and Los Angeles. It's surrounded by green, pristine mountain ranges and filled with a mix of college kids, big-city transplants, dot-com entrepreneurs, and friendly agricultural folk.

The town grew up around an 18th-century mission, and its dozens of historic landmarks, Victorian homes, shops, and restaurants are its primary attractions for visitors. Today, it's still quaint, almost undiscovered, and best ventured on foot. It also makes a good base for an extensive exploration of the region as a whole. To the west of town, a short drive away, are some of the state's prettiest swimming beaches; to the north and south you'll find the Central Coast's Wine Country, home to dozens of respectable wineries and bucolic scenery.

ESSENTIALS

GETTING THERE   U.S. 101, one of the state's primary north-south roadways, runs right through San Luis Obispo; it's the fastest land route here from anywhere. If you're driving down along the coast, Calif. 1 is the way to go for its natural beauty and oceanfront cliffs. If you're entering the city from the east, take Calif. 46 or 41 to U.S. 101, then go south.

VISITOR INFORMATION   The **San Luis Obispo Visitors Center,** 1039 Chorro St. (© **805/781-2777;** www.visitslo.com), is located downtown, between Monterey and Higuera streets. It offers a colorful, comprehensive *Visitors Guide* and the self-guided *Mission Plaza Walking Tour.* The center is open Sunday and Monday from 10am to 5pm, Tuesday and Wednesday from 8am to 5pm, Thursday and Friday from 8am to 8pm, and Saturday from 10am to 8pm.

ORIENTATION   San Luis Obispo is about 10 miles inland, at the junction of Calif. 1 and U.S. 101. The downtown is laid out in a grid, roughly centered on the historic mission and its Mission Plaza (see below). Most of the main tourist sights are around the mission, within the small triangle created by U.S. 101 and Santa Rosa and Marsh streets.

EXPLORING THE TOWN

Before heading downtown, definitely make a pit stop at the perpetually pink **Madonna Inn,** 100 Madonna Rd., off U.S. 101 (© **805/543-3000**), if for no other reason than to use its unique public restrooms (the men's has a waterfall urinal; the women's is a barrage of crimson and pink). Every over-the-top inch of this place is an exercise in excess, from the dining room, complete with pink leather booths, pink table linens, and colored sugar that's—you guessed it— piquantly pink, to the rock-walled, cave-like guest rooms (see p. 408 for a complete review).

Once downtown, you can ride the free trolley that does a repeat loop through the downtown area daily from noon to 5pm. (Stops are well marked.)

Ah Louis Store   Mr. Ah Louis was a Cantonese immigrant who was lured to California by gold fever in 1856. Emerging from the mines empty-handed, he soon began a lucrative career as a labor contractor, hiring and organizing Chinese crews that built the railroad. In 1874, he opened this store. Today, the store is rarely open, but if it is, you can browse the clutter of Asian merchandise. Don't be afraid to call—this is a worthwhile gem!

800 Palm St. (at Chorro St.). © 805/543-4332. Hours vary; serious shoppers phone in advance.

Farmers Market ⚐   If you're lucky enough to be in town on a Thursday, take an evening stroll down Higuera Street, when the county's largest weekly street fair fills 4 downtown city blocks. You'll find much more here than fresh-picked produce—there's an ever-changing array of street entertainment, open-pit barbecues, food stands, and market stalls selling fresh flowers, cider, and other seasonal goodies. Surrounding stores stay open until 9pm.

Higuera St. (between Osos and Nipomo sts.). Thurs 6:30–9pm (rain or shine).

Mission San Luis Obispo de Tolosa   Founded by Father Junípero Serra in 1772, California's fifth mission was built with adobe bricks by Native American Chumash people. It remains one of the prettiest and most interesting structures in the Franciscan chain. Serra chose this valley for the site of his fifth mission based on tales told to him of friendly natives and bountiful food (including grizzly bears). Here the traditional red-tile roof was first used atop a California mission, after the original thatched tule roofs repeatedly fell to hostile Native Americans' burning arrows. The former padres' quarters are now an excellent museum chronicling both Native American and missionary life through all eras of the mission's use. Allow about 30 to 45 minutes to tour the mission and its grounds.

Mission Plaza, a pretty garden with brick paths and park benches fronting a meandering creek in which children love to wade, still functions as San Luis Obispo's town square. It's the focal point for local festivities and activities, from live concerts to poetry readings and dance and theater productions. Check at the visitor center (see "Essentials," above) to find out what's on when you're in town.

At the south end of Mission Plaza, you'll find the **San Luis Obispo Art Center** (© 805/543-8562), whose three galleries display and sell an array of California-made art. Admission is free; hours are Tuesday through Sunday from 11am to 5pm.

751 Palm St. © 805/781-8220. www.oldmissionslo.org. Free admission ($2 donation requested). Summer daily 9am–5pm (sometimes later); winter daily 9am–4pm.

San Luis Obispo Children's Museum *Kids*   This terrific children's museum features a playhouse for toddlers, an authentic reproduction of a Native American Chumash cave dwelling, a music room, a computer corner, a pint-sized bank and post office, and over 20 interactive exhibits rotated on a regular basis. Special events like mask-making, singalongs, and stage-makeup classes are scheduled regularly; call for a list of events.

1010 Nipomo St. (at Monterey St.). © 805/544-KIDS. www.slonet.org/~slokids. Admission $5 adults and children 2 and older, free for children under 2. Tues[nd[Sat 11am–5pm, Sun noon–4pm; open some Mon holidays.

SHOPPING

You'll find SLO resembles a smaller version of Santa Barbara, where unique boutiques and specialty shops are interspersed with recognized names and finer chains. With an influx of new residents, big-name businesses have been popping up all over the place: Look for the Gap, Barnes & Noble, Victoria's Secret, and Starbucks on SLO's charming tree-lined streets. The best place to exercise your credit cards is on the downtown streets surrounding the mission, specifically the 5 blocks of **Higuera Street** from Nipomo to Osos streets, as well as a short stretch of **Monterey Street** between Chorro and Osos streets.

Check out **Hands Gallery,** 777 Higuera St. (© 805/543-1921), which has a playful, bright collection of local and international art. Trinkets range from glass candies to vases, jewelry, and ceramics and can be viewed or purchased Monday through Wednesday from 10am to 6pm, Thursday through Saturday from 10am to 9pm, and Sunday from 11am to 5pm.

ATTRACTIONS OUTSIDE OF TOWN

There are dozens of **wineries** in the area that offer tastings and tours daily and make for a fun country diversion. See "The Central Coast Wine Country: Paso Robles & the Santa Ynez Valley," later in this chapter, for further details. If you don't have time to tour the wineries or would like more information before heading out to taste, you can visit **The Wine Guy,** 1817 Osos St., by the train station (© 805/546-VINO; www.wineguy.net). Local wine guru Ron Rawlinson, who teaches oenology at Cal Poly and even hosts a local radio show devoted to all things wine, is a one-stop source of information, supplies, and anecdotes on the Central Coast wine industry. He also stocks a comprehensive array of bottles, including unknown limited-production gems.

WHERE TO STAY

In addition to what's listed below, there's a pristine branch of **Holiday Inn Express** (℃ 800/465-4329 or 805/544-8600), a reliable **Motel 6** (℃ 800/4-MOTEL-6 or 805/541-6992), and 34 sweet motel-style units at the **Apple Farm Trellis Court** (℃ 800/255-2040 or 805/544-2040).

Adobe Inn   Okay, it's not *actually* adobe—or even remotely close for that matter—but new owners have taken this old motor inn and given it a creatively homey atmosphere at unbeatable prices. Each spotless room is individually decorated in Southwestern style with quirky additions such as playfully painted cupboards or a window-side reading nook. Breakfast is served in a clean dining area that unfortunately faces the street, but coffee snobs will delight in the strong, locally roasted blend. The owners go out of their way to make guests happy and offer a slew of packages that explore the surrounding areas and attractions.

1473 Monterey St., San Luis Obispo, CA 93401. ℃ **800/676-1588** or 805/549-0321. Fax 805/549-0383. www.adobeinns.com. 15 units. $59–$129 double. Rates include breakfast. Extra person $6 in winter, $10 in summer. AE, DISC, MC, V. **Amenities:** Complimentary bikes. *In room:* TV, dataport, kitchenette in some units (no stove), coffeemaker, hair dryer, iron.

Apple Farm Inn 🟊🟊   Ultra-popular, the Apple Farm Inn is a peaceful getaway in a Disney-plantation kind of way. Every square inch of the immaculate Victorian-style farmhouse is cheek-pinchingly cute with floral wallpaper, fresh flowers, and sugar-sweet colorful touches. No two rooms are alike, although each has a gas fireplace, large well-equipped bathroom, pine antiques, lavish country decor, and either a canopy four-poster or brass bed. Some bedrooms open onto cozy turreted sitting areas with romantic window seats; others have bay windows and a view of San Luis Creek, where a working mill spins its huge wheel to power an apple press. The outstanding service here includes nightly turndown and a morning wake-up knock, delivered with complimentary coffee or tea and a newspaper. Other features include complimentary cribs and train and airport shuttle service. Cider is always on hand in the lobby. The hotel shares a name with their on-site restaurant, one of Highway 101's best-loved pit stops.

Those who want the bang without the requisite bucks can opt for the adjoining motel-style **Apple Farm Trellis Court,** which shares the inn's wonderful grounds. Rooms are smaller, but are well decorated and have gas fireplaces. Rates include a continental breakfast and cost just half as much as the inn.

2015 Monterey St., San Luis Obispo, CA 93401. ℃ **800/255-2040** or 805/544-2040. Fax 805/546-9495. www.applefarm.com. 69 units. $179–$359 double. Rates include complimentary morning coffee/tea and afternoon wine reception. AE, DISC, MC, V. **Amenities:** Restaurant; outdoor heated pool; Jacuzzi; room service 6am–11pm; laundry service; dry cleaning. *In room:* A/C, TV w/pay movies, dataport, hair dryer, iron.

Garden Street Inn 🟊   SLO's prettiest (and most-polished) bed-and-breakfast is this gracious Italianate/Queen Anne downtown. Built in 1887 and completely restored in 1990, the house is a monument to gentility and to the good taste of owners Dan and Kathy Smith. Each bedroom and suite is decorated with well-chosen antique armoires, opulent fabric or paper wall coverings, and vintage memorabilia. Choose one with a claw-foot tub, fireplace, whirlpool tub, or private deck—whatever suits your fancy. Breakfast is served in the stained-glass morning room, and each evening wine and cheese are laid out for guests. A well-stocked library is always available.

1212 Garden St. (between Marsh and Pacific), San Luis Obispo, CA 93401. ℃ **800/488-2045** or 805/545-9802. Fax 805/545-9403. www.gardenstreetinn.com. 13 units. $120–$180 double. Rates include full breakfast and evening wine and cheese. AE, MC, V. *In room:* A/C, dataport.

Madonna Inn ⋆ This one you've got to see for yourself. The creative imaginations of owners Alex and Phyllis Madonna gave birth to the wildest—and most superfluously garish—fantasy world this side of Graceland. The only decor consistency throughout the hotel is its color scheme, which is perpetual pink. Beyond that, it's a free-for-all. Although tongue-in-cheek, this place can seem tired and tacky, and some of the rooms could use updating. However, the lobby men's room with its rock-waterfall urinal and clamshell sinks is a must-see. One guest room features a trapezoidal bed—it's 5 feet long on one side and 6 feet long on the other. "Rock" rooms with zebra- or tiger-patterned bedspreads and stone-like showers and fireplaces conjure up thoughts of a Flintstones's Playboy palace. There are also blue rooms, red rooms, and over-the-top Spanish, Italian, Irish, Alps, Currier and Ives, Native American, Swiss, and hunting rooms. The cocktail lounges are also outlandishly ornate. Even if you don't stay here, stop by and check it out. One caveat: The Madonna Inn, surprisingly, lacks a swimming pool.

100 Madonna Rd. (off U.S. 101), San Luis Obispo, CA 93405. ℂ 800/543-9666 or 805/543-3000. Fax 805/543-1800. www.madonnainn.com. 108 units. $147–$248 double; from $210 suite. AE, DISC, MC, V. **Amenities:** Restaurant; coffee shop; 2 lounges. *In room:* A/C, TV, coffeemaker, hair dryer, iron.

WHERE TO DINE

Big Sky Cafe ⋆ AMERICAN The folk-artsy fervor of San Luis really shines at this Southwestern mirage, where local art and a blue, star-studded ceiling surround diners who come for fresh, healthy food. The menu is self-classified "modern food," a category that here means a dizzying international selection including Caribbean shrimp tacos with chipotle-lime yogurt, Thai curry pasta tossed with sautéed tiger shrimp, chilled sesame ginger noodles, and breakfast's red-flannel turkey hash—a beet-fortified ragout topped with basil-Parmesan glazed eggs. Big Sky's owner also runs LA's funky Gumbo Pot, whose Cajun-Creole influences spice up the menu at every turn. In fact, this might be the only Central Coast outlet for decent jambalaya, gumbo, or authentically airy beignets.

1121 Broad St. ℂ 805/545-5401. www.bigskycafe.com. Main courses $9–$17; salads and sandwiches $6–$10; breakfast $5–$9. AE, MC, V. Mon–Sat 7am–10pm, Sun 8am–9pm.

Buona Tavola ⋆⋆ NORTHERN ITALIAN While most choices in town are burger-and-sandwich casual, Buona Tavola offers well-prepared Italian food in a more upscale setting. You can stroll in wearing jeans, but the dining room, with checkerboard floors and original artwork, is warmer and more intimate than other spots in town. There's also backyard-terrace seating where you can enjoy your meal surrounded by magnolias, ficus, and grapevines. The menu boasts a number of salads on the antipasti list. Favorite pastas include *agnolotti de scampi allo zafferano,* which is house-made pockets filled with scampi, then served in a cream-saffron sauce; *linguini fradiavolo* served with Manila clams, mussels, and river shrimp in a spicy tomato sauce; or the classic *timballo di parma,* a vegetarian delight baked with two cheeses. Don't worry—once you've gotten past trying to pronounce your desired dish, the rest of the evening should be both relaxing and satisfying.

1037 Monterey St. ℂ 805/545-8000. Reservations recommended. Main courses $12–$23. AE, DISC, MC, V. Mon–Fri 11:30am–2:30pm; Sun–Thurs 5:30–9:30pm, Fri–Sat 5:30–10pm.

Mondéo Pronto *Value* INTERNATIONAL Mondéo Pronto provides patrons an affordable bite of international fillings in a burrito-type wrap. But unlike most "wrap" restaurants in California, this place goes a step beyond by paying attention to detail with presentation and freshness. Choices range from Americana versions like the Mardi Gras (a tomato tortilla packed with Cajun sausage, rock shrimp, Creole veggies, and jambalaya sauce) to Mediterranean selections like the Sicilian, with grilled portobello mushrooms, herb polenta, veggies, goat cheese, olives, capers, and sun-dried tomato pesto. "Fusion bowls" satisfy non-wrappers with such combinations as basil scampi, a lovely shrimp dish over bow-tie pasta with pesto, marinara, pine nuts, and herbs. Big bonuses: Everything on the kids' menu is under $3, and as the menu states, "Substitutions and sides are no problem."

893 Higuera St. (in the plaza). ℂ 805/544-2956. Most items $5–$7. MC, V. Sun–Wed 11am–9pm, Thurs–Sat 11am–10pm.

Mo's Smokehouse BBQ ✹✹ BARBECUE Just about everyone in SLO is a devotee of this place, whose reputation and great barbecue belie its humble ambience. It's not fancy, but you name it, it's here—pork or baby-back ribs, barbecue beef, and chicken in either a mild or hot sauce, all accompanied by baked beans, bread, potato salad, or coleslaw. To top off this delectable deal, practically everything on the menu is under $10.

970 Higuera St. (at Osos St.). ℂ 805/544-6193. Most items $4.95–$13. AE, MC, V. Sun–Wed 11am–9pm, Thurs–Sat 11am–10pm.

Thai-rrific THAI Although it's located on Higuera Street, Thai-rrific is a bit removed from the downtown action—but once you step inside this cute, ivy-covered building, the aroma will convince you you've made a worthy diversion. Fine examples of authentic Bangkok-style cuisine are the ginger beef, garlic noodles, and my favorite, lemon grass chicken (grilled chicken breasts topped with lemon grass cream sauce, roasted chiles, and peanuts). Don't overlook the great array of tasty appetizers and salads, including the grilled shrimp or beef with cucumber, lime, and chili. An impressive wine list rounds out the offerings. Prices here are a little higher than at most Thai restaurants, but well worth it.

208 Higuera St. ℂ 805/541-THAI. Reservations not accepted. Most dishes $7–$13. MC, V. Mon–Fri 11:30am–2pm; Mon–Sat 5–9pm.

4 Pismo Beach

13 miles S of San Luis Obispo

Just outside San Luis Obispo, on Pismo's 23-mile stretch of prime beachfront, flip-flops are the shoes of choice and surf wear is the dominant fashion. It's all about beach life here, so bring your bathing suit, your board, and a good book.

If building sand castles or tanning isn't your idea of a tantalizing time, you can explore isolated dunes, cliff-sheltered tide pools, and old pirate coves. Bring your dog (Fido's welcome here) and play an endless game of fetch. Or go fishing—it's permitted from Pismo Beach Pier, which also offers arcade entertainment, bowling, and billiards. Pismo is also the only beach in the area that allows all-terrain vehicles on the dunes.

Because the town itself consists of little more than tourist shops and surf-and-turf restaurants, nearby San Luis Obispo is a far more charming place to stay. But if all you want are a few lazy days on a beautiful beach at half the price of an oceanfront room in Santa Barbara, Pismo is the perfect choice.

ESSENTIALS

The **Pismo Beach Chamber of Commerce and Visitors Bureau,** 581 Dolliver St., Pismo Beach, CA 93449 (ℂ **800/443-7778** or 805/773-4382), offers free brochures and information on local attractions, lodging, and dining. The office is open Monday through Saturday from 9am to 5pm and Sunday from 10am to 4pm. You can peruse their information online at **www.classiccalifornia.com**.

WHAT TO SEE & DO

Beaches in Pismo are exceptionally wide, making them some of the best in the state for sunning and playing. The beach north of Grand Avenue is popular with families and joggers. North of Wadsworth Street, the coast becomes dramatically rugged as it rambles northward to Shell Beach and Pirates Cove.

Pismo Beach was once one of the most famous places in America for **clamming,** but the famed "Pismo clam" reached near-extinction in the mid-1980s due to overzealous harvesting. If you'd like to get your feet wet digging for bivalves, you'll need to obtain a license and follow strict guidelines. Or come for the annual **Clam Festival:** Held at the pier each October since 1946, the celebration features a chowder cook-off, sand-sculpture contest, and Miss Pismo Beach pageant.

If **fishing** is more your style, you'll be pleased to know that no license is required to fish from Pismo Beach Pier. Catches here are largely bottom fish like red snapper and lingcod. There's a bait-and-tackle shop on the pier.

Livery Stables, 1207 Silver Spur Place (© **805/489-8100**), in Oceano (about 5 min. south of Pismo Beach), is one of the very few places in the state that rents horses for riding on the beach. Horses go for $20 per hour and can be ridden at your own pace, or you can opt for a guided ride.

You can hike along the **Guadalupe-Nipomo Dunes** year-round. This 18-mile strip of coastline 20 minutes south of Pismo has the highest beach dunes in the West. It's a great place for observing native plants and birds, including the California brown pelican, one of 200 species that migrate here each year.

From late November to February, tens of thousands of migrating **monarch butterflies** take up residence in the area's eucalyptus and Monterey pine-tree groves. The colorful butterflies form dense clusters on the trees, each hanging with its wings over the one below it, providing warmth and shelter for the entire group. During the monarchs' stay, naturalists at Pismo State Beach conduct 45-minute narrative walks every Saturday and Sunday at 11am and 2pm (call © **805/772-2694** for tour information). Most of the "butterfly trees" are located on Calif. 1, between Pismo Beach and Grover Beach, to the south.

WHERE TO STAY

Cottage Inn by the Sea ⋆   One of Pismo Beach's newest cliffside lodgings, the Cottage Inn is a good, moderately priced choice for couples and families alike. With its rounded thatched roofs and Laura Ashley–style decor, the country charm is evident both inside and out. Rooms, which are refreshingly clean and spacious, range both in price and style from traditional to oceanview. All come with the amenities of a romantic inn (including fireplaces) as well as modern conveniences (like in-room microwaves). This seaside retreat is one of the best in town.

2351 Price St., Pismo Beach, CA 93449. © **888/440-8400** or 805/773-4617. Fax 805/773-8336. www. cottage-inn.com. 80 units. Memorial Day to Labor Day $129–$269 double; off-season $89–$189 double. Rates include deluxe continental breakfast. Extra person $10. AE, DC, DISC, MC, V. Pets accepted with $10-per-night fee. **Amenities:** Oceanfront heated pool and Jacuzzi. *In room:* TV w/pay movies and Nintendo, fridge, coffeemaker, hair dryer, iron, safe.

Kon Tiki Inn *Value*   The over-the-top Polynesian architecture of this three-story gem is easy to spot from the freeway, and upon closer examination evokes memories of 1960s Waikiki hotels. Rooms are modest, small, and simply furnished with unremarkable faux bamboo furniture, yet each has an oceanfront balcony or patio. Outside, vast lawns slope gently toward the cliffs, broken only by the windshielded, kidney-shaped swimming pool flanked by twin Jacuzzis. This humble hotel—which is privately owned and does no advertising—has a sandy beach with stairway access, and lacks the highway noise that plagues many neighbors. Room service is provided by Steamers of Pismo next door (see "Where to Dine," below).

1621 Price St., Pismo Beach, CA 93449. ℭ 888/KON-TIKI or 805/773-4833. Fax 805/773-6541. www.kon tikiinn.com. 86 units. $74–$89 double. Extra person $14. AE, DISC, MC, V. **Amenities:** Outdoor heated pool; 2 Jacuzzis; access to adjacent health club; room service; laundry service. *In room:* TV w/pay movies, dataport, fridge, coffeemaker.

The Sea Venture Resort ℛ   If luxury accommodations overlooking the beach and an outdoor spa on your private deck sound like heaven to you, head for SeaVenture, a 7-year-old resort providing the most luxurious accommodations in Pismo. Once in your room, you need only drag your tired traveling feet through the thick forest-green carpeting and past the white country furnishings and feather bed, and turn on your gas fireplace to begin what promises to be a relaxing stay. Then rent a movie from the video library, schedule a massage, or simply bathe your weary bones in your own outdoor hydrotherapy spa tub. With the beach right outside your door, there's not much more you could ask for—although there is, in fact, more provided: plush robes, a wet bar, continental breakfast delivered to your room, and a restaurant on the premises with a lovely brunch. Most rooms have ocean views and many have a private balcony overlooking the beach.

100 Ocean View Ave., Pismo Beach, CA 93449. ℭ 800/662-5545 or 805/773-4994. Fax 805/773-0924. www.seaventure.com. 50 units. $129–$349 double. Rates include continental breakfast. AE, DC, DISC, MC, V. Take U.S. 101 to the Price St. exit and turn W onto Ocean View (at the beach). **Amenities:** Restaurant; outdoor heated pool; massage center; complimentary bikes; room service 5–9pm; laundry service; dry cleaning. *In room:* TV/VCR, dataport, minibar, coffeemaker, hair dryer, iron.

WHERE TO DINE

Local icon **F. McLintocks** has a lock on Pismo with two crowd-pleasing ocean-view eateries: **F. McLintocks Saloon & Dining House,** 750 Mattie Rd. (across Hwy. 101; ℭ 805/773-1892), for stick-to-your-ribs, ranch-style meals in a corny Old West setting; and **Steamers of Pismo,** 1601 Price St. (ℭ 805/773-4711), a warehouse-style space with "Miles of Clams" and plenty for landlubbers too.

Giuseppe's Cucina Italiana ℛ SOUTHERN ITALIAN   This is the region's best southern Italian restaurant—would you believe owner Giuseppe DiFronza started it as his senior project at Cal Poly University? It's true, and DiFronza's love of (and expertise at) cuisine from the Pugliese region (an Adriatic seaport) continues to bring diners a taste of the Italian countryside. Along with the fresh homemade bread baked in a wood-burning oven imported from Italy, Giuseppe's classic fare uses authentic recipes, imported ingredients, and organically grown produce; the extensive menu of antipasti, salads, pizzas, pastas, fish, and steak makes it virtually impossible to not find something you like. Highlights of our meal included linguine with shrimp, scallops, pancetta, and garlic in a vodka cream sauce, and seared ahi with a peppercorn crust and garlic-caper aïoli.

891 Price St. ℭ 805/773-2870. www.giuseppesrestaurant.com. Reservations not accepted. Main courses $6–$10 lunch, $9–$22 dinner. AE, DISC, MC, V. Daily 11:30am–3pm; Sun–Thurs 4:30–10pm, Fri–Sat 4:30–11pm.

Splash Cafe AMERICAN   This beachy burger stand, with a short menu and just a few tables, gets high marks for its award-winning clam chowder, served in a sourdough bread bowl. Fish and chips, burgers, hot dogs, and grilled ahi sandwiches are also available. Far-flung aficionados know that Splash will ship its chowder frozen, overnight, anywhere in the country (sourdough loaves, too).

197 Pomeroy St. (near Pismo Beach Pier). (℃ 805/773-4653. www.splashcafe.com. Most items $3–$7. MC, V. Daily 10am–8pm.

5 The Central Coast Wine Country: Paso Robles & the Santa Ynez Valley

Paso Robles: 29 miles N of San Luis Obispo; Solvang: 60 miles S of San Luis Obispo

When people talk about California wines, you can normally assume they mean those from the Napa and Sonoma regions north of San Francisco. But here in California, and increasingly across the country, wine lovers are becoming more aware of vintages coming from California's Central Coast wineries, located in the dewy green hills and sun-kissed valleys of San Luis Obispo and Santa Barbara counties. The Central Coast is coming into its own as a respected wine region, and offers another excuse to visit some of the state's most beautifully scenic countryside. Wine snobs might tell you that Central Coast wines cannot compare to those from the northern appellations, where precious vintages can age to sublime flavor and astronomical price, but if you're in the market for bottles in the $15-to-$25 range that are ready to drink within a couple of years, then trust me—you'll love what this up-and-comer has to offer.

PASO ROBLES
Welcome to Paso Robles—"pass through the oaks"—so named for the clusters of oak trees liberally scattered throughout the rolling hills of this inland region. The town has a faintly checkered past: It was established in 1870 by Drury James, uncle of outlaw Jesse James (who reportedly hid out in tunnels under the original Paso Robles Inn). In 1913, pianist Ignace Paderewski came to live in Paso Robles, where he brought zinfandel vines for his ranch (zinfandel is now the most successful varietal among area wineries) and played often in the Paso Robles Inn, which today maintains a small exhibit in his honor in the lobby. Paderewski really wasn't here for long, returning to Poland after World War I, but the town today treats him like a native son, and fans gather each year at the Paderewski Festival in March.

ESSENTIALS
GETTING THERE/ORIENTATION   Paso Robles lies along U.S. 101; there's an exit for the town's main business thoroughfare, Spring Street. Calif. 46 intersects, and briefly joins, U.S. 101. Many wineries are located on the winding roads off Calif. 46 on either side—try to cluster your visit according to this destination, visiting one side and then the other. You'll be able to feel how the weather on the western side, which is cooler due to higher elevations and frequent coastal fog, differs from the hotter east side, on a flat plain leading inland; winemakers bicker constantly over which conditions are "better" for wine grapes.

VISITOR INFORMATION   For a complete list of area wineries, tasting rooms, and seasonal events, contact the **Paso Robles Vintners and Growers Association,** 1940 Spring St. (P.O. Box 324), Paso Robles, CA 93447 (℃ **800/ 549-WINE** or 805/239-8463; fax 805/237-6439; www.pasowine.com). Additional information on the area is offered by the **Paso Robles Chamber of**

Commerce, 1225 Park St., Paso Robles, CA 93446 (℘ **800/406-4040** or 805/ 238-0506; fax 805/238-0527; www.pasorobleschamber.com).

TOURING THE LOCAL WINERIES

They've been tending vines in Paso Robles's fertile foothills since the turn of the century—the 19th century, that is. For decades, the area was overlooked by wine aficionados, even though in 1983 it was granted its own "Paso Robles" appellation (the official government designation of a recognized wine-producing region; "Napa Valley" and "Sonoma County" are probably more familiar appellations). But somewhere around 1992, wine grapes surpassed lettuce as San Luis Obispo County's primary cash crop, and there are now almost 40 wineries and more than 100 vineyards (which grow grapes but do not produce their own wine from them).

Wine touring in Paso Robles is reminiscent of another, unhurried time. Because not all wine enthusiasts are wine experts, an advantage of the area is its friendly attitude and small crowds, which make it easy to learn more about the winemaking process as you go along. Enjoy the relaxed rural atmosphere along two-lane country roads, driving leisurely from winery to winery and, more often than not, chatting with the winemaker while tasting his/her product.

Eberle Winery   Owner Gary Eberle, who's been making Paso Robles wine since 1973, is sometimes called the "grandfather of Paso Robles's Wine Country" because many of the recent new vintners in the area honed their craft working under his tutelage. A visit to Eberle Winery includes a tour through its underground caves, where hundreds of aging barrels share space with the Wild Boar Room, site of Eberle's monthly winemaker dinners featuring guest chefs from around the country (always held on Sat nights; the prix-fixe meal is around $80, including wine). Call for a current events schedule.

Hwy. 46 E. (3½ miles E of U.S. 101). ℘ **805/238-9607.** www.eberlewinery.com. Complimentary tastings daily 10am–5pm (until 6pm in summer).

EOS Estate Winery at Arciero Vineyards   Follow the checkered flag to the 800 acres of wine grapes owned by former race-car driver Frank Arciero Sr. Arciero was drawn to the area by its resemblance to his native Italy; he passed through on his way to Laguna Seca, a racetrack near Salinas. (Trivia buffs will know it as James Dean's intended destination in 1955, when he was killed in nearby Cholame while driving his silver Porsche.) The label specializes in Italian varietals (nebbiolo, sangiovese) and blends. The facility includes a self-guided tour, a race-car exhibit, spectacular rose gardens, and a picnic area.

(*Finds*   **Gourmet Picnics, Paso Robles–Style**

You'll find everything you need for a casual snack or sophisticated picnic at Paso Robles's **Odyssey Culinary Provisions,** 1214 Pine St. (℘ **805/237-7516**). A sandwich board features gourmet deli selections on focaccia and other fresh-baked breads, and refrigerated cases yield up inventive salads, cheeses, salami, olives, and other goodies. Mustards, crackers, chocolates, and pastries line the shelves, along with baskets and knapsacks to hold your feast. Odyssey is also the place to come for fresh-brewed coffee and espresso drinks. It's open Sunday through Thursday from 7am to 7pm, Friday and Saturday from 7am to 11pm.

Hwy. 46 E. (6 miles E of U.S. 101). ℭ 805/239-2562. www.eosvintage.com. Complimentary tastings daily 10am–5pm (until 6pm summer weekends).

Justin Vineyards & Winery ★★★ At the end of a scenic country road lies Justin and Deborah Baldwin's boutique winery, and even a casual glance shows how much love and dedication the ex–Los Angelenos have put into their operation. The tasting room, dining room, offices, and even winemaking barns have a stylish Tuscan flair. Justin's flagship wine is Isosceles, a Bordeaux-style blend that's pricier than most area wines but exudes sophistication—and earns *Wine Spectator* raves. Also worth a try is their port-style dessert wine, called Obtuse.

For an extra-special treat, the winery has a three-suite B&B called the **JUST Inn.** Impeccably outfitted, the inn has an undeniable serenity, and you can even have a romantic gourmet dinner prepared for you with advance notice. Room rates are $225 to $275—and worth every precious penny. *Insider tip:* When space permits, Justin's intimate private dining room is also open to the public; if you're celebrating—or just want to have the best meal of your trip—call for advance reservations.

11680 Chimney Rock Rd. (15 miles W of U.S. 101). ℭ 805/237-4150. www.justinwine.com. Tastings daily 10am–5pm. Tasting fee $4, includes souvenir glass.

Meridian Vineyards ★ The local vintner with the largest profile is also the Central Coast's best-known label, producing more cases each year than all the other Paso wineries *combined.* Veteran winemaker Chuck Ortman brought a respected Napa Valley pedigree to Meridian; as a result, here's where you'll get the most Napa-like tasting experience. In addition to a grand tasting room, there's a man-made lake surrounded by rolling lawns, where picnicking is encouraged.

Hwy. 46 E. (7 miles E of U.S. 101). ℭ 805/237-6000. www.meridianvineyards.com. Complimentary tastings daily 10am–5pm.

Summerwood Winery & Inn ★★ There's a spit and polish about this sleek player in the Paso wine game. The former Treana Winery's elegant tasting room (Treana's still in business, crafting wonderful red blends at a different location with no public tastings) now features a gourmet deli for picnickers, plush fireside chairs for relaxed sipping, and the luxurious Summerwood Inn bed-and-breakfast set among the vines (p. 416). With the help of internationally experienced winemaker Scott Hawley, Summerwood is turning out some of the best reds around, including cabernet and syrah from pedigreed estate vineyards.

2175 Arbor Rd. (at Hwy. 46 W., 1 mile W of U.S. 101). ℭ 805/227-1365. www.summerwoodwine.com. Complimentary tastings daily 10am–5pm (till 6pm in summer).

Tobin James Cellars ★★ Winemaker Tobin James is a walking contradiction. A lifelong wine expert who claims to wear the same pair of khaki shorts every day, Toby has patterned his winery in the spirit of local bad boys, the James Gang. The tasting room has a Wild West theme, a 100-year-old saloon bar, and blaring country music, all serving to dispel the wine-snob atmosphere that prevails at so many other wineries. Tobin James's particular expertise lies in the production of a "user-friendly" zinfandel; the late-harvest dessert wine from zinfandel grapes is smooth and spicy.

8950 Union Rd. (at Hwy. 46 E., 8 miles E of U.S. 101). ℭ 805/239-2204. www.tobinjames.com. Complimentary tastings daily 10am–6pm.

York Mountain Winery *Finds* If you're impressed by "firsts" and "onlys," don't miss York Mountain. It was the first winery established in the area (in 1882 by Andrew York, on land originally deeded by President Ulysses S. Grant) and is the oldest continuously operating vintner, as well as the only producer in the "York Mountain" viticulture appellation. In the 100-year-old stone tasting room, look for a dry chardonnay with a complex, spicy aroma, and award-winning cabernet sauvignons, the best of which are the reserve bottlings from hand-chosen grapes.

7505 York Mountain Rd. (off Hwy. 46 W., 7 miles W of U.S. 101). (C) **805/238-3925.** Tasting fee $1. Tastings daily 10am–5pm.

OTHER DIVERSIONS IN THE PASO ROBLES AREA

The fragrance emanating from **Sycamore Farms,** Highway 46 West, several miles west of U.S. 101 ((C) **800/576-5288** or 805/238-5288; www.sycamore farms.com), is that of hundreds of herbs, grown for culinary, medicinal, and decorative purposes. Learn about them at the farm's walk-through garden; it also sells fresh-cut and dried herbs, nursery seedlings to transplant at home, and a bevy of herbal vinegars, olive oils, mustards, herbal soaps, and potpourri. Hours are daily from 10:30am to 5:30pm, except Christmas Day and from January 4 to January 14.

It requires some advance planning, but nothing beats the exhilaration of seeing the Wine Country at sunrise from the serenity of a hot-air balloon. **Seventh Heaven Balloons** ((C) **805/687-8459**) operates on select weekends throughout the year, offering two flights daily followed by champagne brunch. The package price is $139 per person; reservations are suggested at least 4 weeks in advance.

WHERE TO STAY

Adelaide Inn *(Value)* Tended with loving care that's rare among lower-priced accommodations, the Adelaide Inn stands out from other motels. Although it's situated adjacent to freeway-close gas stations and coffee shops, special attention has been given to isolate this quiet, lushly landscaped property from its bustling surroundings. The rooms are clean and comfortable with extra warmth, and the motel has a safe, welcoming ambience. Unexpected comforts include complimentary newspaper and fruit and muffins. Facilities include summertime water diversions and even a putting green.

1215 Ysabel Ave., Paso Robles, CA 93446. (C) **800/549-PASO** or 805/238-2770. Fax 805/238-3497. www. adelaideinn.com. 67 units. $49–$85 double. Extra person $6. Rates include morning coffee and muffins. AE, DC, DISC, MC, V. From U.S. 101, exit Hwy. 46 E. Turn W at 24th St.; the hotel is just W of the freeway. **Amenities:** Heated outdoor pool; Jacuzzi; sauna; coin-op laundry and laundry service; dry cleaning. *In room:* A/C, TV w/pay movies, dataport, fridge, coffeemaker, hair dryer, iron.

Paso Robles Inn This Mission Revival–style inn was built to replace the 1891 Stanford White masterpiece, El Paso De Robles Hotel, that burned to the ground in 1940. Photos of the grand landmark in its heyday line the Spanish-tiled lobby and adjacent dining room and cocktail lounge. A creek meanders through the oak-shaded property, and two-story motel units are scattered across the tranquil and lovely grounds. Well shielded from street noise, these rooms are simple but boast creature comforts (shiny bathrooms, gas fireplaces, and microwaves in many rooms) added in a massive 2000 update that, unfortunately, removed much of their nostalgic charm. The best rooms here are worth the extra bucks: newly built "Spa Rooms" with fireplaces and shielded-for-privacy outdoor Jacuzzis supplied by the property's mineral springs. Convenient carports are located behind each building. Skip the overpriced Hot Springs Grill in favor of the retro-flavored Coffee Shop, both served by the same kitchen. *Insider tip:* Avoid room numbers beginning with 1 or 2—they're too close to the street.

1103 Spring St., Paso Robles, CA 93446. ☎ 805/238-2660. www.pasoroblesinn.com. 100 units. $125–$165 double May–Sept; $95–$115 rest of year. Spa room $175–$235. Extra person $10. Midweek discounts available. AE, DC, DISC, MC, V. **Amenities:** 2 restaurants; lounge; outdoor heated pool; Jacuzzi; business center; room service 7am–8pm; laundry service; dry cleaning. *In room:* A/C, TV w/pay movies, dataport, fridge, coffeemaker, hair dryer, iron.

The Summerwood Inn ⭐ The guest book at this elegant B&B sports more than its share of honeymooners drawn by the splendid setting and luxurious treatment. Located at Summerwood Winery (p. 414), this three-story clapboard house looks like a cross between Queen Anne and Southern-plantation styles, but is furnished in formal English country. It's a contemporary building throughout, so rooms are spacious and bathrooms ultra-modern; the main floor (including two guest rooms) is fully wheelchair accessible. Every room has a private balcony overlooking Summerwood's vineyards, plus a gas fireplace, fresh flowers, and terry robes; morning coffee is left discreetly outside your door in insulated carafes.

2130 Arbor Rd. (P.O. Box 3260), Paso Robles, CA 93447. ☎ 805/227-1111. www.summerwoodinn.com. 9 units. $140–$205 double; $245 suite. Extra person $65. Rates include full breakfast, afternoon wine and hors d'oeuvres, and evening cookies. MC, V. From U.S. 101, exit Hwy. 46 W. Continue 1 mile to Arbor Rd. *In room:* A/C, TV, hair dryer.

WHERE TO DINE

You should also consider Paso's new branch of the San Luis Obispo favorite, **Buona Tavola,** 943 Spring St. (☎ **805/237-0600**), whose house-made pastas and fresh-from-the-fields northern Italian cuisine are a welcome addition to town.

Bistro Laurent ⭐ FRENCH/CALIFORNIA Executive chef Laurent Grangien's sophisticated bistro initially caused quite a stir in this town unaccustomed to such innovations as a chef's tasting menu. But once the dust settled, everyone kept returning for the unpretentious neighborhood atmosphere, delicious recipes, and reasonable (by LA or San Francisco standards) prices. Whet your appetite with a complimentary teaser of hors d'oeuvres (goat-cheese toasts, for example) before plunging into dishes like rosemary-garlic chicken, pork loin bathed in peppercorn sauce, or ahi tuna in red-wine reduction. "Twilight dinners" are served nightly until 6:30pm.

1202 Pine St., Paso Robles. ☎ 805/226-8191. Reservations recommended. Main courses $5–$12 lunch, $15–$23 dinner. MC, V. Mon–Sat 11:30am–2:30pm and 5:30–10pm.

Busi's on the Park CALIFORNIA/ECLECTIC The name may sound snooty and scenic, but Busi's is neither. It's just a comfortable, tavern-like joint across the street from downtown's City Park, but the capable kitchen draws a big local crowd. A short seasonal menu highlights fresh local ingredients. Eclectic offerings include Southwestern chicken salad with refreshing cilantro-lime crema; Chinese stir-fried beef tinged with orange and sesame; pan-roasted salmon with Oriental salsa; and a superior cannelloni that utilizes freshly made basil-egg pasta, roasted tomato sauce, and sautéed spinach. Weekend brunch runs the gamut from French toast or Spanish frittata to Thai noodle salad or saffron mussels.

1122 Pine St., Paso Robles. ☎ 805/238-1390. Reservations recommended on weekends. Main courses $10–$25. AE, MC, V. Tues–Sun 5–9pm; Sat–Sun 10am–2pm.

McPhee's Grill ⭐⭐ *Kids* CALIFORNIA GRILL When Ian McPhee left Ian's restaurant in Cambria and launched this one, it didn't take long for word to get out. McPhee's is worth the short drive to the historic town of Templeton. The converted old saloon features contemporary country decor, an open kitchen, and indoor and outdoor dining. The menu offers a half-dozen appetizers such as a duck quesadilla, artichoke fritters, and a zingy greens-and-grapefruit salad with Maytag bleu cheese and spiced nuts. Gourmet pizza, pasta, an amazing macadamia-crusted salmon, and four varieties of tender, juicy steaks cooked to perfection round out the Americana-with-a-twist style menu. Especially impressive are the prices—it's rare that a restaurant "dedicated to great food and great service" offers the majority of its dishes for under $18. A champagne buffet brunch is offered on Sundays. McPhee's is one of the very best in the region, and families will appreciate the economical kids' menu.

416 Main St., Templeton. ℭ 805/434-3204. www.mcphees.com. Reservations recommended. Main courses $9–$12 lunch, $14–$23 dinner; brunch $19 adults, $8.95 for kids under 10. MC, V. Mon–Sat 8–10:30am; daily 11:30–2pm and 5–9pm; Sun 10am–2pm.

THE SANTA YNEZ VALLEY

Welcome to the Santa Ynez Valley, an idyllic domain of oak-covered hills and uncrowded roads set against a mountain backdrop. This is beautiful country, where the clear blue sky achieves a brilliance unheard of in California's smog-clogged cities. In the Santa Ynez Valley, the pace is a little slower, and the locals a little friendlier. Don't expect to find yokels gnawing on hay, though—this is gentleman-farmer country, where some of the nicest ranches are gated and have video surveillance, and even Disney's Davy Crockett is a respected winemaker. This balance of old-fashioned living and modern sophistication is what makes the area enjoyable: You can wallow in simple pleasures one day and go wine tasting the next.

Los Olivos is a good ol'-fashioned country town right in the middle of the Central Coast Wine Country. There's a big flagpole in the center of the town's intersection, and stretches of boardwalk stand in for sidewalk here and there, giving the town a Wild West air. If you saw TV's *Return to Mayberry*, that was Los Olivos standing in for Andy Griffith's sentimental Southern hamlet. But these days, the town's storefronts feature art galleries, stylish cafes, and wine-tasting rooms; you'll see more Land Rovers than John Deeres in this upscale retreat.

Just minutes away from one another, Los Olivos, Santa Ynez, Ballard, Solvang, and Buellton each make an excellent base for touring the wineries of this fertile area.

ESSENTIALS

GETTING THERE From U.S. 101, take Calif. 246 east 4 miles to reach Solvang, Santa Ynez, and Ballard. Los Olivos is located on Calif. 154 a couple of miles from U.S. 101. Lake Cachuma is also on Calif. 154, traveling southeast toward Santa Barbara.

VISITOR INFORMATION Contact the **Santa Barbara County Vintners' Association,** 3669 Sagunto St., Unit 101 (P.O. Box 1558), Santa Ynez, CA 93460 (ℭ **800/218-0881** or 805/688-0881; www.sbcountywines.com), for its *Winery Touring Map.* Hours are Monday through Friday from 9am to 5pm. The **Solvang Visitors Bureau,** 1511 Mission Dr., at Fifth Street (P.O. Box 70), Solvang, CA 93464 (ℭ **800/GO-SOLVANG** or 805/688-6144; www.solvang usa.com), has additional information on the Santa Ynez Valley. It's open daily from 10am to 4pm.

ORIENTATION U.S. 101, Calif. 246, and Calif. 154 form a triangle enclosing the towns of the Santa Ynez Valley. Calif. 246 becomes Mission Drive within Solvang city limits, then continues east past the mission toward Santa Ynez.

Alamo Pintado Road connects Solvang with Los Olivos, whose commercial stretch is located along 3 blocks of Grand Avenue. Foxen Canyon Road continues north from downtown Los Olivos.

TOURING THE LOCAL WINERIES

Santa Barbara County has a 200-year tradition of growing grapes and making wine—an art originally practiced by Franciscan friars at the area's missions—but only in the past 20 to 30 years have wine-grape fields begun to approach the size of other crops that do so well in these fertile inland valleys.

Geography makes the area well suited for successful vineyards: The Santa Ynez and San Rafael mountain ranges are transverse (east-west) ranges, which allows ocean breezes to flow through, keeping the climate temperate. Variations in temperature and humidity within the valley create many microclimates, and vintners have learned how to cultivate nearly all the classic grape varietals. Today, you'll find about 25 vintners in the Santa Ynez Valley area, most of which have tasting rooms—a few offer tours of their operations as well. If you'd like to start with a winery tour to acquaint yourself with viticulture, Gainey Vineyard or Firestone Vineyard are good bets (see below). And if you'd like to sample wines without driving around, head to **Los Olivos Tasting Room & Wine Shop,** 2905 Grand Ave. (℃ **805/688-7406**), located in the heart of town, or **Los Olivos Wine & Spirits Emporium,** 2531 Grand Ave. (℃ **805/688-4409;** www.sbwines.com), a friendly barn in a field half a mile away. Both offer a wide selection of vintners, including those—such as Au Bon Climat and Qupé—who don't have their own tasting rooms.

The Brander Vineyard   Winemaker Fred Brander has been making a name for himself since 1976; although the winery's production is small, his is a name you'll see frequently on local wine lists. Brander is among the valley's most pleasant wineries, with a friendly family of staff. The best bets are Cuvée Nicolas, which is a 100% sauvignon blanc from low-yielding vines; or choose a high-density cabernet from the cellar for full-bodied perfection.

2401 Refugio Rd., Los Olivos. ℃ 805/688-2455. www.brander.com. Tastings daily 10am–4pm (till 5pm in summer). Tasting fee of $3 includes souvenir glass and is applied toward any purchase.

Fess Parker Winery & Vineyard ⟨★⟩   You loved him as a child, now see what Hollywood's Davy Crockett/Daniel Boone is up to. Fess Parker has made a big name for himself in Santa Barbara County, with resort hotels, cattle ranches, and now an eponymous winery that's turning out some critically acclaimed syrahs, among other varietals. Look for the syrah and chardonnay American Tradition Reserve vintages in the tasting room. Parker's grandiose complex, shaded by the largest oak tree we've ever seen, also features picnic tables on a breezy terrace and an extensive gift shop where you can even buy—you guessed it—coonskin caps!

6200 Foxen Canyon Rd., Los Olivos. ℃ 800/841-1104 or 805/688-1545. www.fessparker.com. Tastings daily 10am–5pm; tours daily at 11am, 1, and 3pm. Tasting fee $3.

Firestone Vineyard   Probably the largest producers in Santa Barbara County, this operation started by Brooks Firestone (of tire-manufacturing fame) now includes two "second" labels. Its wines are affordable and reasonably good, and it's started experimenting with Chilean-grown grapes, some of which can be excellent. Firestone's tasting room and gift shop are a three-ring circus of merchandise, but it offers a quick, worthwhile tour and free tastings.

5000 Zaca Station Rd., Los Olivos. ℃ 805/688-3940. www.firestonewine.com. Tastings daily 10am–5pm; tours hourly Sat–Sun.

The Gainey Vineyard ⭐ This slick operation is one of the most visited wineries in the valley, thanks to its prime location on Calif. 246 and its in-depth tours, offered daily. It has every hallmark of a visitor-oriented winery: a terra-cotta tiled tasting room, plenty of logo merchandise, and a deli case for impromptu lunches at the picnic tables in a secluded vineyard garden. It bottles the most popular varietals—chardonnay, cabernet sauvignon, pinot noir, sauvignon blanc—and offers them at moderate prices.

3950 E. Calif. 246, Santa Ynez. ② 805/688-0558. www.gaineyvineyard.com. Tastings daily 10am–5pm; tours daily 11am, 1, 2, and 3pm. Tasting fee $5, includes souvenir glass.

Sunstone Vineyards and Winery ⭐⭐⭐ Take a rambling drive down to this locally well known winery, whose gracious wisteria-wrapped stone tasting room belies the dirt road you take to reach it. Sunstone is nestled in an oak grove overlooking the river, boasting a splendid view from the lavender-fringed picnic courtyard. Inside, try its flagship merlot or treasured reserve vintages; there's also a fine selection of gourmet foods, logo ware, and cigars. The lovely setting and attractive tasting room, combined with excellent products, make this a quintessentially enjoyable wine-touring experience.

125 Refugio Rd., Santa Ynez. ② 800/313-WINE or 805/688-WINE. www.sunstonewinery.com. Tastings daily 10am–4pm. Tasting fee $3–$5, includes souvenir glass.

Zaca Mesa Winery ⭐⭐ One of the region's old-timers, Zaca Mesa has been in business since 1972, so we can forgive the hippie/New Age mumbo-jumbo pleasantly interwoven with the well-honed vintages. Situated on a unique plateau that the Spanish named *la zaca mesa* (the restful place), this winery's 750 acres are uniquely beautiful—a fact it celebrates with two easy nature trails for visitors. You'll also find picnic tables and a giant lawn chessboard. Inside, look for the usual syrah and chardonnay offerings jazzed up with experimental Rhône varietals like grenache, roussanne, and voignier.

6905 Foxen Canyon Rd., Los Olivos. ② 800/350-7972 or 805/688-9339. www.zacamesa.com. Complimentary tastings daily 10am–4pm; call for tour schedule.

A TASTE OF DENMARK: SOLVANG

The valley's largest town is also one of the state's most popular tourist stops, and Solvang takes a lot of flack for being a Disney-fied version of its founders' vision. Everything here that *can* be Danish *is* Danish: You've never seen so many windmills, cobblestone streets, wooden shoes, and so much gingerbread trim—even the sidewalk trash cans look like little Danish farmhouses with pitched-roof lids.

To reach Solvang from U.S. 101 south, turn east (left) onto Calif. 246 at Buellton. It's a well-marked 20-minute drive along an extremely scenic two-lane road. From Santa Barbara, take U.S. 101 north to Calif. 154, a truly breathtaking 45-minute drive over San Marcos Pass. For a destination guide or hotel information, contact the **Solvang Conference and Visitors Bureau** (② **800/ GO-SOLVANG** or 805/688-6144; www.solvangusa.com).

One way to weed through the unabashed tourism here for a little authentic history is to visit the **Elverhøj Museum,** 1624 Elverhoy Way (② **805/686-1211**), a warm and welcoming place devoted to Danish culture and Solvang history. Set in a traditional handcrafted Scandinavian-style home, and featuring many original old-world furnishings, this little museum can be fully appreciated in 30 minutes or less. Hours are Wednesday through Sunday from 1 to 4pm; a $2 donation is suggested.

Solvang has always been renowned for its traditional and delectable pastries, and the best bakery in town is **Birkholm's Bakery,** 1555 Mission Dr. (© 805/ 688-3872). It's the oldest, opened in 1951 and still family-run. In addition to sticky pastries, sweet rolls, fresh bread, and fresh-brewed coffee, Birkholm's sells its trademark blue-and-white waxed tub of Danish butter cookies ($7.95 each). Hours are daily from 8am to 5:30pm.

Old Mission Santa Ines   Just on the edge of town, and one of the few buildings without a windmill or other Scandinavian fanfare, this Spanish mission was founded by Franciscan friars in 1804 and is still in use for daily services. Most of the original structure, painstakingly constructed of adobe by Native Americans, has been destroyed. The reconstruction features the ornately tiled and painted chapel typical of the Spanish missions, and an extensive museum display of mission artifacts and Franciscan vestment robes.

1760 Mission Dr., Solvang. © 805/688-4815. $3 donation requested, free for children under 16. Summer Mon–Fri 9am–7pm, Sat 9am–4pm, Sun 1:30–5:30pm; winter Sun–Fri 9am–5:30pm, Sat 9am–4pm. From downtown Solvang, take Calif. 246 1 mile E to Mission Dr.

CACHUMA LAKE: A BALD EAGLE HABITAT

Created in 1953 by damming the Santa Ynez River, this picturesque reservoir running along Calif. 154 is the primary water source for Santa Barbara County. It's also the centerpiece of a 6,600-acre county park with a flourishing wildlife population and well-developed recreational facilities. Cachuma has, through both agreeable climate and diligent ranger efforts, become a notable habitat for resident and migratory birds, including rarely sighted bald eagles, which migrate south from as far as Alaska in search of food.

One of the best ways to appreciate this fine-feathered bounty is to take one of the naturalist-led **Eagle Cruises** of the lake, offered between November and February. The 48-foot *Osprey* was specially designed for wildlife observation, with unobstructed views from nearly every seat. During the rest of the year, rangers lead **Wildlife Cruises** around the lake, helping you spot resident waterfowl, grazing deer, and the elusive bobcats and mountain lions that live here. Eagle Cruises depart Wednesday through Sunday at 10am, with additional cruises Friday and Saturday at 2pm. Wildlife Cruises run Friday and Saturday at 3pm, and Saturday and Sunday at 10am. All cruises are 2 hours long. In addition to the park day-use fee of $5 per car, the fare is $10 for adults and $5 for children 12 and under. Reservations are recommended for all cruises; call the **Santa Barbara County Parks Department** (© 805/686-5050; www.sbparks.com).

The recreational opportunities at Cachuma don't stop there: Campers, boaters, and fishermen will find abundant facilities. Contact the **Lake Cachuma Recreation Area** (© 805/686-5054) for more information.

WHERE TO STAY

Ballard Inn ✦✦   This two-story inn may look 100 years old, but it's actually of modern construction, offering both contemporary comforts and charming country details like wicker rockers on a wraparound porch. The entry and parlors are tastefully furnished with a comfortable mix of antiques and reproductions. Sumptuous wallpaper and fabrics lend a cozy touch, and hand-hooked rugs, bent-twig furniture, and vintage accessories lend character to the house. The guest rooms upstairs are similarly unique—some have fireplaces and/or private balconies, and all have well-stocked bathrooms, many featuring a separate antique washbasin in the bedroom. The best (and most expensive) unit is the Mountain Room, a mini-suite decorated in rich forest green and outfitted with a fireplace and private balcony. In addition to cooked-to-order breakfast and a wine-and-hors d'oeuvres reception, you'll be treated to evening coffee and tea, plus addictive chocolate cookies on your nightstand at bedtime.

The inn's restaurant, Cafe Chardonnay, is tucked into a cozy room downstairs by a crackling fire. The California-style seasonal menu can include grilled meats, seafood pastas, and catch-of-the-day specials. *Note:* The inn staff doesn't accept gratuities; instead, a 10% service charge is added at checkout.

2436 Baseline Ave., Ballard, CA 93463. **C** 800/638-2466 or 805/688-7770. Fax 805/688-9560. www. ballardinn.com. 15 units. $195–$275 double. Rates include full breakfast, afternoon wine and hors d'oeuvres, and evening coffee and tea. Packages and midweek discounts available. AE, MC, V. Take Alamo Pintado Rd. to Baseline; the inn is half a block E of the intersection. **Amenities:** Restaurant; bike rental; activities desk; in-room massage. *In room:* A/C, hair dryer, iron.

Inn at Petersen Village ✮ If you think every hotel in Solvang has a kitschy, Danish theme, then step into this quiet, tasteful, and affordable hotel. Rooms are decorated in a European country motif, with print wallpaper, canopy beds, and mahogany-hued furniture. But it's the little touches that impress the most, like lighted magnifying mirrors, bathroom lights controlled by dimmers, free coffee and tea service to your room, and the complimentary food that's nearly always laid out in the hotel's friendly piano lounge. Some rooms overlook a bustling courtyard of shops, while others face Solvang's scenic hills. All are designed so everyone's happy: Smaller units have private balconies, those with noisier views are more spacious, and so on.

1576 Mission Dr., Solvang, CA 93463. **C** 800/321-8985 or 805/688-3121. Fax 805/688-5732. www. peterseninn.com. 42 units. $145–$265 double. Extra person $15. Rates include breakfast buffet, evening wine and hors d'oeuvres, and dessert buffet. Midweek and AAA discounts available. AE, MC, V. **Amenities:** Restaurant; piano/wine bar; room service 7am–11pm. *In room:* A/C, TV, dataport, hair dryer, iron.

Royal Scandinavian Inn If you're looking for a traditional, full-service hotel, this attractive and comfortable mainstay in Solvang is nicely located away from the congested main drag. Popular with business conventions and leisure groups, the Royal Scandinavian Inn has an all-day restaurant and cocktail lounge and is within walking distance of downtown Solvang; the championship Alisal River Golf Course is next door. Rooms are furnished in a vaguely Danish country decor, but are otherwise unremarkable; bathrooms are up-to-date. Ask for a room overlooking the courtyard—the view extends to the foothills beyond.

400 Alisal Rd. (P.O. Box 30), Solvang, CA 93464. **C** 800/624-5572 or 805/688-8000. Fax 805/688-0761. www.solvangrsi.com. 133 units. Mid-Feb to Nov $104–$154 double, from $159 suite; Dec to mid-Feb $99–$134 double, from $149 suite. Extra person $10. Golf packages available. AE, DC, DISC, MC, V. **Amenities:** Restaurant; lounge; outdoor pool; nearby golf; fitness room; Jacuzzi; business center; room service 7am–10pm; laundry service; dry cleaning. *In room:* A/C, TV w/pay movies, fax, fridge, coffeemaker, hair dryer, iron.

WHERE TO DINE

If you're looking for traditional Danish fare in Solvang, head for **Bit o' Denmark,** 473 Alisal Rd. (**C** 805/688-5426). Its smorgasbord may not be the largest in town, but it's the freshest and highest quality; you can also order from the regular menu. It's open daily from 9am to 9pm; the smorgasbord costs $8.95 at lunch, $13 at dinner. **The Hitching Post,** 406 E. Hwy. 246, Buellton (**C** 805/688-0676), is the valley's mecca for meat lovers. Within these Western-themed surroundings, steaks are grilled to perfection over an oak-wood pit, and—fittingly—the house label wine is better than you'd expect.

Mattei's Tavern AMERICAN/CONTINENTAL Mattei's is proud of its stagecoach past, and this rambling white Victorian submerged in climbing

---

Tips Picnicking in the Santa Ynez Valley

You can assemble a picnic lunch at the **Santa Ynez Valley Market,** on Calif. 154 about a mile east of Los Olivos (© **805/688-5115**), where a fresh deli counter prepares simple sandwiches and side salads, plus buckets of fried chicken. With a little advance notice, they'll prepare box lunches that include a sandwich, chips, a piece of fruit, and a cookie, for $7.50 each. The market is open daily from 7am to 8pm.

Los Olivos offers easy-to-carry, eat-at-room-temperature goodies packed up with all the necessary utensils. At **Panino,** 2900 Grand Ave. (© **805/688-9304**), choose from 31 gourmet sandwiches priced from $6 to $8, all served on Panino's fresh-baked, Italian-style bread; varieties include grilled chicken with sun-dried tomatoes, fresh basil, and provolone, or English Stilton with Asian pear on fresh walnut bread. It's open Monday through Friday from 10am to 4pm, Saturday and Sunday from 9am to 5pm.

---

wisteria has successfully retained its historic charm. It's well known throughout the county for fun and good food. Rumors abound of high-stakes poker games in Mattei's back room, where many an early rancher literally "lost the farm." You'll find fine steaks on the menu, along with Australian lobster tail, rainbow trout, burgers, prime-rib chili, a dill-tinged tomato bisque, and chicken piccata, Marsala, or teriyaki.

Calif. 154, Los Olivos. © **805/688-4820**. Reservations recommended on weekends. Dinner $15–$35. MC, V. Daily 5:30–9pm; Sat–Sun noon–2:30pm.

Paula's Pancake House *Kids* AMERICAN/DANISH   Morning means one thing in Solvang, and that's Paula's three-page menu of *just breakfast!* There are wafer-thin Danish pancakes, served plain and simple, sweet and fruity, or with sausage and eggs; plus buttermilk pancakes, whole-wheat/honey pancakes, fresh-baked waffles, sourdough French toast, and every omelet and egg dish imaginable, including some south-of-the-border salsa-fied specials. Paula's is friendly and casual, plunked in the heart of town so that patio diners can watch the whole wacky world go by.

1531 Mission Dr., Solvang. © **805/688-2867**. Most menu items under $7. AE, DISC, MC, V. Daily 6am–3pm.

6 Santa Barbara

45 miles S of Solvang; 105 miles S of San Luis Obispo; 92 miles NW of LA

Santa Barbara is nestled between palm-lined Pacific beaches and the sloping foothills of the Santa Ynez Mountains. This prosperous resort community presents a mosaic of whitewashed stucco and red tile roofs and a gracious, relaxed attitude that has earned it the sobriquet "American Riviera." It's ideal for kicking back on white-sand beaches, prowling the shops and galleries that line the village's pristine, historic streets, and relaxing over a good meal in one of many top-notch cafes and restaurants.

Downtown Santa Barbara is distinctive for its Spanish-Mediterranean architecture. But it wasn't always this way. Santa Barbara had a thriving Native American Chumash population for hundreds, if not thousands, of years. The European era began in the late 18th century, around a Spanish *presidio* (fort) that's been

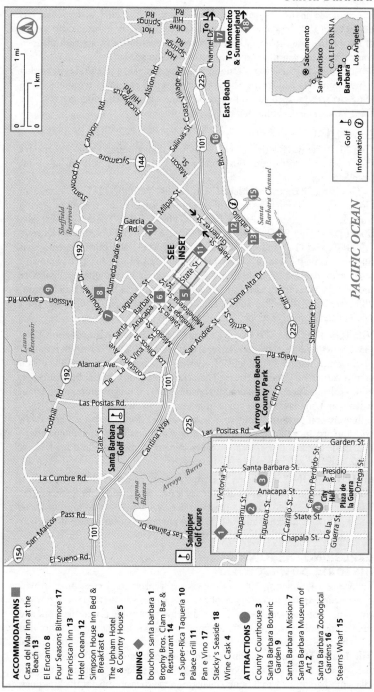

Santa Barbara

CALIFORNIA

Sacramento

San Francisco

Santa Barbara

Los Angeles

PACIFIC OCEAN

Golf
Information ①

To Montecito & Summerland

East Beach

SEE INSET

Santa Barbara Channel

Arroyo Burro Beach County Park

Santa Barbara Golf Club

Sandpiper Golf Course

Garden St.

Santa Barbara St.

Presidio Ave.

Anacapa St.

City Hall

Plaza de la Guerra

State St.

Chapala St.

reconstructed in its original spot. The earliest architectural hodgepodge was destroyed in 1925 by a powerful earthquake that leveled the business district. Out of the rubble rose the Spanish-Mediterranean town of today, a stylish planned community that continues to enforce strict building codes.

Visit Santa Barbara's waterfront on a Sunday and you're sure to see the weekly **Waterfront Arts and Crafts Show,** one of the city's best-loved traditions. Since 1965, artists, craftspeople, and street performers have been lining grassy Chase Palm Park, along Cabrillo Boulevard.

ESSENTIALS

GETTING THERE   By car, U.S. 101 runs right through Santa Barbara. It's the fastest and most direct route from north or south (1½ hr. from LA, 6 hr. from San Francisco).

The **Santa Barbara Municipal Airport** (℃ 805/967-7111) is located in Goleta, about 10 minutes north of downtown Santa Barbara. Airlines serving Santa Barbara include **American Eagle** (℃ 800/433-7300), **AmericaWest Airlines** (℃ 800/235-9292), **United** (℃ 800/241-6522), and **US Airways Express** (℃ 800/428-4322). **Yellow Cab** (℃ 805/965-5111) and other metered taxis line up outside the terminal; the fare is about $22 (without tip) to downtown.

By train, **Amtrak** (℃ **800/USA-RAIL;** www.amtrak.com) offers daily service to Santa Barbara. Trains arrive and depart from the **Santa Barbara Rail Station,** 209 State St. (℃ **805/963-1015**). Fares can be as low as $40 (round-trip) from Los Angeles's Union Station.

VISITOR INFORMATION   The **Santa Barbara Visitor Information Center,** 1 Santa Barbara St., Santa Barbara, CA 93101 (℃ **800/927-4688** for a free destination guide, or 805/965-3021; www.santabarbaraca.com), is on the ocean, at the corner of Cabrillo Street. The center distributes maps, brochures, an events calendar, and information. It's open Monday through Saturday from 9am to 4pm and Sunday from 10am to 4pm.

Be sure you pick up a copy of *The Independent,* Santa Barbara's free weekly, with hip articles and events listings; and *Explore Santa Barbara,* a compact visitors guide published by the local paper, *New-Press.* Both are also available at shops and sidewalk racks throughout town.

ORIENTATION   State Street, the city's primary commercial thoroughfare, is the geographic center of town. It ends at Stearns Wharf and Cabrillo Street; the latter runs along the ocean and separates the city's beaches from touristy hotels and restaurants. Electric shuttles (25¢ fare) provide frequent service along these two routes if you'd rather leave the car behind.

EXPLORING THE TOWN
HISTORIC DOWNTOWN

Following a devastating 1925 earthquake, city planners decreed that all new construction would follow codes of Spanish and mission-style architecture. In time, the adobe-textured walls, rounded archways, artfully glazed tile work and terra-cotta rooftops would come to symbolize the Mediterranean ambience that still characterizes Santa Barbara. The architecture also gave a name to the **Red Tile Tour,** a self-guided walking tour of historic downtown. The visitor center (see "Visitor Information," above) has a map and guide of the tour, which can take anywhere from 1 to 3 hours, including time to visit some of the buildings, and covers about 12 blocks in total. Some of the highlights are destinations in their own right.

Santa Barbara County Courthouse 🖈 Built in 1929, this grand "palace" is considered the local flagship of Spanish colonial-revival architecture. It's certainly the most flamboyant example, with impressive facades, beamed ceilings, striking murals, an 85-foot-high observation clock tower, and formal sunken gardens. Free guided tours are offered on Monday, Tuesday, and Friday at 10:30am and Monday through Saturday at 2pm.

1100 Anacapa St. ✆ 805/962-6464. Mon–Fri 8am–5pm; Sat, Sun, and holidays 10am–4:45pm.

Santa Barbara Museum of Art 🖈 This little jewel of a museum feels more like the private gallery of a wealthy collector. Its leaning is toward early-20th-century Western American paintings and 19th- and 20th-century Asian art, but the best displays might be the antiquities and Chinese ceramics collections. In addition, there are often visiting exhibits featuring small but excellent collections from other establishments. Free docent-led gallery tours are given Tuesday through Saturday at 1pm, and exhibition tours are given Wednesday, Thursday, and Saturday at noon.

1130 State St. ✆ 805/963-4364. www.sbmuseart.org. Admission $6 adults, $4 seniors over age 65, $3 students and children 6–17, free for children under 6. Free for all Thurs and the 1st Sun of each month. Tues–Thurs and Sat 11am–5pm, Fri 11am–9pm, Sun noon–5pm.

ELSEWHERE IN THE CITY

Santa Barbara Botanic Garden *Finds* The Botanic Garden is devoted entirely to indigenous California plants. More than 5½ miles of meandering trails on 65 acres offer glimpses of cacti, redwoods, wildflowers, and much more, many arranged in representational habitats or landscapes. The gardens were established in 1926. You'll catch the very best color and aroma just after spring showers. Docent tours are offered daily at 2pm, with additional tours on Thursday, Saturday, and Sunday at 10:30am.

1212 Mission Canyon Rd. (a short drive uphill from the mission). ✆ 805/682-4726. www.sbbg.org. Admission $5 adults, $3 children 13–18 and seniors over 60, $1 children 5–12, free for children under 5. Mon–Fri 9am–5pm, Sat–Sun 9am–6pm (closing time 1 hr. earlier Nov–Feb).

Santa Barbara Mission 🖈🖈 Established in 1786 by Father Junípero Serra and built by the Chumash Indians, this is a very rare example in physical form of the blending of Indian and Hispanic spirituality. This hilltop structure is called the "Queen of the Missions" for its twin bell towers and graceful beauty. It overlooks the town and the Channel Islands beyond. Brochures are available in six languages, and docent-guided tours can be arranged in advance ($1 extra per person).

Laguna and Los Olivos sts. ✆ 805/682-4149. www.sbmission.org. Admission $4, free for children under 12. Daily 9am–5pm.

Santa Barbara Zoological Gardens *Kids* When you're driving around the bend on Cabrillo Boulevard, look up—you might spot the head of a giraffe poking up through the palms. This zoo is a thoroughly charming, pint-size place, where all 700 animals can be seen in about 30 minutes. Most of the animals live in natural, open settings. There are also a children's Discovery Area, a miniature train ride, and a small carousel. The picnic areas (complete with barbecue pits) are underutilized and especially recommended.

500 Ninos Dr. ✆ 805/962-5339, or 805/962-6310 for a recording. www.santabarbarazoo.org. Admission $8 adults, $6 seniors and children 2–12, free for children under 2. Daily 10am–5pm; last admission 1 hr. prior to closing. Closed Thanksgiving, Dec 25.

Stearns Wharf   California's oldest working wharf attracts visitors for strolling, shopping, and snacking. There's also a Sea Center with aquariums, an outdoor touch-tank, and other exhibits. The wharf has a family-friendly atmosphere, and it's not as touristy as San Francisco's Fisherman's Wharf. Although the wharf no longer functions for passenger and freight shipping as it did when built in 1872 by local lumberman John C. Stearns, you might still see local fishing boats unloading their daily catch. You could also take a narrated sunset harbor cruise aboard the *Harbour Queen* at **Captain Don's** (© **805/969-5217**). Public parking is available on the wharf; it's free with merchant validation.

At the end of State St.

BEACHES

East Beach is Santa Barbara's favorite beach, stretching from the Zoological Gardens to Chase Palm Park and the wharf. Nearer the pier you can enjoy manicured lawns, tall palms, and abundant facilities; to the east are many volleyball courts, plus the Cabrillo Pavilion, a recreational center, bathhouse, and architectural landmark dating from 1925. Picnic areas with barbecue grills, showers, and clean, well-patrolled sands make this beach a good choice for everyone. **West Beach,** between the wharf and the harbor, has recently been dredged to create a kid-friendly water-play lagoon, conveniently located across the street from some of Santa Barbara's best family-choice hotels.

On the other side of Santa Barbara Harbor is **Leadbetter Beach,** which is less sheltered than those to the south, and thus popular with surfers. It's reached by following Cabrillo Boulevard after it turns into Shoreline Drive. This beach is also a great place to watch pleasure boats entering or leaving the harbor. Leadbetter has basic facilities, including restrooms, picnic areas, and a metered parking lot. Two miles west of Leadbetter is the secluded but popular **Arroyo Burro Beach County Park,** also known as "Hendry's Beach." This gem has a grassy park beneath the cliffs and a white crescent beach with great waves for surfing and bodysurfing. There are volleyball nets, picnic areas, restrooms, and a free parking lot.

OUTDOOR ACTIVITIES

BIKING & SURREY CYCLING   A relatively flat, palm-lined 2-mile coastal pathway, perfect for biking, runs along the beach. More adventurous riders can pedal through town (where painted bike lanes line many major routes, including one up to the mission). These routes and many more are outlined in the *Santa Barbara County Bike Map,* a free and comprehensive resource available at the visitor center (see "Essentials," above) or by calling © **805/963-7283.**

Beach Rentals, 22 State St. (© **805/966-6733**), rents well-maintained six-speed cruisers for $6 an hour or $15 for all day. It also has tandem bikes and surrey cycles that can hold as many as four adults and two children; rates vary. The place is open daily from 8am to dusk. Several other operations on the same block rent similar equipment at similar prices.

BOATING   The **Santa Barbara Sailing Center,** in Santa Barbara Harbor (© **800/350-9090** or 805/962-2826; www.sbsailctr.com), rents sailboats from 21 to 50 feet in length. Both skippered and bareboat charters are available by the day or hour. Sailing instruction for all levels of experience is also available. Coastal, island, whale-watching, dinner-cruise, and adventure tours are offered on the 50-foot sailing catamaran *Double Dolphin.*

Finds **Lotusland: Montecito's Hidden, Magical Garden**

For many Southern Californians, it's the stuff of legends: a secret, lavishly landscaped estate—open only to a select few lucky visitors—renowned for spectacular exotic plants and mysterious garden paths. But it's easier than you might expect to gain entry to **Ganna Walska Lotusland,** 695 Ashley Rd. (© **805/969-9990;** www.lotusland.org), as long as you're able to plan ahead.

Named for the estate's vivacious European-born mistress and the romantic, lotus-filled ponds that many associate with her gardens, the late Madame Walska's tony Montecito estate reflects both her eccentricity and the skill of her prestigious gardeners. She was especially fond of succulents and cacti, interspersing them artistically among native plants and decorative objects. Assembled when money was no object and import regulations were lenient (primarily in the 1940s), the garden contains priceless rare specimens, and even prehistoric plants that are extinct in the wild.

Montecito is a 5-minute freeway drive south of downtown Santa Barbara. Two-hour guided tours are conducted from mid-February to mid-November Wednesday through Sunday at 10am and 1:30pm. The tax-deductible admission fee is $15 for adults and $8 for kids ages 2 to 10. Reservations are suggested as much as 6 months in advance.

GOLF   At the **Santa Barbara Golf Club,** 3500 McCaw Ave., at Las Positas Road (© **805/687-7087**), there is a great 6,009-yard, 18-hole course with a driving range. Unlike many municipal courses, the Santa Barbara Golf Course is well maintained and presents a moderate challenge for the average golfer. Greens fees are $25 Monday through Friday and $35 on weekends ($30 for seniors). Optional carts rent for $24 for 18 holes, $14 for 9.

The 18-hole, 7,000-yard course **Sandpiper,** at 7925 Hollister Ave. (© **805/ 968-1541**), a breathtakingly scenic ocean-side course, has a pro shop and driving range. Greens fees are $68 Monday through Thursday and $108 Friday through Sunday. Carts cost $24.

HIKING   The foothill trails in the Santa Ynez Mountains above Santa Barbara are perfect for day hikes. In general, they aren't overly strenuous. Trail maps are available at **Pacific Travelers Supply,** 12 W. Anapamu St. (© **805/963-4438**), at the visitor center (see "Essentials," above), and from **Traffic Solutions** (© **805/963-7283**).

One of the most popular hikes is the **Seven Falls/Inspiration Point Trail,** an easy trek that begins on Tunnel Road, past the mission, and skirts the edge of Santa Barbara's Botanic Garden (which contains some pleasant hiking trails itself). The hike takes about 4 hours if you go all the way to Inspiration Point.

SKATING   The paved beach path that runs along Santa Barbara's waterfront is perfect for skating. **Beach Rentals,** 22 State St. (© **805/966-6733**), located near the path, rents both inline and conventional roller skates. The $5-per-hour fee includes wrist- and kneepads.

WHALE-WATCHING   Whale-watching cruises are offered between late December and late March, when Pacific gray whales pass by on migratory journeys between their breeding lagoons in Baja California, Mexico, and their Alaskan feeding grounds. **Shoreline Park,** west of the harbor, has high bluffs ideal for land-based whale spotting. Sea excursions are offered by both **Captain Don's Harbor Tours,** on Stearns Wharf (*©* **805/969-5217**), and **The Condor,** located on Cabrillo Boulevard at Bath Street (*©* **888/77-WHALE** or 805/963-3564).

SHOPPING

State Street from the beach to Victoria Street is the city's main thoroughfare and has the largest concentration of shops. Many specialize in T-shirts and postcards, but there are a number of boutiques as well. If you get tired of strolling, hop on one of the electric shuttle buses (25¢ fare) that run up and down State Street.

Also check out **Brinkerhoff Avenue** (off Cota St., between Chapala and De La Vina sts.), Santa Barbara's "antiques alley." Most shops here are open Tuesday through Sunday from 11am to 5pm. **El Paseo,** 814 State St., is a picturesque shopping arcade reminiscent of an old Spanish street. It was built around an 1827 adobe home and is lined with charming shops and art galleries. **Paseo Nuevo,** on the other side of State Street, is an equally charming modern outdoor mall, featuring familiar chain stores and inviting cafes, and anchored by an elegant branch of Nordstrom department store.

WHERE TO STAY

Before you even begin calling around for reservations, keep in mind that Santa Barbara's accommodations are expensive—especially in summer. Then decide whether you'd like to stay beachside (even more expensive) or downtown. Santa Barbara is small, but not small enough to happily stroll between the two areas.

The Convention and Visitors Bureau's one-stop reservations service, **Hot Spots** (*©* **800/793-7666** or 805/564-1637), keeps an updated list of availability for about 90% of the area's hotels, motels, inns, and B&Bs. The service will have the latest information on who might be looking to fill last-minute vacancies at reduced rates. Reservationists are available Monday through Saturday from 9am to 9pm and Sunday from 9am to 4pm. There's no charge for using the service.

VERY EXPENSIVE

Four Seasons Biltmore ★★★   This gem of the "American Riviera" manages to adhere to the most elegant standards of hospitality without making anyone feel unwelcome. It's easy to sense the ghosts of golden-age Hollywood celebs like Greta Garbo, Errol Flynn, and Bing Crosby, who used to play croquet or practice putting on the hotel's perfectly manicured lawns and then head over to the private Coral Casino Beach & Cabana Club—because that's exactly what today's privileged guests are *still* doing! In 1987, the Four Seasons company acquired this Spanish-style hacienda (ca. 1927) and tastefully restored the property without spoiling a bit of its historic charm. Rooms have an airy feel, heightened by white plantation shutters, light-wood furnishings, and full marble bathrooms with all the modern amenities. Guests can amuse themselves with a putting green, plus shuffleboard and croquet courts. In addition to two acclaimed dining rooms, the Biltmore offers a no-holds-barred Sunday brunch that draws folks from far away. Afternoon tea and evening cocktails are served in a comfortable lounge, and there's live jazz on Wednesday and Friday nights.

1260 Channel Dr. (at the end of Olive Mill Rd.), Santa Barbara, CA 93108. © 800/332-3442 or 805/969-2261. Fax 805/565-8323. www.fourseasons.com. 217 units. $295–$620 double; suites from $1,050. Extra person $35. Children 18 and under stay free in parents' room. Special midweek and package rates available. AE, DC, MC, V. Valet parking $18; free self-parking. **Amenities:** 2 dining rooms; lounge; 2 outdoor heated pools; 3 lit tennis courts; health club; spa; Jacuzzi; complimentary bikes; salon; 24-hr. room service; laundry service; dry cleaning. *In room:* A/C, TV w/pay movies, dataport, minibar, hair dryer, iron.

EXPENSIVE

El Encanto Hotel & Garden Villas ⚜ This romantic hillside retreat, whose very name means "enchantment," was built in 1915 and is made up of charming Craftsman cottages and Spanish bungalows. Uphill from the mission and surrounded by an exclusive older residential community, El Encanto features a spectacular view, secluded nooks, peaceful gardens and lily ponds, and lush landscaping. The hotel's discreetly attentive service has made it a favorite among privacy-minded celebs. The spacious rooms are tastefully decorated in a European country style, and many have fireplaces, balconies, or patios.

1900 Lasuen Rd., Santa Barbara, CA 93103. © **800/346-7039** or 805/687-5000. Fax 805/687-3903. www.elencantohotel.com. 83 units. $229–$269 double; from $379 suite. AE, DC, MC, V. Valet parking $10. **Amenities:** Restaurant; lounge; outdoor heated pool; outdoor tennis court; access to nearby health club; concierge; business center; room service 6am–10pm; in-room massage; babysitting; laundry service; dry cleaning. *In room:* TV, dataport, minibar, coffeemaker, hair dryer, iron.

Simpson House Inn Bed & Breakfast ⚜⚜ Simpson House is truly something special. Rooms within the 1874 Historic Landmark main house are decorated to Victorian perfection, with extras ranging from a claw-foot tub and antique brass shower to skylight and French doors opening to the masterfully manicured gardens. Romantic cottages are nestled throughout the grounds. The rooms have everything you could possibly need, but most impressive are the extras: the gourmet Mediterranean hors d'oeuvres and Santa Barbara wines served every evening; the enormous video library; and the heavenly full gourmet breakfast (delivered, for detached cottages, on delicate china). Fact is, the Simpson House goes the distance—and then some—to create the perfect stay. Although this property is packed into a relatively small space, it still manages an ambience of country elegance and exclusivity—especially if you book one of the cottages. *Note:* Some rooms don't come with a TV/VCR, but you can have one by request.

121 E. Arrellaga St. (between Santa Barbara and Anacapa sts.), Santa Barbara, CA 93101. © **800/676-1280** or 805/963-7067. Fax 805/564-4811. www.simpsonhouseinn.com. 14 units. $215–$435 double; $500–$550 suite/cottage. 2-night minimum on weekends. Rates include full gourmet breakfast and evening wine and hors d'oeuvres. AE, DISC, MC, V. Free parking. **Amenities:** Complimentary bikes; concierge; in-room massage; laundry service; dry cleaning. *In room:* A/C, TV/VCR, dataport, coffeemaker, minibar, hair dryer, iron.

MODERATE

Casa del Mar Inn at the Beach A half block from the beach (sorry, no views), Casa del Mar is an excellent-value Spanish-architecture motel with one- and two-room suites. The largish rooms have relatively new furnishings, with plenty of pastels. The flower-sprinkled grounds are well maintained, with an attractive sun deck (but no swimming pool), and the staff is eager to please. Many rooms have kitchenettes, and a dozen different room configurations guarantee something to suit your needs (especially families). Guests get discounts at a nearby day spa, and golf packages can be arranged. *Tip:* Despite the hotel's dizzying rate structure, rooms can often be an unexpected bargain. Also check its website for frequent Internet-only specials.

18 Bath St., Santa Barbara, CA 93101. ⓒ **800/433-3097** or 805/963-4418. Fax 805/966-4240. www.casa delmar.com. 21 units. Memorial Day to Labor Day $164–$234 double, $204–$309 suite; Sept–Oct and Mar–May $124–$194 double, $164–$264 suite; Nov–Feb $109–$194 double, $149–$264 suite. Rates include continental breakfast and wine-and-cheese social. Extra person $10. AE, DC, DISC, MC, V. Free parking. From northbound U.S. 101, exit at Cabrillo, turn left onto Cabrillo, and head toward the beach; Bath is the 2nd street on the right after the wharf. From southbound U.S. 101, take the Castillo exit and turn right on Castillo, left on Cabrillo, and left on Bath. Pets accepted with $10 fee. **Amenities:** Jacuzzi; in-room massage; laundry service; dry cleaning. *In room:* TV, fridge and kitchen or kitchenette in some units, coffeemaker, hair dryer, iron.

Hotel Oceana ⭐ New on the scene in 2002, this is the sister property to Santa Monica's Oceana, a sophisticated and upscale boutique hotel. Here they've kicked it down a notch, eschewing ultra-service and amenity-laden suites for a lighter, more beach-friendly feel that still offers a more upscale experience than the surrounding budget motels—but without the expensive price tag. The Oceana "compound"—a low-rise amalgam of four formerly independent motel properties—deftly maintains its vintage-era architecture and charm (including splendid original tile work) while injecting contemporary comforts and a breezy, colorful coastal style. Chic Frette linens and designer furniture unify the diverse layouts of all completely remodeled rooms, and provide a serene counterpoint to the bustle of Cabrillo Boulevard and East Beach outside the front door. (You'll also be walking distance from State St., Stearns Wharf, and the harbor.) Ocean-view rooms come at a premium, but I almost prefer the quieter garden- or poolside rooms. Breakfast is available each morning for a nominal fee, and the original Sambo's coffee shop is just next door for economical breakfast and lunch.

202 W. Cabrillo Blvd., Santa Barbara, CA 93101. ⓒ **800/965-9776** or 805/965-4577. Fax 805/965-9937. www.hoteloceana.com. 122 units. $175–$350 double; $400 suite. Seasonal discounts available based on occupancy. AE, DISC, MC, V. Valet parking $8. **Amenities:** Breakfast room; 2 outdoor pools; Jacuzzi; spa and fitness center; room service 11:30am–9pm; laundry/dry cleaning service. *In room:* TV w/pay movies, CD player, dataport, minibar, hair dryer, iron.

The Upham Hotel and Country House This conveniently located inn combines the intimacy of a B&B with the service of a small hotel. Built in 1871, the Upham is the oldest continuously operating hostelry in Southern California. At some point the management made time for upgrades, though, because guest accommodations are complete with all the other modern comforts. My favorites are the charming cottage rooms, each with a private garden entrance and cozy fireplace. The hotel is constructed of redwood, with sweeping verandas and a Victorian cupola on top. It has a warm lobby, a cozy restaurant, and a resident cat named Henry.

1404 De La Vina St. (at Sola St.), Santa Barbara, CA 93101. ⓒ **800/727-0876** or 805/962-0058. Fax 805/ 963-2825. www.uphamhotel.com. 50 units. $150–$275 double; from $290 suite. Rates include continental breakfast and afternoon wine and cheese. AE, DC, MC, V. Free parking. **Amenities:** Restaurant; laundry service; dry cleaning. *In room:* TV, hair dryer, iron.

INEXPENSIVE

All the best buys fill up fast in the summer months, so be sure to reserve your room in advance—even if you're just planning to stay at the decent, reliable **Motel 6** (ⓒ **800/466-8356** or 805/564-1392) near the beach.

Franciscan Inn *Value* The Franciscan is nestled in a quiet neighborhood just a block from the beach, near Stearns Wharf. This privately owned and meticulously maintained hotel is an affordable retreat with enough frills that you'll still feel pampered. The small but comfy rooms feature a country-tinged decor and finely tiled bathrooms. Services include morning newspaper and free local calls.

Most second-floor rooms have unobstructed mountain views, and some suites feature fully equipped kitchenettes. All in all, the inn stacks up as a great family choice that's classy enough for a romantic weekend too.

109 Bath St. (at Mason St.), Santa Barbara, CA 93101. ℂ 805/963-8845. Fax 805/564-3295. www. franciscaninn.com. 53 units. Summer (mid-May to mid-Sept) $95–$134 double, $145–$250 suite; winter $75–$120 double, $110–$200 suite. Extra person $8. Rates include continental breakfast and afternoon refreshments. AE, DC, MC, V. Free parking. **Amenities:** Heated outdoor pool; Jacuzzi; coin-op laundry; laundry service; dry cleaning. *In room:* A/C, TV/VCR, dataport, kitchenette in some suites, coffeemaker, hair dryer, iron.

WHERE TO DINE
EXPENSIVE

bouchon santa barbara ★★ CALIFORNIA   You can tell this warm and inviting restaurant is passionate about wine just from the name—*bouchon* is the French word for "wine cork." And not just any wines, but those of the surrounding Santa Barbara County. In fact, there are 50 different Central Coast wines available by the glass. Have some fun by enhancing each course with a glass (or half-glass) of wine—knowledgeable servers stand by to help make the perfect match. Chef Charles Fredericks's seasonally composed—and regionally inspired—menu has included dishes such as smoked Santa Barbara albacore "carpaccio," deliciously arranged with a tangy vinaigrette and shaved imported Parmesan; luscious sweetbread and chanterelle ragout cradled in a potato-leek basket; local venison sliced and laid atop cumin spaetzle in a shallow pond of green peppercorn-Madeira demi-glace; or monkfish saddle fragrant with fresh herbs and accompanied by a creamy fennel-Gruyère gratin. Request a table on the romantic patio, and don't miss the mouthwatering signature chocolate soufflé for dessert.

9 W. Victoria St. ℂ 805/730-1160. www.bouchonsantabarbara.com. Reservations recommended. 2- or 3-course prix fixe $38/$45. AE, DC, MC, V. Daily 5:30–10pm.

Wine Cask ★★ CALIFORNIA/ITALIAN   Take an 18-year-old wine shop, a large 1920s landmark dining room with a big stone fireplace, and outstanding Italian fare, and mix them with an attractive staff and clientele, and you've got the Wine Cask—the most popular upscale dining spot in Santa Barbara. Here you'll be treated to such heavenly creations as lamb sirloin with twice-baked au gratin potatoes. Other options include potato and prosciutto-wrapped local halibut in cioppino sauce, or grilled marinated chicken breast in a red-wine reduction with prosciutto, wild mushrooms, fresh rosemary, and sage. The wine list reads like a novel, with more than 1,000 wines (ranging $14–$1,400), and has deservedly received the *Wine Spectator* award for excellence. There's also a happy hour at the beautiful maple bar from 4 to 6pm daily.

In El Paseo Center, 813 Anacapa St. ℂ 805/966-9463. Reservations recommended. Main courses $8–$12 lunch, $18–$29 dinner. AE, DC, MC, V. Mon–Thurs 11:30am–9pm, Fri 11:30am–10pm, Sat 5:30–10pm, Sun 5:30–9pm.

MODERATE

Brophy Bros. Clam Bar & Restaurant ★★ SEAFOOD   This place is best known for its unbeatable view of the marina, but the dependable fresh seafood keeps tourists and locals coming back. Dress is casual, portions are huge, and favorites include New England clam chowder, cioppino, and any one of an assortment of seafood salads. The scampi is consistently good, as is all the fresh fish, which comes with soup or salad, coleslaw, and pilaf or french fries. A nice assortment of beers and wines is also available. *Note:* The wait at this small place can be up to 2 hours on a weekend night.

119 Harbor Way (off Cabrillo Blvd. in the Waterfront Center). © **805/966-4418.** Reservations not accepted. Main courses $9–$18. AE, MC, V. Sun–Thurs 11am–10pm, Fri–Sat 11am–11pm.

Palace Grill CAJUN/CREOLE   Strolling by this restaurant, just a stone's throw from State Street, you'll easily see why descriptions like "rollicking" and "atmosphere as hot as the food" are regularly applied to the Palace Grill. The scene extends to the sidewalk, where waiting diners thirst after Mason-jar Cajun martinis and Caribbean rum punch. Once inside, you'll find yourself part of the loud and fun atmosphere; this is not the place for meaningful dinner conversation. Try a platter of spicy blackened steak and seafood, a rich crawfish étouffée, or Creole jambalaya pasta. Be sure to save room for the renowned Southern desserts, including sweet potato-pecan pie, Florida Key lime pie, and the superstar Louisiana bread-pudding soufflé, laced with Grand Marnier and accompanied by whiskey cream sauce.

8 E. Cota St. © **805/963-5000.** www.palacegrill.com. Reservations recommended; not accepted Fri–Sat. Main courses $5–$13 lunch, $9–$25 dinner. AE, MC, V. Daily 11am–3pm; Sun–Thurs 5:30–10pm, Fri–Sat 5:30–11pm.

Pan e Vino ✦ ITALIAN   The perfect Italian trattoria, Pan e Vino offers food as authentic as you'd find in Rome. The simplest dish, spaghetti topped with basil-tomato sauce, is so delicious it's hard to understand why diners would want to occupy their taste buds with more complicated concoctions. But this kitchen is capable of almost anything. Pasta puttanesca, with tomatoes, anchovies, black olives, and capers, is always tops. Pan e Vino also gets high marks for its reasonable prices, attentive service, and casual atmosphere. Although many diners prefer to eat outside on the intimate patio, some of the best tables are in the charming, cluttered dining room.

1482 E. Valley Rd., Montecito (a 5-min. drive S of downtown Santa Barbara). © **805/969-9274.** Reservations required. Pastas $8–$10; meat and fish dishes $11–$18. AE, MC, V. Mon–Thurs 11:30am–9pm, Fri–Sat 11:30am–9:30pm, Sun 5–9pm.

INEXPENSIVE

La Super-Rica Taqueria ✦✦ MEXICAN   Looking at this street-corner shack, you'd never guess it's blessed with the Nobel Prize of cuisine: an endorsement by Julia Child. The tacos here are no-nonsense, generous portions of filling piled onto fresh, grainy corn tortillas. Try *bistec* (steak), *adobado* (marinated pork), or *gorditas* (thick corn *masa* pockets filled with spicy beans). A dollop of homemade salsa is the only adornment required. You might catch Julia lining up for Sunday's special, *pozole,* a stew of pork and hominy in red chile sauce. On Friday and Saturday, the specialty is freshly made tamales.

622 N. Milpas St. (between Cota and Ortega sts.). © **805/963-4940.** Most menu items $3–$6. No credit cards. Sun–Thurs 11am–9pm, Fri–Sat 11am–9:30pm.

Stacky's Seaside (Value SANDWICHES   Stacky's is an ivy-covered shack filled with fishnets, surfboards, and local memorabilia. The menu of sandwiches is enormous, as are most of their pita pockets, hoagies, and club sandwiches. A sign proudly proclaims HALF OF ANY SANDWICH, HALF PRICE—NO PROBLEM, and Stacky's has made a lot of friends because of it. Choices include the Santa Barbaran (roasted tri-tip and melted jack cheese on sourdough), the Rincon pita (jack and cheddar cheeses, green Ortega chiles, onions, and ranch dressing), and a hot pastrami hoagie with Swiss cheese, mustard, and onions. Stacky's also serves breakfast, featuring scrambled-egg sandwiches and south-of-the-border egg dishes. An order of crispy french fries is enough for two.

2315 Lillie Ave., Summerland (5 min. on the freeway from Santa Barbara). © **805/969-9908.** Most menu items under $6. AE, DISC, MC, V. Mon–Fri 6:30am–7:30pm, Sat–Sun 7am–7:30pm.

SANTA BARBARA AFTER DARK

To find out what's going on while you're in town, check the free weekly *Independent,* or call the following venues: the **Center Stage Theater,** upstairs at the Paseo Nuevo Shopping Center, Chapala and De La Guerra streets (© **805/963-0408**); the **Lobero Theater,** 33 E. Canon Perdido St. (© **805/963-0761**); the **Arlington Theater,** 1317 State St. (© **805/963-4408**); and the **Earl Warren Showgrounds,** at Las Positas Road and U.S. 101 (© **805/687-0766**).

At night, a young crowd spills out of the bars on lower State Street. Unless you're aching to relive your college days, it isn't likely to be your bag.

7 The Ojai Valley

35 miles E of Santa Barbara; 88 miles NW of LA

In a crescent-shaped valley between Santa Barbara and Ventura, surrounded by mountain peaks, lies Ojai (pronounced *O-*hi). It's a magical place, selected by Frank Capra as Shangri-La, the legendary utopia of his 1936 classic *Lost Horizon.* The spectacularly tranquil setting has made Ojai a mecca for artists and a particularly large population of New Age spiritualists, both drawn by the area's mystical beauty.

Life is low-key in the peaceful Ojai Valley. Perhaps the most excitement generated all year happens during the first week of June, when the **Ojai Music Festival** draws world-renowned contemporary jazz artists to perform in the Libbey Bowl amphitheater.

While in Ojai, you're bound to hear folks wax poetically about something called the "pink moment." It's a phenomenon first noticed by the earliest Native American valley dwellers, when the brilliant sunset over the nearby Pacific is reflected onto the mountainside, creating an eerie and beautiful pink glow.

ESSENTIALS

GETTING THERE   The 45-minute drive south from Santa Barbara to Ojai is along two-lane Calif. 150, a beautiful road that's as curvaceous as it is stunning. From Los Angeles, take U.S. 101 north to Calif. 33, which winds through eucalyptus groves to meet Calif. 150—the trip takes about 90 minutes. Calif. 150 is called Ojai Avenue in the town center and is the village's primary thoroughfare.

VISITOR INFORMATION   The **Ojai Valley Chamber of Commerce,** 150 W. Ojai Ave., Ojai, CA 93023 (© **805/646-8126;** www.the-ojai.org), distributes free area maps, brochures, and a *Visitor's Guide to the Ojai Valley,* which lists galleries and current events. It's open Monday through Friday from 9:30am to 4:30pm, Saturday and Sunday from 10am to 4pm. For information on the **Ojai Music Festival,** call © **805/646-2094.**

EXPLORING THE TOWN & VALLEY

Small Ojai is home to more than 35 artists working in a variety of media; most have home studios and are represented in one of several galleries in town. The best for jewelry and smaller pieces is **HumanArts,** 310 E. Ojai Ave. (© **805/646-1525**). It also has a home-accessories annex, **HumanArts Home,** 246 E. Ojai Ave. (© **805/646-8245**). Artisans band together each October for an organized **Artists' Studio Tour** (© **805/646-8126** for information). It's fun to drive from studio to studio at your own pace, meeting various artists and perhaps purchasing some of their work. Ojai's most famous resident is world-renowned Beatrice Wood, who worked up until her death in 1998 at 104 years of age. Her whimsical sculpture and luminous pottery are internationally acclaimed, and her spirit is still a driving force in Ojai.

Strolling the Spanish arcade shops downtown and the surrounding area will yield a treasure trove, including open-air **Bart's Books,** Matilija Street at Canada Street (© **805/646-3755**), an Ojai fixture for many years. Antiques hounds head for **The Antique Collection,** 236 W. Ojai Ave. (© **805/646-6688**), an indoor antiques mall packed to the rafters with treasures, trash, and everything in between.

Residents of the Ojai Valley *love* their equine companions—miles of bridle paths are painstakingly maintained, and horse-crossing signs are everywhere. If you'd like to explore the equestrian way, call the **Ojai Valley Inn's Ranch & Stables** (© **805/646-5511**).

Ojai has long been a haven for several esoteric sects of metaphysical and philosophical beliefs. The **Krotona Institute and School of Theosophy,** Calif. 33 and Calif. 150 at Hermosa Road (© **805/646-2653**), has been in the valley since moving from Hollywood in 1926, and visitors are welcome at their library and bookstore.

In the **Lake Casitas Recreation Area** (© **805/649-2233** for visitor information), the incredibly beautiful Lake Casitas boasts nearly 32 miles of shoreline and was the site of the 1984 Olympic canoeing and rowing events. You can rent rowboats and small powerboats year-round from the **boathouse** (© **805/649-2043**) or enjoy picnicking and camping by the lakeside. Because the lake serves as a domestic water supply, swimming is not allowed. From Calif. 150, turn left onto Santa Ana Road, and then follow the signs to the recreation area.

When Ronald Coleman saw Shangri-La in *Lost Horizon,* he was really admiring the Ojai Valley. To visit the breathtakingly beautiful spot where Coleman stood for his view of **Shangri-La,** drive east on Ojai Avenue, up the hill, and stop at the stone bench near the top—the view is spectacular.

WHERE TO STAY

The Moon's Nest Inn 🞳   Conveniently located a block off Ojai Avenue, this comfortable clapboard B&B was built as a schoolhouse in 1874 and is Ojai's oldest building, newly reborn as a charming bed-and-breakfast. Innkeepers Rich and Joan Assenberg have carefully preserved, replaced, or complemented the inn's historic details, and the building now boasts every modern comfort, including four private balconies. Throughout the house, from a cozy fireplace parlor to the sunny breakfast room, architectural features like crown molding are highlighted by dramatically painted walls, and the entire inn is furnished with a mix of carefully chosen antiques and high-quality contemporary pieces. A once-neglected side lawn has been transformed into a restful, tree-shaded garden retreat, complete with rock-lined pond and large trellised veranda (where breakfast is served on pleasant days). A cottage on the grounds houses a friendly beauty-and-massage salon, and guests enjoy full privileges at the Ojai Valley Athletic Club for a nominal day-use fee.

210 E. Matilija, Ojai, CA 93023. © **805/646-6635.** Fax 805/646-5665. www.moonsnestinn.com. 7 units, 5 with bathroom. $95–$145 double. Rates include breakfast and evening wine and spirits. AE, DC, DISC, MC, V. Small pets accepted with $25-per-night fee. **Amenities:** Nearby health club; bike rental; in-room massage. *In room:* A/C, no phone.

Ojai Valley Inn and Spa 🞳🞳   In 1923, famous Hollywood architect Wallace Neff designed the clubhouse that's now the focal point of this quintessentially

Californian, colonial-Spanish–style resort. The inn has carefully kept a sprawling ranch ambience while providing gracious, elegant service and amenities, along with a beautifully oak-studded Senior PGA Tour golf course. Next to the golf course, the jewel of the resort is pampering Spa Ojai, where stylish spa treatments—many modeled after Native American traditions—are administered inside a beautifully designed and exquisitely tiled Spanish-Moorish complex. Mind- and body-fitness classes, art classes, nifty workout machines, and a sparkling outdoor pool complete the relaxation choices. Many guest rooms have fireplaces, and most have sofas, writing desks, and secluded terraces or balconies that open onto expansive views of the valley and the magnificent Sierra Madre. Take advantage of the scenery with wooded jogging trails and available horseback riding. This chic country inn is worth the trip. (Always check for Internet specials, midweek rates, and AAA discounts, which can almost halve the regular room rates.)

905 Country Club Rd. (off Calif. 33), Ojai, CA 93023. ✆ **800/422-OJAI** or 805/646-5511. Fax 805/646-7969. www.ojairesort.com. 206 units. $275–$390 double; from $390 suite. Golf and spa discount packages available. AE, DC, DISC, MC, V. Free self- and valet parking. Pets accepted with $35-per-night fee, with advance notice. **Amenities:** Formal Maravilla dining room; a casual terrace grill overlooking the golf course; 2 lounges; 2 outdoor heated pools (including a 60-ft. lap pool); championship golf course; 8 tennis courts (4 night-lit); fitness center; full-service spa; Jacuzzi; complimentary bikes; children's programs ("Camp Ojai"); concierge; business center; room service 6am–11pm; in-room massage; babysitting; laundry service; dry cleaning. *In room:* A/C, TV w/pay movies and Nintendo, fax, dataport, minibar, coffeemaker, hair dryer, iron, safe.

Rose Garden Inn This classic ranch-style motel has been well maintained and presents an attractively low-key alternative to the pricey country club around the corner. Situated a few blocks from the heart of town, with rose-filled gardens that border the Ojai equestrian and walking trail, this inn has a lazy, nostalgic feel. Rooms are small but have kitchen alcoves and brand-new beds. A mismatch of functional furniture reflects this place's rustic and inexpensive nature. The Rose Garden's best feature is hidden behind mature hedges: an enormous heated swimming pool (and Jacuzzi) next to a tree-shaded yard complete with hammock. There's even a two-person redwood sauna in a mini-spa facility! Always check for seasonal specials or the "Ghost Stalking" tour package. *Note:* The rooms and cottages in back tend to be quieter than the front rooms near the street.

615 W. Ojai Ave. (at Country Club Dr.), Ojai, CA 93023. ✆ **800/799-1881** or 805/646-1434. Fax 805/640-8455. www.rosegardeninnofojai.com. 18 units. $69–$119 double; $149–$195 cottage. Extra person $10. Rate includes continental breakfast and afternoon snacks. Off-season and other discounts available. AE, DISC, MC, V. **Amenities:** Heated outdoor pool; Jacuzzi; sauna. *In room:* A/C, TV, fridge, hair dryer.

WHERE TO DINE
EXPENSIVE
L'Auberge ✿✿ FRENCH/BELGIAN Possibly the most romantic restaurant in the Ojai Valley, L'Auberge is located in a 1910 mansion with a fireplace, chandeliers, and a charming terrace with an excellent view of Ojai's famous sunset "pink moment." The dinner menu is traditional, featuring scampi, frog legs, poached sole, tournedos of beef, sweetbreads, and duckling à l'orange. The weekend brunch menu offers a selection of crepes. Service is expert and friendly, and this elegant house is an easy walk from downtown.

314 El Paseo (at Rincon St.). ✆ **805/646-2288.** Reservations recommended. Main courses $15–$20. AE, MC, V. Sat–Sun 11am–2:30pm; daily 5:30–9pm.

The Ranch House ★★★ CALIFORNIA   This restaurant has been placing an emphasis on the freshest vegetables, fruits, and herbs since opening its doors in 1965, long before this practice became a national craze. Freshly snipped sprigs from the restaurant's lush herb garden will aromatically transform your simple meat, fish, or game dish into a work of art. From an appetizer of cognac-laced liver paté served with its own chewy rye bread to desserts such as fresh raspberries with sweet Chambord cream, the ingredients always shine through. And you'll dine in a magical setting, for the Ranch House offers alfresco dining year-round on the wooden porch facing the scenic valley, as well as in the romantic garden amid twinkling lights and stone fountains.

S. Lomita Ave. ✆ 805/646-2360. www.theranchhouse.com. Reservations recommended. Main courses $20–$29. AE, DC, DISC, MC, V. Wed–Sat 5:30–8:30pm, Sun 11am–7:30pm. From downtown Ojai, take Hwy. 33 N to El Roblar Dr. Turn left, then left again at Lomita Ave.

MODERATE

Here's another choice for you: **Deer Lodge,** 2261 Maricopa Hwy. (✆ **805/646-4256;** www.ojaideerlodge.com), the latest incarnation of Ojai's favorite hippie-biker hangout on Highway 33, a few minutes north of Ojai. Nestled in the valley's gorgeous foothills, the building dates back to the Depression, when it served as a country store with bait and hunting supplies for local sportsmen, but new owners have been busy sprucing the place up and expanding to include a live stage in the bar, enclosed outdoor dining, and a hearty lodge menu with enough contemporary touches to bring in an upscale—yet adventuresome—clientele.

Suzanne's Cuisine ★★ CONTEMPORARY EUROPEAN   Enjoy a great meal in a comfortably sophisticated setting at this local fave, where every little touch bespeaks a preoccupation with quality details. Ask for a table on the covered outdoor patio, where lush greenery frames a casual setting warmed by a fireplace; when it rains, a plastic curtain descends to keep water out without losing that airy garden feel. Favorites from a seasonally changing menu include the lunch-only Southwest salad (wild, brown, and jasmine rice tossed with smoked turkey, feta cheese, veggies, and green chiles) and pepper-and-sesame encrusted ahi, served at dinner either sautéed or seared (your choice). From seafood specialties to Italian recipes from chef and owner Suzanne Roll's family, everything is fresh and natural. Veggies are crisply al dente, and even the occasional cream sauce tastes light and healthy. Don't skip dessert.

502 W. Ojai Ave. ✆ 805/640-1961. www.suzannescuisine.com. Reservations recommended. Main courses $8–$16 lunch, $12–$28 dinner. MC, V. Wed–Mon 11:30am–3pm and 5:30–8:30pm.

INEXPENSIVE

Boccali's ★ ITALIAN   This small, wood-frame restaurant, set among citrus groves, is a pastoral pleasure spot where patrons eat outside at picnic tables under umbrellas and twisted oak trees, or inside at tables covered with red-and-white checked oilcloths. Pizza is the main dish served here, topped California-style with the likes of crab, garlic, shrimp, and chicken. I think Boccali's lasagna (served piping hot *en casserole*) would win a statewide contest hands down. Fresh lemonade, squeezed from fruit plucked from local trees, is the usual drink of choice. Come hungry, and plan on sharing.

3277 Ojai–Santa Paula Rd. ✆ 805/646-6116. Reservations recommended for dinner. Pizza $9–$23; pasta $7–$15. No credit cards. Mon–Tues 4–9pm, Wed–Sun noon–9pm.

Oak Pit BBQ (Kids) BARBECUE   This stick-to-your-ribs joint on the road between Ojai and Ventura is worth building up an appetite for. The rust-colored shack doesn't have much going for it—just some gingham curtains, a few tables indoors and out, and stacks of wood for firing up the barbecue—but generous portions of slowly oak-smoked meats will have dedicated carnivores coming back for more. Barbecue tri-tip brisket, ham, pork, Cajun sausage, and chicken—they're all served up in sandwiches or full dinners, with available sides of coleslaw, potato salad, french fries, baked beans, and corn on the cob.

820 N. Ventura Ave. (Calif. 33), Oak View. (℃ **805/649-9903.** Reservations not accepted. Sandwiches $6; main courses $9–$13. AE, DISC, MC, V. Tues–Thurs and Sun 11:30am–8:30pm, Fri–Sat 11am–9pm.

8 En Route to Los Angeles: Ventura

15 miles SW of Ojai; 74 miles NW of LA

Nestled between gently rolling foothills and the sparkling blue Pacific Ocean, Ventura may not have the cultural and gastronomic appeal of Los Angeles or even nearby Santa Barbara, but it does boast the picturesque setting and clean sea breezes typical of California coastal towns. Southland antiques hounds know about Ventura's quirky collectible shops, and time-pressed vacationers zip up to charming bed-and-breakfasts just an hour from Los Angeles. Ventura is also the headquarters and main point of embarkation for Channel Islands National Park (see section 9, later in this chapter).

Most travelers don't bother exiting U.S. 101 for a closer look. But think about stopping to wile away a couple of hours around lunchtime. Sleepy Ventura's charm might even convince you to spend a night.

ESSENTIALS

GETTING THERE   If you're traveling northbound on U.S. 101, exit at California Street; southbound, take the Main Street exit. If you're coming west on Calif. 33 from Ojai, there's also a convenient Main Street exit. By the way, don't let the directions throw you off; because of the curve of the coastline, the ocean is not always to the west, but often southward.

VISITOR INFORMATION   For a visitor's guide and genial answers to any questions you might have, stop in at the **Ventura Visitors & Convention Bureau,** 89-C S. California St., Ventura, CA 93001 (℃ **800/333-2989** or 805/648-2075; www.ventura-usa.com).

EXPLORING THE TOWN

Much of Ventura's recent development has taken place inland and to the south, so many folks overlook the charming seaside **Main Street,** the town's historic center, which grew outward from the Spanish mission of San Buenaventura (see below). The best section for strolling is between the mission (to the north) and Fir Street (to the south). Both sides of the street are lined almost entirely with antiques stores, used-book stores, and charity thrift stores, making it perfect for browsing.

Although Ventura stretches south to one of California's most picturesque little harbors (the jumping-off point for the Channel Islands; see section 9), the town has its own simple **pier** at the end of California Street. Exceptionally well maintained and favored by area fishers, the charming wooden pier is the longest of its kind in California.

Mission San Buenaventura   Founded in 1782 (current buildings date from 1815) and still in use for daily services, this whitewashed and red-tile church lent its style to the contemporary civic buildings across the street. Step back in time by touring the mission's inside garden, where you can examine the antique water pump and olive press once essential to daily life here. Good for a quick history fix, the mission is small and near the rest of Ventura's action. Pick up a self-guided tour brochure in the adjacent gift shop for the modest donation of $1 per adult, 50¢ per child.

225 E. Main St. ℂ 805/643-4318. www.anacapa.net/~mission. Free admission; donations appreciated. Mon–Sat 10am–5pm, Sun 10am–4pm.

San Buenaventura City Hall This majestic neoclassical building was constructed in 1912 to serve as the Ventura County Courthouse. It sits on the hillside, regally overlooking old downtown and the ocean. To either side on Poli Street are some of Ventura's best-preserved and most ornate late-19th- and early-20th-century houses. Full of architectural detail (like the carved heads of Franciscan friars adorning the facade) inside and out, City Hall can be fully explored by escorted tour.

501 Poli St. ℂ 805/658-4726. Guided tours $7 adults, free for children 6 and under. 1-hr. tours given May–Sept Sat 11am–1pm.

Ventura County Museum of History & Art This museum is worth visiting for its rich Native American Room, filled with Chumash treasures, and its Pioneer Room, which contains a collection of artifacts from the Mexican-American War (1846–48). The art gallery features revolving exhibits of local painters and photographers, and the museum has an enormous archive (20,000 and counting) of photos depicting Ventura County from its origins to the present. There is also a small archaeological museum across Main Street from the main building. Allow 1 to 2 hours for your visit.

100 E. Main St. ℂ 805/653-0323. www.vcmha.org. Admission $4 adults, $3 seniors 62 and over and AAA members, $1 kids 6–17, free for children under 6. Tues–Sun 10am–5pm.

WHERE TO STAY

Bella Maggiore Inn The Bella Maggiore is an intimate Italian-style small hotel whose simply furnished rooms (some with fireplaces, balconies, or bay-window seats) overlook a romantic courtyard or roof garden. The style is Mediterranean casual, with shuttered windows, ceiling fans, and fresh flowers in every room. An open-air center courtyard is the inn's focal point, with stone fountains and flowering trees. Complimentary breakfast is served downstairs at Nona's Courtyard Cafe, which also offers dinner and weekday lunches. A kind of European elegance pervades all but the reasonable rates here.

67 S. California St. (half a block S of Main St.), Ventura, CA 93001. ℂ **800/523-8479** or 805/652-0277. 24 units. $75–$175 double; $150 suite. Extra person $10. Rates include full breakfast and afternoon refreshments and appetizers. AE, DISC, MC, V. **Amenities:** Restaurant; wine bar; laundry service; dry cleaning. *In room:* TV, dataport.

Holiday Inn Beach Resort *(Kids* One of the nicer Holiday Inns we've seen, this waterfront high-rise enjoys some spectacular views courtesy of its 12 stories. Because there's little else around as tall, nearly every room has a panoramic view of the sea or Ventura's pretty foothills—or both! Situated on the boardwalk that runs between the pier and the fairgrounds, the hotel is also within easy walking distance of historic downtown Ventura. There's excellent beach access, a heated outdoor pool facing the ocean, a couple of nearby restaurants in addition to the hotel's coffee shop, plus bike and surrey rentals right outside the front door. Ride up to the top floor and check out the hotel's circular ballroom; its adjacent cocktail lounge is oh-so-perfect for sunset gazing. Guest rooms are decent and thoroughly renovated but otherwise unremarkable.

450 E. Harbor Blvd. (at California St.), Ventura, CA 93001. ✆ **800/HOLIDAY** or 805/648-7731. Fax 805/653-6202. 260 units. $100–$110 double. AE, DC, DISC, MC, V. **Amenities:** Restaurant; 3 lounges; heated outdoor pool; 24-hr. exercise room; bike rental; game room; business center; room service; coin-op laundry and laundry service; dry cleaning. *In room:* A/C, TV w/pay movies, dataport, hair dryer, iron.

La Mer European Bed & Breakfast ✦ Perfect for a romantic getaway, La Mer is an 1890 Cape Cod–style home with a spectacular view of the ocean from the parlor and two of the five guest rooms, each of which is furnished in a different international style. Whether you choose the "Madame Pompadour" French chamber with wood-burning stove, the "Vienna Woods" Austrian hideaway with sunken bathtub, or one of three other rooms, you'll love this cozy little cottage. It offers generous activity packages for couples, which can include gourmet candlelit dinners, cruises to Anacapa Island, country carriage rides, therapeutic massages . . . or all of the above.

411 Poli St. (W of City Hall), Ventura, CA 93001. ✆ **805/643-3600.** Fax 805/653-7329. www.lamerbnb.com. 5 units (4 with private entrance). $115–$185 double. Rates include full breakfast and complimentary wine in-room. MC, V. No children accepted. **Amenities:** In-room massage. *In room:* No phone.

WHERE TO DINE

Eric Ericsson's SEAFOOD/AMERICAN Having already established a reputation in Ventura for crowd-pleasing seafood, Ericsson's moved to this pier-top spot in 1997. Here scruffy beachgoers mingle with suited business folk at lunch, sports fans and 20-somethings scarf down appetizers at cocktail hour, families come early for generous dinners, and couples on dates linger at window tables until closing. The staggering array of seafood includes clams, oysters, mussels, shrimp, scallops, cod, halibut, lobster, and calamari. Add specialties like Mexican cioppino or traditional clambake, plus plenty of non-fish and vegetarian dishes, and it's impossible to imagine anyone being stumped by this menu.

668 Harbor Blvd. (on the Ventura Pier). ✆ 805/643-4783. Reservations suggested on weekends. Main courses $7–$15 lunch; most full dinners $12–$28. AE, MC, V. Sun–Thurs 11am–10pm, Fri–Sat 11am–11pm.

Rosarito Beach Cafe ✦ MEXICAN The Rosarito Beach Cafe really packs them into this 1938 Aztec Revival Moderne building and its welcoming outdoor patio. In-the-know diners bring their palates for superb Baja-style cuisine (whose tangy elements are borrowed from the Caribbean), delicious handmade tortillas, and a culinary sophistication rare in modest Ventura.

692 E. Main St. (at Fir St.). ✆ 805/653-7343. Reservations recommended. Main courses $10–$19. AE, MC, V. Tues–Sat 11am–3pm; Tues–Thurs and Sun 4:30–9pm, Fri–Sat 4:30–10pm.

71 Palm Restaurant COUNTRY FRENCH Situated in a charmingly restored 1905 Craftsman, this ambitious little restaurant is still working out some of the details, but its country-French menu is a pleasant change of pace in town. Upstairs tables have an ocean view, while downstairs diners are warmed by a crackling fire. Stick with bistro basics like steak au poivre with crispy pommes frites, Provençal lamb stew, or country paté served with crusty bread and tangy cornichons. And don't miss the antique-filled original restrooms.

71 N. Palm St. (between Main and Poli sts.). ✆ 805/653-7222. www.71palm.com. Reservations recommended. Main courses $11–$19. AE, DISC, MC, V. Mon–Fri 11:30am–2pm; Mon–Sat 5–9pm.

9 Channel Islands National Park

Approximately 40 miles W (offshore) of Ventura

There's nothing like a visit to the Channel Islands for discovering the sense of awe explorers must have felt more than 400 years ago. It's miraculous what

25 miles of ocean can do, for compared to the mainland, this is wild and empty land. Whether you approach the islands by sea or air, you'll be bowled over by how untrammeled they remain despite neighboring Southern California's teeming masses.

Channel Islands National Park encompasses the five northernmost islands of the eight-island chain: Santa Barbara, Anacapa, Santa Cruz, Santa Rosa, and San Miguel. The park also protects the ocean 1 nautical mile offshore from each island, thereby prohibiting oil drilling, shipping, and other industrial uses.

The islands are the meeting point of two distinct marine ecosystems: The cold waters of Northern California and the warmer currents of Southern California swirl together here, creating an awesome array of marine life. On land, the relative isolation from mainland influences has allowed distinct species, like the island fox and the night lizard, to develop and survive here. The islands are also the most important seabird nesting area in California and home to the biggest seal and sea-lion breeding colony in the United States.

ESSENTIALS

VISITOR INFORMATION   Each of the five islands is relatively distinct and difficult to reach. Odds are, you're only going to visit one island on a given trip, so it's a good idea to study your options before going. Visit the **Channel Islands National Park Headquarters and Visitor Center,** 1901 Spinnaker Dr., Ventura, CA 93001 (© **805/658-5700;** www.nps.gov/chis), to get acquainted with the various programs and individual personalities of the islands through maps and displays. Rangers run interpretive programs both on the islands and at the center year-round.

GETTING THERE   **Island Packers,** next door to the visitor center at 1867 Spinnaker Dr. (© **805/642-7688** for recorded information, 805/642-1393 for reservations; www.islandpackers.com), is the park's concessionaire for boat transportation to and from the islands.

If you want to get to Santa Rosa in a hurry, **Channel Islands Aviation,** 305 Durley Ave., Camarillo (© **805/987-1678**), will fly you there in one of its small, fixed-wing aircraft. If you just want a quick overflight and maybe a picnic stop with a short hike, **Heli-Tours, Inc.,** at the Santa Barbara Airport (© **805/964-0684**), offers 3- to 4-hour excursions to Santa Cruz Island.

There are no park fees, but getting to the islands is expensive—anywhere from $32 to $120 per person—since you must go by boat or plane. Island Packers will take you on a range of regularly scheduled boat excursions, from 3½-hour non-landing tours of the islands ($24 per person) or full-day tours of individual islands led by naturalists ($32–$49 per person) to 2-day excursions to two islands ($245). Private yachts and commercial dive and tour boats from all over Southern California also visit the park on a regular basis.

THE WEATHER   While the climate is mild, with little variation in temperature year-round, the weather in the islands is always unpredictable. Thirty-mile-per-hour winds can blow for days, or sometimes a fog bank will settle in and smother the islands for weeks at a time. Winter rains can turn island trails into mud baths. In general, plan on wind, lots of sun (bring sunscreen), cool nights, and the possibility of hot days. Water temperatures are in the 50s and 60s (10–20°C) year-round. If you're camping, bring a good tent—if you don't know the difference between a good and a bad tent, the island wind will gladly demonstrate it for you.

CAMPING   Camping is permitted on all the park-owned islands, but is limited to a certain number of campers per night, depending on the island. Fires and pets are prohibited on all the islands. You must bring everything you'll need; there are no supplies on any of the islands. To reserve free camping permits for any of the islands, call © **800/365-CAMP** or log on to http://reservations. nps.gov.

EXPLORING THE ISLANDS

SANTA BARBARA   As you come upon Santa Barbara Island after a typical 3-hour crossing, you'll think that someone took a single, medium-size, grassy hill, ringed it with cliffs, and plunked it down in the middle of the ocean. When you drop anchor, you'll realize that your initial perception is basically on target. Landwise, there's just not a lot here. But the upside is that, of all the islands, Santa Barbara gives you the best sense of what it's like to be stranded on a desert isle. Being on Santa Barbara, far enough out to sea that the mainland is almost invisible, gives you an idea of just how immense the Pacific really is.

Other than the landing cove, there's no access to the water's edge. The snorkeling in the chilly cove is great. You can hike the entire 640-acre island in a few hours; then it's time to stare out to sea. You won't be let down. The cliffs and rocks are home to elephant seals, sea lions, and swarms of seabirds such as you'll never see on the mainland. There's also a small campground, pit toilets, and a tiny museum chronicling island history. Camping is available year-round, but Island Packers only schedules boats to Santa Barbara in summer and fall (see "Essentials," above).

ANACAPA   Most people who visit the park come to Anacapa. It's only 14½ nautical miles from Ventura, an easy half-day trip. At only 1.1 square miles, Anacapa—actually three small islets divided by narrow stretches of ocean—is only marginally larger than Santa Barbara and, consequently, not a place for those who need a lot of space to roam around. Only East Anacapa is open to visitors, as the other two islets are important brown-pelican breeding areas. Several trails on the island will take you to beautiful overlooks of clear-watered coves and wild ocean. **Arch Rock,** a natural land bridge, is visible from the landing cove, where you'll clamber up 154 stairs to the island's flat top.

Camping is allowed on East Anacapa year-round, but don't bring more than you can carry the half mile from the landing cove. Bring earplugs and steer clear of the foghorn, which can cause permanent hearing damage. Most of the waters around the island, including the landing cove, are protected as a National Marine Preserve, where divers can look but not take anything. Pack a good wet suit, mask, fins, and snorkel; you can dive right off the landing-cove dock.

SANTA CRUZ   By far the biggest of the islands—nearly 100 square miles—Santa Cruz is also the most diverse. It has huge canyons, year-round streams, beaches, cliffs, the highest mountain in the Channel Islands (2,400 ft.), now-defunct early cattle and sheep ranches, and Native American Chumash village sites—2,000 Chumash were probably living on the island when Cabrillo first visited in 1542. The island also hosts seemingly endless displays of flora and fauna, including 650 species of plants, nine of which are endemic; 140 land-bird species; and a small group of other land animals, including the island fox.

Most of the island is still privately owned: The Nature Conservancy holds the western nine-tenths. When the park service took over the eastern end from the Gherini family, who had owned a sheep ranch here, it eliminated the island's formerly exorbitant landing and camping fees, but also eliminated the Channel Islands' only non-camping overnight options—lodges that are being converted into interpretive centers.

Valdez Cave (also known as Painted Cave for its colorful rock types, lichens, and algae) is the largest and deepest known sea cave in the world. The huge cave stretches nearly a quarter of a mile into the island and is nearly 100 feet wide. The entrance ceiling rises 160 feet, and in the spring, a waterfall tumbles over the opening. Located on the northwest end of the island, the cave can only be entered via dinghy or kayak.

SANTA ROSA   Windy Santa Rosa also has a strong ranching past—one that ended in 1998 in a storm of controversy that pitted the National Park Service against both environmental groups and the 97-year-old Vail & Vickers cattle ranch. The cows are all gone now, taking with them a slice of history and leaving uncertainty that nature's balance can ever be restored on Santa Rosa. Santa Rosa is home to a large concentration of endangered plant species, 34 of which occur only on the islands. And like Santa Cruz, Santa Rosa is home to the diminutive island fox, a tiny cousin of the gray fox that has become nearly fearless as it has evolved in the predator-free island environment. They'll walk right through your camp if you let them. Santa Rosa also has great beaches, a benefit somewhat outweighed by the nearly constant winds.

SAN MIGUEL   People often argue about what's the wildest place left in the lower 48 states. They bat around names like Montana, Colorado, and Idaho. Curiously, no one ever thinks to consider San Miguel. They should, for this 9,500-acre island is a wild, wild place. The wind blows constantly, and the island can be shrouded in fog for days at a time. Human presence is definitely not the status quo here.

Visitors land at Cuyler Harbor, a half-moon shaped cove on the island's east end. Arriving here is like arriving on earth the day it was made: perfect water, perfect sand, outrageously blue water. Seals bask on the offshore rocks. The island's two most interesting features are the **Caliche Forest,** a sort of petrified forest left when the wind exposed sandstone casts of a forest that once stood on the island, and **Point Bennett,** the outrageous-sounding (and smelling) breeding ground of six separate species of seals and sea lions. In winter, thousands carpet the beach; their barking is deafening.

The waters around San Miguel are the richest and most dangerous of all the islands. The island is exposed to wave action from all sides. Many ships have sunk here. A 3-foot-tall stone cross stands in memory of Juan Rodríguez Cabrillo, the Spanish explorer credited with discovering the Channel Islands in 1542. Although his grave has never been found, Cabrillo is believed to be buried on the island.

Island Packers's schedule to San Miguel is sporadic in summer and almost nonexistent in winter, so call ahead. Primitive camping is allowed near the ranger's residence, but no potable water is available, and fires are prohibited.

THE EXTRA MILE: EXPLORING THE COASTLINE & WATERS OFF THE CHANNEL ISLANDS

DIVING   A good portion of Channel Islands National Park is underwater. In fact, twice as many visitors come annually to dive the waters than ever set foot on the islands. Scuba divers come here from all over the globe for the chance to explore stunning kelp forests, shipwrecks, and underwater caves, all with the best visibility in California. Everything from sea snails and urchins to orcas and great white sharks call these waters home.

Truth Aquatics, in Santa Barbara (© 805/962-1127; www.truthaquatics. com), is the best provider of single- and multi-day dive trips to all the islands. **Ventura Dive & Sport** (© 805/650-6500) also leads trips, including a "Discover Program" that allows novice and uncertified divers to explore the waters accompanied by an instructor. **Channel Islands Scuba** (© 805/644-3483) and **Pacific Scuba** (© 805/984-2566) also lead regular trips, as do boats from San Pedro and other Southern California ports.

SEA KAYAKING   One of the best ways to explore the fascinating coastline of the islands is by kayak. Warren Glaser of **OAARS** (Outdoor and Aquatic Recreation Specialist), based in Ventura (© 805/642-2912), leads small group tours by sea kayak to all five Channel Islands. The trips allow you to explore sea caves and rock gardens. Channel crossing by charter boat, brief lessons, and lunch are included. Fares generally run $125 per person. Three-day adventures to Santa Rosa, with meals, campsite, and guide included, are offered for $295. **Aqua Sports** (© 805/968-7231) and **Paddle Sports** (© 805/899-4925) also lead similar excursions, or trips can be arranged through **Island Packers** (© 805/ 642-7688 for recorded information, 805/642-1393 for reservations; www. islandpackers.com).

13

Los Angeles

by Matthew Richard Poole

The entire world knows what Los Angeles looks like. It's a real-life version of one of those souvenir postcard folders that spill out images accordion-style: tall palm trees sweeping an azure sky; the "Hollywood" sign gleaming huge and white against a shrub-blanketed hillside; freeways flowing like concrete rivers across the landscape; a lone surfer, silhouetted against the sunset's glow, riding the day's last wave. These seductive images are just a few of many that bring to mind the city that just about everyone loves to hate—and should experience, at least once.

Los Angelenos know their city will never have the sophisticated style of Paris or the historical riches of London—but they cheerfully lay claim to living in the most fun city in the United States, maybe the world. Home to the planet's first amusement park, LA regularly feels like one, as the line between fantasy and reality is often obscured. From the unattainable, anachronistic glamour of Beverly Hills to the earthy, often-scary street energy of Venice, each of the city's diverse neighborhoods is like a mini-theme park, offering its own kind of adventure. The colors of this city seem a little bit brighter—and more surreal—than they do in other cities, the angles just a little sharper. Drive down Sunset Boulevard and you'll see what I mean. The billboards are racier, the fashions sexier, the cars fancier, the sun brighter, and the energy higher than anyplace you've ever been. Darlin', you're not in Kansas anymore—you're in La-La Land now.

1 Orientation

ARRIVING
BY PLANE
LAX & the Other Los Angeles–Area Airports

There are five airports in the Los Angeles area. Most visitors fly into **Los Angeles International Airport** (© 310/646-5252; www.lawa.org/lax/laxframe. html), better known as LAX. This behemoth is situated ocean-side, between Marina del Rey and Manhattan Beach. LAX is a convenient place to land; it's located within minutes of Santa Monica and the beaches, and not more than a half-hour from Downtown, Hollywood, and the Westside. Despite its size, the eight-terminal airport has a straightforward, easy-to-understand design. Free blue, green, and white **Airline Connections shuttle buses** (© 310/646-2911) connect the terminals and stop in front of each ticket building. Special minibuses accessible to travelers with disabilities are also available. **Travelers Aid of Los Angeles** (© 310/646-2270; www.tasla.org) operates booths in each terminal. You can find extensive information about LAX—including maps, parking and shuttle-van information, and links to weather forecasts—online at **www. lawa.org**. All car-rental agencies are in the neighborhood surrounding LAX, within a few minutes' drive; each provides a complimentary shuttle to and from the airport.

For some travelers, one of the area's smaller airports might be more convenient than LAX. **Burbank-Glendale-Pasadena Airport,** 2627 N. Hollywood Way, Burbank (© **818/840-8840;** www.burbankairport.com), is the best place to land if you're headed for Hollywood or the valleys—and it's even closer to downtown LA than LAX. The small airport has especially good links to Las Vegas and other southwestern cities. **Long Beach Airport,** 4100 Donald Douglas Dr., Long Beach (© **562/570-2678;** www.lgb.org), south of LAX, is the best place to land if you're visiting Long Beach or northern Orange County and want to avoid LA. **John Wayne Airport,** 19051 Airport Way N., Anaheim (© **949/252-5200;** www.ocair.com), is closest to Disneyland, Knott's Berry Farm, and other Orange County attractions. **Ontario International Airport,** Terminal Way, Ontario (© **909/975-5360;** www.lawa.org/ont/ontframe.html), is not a popular airport for leisure travelers; businesspeople use it to head to San Bernardino, Riverside, and other inland communities. It's convenient if you're heading to Palm Springs, and also a viable choice if you're staying in Pasadena.

Getting into Town from LAX

BY CAR   To reach Santa Monica and other northern beach communities, exit the airport, take Sepulveda Boulevard north, and follow the signs to Calif. 1 (Pacific Coast Hwy., or PCH) north.

To reach Redondo, Hermosa, Newport, and the other southern beach communities, take Sepulveda Boulevard south, then follow the signs to Calif. 1 (Pacific Coast Hwy., or PCH) south.

To reach Beverly Hills or Hollywood, exit the airport via Century Boulevard, then take I-405 north to Santa Monica Boulevard east.

To reach Downtown or Pasadena, exit the airport, take Sepulveda Boulevard south, then take I-105 east to I-110 north.

BY SHUTTLE   Many city hotels provide free shuttles for their guests; ask when you make reservations. **SuperShuttle** (© **800/554-3146** or 310/782-6600; www.supershuttle.com) offers regularly scheduled minivans from LAX to any location in the city. The fare can range from about $15 to $35 per person, depending on your destination. It's cheaper to cab it to most places if you're a group of three or more, but the vans are far more comfortable; you might have to stop at other passengers' destinations before you reach your own. Reservations aren't needed for your arrival, but required for a return to the airport.

BY TAXI   Taxis line up outside each terminal. Rides are metered. Expect to pay about $35 to Hollywood and Downtown, $25 to Beverly Hills, $20 to Santa Monica, and $45 to $60 to the Valley and Pasadena, *including* a $2.50 service charge for rides originating at LAX.

BY RAIL   Budget-minded travelers heading to Downtown, Universal City, or Long Beach can take LA's Metro Rail service from LAX. An airport shuttle can take you to the Green Line light rail station; from there, connections on the Blue and Red Lines can get you where you're headed; it's a good idea to contact your hotel for advice on the closest station. The service operates from 5am to midnight and the combined fare is under $2—but you should be prepared to spend 1 to 2 hours in transit. Contact the **Los Angeles County Metropolitan Transit Authority** (MTA) at © **213/626-4455** or www.mta.net for information.

BY BUS   The city's MTA buses also go between LAX and many parts of the city. MTA's seven direct routes from LAX are much faster than Metrorail. Call

Southern California at a Glance

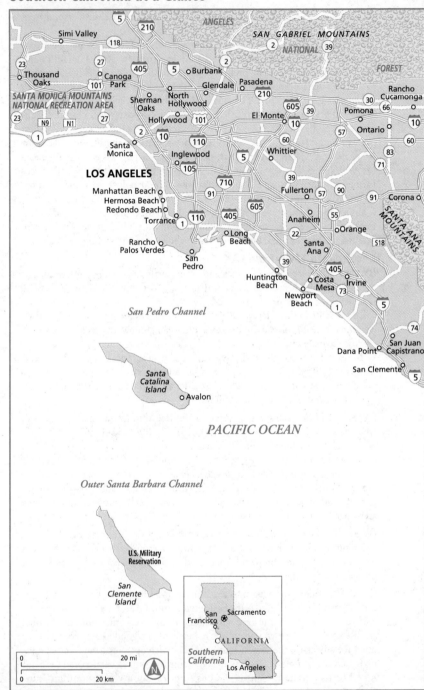

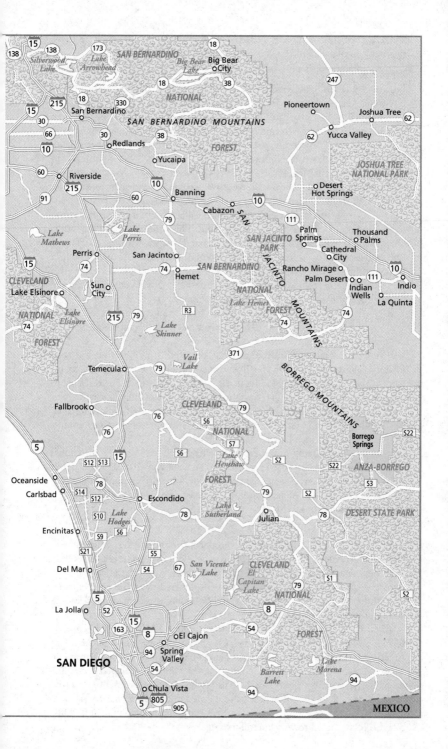

MTA Airport Information at ℂ 213/626-4455 or check their website at www. mta.net for schedules and fares.

BY CAR

Los Angeles is well connected to the rest of the United States by several major highways. Among them are Interstate 5, which enters the state from the north; Interstate 10, which originates in Jacksonville, Florida, and terminates in Los Angeles; and U.S. 101, a scenic route that follows the Western seaboard from Los Angeles north to the Oregon state line. If you're planning to take smaller roads, call the **California Highway Patrol** (ℂ 323/906-3400) to check road conditions before heading out.

If you're driving **from the north,** you have two choices: the quick route, along I-5 through the middle of the state, or the scenic route along the coast. Heading south along I-5, you'll pass a small town called Grapevine. This marks the start of the mountain pass with the same name. Once you've reached the southern end of the pass, you'll be in the San Fernando Valley, which is the start of Los Angeles County. To reach the beach communities and LA's Westside, take I-405 south; to get to Hollywood, take Calif. 170 south to U.S. 101 south (this route is called the Hollywood Fwy. the entire way); I-5 will take you along the eastern edge of Downtown and into Orange County.

If you're taking the **scenic coastal route** from the north, take U.S. 101 to I-405 or I-5, or stay on U.S. 101, following the instructions above to your destination.

If you're approaching **from the east,** you'll be coming in on I-10. For Orange County, take Calif. 57 south. I-10 continues through Downtown and terminates at the beach. If you're heading to the Westside, take I-405 north. To get to the beaches, take Calif. 1 (PCH) north or south, depending on your destination.

From the south, head north on I-5. At the southern end of Orange County, I-405 splits off to the west; take this road to the Westside and beach communities. Stay on I-5 to reach Downtown and Hollywood.

Here are some **driving times:** From Phoenix, it's about 350 miles, or 6 hours (okay, 7, if you drive the speed limit) to Los Angeles via I-10. Las Vegas is 265 miles northeast of Los Angeles (about a 4- or 5-hr. drive). San Francisco is 390 miles north of Los Angeles on I-5 (between 6 and 7 hr.), and San Diego is 115 miles (about 2 hr.) south.

BY TRAIN

Amtrak (ℂ 800/USA-RAIL; www.amtrak.com) connects Los Angeles with about 500 American cities. As with plane travel along popular routes, fares fluctuate depending on season and special promotions. As a general rule, heavily restricted advance tickets are competitive with similar airfares. Remember, however, those low fares are for coach travel in reclining seats; private sleeping accommodations cost substantially more.

The LA train terminus is **Union Station,** 800 N. Alameda (ℂ 213/624-0171), on Downtown's northern edge. Completed in 1939, this was the last of America's great train depots—a unique blend of Spanish Revival and Streamline Moderne architecture. From the station, you can take one of the taxis that line up outside, board the Metro Red Line to Hollywood or Universal City, or the Metro Blue Line to Long Beach. If you're headed to the San Fernando Valley or Anaheim, Metrolink commuter trains leave from Union Station; call ℂ 800/371-LINK or log on to www.metrolinktrains.com.

BY BUS

Bus travel is an inexpensive and often flexible option. **Greyhound** (© **800/ 229-9424;** www.greyhound.com) can get you to LA from anywhere and offers several money-saving multiday passes. The main station for arriving buses is downtown at 1716 E. Seventh St., east of Alameda; it's a seedy section of town, but access to the station is restricted to ticket holders. For additional area terminal locations, contact Greyhound or check their website.

VISITOR INFORMATION
INFORMATION CENTERS

The **Los Angeles Convention & Visitors Bureau** (© **800/366-6116,** events hot line 213/689-8822; www.lacvb.com) is the city's main source for information. In addition to maintaining an informative website and answering telephone inquiries, the bureau provides a **walk-in visitor center** at 685 S. Figueroa St., Downtown. It's open Monday through Friday from 8am to 5pm and Saturday from 8:30am to 5pm.

Many Los Angeles–area communities also have their own information centers, and often maintain detailed and colorful websites. The **Beverly Hills Visitors Bureau,** 239 S. Beverly Dr. (© **800/345-2210** or 310/248-1015; www. bhvb.org), is open Monday through Friday from 9am to 5pm. The **West Hollywood Convention and Visitors Bureau,** 8687 Melrose Ave., M-26, West Hollywood, CA 90096 (© **800/368-6020** or 310/289-2525; www.visitwest hollywood.com), is open Monday through Friday from 8am to 6pm. The **Santa Monica Convention & Visitors Bureau** (© **310/393-7593;** www.santa monica.com), is the best source for information about Santa Monica. Their Palisades Park walk-up center is located near the Santa Monica Pier, at 1400 Ocean Ave. (between Santa Monica Blvd. and Broadway), and is open daily from 10am to 5pm. The **Pasadena Convention and Visitors Bureau,** 171 S. Los Robles Ave. (© **626/795-9311;** www.pasadenavisitor.org), is open Monday through Friday from 8am to 5pm and Saturday from 10am to 4pm.

LOCAL MEDIA SOURCES

Local tourist boards are great for information regarding attractions and special events, but they often fail to keep a finger on the pulse of what's really happening, especially with regard to dining, culture, and nightlife. Several city-oriented newspapers and magazines offer more up-to-date info. *LA Weekly* (www. laweekly.com), a free listings magazine, is packed with information on current

---

Tips LA's California Welcome Center

If you're the type that likes to load up on tourist information before you start exploring a city, you'll want to make a beeline for the **California Welcome Center** (© **310/854-7616**). Located at the Beverly Center (a massive shopping mall) on Beverly Boulevard between La Cienega and San Vicente boulevards near the Hard Rock Cafe, the center offers a wealth of useful tourist information as well as direct and same-day ticket purchases to LA's main attractions, museums, and entertainment venues. But wait, there's more: The "travel counselors" at the center also answer just about any question you have regarding the city, as well as foreign-language assistance and translations, a hotel-reservation service, and maps of LA and California. It's open daily from 10am to 6pm.

events around town. It's available from sidewalk news racks and in many stores and restaurants around the city; it also has a lively website.

The *Los Angeles Times* **"Calendar"** section of the Sunday paper is an excellent guide to the world of entertainment in and around LA, with listings of what's doing and where to do it. The *Times* also maintains a comprehensive website at **www.calendarlive.com**; once there you can find departments with names like "Southland Scenes," "Tourist Tips," "Family & Kids," and "Recreation & Fitness." Information is culled from the newspaper's many departments and is always up-to-date. If you want to check out LA's most immediate news, the *Times*'s main website is **www.latimes.com**.

Los Angeles magazine (www.lamag.com) is a glossy city-based monthly full of real news and pure gossip, plus guides to LA's art, music, and food scenes. Its calendar of events, which has been improving lately, gives an excellent overview of goings-on at museums, art galleries, musical venues, and other places. The magazine is available at newsstands around town and in other major U.S. cities; you can also access stories and listings from the current issue on the Internet. Web surfers should visit @LA's website at **www.at-la.com**; its exceptional search engine (one of my favorite tools) provides links to more than 23,000 sites relating to the LA area, including many destinations covered in chapter 14.

CITY LAYOUT

Los Angeles is not a single compact city, but a sprawling suburbia comprising dozens of disparate communities. Most of the communities are located between mountains and ocean, on the flatlands of a huge basin. Even if you've never visited LA before, you'll recognize the names of many: Hollywood, Beverly Hills, Santa Monica, and Malibu. Ocean breezes push the city's infamous smog inland, toward dozens of less well-known residential communities, and through mountain passes into the sprawl of the San Fernando and San Gabriel valleys.

Downtown Los Angeles—which, by the way, isn't where most tourists go—is in the center of the basin, about 12 miles east of the Pacific Ocean. Most visitors spend the bulk of their time either on the coast or on the city's Westside. (See "Neighborhoods in Brief," below, for details on all the city's sectors.)

MAIN ARTERIES & STREETS

LA's extensive system of toll-free, high-speed freeways connects the city's patchwork of communities. The system works well to get you where you need to be, although rush-hour (roughly 7–9am and 4–6pm) traffic can be bumper-to-bumper. Here's an overview (best read with an LA map in hand):

U.S. 101, called the "Ventura Freeway" in the San Fernando Valley and the "Hollywood Freeway" in the city, runs across LA in a roughly northwest-southeast direction, from the San Fernando Valley to the center of Downtown.

Calif. 134 continues as the "Ventura Freeway" after U.S. 101 turns into the city and becomes the Hollywood Freeway. This branch of the Ventura Freeway continues directly east, through the valley towns of Burbank and Glendale, to I-210 (the "Foothill Fwy."), which takes you through Pasadena and out toward the eastern edge of Los Angeles County.

I-5, otherwise known as the "Golden State Freeway" north of I-10 and the "Santa Ana Freeway" south of I-10, bisects Downtown on its way from Sacramento to San Diego.

I-10, labeled the "Santa Monica Freeway" west of I-5 and the "San Bernardino Freeway" east of I-5, is the city's major east-west freeway, connecting the San Gabriel Valley with Downtown and Santa Monica.

I-405, known as the "San Diego Freeway," runs north-south through LA's Westside, connecting the San Fernando Valley with LAX and southern beach areas. This is one of the area's busiest freeways.

I-105, Los Angeles's newest freeway—called the "Century Freeway"—extends from LAX east to I-605.

I-110, commonly known as the "Harbor Freeway," starts in Pasadena as Calif. 110 (the "Pasadena Fwy."); it becomes an interstate in Downtown Los Angeles and runs directly south, where it dead-ends in San Pedro. The section that is now the Pasadena Freeway was Los Angeles's first freeway, known as the Arroyo Seco when it opened in 1940.

I-710, aka the "Long Beach Freeway," runs in a north-south direction through East Los Angeles and dead-ends at Long Beach.

I-605, the "San Gabriel River Freeway," runs roughly parallel to the I-710 farther east, through the cities of Hawthorne and Lynwood and into the San Gabriel Valley.

Calif. 1—called "Highway 1," the "Pacific Coast Highway," or simply "PCH"—is really more of a scenic parkway than a freeway. It skirts the ocean, linking all of LA's beach communities, from Malibu to the Orange Coast.

A complex web of surface streets complements the freeways. From north to south, the major east-west thoroughfares connecting Downtown to the beaches are **Sunset Boulevard, Santa Monica Boulevard, Wilshire Boulevard,** and **Olympic, Pico,** and **Venice boulevards.** The section of Sunset Boulevard from Crescent Heights Boulevard to Doheny Drive is the famed **Sunset Strip.**

NEIGHBORHOODS IN BRIEF

Los Angeles is a very confusing city, with fluid neighborhood lines and equally elastic labels. I've found that the best way to grasp the city is to break it into six regions—Santa Monica & the Beaches, Westside LA & Beverly Hills, Hollywood, Downtown, the San Fernando Valley, and Pasadena & Environs—each of which encompasses a more-or-less distinctive patchwork of city neighborhoods and independently incorporated communities.

Santa Monica & the Beaches

These are nearly everyone's favorite LA communities. The 60-mile beachfront stretching from Malibu to the Palos Verdes Peninsula has milder weather and less smog than the inland communities, and traffic is nominally lighter, except on summer weekends. The towns along the coast all have a distinct mood and charm. They're listed below from north to south:

Malibu, at the northern border of Los Angeles County, 25 miles from Downtown, was once a privately owned ranch—purchased in 1857 for 10¢ an acre. Today its wide beaches, sparsely populated hills, and relative remoteness from the inner city make it popular with rich recluses. Indeed, the resident lists of Malibu Colony and nearby Broad Beach—oceanfront strips of closely packed mansions—read like a who's who in Hollywood. With plenty of green space and dramatic rocky outcroppings, Malibu's rural beauty is unsurpassed in LA and surfers flock to "The 'Bu" for great, if crowded, waves.

Pretty **Santa Monica,** Los Angeles's premier beach community, is known for its long ocean pier, artsy atmosphere, and somewhat wacky residents. It's also noted for its acute homelessness problem. The city has taken great pains to alleviate the situation and the Third Street Promenade, a pedestrian-only outdoor mall lined with excellent shops and

Santa Monica & the Beaches

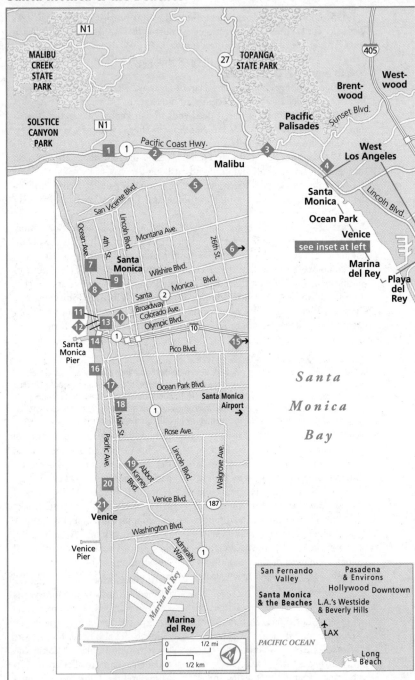

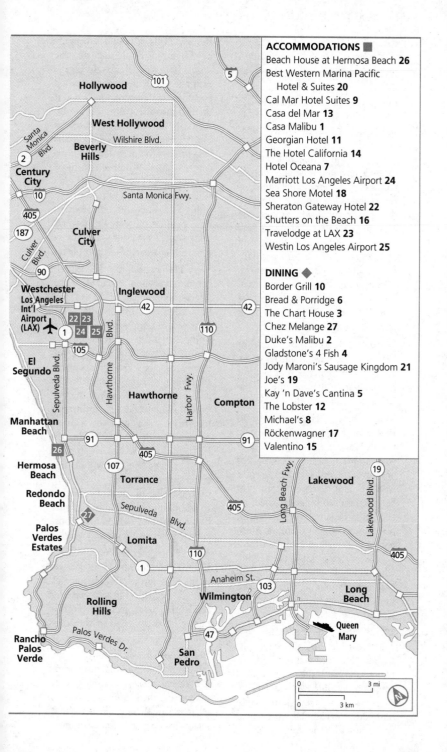

ACCOMMODATIONS ■
Beach House at Hermosa Beach **26**
Best Western Marina Pacific
    Hotel & Suites **20**
Cal Mar Hotel Suites **9**
Casa del Mar **13**
Casa Malibu **1**
Georgian Hotel **11**
The Hotel California **14**
Hotel Oceana **7**
Marriott Los Angeles Airport **24**
Sea Shore Motel **18**
Sheraton Gateway Hotel **22**
Shutters on the Beach **16**
Travelodge at LAX **23**
Westin Los Angeles Airport **25**

DINING ◆
Border Grill **10**
Bread & Porridge **6**
The Chart House **3**
Chez Melange **27**
Duke's Malibu **2**
Gladstone's 4 Fish **4**
Jody Maroni's Sausage Kingdom **21**
Joe's **19**
Kay 'n Dave's Cantina **5**
The Lobster **12**
Michael's **8**
Röckenwagner **17**
Valentino **15**

restaurants, is one of the country's most successful revitalization projects.

Venice, a planned community in the spirit of its Italian forebear, was constructed with a series of narrow canals connected by quaint one-lane bridges. It had become infested with grime and crime, but gentrification is now in full swing, bringing scores of great restaurants and boutiques and rising property values for the quaint canal-side homes and apartment duplexes. Some of LA's most innovative and interesting architecture lines funky Main Street. But without question, Venice is best known for its Ocean Front Walk, a nonstop circus of skaters, vendors, and poseurs of all ages, colors, types, and sizes.

Marina del Rey, just south of Venice, is a somewhat quieter, more upscale community best known for its small-craft harbor, one of the largest of its kind in the world.

Manhattan, Hermosa, and **Redondo beaches** are laid-back, mainly residential neighborhoods with modest homes (except for oceanfront real estate), mild weather, and residents happy to have fled the LA hubbub. There are excellent beaches for volleyball players, surfers, and sun worshippers here, but when it comes to cultural activities, pickings can be slim. The restaurant scene, while limited, has been improving steadily and some great new bars and clubs have opened near their respective piers.

LA's Westside & Beverly Hills

The **Westside,** an imprecise, misshapen L, sandwiched between Hollywood and the city's coastal communities, includes some of Los Angeles's most prestigious neighborhoods, virtually all with names you're sure to recognize:

Beverly Hills is bounded roughly by Olympic Boulevard on the south, Robertson Boulevard on the east, and the districts of Westwood and Century City on the west; it extends into the hills to the north. Politically distinct from the rest of Los Angeles, this famous enclave is best known for its palm-tree-lined streets of palatial homes and high-priced shops. But it's not all glitz and glamour; the healthy mix of filthy rich, wannabes, and tourists that peoples downtown Beverly Hills creates a unique—and sometimes snobby-surreal—atmosphere.

West Hollywood is a key-shaped community whose epicenter is the intersection of Santa Monica and La Cienega boulevards. It's bounded on the west by Doheny Drive and on the south roughly by Melrose Avenue. The tip of the key extends east for several blocks north and south of Santa Monica Boulevard as far as La Brea Avenue, but West Hollywood is primarily located to the west of Fairfax Avenue. Nestled between Beverly Hills and Hollywood, this politically independent town can feel either tony or tawdry, depending on which end of the city you're in. In addition to being home to some of the area's best restaurants, shops, and art galleries, West Hollywood is the center of LA's gay community.

Bel Air and **Holmby Hills,** located in the hills north of Westwood and west of Beverly Hills, are wealthy residential areas featured prominently on most maps to the stars' homes.

Brentwood is best known as the famous backdrop to the O. J. Simpson melodrama. If Starbucks ever designed a neighborhood, this is what it would look like—a quiet, relatively upscale mix of homes,

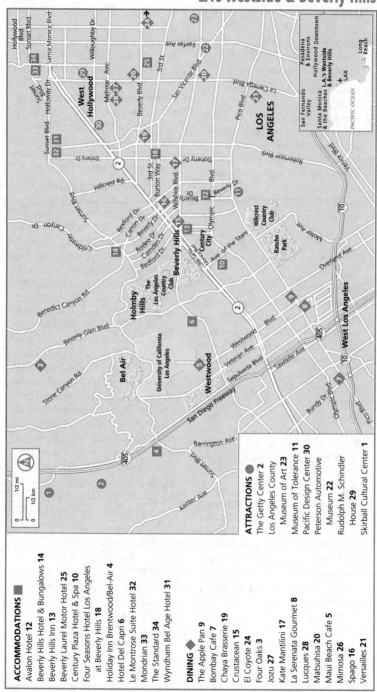

LA's Westside & Beverly Hills

ACCOMMODATIONS

Avalon Hotel **12**
Beverly Hills Hotel & Bungalows **14**
Beverly Hills Inn **13**
Beverly Laurel Motor Hotel **25**
Century Plaza Hotel & Spa **10**
Four Seasons Hotel Los Angeles
at Beverly Hills **18**
Holiday Inn Brentwood/Bel-Air **4**
Hotel Del Capri **6**
Le Montrose Suite Hotel **32**
Mondrian **33**
The Standard **34**
Wyndham Bel Age Hotel **31**

DINING

The Apple Pan **9**
Bombay Cafe **7**
Chaya Brasserie **19**
Crustacean **15**
El Coyote **24**
Four Oaks **3**
Jozu **27**
Kate Mantilini **17**
La Serenata Gourmet **8**
Lucques **28**
Matsuhisa **20**
Maui Beach Cafe **5**
Mimosa **26**
Spago **16**
Versailles **21**

ATTRACTIONS

The Getty Center **2**
Los Angeles County
Museum of Art **23**
Museum of Tolerance **11**
Pacific Design Center **30**
Peterson Automotive
Museum **22**
Rudolph M. Schindler
House **29**
Skirball Cultural Center **1**

restaurants, and strip malls. It's west of I-405 and north of Santa Monica and West Los Angeles. The Getty Center looms over Brentwood from its hilltop perch next to I-405.

Westwood, an urban village that is home to the University of California at Los Angeles (UCLA), is bounded by I-405, Santa Monica Boulevard, Sunset Boulevard, and Beverly Hills. It used to be a hot destination for a night on the town, but has lost much of its appeal due to overcrowding, general rudeness, and even some minor street violence. There's still a high concentration of movie theaters here, but I'm waiting for Westwood to regain its old charm.

Century City is a compact, busy, rather bland high-rise area sandwiched between West Los Angeles and Beverly Hills. It was once the back lot of 20th Century Fox studios. The primary draws here are the Shubert Theatre and the Century City Marketplace, a pleasant (though ugly) open-air mall. Century City's three main thoroughfares are Century Park East, Avenue of the Stars, and Century Park West; the area is bounded on the north by Santa Monica Boulevard and on the south by Pico Boulevard.

West Los Angeles is a label that generally applies to everything that isn't one of the other Westside neighborhoods. It's basically the area south of Santa Monica Boulevard, north of Venice Boulevard, east of Santa Monica and Venice, and west and south of Century City.

Hollywood

Yes, they still come. Young hopefuls with stars in their eyes are attracted to this town like moths fluttering to the glare of neon lights. But Hollywood is much more a state of mind than a glamour center. Many of the neighborhood's former movie studios have moved to more spacious venues in Burbank, on the Westside, and in other parts of the city.

For our purposes, the label "Hollywood" extends beyond the worn central area of Hollywood itself to the surrounding neighborhoods. It encompasses everything between Western Avenue to the east and Fairfax Avenue to the west and from the Hollywood Hills south.

Hollywood itself, which centers on Hollywood and Sunset boulevards (between La Brea and Vine), is the historic heart of LA's movie industry. Visitors have always flocked to see landmark attractions like the star-studded Walk of Fame and Mann's Chinese Theatre. Hollywood Boulevard is showing signs of rising out of a seedy slump, with refurbished movie houses and stylish restaurants and clubs making a fierce comeback. The centerpiece "Hollywood & Highland" complex anchors the neighborhood, with shopping, entertainment, and a luxury hotel built around the beautiful new Kodak Theater designed to host the Academy Awards (really, you'll want to poke your head into this theater).

Melrose Avenue, scruffy but fun, is the city's funkiest shopping district, catering to often-raucous youths with secondhand- and avant-garde clothing shops—there are also several appealing restaurants in between.

The stretch of Wilshire Boulevard running through the southern part of Hollywood is known as the **Mid-Wilshire** district, or Miracle Mile. It's lined with contemporary apartment houses and office buildings. The section just east of Fairfax Avenue, known as Museum Row, is home to almost a dozen museums, including the Los Angeles County

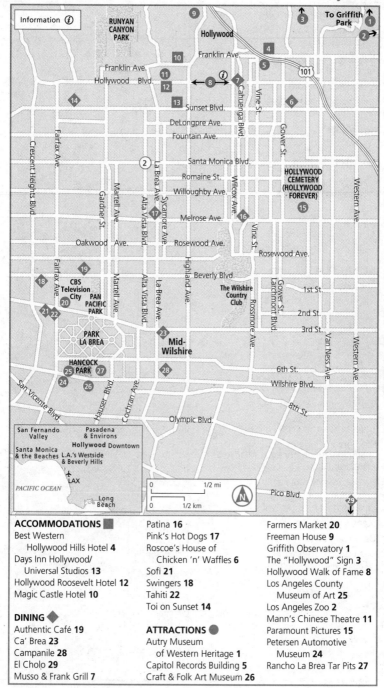

Hollywood

Information ⓘ

RUNYAN CANYON PARK

To Griffith Park

Hollywood

Franklin Ave.

Franklin Ave.
Hollywood Blvd.

Sunset Blvd.

DeLongpre Ave.

Fountain Ave.

Santa Monica Blvd.

Romaine St.

Willoughby Ave.

Melrose Ave.

Rosewood Ave.

Oakwood Ave.

Rosewood Ave.

Beverly Blvd.

HOLLYWOOD CEMETERY (HOLLYWOOD FOREVER)

CBS Television City

PAN PACIFIC PARK

The Wilshire Country Club

1st St.

2nd St.

3rd St.

PARK LA BREA

Mid-Wilshire

HANCOCK PARK

6th St.

Wilshire Blvd.

8th St.

Olympic Blvd.

San Fernando Valley

Pasadena & Environs

Santa Monica & the Beaches

Hollywood Downtown

L.A.'s Westside & Beverly Hills

PACIFIC OCEAN

LAX

Long Beach

Pico Blvd.

0   1/2 mi
0   1/2 km

Fairfax Ave.
Crescent Heights Blvd.
Gardner St.
Martell Ave.
La Brea Ave.
Alta Vista Blvd.
Sycamore Ave.
Highland Ave.
Cahuenga Blvd.
Vine St.
Wilcox Ave.
Vine St.
Rossmore Ave.
Gower St.
Larchmont Blvd.
Gower St.
Van Ness Ave.
Western Ave.
Western Ave.
Hauser Blvd.
Cochran Ave.
San Vicente Blvd.

ACCOMMODATIONS ▪

Best Western
  Hollywood Hills Hotel **4**
Days Inn Hollywood/
  Universal Studios **13**
Hollywood Roosevelt Hotel **12**
Magic Castle Hotel **10**

DINING ◆

Authentic Café **19**
Ca' Brea **23**
Campanile **28**
El Cholo **29**
Musso & Frank Grill **7**

Patina **16**
Pink's Hot Dogs **17**
Roscoe's House of
  Chicken 'n' Waffles **6**
Sofi **21**
Swingers **18**
Tahiti **22**
Toi on Sunset **14**

ATTRACTIONS ●

Autry Museum
  of Western Heritage **1**
Capitol Records Building **5**
Craft & Folk Art Museum **26**

Farmers Market **20**
Freeman House **9**
Griffith Observatory **1**
The "Hollywood" Sign **3**
Hollywood Walk of Fame **8**
Los Angeles County
  Museum of Art **25**
Los Angeles Zoo **2**
Mann's Chinese Theatre **11**
Paramount Pictures **15**
Petersen Automotive
  Museum **24**
Rancho La Brea Tar Pits **27**

Downtown Los Angeles

ACCOMMODATIONS ■

Hotel Figueroa **23**

Hotel Stillwell **21**

Millennium Biltmore Hotel Los Angeles **18**

Westin Bonaventure Hotel & Suites **16**

Wyndham Checkers Hotel **19**

DINING ◆

Cha Cha Cha **1**

Ciudad **15**

The Original Pantry Cafe **22**

Philippe the Original **4**

R23 **9**

Traxx **6**

Water Grill **20**

ATTRACTIONS ●

Angelino Heights **2**

The Bradbury Building **13**

California Science Center **25**

Central Library **17**

Chinatown **3**

City Hall **10**

El Pueblo de Los Angeles Historic District (Olvera Street) **5**

Grand Central Market **14**

Japanese American National Museum **8**

Museum of Contemporary Art/
Geffen Contemporary at MOCA **7**
Main Building **12**

Natural History Museum of Los Angeles County **25**

Performing Arts Center of L.A. County **11**

Staples Center **24**

Union Station **6**

University of Southern California (USC) **25**

W. Temple St.
2
1
S. Virgil Ave.
Commonwealth Ave.
Hoover St.
Benton Way
Rampart Blvd.
LAFAYETTE PARK
MACARTHUR PARK
Westmoreland Ave.
S. Hoover St.
W. 8th St.
W. 9th St.
San Marino St.
Westlake Ave.
S. Burlington Ave.
Bonnie Brae St.
S. Union Ave.
W. 11th St.
W. 12th St.
W. Pico Blvd.
Magnolia Ave.
W. Venice Blvd.
W. Washington Blvd.
W. 20th St.
10
Santa Monica Freeway
110
W. 23rd St.
Information
Parking P
0
1/2 mi
0
.5 km
N
25

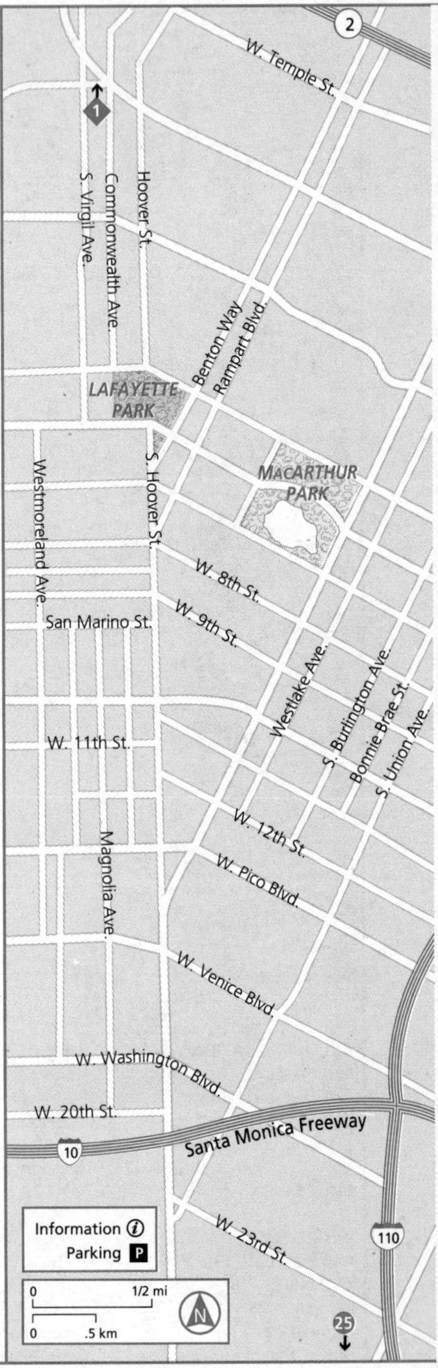

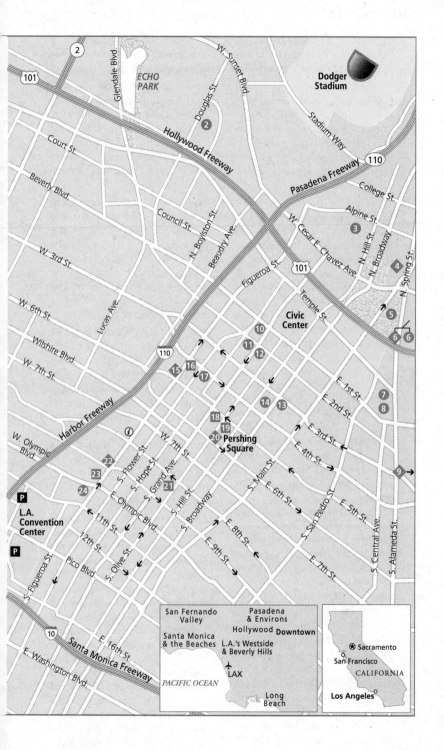

Museum of Art, the La Brea Tar Pits, and that shrine to LA car culture, the Petersen Automotive Museum.

Griffith Park, up Western Avenue in the northernmost part of Hollywood, is one of the country's largest urban parks, home to the Los Angeles Zoo, the famous Griffith Observatory, and the outdoor Greek Theater.

Downtown

Roughly bounded by the U.S. 101, I-110, I-10, and I-5 freeways, LA's Downtown is home to a tight cluster of high-rise offices, the El Pueblo de Los Angeles Historic District, and the neighborhoods of Koreatown, Chinatown, and Little Tokyo. The construction of skyscrapers—bolstered by earthquake-proof technology—transformed Downtown into the business center of the city. Despite the relatively recent construction of numerous cultural centers (such as the Music Center and the Museum of Contemporary Art) and a few hip restaurants, it isn't the hub that it would be in most cities. The Westside, Hollywood, and the beach communities are all far more popular.

For our purposes, the residential neighborhoods of Silver Lake and Los Feliz, Exposition Park (home to Los Angeles Memorial Coliseum, the LA Sports Arena, and several Downtown museums), and East and South Central LA, the city's famous barrios, all fall under the Downtown umbrella.

El Pueblo de Los Angeles Historic District, a 44-acre ode to the city's early years, is worth a visit. **Chinatown** is small and touristy, but can be plenty of fun for souvenir hunting or traditional dim sum. **Little Tokyo,** on the other hand, is a genuine gathering place for the South-

land's Japanese population, with a wide array of shops and restaurants with an authentic flair.

Silver Lake, a residential neighborhood just north of Downtown, and adjacent **Los Feliz,** just to the west, have arty areas with unique cafes, theaters, graffiti, and art galleries— all in equally plentiful proportions. The local music scene has been burgeoning of late.

Exposition Park, south and west of Downtown, is home to the Los Angeles Memorial Coliseum and the L.A. Sports Arena, as well as the Natural History Museum, African-American Museum, and the California Science Center. The University of Southern California (USC) is next door.

East and **South Central LA,** just east and south of Downtown, are home to the city's large barrios. This is where the 1992 LA riots were centered. These neighborhoods are, without question, quite unique, though they contain few tourist sites (the Watts Towers being a notable exception). This can be a rough part of town, so be smart and alert if you decide to visit, particularly at night.

The San Fernando Valley

The San Fernando Valley, known locally as "the Valley," was nationally popularized in the 1980s by the notorious mall-loving "Valley Girl" stereotype. Snuggled between the Santa Monica and San Gabriel mountain ranges, most of the Valley is residential and commercial and off the beaten track for tourists. But some of its attractions are bound to draw you over the hill. **Universal City,** located west of Griffith Park between U.S. 101 and Calif. 134, is home to Universal Studios Hollywood and the trippy shopping-and-entertainment complex CityWalk. And you may make

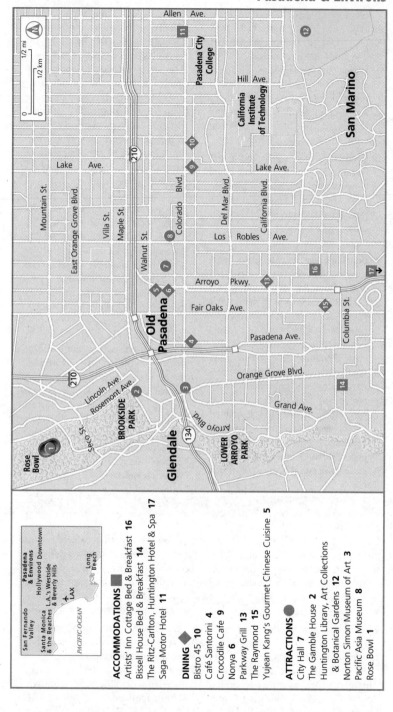

Pasadena & Environs

Allen Ave.

Pasadena City College

Hill Ave.

California Institute of Technology

San Marino

Lake Ave.

210

Lake Ave.

Mountain St.

East Orange Grove Blvd.

Villa St.

Maple St.

Colorado Blvd.

Del Mar Blvd.

California Blvd.

Los Robles Ave.

Walnut St.

Arroyo Pkwy.

Fair Oaks Ave.

Columbia St.

Old Pasadena

Pasadena Ave.

Orange Grove Blvd.

Lincoln Ave.

Rosemont Ave.

BROOKSIDE PARK

Seco St.

Grand Ave.

Arroyo Blvd.

LOWER ARROYO PARK

210

134

Glendale

Rose Bowl

1/2 mi

1/2 km

San Fernando Valley

Santa Monica & the Beaches

L.A.'s Westside & Beverly Hills

Hollywood Downtown

Pasadena & Environs

PACIFIC OCEAN

LAX

Long Beach

ACCOMMODATIONS ■
Artists' Inn Cottage Bed & Breakfast **10**
Bissell House Bed & Breakfast **16**
The Ritz-Carlton, Huntington Hotel & Spa **17**
Saga Motor Hotel **11**

DINING ◆
Bistro 45 **7**
Café Santorini **4**
Crocodile Cafe **9**
Nonya **6**
Parkway Grill **13**
The Raymond **15**
Yujean Kang's Gourmet Chinese Cuisine **5**

ATTRACTIONS ●
City Hall **7**
The Gamble House **2**
Huntington Library, Art Collections
& Botanical Gardens **12**
Norton Simon Museum of Art **3**
Pacific Asia Museum **8**
Rose Bowl **1**

a trip to **Burbank,** west of these other suburbs and north of Universal City, to see one of your favorite TV shows being filmed at NBC or Warner Brothers Studios. There are also a few good restaurants and shops along Ventura Boulevard, in and around Studio City. (See the "Universal City & Burbank" map, on p. 525.)

Glendale is a largely residential community north of Downtown between the Valley and Pasadena. Here you'll find Forest Lawn, the final act for numerous Hollywood stars.

Pasadena & Environs

Best known as the site of the Tournament of Roses Parade each New Year's Day, **Pasadena** was spared from the tear-down epidemic that swept LA, so it has a refreshing old-time feel. Once upon a time, Pasadena was every Angeleno's best-kept secret—a quiet community whose slow and careful regentrification meant excellent, unique restaurants and boutique shopping without the crowds, in a revitalized downtown respectful of its old brick and stone commercial buildings. Although the area's natural and architectural beauty still shines

through—so much so that Pasadena remains Hollywood's favorite backyard location for countless movies and TV shows— Old Town has become a pedestrian mall similar to Santa Monica's Third Street Promenade, complete with huge crowds, midrange chain eateries, and standard-issue mall stores. It still gets my vote as a scenic alternative to the congestion of central LA, but it has lost much of its small-town charm.

Pasadena is also home to the famous California Institute of Technology (Caltech), which boasts 22 Nobel Prize winners among its alumni. The Caltech-operated Jet Propulsion Laboratory was the birthplace of America's space program, and Caltech scientists were the first to report earthquake activity worldwide.

The residential neighborhoods in Pasadena and its adjacent communities—**Arcadia, La Cañada-Flintridge, San Marino,** and **South Pasadena**—are renowned for well-preserved historic homes, from humble bungalows to lavish mansions. These areas feature public gardens, historic neighborhoods, house museums, and bed-and-breakfast inns.

2 Getting Around

BY CAR

Need I tell you that Los Angeles is a car city? You're really going to need one to easily get around. An elaborate network of well-maintained freeways connects this urban sprawl, but you have to learn how to make sense of the system and cultivate some patience for dealing with the traffic. The golden rule of driving in Los Angeles is this: Always allow more time to get to your destination than you think you might need, especially during morning and evening rush hours.

RENTALS   Los Angeles is one of the cheaper places in America to rent a car. Major national car-rental companies usually rent economy- and compact-class cars for about $35 per day and $120 per week with unlimited mileage.

All the major car-rental agencies have offices at LAX and in the larger hotels. Among the national firms operating in LA are **Alamo** (© 800/462-5866), **Avis** (© 800/230-4898), **Budget** (© 800/527-0700), **Dollar** (© 800/800-3665), **Hertz** (© 800/654-3131), **National** (© 800/227-7368), and **Thrifty**

(© 800/847-4389). If you're thinking of splurging, the place to call is **Budget Beverly Hills Car Collection,** 9815 Wilshire Blvd. (© **800/227-7117** or 310/ 274-9173), which rents SUVs, exotics, and luxury cars for $130 to $600 a day (an Audi TT roadster will set you back $250).

BY PUBLIC TRANSPORTATION

There are visitors who successfully tour Los Angeles entirely by public transportation, but I can't honestly recommend that plan for most travelers. LA is a metropolis that's grown up around the automobile, and many areas are inaccessible without one. As a result, an overwhelming number of visitors rent a car for their stay. Still, if you're in the city for only a short time, are on a very tight budget, or don't expect to be moving around a lot, public transport might be for you. The city's trains and buses are operated by the **Los Angeles County Metropolitan Transit Authority** (MTA; © **213/922-2000;** www.mta.net), and MTA brochures and schedules are available at every area visitor center.

BY BUS OR SHUTTLE

Spread-out sights, sluggish service, and frequent transfers make extensive touring by bus impractical. For short hops and occasional jaunts, however, buses are economical (and environmentally correct). However, I don't recommend riding buses late at night.

The basic bus fare is $1.35 for all local lines, with transfers costing 25¢. Express buses, which travel along the freeways, and buses on inter-county routes charge higher fares; call the MTA for information.

The **Downtown Area Short Hop** (DASH) shuttle system operates buses throughout Downtown and the Westside. Service runs every 5 to 20 minutes, depending on the time of day, and costs just 25¢. Contact the Department of Transportation (© **213/808-2273;** www.ladottransit.com) for schedules and route information.

BY RAIL & SUBWAY

The **MetroRail** system is a sore subject around town. For years the MTA has been digging up the city's streets, sucking huge amounts of tax money, and pushing exhaust vents up through peaceful parkland—and for what? Let's face it, LA will never have New York's subway system or San Francisco's BART. Today, the system is still in its infancy, mainly popular with commuters from outlying suburbs. Here's an overview of what's currently in place:

The **Metro Blue Line,** an aboveground rail line, connects downtown Los Angeles with Long Beach. Trains operate daily from 6am to 9pm; the fare is $1.35.

The **Metro Red Line,** LA's first subway, has been growing since 1993 and opened a highly publicized Hollywood–Universal City extension in 2000. The line begins at Union Station, the city's main train depot, and travels west underneath Wilshire Boulevard, looping north into Hollywood and the San Fernando Valley. The fare is $1.35; discount tokens are available at Metro service centers and many area convenience stores.

The **Metro Green Line,** opened in 1995, runs for 20 miles along the center of the new I-105, the Glenn Anderson (Century) Freeway, and connects Norwalk in eastern Los Angeles County to LAX. A connection with the Blue Line offers visitors access from LAX to downtown LA or Long Beach. The fare is $1.35.

Call the **MTA** (© **213/922-2000;** www.mta.net) for information on the Metro, including construction updates and details on purchasing tokens or passes.

BY TAXI

Distances are long in Los Angeles, and cab fares are high; even a short trip can cost $10 or more. Taxis charge $1.90 at the flag drop, plus $1.60 per mile. A service charge is added to fares originating at LAX.

Except in the heart of Downtown, cabs will usually not pull over when hailed. Cabstands are located at airports, at Downtown's Union Station, and major hotels. To ensure a ride, order a taxi in advance from **Checker Cab** (© 323/654-8400), **L.A. Taxi** (© 213/627-7000), or **United Taxi** (© 213/483-7604).

 FAST FACTS: **Los Angeles**

American Express In addition to those at 327 N. Beverly Dr., Beverly Hills (© 310/274-8277), and at the Beverly Connection, 8493 W. Third St., Los Angeles (© 310/659-1682), offices are located throughout the city. To locate the one nearest you, call © 800/221-7282.

Area Codes Within the past 20 years, LA has gone from having a single (213) area code to a whopping seven—with more promised by 2003. Even residents can't keep up. As of press time, here's the basic layout: Those areas west of La Cienega Boulevard, including Beverly Hills and the city's beach communities, use the **310** area code. Portions of Los Angeles County east and south of the city, including Long Beach, are in the **562** area. The San Fernando Valley has the **818** area code, while points east—including parts of Burbank, Glendale, and Pasadena—use the newly created **626** code. What happened to 213, you ask? The Downtown business area still uses **213**. All other numbers, including Griffith Park, Hollywood, and parts of West Hollywood (east of La Cienega Blvd.) now use the new area code **323**. If it's all too much to remember, just call directory assistance at © **411**.

Babysitters If you're staying at one of the larger hotels, the concierge can usually recommend a reliable babysitter. If not, contact the **Baby-Sitters Guild** in Glendale (© **323/658-8792** or 818/552-2229), LA's oldest and largest babysitting service.

Camera Repair On-site repairs are the specialty at family-owned **General Camera Repair**, 2218 E. Colorado Blvd., Pasadena (© **626/449-4533**); they opened in 1964 at this spot on the Rose Parade route.

Dentists For a recommendation in the area, call the **Dental Referral Service** (© **800/422-8338**).

Doctors Contact the **Uni-Health Information and Referral Hotline** (© 800/922-0000) for a free, confidential physician referral.

Emergencies For police, fire, or highway patrol, or in case of life-threatening medical emergencies, dial © **911**.

Hospital The centrally located (and world-famous) **Cedars-Sinai Medical Center**, 8700 Beverly Blvd., Los Angeles (© 310/855-5000), has a 24-hour emergency room staffed by some of the country's finest MDs.

Hot Lines Alcoholics Anonymous © **323/936-4343**; Poison Hotline © 800/876-4766; National AIDS Hotline © 800/342-AIDS; Rape/Domestic Violence Hotline (L.A. Commission on Assault Against Women) © 213/626-3393; Suicide Crisis Line © **310/391-1253**.

Liquor Laws Liquor and grocery stores can sell packaged alcoholic beverages between 6am and 2am. Most restaurants, nightclubs, and bars are licensed to serve alcoholic drinks during the same hours. The legal age for purchase and consumption is 21; proof of age is required.

Newspapers & Magazines **World Book & News Co.**, at 1652 N. Cahuenga Blvd., near Hollywood and Vine and Mann's Chinese Theatre, stocks lots of out-of-town and foreign papers and magazines. No one minds if you browse through the magazines, but you'll be reprimanded for thumbing through the newspapers. It's open 24 hours.

Pharmacies **Horton & Converse** has locations around LA, including 2001 Santa Monica Blvd., Santa Monica (② **310/829-3401**); 9201 Sunset Blvd., Beverly Hills (② **323/272-0488**); and 11600 Wilshire Blvd., West Los Angeles (② **310/478-0801**). Hours vary, but the West LA location is open until 2am.

Police In an emergency, dial ② **911**. For nonemergency police matters, call ② **213/485-2121**; in Beverly Hills, dial ② **310/550-4951**.

Post Office Call ② **800/ASK-USPS** to find the one closest to you.

Taxes The combined Los Angeles County and California state sales taxes amount to 8.25%; hotel taxes add 12% to 17% to room tariffs.

Taxis See "Getting Around," above.

Time Zone Los Angeles is in the Pacific time zone, which is 8 hours behind Greenwich mean time and 3 hours behind Eastern time. Call ② **853-1212** for the correct time (operates in all local area codes).

Weather Call **Los Angeles Weather Information** at ② **213/554-1212** for the daily forecast. For beach conditions, call the **Zuma Beach Lifeguard** at ② **310/457-9701** for recorded information.

3 Where to Stay

Due to space considerations, I've had to limit the number of hotels included here. If you'd like a larger selection, check out *Frommer's Los Angeles 2003,* which has dozens of additional options.

CHOOSING A LOCATION In sprawling Los Angeles, location is everything. Choosing the right neighborhood as a base can make or break your vacation; if you plan to wile away a few days at the beach but base yourself Downtown, for example, you're going to lose a lot of valuable relaxation time on the freeway. Take into consideration where you'll want to spend your time before you commit yourself to a base. But wherever you stay, count on doing a good deal of driving—no hotel in Los Angeles is convenient to everything.

In general, **Downtown** hotels are business-oriented; they're sometimes popular with groups but are largely ignored by independent tourists. The top hotels here are very good, but cheaper ones can be downright nasty. If you're on a budget, locate elsewhere.

Hollywood, which is centrally located between Downtown and Beverly Hills and within easy reach of Santa Monica, makes a great base if you're planning to do a lot of sightseeing—but there are fewer hotels here than you'd expect. The accommodations in Hollywood are usually moderately priced and generally well maintained, but otherwise unspectacular.

Most visitors stay on the city's **Westside,** a short drive from the beach and close to many of LA's most colorful sights. The city's most elegant—and expensive— accommodations are in Beverly Hills and Bel Air. You'll find the city's best hotel values in West Hollywood, an exciting and convenient place to settle in.

Trendy, relatively smogless **Santa Monica** and its coastal neighbors are home to lots of hotels; book ahead because they fill up quickly in the summer, when everyone wants to be by the water. Santa Monica also enjoys convenient freeway access to the popular inland tourist sights. Malibu and the South Bay communities (Manhattan, Hermosa, and Redondo Beaches) are more out of the way, and hence quieter.

Families might want to head to the **San Fernando Valley** to be near Universal Studios, or straight to Anaheim or Buena Park for easy access to Disneyland and Knott's Berry Farm (see chapter 14). **Pasadena** is a charming community with some unique accommodations, but it's not a good choice if you'll need to get back and forth across town.

To locate the hotels reviewed below, see the individual neighborhood maps in section 1, "Orientation."

RATES & RESERVATIONS   The hotels listed below are categorized first by area, then by price. Rates given are the rack rates for a standard room for two people with a private bathroom (unless otherwise noted); you can often do better. Ask about weekend packages and discounts, ACCOMMODATIONS or AARP discounts, corporate rates, family plans, and any other special rates that might be available. The prices given do not include state and city hotel taxes, which run from 12% to a whopping 17%, depending on which community you're in. Be aware that many hotels charge extra for parking (with in-and-out privileges, except where noted), and some levy heavy surcharges for telephone use.

Reservations services usually work as consolidators, buying up or reserving rooms in bulk and then dealing them out to customers. They sometimes garner special rates that range from 10% to 50% off rack rates. If you don't like bargaining, this is certainly a viable option. Among the more reputable reservations services, offering both telephone and online bookings, are: **Accommodations Express** (✆ 800/950-4685; www.accommodationsexpress.com); **Hotel Reservations Network** (✆ 800/715-7666; www.hoteldiscounts.com or www.1800 96HOTEL.com); **Quikbook** (✆ 800/789-9887, includes fax-on-demand service; www.quikbook.com). You can also try booking your hotel online through **Frommers.com** (www.frommers.com) or **Expedia** (www.expedia.com).

SANTA MONICA & THE BEACHES
VERY EXPENSIVE

Casa del Mar ⭐⭐⭐   Housed in a former 1920s Renaissance Revival beach club, this Art Deco stunner is a real dream of a resort hotel, equal in every respect to big sister Shutters just down the beach (see below). Which one you prefer depends on your personal sense of style. While Shutters is outfitted like a chic, contemporary beach house, this impeccable, U-shaped villalike structure radiates period glamour. The building's shape awards ocean views to most of the guest rooms; unfortunately, windows don't open more than an inch or two (which gives Shutters, whose rooms have floor-to-ceiling windows and balconies, a slight advantage). You're unlikely to be too disappointed thanks to the gorgeous summery European-inspired decor in golds and sea-grass hues, plus abundant luxuries that include sumptuously dressed beds, big Italian marble bathrooms with extra-large whirlpool tubs and separate showers; rubber duckies and turndown teddies are playful treats. Rooms are laid out for relaxation, not business, so travelers with work on their minds should stay elsewhere.

Downstairs you'll find a big, elegant living room with ocean views, a stylish lounge, and the Oceanfront restaurant, which has earned justifiable kudos (and more than a few celebrity fans) for its lovely setting, great service, and seafood-heavy California cuisine. Outdoors, the Mediterranean-evocative Palm Terrace boasts a gorgeous Roman-style pool and Jacuzzi with spectacular ocean views.

1910 Ocean Way (next to the Santa Monica Pier), Santa Monica, CA 90405. ⓒ 800/898-6999 or 310/581-5533. Fax 310/581-5503. www.hotelcasadelmar.com. 129 units. $345–$625 double; from $875 suite. AE, DC, DISC, MC, V. Valet parking $21. **Amenities:** Restaurant; lounge; cafe; heated outdoor Roman-style pool and plunge pool; Jacuzzi; state-of-the-art health club with spa services; 24-hr. concierge; business center; 24-hr. room service; laundry service; dry cleaning. *In room:* A/C, TV/VCR, CD player, dataport, minibar, hair dryer, iron, safe.

Hotel Oceana ★★ *(Kids)*   Located right across the street from the ocean, this all-suite hotel sits alongside low-rise, high-rent condos on a gorgeous stretch of Ocean Avenue, several blocks north of the Santa Monica hubbub. With their bright Matisse-style interiors and cushy IKEA-ish furniture, the wonderful apartment-like suites are colorful, modern, and amenity laden: Goodies run the gamut from comfy robes and multiple TVs to full gourmet kitchens stocked with Wolfgang Puck microwavable pizzas, Häagen-Dazs pints, and bottles of California merlot. The enormous size of the suites—even the studios are huge—makes the Oceana terrific for families or shares. Oceanview suites feature balconies and two-person whirlpool tubs in the mammoth bathrooms, but don't feel the need to stretch your budget for a view, as all units sit garden-style around the darling courtyard, with its cushiony chaises and cute boomerang-shaped pool. Everything is fresh, welcoming, and non-institutional—the primary colors and playful modern style suits the beach location perfectly, and service is excellent—so it's no wonder advertising execs and others who could stay anywhere make the Oceana their choice for long-term stays.

849 Ocean Ave. (S of Montana Ave.), Santa Monica, CA 90403. ⓒ 800/777-0758 or 310/393-0486. Fax 310/309-2762 (reservations) or 310/458-1182. www.hoteloceana.com. 63 units. $380 studio suite; $390–$500 1-bedroom suite; $750–$800 2-bedroom suite. AE, DC, DISC, MC, V. Valet parking $21. **Amenities:** Outdoor heated pool; exercise room; access to nearby health club; watersports equipment; concierge; business center; 24-hr. room service for extended breakfast, lunch, or dinner, 7am–10pm from Wolfgang Puck Cafe; in-room massage; babysitting; laundry service; dry cleaning. *In room:* A/C, TV/VCR w/pay movies and Sega Genesis, CD player, dataport, kitchen, minibar, fridge, coffeemaker, hair dryer, iron, safe.

Shutters on the Beach ★★★   This Cape Cod–style luxury hotel enjoys one of the city's most prized locations: directly on the beach, a block from the Santa Monica Pier. Only relative newcomer Casa del Mar (see above) can compete, but Shutters bests the Casa by attaching alfresco balconies to every guest room. The beach-cottage rooms overlooking the sand are more desirable and no more expensive than those in the towers. The views and sounds of the ocean are the most outstanding qualities of the spacious, luxuriously outfitted, Cape Cod–inspired rooms, some of which have fireplaces and/or whirlpool tubs; all have floor-to-ceiling windows that open. The elegant marble bathrooms come with generous counter space and whimsies that include waterproof radios and toy whales.

A relaxed and elegant ambience pervades the contemporary art-filled public spaces, which feel like the common areas of a deluxe Montauk beach house. The small swimming pool and the sunny lobby lounge overlooking the sand are two great perches for spotting the celebrities who swear by Shutters as an alternative hangout to smoggy Hollywood. One Pico, the hotel's premier restaurant, serves modern American cuisine in a seaside setting. The best meals at the more casual Pedals Cafe come from the wood-burning grill.

1 Pico Blvd., Santa Monica, CA 90405. ℂ **800/334-9000** or 310/458-0030. Fax 310/458-4589. www. shuttersonthebeach.com. 198 units. $380–$615 double; from $895 suite. AE, DC, DISC, MC, V. Valet parking $22. **Amenities:** Restaurant; cafe; lounge; outdoor heated pool; Jacuzzi; health club with spa services; sauna; extensive beach-equipment rentals; concierge; activities desk; courtesy car; business center with secretarial services; 24-hr. room service; babysitting; laundry service; dry cleaning. *In room:* A/C, TV/VCR, CD player, dataport, hair dryer, iron, safe.

EXPENSIVE

Beach House at Hermosa Beach ★★ *(Finds)* Sporting a Cape Cod style that suits the on-the-sand location, this luxurious, romantic inn is comprised of beautifully designed and outfitted split-level studio suites. Every unit boasts a plush, furnished living room with wood-burning fireplace (Duraflame logs provided) and entertainment center; a micro-kitchen with china and flatware for four; an elevated sleeping niche with a down-dressed king bed, a second TV, and a generous work area; an extra-large bathroom with extra-deep soaking tub, a separate shower, cotton robes, and Aveda products; and a furnished balcony, many of which overlook the beach. (While sofas convert into second beds, the unit configuration is best suited to couples rather than families; more than three is too many.) Despite the summertime carnival atmosphere of the Strand, the Beach House keeps serene with double-paned windows and noise-insulated walls. The attentive staff has an easygoing attitude that suits the property perfectly. While LA's city center is an easy half-hour's drive away, charming Hermosa is airport-convenient and ideal for a beach getaway.

1300 The Strand, Hermosa Beach, CA 90254. ℂ **888/895-4559** or 310/374-3001. Fax 310/372-2115. www. beach-house.com. 96 units. $209–$349 double. Rates include continental breakfast. AE, DC, DISC, MC, V. Valet parking $17. **Amenities:** Room service from nearby restaurant; concierge; laundry service; dry cleaning. *In room:* A/C, TV, CD player, dataport, stocked kitchenette, coffeemaker, fridge, hair dryer, iron.

Georgian Hotel ★ *(Finds)* This eight-story Art Deco beauty boasts luxury comforts, loads of historic charm, and a terrific location, just across the street from Santa Monica's beach and pier, with prime Ocean Avenue dining just steps away. Established in 1933, the former Lady Windermere was popular among Hollywood's Golden Age elite; it even had its own speakeasy, rumored to have been established by Bugsy Siegel (guests now enjoy breakfast in the historic room). Today, the elegant Classical Revival architecture is beautifully accented with a well-chosen palette of bold pastels (à la Miami Beach's hotels of the same era). A wonderful veranda with cushy wicker chaises and unobstructed ocean views opens onto a light and airy lobby with comfortable seating nooks.

An attended elevator leads to beautifully designed guest rooms that are an ideal blend of nostalgic style and modern-day amenities. Fittings include furnishings upholstered in gorgeous nubby textiles, mattresses dressed in goosedown comforters, ceiling fans, and terry robes; suites have sleeper sofas and CD players as well. The hotel has an unobstructed coastal vista, so most rooms have at least a partial or full ocean view; the best views are above the third floor. Front rooms can be a bit noisy, so ask for a Malibu view for the best of both worlds. Back-facing rooms have city views that are more attractive than you'd expect, so nobody loses; these rooms are best for light sleepers.

1415 Ocean Ave. (between Santa Monica Blvd. and Broadway), Santa Monica, CA 90401. ℂ **800/538-8147** or 310/395-9945. Fax 310/656-0904. www.georgianhotel.com. 84 units. $235–$310 double; from $350 suite. Inquire about packages. AE, DC, DISC, MC, V. Valet parking $18. **Amenities:** Restaurant for breakfast; lobby bar; exercise room; concierge; activities desk; room service 6:30am–10:30pm; laundry service; dry cleaning. *In room:* TV w/pay movies and Nintendo, fax, dataport, minibar, coffeemaker, hair dryer, iron, safe.

MODERATE

Casa Malibu ★★ *Finds*   Sitting right on its very own beach, this leftover jewel from Malibu's golden age doesn't try to play the sleek resort game (and what a refreshing exception). Instead, the modest, low-rise inn sports a traditional-California-beach-cottage look that's cozy and timeless.

Wrapped around a palm-studded inner courtyard brightened with well-tended flowerbeds and climbing *cuppa d'oro* vines, the 21 rooms are comfortable, charming, and thoughtfully outfitted. Many have been upgraded with Mexican-tile bathrooms, air-conditioning, and VCRs, but even the older ones are in great shape and boast top-quality bedding and bathrobes. Depending on which you choose, you might also find a fireplace, a kitchenette (in a half-dozen or so), a CD player (in suites), a tub (instead of shower only), and/or a private deck over the sand. The upstairs Catalina Suite (Lana Turner's old hideout) has the best view, while the gorgeous Malibu Suite—the best room in the house, and, like the Beachfront rooms, located right on the beach—offers state-of-the-art pampering. More than half have ocean views, but even those facing the courtyard are quiet and offer easy beach access via wooden stairs to the private stretch of beach, which is raked smooth each morning. There's also a handsome, wind-shielded brick sun deck that extends directly over the sand, allowing everyone to enjoy the blue Pacific even in cool months. Book well ahead for summer—this one's a favorite of locals and visitors alike.

22752 Pacific Coast Hwy. (about ¼ mile S of Malibu Pier), Malibu, CA 90265. © **800/831-0858** or 310/456-2219. Fax 310/456-5418. www.casamalibu.com. 21 units. $99–$169 garden- or oceanview double; $199–$229 beachfront double; $229–$349 suite. Rates include continental breakfast. Extra person $15. AE, MC, V. Free parking. **Amenities:** Access to nearby private health club; room service for lunch and dinner; in-room massage; laundry service; dry cleaning. *In room:* TV, dataport, fridge, coffeemaker, hair dryer, iron.

The Hotel California ★ *Finds*   This former backpackers' flophouse has been remade into a clean, welcoming hacienda-style beachfront motel that reflects the owner's love of surfing and California beach nostalgia. Boasting an enviable location on Ocean Avenue—right next door to the behemoth Loews—this place embodies the ocean ambience everyone wants from Santa Monica. The well-tended complex offers excellent views and direct access to the sand via a 5-minute walk along a pretty stepped path. Fully renovated in 2000, the inn offers small, comfortable rooms with beds with down comforters, refinished woodwork, retiled bathrooms, and lovingly tended landscaping. Five one-bedroom suites also have kitchenettes and pullout sofas that make them great for families or longer stays; all rooms have minifridges and ceiling fans. The suites and some rooms have partially obstructed ocean views. A handful of rooms have showers-only in the bathrooms, so be sure to request a room with a tub from the friendly front-desk staff if it matters to you. *Tip:* Pay a few bucks extra for a courtyard view, as the cheapest rooms face the parking lot and noisy Ocean Avenue.

1670 Ocean Ave. (S of Colorado Ave.), Santa Monica, CA 90401. © **866/571-0000** or 310/393-2363. Fax 310/393-1063. www.hotelca.com. 26 units. $169–$279 double or suite. AE, DISC, MC, V. Self-parking $9. **Amenities:** Jacuzzi; activities desk; discount car-rental desk; high-speed Internet access, fax/copier, and coffeemaker in front office. *In room:* TV/VCR, dataport, fridge, hair dryer, iron.

INEXPENSIVE

Best Western Marina Pacific Hotel & Suites ★ *Kids*   This bright, recently renovated four-story hotel is a haven of smart value just off the newly renovated

Venice Boardwalk. A simple, contemporary lobby leads to spacious rooms brightened with beachy colors and new chain-standard furnishings and two-line phones. The one-bedroom suites are terrific for families, boasting master bedrooms with king-size beds, fully outfitted kitchens with microwave and dishwasher, dining areas, queen-size sofa sleepers, balconies and fireplaces, plus (if needed) a connecting door that can form a well-priced two-bedroom, two-bathroom suite. Photos of local scenes and rock 'n' roll legends, plus works by local artists, lend the public spaces a wonderful vibe, and many rooms have at least partial ocean views. Additional incentives include complimentary upscale continental breakfast, free local shuttle service, and secured indoor parking. Stay elsewhere if you need a lot in the way of service or if you won't relish the party-hearty human carnival of Venice Beach (Santa Monica is generally quieter and more refined).

1697 Pacific Ave. (at 17th Ave.), Venice, CA 90291. © **800/780-7234** (Best Western reservations), 800/421-8151 (direct), or 310/452-1111. Fax 310/452-5479. www.mphotel.com or www.bestwestern.com. 88 units. $109–$159 double; $169–$269 suite. Rates include continental breakfast. Extra person $10. Children 12 and under stay free in parents' room. Ask about AAA, senior, and other discounts; weekly and monthly rates also available. AE, DC, DISC, MC, V. Self-parking $9. **Amenities:** Free shuttle to Santa Monica and Marina del Rey; coin-op laundry and laundry service; dry cleaning. *In room:* A/C, TV, dataport, fridge, coffeemaker, hair dryer, iron.

Cal Mar Hotel Suites ✷ *Value* Tucked away in a beautiful residential neighborhood just 2 blocks from the ocean, this garden-apartment complex is lovingly cared for and delivers a lot of bang for your vacation buck. Each unit is an apartment-style suite with a living room with a pullout sofa, a full-size kitchen, and a separate bedroom; most are spacious enough to accommodate four in comfort. The building was constructed in the 1950s with an eye for quality (attractive tile work, large closets). While the furnishings aren't luxurious and fixtures are from a couple of decades past, everything is well kept and every need is provided for. It's easy to be comfortable here for stays of a week or more. The staff is attentive and courteous, which helps account for the high rate of repeat guests. The garden courtyard boasts a nice swimming pool and plenty of chaises for lounging.

220 California Ave., Santa Monica, CA 90403. © **800/776-6007** or 310/395-5555. Fax 310/451-1111. www.calmarhotel.com. 36 units. $109–$169 suite. Extra person $10. Children 9 and under stay free in parents' room. AE, DC, DISC, MC, V. Free parking. **Amenities:** Heated outdoor pool; coin-op laundry. *In room:* TV, kitchen, fridge, coffeemaker, hair dryer, iron.

Sea Shore Motel ✷✷ *Finds* Located in the heart of Santa Monica's best dining and shopping action, this small, friendly, family-run motel is the bargain of the beach. The Sea Shore is such a well-kept secret that most denizens of stylish Main Street are unaware of the incredible value in their midst. A recent total upgrade of the property—furnishings, fixtures, and exterior—has made the entire place feel fresh. Arranged around a parking courtyard, rooms are small and unremarkable, but the conscientious management has done a nice job with them, installing attractive terra-cotta floor tiles, granite countertops, and conveniences like voice mail and data-jack phones. Boasting a sitting room and microwave, the suite is a phenomenal deal; book it as far in advance as possible. With a full slate of restaurants out the front door, and the Santa Monica Pier and beach just a couple of blocks away, this is a terrific bargain base for exploring the sandy side of the city. A cute deli is attached, selling morning muffins and sandwiches and homemade soup at lunchtime, and a laundromat is next door. A real find!

2637 Main St. (S of Ocean Park Blvd.), Santa Monica, CA 90405. (C) 310/392
www.seashoremotel.com. 20 units. $75–$95 double; $100–$120 suite. Extra p
under stay free in parents' room. Midweek discounts available. AE, DISC, MC, V.
with $10-per-night fee. **Amenities:** Deli; coin-op laundry. *In room:* TV, coffeemal

NEAR LAX

If you have an early-morning flight and you need an airport hotel, the **Westin Los Angeles Airport,** 5400 W. Century Blvd. ((C) **800/WESTIN-1** or 310/216-5858; www.westin.com), is a cut above the rest, with its patented Westin "Heavenly Beds." Two good, moderately priced choices are **Sheraton Gateway Hotel,** 6101 W. Century Blvd., near Sepulveda Boulevard ((C) **800/325-3535** or 310/642-1111; www.sheraton.com), a comfortable, California-style hotel that literally overlooks the runway; and the **Marriott Los Angeles Airport,** 5855 Century Blvd. ((C) **800/228-9290** or 310/641-5700; www.marriott.com), a reliable choice for travelers on-the-fly.

If you're looking for an inexpensive option, try the **Travelodge at LAX,** 5547 W. Century Blvd. ((C) **800/421-3939** or 310/649-4000; www.travelodgelax. com), an otherwise standard member of the reliable chain with a surprisingly beautiful tropical garden surrounding the pool area.

LA'S WESTSIDE & BEVERLY HILLS
VERY EXPENSIVE

Beverly Hills Hotel & Bungalows ★★★ Behind the famous facade (pictured on the Eagles' *Hotel California*) lies this star-studded haven where legends were, and still are, made: The "Pink Palace" was center stage for both deal- and star-making in Hollywood's golden days. Today, stars and industry hotshots can still be found around the Olympic-size pool, into which Katharine Hepburn once dove fully clothed, and digging into Dutch apple pancakes in the iconic Polo Lounge, where Hunter S. Thompson kicked off his adventure to Las Vegas. Following a $100 million restoration a few years ago, the hotel's grand lobby and impeccably landscaped grounds retain their over-the-top glory, while the lavish guest rooms boast every state-of-the-art luxury, including extra-large bathrooms with double Grecian marble sinks and TVs. The best original touches have been retained, like butler service at the touch of a button. Many rooms feature private patios, Jacuzzi tubs, kitchens, and/or dining rooms. The bungalows are more luxurious than ever—and who knows who your neighbor might be?

9641 Sunset Blvd. (at Rodeo Dr.), Beverly Hills, CA 90210. (C) 800/283-8885 or 310/276-2251. Fax 310/281-2905. www.beverlyhillshotel.com. 203 units. $345–$375 double; from $745 suite or bungalow. AE, DC, MC, V. Parking $23. Pets accepted in bungalows only. **Amenities:** 3 restaurants (Polo Lounge, Fountain Coffee Shop, alfresco Cabana Club Cafe); 2 lounges (Sunset Lounge for high tea and cocktails, bar in Polo Lounge); Olympic-size outdoor heated pool; Jacuzzi; fitness center; 2 lit tennis courts; concierge; car-rental desk; courtesy limo; business center with computers; salon services; 24-hr. room service; in-room or poolside massage; babysitting; laundry service; dry cleaning. *In room:* A/C, TV/VCR, CD player, DSL dataport, fax/copier/scanner, minibar, hair dryer, safe.

Century Plaza Hotel & Spa ★★ Despite the almost-foreboding scale, I love this place. The recently renovated guest rooms are more beautiful than you'd expect, with designer furnishings, gorgeous warm-hued textiles, attractive contemporary prints, big closets with terry robes, and almost universally impressive views from the small deck. The beautiful Italian-tile-and-glass bathrooms are some of LA's best. Westin's celestial Heavenly Bed—touted as "10 layers of heaven"—is a treat, and the cushioned headboards are a nice finishing touch. Guest office rooms add a fax/printer/copier, an ergonomic desk chair, glare-free

lighting, a coffeemaker, late checkout, and continental breakfast for a few
extra dollars.

Now open for business is the much-anticipated 35,000-square-foot, Asian-
inspired Spa Mystique, the largest in LA. Its features include an epic menu of
traditional and Eastern treatments, 27 indoor treatment rooms and four outdoor cabanas, impressive hydrotherapy features (including two Japanese *furo*
pools), salon services, and a fitness center with cardio machines that let you surf
the Web as you pump, plus a meditation garden and alfresco spa cafe. Even if
you're not staying at the hotel, it's worth a splurge to pamper yourself at this
amazing spa. Recently opened Breeze, the hotel's 250-seat restaurant and raw bar
designed by architect-of-the-moment Stephen Jacobs, is worth a look.

2025 Ave. of the Stars (S of Santa Monica Blvd.), Century City, CA 90067. © **800/WESTIN-1** or 310/
277-2000. Fax 310/551-3355. www.centuryplazala.com or www.westin.com. 724 units. $350–$415 double;
from $500 suite. Weekend, off-season, and other discounts available (from $279 at press time). AE, DC, DISC,
MC, V. Valet parking $23; self-parking $15. Pets accepted with $50 deposit. **Amenities:** Restaurant and
lounge; spa cafe; lobby bar; outdoor heated pool and Jacuzzi; Spa Mystique health club and sauna; Westin
Kids Club; concierge; Hertz car-rental desk; business center; salon; 24-hr. room service; in-room massage;
laundry service; dry cleaning. *In room:* A/C, TV w/pay movies, dataport, minibar, coffeemaker, hair dryer, iron,
safe.

Four Seasons Hotel Los Angeles at Beverly Hills ★★   This intimate-feel-
ing 16-story hotel attracts a mix of A-list jet-setters loyal to the Four Seasons
brand, and an LA showbiz crowd who cherish the hotel as an après-event gathering place. The small marbled lobby is anchored by an always-stunning floral
extravaganza, and lovely gardens will help you forget you're in the heart of the
city. Four Seasons operates terrific hotels, with a concierge that's famously well
connected and service that goes the distance. Guest rooms are sumptuously furnished in traditional style and pastel hues. Luxuries include custom extra-stuffed
Sealy mattresses with heavenly linens and pillows, marble bathrooms with vanity TVs, and French doors leading to private balconies. Room rates rise with the
elevator, so bargain hunters sacrifice the view; ask for a corner room to get extra
space at no additional cost. The hotel has a petite but first-rate full-service spa.
The view-endowed fourth-floor deck features a lap pool, poolside grill, and
glass-walled fitness center. Gardens is a refined and excellent California-French
restaurant often overlooked by locals.

300 S. Doheny Dr. (at Burton Way), Los Angeles, CA 90048. © **800/819-5053**, 800/332-3442, or 310/
273-2222. Fax 310/859-3824. www.fourseasons.com. 285 units. $370–$470 double; from $600 suite. AE, DC,
DISC, MC, V. Valet parking $21; free self-parking. Pets under 15 lb. accepted (no charge). **Amenities:** Restau-
rant and lounge; poolside grill; rooftop heated pool; exercise room; full-service spa; Jacuzzi; children's program; concierge; courtesy limo within 5-mile radius; business center; 24-hr. room service; in-room massage;
laundry service; dry cleaning. *In room:* A/C, TV/VCR w/pay movies (suites have DVD), CD player, dataport,
minibar, hair dryer, iron, safe.

Mondrian ★★   Theatrical, enchanted, sophisticated—this is the kind of place
super-hotelier Ian Schrager has created from a once-drab apartment building.
Working with his regular partner, *enfant terrible* French designer Philippe Starck
(as he successfully did at Miami's Delano and Manhattan properties like the
Royalton and Hudson), Schrager used the Mondrian's breathtaking views (from
every room) as the starting point for his vision of a "hotel in the clouds." Pur-
posely underlit hallways lead to bright, clean rooms done in shades of white,
beige, and pale gray and outfitted with simple furniture casually slip-covered in
white; about three-quarters of the rooms and suites have fully outfitted kitchenettes. Truthfully, the accommodations themselves are only secondary—stay

here if you want to be part of a superhip, star-studded scene. Set poolside and in a magical treehouse, Skybar is still one of LA's hottest watering holes, and booking a room guarantees admission. (Soundproof windows on the entire south side of the building have already dealt with a troublesome noise problem in rooms overlooking the raucous late-night scene.) In addition to its terrific—and ultra-hip—Asian-Latin fusion restaurant Asia de Cuba, light meals and sushi are served at a quirky communal table in the lobby. The beautiful-people staff isn't strong on service, but so what? They look great.

8440 Sunset Blvd., West Hollywood, CA 90069. ✆ **800/525-8029** or 323/650-8999. Fax 323/650-5215. www.ianschragerhotels.com. 238 units. $310–$560 double; from $385 suite. Weekend rates available. AE, DC, DISC, MC, V. Valet parking $23. **Amenities:** Restaurant; bar; outdoor pool; exercise room with sauna and Jacuzzi; concierge; business center; 24-hr. room service; in-room massage; laundry service; dry cleaning. *In room:* A/C, TV/VCR, CD player, dataport, minibar, coffeemaker, hair dryer, iron, safe.

EXPENSIVE

Avalon Hotel ★★ *Finds*   The first style-conscious boutique hotel on the LA scene, this marvelous midcentury-inspired gem in the heart of Beverly Hills still leads the pack. Boasting a soothing sherbet-hued palette and classic Atomic Age furnishings—Eames cabinets, Heywood-Wakefield chairs, Nelson bubble lamps—mixed with smart custom designs, every room looks as if it could star in a *Metropolitan Home* photo spread. But fashion doesn't forsake function at this beautifully designed hotel, which boasts enough luxury comforts and amenities to please design-blind travelers, too.

The property is comprised of the former Beverly-Carlton (seen on *I Love Lucy* and once home to Marilyn Monroe and Mae West) as well as two neighboring 1950s-era apartment houses. The main building is the hub of a chic but low-key scene, but I prefer the quieter Canon building, where many of the units have kitchenettes and/or furnished terraces. No matter which one you end up in, you'll find a gorgeous, restful cocoon with terry bathrobes, and top-of-the-line bedding that includes a cozy, nubby throw. You'll also have easy access to the sunny courtyard with its retro-hip amoeba-shaped pool, the fitness room, and the groovy *Jetsons*-style restaurant and bar, which shakes a terrific green-apple martini. Service is friendlier than you'll find in other style-minded hotels.

9400 W. Olympic Blvd. (at Beverly Dr.), Beverly Hills, CA 90212. ✆ **800/535-4715** or 310/277-5221. Fax 310/277-4928. www.avalon-hotel.com. 88 units. $199–$289 double; from $249 junior or 1-bedroom suite. Extra person $25. AE, DC, MC, V. Valet parking $17. **Amenities:** Restaurant; bar; courtyard pool; concierge; 24-hr. room service; in-room massage; laundry service; dry cleaning. *In room:* A/C, TV/VCR w/pay movies and Nintendo, CD, fax, dataport, minibar, coffeemaker, hair dryer, iron, safe.

Le Montrose Suite Hotel ★ *Value*   Nobody pays rack at this terrific all-suite hotel, which offers money-saving specials of every stripe for travelers who want more than a standard room for their accommodations dollars. Nestled on a quiet street just 2 blocks from the red-hot Sunset Strip, cozy Le Montrose features large split-level studio and one-bedroom apartments that feel more like comfortable, upscale condos than hotel rooms. Each contemporary-styled suite has a sizable living room with gas fireplace, a dining area, a comfortable sleeping nook (or dedicated bedroom), and a very nice bathroom. Executive and one-bedroom suites have kitchenettes (which can be stocked upon request). The two-bedrooms are a great deal for families or sharing friends. You have to go up to the roof for anything resembling a view, but once you're up there, you can swim in the pool, soak in the Jacuzzi, or brush up on your tennis game. This place is a favorite for long-term stays among the music and film crowds, so don't be surprised if you spot a famous face in the pleasant Library restaurant during the breakfast hour.

900 Hammond St., West Hollywood, CA 90069. ✆ **800/776-0666** or 310/855-1115. Fax 310/657-9192. www.lemontrose.com. 132 units. $295–$575 suite. Money-saving deals abound; AAA, AARP, seasonal, and weekend rates as low as $159 at press time; breakfast (from $199), car, and Disneyland- and Universal Studios–inclusive packages also available. AE, DC, DISC, MC, V. Valet and self-parking $18. Pets accepted with $100-per-pet nonrefundable fee. **Amenities:** Restaurant; outdoor heated pool; Jacuzzi; lit tennis court; exercise room with sauna; complimentary bikes; concierge; car-rental desk; business center; secretarial services; 24-hr. room service; coin-op laundry and laundry service; dry cleaning; executive-level rooms. *In room:* A/C, TV/VCR and DVD w/pay movies and Nintendo, CD player, fax/copier/scanner, dataport, minibar, coffeemaker, hair dryer, iron, safe.

Wyndham Bel Age Hotel ★★ *Kids* *Value*   This high-rise all-suite hotel is one of West Hollywood's best. The Bel Age has it all: huge, amenity-laden suites, excellent service, terrific rooftop sun deck with pool and Jacuzzi, and A-1 location just 1½ blocks off the Sunset Strip, but removed from the congestion and noise. What's more, thanks to an excellent art collection (assembled by the hotel's original owners) that fills the public spaces and guest rooms, the hotel has far more personality than your average chain hotel.

Accommodations hardly get better for the money. The monster-size suites boast contemporary decor with a few classic touches and a serious, soothing palette of navy, burgundy, and gray. Selected to suit every need—including those of families and business travelers—luxuries include pillow-top mattresses with cushioned headboards and plush bedding, a sleeper sofa in the living area that opens into a queen bed, plus an excellent work desk with an ergonomically correct Herman Miller desk chair. The bathrooms boast generous counter space and robes. The best rooms face south; on a clear day, you can see all the way to the Pacific. Be sure to make reservations before you leave home for a special meal at the Franco-Russian Diaghilev restaurant. The pretty Brasserie offers good Cal-Tuscan cuisine and top-flight jazz on Friday and Saturday nights.

1020 N. San Vicente Blvd. (between Sunset and Santa Monica boulevards), West Hollywood, CA 90069. ✆ **800/WYNDHAM** or 310/854-1111. Fax 310/854-0926. www.wyndham.com. 200 units. $199–$339 suite (accommodates up to 4 at no extra charge). Ask about weekend rates, holiday specials, and discounts on longer stays. AE, DC, DISC, MC, V. Valet parking $18. **Amenities:** Restaurant; bar and grill with live entertainment; rooftop outdoor heated pool; Jacuzzi; exercise room; concierge; salon; room service 6am–2am; laundry service; dry cleaning. *In room:* A/C, TV/VCR w/pay movies and Sony PlayStation, CD player, dataport, minibar, coffeemaker, hair dryer, iron.

MODERATE

Beverly Hills Inn ★ *Value*   This hotel is a real coup for those who want a gold-plated address at a moderate price. The excellent location (just south of prime Beverly Hills shopping territory), premium comforts, and across-the-board quality add up to one of Beverly Hills's best values. The 50-room hotel is attractively done in a rich European style and boasts extras that usually cost more, like a fitness room with dry sauna, an eager-to-please staff, and a small but well-tended pool. All add up to a very good deal in a high-rent neighborhood. A 2002 renovation should be complete by the time you arrive, and will increase the good value even more.

125 S. Spalding Dr., Beverly Hills, CA 90212. ✆ **800/463-4466** or 310/278-0303. Fax 310/278-1728. www.innatbeverlyhills.com. 50 units. $189–$259 double; from $269 suite. AE, DC, MC, V. Free parking. **Amenities:** Restaurant; bar; heated outdoor pool; exercise room with sauna; tour desk; room service until 10pm; laundry service; dry cleaning. *In room:* A/C, TV, dataport, fridge, hair dryer, iron.

Holiday Inn Brentwood/Bel-Air   This LA landmark is the last of a vanishing breed of circular hotels from the 1960s and '70s. It's perched beside the city's busiest freeway a short hop from the popular Getty Center and centrally located between the beaches, Beverly Hills, and the San Fernando Valley. Completely refurbished in 2000, each pie-shaped room boasts a private balcony and double-paned glass to keep the noise out; little extras like Nintendo games, in-room bottled water, and great views add panache to otherwise unremarkable chain-style accommodations. You'll also enjoy a million-dollar 360° view from the hotel's top-floor Brentwood Terrace restaurant, which serves a casual, please-all cuisine. The adjoining cocktail lounge features live piano nightly. Popular with older travelers and museum groups, the hotel provides complimentary pickup and drop-off service to the Getty Center and Westwood.

170 N. Church Lane (at intersection of Sunset Blvd. and I-405), Los Angeles, CA 90049. *Ⓒ* **800/HOLIDAY** or 310/476-6411. Fax 310/472-1157. www.holiday-inn.com/brentwood-bel. 211 units. $149–$189 double; from $275 suite. Inquire about AAA and AARP discounts, breakfast packages, and "Great Rates," often as low as $119. AE, DC, DISC, MC, V. Valet parking $10; self-parking $8. Small pets accepted with $50-per-pet nonrefundable fee. **Amenities:** Rooftop restaurant and lounge; heated outdoor pool; Jacuzzi; exercise room; concierge; activities desk; free shuttle to Getty Center and within a 3-mile radius; room service 6am–10pm; coin-op laundry and laundry service; dry cleaning. *In room:* A/C, TV w/pay movies and Nintendo, dataport, coffeemaker, hair dryer, iron.

The Standard ★★

If Andy Warhol had gone into the hotel business, the Standard would've been the end result. Designed to appeal to the under-35 "it" crowd, Andre Balazs's swank West Hollywood neo-motel is sometimes silly, sometimes brilliant, and always provocative (not to mention crowded!). It's a scene worthy of its Sunset Strip location: shag carpeting on the lobby ceiling, blue Astroturf around the swimming pool, and a DJ spinning ambient sounds while a performance artist showing more skin than talent poses in a display case behind the check-in desk. This place is definitely left of center.

The good news is that the Standard is more than just a pretty (wild) face. Look past the retro clutter and often-raucous party scene and you'll find a level of service more often associated with hotels costing twice as much. Constructed from the bones of a vintage 1962 motel, it boasts comfortably sized rooms outfitted with cobalt blue indoor-outdoor carpeting, silver beanbag chairs, orange tiles in the bathrooms, and Warhol's Poppy-print curtains, plus private balconies, and minibars whose contents include goodies like sake, condoms, and animal crackers. On the downside, the cheapest rooms face noisy Sunset Boulevard, and the relentless scene can get tiring if you're not into it.

Note: Set to open by the time you read this is **Downtown Standard,** 550 S. Flower St. (*Ⓒ* **213/892-8080**), which will bring a similar dose of Generation Y–targeted cheap-cool style and tattooed attitude to suit-jacketed downtown LA.

8300 Sunset Blvd. (at Sweetzer Ave.), West Hollywood, CA 90069. *Ⓒ* **323/650-9090.** Fax 323/650-2820. www.standardhotel.com. 139 units. $99–$225 double; from $450 suite. AE, DC, DISC, MC, V. Valet parking $18. Pets under 30 lb. accepted with $100-per-pet fee. **Amenities:** 24-hr. coffee shop; poolside cafe; bar/lounge; outdoor heated pool; access to nearby health club; concierge; business center; barbershop; 24-hr. room service; in-room massage; babysitting; laundry service; dry cleaning. *In room:* A/C, TV/VCR w/pay movies, CD player, dataport, minibar.

INEXPENSIVE

Beverly Laurel Motor Hotel *Value*

The Beverly Laurel is a great choice for wallet-watching travelers who want a central location and a room with more style than your average motel. Overlooking the parking lot, the basic but well-kept rooms are smartened up with diamond-print spreads and eye-catching artwork; other features include a minifridge, microwave, and ample closet space, and a large kitchenette for an extra 10-spot. The postage-stamp-size outdoor pool is a little public for carefree sunbathing, but it does the job on hot summer days. Best of all is the motel's own excellent coffee shop, Swingers (p. 497)—nobody serves burgers and malts better, and you may even spot your favorite alt-rocker tucking into a 3pm breakfast in the vinyl booth next to yours.

8018 Beverly Blvd. (between La Cienega Blvd. and Fairfax Ave.), Los Angeles, CA 90048. ✆ **800/962-3824** or 323/651-2441. Fax 323/651-5225. 52 units. $79–$84 double; $89 double with kitchenette. AAA and senior discounts may be available. AE, DC, MC, V. Free parking. **Amenities:** Heated outdoor pool; access to nearby health club; car-rental desk; laundry service. *In room:* A/C, TV, dataport, fridge, hair dryer.

Hotel Del Capri ★ *Kids*   This well-located and well-kept Westwood hotel/motel is hugely popular with returning guests, thanks to spacious rooms, a helpful staff, and retro pricing. There are two parts to the Eisenhower-era property: a four-story tower and a charming two-story motel with white louver shutters and flowering vines, whose units surround a pleasant pool that's open 24 hours. All guest rooms are clean and well cared for, but the decidedly discount decor won't be winning any style awards, and the basic bathrooms could use some upgrading (not to mention quieter fans). Still, every one is comfortable and well worth the money. Free continental breakfast (delivered to your room) and free parking make a good value even better. The most notable room feature is electrically adjustable beds, a novel touch. More than half of the units are one- or two-bedroom suites with kitchenettes, and some units have whirlpool tubs. Nothing is within walking distance of the ritzy high-rise neighborhood, but it's hard to be more freeway-convenient or centrally located. No room service, but nearly 50 restaurants will deliver.

10587 Wilshire Blvd. (at Westholme Ave.), Los Angeles, CA 90024. ✆ **800/44-HOTEL** or 310/474-3511. Fax 310/470-9999. www.hoteldelcapri.com. 79 units. $110–$125 double; from $135 suite. Extra person $10. Rates include continental breakfast ($1 gratuity). Price breaks for almost everybody—AAA members, seniors, UCLA grads, military members, and more—so be sure to ask. AE, DC, MC, V. Free parking. **Amenities:** Pool with deck chairs; tour desk; free shuttle service to UCLA, Westwood, Beverly Hills, and Century City with advance notice; coin-op laundry and laundry service; dry cleaning. *In room:* A/C, TV, kitchenette in some units, hair dryer and iron upon request.

HOLLYWOOD
MODERATE

Hollywood Roosevelt Hotel ★ *Kids* *Value*   This 12-story movie-city landmark is located on an unabashedly touristy section of Hollywood Boulevard, across from Mann's Chinese Theatre and just down the street from the Walk of Fame. This Tinseltown legend—host to the first Academy Awards, not to mention a few famous-name ghosts—is a great value, since you get a prime location and buckets of Hollywood history, plus comforts and services that usually cost twice the price. A complete renovation in 2002—down to the plumbing and electrical—has jacked up the rates about 20%, but the stylish new Pan-Asian design is worlds better than the old, unappealing guest rooms. Those on the upper floors have unbeatable skyline views, while cabana rooms have a balcony or patio overlooking the Olympic-size pool, whose mural was painted by David Hockney, and poolside bar. The specialty suites are named after stars who stayed in them during the glory days; some have grand verandas. The Cinegrill supper club draws locals with live jazz and top-notch cabaret entertainment. A new bar/lounge and spa should be completed by the time you read this.

7000 Hollywood Blvd., Hollywood, CA 90028. ✆ **800/950-7667** or 323/466-7000. Fax 323/462-8056. www.hollywoodroosevelt.com. 330 units. $199–$269 double; from $289 suite. Ask about AAA, senior, business, government, and other discounted rates (as low as $149 at press time). Children 17 and under stay free in parents' room. AE, DC, DISC, MC, V. Valet parking $18. **Amenities:** Restaurant; cocktail lounge; Cinegrill cabaret and nightclub; coffee bar; poolside bar; outdoor pool and Jacuzzi; exercise room; concierge; activities

Kids Family-Friendly Hotels

Best Western Marina Pacific Hotel & Suites (p. 469) now gives families a place to stay just off the carnival-like Venice Boardwalk. The suites are a terrific choice for the brood, since each features a full kitchen, a dining area, a pullout sofa, and a connecting door to an adjoining room that lets you form an affordable two-bedroom, two-bathroom suite.

Beverly Garland's Holiday Inn (p. 481) is a terrific choice for wallet-watching families: Rates are low, the North Hollywood location is close to Universal Studios (a free shuttle ride away), and kids stay and eat free.

Hollywood Roosevelt Hotel (p. 476) welcomes kids under 18 for free with their parents. The heart-of-gentrified-Hollywood location makes an excellent base for families who want easy access to the touristy but fun Walk of Fame.

Hotel Del Capri (p. 476) offers spacious, retro-priced rooms and suites to families with kids—and anybody who wants a big bang for their buck. You can even hop a free shuttle to Westwood to stroll, shop, and maybe even watch a few celebs walk the red carpet into their latest movie premiere.

Hotel Oceana (p. 467) offers big apartment-style suites outfitted with all the conveniences of home. Kids will love the bright colors, the cushy furniture, the video games, and the location—across the street from the beach.

Magic Castle Hotel (p. 478) is a good budget choice, with roomy apartment-style suites and its proximity to Hollywood Boulevard's family-friendly attractions.

Sheraton Universal Hotel (p. 481) enjoys a terrifically kid-friendly location, adjacent to Universal Studios and the fun CityWalk mall. Babysitting services are available, and there's a game room on the premises.

Wyndham Bel Age Hotel (p. 474) is a terrific all-suite hotel whose megasize suites feature everything a family requires, including a sleeper sofa in the living area that opens into a second king bed, VCR and Sony PlayStation, and a wet bar with fridge that allows for easy prep of morning cereal. There's no extra-person charge for kids (rates include up to four per unit), which improves the value-for-dollar ratio even more.

desk; Thrifty car-rental desk; business center; room service 6am–11pm; babysitting; laundry service; dry cleaning; executive-level rooms. *In room:* A/C, TV w/pay movies and Nintendo, dataport, minibar, coffeemaker, hair dryer, iron, safe.

INEXPENSIVE

Best Western Hollywood Hills Hotel ✦ Location is a big selling point for this family-owned (since 1948) member of the reliable Best Western chain: It's just off U.S. 101 (the Hollywood Fwy.), a Metro Line stop just 3 blocks away means easy car-free access to Universal Studios, and the famed Hollywood and

Vine intersection is just a walk away. The walls showcase images from the golden age of movies, and the front desk offers an endless variety of arranged tours. Rooms are plain and clean but lack warmth—outer walls are painted cinder block, and closets are hidden behind institutional metal accordion doors. Still, management is constantly striving to improve the hotel, and all rooms have extras like a microwave and free movies. Rooms in the back building are my favorites, as they sit well back from busy Franklin Avenue, face the gleaming blue-tiled, heated outdoor pool, and have an attractive view of the neighboring hillside. The bathrooms are jazzier in the front building, though. A major convenience is the 101 Hills Coffee Shop located off the lower lobby.

6141 Franklin Ave. (between Vine and Gower sts.), Hollywood, CA 90028. © **800/287-1700** in Calif. only, or 323/464-5181. Fax 323/962-0536. www.bestwestern.com/hollywoodhillshotel. 86 units. $79–$129 double. AAA and AARP discounts available. AE, DISC, MC, V. Free covered parking. Small pets accepted with $25-per-night fee. **Amenities:** Coffee shop; heated outdoor pool; access to nearby health club; tour desk; coin-op laundry. *In room:* A/C, TV, fridge, coffeemaker, hair dryer, dataport, iron.

Days Inn Hollywood/Universal Studios While it's east of the prime Sunset Strip action, this freshly renovated motel is safe and convenient, and extras like free underground parking and continental breakfast make it an especially good value. Double-doubles are large enough for families. It's usually easy to snare an under-$100 rate; for maximum bang for your buck, ask for a room overlooking the pool.

7023 Sunset Blvd. (between Highland and La Brea aves.), Hollywood, CA 90028. © **800/544-8313,** 800/346-7723, or 323/464-8344. Fax 323/962-9748. www.daysinn.com. 72 units. $82–$160 double; $125–$200 Jacuzzi suite. Rates include continental breakfast. Ask about AAA, AARP, and other discounted rates (as low as $73 at press time). AE, DC, DISC, MC, V. Free secured parking. **Amenities:** Heated outdoor pool; laundry service; dry cleaning. *In room:* A/C, TV, fridge and coffeemaker in some units, hair dryer and iron upon request.

Magic Castle Hotel ✫ *Kids* *Value* Located a stone's throw Hollywood Boulevard's attractions, this garden-style hotel/motel at the base of the Hollywood Hills offers LA's best cheap sleeps. You won't see the Magic Hotel in a shelter mag spread—the rooms are done in high Levitz style—but the newly refurbished units are spacious, comfortable, and well kept. Named for the Magic Castle, the illusionist club just uphill, the hotel was once an apartment building; it still feels private and insulated from Franklin Avenue's constant stream of traffic. The units are situated around a swimming-pool courtyard ensconced with trees. Most are full, extra-large apartments, with fully equipped kitchens with microwaves (grocery shopping service is available as well). Several units have balconies overlooking the large heated pool. Ideal for wallet-watching families or long-term stays.

7025 Franklin Ave. (between La Brea and Highland), Hollywood, CA 90028. © **800/741-4915** or 323/851-0800. Fax 323/851-4926. www.magiccastlehotel.com. 49 units. $79 double; $89–$169 suite. Extra person $10. Off-season and other discounts available. AE, DC, DISC, MC, V. Free secured parking. **Amenities:** Heated outdoor pool; coin-op laundry and laundry service. *In room:* A/C, TV, dataport, kitchen, coffeemaker, hair dryer, iron, safe.

DOWNTOWN
EXPENSIVE/MODERATE

How much you'll pay at any of the following hotels largely depends on when you come. All become quite affordable once the business travelers go home; more often than not, rooms go for a relative song over holidays and weekends. Some even offer good-value weekday rates to leisure travelers during periods when rooms would otherwise sit open.

Millennium Biltmore Hotel Los Angeles ★★ Built in 1923 and encompassing an entire square block, this Italian-Spanish Renaissance landmark is the grande dame of LA's hotels. You've seen the Biltmore in many movies, including *The Fabulous Baker Boys, Beverly Hills Cop,* and Barbra Streisand's *A Star Is Born;* the hotel lobby appeared upside-down in *The Poseidon Adventure.* Always in fine shape and host to world leaders and luminaries, the former Regal Biltmore is now under the guiding hand of the Millennium Hotels and Resorts group, and the sense of refinement and graciousness endures. The large guest rooms aren't quite as eye-popping, but they've recently undergone a sumptuous redecorating that suits the hotel's vibe beautifully. Bathrooms are on the small side, but peach-toned marble and plush robes add a luxurious edge.

A range of dining and cocktail outlets includes Sai Sai for Japanese cuisine. Pretty, casual Smeraldi's serves homemade pastas and lighter California fare. Off the lobby is the stunning Gallery Bar, named by *Los Angeles* magazine as one of the sexiest cocktail lounges in LA. Afternoon tea and cocktails are served in the Rendezvous Court (the hotel's original lobby). Spend the few bucks to appreciate the Art Deco health club, with its gorgeous Roman-style pool.

506 S. Grand Ave. (between 5th and 6th sts.), Los Angeles, CA 90071. © 800/245-8673 or 213/624-1011. Fax 213/612-1545. www.millennium-hotels.com. 683 units. $174–$319 double; from $459 suite. Weekend discount packages available. AE, DC, DISC, MC, V. Parking $22. **Amenities:** 3 restaurants; 2 lounges; health club with original 1923 inlaid pool, Jacuzzi, steam, sauna; concierge; Enterprise car-rental desk; courtesy car; business center; salon; 24-hr. room service; in-room massage; babysitting; laundry service; dry cleaning; executive-level rooms. *In room:* A/C, TV w/pay movies, dataport, minibar, hair dryer, safe.

Westin Bonaventure Hotel & Suites ★★ This 35-story, 1,354-room monolith is the hotel that locals love to hate. The truth is that the Bonaventure is a terrific hotel. It's certainly not for travelers who want intimacy or personality in their accommodations—but with more than 20 restaurants and bars, a full-service spa, a monster health club, a Kinko's-size business center, and much more on hand, you'll be hard-pressed to want for anything here (except maybe some individualized attention). And with a recently completed $35 million renovation, this convention favorite has never looked better or felt fresher.

The hotel's five gleaming glass silos encompass an entire square block and form one of Downtown's most distinctive landmarks. The six-story lobby houses fountains and trees (and, surprise, a Starbucks). A tangle of concrete ramps and 12 high-speed glass elevators lead to the extensive array of shops and services. Among the highlights is the rooftop L.A. Prime steakhouse and revolving Bona-Vista lounge, both offering unparalleled views; the Bonaventure Chowder Bar for live entertainment; and even a Krispy Kreme Donut Stand (well, that settles it!).

The pie-shaped guest rooms are on the small side, but a wall of windows offering great views, nice contemporary furnishings, and Westin's unparalleled Heavenly Bed make for a very comfortable cocoon. With an executive workstation, fax, and wet bar, guest office suites are great for business travelers, while tower suites—with a living room, an extra half-bathroom, minifridge, microwave, and two TVs—are ideal for families.

404 S. Figueroa St. (between 4th and 5th sts.), Los Angeles, CA 90071. © 800/WESTIN-1 or 213/624-1000. Fax 213/612-4800. www.westin.com. 1,354 units. $227–$279 double; from $287 suite. Ask about theater packages. AE, DC, DISC, MC, V. Valet parking $19. **Amenities:** 17 restaurants and fast-food outlets; 5 bars and lounges; outdoor heated lap pool; 15,000-sq.-ft. full-service spa with exercise room, running track, and access to adjacent 85,000-sq.-ft. health club; Westin Kids Club; concierge; tour desk; car-rental desk; full-service business and copy center; shopping arcade; salon; 24-hr. room service; babysitting; laundry service; dry cleaning; executive-club level. *In room:* A/C, TV w/pay movies and Nintendo, dataport, coffeemaker, hair dryer, iron, safe.

Wyndham Checkers Hotel ★★ The atmosphere at this boutique version of the Biltmore is as removed from "Hollywood" as a top LA hotel can get. Built in 1927, the 12-story hotel is a Historic Cultural Monument. Plenty of polished brass complements the neutral sand-colored decor; both accentuate the splendid architectural features that remain intact, despite a complete update over the past couple of years (which included a total guest-room overhaul in 2001). Your room is a pristine temple, warmly radiant and immaculately outfitted. Checkers is a European-styled hotel, without a lot of flashy amenities—but first-class all the way. Spacious marble bathrooms feature plush terry bathrobes. Public areas include a wood-paneled library, a bar stocked with fine cigars and an impressive collection of single-malt scotches and cognacs, and serene corridors punctuated with Asian antiques. Checkers Restaurant is one of Downtown's finest dining rooms, with a weekend brunch worth planning for in advance. *Tip:* Be sure to check their website for terrific "E-Specials" such as $99 Romantic Weekends rates.

535 S. Grand Ave. (between 5th and 6th sts.), Los Angeles, CA 90071. © **800/423-5798** or 213/624-0000. Fax 213/626-9906. 188 units. $199–$289 double; from $500 suite. www.checkershotel.com or www. wyndham.com. Weekend specials, often as low as $109. AE, DC, DISC, MC, V. Valet parking $23; self-parking (off-site) $20. **Amenities:** Restaurant and lounge; rooftop heated lap pool; Jacuzzi; exercise room with sauna and massage services; concierge; courtesy car; secretarial services; 24-hr. room service; in-room massage; babysitting; laundry service; dry cleaning. *In room:* A/C, TV w/pay movies, dataport, minibar, coffeemaker, hair dryer, iron.

INEXPENSIVE

Hotel Figueroa ★★ *Finds* With an artistic eye and a heartfelt commitment to budget travelers, owner Uno Thimansson has transformed a 1925-vintage former YWCA residence into LA's best budget hotel. This enchanting 12-story property sits in a nicely gentrified corner of Downtown, within shouting distance of the Staples Center and a block from the Original Pantry Cafe, the landmark 24-hour breakfast house.

The big, airy lobby exudes a romantic Spanish Colonial–Gothic vibe with beamed ceilings and soaring columns, Moroccan chandeliers, and medievalist furnishings. Elevators lead to equally artistic guest rooms. Even the smallest ones are a good size and comfortable. Each boasts terra cotta–sponged walls, a firm, well-made bed with a wrought-iron headboard or canopy and a Georgia O'Keeffe–reminiscent spread, a Mexican-tiled bathroom, and Indian fabrics that double as blackout drapes. My favorite is no. 1130, a large double-queen with a Spanish terra-cotta-print chaise, but you can't go wrong with any room. The Casablanca Suite is a Moroccan pleasure den, ideal for romance. Out back you'll find a gorgeous desert-garden deck with mosaic-tiled pool and Jacuzzi.

939 S. Figueroa St. (at Olympic Blvd.), Los Angeles, CA 90015. © **800/421-9092** or 213/627-8971. Fax 213/689-0305. www.figueroahotel.com. 285 units. $94–$124 double; $195 Casablanca suite. AE, DC, MC, V. Parking $8. **Amenities:** Restaurant; bar; outdoor pool; Jacuzzi; laundry service; dry cleaning. *In room:* A/C, TV, dataport, fridge.

Hotel Stillwell The Stillwell is far from fancy, but its modestly priced rooms are a good option in a generally pricey neighborhood. Built in 1906, this once-elegant 250-room hotel is conveniently located, close to Staples Center, the Civic Center, and the Museum of Contemporary Art. Rooms are clean, basic, and simply decorated with decent furnishings. Much-needed new paint and carpeting were installed in 2000, but the ancient TVs still look like something from great-uncle Horace's rumpus room. The hotel is quiet, though, and hallways feature East Indian artwork. That said, I much prefer the Hotel Figueroa (see above), but this is a less eccentric and perfectly reasonable choice. The lobby-level Indian restaurant is a popular lunch spot for Downtown office work-ers; other options include a casual Mexican restaurant and so-old-it's-retro Hank's Bar for cocktails.

838 S. Grand Ave. (between 8th and 9th sts.), Los Angeles, CA 90017. ✆ **800/553-4774** or 213/627-1151. Fax 213/622-8940. www.stillwell-la.com. 250 units. $59 double; $75–$95 suite. AE, DC, DISC, MC, V. Parking $4. **Amenities:** 2 restaurants; lounge; activities desk; business center; coin-op laundry and laundry service; dry cleaning. In room: A/C, TV, fridge, fax, iron.

SAN FERNANDO VALLEY
EXPENSIVE

Hilton Universal City & Towers ⊛   Although this shiny 24-story hotel sits right outside Universal Studios, there's more of a conservative business-traveler feel here than the raucous family-with-young-children vibe you might expect. Still, free tram service to the theme park and adjacent Universal CityWalk for shopping and dining means that it's hard for families to be better situated. The polished brass and upscale attitude set the businesslike tone, and a light-filled glass lobby leads to a seemingly endless series of conference and banquet rooms, the hotel's bread and butter. The oversize guest rooms are tastefully decorated and constantly refurbished, and have exceptional views (even if the modern, mirror-surfaced windows don't actually open). I prefer the adjacent Sheraton Universal Hotel (see below) for leisure stays, but go for the best rate.

555 Universal Terrace Pkwy., Universal City, CA 91608. ✆ **800/HILTONS** or 818/506-2500. Fax 818/ 509-2031. www.universalcity.hilton.com. 483 units. $225–$260 double; from $350 suite. Weekend and other discounts often available. AE, DC, DISC, MC, V. Valet parking $16; self-parking $11. **Amenities:** Cafe-style restaurant; outdoor heated pool; Jacuzzi; exercise room; concierge; activities desk; car-rental desk; business center; 24-hr. room service; babysitting; laundry service; dry cleaning; executive-level rooms. In room: A/C, TV w/pay movies and Nintendo, dataport, minibar, coffeemaker, hair dryer, iron, safe.

MODERATE

Beverly Garland's Holiday Inn (Kids)   The "Beverly Garland" in this 258-room hotel's name is the actress who played Fred MacMurray's wife on *My Three Sons*. Grassy areas and greenery abound at this North Hollywood Holiday Inn, a virtual oasis in the concrete jungle. The mission-influenced buildings are a bit dated, but if you grew up with *Brady Bunch* reruns, this only adds to the charm—the spread looks like something Mike Brady would have designed. Southwestern-themed fabrics complement the natural-pine furnishings in the spacious guest rooms, attracting your attention away from the somewhat unfor-tunate painted cinder-block walls. On the upside, all of the well-outfitted rooms have balconies overlooking the pleasant grounds, and a nice pool and lit tennis courts are on hand. With Universal Studios just down the street and a free shut-tle to the park, the location can't be beat for families. Since proximity to the 101 and 134 freeways also means the constant buzz of traffic, ask for a room facing Vineland Avenue for maximum quiet.

4222 Vineland Ave., North Hollywood, CA 91602. ✆ **800/BEVERLY** or 818/980-8000. Fax 818/766-0112. www.beverlygarland.com. 255 units. $149–$179 double; from $209 suite. Ask about AAA, AARP, corporate, military, Great Rates, weekend, and other discounted rates (from $109 at press time). Kids 12 and under stay free in parents' room and eat free. AE, DC, DISC, MC, V. Free parking. **Amenities:** Restaurant; heated outdoor pool; 2 lit tennis courts; sauna; car-rental desk; complimentary shuttle to Universal Studios. In room: A/C, TV, coffeemaker, hair dryer, iron.

Sheraton Universal Hotel ⊛ (Kids)   Despite the addition of the sleekly mod-ern Hilton just uphill, the 21-story Sheraton is still considered "the" Universal City hotel of choice for tourists, businesspeople, and industry folks visiting the studios' production offices. Located on the back lot of Universal Studios, it has a spacious 1960s feel, with updated styling and amenities. Although the Sheraton does its share of convention/event business, the hotel feels more leisure-oriented than the Hilton next door (an outdoor elevator connects the two properties). Choose a Lanai room for balconies that overlook the lushly planted pool area, or a Tower room for stunning views and solitude. The hotel is very close to the Hollywood Bowl, and you can practically roll out of bed and into the theme park (via a continuous complementary shuttle). An extra $35 per night buys a Club Level room—worth the money for the extra in-room amenities, plus free continental breakfast and afternoon hors d'oeuvres. Business rooms also feature a moveable workstation and a fax/copier/printer.

333 Universal Dr., Universal City, CA 91608. ℂ 800/325-3535 or 818/980-1212. Fax 818/985-4980. www.sheraton.com. 436 units. $149–$219 double; from $350 suite. Children under 18 stay free in parents' room. Ask about AAA, AARP, and corporate discounts; also inquire about packages that include theme-park admission. AE, DC, DISC, MC, V. Valet parking $16; self-parking $11. **Amenities:** Casual indoor/outdoor restaurant; lobby lounge with pianist; outdoor pool; Jacuzzi; health club; game room; concierge; free shuttle to Universal Studios every 15 min.; business center; room service 6am–midnight; babysitting; laundry service; dry cleaning; executive-level rooms. *In room:* A/C, TV w/pay movies, dataport, minibar, hair dryer and iron in club-level rooms, safe.

INEXPENSIVE

Best Western Mikado Hotel   This nice Asian-flavored garden hotel has been a Valley fixture for 40-plus years. A 1999 renovation muted but didn't obliterate the kitsch value, which extends from the pagoda-style exterior to the sushi bar (the Valley's oldest) across the driveway. Two-story motel buildings face two well-maintained courtyards, one with a koi pond and wooden footbridge, the other with a shimmering blue-tiled pool and hot tub. The facelift stripped most of the Asian vibe from guest rooms, which are fresh feeling, comfortable, and well outfitted. Furnished in 1970s-era chic (leather sofas, earth tones), the one-bedroom apartment is a steal, with enormous rooms and a full-size kitchen.

12600 Riverside Dr. (between Whitsett and Coldwater Canyon), North Hollywood, CA 91607. ℂ **800/826-2759** or 800/433-2239 in Calif., or 818/763-9141. Fax 818/752-1045. www.bestwestern.com/mikadohotel. 58 units. $129–$139 double; $175 1-bedroom apt. Rates include full breakfast. Ask about AAA, senior, and other discounted rates (as low as $98 at press time). Extra person $10. Children 11 and under stay free in parents' room. Rates include full American breakfast. AE, DC, DISC, MC, V. Free parking. **Amenities:** Japanese restaurant and sushi bar; cocktail lounge; outdoor pool; Jacuzzi; fax and copying services at front desk. *In room:* A/C, TV, dataport, coffeemaker, hair dryer, iron.

Safari Inn 𝒦 *Finds*   This 1957 vintage motel is so retro that it—and its landmark neon sign—have starred in such films as *Apollo 13* and *True Romance.* The exterior is still gloriously intact (note the groovy wrought-iron railings and the floating stone fireplace in the lobby), while the interiors have been upgraded with a smart, colorful SoCal look and all the modern comforts. Everything within is 21st-century new, including the attractive IKEA-style furniture, the bright contemporary textiles and wall prints, and the modern bathrooms; about 10 rooms also have "micro kitchens" (basically wet bars) with a microwave. Everything is clean, fresh, and pleasing. Attention families: Book now to snare one of the two suites, which have pullout sofas, huge closets, full kitchens, and a second TV.

Located just down the street from the movie studios, the neighborhood is modest but quiet and nice, convenient for those interested in studio tours, TV-show tapings, and easy freeway access to Universal Studios. In classic motor-lodge style, a petite pool sits in a gated corner of the parking lot, but it's attractive and inviting on hot Valley days. Other amenities that elevate the Safari above the motel standard include an exercise room, room service from the modest but surprisingly good restaurant at the Anabelle Hotel (the Safari's sister property) next door, and valet service, as well as self-serve laundry.

1911 W. Olive Ave., Burbank, CA 91506. © **818/845-8586**. Fax 818/845-0054. 55 units. $109–$119 double; $168 suite. AAA and corporate rate $95. Extra person $10. AE, DC, DISC, MC, V. Free parking. Pets accepted with $100 deposit. **Amenities:** Restaurant and martini bar (in hotel next door); heated outdoor pool; exercise room; limited room service; coin-op laundry and laundry service; dry cleaning. *In room:* TV w/pay movies, dataport, coffeemaker, fridge, iron, hair dryer.

PASADENA & ENVIRONS
VERY EXPENSIVE

The Ritz-Carlton, Huntington Hotel & Spa ★★★ Originally built in 1906, the opulent Huntington Hotel was one of America's grandest hotels, but not the most earthquake-proof. No matter—the hotel was rebuilt and opened on the same spot in 1991, and the astonishing authenticity (including reinstallation of many decorative features) even fools patrons from the resort's early days. This Spanish-Mediterranean beauty sits on 23 spectacularly landscaped acres that seem a world apart from LA, though Downtown is only 20 minutes away. Each oversize guest room is dressed in conservatively elegant Ritz-Carlton style, softened by ultrapretty English garden textiles and a beautiful palette of celadon, cream, and butter yellow. Luxuries include beds dressed in Frette, marble bathrooms, thick carpets, and terry-cloth robes. You might consider spending a few extra value-wise dollars on a club-level room, which also features featherbeds, down comforters, CD players, morning coffee delivered with your wakeup call, and access to the club lounge with dedicated concierge and complimentary gourmet spreads all day (including breakfast).

The 12,000-square-foot full-service Ritz-Carlton Spa makes the Huntington an ideal place for a pampering getaway. Both guests and locals enjoy dining in the casual elegance of The Grill, but I prefer the more casual California-style Terrace Restaurant, which also serves at umbrella-covered tables by the Olympic-size pool (Southern California's first). High tea is served in the Lobby Lounge.

1401 S. Oak Knoll Ave., Pasadena, CA 91106. © **800/241-3333** or 626/568-3900. Fax 626/568-3700. www.ritzcarlton.com. 392 units. $310–$420 double; from $415 suite. Discount packages always available. AE, DC, MC, V. Valet parking $21. Pets accepted. **Amenities:** 2 restaurants; 2 lounges; Olympic-size heated outdoor pool and Jacuzzi; 3 lit tennis courts; full-service spa with Jacuzzi, sauna, and steam room; fitness center; concierge; business center; 24-hr. room service; salon; in-room massage; babysitting; laundry service; dry cleaning. *In room:* A/C, TV w/pay movies, dataport, minibar, hair dryer, iron, safe.

MODERATE

Artists' Inn & Cottage Bed & Breakfast Pleasantly unpretentious and furnished with wicker throughout, this yellow-shingled Victorian-style inn was built in 1895 as a farmhouse and expanded to include a neighboring 1909 home. Each room is decorated to reflect the style of a particular artist or period. Among the artistically inspired choices are the country-cozy New England–style Grandma Moses room; the soft, pastel-hued Degas suite; and the bold-lined, primary-hued Expressionist suite, a nod to such artists as Picasso and Dufy. Every room is thoughtfully arranged and features a private bathroom (many with period fixtures, three with Jacuzzi tubs), fresh roses from the front garden, port wine, and chocolates. Most rooms have TVs; if yours doesn't, friendly innkeeper Janet Marangi will provide one if you want it. She's constantly improving the home—a 30-foot Seurat-inspired mural was added in 2000—so you can expect everything to be in tip-top shape. The quiet residential location is just 5 minutes from the heart of Old Town Pasadena.

1038 Magnolia St., South Pasadena, CA 91030. ☎ **888/799-5668** or 626/799-5668. Fax 626/799-3678. www.artistsinns.com. 10 units. $115–$205 double. Rates include full breakfast and afternoon tea. Check for midweek specials. Extra person $20. AE, MC, V. Free parking. *In room:* A/C, TV (upon request in some units), dataport, hair dryer.

Bissell House Bed & Breakfast ✦ If you enjoy the true B&B experience, you'll love the Bissell House. Hidden behind hedges that carefully isolate it from busy Orange Grove Avenue, this antique-filled 1887 gingerbread Victorian—the former home of the vacuum heiress and now owned by hosts Russell and Leonore Butcher—offers a unique taste of life on what was once Pasadena's "Millionaire's Row." Outfitted in a traditional chintz-and-cabbage roses style, all individually decorated rooms have private bathrooms (one with an antique claw-foot, one with a whirlpool tub, two with shower only), individual heating and air-conditioning (a B&B rarity), Internet access, and very comfortable beds. If you don't mind stairs, request one of the more spacious top-floor rooms. The modern world doesn't interfere with the mood in these romantic sanctuaries, but the downstairs library features a TV with VCR and a telephone/fax machine for guests' use. The beautifully landscaped grounds boast an inviting pool, Jacuzzi, and a deck with lounge chairs. Included in the room rate is an elaborately prepared breakfast served in the large dining room, as well as an afternoon tea, cookie, and wine service.

201 Orange Grove Ave. (at Columbia St.), South Pasadena, CA 91030. ☎ **800/441-3530** or 626/441-3535. Fax 626/441-3671. www.bissellhouse.com. 6 units (2 with shower only). $125–$185 double. Rates include full breakfast. AE, MC, V. Free parking. **Amenities:** Outdoor pool; Jacuzzi. *In room:* A/C, hair dryer, iron.

INEXPENSIVE

Saga Motor Hotel *Value* This 1950s relic of old Route 66 has far more character than most other motels in its price range. The rooms are small, clean, and simply furnished with the basics. The double-doubles are spacious enough for shares, but budget-minded families will prefer the extra-large configuration dedicated to them, which has a king and two doubles. The best rooms are in the front building surrounding the gated swimming pool, shielded from the street and inviting in warm weather. The grounds are attractive and well kept, if you don't count the Astroturf "lawn" on the pool deck. The location is very quiet and very good, just off the Foothill Freeway (I-210) about a mile from the Huntington Library and within 10 minutes of both the Rose Bowl and Old Pasadena.

1633 E. Colorado Blvd. (between Allen and Sierra Bonita aves.), Pasadena, CA 91106. ☎ **800/793-7242** or 626/795-0431. Fax 626/792-0559. www.thesagamotorhotel.com. 70 units. $65–$89 double; $99 family suite. Rates include continental breakfast. AE, DC, DISC, MC, V. Free parking. **Amenities:** Outdoor heated pool; free self-serve laundromat; laundry service; dry cleaning. *In room:* A/C, TV, dataport.

4 Where to Dine

Since the advent of California cuisine—now a staple across the country—trend-watchers have looked to LA restaurants for culinary fashion tips. LA gourmands have lately embraced New American fare, where the meat-and-potatoes appear both haute and humble. But jazzed-up comfort food is only part of the story. The 2000 Census painted a multiethnic portrait of a Los Angeles with more minorities than majorities, a diversity reflected in a rainbow of Argentinean, Armenian, Cajun/Creole, Caribbean, Cuban, Ethiopian, Indian, Korean, Lebanese, Oaxacan, Peruvian, Spanish, Thai, and Vietnamese dining choices.

The restaurants below are categorized first by geographic area, then by price. Keep in mind that many of the restaurants listed as "Expensive" are moderately priced at lunch. Reservations are recommended almost everywhere, particularly on weekends and during peak lunch (noon–1:30pm) and dinner (7–8:30pm) hours.

Limited space forced me to make tough choices; for a greater selection of reviews, see *Frommer's Los Angeles 2003*. For additional late-night dining options, see "Late-Night Bites" under "Los Angeles After Dark," later in this chapter. To locate the restaurants reviewed below, see the individual neighborhood maps in section 1, "Orientation."

SANTA MONICA & THE BEACHES
EXPENSIVE

The Lobster ⭐ SEAFOOD   There's been a seafood shack called The Lobster on the Santa Monica Pier since 1923—almost as long as the pier's been standing—but a 2000 revival brought a new sophistication to the old favorite. The interior is completely rebuilt, but still accentuates a seaside ambience and million-dollar ocean view. The menu has been revamped by chef Allyson Thurber, who brings an impressive culinary pedigree (including Downtown's Water Grill, p. 497) to the kitchen. Although the namesake crustacean is a great choice, the menu consistently presents a multitude of ultrafresh fish with thoughtful and creative preparation. Specialties range from spicy Louisiana prawns and Jumbo Lump Crab Cakes to an excellent sautéed North Carolina black bass luxuriating in white truffle sauce accompanied by lobster salad. Creative appetizers include ahi carpaccio with tangy tobiko wasabi, steamed mussels and Manila clams with apple-wood bacon, and oysters plain or fancy. For something truly decadent, try the Kasu-marinated Chilean sea bass and pick a bottle of dry chardonnay from the well-stocked cellar. The menu offers a couple of fine steaks for landlubbers, and there's a practiced bar for dedicated locals.

1602 Ocean Ave. (at Colorado Ave.), Santa Monica. © **310/458-9294.** www.thelobster.com. Reservations recommended. Main courses $15–$32. AE, MC, V. Daily 11:30am–3pm and 5–10pm. Self-parking $3–$6.

Michael's ⭐⭐ CALIFORNIA   Owner Michael McCarty, LA's answer to Alice Waters, is considered by many to be the father of California cuisine. Since Michael's opened in 1979 (when McCarty was only 25), several top LA restaurants have caught up to it, but this fetching Santa Monica venue remains one of the city's best. The dining room is filled with contemporary art by Michael's wife, Kim McCarty, and the restaurant's beloved garden is a relaxed setting for always-inventive menu choices like Baqueta sea bass with a chanterelle-mushroom ragout and fresh Provençal herbs; seared Hawaiian ahi accented with braised enoki mushrooms and earthy-tangy sesame wasabi ponzu sauce; or grilled pork chop sweetened with sweet-potato purée and anise–pinot noir sauce. Don't miss Michael's famous warm mushroom salad, tossed with crumbled goat cheese, watercress, caramelized onion, and mustard-sage vinaigrette. *Note:* Michael's automatically adds a 15% service charge to the check.

1147 3rd St. (N of Wilshire Blvd.), Santa Monica. © **310/451-0843.** Reservations recommended. Main courses $13–$23 lunch, $27–$34 dinner. AE, DC, DISC, MC, V. Mon–Fri 11:30am–2:30pm; Mon–Sat 6–10:30pm. Valet parking $4.50.

Röckenwagner ⭐⭐⭐ CALIFORNIA   Set in Frank Gehry's starkly modern Edgemar complex (itself a work of art), chef Hans Röckenwagner's eponymous restaurant continues the motif by presenting edible sculpture amid a gallery-like decor. Although it sits in the midst of a popular shopping area, the space manages to be refreshingly quiet. Röckenwagner takes his art—and his food—very seriously, once orchestrating an entire menu around German white asparagus at the height of its short season. The unpretentious staff serves deliciously pretentious dishes fusing Pacific Rim ingredients with traditional European preparations; a good example is the langoustine ravioli with mangoes in port-wine reduction and curry oil. The menu tastes as good as it reads—seared foie gras on raisin toast with tangerines, panko-crusted petrale sole with haricot vert tempura—and desserts are to die for. Don't overlook the lunch bargains, the unique European-style breakfast of bread and cheese, or the informal Wunder-BAR Wine and Snack Bar for a quick drop-in bite.

2435 Main St. (N of Ocean Park Blvd.), Santa Monica. ℂ 310/399-6504. www.rockenwagner.com. Reservations recommended. Main courses $22–$31. AE, DC, MC, V. Mon–Fri 6–10pm, Sat 5:30–11pm, Sun 10am–2:30pm and 5:30–10pm. Valet parking $4.

Valentino 🐸🐸 NORTHERN ITALIAN   Valentino is a good choice if you're splurging on just one special dinner. Charming owner Piero Selvaggio oversees two other restaurants, but his distinctive touch still pervades this 26-year-old flagship. This elegant spot continues to maintain its position as *Wine Spectator* magazine's top wine cellar, and former *New York Times* food critic Ruth Reichl calls this the best Italian restaurant in the United States. The creations of Selvaggio and his brilliant Italian-born chef, Angelo Auriana, make dinners here lengthy multicourse affairs (often involving several bottles of wine). You might begin with a crisp pinot grigio paired with caviar-filled cannoli, or *crespelle*— thin little pancakes with fresh porcini mushrooms and a rich melt of fontina cheese. A rich Barolo is the perfect accompaniment to rosemary-infused roasted rabbit. The fantastically fragrant risotto with white truffles is one of the most magnificent dishes I've ever had. Jackets are all but required in the elegant dining room.

3115 Pico Blvd. (W of Bundy Dr.), Santa Monica. ℂ **310/829-4313**. www.welovewine.com. Reservations required. Jacket advised for men. Main courses $22–$32. AE, DC, MC, V. Mon–Thurs 5:30–10:30pm, Fri 11:30am–2:30pm and 5:30–11pm, Sat 5:30–11pm. Valet parking $4.

MODERATE

Border Grill 🐸🐸🐸 MEXICAN   Before Mary Sue Milliken and Susan Feniger spiced up cable TV as *Too Hot Tamales*, they started this restaurant in West Hollywood. Now Border Grill has moved to a boldly painted, cavernous (read: loud) space in Santa Monica, and the gals aren't in the kitchen very much at all (though cookbooks and paraphernalia from their Food Network show are displayed prominently for sale). But their influence on the inspired menu is enough to maintain the cantina's popularity with folks who swear by the authentic flavor of Yucatán fish tacos, rock shrimp with ancho chiles, and meaty *ropa vieja,* the traditional Latin stew. The best meatless dish is *mulitas de hongos,* a layering of portobello mushrooms, poblano chiles, black beans, cheese, and guacamole, spiced up with roasted garlic and seared red chard. Distracting desserts are displayed prominently near the entrance, so you may spend the meal fantasizing about the yummy coconut flan or Key lime pie.

1445 4th St. (between Broadway and Santa Monica Blvd.), Santa Monica. ℂ **310/451-1655**. www. bordergrill.com. Reservations recommended. Main courses $10–$21. AE, DC, DISC, MC, V. Mon 5–10pm, Tues–Thurs and Sun 11:30am–10pm, Fri–Sat 11:30am–11pm. Metered parking lots; valet parking $4.

Chez Melange 🐸🐸 CALIFORNIA   Located inside the modest Palos Verdes Inn, this well-regarded brasserie has been presenting artful California cuisine for so long that it's become a South Bay institution. Though the menu is no longer cutting-edge, it does seem to get more and more eclectic, moving seamlessly from Japanese to Cajun, Italian to Chinese, and keeping up-to-date with premium vodkas and a mouthwatering oyster-and-seafood bar. The decor has a dated, late 1980s feel, but the conservative, moneyed crowd here doesn't mind. Each meal begins with a basket of irresistible breads before moving on to international dishes like shrimp and chicken in orange vindaloo curry over basmati rice with sweet, chunky chutney; rosemary laced pork tenderloin and shallot-sherry cream sauce; Parmesan-crusted albacore with Greek feta salad and tabbouleh; or spicy blackened halibut sauced with horseradish and served with seafood gumbo. Spa cuisine selections are available at every meal.

1716 Pacific Coast Hwy. (between Palos Verdes Blvd. and Prospect Ave.), Redondo Beach. ℂ 310/540-1222. www.chezmelange.com. Reservations recommended. Main courses $8–$13 lunch, $13–$19 dinner. AE, DISC, MC, V. Mon–Thurs 8am–10pm, Fri–Sat 8am–11pm, Sun 8am–10pm. Free parking.

Joe's ★★ *(Value* AMERICAN ECLECTIC   This is one of LA's best dining bargains. Chef/owner Joeseph Miller excels in simple New American cuisine, particularly grilled fish and roasted meats accented with piquant herbs. Formerly a tiny, quirky storefront with humble elbow room, Joe gutted and completely remodeled the entire restaurant, adding a far more spacious dining room and display wine room (though the best tables are still tucked away on the trellised outdoor patio, complete with a gurgling waterfall). But don't let the upscale additions dissuade your budgeted appetite—Joe's remains a hidden treasure for those with a champagne palate but a seltzer pocketbook. Case in point: For lunch, an autumn vegetable platter of butternut-squash purée, braised greens, grilled portobello mushrooms, and Brussels-sprout leaves wilted with truffle oil and wild mushrooms goes for a mere $11. And this *includes* a fresh mixed green salad or one of Miller's exquisite soups. Dinner entrees are equally sophisticated: fallow deer wrapped in bacon (served in a black-currant sauce with a side of roasted root vegetables), monkfish in a saffron broth, wild striped bass with curried cauliflower coulis. A double whammy is Joe's grilled ahi tuna *and* Hudson Valley foie gras appetizer served with Rosti potatoes and a red-wine herb sauce, and the desserts are equally fantastic. Two four-course prix-fixe menus are offered as well—a real bargain for under $40.

1023 Abbot Kinney Blvd., Venice. ℂ 310/399-5811. www.joesrestaurant.com. Reservations required. Main courses $8–$15 lunch, $18–$25 dinner. AE, MC, V. Tues–Fri 11:30am–2:30pm and 6–10pm, Sat–Sun 11am–2:30pm and 6–11pm. Free street parking.

INEXPENSIVE

Bread & Porridge ★ INTERNATIONAL/BREAKFAST   A dozen tables are all that compose this neighborhood cafe, but steady streams of locals mill outside, reading their newspapers and waiting for a vacant seat. Once inside, surrounded by the vintage fruit-crate labels adorning the walls and tabletops, you can sample the delicious breakfasts, fresh salads and sandwiches, and superaffordable entrees. There's a vaguely international twist to the menu, which leaps from breakfast quesadillas and omelets—all served with black beans and salsa—to the Southern comfort of Cajun crab cakes and coleslaw to typical Italian pastas adorned with Roma tomatoes and plenty of garlic. All menu items are cheap—truck-stop cheap—but with an inventive elegance that truly makes this a best-kept secret. Get a short stack of one of five varieties of pancakes with any meal—this place thoughtfully serves breakfast all day.

2315 Wilshire Blvd. (3 blocks W of 26th St.), Santa Monica. ℂ 310/453-4941. Main courses $6–$9. AE, MC, V. Mon–Fri 7am–2pm, Sat–Sun 7am–3pm. Metered street parking.

Sea Breezes & Sunsets: Oceanview Dining in Malibu

Despite fires, mudslides, and high rents, Malibu residents remain enamored of their precious parcel of beachfront paradise. There really is a beautifully calm, on-vacation vibe to this upscale stretch of coast. One of the best ways to sample a slice of this happiness pie is to (literally) turn your back on the frenzy of LA and gaze upon the sparkling Pacific—at least for the duration of a meal. From south to north, numerous restaurants dot the coastline, all exploiting as much ocean view as their property lines allow. Here are three of my favorites:

Gladstone's 4 Fish, 17300 Pacific Coast Hwy., at Sunset Boulevard (© 310/454-3474), is totally immersed in the Malibu scene. It shares a parking lot with a public beach, so the restaurant's wood deck has a constant view of surfers, bikini-clad sunbathers, and other frolicking beachgoers. At busy times, Gladstone's even sets up picnic-style tables on the sand. Prices are moderate, and the atmosphere is casual. The menu offers several pages of fresh fish and seafood, augmented by a few salads and other meals for landlubbers—it's mostly fried tourist food, but it gets the job done. Gladstone's is popular for afternoon/evening drinking and offers nearly 20 seafood appetizer platters; it's also known for decadent chocolate desserts large enough for the whole table. Open Monday through Thursday from 11am to 11pm, Friday from 11am to midnight, Saturday from 7am to midnight, and Sunday from 7am to 11pm. Parking costs $3.50.

The Malibu branch of **The Chart House,** 18412 Pacific Coast Hwy., south of Topanga Canyon (© 310/454-9321), lets its dramatic location steal the attention from its unique architecture. Built on a rocky point,

Jody Maroni's Sausage Kingdom ★ *Finds* SANDWICHES/SAUSAGES Your cardiologist might not approve, but Jody Maroni's all-natural, preservative-free "haut dogs" are some of the best wieners served anywhere. The grungy walk-up counter looks fairly foreboding—you wouldn't know there was gourmet fare behind that aging hot dog–stand facade, from which at least 14 different grilled-sausage sandwiches are served up. Bypass the traditional hot Italian and try the Toulouse garlic, Bombay curried lamb, all-chicken apple, or orange-garlic-cumin. Each is served on a freshly baked onion roll and smothered with onions and peppers. Burgers, BLTs, and rotisserie chicken are also served, but why bother?

Other locations include the Valley's Universal CityWalk (© 818/622-5639), and inside LAX Terminals 3, 4, and 6, where you can pick up some last-minute vacuum-packed sausages for home. Having elevated sausage-worship to an art form, Jody's now boasts a helpful and humorous cookbook, plus its own website offering franchising opportunities.

2011 Ocean Front Walk (N of Venice Blvd.), Venice. © 310/822-5639. www.maroni.com. Sandwiches $4–$6. No credit cards. Daily 10am–sunset.

Kay 'n Dave's Cantina *Kids* HEALTHY MEXICAN A beach community favorite for "really big portions of really good food at really low prices," Kay 'n suspended over the sand, and often perilously close to the breaking surf, The Chart House's dining room is terraced so every table has a great view. The interior is dark and woody, with a cozy bar and the glimmer of copper hoods from the exposed kitchen. There are some outdoor tables, but most seating is inside. The menu, though predictable (prime rib, steaks, lobsters, seafood), is first-class. Prices are moderate to expensive but include a generous meal's worth of food. Lunch portions provide a more affordable option. Open Monday and Tuesday from 5 to 9:30pm, Wednesday and Thursday from 11:30am to 9:30pm, Friday and Saturday from 11:30am to 10:30pm, and Sunday from 11am to 9:30pm. Complimentary valet parking is available.

Lovers of Hawaii and all things Polynesian will thrive in **Duke's Malibu** 🎯, 21150 Pacific Coast Hwy., at Las Flores Canyon (📞 **310/317-0777**), an outpost of the Hawaiian chain. Imagine a South Pacific T.G.I. Fridays where the food is secondary to the decor, then add a rocky perch atop breaking waves, and you have this surfing-themed crowd-pleaser. It's worth a visit for the memorabilia alone—the place is named for Hawaiian surf legend "Duke" Kahanamoku. Duke's offers up pretty good food at inflated, but not outrageous, prices. You'll find plenty of good-quality fresh fish prepared in the Hawaiian regional style, hearty surf and turf, a smattering of chicken and pasta dishes, and plenty of finger-lickin' appetizers to accompany Duke's Day-Glo tropical cocktails. Open Monday through Thursday from 11:30am to 10pm, Friday and Saturday from 11:30am to 10:30pm, and Sunday from 10am to 10pm. Valet parking $2 (dinner and weekends only, otherwise free self-parking).

Dave's cooks with no lard and has a vegetarian-friendly menu with plenty of meat items, too. Come early (and be prepared to wait) for breakfast, as local devotees line up for five kinds of fluffy pancakes, zesty omelets, or one of the best breakfast burritos in town. Grilled tuna Veracruz, spinach and chicken enchiladas in tomatillo salsa, seafood fajitas tostada, vegetable-filled corn tamales, and other Mexican specialties are served in huge portions, making this mostly locals' mini-chain a great choice to energize for (or reenergize after) an action-packed day of sightseeing. Bring the family—there's a kids' menu and crayons on every table.

262 26th St. (S of San Vicente Blvd.), Santa Monica. 📞 **310/260-1355**. Reservations not accepted. Main courses $5–$10. AE, MC, V. Mon–Thurs 11am–9:30pm, Fri 11am–10pm, Sat 8:30am–10pm, Sun 8:30am–9:30pm. Metered street parking.

LA'S WESTSIDE & BEVERLY HILLS
EXPENSIVE

Crustacean 🎯🎯 VIETNAMESE   It's an amazing story how this Beverly Hills restaurant came to be. Helene An, matriarch and executive chef of the An Family restaurants, is by title a Vietnamese princess, great-granddaughter of the Vice-King of Vietnam. When she and her family fled from Saigon penniless in

1975, they relocated in San Francisco, purchased a small deli, and introduced the city to their now-legendary recipe: An Family's Famous Roast Crab and Garlic Noodles. From this single dish spawned a Horatio Alger story and a family restaurant dynasty. The Beverly Hills location is pure drama from the moment you walk in: You're immediately scrutinized by the patrons to see 1) if you're a somebody and 2) what you're wearing, but you're too busy admiring the Indochina-themed decor—curvaceous copper bar, balcony seating, bamboo garden, waterfall, and an 80-foot-long "stream" topped with glass and filled with exotic koi—to notice. What you won't see is the Secret Kitchen (literally, it's off-limits to most of the staff), where the An family's signature dishes such as tiger prawns with garlic noodles, roasted lobster in tamarind sauce, and roast Dungeness crab are prepared. Although all these dishes are quite good, they're also heavy on the butter—I prefer the lighter sea bass dish with ginger and garlic-black bean sauce. On weekend nights, Helene (a real sweetheart and timeless beauty) is often holding court, making sure your dining experience is faultless.

9646 Little Santa Monica Blvd. (at Bedford St.), Beverly Hills. ☎ 310/205-8990. Reservations recommended. Main courses $19–$26. AE, DC, DISC, MC, V. Mon–Fri 11:30am–2:30pm; Mon–Tues and Thurs–Fri 5:30–10:30pm; Wed and Sat 5:30–11:30pm. Valet parking $4.50.

Four Oaks ✦✦✦ CALIFORNIA   The country-cottage ambience and chef Peter Roelant's superlative blend of fresh ingredients with luxurious continental flourishes make a meal at the Four Oaks one of my favorite luxuries. Dinner is served beneath trees festooned with twinkling lights. Appetizers like lavender-smoked salmon with crisp potatoes and horseradish crème fraîche complement mouthwatering dishes like roasted chicken with sage, Oregon forest mushrooms, artichoke hearts, and port-balsamic sauce. If you're looking for someplace special, head to this canyon hideaway.

2181 N. Beverly Glen Blvd., Los Angeles. ☎ 310/470-2265. www.fouroaksrestaurant.com. Reservations required. Main courses $22–$29. AE, DISC, MC, V. Tues–Sat 11:30am–2pm, Sun 10:30am–2pm; daily 6–10pm. Valet parking $4.

Jozu ✦✦ PACIFIC RIM/CALIFORNIA   *Jozu* means "excellent" in Japanese, and the word describes everything about this tranquil restaurant. All meals begin with complimentary sake from Jozu's premium sake list. Chef Hisashi Yoshiara's menu presents Asian flavors interpreted with an international inventiveness. Outstanding dishes include delicately roasted sea bass on a bed of crunchy cabbage, accented with tangy ponzu sauce; albacore tuna wrapped in a crispy potato nest and bathed in soy butter; and rack of lamb perfectly charbroiled and presented over a warm bell-pepper and arugula ragout. Appetizers range from shrimp sui-mai in rich lobster sauce to spicy halibut sashimi. The dessert of choice is Asian pear tart, lightly caramelized fruit laid in a buttery crust. The restaurant's interior is warmly comfortable and subtly lit; plenty of beautiful Hollywood types dine here, but it's quiet enough for real dinner conversation.

8360 Melrose Ave. (at Kings Rd.), West Hollywood. ☎ 323/655-5600. www.jozu.com. Reservations recommended. Main courses $16–$25. AE, MC, V. Mon–Fri 6–10:30pm, Sat–Sun 5:30–10:30pm. Valet parking $3.50.

Lucques ✦✦ FRENCH/MEDITERRANEAN   Once Los Angeles became accustomed to this restaurant's unusual name—"Lucques" is a variety of French olive, pronounced "Luke"—local foodies fell hard for this quietly and comfortably sophisticated home of former Campanile chef Suzanne Goin. The old brick building, once silent star Harold Lloyd's carriage house, is decorated in mute, clubby colors with subdued lighting that extends to the handsome enclosed patio. Goin cooks with bold flavors, fresh-from-the-farm produce, and an instinctive feel for the food of the Mediterranean. The short and oft-changed menu makes the most of unusual ingredients like salt cod and oxtails. Standout dishes include Tuscan bean soup with tangy greens and pistou, grilled chicken served alongside spinach sautéed with pancetta and shallots, rustic mascarpone polenta topped with wild-mushroom ragout and wilted greens, and perfect vanilla *pòt de crème* for dessert. Lucques's bar menu, featuring steak frites béarnaise, omelets, and tantalizing hors d'oeuvres (olives, warm almonds, sea salt, chewy bread), is a godsend for late-night diners. *Tip:* On Sundays, Lucques offers a bargain $30 prix-fixe three-course dinner from a weekly changing menu.

8474 Melrose Ave. (E of La Cienega), West Hollywood. ✆ 323/655-6277. Reservations recommended. Main courses $18–$30. AE, DC, MC, V. Tues–Sat noon–2:30pm and 6pm–1:30am; Sun 5:30pm–midnight. Closed the last 2 weeks of Aug. Metered street parking or valet ($3.50).

Matsuhisa ★★★ JAPANESE/PERUVIAN   Japanese chef/owner Nobuyuki Matsuhisa arrived in Los Angeles via Peru and opened what may be the most creative restaurant in the city. A true master of fish cookery, Matsuhisa creates fantastic dishes by combining Japanese flavors with South American spices and salsas. Broiled sea bass with black truffles, sautéed squid with garlic and soy, and Dungeness crab tossed with chiles and cream are examples of the masterfully prepared delicacies that are available in addition to thickly sliced nigiri and creative sushi rolls. Matsuhisa is perennially popular with celebrities and hard-core foodies, so reserve early for those hard-to-get tables. The small, crowded main dining room suffers from poor lighting and precious lack of privacy; many big names are ushered through to private dining rooms. If you dare, ask for *omakase*, and the chef will personally compose a selection of eccentric dishes.

129 N. La Cienega Blvd. (N of Wilshire Blvd.), Beverly Hills. ✆ 310/659-9639. Reservations recommended. Main courses $14–$26; sushi $4–$13 per order; full omakase dinner from $65. AE, DC, MC, V. Mon–Fri 11:45am–2:15pm; daily 5:45–10:15pm. Valet parking $3.50.

Mimosa ★ FRENCH PROVENÇAL   Decked out in traditional bistro garb (butter-yellow walls, artistic photos, French posters), Mimosa attracts plenty of French expatriates and Euro-style denizens with a truly authentic menu. You won't get the classic French of caviar and truffles, but rather regional peasant specialties like rich veal daube, *andouillette* (tripe sausage), perfect steak fries, and a slow-cooked pork roast with horseradish lentils. The appetizer list usually includes a splendid terrine, and bowls of house-cured cornichons and spicy Dijon mustard accompany bread to every table. Despite the occasional tinge of trendy attitude—usually precipitated by the presence of habitués like Tom Cruise, Jennifer Aniston, and Brad Pitt—Mimosa should be appreciated for its casual, comforting bistro fare.

8009 Beverly Blvd. (W of Fairfax), West Hollywood. ✆ 323/655-8895. Reservations recommended. Main courses $13–$24. AE, MC, V. Mon–Fri 11:30am–3pm; daily 5:30pm–midnight. Metered street parking.

Spago ★★★ CALIFORNIA   Wolfgang Puck is more than a great chef, he's also a masterful businessman and publicist who has made Spago one of the best-known restaurants in the United States. Despite all the hoopla—and almost 20 years of service—Spago remains one of LA's top-rated restaurants. Talented Puck henchman Lee Hefter presides over the kitchen, delivering the culinary sophistication demanded by an upscale Beverly Hills crowd. This high-style indoor/outdoor space glows with the aura of big bucks, celebrity, and the pe fectly honed California cuisine that can honestly take credit for setting the s dard. Spago is also one of the last places in LA where men will fee comfortable in jacket and tie (suggested, but not required). All eyes the romantically twinkle-lit outdoor patio (the most coveted tables), but the food takes center stage. You simply can't choose wrong—highlights include the appetizer of foie gras "three ways"; savory duck either honey-lacquered and topped with foie gras, or Cantonese-style with a citrus tang; and rich Austrian dishes from "Wolfie's" childhood, like spicy beef goulash or perfect veal schnitzel.

176 N. Canon Dr. (N of Wilshire Blvd.), Beverly Hills. ✆ 310/385-0880. www.wolfgangpuck.com. Reservations required. Jacket advised for men. Main courses $18–$34; tasting menu $85. AE, DC, DISC, MC, V. Mon–Fri 11:30am–2:30pm, Sat noon–2:30pm; daily 5:30–10:30pm. Valet parking $4.50.

MODERATE

Bombay Café ★★ INDIAN   This friendly sleeper may be LA's best Indian spot, serving excellent curries and kurmas typical of South Indian street food. Once seated, immediately order *sev puri* for the table; these crispy little chips topped with chopped potatoes, onions, cilantro, and chutneys are the perfect accompaniment to what's sure to be an extended menu-reading session. Also recommended are the burrito-like "frankies," juicy little bread rolls stuffed with lamb, chicken, or cauliflower. The best dishes come from the tandoor and include spicy yogurt-marinated swordfish, lamb, and chicken. While some dishes are authentically spicy, plenty of others have a mellow flavor for less incendiary palates. This restaurant is phenomenally popular and gets its share of celebrities.

12021 W. Pico Blvd. (at Bundy Dr.), West Los Angeles. ✆ 310/473-3388. Reservations recommended for dinner. Main courses $9–$17. AE, MC, V. Mon–Fri 11:30am–3pm; Sun–Thurs 5–10pm, Fri–Sat 5–11pm. Metered street parking (lunch); valet parking $3.50 (dinner).

Chaya Brasserie ★★ FRENCH/JAPANESE   Now open for 2 decades, Chaya has become ensconced as one of Los Angeles's finest restaurants. This Continental bistro with Asian overtones is popular with film agents during lunch and a particularly beautiful assembly of stars at night (spotted recently: George Clooney, Mark Wahlberg, the Baldwin brothers). The place is loved for its exceptionally good food and unpretentious atmosphere. Despite a high noise level, the stage-lit dining room feels sensuous and swoony. On warm afternoons and evenings, the best tables are on the outside terrace, overlooking the busy street. Chaya is best known for superb grilled fish and meats, like seared soy-marinated Hawaiian tuna and Long Island duckling. Chef Shigefumi Tachibe's lobster ravioli with pesto-cream sauce is both stylish and delicious, as is tangy grilled chicken Dijon, a house specialty. Chaya is also a hot late-night rendezvous, with a short but choice supper menu served until 12:15am Tuesday through Saturday.

8741 Alden Dr. (E of Robertson Blvd.), Beverly Hills. ✆ 310/859-8833. Reservations recommended on weekends. Main courses $10–$16 lunch, $15–$27 dinner. AE, DC, MC, V. Mon–Fri 11am–2:30pm; Mon–Thurs 6–10:30pm; Fri–Sat 6–11pm; Sun 6–10pm. Valet parking $3.50.

El Coyote ★ *Value* MEXICAN   Everyone from 20-something hipsters to slick showbiz player-types, rockers, movie stars, and families can be found at this local ⸺⸺. The rowdy bar scene alone is a great reason to hang out at this highly ⸺ ⸺et eminently affordable) Mexican restaurant. During prime dining ⸺ ⸺staurant's bustling atmosphere spills over into the bar, which is fre-⸺ ⸺ed to capacity. Settle in by sampling from the grande-size menu ⸺ ⸺h as taquitos, quesadillas, and nachos, and be sure to wash them ⸺ ⸺le of cheap and tasty margaritas. The fare is traditional Mexi-⸺ ⸺ared, with a wide array of taco, enchilada, and burrito combi-⸺ ⸺ng fajita platters.

7312 Beverly Blvd. (at La Brea Ave.), West Hollywood. ✆ 323/939-2255. Main courses $8–$10. AE, MC, V. Mon–Thurs 11am–10pm, Fri–Sat 11am–11pm.

Kate Mantilini ☆ AMERICAN   It's rare to find a restaurant that feels comfortably familiar yet cutting-edge trendy at the same time—and also happens to be one of LA's few late-night eateries. Kate Mantilini fits the bill perfectly. One of the first to bring meatloaf back into fashion, Kate's offers a huge menu of upscale truck-stop favorites like "white" chili (made with chicken, white beans, and Jack cheese), grilled steaks and fish, a few token pastas, and just about anything you might crave. At 2am, nothing quite beats a steaming bowl of lentil-vegetable soup and some garlic-cheese toast, unless your taste runs to fresh oysters and a dry martini—Kate's has it all. The huge mural of the Hagler-Hearns boxing match that dominates the stark, open interior provides the only clue to the namesake's identity: Mantilini was an early female boxing promoter, around 1947.

9101 Wilshire Blvd. (at Doheny Dr.), Beverly Hills. ✆ 310/278-3699. Reservations accepted only for parties of 6 or more. Main courses $7–$16. AE, MC, V. Mon–Thurs 7:30am–1am, Fri 7:30am–2am, Sat 11am–2am, Sun 10am–midnight. Validated valet parking.

La Serenata Gourmet ☆☆ MEXICAN   Westsiders rejoiced when this branch of Boyle Heights's award-winning La Serenata de Girabaldi began serving its authentic, but innovative, Mexican cuisine just a block away from the Westside Pavilion shopping center. This place is casual, fun, and intensely delicious. Specialties like shrimp enchiladas, fish tacos, and pork *gorditas* are all accented with hand-patted corn tortillas, fresh chips dusted with *añejo* cheese, and flavorful fresh salsas. Though it's always packed to capacity despite an expansion in 1998, you should try to avoid the prime lunch and dinner hours nevertheless.

10924 W. Pico Blvd., West LA. ✆ 310/441-9667. Main courses $8–$13. AE, MC, V. Daily 11am–3:30pm; Sun–Thurs 5–10pm, Fri–Sat 5–10:30pm. Metered street parking.

INEXPENSIVE

The Apple Pan ☆☆ SANDWICHES/AMERICAN   There are no tables, just a U-shaped counter, at this classic American burger shack and LA landmark. Open since 1947, The Apple Pan is a diner that looks—and acts—the part. It's famous for juicy burgers, speedy service, and an authentic frills-free atmosphere. The hickory burger is best, though the tuna sandwich also has its share of fans. Ham, egg-salad, and Swiss-cheese sandwiches round out the menu. Definitely order fries and, if you're in the mood, the home-baked apple pie too.

10801 Pico Blvd. (E of Westwood Blvd.), West LA. ✆ 310/475-3585. Most menu items under $6. No credit cards. Tues–Thurs and Sun 11am–midnight; Fri–Sat 11am–1am. Free parking.

Versailles ☆ *Value* CUBAN   Outfitted with Formica tabletops and looking something like an ethnic IHOP, Versailles feels much like any number of Miami restaurants that cater to the Cuban community. The menu reads like a veritable survey of Havana-style cookery and includes specialties like "Moors and Christians" (flavorful black beans with white rice), *ropa vieja* (a stringy beef stew), *eastin lechón* (suckling pig with sliced onions), and fried whole fish (usually sea bass). Shredded roast pork is particularly recommendable, especially when tossed with the restaurant's trademark garlic-citrus sauce. But what everyone comes for is the chicken—succulent, slow roasted, smothered in onions and either garlic-citrus sauce or barbecue sauce. Almost everything is served with black beans and rice; wine and beer are available. Because meals are good, bountiful, and cheap, there's often a wait.

Another Versailles restaurant is located in Culver City at 10319 Venice Blvd. (© **310/558-3168**).

1415 S. La Cienega Blvd. (S of Pico Blvd.), West Hollywood. © **310/289-0392**. Main courses $5–$11. AE, MC, V. Daily 11am–10pm. Free parking.

HOLLYWOOD
EXPENSIVE
Campanile ★★ CALIFORNIA/MEDITERRANEAN   Built as Charlie Chaplin's private offices in 1928, this lovely building has a multilevel layout with flower-bedecked interior balconies, a bubbling fountain, and a skylight through which diners can see the *campanile* (bell tower). The kitchen, headed by Spago alumnus chef/co-owner Mark Peel, gets a giant leg up from pastry chef/co-owner (and wife) Nancy Silverton, who also runs the now-legendary La Brea Bakery next door. Meals here might begin with fried zucchini flowers drizzled with melted mozzarella or lamb carpaccio surrounded by artichoke leaves—a dish that arrives looking like one of van Gogh's sunflowers. Chef Peel is particularly known for his grills and roasts; try the grilled prime rib smeared with black-olive tapenade or papardelle with braised rabbit, roasted tomato, and collard greens. And don't skip dessert—the restaurant's many sweets fans have turned Nancy's dessert book into a bestseller. The weekend brunch is a surprising crowd-pleaser and a terrific way to appreciate this beautiful space on a budget.

624 S. La Brea Ave. (N of Wilshire Blvd.). © **323/938-1447**. www.campanilerestaurant.com. Reservations required. Main courses $26–$38. AE, DC, DISC, MC, V. Mon–Fri 11:30am–2:30pm, Sat–Sun 9:30am–1:30pm; Mon–Thurs 6–10pm, Fri–Sat 5:30–11pm. Valet parking $3.50.

Patina ★★★ CALIFORNIA/FRENCH   Joachim Splichal, arguably LA's very best chef, is also a genius at choosing and training top chefs to cook in his kitchens while he jets around the world. Patina routinely wins the highest praise from demanding gourmands, who are happy to empty their bank accounts for unbeatable meals. The dining room is straightforwardly attractive, low-key, well lit, and professional, without a hint of stuffiness. The menu is equally disarming: "Mallard Duck with Portobello Mushrooms" gives little hint of the brilliant colors and flavors that appear on the plate. The seasonal menu features partridge, pheasant, venison, and other game in winter and spotlights exotic local vegetables in warmer months. Seafood is always available; if Maine lobster cannelloni or asparagus-wrapped John Dory is on the menu, order it. Patina is justifiably famous for its mashed potatoes and potato-truffle chips; be sure to include one (or both) with your meal.

5955 Melrose Ave. (W of Cahuenga Blvd.). © **323/467-1108**. www.patinagroup.com. Reservations required. Main courses $18–$30. AE, DC, DISC, MC, V. Mon–Fri 6–10pm, Sat 5:30–10:30pm; Fri noon–2pm. Valet parking $4.

MODERATE
Authentic Café ★ SOUTHWESTERN/ECLECTIC   True to its name, this restaurant serves authentic Southwestern food in a casual atmosphere. It's a winning combination that made this place an LA favorite, although popularity has dropped off recently due to the rush for the next big thing. But Authentic Café still has a loyal following of locals who appreciate generous portions and lively flavor combinations. You can sometimes find an Asian flair to chef Roger Hayot's dishes. Look for brie, papaya, and chili quesadillas; other worthwhile dishes are the chicken casserole with a cornbread crust, fresh corn and red peppers in chile-cream sauce, and meatloaf with caramelized onions.

7605 Beverly Blvd. (at Curson Ave.). ⓒ **323/939-4626.** Reservations accepted only fo
Main courses $9–$19. AE, MC, V. Mon–Thurs 11:30am–11pm, Fri 11:30am–midnight, Sï
Sun 10:30am–11pm. Metered street parking or evening valet parking $3.50.

Ca' Brea ⚝⚝ NORTHERN ITALIAN   When Ca' Brea ope
talented chef/owner Antonio Tommasi was catapulted into a public spotlight
shared by only a handful of LA chefs—Wolfgang Puck, Michel Richard, and
Joachim Splichal. Since then, Tommasi has opened two other celebrated restaurants, Locanda Veneta in Hollywood and Ca' Del Sole in the Valley, but, for
many, Ca' Brea remains tops. The restaurant's refreshingly bright two-story dining room is a happy place, hung with colorful, oversize contemporary paintings
and backed by an open prep-kitchen where you can watch as your seafood cakes
are sautéed and your Napa cabbage braised. Booths are the most coveted seats;
but with only 20 tables in all, be thankful you're sitting anywhere. Detractors
might complain that Ca' Brea isn't what it used to be since Tommasi began split-
ting his time between three restaurants, but Tommasi stops in daily and keeps a
very close watch over his handpicked staff. Consistently excellent dishes include
the roasted pork sausage, the butternut squash–stuffed ravioli, and a different
risotto each day—always rich, creamy, and delightfully indulgent.

346 S. La Brea Ave. (N of Wilshire Blvd.). ⓒ **323/938-2863.** Reservations recommended. Main courses
$7–$20 lunch, $9–$21 dinner. AE, DC, MC, V. Mon–Fri 11:30am–2:30pm; Mon–Thurs 5:30–10:30pm; Fri–Sat
5:30–11pm; Sun 5:30–10pm. Valet parking $3.50.

Musso & Frank Grill ⚝ AMERICAN/CONTINENTAL   A survey of Hollywood restaurants that leaves out Musso & Frank is like a study of Las Vegas
singers that fails to mention Wayne Newton. As LA's oldest eatery (since 1919),
Musso & Frank is the paragon of Old Hollywood grillrooms. This is where
Faulkner and Hemingway drank during their screenwriting days and where
Orson Welles used to hold court. The restaurant is still known for its bone-dry
martinis and perfectly seasoned Bloody Marys. The setting is what you'd expect:
oak-beamed ceilings, red-leather booths and banquettes, mahogany room
dividers, and chandeliers with tiny shades. The extensive menu is a veritable survey of American/Continental cookery. Hearty dinners include veal scaloppini
Marsala, roast spring lamb with mint jelly, and broiled lobster. Grilled meats are
a specialty, as is the Thursday-only chicken potpie. Regulars also flock in for
Musso's trademark "flannel cakes," crepe-thin pancakes flipped to order.

6667 Hollywood Blvd. (at Cherokee Ave.). ⓒ **323/467-7788.** Reservations recommended. Main courses
$13–$32. AE, DC, MC, V. Tues–Sat 11am–11pm. Self-parking $2.25 with validation.

Sofi ⚝ *(Finds)* GREEK   Look for the simple black awning over the narrow pas-
sageway that leads from the street to this hidden Aegean treasure. Be sure to ask
for a table on the romantic patio amid twinkling lights, and immediately order
a plate of their thick, satisfying *tsatziki* (yogurt-cucumber-garlic spread) accompanied by a basket of warm pitas for dipping. Other specialties (recipes courtesy
of Sofi's grandmother) include herbed rack of lamb with rice, fried calamari
salad, *saganaki* (kasseri cheese flamed with ouzo), and other hearty taverna
favorites. Sofi's odd, off-street setting, near the Farmers Market in a popular part
of town, has made it an insiders' secret.

8030¾ W. 3rd St. (between Fairfax Ave. and Crescent Heights Blvd.). ⓒ **323/651-0346.** Reservations recommended. Main courses $7–$14. AE, DC, MC, V. Mon–Sat noon–3pm; daily 5:30–11pm. Metered street
parking or valet parking $3.

Tahiti ⚝ INTERNATIONAL   Tahiti has a rapidly growing fan base of showbiz types and artists who inhabit the eclectic surrounding neighborhood.

⊃hef/owner Tony DiLembo's distinctive "world cuisine" is a provocative mix of influences that produces diverse specialties like rare ahi tuna drizzled with lime-ginger butter, sprinkled with toasted sesame seeds, and served with wasabi horse-radish and papaya garnish; Argentinean-style T-bone with chimichurri dipping sauce; sherry-sautéed chicken and spinach pot stickers accented with mint; and perennial standout rosemary chicken strips with fettuccine in sun-dried tomato/cream sauce. The relaxing decor is sophisticated South Seas with a mod-ern twist, incorporating thatch, batik, rattan, and palm fronds. In the adjacent Tiki Lounge (open daily 6pm–2am, with happy hour 6–8pm), tropical concoc-tions contribute to the island ambience. If the weather is nice, try to get a table on the patio. And don't forget to save room for Tahiti's tropical-tinged desserts.

7910 W. 3rd St. (at Fairfax). ℭ 323/651-1213. Reservations recommended. Main courses $11–$17. AE, MC, V. Mon–Fri 11:30am–2:30pm; Mon–Thurs 6–10pm, Fri–Sat 6–11pm, Sun 5–9pm. Valet parking $3.50.

INEXPENSIVE

El Cholo ✿ MEXICAN   There's authentic Mexican and then there's tradi-tional Mexican—El Cholo is comfort food of the latter variety, south-of-the-border cuisine regularly craved by Angelenos. They've been serving it up in this pink adobe hacienda since 1927, even though the once-outlying mid-Wilshire neighborhood around them has turned into Koreatown. El Cholo's expertly blended margaritas, invitingly messy nachos, and classic combination dinners don't break new culinary ground, but the kitchen has perfected these standards over 70 years. I wish they bottled their rich enchilada sauce! Other specialties include seasonally available green-corn tamales and creative sizzling vegetarian fajitas that go way beyond just eliminating the meat. The atmosphere is festive, as people from all parts of town dine happily in the many rambling rooms that compose the restaurant. There's valet parking as well as a free self-parking lot directly across the street.

Westsiders head to El Cholo's Santa Monica branch at 1025 Wilshire Blvd. (ℭ **310/899-1106**).

1121 S. Western Ave. (S of Olympic Blvd.). ℭ **323/734-2773**. www.elcholo.com. Reservations suggested. Main courses $8–$14. AE, DC, DISC, MC, V. Mon–Thurs 11am–10pm, Fri–Sat 11am–11pm, Sun 11am–9pm. Free self-parking or valet parking $3.

Pink's Hot Dogs ✿ *Kids* HOT DOGS   Pink's isn't your usual guidebook rec-ommendation, but then again, this crusty corner stand isn't your usual dog cart either. The heartburn-inducing chilidogs ("World's Best!") are craved by even the most upstanding, health-conscious Angelenos. Bruce Willis reportedly pro-posed to Demi Moore at the 63-year-old shack that grew around the late Paul Pink's 10¢ wiener cart. Pray the bulldozers stay away from this little nugget of a place. Cool website, too.

709 N. La Brea Ave. (at Melrose Ave.). ℭ **323/931-4223**. www.pinkshollywood.com. Hot dogs $2.10. No credit cards. Sun–Thurs 9:30am–2am, Fri–Sat 9:30am–3am.

Roscoe's House of Chicken 'n' Waffles ✿ SOUTHERN/BREAKFAST   It sounds like a bad joke: Only chicken and waffle dishes are served here, a rubric that also encompasses eggs and chicken livers. Its close proximity to CBS Tele-vision City has turned this simple restaurant into a kind of de facto commissary for the network. A chicken-and-cheese omelet isn't everyone's ideal way to begin the day, but it's de rigueur at Roscoe's. At lunch, few calorie-unconscious diners can resist the chicken smothered in gravy and onions, a house specialty that's served with waffles or grits and biscuits. Large chicken-salad bowls and chicken sandwiches also provide plenty of cluck for the buck. Homemade cornbread, sweet-potato pie, homemade potato salad, and corn on the cob are available as side orders, and wine and beer are available.

Roscoe's can also be found at 106 W. Manchester St. (at Main St.; ✆ **323/ 752-6211**), and 5006 W. Pico Blvd. (at La Brea Ave.; ✆ **323/934-4405**).

1514 N. Gower St. (at Sunset Blvd.). ✆ **323/466-7453.** Main courses $4–$11. No credit cards. Sun–Thurs 9am–midnight, Fri–Sat 9am–4am. Metered street parking.

Swingers ⭐ DINER/AMERICAN   Resurrected from a motel coffee shop, Swingers was transformed by a couple of LA hipster nightclub owners into a 1990s version of comfy Americana. The interior seems like a slice of the 1950s until you notice the plaid upholstery and Warholesque graphics, which contrast nicely with the retro red-white-and-blue "Swingers" logo adorning *everything*. Guests at the attached Beverly Laurel Motor Hotel (p. 475) chow down alongside body-pierced industry hounds from nearby record companies, while a soundtrack that runs the gamut from punk rock to "Schoolhouse Rock" plays in the background. It's not all attitude, though—you'll enjoy a menu of high-quality diner favorites with trendy crowd-pleasers: Steel-cut Irish oatmeal, challah French toast, grilled Jamaican jerk chicken, and a selection of tofu-enhanced vegetarian dishes are just a few of the eclectic offerings. Sometimes I just "swing" by for a malt or milkshake to go—they're among the best in town.

8020 Beverly Blvd. (W of Fairfax Ave.). ✆ **323/653-5858.** Most items less than $8. AE, DISC, MC, V. Sun–Thurs 6am–2am, Fri–Sat 9am–4am. Metered street parking.

Toi on Sunset ⭐ *Value* THAI   Because they're open *really* late, Toi has become an instant fave of Hollywood hipsters like Sean Penn and Woody Harrelson, who make post-clubbing excursions to this rock 'n' roll eatery a few blocks from the Sunset Strip. After all the hype, I was surprised to find possibly LA's best bargain Thai food, authentically prepared and served in portions so generous the word "enormous" seems inadequate. Menu highlights include hot-and-sour chicken, coconut soup, and the house specialty: chicken curry *somen,* a spicy dish with green curry and mint sauce spooned over thin Japanese rice noodles. Vegetarians will be pleased with the vast selection of meat-free items like *pad kee mao,* rice noodles served spicy with tofu, mint, onions, peppers, and chili. The interior is a noisy amalgam of cultish movie posters, rock 'n' roll memorabilia, and haphazardly placed industrial-issue dinette sets; and the plates, flatware, and drinking glasses are cheap coffee-shop issue. In other words, it's all about the food and the scene—neither will disappoint.

Westsiders can opt for **Toi on Wilshire,** 1120 Wilshire Blvd., Santa Monica (✆ **310/394-7804**). It's open daily from 11am to 3am.

7505½ Sunset Blvd. (at Gardner). ✆ **323/874-8062.** Reservations accepted only for parties of 6 or more. Main courses $6–$11. AE, DISC, MC, V. Daily 11am–4am.

DOWNTOWN
EXPENSIVE

Water Grill ⭐⭐⭐ SEAFOOD   This restaurant is popular with the suit-and-tie crowd at lunch and with concertgoers en route to the Music Center at night. The dining room is a stylish and sophisticated fusion of wood, leather, and brass, but gets a lighthearted lift from cavorting papier-mâché fish that play against an aquamarine ceiling painted with bubbles. Water Grill, considered by many to be LA's best seafood house, is known for its shellfish; among the appetizers are a dozen different oysters. Main courses are imaginative dishes influenced by the cuisines of Hawaii, the Pacific Northwest, New Orleans, and New England. Try the appetizer seafood platter, a mouthwatering assortment served with well-made aïoli; bluefin tuna tartare; Santa Barbara spot prawns paired with fingerling potato salad; Maine lobster stuffed with Dungeness crab; perfectly pan-roasted Alaskan halibut; and simple desserts like mascarpone with figs and cherries.

544 S. Grand Ave. (between 5th and 6th sts.). © 213/891-0900. Reservations recommended. Main courses $19–$31. AE, DC, DISC, MC, V. Mon–Tues 11:30am–9pm, Wed–Fri 11:30am–10pm, Sat 5–10pm, Sun 4:30–9pm. Valet parking $4.

MODERATE

Cha Cha Cha 🌟🌟 CARIBBEAN   Cha Cha Cha serves the West Coast's best Caribbean food in a fun and funky space on the seedy fringe of Downtown. The restaurant is a festival of flavors and colors both upbeat and offbeat. It's impossible to feel down when you're part of this eclectic hodgepodge of pulsating Caribbean music, wild decor, and kaleidoscopic clutter; still, the intimate dining rooms cater to lively romantics, not the obnoxious types. Claustrophobes should choose seats in the airy covered courtyard. The very spicy black-pepper jumbo shrimp gets top marks, as does the paella, a generous mixture of chicken, sausage, and seafood blended with saffron rice. Other Jamaican-, Haitian-, Cuban-, and Puerto Rican–inspired recommendations include jerk pork and mambo gumbo, a zesty soup of okra, shredded chicken, and spices. Hard-core Caribbeanites might visit for breakfast, when the fare ranges from plantain, yucca, onion, and herb omelets to scrambled eggs with fresh tomatillos served on hot grilled tortillas.

656 N. Virgil Ave. (at Melrose Ave.), Silver Lake. © 323/664-7723. Reservations recommended. Main courses $8–$15. AE, DC, DISC, MC, V. Sun–Thurs 8am–10:30pm, Fri–Sat 8am–11:30pm. Valet parking $3.50.

Ciudad 🌟🌟 LATIN   The latest venture of TV's *Too Hot Tamales*—Susan Feniger and Mary Sue Milliken—is this intriguing restaurant in the heart of Downtown. *Ciudad* means "city" in Spanish, and is a nod to the partners' long-ago venture City Restaurant. Here, amidst juicy sherbet pastel walls and 1950s geometric abstract designs, exuberant crowds gather to revel in a menu that brings together cuisines from the world's great Latin urban centers: Havana, Rio de Janeiro, Barcelona, and so on. Standout dishes include Honduran ceviche presented in a martini glass and accented with tropical coconut and pineapple, Argentine rib eye stuffed with jalapeño chiles and whole garlic cloves, and citrus-roasted Cuban-style chicken served with Puerto Rican rice and fried plantains. Between 3 and 7pm on weekdays, Ciudad presents *cuchifrito,* traditional Latin snacks served at the bar; it's easy to make a meal of several, choosing from sweet-savory pork-stuffed green tamales, *papas rellenos* (mashed-potato fritters stuffed with oxtail stew), plantain gnocchi in tomatillo sauce, and more. As with the pair's Border Grill (p. 486), desserts are worth saving room for, and large enough to share.

445 S. Figueroa St. © 213/486-5171. Reservations recommended. Main courses $12–$23; *cuchifrito* $5–$8. AE, MC, V. Mon–Fri 11:30am–10pm, Sat–Sun 5–10pm. Free parking during the day; valet parking after 5pm $3.50.

R23 🌟🌟 JAPANESE/SUSHI   This gallery-like space in Downtown's out-of-the-way warehouse/artist-loft district has been the secret of sushi connoisseurs since 1991. At the back of R23's single, large dining room, the 12-seat sushi bar shines like a beacon; what appear at first to be ceramic wall ornaments are really stylish sushi platters hanging in wait for large orders. More functional art reveals itself in the corrugated cardboard chairs—they're funky, yet far more comfortable than wood! Genial sushi wizards stand in wait, cases of the finest fish before them. Salmon, yellowtail, shrimp, tuna, and scallops are among the always-fresh selections; an excellent and unusual offering is seared *toro,* where the rich belly tuna absorbs a faint and delectable smoky flavor from the grill. Though R23's sublimely perfect sushi is the star, the short but inventive menu also includes pungent red miso soup, creamy baked scallops, finely sliced beef "sashimi," and several other choices. Their latest addition is a wide selection of premium wines and sakes (try the addictively sweet nigori).

923 E. 2nd St. (between Alameda St. and Santa Fe Ave.). ✆ 213/687-7178. Reservations recommended. Main courses $12–$20; sushi $4–$8. AE, DC, DISC, MC, V. Mon–Fri 11:45am–2pm; Mon–Sat 5:45–10pm. Free parking.

Traxx ★ *Finds* CALIFORNIA   There's always been a restaurant—of some sort—inside the Union Station passenger concourse, but Traxx is the first to do justice to its grand, historic setting. Boasting the right mix of retro-evocative Art Deco character with sleek contemporary touches, the interior blends seamlessly with the station's architecture, a unique fusion of Spanish Colonial Revival and Streamline Moderne. Elegant enough for a romantic dinner, yet welcoming to the casual commuter in search of a stylish lunch or sit-down snack, Traxx features a menu with the same cosmopolitan flavor as the station itself. Samples range from "small plates" of ahi tuna Napoleon with crispy wonton or "Really Good" (and they are) crab cakes with a chipotle kick, to main dishes like grilled salmon with a Mediterranean flair or the much-talked-about Gorgonzola-crusted beef tenderloin presented atop crispy and mashed potatoes surrounded by a pool of demi-glace/herb reduction.

In Union Station, 800 N. Alameda St. (at Cesar E. Chavez Ave.). ✆ 213/625-1999. Reservations suggested for dinner. Main courses $10–$15 lunch, $10–$25 dinner. AE, MC, V. Mon–Fri 11am–10pm, Sat 6–10pm. Free valet parking with validation.

INEXPENSIVE

The Original Pantry Cafe *Value* AMERICAN/BREAKFAST   An LA institution if ever there was one, this place has been serving huge portions of comfort food around the clock for more than 60 years. In fact, there isn't even a key to the front door. Owned by former LA mayor and botched governor contender Richard Riordan, the Pantry is popular with politicos, who come here for weekday lunches, and with conferencegoers en route to the nearby L.A. Convention Center. The well-worn restaurant is also a welcoming beacon to clubbers after hours, when Downtown becomes a virtual ghost town. A bowl of celery stalks, carrot sticks, and whole radishes greets you at your Formica table, and creamy coleslaw and sourdough bread come free with every meal. Famous for quantity rather than quality, the Pantry serves huge T-bone steaks, densely packed meatloaf, macaroni and cheese, and other American favorites. A typical breakfast (served all day) might consist of a huge stack of hotcakes, a big slab of sweet cured ham, home fries, and coffee.

877 S. Figueroa St. (at 9th St.). ✆ 213/972-9279. Main courses $6–$11. No credit cards. Daily 24 hr. Free parking with validation.

Philippe the Original SANDWICHES   Good old-fashioned value is what this legendary landmark cafeteria is all about. Popular with both South Central residents and Beverly Hills elite, Philippe's unspectacular dining room is one of the few places in LA where everyone can get along. Philippe's claims to have invented the French-dipped sandwich at this location in 1908; it remains the most popular menu item. Patrons push trays along the counter and watch while their choice of beef, pork, ham, turkey, or lamb is sliced and layered onto crusty

French bread that's been dipped in meat juices. Other menu items include homemade beef stew, chili, and pickled pigs' feet. A hearty breakfast, served daily until 10:30am, is worthwhile if only for Philippe's uncommonly good cinnamon-dipped French toast. Beer and wine are available. *Tip:* For added entertainment, request a booth in the new Train Room, which houses the nifty Model Train Museum.

1001 N. Alameda St. (at Ord St.). ℂ 213/628-3781. www.philippes.com. Most menu items under $7. No credit cards. Daily 6am–10pm. Free parking.

THE SAN FERNANDO VALLEY
EXPENSIVE
Pinot Bistro ✦✦ *Kids* CALIFORNIA/FRENCH   When the Valley crowd doesn't want to make the drive to Patina, they pack into Pinot Bistro, one of Joachim Splichal's other successful restaurants. The Valley's only great bistro is designed with dark woods, etched glass, and cream-colored walls that scream "trendy French" almost as loudly as the rich, straightforward cooking. The menu, a symphony of California and Continental elements, includes a beautiful warm potato tart with smoked whitefish, and baby lobster tails with creamy polenta—both studies in culinary perfection. The most popular dish here is the Frenchified Tuscan bean soup, infused with oven-dried tomatoes and roasted garlic and served over crusty *ciabatta* bread. The generously portioned main dishes continue the gourmet theme: baby lobster risotto, braised oxtail with parsley gnocchi, and puff pastry stuffed with bay scallops, Manila clams, and roast duck. The service is good, attentive, and unobtrusive. Many regulars prefer Pinot Bistro at lunch, when a less expensive menu is served to a more easygoing crowd.

12969 Ventura Blvd. (W of Coldwater Canyon Ave.), Studio City. ℂ 818/990-0500. www.patinagroup.com. Reservations required. Main courses $7–$13 lunch, $16–$22 dinner. AE, DC, DISC, MC, V. Mon–Fri noon–2pm; Mon–Thurs 6–10pm, Fri 6–10:30pm, Sat 5:30–10:30pm, Sun 5:30–9:30pm. Valet parking $3.50.

MODERATE
Jerry's Famous Deli ✦ *Kids* DELI   Here's a simple yet sizable deli where all the Valley's hipsters go to relieve their late-night munchies. This place probably has one of the largest menus in America—a tome that spans cultures and continents, from Central America to China to New York. From salads to sandwiches to steak-and-seafood platters, everything—including breakfast—is served all day. Jerry's is consistently good at lox and eggs, pastrami sandwiches, potato pancakes, and all the deli staples. It's also an integral part of LA's cultural landscape and a favorite of the show-business types who populate the adjacent foothill neighborhoods. It even has a full bar.

12655 Ventura Blvd. (just E of Coldwater Canyon Ave.), Studio City. ℂ 818/980-4245. Dinner main courses $9–$14; breakfast $2–$11; sandwiches and salads $4–$12. AE, MC, V. Daily 24 hr. Free parking.

Miceli's *Kids* ITALIAN   Mostaccioli marinara, lasagna, thin-crust pizza, and eggplant parmigiana are indicative of the Sicilian-style fare at this cavernous, stained-glass-windowed Italian restaurant adjacent to Universal City. The wait staff sings show tunes or opera favorites in between serving dinner (and sometimes instead of); make sure you have enough Chianti to get into the spirit of it all. This is a great place for kids, but too rollicking for romance.

   If you're near Hollywood Boulevard, visit the original (since 1949) Miceli's at 1646 N. Las Palmas (ℂ 323/466-3438).

3655 Cahuenga Blvd. (E of Lankershim), Los Angeles. ℂ 818/508-1221. Main courses $7–$12; pizza $9–$15. AE, DC, MC, V. Mon–Thurs 5pm–midnight, Fri 5pm–1am, Sat 4pm–1am, Sun 4–11pm. Parking $2.50.

Paul's Café ☆ CALIFORNIA/FRENCH   One of the Valley's hardest reservations (hint: call early, dine early, or both) is at this midsize neighborhood bistro, where a quietly elegant setting belies the friendly prices that have made Paul's a big success. Expect Chef Ricardo Macchi's seasonal menu to include plenty of seafood (roasted sea bass laid atop spinach with a mushroom vinaigrette, sautéed sea scallops with saffron risotto and lobster sauce), hearty meats (filet mignon with port sauce accompanied by a creamy sweet potato–Gorgonzola gratin, garlic-rubbed rack of lamb sweetened with mint), and appetizers that ought to be main courses (pepper-crusted seared ahi drizzled with scallion vinaigrette, crab cakes with lobster aïoli). Soup or a small salad is only $1 with any dinner, and locals love the mere $2 corkage fee. Paul's manages to be intimate enough for lovers (though I've received complaints about the "dark as a coal mine" dining room) yet also welcoming for families—its success is no surprise.

13456 Ventura Blvd. (between Dixie Canyon and Woodman Ave.), Sherman Oaks. ☎ 818/789-3575. Main courses $8–$11 lunch, $12–$17 dinner. AE, MC, V. Mon–Fri 11:30am–2:30pm; Mon–Thurs 5:30–10pm, Fri 5:30–11pm, Sat 5–11pm, Sun 5–9:30pm. Metered street parking or valet parking $4.

INEXPENSIVE

Du-par's Restaurant & Bakery ☆ AMERICAN/DINER   It's been called a "culinary wax museum," the last of a dying breed, the kind of coffee shop Donna Reed took the family to for blue-plate specials. This isn't a trendy new theme place, it's the real deal—and that motherly waitress who calls everyone under 60 "hon" has probably been slinging hash here for 20 or 30 years. Du-par's is popular among old-timers who made it part of their daily routine decades ago, show-business denizens who eschew the industry watering holes, a new generation that appreciates a tasty, cheap meal . . . well, everyone, really. It's common knowledge that Du-par's makes the best buttermilk pancakes in town, though some prefer the eggy, perfect French toast (extra-crispy around the edges, please). Mouthwatering pies (blueberry cream cheese, coconut cream, and more) line the front display case and can be had for a song.

West Hollywood denizens can visit the branch of Du-par's in the Ramada Hotel, 8571 Santa Monica Blvd., west of La Cienega (☎ 310/659-7009); they're open until 3am on weekends *and* have a full bar. There's another Du-par's in Los Angeles at the Farmers Market, 6333 W. Third St., at Fairfax St. (☎ 323/933-8446), but it doesn't stay open as late.

12036 Ventura Blvd. (1 block E of Laurel Canyon Blvd.), Studio City. ☎ 818/766-4437. www.dupars.com. All items under $11. AE, DC, DISC, MC, V. Sun–Thurs 6am–1am, Fri–Sat 6am–4am. Free parking.

PASADENA & ENVIRONS

During the past decade or so, Pasadena has grown into one of the premier dining destinations for Angelenos in the know. It's now packed with restaurants ranging from elegant art-food dining to casual sidewalk cafes, and Pasadena is no longer anybody's secret.

EXPENSIVE

Bistro 45 ☆☆ CALIFORNIA/FRENCH   All class, yet never stuffy, Bistro 45 is a favorite among Pasadena's old guard and nouvelle riche alike. The restaurant's warm, light ambience and gallery-like decor are an unexpected surprise after the ornately historic Art Deco exterior (the building is a former bank), but provide a perfect backdrop for owner Robert Simon's refreshing cuisine. The seasonally inspired menu changes frequently; dishes might include salmon and tuna tartares flavored with cilantro, rock-shrimp risotto with saffron, pan-roasted monkfish with garlic polenta, roasted veal loin filled with Roquefort,

Fanny Bay oyster salad, and Nebraska pork with figs. For dessert, try the "choco-late soup," a creamy soufflé served with chocolate-kirsch sauce and vanilla ice cream. The knowledgeable wait staff can answer questions about the excellent wine list; Bistro 45 appears regularly on *Wine Spectator's* "best of" lists, and hosts special-event wine dinners.

45 S. Mentor Ave. (between Colorado Blvd. and Green), Pasadena. ✆ 626/795-2478. Reservations recommended. Main courses $11–$16 lunch, $17–$27 dinner. AE, MC, V. Tues–Fri 11:30am–2:30pm; Tues–Thurs 6–10pm, Fri–Sat 6–11pm, Sun 5–9pm. Valet parking $4.

Parkway Grill ✿ CALIFORNIA ECLECTIC This vibrant, quintessentially Southern California restaurant has been one of the LA area's top-rated spots since 1985, quickly gaining a reputation for avant-garde flavor combinations and gourmet pizzas to rival Spago's. Although some critics find many dishes too fussy, others thrill to appetizer innovations like lobster-stuffed cocoa crepes or Dungeness crab cakes with ginger cream and two salsas. The stars of the menu are meat and game from the iron mesquite grill, followed by richly sweet (and substantial) desserts. Located where the old Arroyo Seco Parkway glides into an ordinary city street, the Parkway Grill is within a couple of minutes' drive from Old Pasadena and thoughtfully offers free valet parking.

510 S. Arroyo Pkwy. (at California Blvd.), Pasadena. ✆ 626/795-1001. Reservations recommended. Main courses $8–$27. AE, DC, MC, V. Mon–Fri 11:30am–2:30pm; Mon–Thurs 5:30–11pm, Fri–Sat 5pm–midnight, Sun 5–11pm. Free valet parking.

The Raymond ✿✿ NEW AMERICAN/CONTINENTAL With its easy-to-miss setting in a sleepy part of Pasadena, the Raymond is a jewel few locals even know about. This Craftsman cottage was once the caretaker's house for a grand Victorian hotel called The Raymond. Though the city has grown to surround it, the place maintains an enchanting air of seclusion and serenity. Chef/owner Suzanne Bourg brings a romantic sensibility and impeccable culinary instincts to dishes that are mostly haute American—with an occasional European flair. The menu changes weekly. One night a grilled rack of lamb is sauced with orange, Grand Marnier, and peppercorns; another night it comes with a creamy white wine and chèvre sauce with dried cherries. Bourg's soups are always heav-enly (the restaurant gladly gives out the recipes), and desserts are inspired. Tables are scattered throughout the house and in the lush English garden, and there's plenty of free, nonvalet parking. (You wouldn't find *that* on the Westside!)

1250 S. Fair Oaks Ave. (at Columbia St.), Pasadena. ✆ 626/441-3136. www.theraymond.com. Reservations required. Main courses $13–$20 lunch, $30–$34 dinner; prix-fixe 3-course dinner $36 (including wine), 4-course dinner $45–$49. AE, DC, DISC, MC, V. Tues–Thurs 11:30am–2:30pm and 6–9:30pm; Fri 11:30am–2:30pm and 5:45–10pm; Sat 11am–2:30pm and 5:45–10pm; Sun 10am–2:30pm and 4:30–8pm; afternoon tea Tues–Fri noon–4pm and Sat–Sun noon–3pm. Free parking.

MODERATE

Café Santorini ✿ MEDITERRANEAN Located at the center of Pasadena's crowded Old Town shopping mecca, this second-story gem has a secluded Mediterranean ambience, due in part to its historic brick building with splendid patio tables overlooking, but insulated from, the plaza below. In the evening, light-ing is subdued and romantic, but ambience is casual; many diners are coming from or going to an adjacent movie-theater complex. The food is outstanding and affordable, featuring grilled meats and kebobs, pizzas, fresh and tangy hummus, plenty of warm pitas, and other staples of Greek cuisine. The menu includes regional flavors like lamb, feta cheese, spinach, or Armenian sausage; the vegetar-ian baked butternut squash is filled with fluffy rice and smoky roast vegetables.

64 W. Union St. (main entrance at the shopping plaza at the corner of Fair Oaks Ave. and Colorado Blvd.), Pasadena. © **626/564-4200.** www.cafesantorini.com. Reservations recommended on weekends. Main courses $9–$22. AE, DC, DISC, MC, V. Sun–Thurs 11am–11pm, Fri–Sat 11am–midnight. Valet or self-parking $4.

Nonya ★★ *(Finds* PERANAKAN   It's a rare day in a travel writer's career when he enjoys a cuisine he's never even heard of. Peranakan cuisine (aka Nonya) was developed in the 15th century by Peranakans, a people whose heritage stems from the intermarriage between Chinese settlers of Singapore and the local Malaysians. It's a complex and sophisticated style of cooking, involving exotic ingredients and a layering of flavors, and there are only a few chefs in the Western world—including Nonya's executive chef Tony Pat, a Hong Kong native—who know the authentic techniques to make it. Use of pungent roots such as ginger, *tumeric,* and galangal are used liberally along with aromatic and often spicy seasonings to an eclectic and wondrous effect. Case in point: It's a sure bet you haven't had a *mangga ikan* salad—a light yet flavorful dish made with fresh mango, tender halibut, thinly sliced red onions and a lemon grass–lime vinaigrette. Nor are you familiar with *khaj panggang,* thin slices of chicken breast marinated in chili and grilled in banana leaves. The seafood dishes are equally enticing: red snapper spiced with *tumeric* and tamarind, cooked in banana leaves and served with house-pickled vegetables; and whole Dungeness crab sautéed with curry leaves and black pepper. Owner Simon Tong, who owned Asian restaurants in London for 25 years until recently settling in Pasadena, hired designer Dodd Mitchell to create a gorgeous dining room, replete with glimmering hardwoods, metals, and lush foliage that surround a tranquil elevated pond. It's both sexy and soothing, the perfect date place.

61 N. Raymond St. (at Union St.), Pasadena. © **626/583-8398.** Reservations recommended. Main courses $9–$42. AE, MC, V. Daily 11am–2:30pm; Sun–Thurs 5–10pm, Fri–Sat 5–11pm. Valet parking $4.

Yujean Kang's Gourmet Chinese Cuisine ★★ CONTEMPORARY CHINESE   Many Chinese restaurants put the word "gourmet" in their name, but few really mean it—or deserve it. Not so at Yujean Kang's, where Chinese cuisine is taken to an entirely new level. A master of "fusion" cuisine, the eponymous chef/owner snatches bits of techniques and flavors from both China and the West, commingling them in an entirely fresh way. Can you resist such provocative dishes as "Ants on Tree" (beef sautéed with glass noodles in chili and black sesame seeds), or lobster with caviar and fava beans, or Chilean sea bass in passion-fruit sauce? Kang is also a wine aficionado and has assembled a magnificent cellar of California, French, and German wines. Try pairing a German Spätlese with tea-smoked duck salad. The red-wrapped dining room is less subtle than the food, but just as elegant.

67 N. Raymond Ave. (between Walnut St. and Colorado Blvd.), Pasadena. © **626/585-0855.** Reservations recommended. Main courses $8–$19. AE, MC, V. Daily 11:30am–2:30pm and 5–10pm. Street parking.

INEXPENSIVE

Crocodile Cafe CASUAL ECLECTIC   Casual and colorful, this offshoot of Pasadena's groundbreaking Parkway Grill (p. 502) builds a menu around simple crowd-pleasers (pizza, pasta, burgers, salads) prepared with fresh ingredients and jazzed up with creative marinades, vinaigrettes, and salsas. It's a formula that works; this Lake Avenue branch is the original location, but siblings have sprung up throughout the San Fernando and San Gabriel valleys—even as far away as Santa Monica. Favorite selections include the oak-grilled burger with curly french fries, the Croc's signature blue-corn chicken tostada with warm black beans and fresh guacamole, wood-grilled gourmet pizzas in the California Pizza Kitchen style, zesty tortilla soup, and ooey-gooey desserts.

Other branches include 88 W. Colorado Blvd. in Old Town Pasadena (© **626/568-9310**); 626 N. Central Ave. in Glendale (© **818/241-1114**); and 101 Santa Monica Blvd. in Santa Monica (© **310/394-4783**).

140 S. Lake Ave., Pasadena. © **626/449-9900**. www.crocodilecafe.com. Main courses $8–$18. AE, MC, V. Sun–Thurs 11am–10pm, Fri–Sat 11am–midnight. Free self-parking.

5 The Top Attractions

To locate these attractions, see the individual neighborhood maps in section 1, "Orientation."

SANTA MONICA & THE BEACHES

Venice Ocean Front Walk ★★ *Kids*　This has long been one of LA's most colorful areas. Founded at the turn of the 20th century, Venice was a development inspired by its Italian namesake. Authentic gondolas plied miles of inland waterways lined with rococo palaces. In the 1950s, Venice became the stomping grounds of Jack Kerouac, Allen Ginsberg, William S. Burroughs, and other beats. In the '60s, this was the epicenter of LA's hippie scene.

Today, Venice is still one of the world's most engaging bohemian locales. It's not an exaggeration to say that no visit to LA would be complete without a stroll along the famous beach path, an almost-surreal assemblage of every LA stereotype—and then some. Among stalls and stands selling cheap sunglasses and Mexican blankets swirls a carnival of humanity that includes bikini-clad in-line skaters, tattooed bikers, muscle-bound pretty boys, panhandling vets, beautiful wannabes, and plenty of tourists and gawkers. On any given day, you're bound to come across all kinds of performers: mimes, break-dancers, buskers, chainsaw jugglers, talking parrots, or an occasional apocalyptic evangelist.

On the beach, between Venice Blvd. and Rose Ave, Venice. www.venicebeach.com.

LA'S WESTSIDE & BEVERLY HILLS

J. Paul Getty Museum at the Getty Center ★★ *Kids*　Since opening in 1997, the Richard Meier–designed Getty Center has quickly assumed its place in the LA landscape (literally and figuratively) as a cultural cornerstone and international mecca. Headquarters for the Getty Trust's research, education, and conservation concerns, the complex is most frequently visited for the museum galleries displaying collector J. Paul Getty's enormous collection of art. Always known for antiquities, expanded galleries now allow the display of Impressionist paintings, truckloads of glimmering French furniture and decorative arts, fine illuminated manuscripts, contemporary photography, and previously overlooked graphic arts. The area that's open to the public consists of five two-story pavilions set around an open courtyard, and each gallery within is specially designed to complement the works on display. A sophisticated system of programmable window louvers allows many outstanding works (particularly paintings) to be displayed in the natural light they were created in for the first time in the modern era. One of these is van Gogh's *Irises,* one of the museum's finest holdings. Trivia buffs will enjoy knowing that the museum spent $53.9 million to acquire this painting; it's displayed in a complex that cost roughly $1 *billion* to construct.

Visitors to the center park at the base of the hill and ascend via a cable-driven electric tram. On clear days, the sensation is of being in the clouds, gazing across

Los Angeles and the Pacific Ocean (and into a few chic Brentwood backyards). If you're like me and don't remember a thing from your college Art Appreciation class, plunk down $3 for a self-guided audio tour that gives a brief overview of the 250+ works in the collection. The 45-minute architectural tours, offered throughout the day, are also worth looking into. Dining options include several espresso/snack carts, a cafeteria, a self-service cafe, and the elegant (though informal) Restaurant offering table service for lunch (Tues–Sun) and dinner (Fri–Sat) with breathtaking views overlooking the ocean and mountains (reservations are recommended, though walk-ins are accepted; call © **310/440-7300** or make reservations online at www.getty.edu).

Realizing that fine-art museums are usually dreadfully boring for kids, the center provides several clever programs for kids, including exploratory games such as "Perplexing Paintings" and "The Getty Art Detective"; a Family Room filled with puzzles, computers, picture books, and games; mythical storytelling sessions on weekends at 11am, noon, and 1pm; weekend family workshops; and self-guided audio tours made specifically for families.

Entrance to the Getty Center is free—they don't need your money—but parking reservations are required weekdays (though I've heard of people getting in without one on slow days). College students with current ID and those arriving by public transportation, motorcycle, or bicycle do not require reservations. Reservations are not required after 4pm and all day Saturday and Sunday. Cameras and video cams are permitted but only if you use existing light (flash units are verboten). *Tip:* Avoid the crowds by visiting in the late afternoon or evening; the center is open until 9pm Friday and Saturday, the nighttime view is breathtaking, and you can finish with a late dinner on the Westside.

1200 Getty Center Dr., Los Angeles. © **310/440-7300**. www.getty.edu. Free admission. Tues–Thurs and Sun 10am–6pm, Fri–Sat 10am–9pm. Closed major holidays. Parking $5; reservations required weekdays (see above).

HOLLYWOOD

Farmers Market ✮ *Kids*   The original market was little more than a field with stands set up by farmers during the Depression so they could sell directly to city dwellers. Eventually, permanent buildings grew up, including the trademark shingled 10-story clock tower. Today the place has evolved into a sprawling marketplace with a carnival atmosphere, a kind of "turf" version of San Francisco's Fisherman's Wharf. About 100 restaurants, shops, and grocers cater to a mix of workers from the CBS Television City complex, locals, and tourists, brought here by the busload. Retailers sell greeting cards, kitchen implements, candles, and souvenirs; but everyone comes for the food stands, which offer oysters, Cajun gumbo, fresh-squeezed orange juice, roast-beef sandwiches, fresh-pressed peanut butter, and all kinds of international fast foods. You can still buy produce here—it's no longer a farm-fresh bargain, but the selection's better than at the grocery store. Don't miss **Kokomo** (© **323/933-0773**), a "gourmet" outdoor coffee shop that has become a power-breakfast spot for showbiz types. Red turkey hash and sweet-potato fries are the dishes that keep them coming back.

6333 W. 3rd St. (at Fairfax Ave.), Hollywood. © **323/933-9211**. www.farmersmarketla.com. Mon–Fri 9am–9pm, Sat 9am–8pm, Sun 10am–7pm.

Griffith Observatory   Made world-famous in the film *Rebel Without a Cause,* Griffith Observatory's bronze domes have been Hollywood Hills landmarks since 1935. Most visitors don't actually go inside; they come to this spot on the south slope of Mount Hollywood for unparalleled city views. On warm nights, with the lights twinkling below, this is one of the most romantic places in LA.

The main dome houses a planetarium, where narrated projection shows reveal the stars and planets that are hidden from the naked eye by the city's lights and smog. Other shows take you on excursions into space to search for extraterrestrial life, or examine the causes of earthquakes and moonquakes.

The adjacent Hall of Science holds exhibits on galaxies, meteorites, and other cosmic objects, including a telescope trained on the sun, a Foucault pendulum, and earth and moon globes 6 feet in diameter. On clear nights you can gaze at the heavens through the powerful 12-inch telescope.

Note: The entire Griffith Observatory area is closed for a major renovation and expansion and will not reopen until May 2005. An "Observatory Satellite Temporary Facility" with public access is scheduled to open by the time you read this, near the Los Angeles Zoo. Call ℭ **323/664-1191** for more information.

2800 E. Observatory Rd. (in Griffith Park, at the end of Vermont Ave.). ℭ **323/664-1191**, or 323/663-8171 for the Sky Report, a recorded message on current planet positions and celestial events. www.griffith observatory.org.

The "Hollywood" Sign ⭐

These 50-foot-high white sheet-metal letters have come to symbolize the movie industry and the city itself. The sign was erected in 1923 as an advertisement for a real-estate development. The full text originally read HOLLYWOODLAND. The sign gained dubious notoriety when actress Peg Entwistle leapt to her death from the "H" in 1932. The installation of motion detectors around the sign made this graffiti tagger's coup a target even more worth boasting about. A thorny hiking trail leads toward the sign from Durand Drive near Beachwood Drive, but the best view is from down below, at the corner of Sunset Boulevard and Bronson Avenue.

At the top of Beachwood Dr., Hollywood.

Hollywood Walk of Fame ⭐ *Kids*

More than 2,500 celebrities are honored along the world's most famous sidewalk. Each bronze medallion, set into the center of a granite star, pays homage to a famous television, film, radio, theater, or recording personality. Although about a third of them are just about as obscure as Andromeda—their fame simply hasn't withstood the test of time— millions of visitors are thrilled by the sight of famous names like James Dean (1719 Vine St.), John Lennon (1750 Vine St.), Marlon Brando (1765 Vine St.), Rudolph Valentino (6164 Hollywood Blvd.), Marilyn Monroe (6744 Hollywood Blvd.), Elvis Presley (6777 Hollywood Blvd.), Greta Garbo (6901 Hollywood Blvd.), Louis Armstrong (7000 Hollywood Blvd.), and Barbra Streisand (6925 Hollywood Blvd.). Gene Autry's all over the place: The singing cowboy earned five different stars (a sidewalk record), one in each category.

The sight of bikers, metalheads, druggies, hookers, and hordes of disoriented tourists all treading on memorials to Hollywood's greats makes for quite a bizarre tribute. But the Hollywood Chamber of Commerce has been doing a terrific job sprucing up the pedestrian experience with filmstrip crosswalks, swaying palms, and more. And at least one weekend a month, a group of fans calling themselves Star Polishers busy themselves scrubbing tarnished medallions.

The legendary sidewalk is continually adding new names. The public is invited to attend dedication ceremonies; the honoree—who pays a whopping $15,000 for the eternal upkeep—is usually in attendance. Contact the

Stargazing in LA: Top Spots for Sighting Celebrities

Celebrities pop up everywhere in LA. If you spend enough time here, you'll surely bump into a few of them. If you're in the city for only a short time, however, it's best to go on the offensive.

Restaurants are your surest bet. Dining out is such a popular recreation among Hollywood's elite that you sometimes wonder whether frequently sighted folks like Johnny Depp, Nicole Kidman, Bridget Fonda, Nicolas Cage, Brad Pitt, or Cindy Crawford ever actually eat at home. **Matsuhisa, Locanda Veneta** (at 8638 W. Third St.)**, Mimosa, Jozu, Maple Drive** (at 345 N. Maple Dr.), and **Lola's** (at 945 N. Fairfax Ave.) can almost guarantee sightings any night of the week. The city's stylish hotels can also be good bets—the **Mondrian** draws stars galore to its dining room **Asia de Cuba,** as well as the elite **Sky Bar;** and **Shutters's** lobby lounge is the rendezvous of choice for famous faces heading to dinner at the hotel's **One Pico** restaurant. The trendiest clubs and bars—**Whiskey Bar** (in the Sunset Marquis Hotel & Villas at 1200 N. Alta Loma Rd.), **House of Blues, Viper Room,** and Sky Bar—are all good for star sightings, but cover charges can be astronomical and the velvet-rope gauntlet oppressive. And it's not always Mick and Quentin and Madonna; a recent night on the town turned up only Yanni, Ralph Macchio, and Dr. Ruth.

Often, the best places to see members of the A-list aren't as obvious as a back-alley stage door or the front room of Spago. Shops along Sunset Boulevard, like **Tower Records** and the **Virgin Megastore,** are often star-heavy, as are chichi shops within the **Beverly Center** mall. **Book Soup,** that browser's paradise across the street from Tower, is usually good for a star or two. A midafternoon stroll along **Melrose Avenue** might also produce a familiar face; likewise the chic European-style shops of **Sunset Plaza.**

Or you can seek out the celebrities on the job. It's not uncommon for star-studded movie productions to use LA's diverse cultural landscape for **location shots;** in fact, it's such a regular occurrence that locals are usually less impressed with an A-list presence than perturbed about the precious parking spaces lost to all those equipment trucks and dressing-room trailers. On-the-street movie shoots are part of what makes LA unique, and onlookers gather wherever hastily scrawled production signs point to a hot site. For the inside track on where the action is, check the **"Daily Shoot Sheet"** at www.eidc.com. This isn't some word-of-mouth groupie posting: This is a strictly legit online listing of every filming permit applied for within the city limits. Entries are classified by type (commercial advertisement, feature film, student film, TV program) and working title, and the site lists production hours and exact street addresses.

Keep your eyes peeled for celebrities—everyone does in LA—and you'll more than likely be rewarded. And don't forget to peer through the windows of any Land Rover or Mercedes driving by; even mo<del></del> stars have errands to run.

Hollywood Chamber of Commerce, 6255 Sunset Blvd., Suite 911, Hollywood, CA 90028 (✆ **323/469-8311**), for information on who's being honored this week.

· Hollywood Blvd., between Gower St. and La Brea Ave.; and Vine St., between Yucca St. and Sunset Blvd.

Mann's Chinese Theatre ✿
This is one of the world's great movie palaces and one of Hollywood's finest landmarks. The theater was opened in 1927 by impresario Sid Grauman, a brilliant promoter who's credited with originating the idea of the paparazzi-packed movie "premiere." Outrageously conceived, with both authentic and simulated Chinese embellishments, Grauman's theater was designed to impress. Original Chinese heavenly doves top the facade, and two of the theater's columns once propped up a Ming Dynasty temple.

Visitors by the millions flock to the theater for its famous entry court, where stars like Elizabeth Taylor, Paul Newman, Ginger Rogers, Humphrey Bogart, Frank Sinatra, Marilyn Monroe, and about 160 others set their signatures and hand/foot prints in concrete. It's not always hands and feet: Betty Grable made an impression with her shapely leg; Gene Autry with the hoof-prints of his horse, Champion; and Jimmy Durante and Bob Hope with their trademark noses.

6925 Hollywood Blvd. (1 block W of Highland Ave.). ✆ **323/464-MANN** or 323/461-3331. Movie tickets $9. Call for showtimes.

Rancho La Brea Tar Pits ✿ *Kids*
An odorous swamp of congealed oil oozes to the earth's surface in the middle of Los Angeles. No, it's not a low-budget horror-movie set—it's the La Brea Tar Pits, an awesome, primal pool on Museum Row, where hot tar has been bubbling from the earth for over 40,000 years. The glistening pools, which look like murky water, have enticed thirsty animals throughout history. Thousands of mammals, birds, amphibians, and insects—many of which are now extinct—crawled into the sticky sludge, got stuck in the worst way, and stayed forever. In 1906, scientists began a systematic removal and classification of entombed specimens, including ground sloths, giant vultures, mastodons, camels, bears, lizards, and even prehistoric relatives of today's super-rats. The best finds are on display in the adjacent George C. Page Museum of La Brea Discoveries, where an entertaining 15-minute film documenting the recoveries is also shown. Archaeological work is ongoing; you can watch as scientists clean, identify, and catalog new finds in the Paleontology Laboratory.

5801 Wilshire Blvd. (E of Fairfax Ave.), Los Angeles. ✆ **323/934-PAGE.** www.tarpits.org. Admission $6 adults, $3.50 seniors 62 and older and students with ID, $2 children 5–12, free for kids 4 and under; free for everyone 1st Tues of every month. Mon–Fri 9:30am–5pm, Sat–Sun 10am–5pm (museum).

DOWNTOWN

El Pueblo de Los Angeles Historic Monument ✿
This historic district was built in the 1930s, on the site where the city was founded, as an alternative to the razing of a particularly unsightly slum. The result is a contrived nostalgic fantasy of the city's beginnings, a kitschy theme park portraying Latino culture in a Disneyesque fashion. Nevertheless, El Pueblo has proven wildly successful, adopted it as an important cultural monument.

ithout authenticity. Some of LA's oldest buildings are here,
bes exude the ambience of old Mexico. At its core is a Mex-
e on old Olvera Street. The carnival of sights and sounds is
chis, piñatas, and more-than-occasional folkloric dancing.
trict's primary pedestrian street, and adjacent Main Street
wo dozen 19th-century buildings; one houses a Mexican
drina. A self-guided-tour brochure describing the historic

buildings is available at the Information Desk in the Plaza, or at the El Pueblo Visitors Center (© **213/628-1274;** open Mon–Sat 10am–3pm), located in the Sepulveda house midway down Olvera Street on the west side. Don't miss the **Avila Adobe,** at E-10 Olvera St. (open Mon–Sat 10am–5pm; free admission); built in 1818, it's the oldest building in the city. Enter on Alameda Street across from Union Station.

© **213/628-3562.** www.cityofla.org/elp.

THE SAN FERNANDO VALLEY

Universal Studios Hollywood ★★★ *Kids*   Believing that filmmaking itself is a bona fide attraction, Universal Studios began offering tours to the public in 1964. The concept worked. Today Universal is more than just one of the largest movie studios in the world—it's one of the biggest amusement parks.

The main attraction continues to be the **Studio Tour,** a 1-hour guided tram ride around the company's 420 acres. En route you pass stars' dressing rooms and production offices before visiting famous back-lot sets that include an eerily familiar Old West town, a clean New York City street, the famous town square from the *Back to the Future* films, and newer sets such as *Curse of the Mummy's Tomb, Jurassic Park III,* and *The Grinch.* Along the way the tram encounters several staged "disasters," which I won't divulge here lest I ruin the surprise.

Other attractions are more typical of high-tech theme-park fare, but all have a film-oriented slant. On **Back to the Future—The Ride,** you're seated in a mock time-traveling DeLorean and thrust into a fantastic multimedia roller-coasting extravaganza—it's far and away Universal's best ride. The **Waterworld** live-action stunt show is thrilling to watch (and probably more successful than the film that inspired it), while the special-effects showcase **Jurassic Park—The Ride** is short in duration but long on dinosaur illusions and computer magic lifted from the Universal blockbuster. The latest thrills are the **Mummy Returns Chamber of Doom** ride *(scarrrrrrryyyy)* and **Terminator 2 3-D,** a virtual adventure utilizing triple-screen technology to impact all the senses. **Totally Nickelodeon** is an interactive live show from the kids' TV network, providing adventure and gallons of green slime, and the new **Animal Planet Live!** stars trained monkeys and other animals doing various entertaining tricks.

Located just outside the gate of Universal Studios Hollywood is the shiny new **Universal CityWalk** (© **818/622-4455**), Universal Studio's version of Downtown Disney. If you have any money left from the amusement park, you can spend it here among the 30 stores selling brand-name everything, 25 restaurants (Hard Rock Cafe, Daily Grill, Jerry's Famous Deli, and so forth), eight nightclubs (including Blues at B. B. King's, Howl at the Moon dueling piano bar, Rumba Room Latin dance club), a six-story 3-D IMAX theater, NASCAR virtual racing, and even a bowling alley.

Universal Studios is a really fun place, but just as in any theme park, lines can be brutally long; the wait for a 5-minute ride can sometimes last more than an hour. In summer, the stifling Valley heat can dog you all day. To avoid the crowds, skip weekends and school vacations.

Hollywood Fwy. (Universal Center Dr. or Lankershim Blvd. exits), Universal City. © **818/662-3801.** www. universalstudios.com. Admission $45 adults, $35 children 3–9, free for kids under 3. Weekdays 10am–6pm, weekends 9am–7pm. Parking $7.

PASADENA & ENVIRONS

Huntington Library, Art Collections & Botanical Gardens ★★   The Huntington Library is the jewel in Pasadena's crown. The 207-acre hilltop estate was once home to industrialist and railroad magnate Henry E. Huntington (1850–1927), who bought books on the same massive scale on which he acquired businesses. The continually expanding collection includes dozens of Shakespeare's first editions, Benjamin Franklin's handwritten autobiography, a Gutenberg Bible from the 1450s, and the earliest known manuscript of Chaucer's *Canterbury Tales*. Although some rare works are available only to visiting scholars, the library has a regularly changing (and always excellent) exhibit showcasing different items in the collection.

If you prefer canvas to parchment, Huntington also put together a terrific 18th-century British and French art collection. The most celebrated paintings are Gainsborough's *The Blue Boy*, and *Pinkie*, a companion piece by Sir Thomas Lawrence depicting the youthful aunt of Elizabeth Barrett Browning. These and other works are displayed in the stately Italianate mansion on the crest of this hillside estate, so you can also get a glimpse of its splendid furnishings. American art and Renaissance paintings are exhibited in two additional galleries.

But it's the **botanical gardens** that draw most locals to the Huntington. The Japanese Garden comes complete with a traditional open-air Japanese house, koi-filled stream, and serene Zen garden. The cactus garden is exotic, the jungle garden is intriguing, the lily ponds are soothing—and there are many benches scattered about so you can sit and enjoy the surroundings.

Because the Huntington surprises many with its size and wealth of activities from which to choose, first-timers might want to start with a tour. One-hour garden tours are offered daily; no reservations or additional fees required. Times vary, so check at the Information Desk on arrival. I also recommend that you tailor your visit to include the popular English high tea served Tuesday through Friday from noon to 4:30pm, and Saturday and Sunday from 10:45am to 4:30pm (last seating at 3:30pm). The charming **tearoom** overlooks the Rose Garden (home to 1,000 varieties displayed in chronological order of their breeding), and since the finger sandwiches and desserts are served buffet-style, it's a genteel bargain even for hearty appetites at $13 per person (please note that museum admission is a separate required cost). Phone ✆ **626/683-8131** for tearoom reservations.

1151 Oxford Rd., San Marino. ✆ **626/405-2100**. www.huntington.org. Admission $10 adults, $8.50 seniors 65 and over, $7 students and children 12 and over, free to children under 12; free to all 1st Thurs of each month. Sept–May Tues–Fri noon–4:30pm, Sat–Sun 10:30am–4:30pm; June–Aug Tues–Sun 10:30am–4:30pm. Closed major holidays.

6 Exploring the City

To locate the attractions discussed below, see the individual neighborhood maps in section 1, "Orientation."

ARCHITECTURAL HIGHLIGHTS

Los Angeles is a veritable Disneyland of architecture. The city is home to an amalgam of distinctive styles, from Art Deco to Spanish Revival to coffee-shop kitsch to suburban ranch to postmodern—and much more. Cutting-edge, over-the-top styles that would be out of place in other cities, from the oversize hot dog that is Tail o' the Pup to the mansions lining the streets of Beverly Hills, are perfectly at home in movie city.

SANTA MONICA & THE BEACHES

When you're strolling the historic canals and streets of Venice, be sure to check out the **Chiat/Day** offices at 340 Main St. What would otherwise be an unspectacular contemporary office building is made fantastic by a **three-story pair of binoculars** that frames the entrance. The sculpture is modeled after a design created by Claes Oldenburg and Coosje van Bruggen.

When you're on your way in or out of LAX, be sure to stop for a moment to admire the **Control Tower** and **Theme Building.** The spacey *Jetsons*-style Theme Building, which has always loomed over LAX, has been joined by a more recent silhouette. The main control tower, designed by local architect Kate Diamond to evoke a stylized palm tree, is tailored to present Southern California in its best light. You can go inside to enjoy the view from the Theme Building's observation deck, or have a space-age cocktail at the Technicolor bachelor pad that is the **Encounter LAX** restaurant.

LA'S WESTSIDE & BEVERLY HILLS
In addition to the sights below, don't miss the **Beverly Hills Hotel** (p. 471), and be sure to wind your way through the streets of Beverly Hills off Sunset Boulevard.

Pacific Design Center   The bold architecture and overwhelming scale of the Pacific Design Center, designed by Argentinean architect Cesar Pelli, aroused controversy when it was erected in 1975. Sheathed in gently curving cobalt-blue glass, the seven-story building houses over 750,000 square feet of wholesale interior-design showrooms and is known to locals as "the blue whale." When the property for the design center was acquired in the 1970s, almost all of the small businesses that lined this stretch of Melrose Avenue were demolished. Only Hugo's Plating, which still stands in front of the center, successfully resisted the wrecking ball. In 1988, a second boxlike structure, dressed in equally dramatic Kelly green, was added to the design center and surrounded by a protected outdoor plaza.
8687 Melrose Ave., West Hollywood. © 310/657-0800.

Schindler House ✦   A protégé of Frank Lloyd Wright and contemporary of Richard Neutra, Austrian architect Rudolph Schindler designed this innovative modern house for himself in 1921–22. It's now home to the Los Angeles arm of Austria's Museum of Applied Arts (MAK). The house is noted for its complicated interlocking spaces; the interpenetration of indoors and out; simple, unadorned materials; and technological innovations. Docent-guided tours are conducted at no additional charge on weekends only.

The MAK Center offers guides to LA-area buildings by Schindler and other Austrian architects, and presents visiting related exhibitions and creative arts programming. Call for schedules.
835 N. Kings Rd. (N of Melrose Ave.), West Hollywood. © 323/651-1510. www.makcenter.com. Admission $5 adults, free to children 12 and under. Free to all on Sept 10 (Schindler's birthday), May 24 (International Museum Day), Dec 1, and every Fri after 4pm. Daily 11am–6pm.

Tail o' the Pup   At first glance, you might not think twice about this hot dog–shaped bit of kitsch just across from the Beverly Center. But locals adored this closet-size wiener dispensary so much that when it was threatened by the developer's bulldozer, they spoke out en masse to save it. One of the last remaining examples of 1950s representational architecture, the "little dog that could" serves up an "only in LA" experience to go with its great Baseball Special.
329 N. San Vicente Blvd. (between Beverly Blvd. and Melrose Ave.), West Hollywood. © 310/652-4517.

HOLLYWOOD
In addition to the buildings listed below, don't miss the **Griffith Observatory** (p. 505) **Mann's Chinese Theatre** (p. 508), the **Hollywood Roosevelt Hotel**

Stargazing, Part II: The Less-than-Lively Set

Almost everybody who visits LA hopes to see a celebrity—they are, after all, our most common export. But celebrities usually don't cooperate, failing to gather in readily viewable herds. There is, however, an absolutely guaranteed method to approach within 6 feet of many famous stars. Cemeteries are *the* place for star- (or at least headstone-) gazing: The star is always available, and you're going to get a lot more up close and personal than you probably would to anyone who's actually alive. Here is a guide to the most fruitful cemeteries, listed in order of their friendliness to stargazers.

Weathered Victorian and Deco memorials add to the decaying charm of **Hollywood Forever** (formerly Hollywood Memorial Park), 6000 Santa Monica Blvd., Hollywood (© **323/469-1181**). Fittingly, there's a terrific view of the HOLLYWOOD sign over the graves, as many of the founders of the community rest here. The most notable tenant is Rudolph Valentino, who rests in an interior crypt. Outside are Tyrone Power Jr.; Douglas Fairbanks Sr. and Jr.; Cecil B. DeMille (facing Paramount, his old studio); Carl "Alfalfa" Switzer from *The Little Rascals* (the dog on his grave is not Petey); Hearst mistress Marion Davies; John Huston; a headstone for Jayne Mansfield (she's really buried in Pennsylvania with her family); and Dee Dee Ramone.

Catholic **Holy Cross Cemetery,** 5835 W. Slauson Ave., Culver City (© **310/670-7697**), hands out maps to the stars' graves. In one area, within mere feet of one another, lie Bing Crosby, Bela Lugosi (buried in his Dracula cape), and Sharon Tate; not far away are Rita Hayworth and Jimmy Durante. Also here are "Tin Man" Jack Haley and "Scarecrow" Ray Bolger, Mary Astor, John Ford, and Gloria Morgan Vanderbilt. More recent arrivals include John Candy and Audrey Meadows.

The front office at **Hillside Memorial Park,** 6001 Centinela Ave., Baldwin Hills (© **310/641-0707**), can provide a guide to this Jewish cemetery, which has an LA landmark: the behemoth tomb of Al Jolson. His rotunda, complete with a bronze reproduction of Jolson and cascading fountain, is visible from I-405. Also on hand are Jack Benny, Eddie Cantor, Vic Morrow, and Michael Landon.

You just know developers get stomachaches looking at **Westwood Memorial Park,** 1218 Glendon Ave., Westwood (© **310/474-1579**; the staff can direct you around), smack-dab in the middle of some of LA's

(p. 476), and the **Egyptian Theatre,** 6712 Hollywood Blvd (© **323/466-FILM;** www.egyptiantheatre.com). Conceived by grandiose Sid Grauman, the Egyptian Theatre is just down the street from the better-known Chinese Theatre, but it remains less altered from its 1922 design, which was based on the then-headline-news discovery of hidden treasures in Pharaohs' tombs. The building recently underwent a sensitive restoration by American Cinematheque, which now screens rare, classic, and independent films.

priciest real estate. But it's not going anywhere. Especially when you consider its most famous resident: Marilyn Monroe. It's also got Truman Capote, John Cassavetes, Armand Hammer, Walter Matthau, Donna Reed, and Natalie Wood.

Forest Lawn Glendale, 1712 S. Glendale Ave. (© **323/254-3131**), likes to pretend it has no celebrities. The most prominent of LA cemeteries, it's also the most humorless. The place is full of bad art, all part of the continuing vision of founder Huburt Eaton, who thought cemeteries should be happy places. So he banished those gloomy upright tomb-stones and monuments in favor of flat, pleasant, character-free, flush-to-the-ground slabs. Contrary to urban legend, Walt Disney was *not* frozen and placed under Cinderella's castle at Disneyland; his cremated remains are in a little garden to the left of the Freedom Mausoleum. Turn around, and just behind you are Errol Flynn and Spencer Tracy. In the Freedom Mausoleum itself are Nat "King" Cole, Chico Marx, Gummo Marx, Gracie Allen, and George Burns. In a columbarium near the Mystery of Life is Humphrey Bogart. Unfortunately, some of the best celebs—such as Clark Gable, Carole Lombard, and Jean Harlow—are in the Great Mausoleum, which you often can't get into unless you're visiting a relative.

You'd think a place that encourages people to visit for fun would understand what the attraction is. But no—Forest Lawn Glendale won't tell you where any of their illustrious guests are, so don't ask. This place is immense—and, frankly, dull in comparison to the previously listed cemeteries, unless you appreciate the kitsch value of the Forest Lawn approach to art.

Forest Lawn Hollywood Hills, 6300 Forest Lawn Dr. (© **800/204-3131**), is slightly less anal than the Glendale branch, but the same basic attitude prevails. On the right lawn, near the statue of George Wash-ington, is Buster Keaton. In the Courts of Remembrance are Lucille Ball, Charles Laughton, and the not-quite-gaudy-enough tomb of Liberace. Outside, in a vault on the Ascension Road side, is Andy Gibb. Bette Davis's sarcophagus is in front of the wall, to the left of the entrance to the Courts. Gene Autry was also buried here, almost within earshot of the museum that bears his name.

Capitol Records Building   Opened in 1956, this 12-story tower, just north of the legendary intersection of Hollywood and Vine, is one of the city's most recognizable buildings. This circular tower is often incorrectly said to have been made to resemble a stack of 45s under a turntable stylus (it kinda does, though). Nat "King" Cole, songwriter Johnny Mercer, and other 1950s Capitol artists populate a giant exterior mural.

1750 Vine St. © 323/462-6252.

Freeman House   Frank Lloyd Wright's Freeman House, built in 1924, was designed as an experimental prototype of mass-produced affordable housing. The home's richly patterned "textile-block" exterior was Wright's invention and is the most famous aspect of the home's design. Situated on a dramatic site overlooking Hollywood, Freeman House is built with the world's first glass-to-glass corner windows. Dancer Martha Graham, bandleader Xavier Cugat, art collector Galka Sheye, photographer Edward Weston, and architects Philip Johnson and Richard Neutra all lived or spent significant time at this house, which became known as an avant-garde salon. The house was closed for restoration at press time; call ahead to see if it's open.

1962 Glencoe Way (off Hillcrest, near Highland and Franklin aves.). ℭ 323/851-0671.

DOWNTOWN

For a taste of what Downtown's Bunker Hill was like before the bulldozers, visit the residential neighborhood of **Angelino Heights,** near Echo Park. Entire streets are still filled with stately gingerbread Victorian homes; most still enjoy the splendid views that led early LA's elite to build here. The 1300 block of Carroll Avenue is the best preserved. Don't be surprised if a film crew is scouting locations while you're there—these blocks appear often on the silver screen.

The Bradbury Building   This National Historic Landmark, built in 1893, is Los Angeles's oldest commercial building and one of the city's most revered architectural achievements. Capped by a magical five-story skylight, Bradbury's courtyard combines glazed brick, Mexican tile, rich Belgian marble, handsome oak paneling, and lacelike wrought-iron railings. The glass-topped atrium is often used as a movie and TV set; you've seen it in *Chinatown* and *Blade Runner.*

304 S. Broadway (at 3rd St.). ℭ 213/626-1893. Mon–Fri 9am–6pm, Sat–Sun 9am–5pm.

Central Library ★★   This is one of LA's early architectural achievements. The city rallied to save the library when arson nearly destroyed it in 1986; the triumphant restoration has returned much of its original splendor. Working in the early 1920s, architect Bertram G. Goodhue employed the Egyptian motifs and materials popularized by the recent discovery of King Tut's tomb, and combined them with a more modern use of concrete block to great effect. *Warning:* Parking in this area can involve a heroic effort. Try visiting on the weekend and using the Flower Street parking entrance; the library will validate your ticket and you can escape for only $2.

630 W. 5th St. (between Flower St. and Grand Ave.). ℭ 213/228-7000. www.lapl.org.

City Hall   Built in 1928, the 27-story triangular Los Angeles City Hall was the tallest building in the city for over 30 years. The structure's distinctive ziggurat roof was featured in the film *War of the Worlds,* but it is probably best known as the headquarters of the *Daily Planet* in the *Superman* TV series. When it was built, City Hall was the sole exception to an ordinance outlawing buildings taller than 150 feet. On a clear day (yeah right), the top-floor observation deck offers views to Mount Wilson, 15 miles away.

200 N. Spring St. ℭ 213/485-2121. www.lacityhall.org. Observation deck open Mon–Fri 10am–4pm.

El Alisal ★   El Alisal is a small, rugged, two-story "castle," built between 1889 and 1910 from large rocks and telephone poles purchased from the Santa Fe Railroad. The architect and creator was Charles F. Lummis, a Harvard graduate, archaeologist, and writer, who walked from Ohio to California and coined the slogan "See America First." A fan of Native American culture, Lummis is credited with popularizing the concept of the "Southwest," referring to New Mexico and Arizona. He often lived the lifestyle of the Indians, and he founded the nearby Southwest Museum, a repository of Indian artifacts. Lummis held fabulous parties for the theatrical, political, and artistic elite; his guest list often included Will Rogers and Teddy Roosevelt. The outstanding feature of his house is the fireplace, which was carved by Mount Rushmore creator Gutzon Borglum. The lawn has been turned into an experimental garden of water-conserving plants.

200 E. Avenue 43, Highland Park. ✆ 323/222-0546. www.socalhistory.org. Free admission. Fri–Sun noon–4pm.

Union Station ⊛   Union Station, completed in 1939, is one of the finest examples of California mission-style architecture. It was built with the opulence and attention to detail that characterize 1930s WPA projects. The cathedral-size, richly paneled ticket lobby-and-waiting area of this fantastic cream-colored structure stand sadly empty most of the time, but the MTA does use Union Station for Blue Line commuter trains. When you're strolling through these grand historic halls, it's easy to imagine the glamorous movie stars who once boarded *The City of Los Angeles* and *The Super Chief* to journey back east during the glory days of rail travel; I also like to picture the many joyous reunions between returning soldiers and loved ones following the victorious end to World War II, in the station's heyday. There's always been a restaurant in the station; the latest to occupy this unusually beautiful setting is Traxx (p. 499).

Alameda St. (at Cesar E. Chavez Ave.).

Watts Towers & Art Center   Watts became notorious as the site of riots in the summer of 1965, during which 34 people were killed and more than 1,000 injured. Today, a visit to Watts is a lesson in inner-city life. It's a high-density land of gray strip malls, well-guarded check-cashing shops, and fast-food restaurants; but it's also a neighborhood of hardworking families struggling to survive in the midst of gangland. Although there's not much for the casual tourist here, the Watts Towers are truly a unique attraction, and the adjoining art gallery illustrates the fierce determination of area residents to maintain cultural integrity.

The Towers are colorful, 99-foot-tall cement and steel sculptures ornamented with mosaics of bottles, seashells, cups, plates, pottery, and ceramic tiles. They were completed in 1954 by folk artist Simon Rodia, an immigrant Italian tile-setter who worked on them for 33 years in his spare time. True fans of decorative ceramics will enjoy the fact that Rodia's day job was at the legendary Malibu Potteries (are those fragments of valuable Malibu tile encrusting the Towers?). Closed in 1994 due to earthquake damage, the towers were triumphantly reopened in 2001. At press time, tour schedules were limited due to restoration projects; call ahead for the latest information.

Note: Next to these designated Cultural Landmarks is the Art Center, which has a fascinating collection of ethnic musical instruments as well as several visiting art exhibits throughout the year.

1765 E. 107th St., Los Angeles. ✆ 213/847-4646. www.culturela.org. Gallery open Tues–Sat 10am–4pm and Sun noon–4pm; call for tower tour schedule and directions.

PASADENA & ENVIRONS

For a quick but profound architectural fix, stroll past Pasadena's grandiose and baroque **City Hall,** 100 N. Garfield Ave., 2 blocks north of Colorado Boulevard. Closer inspection will reveal its classical colonnaded courtyard, formal gardens, and spectacular tiled dome.

Value **CityPass Money Saver**

If you're the type who loves to cram in as many tourist attractions as possible in one trip, then you need a **CityPass** (© 707/256-0490; www.city pass.com). This money-saving booklet includes tickets to six popular attractions, a 2-hour bus tour of Beverly Hills and celebrity homes from **Starline Tours,** and savings coupons for Beverly Center shopping. The main draw, and the primary reason to purchase CityPass, is **Universal Studios Hollywood;** the rest are the **Hollywood Entertainment Museum, American Cinematheque at the Egyptian Theatre, Museum of Television and Radio, Petersen Automotive Museum,** and **Autry Museum of Western Heritage.** Purchase the pass at any of the seven attractions, or visit the website to buy advance passes online, find links to the attraction websites, and peruse hotel packages that include CityPass. The pass costs $59 for adults ($39 for kids 3–11) and will expire 30 days from the first use. Is it a good deal? If you use all the tickets, you end up saving 45% over individual, full-price admissions.

The Gamble House ✶✶   The huge two-story Gamble House, built in 1908 as a California vacation home for the wealthy family of Procter and Gamble fame, is a sublime example of Arts and Crafts architecture. The interior, designed by the famous Pasadena-based Greene & Greene architectural team, abounds with handcraftsmanship, including intricately carved teak cornices, custom-designed furnishings, elaborate carpets, and a fantastic Tiffany glass door. No detail was overlooked. Every oak wedge, downspout, air vent, and switch plate contributes to the unified design. Admission is by 1-hour guided tour only, which departs every 15 minutes. No reservations are necessary.

If you can't fit the tour into your schedule but have a love of Craftsman design, visit the well-stocked bookstore and museum shop located in the former garage (you can also see the exterior and grounds of the house this way). The bookstore is open Tuesday through Saturday from 10am to 5pm and Sunday from 11:30am to 5pm.

Additional elegant Greene & Greene creations (still privately owned) abound 2 blocks away along **Arroyo Terrace,** including nos. **368, 370, 400, 408, 424,** and **440.** The Gamble House bookstore can give you a walking-tour map and also conducts guided neighborhood tours by appointment.

4 Westmoreland Place (in the 300 block of N. Orange Grove Blvd.), Pasadena. © **626/793-3334.** www. gamblehouse.org. Admission $8 adults, $5 students with ID and seniors 65 and over, free for children under 12. Thurs–Sun noon–3pm. Closed holidays.

MUSEUMS & GALLERIES
SANTA MONICA & THE BEACHES

Museum of Flying ✶ *Kids*   Once headquarters of the McDonnell Douglas corporation, the Santa Monica Airport is the birthplace of the DC-3 and other pioneers of commercial aviation. The museum celebrates this bit of local history with 24 authentic aircraft displays and some interactive exhibits. In addition to antique Spitfires and Sopwith Camels, there's a kid-oriented learning area, where hands-on exhibits detail airplane parts, pilot procedures, and the properties of air and aircraft design. The museum shop is full of scale models of World War II birds; the coffee-table book *The Best of the Past* beautifully illustrates 50 years of aviation history.

At Santa Monica Airport, 2772 Donald Douglas Loop N., Santa Monica. ℂ 310/392-8822. www.museum offlying.com. Suggested contribution $8 adults, $6 seniors, $4 children 3–17, free for children under 3. Wed–Sun 10am–5pm.

LA'S WESTSIDE & BEVERLY HILLS

Museum of Tolerance ⭐ The Museum of Tolerance is designed to expose prejudices and to teach racial and cultural tolerance. It's located in the Simon Wiesenthal Center, an institute founded by the legendary Nazi-hunter. While the Holocaust figures prominently here, this is not just a Jewish museum—it's an academy that broadly campaigns for a live-and-let-live world. Tolerance is an abstract idea that's hard to display, so most of this $50 million museum's exhibits are high-tech and conceptual in nature. Fast-paced interactive displays are designed to touch the heart as well as the mind, and engage both serious investigators and the MTV crowd. One of two major museums in America that deal with the Holocaust, the Museum of Tolerance is considered by many to be inferior to its Washington, D.C., counterpart. *Note:* Visitors might be frustrated by the museum's policy of insisting that you follow a prescribed 2½-hour route through the exhibits.

9786 W. Pico Blvd. (at Roxbury Dr.). ℂ 310/553-8403. www.wiesenthal.com/mot. Admission $9 adults, $7 seniors 62 and over, $5.50 students w/ID, $5.50 children 3–10, free for children 2 and under. Advance purchase recommended; photo ID required for admission. Mon–Thurs 11:30am–4pm, Fri 11:30am–3pm (to 1pm Nov–Mar), Sun 11am–5pm. Closed many Jewish and secular holidays.

Skirball Cultural Center ⭐ This strikingly modern museum/cultural center is quick to remind us that Jewish history is about more than the Holocaust. Nestled in the Sepulveda Pass uphill from the Getty Center, the Skirball explores American Jewish life, American democratic values, and the pursuit of the American Dream—a theme shared by many immigrant groups. The Skirball's core exhibits chronicle the journey of the Jewish people through the ages, with emphasis on American Jewry. Related events are held here throughout the year; one recent highlight was a rollicking festival of klezmer music (a traditional Jewish folk style). Call for free docent-led tour times.

2701 N. Sepulveda Blvd. (at Mulholland Dr.). ℂ 310/440-4500. www.skirball.org. Admission $8 adults, $6 students with ID and seniors 65 and over, free for kids under 12. Tues–Sat noon–5pm, Sun 11am–5pm. Free parking. From I-405, exit at Skirball Center Dr./Mulholland Dr.

HOLLYWOOD

Autry Museum of Western Heritage ⭐⭐ If you're under the age of 45, you might not be familiar with Gene Autry, a Texas-born actor who starred in 82 westerns and became known as the "Singing Cowboy." Located north of Downtown in Griffith Park, his eponymous museum is one of California's best, a collection of art and artifacts of the European conquest of the West, remarkably comprehensive and intelligently displayed. Evocative exhibits illustrate the everyday lives of early pioneers, not only with antique firearms, tools, saddles, and the like, but with many hands-on displays that successfully stir the imagination and the heart. You'll find footage from Buffalo Bill's Wild West Show, movie clips from the silent days, contemporary films, the works of Wild West artists, and plenty of memorabilia from Autry's own film and TV projects. The "Hall of Merchandising" displays Roy Rogers bedspreads, Hopalong Cassidy radios, and other items from the collective consciousness—and material collections—of baby boomers. Provocative visiting exhibits (whose banners are visible from Interstate 5) usually focus on cultural or domestic regional history. Allow about an hour to see it all.

4700 Western Heritage Way (in Griffith Park). © 323/667-2000. www.autry-museum.org. Admission $7.50 adults, $5 seniors 60 and over and students 13–18, $3 children 2–12, free for kids under 2. Tues–Wed and Fri–Sun 10am–5pm, Thurs 10am–8pm. Free to all 2nd Tues of each month.

Craft & Folk Art Museum   This gallery, housed in a prominent Museum Row building, has grown into one of the city's largest. "Craft and folk art" encompasses everything from clothing, tools, religious artifacts, and other everyday objects to woodcarvings, papier-mâché, weaving, and metalwork. The museum displays folk objects from around the world, but its strongest collection is masks from India, America, Mexico, Japan, and China. The museum is also known for its annual International Festival of Masks, held each October in Hancock Park, across the street. Be sure to stop in the funky, eclectic Museum Shop to peruse the wearable art, folk-art books, and various crafts.

5814 Wilshire Blvd. (at Curson Ave.). © 323/937-4230. Admission $3.50 adults, $2.50 seniors and students, free for children under 12, free to all 1st Wed of each month. Museum Wed–Sun 11am–5pm; Museum Shop Tues–Sun 11am–5pm.

Los Angeles County Museum of Art 🖈🖈   This is one of the finest art museums around, housing works by Degas, Rembrandt, Hockney, and Monet. The huge complex was designed by three very different architects over a span of 30 years. The architectural fusion can be migraine inducing, but this city landmark is well worth delving into.

The newest wing is the **Japanese Pavilion,** which has exterior walls made of Kalwall, a translucent material that, like shoji screens, permits the entry of soft natural light. Inside is a collection of Japanese Edo paintings that's rivaled only by the holdings of the emperor of Japan. The **Anderson Building,** the museum's contemporary wing, is home to 20th-century painting and sculpture. Here you'll find works by Matisse, Magritte, and a good number of Dada artists. The **Ahmanson Building** houses the rest of the museum's permanent collections. You'll find everything from 2,000-year-old pre-Columbian Mexican ceramics to 19th-century portraiture to a unique glass collection spanning the centuries. Other displays include one of the nation's largest holdings of costumes and textiles, and an important Indian and Southeast Asian art collection. The **Hammer Building** is primarily used for major special-loan exhibitions. Free guided tours covering the museum's highlights depart on a regular basis from here.

The museum recently took over the former May Company department store 1 block away, converting the historic Art Deco building into gallery space.

5905 Wilshire Blvd. © 323/857-6000. www.lacma.org. Admission $7 adults, $5 students and seniors 62 and over, $1 children 6–17, free for kids 5 and under; regular exhibitions free for everyone 2nd Tues of each month. Mon–Tues and Thurs noon–8pm, Fri noon–9pm, Sat–Sun 11am–8pm. Parking $5.

Petersen Automotive Museum 🖈   When the Petersen opened in 1994, many locals were surprised that it had taken this long for the City of Freeways to salute its most important shaper. Indeed, this museum says more about the city than probably any other in LA. Named for Robert Petersen, the publisher responsible for *Hot Rod* and *Motor Trend* magazines, the four-story museum displays more than 200 cars and motorcycles, from the historic to the futuristic. Cars on the first floor are exhibited chronologically, in period settings. Other floors are devoted to frequently changing shows of race cars, early motorcycles, and famous movie vehicles. Past shows have included a comprehensive exhibit of "woodies" and surf culture, and displays of the Flintstones' fiberglass-and-cotton movie car and of a three-wheeled scooter that folds into a Samsonite briefcase (created in a competition by a Mazda engineer).

6060 Wilshire Blvd. (at Fairfax Ave.). © 323/930-CARS. www.petersen.org. Admission $7 adults, $6 seniors and students, $5 children 5–12, free for kids 4 and under. Tues–Sun 10am–6pm. Parking $6.

DOWNTOWN

California Science Center ★★ *Kids*   A $130 million renovation—reinvention, actually—has turned the former Museum of Science and Industry into Exposition Park's newest attraction. Using high-tech sleight-of-hand, the center stimulates kids of all ages with questions, answers, and lessons about the world. One of the museum's highlights is Tess, a 50-foot animatronic woman whose muscles, bones, organs, and blood vessels are revealed, demonstrating how the body reacts to a variety of external conditions and activities. (Appropriate for children of all ages, Tess doesn't possess reproductive organs.)

There are nominal fees, ranging from $2 to $5, to enjoy the science center's more thrilling attractions. You can pedal a bicycle across a high-wire suspended 43 feet above the ground (demonstrating the principle of gravity and counterweights) or get strapped into the Space Docking Simulator for a virtual-reality taste of zero gravity. There's plenty more, and plans for expansion in the works. The IMAX theater boasts a screen seven stories high and 90 feet wide, with state-of-the-art surround sound and 3-D technology. Films are screened throughout the day until 9pm and are nearly always breathtaking, even the ones in 2-D.

700 State Dr., Exposition Park. © 213/SCIENCE, or 213/744-7400; IMAX theater © 213/744-2014. www.casciencectr.org. Free admission to the museum; IMAX theater $7 adults, $5.25 seniors over 60 and children 13–17, $4.25 kids 4–12. Multishow discounts available. Parking $6. Daily 10am–5pm. Closed Thanksgiving, Dec 25, and Jan 1.

Japanese American National Museum ★   Located in an architecturally acclaimed modern building in Little Tokyo, this museum is a private nonprofit institute created to document and celebrate the history of the Japanese in America. Its fantastic permanent exhibition chronicles Japanese life in the United States, while temporary exhibits highlight distinctive aspects of Japanese-American culture, from the internment camp experience to the lives of Japanese-Americans in Hawaii. Don't miss the museum store, which carries everything from hand-fired sake sets to mini-Zen gardening kits.

369 E. 1st. St. (at Central Ave.). © 213/625-0414. www.janm.org. Admission $6 adults, $5 seniors, $3 students and kids 6–17, free for kids 5 and under; free to all 3rd Thurs of each month, and every Thurs after 5pm. Tues–Wed and Fri–Sun 10am–5pm, Thurs 10am–8pm.

Museum of Contemporary Art/Geffen Contemporary at MOCA ★★   MOCA is Los Angeles's only institution devoted to art from 1940 to the present. Displaying works in a variety of media, it's strong in works by Cy Twombly, Jasper Johns, and Mark Rothko, and shows are often superb. For many experts, MOCA's collections are too spotty to be considered world-class, and the conservative museum board blushes when offered controversial shows (they passed on a Whitney exhibit that included photographs by Robert Mapplethorpe). Nevertheless, I've seen some excellent exhibitions here.

MOCA is housed in three buildings: The main building at 250 S. Grand Ave. is a contemporary red sandstone structure by renowned Japanese architect Arata Isozaki. The museum restaurant, **Patinette** (© 213/626-1178), located here, is the casual-dining creation of celebrity chef Joachim Splichal (see Patina on p. 494); it's open daily from 11am to 4pm. The museum's second space, at 152 N. Central Ave. in Little Tokyo, was the "temporary" Contemporary while the Grand Avenue structure was being built; it now houses a superior permanent collection in a warehouse-type space recently renamed for entertainment mogul and art collector David Geffen. An added feature is a detailed timeline corresponding to the progression of works. Unless there's a visiting exhibit of great interest at the main museum, I recommend that you start at the Geffen building, where it's also easier to park. The third gallery, which opened in January 2001, is in the compact building next to the Pacific Design Center at 8687 Melrose Ave. in West Hollywood. Unlike the other two, admission to this galley is only $3, and emphasis is on contemporary architecture and design, as well as new work by emerging and established artists.

Main MOCA information line ℭ **213/626-6222.** www.moca-la.org. Admission $8 adults, $5 seniors 65 and over and students, free for children 11 and under. Tues–Wed and Fri–Sun 11am–5pm, Thurs 11am–8pm.

Natural History Museum of Los Angeles County *Kids*   The "Fighting Dinosaurs" are not a high-school football team but the trademark symbol of this massive museum: Tyrannosaurus rex and Triceratops skeletons poised in a stance so realistic that every kid feels inspired to imitate their Jurassic Park bellows. Opened in 1913 in a beautiful domed Spanish renaissance building, this museum is a 35-hall warehouse of earth's history, chronicling the planet and its inhabitants from 600 million years ago to the present day. There's a mind-numbing number of exhibits of prehistoric fossils, bird and marine life, rocks and minerals, and North American mammals. The best permanent displays include the world's rarest shark, a walk-through vault of priceless gems, and an insect zoo. You'll need at least 3 hours to see everything here.

The Dinosaur Shop sells ant farms and exploding-volcano and model kits. The Ethnic Arts Shop has one-of-a-kind folk art and jewelry from around the world. The bookstore has an extensive selection of scientific titles and hobbyists' field guides.

900 Exposition Blvd., Exposition Park. ℭ **213/763-DINO.** www.nhm.org. Admission $8 adults; $5.50 children 13–17, seniors, and students with ID; $2 children 5–12; free for kids under 5; free to all 1st Tues of each month. Daily 10am–5pm.

PASADENA & ENVIRONS

Norton Simon Museum of Art ★★ *Finds*   Named for a food-packing king and financier who reorganized the failing Pasadena Museum of Modern Art, this has become one of California's most important museums. Comprehensive collections of masterpieces by Degas, Picasso, Rembrandt, and Goya are augmented by sculptures by Henry Moore and Auguste Rodin, including *The Burghers of Calais,* which greets you at the gates. The "Blue Four" collection of works by Kandinsky, Jawlensky, Klee, and Feininger is impressive, as is a superb collection of Southeast Asian sculpture. *Still Life with Lemons, Oranges, and a Rose* (1633), an oil by Francisco de Zurbarán, is one of the museum's most important holdings. One of the most popular pieces is *The Flower Vendor/Girl with Lilies* by Diego Rivera. Architect Frank Gehry recently helped remodel the galleries. Allow 2 hours for your visit.

411 W. Colorado Blvd., Pasadena. ℭ **626/449-6840.** www.nortonsimon.org. Admission $6 adults, $3 seniors, free for students and kids 12 and under. Wed–Thurs and Sat–Mon noon–6pm, Fri noon–9pm. Free parking.

Pacific Asia Museum   The most striking aspect of this museum is the building itself. Designed in the 1920s in Chinese Imperial Palace style, it's rivaled in flamboyance only by Mann's Chinese Theatre in Hollywood (p. 508). Rotating exhibits of Asian art span the centuries, from 100 B.C. to the current day. This manageably sized museum is worth a visit; plan to spend about 2 hours here.

46 N. Los Robles Ave., Pasadena. (C) **626/449-2742**, ext. 10. www.pacificasiamuseum.org. Admission $5 adults, $3 students and seniors, free for children under 12; free to all 3rd Sat of each month. Wed–Thurs and Sat–Sun 10am–5pm, Fri 10am–8pm. Free parking.

PARKS

Griffith Park ★★ *Kids* Mining tycoon Griffith J. Griffith donated these 4,000 acres to the city in 1896. Today, Griffith Park is the largest city park in America. There's a lot to do here, including hiking, horseback riding, golfing, swimming, biking, and picnicking (see "Outdoor Pursuits," later in this chapter). For a general overview of the park, drive the mountainous loop road that winds from the top of Western Avenue, past Griffith Observatory, and down to Vermont Avenue. For a more extensive foray, turn north at the loop road's midsection, onto Mt. Hollywood Drive. To reach the golf courses, the **Autry Museum,** or **Los Angeles Zoo,** take Los Feliz Boulevard to Riverside Drive, which runs along the park's western edge.

Near the zoo, in a particularly dusty corner of the park, you can find the **Travel Town Transportation Museum,** 5200 Zoo Dr. (C) **323/662-5874;** www.cityofla.org/RAP/grifmet/tt), a little-known outdoor museum with a small collection of vintage locomotives and old airplanes. Kids love it. It's open Monday through Friday from 10am to 4pm and Saturday and Sunday from 10am to 5pm; admission is free.

Griffith Park entrances are along Los Feliz Blvd., at Riverside Dr., Vermont Ave., and Western Ave. (Hollywood). (C) **323/913-4688.** www.cityofla.org/rap/grifmet/gp.

Will Rogers State Historic Park Will Rogers State Historic Park was once Will Rogers's private ranch and grounds. Willed to the state of California in 1944, the 168-acre estate is now both a park and a historic site, supervised by the Department of Parks and Recreation. Visitors may explore the grounds, the former stables, and the 31-room house filled with the original furnishings, including a porch swing in the living room and many Native American rugs and baskets. Charles Lindbergh and his wife, Anne Morrow Lindbergh, hid out here in the 1930s during part of the craze that followed the kidnap and murder of their first son. There are picnic tables, but no food is sold.

Will Rogers (1879–1935) was born in Oklahoma and became a cowboy in the Texas Panhandle before drifting into a Wild West show as a folksy, speechifying roper. The "cracker-barrel philosopher" performed lariat tricks while carrying on a humorous deadpan monologue on current events. The showman moved to Los Angeles in 1919, where he became a movie actor as well as the author of numerous books detailing his down-home "cowboy philosophy."

1501 Will Rogers State Park Rd., Pacific Palisades (between Santa Monica and Malibu). (C) **310/454-8212.** Park entrance $6 per vehicle. Daily 8am–sunset. House opens daily 10am–5pm; guided tours can be arranged for groups of 10 or more. From Santa Monica, take the Pacific Coast Hwy. (Calif. 1) N, turn right onto Sunset Blvd., and continue to the park entrance.

PIERS

Santa Monica Pier ★★ Piers have been a tradition in Southern California since the area's 19th-century seaside resort days. Many have long since disappeared, and others have been shortened by battering storms and are now mere shadows (or stumps) of their former selves, but you can still get a chance to experience those halcyon days of yesteryear at world-famous Santa Monica Pier.

Built in 1909 for passenger and cargo ships, the Santa Monica Pier does a pretty good job of recapturing the glory days of Southern California. The wooden wharf is now home to seafood restaurants and snack shacks, a touristy

Mexican cantina, and a gaily colored indoor wooden carousel (which Paul Newman operated in *The Sting*). Summer evening concerts, which are free and range from big band to Miami-style Latin, draw crowds, as does the small amusement area perched halfway down. Its name, **Pacific Park** (© **310/260-8744;** www.pacpark.com), hearkens back to the granddaddy pier amusement park in California, Pacific Ocean Park. This updated version has a roller coaster and other rides, plus a high-tech arcade shoot-out. But anglers still head to the end to fish, and nostalgia buffs to view the photographic display of the pier's history. This is the last of the great pleasure piers, offering rides, romance, and perfect panoramic views of the bay and mountains.

The pier is about a mile up Ocean Front Walk from Venice; it's a great round-trip stroll. Parking is available for $6 to $8 on both the Pier Deck and the Beachfront nearby. Limited short-term parking is also available. For information on twilight concerts (generally held Thurs between mid-June and the end of Aug), call © **310/458-8900** or visit www.santamonicapier.org.

Ocean Ave. at the end of Colorado Blvd., Santa Monica.

THEME PARKS

You'll find LA's most famous theme park, **Universal Studios Hollywood,** on p. 509.

Six Flags California (Magic Mountain and Hurricane Harbor) ★★

What started as a countrified little amusement park with a couple of relatively tame roller coasters in 1971 has been transformed by Six Flags into a thrill-a-minute daredevil's paradise now called "The Xtreme Park." Located about 20 to 30 minutes north of Universal Studios, Six Flags Magic Mountain is one of the few 38 Six Flags parks that are open year-round. The world-class roller coasters make it enormously popular with teenagers and young adults and a recently renovated children's playland—Bugs Bunny World—creates excitement for the pint-size set (kids that are under 48 in. tall.) Bring an iron constitution: Rides with names like Goliath, Déjà Vu, Ninja, Viper, Colossus, and Psyclone will have your cheeks flapping with the G-force and queasy expressions are common at the exit. But where else can you experience zero gravity weightlessness, careen down vertical tracks into relentless hairpin turns, or "race" another train on a side-by-side wooden roller coaster? Some rides are themed to action-film characters, like Superman the Escape and The Riddler's Revenge; others are loosely tied to their themed surroundings, like a Far East pagoda or gold-rush mining town. Arcade games and summer-only entertainment (stunt shows, animal shows and parades) round out the park's attractions.

Hurricane Harbor is Six Flags's tropical paradise, which is located right next door to Magic Mountain. You really can't see both in 1 day—combo tickets allow you to return sometime before the end of the season. Bring your own swimsuit; the park has changing rooms with showers and lockers. Like Magic Mountain, areas have themes like a tropical lagoon or an African river (complete with ancient temple ruins). The primary activities are swimming, water slides, rafting, volleyball, and lounging; many areas are designed especially for the little "buccaneer."

Magic Mountain Pkwy. (off Golden State Fwy./I-5 N), Valencia. © **661/255-4100** or 818/367-5965. www.sixflags.com. Magic Mountain $43 adults, $27 seniors 55 and older and children age 2 to 48 in. high, free for kids under 2; Hurricane Harbor $22 adults, $15 seniors and children; combo ticket $53. Magic Mountain is open daily Apr to Labor Day and weekends and holidays the rest of the year. Hurricane Harbor daily Memorial Day to Labor Day; weekends-only May and Sept; closed Oct–Apr. Both parks open at 10am; closing hours vary between 6pm–midnight. Parking $7. All prices and hours are subject to change without notice, so call before you arrive.

THE ZOO

Los Angeles Zoo ⋆ *Kids*   The LA Zoo, which shares its parking lot with the Autry Museum, has been welcoming visitors and busloads of schoolkids since 1966. In 1982, the zoo inaugurated a display of cuddly koalas, still one of its biggest attractions. Although it's quite a bit smaller than the world-famous San Diego Zoo, the LA Zoo is surprisingly enjoyable and easy to fully explore. As much an arboretum as a zoo, the grounds are thick with mature shade trees from around the world that help cool the once-barren grounds, and new habitats are light-years ahead of the cruel concrete roundhouses originally used to exhibit animals (though you can't help feeling that, despite the fancy digs, all the creatures would rather be in their natural habitat). Highlights include the **Chimpanzees of the Mahale Mountains** habitat, where visitors can see plenty of primate activity; the **Red Ape Rain Forest,** a natural orangutan habitat; the entertaining **World of Birds** show; and the silverback gorilla exhibit. The gargantuan Andean condor had me enthralled as well (the facility is renowned in zoological circles for the successful breeding and releasing of California condors, and occasionally it has some of these majestic and endangered birds on exhibit).

The zoo's latest attraction (and one they're rightfully proud of) is the **Winnick Family Children's Zoo,** a fantastic and forward-thinking children's zoo that contains a petting area, exhibition animal-care center, "Adventure Theater" storytelling and puppet show, and other kid-hip exhibits and activities. *Tip:* To avoid the busloads of rambunctious school kids, arrive after noon.

5333 Zoo Dr., Griffith Park. © 323/644-6400. www.lazoo.org. Admission $8.25 adults, $3.25 kids 2–12, $5.25 seniors 65 and over, free to children under 2. Daily 10am–5pm. Closed Dec 25. Free parking.

ORGANIZED TOURS
STUDIO TOURS

NBC Studios ⋆   According to a security guard, John Wayne and Redd Foxx once got into a fight here after Wayne refused to ride in the same limo as Foxx, who called the movie star a "redneck." Well, your NBC tour will probably be a bit more docile than that. The guided 70-minute tour includes a behind-the-scenes unstaged look at *The Tonight Show with Jay Leno* set; wardrobe, makeup, and set-building departments; and several sound studios. The tour also includes some cool video demonstrations of high-tech special effects. *Note:* Tours are sold on a first-come, first-served basis and sell out early during peak vacation season.

3000 W. Alameda Ave., Burbank. © 818/840-3537. Tours $7.50 adults, $6.75 seniors 60 and over, $4 children 5–12, free for children under 5. Mon–Fri 9am–3pm (open weekends and extended hr. during summer and holiday season).

Paramount Pictures ⋆   Paramount's 2-hour walking tour around its Hollywood headquarters is both a historical ode to filmmaking and a real-life look at a working studio—it's the only major movie studio still located in Hollywood. Tours depart hourly; the itinerary varies, depending on what productions are in progress. Visits might include a walk through the soundstages of TV shows or feature films, though you can't enter while taping is taking place. Cameras, recording equipment, and children under 10 are not allowed.

5555 Melrose Ave., Hollywood. © 323/956-5575. www.paramount.com. Tours $15 per person. Mon–Fri 9am–2pm.

Sony Pictures Studio Tour   Although it doesn't have quite the historical cachet as Warner Brothers or Paramount, a lot of movie history was made at this Culver City lot. The 2-hour walking tour includes stops at classic stage scenes such as the Yellow Brick Road winding through Munchkinland, sets from modern thrillers like *Men in Black*, and an opportunity to drop in on the *Jeopardy!* set to test your trivia prowess. But the main reason for the tour is the chance to catch a glimpse at the stars who work here (it's one of the busiest studio lots in the world).

Sony Picture Studios, 10202 W. Washington Blvd., Culver City. (© 323/520-TOUR. Advance reservations highly recommended; children under 12 not admitted. Tours $20 per person, departing Mon–Fri at 9:30am, 11am, noon, and 2:30pm. Photo ID required.

Warner Brothers Studios ★★   Warner Brothers offers the most comprehensive—and the least theme park–like—of the studio tours. The tour takes visitors on a 2-hour informational drive-and-walk jaunt around the studio's faux streets. After a brief introductory film, you'll pile into glorified golf carts and cruise past parking spaces marked "Clint Eastwood," "Michael Douglas," and "Sharon Stone," then walk through active film and television sets. Whether it's an orchestra scoring a film or a TV show being taped or edited, you'll get a glimpse of how it's done (nothing is staged for the tour). Stops include the wardrobe department or the mills where sets are made. Whenever possible, you can also visit working sets to watch actors filming actual productions. Reservations are required; children under 8 are not admitted.

WB Studio Gate 3, 4301 W. Olive Ave. (at Hollywood Way), Burbank. (© 818/972-TOUR; www.wbstudio tour.com. Advance reservations recommended. Tours $32 per person, departing on the half-hr. Mon–Fri 9am–4pm (9am–3pm winter).

SIGHTSEEING TOURS

L.A. Tours (© 323/993-0093; www.la-tours.com) operates regularly scheduled tours of the city. Plush shuttle buses (27 passengers maximum) pick up riders from major hotels for morning or afternoon tours of the Sunset Strip, the movie studios, Farmers Market, Hollywood, homes of the stars, and other attractions. Different itineraries are available, if you're interested in Downtown and the Music Center, for example, or want to spend your time exploring the beaches and shopping in Santa Monica. Tours vary in length from a half day to a full day and cost $42 to $58 for adults. There are discounts for kids; book online for a $4-per-person discount. Advance reservations are required.

The **L.A. Conservancy** (© 213/623-2489; www.laconservancy.org) conducts a dozen fascinating walking tours of historic downtown LA, seed of today's sprawling metropolis. (See "Architectural Highlights" earlier in this chapter). In Pasadena, **Pasadena Heritage** (© 626/441-6333; www.pasadenaheritage.org) offers various tours spotlighting neighborhoods and their wealthy estates. Call for a schedule of guided tours, or pick up one of the self-guided-walking or -driving maps available at the **Pasadena Convention and Visitors Bureau,** 171 S. Los Robles Ave. (© 626/795-9311).

For a more aerobic way to see LA, sign up with **LA Bike Tours** (© 888/775-BIKE or 323/466-5890; www.labiketours.com), who offers guided rides of Hollywood or Beverly Hills, plus longer excursions to the Getty Center, Venice Beach, Griffith Park, and Topanga's Redrock Canyon. Most tours last around 3 hours; prices range from $40 to $50 and include bike rental plus safety gear, snacks, and bottled water.

Off 'N Running Tours (© 800/523-TOUR or 310/246-1418) combines sporting with sightseeing, taking joggers on guided runs through Los Angeles. One-on-one tours are customized to take in the most beautiful areas around your hotel and can accommodate any skill level for 4 to 12 miles. It's a fun way

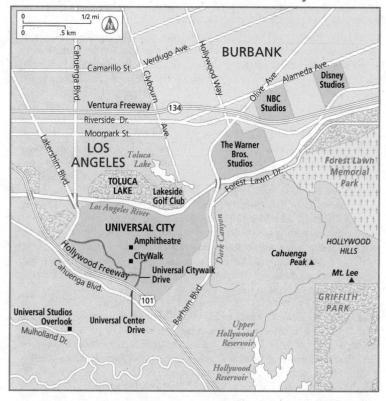

to get the most out of your morning jog. Tours cost about $45 and include a T-shirt and runner's breakfast.

7 TV Tapings

Being part of the audience for the taping of a television show might be the quintessential LA experience. This is a great way to see Hollywood at work, to find out how your favorite sitcom or talk show is made, and to catch a glimpse of your favorite TV personalities. Timing is important—remember that most series go on hiatus between March and July. And tickets to the top shows, like *Friends* and *Everybody Loves Raymond,* are in greater demand than others, so getting your hands on them takes advance planning—and possibly some waiting in line.

Request tickets as far in advance as possible. Several episodes may be shot on a single day, so you may be required to remain in the theater for up to 4 hours (in addition to the recommended 1-hr. early check-in). If you phone at the last moment, you may luck into tickets for your top choice. More likely, however, you'll be given a list of shows that are currently filming, and you won't recognize many of the titles; studios are always taping pilots, few of which end up on the air. But you never know who may be starring in them—look at all the famous faces that have launched new sitcoms in the past couple of years. Tickets are always free, usually limited to two per person, and are distributed on a first-come, first-served basis. Many shows don't admit children under the age of 10; in some cases no one under the age of 18 is admitted.

Tickets are sometimes given away to the public outside popular tourist sites like Mann's Chinese Theatre in Hollywood and Universal Studios in the Valley; LA's visitor information centers in Downtown and Hollywood often have tickets as well. But if you're determined to see a particular show, contact the following suppliers:

Audiences Unlimited, Inc. (© **818/753-3470;** www.tvtickets.com) is a good place to start. It distributes tickets for most of the top sitcoms, including *Friends, That '70s Show, Will & Grace, The Drew Carey Show, Everybody Loves Raymond,* and many more. This service is organized and informative (as is their website), and fully sanctioned by production companies and networks. ABC, for example, no longer handles ticket distribution directly, but refers all inquiries to Audiences Unlimited, Inc. **Television Tickets** (© **323/467-4697**) distributes tickets for numerous talk and game shows, including *Jeopardy!,* as does **TVTIX.COM** (© **323/653-4105;** www.tvtix.com).

You also may want to contact the networks for information on a specific show, including some whose tickets are not available at the above agencies. At **ABC,** all ticket inquiries are referred to Audiences Unlimited (see above), but you may want to check out ABC's website at **www.abc.com** for a colorful look at their lineup and links to specific shows' sites.

For **CBS Television City,** 7800 Beverly Blvd., Los Angeles, CA 90036, call © **323/575-2458** to see what's being filmed while you're in town. Tickets for CBS tapings are distributed on a first-come, first-served basis; you can write in advance to reserve them or pick them up at the studio up to an hour before taping. Tickets for many CBS sitcoms, including *Everybody Loves Raymond,* are also available from Audiences Unlimited (see above). For tickets to *The Price Is Right,* call the 24-hour ticket hot line at © **323/575-2449.** For a virtual visit to CBS's shows, log on to **www.cbs.com**.

For **NBC,** 3000 W. Alameda Ave., Burbank, CA 91523 (© **818/840-3537**), call to see what's on while you're in LA. Tickets for NBC tapings, including *The Tonight Show with Jay Leno* (minimum age to attend this show is 16), can be obtained in two ways: Either pick them up at the NBC ticket counter on the day of the show (they're distributed on a first-come, first-served basis at the ticket counter off California Ave.), or, at least 6 weeks before your visit, send a self-addressed stamped envelope with your ticket request to the address above. Be sure to include show name, number of tickets (four per request), and dates desired. All the NBC shows are represented online at **www.nbc.com**.

8 Beaches

Los Angeles County's 72-mile coastline sports over 30 miles of beaches, most of which are operated by the **Department of Beaches & Harbors,** 13837 Fiji Way, Marina del Rey (© **310/305-9503**). County-run beaches usually charge for parking ($4–$8). Alcohol, bonfires, and pets are prohibited. For recorded **surf conditions** (and coastal weather forecast), call © **310/457-9701.** The following are the county's best beaches, listed from north to south.

EL PESCADOR, LA PIEDRA & EL MATADOR BEACHES *Finds* These rugged and isolated beaches front a 2-mile stretch of the Pacific Coast Highway (Calif. 1) between Broad Beach and Decker Canyon roads, a 10-minute drive from the Malibu Pier. Picturesque coves with unusual rock formations are great for sunbathing and picnicking, but swim with caution as there are no lifeguards. The beaches can be difficult to find; only small signs on the highway mark them. There are a limited number of parking spots atop the bluffs. Descend to the beach via stairs that cling to the cliffs.

ZUMA BEACH COUNTY PARK ⭐ Jam-packed on warm weekends, Los Angeles County's largest beach park is located off the Pacific Coast Highway (Calif. 1), a mile past Kanan Dume Road. While it can't claim to be the loveliest beach in the Southland, Zuma has the most comprehensive facilities: plenty of restrooms, lifeguards, playgrounds, volleyball courts, and snack bars. The southern stretch, toward Point Dume, is Westward Beach, separated from the noisy highway by sandstone cliffs. A trail leads over the point's headlands to Pirate's Cove, once a popular nude beach.

PARADISE COVE This private beach in the 28000 block of the Pacific Coast Highway (Calif. 1) charges $15 to park and $5 per person if you walk in. Changing rooms and showers are included in the price. The beach is often full by noon on weekends.

MALIBU LAGOON STATE BEACH ⭐⭐ Not just a pretty white-sand beach but an estuary and wetlands area as well, Malibu Lagoon is the historic home of the Chumash Indians. The entrance is on the Pacific Coast Highway (Calif. 1) south of Cross Creek Road, and there's a small admission charge. Marine life and shorebirds teem where the creek empties into the sea, and the waves are always mild. The historic **Adamson House** is here, a showplace of Malibu tile now operating as a museum.

SURFRIDER BEACH Without a doubt, LA's best waves roll ashore here. One of the city's most popular surfing spots, this beach is located between the Malibu Pier and the lagoon. Few "locals-only" wave wars are ever fought here—surfing is not as territorial here as it can be in other areas, where out-of-towners can be made to feel unwelcome. Surfrider is surrounded by all of Malibu's hustle and bustle; don't come here for peace and quiet, and the surf is always crowded.

TOPANGA STATE BEACH Highway noise prevents solitude at this short, narrow strip of sand located where Topanga Canyon Boulevard emerges from the mountains. Why go? Ask the surfers who wait in line to catch Topanga's excellent right point breaks. There are restrooms and lifeguard services here, and across the street you'll find one of the best fresh-fish restaurants around.

WILL ROGERS STATE BEACH Three miles along the Pacific Coast Highway (Calif. 1), between Sunset Boulevard and the Santa Monica border, are named for the American humorist whose ranch-turned-state-historic-park is nestled above the palisades that provide the backdrop for this popular beach. A pay parking lot extends the entire length of Will Rogers, and facilities include restrooms, lifeguards, and a snack hut in season. While the surfing is not the best, the waves are friendly for swimmers and there are always competitive volleyball games to be found.

SANTA MONICA STATE BEACH *(Kids)* The beaches on either side of the Santa Monica Pier (p. 521) are popular for their white sands and accessibility. There are big parking lots, eateries, and lots of well-maintained restrooms. A paved beach path runs along here, allowing you to walk, bike, or skate to Venice and points south. Colorado Boulevard leads to the pier; turn north on the Pacific Coast Highway (Calif. 1) below the coastline's bluffs, or south along Ocean Avenue; you can find parking in both directions.

LA's Beaches & Coastal Attractions

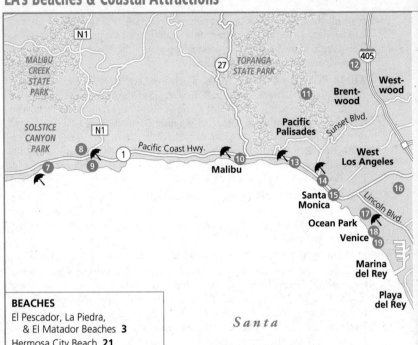

BEACHES
El Pescador, La Piedra,
   & El Matador Beaches **3**
Hermosa City Beach **21**
Leo Carrillo Beach **2**
Malibu Lagoon State Beach **7**
Manhattan State Beach **20**
North County Line Beach **1**
Paradise Cove **6**
Point Dume Beach **5**
Redondo State Beach **22**
Santa Monica State Beach **14**
Surfrider Beach **9**
Topanga State Beach **10**
Venice Beach **18**
Will Rogers State Beach **13**
Zuma Beach County Park **4**

SIGHTS & ATTRACTIONS
Aquarium of the Pacific **23**
Chiat/Day Headquarters **17**
Getty Center **12**
Museum of Flying **16**
Pepperdine University **8**
Queen Mary **24**
Venice Ocean Front Walk **19**
Will Rogers State Historic Park **11**
Santa Monica Pier **15**

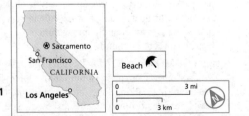

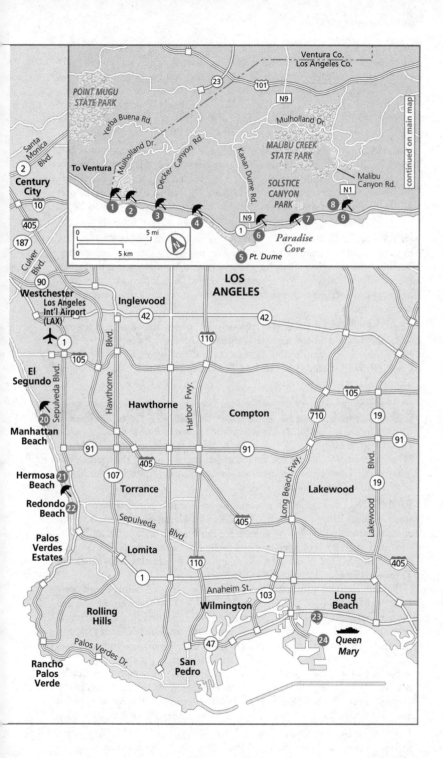

continued on main map

Ventura Co.
Los Angeles Co.

POINT MUGU
STATE PARK

Yerba Buena Rd.

Mulholland Dr.

Santa
Monica
Blvd.

2

Century
City

10

405

187

N9

Mulholland Dr.

MALIBU CREEK
STATE PARK

Decker Canyon Rd.

Kanan Dume Rd.

SOLSTICE
CANYON
PARK

Malibu
Canyon Rd.

N1

8

To Ventura

1

2

3

4

1

N9

6

7

9

Paradise
Cove

5 Pt. Dume

0   5 mi
0   5 km

N

LOS
ANGELES

Culver Blvd.

90

Westchester
Los Angeles
Int'l Airport
(LAX)

Inglewood

42

42

110

Sepulveda Blvd.

1

105

Hawthorne Blvd.

Harbor Fwy.

105

El
Segundo

Hawthorne

Compton

710

19

91

20

Manhattan
Beach

91

405

91

91

19

Hermosa
Beach

21

107

Torrance

Long Beach Fwy.

Lakewood

Lakewood Blvd.

19

Redondo
Beach

22

405

Palos
Verdes
Estates

Sepulveda Blvd.

Lomita

405

1

110

Rolling
Hills

Anaheim St.

103

Wilmington

Long
Beach

23

Palos Verdes Dr.

47

Queen
Mary

24

Rancho
Palos
Verde

San
Pedro

529

VENICE BEACH 🏖🏖 Moving south from the city of Santa Monica, the paved pedestrian Promenade becomes Ocean Front Walk and gets progressively weirder until it reaches an apex at Washington Boulevard and the Venice fishing pier. Although there are people who swim and sunbathe, Venice Beach's character is defined by the sea of humanity on the Ocean Front Walk, plus the bevy of boardwalk vendors and old-fashioned pedestrian streets a block away. Park on the side streets or in the plentiful lots west of Pacific Avenue.

MANHATTAN STATE BEACH   The Beach Boys used to hang out at this wide, friendly beach backed by beautiful oceanview homes. Plenty of parking on 36 blocks of side streets (between Rosecrans Ave. and the Hermosa Beach border) draws weekend crowds from the LA area. Manhattan has some of the best surfing around, restrooms, lifeguards, and volleyball courts. Manhattan Beach Boulevard leads west to the fishing pier and adjacent seafood restaurants.

HERMOSA CITY BEACH 🏖 A very, very wide white-sand beach with tons to recommend it, Hermosa extends to either side of the pier and includes the Strand, a pedestrian lane that runs its entire length. Main access is at the foot of Pier Avenue, which is lined with interesting shops. There is plenty of street parking, as well as restrooms, lifeguards, volleyball courts, a fishing pier, playgrounds, and good surfing.

REDONDO STATE BEACH   Popular with surfers, bicyclists, and joggers, Redondo's white sand and ice plant–carpeted dunes are just south of tiny King Harbor, along "the Esplanade" (S. Esplanade Dr.). Get there via the Pacific Coast Highway (Calif. 1) or Torrance Boulevard. Facilities include restrooms, lifeguards, and volleyball courts.

9 Outdoor Pursuits

Bisected by the Santa Monica Mountains and fronted by long stretches of beach, Los Angeles is one of the best cities in the world for nature and sports lovers. Where else can you hike in the mountains, in-line skate along the beach, swim in the ocean, enjoy a gourmet meal, and then take in a basketball, ice-hockey, or baseball game—all in the same day?

BICYCLING   Los Angeles is great for biking. If you're into distance pedaling, you can do no better than the flat 22-mile paved **Ocean Front Walk** that runs along the sand from Pacific Palisades in the north to Torrance in the south. The path attracts all levels of riders and gets pretty busy on weekends. For information on this and other city bike routes, call the **Los Angeles Department of Transportation** at ℂ 213/485-9957.

The best place to mountain-bike is along the trails of **Malibu Creek State Park** (ℂ 818/880-0367), in the Santa Monica Mountains between Malibu and the San Fernando Valley in Calabasas. Fifteen miles of trails rise to a maximum of 3,000 feet and are appropriate for intermediate to advanced bikers. Pick up a trail map at the park entrance, 4 miles south of U.S. 101 off Las Virgenes Road, just north of Mulholland Highway. Park admission is $5 per car.

Spokes 'n' Stuff Bike Rental has two locations: 4175 Admiralty Way, Marina del Rey (ℂ 310/306-3332), and 1715 Oceanfront Walk, behind Loews Hotel, Santa Monica (ℂ 310/458-6700). They rent 10-speed cruisers for $7 per hour and $16 per day; 15-speed mountain bikes rent for $8 per hour and $20 per day.

FISHING   Del Rey Sportfishing, 13759 Fiji Way (ℂ 310/822-3625; www. marinadelreysportfishing.com), has four deep-sea boats departing daily on half- and full-day ocean fishing trips. Of course, it depends on what's running when you're out, but bass, barracuda, halibut, and yellowtail are the most common catches on these party boats. Excursions cost from $22 to $30; tackle rental is available. Call for reservations.

No permit is required to cast from shore or drop a line from a pier. Local anglers will hate me for giving away their secret spot, but the **best saltwater fishing spot** in all of LA is at the foot of Torrance Boulevard in Redondo Beach.

GOLF   The greater Los Angeles area has more than 100 golf courses, which vary in quality from abysmal to superb. Most of the city's public courses are administered by the Department of Recreation and Parks, which follows a complicated registration/reservation system for tee times. While visitors cannot reserve start times in advance, you're welcome to play any of the courses by showing up and getting on the call sheet. Expect to wait for the most popular tee times, but try to use your flexible vacationer status to your advantage by avoiding the early-morning rush.

Of the city's seven 18-hole and three 9-hole courses, you can't get more central than the **Rancho Park Golf Course,** 10460 W. Pico Blvd. (℃ **310/838-7373**), located smack-dab in the middle of LA's Westside. The par-71 course has lots of tall trees, but not enough to blot out the towering Century City buildings next door. Rancho also has a nine-hole, par-3 course.

For a genuinely woodsy experience, try one of the three courses inside Griffith Park (p. 521), northeast of Hollywood. The courses are extremely well maintained, challenging without being frustrating, and (despite some holes alongside I-5) a great way to leave the city behind. Bucolic pleasures abound, particularly on the nine-hole **Roosevelt,** on Vermont Avenue across from the Greek Theatre; early-morning wildlife often includes deer, rabbits, raccoons, and skunks (fore!). **Wilson** and **Harding** are each 18 holes and start from the main clubhouse off Riverside Drive, the park's main entrance.

Greens fees on all city courses are $18 Monday through Friday and $25 on weekends and holidays; nine-hole courses cost $11 weekdays, $14 on weekends and holidays. For details on other city courses, or to contact the starter directly by phone, call the Department of Recreation and Parks at ℃ **888/527-2757.**

Industry Hills Golf Club, 1 Industry Hills Pkwy., City of Industry (℃ **626/810-4653**), has two 18-hole courses designed by William Bell. Together they encompass eight lakes, 160 bunkers, and many long fairways. The Eisenhower Course, consistently ranked among *Golf Digest*'s top 25 public courses, has extra-large undulating greens and the challenge of thick Kikuyu rough. An adjacent driving range is lit for night use. Greens fees are $59 Monday through Thursday and $89 Friday through Sunday, including cart; call in advance for tee times.

HIKING   The **Santa Monica Mountains,** a small range that runs only 50 miles from Griffith Park to Point Mugu, on the coast north of Malibu, makes Los Angeles a great place for hiking. The mountains, which peak at 3,111 feet, are part of the Santa Monica Mountains National Recreation Area, a contiguous conglomeration of 350 public parks and 65,000 acres. Many animals live in this area, including deer, coyote, rabbit, skunk, rattlesnake, fox, hawk, and quail. The hills are also home to almost 1,000 drought-resistant plant species, including live oak and coastal sage.

Hiking is best after spring rains, when the hills are green, flowers are in bloom, and the air is clear. Summers can be very hot; hikers should always carry fresh water. Beware of poison oak, a hearty shrub that's common on the West Coast. Usually found among oak trees, poison oak has leaves in groups of three, with waxy surfaces and prominent veins. If you come into contact with this itch-producing plant, bathe yourself in calamine lotion or the ocean.

For trail maps and more information, contact the **National Park Service** (© 818/597-1036), or stop by its visitor center at 30401 Agoura Rd., Suite 100, in Agoura Hills. It's open Monday through Friday from 8am to 5pm, and Saturday and Sunday from 9am to 5pm. Some areas are administered by the **California Department of Parks** (© 800/275-8777); the offices are located in Calabasas at 1925 Las Virgenes Rd.

Santa Ynez Canyon, in Pacific Palisades, is a long and difficult climb that rises steadily for about 3 miles. At the top, hikers are rewarded with fantastic views over the Pacific. At the top is **Trippet Ranch,** a public facility providing water, restrooms, and picnic tables. From Santa Monica, take Pacific Coast Highway (Calif. 1) north. Turn right onto Sunset Boulevard, then left onto Palisades Drive. Then continue for 2½ miles, turn left onto Verenda de la Montura, and park at the cul-de-sac at the end of the street, where you can find the trail head.

Temescal Canyon, in Pacific Palisades, is far easier than the Santa Ynez trail and, far more popular, especially among locals. This is one of the quickest routes into the wilderness. Hikes here are anywhere from 1 to 5 miles. From Santa Monica, take Pacific Coast Highway (Calif. 1) north; turn right onto Temescal Canyon Road, and follow it to the end. Sign in with the gatekeeper, who can also answer your questions.

Will Rogers State Historic Park (p. 521), Pacific Palisades, is also a terrific place for hiking. An intermediate-level hike from the park's entrance ends at Inspiration Point, a plateau from which you can see a good portion of LA's Westside.

HORSEBACK RIDING   The **Griffith Park Livery Stable,** 480 Riverside Dr. (in the Los Angeles Equestrian Center), Burbank (© 818/840-8401), rents horses by the hour for western or English riding through Griffith Park's hills. There's a 200-pound weight limit, and children have to be at least 6 years old and at least 4 feet tall. Horse rental costs $20 per hour; maximum rental is 2 hours. You can also arrange for private 1-hour lessons by calling © 818/569-3666. The stables are open daily from 8am to 5pm, and cash is required for payment.

SEA KAYAKING   Sea kayaking is all the rage in Southern California; if you've ever tried it, you know why. Unlike river kayaks, in which your legs are actually inside the boat's hull, paddlers sit on top of sea kayaks, which can be maneuvered more easily than canoes.

Southwind Kayak Center (© 800/768-8494 or 949/261-0200; www.southwindkayaks.com) rents sea kayaks for use in the bay or open ocean at rates of $12 to $16 per hour; instructional classes are available on weekends only. The center also conducts bird-watching kayak expeditions into Upper Newport Bay Ecological Reserve at rates of $50 to $65.

SKATING   The 22-mile-long Ocean Front Walk that runs from Pacific Palisades to Torrance is one of the premiere skating spots in the country. In-line skating is especially popular, but conventional skates are often seen here, too. Skating is allowed just about everywhere bicycling is, but be advised that cyclists have the right of way. **Spokes 'n' Stuff,** 4175 Admiralty Way, Marina del Rey (© 310/306-3332), is just one of many places to rent wheels near the Venice portion of Ocean Front Walk. In the South Bay, in-line skate rentals are available

Spectator Sports

The **Los Angeles Dodgers** play at Dodger Stadium, 1000 Elysian Park, near Sunset Boulevard (© **323/224-1HIT**). The team's slick, interactive website (**www.dodgers.com**) offers everything from game schedules to souvenir merchandise online.

Los Angeles has two NBA franchises, the **LA Lakers** (www.nba.com/lakers) and the **LA Clippers** (www.nba.com/clippers). Both teams play in the $300 million Staples Center in downtown LA, 1111 S. Figueroa St. (© **213/742-7155**; www.staplescenter.com). Celebrity fans like Jack Nicholson and Dyan Cannon have the best tickets, but this 20,000-seater should have room for you, too.

The **LA Sparks** (© **310/330-2434**; www.wnba.com/sparks), who claimed their second WNBA Championship in 2002, play at the Staples Center May through August. The Sparks are especially proud of star center Lisa Leslie.

Los Angeles suffers from an absence of major-league football, but is blessed with two popular college teams and an Arena League team. The college season runs September through November; if you're interested in checking out a game, contact **UCLA Bruins Football** (© **310/825-2101**; www.uclabruins.fansonly.com) or **USC Trojan Football** (© **213/740-2311**; www.usctrojans.com).

1 block from the Strand at **Hermosa Cyclery,** 20 13th St. (© **310/374-7816**). Skates cost around $6 per hour ($18 max); kneepads and wrist guards come with every rental.

SURFING   Surfing was invented by the Polynesians; Captain Cook made note of it in Oahu in 1778. George Freeth (1883–1918), who first surfed Redondo Beach in 1907, is widely credited with introducing the sport to California. But surfing didn't catch on until the 1950s, when Caltech graduate Bob Simmons invented a more maneuverable lightweight fiberglass board. The Beach Boys and other surf-music groups popularized Southern California in the minds of beach-babes and -dudes everywhere, and the rest, as they say, is history. See "Beaches," earlier in this chapter, for beach and point-break suggestions. You'll also find some great surf an hour or two down the coast in the Huntington Beach and Newport areas of Orange County.

If you're a first-timer eager to learn the sport, contact **Pure Surfing Experience** (© **310/546-4451;** www.campsurf.com) in Manhattan Beach. This highly respected school features a team of experienced instructors and will supply all necessary equipment. Single lessons are $80, but subsequent follow-ups are deeply discounted. Call for reservations (also available online).

Boards are available for rent at shops near all top surfing beaches in the LA area. **Zuma Jay Surfboards,** 22775 Pacific Coast Hwy., Malibu (© **310/456-8044**), is about ¼ mile south of Malibu Pier. Rentals are $20 per day, plus $8 for wet suits in winter.

TENNIS   While soft-surface courts are more popular on the East Coast, hard surfaces are most common in California. If your hotel doesn't have a court and can't suggest any courts nearby, try the well-maintained, well-lit **Griffith Park Tennis Courts,** on Commonwealth Road, just east of Vermont Avenue (© 323/662-7772). Or call the **City of Los Angeles Department of Recreation and Parks** (© 888/527-2757) to make a reservation at a municipal court near you.

10 Shopping

Here's a rundown of the primary shopping areas, along with descriptions of a few of their best stores. The sales tax in Los Angeles is 8%, but savvy out-of-state shoppers know how to have more expensive items shipped directly home, thereby avoiding the tax.

SANTA MONICA & THE BEACHES

Bergamot Station _Finds_   Once a station for the Red Car trolley line, this industrial space is now home to the **Santa Monica Museum of Art,** plus two dozen art galleries, a cafe, a bookstore, and offices. Most of the galleries are closed Monday. The train yard is located at the terminus of Michigan Avenue, west of Cloverfield Boulevard.

Exhibits change often and vary widely, ranging from a Julius Shulman black-and-white-photo retrospective of LA's Case Study Houses to a provocative exhibit of Vietnam War propaganda posters from the United States and Vietnam, to whimsical furniture constructed entirely of corrugated cardboard. A sampling of offerings includes the **Gallery of Functional Art** (© 310/829-6990), which features one-of-a-kind and limited-edition furniture, lighting, bathroom fixtures, and other functional art pieces, as well as smaller items like jewelry, flatware, ceramics, and glass. **The Rosamund Felson Gallery** (© 310/828-8488) is well known for showcasing LA-based contemporary artists; this is a good place to get a taste of current trends. **Track 16 Gallery** (© 310/264-4678) has exhibitions that range from pop art to avant-garde inventiveness—try to see what's going on here. 2525 Michigan Ave. (E of Cloverfield Blvd.), Santa Monica. © 310/829-5854.

Main Street   An excellent street for strolling, Main Street boasts a healthy combination of mall standards as well as upscale, left-of-center individual boutiques. You can also find plenty of casually hip cafes and restaurants. The primary strip connecting Santa Monica and Venice, Main Street has a relaxed, beach-community vibe that sets it apart from similar strips. The stores here straddle the fashion fence between upscale trendy and beach-bum edgy. Highlights include **C.P. Shades,** 2937 Main St. (between Ashland and Pier sts.; © 310/392-0949), a San Francisco ladies' clothier whose loose and comfy cotton and linen line is carried by many department stores and boutiques. **Horizons West,** 2011 Main St. (south of Pico Blvd.; © 310/392-1122), sells brand-name surfboards, wet suits, leashes, magazines, waxes, lotions, and everything else you need to catch the perfect wave. Stop in and say hi to Randy, and pick up a free tide table. If you're looking for some truly sophisticated, finely crafted eyewear, friendly **Optical Shop of Aspen,** 2904 Main St. (between Ashland and Pier sts.; © 310/392-0633), is for you. Ask for frames by cutting-edge LA designers Bada and Koh Sakai. If you're lucky enough to have perfect vision, consider some stylish shades. Outdoors types will get lost in 5,600-square-foot **Patagonia,** 2936 Main St. (© 310/314-1776; www.patagonia.com), where climbers, surfers, skiers, and hikers can gear up in the functional, colorful duds that put this environmentally friendly firm on the map. Between Pacific St. and Rose Ave., Santa Monica and Venice blvds.

Montana Avenue   This breezy stretch of slow-traffic Montana is one of my favorite regentrified parts of the city. It's gotten a lot pricier than in the late 1970s when tailors and laundromats ruled the roost, but the specialty shops still outnumber the chains. Look around and you can see upscale moms with strollers and cellphones shopping for designer fashions, country-home decor, and gourmet takeout.

Montana is still original enough for residents from across town to make a special trip here, seeking out distinctive shops like **Shabby Chic,** 1013 Montana Ave. (© 310/394-1975), a much-copied purveyor of slip-covered sofas and flea-market furnishings, while clotheshorses shop for designer wear at minimalist **Savannah,** 706 Montana Ave. (© 310/458-2095); ultra-hip **Jill Roberts,** 920 Montana Ave. (© 310/260-1966); and sleekly professional **Weathervane,** 1209 Montana Ave. (© 310/393-5344). Upscale moms can find tiny fashions at **Real Threads,** 1527 Montana Ave. (© 310/393-3175). For more grown-up style, head to **Ponte Vecchio,** 702 Montana Ave. (© 310/394-0989), which sells Italian hand-painted dishes and urns, or to **Cinzia,** 1129 Montana Ave. (© 310/393-7751), which features a smattering of both Tuscan and English home accessories. If Valentine's Day is approaching, duck into **Only Hearts,** 1407 Montana Ave. (© 310/393-3088), for heart-themed gifts and seductively comfortable intimate apparel. The stylish choice for lunch is **Wolfgang Puck Cafe,** 1323 Montana Ave. (© 310/393-0290). Between 7th and 17th sts., Santa Monica.

Third Street Promenade   Packed with chain stores and boutiques as well as dozens of restaurants and a large movie theater, Santa Monica's pedestrians-only section of Third Street is one of the most popular shopping areas in the city. The Promenade bustles on into the evening with a seemingly endless assortment of street performers and shoppers. Stores stay open late (often until 1 or 2am on the weekends) for the movie-going crowds. There's plenty of metered parking in structures on the adjacent streets, so bring lots of quarters!

Highlights include **Hennessey & Ingalls,** 1254 Third Street Promenade (© 310/458-9074), a bookstore devoted to art and architecture, from magnificent coffee-table photography books to graphic-arts titles and obscure biographies of artists and art movements; **Midnight Special Bookstore,** 1318 Third Street Promenade (© 310/393-2923), a medium-size general bookshop known for its good small-press selection and regular poetry readings; **Restoration Hardware,** 1221 Third Street Promenade (© 310/458-7992), the retro-current source for reproduction home furnishings and accessories; and **Puzzle Zoo,** 1413 Third Street Promenade (© 310/393-9201), where you'll find the double-sided World's Most Difficult Puzzle, the Puzzle in a Bottle, and many other brain-teasing challenges. Book lovers may also want to stop by the local **Barnes & Noble,** 1201 Third Street Promenade (© 310/260-9110), which carries thousands of titles; or **Borders,** which has a branch across town at 330 S. La Cienega Blvd., at Third Street (© 310/659-4045). 3rd St., from Broadway to Wilshire Blvd., Santa Monica. www.thirdst.com.

LA'S WESTSIDE & BEVERLY HILLS

La Brea Avenue   This is LA's artsiest shopping strip. Anchored by the giant **American Rag, Cie.** alterna-complex, 150 S. La Brea Ave. (© 323/935-3157), La Brea is home to lots of great urban antiques stores dealing in Deco, Arts and

Crafts, 1950s modern, and the like. You'll also find vintage clothiers, furniture galleries, and other warehouse-size stores, as well as some of the city's hippest restaurants, such as Campanile (p. 494).

Bargain hunters find flea-market furnishings at **Nick Metropolis,** 100 S. La Brea Ave. (© **323/934-3700**), while more upscale seekers of home decor head to **Mortise & Tenon,** 446 S. La Brea Ave. (© **323/937-7654**), where hand-crafted heavy wood pieces sit next to overstuffed velvet-upholstered sofas and even vintage steel desks. Stuffed to the rafters with hardware and fixtures of the last 100 years, **Liz's Antique Hardware,** 453 S. La Brea Ave. (© **323/939-4403**), thoughtfully keeps a canister of wet-wipes at the register—believe me, you'll need one after sifting through bags and crates of doorknobs, latches, finials, and any other home hardware you can imagine needing. Perfect sets of Bakelite drawer pulls and antique ceramic bathroom fixtures are some of the more intriguing items. Be prepared to browse for hours, whether you're redeco-rating or not!

Although the art of millinery often seems to have gone the way of white after-noon gloves for ladies, inventive **Drea Kadilak,** 463 S. La Brea Ave., at Sixth Street (© **323/931-2051**), charms visitors with her tiny hat shop. Designing in straw, cotton duck, wool felt, and a number of more unusual fabrics, she does her own blocking, will cheerfully take measurements for custom ladies' head-wear, is reasonably priced, and gives away signature hatboxes with your pur-chase.

The best place for a snack is Nancy Silverton's **La Brea Bakery,** 624 S. La Brea Ave. (© **323/939-6813**), which foodies know from gourmet markets and the attached Campanile restaurant. Hipsters also head up the street to **Yellow-stone,** 712 N. La Brea Ave. (© **323/931-6616**), for vintage duds, and souvenir seekers know to visit **Moletown,** 900 N. La Brea Ave. (© **800/851-7221**), for studio merchandise featuring logo graphics from the hottest new movies. N of Wilshire Blvd.

Rodeo Drive & Beverly Hills' Golden Triangle

Everyone knows about Rodeo Drive, the city's most famous shopping street. Couture shops from high fashion's old guard are located along these 3 hallowed blocks, along with plenty of newer high-end labels. And there are two examples of the Beverly Hills ver-sion of minimalls, albeit more insular and attractive—the **Rodeo Collection,** 421 N. Rodeo Dr.; and **Two Rodeo,** at Wilshire Boulevard. The 16-square-block area surrounding Rodeo Drive is known as the "Golden Triangle." Shops off Rodeo are generally not as name-conscious as those on the strip (and you might actually be able to afford something), but they're nevertheless plenty upscale. Little Santa Monica Boulevard has a particularly colorful line of spe-cialty stores, and Brighton Way is as young and hip as relatively staid Beverly Hills gets.

The big names to look for here are **Giorgio Beverly Hills,** 327 N. Rodeo Dr. (© **800/GIORGIO**); **Gucci,** 347 N. Rodeo Dr. (© **310/278-3451**); **Hermès,** 434 N. Rodeo Dr. (© **310/278-6440**); **Louis Vuitton,** 295 N. Rodeo Dr. (© **310/859-0457**); **Polo/Ralph Lauren,** 444 N. Rodeo Dr. (© **310/281-7200**); and **Tiffany & Co.,** 210 N. Rodeo Dr. (© **310/273-8880**). The newest arrival is **Niketown,** corner of Wilshire Boulevard and Rodeo Drive (© **310/275-9998**), a behemoth shrine to the reigning athletic-gear king.

Wilshire Boulevard is also home to New York–style department stores (each in spectacular landmark buildings) like **Saks Fifth Avenue,** 9600 Wilshire Blvd.

(© **310/275-4211**), **Barney's New York,** 9570 Wilshire Blvd. (© **310/276-4400**), and **Neiman Marcus,** 9700 Wilshire Blvd. (© **310/550-5900**). Between Santa Monica Blvd., Wilshire Blvd., and Crescent Dr.

Sunset Strip   The monster-size billboards advertising the latest rock god make it clear that this is rock 'n' roll territory. So it makes sense that you'll find legendary **Tower Records,** 8801 W. Sunset Blvd. (© **310/657-7300;** www. towerrecords.com), in the heart of the action. Tower insists that it has LA's largest selection of CDs—over 125,000 titles—despite the Virgin Megastore's contrary claim. Even if Virgin has more, Tower's collection tends to be more interesting and browser-friendly. And the shop's enormous blues, jazz, and classical selections are definitely better than the competition's. It's open 365 days a year. At the east end of the strip sits the gigantic **Virgin Megastore,** 8000 Sunset Blvd., at Crescent Heights (© **323/650-8666**). Some 100 CD-listening posts and an in-store radio station make this megastore a music lover's paradise. Virgin claims to stock 150,000 titles, including an extensive collection of hard-to-find artists.

The "Strip" is lined with trendy restaurants, industry-oriented hotels, and dozens of shops offering outrageous fashions and chunky stage accessories. One anomaly is **Sunset Plaza,** an upscale cluster of Georgian-style shops resembling Beverly Hills at its snootiest. Here's where you'll find **Billy Martin's,** 8605 Sunset Blvd. (© **310/289-5000**), which was founded by the legendary Yankee manager in 1978. This chic men's Western shop—complete with fireplace and leather sofa—stocks hand-forged silver and gold belt buckles, Lucchese and Liberty boots, and stable staples like flannel shirts. **Book Soup,** 8818 Sunset Blvd. (© **310/659-3110;** www.booksoup.com), has long been one of LA's most celebrated bookshops, selling both mainstream and small-press books and hosting regular book signings and author nights. A great browsing shop, it has a large selection of showbiz books and an extensive outdoor news- and magazine stand on one side. Between La Cienega Blvd. and Doheny Dr., West Hollywood.

West Third Street   You can shop till you drop on this trendy strip, anchored on the east end by the Farmers Market (p. 505). Many of Melrose Avenue's shops have relocated here, alongside some terrific up-and-comers and several cafes. "Fun" is more the catchword here than "funky," and the shops (including the vintage-clothing stores) tend a bit more to the refined than do those along Melrose.

The **Cook's Library,** 8373 W. Third St. (© **323/655-3141;** www.cooks library.com), is where the city's top chefs find both classic and deliciously offbeat cookbooks and other food-oriented tomes. Browsing is welcomed, even encouraged, with tea, tasty treats, and rocking chairs. **Traveler's Bookcase,** 8375 W. Third St. (© **323/655-0575;** www.travelbooks.com), is truly one of the best travel-book shops in the West, stocking a huge selection of guidebooks and travel literature, as well as maps and travel accessories. A quarterly newsletter chronicles the travel adventures of the genial owners, who know firsthand the most helpful items to carry.

There's a lot more to see along this always-growing street, enough to take up several hours. Refuel at **Chado Tea Room** ✲, 8422 W. Third St. (© **323/655-2056**), a temple for tea lovers. Chado is designed with a nod to Paris's renowned Mariage Frères tea purveyor; one wall is lined with nooks whose recognizable brown tins are filled with over 250 different varieties of tea from around the world. Among the choices are 15 kinds of Darjeeling, Indian teas blended with rose petals, and ceremonial Chinese and Japanese blends. You can also get tea meals here, featuring delightful sandwiches and individual pots of any loose tea in the store. Between Fairfax Ave. and Robertson Blvd.

HOLLYWOOD

Hollywood Boulevard   One of Los Angeles's most famous streets is, for the most part, a sleazy strip. But along the Walk of Fame, between the T-shirt shops and greasy pizza parlors, you'll find some excellent poster shops, souvenir stores, and Hollywood-memorabilia dealers that are worth getting out of your car for—especially if there's a chance of getting your hands on that long-sought-after Ethel Merman autograph or *200 Motels* poster. Between Gower St. and La Brea Ave.

Melrose Avenue   Melrose is showing some wear—some stretches have become downright ugly—but this is still one of the most exciting shopping streets in the country for cutting-edge fashions—and some eye-popping people-watching to boot. There are scores of shops selling the latest in clothes, gifts, jewelry, and accessories. Melrose is a playful stroll, dotted with plenty of hip restaurants and funky shops that are sure to shock. Where else could you find green patent-leather cowboy boots, a working 19th-century pocket watch, an inflatable girlfriend, and glow-in-the-dark condoms in the same shopping spree? From east to west, here are some highlights:

l.a. Eyeworks, 7407 Melrose Ave. (© 323/653-8255), revolutionized eyeglass designs from medical supply to stylish accessory, and now their brand is sold nationwide. **Retail Slut,** 7308 Melrose Ave. (© 323/934-1339), is a famous rock 'n' roll shop carrying new clothing and accessories for men and women. The unique designs are for a select crowd (the name says it all), so don't expect to find anything for your next PTA meeting here. **Betsey Johnson Boutique,** 7311 Melrose Ave. (© 323/931-4490), is a favorite among the young and pencil-thin; the New York–based designer has brought her brand of fashion—trendy, cutesy, body-conscious women's wear in colorful prints and faddish fabrics—to LA. It's also in Santa Monica at 2929 Main St. (© 310/452-7911).

Across the street, **Off the Wall,** 7325 Melrose Ave. (© 323/930-1185), is filled with neon-flashing, bells-and-whistles kitsch collectibles, from vintage Wurlitzer jukeboxes to life-size fiberglass cows. The LA branch of a Bay Area hipster hangout, **Wasteland,** 7428 Melrose Ave. (© 323/653-3028), has an enormous steel-sculpted facade. There's a lot of leather, denim, and some classic vintage—but mostly funky 1970s garb, both vintage and contemporary. This ultra-trendy store is packed with the flamboyantly colorful polyester halters and bell-bottoms from the decade some of us would rather forget. More racks of vintage treasures (and trash) are found at **Aardvark's Odd Ark,** 7579 Melrose Ave. (© 323/655-6769), which stocks everything from suits and dresses to neckties, hats, handbags, and jewelry. This place also manages to anticipate some of the hottest new street fashions. There's another Aardvark's at 85 Market St., Venice (© 310/392-2996). Between Fairfax and La Brea aves.

DOWNTOWN

Since the late, lamented department store Bullock's closed in 1993 (its Deco masterpiece salons rescued to house the Southwestern Law School's library), Downtown has become less of a shopping destination than ever. Although many of the once-splendid streets are lined with cut-rate luggage and electronics stores, shopping here can be a rewarding if gritty experience for the adventuresome.

Savvy Angelenos still go for bargains in the garment and fabric districts; florists and bargain hunters arrive at the vast Flower Mart before dawn for the city's best selection of fresh blooms; and families of all ethnicities stroll the **Grand Central Market,** 317 S. Broadway (between 3rd and 4th sts.; © **213/ 624-2378;** www.grandcentralsquare.com). Opened in 1917, this bustling market has watched the face of downtown LA change while changing little itself. Today, it serves Latino families, enterprising restaurateurs, and cooks in search of unusual ingredients and bargain-priced produce. On weekends you'll be greeted by a mariachi band at the Hill Street entrance, near my favorite market feature: the fruit-juice counter, which dispenses 20 fresh varieties from wall spigots, and blends the tastiest, healthiest "shakes" in town. Farther into the market you'll find produce sellers and prepared-food counters, spice vendors who seem straight out of a Turkish bazaar, and a grain-and-bean seller who'll scoop out dozens of exotic rices and dried legumes.

11 Los Angeles After Dark

The *LA Weekly* (www.laweekly.com), a free weekly paper available at sidewalk stands, shops, and restaurants, is the best place to find up-to-date news on what's happening in Los Angeles's playhouses, cinemas, museums, and live-music venues. The "Calendar" section of the *Los Angeles Times* (www.calendarlive.com) is also a good place to see what's going on after dark.

Ticketmaster (© **213/480-3232;** www.ticketmaster.com) is the major charge-by-phone ticket agency in the city, selling tickets to concerts, sporting events, plays, and special events. I also recommend logging on to either **www.localmusic2.com,** which provides 2 weeks' worth of schedules organized by neighborhood and/or style, or the concert business trade publication **Pollstar** (**www.pollstar.com**). Sometimes tickets may come available at the box office before shows, or when all else fails, try "negotiating" with some of the locals in front of the venue.

THEATER

Tickets for most plays usually cost $10 to $35, although big-name shows at the major theaters can fetch up to $75 for the best seats. **Theatre League Alliance** (© **213/614-0556**), an association of live theaters and producers in Los Angeles (they also put on the yearly Ovation Awards, LA's theater awards), offers same-day, half-price tickets via **Web Tix,** an Internet-only service at www.theatrela.org. Tickets are available Tuesday through Saturday from 4am to 11pm; purchase them online with a credit card and they'll be waiting for you at the box office. The site features a frequently updated list of shows and availability; you can also sign up for e-mail alerts.

MAJOR THEATERS & COMPANIES

The all-purpose **Performing Arts Center of Los Angeles County,** 135 N. Grand Ave., Downtown (formerly known as the Music Center), houses the **Ahmanson Theatre** and **Mark Taper Forum** (© **213/628-2772;**

Finds Free Morning Music at Hollywood Bowl

It's not widely known, but the Bowl's morning rehearsals are open to the public (and absolutely free). On Tuesday, Thursday, and Friday from 9:30am to 12:30pm, you can see the program scheduled for that evening. So grab some coffee and donuts (the concession stands aren't open) and enjoy the best seats in the house.

www.taperahmanson.com), as well as the **LA Philharmonic** and **LA Opera.** The Ahmanson Theatre is an active year-round theater, with shows produced by the in-house Center Theatre Group or with traveling productions, often Broadway- or London-bred. Each season has guaranteed a handful of high-profile shows, such as Mel Brooks's *The Producers,* Lily Tomlin's *The Search for Signs of Intelligent Life in the Universe,* and *Bring in 'Da Noise, Bring in 'Da Funk* featuring Savion Glover. The Ahmanson is so huge that you'll want seats in the front third or half of the theater.

The Mark Taper Forum is a more intimate, circular theater staging contemporary works by international and local playwrights. Federico García Lorca's *The House of Bernarda Alba* and Tony Kushner's *Homebody/Kabul* are two recent productions, each ideally suited to this intimate setting. Ticket prices vary depending on the performance. *Tip:* Two hours prior to curtain time, the Mark Taper Forum offers specially priced $12 tickets, which must be purchased in person with cash.

Across town, the moderately sized **Geffen Playhouse,** 10886 Le Conte Ave., Westwood (© **310/208-5454;** www.geffenplayhouse.com), presents dramatic and comedic work by prominent and emerging writers. UCLA purchased the theater—which was originally built as a Masonic temple in 1929, and later served as the Westwood Playhouse—back in 1995 with a little help from philanthropic entertainment mogul David Geffen. This charming venue is often the West Coast choice of many acclaimed off-Broadway shows, and also attracts locally based TV and movie actors eager for the immediacy of stage work. One recent production featured Maria Conchita Alonso and John Larroquette in Neil Simon's *Oscar and Felix, A New Look at the Odd Couple.* Always audience-friendly, the Playhouse prices tickets in the $25-to-$38 range.

The recently restored **Pantages Theatre,** 6233 Hollywood Blvd., between Vine and Argyle (© **323/463-4367**), reflects the full Art Deco glory of LA's theater scene, features musicals on the level of *Cats,* and just finished a multiyear run of Disney's *The Lion King.*

Located at the foot of the Hollywood Hills, the 1,245-seat outdoor **John Anson Ford Amphitheatre** (© **213/974-1343;** www.lacountyarts.org/ford. html) is located in a county regional park and is set against a backdrop of cypress trees and chaparral. It is an intimate setting with no patron more than 96 feet away from the stage. Music, dance, film, theater, and family events run May through September. The cozy, 87-seat indoor theater space, which was extensively renovated in 1998 and re-named **[Inside] The Ford,** features live music and theater year-round.

One of the most highly acclaimed professional theaters in LA, the **Pasadena Playhouse,** 39 S. El Molino Ave., near Colorado Boulevard, Pasadena (© **626/ 356-7529;** www.pasadenaplayhouse.org), is a registered historic landmark that has served as the training ground for many theatrical, film, and TV stars, including William Holden and Gene Hackman. Productions are presented on the main theater's elaborate Spanish Colonial revival stage.

For a schedule at any of the above theaters, check the listings in *Los Angeles Magazine,* available at most area newsstands, or the "Calendar" section of the Sunday *Los Angeles Times,* or call the box offices at the numbers listed above.

SMALLER PLAYHOUSES & COMPANIES

On any given night, there's more live theater to choose from in Los Angeles than in New York City, due in part to the surfeit of ready actors and writers chomping at the bit to make it in Tinseltown. Many of today's familiar faces from film and TV spent plenty of time cutting their teeth on LA's busy theater circuit, which is home to nearly 200 small- and medium-size theaters and theater companies, ranging from the 'round-the-corner, neighborhood variety to high-profile, polished troupes of veteran actors. With so many options, navigating the scene to find the best work can be a monumental task. A good bet is to choose one of the theaters listed below, which have established excellent reputations for their consistently high quality productions; otherwise, consult *LA Weekly*, which advertises most current productions, or call **Theatre LA** (© 213/688-2787) for up-to-date performance listings.

The **Colony Studio Theatre,** 555 N. Third Street, Burbank (© 818/558-7000; www.colonytheatre.org), was formed in 1975 and has developed from a part-time ensemble of TV actors longing for their theatrical roots into a nationally recognized company. The company produces plays in all genres at the 276-seat Burbank Center Stage, which is shared with other performing-arts groups.

Actors Circle Theater, 7313 Santa Monica Blvd., West Hollywood (© 323/882-8043), is a 47-seater that's as acclaimed as it's tiny. Look for original contemporary works throughout the year.

The Actors' Gang Theater, 6201 Santa Monica Blvd., Hollywood (© 323/465-0566; www.theactorsgang.com), is not one to shy from irreverence. Back in 1997, the in-house company, a group of UCLA alums, presented *Bat Boy: The Musical,* based on a story in the bizarre tabloid *Weekly World News.* The theater has also co-produced Eric Bogosian's *Suburbia* with the Namaste Theatre Company, and Roger Guenvere Smith's *A Huey P. Newton Story.*

The classical theater company **A Noise Within,** 5151 State University Dr. (© 323/224-6320; www.anoisewithin.org), has performed everything from Shakespeare to Coward to Molière. In 1999, the company moved to the Luckman Fine Arts Complex on the campus of Cal State Los Angeles, located northeast of Downtown. Recent highlights included Shakespeare's *Love's Labour's Lost* and Ibsen's *The Wild Duck.*

Founded in 1965, **East West Players,** 120 N. Judge John Aiso St., Los Angeles (© 323/625-7000; www.eastwestplayers.com), is now the oldest Asian-American theater company in the United States. It's been so successful that the company moved from a 99-seat venue to the 200-seat David Henry Huang Theater in downtown LA in 1998. To commemorate the massacre in Tiananmen square, EWP presented the musical *Beijing Spring* in 1999, and in 2002 staged Derek Nguyen's *Monster,* a winning play from the theater's Y2K Playwriting Competition.

The 25-year-old **L.A. Theatre Works** (© 310/827-0889; www.latw.org) is renowned for its marriage of media and theater and has performed more than 200 plays and logged over 350 hours of on-air programming. Performances are held at the wonderful Skirball Cultural Center (p. 517), nestled in the Sepulveda Pass near the Getty Center. In the past, personalities such as Richard Dreyfuss, Julia Louis-Dreyfuss, Jason Robards, Annette Bening, and John Lithgow have given award-winning performances of plays by Arthur Miller, Neil Simon, Joyce Carol Oates, and more. For 7 years now, the group has performed simultaneously for viewing and listening audiences in its radio theater series. In 2002, L.A. Theatre Works presented the West Coast premiere of *The Credeaux Canvas,* starring Hilary Swank. Tickets are usually around $35.

Founded in 1981, **West Coast Ensemble Theater,** 522 N. La Brea Ave., between Melrose and Beverly, Hollywood (© 323/876-8723; www.wcensemble. org), is a nonprofit multiethnic assemblage of professional actors, writers, and directors. The ensemble has collected accolades from local critics, as well as many awards for its excellent production quality. Expect to see well-written, well-directed, and socially relevant plays performed by talented and professional casts. Ticket prices range from $15 to $22.

CLASSICAL MUSIC & OPERA

While best known for its pop realms (see above), other types of music in Los Angeles consist of top-flight orchestras and companies, both local and visiting, to fulfill the most demanding classical-music appetites; scan the papers to find out who's performing while you're in the city.

The world-class **Los Angeles Philharmonic** (© 323/850-2000; www. laphil.org) is the only major classical-music company in Los Angeles. Finnish-born music director Esa-Pekka Salonen concentrates on contemporary compositions; despite complaints from traditionalists, he does an excellent job attracting younger audiences. Tickets can be hard to come by when celebrity players like Itzhak Perlman, Isaac Stern, Emanuel Ax, or Yo Yo Ma are in town. In addition to performances at the **Dorothy Chandler Pavilion** in the all-purpose Music Center, 135 N. Grand Ave., Downtown, the Philharmonic also plays a summer season at the **Hollywood Bowl** (see below), and a chamber-music series at the **Skirball Cultural Center** (p. 517). The philharmonic and the master choral will have a new home as of 2003, the Walt Disney Concert Hall; designed by world-renowned architect Frank O. Gehry, this exciting addition to the Music Center of LA includes a 2,273-seat concert hall, outdoor park, restaurant, cafe, bookstore, and gift shop.

Slowly but surely, the **Los Angeles Opera** (© 213/972-8001; www.los angelesopera.com), which performs at the Dorothy Chandler Pavilion, is gaining respect and popularity with inventive stagings of classic pieces, modern operas, visiting divas, and the contributions from high-profile artistic director Plácido Domingo. The 120-voice Los Angeles Master Chorale sings a varied repertoire that includes classical and pop compositions. Concerts are usually held at the Performing Arts Center of Los Angeles County (© 213/972-7200) October through June.

The **UCLA Center for the Performing Arts** (© 310/825-2101; www. performingarts.ucla.edu) has presented music, dance, and theatrical performances of unparalleled quality for over 60 years, and continues to be a major presence in the local and national cultural landscape. Presentations occur at several different theaters around Los Angeles, both on and off campus. UCLA's Royce Hall is the center's pride; it has even been compared to New York's Carnegie Hall. Recent standouts from the center's busy calendar included the famous Gyuto Monks Tibetan Tantric Choir and the Cinderella story *Cendrillon* with an original score by Sergei Prokofiev.

CONCERTS UNDER THE STARS

Hollywood Bowl   Built in the early 1920s, the Hollywood Bowl is an elegant Greek-style natural outdoor amphitheater cradled in a small mountain canyon. This is the summer home of the Los Angeles Philharmonic Orchestra. Internationally known conductors and soloists often sit in on Tuesday and Thursday nights. Friday and Saturday concerts often feature orchestral swing or pops concerts. The summer season also includes a jazz series; past performers have included Natalie Cole, Dionne Warwick, and Chick Corea. Other events, from rock acts like Radiohead to Garrison Keillor programs, summer fireworks galas, and the annual Mariachi Festival, are often on the season's schedule.

To round out an evening at the Bowl, many concertgoers use the occasion to enjoy a picnic dinner and a bottle of wine—it's one of LA's grandest traditions. You can prepare your own, or order a picnic basket with a choice of hot and cold dishes and a selection of wines and desserts from Patina's on-site catering department, who also provide delivery to box seats. Call ☎ **323/850-1885** by 4pm the day before you go to place your food order. 2301 N. Highland Ave. (at Pat Moore Way), Hollywood. ☎ 323/850-2000. www.hollywoodbowl.org.

THE CLUB & MUSIC SCENE

Let's face it: Los Angeles is more or less the center of the entertainment industry. So, on any given night, finding something to satisfy any musical fancy can be a snap. From acoustic rock to jazz fusion, from Judas Priest cover bands to Latin funk, from the up-and-coming to the already gone, LA's got something for everyone. For a listing of shows closer to the date of your arrival, check the websites of the *LA Weekly* (www.laweekly.com) and the *Los Angeles Times* "Calendar" section (www.calendarlive.com).

B. B. King's Blues Club   Nestled away in Universal CityWalk's commercial plaza, this three-level club/restaurant—the ribs alone are worth the trip—hosts plenty of great local and touring national blues acts and is a testament to the establishment's venerable namesake. There's no shortage of good seating, but if you find yourself on the top two levels, it's best to grab a table adjacent to the railing to get an ideal view of the stage. CityWalk, Universal City. ☎ 818/622-5464.

Dragonfly   Not one to miss a trend, Dragonfly went from being a dance club that offered live music to becoming a live stage that offers dancing. From "surprise" shows by top-notch "local" acts such as the Red Hot Chili Peppers and Social Distortion to national acts like Alanis Morissette, Dragonfly is soaring. Overheated guests and smokers also enjoy its cool outdoor patio. 6510 Santa Monica Blvd., Hollywood. ☎ 323/466-6111. www.dragonfly.com.

House of Blues   With three great bars, cutting-edge Southern art, and a key Sunset Strip location, there are plenty of reasons music fans and industry types keep coming back to House of Blues. Night after night, audiences are dazzled by performances from nationally and internationally acclaimed acts as diverse as the B-52's, Eric Clapton, and Third World. The food in the upstairs restaurant can be great (reservations are a must), and the Sunday gospel brunch, though a bit pricey, promises a rollicking time. 8430 Sunset Blvd., West Hollywood. ☎ 323/848-5100. www.hob.com.

Jazz Bakery   Ruth Price's nonprofit venue is renowned for attracting some of the most important names in jazz—and for the restored Helms bakery factory that houses the club and inspires its name. Hers is a no-frills, all-about-the-music affair, and the place is pretty much BYO in the drinks department. Drummer Jimmy Cobb, the last remaining member of Miles Davis's "Kind of Blue" band, had a 4-night stint at JB recently. 3233 Helms Ave., Culver City. ☎ 310/271-9039. www.jazzbakery.org. All ages. Cover $10–$25.

The Knitting Factory   Straight from the New York City legend, a West Coast branch of the famous Knitting Factory has arrived in the redeveloping Hollywood Boulevard nightlife district. The Main Stage was inaugurated by a Posies performance, and sees such diverse bookings as Kristin Hersh, Pere Ubu, and Jonathan Richman; a secondary AlterKnit stage has sporadic shows. The Factory is totally wired for digital, including interactive online computer stations throughout the club. 7021 Hollywood Blvd., Hollywood. ☎ 323/463-0204. www.knittingfactory.com/KFLA.

The Mint   Once a shotgun shack serving fried chicken and blues in a beer-only bar, the Mint has reemerged as a gloriously loungey hangout for rock/pop/blues devotees. The clientele—ranging from youthful scenesters to middle-aged moms—packs the place to catch regular performances by such diverse artists as G. Love & Special Sauce, Gwen Stefani, and Duke Robillard. 6010 W. Pico Blvd., Los Angeles. ✆ 323/954-9630. www.theminthollywood.com. Cover $5–$10.

Moomba   This branch of New York's hot spot opened in 2001, promising New American cuisine, hip supper-club entertainment, and several satellite bars for lounging. The nightclub, in the former LunaPark space in WeHo's club zone, was completely overhauled with "cruelty-free" and environmentally chic interiors. Proprietor Jeff Gossett is ensuring that, as in NYC, Moomba will be as much a restaurant destination as nightspot—he's garnered a heavy-hitting San Francisco chef de cuisine and former Spago manager. 665 N. Robertson Blvd., West Hollywood. ✆ 310/652-6364.

Roxy   Veteran record producer/executive Lou Adler opened this Sunset Strip club in the mid-1970s with concerts by Neil Young and a lengthy run of the pre-movie *The Rocky Horror Show.* Since then, it's remained among the top showcase venues in Hollywood—although the revitalized Troubadour and such new entries as the House of Blues challenge its preeminence among cozy clubs. 9009 Sunset Blvd. ✆ 310/276-2222.

Spaceland   The wall-to-wall mirrors and shiny brass posts decorating the interior create the feeling that, in a past life, Spaceland must've been a seedy strip joint, but the club's current personality offers something entirely different. Having hosted countless performances by artists such as Pavement, Mary Lou Lord, Grant Lee Buffalo, Elliot Smith, and the Eels, this hot spot on the fringe of east Hollywood has become one of the most important clubs on the LA circuit. 1717 Silver Lake Blvd., Silver Lake. ✆ 323/661-4380.

The Troubadour   This West Hollywood mainstay radiates rock history—from the 1960s to the 2000s, the Troub really has seen 'em all. Audiences are consistently treated to memorable shows from the already-established or young-and-promising acts that take the Troubadour's stage. But bring your earplugs—this beer- and sweat-soaked club likes it loud. 9081 Santa Monica Blvd., West Hollywood. ✆ 310/276-6168. www.troubadour.com. All ages.

Viper Room   This world-famous club on the Strip has been king of the hill since it was first opened by actor Johnny Depp and co-owner Sal Jenco back in 1993. With an intensely electric and often star-filled scene, the intimate club is also known for unforgettable, late-night, surprise performances from such powerhouses as Johnny Cash, Iggy Pop, Tom Petty, Nancy Sinatra, and Everclear (to name but a few) after headline gigs elsewhere in town. 8852 Sunset Blvd., West Hollywood. ✆ 310/358-1880. www.viperroom.com.

DANCE CLUBS

The Coconut Club   Master of entertainment Merv Griffin, remembering the legendary Coconut Grove ballroom in the now-abandoned Ambassador Hotel, has lavishly re-created its classy swank with this A-list dine-and-dance club in the Beverly Hilton. It offers some of the city's very best in Latin and swing dance on Fridays and Saturdays. This is a great place to bring your guy or doll to reenact the romantic splendor of Hollywood past. Entrance to Chimps Cigar Club is also included in the cover charge. 9876 Wilshire Blvd., Beverly Hills. ✆ 310/285-1358. Cover $10.

The Conga Room   Attracting such Latin-music luminaries as Pucho & The Latin Soul Brothers, this one-time health club on the Miracle Mile has quickly become *the* nightspot for live salsa and merengue. Break up the evening of heart-melting, sexy Latin dancing with a trip to the dining room, where the chef serves up savory Cuban fare in a setting that conjures the romance of pre-Castro Cuba, or indulge yourself in the Conga Room's stylish cigar lounge. 5364 Wilshire Blvd., Los Angeles. © 323/938-1696. www.congaroom.com.

The Derby   This class-A east-of-Hollywood club has been at the center of the swing revival since the very beginning. Located at a former Brown Derby site, the club was restored to its original luster and detailed with a heavy 1940s edge. With Big Bad Voodoo Daddy as the onetime house band and regular visits from Royal Crown Revue, hep guys and dolls knew that the Derby was money even before *Swingers* transformed it into one of the city's most happenin' hangs. But if you come on the weekends, expect a wait to get in, and once you're inside, dance space is at a premium. 4500 Los Feliz Blvd., Los Feliz. © 323/663-8979. www.the-derby.com. Cover $7–$10.

El Floridita   This tiny Cuban restaurant-and-salsa club is hot. Despite its modest strip-lot locale, it draws the likes of Jennifer Lopez, Sandra Bullock, Jimmy Smits, and Jack Nicholson, in addition to a festive crowd of Latin-dance devotees who groove well into the night. The hippest nights continue to be Mondays, when Johnny Polanco and his swinging New York–flavored salsa band get the dance floor jumpin'. 1253 N. Vine St., Hollywood. © 323/871-8612. Cover $10.

Hollywood Athletic Club   Built in 1924, this pool hall, restaurant, and nightclub is home to some groovin' dance clubs. Saturdays feature a lively mix of progressive house music spun by DJs Drew Down and Dave Audé. On Sundays, the sounds of Latin house, merengue, hip-hop, and salsa fill the air. Hollywood Athletic Club also hosts concerts from internationally known DJs and bands. 6525 Sunset Blvd., Hollywood. © 323/462-6262 or 323/957-0722. Cover $10–$20.

The Palace   Weekend nights this Hollywood landmark music hall turns the power of its 20,000-watt sound system on the dancing set. Fridays feature DJs upstairs and down, plus a cash-reward dance contest. Hip-hop, house, and pop are the order of the day on Saturdays, when Klub KIIS takes control of the turntables while also broadcasting live from the club. 1735 N. Vine Ave., Hollywood. © 323/462-3000. www.hollywoodpalace.com. 18 and over. Cover $10–$12.

sixteen fifty   Formerly Vynyl, this big open room, located on a Hollywood side street in the former home of a divey rock 'n' roll club, has theatrical—almost gothic—overtones. A trendy dance club with DJs (including occasional big-name guests) spinning house and electronica, they also feature concerts by local and visiting bands that range from jazz to glam to contemporary. There's an elevated stage above the dance floor for people-watching or checking out the go-go dancers in action. Though the crowd naturally varies according to what's on the night's schedule, it's a bit more upscale than trashy, with a look-like-you-mean-it dress code. 1650 Schrader Blvd., Hollywood. © 323/465-7449.

BARS & COCKTAIL LOUNGES

Beauty Bar   It's a proven concept in New York and San Francisco: a cocktail lounge/beauty salon. Decorated with vintage salon gear and sporting a hip-retr⟩ vibe, the Beauty Bar is campy, fun, and trendy all at once. Where else can actually get a manicure while sipping cocktails with names like Blue (made with Blue Curacao) or Prell (their version of a grasshopper)? 1638 N. Cahuenga Blvd., Hollywood. ℭ 323/464-7676. www.beautybar.com.

The Dresden Room   Hugely popular with LA hipsters because of its longevity, location, often-overlooked cuisine, and elegant ambience, "The Den" has been pushed into the mainstream of LA nightlife thanks to its inclusion in the movie *Swingers*. But it's the timeless lounge act of Marty and Elayne (the couple has been performing there up to 5 nights a week since 1982) has proven that fad or no fad, this place is always cool. Sidle up to the bar, where blue glasses are seen before patrons as they sip the house classic, Blood and Sand, a space-age margarita of sorts and, of course, the ubiquitous martinis and Manhattans. Separated from the lounge by frosted Art Deco glass is a cozy dining area serving up excellent food, including mouthwatering steaks and great Italian food. 1760 N. Vermont Ave., Hollywood. ℭ 323/665-4294.

Good Luck Bar   Until they installed a flashing neon sign outside, only locals and hipsters knew about this Kung Fu–themed room in the Los Feliz/Silver Lake area. The dark-red windowless interior boasts Oriental ceiling tiles, fringed Chinese paper lanterns, sweet-but-deadly drinks like the "Yee Mee Loo" (translated as "blue drink"), and a jukebox with selections ranging from Thelonius Monk to Cher's "Half Breed." The spacious sitting room, furnished with mismatched sofas, armchairs, and banquettes, provides a great atmosphere for conversation or romance. Arrive early to avoid the throngs of LA scenesters. 1514 Hillhurst Ave. (between Hollywood and Sunset blvds.), Los Angeles. ℭ 323/666-3524.

Skybar   Since its opening in hotelier Ian Schrager's refurbished Sunset Strip hotel, Skybar has been a favorite among LA's most fashionable of the fashionable set. This place is so hot that even the agents to the stars need agents to get in. (Rumor has it that one agent was so desperate to get in, he promised one of the servers a contract.) Nevertheless, a little image consulting—affect the right look, strike the right pose, and look properly disinterested—might get you in to rub elbows with some of the faces that regularly appear on the cover of *People* (but please don't stare). 8440 W. Sunset Blvd., in the Mondrian hotel, West Hollywood. ℭ 323/ 848-6025.

360   This 19th-story, penthouse-perched restaurant and lounge is a perfect place to romance your special someone. It's all about the view here—all 360° of it. The understated and softly lit sleek interior emphasizes the scene outside the plentiful windows, including a spectacular vista of the famed HOLLYWOOD sign. 6290 Sunset Blvd., Hollywood. ℭ 323/871-2995. www.360hollywood.com.

COMEDY & CABARET

The Cinegrill   The Cinegrill, located in one of LA's most historic hotels, draws locals with a zany cabaret show and guest chanteuses ranging from Eartha Kitt to Cybill Shepherd. Some of the country's best cabaret singers pop up here regularly. 7000 Hollywood Blvd., in the Hollywood Roosevelt Hotel, Hollywood. ℭ 323/ 466-7000. www.cinegrill.com.

You can't go wrong here: New comics develop their material, ...es work out their kinks, at this landmark owned by Mitzi ...). The Best of the Comedy Store Room, which seats 400, ...l stand-ups continuously on Friday and Saturday nights. Sev-...always featured, each doing about a 15-minute stint. The tal-...ate and includes comics who regularly appear on the *Tonight*

Show and other shows. The Original Room features a dozen or so comedians back-to-back nightly. Sunday night is amateur night: Anyone with enough guts can take the stage for 3 minutes, so who knows what you'll get? 8433 Sunset Blvd., West Hollywood. © 323/650-6268. www.comedystore.com.

Groundling Theater LA's answer to Chicago's Second City has been around for over 25 years, yet it remains the most innovative and funny group in town. The skits change every year or so, but they take new improvisational twists every night and the satire is often savage. The Groundlings were the springboard to fame for Pee-Wee Herman, Elvira, and former *Saturday Night Live* stars Jon Lovitz, the late Phil Hartman, and Julia "It's Pat" Sweeney. You haven't laughed this hard in ages. Call for showtimes and reservations. 7307 Melrose Ave., Los Angeles. © 323/934-9700. www.groundlings.com. Tickets $10–$20.

The Improv A showcase for top stand-ups since 1975, the Improv offers something different each night. Although it used to have a fairly active music schedule, the place is now mostly doing what it does best—showcasing comedy. Owner Budd Freedman's buddies—like Jay Leno, Billy Crystal, and Robin Williams—hone their skills here more often than you would expect. But even if the comedians on the bill are all unknowns, they won't be for long. Shows are at 8pm Sunday and Thursday, at 8:30 and 10:30pm Friday and Saturday. 8162 Melrose Ave., West Hollywood. © 323/651-2583. www.improvclubs.com.

LATE-NIGHT BITES

The Apple Pan This classic American burger shack, an LA landmark, hasn't changed much since 1947—and its burgers and pies continue to hit the spot. Open until 1am Friday and Saturday, until midnight other nights; closed Monday. See p. 493 for a full restaurant review. 10801 W. Pico Blvd., West LA. © 310/475-3585.

Canter's Fairfax Restaurant, Delicatessen & Bakery This 24-hour Jewish deli has been a winner with late-nighters since it opened more than 65 years ago. If you show up after the clubs close, you're sure to spot a bleary-eyed celebrity or two alongside the rest of the after-hours crowd, chowing down on a giant pastrami sandwich, matzo-ball soup, potato pancakes, or other deli favorites. Try a potato knish with a side of brown gravy—trust me, you'll love it. 419 N. Fairfax Ave., West Hollywood. © 323/651-2030.

Dolores's One of LA's oldest surviving coffee shops, Dolores's offers just what you might expect: Naugahyde, laminated counters, and linoleum, with a comforting predictability. Scores of late-night moviegoers head here after an evening at the nearby Nuart theaters. Expect the usual coffee-shop fare of pancakes, burgers, and eggs at this 24-hour joint. 11407 Santa Monica Blvd., Los Angeles. © 310/477-1061.

Du-par's Restaurant & Bakery During the week, this popular Valley coffee shop serves up blue-plate specials until 1am; come the weekend, they're slingin' hash until 4am. The West Hollywood location, in the Ramada Hotel at 8571 Santa Monica Blvd., west of La Cienega (© 310/659-7009), is open till 3am on weekends. See p. 501 for a full restaurant review. 12036 Ventura Blvd. (1 block E of Laurel Canyon), Studio City. © 818/766-4437.

Fred 62 Silver Lake/Los Feliz hipsters hankering for a slightly demented take on classic American comfort grub skulk into Fred around the clock. 1850 N. Vermont. © 323/667-0062.

Jerry's Famous Deli Valley hipsters head to 24-hour Jerry's to satiate the late-night munchies. See p. 500 for a full restaurant review. 12655 Ventura Blvd. (E of Coldwater Canyon Ave.), Studio City. ℂ 818/980-4245.

Kate Mantilini Kate's serves stylish nouveau comfort food in a striking setting, and it's open till 1am Sunday through Thursday, till 2am Friday and Saturday. See p. 493 for a full restaurant review. 9101 Wilshire Blvd. (at Doheny Dr.), Beverly Hills. ℂ 310/278-3699.

Mel's Drive-in Straight from an episode of *Happy Days*, this 24-hour 1950s diner on the Sunset Strip attracts customers ranging from chic shoppers during the day to rock-and-rollers at night. The fries and shakes here are among the best in town. 8585 Sunset Blvd. (W of La Cienega), West Hollywood. ℂ 310/854-7200.

Operetta This French bakery and cafe is a welcome sight to LA night owls. Although the kitchen stops serving sandwiches and other light fare at midnight, Operetta's mouthwatering pastries and breads are available around the clock. 8223 W. 3rd St. (near Harper St.), Beverly Hills. ℂ 213/627-7898.

Original Pantry Cafe Owned by former Los Angeles mayor Richard Riordan, this Downtown diner has been serving huge portions of comfort food around the clock for more than 60 years; in fact, they don't even have a key to the front door. See p. 499 for a full restaurant review. 877 S. Figueroa St. (at 9th St.), Downtown. ℂ 213/972-9279.

Pink's Hot Dogs Many a woozy hipster has awakened with the telltale signs of a post-cocktailing trip to this greasy street-side hot-dog stand—the oniony morning-after breath and chili stains on your shirt are dead giveaways. Open Friday and Saturday until 3am, all other nights until 2am. See p. 496 for a full review. 709 N. La Brea Ave., Hollywood. ℂ 323/931-4223.

Swingers This hip coffee shop keeps LA scene-stealers happy with its retro comfort food. Open Friday and Saturday until 2am, all other nights until 1am. See p. 497 for a full review. 8020 Beverly Blvd. (W of Fairfax Ave.), Hollywood. ℂ 323/653-5858.

Toi on Sunset Those requiring a little more oomph from their late-night snack should come here. At this colorful and *loud* hangout, garbled pop culture metaphors mingle with the tastes and aromas of "rockin' Thai" cuisine in delicious ways, until 3am nightly. See p. 497 for a full review. 7505 Sunset Blvd. (at Gardner), Hollywood. ℂ 323/874-8062.

MOVIES

Promoting moving pictures as this country's great art form, **The American Cinematheque** (ℂ 323/466-3456; www.egyptiantheatre.com), presents not-readily-seen videos and films, ranging from the wildly arty to the old classics. Since relocating to the historic and beautifully refurbished 1923 **Egyptian Theatre** (6712 Hollywood Blvd., in Hollywood), American Cinematheque has hosted several film events, including a celebration of contemporary flicks from Spain, a tribute to the femme fatales of film noir, and a retrospective of the films of William Friedkin. Events highlighting a specific individual are usually accompanied by at least one in-theater audience Q&A session with the honoree.

The **Leo S. Bing Theater** at the **Los Angeles County Museum of Art**, 5905 Wilshire Blvd. (ℂ 323/857-6010), presents a themed film series each month. Past subjects have ranged from 1930s blonde bombshell films to Cold War propaganda flicks to contemporary British satire (complete with a 3-day *Monty Python's Flying Circus* marathon).

Laemmle's Sunset 5, 8000 Sunset Blvd., West Hollywood (© **323/848-3500**), despite being a multiplex in a bright outdoor mall, features films that most theaters of its ilk won't even touch. This is the place to come to see interesting independent art films. There's often a selection of gay-themed movies.

The Nuart Theater, 11272 Santa Monica Blvd. (© **310/478-6379**), digs deep into its archives for real classics, ranging from campy to cool. They also feature frequent in-person appearances and Q&A sessions from stars and filmmakers, and screen *The Rocky Horror Picture Show* (yes, still!) every Saturday at midnight.

Fans of silent-movie classics might already know about the renowned **Silent Movie Theatre,** 611 N. Fairfax Ave. (½ block south of Melrose), near the Miracle Mile (© **323/655-2520** for recorded program information, 323/655-2510 for main office; www.silentmovietheatre.com). This silent-movie shrine for over 60 years was itself silent following the tragic murder, in 1996, of the longtime owner. It reopened in November 1999 to crowds eager to step inside, where Charlie Chaplin's appeal, Clara Bow's sexuality, and Edward G. Robinson's menace are once again bigger than life. Live music accompanies the silents (classic "talkies" are shown Tues nights); the theater is open Tuesday through Sunday, and tickets are $8 ($6 for kids and seniors).

If TV's more your thing, the **Museum of Radio and Television,** 465 N. Beverly Drive, Beverly Hills (© **310/786-1000**), celebrates this country's long relationship with the tube. The museum often features a movie of the month, and it also shows selections from past television programs. I'm still hoping for a retrospective on the wonderful women of *The Avengers*.

14

Side Trips from Los Angeles

by Matthew Richard Poole

The area within a 100-mile radius of Los Angeles is one of the most diverse regions in the world. Here, you can find arid deserts, rugged mountains, historic towns, alpine lakes, and even an island paradise. In the following pages, I've included a wide variety of the best attractions outside of Los Angeles County, such as the smog-free mountain communities of Big Bear and Lake Arrowhead, the world-famous Disneyland and Knott's Berry Farm amusement parks, sun-filled SoCal beach towns like Newport and Huntington Beach, and the ultimate LA weekend getaway, Catalina Island. From LA, you can reach most of these scenic side trips in less than an hour by car or boat—an easy and refreshing diversion from the big city scene.

1 Long Beach & the *Queen Mary*

21 miles S of downtown LA

The fifth-largest city in California, Long Beach is best known as the permanent home of the former cruise liner *Queen Mary* and the Long Beach Grand Prix, whose star-studded warm-up race sends the likes of hipster Jason Priestley and perennial racer Paul Newman burning rubber through the streets of the city in mid-April. A sleek aquarium recently joined Long Beach's many waterfront attractions. Still, if you're not into seeing the *Queen Mary*, there's really no pressing reason to spend much time here.

ESSENTIALS

GETTING THERE   Driving from Los Angeles, take either I-5 or I-405 to I-710 south, which leads directly to both downtown Long Beach and the *Queen Mary* Seaport. With minimum traffic, the drive takes about 20 minutes.

ORIENTATION   Downtown Long Beach is at the eastern end of the vast Port of Los Angeles; Pine Avenue is the central restaurant and shopping street, which extends south to Shoreline Park and the Aquarium. The *Queen Mary* is docked just across the waterway, gazing south toward tiny Long Beach marina and Naples Island.

VISITOR INFORMATION   Contact the **Long Beach Area Convention & Visitors Bureau,** One World Trade Center, Suite 300 (© **800/4LB-STAY** or 562/436-3645; www.golongbeach.org). For information on the **Long Beach Grand Prix,** call © **562/981-2600** or check out www.longbeachgp.com.

WHAT TO SEE & DO
THE MAJOR ATTRACTIONS

Aquarium of the Pacific ★★ *(Kids*   This enormous aquarium is the cornerstone of Long Beach's waterfront. Figuring that what stimulated flagging economies in Monterey and Baltimore would work in Long Beach, planners gave their all to this project, creating a crowd-pleasing attraction just across the harbor from Long Beach's other mainstay, the *Queen Mary* (see below). The vast facility—it has enough exhibit space to fill three football fields—re-creates three areas of the Pacific: the warm Baja and Southern California regions, the Bering Sea and chilly northern Pacific, and faraway tropical climes, including stunning re-creations of a lagoon and barrier reef. There are more than 12,000 creatures in all, from sharks and sea lions to delicate sea horses, moon jellies, and gaggles of tropical birds within the Loriket Forest. Learn little-known aquatic facts at the many educational exhibits, or come nose-to-nose with sea lions, eels, sharks, and other inhabitants of giant, three-story-high tanks.

100 Aquarium Way, off Shoreline Dr., Long Beach. ℭ 562/590-3100. www.aquariumofpacific.org. Admission $17 adults, $14 seniors 60 and over, $9.95 children 3–11, free for kids under 3. Daily 9am–6pm. Closed Dec 25 and Toyota Grand Prix weekend (mid-Apr). Parking $7 maximum.

The *Queen Mary* ⭐   It's easy to dismiss this old cruise ship/museum as a barnacle-laden tourist trap, but it's the only surviving example of this particular kind of 20th-century elegance and excess. From the staterooms paneled lavishly in now-extinct tropical hardwoods to the perfectly preserved crew quarters and the miles of hallway handrails made of once-pedestrian Bakelite, wonders never cease aboard this 81,237-ton Deco luxury liner. Stroll the teakwood decks with just a bit of imagination and you're back in 1936 on the maiden voyage from Southampton, England. Don't miss the Streamline Moderne observation lounge, featured often in period motion pictures, and have drinks and listen to some live jazz. Kiosk displays of photographs and memorabilia are everywhere—following the success of the movie *Titanic,* the *Queen Mary* even hosted an exhibit of artifacts from its less fortunate cousin. The Cold War–era Soviet submarine *Scorpion* resides alongside; separate admission is required to tour the sub. Buy both tickets and you'll also get a behind-the-scenes guided tour, peppered with worthwhile anecdotes and details.

1126 Queen's Hwy. (end of I-710), Long Beach. ℭ 562/435-3511. www.queenmary.com. Admission $19 adults, $17 seniors 55 and over and military, $15 children 3–11, free for kids under 3. Daily 10am–6pm (last entry at 5:30pm), with extended summer hours. Parking $8.

OTHER WATERFRONT DIVERSIONS

A different kind of nautical excursion awaits at the **Tall Ship *Californian,*** the flagship of the Nautical Heritage Society. At 145 feet long, this two-masted wooden cutter-class vessel offers barefooters the opportunity to help raise and lower eight sails, steer by compass, and generally experience the "romance of the high seas." Landlubbers might want to choose the 4-hour day sail for $75 ($113 for 2), including lunch, while old salts can take 2-, 3-, or 4-day cruises out to Catalina or the Channel Islands at $140 per person per day. The *Californian* sails from Long Beach between late August and mid-April (it's based in Northern California in summer). Call ℭ 800/432-2201 for schedule and reservations.

Take to the waterways Italian-style at nearby Naples Island with **Gondola Getaway,** 5437 E. Ocean Blvd. (ℭ 562/433-9595; www.gondolagetawayinc.com). Since 1982, these authentic Venetian gondolas have been snaking around the man-made canals of Naples Island, under gracefully arched bridges and past the gardens of resort cottages. Perhaps your traditionally clad oarsman will sing an Italian aria or relate the many tales of marriage proposals (some not so successful) made by romance-minded passengers. You'll also get a nice basket of bread, cheese, and salami, plus wineglasses and a full ice bucket; feel free to bring your beverage of choice. Gondola Getaway operates daily between 11am and 11pm; a 1-hour cruise for two costs $60.

WHERE TO STAY

Hotel Queen Mary ★ *Finds*   The *Queen Mary* isn't only a piece of maritime history; it's also a hotel. But although the historic ocean liner is considered the most luxurious vessel ever to sail the Atlantic, with some of the largest rooms built aboard a ship, the quarters aren't exceptional when compared to those on terra firma today, nor are the amenities. The idea is to enjoy the novelty and charm of features like the original bathtub watercocks ("cold salt," "cold fresh," "hot salt," "hot fresh"). The beautifully carved interior is a feast for the eye and fun to explore, and the weekday rates are hard to beat. Three onboard restaurants are overpriced but convenient, and the shopping arcade has a decidedly British feel (one shop sells great *Queen Mary* souvenirs). An elegant Sunday champagne brunch—complete with ice sculpture and harpist—is served in the ship's Grand Salon, and it's always worth having a cocktail in the Art Deco Observation Bar. If you're too young to have traveled on the old luxury liners, this is the perfect opportunity to experience the romance of an Atlantic crossing—with no seasickness, cabin fever, or week of formal dinners.

1126 Queen's Hwy. (end of I-710), Long Beach, CA 90802-6390. *(C)* **800/437-2934** or 562/435-3511. Fax 562/437-4531. www.queenmary.com. 365 units. $109 inside cabin, $219 deluxe cabin; from $450 suite. Many packages available. AE, DC, MC, V. Valet parking $12; self-parking $8. **Amenities:** 3 restaurants; spa; shopping arcade. *In room:* A/C, TV.

Lord Mayor's Inn ★   Situated in a once elite residential neighborhood downtown, this impeccably restored Edwardian home was built in 1904 and belonged to Long Beach's first mayor, Charles H. Windham. The main house offers five charming guest rooms, each furnished with antiques, luxurious high-quality linens, and heirloom bedspreads and accessories (but no phone). All boast private bathrooms cleverly re-created with vintage fixtures and painstakingly matched materials (the original home had only one bathroom). Seven more rooms—four with private bathrooms—are available in two less-formal adjacent cottages, also dating from the early 20th century; they offer a private option for families or those seeking seclusion and independence. Guests gather at their leisure in the main-house dining room for innkeeper Laura Brasser's lavish breakfasts, which include specialties like old-world pancakes with fried apples, delicate asparagus eggs, and hearty stuffed French toast.

435 Cedar Ave., Long Beach, CA 90802. *(C)* **562/436-0324.** www.lordmayors.com. 12 units. $85–$140 double. Rates include full breakfast. AE, DISC, MC, V. *In room:* TV and kitchenette in Garden House, fridge in Apple and Cinnamon House.

WHERE TO DINE

The Madison Restaurant & Bar ★ STEAKS/SEAFOOD   This elegant 1920s-style supper club offers fine dining reminiscent of majestic ocean-liner dining salons. A beautifully restored historic bank building (and dinner music from the 1940s) provides the backdrop for service that's deferential without being stuffy. The Madison serves exceptional dry aged beef broiled and accompanied by a la carte sides like buttery garlic potatoes or perfectly seasoned creamed spinach. The menu also includes seafood dishes like grilled salmon atop mussels and clams with a creamy ginger-citrus sauce, or oyster-stuffed sole breaded and drizzled with beurre blanc and fragrant fresh dill. Desserts are artistic renditions of reliable favorites—a s'mores sundae or sugary apple crumble.

102 Pine Ave., Long Beach. 🕐 **562/628-8866.** www.madisonsteakhouse.com. Reservations recommended. Main courses $10–$22 lunch, $18–$29 dinner. AE, MC, V. Mon–Thurs 11am–11pm, Fri 11am–midnight, Sat 5pm–midnight, Sun 5–11pm. Valet parking $3.

Shenandoah Cafe 🎯🎯 AMERICAN/SOUTHERN   Here's a place where "American" food means regional home-style meals served in a high-ceilinged parlor equal parts New Orleans mansion and Grandma's house. It's not for vegetarians or light eaters; even fresh fish specialties are given rich, heavy Southern treatments, and meats take up most of the menu. Start by nibbling on fresh-from-the-oven apple fritters, and prepare for an enormous meal that includes soup or salad and sides. Specialties include Texas-size chicken-fried steak with country gravy, Santa Fe–style baby-back ribs glazed with smoky chipotle, Cajun blackened fresh catch of the day, and Granny's deep-fried chicken.

4722 E. 2nd St. (at Park Ave.), Long Beach (Belmont Shore). 🕐 **562/434-3469.** www.shenandoahcafe.com. Reservations recommended. Main courses $13–$25. AE, DC, MC, V. Mon–Thurs 5–10pm, Fri 5–11pm, Sat 4:30–11pm, Sun 10am–2pm and 4:30–10pm.

Yard House 🎯 AMERICAN ECLECTIC   Not only does it have one of the best outdoor dining venues in Long Beach, the Yard House also features one of the *world's* largest selection of draft beers. The keg room houses more than 1,000 gallons of beer, all visible through a glass door where you can see the golden liquids transported to a signature oval bar via miles of nylon tubing to the dozens of taps. The restaurant takes its name from the early colonial tradition of serving beer in 36-inch-tall glasses—or yards—to weary stagecoach drivers. Customers are encouraged to partake in this tradition and can drink from the glass yards, as well as half yards and traditional pint glasses. Signature dishes range from the torte-like California roll to the crab-cake hoagie and an impressive selection of steaks and chops. There's also an extensive list of appetizers, salads, and pasta and rice dishes, as well as sandwiches and individual pizzas (the Thai chicken pizza is excellent). On sunny days be sure to request a table on the deck overlooking the picturesque harbor.

401 Shoreline Village Dr., Long Beach. 🕐 **562/628-0455.** www.yardhouse.com. Reservations not accepted. Main courses $10–$30. AE, DC, MC, V. Mon–Thurs 11:30am–midnight, Fri and Sat 11am–2am, Sun 11am–midnight.

2 Santa Catalina Island

22 miles W of mainland LA

After an unhealthy dose of the mainland's soupy smog and freeway gridlocks, you'll appreciate an excursion to Santa Catalina Island with its clean air, crystal-clear water, and the blissful absence of traffic. In fact, there isn't a single traffic light on the entire island. Conditions like these can fool you into thinking that you're miles away from the hustle and bustle of the city, but the reality is that you're only 22 miles off the Southern California coast and *still* in Los Angeles County.

Because of its relative isolation, out-of-state tourists tend to ignore Santa Catalina—which everyone calls simply Catalina—but those who do make the crossing have plenty of elbow room to boat, fish, swim, scuba, and snorkel. There are also miles of hiking and biking trails, plus golf, tennis, and horseback riding.

ESSENTIALS

GETTING THERE   The most common way to get to and from the island is via the **Catalina Express** ferryboat (🕐 **800/481-3470** or 562/519-1212;

www.catalinaexpress.com), which operates up to 30 daily departures year-round from San Pedro and Long Beach. The trip takes about an hour. Round-trip fares are $40 for adults, $37 for seniors 55 and over, $31 for children ages 2 to 11, and $2 for infants. In San Pedro, the Catalina Express departs from the **Sea/Air Terminal,** Berth 95; take the Harbor Freeway (I-110) south to the Harbor Boulevard exit, then follow signs to the terminal. In Long Beach, boats leave from the **Queen Mary Landing;** take the Long Beach Freeway (I-710) south, following the QUEEN MARY signs to the Catalina Express port. Call ahead for reservations. *Note:* Luggage is limited to 50 pounds per person; reservations are necessary for bicycles, surfboards, and dive tanks; and there are restrictions on transporting pets. You can leave your car at designated lots at each departure terminal; the parking fee is around $8 per 24-hour period.

Island Express Helicopter Service, 900 Queens Way Dr., Long Beach (© **800/2-AVALON** or 310/510-2525; www.islandexpress.com), flies from Long Beach or San Pedro to Avalon in about 15 minutes. The expense is definitely worth the thrill and convenience (particularly if you're prone to seasickness) from either Long Beach or San Pedro. It flies on demand between 8am and sunset year-round, charging $67 each way. The weight limit for luggage, however, is a mere 25 pounds. It also offers brief air tours over the island; prices vary. The heliport is located a few hundred yards southwest of the Queen Mary.

Tip: **Elite Airport Transportation** (© 310/831-1369) offers shuttle service from LAX to the Catalina Express ferry and Island Express Helicopter Service.

VISITOR INFORMATION The **Catalina Island Chamber of Commerce and Visitors Bureau,** P.O. Box 217, Avalon, CA 90704 (© **310/510-1520;** fax 310/510-7606), located on the Green Pleasure Pier, distributes brochures and information on island activities, hotels, and transportation. Call for a free 100-page visitors' guide. Its colorful website, **www.catalina.com**, offers current news from the *Catalina Islander* newspaper in addition to updated activities, events, and general information.

ORIENTATION The picturesque town of **Avalon** is both the port of entry for the island and the island's only city. From the ferry dock, you can wander along Crescent Avenue, the main road along the beachfront, and easily explore adjacent side streets.

Northwest of Avalon is the village of **Two Harbors,** accessible by boat or shuttle bus. Its twin bays are favored by pleasure yachts from LA's various marinas, so there's more camaraderie and a less touristy ambience overall.

GETTING AROUND Once in Avalon, take a taxi **Catalina Cab Company** (© 310/510-0025) from the heliport or dock to your hotel and enjoy the quick and colorful trip through town (don't blink or you'll miss it). Only a limited number of cars are permitted on the island; visitors are not allowed to drive cars on the island, and most residents motor around in golf carts (many of the homes only have golf cart–size driveways). Don't worry, though—you'll be able to get everywhere you want to go by renting a cart yourself or just hoofing it, which is what most visitors do.

If you want to explore the area around Avalon beyond where your feet can comfortably carry you, try renting a mountain bike or tandem from **Brown's Bikes,** 107 Pebbly Beach Rd. (© 310/510-0986). If you'll be doing a lot of exploring, you'll want to rent a gas-powered golf cart from **Cartopia Golf Cart Rentals** on Crescent Avenue at Pebbly Beach Road (© 310/ 510-2493), or **Island Rentals** (© 310/510-1456) across from the boat

Catalina's Grand Casino

No trip to Catalina is complete without taking the **Casino Tour.** The Casino Building, Avalon's world-famous Art Deco landmark, is not—and never was—a place to gamble your vacation money away ("casino" is an Italian word for a place of entertainment or gathering). Rather, the incredibly ornate structure (the craftsmanship inside and out is spectacular) is home to the island's only movie theater and the world's largest circular ballroom. Virtually every big band in the 1930s and '40s played in the 158-foot-diameter ballroom, carried over CBS radio since its grand opening in May 1929. Today it's a coveted venue for elaborate weddings, dances, gala dinners, and the Catalina Jazz and Blues Festivals. **The Blues Festival (℃ 888/25-EVENT;** www.catalina blues.com) takes place in May and the 3-week **JazzTraxx Festival** (℃ **888/330-5252;** www.jazztrax.com) takes place every October. Both are extremely popular and make finding hotel rooms nearly impossible. To experience either festival, be sure to book your tickets and accommodations as far in advance as possible.

terminal. Both companies offer a detailed map of town for a self-guided tour. Rates are about $30 per hour.

WHAT TO SEE & DO
EXPLORING THE ISLAND
ORGANIZED TOURS   The Santa Catalina Island Company's **Discovery Tours** (℃ **800/626-7489** or 310/510-TOUR; www.scico.com) has a ticket and information office on Crescent Avenue across from the Green Pier. It offers the greatest variety of excursions from Avalon; many last just a couple of hours, so you don't have to tie up your whole day. Tours are available in money-saving combo packs; inquire when you call.

Noteworthy excursions include the **Undersea Tour,** a slow 1-hour cruise of Lover's Cove Marine Preserve in a semi-submerged boat that allows you to sit 5 feet under the water in a climate-controlled cabin where you comfortably observe Catalina's kelp forests by day or night ($21 for adults and $13 for kids); the **Casino Tour,** a fascinating 1-hour look at the style and inventive engineering of this elegant ballroom (see "Catalina's Grand Casino," above; $8.50 adults, $4.25 kids); nighttime **Flying Fish Boat Trips,** a 70-minute Catalina tradition in searchlight-equipped open boats ($8.50 adults, $4.25 kids); and the **Inland Motor Tour,** a 32-mile, 4-hour jaunt through the island's rugged interior, including a stop at the **Airport-in-the-Sky, Little Harbor,** on Catalina's west coast (my favorite locale for camping, hiking, and swimming), and Wrigley's **El Rancho Escondido,** a working ranch where some of America's finest Arabian horses are raised and trained ($30 adults, $15 kids).

IN AVALON   Walk along horseshoe-shaped Crescent Avenue, past private yachting and fishing clubs, toward the landmark **Casino** building. You can see the Art Deco **theater** for the price of a movie ticket any night. Also on the ground floor is the **Catalina Island Museum** (℃ **310/510-2414**), which features exhibits on island history, archaeology, and natural history. The museum has a contour relief map of the island that's helpful to hikers. Admission is $1.50 for adults, 50¢ for kids; it's included in the price of Discovery's Casino Tour (see "Organized Tours" above).

Around the point from the Casino lies **Descanso Beach Club** (© 310/510-7410), a mini–Club Med in a private cove. While you can get on the beach year-round, the club's facilities (including showers, restaurant/bar, volleyball lawns, and thatched beach umbrellas) are only open from Easter to September 30. Admission is $1.50.

About 1½ miles from downtown Avalon is the **Wrigley Memorial and Botanical Garden** (© 310/510-2288), an invigorating walk or short taxi ride. The specialized gardens, a project of Ada Wrigley, showcase plants endemic to California's coastal islands. Open daily from 8am to 5pm; admission is $1.

DIVING, SNORKELING & SEA KAYAKING ✦

Snorkeling, scuba diving, and sea kayaking are among the main reasons main-landers head to Catalina. Catalina Island's naturally clean water and giant kelp forests teeming with marine life have made it a renowned diving destination that attracts expert and beginning divers alike. **Casino Point Marine Park,** South-ern California's first city-designated underwater park, established in 1965, is located behind the Casino. Due to its convenient location, it can get outra-geously crowded in the summer (just like everything else at that time of year). The three best locations for snorkeling are **Lover's Cove Marine Preserve,** Casino Point Marine Park, and **Descanso Beach Club.**

Catalina Divers Supply (© 800/353-0330) offers a full-service dive shop from a large trailer that sits right at the Casino's edge. For guided half-day to 2-day snorkel and scuba tours with certified instructors, as well as equipment sales and rentals, try **Scuba Luv** (© 800/262-DIVE or 310/510-2350; www.scubaluv.com) on Catalina Avenue. **Catalina Snorkeling Adventures,** at Lover's Cove (© 877/SNORKEL), offers snorkel gear rental. Snorkeling trips that take you outside of Avalon depart from **Joe's Rent-a-Boat** (© 310/510-0455) on the Green Pier.

At Two Harbors, stop by **West End Dive Center** (© 310/510-2800). Excur-sions range from half-day introductory dives to complete certification courses to multi-day dive packages. It also rents snorkel gear and offers kayak rental, instruction, and excursions.

HIKING & BIKING

When the summer crowds become overwhelming, it's time to head on foot for the peacefulness of the interior, where secluded coves and barren rolling hills soothe frayed nerves. Visitors can obtain a free hiking permit at the **Conser-vancy Office,** 125 Claressa Ave. (© 310/510-2595; www.catalinaconservancy.org), where you'll find maps, wildlife information, and friendly assistance from staffers who love to share their knowledge of the interior. It's open daily from 9am to 5pm; on weekends it's closed for lunch. Among the sights you may see are the many giant buffalo roaming the hills, scions of movie extras that were left behind in 1929 and have since flourished.

Mountain biking is allowed on the island's designated dirt roads, but requires a $50-per-person permit ($75 family) that must be purchased in person at the Conservancy Office.

BEACHES

Believe it or not, Avalon's beaches leave much to be desired. The town's central beach, located on Crescent Avenue, is small and completely congested in the busy season. Be sure to claim your spot early in the morning before it's full. **Descanso Beach Club** offers the best beach in town but also gets crowded very quickly. Your best bet is to kayak out to a secluded cove where you virtually have the beach to yourself.

WHERE TO STAY

If you're having trouble finding a vacancy, try calling the **Convention and Visitors Bureau** (② 310/510-1520); they keep tabs on last-minute cancellations. **Catalina Island Accommodations** (② 310/510-3000) might be able to help you out in a pinch; it's a reservations service with updated information on the whole island. When booking, ask the hotel agent about money-saving packages that offer discounted room rates, boat or helicopter fare, and tours.

EXPENSIVE

The Inn on Mt. Ada ★★   When William Wrigley Jr. purchased Catalina Island in 1921, he built this ornate hilltop Georgian colonial mansion as his summer vacation home; it's now one of the finest small hotels in California. The opulent inn—considered to be the best in town for its luxury accommodations and views—has several ground-floor salons, a club room with fireplace, a deep-seated formal library, and a sunroom where tea, cookies, and fruit are always available. The best guest room is the Grand Suite, fitted with a fireplace and a large private patio. Amenities include bathrobes and the use of a golf cart during your stay. A hearty full breakfast, a light deli-style lunch, and a beautiful multi-course dinner complemented by a limited wine selection are included in the tariff. *Tip:* Even if you find that they're sold out or too pricey to fit your budget, make a lunch reservation and enjoy amazing views from the inn's spectacular balcony.

398 Wrigley Rd. (P.O. Box 2560), Avalon, CA 90704. ② **800/608-7669** or 310/510-2030. Fax 310/510-2237. www.catalina.com/mtada. 6 units. Nov–May Mon–Thurs $280–$350 double; $350–$455 suite. June–Oct and Fri–Sun year-round $300–$475 double; $475–$620 suite. Rates include 3 meals daily. DC, MC, V. **Amenities:** Courtesy car. *In room:* TV upon request, hair dryer, iron, no phone.

MODERATE

Hotel Villa Portofino ★   European flair sets this hotel apart from the rest, along with its efficient, friendly staff, and recently renovated rooms with beautiful marble bathrooms and fantastic views overlooking the bay from the hotel suites' private balconies. There's a rooftop deck overlooking the harbor, and some rooms have luxurious touches like fireplaces and deep soaking tubs. Just outside the front door is all of Avalon Bay's activity.

111 Crescent Ave. (P.O. Box 127), Avalon, CA 90704. ② 310/510-0555. Fax 310/510-0839. www.hotel villaportofino.com. 35 units. May–Oct $85–$209 double; from $245 suite. Winter $75–$105 double; from $140 suite. Rates include continental breakfast. AE, MC, V, DC. **Amenities:** Award-winning restaurant. *In room:* A/C, TV, fridge, coffeemaker, hair dryer.

Hotel Vista Del Mar   Located smack-dab in the middle of town, there's nothing fancy about this well-maintained 15-room hotel, but its open-air atrium garden courtyard, huge fish tank, freshly baked cookies and milk each evening, and friendly staff make it an island favorite. The oceanview suites are fantastic but hard to secure, as there are only two and they are booked by regulars almost year-round.

417 Crescent Ave. (P.O. Box 1979), Avalon, CA 90704. ② 310/510-1452. www.hotel-vistadelmar.com. 15 units. May–Oct $125–$350 double; Nov–Apr $105–$300 double. Winter discounts and midweek rates available. Rates include continental breakfast. AE, DISC, MC, V. **Amenities:** Jacuzzi. *In room:* A/C, TV/VCR, fridge, coffeemaker.

INEXPENSIVE

My recommended choices for inexpensive lodgings are: the **Pavilion Lodge** (© **800/414-2754** or 310/510-2500), whose rooms are extremely basic but affordable and clean (a great alternative when budgets and availability are tight); **Hotel Catalina** (© **800/540-0184** or 310/510-0027), a well-maintained Victorian-style hotel just a half block from the beach with tons of charm, family cottages, a courtyard with beautiful stained glass, and large verandas with bay views; and **Zane Grey** (© **310/510-0966**), a 1926 Hopi-style pueblo and former home of author Zane Grey, situated above town and equipped with a cozy living room with fireplace and piano, free shuttle service, and a swimming pool.

Hermit Gulch Campground (© **310/510-7254**) is Avalon's only campground, and it can be crowded and noisy in peak season. Campsites can be tough to secure, especially when hotels are booked, so it's a good idea to make reservations in advance. The walk to town and back can be draining, so hop on the green-and-white tram that runs you back and forth to town for $1 each way.

WHERE TO DINE

Along with the choices below, recommended Avalon options include **The Busy Bee** on Crescent Avenue (© **310/510-1983**), an always-crowded waterfront diner with a heated and wind-protected patio. On the Two Harbors side of the island, **Doug's Harbor Reef** (© **310/510-7265**), a nautical- and tropical-themed saloon/restaurant, is the place to eat.

EXPENSIVE

Clubhouse Bar & Grille ⭐ CALIFORNIA   You'll find some of Avalon's most elegant meals at this landmark Catalina Country Club, whose stylish Spanish-Mediterranean clubhouse was built by William Wrigley Jr. during the 1920s. Recently restored, it exudes a chic and historic atmosphere; the menu is peppered with archival photos and vintage celebrity anecdotes. Sit outdoors in an elegant tiled courtyard, or inside the intimate, clubby dining room. Much of the menu is served throughout the afternoon, including gourmet pizzas, international appetizer samplers, and soups (fisherman's bisque or French onion, both available in a sourdough bowl). Dinner offerings follow a fusion style, such as New Zealand lamb accented with a piquant mango-mint chutney; cioppino and pad Thai both appear on the menu. The club is a few blocks uphill, so shuttle service is available from Island Plaza (on Sumner Ave.) on weekends.

1 Country Club Dr. (above Sumner Ave.). © **310/510-7404.** Reservations recommended. Main courses $10–$30. AE, DISC, MC, V. Daily 11:30am–2:30pm and 5–9pm (closing hours vary seasonally).

MODERATE

The Landing Bar and Grill AMERICAN   With a secluded deck overlooking the harbor, The Landing is generally agreed to be the most romantic dining spot in Avalon. It boasts beautiful Spanish-style architecture located in the historical El Encanto Center that manages to attract as many jeans-clad vacationers as dressed-up islanders. The menu is enticing, with local seafood offerings, pasta, Mexican cuisine, and gourmet pizzas that can be delivered to your hotel room if you wish.

At the intersection of Crescent and Marilla. © **310/510-1474.** Reservations recommended. Main courses $11–$22. AE, DISC, MC, V. Daily 11am–3pm and 4–10pm (subject to changes in winter).

Steve's Steakhouse AMERICAN   Step up above the busy bay-side promenade into a fantastic collage of murals, a tribute to the film classic *Casablanca*. This setting overlooking Avalon Bay feels just right for the hearty menu of steaks, seafood, and pasta. Catalina swordfish is their specialty, along with excellent cuts of meat. You can also make a respectable repast from the many appetizer selections, especially the fresh oysters.

417 Crescent Ave. (directly across from the Green Pier, upstairs). © **310/510-0333.** Reservations recommended on weekends. Main courses $7–$15 lunch, $15–$25 dinner. AE, DISC, MC, V. Daily 11am–3pm and 5–10pm.

INEXPENSIVE

My three favorite places for a low-bucks meal in Avalon are **Rosie's Fish and Chips** (© **310/510-0197**), an Avalon classic located on the Green Pier that serves fresh seafood favorites; **Casino Dock Café** (© **310/510-2755**) because nothing beats the cafe's live entertainment, marina views from the sun-drenched deck, and delicious breakfast burrito loaded with homemade salsa and served with a Bloody Mary (or wait till the outdoor bar opens and the lunch menu rolls out with fresh burgers and addictive fish tacos); and **Lori's Good Stuff** (© **310/510-2489**), a tiny restaurant that serves the best sandwiches, smoothies, and milkshakes around. Their fresh and healthy fare is a nice alternative to the heavy burgers, burritos, and pizza offered elsewhere. All three of these restaurants are within a stone's throw of each other on Crescent Avenue.

AVALON AFTER DARK

Avalon's bar scene offers a slew of watering holes from which to choose, most with good food and live entertainment. The following bars are all within stumbling distance of each other on Crescent Avenue.

The **Chi Chi Club** (© **310/510-2828**), the "noisy bar in Avalon" referred to in Crosby, Stills and Nash's song "Southern Cross," is the island's only dance club. It's quite a scene on summer weekend evenings—the DJ spins an eclectic mixture of dance tunes for the islanders and tourists get their mai tai cocktail groove on. **Luau Larry's** (© **310/510-1919**) is Avalon's signature bar that everyone must visit; its tacky tiki theme kicks you into island mode as soon as you step inside. Many a tourist has gotten their "Wicky Wacked" (the bar's signature drink) in Luau's famous cave. Don't leave without the straw hat sitting lopsided on your head and a Wicky Wacker bumper sticker proudly affixed. You can also go where the locals go and swill beers at **The Marlin Club** (© **310/510-0044**), Avalon's eldest drinking hole; catch a Dodgers game at **J.L.'s Locker Room** (© **310/510-0258**); and recover from your hangover with a spicy Bloody Mary at the rustic bar inside **The Busy Bee** (© **310/510-1983**).

3 Big Bear Lake & Lake Arrowhead

100 miles NE of LA

These two deep-blue lakes lie close to each other in the San Bernardino Mountains and have long been favorite year-round alpine playgrounds for city-weary Angelenos.

Big Bear Lake has always been popular with skiers as well as avid boaters (it's much larger than Arrowhead, and equipment rentals abound), and in the past decade the area has been given a much-needed face-lift. Big Bear Boulevard was substantially widened to handle high-season traffic, and downtown Big Bear Lake (the "Village") was spiffed up without losing its woodsy charm. In addition to two excellent ski slopes less than 5 minutes from town, you can enjoy the comforts of a real supermarket and several video-rental shops, all especially convenient if you're staying in a cabin. Most people choose Big Bear over Arrowhead because there's so much more to do, from boating, fishing, and hiking to snow sports, mountain biking, and horseback riding. The weather is nearly always perfect at this 7,000-foot-plus elevation: If you want proof, ask Caltech, which operates a solar observatory here to take advantage of nearly 300 days of sunshine per year.

Lake Arrowhead has always been privately owned, as is immediately apparent from the affluence of the surrounding homes, many of which are gated estates rather than rustic mountain cabins. The lake and the private docks lining its shores are reserved for the exclusive use of homeowners, but visitors can enjoy Lake Arrowhead by boat tour or use of the summer-season beach clubs, a privilege included in nearly all private-home rentals. Reasons to choose a vacation at Lake Arrowhead? The roads up are less grueling than the winding ascent to Big Bear Lake and, being at a lower elevation, Arrowhead gets little snow (you can forget those pesky tire chains). It's very easy and cost effective to rent a luxurious house from which to enjoy the spectacular scenery, crisp mountain air, and relaxed resort atmosphere—and if you do ski, the slopes are only a half-hour away.

ESSENTIALS

GETTING THERE   Lake Arrowhead is reached by taking Calif. 18 from San Bernardino. The last segment of this route takes you along the aptly named **Rim of the World Highway,** offering a breathtaking panoramic view out over the valley below on clear days. Calif. 18 then continues east to Big Bear Lake, but to get to Big Bear Lake it's quicker to bypass Arrowhead by taking Calif. 330 from Redlands, which meets Calif. 18 in Running Springs. During heavy-traffic periods, it can be worthwhile to take scenic Calif. 38, which winds up from Redlands through mountain passes and valleys to approach Big Bear from the other side.

Note: Nostalgia lovers can revisit legendary **Route 66** on the way from Los Angeles to the mountain resorts, substituting scenic motor courts and other relics of the "Mother Road" in place of impersonal I-10. For a complete driving tour, see "Get Your Kicks on Historic Route 66" in chapter 15.

VISITOR INFORMATION   National ski tours, mountain-bike races, and one of Southern California's largest Oktoberfest gatherings are just some of the many events held here year-round—which may either entice or discourage you from visiting when they're on. Contact the **Big Bear Lake Resort Association,** 630 Bartlett Rd., Big Bear Lake Village (℗ **800/4BIG-BEAR** or 909/866-7000; www.bigbearinfo.com), for schedules and information. They also provide information on sightseeing and lodging and will send you a free visitors' guide.

In Lake Arrowhead, contact the **Lake Arrowhead Communities Chamber of Commerce** (℗ **800/337-3716** for the Lodging Information Line, or 909/337-3715; www.lakearrowhead.net). The visitor center is located in the Lake Arrowhead Village lower shopping center.

ORIENTATION   The south shore of Big Bear Lake was the first resort area to be developed and remains the most densely populated. Calif. 18 passes first through the city of Big Bear Lake and its downtown village; then, as Big Bear Boulevard, it continues east to Big Bear City, which is more residential and suburban. Calif. 38 traverses the north shore, home to pristine national forest and great hiking trails, as well as a couple of small marinas and a lakefront bed-and-breakfast inn (see the Windy Point Inn on p. 566).

Big Bear Lake & Lake Arrowhead

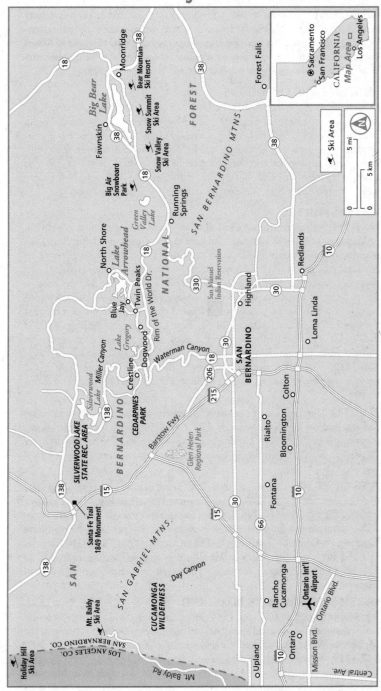

Arrowhead's main town is Lake Arrowhead Village, located on the south shore at the end of Calif. 173. The village's commercial center is home to factory-outlet stores, about 40 chain and specialty shops, and the Lake Arrowhead Resort (p. 567). Minutes away is the town of Blue Jay (along Calif. 189), where the Blue Jay Ice Castle skating rink is located (see "Winter Fun," below).

ENJOYING THE OUTDOORS

In addition to the activities described below, there's a great recreation spot for families near the heart of Big Bear Lake: **Magic Mountain,** on Calif. 18/Big Bear Boulevard (✆ **909/866-4626;** www.bigbear.com/alpineslide), has a year-round bobsled-style Alpine Slide, a splashy double water slide open from mid-June to mid-September, and bunny slopes for snow tubing from November to Easter. The dry Alpine Slide is $4 a ride, the water slide is $1 (or $12 for a day pass), and snow play costs $18 per day including tube and rope tow.

WATERSPORTS

BOATING You can rent all kinds of boats—including speedboats, rowboats, paddleboats, pontoons, sailboats, and canoes—at a number of Big Bear Lake marinas. Rates vary only slightly from place to place: A 14-foot dinghy with an outboard runs around $12 per hour or $30 for a half day; pontoon (patio) boats that can hold large groups range in size and price from $25 to $45 per hour or $80 to $150 for a half day. **Pine Knot Landing** (✆ **909/866-BOAT;** www.pine knotlanding.com) is the most centrally located marina, behind the post office at the foot of Pine Knot Boulevard in Big Bear Lake. **Gray's Landing** (✆ **909/866-2443**) is just across the dam on the north shore and offers the best prices and the least attitude. **Big Bear Marina,** Paine Road at Lakeview (✆ **909/866-3218;** www.bigbearmarina.com), is also close to Big Bear Lake Village and provides take-along chicken dinners when you rent a pontoon boat for a sunset cruise.

FISHING Big Bear Lake brims with rainbow trout, bass, and catfish in spring and summer, the best fishing seasons. Call ✆ **310/590-5020** for recorded stocking information. Pine Knot Landing, Gray's Landing, and Big Bear Marina (see "Boating," above) all rent fishing boats and have bait-and-tackle shops that sell licenses.

JET-SKIING Personal Water Craft (PWCs) are available for rent at **Big Bear Marina** (see "Boating," above) and **Pleasure Point Landing,** 603 Landlock Landing Rd. (✆ **909/866-2455**), where you can rent a single-rider Sea-Doo for $35 an hour, or opt for a two-seat WaveRunner at $55 per hour. **North Shore Landing,** on Calif. 38, 2 miles west of Fawnskin (✆ **909/878-4FUN**), rents jet skis and two- and three-person WaveRunners at rates ranging from $55 to $65 per hour. Call ahead to reserve your craft and check age and deposit requirements.

WATER-SKIING & WAKE BOARDING Big Bear Lake, Pine Knot Landing, North Shore Landing, and Big Bear Marina (see above) all offer water-ski and wake-board lessons and speedboat rentals. Lake Arrowhead is home to the **McKenzie Water Ski School,** dockside in Lake Arrowhead Village (✆ **909/337-3814;** www.mckenzieskischool.com), famous for teaching Kirk Douglas, George Hamilton, and other Hollywood stars to ski. It's open from Memorial Day to the end of September and offers group lessons for $45 per hour, short pulls for $35, and boat charters (including driver) for $135 an hour.

OTHER WARM-WEATHER ACTIVITIES

GOLF   The **Bear Mountain Golf Course,** Goldmine Drive, Big Bear Lake
(© **909/585-8002**), is a nine-hole, par-35, links-style course that winds
through a gently sloping meadow at the base of the Bear Mountain Ski Resort.
The course is open daily April through November. Weekend greens fees are $28
and $35 for 9 and 18 holes, respectively. Both riding carts and pull carts are
available. Call ahead for tee times.

HIKING   Hikers will love the **San Bernardino National Forest.** The gray
squirrel is a popular native so you may see them scurrying around gathering
acorns or material for their nests. You can sometimes spot deer, coyotes, and
American bald eagles, which come here with their young in winter. The black-
crowned Steller's jay and the talkative red, white, and black acorn woodpecker
are the most common of the great variety of birds in this pine forest.

The best choice for a short mountain hike is the **Woodland Trail,** which
begins near the ranger station. The best long hike is a section of the **Pacific
Crest Trail,** which travels 39 miles through the mountains above Big Bear and
Arrowhead lakes. The most convenient trail head is located at Cougar Crest, a
half mile west of the Big Bear Ranger Station.

The best place to begin a hike in Lake Arrowhead is at the **Arrowhead
Ranger Station** (© **909/337-2444**), located in the town of Skyforest on Calif.
18 a quarter mile east of the Lake Arrowhead turnoff (Calif. 173). The staff will
provide you with maps and information on the best area trails, which range from
easy to difficult. The **Enchanted Loop Trail,** near the town of Blue Jay, is an
easy half-hour hike. The **Heaps Peak Arboretum Trail** winds through a grove
of redwoods; the trail head is on the north side of Calif. 18, at an auxiliary
ranger kiosk west of Running Springs.

The area is home to a **National Children's Forest,** a 20-acre area developed
so that children, the wheelchair-bound, and the visually impaired could enjoy
nature. To get to the Children's Forest from Lake Arrowhead, take Calif. 330 to
Calif. 18 east, past Deer Lick Station; when you reach a road marked IN96
(open only in summer), turn right and go 3 miles.

HORSEBACK RIDING   Horses are permitted on all the mountain trails
through the national forest. **Rockin' K Riding Stables** (© **909/878-4677**),
offers trail rides through Big Bear's national forest as well as pony rides for the
kids. The stables, located at 731 Tulip Lane near Big Bear Boulevard, are open
daily from 9am to 5pm; call for reservations. **Baldwin Lake Stables,** southeast
of Big Bear City (© **909/585-6482;** www.baldwinlakestables.com), conducts
hourly, lunch, and sunset rides in addition to offering lessons.

MOUNTAIN BIKING   Big Bear Lake has become a mountain-biking center,
with most of the action around the Snow Summit ski area (see "Winter Fun,"
below), where an $8 lift ticket will take you and your bike to a scenic web of
trails, fire roads, and meadows at about 8,000 feet. Call its **Summer Activities
Hotline** (© **909/866-4621**). The lake's north shore is also a popular biking destination; the forest-service ranger stations (see "Hiking," above) have maps to
the historic gold rush–era Holcomb Valley and the 2-mile Alpine Pedal Path (an
easy lakeside ride).

Big Bear Bikes, 41810 Big Bear Blvd. (© **909/866-6588**), rents quality
mountain bikes for about $9 an hour or $50 a day, as does **Bear Valley Bikes,**
40298 Big Bear Blvd. (© **909/866-8000;** www.bearvalleybikes.com). **Team Big**

Bear is located at the base of Snow Summit (© **909/866-4565;** www.team bigbear.com); it rents bicycles and provides detailed maps and guides for all Big Bear–area trails.

At Lake Arrowhead, bikes are permitted on all hiking trails and back roads except the Pacific Crest Trail. See the local ranger station for an area map. Gear can be rented from the **Lake Arrowhead Resort** (© **909/336-1511**) or **Above & Beyond Sports,** 32877 Calif. 18, Running Springs (© **909/867-5517**).

WINTER FUN

SKIING & SNOWBOARDING   When the LA basin gets wintertime rain, skiers everywhere rejoice, for they know snow is falling up in the mountains. The last few seasons have seen abundant natural snowfall at Big Bear, augmented by sophisticated snowmaking equipment. While the slopes can't compare with those in Utah or Colorado, they do offer diversity, difficulty, and convenience.

Snow Summit at Big Bear Lake (© **909/866-5766;** www.snowsummit.com) is the skiers' choice, especially because it installed its second high-speed quad express from the 7,000-foot base to the 8,200-foot summit. Another nice feature is green (easy) runs even from the summit, so beginners can also enjoy the Summit Haus lodge and breathtaking lake views from the top. Advanced risk-takers will appreciate three double black-diamond runs. Lift tickets range from $35 to $47. The resort offers midweek, beginner, half-day, night, and family specials, as well as ski and snowboard instruction. Hey, you can even ski free on your birthday here! Other helpful Snow Summit phone numbers include advance lift-ticket sales (© **909/866-5841**), the ski school (© **909/866-4546**), and a snow report (© **888/SUMMIT-1**).

The **Bear Mountain Resort** at Big Bear Lake (© **800/BEAR-MTN** or 909/585-2519; www.bearmtn.com) has the largest beginner area, but experts flock to the double-black-diamond "Geronimo" run from the 8,805-foot Bear Peak. Natural-terrain skiers and snowboarders will enjoy legal access to off-trail canyons, but the limited beginner slopes and kids' areas get pretty crowded in season. One of two high-speed quad expresses rises from the 7,140-foot base to 8,440-foot Goldmine Mountain; most runs from here are intermediate. Bear Mountain has a ski-and-snowboard school, abundant dining facilities, and a well-stocked ski shop.

The **Snow Valley Ski Resort** in Arrowbear, midway between Arrowhead and Big Bear (© **800/680-SNOW** or 909/867-2751; www.snow-valley.com), has improved its snowmaking and facilities to be competitive with the other two major ski areas, and is the primary choice of skiers staying at Arrowhead. From a base elevation of 6,800 feet, Snow Valley's 13 chairlifts (including five triples) can take you from the beginner runs all the way up to black-diamond challenges at the 7,898-foot peak. Lift tickets cost $37 to $42 for adults; children's programs, night skiing, and lesson packages are available.

ICE-SKATING   The **Blue Jay Ice Castle,** at North Bay Road and Calif. 189 (© **909/33-SKATE;** www.ice-castle.com), near Lake Arrowhead Village, is a training site for world champion Michelle Kwan and boasts Olympic gold medalist Robin Cousins on its staff. Several public sessions each day—as well as hockey, broomball, group lessons, and book-in-advance private parties—give non-pros a chance to enjoy this impeccably groomed "outdoor" rink (it's open on three sides to the scenery and fresh air).

ORGANIZED TOURS

FOREST TOURS   **Big Bear Jeep Tours** (℃ 909/878-JEEP; www.bigbear jeeptours.com) journeys into Big Bear Lake's backcountry, including historic Holcomb Valley, relic of the gold rush, plus the panoramic viewpoint Butler Peak. These off-road adventures range in length from 1½ to 4½ hours, and cost from $40 to $85 per person. Bring your own snack, though, because although the guide carries ample water, the longer excursions include short but appetite-building hikes. Call for reservations, particularly on weekends and holidays (no tours are offered in winter).

LAKE TOURS   The *Big Bear Queen* (℃ 909/866-3218; www.bigbear marina.com), a midget Mississippi-style paddle-wheeler, cruises Big Bear Lake on 90-minute tours daily from late April to the end of November. The boat departs from Big Bear Marina (at the end of Paine Ave.). Tours are $10 for adults, $8.50 for seniors 65 and older, $5.50 for children ages 3 to 12, and free for kids under 3. Call for reservations and information on the special Sunday brunch, champagne sunset, and dinner cruises.

Fifty-minute tours of Lake Arrowhead are offered year-round on the *Arrowhead Queen* (℃ 909/336-6992), a sister ship that departs hourly each day between 10am and 6pm from Lake Arrowhead Village. Tours are $10 for adults, $8.50 for seniors, $6.50 for children 2 to 12, and free for kids under 2. It's about the only way to really see this alpine jewel, unless you know a resident with a boat.

WHERE TO STAY

BIG BEAR LAKE

Vacation rentals are plentiful in the area, from cabins to condos to private homes. Some can accommodate up to 20 people and can be rented on a weekly or monthly basis. For a wide range of rental properties, all pictured in detail online, contact **Big Bear Mountain Rentals** (℃ 909/878-2233; www.bigbear mountainrentals.com). The **Village Reservation Service** (℃ 909/866-8583; www.bigbear.com/villageres) can arrange for everything from condos to lake-front homes, or call the **Big Bear Lake Resort Association** (℃ 909/866-7000) for information and referrals on all types of lodgings.

Besides the places below, other choices I recommend are **Apples Bed & Breakfast Inn,** 42430 Moonridge Rd. (℃ 909/866-0903; www.applesbedand breakfast.com), a crabapple-red New England–style clapboard that blends hotel-like professionalism with B&B amenities (and lots of frilly touches); and **Gold Mountain Manor,** 1117 Anita Ave. (℃ 800/509-2604 or 909/585-6997; www.goldmountainmanor.com), a woodsy 1920s lodge that's now an ultra-cozy (and affordable) B&B.

Grey Squirrel Resort (*Kids*   This is the most attractive of the many cabin cluster–type motels near the city of Big Bear Lake, offering a wide range of rustic cabins, most with fireplace and kitchen. They're adequately, if not attractively, furnished—the appeal here is the flexibility and privacy afforded large or long-term parties. Facilities include a heated pool that's enclosed in winter, a fire pit and barbecues, volleyball and basketball courts, and completely equipped kitchens.

39372 Big Bear Blvd., Big Bear Lake, CA 92315. ℃ 800/381-5569 or 909/866-4335. Fax 909/866-6271. www.greysquirrel.com. 18 cabins. $85–$115 1-bedroom cabin; $115–$145 2-bedroom cabin; $155–$275 3-bedroom cabin. Value rates available. Higher rates on holidays. AE, DISC, MC, V. Pets accepted with $10-per-day fee. **Amenities:** Heated indoor/outdoor pool; Jacuzzi; coin-op laundry. *In room:* TV/VCR, kitchen in some units.

Holiday Inn Big Bear Chateau   This European-flavored property is one of only two traditional full-service hotels in Big Bear. Its highly visible location—just off Big Bear Boulevard at the base of the road to Bear Mountain—makes the Chateau a popular choice for skiers and families. The rooms are modern but more charming than your average Holiday Inn, with tapestries, brass beds, antique furniture, gas fireplaces, and lavish marble bathrooms, all with heated towel racks and many with whirlpool tubs. The entire compound is surrounded by tall forest. The restaurant (which also provides room service) is advertised as "casually elegant," which means you can enjoy upscale Continental/American cuisine even in après-ski duds.

42200 Moonridge Rd. (P.O. Box 1814), Big Bear Lake, CA 92315. ℂ **800/232-7466** or 909/866-6666. Fax 909/866-8988. 80 units. Winter $99–$180 double; summer $79–$160 double. Children 17 and under stay free in parents' room. Extra person $10. Winter-ski and summer-fun packages available. AE, DISC, MC, V. **Amenities:** Restaurant; lounge; heated outdoor pool; Jacuzzi; children's activities; limited room service. *In room:* A/C, TV, dataport, coffeemaker, hair dryer, iron.

Knickerbocker Mansion Country Inn ⚘   Innkeepers Thomas Bicanic and Stan Miller faced quite a task reviving this landmark log house; when they moved in, it was empty of all furnishings and suffered from years of neglect at the hands of the former B&B owners. But Knickerbocker Mansion has risen to become the most charming and sophisticated inn on the lake's south side; chef Bicanic, who honed his craft in LA's culinary temple Patina restaurant, even has plans to begin serving intimate gourmet dinners. The pair scoured antiques stores in Big Bear and Los Angeles for vintage furnishings, creating a warm and relaxing ambience in the grand-yet-quirky, hand-built house of legendary local character Bill Knickerbocker, who assembled it by hand almost 90 years ago. Today's guest rooms are a cedar-paneled dream, with luxury bed linens, cozy bathrobes, modern marble bathrooms with deluxe Australian showerheads, and refreshing mountain views. After Bicanic's stunning breakfast, you can spend the day relaxing on veranda rockers or garden hammocks; Big Bear's village is also an easy walk away.

869 Knickerbocker Rd. (P.O. Box 1907), Big Bear Lake, CA 92315. ℂ **800/388-4179** or 909/878-9190. Fax 909/878-4248. www.knickerbockermansion.com. 11 units. $110–$155 double; $200–$225 suite. Rates include full gourmet breakfast and all-day refreshments and snacks. AE, DISC, MC, V. *In room:* TV/VCR, dataport, iron, hair dryer.

Windy Point Inn ⚘⚘   A contemporary architectural showpiece on the scenic north shore, the Windy Point is the only shorefront B&B in Big Bear; ergo, all guest rooms have a view of the lake. Hosts Val and Kent Kessler's attention to detail is impeccable—if you're tired of knotty pine and Victorian frills, here's a grown-up place for you, with plenty of romance and all the pampering you can stand. Every room has a wood-burning fireplace, feather bed, private deck, and DVD player (borrow DVDs from the inn's plentiful collection); some also feature whirlpool tubs and luxurious state-of-the-art bathrooms. The welcoming Great Room features a casual sunken fireplace nook with floor-to-ceiling windows overlooking the lake, a telescope for stargazing, a baby grand, and up-to-date menus for every local eatery. You might not want to leave the cocoon of your room after Kent's custom gourmet breakfast, but if you do, you'll find a wintertime bald-eagle habitat is just up the road, and the city of Big Bear Lake is only a 10-minute drive around the lake.

39015 North Shore Dr., Fawnskin, CA 92333. ℂ **909/866-2746.** Fax 909/866-1593. www.windypointinn. com. 5 units. $135–$255 double. Rates include welcome cookies, lavish full breakfast, and afternoon hors d'oeuvres. Midweek discounts available. AE, DISC, MC, V. *In room:* TV/DVD, CD player in some units, coffeemaker, fridge, hair dryer, no phone.

LAKE ARROWHEAD

There are far more private homes than tourist accommodations in Arrowhead, but rental properties abound, from cozy cottages to palatial mansions; many can be surprisingly economical for families or other groups. Two of the largest agencies are **Arrowhead Cabin Rentals** (© **800/244-5138** or 909/337-2403; www.arrowheadrent.com) and **Arrowhead Mountain Resorts Rentals** (© **800/743-0865** or 909/337-4413; www.lakearrowheadrentals.com). Overnight guests in rental properties enjoy some resident lake privileges—be sure to ask when you reserve.

Two other options are **Chateau du Lac,** 911 Hospital Rd. (© **800/601-8722** or 909/337-6488; www.lakearrowhead.com/chateaudulac), an elegant and contemporary five-room B&B with stunning views of the lake; and the **Saddleback Inn,** 300 S. Calif. 173 (© **800/858-3334** or 909/336-3571; www.lake arrowhead.com/saddleback), an inn and restaurant that still boasts historic charm while offering up-to-date amenities, all at a prime location in the center of the village.

Bracken Fern Manor (★ (Finds Billing itself as a "House of Now Fine Repute," this off-the-beaten-path inn boasts a registered historical marker as well as a checkered past. The present owners work hard at evoking its 1930s heyday: They've preserved the downstairs public rooms, along with many well-maintained antiques, and named each guest room for one of the "girls." There are many quiet corners for relaxing, including a game room, hidden library, whirlpool gazebo, and wood-lined sauna. Rooms are decorated in a fresh country style and have private bathrooms, a feature not originally included in the house. A detached cottage sleeps four and rents for $380 for 2 nights.

815 Arrowhead Villas Rd. (P.O. Box 1006), Lake Arrowhead, CA 92352. © 888/244-5612 or 909/337-8557. Fax 909/337-3323. www.brackenfernmanor.com. 10 units. $80–$185 double. Rates include full breakfast. MC, V. Located ½ mile N of Calif. 18. **Amenities:** Jacuzzi; sauna. *In room:* No phone.

Lake Arrowhead Resort (Kids This sprawling resort has been upgraded somewhat since it was part of the Hilton chain, but location is still its most outstanding feature, coupled with unparalleled (for the mountains) service and facilities. Situated on the lakeshore adjacent to Lake Arrowhead Village, the hotel has its own beach, plus docks that are ideal for fishing. The rooms are fitted with good-quality, bulk-purchased contemporary furnishings, and most have balconies, king-size beds, and fireplaces. The suites, some in private cottages, are equipped with full kitchens and whirlpool tubs.

The hotel caters primarily to groups, and sports a business-like ambience during the week. A full program of supervised children's activities, ranging from nature hikes to T-shirt painting, is offered on weekends year-round.

27984 Hwy. 189, Lake Arrowhead, CA 92352. © 800/800-6792 or 909/336-1511. Fax 909/336-1378. www.lakearrowheadresort.com. 177 units. $109–$229 double; $325–$475 suite. Inquire about auto-club discounts. AE, DC, DISC, MC, V. **Amenities:** 2 restaurants; outdoor pool (heated summer only); 2 lit rooftop tennis courts; health club; Jacuzzi; children's programs; video arcade; business center; salon; babysitting; laundry service; dry cleaning. *In room:* A/C, TV w/pay movies, dataport, minibar, coffeemaker, hair dryer.

Pine Rose Cabins (Kids The only place of its kind in Lake Arrowhead, Pine Rose Cabins is a good choice for families. Situated on 5 forested acres about 3 miles from the lake, the wonderful freestanding cabins offer lots of privacy.

Innkeeper Tricia Dufour has 15 cabins, ranging in size from romantic studios to a large five-bedroom lodge, each decorated in a different theme: The Indian cabin has a tepee-like bed; the bed in Wild Bill's cabin is covered like a wagon. Multi-bedroom units have fully stocked kitchens and separate living areas; for all cottages, daily maid service is available at an additional charge. There are plenty of fun-and-games on the premises, including swing sets, croquet, tetherball, and Ping-Pong.

25994 Calif. 189 (P.O. Box 31), Twin Peaks, CA 92391. ℂ 800/429-PINE or 909/337-2341. Fax 909/337-0258. www.lakearrowheadcabins.com. 19 units. $59–$179 studio for 2; $69–$179 1-, 2-, and 3-bedroom cabins for up to 10 people; $395–$450 large-group lodges. Ski packages available. AE, DISC, MC, V. Pets accepted with $10 fee per night and $100 refundable deposit. **Amenities:** Outdoor heated pool; Jacuzzi. *In room:* TV/VCR, kitchen, coffeemaker.

WHERE TO DINE
BIG BEAR LAKE
Another very reliable option for all-day dining is **Stillwell's,** 40650 Village Dr. (ℂ **909/866-3121,** ext. 7885). You might otherwise pass right by, because Stillwell's is the dining room for convention-friendly Northwoods Resort at the edge of the village; despite the unmistakable hotel feel, though, its something-for-everyone American/Continental menu is surprisingly good, with noted attention to detail and fair prices (rare in this mountain resort town).

The Captain's Anchorage STEAK/SEAFOOD Historic and rustic, this knotty-pine restaurant has been serving fine steaks, prime rib, seafood, and lobster since 1947. Inside, the dark, nautical decor and fire-warmed bar are just right on blustery winter nights. It's got one of those mile-long soup-and-salad bars, plus some great early-bird and weeknight specials.

Moonridge Way at Big Bear Blvd., Big Bear Lake. ℂ **909/866-3997.** Reservations recommended. Full dinners $15–$29. AE, MC, V. Sun–Thurs 4:30–9pm, Fri–Sat 4:30–10pm.

Madlon's AMERICAN/CONTINENTAL One of the few non-retro-fare dining rooms at the mountain resorts, Madlon's brings a bit of European flair to this fairy-tale cottage. A variety of creative croissant sandwiches at lunch are complemented by dinner selections like black-pepper filet mignon with mushroom-and-brandy sauce, and lemon-pepper-marinated chicken breast over pasta, all of which are prepared with a sophisticated touch.

829 W. Big Bear Blvd., Big Bear City. ℂ **909/585-3762.** Reservations recommended. Main courses $12–$25. DC, DISC, MC, V. Sat–Sun 8am–2pm, Tues–Fri 11am–2pm; Tues–Sun 5–9pm.

Mozart's Bistro CALIFORNIA At last, a trendy Big Bear restaurant (the regular weekenders from LA must have been complaining). Mozart's isn't perfect—at these prices, the service could be more polished, the bar better stocked, and some grouse about seriously "off" nights—but its immediate surge in popularity shows how starved the community was for a sophisticated menu incorporating American-based fusion and Pacific Rim cuisine. The house specialty is rack of pork glazed with hard-cider molasses sauce served with chayote squash and garlic mashed potatoes. Other seasonal choices include mahimahi in a macadamia-coconut crust on a pool of honey-lime beurre blanc, and breaded veal schnitzel with lingonberry port-wine sauce—a nod to the Bavarian flavor of the building (which was formerly Hansel's Cottage).

40701 Village Dr., Big Bear Lake. ℂ **909/866-9497.** Main courses $7–$10 lunch; $14–$25 dinner. AE, DISC, MC, V. Daily 11:30am–3pm; Mon–Thurs and Sun 5:30–9pm, Fri–Sat 5:30–10pm.

Old Country Inn DINER/GERMAN   The Old Country Inn has long been a favorite for hearty pre-ski breakfasts and stick-to-your-ribs old-world dinners. The restaurant is casual and welcoming, and the adjacent cocktail lounge is raucous on weekends. At breakfast, enjoy German apple pancakes or colossal omelets, while lunch choices include salads, sandwiches, and burgers. At lunch or dinner, feast on Wiener schnitzel, sauerbraten, and other gravy-topped German standards, along with grilled steaks and chicken.

41126 Big Bear Blvd., Big Bear Lake. © **909/866-5600.** Main courses $6–$28. AE, DC, DISC, MC, V. Sun–Thurs 8am–9pm, Fri–Sat 8am–10pm.

LAKE ARROWHEAD

For an affluent residential community, there are surprisingly few dining options around Lake Arrowhead. But not surprisingly, what there is tends to run toward pricey elegance—elegant for a rustic mountain resort, that is. Although there are both a California/Continental restaurant and a casual family eatery in the Lake Arrowhead Resort (p. 567), you might want to venture out to some of the locals' choices. These include the **Chef's Inn & Tavern,** 29020 Oak Terrace, Cedar Glen (© **909/336-4488**), a moderate to expensive Continental restaurant in a former bordello; the **Antler's Inn,** 26125 Calif. 189, Twin Peaks (© **909/ 337-4020**), serving prime rib, seafood, and buffalo in a historic log lodge; the **Royal Oak,** 27187 Calif. 189, Blue Jay Village (© **909/337-6018**), an expensive American/Continental steakhouse with a pub; and **Belgian Waffle Works,** dockside at Lake Arrowhead Village (© **909/337-5222**), an inexpensive coffee shop with Victorian decor, known for its generous, crispy waffles with tasty toppings.

4 The Disneyland Resort ★★★

30 miles SE of downtown LA

The sleepy Orange County town of Anaheim grew up around Disneyland, the West's most famous theme park. Now, even beyond the park that bills itself the Happiest Place on Earth, the city and its neighboring communities are kid central. Otherwise unspectacular, sprawling suburbs have become a playground of family hotels and restaurants, and unabashedly tourist-oriented attractions.

ESSENTIALS

GETTING THERE   From Los Angeles, take I-5 south till you see signs for Disneyland; dedicated off-ramps from both directions lead to the attraction's parking lots and surrounding streets. The drive from downtown LA takes approximately 45 minutes.

If Anaheim is your first—or only—destination, and you want to avoid LA altogether, try flying directly into **John Wayne Airport** in Santa Ana (© **949/252-5200;** www.ocair.com), Orange County's largest airport. It's about 15 miles from Disneyland. Check to see if your hotel has a free shuttle to and from either this airport or LAX (some will pick you up at LAX, 30 min. away), or call one of the following commercial shuttle services (fares are generally $10 one-way from John Wayne): **L.A. Xpress** (© **800/I-ARRIVE**), **Prime Time** (© **800/262-7433**), or **SuperShuttle** (© **714/517-6600**). Car-rental agencies located at the John Wayne Airport include **Budget** (© **800/221-1203**) and **Hertz** (© **800/654-3131**).

VISITOR INFORMATION   The **Anaheim/Orange County Visitor and Convention Bureau,** 800 W. Katella Ave. (© **714/765-8888;** www.anaheimoc.org), can fill you in on area activities and shopping shuttles. It's across the street from Disneyland inside the Convention Center, next to the dramatic cantilevered arena. It's open Monday through Friday from 8:30am to 5:30pm. The **Buena Park Convention and Visitors Office,** 6280 Manchester Blvd., Suite 103 (© **800/541-3953** or 714/562-3560; www.buenapark.com/cvo), provides specialized information on the area, including Knott's Berry Farm.

THE DISNEY EXPERIENCE

It's not called "The Happiest Place on Earth" for nothing. Disney sister parks have sprung up in Florida, Tokyo, and even France, but there's still nothing to compare with the original. Smaller than Walt Disney World, Disneyland has always capitalized on being the original—and the world's first family-oriented mega theme park. Nostalgia is a big part of the appeal, and despite many advancements, changes, and expansions over the years, Disneyland remains true to the original vision of founder Walt Disney.

In 2001, Disney unveiled a brand-new theme park **(Disney's California Adventure),** a new shopping/dining/entertainment district **(Downtown Disney),** and a third on-site hotel **(Disney's Grand Californian Hotel).** They also revamped their own name to "The Disneyland Resort," reflecting a greatly expanded array of entertainment options. What does this all mean for you? Well, first of all, you might want to think seriously about budgeting more time (and yes, more money) for your Disney visit—you'll need at least 3 full days to see it all. If you have limited time, plan carefully so you don't skip what's important to you. In the pages ahead, I describe what to expect throughout the resort. And, most of all, get ready to have fun—there's lots of great new stuff to check out!

ADMISSION, HOURS & INFORMATION   Admission to *either* Disneyland or Disney's California Adventure, including unlimited rides and all festivities and entertainment, is $43 for adults and children over 11, $41 for seniors 60 and over, $33 for children 3 to 11, and free for children under 3. Parking costs $7. Three- and 4-day passports are available; you can see both parks this way, but you can only enter one park *each* day. Prices for adults/children are $111/$87 (3-day) and $137/$107 (4-day). In addition, some area accommodations offer lodging packages that include admission for 1 or more days.

Disneyland and Disney's California Adventure are open every day of the year, but operating hours vary, so I recommend that you call for information that applies to the specific day(s) of your visit (© **714/781-7290**). The same information, including ride closures and show schedules, can also be found online at **www.disneyland.com**. Generally speaking, the parks are open from 9 or 10am to 6 or 7pm on weekdays, fall to spring; and from 8 or 9am to midnight or 1am on weekends, holidays, and during winter, spring, or summer vacation periods.

If you plan on arriving during a busy time (when the gates open in the morning, or between 11am and 2pm), purchase your tickets in advance and get a jump on the crowds at the ticket counters. Advance tickets may be purchased through Disneyland's website (www.disneyland.com), at Disney stores in the United States, or by calling the ticket mail-order line (© **714/781-4043**).

WHEN TO GO   Disneyland is busiest from mid-June to mid-September and on weekends and school holidays year-round. Peak hours are from noon to 5pm; visit the most popular rides before and after these hours and you'll cut your waiting times substantially.

Attendance falls dramatically during the winter, so the park offers discounted (about 25% off) admission to Southern California residents, who may buy up

Anaheim Area & Orange Coast Attractions

Balboa Pavilion **7**	International Surfing Museum **4**
Bolsa Chica Ecological Reserve **3**	Knott's Berry Farm **1**
Dana Point **9**	Mission San Juan Capistrano **5**
Disneyland Resort **2**	Monarch Beach Golf Links **9**
Doheny State Beach **9**	Pelican Hill Golf Club **8**
Fashion Island Newport Beach **6**	Salt Creek Beach **9**

Beach ⌐
Information ⓘ

to five tickets per ZIP code verification. If you'll be visiting the park with someone who lives here, be sure to take advantage of this "Resident Salutes" promotion.

Once in the park, many visitors tackle Disneyland (or California Adventure) systematically, beginning at the entrance and working their way clockwise around the park. My advice: Arrive early and run to the most popular rides—in **Disneyland,** they are the Indiana Jones Adventure, Star Tours, Space Mountain, Big Thunder Mountain Railroad, Splash Mountain, the Haunted Mansion, and Pirates of the Caribbean; and in **California Adventure,** make a beeline for Soarin' Over California, California Screamin', Grizzly River Run, and It's Tough to Be a Bug.

Waits for these can last an hour or more in the middle of the day. This time-honored plan of attack may eventually become obsolete, thanks to the new **Fast-Pass** system. Here's how it works: Say you want to ride Space Mountain, but the line is long—*so* long the wait sign indicates a 75-minute standstill! Now you can head to the Automated FastPass ticket dispensers, which allow you to swipe the magnetic strip of your Disneyland entrance ticket, get a FastPass for later that day, and return to use the reduced-wait FastPass entrance (to the envy of everyone in the slowpoke line). At press time, about a dozen Disneyland rides were equipped with FastPass; several more will be added by the time you read this. The hottest features at California Adventure had FastPass built in from the start; for a complete list for each park, check your official map/guide when you enter.

TOURING DISNEYLAND

Disneyland is divided into several theme "lands," each of which has a number of rides and attractions that are, more or less, related to that land's theme.

MAIN STREET U.S.A.   At the park's entrance, Main Street U.S.A. is a cinematic version of early-20th-century small-town America. The whitewashed Rockwellian fantasy is lined with gift shops, candy stores, a soda fountain, and a silent theater that continuously runs early Mickey Mouse films. Here you can find the practical things you might need, such as stroller rentals and storage lockers.

Because there are no rides, it's best to tour Main Street during the middle of the afternoon, when lines for rides are longest, and in the evening, when you can rest your feet in the theater that features "Great Moments with Mr. Lincoln," a patriotic (and audio-animatronic) look at America's 16th president delivering the Gettysburg Address and other Civil War–related themes. There's always something happening on Main Street; stop in at the information booth to the left of the main entrance for a schedule of the day's events.

ADVENTURELAND   Inspired by the most exotic regions of Asia, Africa, India, and the South Pacific, Adventureland is home to several popular rides. Here's where you can cavort inside **Tarzan's Treehouse,** a climb-around attraction based on the animated film. Its African-themed neighbor is the **Jungle Cruise,** where passengers board a large authentic-looking Mississippi River paddleboat and float along an Amazon-like river; a spear's throw away is the **Enchanted Tiki Room,** one of the most sedate attractions in Adventureland. Inside, you can sit down and watch a 20-minute musical comedy featuring electronically animated tropical birds, flowers, and "tiki gods."

The **Indiana Jones Adventure** is Adventureland's star ride. Based on the Steven Spielberg films, this ride takes adventurers into the Temple of the Forbidden Eye, in joltingly realistic all-terrain vehicles. Riders follow Indy and experience the perils of bubbling lava pits, whizzing arrows, fire-breathing serpents, collapsing bridges, and the familiar cinematic tumbling boulder (an effect that's very realistic in the front seats!).

NEW ORLEANS SQUARE   A large, grassy green dotted with gas lamps, New Orleans Square is home to the **Haunted Mansion,** the most high-tech ghost house I've ever seen; the clever events inside are as funny as they are scary.

Even more fanciful is **Pirates of the Caribbean,** one of Disneyland's most popular rides. Visitors float on boats through mock underground caves, entering an enchanting world of swashbuckling, rum-running, and buried treasure. Even in the middle of the afternoon you can dine by the cool moonlight and to the sound of crickets in the **Blue Bayou** restaurant, situated in the middle of the ride itself.

CRITTER COUNTRY   An ode to the backwoods, Critter Country is a sort of Frontierland without those pesky settlers. Older kids and grown-ups head straight for **Splash Mountain,** one of the largest water flume rides in the world. Loosely based on the Disney movie *Song of the South,* the ride is lined with about 100 characters that won't stop singing "Zip-A-Dee-Doo-Dah." Be prepared to get wet, especially if someone sizable is in the front seat of your log-shaped boat.

FRONTIERLAND   Inspired by 19th-century America, Frontierland features a raft to **Tom Sawyer's Island,** a do-it-yourself play area with balancing rocks, caves, and a rope bridge, and from there you can board the **Big Thunder Mountain Railroad,** a runaway roller coaster that races through a deserted 1870s gold mine. You can also find a petting zoo and an Abe Lincoln–style log cabin here; both are great for exploring with the little ones.

On Saturdays, Sundays, and holidays, and during vacation periods, head to Frontierland's **Rivers of America** after dark to see the FANTASMIC! show. It mixes magic, music, live performers, and sensational special effects. Just as he did in *The Sorcerer's Apprentice,* Mickey Mouse appears and uses his magical powers to create giant water fountains, enormous flowers, and fantasy creatures. There's plenty of pyrotechnics, lasers, and fog, as well as a 45-foot-tall dragon that breathes fire and sets the water of the Rivers of America aflame.

MICKEY'S TOONTOWN   This is a colorful, whimsical world inspired by the "Roger Rabbit" films—a wacky, gag-filled land populated by 'toons. There are several rides, including **Roger Rabbit's CarToonSpin,** but they take a back seat to Toontown itself—a smile-inducing world without a straight line or right angle in sight.

FANTASYLAND   With a storybook theme, this is the catch-all "land" for stuff that doesn't quite fit anywhere else. Most of the rides are geared to the under-6 set, including the **King Arthur Carousel, Dumbo the Flying Elephant ride,** and the **Casey Jr. Circus Train.** Some, like **Mr. Toad's Wild Ride** and **Peter Pan's Flight,** appeal to grown-ups as well. You'll also find **Alice in Wonderland, Snow White's Scary Adventures, Pinocchio's Daring Journey,** and more.

The most lauded attraction is **"it's a small world,"** a slow-moving indoor river ride through a saccharine nightmare of all the world's children singing the song everybody loves to hate. For a different kind of thrill, try the **Matterhorn Bobsleds,** a zippy roller coaster through chilled caverns and drifting fog banks. It's one of the park's most popular rides.

TOMORROWLAND   Conceived as an optimistic look at the future, Tomorrowland employs an angular, metallic look popularized by futurists like Jules

Verne. Longtime Tomorrowland favorites include **Space Mountain** (a pitch-black indoor roller coaster that assaults your equilibrium and ears), and **Star Tours,** the original Disney–George Lucas joint venture. It's a 40-passenger Star-Speeder that encounters a space-load of misadventures on the way to the Moon of Endor, achieved with wired seats and video effects—not for the queasy.

DISNEY'S CALIFORNIA ADVENTURE ★★

With a grand entrance designed to resemble one of those "Wish you were here" scenic postcards, California Adventure starts out with a bang. Beneath a scale model of the Golden Gate Bridge (watch carefully, the monorail passes overhead), handmade tiles of across-the-state scenes glimmer on either side. Just inside, an enormous gold titanium "sun" shines all day, illuminated by computerized heliostats that follow the real sun's path. From this point, visitors can head into three distinct themed areas, each containing rides, interactive attractions, live-action shows, and plenty of dining, snacking, and shopping opportunities.

THE GOLDEN STATE   This multi-dimensional area represents California's history, heritage, and physical attributes. Sound boring? Actually, the park's splashiest attractions are here. "Condor Flats" is a tribute to daring aviators; inside a weathered corrugated test-pilots' hangar is **Soarin' Over California,** the ride that immediately rose to the top on everyone's "ride first" list (it's equipped with FastPass and I highly recommend using it). It uses cool cutting-edge technology to combine suspended seats with a spectacular IMAX-style surround-movie—so riders literally "soar" over California's scenic wonders.

Nearby, California Adventure's iconic "Grizzly Peak" towers over the **Grizzly River Run,** a splashy gold-country ride through caverns, mineshafts, and water-slides; it culminates with a wet plunge into a spouting geyser. Kids can cavort nearby on the **Redwood Creek Challenge Trail,** a forest playground with smoke-jumper cable slides, net climbing, and swaying bridges.

Pacific Wharf was inspired by Monterey's Cannery Row, and features mouth-watering demonstration attractions by **Boudin Sourdough Bakery, Mission Tortillas,** and **Lucky Fortune Cookies.** If you get hungry, each has a food counter where you can enjoy soup-in-a-sourdough-bowl; tacos, burritos, and enchiladas; and teriyaki bowls, egg rolls, and wonton soup.

Straight from the imagination of Disney CEO Michael Eisner comes the "Bountiful Farm," constructed to pay tribute to California's rich agriculture. The Robert Mondavi **Golden Vine Winery** boasts a demonstration vineyard, mission-style "aging room" (with a presentation on the art of winemaking), wine bars, and the park's most upscale eatery, **Vineyard Room** (see "Where to Dine," below). Next to a demonstration produce garden lies another California Adventure "E ticket," the interactive film *It's Tough to Be a Bug.* Using next-generation 3-D technology, *A Bug's Life* characters Flik and Hopper lead the audience on an underground romp with bees, termites, grasshoppers, stink bugs, spiders, and a few surprises that keep everyone hopping, ducking, and laughing along (I could see how little kids might find the show rather terrifying, however).

PARADISE PIER   Journey back to the glory days of California's beachfront amusement piers—remember Santa Monica, Santa Cruz, Belmont Park?—on this fantasy boardwalk. Highlights include **California Screamin',** a classic roller coaster that replicates the whitewashed wooden white-knucklers of the past—but with state-of-the-art steel construction and a smooth, computerized ride.

There's also the **Maliboomer,** a trio of towers (giant strongman sledgehammer tests) that catapult riders to the tip-top bell, then lets them down bungee-style with dangling feet; the **Orange Stinger,** a whooshing swing ride inside an enormous orange, complete with orange scent piped in; **Mulholland Madness,** a wacky wild trip along LA's precarious hilltop street; and the **Sun Wheel Carousel,** featuring unique zigzagging cars that bring new meaning to the familiar ride.

There are all the familiar boardwalk games (complete with stuffed prizes), guilty pleasure fast foods like pizza, corn dogs, and burritos, plus a full-service over-water restaurant by Wolfgang Puck, **Avalon Cove.**

HOLLYWOOD PICTURES BACKLOT   If you've visited Disney in Florida, you might recognize many elements of this trompe l'oeil re-creation of a Hollywood movie-studio lot. Pass through a classic studio archway flanked by gigantic golden elephants, and you'll find yourself on a surprisingly realistic "Hollywood Boulevard." In the **Disney Animation** building, visitors can participate in six different interactive galleries—learn how stories become animated features; watch Robin Williams become an animated character; listen to a Disney illustrator invent "Mushu," from *Mulan;* and even take a computerized personality test to see which Disney character you resemble most.

At the end of the street, the replica movie palace **Hyperion Theater** presents a live-action tribute to classic Disney films. Across the way, step aboard the **Superstar Limo,** where you're cast as a hot new star being chauffeured around Hollywood to sign a big movie deal; the wacky but tame ride winds through Malibu, Rodeo Drive, Beverly Hills, and the Sunset Strip. The latest attraction is **"Who Wants to Be a Millionaire—Play It!",** an interactive, high-energy mockup of the game show. It's re-created to look and feel as it does on television, complete with the dramatic lighting and high-tech set.

The Backlot's main attraction is **Jim Henson's MuppetVision 3D,** an onscreen blast from the past featuring Kermit, Miss Piggy, Gonzo, Fozzie Bear—and even hecklers Waldorf and Statler. Although it's not nearly as entertaining as *It's Tough to Be a Bug,* it has its moments and won't scare the bejeezus out of little kids. A bevy of dining options is led by the **ABC Soap Opera Bistro,** where you can dine in replica sets from your favorite soap operas.

DOWNTOWN DISNEY ⊛

Borrowing a page from central Florida's successful Disney compound, **Downtown Disney** is filled with restaurants, shops, and entertainment for all ages. Whether you want to stroll with kids in tow, have an upscale dinner for two, or party into the night, this colorful and sanitized "street scene" fills the bill.

The promenade begins at the amusement park gates and stretches toward the Disneyland Hotel; there are nearly 20 shops and boutiques, and a dozen-plus restaurants, live-music venues, and entertainment options.

Highlights include **House of Blues,** the blues-jazz restaurant/club that features Delta-inspired cuisine and big-name music; **Ralph Brennan's Jazz Kitchen,** a spicy mix of New Orleans traditional foods and live jazz; **ESPN Zone,** the ultimate sports dining-and-entertainment experience, including an interactive game room; **Y Arriba! Y Arriba!,** where Latin cuisine combines with spicy entertainment and dancing; and **World of Disney,** one of the biggest Disney shopping experiences anywhere, with a vast and diverse range of toys, souvenirs, and collectibles. There is also a 12-screen multiplex, LEGO Imagination Center, Sephora cosmetics store, and much more.

Even if you're not staying at a Disney hotel, Downtown Disney is worth a visit. Locals and day shoppers take advantage of the free entry and validated Downtown Disney parking lots (3 hr. free; 5 hr. with restaurant or theater validation).

WHERE TO STAY
EXPENSIVE

The Disneyland Hotel ★★ *Kids*   The holy grail of Disney-goers has always been this, the "Official Hotel of the Magic Kingdom." A monorail connection via Downtown Disney means you'll be able to return to your room anytime, whether to take a much-needed nap or to change your soaked shorts after your Splash Mountain or Grizzly Peak adventure. The theme hotel is an attraction unto itself, and the best choice for families with small children. The rooms aren't fancy, but they're comfortably and attractively furnished, like a good-quality business hotel, and all have balconies. In-room amenities include movie channels (with free Disney Channel, naturally) and cute-as-a-button Disney-themed toiletries and accessories. This all-inclusive resort offers over 10 combined restaurants, snack bars, and cocktail lounges; every kind of service desk imaginable; a fantasy swimming lagoon with white-sand beach; and video-game center. The complex includes the adjoining Paradise Pier Hotel, which offers a Disney version of Asian tranquillity; adults and older kids looking to escape the frenetically colorful Disney atmosphere will appreciate this option.

Best of all, hotel guests get to enter the park early almost every day and enjoy the major rides before the lines form. The amount of time varies from day to day, but usually you can enter 1½ hours early. Call ahead to check the schedule.

When you're planning your trip, inquire about multi-day packages that allow you to take on the park at your own pace and usually include free parking.

1150 Magic Way, Anaheim, CA 92802. ℂ 714/956-MICKEY (central reservations), 714/778-6600 (Disneyland Hotel), or 714/999-0990 (Paradise Pier Hotel). Reservations fax 714/956-6582. 990 units. $170–$310 double; from $265 suite. AE, MC, V. Parking $10. **Amenities:** 4 restaurants; 3 lounges; 3 outdoor pools; health club; Jacuzzi; children's programs; game room; concierge; shopping arcade; salon; room service; babysitting; laundry service; dry cleaning. *In room:* A/C, TV w/pay movies, dataport, minibar, coffeemaker, hair dryer, safe.

Disney's Grand Californian Hotel ★★ *Kids*   Disney didn't miss the details when constructing this enormous version of an Arts and Crafts–era lodge (think Yosemite's Ahwahnee, Pasadena's Gamble House), hiring craftspeople throughout the state to contribute one-of-a-kind tiles, furniture, sculptures, and artwork. Taking inspiration from California's redwood forests, mission pioneers, and plein-air painters, designers managed to create a nostalgic yet state-of-the-art high-rise hotel.

Guest rooms are spacious and smartly designed, carrying through the Arts and Crafts theme surprisingly well considering the hotel's grand scale. The best ones overlook the park (but you'll pay for that view). Despite the sophisticated air of the Grand Californian, this is a hotel that truly caters to families, with a bevy of room configurations including one with a double bed plus bunk-beds-with-trundle. Since the hotel provides sleeping bags (rather than rollaways) for kids, this standard-size room will sleep a family of six—but you have to share the bathroom.

1600 S. Disneyland Dr., Anaheim, CA 92802. ℂ 714/956-MICKEY (central reservations) or 714/635-2300. Fax 714/956-6099. www.disneyland.com. 751 units. $205–$335 double; from $345 suite. AE, DC, DISC, MC, V. Free self-parking; valet $6. **Amenities:** 3 restaurants; lounge; 2 outdoor pools; health club and spa; Jacuzzi; children's center; game room/arcade; concierge; business center; 24-hr. room service; laundry service; dry cleaning; concierge-level rooms. *In room:* A/C, TV w/pay movies, dataport, minibar, coffeemaker, hair dryer, iron, safe.

Sheraton Anaheim Hotel 🅐 This hotel rises to the festive theme-park occasion with its fanciful English Tudor architecture; it's a castle that lures business conventions, Disney-bound families, and local high-school proms. The public areas are quiet and elegant—intimate gardens with fountains and koi ponds, plush lobby and lounges—which can be a pleasing touch after a frantic day at the amusement park. The rooms are modern and unusually spacious, but otherwise not distinctive. A large swimming pool sits in the center of the complex, surrounded by attractive landscaping. Don't be put off by the high rack rates; rooms commonly go for $100 to $130, even on busy summer weekends.

1015 W. Ball Rd. (at I-5), Anaheim, CA 92802. ✆ 800/325-3535 or 714/778-1700. Fax 714/535-3889. 489 units. $190–$225 double; $290–$360 suite. AE, DC, MC, V. Parking $10; free Disneyland shuttle. **Amenities:** 2 restaurants; lounge; outdoor pool; fitness center; Jacuzzi; concierge; 24-hr. room service; coin-op laundry and laundry service; dry cleaning. *In room:* A/C, TV w/pay movies, dataport, minibar, coffeemaker, hair dryer, iron.

MODERATE

Anaheim Vagabond Hotel 🅐 *Value* You can easily cross the street to Disneyland's main gate, or take the Anaheim Plaza's free shuttle. Once you return, you'll appreciate the way this 32-year-old hotel's clever design shuts out the noisy world. In fact, the seven two-story garden buildings remind me more of 1960s Waikiki than busy Anaheim. The Olympic-size heated outdoor pool and whirlpool are unfortunately surrounded by Astroturf, and the plain motel-style furnishings are beginning to look a little tired. On the plus side, nothing's changed about the light-filled modern lobby, nor the friendly rates, which often drop as low as $49.

1700 S. Harbor Blvd., Anaheim, CA 92802. ✆ 800/228-1357 or 714/772-5900. Fax 714/772-8386. 300 units. $79–$150 double; from $185 suite. Rates include continental breakfast. AE, DC, DISC, MC, V. Free parking and Disneyland shuttle. **Amenities:** Restaurant; lounge; outdoor pool; Jacuzzi; room service 8am–11pm; coin-op laundry and laundry service; dry cleaning. *In room:* A/C, TV, coffeemaker.

Candy Cane Inn 🅐/🅐 *Value* Take your standard U-shaped motel court with outdoor corridors, spruce it up with cobblestone drives and walkways, old-time street lamps, and flowering vines engulfing the balconies of attractively painted rooms, and you have the Candy Cane. The face-lift worked, making this gem near Disneyland's main gate a treat for the stylish bargain hunter. The rooms are decorated in bright floral motifs with comfortable furnishings, including queen beds and a separate dressing and vanity area. Breakfast is served in the courtyard, where you can also splash around in a heated pool, spa, or kids' wading pool.

1747 S. Harbor Blvd., Anaheim, CA 92802. ✆ 800/345-7057 or 714/774-5284. Fax 714/772-5462. 173 units. $84–$129 double. Rates include expanded continental breakfast. AAA discount available. AE, DC, DISC, MC, V. Free parking and Disneyland shuttle. **Amenities:** Outdoor pool; Jacuzzi; coin-op laundry and laundry service; dry cleaning. *In room:* A/C, TV, coffeemaker, hair dryer.

INEXPENSIVE

Best Western Anaheim Stardust Located on the back side of Disneyland, this modest hotel appeals to the budget-conscious traveler who isn't willing to sacrifice everything. Each room has a refrigerator and microwave, breakfast is served in a refurbished train dining car, and you can relax by the large outdoor heated pool and spa while using the laundry room. The extra-large family rooms accommodate virtually any brood, and shuttles run regularly to the park.

1057 W. Ball Rd., Anaheim, CA 92802. ✆ 800/222-3639 or 714/774-7600. Fax 714/535-6953. 121 units. $64–$89 double; $105 family room. Rates include full breakfast. AE, DC, DISC, MC, V. Free parking and Disneyland shuttle. **Amenities:** Restaurant; outdoor pool; Jacuzzi; coin-op laundry. *In room:* A/C, TV, fridge.

WHERE TO DINE

If you're visiting the Disneyland Resort, chances are you'll probably eat at one of the many choices inside the theme parks or at Downtown Disney; there are plenty of restaurants from which to choose for all tastes and budgets. At Disneyland, in the Creole-themed **Blue Bayou,** you can sit under the stars inside the Pirates of the Caribbean ride—no matter what time of day it is. California Adventure features two bona fide sit-down options: **Avalon Cove** is a Wolfgang Puck seafood restaurant overlooking a boardwalk amusement zone, and the Robert Mondavi–backed **Vineyard Room** offers upscale prix-fixe Wine Country cuisine matched to Mondavi wines (the more casual Golden Vine Terrace is downstairs). Make reservations early in the day for dinner, as they all fill up pretty quickly.

I also list some of the best bets in the surrounding area, including nearby **Orange,** whose charming historic downtown is home to several of the region's best dining options, if you're willing to drive 10 to 15 minutes.

Anaheim White House ★★ ITALIAN/FRENCH   Once surrounded by orange groves, this stately 1909 colonial-style mansion now sits on a wide industrial street just 5 minutes from Disneyland. It's set back, though, framed by lawns and gardens, and exudes gentility and nostalgia. The home is nicely restored inside and out; the restaurant opened in 1981, named after its stylistic cousin in Washington, D.C. Owner Bruno Serato maintains this architectural treasure, serving northern Italian cuisine—with a French accent—in elegant white-on-white rooms on the main and second floors. Dinner courses are whimsically named for fashion giants (Versace whitefish, Prada rack of lamb), and sometimes arrive on oddly shaped platters that work better as artwork than dishware. But chef David Libby knows what he's doing, applying just the right amount of sauce to pastas both formal (gnocchi in velvety Gorgonzola sauce) and rustic (linguine with chunky garlic, roasted peppers, and olives). Prices tend to reflect the expense account and well-heeled retiree crowd, but lunch prices (including a terrific prix fixe) deliver the same bang for fewer bucks.

887 Anaheim Blvd. (N of Ball Rd.), Anaheim. ℂ 714/772-1381. www.anaheimwhitehouse.com. Reservations recommended at dinner. Main courses $10–$16 lunch, $18–$28 dinner. AE, MC, V. Mon–Fri 11:30am–2pm; daily 5–10pm.

Citrus City Grille ★★ CALIFORNIA   Though housed in Orange's second-oldest brick building, this sophisticated crowd-pleaser is furnished without an antique in sight, paying homage to the town's agricultural (citrus) legacy with a bold industrial chic. World-inspired appetizers range from Hawaiian-style *ahi poke* (raw tuna salad) to southeast Asian coconut shrimp tempura accented with spiced apricots. Main courses come from the Mediterranean (pasta and risotto), Mexico (carne asada with avocado-corn relish), the American South (authentic Louisiana gumbo), and your Mom's kitchen (meatloaf smothered in gravy and fried onions). Gleaming bar shelves house myriad bottles for the extensive martini menu, and outdoor foyer tables are nicely protected from the street.

122 N. Glassell St. (½ block N of Chapman), Orange. ℂ 714/639-9600. Reservations recommended. Main courses $8–$13 lunch, $12–$24 dinner. AE, DC, MC, V. Tues–Sat 11:30am–3pm and 5–10pm.

Felix Continental Cafe ★ CUBAN/SPANISH   If you like the re-created Main Street in the Magic Kingdom, you'll love the historic 1886 town square in the city of Orange, on view from the cozy sidewalk tables outside the Felix Continental Cafe. Dining on traditional Cuban specialties (such as citrus-marinated chicken, black beans and rice, and fried plantains) and watching traffic spin around the magnificent fountain and rose bushes of the plaza evokes old Havana or Madrid rather than the cookie-cutter Orange County communities just blocks away. The food is praised by restaurant reviewers and loyal locals alike.

36 Plaza Sq. (at the corner of Chapman and Glassell), Orange. ℭ 714/633-5842. Reservations recommended for dinner. Main courses $6–$14. AE, DC, MC, V. Mon–Thurs 7am–9pm, Fri 7am–10pm, Sat 8am–10pm, Sun 8am–9pm.

5 Knott's Berry Farm

30 miles SE of downtown LA

Cynics say that Knott's Berry Farm is for people who aren't smart enough to find Disneyland. The reality is that Knott's simply can't compete with the Disney allure, but instead focuses on newer and faster thrill rides that target Southern California youths and families instead.

Like Disneyland, Knott's Berry Farm is not without historical background. Rudolph Boysen crossed a loganberry with a raspberry, calling the resulting hybrid the boysenberry. In 1933, Buena Park farmer Walter Knott planted the boysenberry and launched Knott's berry farm on 10 acres of leased land. When things got tough during the Depression, Mrs. Knott set up a roadside stand, selling pies, preserves, and home-cooked chicken dinners. Within a year she was selling 90 meals a day. Lines became so long that Walter decided to create an Old West Ghost Town as a diversion for waiting customers.

Today the amusement park offers a whopping 165 shows, attractions, and high-tech rides that are far more thrilling than most rides at the Disneyland Resort. Granted, it doesn't have nearly the magical appeal of Disneyland, but if you're more into fast-paced amusement rides than swirling tea cups, spend your money here.

ESSENTIALS

GETTING THERE Knott's Berry Farm is at 8039 Beach Blvd. in Buena Park. It's a 10-minute ride north on I-5 from Disneyland. From I-5 or Calif. 91, exit south onto Beach Boulevard. The park is about half a mile south of Calif. 91.

ADMISSION, HOURS & INFORMATION Admission to the park, including unlimited access to all rides, shows, and attractions, is $40 for adults and children 12 and over, $30 for seniors over 60, kids 3 to 11, nonambulatory visitors, and expectant mothers; children under 3 are admitted free. Admission is $20 for adults and $15 for kids 3 to 11 after 4pm on days when the park is open past 6pm. Parking is $7. Like Disneyland, Knott's offers discounted admission for Southern California residents during the off-season, so if you're bringing local friends or family members along, be sure to take advantage of the bargain. Also like Disneyland, Knott's Berry Farm's hours vary both during the week and week to week, so call ahead. The park is generally open during the summer daily from 9am to midnight. The rest of the year, it opens at 10am and closes at 6 or 8pm, except Saturday, when it stays open till 10pm. Knott's is closed December 25. Special hours and prices are in effect during Knott's Scary Farm in late October (a hugely popular event). Stage shows and special activities are scheduled throughout the day. Pick up a schedule at the ticket booth.

For more information, call ℭ 714/220-5200 or log on to **www.knotts.com**.

TOURING THE PARK

Despite all the new multimillion-dollar rides, Knott's Berry Farm still maintains much of its original Old West motif, and is divided into six themed areas spread across 150 acres. The newest attraction is the **Xcelerator,** which launches you from 0 to 82 mph in 2.3 seconds. Other new attractions include the **California MarketPlace,** the Farm's version of Downtown Disney, and **Knott's Soak City U.S.A.,** a 21-ride water adventure park located right next to Knott's Berry Farm (separate admission required).

GHOST TOWN   The park's original attraction is a collection of refurbished 19th-century buildings relocated from deserted Old West towns. You can pan for gold, ride an authentic stagecoach, take rickety train cars through the Calico Mine, get held up aboard the Denver and Rio Grande Calico Railroad, and hiss at the villain during a melodrama in the Birdcage Theater. If you love wooden roller coasters, don't miss the clackity GhostRider.

FIESTA VILLAGE   Here you'll find a south-of-the-border theme. That means festive markets, strolling mariachis, and wild rides like Montezooma's Revenge and Jaguar, a roller coaster that includes two heart-in-the-mouth drops and a loop that turns you upside down.

WILD WATER WILDERNESS   This 3½-acre attraction is styled like a early-20th-century California wilderness park. The top ride is a white-water adventure called Bigfoot Rapids, with a long stretch of artificial rapids; it's the longest ride of its kind in the world. You can also look Mystery Lodge right in the eye—it's a truly amazing high-tech, trick-of-the-eye attraction based on the legends of local Native Americans. Don't miss this wonderful theater piece.

CAMP SNOOPY   This will probably be the youngsters' favorite area. It's meant to re-create a wilderness camp in the picturesque High Sierra. Its 6 rustic acres are the playgrounds of Charles Schulz's beloved beagle and his pals, Charlie Brown and Lucy, who greet guests and pose for pictures. The rides here, including the new Charlie Brown Speedway and Beary Tales Playhouse, are tailor-made for the 6-and-under set.

INDIAN TRIALS   A nod to Native Americans is this Native American interpretive center on the outskirts Ghost Town. Exhibits include authentic tepees, hogans, and big houses. There are also daily educational events such as native craftmaking, storytelling, music, and dance.

THE BOARDWALK   This theme area is a salute to Southern California's beach culture. The main attractions are the 30-story Supreme Scream, one of the tallest (and scariest) thrill rides in the world, and a white-water adventure called Perilous Plunge, the world's tallest, steepest (think four-story waterfall), and wettest water ride.

WHERE TO STAY

Radisson Resort Knott's Berry Farm ⭐ (Kids)   Within easy walking distance of Knott's Berry Farm, this spit-shined Radisson (the former Buena Park Hotel) also offers a free shuttle to Disneyland, 7 miles away. The pristine lobby has the look of a business-oriented hotel, and that it is. But vacationers can also benefit from the elevated level of service. Ask about "Super Saver" rates (as low as $99—with breakfast—at press time), plus Knott's or Disneyland package deals. The rooms in the nine-story tower were tastefully redecorated when Radisson took over. Doting parents can even treat their kids to a Peanuts-themed room with Snoopy turndown service.

7675 Crescent Ave. (at Grand), Buena Park, CA 90620. © **800/333-3333** or 714/995-1111. Fax 714/828-8590. www.radisson.com/buenaparkca. 320 units. $129–$139 double; $159–$299 suite. Discounts and packages available. AE, DC, DISC, MC, V. Free parking and Disneyland shuttle. **Amenities:** 2 restaurants; lounge; outdoor pool; lit tennis court; fitness center; Jacuzzi; video arcade; concierge; 24-hr. room service; coin-op laundry and laundry service; dry cleaning. *In room:* A/C, TV w/pay movies, fax, dataport, coffeemaker, hair dryer, iron, safe.

WHERE TO DINE

Mrs. Knott's Chicken Dinner Restaurant ★ *Kids* AMERICAN   Knott's Berry Farm got its start as a down-home diner in 1934, and you can still get a hearty all-American meal without even entering the theme park. The restaurant that started it all, descended from Cordelia Knott's Depression-era farmland tea-room, stands just outside the park's entrance, with plenty of free parking for patrons. Looking just as you'd expect—country cute, with window shutters and paisley aplenty—the restaurant's featured attraction is the original fried-chicken dinner, complete with soup, salad, buttermilk biscuits, mashed potatoes and gravy, and a slice of famous pie. Country fried steak, pot roast, roast turkey, and pork ribs are options, as well as sandwiches, salads, and a terrific chicken potpie. Boysenberries abound (of course!), from breakfast jam to traditional double-crust pies, and there's even an adjacent takeout shop that's always crowded.

8039 Beach Blvd. (near La Palma), Buena Park. © **714/220-5080.** Reservations not accepted. Main courses $5–$7; complete dinners $11. AE, DC, DISC, MC, V. Sun–Thurs 7am–8:30pm, Fri 7am–9pm, Sat 7am–9:30pm.

6 The Orange Coast

Huntington Beach: 39 miles S of LA; Newport Beach: 49 miles S of LA; Dana Point: 65 miles S of LA

Whatever you do, don't say "Orange County" here. The mere name evokes images of smoggy industrial parks, cookie-cutter housing developments, and the staunch Republicanism that prevails behind the so-called "orange curtain." We're talking instead about the Orange Coast, one of Southern California's best-kept secrets, a string of seaside jewels that have been compared with the French Riviera or the Costa del Sol. Here, 42 miles of beaches offer pristine stretches of sand, tide pools teeming with marine life, ecological preserves, charming secluded coves, quaint pleasure-boat harbors, and legendary surfers carving nec-tar waves. Whether your bare feet want to stroll a funky wooden boardwalk or your gold card gravitates toward a yacht club, you've come to the right place.

ESSENTIALS

GETTING THERE   By car from Los Angeles, take I-5 or I-405 south. The scenic, shore-hugging Pacific Coast Highway (Calif. 1, or just PCH to the locals) links the Orange Coast communities from Seal Beach in the north to Capistrano Beach just south of Dana Point, where it merges with I-5. To reach the beach communities directly, take the following freeway exits: **Seal Beach,** Seal Beach Boulevard from I-405; **Huntington Beach,** Beach Boulevard/Calif. 39 from either I-405 or I-5; **Newport Beach,** Calif. 55 from either I-405 or I-5; **Laguna Beach,** Calif. 133 from I-5; **San Juan Capistrano,** Ortega Highway/ Calif. 74 from I-5; and **Dana Point,** Pacific Coast Highway/Calif. 1 from I-5.

VISITOR INFORMATION   The **Seal Beach Chamber of Commerce,** 311 Main St., #14A, at Electric (© **562/799-0179;** www.sealbeachchamber.com), is open Monday through Friday from 10am to 4pm.

The **Huntington Beach Conference & Visitors Bureau,** 417 Main St., Suite A-2 (© **800/SAY-OCEAN** or 714/969-3492; www.hbvisit.com), enthusiastically offers tons of information and personal anecdotes. Open Monday through Friday from 9am to 5pm.

The **Newport Beach Conference & Visitors Bureau,** 3300 W. Coast Hwy. (② **800/94-COAST** or 949/722-1611; www.newportbeach-cvb.com), distributes brochures, sample menus, a calendar of events, and the free *Visitor's Guide.* Call or stop in Monday through Friday from 8am to 5pm (plus weekends in summer).

The **Laguna Beach Visitors Bureau,** 252 Broadway (② **800/877-1115** or 949/497-9229; www.lagunabeachinfo.org), is in the heart of town and distributes lodging, dining, and art-gallery guides. It's open Monday through Friday from 9am to 5pm and on Saturday from 10am to 4pm (plus Sun in summer).

The **San Juan Capistrano Chamber of Commerce,** Franciscan Plaza, 31781 Camino Capistrano, Suite 306 (② **949/493-4700;** www.sanjuancapistrano. com), is within walking distance of the mission and offers a walking-tour guide to historic sites. Open Monday through Friday from 8:30am to 4pm.

The **Dana Point Chamber of Commerce,** 24681 La Plaza, Suite 120 (② **800/290-DANA** or 949/496-1555; www.danapoint-chamber.com), is open Monday through Friday from 9am to 4:30pm and carries some restaurant and lodging information as well as a comprehensive recreation brochure.

DRIVING THE ORANGE COAST

You'll most likely be exploring the coast by car, so I cover the beach communities in order, from north to south. Keep in mind, however, that if you're traveling between Los Angeles and San Diego, the Pacific Coast Highway (Calif. 1) is a fantastic scenic detour that adds less than an hour to the commute—so pick out a couple of destinations and go for it.

Seal Beach, on the border between Los Angeles and Orange counties and a neighbor to Long Beach's Naples Harbor, is geographically isolated by both the adjacent U.S. Naval Weapons Station and the self-contained Leisure World retirement community. As a result, the charming beach town appears untouched by modern development—it's Orange County's version of small-town America. Take a stroll down Main Street for a walk back in time, culminating in the Seal Beach Pier. Although the clusters of sunbathing, squawking seals that gave the town its name aren't around anymore, old-timers still fish, lovers still stroll, and families still cavort by the seaside, enjoying great food and retail shops or having a cold drink at Hennessey's tavern.

Huntington Beach ✦, or "Surf City" as it's known, is probably the largest Orange Coast city; it stretches quite a ways inland and has seen the most urbanization. To some extent this has changed the old boardwalk and pier to a modern outdoor mall where cliques of gang kids coexist with families and the surfers who continue to flock here, drawn by Huntington's legendary place in surf lore. Hawaiian-born George Freeth is credited with bringing the sport here in 1907, and some say the breaks around the pier and Bolsa Chica are the best in California. The world's top wave riders flock to Huntington each August for the rowdy but professional **U.S. Open of Surfing.** If you're around at Christmastime, try to see the gaily decorated marina homes and boats in Huntington Harbor by taking the **Cruise of Lights,** a 45-minute narrated sail through and around the harbor islands. The festivities generally last from mid-December until Christmas; call ② **714/840-7542** for schedules and ticket information.

The name **Newport Beach** ✦ conjures comparisons to Rhode Island's Newport, where the well-to-do enjoy seaside living with all the creature comforts.

That's the way it is here, too, but on a less grandiose scale. From the million-dollar Cape Cod–style cottages on sunny Balboa Island in the bay to elegant shopping complexes like Fashion Island and South Coast Plaza (an über-mall with valet parking, car detailing, limo service, and concierge), this is where fashionable socialites, right-wing celebrities, and business mavens can all be found. Alternatively, you could explore **Balboa Peninsula**'s historic Pavilion and old-fashioned pier or board a passenger ferry to Catalina Island.

Laguna Beach, whose breathtaking geography is marked by bold elevated headlands, coastal bluffs, and pocket coves, is known as an artists' enclave, but the truth is that Laguna has become so *in* (read: expensive) that it's driven most of the true bohemians *out*. Their legacy remains with the annual **Festival of Arts & Pageant of the Masters,** as well as a proliferation of art galleries mingling with high-priced boutiques along the town's cozy streets. In warm weather, Laguna Beach has an overwhelming Mediterranean-island ambience, which makes *everyone* feel beautifully, idly rich.

San Juan Capistrano, in the verdant headlands inland from Dana Point, is defined by Spanish missions and its loyal swallows. The mission architecture is authentic, and history abounds. Consider San Juan Capistrano a compact, life-size diorama illustrating the evolution of a small Western town from Spanish-mission era to secular rancho period, into statehood and the 20th century. Ironically, **Mission San Juan Capistrano** (p. 586) is once again the center of the community, just as the founding friars intended 200 years ago.

Dana Point ⍟, the last town south, has been called a "marina development in search of a soul." Overlooking the harbor stands a monument to 19th-century author Richard Henry Dana, who gave his name to the area and described it in *Two Years Before the Mast*. Activities generally center around yachting and Dana Point's lovely harbor. Nautical themes are everywhere, particularly the streets named for old-fashioned shipboard lights—a hodgepodge that includes "Street of the Amber Lantern," ". . . the Violet Lantern," ". . . the Golden Lantern," and so on. Bordering the harbor is Doheny State Beach (see "Beaches & Nature Preserves," below), which wrote the book on seaside park and camping facilities.

ENJOYING THE OUTDOORS

BEACHES & NATURE PRESERVES   The **Bolsa Chica Ecological Reserve,** in Huntington Beach (© **714/840-1575**), is a 300-acre restored urban salt marsh that's a haven to more than 200 bird species, as well as a wide variety of protected plants and animals. Naturalists come to spot herons and egrets as well as California horn snails, jackknife clams, sea sponges, common jellyfish, and shore crabs. An easy 1½-mile loop trail begins from a parking lot on the Pacific Coast Highway (Calif. 1) a mile south of Warner Boulevard; docents lead a narrated walk the first Saturday of every month. The trail heads inland, over Inner Bolsa Bay and up Bolsa Chica bluffs. It then loops back toward the ocean over a dike that separates the Inner and Outer Bolsa bays and traverses a coastal sand-dune system. This beautiful hike is a terrific afternoon adventure. The Bolsa Chica Conservancy has been working since 1978 on reclaiming the wetlands from oil companies that began drilling here 70 years ago. It's an ongoing process, and you can still see those "seesaw" drills dotting the outer areas of the reserve.

Huntington City Beach, adjacent to Huntington Pier, is a haven for volleyball players and surfers; dense crowds abound, but so do amenities like outdoor showers, beach rentals, and restrooms. Just south of the city beach is 3-mile-long

Huntington State Beach. Both popular beaches have lifeguards and concession stands seasonally. The state beach also has restrooms, showers, barbecue pits, and a waterfront bike path. The main entrance is on Beach Boulevard, and there are access points all along the Pacific Coast Highway (Calif. 1).

Newport Beach runs for about 5 miles and includes both Newport and Balboa piers. It has outdoor showers, restrooms, volleyball nets, and a vintage boardwalk that just may make you feel as though you've stepped 50 years back in time. **Balboa Bike and Beach Stuff** (© 949/723-1516), at the corner of Balboa and Palm near the pier, rents a variety of items, from pier fishing poles to bikes, beach umbrellas, and body boards. The **Southwind Kayak Center,** 2801 W. Pacific Coast Hwy. (© **800/768-8494** or 949/261-0200; www.south windkayaks.com), rents sea kayaks for use in the bay or open ocean at rates of $10 to $14 per hour; instructional classes are available on weekends, with some midweek classes in summer. It also offers winter bird-watching kayak expeditions into the Upper Newport Bay Ecological Reserve at rates of $40 to $65.

Crystal Cove State Park, which covers 3 miles of coastline between Corona del Mar and Laguna Beach and extends into the hills around El Moro Canyon, is a good alternative to the more popular beaches for seekers of solitude. (There are, however, lifeguards and restrooms.) The beach is a winding, sandy strip, backed with grassy terraces; high tide sometimes sections it into coves. The entire area offshore is an underwater nature preserve. There are four entrances, including Pelican Point and El Moro Canyon. For information, call © **949/ 494-3539.**

Salt Creek Beach Park lies below the palatial Ritz-Carlton Laguna Niguel (p. 586). Guests who tire of the pristine swimming pool can venture down the staircase on Ritz-Carlton Drive to wiggle their toes in the sand. The setting is marvelous, with wide white-sand beaches looking out toward Catalina Island (why do you think the Ritz-Carlton was built here?). The park has lifeguards, restrooms, a snack bar, and convenient parking near the hotel.

Doheny State Beach in Dana Point, just south of lovely Dana Point Marina (enter off Del Abispo St.), has long been known as a premier surfing spot and camping site. Doheny has the friendly vibe of beach parties in days gone by: tree-shaded lawns give way to wide beaches, and picnicking and beach camping are encouraged. There are 121 sites for both tents and RVs, plus a state-run visitor center featuring several small aquariums of sea and tide-pool life. For more information and camping availability, call © **949/492-0802.**

BICYCLING Biking is the most popular beach activity up and down the coast. A slower-paced alternative to driving, it allows you to enjoy the clean, fresh air and notice smaller details of these laid-back beach towns and harbors. The Newport Beach visitor center (see "Visitor Information," above) offers a free *Bike Ways* map of trails throughout the city and harbor. Bikes and equipment can be rented at **Balboa Bike & Beach Stuff,** 601 Balboa Blvd., Newport Beach (© **949/723-1516**); **Laguna Beach Cyclery,** 240 Thalia St. (© **949/ 494-1522**); and **Dana Point Bicycle,** 34155 Pacific Coast Hwy. (© **949/661- 8356**).

GOLF Many golf-course architects have used the geography of the Orange Coast to its full advantage, molding challenging and scenic courses from the rolling bluffs. Most courses are private, but two outstanding ones are open to the public. **The Links at Monarch Beach,** 33033 Niguel Rd., Dana Point (© **949/ 240-8247**), is particularly impressive. This hilly, challenging course, designed by

Robert Trent Jones Jr., offers great ocean views. Afternoon winds can sneak up, so accuracy is essential. Weekend greens fees are $145 ($115 weekdays).

Another challenge is the **Pelican Hill Golf Club,** 22651 Pelican Hill Rd. S., Newport Beach (© **949/760-0707** starter, 949/640-0238 pro shop; www. pelicanhill.com), with two Tom Fazio–designed courses. The Ocean North course is heavily bunkered, while the Ocean South course features canyons and ravines; both have large, multi-tier greens. Weekend greens fees are $250; weekdays $175. And remember: When putting near the ocean, the break is always toward the water.

SEEING THE SIGHTS

Beyond the sights listed below, an excellent attraction is **Balboa Island.** The charm of this pretty little neighborhood isn't diminished by knowing that the island was man-made—and it certainly hasn't affected the price of real estate. Tiny clapboard cottages in the island's center and modern houses with two-story windows and private docks along the perimeter make a colorful and romantic picture. You can drive onto the island on Jamboree Road to the north or take the three-car ferry from Balboa Peninsula (about $1.50 per vehicle). It's generally more fun to park and take the ferry as a pedestrian, since the island is crowded and lacks parking, and the tiny alleys they call streets are more suitable for strolling. **Marine Avenue,** the main commercial street, is lined with small shops and cafes that evoke a New England fishing village. Refreshing shaved ices sold by sidewalk vendors will relieve the heat of summer.

Balboa Pavilion ⚓ *(Kids)*   This historic cupola-topped structure, a California Historical Landmark, was built in 1905 as a bathhouse for swimmers in their ankle-length bathing costumes. Later, during the Big Band era, dancers rocked the Pavilion doing the "Balboa Hop." Now it serves as the terminal for Catalina Island passenger service, harbor and whale-watching cruises, and fishing charters. The surrounding boardwalk is the Balboa Fun Zone, a collection of carnival rides, game arcades, and vendors of hot dogs and cotton candy. For Newport Harbor or Catalina cruise information, call © **949/673-5245;** for sport fishing and whale-watching, call © **949/673-1434.**

400 Main St., Balboa, Newport Beach. © **714/960-3483.** From Calif. 1, turn S onto Newport Blvd. (which becomes Balboa Blvd. on the peninsula); turn left at Main St.

International Surfing Museum   Nostalgic Gidgets and Moondoggies shouldn't miss this monument to the laid-back sport that has become synonymous with California beaches. You'll find gargantuan long boards from the sport's early days, memorabilia of Duke Kahanamoku and the other surfing greats represented on the "Walk of Fame" near Huntington Pier, and a gift shop where a copy of the *"Surfin'ary"* can help you bone up on your surfer slang even if you can't hang 10.

411 Olive Ave., Huntington Beach. © **714/960-3483.** www.surfingmuseum.org. Admission $2 adults, $1 students, free for kids 6 and under. Mid-June to late Sept daily noon–5pm; rest of the year Wed–Sun noon–5pm.

Laguna Art Museum   This beloved local institution is working hard to position itself as the artistic cornerstone of the community. In addition to a small but interesting permanent collection, the museum presents installations of regional works definitely worth a detour. Past examples include a display of surf photography from the coast's 1930s and 1940s golden era, and dozens of plein-air Impressionist paintings (ca. 1900–30) by the founding artists of the original colony. The museum is also open during Laguna Beach Artwalk, the first Thursday each month, when all are admitted free.

307 Cliff Dr., Laguna Beach. © 949/494-8971. www.lagunaartmuseum.org. Admission $5 adults, $4 students and seniors, free for kids under 12. Tues–Sun 11am–5pm.

Mission San Juan Capistrano   The 7th of the 21 California coastal missions, Mission San Juan Capistrano is continually being restored. The mix of old ruins and working buildings is home to small museum collections and various adobe rooms that are as quaint as they are interesting. The intimate mission chapel with its ornate baroque altar is still used for religious services, and the mission complex is the center of the community, hosting performing arts, children's programs, and other cultural events year-round.

This mission is best known for its **swallows,** which are said to return to nest each year at their favorite sanctuary. According to legend, the birds wing their way back to the mission annually on March 19, St. Joseph's Day, arriving at dawn; they are said to take flight again on October 23, after bidding the mission farewell. In reality, you can probably see the well-fed birds here any day of the week, winter or summer.

Ortega Hwy. (Calif. 74), San Juan Capistrano. © 949/234-1300. www.missionsjc.com. Admission $6 adults, $5 seniors, $4 children. Daily 8:30am–5pm.

WHERE TO STAY

Also consider the **Seal Beach Inn,** 212 Fifth St., Seal Beach (© **800/HIDE-AWAY** or 562/493-2416; http://sealbeachinn.com), a romantic 23-room bed-and-breakfast inn 1 block from the beach in a charming residential neighborhood.

VERY EXPENSIVE

Ritz-Carlton Laguna Niguel ✦✦✦   The Old World meets the Pacific Rim at this glorious hotel, set among terraces and fountained gardens on a 150-foot-high bluff above a 2-mile-long beach. There's a beautiful marble fireplace in the silk-lined lobby, and lush foliage abounds throughout the interior. A ravishingly arched lounge is perfect for watching the sun set over the Pacific. The service, in Ritz-Carlton style, is unassuming and impeccable. The spacious rooms are outfitted with sumptuous furnishings and fabrics, and all come with a terrace, an Italian marble bathroom equipped with double vanity, three phones (with voice mail), and a shoe polisher. Some suites even have fireplaces.

1 Ritz-Carlton Dr., Dana Point, CA 92629. © 800/241-3333 or 949/240-2000. Fax 949/240-0829. 393 units. From $325 garden/pool-view double; $475 oceanview double; from $525 suite. Children 17 and under stay free in parents' room. Midweek and special packages available. AE, DC, DISC, MC, V. Parking $25. **Amenities:** 4 restaurants; 2 lounges; 4 outdoor tennis courts; health club; Jacuzzi; sauna; children's programs; concierge; regular shuttle to/from the beach and the golf course; business center; 24-hr. room service; in-room massage; babysitting; laundry service; dry cleaning; executive-level rooms. *In room:* A/C, TV w/pay movies, minibar, hair dryer, iron, safe.

St. Regis Monarch Beach Resort & Spa ✦✦✦   Let's cut to the chase: The St. Regis Monarch Beach Resort is the finest luxury hotel I have ever had the pleasure of reviewing—and I've reviewed a *lot* of luxury hotels. They nailed it with this one, setting a standard for all other resort hotels to follow. Everything oozes with indulgence here, from the stellar service to the striking artwork, high-tech electronics, absurdly comfortable beds, and a spa that will blow your mind. The $240-million, 172-acre resort opened in July 2001, with a massive star-studded gala, and has since been wooing the wealthy with its gorgeous Tuscan-inspired architecture and soothing ocean views.

Perfection is all in the details, and the St. Regis is full of them: a three-lane lap pool with an underwater sound system; a yoga, spinning, and "movement" studio; a full-service Vogue salon; private poolside cabanas; star chef Michael Mina's Aqua restaurant; 24-hour butler service; couples spa treatment rooms with whirlpool bathtubs and fireplaces; an 18-hole Robert Trent Jones Jr. golf course; even a private beach club. Then there are the guest rooms, each loaded with beautiful custom-designed furniture, 32-inch Sony Wega flat-screen TV with CD-DVD audio systems and a 300 DVD library, huge marble-laden bathroom with glass shower door that must weigh 100 pounds, and the most comfortable bathrobe I've ever worn. Even if it's a bit beyond your price range, give yourself one heckuva birthday present this year and book a room and spa treatment at the gorgeous St. Regis resort.

1 Monarch Beach Rd., Dana Point, CA 92629. ℂ **800/325-3589** or 949/234-3200. Fax 949/234-333. www.stregismonarchbeach.com. From $355 resort-view double; from $496 oceanview double; from $1,000 suites. Golf and spa packages available. AE, DC, DISC, MC, V. Valet parking $23. **Amenities:** 4 restaurants; lounge; wine-cellar tasting room; 3 pools; 2 hot tubs; 3 lit tennis courts; spa and fitness center; 18-hole golf course; 24-hr. room service; concierge; complimentary local shuttle; 24-hr. business center; in-room massage; babysitting; laundry service; dry cleaning; executive-level rooms. *In room:* A/C, TV/DVD, CD player, minibar, hair dryer, safe.

Surf and Sand Resort 🌟🌟 The fanciest hotel in Laguna Beach has come a long way since it started in 1937 as a modest little inn with 13 units. Still occupying the same fantastic ocean-side location, it now features dozens of top-of-the-line rooms that, despite their standard size, feel enormously decadent. They're very bright and beachy; every one is done entirely in white and has a private balcony with an ocean view, a marble bathroom, and plush robes. Some have whirlpool tubs. Try to get a deluxe corner room. Stunning Splashes restaurant serves three meals daily in a beautiful oceanfront setting; the Mediterranean cuisine is perfect against a backdrop of sunlight and crashing waves.

1555 S. Coast Hwy. (S of Laguna Canyon Rd.), Laguna Beach, CA 92651. ℂ **888/869-7569** or 949/497-4477. Fax 949/494-2897. www.surfandsandresort.com. 164 units. Apr–Oct $290–$440 double; from $475 suite. Nov–Mar $275–$350 double; from $450 suite. AE, DC, DISC, MC, V. **Amenities:** Restaurant; bar; outdoor heated pool; spa; Jacuzzi; summer children's programs; concierge; business center; room service 6:30am–10pm; in-room massage; babysitting; laundry service; dry cleaning; concierge-level rooms. *In room:* TV w/pay movies, minibar, hair dryer, iron, safe.

EXPENSIVE

Portofino Beach Hotel 🌟 This oceanfront inn, built in a former seaside rail station, is steps away from the Newport Pier, along a stretch of bars and equipment-rental shacks; the beach is across the parking lot. The place maintains a calm, European air even in the face of the midsummer beach frenzy. Although it can get noisy in summer, there are advantages to being at the center of the action. The hotel has its own enclosed parking, and sunsets are spectacular viewed from a plush armchair in the upstairs parlor. Guest rooms, furnished with antique reproductions, are on the second floor—the first is occupied by a guests-only bar and several cozy sitting rooms—and most have luxurious sky-lit bathrooms.

2306 W. Ocean Front, Newport Beach, CA 92663. ℂ **800/571-8749** or 949/673-7030. Fax 949/723-4370. www.portofinobeachhotel.com. 20 units. $159–$279 double. Rates include continental breakfast. Free parking. AE, DC, DISC, MC, V. **Amenities:** Jacuzzi; coin-op laundry and laundry service; dry cleaning. *In room:* A/C, TV.

MODERATE

Blue Lantern Inn 🌟 A three-story New England-style gray clapboard inn, the Blue Lantern is a pleasant cross between romantic B&B and sophisticated small hotel. Almost all the rooms, which are decorated with reproduction traditional furniture and plush bedding, have a balcony or deck overlooking the harbor. Each has a fireplace and whirlpool tub. You can have your breakfast here in private (clad in the fluffy robe provided), or go downstairs to the sunny dining room that also serves complimentary afternoon tea. There is an exercise room and a cozy lounge with menus for many area restaurants. The friendly staff welcomes you with home-baked cookies at the front desk.

34343 St. of the Blue Lantern, Dana Point, CA 92629. ⓒ 800/950-1236 or 949/661-1304. Fax 949/496-1483. www.foursisters.com. 29 units. $150–$500 double. Rates include full breakfast and afternoon wine and hors d'oeuvres. AE, DC, MC, V. **Amenities:** Jacuzzi; exercise room; complimentary bikes; laundry service; dry cleaning. *In room:* A/C, TV/VCR, minibar, coffeemaker, hair dryer.

Casa Laguna ⭐ Once you see this romantic terraced complex of Spanish-style cottages amid lush gardens and secluded patios—which offers all the amenities of a B&B *and* affordable prices—you might wonder: What's the catch? Well, the noise of busy PCH wafts easily into Casa Laguna, which might prove disturbing to sensitive ears and light sleepers. Still, the Casa has been a favorite hideaway since Laguna's early days, and now glows under the watchful eye of a terrific owner, who's been upping the comfort ante. Some rooms—especially the suites—are downright luxurious, with fireplace, kitchen, bathrobes, CD player, VCR, and other in-room goodies. Throughout the property, Catalina tile adorns fountains and bougainvillea spills into paths; each room has an individual charm. Breakfast is served in the sunny morning room of the Craftsman-style Mission House, where a cozy living room also invites relaxation and conversation.

2510 S. Coast Hwy., Laguna Beach, CA 92651. ⓒ 800/233-0449 or 949/494-2996. Fax 949/494-5009. 21 units. $120–$195 double; $195–$295 suite. Rates include breakfast, afternoon wine, and hors d'oeuvres. Off-season and midweek discounts available. AE, DISC, MC, V. **Amenities:** Heated outdoor pool; Jacuzzi. *In room:* TV.

Doryman's Inn Bed & Breakfast The rooms at Doryman's Inn are both luxurious and romantic, making this one of the nicest B&Bs to be found anywhere. The rooms are outfitted with French and American antiques, floral textiles, beveled mirrors, and cozy furnishings. Every room has a working fireplace and a sunken marble tub (some have whirlpool jets). King- or queen-size beds, lots of plants, and good ocean views round out the decor. The location, directly on the Newport Beach Pier Promenade, is also enviable, though some may find it a bit too close to the action. Breakfast includes fresh pastries and fruit, brown eggs, yogurt, cheeses, and international coffees and teas.

2102 W. Ocean Front, Newport Beach, CA 92663. ⓒ 949/675-7300. www.dorymansinn.com. 10 units. $175–$295 double; from $325 suite. Rates include continental breakfast. AE, MC, V. Free parking. **Amenities:** Restaurant. *In room:* A/C, TV.

WHERE TO DINE

Options in Seal Beach are limited, but a good choice for seafood is **Walt's Wharf,** 201 Main St. (ⓒ **562/598-4433**), a bustling, polished restaurant featuring market-fresh selections either plain or with Pacific Rim accents.

EXPENSIVE

5'0" (Five Feet) ⭐⭐ CALIFORNIA/ASIAN While 5'0" may no longer break culinary ground, the kitchen still combines the best in California cuisine with Asian technique and ingredients. The restaurant has a minimalist, almost-industrial decor that's brightened by a friendly staff and splendid cuisine. Menu selections run the gamut from tea-smoked filet mignon topped with Roquefort cheese and candied walnuts to a hot Thai-style mixed grill of veal, beef, lamb, and chicken stir-fried with sweet peppers, onions, and mushrooms in curry-mint sauce. The menu changes daily, but you can always find the house specialty, whole braised catfish. ©

328 Glenneyre, Laguna Beach. © **949/497-4955**. Reservations recommended. Main courses $18–$30. AE, DC, DISC, MC, V. Sun–Thurs 5–10pm, Fri–Sat 5–11pm.

Roy's of Newport Beach ⭑ HAWAIIAN REGIONAL/PACIFIC RIM   Any foodie who's been to Hawaii in the past decade knows the name Roy Yamaguchi, father of Hawaiian Regional Cuisine (HRC) and the islands' answer to Wolfgang Puck. Roy's empire expanded to Southern California in 1999, with the opening of this dinner-only restaurant on the fringe of Fashion Island shopping center. Yamaguchi developed a menu that represents his groundbreaking East/West/Polynesian cuisine but can be reliably executed by chefs in far-flung kitchens. Most of each night's specials are fresh Pacific fish, given the patented HRC touch with Japanese, Thai, and even Latin accents. Signature dishes include island-style ahi poke, spicy Mongolian-glazed rack of lamb, and blackened yellowfin tuna in soy-mustard-butter sauce. The bar whips up "vacation" cocktails in tropical colors, and there's a to-die-for chocolate soufflé dessert.

453 Newport Center Dr., Fashion Island. © **949/640-ROYS**. Reservations suggested. Main courses $16–$29. AE, DC, DISC, MC, V. Mon–Thurs 5–10pm, Fri–Sat 5–11pm.

MODERATE

Crab Cooker SEAFOOD   Since 1951, folks in search of fresh, well-prepared seafood have headed to this bright-red former bank building. Also a fish market, the Crab Cooker has a casual atmosphere of humble wooden tables, uncomplicated smoked and grilled preparations, and meticulously selected fresh fare. The place is especially proud of its Maryland crab cakes; clams and oysters are also part of the repertoire.

2200 Newport Blvd., Newport Beach. © **949/673-0100**. Main courses $8–$19 lunch, $10–$25 dinner. AE, MC, V. Sun–Thurs 11am–9pm, Fri–Sat 11am–10pm.

Harbor Grill SEAFOOD/STEAK   Located in a business/commercial mall right in the center of the pretty Dana Point Marina, the Harbor Grill is enthusiastically recommended by locals for mesquite-broiled, ocean-fresh seafood. Hawaiian mahimahi with a mango-chutney baste is on the menu, along with Pacific swordfish, crab cakes, and beef steaks.

34499 St. of the Golden Lantern, Dana Point. © **949/240-1416**. www.harborgrill.com. Reservations recommended. Main courses $10–$20. AE, DC, DISC, MC, V. Mon–Sat 11:30am–10pm, Sun 9am–10pm.

Las Brisas *Moments* MEXICAN SEAFOOD   Las Brisas' breathtaking view of the Pacific (particularly at sunset) and potent margaritas are a sure-fire combination for a *muy romantico* evening. In fact, it's so popular that it can get pretty crowded during the summer months, so be sure to make reservation. Affordable during lunch but pricey at dinner, the menu consists mostly of seafood recipes from the Mexican Riviera. Even the standard enchiladas and tacos get a zesty update with crab or lobster meat and fresh herbs. Calamari steak is sautéed with bell peppers, capers, and herbs in a garlic-butter sauce, and king salmon is mesquite broiled and served with a creamy lime sauce. Although a bit on the touristy side, Las Brisas can be a fun part of the Laguna Beach experience.

361 Cliff Dr. (off the Calif. 1 N of Laguna Canyon), Laguna Beach. © **949/497-5434**. Reservations recommended. Main courses $10–$24. AE, DC, DISC, MC, V. Mon–Sat 8am–10:30pm, Sun 9am–10:30pm.

INEXPENSIVE

Ramos House Cafe 🎃🎃 REGIONAL AMERICAN   Hidden away in the historic Rios district next to the train tracks, this converted 1881 cottage brings the flavor of a simpler time to busy Orange County. The small seasonal menu of regional American favorites utilizes garden-grown herbs, house-baked breads, and hand-turned ice cream. The all-purpose breakfast/lunch menu (dinner only for special events) features warmly satisfying cinnamon-apple beignets, wild-mushroom and sun-dried-tomato omelets, fried green tomatoes sauced with goat cheese, Southern fried chicken salad bathed in pumpkin seed–buttermilk dressing, shrimp and sourdough bread pudding, an always changing but always superb fresh soup, and more comfort-food faves with a Southern flair. Seating is outside, on a tree-shaded brick garden patio that invites leisure.

31752 Los Rios St. (off Del Obispo St.), San Juan Capistrano. © **949/443-1342.** Main courses $5–$10. AE, DC, DISC, MC, V. Tues–Sun 8am–3pm.

15

The Southern California Desert

by Stephanie Avnet Yates

To the casual observer, Southern California's desert seems desolate—nothing but vast landscapes baking under a relentless sun. Its splendor is subtle, though; you have to discover its beauty in your own time. For some travelers it will be the surprising lushness of trees, flowering cacti, fragrant shrubs, and other plants—many of them unique to the region—that have adapted ingeniously to the harsh climate. The unique Joshua tree, which some deem majestic and others call ugly, thrives in the upper Mojave Desert. Each spring, the ground throughout the Lancaster area is carpeted with the brilliant golds and oranges of the poppy, California's state flower. Like the autumn leaves in New England, the poppies draw seasonal tourists in droves.

If it looks as though nothing except insects could survive here, look again: You're bound to see a speedy roadrunner or a tiny gecko dart across your path. Close your eyes and listen for the cry of a hawk or an owl. Check the ground for coyote or bobcat tracks. Notice the sparkle of fish in the streams running through flourishing palm oases. Check the road signs, which warn of desert tortoise crossings. The tortoise is just one of the many endangered species found only here; fortunately, most of the Southern California desert's flora and fauna is protected by the federal government in a wildlife sanctuary.

Perhaps the beauty you seek is that of personal renewal in the spectacular desert landscape. Whether it's in the shadow of purple-tinged mountains, amid otherworldly rock formations, or beside a sparkling swimming pool, you'll find as much or as little to occupy your time as you desire. Destinations range from gloriously untouched national parks to ultra-luxurious resorts—and it's a rare day when the sun doesn't shine out here.

1 En Route to the Palm Springs Resorts

If you're making the drive from Los Angeles via I-10, your first hour or so will be spent just, well, getting out of the LA metropolitan sprawl. Soon you'll leave the Inland Empire auto plazas behind, sail past the last of the bedroom-community shopping malls, and edge ever closer to the snowcapped (if you're lucky) San Bernardino and San Jacinto mountain ranges. (Coming from San Diego via I-15, the area discussed below is east of the junction with I-10.)

For frequent travelers on this stretch of highway, there are certain unmistakable signposts. Roadside attractions are part of what makes every moment of the vacation enjoyable. Below are three of my favorites.

Desert Hills Premium Outlets   Factory-outlet malls are all the rage among bargain-hunters, and this one is truly a cut above the rest—or maybe it's just so

---

Fun Fact   *Jurassic Park* **in the Desert**

As the cities give way to pale, dry desert, keep your eyes peeled for the dinosaurs that stand guard over the **Wheel Inn Restaurant** (② **760/ 849-7012**), in Cabazon. That's right, a four-story-tall brontosaurus and his Tyrannosaurus rex pal. You can even climb into the belly of the larger one, where you'll find a remarkably spacious gift shop.

---

massive, the schlock gets lost in the shuffle. Pick up a map to help navigate this two-part behemoth, or you may find yourself browsing Timberland when you'd rather be shopping the Gap. Some of my faves: Kenneth Cole, J. Crew, Eddie Bauer, Coach, Barney's New York, A/X Armani Exchange, Banana Republic, Donna Karan DKNY, Max Studio, Nike, and Quiksilver. The list goes on; there are 15 shoe stores alone here.

But wait, there's more: The newer—but smaller—**Cabazon Outlets** (② 909/ 922-3000; www.cabazonoutlet.com) next door is worth a visit for the Crate & Barrel outlet and others including Adidas and Puma.

48400 Seminole Dr. (off I-10), Cabazon. ② **909/849-6641.** www.premiumoutlets.com. Sun–Thurs 10am–8pm, Fri 10am–9pm, Sat 9am–9pm.

Hadley's Fruit Orchards   This friendly emporium has been a fixture here since 1931. It's always packed with folks shopping for dates, dried fruits, nuts, honey, preserves, and other regional products. A snack bar serves the beloved date shake; there are also plenty of gift-packed treats to carry (or ship) home. (For more about the date mystique, see "Sweet Treat of the Desert: The Coachella Valley Date Gardens" on p. 606.)

48190 Seminole Dr. (off I-10), Cabazon. ② **800/854-5655** or 909/849-5255. www.hadleys.com. Mon–Thurs 8am–8pm, Fri–Sun 8am–9pm.

Windmill Tours   For years, travelers through the San Gorgonio Pass have been struck by an awesome and otherworldly sight: never-ending windmill fields that harness the powerful force of the wind gusting through this passage and convert it to electricity to power air conditioners throughout the Coachella Valley. If you really get a charge from them, consider a unique guided tour offering a look into this alternative energy source. Learn how designers have improved the efficiency of wind turbines (technically they're not windmills, which are used in the production of grain) over the years, and measure those long rotors against the average human height (about 10 people could lie along one span).

Interstate 10 (Indian Ave. exit), Palm Springs. ② **877/449-WIND** or 760/251-1997. www.windmilltours.com. Admission $23 adults, $20 seniors, $15 students, $10 kids under 14. Tours Mon–Sat at 9am, 11am, 1pm, and 3pm (varies seasonally).

2 Get Your Kicks on Historic Route 66

There's a way for nostalgia buffs to take a detour down memory lane on their way to desert destinations: Just eschew the fast-paced, faceless I-10 for a very special interstate highway—Route 66.

It's been immortalized in film, song, literature, memory, and the popular imagination. But is anything really left of this great snaking highway, this dependable, comforting spirit John Steinbeck called "the Mother Road?" What of the path to adventure traveled by Tod and Buz in their trademark red Corvette on the namesake 1960s TV series?

The answer is, yes, it's still there. You just have to be willing to look for it.

Until the final triumph of the multi-lane superslab in the early 1960s, Route 66 was the only automobile route between the windy Chicago shores of Lake Michigan and LA's golden Pacific beaches. "America's Main Street" rambled through eight states, and today, in each one, there are enthusiastic organizations dedicated to preserving its remnants. California is fortunate to have a lengthy stretch of the original highway, many miles of which still proudly wear the designation "California State Highway 66." It's not just weed-split abandoned blacktop, either. These are active streets, often the main commercial drag of the community. Many stretches have become clusters of new home developments, stucco shopping centers, and fast-food chains. Pretty mundane—until you round a curve and unexpectedly see a vintage wood-frame house, perhaps from a pre–Great Depression ranch. There's poignancy here: That house was probably set way back from the road, amidst a shady grove, before highway workers buried the front yard under asphalt.

Other picturesque relics of that bygone era—single-story motels, friendly two-pump gas stations—exist beside their modern neighbors, inviting nostalgia for a slower, simpler time, a time when the vacation began the moment you backed out of the driveway.

ESSENTIALS

THE ROUTE   Our drive begins in Pasadena and ends in downtown San Bernardino, 56 miles west of Palm Springs. In San Bernardino, I-215 intersects Route 66; take it 4 miles south to rejoin I-10 and continue east.

Note: This detour works equally well if your destination is Lake Arrowhead or Big Bear Lake; take I-215 north 3 miles to Calif. 30 and continue into the mountains. For more information, see chapter 14, "Side Trips from Los Angeles." The drive will add anywhere from 30 minutes to 3 hours to your trip, depending on how many relics and photo opportunities you stop to enjoy. Some suitably retro meal suggestions are included in case you want to incorporate lunch into your drive.

VISITOR INFORMATION   For more information, contact the **National Historic Route 66 Federation,** headquartered in the Los Angeles area (© 818/ 352-7232; www.national66.com). There's also a quarterly *Route 66 Magazine;* for information, call © 520/635-4322 or visit www.route66magazine.com.

LET'S HIT THE ROAD!

Although Route 66 officially ended at the picturesque Pacific, there are very few reminders left in the heart of LA. Besides, I assume you've already seen the city, so Pasadena is the best point to begin your time-warp experience.

One of my favorite places is the **Fair Oaks Pharmacy,** Fair Oaks Avenue and Mission Street, 1½ miles south of Colorado Boulevard (© **626/799-1414**), a fixture on this street corner since 1915. If you're in the mood for a treat, try an authentic ice-cream soda, a sparkling phosphate, a "Route 66" sundae, or an old-fashioned malt (complete with the frosty mixing can), all served by fresh-faced soda jerks from behind the marble counter. They also serve soup, sandwiches, and other snacks. The Fair Oaks is still a dispensing pharmacy and offers a variety of charming gifts, including an abundance of Route 66–themed items. It's open Monday through Saturday from 9am to 6pm, Sunday from 11am to 6pm.

Perhaps you'd like some appropriate driving music, or a souvenir to help you reminisce about your Route 66 experience later. If so, there's no better place than **Canterbury Records,** 805 E. Colorado Blvd., a block west of Lake Avenue

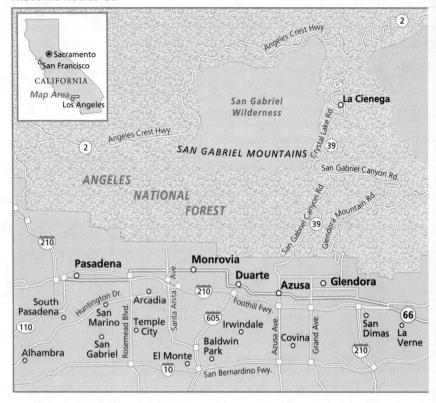

(☎ **626/792-7184**). It has LA's finest selection of big bands and pop vocalists on CD and cassette; perhaps you'll choose one of the many renditions of Bobby Troup's homage, "(Get Your Kicks on) Route 66." The store is open Monday through Friday from 9am to 8pm, Saturday from 9am to 6pm, and Sunday from 10am to 5pm.

As you continue east on Colorado Boulevard, keep your eyes peeled for **motels** like the Saga Motor Hotel, Swiss Lodge, Siesta Inn, Astro (fabulous *Jetsons*-style architecture), and Hi-Way Host. In fact, lodgings have proven the hardiest post-66 survivors, and you'll be seeing many unique frozen-in-time motor courts along the way.

Turn left on Rosemead Boulevard, passing under the freeway (boo, hiss) to Foothill Boulevard. Turning right, you'll soon be among the tree-lined residential streets of **Arcadia,** home to the Santa Anita Racetrack and the Los Angeles Arboretum, the picturesque former estate of "Lucky" Baldwin, whose Queen Anne cottage has been the setting for many movies and TV shows. Passing into Monrovia, look for the life-size plastic cow on the southeast corner of Mayflower. It marks the drive-thru called **Mike's Dairy**—a splendid example of this auto-age phenomenon. If you're observant, you'll see many drive-thru dairies along my route (mostly Alta-Dena brand). Mike's has all the typical features, including the refrigerated island display case still bearing a vintage DRIFTWOOD DAIRY PRODUCTS price sign.

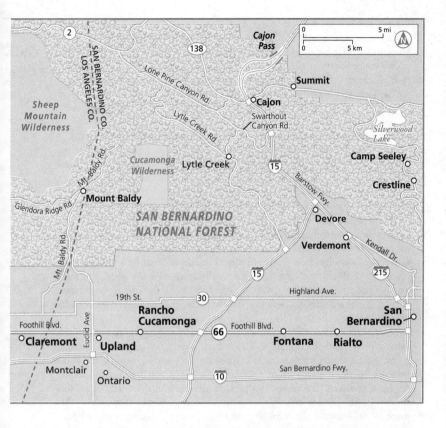

Next, look for Magnolia Avenue and the outrageous **Aztec Hotel** on the northwest corner. Opened in 1925, the Aztec was a local showplace, awing guests with its overscale, dark, Native American–themed lobby; garish Mayan murals; and exotic Brass Elephant bar. An arcade of shops once held the city's most prominent barbershop, beauty salon, and pharmacy. Little has changed about the interior, and a glance behind the front desk will reveal the original cord-and-plug telephone switchboard still in use. If you care to wet your whistle, stop into the bar before continuing on.

Leaving the Aztec, you'll pass some splendid Craftsman bungalows and other historic homes. The street dead-ends at Mountain Avenue; turn right to catch up with the 1930s alignment of Route 66. Make a left turn on Huntington Drive, and look out for **The Trails,** a prime example of the "wagon wheel–Wild West" theme restaurants. Its super-tall DINING sign will let you know when you're getting close. Now you're in **Duarte,** where Huntington Drive is lit by graceful and ornate double street lamps on the center median. This stretch also has many fabulous old motor courts; see if you can spot the Filly, Ranch Inn, Evergreen, and Capri.

Crossing over the wide but nearly dry San Gabriel River, glance right from the bridge to see cars streaming along the interstate that supplanted Route 66. In Irwindale—which smells just like the industrial area it is, with manufacturing plants ranging from a Miller brewery to Health Valley Foods—the street resumes the Foothill Boulevard name, and you'll pass into Azusa. Look for the elegant 1932 **Azusa City Hall and Auditorium,** whose vintage lampposts and Moorish fountain enhance a charming courtyard.

Our route swerves right onto Alosta Avenue at the **Foothill Drive-In Theater,** Southern California's last single-screen drive-in. As you cruise by, think of the days when our cars were an extension of our living rooms (with the great snacks Mom wouldn't allow at home), and the outdoor theaters were filled every summer evening by dusk.

Continuing on Alosta, you'll enter Glendora, named in 1887 by founder George Whitcomb for his wife, Ledora. Look for the **Palm Tropics,** one of the best-maintained old motels along the route. On the northeast corner of Grand Avenue stands the "world-famous" **Derby East** restaurant. It's not affiliated with the legendary Hollywood watering hole, but was clearly built in the 1940s to capitalize on both its famous namesake and the nearby Santa Anita Racetrack. Farther along on the left-hand side is the **Golden Spur,** which began 70 years ago as a ride-up hamburger stand for the equestrian crowd. Unfortunately, the restaurant has been remodeled in boring stucco, leaving only the original sign, with its neon cowboy boot, as a reminder of its colorful past. In a block or two, you'll pass briefly through San Dimas, a ranch-like community where you must pay attention to the HORSE CROSSING street signs. At the corner of Cataract Avenue, a covered wagon announces the **Pinnacle Peak** restaurant, guarded by a giant steer atop the roof.

Don't blink, because almost immediately the street rejoins Foothill Boulevard, passing underneath the ramps to I-210 (boo, hiss); now you're in La Verne, home of **La Paloma** Mexican cafe, a fixture on the route for many years. Continue on to the community of Claremont, known these days for the highly respected group of **Claremont Colleges.** You'll pass several of them along this eucalyptus-lined boulevard. In days gone by, drivers would cruise along this route for mile upon mile, through orchards and open fields, the scenery punctuated only by ambling livestock or a rustic wood fence.

At Benson Avenue in Upland, a classic **1950s-style McDonald's** stands on the southeast corner, its golden arches flanking a low, white, walk-up counter with outdoor stools. The fast-food chain has its roots in this region: Richard and Maurice McDonald opened their first burger joint in San Bernardino in 1939. The successful brothers expanded their business, opening locations throughout Southern California, until entrepreneur Ray Kroc purchased the chain in 1955 and franchised McDonald's nationwide. Farther along, look north at the intersection of Euclid Avenue for the regal **monument to pioneer women.**

Pretty soon you'll be cruising through Rancho Cucamonga, whose fertile soil still yields a reliable harvest. You might see impromptu **produce stands** springing up by the side of the road; stop and pick up a fresh snack. If you're blessed with clear weather, gaze north at the gentle slope of the **San Gabriel Mountains** and you'll understand how Foothill Boulevard got its name. The construction codes in this community are among the most stringent in California, designed to respect the region's heritage and restrict runaway development. All new buildings are Spanish-Mediterranean in style and amply landscaped. At the corner of San Bernardino Road, the playful architectural bones of a wonderful old service station can't be obscured by the flashy car-stereo/cellphone store that inhabits it now. Across the street is the **Sycamore Inn,** nestled in a grove of trees and looking very much like an old-style stagecoach stop. This reddish-brown wooden house, dating from 1848, has been a private home and gracious inn; today, it serves the community of Cucamonga as a restaurant and civic hall.

Rancho Cucamonga has earnestly preserved two historic wineries. First you'll see the **Thomas Vineyards,** at the northeast corner of Vineyard Avenue, established in 1839. Legend holds that the first owner mysteriously disappeared, leaving hidden treasure still undiscovered on the property. The winery's preserved structures now hold two eateries, a country crafts store, and a bookstore housed in the former brandy still. Take a minute to stop into the shopping mall behind the Thomas Winery to tour the **Route 66 Territory Museum and Visitor's Bureau** (© 909/592-2090), a mini-museum and gift shop. You'll see lovingly tended exhibits of old gas pumps, road signs, and other relics, plus an array of books, maps, glassware, garments, jewelry, and other souvenirs. Many items bear the original black-on-white Route 66 shield, the ubiquitous highway marker purged from the old route by state transportation officials in 1984. The brown markers you see today were subsequently placed by the historical associations.

Continuing on to Hellman Avenue, look for the **New Kansan Motel** (on the northeast corner). With that name, it must have seemed welcoming to Dust Bowl refugees. Near the northwest corner of Archibald Avenue, you'll find lonely remnants of a **1920s-era gas station.** Empty now, those service bays have seen many a Ford, Studebaker, and Packard in need of a helping hand. Next you'll pass the **Virginia Dare Winery,** at the northwest corner of Haven Avenue, whose structures now house part of a large business park/shopping mall, but retain the flourish of the original (1830s) winery logo.

Soon you'll pass the I-15 junction and be driving through Fontana, whose name in Italian means "fountain city." There isn't too much worth stopping for along this stretch, but definitely slow down to have a look at the **motor-court hotels** lining both sides of the road. They're of various vintages, all built to cater to the once-vigorous stream of travelers passing through. Although today they're dingy, the melody of their names conjures up those glory days: Ken-Tuck-U-Inn, Rose Motel, Moana, Dragon, Sand & Sage, Sunset, 40 Winks, and Redwing.

After entering Rialto, be on the lookout for Meriden Avenue, site of the fanciful **Wigwam Motel.** Built in the 1950s (along with an identical twin motor court in Holbrook, Ariz.), the whimsy of these stucco tepees lured many a road-weary traveler in for the night. Its catchy slogan, "Sleep in a wigwam, get more for your wampum," has been supplanted today by the more to-the-point "Do it in a teepee." But, as with many of the motor courts we'll pass on this drive, you need only picture a few large, shiny Buicks, T-bird convertibles, and "woodie"

Take a Break

If all this driving has made you hungry, consider the **Magic Lamp Inn,** 8189 Foothill Blvd. (© **909/981-8659),** open for lunch and dinner Tuesday through Friday and dinner only on Saturday and Sunday. Built in 1957, the Magic Lamp offers excellent Continental cuisine (nothing nouvelle about Route 66!) in a setting that's part manor house and part *Aladdin* theme park. Dark, stately dining rooms lurk behind a funky banquette cocktail lounge punctuated by a psychedelic fountain/fire pit and a panoramic view. The genie-bottle theme is everywhere, from the restaurant's dinnerware to the plush carpeting, which would be right at home in a Las Vegas casino. Lovers of kitsch and hearty retro fare shouldn't pass this one up.

station wagons pulling in for the night and your imagination will drift back to days gone by.

Soon Foothill Boulevard will become Fifth Street, a sign that you're nearing **San Bernardino,** which must have been a welcome sight for hot and weary westbound travelers emerging from the Mojave Desert. Route 66 wriggled through the steep Cajon Pass into a land fragrant with orange groves, where agricultural prosperity had quickly earned this region a lasting sobriquet: "the Inland Empire."

The year 1928 saw the grand opening of an elegant movie palace, the **California Theatre,** 562 W. Fourth St., only a block from Route 66. From Fifth Street east, turn right at E Street, then make a right on Fourth Street, where you can pull over to view the theater. Lovingly restored and still popular for nostalgic live entertainment and the rich tones of its original Wurlitzer pipe organ, the California was a frequent site of Hollywood "sneak previews." Humorist Will Rogers made his last public appearance here, in 1935. (Following his death, the highway was renamed the "Will Rogers Memorial Hwy." in his honor, but it remained popularly known as Route 66.) Notice the intricate relief of the theater's stone facade, and peek into the lobby to see the red velvet draperies, rich carpeting, and gold-banistered double staircase leading up to the balcony.

The theater is the last stop on your time-warp driving tour. Continue west on Fourth Street to the superslab highway only 2½ blocks away—that's I-215, your entry back to the present (see "Essentials," above).

3 The Palm Springs Desert Resorts

120 miles E of LA; 135 miles NE of San Diego

Palm Springs had been known for years as a golf-course-studded retirement mecca that's invaded annually by raucous hordes of libidinous college kids on spring break. Well, the city of Palm Springs has been quietly changing its image and attracting a whole new crowd. Former mayor Sonny Bono's revolutionary "anti-thong" ordinance in 1991 put a lightning-quick halt to the spring-break migration by eliminating public display of the bare coed derrière, and the upscale fairway-condo crowd has decided to congregate in the tony outlying resort cities of Rancho Mirage, Palm Desert, Indian Wells, and La Quinta.

These days, there are no billboards allowed in Palm Springs itself, all the palm trees in the center of town are appealingly backlit at night, and you won't see the word "motel" on any establishment. Senior citizens are everywhere, dressed to the nines in brightly colored leisure suits and keeping alive the retro-kitsch establishments from the days when Elvis, Liberace, and Sinatra made the balmy desert a swingin' place. But they're not alone: Baby boomers and yuppies nostalgic for the kidney-shaped swimming pools and backyard luaus of the Eisenhower/Kennedy glory years are buying ranch-style vacation homes and restoring them to their 1950s splendor. Hollywood's young glitterati are returning, too. Today, the city fancies itself a European-style resort with a dash of good ol' American small town thrown in for good measure—think *Jetsons* architecture and the crushed-velvet vibe of piano bars with the colors and attitude of a laid-back Aegean island village. One thing hasn't changed: Swimming, sunbathing, golfing, and playing tennis are still the primary pastimes in this convenient little oasis.

Another important presence in Palm Springs has little to do with socialites and Americana. The Agua Caliente band of Cahuilla Indians settled in this area

The Palm Springs Desert Resorts

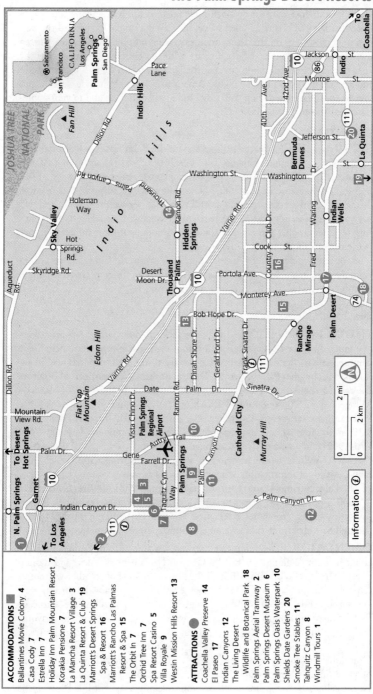

1,000 years before the first golf ball was ever teed up. Recognizing the beauty and spirituality of this wide-open space, they lived a simple life around the natural mineral springs on the desert floor, migrating into the cool canyons during the hot summer months. Under a treaty with the railroad companies and the U.S. government, the tribe owns half the land on which Palm Springs is built and actively works to preserve Native American heritage. It's easy to learn about the American Indians during your visit, and it will definitely add to your appreciation of this part of California.

ESSENTIALS

GETTING THERE   Several airlines service the **Palm Springs Regional Airport,** 3400 E. Tahquitz Canyon Way (© 760/323-8161), including **Alaska Airlines** (© 800/426-0333; www.alaskaair.com), **America West** (© 800/235-9292; www.americawest.com), **Delta/Skywest** (© 800/453-9417; www.delta.com), **United Express** (© 800/241-6522; www.united.com), and **US Airways Express** (© 800/428-4322; www.usairways.com). Flights from Los Angeles International Airport take about 40 minutes. For more information, see "Orientation," in chapter 13, "Los Angeles."

If you're driving from Los Angeles, take I-10 east to the Calif. 111 turnoff to Palm Springs. You'll breeze into town on North Palm Canyon Drive, the main thoroughfare. The trip from downtown Los Angeles takes about 2 hours. If you're driving from San Diego, take I-15 north to I-10 east; it takes a little more than 2 hours.

VISITOR INFORMATION   Be sure to pick up *Palm Springs Life* magazine's free monthly, *Desert Guide.* It contains tons of visitor information, including a comprehensive calendar of events. Copies are distributed in hotels and newsstands and by the **Palm Springs Desert Resorts Convention & Visitors Bureau,** in the Atrium Design Centre, 69930 Calif. 111, Suite 201, Rancho Mirage, CA 92270 (© **800/41-RELAX** or 760/770-9000). The bureau's office staff can help with maps, brochures, and advice Monday through Friday from 8:30am to 5pm. They also operate a 24-hour information line (© **760/770-1992**) and a website (www.palmspringsusa.com).

Another website worth browsing is **www.inpalmsprings.com**, which contains a wealth of information designed for locals as well as visitors.

The **Palm Springs Visitors Information Center,** 2781 N. Palm Canyon Dr. (© **800/34-SPRINGS;** www.palm-springs.org), offers maps, brochures, advice, souvenirs, and a free hotel reservation service. The office is open Monday through Saturday from 9am to 5pm and Sunday from 8am to 4pm.

ORIENTATION   The commercial downtown area of Palm Springs stretches about half a mile along North Palm Canyon Drive between Alejo and Ramon streets. The street is one-way through the heart of town, but its other-way counterpart is Indian Canyon Drive, 1 block east. The mountains lie directly west and south, while the rest of Palm Springs is laid out in a grid to the southeast. Palm Canyon forks into South Palm Canyon (leading to the Indian Canyons) and East Palm Canyon (the continuation of Calif. 111) traversing the resort towns of Cathedral City, Rancho Mirage, Palm Desert, Indian Wells, and La Quinta before looping up to rejoin I-10 at Indio. Desert Hot Springs is north of Palm Springs, straight up Gene Autry Trail. Tahquitz Canyon Way creates North Palm Canyon's primary intersection, tracking a straight line between the airport and the heart of town.

WHAT TO SEE & DO
GREAT GOLF COURSES

The Palm Springs desert resorts are world-famous meccas for golfers (see "Fairways & Five-Irons, Desert Style," below). There are nearly 100 public, semiprivate, and private courses in the area. If you're the kind who starts polishing your irons the moment you begin planning your vacation, you're best off staying at one of the valley's many golf resorts, where you can enjoy the proximity of your hotel's facilities as well as smart package deals that can give you a taste of country-club membership. If, on the other hand, you'd like to fit a round of golf into an otherwise varied trip and you aren't staying at a hotel with its own links, there are courses at all levels open to the general public, mostly in Palm Springs. Call ahead to see which will rent clubs or other equipment to the spontaneous player.

Beginners will enjoy **Tommy Jacobs' Bel-Air Greens,** 1001 El Cielo, Palm Springs (© 760/322-6062), a scenic nine-hole, par-32 executive course that has some water- and sand-trap challenges but also allows for a few confidence-boosting successes. Generally flat fairways and mature trees characterize the relatively short (3,350-yd.) course. The complex also offers an 18-hole miniature golf course. Greens fees range from $17 to $19.

Slightly more intermediate amateurs will want to check out the **Tahquitz Creek Golf Resort,** 1885 Golf Club Dr., Palm Springs (© 760/328-1005), whose two diverse courses both appeal to mid-handicappers. The "Legend's" wide, water-free holes will appeal to anyone frustrated by the "target" courses popular with many architects, while the Ted Robinson–designed "Resort" course offers all those accuracy-testing bells and whistles more common to lavish private clubs. Greens fees, including cart, range from $55 to $100, depending on the day of the week.

The **Palm Springs Country Club,** 2500 Whitewater Club Dr. (© 760/323-8625), is the oldest public-access golf course within the city of Palm Springs, and is especially popular with budget-conscious golfers, as greens fees are only $35 to $60, including the required cart. The challenge of bunkers and rough can be amplified by the oft-blowing wind along the 5,885 yards of this unusually laid-out course.

The **Westin Mission Hills Resort Course,** Dinah Shore and Bob Hope drives, Rancho Mirage (© 760/328-3198), is somewhat more forgiving than most of legendary architect Pete Dye's courses, but don't play the back tees unless you've got a consistent 220-yard drive and won't be fazed by the Dye-trademark giant sand bunkers and elevated greens. Water only comes into play on four holes, and the scenery is an exquisite reward for low-handicappers. Non-guest greens fees are $150 to $175, including cart.

One of my favorite desert courses is the **PGA West TPC Stadium Course,** La Quinta Resort & Club, 49499 Eisenhower Dr., La Quinta (© 760/564-4111), which received *Golf* magazine's 1994 Gold Medal Award for the total golf-resort experience. The par-three 17th has a picturesque island green where Lee Trevino made Skins Game history with a spectacular hole-in-one. The rest of Pete Dye's 7,261-yard design is flat, with huge bunkers, lots of water, and severe mounding throughout. Also open for semiprivate play is the **Mountain Course at La Quinta,** another Dye design that regularly appears on U.S. top-100 lists. It's set dramatically against the rocky mountains, which thrust into fairways to create tricky doglegs, and its small Bermuda greens are well guarded by boulders and deep bunkers. Greens fees for non-guests vary seasonally, from $85 to $225, at both La Quinta courses.

Fairways & Five-Irons, Desert Style

Two hours outside of Los Angeles in the Coachella Valley, strung like ripe dates from I-10, lie the resort cities of Palm Springs, Rancho Mirage, Palm Desert, Indian Wells, and La Quinta. This all-season golfer's paradise boasts close to 100 courses, their lush fairways and velvety greens incongruously carved from the arid desert scruff. Both public and resort/semiprivate courses range in difficulty to accommodate low-handicappers and weekend duffers alike, and every imaginable service is available nearby.

If you'd like to sharpen your game, all the principal clubs have resident pros, and there are several schools and clinics, including the **Indian Wells Golf School** at Indian Wells Resort (© 800/241-5782 or 760/346-4653), the **Golf Center at Palm Desert** (© 760/779-1877), and the **Leadbetter Golf Academy** at PGA West in La Quinta (© 800/424-3542 or 760/564-0777). If you're looking to pick up new equipment or some stylish attire, try **Nevada Bob's Discount Golf** in Palm Springs (© 760/324-0196) and Indian Wells (© 760/346-6166), the **Roger Dunn Golf Shop** in Palm Desert (© 760/345-3133) and Cathedral City (© 760/324-1160), and **Lady Golf** in Rancho Mirage (© 760/773-4949).

Many fine resorts offer generous golf packages, among them **Marriott's Desert Springs Spa & Resort** in Palm Desert (© 760/341-2211), **Marriott's Rancho Las Palmas Resort & Spa** in Rancho Mirage (© 760/568-2727), the **Hyatt Grand Champions** in Indian Wells (© 760/341-1000), **La Quinta Resort & Club** in La Quinta (© 760/346-2904), and the **Estrella Inn** (© 800/237-3687 or 760/320-4417).

Tee times at many courses cannot be booked more than a few days in advance for non-guests, but **Golf à la Carte** (© 877/887-6900 or

A complete **golfer's guide** is available from the Palm Springs Desert Resorts Convention & Visitors Bureau (see "Visitor Information," above).

MORE OUTDOOR FUN

The Coachella Valley Desert is truly a playground, and what follows is but a sampling of the opportunities to enjoy the abundant sunshine during your vacation here. But the strong sun and dry air that are so appealing can also sneak up on you in the form of sunburn and heat exhaustion. Especially during the summer, but even in milder times, always carry and drink plenty of water.

BALLOONING   This is perhaps the most memorable way to see the desert: floating above the landscape in a colorful hot-air balloon. Choose from specialty themes like sunrise, sunset, or romantic champagne flights. Rides are offered by **Dream Flights** (© 800/933-5628 or 760/321-5154; www.dreamflights.com), and **Fantasy Balloon Flights** (© 800/GO-ABOVE or 760/568-0997). Rates range from $145 to $160 per person.

BICYCLING   The clean, dry air just cries out to be enjoyed—what could be better than to pedal your way around town or into the desert? **Adventure Bike Tours** (© 760/328-0282) will outfit you with a bike, helmet, souvenir water bottle, and certified guide. Tours, which meet at local hotels, start at about $40,

760/320-8713; www.palmspringsgolf.com) is able to make arrangements several months earlier and even construct a custom package for you with accommodations, golf, meals, and other extras. A valuable service for the budget traveler is **Stand-By Golf** (© **866/244-2665** or 760/321-2665; www.stand-bygolf.com), which helps more than 35 area courses—including prestigious semi-private and resort courses—fill their bookings by offering players a last-minute discount of up to 50%. Most tee times are for the same or next day; call between 7am and 9pm daily.

For the non-playing spectator (or anyone longing to see the pros make it look *so* easy), there are dozens of golf tournaments year-round, including many celebrity and pro-am events in addition to regular PGA, LPGA, and Senior Tour stops. February brings the PGA Tour's **Bob Hope Chrysler Classic** at the Bermuda Dunes Country Club and the **Frank Sinatra Celebrity Invitational** at Marriott's Desert Springs Resort & Spa. In March, catch the LPGA Tour's **Kraft Nabisco Championship** at the Mission Hills Country Club; in April, the Senior PGA's **Liberty Mutual Legends of Golf** comes to PGA West. November brings two of the desert's longest-running charity events: the **24th Annual Frostig Center/Chris Korman Celebrity Tournament,** at the Westin Mission Hills; and the **Billy Barty/7-Up Celebrity Golf Classic,** at the Mesquite Country Club in Palm Springs. Also in November, check out the wacky **Palm Desert Golf Cart Parade** along El Paseo.

For more information, you can call the Palm Springs Desert Resorts Convention and Visitors Bureau (© **800/41-RELAX** or 760/770-9000; www.palmspringsusa.com). The bureau also maintains an activities hot line (© **760/770-1992**).

and bike rentals are $10 per hour or $28 for the day. If you're just looking to rent some wheels and a helmet, **Mac's Bicycle Rental,** 79953 Calif. 111, between Country Club and Frank Sinatra drives (© **760/321-9444**), rents bikes for the hour ($7), the day ($19), or the week ($65), and offers children's and mountain models. The **Bighorn Bicycle Rental & Tour Company,** 302 N. Palm Canyon (© **760/325-3367**), has hourly ($7) and daily ($27) rental rates in addition to guided bike treks (a 4-hr. guided ride/hike is $45 per person including all equipment and snacks).

A FAMILY WATER PARK   **Palm Springs Oasis Waterpark,** off I-10 south on Gene Autry Trail between Ramon Road and East Palm Canyon Drive (© **760/325-7873;** www.oasiswaterresort.com), is a water playground with 12 water slides, body- and board surfing, an inner-tube ride, and more. Dressing rooms, lockers, and private beach cabanas (with food service) are available. Admission is $19 for visitors over 5 feet tall, $12 for kids 3 to 5 feet, and free for kids under 3 feet ($11 for seniors). The park is open from mid-March to Labor Day daily from 11am to 6pm, plus weekends through all of October.

GUIDED JEEP & WAGON EXCURSIONS   Desert Adventures (© **888/ 440-JEEP** or 760/324-JEEP; www.red-jeep.com) offers four-wheel-drive ecotours led by experienced naturalist guides. Your off-road adventure may take you to a replica of an ancient Cahuilla village, the rugged Santa Rosa Mountain roads overlooking the Coachella Valley, or picturesque ravines on the way to the San Andreas Fault. Tours range in duration from 2 to 4 hours and in price from $79 to $129. Advance reservations are required. The company's trademark red Jeeps depart from the Desert Adventures Ranch on South Palm Canyon near the entrance to the Indian Canyons, but most of the longer excursions include hotel pickup and return.

Covered Wagon Tours (① 800/367-2161 or 760/347-2161; www.covered wagontours.com) embraces the pioneer spirit with a 2-hour ride through the Coachella Valley Nature Preserve followed by a good old-fashioned barbecue and live country music. The tours take place 7 days a week from October to mid-May; the cost is $55 for adults, $28 for children ages 7 to 16, and free for kids under 7. Without the "grub," the charge is $40 per adult and $20 per child. Advance reservations are required.

HIKING   The most popular spot for hiking is the nearby **Indian Canyons** (① 760/325-5673 for information). The Agua Caliente tribe made their home here centuries ago, and remnants of their simple lifestyle can be seen among the streams, waterfalls, and astounding palm groves in Andreas, Murray, and Palm canyons. Striking rock formations and herds of bighorn sheep and wild ponies will probably be more appealing than the "Trading Post" in Palm Canyon, but it does sell detailed trail maps. This is Indian land, and the Tribal Council charges admission of $6 per adult, with discounts for seniors, children, students, and military. The canyons are closed to visitors from late June to early September.

Don't miss the opportunity to explore the newly re-opened **Tahquitz Canyon** (500 W. Mesquite, west of Palm Canyon Dr.), also an Agua Caliente territory. This incredibly scenic canyon, which features the waterfall filmed for the classic *Lost Horizon,* was closed to the public for nearly 30 years after it became an all-night party zone for hippies, who vandalized land considered sacred—serious injuries also plagued careless canyon squatters. But now the vegetation is renewed and decades' worth of dumping cleaned up, and in 2001 the tribe began offering 2-hour ranger-led hikes into their most spiritual and beautiful place. The canyon is open daily from 7:30am to 5pm, with hikes departing hourly from 8am until 3pm. The fee is $12.50; call ① **760/416-7044** for information and reservations.

Ten miles east of Palm Springs is the 13,000-acre **Coachella Valley Preserve** (① **760/343-1234**), which is open daily from sunrise to sunset. There are springs, mesas, both hiking and riding trails, the Thousand Palms Oasis, a visitor center, and picnic areas.

If you're heading up to Joshua Tree National Park (see section 4, later in this chapter), consider stopping at the **Big Morongo Canyon Preserve** (① **760/ 363-7190**), which was once an Indian village and later a cattle ranch. It's open to visitors Wednesday through Sunday from 7:30am to sundown. The park's high water table makes it a magnet for birds and other wildlife; the lush springs and streams are an unexpected desert treat.

HORSEBACK RIDING   Equestrians from novice to advanced can experience the natural solitude and quiet of the desert on horseback at **Smoke Tree Stables** (① **760/327-1372**). Located south of downtown and ideal for exploring the nearby Indian Canyon trails, Smoke Tree offers guided rides for $25 per hour. But don't expect your posse leader to be primed with facts on the nature you'll encounter—this is strictly a do-it-yourself experience.

Here's the Rub: Two Bunch Palms Desert Spa

Since the time of the Native American Cahuilla, who knew how great it felt to soak in the Coachella Valley's natural hot springs, this desert has drawn stressed-out masses seeking relaxation, rejuvenation, and the pure sigh-inducing pleasure only a health spa can deliver. My number-one, I-can't-recommend-it-enough choice is heavenly **Two Bunch Palms.** Posh yet intimate, this spiritual sanctuary in Desert Hot Springs (about 20 min. north of Palm Springs) has been drawing weary city dwellers since Chicago mobster Al Capone hid out here in the 1930s. Two Bunch Palms later became a playground for the movie community, but today it's a friendly and informal haven offering renowned spa services, quiet bungalows nestled on lush grounds, and trademark lagoons of steaming mineral water. Service is famously—and excellently—discreet; and legions of return guests will attest that the outstanding spa treatments (nine varieties of massage, mud baths, body wraps, facials, salt rubs, and more) and therapeutic waters are what make the luxury of Two Bunch Palms irresistible. Room rates start at $175 (including breakfast) in the high season, with midweek and substantial seasonal discounts available. Spa treatments typically cost between $75 to $100 per hour, and money-saving room/meal/spa packages are always offered. Don't want to stay over? Then book one of Two Bunch's new 6-hour Day Spa packages. The resort is located off Palm Drive (Gene Autry Trail) at 67425 Two Bunch Palms Trail (© 800/472-4334 or 760/329-8791; www.twobunchpalms.com).

TENNIS   Virtually all the larger hotels and resorts have tennis courts; but if you're staying at a B&B, you might want to play at the **Tennis Center,** 1300 Baristo Rd., Palm Springs (© **760/320-0020**), which has nine courts and offers day and evening clinics for adults, juniors, and seniors, as well as ball machines for solo practice. USPTA pros are on hand.

If you'd like to play for free, the night-lit courts at **Palm Springs High School,** 2248 E. Ramon Rd., are open to the public on weekends, holidays, and in summer. There are also eight free night-lit courts in beautiful **Ruth Hardy Park** at Tamarisk and Caballero streets.

EXPLORING THE AREA

The Living Desert Wildlife and Botanical Park 🄰 *Kids*   This 1,200-acre desert reserve, museum, zoo, and educational center is designed to acquaint visitors with the unique habitats that make up the Southern California deserts. You can walk or take a tram tour through sectors that re-create life in several distinctive desert zones. See and learn about a dizzying variety of plants, insects, and wildlife, including bighorn sheep, mountain lions, rattlesnakes, lizards, owls, golden eagles, and the ubiquitous roadrunner. It's a non-stuffy learning experience for kids, and an interesting way for anyone to learn about the surrounding landscape.

47900 Portola Ave., Palm Desert. © 760/346-5694. www.livingdesert.org. Admission $8.50 adults, $7.50 seniors age 62 and over, $4.25 children 3–12, free for kids under 3. Reduced summer rates available. Daily 9am–5pm (last entrance 4:30pm); summer (June 16–Aug) 8am–1pm. Closed Dec 25.

Sweet Treat of the Desert: The Coachella Valley Date Gardens

In a splendid display of both wishful thinking and clever engineering, the Coachella Valley has grown into a rich agricultural region, known internationally for grapefruit, figs, and grapes—but mostly for dates. Entrepreneurs, fascinated with Arabian lore and fueled by the Sahara-like conditions of the desert around Indio, planted the area's date palm groves in the 1920s. Launched with just a few parent trees imported from the Middle East, the groves now produce 95% of the world's date crop.

Farmers hand-pollinate the trees, and the resulting precious fruit is bundled in wind-protective paper while still on the tree, which makes an odd sight indeed. You'll see them along Calif. 111 through Indio, where the road is sometimes referred to as the "Date Highway."

For decades, **Shields Date Gardens**, 80225 Calif. 111 (© **760/347-0996**; www.shieldsdates.com), has been enticing visitors into its splendid 1930s Moderne building with banners proclaiming free admission to the continuously running film *The Romance and Sex Life of the Date*. (Fair warning: Its racy title is the best part.) Even if you're not interested in the flick, stop by the lunch counter (date shake, anyone?) and store (which sells an endless variety of dates and related goodies) and sample some date ice cream or date crystals, a mysterious sweet product that seems to have many practical uses—until you actually get it home. But the quality and selection of fresh-harvested dates is superb; I guarantee you'll find yourself snacking on them before long. Open daily from 8am to 6pm.

There's no more picturesque place in the valley to sample dates than **Oasis Date Gardens**, 59111 Calif. 111 (© **800/827-8017** or 760/399-5665), started in 1912 with nine Moroccan trees and now one of the largest commercial date groves in the United States. It's a drive—about 40 minutes from downtown Palm Springs—but there's a lot to do here. Picnic tables dot an inviting lawn, videos illustrate the history and art of date cultivation, and there's a cool palm arboretum and cactus exhibit, plus a petting zoo for impatient youngsters. Many varieties of dates are laid out for free tasting; Oasis also sells date shakes, ice cream, chewy date pie by the slice, homemade chili and sandwiches, and gourmet food gifts from all over the Southwest. Open daily (except Christmas) from 6am to 5:30pm.

Palm Springs Aerial Tramway 🦆🦆 To gain a bird's-eye perspective on the Coachella Valley, take this 14-minute ascent up nearly 5,900 feet to the top of Mount San Jacinto. While the Albert Frey–designed boarding stations retain their 1960s ski-lodge feel, newly installed Swiss funicular cars are sleekly modern and rotate during the trip to allow each passenger a panoramic view. There's a whole other world once you arrive: alpine scenery, a ski lodge–flavored restaurant and gift shop, and temperatures typically 40°F (4°C) cooler than the desert floor. The most dramatic contrast is during the winter, when the mountaintop is a snowy wonderland, irresistible to hikers and bundled-up kids with saucers. The excursion might not be worth the expense during the rest of the year. Guided mule rides and cross-country ski equipment are available at the top.

Tramway Rd. off Hwy. 111, Palm Springs. © **888/515-TRAM** or 760/325-1391. www.pstramway.com. Tickets $21 adults, $19 seniors, $14 children ages 3–12, free for kids under 3; Ride 'n' Dine combination (available after 2:30pm, dinner served after 4pm) $28 adults, $19 children. Mon–Fri 10am–8pm, Sat–Sun 8am–8pm.

Palm Springs Desert Museum ⚑   Unlikely though it may sound, this well-endowed museum is a must-see. Exhibits include world-class Western and Native American art collections, the natural history of the desert, and an outstanding anthropology department, primarily representing the local Cahuilla tribe. Traditional Indian life as it was lived for centuries is illustrated by tools, baskets, and other relics. Check local schedules to find out about visiting exhibits (which are usually excellent). Plays, lectures, and other events are presented in the museum's Annenberg Theater.

101 Museum Dr. (just W of the Palm Canyon/Tahquitz intersection), Palm Springs. © 760/325-7186. www.psmuseum.org. Admission $7.50 adults, $6.50 seniors age 62 and over, $3.50 military and children 6–17, free for children under 6; free to all 1st Fri of each month. Tues–Sat 10am–5pm, Sun noon–5pm.

SHOPPING

Downtown Palm Springs revolves around **North Palm Canyon Drive;** many art galleries, souvenir shops, and restaurants are located here, along with a couple of large-scale hotels and shopping centers. This wide, one-way boulevard is designed for pedestrians, with many businesses set back from the street itself—don't be shy about poking around the little courtyards you'll encounter. On Thursday night from 6 to 10pm, the blocks between Amado and Baristo roads are transformed into **VillageFest,** a street-fair tradition celebrating its sixth anniversary. Handicrafts vendors and aromatic food booths compete for your attention with wacky street performers and even wackier locals shopping at the mouthwatering fresh-produce stalls.

The northern section of Palm Canyon is becoming known for vintage collectibles and is being touted as the **Antique and Heritage Gallery District.** Check out **John's Resale Furnishings,** 891 N. Palm Canyon Dr. (© 760/416-8876), for a glorious collection of midcentury modern furnishings; **Bandini Johnson Gallery,** 895 N. Palm Canyon Dr. (© 760/323-7805), a cramped warren of eclectic treasures; and the **Antiques Center,** 798 N. Palm Canyon Dr. (© 760/323-4443), a discriminating mall-style store whose 35 dealers display wares ranging from vintage linens to handmade African crafts to prized Bakelite jewelry.

Down in Palm Desert lies the delicious excess of **El Paseo,** a glitzy cornucopia of high-rent boutiques, salons, and upscale eateries reminiscent of Rodeo Drive in Beverly Hills, along with a dozen or more major shopping malls just like back home.

Factory-outlet shopping is 20 minutes away in Cabazon (see "En Route to the Palm Springs Resorts," earlier in this chapter).

GAY & LESBIAN LIFE IN PALM SPRINGS

Don't think the local chamber of commerce doesn't recognize that the Palm Springs area is among the current top-three American destinations for gay and lesbian travelers. After just a short while in town, it's easy to see how the gay tourism dollar is courted as aggressively as straight spending. Real-estate agents cater to gay shoppers for vacation properties, while entire condo communities are marketed toward the gay resident. Advertisements for these and scores of other gay-owned businesses can be found in *The Bottom Line,* the desert's free biweekly magazine of articles, events, and community guides for the gay reader, which is available at hotels, at newsstands, and from select merchants.

Throughout the year, events are held that transcend the gay community to include everyone. In March, the **Desert AIDS Walk** benefits the Desert AIDS Project, while the world's largest organized gathering of lesbians coincides with the **Kraft Nabisco Championship.**

Be sure to visit **Village Pride,** 214 E. Arenas Rd. (© 760/323-9120), a coffeehouse and local gathering place. Besides offering a selection of gay- and lesbian-oriented reading material, Village Pride also serves as the lobby for the **Top Hat Playhouse.** This short block of Arenas is home to a score of gay establishments, including **Streetbar** (© 760/320-1266), a neighborhood gathering spot for tourists and locals alike.

Just a few blocks away is a cozy neighborhood of modest homes and small hotels, concentrated on Warm Sands Drive south of Ramon. Known simply as **"Warm Sands,"** this area holds the very nicest "private resorts"—mostly discreet and gated B&B-style inns. Locals recommend the co-ed **El Mirasol,** 525 Warm Sands Dr. (© **800/327-2985** or 760/326-5913), a charming historic resort; or **Sago Palms,** 595 Thornhill Rd. (© **800/626-7246** or 760/323-0224), which is small, quiet, and affordable. The **Bee Charmer,** 1600 E. Palm Canyon Dr. (© **888/321-5699;** www.beecharmer.com), is one of the few all-women resorts in town.

Gay nightlife is everywhere in the valley, and especially raucous on holiday weekends. Pick up *The Bottom Line* for the latest restaurant, nightclub, theater, and special-events listings.

WHERE TO STAY

The city of Palm Springs offers a wide range of accommodations, but I particularly like the inns that have opened as new owners renovate the many fabulous 40- to 60-year-old cottage complexes in the wind-shielded "Tennis Club" area west of Palm Canyon Drive. The other desert-resort cities offer mostly sprawling complexes, many boasting world-class golf, tennis, or spa facilities and multiple on-site restaurants. Most are destinations in and of themselves, offering activities for the whole family (including a whole lot of relaxing and being pampered). So if you're looking for a good base from which to shop or sightsee, Palm Springs is your best bet.

Regardless of your choice, remember that the rates given below are for high season (winter, generally Oct–May). During the hotter summer months, it's common to find $300 rooms going for $99 or less as part of off-season packages. Even in high season, midweek and golf packages are common, so always ask when making your reservation.

PALM SPRINGS
Expensive

La Mancha Resort Village ✦ The security-gated entry makes La Mancha look like a private community, and it was designed that way. Once you're inside, though, a warmly respectful staff will pamper you, just the way they've coddled the countless celebs who've lent their names to the brochure. What distinguishes La Mancha from other resorts is its quiet elegance and service, not its modern but unoriginal furnishings. Most units are suites with TV/VCRs (they'll even provide Nintendo for the kids). Many guests opt for the villas, which have private pools, fireplaces, and wet bars. Fruit baskets welcome guests on arrival. A private fleet of rental cars stands ready should you want to venture the half mile into town, or you can simply relax the days away—how about a massage on your personal patio?

444 Avenida Caballeros, Palm Springs, CA 92262. ✆ **888/PRIVACY** or 760/323-1773. www.la-mancha.com. 66 units. $150–$245 double; villas from $295. AE, DC, DISC, MC, V. Free parking. Dogs accepted with $200 fee. **Amenities:** Restaurant; lounge; outdoor heated pool; 5 lit tennis courts; fitness center w/spa; Jacuzzi; complimentary bikes; room service 7am–11pm; in-room massage. *In room:* A/C, TV/VCR, fridge, coffeemaker, hair dryer, iron, safe.

Spa Resort Casino   This is one of the more unusual choices in town. It's located on the Indian-owned parcel of land containing the original mineral springs for which Palm Springs was named. The Cahuilla claimed that the springs had magical powers to cure illness. Today's travelers still come here to pamper both body and soul by "taking the waters," though now the facility is sleekly modern. There are three pools on the premises: One is a conventional outdoor swimming pool; the other two are filled from the underground natural springs brimming with revitalizing minerals. Inside the hotel's extensive spa are private sunken marble swirl-pools fed by the springs. After your bath, you can avail yourself of the many other pampering treatments offered. Despite the addition of an adjoining Vegas-style casino, the Cahuilla have truly managed to integrate modern hotel comforts with the ancient healing and Indian spirit this land represents.

100 N. Indian Canyon Dr., Palm Springs, CA 92263. ✆ **800/854-1279** or 760/325-1461. Fax 760/325-3344. www.sparesortcasino.com. 230 units. $159–$239 double; $219–$279 suite. AE, DC, MC, V. Free parking. **Amenities:** 2 restaurants; 2 bars; 3 outdoor heated pools; full-service spa; fitness center; concierge; car-rental desk; 24-hr. room service. *In room:* A/C, TV, minibar, hair dryer, iron.

Moderate

Ballantines Movie Colony ⭐⭐   Take one classic 1930s hotel designed by prolific and renowned area architect Albert Frey, add a warehouse's worth of barely-used, midcentury furnishings and repro classics (cleverly grouped to create mini–theme rooms), sprinkle generously with stylish vacationers and flavor-of-the-month celebs, and you've got a retro-chic boutique motel in groovy Technicolor. Situated off the town's main drag in a neighborhood once favored by golden-age celebs (hence the name), Ballantine's offers a quietly hip, highly personalized experience in a setting marked by scrupulous detail and tantalizing colors; the swimming pool is edged in brilliant lime, the "Sinatra" room is boldly orange (Frank's favorite color), and the made-to-look-old rotary (!) phones are jelly-bean bright.

The same brilliant owners have a similarly outfitted property a few blocks away; **Ballantines Original,** 1420 N. Indian Canyon Dr. (✆ **760/320-2449**), has fewer rooms and a more discreet facade, while still boasting the same fabulous amenities, including a pool with fire pit and outdoor bar, meticulous midcentury furnishings, and personal service.

726 N. Indian Canyon Dr., Palm Springs, CA 92262. ✆ **800/780-3464** or 760/320-1178. Fax 760/320-5308. www.ballantineshotels.com. 18 units. High season $149–$260 double. Rates include continental breakfast and evening cocktail. Midweek and summer discounts available (as low as $89). AE, MC, V. Free parking. **Amenities:** Outdoor heated pool; Jacuzzi; massage. *In room:* A/C, TV, fridge, hair dryer, iron.

Estrella Inn ⭐   Once the choice of Hollywood celebrities, this outstanding historic hotel is quiet and secluded, yet wonderfully close to the action. It's composed of three distinct properties from three different eras, which at press time were being completely refitted in a unified style—sort of a Grecian-meets-modern Regency style popular during Palm Springs's golden era. Lavish landscaping completes the elegant ambience, but only time will tell whether this chic transformation will usher in price hikes. Guest rooms vary widely in terms of size and amenities—some have fireplaces and/or full kitchens, others have wet bars or private balconies—so be sure to enlist the reservationist's help to find your favorite. The real deals are the studio bungalows, even though they have tiny 1930s bathrooms. The Estrella has an outdoor barbecue, plus a lawn with games equipment. Ask about attractive golf packages that include play at one of several nearby courses.

415 S. Belardo Rd. (S of Tahquitz Way), Palm Springs, CA 92262. © **800/237-3687** or 760/320-4117. Fax 760/323-3303. www.estrellapalmsprings.com. 77 units. $150 double; $225–$275 1- or 2-bedroom suite; $250–$350 1- or 2-bedroom bungalow. Rates include continental breakfast. Monthly rates available. AE, DC, MC, V. Free parking. Pets accepted in tile-floored units for $20 fee. **Amenities:** 3 outdoor heated pools (including 1 children's pool); 2 Jacuzzis; fitness room; coin-op laundry. *In room:* A/C, TV, fridge, coffeemaker, hair dryer.

Korakia Pensione ★★ If you can work within the Korakia's rigid deposit-cancellation policy, you're in for a special stay at this Greek-Moroccan oasis just a few blocks from Palm Canyon Drive. This former artist's villa from the 1920s draws a hip international crowd of artists, writers, and musicians. The simply furnished rooms and unbelievably spacious suites are peaceful and private, surrounded by flagstone courtyards and flowering gardens. Rooms are divided between the main house, a second restored villa across the street, and surrounding guest bungalows. Most have kitchens; many have fireplaces. All beds are blessed with thick feather duvets, and the windows are shaded by flowing white canvas, Mediterranean-style draperies. You also get a sumptuous breakfast served in your room or poolside. *Korakia* is Greek for "crow," and a tile mosaic example graces the pool bottom. *Note:* You must pay a deposit when booking a room, and you have to give at least 2 weeks advance cancellation notice (45 days advance notice for holidays) or you'll lose your deposit.

257 S. Patencio Rd., Palm Springs, CA 92262. © **760/864-6411.** Fax 760/864-4147. www.korakia.com. 26 units. $119–$279 double. Rates include breakfast. MC, V. Free parking. **Amenities:** 2 outdoor heated pools; in-room massage. *In room:* A/C, fridge, coffeemaker, safe, hair dryer and iron on request.

The Orbit In ★★ This much-hyped renovation of a classic 1950s motel gets my vote as grooviest digs in town, exceeding everyone's expectations with a mix of streamlined midcentury style, cocktails-by-the-pool Rat Pack aesthetic, and almost scholarly appreciation of the architects and designers responsible for Palm Springs's reign as a mecca of vintage modernism. Serious connoisseurs of interior design will find a museum's worth of furnishings in these rooms, each of which adheres to its theme (Martini Room, Bertoia's Den, Atomic Paradise, and so on) right down to customized lounge-music CDs for your in-room listening pleasure. Contemporary comforts are impeccably provided, from cushy double pillow-top mattresses to poolside misters that create an oasis of cool even during midsummer scorchers. Kitchenettes all boast charming restored fixtures, as do the candy pink–tiled original bathrooms, which have only stall showers, but make up for the lack of tubs by being surprisingly spacious—and naturally sunlit. Guests gather at the poolside "boomerang" bar, or in the Albert Frey lounge (homage to the late, great architect whose unique home sits midway up the mountain backdrop); a central "movies, books, and games" closet encourages old-fashioned camaraderie amidst this chic atmosphere.

562 W. Arenas Rd., Palm Springs, CA 92262. © **877/99-ORBIT** or 760/323-3585. Fax 760/323-3599. www.orbitin.com. 10 units. $209–$249 double. Midweek and off-season discounts as low as $149. Rates include deluxe continental breakfast and evening hors d'oeuvres. AE, DISC, MC, V. Free parking. **Amenities:** Outdoor heated pool; Jacuzzi; complimentary Schwinn cruiser bikes. *In room:* A/C, TV/VCR, CD player, dataport, kitchenette, fridge, coffeemaker, hair dryer, iron, safe.

Villa Royale ✦ This charming inn, 5 minutes from the hustle and bustle of downtown Palm Springs, evokes a European cluster of villas, complete with climbing bougainvillea and rooms filled with international antiques and artwork. Villa Royale's reputation had been suffering due to indifferent management, but new ownership has brought renovation and a renewed dedication to service. Uniform luxuries (down comforters and other pampering touches) appear throughout. Rooms vary widely in size and ambience; larger isn't always better, as some of the inn's most appealing rooms are in the smaller, more affordable range. Many rooms have fireplaces, private patios with Jacuzzis, full kitchens, and a variety of other amenities. A continental breakfast is served in an intimate garden setting surrounding the main pool. The hotel's romantic restaurant, Europa (p. 614), is a sleeper, offering some of Palm Springs's very best meals.

1620 Indian Trail (off E. Palm Canyon), Palm Springs, CA 92264. © **800/245-2314** or 760/327-2314. Fax 760/322-3794. www.villaroyale.com. 31 units. High season (Oct–May) $139–$199 double; $249–$299 suite. Summer $119–$179 double; $229–$279 suite. Rates include full breakfast. Extra person $25. AE, DC, DISC, MC, V. Free parking. **Amenities:** Restaurant; 2 outdoor heated pools; Jacuzzi; concierge; in-room massage. *In room:* A/C, TV, dataport, hair dryer, iron.

Inexpensive

Casa Cody ✦ Once owned by "Wild" Bill Cody's niece, this 1920s casa with a double courtyard (each with swimming pool) has been restored to fine condition. It now sports a vaguely Southwestern decor and peaceful grounds marked by large lawns and mature, blossoming fruit trees. You'll feel more like a houseguest than a hotel client at the Casa Cody. It's located in the primarily residential "Tennis Club" area of town, a couple of easy blocks from Palm Canyon Drive. Many units here have fireplaces and full-size kitchens. Breakfast is served poolside, as are complimentary wine and cheese on Saturday afternoons.

175 S. Cahuilla Rd. (between Tahquitz Way and Arenas Rd.), Palm Springs, CA 92262. © **760/320-9346.** Fax 760/325-8610. www.palmsprings.com/hotels/casacody. 23 units. $79–$99 double; $99–$159 studio; $149–$259 suite; 2-bedroom adobe $299–$359. Rates include expanded continental breakfast. AE, DC, DISC, MC, V. Pets accepted for $10-per-night fee. **Amenities:** 2 outdoor heated pools; Jacuzzi; in-room massage. *In room:* A/C, TV, fridge.

Holiday Inn Palm Mountain Resort *Kids* Within easy walking distance of Palm Springs's main drag, this Holiday Inn (like most in the chain) welcomes kids under 18 free in their parents' room, making it a terrific choice for families. The rooms are in the two- or the three-story wing, and many have a patio or balcony, with a view of the mountains or the large Astroturf courtyard. Midweek and summer rates can be as low as $59. For the best rates, book online or ask for "Great Rates."

155 S. Belardo Rd., Palm Springs, CA 92262. © **800/622-9451** or 760/325-1301. Fax 760/323-8937. www.palmmountainresort.com. 122 units. High season $89–$169 double. Children 17 and under stay free in parents' room. AE, DC, DISC, MC, V. Free parking. **Amenities:** Restaurant; lounge; poolside bar; heated outdoor pool. *In room:* A/C, TV, fridge, coffeemaker.

Orchid Tree Inn Billed as a "1930s desert garden retreat," the Orchid Tree is a sprawling complex of buildings from the 1920s to 1950s, located just a block from Palm Canyon Drive in the historic "Tennis Club" district. Dedicated family ownership ensures that the place is impeccably maintained. The inn truly feels like a retreat. The grounds are rich with flowering shrubs, mature citrus trees, and multitudes of twittering hummingbirds, sparrows, and quail drawn by bird feeders and birdbaths. The rooms are nicer than you'd expect at this price, in keeping with the overall grace and excellence of the entire neighborhood. Room types range from simple, hotel-style doubles to charming bungalows to pool-front studios with sliding-glass doors.

261 S. Belardo Rd. (at Baristo Rd.), Palm Springs, CA 92262. ✆ **800/733-3435** or 760/325-2791. Fax 760/325-3855. www.orchidtree.com. 40 units. Nov–May $110–$185 double; $150–$395 suite. Summer $65–$125 double; $105–$285 suite. Extra person $15. Rates include expanded continental breakfast (Nov–May only). AE, DC, DISC, MC, V. **Amenities:** 3 swimming pools; 2 Jacuzzis. *In room:* A/C, TV, hair dryer.

RANCHO MIRAGE

Marriott's Rancho Las Palmas Resort & Spa ★★ The early-California charm of this relaxing Spanish hacienda makes Rancho Las Palmas one of the less pretentious luxury resorts in the desert. Dedicated golfers come to play on the adjoining country club's 27 holes of golf; tennis buffs flock to the 25 hotel courts (3 of them red clay); everybody enjoys the world-class health spa plus a separate pool with water slide. Guest rooms are arranged in a complex of low-rise, tile-roofed structures, and the public areas have an easygoing elegance, filled with flower-laden stone fountains, smooth terra-cotta tile floors, and rough-hewn wood trim. Each room has a balcony or patio.

41000 Bob Hope Dr., Rancho Mirage, CA 92270. ✆ **800/I-LUV-SUN** or 760/568-2727. Fax 760/568-5845. www.rancholaspalmas.com. 450 units. Sept–May $250–$425 double; Memorial Day to Labor Day $160–$255 double. Children 17 and under stay free in parents' room. Packages and off-season discounts available. AE, DISC, MC, V. Free valet and self-parking. **Amenities:** 4 restaurants (ranging from casual patio dining to dressy dinner fare); cocktail lounge; 2 outdoor heated pools; 2 Jacuzzis; night-lit outdoor tennis courts; health club; full-service spa; children's programs; concierge; activities desk; business center; room service 6am–midnight; babysitting; laundry/dry cleaning service. *In room:* A/C, TV w/pay movies, dataport, minibar, coffeemaker, hair dryer, iron, safe.

Westin Mission Hills Resort ★★ Designed to resemble a Moroccan palace surrounded by pools, waterfalls, and lush gardens, this self-contained resort stands on 360 acres. It's an excellent choice for families and for travelers who take their golf game seriously. (Regular desert visitors will note the Westin is ideally situated so Palm Springs and Palm Desert are equally accessible without driving on congested Hwy. 101.) Rooms are arranged around the grounds in a series of two-story buildings, with accommodations that range from basic to palatial. All have terraces and come with an array of creature comforts befitting this price range—including the Westin trademark "Heavenly Bed," an ultra-comfy white confection so popular many guests order one for home.

Though the Westin has the business demeanor of a practiced group-and-meeting hotel, it offers a multitude of recreation options for leisure travelers, gamblers attracted to the nearby Agua Caliente Casino, or professionals after the day's business is concluded. In addition to their championship golf course, you'll find a running track, bike trails, lawn games, and the freshly expanded Spa at Mission Hills, a stylishly boutique-like oasis whose treatments range from sports massage to pampering Hawaiian body treatments.

71-333 Dinah Shore Dr. (at Bob Hope Dr.), Rancho Mirage, CA 92270. ✆ **800/WESTIN-1** or 760/328-5955. Fax 760/321-2955. www.starwood.com. 512 units. Jan–Apr $470–$515 double; May and Sept–Dec $360–$415 double; Memorial Day to Labor Day $219–$249 double. Extra person $35. Children under 18 stay free in parents' room. Golf, spa, and family packages available. AE, DC, DISC, MC, V. Free valet and self-parking. **Amenities:** Excellent restaurant serving breakfast all day; 2 lounges; 3 poolside cabana bars; multiple outdoor heated pools and Jacuzzis; night-lit outdoor tennis courts; health club; full-service spa; bike rental; children's activity center; concierge; business center; 24-hr. room service; in-room massage; babysitting; dry cleaning/laundry service. *In room:* A/C, TV w/pay movies, dataport, minibar, coffeemaker, hair dryer, iron, safe.

PALM DESERT

Marriott's Desert Springs Spa & Resort ★★ A tourist attraction in its own right, Marriott's Desert Springs Resort is worth a peek even if you're not lucky enough to stay here. Most of the guests are attracted by the excellent golf and tennis facilities, and the huge, luxurious, full-service spa is an added perk. Visitors enter this artificial desert oasis via a sweeping palm tree–lined road wending its way past a small pond that's home to a gaggle of pink flamingos. Once inside, guests are greeted by a shaded marble lobby "rain forest" replete with interior moat and the squawk of tropical birds; gondolas even ply the lobby's waterways.

While the rooms here are not as fancy as the lobby would lead you to believe, they're exceedingly comfortable, decorated with muted pastels and contemporary furnishings. All have terraces with views of the golf course and the San Jacinto Mountains. Recreational options include a jogging trail, 36 holes of golf, driving range, unique 18-hole putting range, basketball courts, lawn croquet, and a sunbathing "beach" with volleyball court—I guarantee you don't have to ever leave the perimeter if you don't want to.

74855 Country Club Dr., Palm Desert, CA 92260. © **800/331-3112** or 760/341-2211. Fax 760/341-1872. www.desertspringsresort.com. 884 units. Sept–May $290–$550 double; Memorial Day to Labor Day $195–$385 double. Children 17 and under stay free in parents' room. Packages and off-season discounts available. AE, DC, DISC, MC, V. **Amenities:** 6 restaurants; 4 snack bars; 2 lounges (1 with live entertainment); 4 heated outdoor pools; 3 outdoor Jacuzzis; 20 tennis courts (hard, clay, and grass; 7 lit); full-service spa and health club; bike rental; children's programs; game room; concierge; tour desk; car-rental desk; business center; shopping arcade; salon; 24-hr. room service; in-room massage; babysitting; dry cleaning/laundry service. *In room:* A/C, TV w/pay movies, dataport, minibar, coffeemaker, hair dryer, iron, safe.

LA QUINTA

La Quinta Resort & Club ★★★ A luxury resort set amid citrus trees, towering palms, cacti, and desert flowers at the base of the rocky Santa Rosa Mountains, La Quinta is *the* place to be if you're serious about your golf or tennis game. The resort is renowned for its five championship golf courses—including one of California's best, Pete Dye's PGA West TPC Stadium Course. All guest rooms are in comfortable single-story, Spanish-style buildings scattered throughout the grounds. Each has its own patio and access to one of several dozen small pools, enhancing the feeling of privacy at this retreat. Some units have a fireplace

A La Quinta Bed & Breakfast Hideaway

Devotees of bed-and-breakfasts or boutique inns might find the La Quinta Resort's 900-plus rooms a little daunting, but there's a way to enjoy this quiet, affluent end of the valley with a little more intimacy. Check out the hidden-secret **Lake La Quinta Inn,** 78-120 Caleo Bay (© **888/226-4546** or 760/564-7332; www.lakelaquintainn.com), a 12-room Norman-style bed-and-breakfast on the shores of a man-made lake (surrounded by equally luxurious homes) just blocks from the famous resort. Exquisitely outfitted rooms, delightful knowledgeable hosts, on-site massage, and a 24-hour pool and Jacuzzi complete the fantasy. Rates range from $189 to $329 in season, with off-season discounts as low as $99; golf, romance, and dinner packages are available.

or private Jacuzzi. The tranquil lounge and library in the unaltered original hacienda hearkens back to the early days of the resort, when Clark Gable, Greta Garbo, Frank Capra, and other luminaries chose La Quinta as their hideaway. The resort includes Spa La Quinta, a deluxe mission-style complex with 35 treatment rooms for every pampering luxury.

49499 Eisenhower Dr., La Quinta, CA 92253. ⓒ **800/598-3828** or 760/564-4111. Fax 760/564-7656. www.laquintaresort.com. 919 units. High-season $340–$460 double; mid-June to Sept $170–$290 double. Extra person $15. Children 17 and under stay free in parents' room. Packages available. AE, MC, V. Free self parking; valet parking $3 ($12 overnight). Pets accepted with $250 refundable deposit. **Amenities:** 5 restaurants (including Montanas, which serves outstanding Mediterranean fare); 3 bars (2 featuring entertainment); 42 outdoor pools w/Jacuzzis; 23 outdoor tennis courts (10 night-lit); full-service spa; bike rental; children's programs; concierge; business center; 24-hr. room service; in-room massage; babysitting; laundry service. *In room:* A/C, TV/VCR w/pay movies, dataport, minibar, coffeemaker, hair dryer, iron, safe.

WHERE TO DINE
PALM SPRINGS
Expensive

Europa Restaurant 𝆑𝆑 CALIFORNIA/CONTINENTAL   Long advertised as the "most romantic dining in the desert," Europa is a sentimental favorite of many regulars among an equally gay and straight clientele. This European-style hideaway exudes charm and ambience. Whether you sit under the stars on Europa's garden patio or in subdued candlelight indoors, you'll savor dinner prepared by one of Palm Springs's most dedicated kitchens and served by a discreetly attentive staff. Standout dishes include deviled crab fritters on mango-papaya chutney, filet mignon on a bed of crispy onions with garlic butter, and a show-stopping salmon baked in parchment with crème fraîche and dill. For dessert, don't miss the signature chocolate mousse—smooth, grainy, and addictive.

1620 Indian Trail (at the Villa Royale). ⓒ 760/327-2314. Reservations recommended. Main courses $18–$32. AE, DC, DISC, MC, V. Tues–Sat 5:30–10pm; Sun 11:30am–2pm and 5:30–10pm.

Palmie 𝆑 CLASSIC FRENCH   You can't see Palmie from the street, and once you're seated inside its softly lit, lattice-enclosed dining patio, you won't see the bustle outside anymore, either. Martine and Alain Clerc's cozy bistro is filled with Art Deco posters of French seaside resorts. Chef Alain sends out masterful traditional French dishes such as bubbling cheese soufflé, green lentil salad dotted with pancetta, steak au poivre rich with cognac sauce, and lobster raviolis garnished with caviar. In fact, every carefully garnished plate is a work of art. To the charming background strains of French chanteuses, hostess and manager Martine circulates between tables, determined that visitors should enjoy their meals as much as do the loyal regulars she greets by name. Don't leave without sampling dessert: My favorite is the trio of petite crème brûlées, flavored with ginger, vanilla, and Kahlúa.

276 N. Palm Canyon Dr. ⓒ 760/320-3375. Reservations recommended. Main courses $12–$26. AE, DC, MC, V. Mon–Sat 5:30–9:30pm.

Moderate

La Provence 𝆑𝆑 COUNTRY FRENCH   The casually elegant La Provence is a favorite of locals and often gets recommended by knowledgeable innkeepers. The second-story terrace sets a lovely mood on balmy desert evenings. This restaurant eschews heavy traditional French cream sauces in favor of carefully combined herbs and spices. The menu offers some expected items (escargots in mushroom caps, bouillabaisse, steak au poivre) as well as inventive pastas, like wild-mushroom raviolis in a sun-dried-tomato-and-sweet-onion sauce. Foodies will note with pleasure that executive chef Clay Arkless comes by way of New York City's River Cafe.

254 N. Palm Canyon Dr. (upstairs). © **760/416-4418**. Reservations recommended. Main courses $12–$24. AE, DC, DISC, MC, V. Daily 5–10:30pm.

Las Casuelas Terraza CLASSIC MEXICAN   The original Las Casuelas, a tiny storefront several blocks away, is still open, but the bougainvillea-draped front patio here is a much better place to people-watch. You can order Mexican standards like quesadillas, enchiladas, and mountainous nachos, as well as equally supersize margaritas. Inside, the action heats up with live music and raucous happy-hour crowds. During hot weather, the patio and even sidewalk passersby are cooled by the restaurant's well-placed misters, making this a perfect late-afternoon or early-evening choice.

222 S. Palm Canyon Dr. © **760/325-2794**. Reservations recommended on weekends. Main courses $7–$13. AE, DC, DISC, MC, V. Mon–Thurs 11am–10pm, Fri–Sat 11am–11pm, Sun 10am–10pm.

Inexpensive

Edgardo's Café Veracruz ⭐ *(Value)* MEXICAN   The pleasant but humble ambience at Edgardo's is a welcome change from touristy Palm Springs. The expert menu features authentic Mayan, Huasteco, and Aztec cuisine. The dark interior boasts an array of colorful masks and artwork from Central and South America, but the postage stamp–size front patio with a trickling fountain is the best place to sample Edgardo's tangy quesadillas, desert cactus salad, and traditional poblano chiles rellenos—and perhaps even an oyster-tequila shooter from the oyster bar!

494 N. Palm Canyon (at W. Alejo Rd.). © **760/320-3558**. Reservations recommended for weekend dinner. Main courses $3.50–$15. AE, DC, DISC, MC, V. Mon–Fri 11am–3pm and 5:30–9:30pm; Sat–Sun 8am–10pm (sometimes later). Free parking.

Mykonos GREEK   Locals have been enjoying authentic Greek specialties at this family-run spot for 10 years. Mykonos is supercasual, offering simple, candlelit tables (with vinyl tablecloths and the like) in an off-street brick courtyard, but it's a pleasant treat. Traditional lamb shanks over rice, dolmades (stuffed grape leaves), tangy salads with crumbled feta cheese, and sweet, sticky baklava are among the best items.

139 Andreas (just off Palm Canyon). © **760/322-0223**. Most items under $10. MC, V. Wed–Mon 11am–10pm.

PALM DESERT

Doug Arango's ⭐ NORTHERN ITALIAN   With so many Italian restaurants that are either old-world lasagna joints or pricey resort trattorias, it's no wonder Doug's is always packed with locals thankful for an affordable, stylish choice offering northern Italian fare without pretension. The decor is understated, with black-and-white tiles, glass urns of marinating delicacies, and an open kitchen you can gaze into from the large, oval bar. Expect a friendly, noisy clatter when it's full, and beware: The kitchen can be heavy-handed with the garlic. Crispy, thin-crust individual pizzas are one specialty, and everyone raves about the appetizer of zucchini pancakes with scallion sour cream.

73520 El Paseo. © **760/341-4120**. www.dougarangos.com. Reservations recommended. Main courses $18–$35. AE, MC, V. Tues–Sat 11:30am–2:30pm (Oct–May); Tues–Sun 5:30–10pm (year-round).

Louise's Pantry ⭐ COFFEE SHOP/DINER   A real old-fashioned diner, Louise's was a fixture in Palm Springs since opening as a drugstore lunch counter in 1945. The original location on Palm Canyon Drive fell victim to skyrocketing property values, but not before establishing this welcome offshoot decorated with vintage photos of Louise's heyday. Devoted patrons—young and old—still flock in for premium-quality comfort foods such as Cobb salad, Reuben and French dip sandwiches, chicken and dumplings, hearty breakfasts with biscuits and gravy, and tasty fresh-baked pies.

44491 Town Center Way (at Fred Waring Dr. N of Hwy. 111). (℡ **760/346-9320.** Reservations not accepted. Most menu items under $10. MC, V. Daily 7am–3pm.

Palomino CALIFORNIA/MEDITERRANEAN   Opened by the Seattle team responsible for other upscale "chains" like Kincaid's, this local branch of their "Euro Bistro" provides just the right blend of casual, trendy, and good value. The menu reads better than it eats, because the assembly-line kitchen is better suited for pared-down dishes than some of the more complex or delicate preparations. Stick with the creative pizzas, daily fresh seafood (like cedar-plank salmon from the Northwest), and meats from the Italian spit-roaster. Portions are enormous, the atmosphere is divided between the high-style designer setting and the low-key, and chatty service is provided by a youthful staff. This place is a happening scene most nights in season, so prepare for a buzz of noise from other diners—and the attached bar. Forego valet parking for a space in the lot behind Palomino.

73101 Hwy. 111 (at Monterey Ave.). (℡ **760/773-9091.** Reservations recommended in high season. Main courses $14–$27. AE, MC, V. Sun–Thurs 5–10pm, Fri–Sat 5–11pm.

Tommy Bahama's Tropical Cafe CARIBBEAN   If all this desert makes you long for *de islands, mon,* step upstairs from fashionable Tommy Bahama's boutique for a dose of Caribbean relaxation. The decor alone is worth a visit: a fantasy port of call, around 1940, with ceiling fans, plenty of rattan and palms, and upholstery in TB's signature tropical prints. Enormous umbrellas shade patio seating with valley views, and spacious indoor booths make for easy relaxing over a series of sweet umbrella drinks. The food is a delicious change of pace, its Caribbean zing not overly spiced; check out coconut shrimp with mango dip, conch fritters, mango shrimp salad, Boca Chica chicken, Jamaican jerk pork, and Key lime pie for dessert. Diners are an entertaining mix of fresh-from-the-courts socialites, always-on-vacation retirees, and well-heeled shoppers.

73595 El Paseo (at Larkspur Ave.). (℡ **760/836-0188.** http://tommybahama.com. Reservations recommended in season. Main courses $8–$12 lunch, $16–$26 dinner. AE, MC, V. Daily 11am–10pm.

THE DESERT RESORTS AFTER DARK

Every month a different club or disco is the hot spot in the Springs, and the best way to tap into the trend is by consulting *The Desert Guide, The Bottom Line* (see "Gay & Lesbian Life in Palm Springs," earlier in this chapter), or one of the many other free newsletters available from area hotels and merchants. **Village-Fest** (see "Shopping," earlier in this chapter) turns Palm Canyon Drive into an outdoor party every Thursday night. Below, I've described a couple of the enduring arts and entertainment attractions around the desert resorts.

The **Fabulous Palm Springs Follies,** at the Plaza Theatre, 128 S. Palm Canyon Dr., Palm Springs (℡ **760/327-0225;** www.psfollies.com), a vaudeville-style show filled with lively production numbers, is celebrating its 12th year in the historic Plaza Theatre in the heart of town. With a cast of energetic retired showgirls, singers, dancers, and comedians, the revue has been enormously popular around town. Call for show schedule. Tickets range from $37 to $75.

The **McCallum Theatre for the Performing Arts,** 73000 Fred Waring Dr., Palm Desert (© **760/340-ARTS**), offers the only cultural high road around. Frequent symphony performances with visiting virtuosos such as conductor Seiji Ozawa or violinist Itzhak Perlman, musicals like *Grease* or *A Chorus Line* revival, and pop performers like the Captain and Tennille or the Ink Spots are among the theater's recent offerings. Call for upcoming event information.

CASINOS

Native American gaming has been around in the desert for many years now, but recently the industry seems to have joined the major leagues, with a professionalism and polish that create a "virtual Vegas."

The best-known and most centrally located casino is the **Spa Resort Casino** in the heart of Palm Springs (p. 609). The gaming rooms that used to be almost an afterthought now share the spotlight along with the historic hot springs. Attendees at the hotel's conference center can often be found playing hooky from business at one or both!

You can't help but be impressed by the brilliant neon fireballs of the **Agua Caliente Casino,** 32-250 Bob Hope Dr., Rancho Mirage (© **760/321-2000;** www.hotwatercasino.com), down the street from the Westin Mission Hills. The complex already boasts a full house of dining options plus musical entertainers and prestigious boxing matches; it will also eventually include an on-site hotel of its own.

And it was only a matter of time before savvy investor Donald Trump came to mine gold in the California desert: Check out his latest venture, the **Trump 29 Casino,** 46-200 Harrison Place, Coachella (© **866/TRUMP-29;** www.trump29.com), about a half-hour from Palm Springs. The land may be tribal-owned, but this sophisticated complex is Vegas all the way, from the big-name shows and a high-roller players club to 24-hour fine dining and even one of those all-you-can-eat prime-rib buffets.

4 Joshua Tree National Park

40 miles NE of Palm Springs; 128 miles E of LA

The Joshua trees in this national park are merely a jumping-off point for exploring this seemingly barren desert. Viewed from the roadside, the dry land only hints at hidden vitality, but closer examination reveals a giant mosaic of intense beauty and complexity. From lush oases teeming with life to rusted-out relics of man's attempts to tame the wilderness, from low plains of tufted cacti to mountains of exposed, twisted rock, the park is much more than a tableau of the curious tree for which it is named.

The Joshua tree is said to have been given its name by early Mormon settlers traveling west, for its upraised limbs and bearded appearance reminded them of

---

Tips **Load Up**

No restaurants, lodging, gas stations, or stores are found within Joshua Tree National Park. In fact, water is only available at four park locations: Cottonwood Springs, the Black Rock Canyon Campground, the Indian Cove Ranger Station, and the Oasis Visitor Center. Twentynine Palms and Yucca Valley have lots of restaurants, markets, motels, and B&Bs.

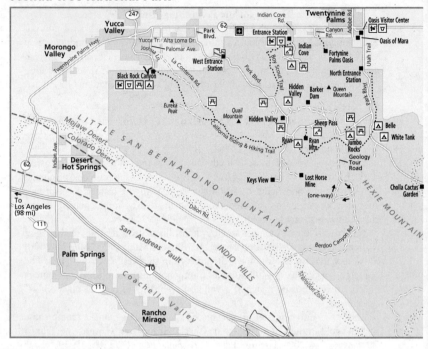

the prophet Joshua leading them to the promised land. Other observers were not so kind. Explorer John C. Frémont called it "the most repulsive tree in the vegetable kingdom." Nature writer Charles Francis Saunders opined: "The trees themselves were as grotesque as the creations of a bad dream; the shaggy trunks and limbs were twisted and seemed writhing as though in pain, and dagger-pointed leaves were clenched in bristling fists of inhospitality."

Harsh criticism for this hardy desert dweller, which is really not a tree but a variety of yucca and member of the lily family. The relationship is apparent when pale-yellow, lily-like flowers festoon the limbs of the Joshuas when they bloom in March, April, or May (depending on rainfall). When Mother Nature cooperates, the park also puts on quite a wildflower display, and you can get an updated report on prime viewing sites by calling the park ranger (see "Essentials," below).

The park, which reaches the southernmost boundary of this special tree's range, straddles two desert environments. There's the mountainous, Joshua tree–studded Mojave Desert forming the northwestern part of the park, while the Colorado Desert—hotter, drier, lower, and characterized by a wide variety of desert flora, including cacti, cottonwood, and native California fan palms—comprises the southern and eastern sections of the park. Between them runs the "transition zone," displaying characteristics of each.

The area's geological timeline is fascinating, stretching back eight million years to a time when the Mojave landscape was one of rolling hills and flourishing grasslands; horses, camels, and mastodons abounded, preyed upon by saber-toothed tigers and wild dogs. Displays at the Oasis Visitor Center show how resulting climatic, volcanic, and tectonic activity have created the park's signature cliffs and boulders and turned Joshua Tree into the arid desert you see today.

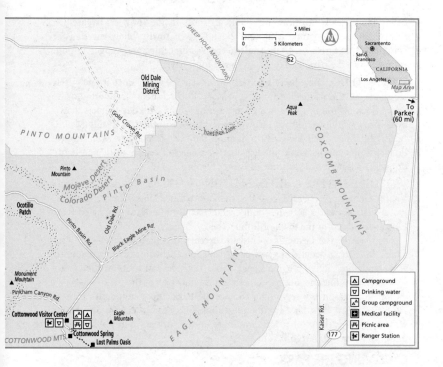

Human presence has been traced back nearly 10,000 years with the discovery of Pinto Man, and evidence of more recent habitation can be seen in the form of Native American pictographs carved into rock faces throughout the park. Miners and ranchers began coming in the 1860s, but the boom went bust by the turn of the 20th century. Then a Pasadena doctor, treating World War I veterans suffering from respiratory and heart ailments caused by mustard gas, prescribed the desert's clean, dry air—and the modern town of Twentynine Palms was (re)born.

In the 1920s, a worldwide fascination with the desert emerged, and cactus gardens were very much in vogue. Entrepreneurs hauled truckloads of desert plants into Los Angeles for quick sale or export, and souvenir hunters removed archaeological treasures. Incensed that the beautiful Mojave was in danger of being picked clean, Los Angeles socialite Minerva Hoyt organized a desert conservation movement and successfully lobbied for the establishment of Joshua Tree National Monument in 1936.

In 1994, under provisions of the federal California Desert Protection Act, Joshua Tree was "upgraded" to national-park status and expanded to nearly 800,000 acres. The park is popular with everyone from rock climbers and campers to wildflower lovers and even RV-ers just cruising through. It's a must-see for nature and geology lovers visiting during temperate weather, and more "user-friendly" than the other two hard-core desert parks.

ESSENTIALS
GETTING THERE From metropolitan Los Angeles, the usual route to the Oasis Visitor Center in Joshua Tree National Park is via I-10 to its intersection with Calif. 62 (some 92 miles east of downtown). Calif. 62 (the Twentynine

Palms Hwy.) leads northeast for about 43 miles to the town of Twentynine Palms. Total driving time is around 2½ hours. In town, follow the signs at National Park Drive or Utah Trail to the visitor center and ranger station. Admission to the park is $10 per car (good for 7 days).

WHEN TO GO The park is busiest—relatively speaking, since it rarely feels crowded—in the winter months (Nov–Mar). Rock climbers from around the world flock to Joshua Tree in winter and spring, along with day-trippers drawn by brilliant wildflower displays (if winter rainfall was sufficient) during March, April, and May. Even the sizzling summer months are popular with international visitors curious about the legendary extremes of temperature, and hardy campers looking for the solitude of balmy evenings.

VISITOR CENTERS & INFORMATION In addition to the main **Oasis Visitor Center** (© 760/367-5500) at the Twentynine Palms entrance, **Cottonwood Visitor Center** is at the south entrance, and the privately operated **Park Center** is located in the town of Joshua Tree.

The Oasis Visitor Center is open daily (except Christmas) from 8am to 5pm. Check here for a detailed map of park roads, plus schedules of ranger-guided walks and interpretive programs. Ask about the weekend tours of the Desert Queen Ranch, once a working homestead and now part of the park.

For information before you go, contact the **Park Superintendent's Office,** 74485 National Park Dr., Twentynine Palms, CA 92277 (© 760/367-5500; www.nps.gov/jotr). Another terrific website on the park and surrounding communities is **www.desertgold.com**.

EXPLORING THE PARK

An excellent first stop, outside the park's north entrance, is the main **Oasis Visitor Center,** located alongside the Oasis of Mara, also known as the Twentynine Palms Oasis. For many generations, the native Serrano tribe lived at this "place of little springs and much grass." Get maps, books, and the latest in road, trail, and weather conditions before beginning your tour.

From the Oasis Center, drive south to **Jumbo Rocks,** which captures the complete essence of the park: a vast array of rock formations, a Joshua tree forest, and the yucca-dotted desert, open and wide. Check out Skull Rock (one of the many rocks in the area that appear to resemble humans, dinosaurs, monsters, cathedrals, or castles) via a 1½-mile nature trail that provides an introduction to the park's flora, wildlife, and geology.

At Cap Rock Junction, the main park road swings north toward the **Wonderland of Rocks,** 12 square miles of massive jumbled granite. This curious maze of stone hides groves of Joshua trees, trackless washes, and several small pools of water. To the south is Keys View Road, which dead-ends at mile-high **Keys View.** From the crest of the Little San Bernardino Mountains, enjoy grand desert views that encompass both the highest (Mount San Gorgonio) and lowest (Salton Sea) points in Southern California.

Don't miss the contrasting Colorado Desert terrain found along Pinto Basin Road—to conserve time, you might plan to exit the park via this route, which ends up at I-10. You'll pass both the **Cholla Cactus Garden** and spindly **Ocotillo Patch** on your way to vast, flat **Pinto Basin,** a barren lowland surrounded by austere mountains and punctuated by trackless sand dunes. The dunes are an easy 2-mile round-trip hike from the backcountry camping board (one of the few man-made markers along this road and one of the only designated parking areas), or simply continue to **Cottonwood Springs,** near the

---

Tips Desert Queen Ranch Tours

Combine your outdoor adventure with the fascinating history of the Keys family, rugged pioneers who in 1919 settled a desert homestead that's now part of the national park, then for 60 years lived, worked, and raised five children in this remote location. Located in a remote, rocky canyon, admission to the ranch is restricted to guided walking tours. The half-mile, 90-minute tours are offered from October to May daily at 10am and 1pm; summer tours are daily at 8am and 6pm. You may book tours up to 5 months in advance by calling ☎ **760/367-5555**. The tour is $5 for adults, $2.50 for children 6 to 12, and free for kids under 6.

---

southern park entrance. Besides a small ranger station and well-developed campground, Cottonwood has a cool, palm-shaded oasis that is the trail head for a tough hike to Lost Palms Oasis.

HIKING, BIKING & CLIMBING

HIKING & NATURE WALKS   The national park holds a variety of nature trails ranging in difficulty from strenuous challenges to kid-friendly interpretive walks—two of these (**Oasis of Mara** and **Cap Rock**) are paved and wheelchair-accessible. My favorite of the 11 short interpretive trails is **Cholla Cactus Garden,** smack-dab in the middle of the park, where you stroll through dense clusters of the deceptively fluffy-looking "teddy bear cactus."

For the more adventurous, **Barker Dam** is an easy 1-mile loop accessible by a graded dirt road east of Hidden Valley. A small, man-made lake is framed by the majestic Wonderland of Rocks. In addition to scrambling atop the old dam, it's fun to search out Native American petroglyphs carved into the base of cliffs lining your return to the trail head.

The moderately challenging **Lost Horse Mine Trail** near Keys View leads through rolling hills to the ruins of a successful gold-mining operation; once here, a short, steep hike leads uphill behind the ruins for a fine view into the heart of the park.

When you're ready for a strenuous hike, try the **Fortynine Palms Oasis Trail,** accessible from Canyon Road in Twentynine Palms. After a steep, harsh ascent to a cactus-fringed ridge, the rocky canyon trail leads to a spectacular oasis, complete with palm-shaded pools of green water and abundant birds and other wildlife. Allow 2 to 3 hours for the 3-mile round-trip hike.

Another lush oasis lies at the end of **Lost Palms Oasis Trail** at Cottonwood Springs. The first section of the 7½-mile trail is moderately difficult, climbing slowly to the oasis overlook; from here, a treacherous path continues to the canyon bottom, a remote spot that the elusive bighorn sheep find attractive.

MOUNTAIN BIKING   Much of the park is designated wilderness, meaning that bicycles are limited to roads (they'll damage the fragile ecosystem if you venture off the beaten track). None of the paved roads have bike lanes, but rugged mountain bikes are a great tool to explore the park via unpaved roads, where distraction from autos is light.

Try the 18-mile **Geology Tour Road,** which begins west of Jumbo Rocks. Dry lake beds contrast with towering boulders along this sandy downhill road, and you'll also encounter abandoned mines.

A shorter but still rewarding ride begins at the **Covington Flats** picnic area. A steep 4-mile road climbs through Joshua trees, junipers, and pinyon pines to Eureka Peak, where you'll be rewarded with a panoramic view.

For other bike-friendly unpaved and four-wheel-drive roads, consult the official park map.

ROCK CLIMBING From Hidden Valley to the Wonderland of Rocks, the park has emerged as one of the world's premier rock-climbing destinations. The park offers some 4,000 climbing routes, ranging from the easiest of bouldering to some of the sport's most difficult technical climbs. November through May is the prime season to watch lizard-like humans scale sheer rock faces with impossible grace. Even beginners can get into the act: At **First Ascent** (© **800/325-5462**), certified guides start the day with detailed instruction, then stay with you, providing guidance as you learn the ropes. All equipment is provided, and prices start at $75.

WHERE TO STAY

If you're staying in the Palm Springs area, it's entirely possible to make a day trip to the national park. But if you'd like to stay close by and spend more time here, Twentynine Palms, just outside the north boundary of the national park on Calif. 62, offers budget-to-moderate lodging. For a complete listing of Twentynine Palms lodging, contact the **29 Palms Chamber of Commerce,** 5672 Historic Plaza, Twentynine Palms, CA 92277 (© **760/367-3445;** www.29chamber.com).

Near the visitor center in the Oasis of Mara is the rustic **29 Palms Inn** (© **760/367-3505;** www.29palmsinn.com), a cluster of adobe cottages and old cabins dating from the 1920s; its garden-fresh restaurant is the best in town. There's also the 100-room **Best Western Garden Inn** (© **760/367-9141;** www. bestwestern.com), a comfortable base from which to maximize your outdoor time.

Nine **campgrounds** scattered throughout the park offer pleasant though often spartan accommodations, with just picnic tables and pit toilets for the most part. Only two—**Black Rock Canyon** and **Cottonwood Springs**—have potable water and flush toilets, plus a $10 overnight fee. You can make campground reservations online at **http://reservations.nps.gov** or by calling © **800/365-2267.**

5 Mojave National Preserve

180 miles E of LA; 75 miles SW of Las Vegas

Two decades of park politicking finally ended in 1994 when President Clinton signed into law the California Desert Protection Act, which created the Mojave National Preserve. Thus far, the Mojave's elevated status has not attracted hordes of sightseers, and devoted visitors are happy to keep it that way. Unlike a fully protected national park, the "national preserve" designation allows certain commercial land uses, and the continued grazing and mining within the preserve's boundaries are a sore spot for ardent environmentalists.

To most Americans, the East Mojave is that vast, bleak, interminable stretch of desert to be crossed as quickly as possible while leaving California via I-15 or I-40. Few realize that these highways are the boundaries of what some have long considered the crown jewel of the California desert.

This land is hard to get to know—unlike more developed desert parks, it has no lodgings or concessions, few campgrounds, and only a handful of roads suitable for the average passenger vehicle. But hidden within this natural fortress

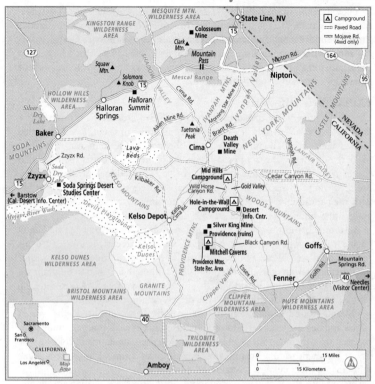

are some true gems—the preserve's 1.4 million acres include the world's largest Joshua tree forest; abundant wildlife; spectacular canyons, caverns, and volcanic formations; nationally honored scenic back roads and footpaths to historic mining sites; tabletop mesas; and a dozen mountain ranges.

ESSENTIALS

GETTING THERE   I-15, the major route taken between the Southern California metropolis and the state line by Las Vegas–bound travelers, extends along the northern boundary of Mojave National Preserve. I-40 is the southern access route to the East Mojave. It's a 2½-hour drive from Los Angeles to the Oasis Visitor Center, 2 hours to the southern entrance (Cottonwood Visitor Center).

WHEN TO GO   Spring is a splendid time to visit this desert (autumn is another). From March to May, the temperatures are mild, the Joshua trees are in bloom, and the lower Kelso Dunes are bedecked with yellow and white desert primrose and pink sand verbena.

VISITOR CENTERS & INFORMATION   You can visit the preserve online at **www.nps.gov/moja**. The best source for up-to-date weather conditions and a free topographical map is the **Mojave Desert Information Center,** 72157 Baker Blvd. (under the "World's Tallest Thermometer"), Baker, CA 92309 (© **760/733-4040**), which is open daily from 9am to 5pm and also has a superior selection of books for sale. Additional information and maps are available inside the preserve at the **Hole-in-the-Wall Campground's Visitor Center** (© **760/928-2572**), which is open seasonally (as staffing allows).

Those coming in on I-40 should stop in Needles, where the **Needles Information Center,** 707 W. Broadway (📞 **760/326-6322**), is open Tuesday through Sunday from 8am to 4pm. There's also the **California Desert Information Center,** 831 Barstow Rd., Barstow (📞 **760/255-8760**), which has a mini-museum and educational displays on the history and characteristics of the desert. It's open daily from 9am to 5pm.

EXPLORING THE PARK

One of the preserve's spectacular sights is the **Kelso Dunes,** the most extensive dune field in the West. The 45-square-mile formation of magnificently sculpted sand is famous for "booming": Visitors' footsteps cause mini-avalanches and make the dunes go "sha-boom-sha-boom-sha-boom." Geologists speculate that the extreme dryness of the East Mojave Desert, combined with the wind-polished, rounded nature of the individual sand grains, has something to do with their musicality. Sometimes the low rumbling sound resembles a Tibetan gong; other times it sounds like a 1950s doo-wop musical group.

A 10-mile drive from the Kelso Dunes is **Kelso Depot,** built by the Union Pacific in 1924. The Spanish Revival–style structure was designed with a red-tile roof, graceful arches, and a brick platform. The depot continued to be open for freight-train crew use through the mid-1980s, although it ceased to be a railroad stop for passengers after World War II. The National Park Service is considering refurbishing the building for use as the preserve's visitor center.

On and around **Cima Dome,** a rare geological anomaly, grows the world's largest and densest Joshua tree forest. Botanists say Cima's Joshuas are more symmetrical than their cousins elsewhere in the Mojave. The dramatic colors of the sky at sunset provide a breathtaking backdrop for Cima's Joshua trees, some more than 25 feet tall and several hundred years old.

Tucked into the Providence Mountains, in the southern portion of the preserve, is a treat everyone should try to see. The **Mitchell Caverns** 🐾, contained in a state recreation area within the national preserve, are a geological oddity exploited for tourism but still quite fascinating. Regular tours are conducted of these cool rock "rooms"; in addition to showcasing marvelous stalactites, stalagmites, and other limestone formations, the caves have proven to be rich in Native American archaeological finds.

Hole-in-the-Wall and **Mid Hills** are the centerpieces of Mojave National Preserve. Both locales offer diverse desert scenery, fine campgrounds, and the feeling of being in the middle of nowhere—because you are. The preserve's best drive links the two sites. In 1989, **Wildhorse Canyon Road,** which loops from Mid Hills Campground to Hole-in-the-Wall Campground, was declared the nation's first official "Back Country Byway," an honor federal agencies bestow upon America's most scenic back roads. The 11-mile, horseshoe-shaped road crosses wide-open country dotted with cholla and, in season, delicate purple, yellow, and red wildflowers. Dramatic volcanic slopes and flattop mesas tower over the low desert.

Mile-high Mid Hills, so named because of its location halfway between the Providence and New York mountains, recalls the Great Basin Desert topography of Nevada and Utah. Mid Hills Campground offers a grand observation point from which to gaze out at the creamy, coffee-colored Pinto Mountains to the north and the rolling Kelso Dunes shining on the western horizon.

Hole-in-the-Wall is the kind of place Butch Cassidy and the Sundance Kid would have chosen as a hideout. This twisted maze of rhyolite rocks is a form of crystallized red-lava rock. A series of iron rings aids descent into Hole-in-the-Wall; they're not particularly difficult for those who are reasonably agile and take their time.

Kelso Dunes, Mitchell Caverns, Cima Dome, and Hole-in-the-Wall are highlights of the preserve that can be viewed in a weekend. But you'll need a week just to see all the major sights, and maybe a lifetime to really get to know the East Mojave. And right now, without much in the way of services, the traveler to this desert must be well prepared and self-reliant. For many, this is what makes a trip to the East Mojave an adventure.

If Mojave National Preserve attracts you, you'll want to return again and again to see the wonders of this desert, including **Caruthers Canyon,** a "botanical island" of pinyon pine and juniper woodland, and **Ivanpah Valley,** which supports the largest desert tortoise population in the California desert.

HIKING & BIKING

HIKING   The free-form ambling climb to the top of the **Kelso Dunes** is 3 miles round-trip. A cool, inviting pinyon pine/juniper woodland is explored by the **Caruthers Canyon Trail** (3 miles round-trip). The longest pathway is **Mid Hills to Hole-in-the-Wall Trail,** a grand tour of basin and range tabletop mesas, large pinyon trees, and colorful cacti; it's 8 miles one-way. If you're not up for a long day hike, the 1-mile trip from **Hole-in-the-Wall Campground** to **Banshee Canyon** and the 5-mile jaunt to **Wildhorse Canyon** offer some easier alternatives. Be sure to pick up trail maps at one of the visitor centers.

MOUNTAIN BIKING   Opportunities are as extensive as the preserve's hundreds of miles of lonesome dirt roads. The 140-mile historic **Mojave Road,** a rough four-wheel-drive route, visits many of the most scenic areas in the East Mojave; sections of this road make excellent bike tours. Prepare well: The Mojave Road and other dirt roads are rugged routes through desert wilderness.

CAMPING

The **Mid Hills Campground** is located in a pinyon-pine/juniper woodland and offers outstanding views. This mile-high camp is the coolest in the East Mojave. Nearby **Hole-in-the-Wall Campground** is perched above two dramatic canyons. Both campgrounds have pit toilets and potable water but no utility hookups. *Warning:* The washboard dirt road between the two might be too jarring for many two-wheel-drive passenger cars.

There are also some sites at **Providence Mountain State Recreation Area** (Mitchell Caverns; see "Exploring the Park," above).

One of the highlights of the East Mojave Desert is camping in the open desert all by your lonesome, but certain rules apply. Call the **Mojave Desert Information Center** (© 760/733-4040) for suggestions.

NEARBY TOWNS WITH TOURIST SERVICES

BARSTOW   This sizable town has a great many restaurants and motels, and is roughly a 1-hour drive from the center of the preserve. Of the dozen motels in town, the most reliable are the **Best Western Desert Villa,** 1984 E. Main St., Barstow, CA 92311 (© 760/256-1781), and the **Holiday Inn,** 1511 E. Main St., Barstow, CA 92311 (© 760/256-5673).

BAKER   Accommodations and food are available in this small desert town, which is a good place to fill up your gas tank and purchase supplies before entering Mojave National Preserve. Inexpensive lodging can be secured at the **Bun**

Boy Motel, P.O. Box 130, Baker, CA 92309 (© **760/733-4363**). The Bun Boy Coffee Shop is open 24 hours. For a tasty surprise, stop at the **Mad Greek** (© **760/733-4354**). Order a Greek salad, souvlaki, or baklava, and marvel at your good fortune for finding such tasty food and pleasant surroundings in the middle of nowhere.

NIPTON   This tiny, charming town boasts a "trading post" that stocks snacks, maps, ice, and native jewelry; and the **Hotel Nipton** (© **760/856-2335**), a B&B with a sitting room, two bathrooms down the hall, and four guest rooms, each going for $60 a night. Jerry Freeman, a former hard-rock miner who purchased the entire town in 1984, says hotel occupancy is up 80% since the East Mojave became a national preserve. He and his wife, Roxanne, moved from the famous sands of Malibu to the abandoned ghost town and have gradually brought it back to life. Nipton is located on Nipton Road, a few miles from I-15 near the Nevada state line.

PRIMM (FORMERLY STATELINE)   This privately owned town on the California–Nevada border features three hotel/casinos—Whiskey Pete's, Buffalo Bill's, and Primadonna—each as large and garish as an amusement park and all managed by the same company. Rooms here are pretty nice, really cheap, and (if you have a twisted sense of humor) an ironic counterpoint to the wilderness you came for. With a dozen restaurants, including those low-cost Vegas-style buffets, Primm might also be your best dining bet. For reservations, call © **800/FUN-STOP.**

6 Death Valley National Park

115 miles N of Baker; 290 miles NE of LA

Park? Death Valley National Park? The Forty-Niners, whose suffering gave the valley its name, would have howled at the notion. To them, other four-letter words would have been more appropriate: gold, mine, heat, lost, dead. And the four-letter words shouted by teamsters who drove the 20-mule-team borax wagons need not be repeated here.

Americans looking for gold in California's mountains in 1849 were forced to cross the burning sands to avoid severe snowstorms in the nearby Sierra Nevada. Some perished along the way, and the land became known as Death Valley.

Mountains stand naked, unadorned. The bitter waters of saline lakes evaporate into bizarre, razor-sharp crystal formations. Jagged canyons jab deep into the earth. Oven-like heat, frigid cold, and the driest air imaginable combine to make this one of the most inhospitable locations in the world.

But, human nature being what it is, it's not surprising that people have long been drawn to challenge the power of Mother Nature, even in this, her home court. Man's first foray into tourism began in 1925, a scant 76 years after the Forty-Niners' harrowing experiences (which would discourage most sane folks from ever returning!). It probably would have begun sooner, but the valley had been consumed with lucrative borax mining since the late 1880s.

Death Valley is raw, bare earth, the way it must have looked before life began. Here, forces of the earth are exposed to view with dramatic clarity; just looking out on the landscape, it's impossible to know what year—or what century—it is. It's no coincidence that many of Death Valley's topographical features are associated with hellish images—the Funeral Mountains, Furnace Creek, Dante's View, Coffin Peak, and the Devil's Golf Course. But it can be a place of serenity.

Death Valley National Park

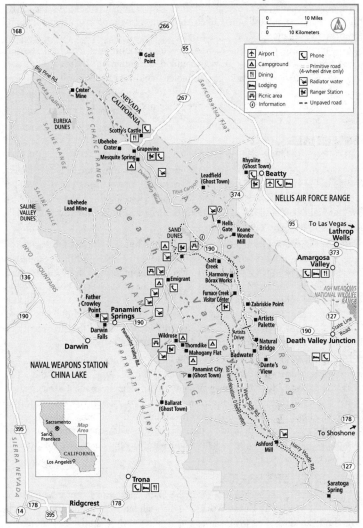

In one of his last official acts, President Herbert Hoover signed a proclamation designating Death Valley a national monument on February 11, 1933. With the stroke of a pen, he not only authorized the protection of a vast and wondrous land, but also helped to transform one of the earth's least hospitable spots into a popular tourist destination.

The naming of Death Valley National Monument came at a time when Americans began to discover the romance of the desert. Land that had previously been considered hideously devoid of life was now celebrated for its spare beauty; places that had once been feared for their harshness were now admired for their uniqueness. In 1994, when President Clinton signed the California Desert Protection Act, Death Valley National Park became the largest national park outside Alaska, with over 3.3 million acres. Though remote, it's one of the most heavily visited, and you're likely to hear less English spoken than German, French, and Japanese.

Today's visitor to Death Valley drives in air-conditioned comfort, stays in comfortable hotel rooms or at well-maintained campgrounds, orders meals and provisions at park concessions, even quaffs a cold beer at the local saloon. You can take a swim in the Olympic-size pool, tour a Moorish castle, shop for souvenirs, and enjoy the desert landscape while hiking along a nature trail with a park ranger.

ESSENTIALS

GETTING THERE   There are several routes into the park, all of which involve crossing one of the steep mountain ranges that isolate Death Valley from, well, everything. Perhaps the most scenic entry to the park is via Calif. 190, east of Calif. 178 from Ridgecrest. Another scenic drive to the park is by way of Calif. 127 and Calif. 190 from Baker. You'll be required to pay a $10-per-car entrance fee, valid for 7 days.

WHEN TO GO   Death Valley is popular year-round, with the greatest number of visitors during the temperate winter and spring (Nov–Mar). But the park is never deserted, not even in the truly scorching months of July, August, and September, as international visitors and extreme heat–seekers come in ever-increasing numbers to experience record-breaking temperatures. Even during the "cool" months (when evenings can actually become quite chilly), it's essential to wear sunscreen to protect against unfiltered rays, and to drink plenty of water to avoid become dehydrated in the ultra-arid climate.

VISITOR CENTER & INFORMATION   For information before you go, contact the Superintendent, Death Valley National Park, Death Valley, CA 92328 (© **760/786-2331;** www.nps.gov/deva). The **Furnace Creek Visitor Center & Museum,** 15 miles inside the eastern park boundary on Calif. 190 (© **760/786-2331**), offers interpretive exhibits and an hourly slide program. Ask at the information desk for ranger-led nature walks and evening naturalist programs. The center is open daily from 8am to 6pm in winter (to 5pm in summer).

EXPLORING THE PARK

A good first stop after checking in at the main park visitor center in Furnace Creek is the **Harmony Borax Works**—a rock-salt landscape as tortured as you'll ever find. Death Valley prospectors called borax "white gold," and though it wasn't exactly a glamorous substance, it was a profitable one. From 1883 to 1888, more than 20 million pounds of borax were transported from the Harmony Borax Works, and borax mining continued in Death Valley until 1928. A short trail with interpretive signs leads past the ruins of the old borax refinery and some outlying buildings. Transport of the borax was the stuff of legends, too. The famous 20-mule teams hauled the huge loaded wagons 165 miles to the rail station at Mojave. To learn more about this colorful era, visit the Borax Museum at Furnace Creek Ranch and the park visitor center, also located in Furnace Creek.

Badwater—at 282 feet below sea level, the lowest point in the Western Hemisphere—is also one of the hottest places in the world, with regularly recorded summer temperatures of 120°F (49°C). Badwater is mostly a curiosity, and really not that much hotter or more brutal than the rest of Death Valley;

most folks like to make a brief detour to see the otherworldly landscape and to say they were there.

Salt Creek is the home of the **Salt Creek pupfish,** found nowhere else on earth. This little fish, which has made some amazing adaptations to survive in this arid land, can be glimpsed from a wooden-boardwalk nature trail. In spring, a million pupfish might be wriggling in the creek, but by summer's end only a few thousand remain.

Before sunrise, photographers set up their tripods at **Zabriskie Point** and aim their cameras down at the magnificent panoramic view of Golden Canyon's pale mudstone hills and the great valley beyond. For another spectacular vista, check out **Dante's View,** a 5,475-foot viewpoint looking out over the shimmering Death Valley floor, backed by the high Panamint Mountains.

Just south of Furnace Creek is the 9-mile loop of **Artists Drive,** an easy must-see for visitors (except those in RVs, which can't negotiate the sharp, rock-bordered curves in the road). From the highway, you can't see the splendid palette of colors splashed on the rocks behind the foothills; once inside, though, stop and climb a low hill that offers an overhead view, then continue through to aptly named **Artists Palette,** where an interpretive sign explains the source of nature's rainbow.

Scotty's Castle & the Gas House Museum (© 760/786-2392), the Mediterranean hacienda in the northern part of the park, is unabashedly Death Valley's premier tourist attraction. Visitors are wowed by the elaborate Spanish tiles, well-crafted furnishings, and innovative construction that included solar water heating. Even more compelling is the colorful history of this villa in remote Grapevine Canyon, brought to life by park rangers dressed in 1930s period clothing. Don't be surprised if the castle cook or a friend of Scotty's gives you a special insight into castle life.

Construction of the "castle"—more officially, Death Valley Ranch—began in 1924. It was to be a winter retreat for eccentric Chicago millionaire Albert Johnson. The insurance tycoon's unlikely friendship with prospector, cowboy, and spinner-of-tall-tales Walter Scott put the $2.3-million structure on the map and captured the public's imagination. Scotty greeted visitors and told them fanciful stories from the early hard-rock mining days of Death Valley.

The 1-hour walking tour of Scotty's Castle is excellent, both for its inside look at the mansion and for what it reveals about the eccentricities of Johnson and Scotty. Tours fill up quickly; arrive early for the first available spots (there's an $8 fee). A snack bar and gift shop make the wait more comfortable. To learn more about the castle grounds, pick up the pamphlet *A Walking Tour of Scotty's Castle,* which leads you on an exploration from stable to swimming pool, from bunkhouse to powerhouse.

Near Scotty's Castle is **Ubehebe Crater.** It's known as an explosion crater—one look and you'll know why. When hot magma rose from the depths of the earth to meet the groundwater, the resultant steam blasted out a crater and scattered cinders.

BIKING & HIKING

BIKING   Because most (94%) of the park is federally designated wilderness, cycling is allowed only on roads used by cars. Cycling is not allowed on hiking trails.

Good routes for bikers include Racetrack (28 miles, mainly level), Greenwater Valley (30 miles, mostly level), Cottonwood Canyon (20 miles), and West

Side Road (40 miles, fairly level with some washboard sections). Artists Drive is 8 miles long and paved, with some steep uphills. A favorite is Titus Canyon (28 miles on a hilly road—it's highly recommended that you make this a one-way descent).

HIKING The trails in Death Valley range from the half-mile **Salt Creek Nature Trail,** an easy boardwalk path suitable for everyone in the family, to the grueling **Telescope Peak Trail** (14 miles round-trip), an all-day challenge. Telescope Peak is a strenuous, 3,000-foot climb to the 11,049-foot summit, where you'll be rewarded by the view described by one pioneer: "You can see so far, it's just like looking through a telescope." Snow-covered during the winter, the peak is best climbed between May and November.

But there are lots of levels in between. I like the trail into **Mosaic Canyon,** near Stovepipe Wells, where water has polished the marble rock into white, gray, and black mosaics. It's a relatively easy 2½-mile scramble through long, narrow walls that seem quite "gallery-like"—and provide welcome shade at every turn.

Romping among the **Sand Dunes** on the way to Stovepipe Wells is also fun, particularly for kids. It's a free-form adventure, and the dunes aren't particularly high—but the sun can be merciless. The sand in the dunes is actually tiny pieces of rock, most of them quartz fragments. As with all desert activities, your water supply is crucial.

Near the park's eastern border, two trails lead from the **Keane Wonder Mill,** site of a successful gold mine. The first is a steep and strenuous 2-mile challenge leading to the mine itself, passing along the way the solid, efficient wooden tramway that carried ore out of the mountain.

If that's beyond your fitness level, try the **Keane Wonder Spring Trail,** leading in another direction. This 2-mile walk is much easier, and the spring that supplied water for the Keane Wonder operation will announce itself with a sulfur smell and piping birdcalls.

If you're visiting **Ubehebe Crater,** there's a steep but plain trail leading from the parking area up to the crater's lip and around some of the contours. Fierce winds can hamper your progress, but you'll get the exhilarating feeling that you're truly on another planet.

Park rangers can provide topographical maps and detailed directions to these and a dozen other hiking trails within the national park.

WHERE TO STAY

The park's nine campgrounds are located at elevations ranging from below sea level to 8,000 feet. In Furnace Creek, **Sunset** offers 1,000 spaces with water and flush toilets. **Furnace Creek Campground** has 200 similarly appointed spaces. **Stovepipe Wells** has 200 spaces with water and flush toilets. Camping reservations can be made online at **http://reservations.nps.gov** or by calling ✆ **800/ 365-2267.**

The **Furnace Creek Ranch** (✆ 760/786-2345; www.furnacecreekresort. com) has 224 no-frills cottage units with air-conditioning and showers. The swimming pool is a popular hangout for tired lodgers. Nearby are a coffee shop, saloon, steakhouse, and general store. **Stove Pipe Wells Village** (✆ 760/786-2387) has 74 modest rooms with air-conditioning and showers, plus a casual dining room that closes between meals.

The only lodging within the park not operated by the official concessionaire is the **Panamint Springs Resort** (✆ 702/482-7680; www.deathvalley.com), a truly charming rustic motel, cafe, and snack shop about an hour east of Furnace Creek.

Because accommodations in Death Valley are both limited and expensive, you might consider the money-saving (but inconvenient) option of spending a night at one of the two gateway towns: **Lone Pine,** on the west side of the park, or **Baker,** on the south. **Beatty, Nevada,** which has inexpensive lodging, is an hour's drive from the park's center. The restored **Amargosa Hotel** (✆ **760/852-4441**) in Death Valley Junction offers 14 rooms in a historic, out-of-the-way place, 40 minutes from Furnace Creek.

Tip: Meals and groceries are exceptionally costly due to the remoteness of the park. If possible, consider bringing a cooler with some snacks, sandwiches, and beverages to last the duration of your visit. Ice is easily obtainable, and you'll also be able to keep water chilled.

Furnace Creek Inn   Like an oasis in the middle of stark Death Valley, the inn's red-tiled roofs and sparkling blue mineral-spring-fed swimming pool hint at the elegance within. The hotel has equipped its 66 deluxe rooms and suites with every modern amenity while successfully preserving the charm of this 1930s resort. Stroll the lush, palm-shaded gardens before sitting down to a meal in the elegant Dining Room, where the food is excellent but the formality a bit out of place. Don tennis whites for a match in the midwinter sunshine, enjoy 18 holes of golf nearby, take an excursion on horseback—there's even a shuttle from the Furnace Creek private airstrip for well-heeled clientele. Reserve early: The inn is booked solid year-round with American and European guests who appreciate a little pampering after a day spent in the park.

Hwy. 190 (P.O. Box 1), Death Valley, CA 92328. ✆ **800/236-7916** or 760/786-2345. Fax 760/786-2307. www.furnacecreekresort.com. 66 units. Oct–May $235–$350 double; $345–$365 suite. Off-season $155–$210 double; $225 suite. Extra person $15. AE, DC, DISC, MC, V. **Amenities:** Restaurant; lounge; naturally heated outdoor pool; 4 night-lit tennis courts; nearby golf course; room service 7am–10pm; in-room massage. *In room:* A/C, TV w/pay movies, fridge, hair dryer, iron.

16

San Diego & Environs

by Stephanie Avnet Yates

San Diego is best known for its benign climate and fabulous beaches, attributes that make the city one big outdoor playground on sunny days. With 70 miles of sandy coastline—plus pretty, sheltered Mission Bay—you can choose from swimming, snorkeling, windsurfing, kayaking, bicycling, skating, and tons of other fun in or near the water. The city is also home to top-notch attractions, including three world-famous animal parks and splendid Balboa Park, a cultural and recreational jewel that's one of the finest urban parks in the country. Once dismissed as a slow-growth, conservative Navy town, San Diego has been expanding steadily over the past 2 decades, and now boasts an almost Los Angeles–like diversity of neighborhoods and residents. A heightened sensitivity to historical preservation means formerly seedy downtown neighborhoods and architecturally rich suburbs are being carefully restored; they draw a stylish young crowd that's updating the face of San Diego dining, shopping, and entertainment. California's first city, San Diego reflects its Spanish-Mexican heritage in every corner—in fact, bustling Tijuana is just across the border, less than 30 minutes away. So pack a laid-back attitude along with your sandals and swimsuit, and welcome to California's grown-up beach town.

1 Orientation

ARRIVING

BY PLANE

San Diego International Airport, 3707 N. Harbor Dr. (© **619/231-2100**), locally known as Lindbergh Field, is just 3 miles from downtown. Most of the major carriers fly here. Lindbergh Field consists of three adjacent passenger buildings: Terminal 1, Terminal 2, and the Terminal 2 Expansion. Short local flights use the Commuter Terminal, which is a half mile away and can be reached from the main airport by the free "red bus" shuttle.

TRANSPORTATION FROM THE AIRPORT All the major car-rental agencies have offices at the airport, including **Avis** (© **800/230-4898**), **Budget** (© **800/527-0700**), **Dollar** (© **800/800-3665**), and **Hertz** (© **800/654-3131**). If you're driving to downtown from the airport, take Harbor Drive south to Broadway, the main east-west thoroughfare, and turn left. To reach Hillcrest or Balboa Park, exit the airport toward I-5, and follow the signs for Laurel Street. To reach Mission Bay (home of SeaWorld), take I-5 north to I-8 west. To reach La Jolla, take I-5 north to the Ardath Road exit, turning onto Torrey Pines Road.

    Metropolitan Transit System (MTS) (© **619/233-3004;** www.sdcommute. com) bus route no. 992 provides service between the airport and downtown San Diego. Route no. 992 bus stops are located at each of the three terminals. The

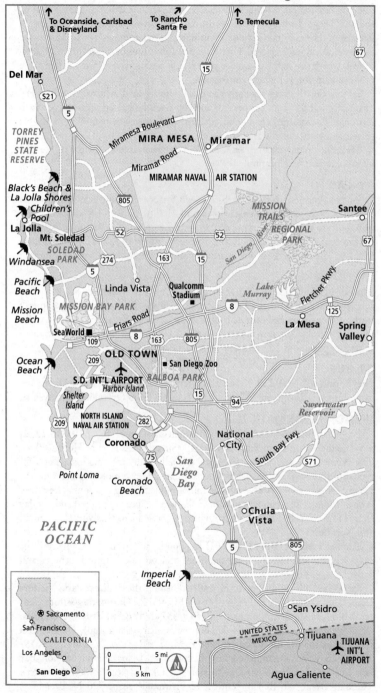

To Oceanside, Carlsbad & Disneyland

To Rancho Santa Fe

To Temecula

67

15

Del Mar

S21

5

TORREY PINES STATE RESERVE

MIRA MESA

Miramesa Boulevard

Miramar

Miramar Road

MIRAMAR NAVAL AIR STATION

805

Black's Beach & La Jolla Shores

Children's Pool

MISSION TRAILS

Santee

La Jolla

Mt. Soledad

SOLEDAD PARK

52

52

REGIONAL PARK

San Diego River

67

Windansea

274

5

Linda Vista

163

15

Lake Murray

Fletcher Pkwy.

125

Pacific Beach

Qualcomm Stadium

8

La Mesa

Spring Valley

MISSION BAY PARK

Friars Road

8

163

805

Mission Beach

SeaWorld

109

OLD TOWN

San Diego Zoo

Ocean Beach

209

S.D. INT'L AIRPORT

Harbor Island

BALBOA PARK

94

15

Shelter Island

Sweetwater Reservoir

NORTH ISLAND NAVAL AIR STATION

209

282

National City

Coronado

75

San Diego Bay

South Bay Fwy.

S71

Point Loma

Coronado Beach

Chula Vista

PACIFIC OCEAN

5

805

Imperial Beach

⊛ Sacramento

San Francisco

CALIFORNIA

Los Angeles

San Diego

San Ysidro

UNITED STATES
MEXICO

Tijuana

TIJUANA INT'L AIRPORT

0   5 mi

0   5 km

N

Agua Caliente

one-way fare is $2.25. Request a transfer if you're connecting to another bus or the San Diego Trolley route downtown. Downtown, route no. 992 stops on Broadway. The ride takes about 15 minutes; buses come at 10- to 15-minute intervals. At Broadway and First Avenue is the **Transit Store** (© **619/234-1060**), where the staff can answer your transit questions and provide free route maps to help you get where you're going.

Several **shuttles** run regularly from the airport to downtown hotels. They charge around $5 to $9 per person, and you'll see designated areas outside each terminal. The shuttles are a good deal for single travelers; two or more people traveling together might as well take a taxi.

Taxis line up outside both terminals and charge around $8 (before tip) to take you to a downtown location.

BY CAR

From Los Angeles, you'll enter San Diego via coastal route I-5. From points northeast of the city, you'll come down on I-15 (link up with I-8 west and Calif. 163 south to drive into downtown). From the east, you'll come in on I-8, connecting with Calif. 163 south (Calif. 163 turns into 10th Ave.). From the south, take I-5. The freeways are well marked, pointing the way to downtown streets.

BY TRAIN

Amtrak (© **800/USA-RAIL;** www.amtrak.com) trains connect San Diego to Los Angeles and the rest of the country. Trains pull into San Diego's pretty mission-style **Santa Fe Station,** 1850 Kettner Blvd. (at Broadway), within walking distance of many downtown hotels and 1½ blocks from the Embarcadero. Expect to pay about $27 one-way from Los Angeles.

BY BUS

Greyhound (© **800/229-9424;** www.greyhound.com) serves San Diego; the bus terminal is downtown, on Broadway between Front Street and First Avenue.

VISITOR INFORMATION

The official **International Visitor Information Center** (© **619/236-1212;** www.sandiego.org) is on First Avenue at F Street, street level at Horton Plaza. The glossy *San Diego Visitors Planning Guide* includes information on accommodations, dining, activities, attractions, tours, and transportation. Ask for the *Super Savings Coupon Book,* which is full of money-saving coupons. The center is open Monday through Saturday from 8:30am to 5pm year-round and Sunday from 11am to 5pm June through August; it's closed Thanksgiving, Christmas, and New Year's Day.

Traveler's Aid (© **619/231-7361**) has booths at Terminals 1 and 2 and the train station. Volunteers answer questions and provide helpful brochures and maps.

Specialized visitor information outlets include the **Balboa Park Visitors Center,** located at 1549 El Prado (© **619/239-0512**); **Coronado Visitors Center,** 1100 Orange Ave., Coronado (© **619/437-8788**); and **Promote La Jolla,** 1150 Silverado St. (© **858/454-5718;** www.lajollabythesea.com). The **Mission Bay Visitor Information Center,** 2688 E. Mission Bay Dr., San Diego (© **619/276-8200;** www.infosandiego.com), is conveniently located on Mission Bay next to I-5 (exit Clairemont Dr./Mission Bay Dr. and head toward the water). The **San Diego North Convention & Visitors Bureau,** 720 N. Broadway, Escondido (© **800/848-3336** or 760/745-4741; www.sandiegonorth.com), can provide information on excursion areas in San Diego County, including Del Mar, Carlsbad, Escondido, Julian, and Anza-Borrego Desert State Park.

To find out what's on at the theater and who's playing in the clubs during your visit, pick up a copy of the *San Diego Reader,* a free weekly newspaper available all over the city. There's also a Thursday entertainment supplement called **"Night & Day"** in the *San Diego Union-Tribune.*

CITY LAYOUT

San Diego has a clearly defined downtown, which is surrounded by a dozen or more separate neighborhoods—each with its own personality, but all legally part of the city. The street system is straightforward, so getting around is fairly easy.

MAIN ARTERIES & STREETS   I-5 runs south to the United States–Mexico border and north to Old Town, Mission Bay, La Jolla, and beyond. It's the most important thoroughfare in San Diego, connecting the city's divergent parts with one another and the entire region with the rest of the state. Access to the Coronado Bay Bridge is via I-5. Balboa Park is most easily accessible via 12th Avenue, which becomes Park Boulevard. Fifth Avenue leads to the Hillcrest/ Uptown area.

Downtown, Broadway is the main street. Located in the heart of the central business district, it's intersected by Fourth and Fifth avenues (running south and north, respectively). Harbor Drive, hugging the waterfront (Embarcadero), connects downtown with the airport to the northwest and the Convention Center to the south.

NEIGHBORHOODS IN BRIEF

Downtown   The business, shopping, dining, and entertainment heart of the city, it includes Horton Plaza, the Gaslamp Quarter, the Embarcadero (waterfront), and the distinctive Convention Center. Visitors with business to conduct in the city center would be wise to stay downtown. The **Gaslamp Quarter** is the center of a massive redevelopment kicked off in the mid-1980s with the opening of **Horton Plaza,** a colorful multi-level 6-block shopping mall that's a major attraction in itself. Now the once-seedy area is filled with trendy boutiques, chic restaurants, and swingin' nightspots.

Hillcrest/Uptown   Despite the cachet of being adjacent to **Balboa Park**—home to the **San Diego Zoo** and numerous splendid museums— this once-elite suburban area north of downtown fell into neglect during the 1960s and '70s. However, Hillcrest's charms have been restored by legions of preservation-minded residents—including a very active gay community—and is the local equivalent of LA's West Hollywood. Centrally located and packed with the latest in stylish restaurants and avant-garde boutiques, Hillcrest also offers less expensive and more personalized accommodations than anywhere else in the city.

Old Town & Mission Valley   This area encompasses the Old Town State Historic Park, Presidio Park, Heritage Park, and numerous museums harking back to the early 1900s and the city's beginnings. There's shopping and dining here, too, all aimed at tourists. Not far from Old Town lies the vast suburban sprawl of Mission Valley, home to San Diego's gigantic shopping centers. Between them is **Hotel Circle,** adjacent to I-8, where a string of midprice and budget hotel options offer an alternative to more desirable neighborhoods.

Mission Bay & the Beaches
Mission Bay is a watery playground perfect for water-skiing, sailing, and windsurfing. The adjacent communities of Ocean Beach, Mission Beach, and Pacific Beach are known for their wide stretches of sand fronting the Pacific, active nightlife, and California-casual dining. The **boardwalk,** which runs from South Mission Beach through North Mission Beach to Pacific Beach, is a popular place for in-line skating, bike riding, and watching sunsets.

La Jolla With an atmosphere that's a cross between Rodeo Drive and a Mediterranean village, this seaside community is home to an inordinate number of wealthy folks who could live anywhere but choose to live here, surrounded by the beach, the University of California at San Diego, outstanding restaurants, pricey and traditional shops, and some of the world's best medical facilities. The name is a compromise between Spanish and American Indian, as is the pronunciation—La *Hoy*-ya—and it has come to mean "the jewel."

Coronado The "island" of Coronado is actually a peninsula, home to the U.S. Naval Air Station and a town filled with charming cottages, quaint shops along Orange Avenue (the main street), and ritzy hotels and resorts that include the landmark **Hotel del Coronado.** Coronado has a lovely duned beach; it's also home to more retired admirals than any other community in the country.

2 Getting Around

BY CAR

San Diego has its fair share of traffic, concentrated in the downtown area, and heaviest during the morning and evening commuting hours. Aside from that, it's a very car-friendly town and easy to navigate.

Downtown, many streets run one way, and finding a parking space can be tricky—but some reasonably priced parking lots are centrally located.

RENTALS All the large, national car-rental firms have rental outlets at the airport (see "Arriving," above), in the major hotels, and at other locations around the city. **Avis** (© **800/230-4898**), like several other companies, will allow its cars into Mexico as far as Ensenada, providing that you stop before crossing the border and buy Mexican auto insurance. You would also be wise to buy insurance if you drive your own car south of the border.

PARKING Parking meters are plentiful in most San Diego areas: Posted signs indicate operating hours—generally between 8am and 6pm, even on weekends—and most meters accept only quarters. In the popular Gaslamp Quarter, consider parking in Horton Plaza's garage (G St. and Fourth Ave.), which is free to shoppers for the first 3 hours, $1 for every additional half-hour.

BY PUBLIC TRANSPORTATION

Both city buses and the **San Diego Trolley**—which runs to the Mexican border, Old Town, and East County—are operated by the **San Diego Metropolitan Transit System** (MTS) (© **619/233-3004;** www.sdcommute.com). The system's **Transit Store,** 102 Broadway at First Avenue (© **619/234-1060**), is a complete public-transportation information center, supplying travelers with passes, tokens, timetables, maps, and brochures. It's open Monday through Friday from 8:30am to 5:30pm, Saturday and Sunday from 10am to 4pm. Request a copy of the useful brochure, *Your Open Door to San Diego,* which details the city's most popular tourist attractions and the buses that take you to them. For **bus route information** (and other transit FAQ), you can also call ℂ **619/685-4900** 24 hours a day.

The $5 **Day-Tripper pass** allows for 1 day of unlimited rides on the public transit system; you can also get a 4-day pass for $12. Passes are available from the Transit Store and at all Trolley Station automatic ticket vending machines.

BY BUS Bus stops are marked by rectangular blue signs, every other block or so on local routes. More than 20 bus routes traverse downtown. Most fares range from $1.50 to $2.50, depending on the distance and type of service (local or express). Buses accept dollar bills, but the driver can't give change. Most buses run every half-hour. Transfers should be obtained from the driver when boarding.

The **Coronado Shuttle,** route no. 904, runs between the Coronado Island Marriott and the Old Ferry Landing along Orange Avenue to the Hotel del Coronado, Glorietta Bay, Loews Coronado Bay Resort, and back again. It costs only $1 per person. Route no. 901 goes to Coronado from downtown San Diego; the fare is $2 for adults, $1 for seniors and children. Call ℂ **619/233-3004** for more information.

BY TROLLEY The San Diego Trolley system runs south to the Mexican border (a 40-min. trip), north to Old Town, and east to the city of Santee. Within the city, trolleys stop at many popular locations; fares range from $1.25 to $2.50. Children under 5 ride free; seniors and riders with disabilities pay only 75¢. For **recorded trolley information,** call ℂ **619/685-4900.** To talk to a real person, you can call ℂ **619/233-3004** from 5:30am to 8:30pm Monday through Friday.

Trolleys operate on a self-service fare-collection system; riders purchase tickets from machines in stations before boarding, and fare inspectors board trains at random to check tickets. The bright-red trains run every 15 minutes during the day (every half-hour at night) and stop for only 30 seconds at each stop. To board, push the lighted green button beside the doors; to exit the car, push the lighted white button.

Trolleys generally operate daily from 5am to about 12:30am, although the Blue Line, which goes to the border, runs around the clock on Saturday.

BY TRAIN Within the San Diego area, **Amtrak** (ℂ **800/USA-RAIL;** www.amtrak.com) stops downtown, in Solana Beach, and in Oceanside. Fares range from $5 to $15 each way, depending on how far you go. You can also get to Disneyland in Anaheim (see chapter 14, "Side Trips from Los Angeles") via the train; call for details.

San Diego's express rail commuter service, **The Coaster** (ℂ **800/COASTER**), travels between downtown and Oceanside with stops en route at Old Town, Sorrento Valley, Solana Beach, Encinitas, and Carlsbad.

BY FERRY & WATER TAXI There's regularly scheduled **ferry service** (ℂ **619/234-4111**) between San Diego and Coronado. Ferries leave from the Broadway Pier on the hour from 9am to 9pm daily (until 10pm Fri–Sat), and return from the Old Ferry Landing in Coronado to the Broadway Pier every hour on the 42-minute mark from 9:42am to 9:42pm daily (until 10:42pm Fri–Sat). Ferries also run from the Fifth Avenue Landing near the Convention Center to the Old Ferry Landing at 1-hour intervals during roughly the same time period. The fare is $2 for each leg of the journey (50¢ extra if you bring your bike). Purchase tickets in advance at the Harbor Excursion kiosk on the Broadway Pier, at the Fifth Avenue Landing in San Diego, or at the Old Ferry Landing in Coronado.

Water taxis (© 619/235-TAXI) will take you around most of San Diego Bay for $5. If you want to go to the southern part of the bay (to Loews Coronado Bay Resort, for example), you'll be charged a flat fee of $25.

BY TAXI

Cab companies don't have standardized rates, except from the airport into town, which costs about $9 with tip. It's uncommon to find taxis cruising for passengers; phone for a guaranteed pickup. Companies include **Orange Cab** (© 619/291-3333), **San Diego Cab** (© 619/226-TAXI), and **Yellow Cab** (© 619/234-6161). The **Coronado Cab Company** (© 619/435-6211) serves Coronado. In La Jolla, call **La Jolla Cab** (© 858/453-4222).

BY ORGANIZED TOUR

The **Old Town Trolley Tours** (© 619/298-TOUR; www.trolleytours.com) aren't by trolley at all; rather, it's a privately operated open-air tour bus that travels in a continuous loop around the city, stopping at sightseeing highlights. It stops at more than a dozen places around the city, and you can hop on and off as many times as you please during one entire loop (but once you've completed the circuit, you can't go around again). A nonstop tour takes 90 minutes and is accompanied by a fast-moving live commentary on city history and sights. Major stops include Old Town, Presidio Park, Bazaar del Mundo, Balboa Park, the San Diego Zoo, the Embarcadero, Seaport Village, and the Gaslamp Quarter. Tours operate daily from 9am to 5pm; they cost $24 for adults and $12 for children ages 4 to 12; kids under 4 ride free.

Gray Line San Diego (© 800/331-5077 or 619/491-0011; www.grayline sandiego.com) offers city sightseeing, including tours of Cabrillo National Monument, SeaWorld, and La Jolla. Other trips go farther afield, to the Wild Animal Park, Wine Country, and Tijuana and Ensenada, Mexico. Prices range from $24 to $56 for adults and $10 to $35 for children. **Contact Tours** (© 800/235-5393 or 619/477-8687; www.contacttours.com) offers city sightseeing tours, including a "Grand Tour" that covers San Diego, Tijuana, and a 1-hour harbor cruise. It also runs trips to the San Diego Zoo, SeaWorld, Disneyland, Universal Studios, Rosarito Beach, and Ensenada. Prices range from $26 to $62 for adults, $14 to $44 for children under 12, and include admissions.

BY BICYCLE

San Diego is great for bikers. It's relatively flat and many roads have designated bike lanes. If you didn't bring your own wheels, you can rent from **Bike Tours San Diego,** 509 Fifth Ave. (© 619/238-2444), or **Hamel's Action Sports Center,** 704 Ventura Place, off Mission Boulevard in Mission Beach (© 619/488-8889). In Coronado, there's **Bikes & Beyond** at the Old Ferry Landing (© 619/435-7180). Expect to pay $6 per hour for bicycles, $15 to $25 for surreys (pedal-powered carriages).

The **San Diego Region Bike Map** is available at visitor centers; to receive a copy in advance, call © 619/231-BIKE.

If a bus stop has a bike-route sign attached (not all of them do), you can place your bike on the bus's bike rack for free while you ride. The San Diego Trolley also allows bikes onboard for free. You just need a bike permit, which is available for $4 from the Transit Store, 102 Broadway at First Avenue (© 619/234-1060). Bikes can also be brought aboard the San Diego–Coronado ferry.

FAST FACTS: San Diego

American Express A full-service office is located downtown at 258 Broadway, at Third Avenue (☎ **619/234-4455**).

Area Codes In the past couple of years, San Diego County's area-code layout has become more complicated. The main area code, 619, is now used primarily by the core city, including downtown, uptown, Mission Valley, and Point Loma. Northern and coastal areas, including Mission Beach, Pacific Beach, La Jolla, Del Mar, Rancho Santa Fe, and Rancho Bernardo, use the area code 858. The vast southeastern portion of the city, primarily bedroom communities like El Cajon, La Mesa, National City, and Chula Vista, now use 935. Use 760 to reach the remainder of San Diego County, including Encinitas, Carlsbad, Oceanside, Escondido, Ramona, Julian, and Anza-Borrego.

Babysitters **Marion's Childcare** (☎ **619/582-5029**) has bonded babysitters available to come to your hotel room.

Dentist/Doctor For dental referrals, contact the **San Diego County Dental Society** at ☎ **800/201-0244** or 800/DENTIST. **Hotel Docs** (☎ **800/468-3537** or 619/275-2663) is a 24-hour network of physicians, dentists, and chiropractors who claim they'll come to your hotel room within 35 minutes of your call. They accept credit cards, and their services are covered by most insurance policies.

Emergencies For police, fire, highway patrol, or life-threatening medical emergencies, dial ☎ **911** from any phone. No coins are required.

Hospitals The most conveniently located emergency room is at **UCSD Medical Center–Hillcrest,** 200 W. Arbor Dr. (☎ 619/543-6400). In Coronado, head to **Coronado Hospital,** 250 Prospect Place (☎ 619/435-6251). In La Jolla, **Thornton Hospital,** 9300 Campus Point Dr. (☎ 858/657-7600), has a good emergency room.

Police For nonemergency matters, contact the downtown precinct at 1401 Broadway (☎ **619/531-2000**).

Post Office Post offices are located downtown, at 815 E St.; at 51 Horton Plaza, beside the Westin Hotel; and toward Point Loma, at 2535 Midway Dr. They are generally open Monday through Friday during regular business hours, plus Saturday mornings. For specific branch information, call ☎ **800/ASK-USPS** or log on to www.usps.gov.

Safety As cities go, San Diego is pretty safe. But use particular caution on beaches after dark, and stay on designated walkways and away from secluded areas in Balboa Park—night or day. In the Gaslamp Quarter, try to stay west of Fifth Avenue. Take particular care to lock your car and park in well-lit areas; San Diego's proximity to the border contributes to its high rate of auto theft.

Taxes A 7.5% sales tax is added at the register for all goods and services purchased in San Diego. The city hotel tax is 10.5%.

Useful Telephone Numbers For the correct time, call ☎ **853-1212** (works in all area codes). For local **weather**, call ☎ **619/289-1212.**

3 Where to Stay

The rates listed below are all "rack," or official rates—you can often do better. Rates tend to be highest in summer (especially true of beach hotels) and when there's a big convention in town. Remember to factor in the city's 10.5% hotel tax.

For good prices in all accommodation categories, contact **San Diego Hotel Reservations** (© **800/SAVE-CASH** or 619/627-9300; www.sandiegohotelres.com). Bed-and-breakfasts are growing in popularity, and several are listed below. For additional choices, contact the **San Diego Bed & Breakfast Guild** (© **619/523-1300;** www.bandbguildsandiego.org).

DOWNTOWN

The downtown area is very convenient for business travelers, but also includes hotels in the stylish Gaslamp Quarter, as well as those located near the harbor and other leisure attractions.

EXPENSIVE

Embassy Suites ⭐⭐   What might seem like an impersonal business hotel is actually one of the better deals in town. It provides modern accommodations with lots of room for families or claustrophobes. Built in 1988, this neoclassical high-rise is topped with a distinctive neon bull's-eye that's visible from far away. Every room is a suite, with sofa beds in the living-dining areas and convenient touches like microwaves in the kitchenette. All rooms open onto a 12-story atrium filled with palm trees, koi ponds, and a bubbling fountain; each also has a city or bay view. One block from Seaport Village and 5 blocks from downtown, the Embassy Suites is the second choice of Convention Center groups (after the pricier Hyatt Regency), and as a result it can be fully booked at unexpected times.

601 Pacific Hwy. (at N. Harbor Dr.), San Diego, CA 92101. © **800/EMBASSY** or 619/239-2400. Fax 619/239-1520. 337 suites. $189–$300 suite. Rates include full breakfast and afternoon cocktail. Children 17 and under stay free in parents' room. AE, DC, DISC, MC, V. Valet parking $14; indoor self-parking $11. Bus: 7. Trolley: Seaport Village. **Amenities:** 2 restaurants; indoor pool; tennis court; exercise room; Jacuzzi; concierge; car-rental desk; babysitting; laundry service; self-service laundry; VIP rooms. *In room:* A/C, TV w/pay movies, dataport, kitchenette, fridge, coffeemaker, hair dryer, iron.

Holiday Inn on the Bay ⭐⭐ *Kids*   With a location and list of services that make it ideal for business gatherings, vacationing families, and airport stopovers, this better-than-average Holiday Inn is reliable and nearly always offers great deals. The multi-building high-rise complex is located on the Embarcadero across from the harbor and the Maritime Museum—this scenic spot is only 1½ miles from the airport (you can watch planes landing and taking off), and 2 blocks from the train station and trolley. Rooms, while basic, always seem to sport clean new furnishings and plenty of thoughtful comforts. Choose your room carefully; while the bay views are astounding, city views can be depressing. In either case, request the highest floor possible.

1355 N. Harbor Dr. (at Ash St.), San Diego, CA 92101-3385. © **800/HOLIDAY** or 619/232-3861. Fax 619/232-4924. 600 units. $189–$209 double; from $400 suite. Children 17 and under stay free in parents' room. Terrific packages are available, as well as AARP and AAA rates as low as $99–$139. AE, DC, MC, V. Parking $13 (self) or $18 (valet). Bus: 22, 23, or 992. Pets accepted with $25 fee and $75 deposit. **Amenities:** 4 restaurants; lounge; outdoor heated pool; exercise room; concierge; business center; room service 6–11am and 5–11pm; babysitting; laundry service; self-service laundry. *In room:* A/C, TV w/pay movies, dataport, coffeemaker, hair dryer, iron.

U.S. Grant Hotel ⭐⭐⭐   In 1910, Ulysses S. Grant Jr. opened this stately hotel, now on the National Register of Historic Places, in honor of his father.

Famous guests have included Albert Einstein, Charles Lindbergh, FDR, and JFK. Resembling an Italianate palace, the hotel is of a style more often found on the East Coast. An elegant atmosphere prevails, with age-smoothed marble, wood paneling, crystal chandeliers, and formal room decor that verges on stuffy. Guest rooms are quite spacious, as are the richly outfitted bathrooms. Extras in the suites make them worth the splurge; each has a fireplace and Jacuzzi tub, and suite rates include continental breakfast and afternoon cocktails and hors d'oeuvres. Afternoon tea is served in the lobby Tuesday through Saturday with soft piano music as a backdrop. While the hotel has preserved a nostalgic formality, the surrounding neighborhood has become a hodgepodge of chic bistros, wandering panhandlers, and the visually loud Horton Plaza shopping center (which looms large right across the street.)

326 Broadway (between 3rd and 4th aves.), San Diego, CA 92101. © 800/237-5029 or 619/232-3121. Fax 619/232-3626. 340 units. $195–$215 double; from $275 suite. Children 11 and under stay free in parents' room. AAA, off-season, and weekend rates ($139–$179 double) available. Off-season packages available. AE, DC, MC, V. Parking $17. Bus: 2. Trolley: Civic Center (C St. and 3rd Ave.). Pets accepted. **Amenities:** Restaurant; jazz lounge; 24-hr. fitness center; in-room exercise bike/rowing machine rental; concierge; courtesy airport shuttle; business center; 24-hr. room service; babysitting; laundry service; dry cleaning. In room: A/C, TV w/pay movies, dataport, minibar, hair dryer.

MODERATE

Other reliable choices include the colorful and modern **Bristol Hotel,** 1055 First Ave., between Broadway and C St. (© **800/662-4477** or 619/232-6141; www.bristolhotelsandiego.com), adjacent to downtown and the Gaslamp Quarter. The **Best Western Bayside Inn,** 555 W. Ash St., at Columbia Street (© **800/341-1818** or 619/233-7500; www.baysideinn.com), is popular with business travelers and boasts magnificent views.

Gaslamp Plaza Suites ★★ (Value) You can't get closer to the center of the vibrant Gaslamp Quarter than this impeccably restored late Victorian. At 11 stories, it was San Diego's first skyscraper in 1913. Built (at great expense) of Australian gumwood, marble, brass, and exquisite etched glass, this splendid building originally housed San Diego Trust & Savings. Various other businesses (jewelers, lawyers, doctors, photographers) set up shop here until 1988, when the elegant structure was placed on the National Register of Historic Places and reopened as a boutique hotel.

You'll be surprised at the timeless elegance, from the dramatic lobby and wide corridors to guest rooms furnished with European flair. Each bears the name of a writer (Emerson, Swift, Zola, Shelley, Fitzgerald, and so on). Most rooms are spacious and offer luxuries rare in this price range, like pillow-top mattresses and premium toiletries, microwave ovens and dinnerware, and impressive bathrooms. Beware of the few cheapest rooms, however; they are uncomfortably small (although they do have regular-size bathrooms).

Despite the welcome recent addition of new, noise-muffling windows, don't be surprised to hear a hum from the street below, especially when the Quarter gets rockin' on the weekends.

520 E St. (corner of 5th Ave.), San Diego, CA 92101. © **619/232-9500.** Fax 619/238-9945. www.gaslamp plaza.com. 64 units. $89–$159 double; $179–$259 suite. Rates include continental breakfast. AE, DC, DISC, MC, V. Valet parking $18. Bus: 1, 3, or 25. Trolley: 5th Ave. **Amenities:** Restaurant; access to nearby health club; rooftop Jacuzzi. In room: A/C, TV/VCR, dataport, fridge, coffeemaker, hair dryer, iron, safe.

Horton Grand ★★ A cross between an elegant hotel and a charming inn, the Horton Grand combines two hotels that date from 1886—the Horton Grand (once an infamous red-light establishment) and the Brooklyn Hotel (which for

San Diego Accommodations & Dining

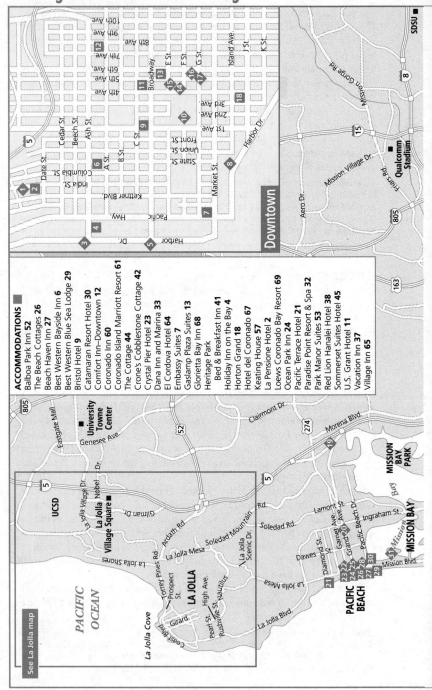

ACCOMMODATIONS

Balboa Park Inn **52**
The Beach Cottages **26**
Beach Haven Inn **27**
Best Western Bayside Inn **6**
Best Western Blue Sea Lodge **29**
Bristol Hotel **9**
Catamaran Resort Hotel **30**
Comfort Inn–Downtown **12**
Coronado Inn **60**
Coronado Island Marriott Resort **61**
The Cottage **44**
Crone's Cobblestone Cottage **42**
Crystal Pier Hotel **23**
Dana Inn and Marina **33**
El Cordova Hotel **64**
Embassy Suites **7**
Gaslamp Plaza Suites **13**
Glorietta Bay Inn **68**
Heritage Park
Bed & Breakfast Inn **41**
Holiday Inn on the Bay **4**
Horton Grand **18**
Hotel del Coronado **67**
Keating House **57**
La Pensione Hotel **2**
Loews Coronado Bay Resort **69**
Ocean Park Inn **24**
Pacific Terrace Hotel **21**
Paradise Point Resort & Spa **32**
Park Manor Suites **53**
Red Lion Hanalei Hotel **38**
Sommerset Suites Hotel **45**
U.S. Grant Hotel **11**
Vacation Inn **37**
Village Inn **65**

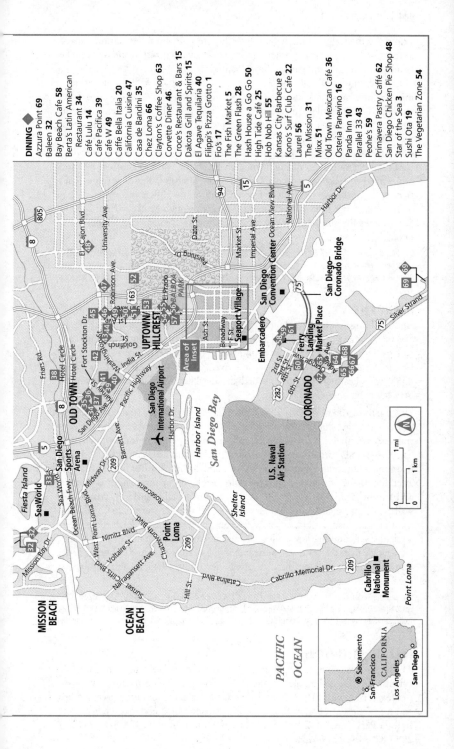

a time was the Kahle Saddlery Shop). Both were saved from demolition, moved to this spot, and connected by an airy atrium lobby filled with white wicker. The facade, with its graceful bay windows, is original.

Each room is utterly unique. All were renovated in 2000 with vintage furnishings, gas fireplaces, and business-savvy features. Bathrooms are resplendent with reproduction floor tiles, fine brass fixtures, and genteel appointments. Rooms overlook either the city or the fig tree–filled courtyard—they're divided between the clubby and darker "saddlery" side and the pastel-toned and Victorian "brothel" side. The suites (really just large studio-style rooms) are located in a newer wing; choosing one means sacrificing historic character for a sitting area/sofa bed and minibar with microwave oven. With all these offerings, there's a room that's right for everyone, so query your reservationist on the different features.

The Palace Bar serves afternoon tea Tuesday through Saturday from 2:30 to 5pm; there's live music Thursday through Saturday evenings and Sunday afternoons.

311 Island Ave. (at 4th Ave.), San Diego, CA 92101. ✆ 800/542-1886 or 619/544-1886. Fax 619/544-0058. www.hortongrand.com. 132 units. $139–$199 double; $259 suite. Children 17 and under stay free in parents' room. Packages available. AE, DC, MC, V. Valet parking $15. Bus: 1. **Amenities:** Restaurant; lounge. *In room:* A/C, TV, dataport, hair dryer.

INEXPENSIVE

Another budget-conscious choice is **Comfort Inn–Downtown,** 719 Ash St., at Seventh Avenue (✆ 800/228-5150 or 619/232-2525; www.comfortinnsandiego. com), offering clean and safe accommodations in a quieter corner of downtown. Or try **Keating House,** 2331 Second Ave. (✆ 800/995-8644 or 619/239-8585; www.keatinghouse.com), a bed-and-breakfast set in a restored mansion between downtown and Hillcrest.

La Pensione Hotel ☆ *(Value)* This place has a lot going for it: modern amenities, remarkable value, a convenient location within walking distance of the central business district, a friendly staff, and parking (a premium for small hotels in San Diego). The three-story La Pensione is built around a courtyard and feels like a small European hotel; in fact, it's the number-one choice of foreign students attending the downtown Language Institute. The decor throughout is modern and streamlined, with plenty of sleek black and metallic surfaces, crisp white walls, and minimal furniture. Guest rooms, while not overly large, make the most of their space and leave you with room to move around. Each room offers a tub-shower combination, ceiling fan, and microwave oven; try for a bay or city view rather than the concrete courtyard view. La Pensione is in San Diego's Little Italy and within walking distance of eateries (mostly Italian) and nightspots; there are two restaurants directly downstairs.

606 W. Date St. (at India St.), San Diego, CA 92101. ✆ 800/232-4683 or 619/236-8000. Fax 619/236-8088. www.lapensionehotel.com. 80 units. $60–$80 double. AE, DC, DISC, MC, V. Limited free underground parking. Trolley: County Center/Little Italy. **Amenities:** Access to nearby health club; bike rental; self-service laundry. *In room:* TV, dataport, fridge.

HILLCREST/UPTOWN

The regentrified historic neighborhoods north of downtown are something of a bargain: Well located to take advantage of Balboa Park (yet providing easy access to the rest of town), they're also filled with chic casual restaurants, eclectic shops and movie theaters, and sizzling nightlife. An additional park-side choice is the **Balboa Park Inn,** 3402 Park Blvd., at Upas Street (✆ 800/938-8181 or 619/ 298-0823; www.balboaparkinn.com).

MODERATE

Park Manor Suites ★ *Value*   Popular with actors appearing at the Old Globe Theatre in neighboring Balboa Park, this eight-floor Italianate masterpiece was built as a full-service luxury hotel in 1926 on a prime corner overlooking the park. One of the original investors was the family of child actor Jackie Coogan. The Hollywood connection continued—the hotel became a popular stopping-off point for celebrities headed for Mexican vacations in the 1920s and 1930s. Guest rooms are spacious and comfortable, featuring full kitchens, dining rooms, living rooms, and bedrooms with a separate dressing area. A few have glassed-in terraces; request one when you book. The overall feeling is that of a pre-war East Coast apartment building, complete with steam heat and lavish moldings. Park Manor Suites does have its weaknesses: Bathrooms have mostly original fixtures and could use some renovation; and the rooftop banquet room, where a simple continental breakfast buffet is served, suffers from bad '80s decor (though the view is spectacular). But prices are quite reasonable for the trendy Hillcrest neighborhood. There's a darkly old-world restaurant on the ground floor.

525 Spruce St. (between 5th and 6th aves.), San Diego, CA 92103. (℃) **800/874-2649** or 619/291-0999. Fax 619/291-8844. www.parkmanorsuites.com. 80 units. $99–$129 studio; $139–$179 1-bedroom suite; $199–$239 2-bedroom suite. Rates include continental breakfast. Children under 12 stay free in parents' room. Extra person $15. Weekly rates available. AE, DC, DISC, MC, V. Free parking. Bus: 1, 3, or 25. **Amenities:** Restaurant; bar; access to nearby health club; bike rental; laundry service; dry cleaning; self-service laundry. *In room:* TV, dataport, kitchen, coffeemaker, hair dryer, iron.

Sommerset Suites Hotel ★★   This all-suite hotel on a busy street was originally built as apartment housing for interns at the hospital nearby. It retains a residential ambience and unexpected amenities such as huge closets, medicine cabinets, and fully equipped kitchens in all rooms (executive suites even have dishwashers). Poolside barbecue facilities encourage warm-weather mingling. The hotel has a personal, welcoming feel, from the friendly, helpful staff to the snacks, soda, beer, and wine served each afternoon. You'll even get a welcome basket with cookies and microwave popcorn. Rooms are comfortably furnished, and each has a private balcony. Be prepared for noise from the busy thoroughfare below, though. Several blocks of Hillcrest's chic restaurants and shops (plus a movie multiplex) are within easy walking distance. Guest services include a courtesy van to the airport, SeaWorld, the zoo, and other attractions within a 5-mile radius.

606 Washington St. (at 5th Ave.), San Diego, CA 92103. (℃) **800/962-9665** or 619/692-5200. Fax 619/692-5299. www.sommersetsuites.com. 80 units. $109–$195 double. Rates include continental breakfast and afternoon refreshments. Children under 12 stay free in parents' room. AE, DC, DISC, MC, V. Free covered parking. Take Washington St. exit off I-5. Bus: 16 or 25. **Amenities:** Outdoor pool; Jacuzzi; coin-op laundry. *In room:* A/C, TV, dataport, coffeemaker, hair dryer, iron.

INEXPENSIVE

Two extremely cozy and welcoming bed-and-breakfasts around $100 are **The Cottage,** 3829 Albatross St., off Robinson (℃ **619/299-1564**), and **Crone's Cobblestone Cottage,** 1302 Washington Place, 2½ blocks west of Washington Street at Ingalls Street (℃ **619/295-4765**).

OLD TOWN & MISSION VALLEY

Old Town is a popular area for families because of its proximity to Old Town State Historic Park and other attractions within walking distance. Hotel Circle, on the way to Mission Valley, offers easy freeway access to a bevy of mostly chain hotels convenient for sports fans or bargain seekers.

MODERATE

Heritage Park Bed & Breakfast Inn 🎯🎯 This exquisite 1889 Queen Anne mansion is set in a Victorian park—an artfully arranged cobblestone cul-de-sac lined with historic buildings saved from the wrecking ball and assembled here, near Old Town, as a tourist attraction. Most of the inn's rooms are in the main house, with a handful of equally appealing choices in an adjacent 1887 Italianate companion. Owner Nancy Helsper is an amiable and energetic innkeeper with an eye for every necessary detail; she's always eager to share tales of these homes' fascinating history. A stay here is about surrendering to the pampering of afternoon tea, candlelight breakfast, and a number of romantic extras (champagne and chocolates, private in-room dinner) available for special celebrations. Like the gracious parlors and porches, each room is outfitted with meticulous period antiques and luxurious fabrics; the practiced staff provides turndown service and virtually anything else you might require. Although the fireplaces are all ornamental, some rooms have Jacuzzis. In the evenings, vintage films are shown in the Victorian parlor.

2470 Heritage Park Row, San Diego, CA 92110. (C) **800/995-2470** or 619/299-6832. Fax 619/299-9465. www.heritageparkinn.com. 12 units. $120–$250 double. Rates include full breakfast and afternoon tea. Extra person $20. AE, DC, DISC, MC, V. Free parking. Take I-5 to Old Town Ave., turn left onto San Diego Ave., then turn right onto Harney St. *In room:* A/C, hair dryer, iron.

Red Lion Hanalei Hotel 🎯 My favorite hotel on Hotel Circle has a Polynesian theme and comfort-conscious sophistication that sets it apart from the rest of the pack. Rooms are split between two high-rise towers, set far away from the freeway and cleverly positioned so that the balconies open onto the tropically landscaped pool courtyard or the luxurious links of a formerly private golf club on the Mission Valley floor. The heated outdoor pool is large enough for any luau, as is the oversized Jacuzzi beside it. The hotel boasts an unmistakable 1960s vibe and Hawaiian ambience—the restaurant and bar have over-the-top kitschy decor, with waterfalls, outrigger canoes, and more. But guest rooms sport contemporary furnishings and conveniences; some have microwaves and refrigerators. Services include a free shuttle to Old Town and other attractions, plus extensive meeting facilities.

2270 Hotel Circle N., San Diego, CA 92108. (C) **800/RED-LION** or 619/297-1101. Fax 619/297-6049. www.redlion.com. 416 units. $109–$159 double; $275–$375 suite. Off-season, AARP, and AAA discounts and golf packages available. Extra person $10. AE, DISC, MC, V. Parking $8. From I-8, take Hotel Circle exit, follow signs for Hotel Circle N. Bus: 6. Pets accepted with $25 fee. **Amenities:** 2 restaurants; lounge; outdoor pool; nearby golf; fitness center; Jacuzzi; game room; activities desk; 24-hr. business center; room service 6am–10pm; self-service laundry; laundry service; dry cleaning. *In room:* A/C, TV w/pay movies, dataport, coffeemaker, hair dryer, iron.

Vacation Inn 🎯 Just a couple of easy walking blocks from the heart of Old Town, the Vacation Inn has a colonial Spanish exterior that suits the neighborhood's theme. Inside you'll find better-than-they-have-to-be contemporary furnishings and surprising small touches that make this hotel an affordable option favored by business travelers and families alike. There's nothing scenic on the adjacent streets, so the hotel is smartly oriented toward the inside; request a room whose patio or balcony opens onto the pleasant courtyard. Rooms are thoughtfully and practically appointed, with extras like microwave ovens and writing tables. The lobby, surrounded by French doors, features a large fireplace, several sitting areas, and a TV. The hotel entrance, on Jefferson Street, is hard to find but definitely worth the search.

3900 Old Town Ave., San Diego, CA 92110. © 800/451-9846 or 619/299-7400. Fax 619/299-1619. 124 units. June–Sept $119–$129 double; $130–$175 suite. Oct–May $89–$109 double; $99–$165 suite. Rates include continental breakfast and afternoon refreshments. Children 17 and under stay free in parents' room. Extra person $10. AE, DC, DISC, MC, V. Free parking. Bus: 5 or 5A. **Amenities:** Outdoor pool; Jacuzzi; laundry service; dry cleaning. *In room:* A/C, TV, fridge, coffeemaker.

INEXPENSIVE

Room rates at properties on Hotel Circle are significantly cheaper than those in many other parts of the city. You'll find a cluster of inexpensive chain hotels and motels, including **Best Western Seven Seas** (© **800/421-6662** or 619/291-1300), **Comfort Inn & Suites** (© **800/647-1903** or 619/291-7700), **Mission Valley Center Travelodge** (© **800/255-3050** or 619/297-2271), **Ramada Inn** (© **800/532-4241** or 619/291-6500), and **Vagabond Inn** (© **800/522-1555** or 619/297-1691).

MISSION BAY & THE BEACHES

If you plan to enjoy the beach and aquatic activities during your visit (including SeaWorld), staying in this part of town will set you up in the right spot.

VERY EXPENSIVE

Pacific Terrace Hotel ★★   The best modern hotel on the boardwalk recently emerged from a multimillion-dollar renovation sporting a soothing South Seas ambience—rattan fans caress the lobby and hint at the sunny Indonesian-inspired decor in guest rooms. Hands-on owners kicked the luxury factor (and prices) up a notch, resulting in an upscale atmosphere and relaxed ambience that stand apart from the casual beach pads in the area.

Large, comfortable guest rooms each come with a balcony or terrace and a fancy wall safe. About half the rooms have kitchenettes, and top-floor rooms in this three-story hotel enjoy particularly nice views—you'll find yourself mesmerized by the rhythmic waves and determined surfers below. Management keeps popcorn, coffee, and lemonade at the ready throughout the day; the lushly landscaped pool and Jacuzzi face a relatively quiet stretch of beach with fire rings for bonfires or barbecues. Several local restaurants allow meals to be billed to the hotel but there's no restaurant on the premises.

610 Diamond St., San Diego, CA 92109. © 800/344-3370 or 858/581-3500. Fax 858/274-3341. www.pacific terrace.com. 75 units. $269 standard double; $369 oceanfront double; from $395 suite. Rates include continental breakfast. 10% AAA discount June 15–Sept 15 (25% Sept 16–June 14). AE, DC, DISC, MC, V. Parking $5. Take I-5 to Grand/Garnet exit and follow Grand or Garnet W to Mission Blvd., turn right (N), then left (W) onto Diamond; hotel is at the end of the street on the right. Bus: 34 or 34A. **Amenities:** Oceanview outdoor pool; access to nearby health club; Jacuzzi; bike rental nearby; activities desk; room service 7am–midnight; in-room massage; laundry service; dry cleaning; coin-op laundry. *In room:* A/C, TV w/pay movies, dataport, minibar, coffeemaker, hair dryer, iron.

EXPENSIVE

Catamaran Resort Hotel ★★ *Kids*   Ideally situated right on Mission Bay, the Catamaran has its own bay and ocean beaches with watersports facilities. Built in the 1950s, the hotel has been fully renovated to modern standards without losing its trademark Polynesian theme; the atrium lobby holds a 15-foot waterfall and full-size dugout canoe, and koi-filled lagoons meander through the property. After dark, torches blaze throughout the grounds, with numerous varieties of bamboo and palms sprouting; during the day, the resident tropical birds chirp away. Guest rooms—in a 13-story building or one of the six two-story buildings—have subdued South Pacific decor, and each has a balcony or patio.

Tower rooms have commanding views of the bay, the San Diego skyline, La Jolla, and Point Loma. Studios and suites have the added convenience of kitchenettes. The Catamaran is within walking distance of Pacific Beach's restaurant and nightlife. It's also steps away from the bay's exceptional jogging and biking path; runners with tots-in-tow can rent jogging strollers at the hotel.

3999 Mission Blvd. (4 blocks S of Grand Ave.), San Diego, CA 92109. © **800/422-8386** or 858/488-1081. Fax 858/488-1619. www.catamaranresort.com. 313 units. $195–$265 double; from $400 suite. Children 11 and under stay free in parents' room. Off-season discounts and packages available. AE, DC, DISC, MC, V. Valet parking $10; self-parking $8. Take Grand/Garnet exit off I-5 and go W on Grand Ave., then S on Mission Blvd. Bus: 34 or 34A/B. **Amenities:** Restaurant; nightclub; piano bar; outdoor pool; health club; Jacuzzi; watersports equipment rental; bike rental; children's programs; concierge; activities desk; car-rental desk; room service 5am–11pm; in-room massage; babysitting; laundry service; dry cleaning. *In room:* A/C, TV w/pay movies, dataport, fridge, coffeemaker, hair dryer, iron.

Paradise Point Resort & Spa ★★★ *Kids*   Smack-dab in the middle of Mission Bay, this hotel complex is as much a theme park as its closest neighbor, SeaWorld (a 3-min. drive). Single-story accommodations are spread across 44 acres of duck-filled lagoons, tropical gardens, and swim-friendly beaches; all have private lanais (patios) and plenty of thoughtful conveniences. Recently updated to keep its low-tech 1960s charm but lose tacky holdovers—for example, rooms now sport a refreshingly colorful beach cottagey decor—the resort offers so much fun and recreation, you may never want to leave! And despite daunting high-season rack rates, there's usually a deal to be had here. In 2000, the resort unveiled its upscale waterfront Baleen restaurant (excellent fine dining in a contemporary, fun space), followed in 2001 by a stunning Indonesian-inspired spa that offers cool serenity and aroma-tinged Asian treatments—this spa is a vacation in itself!

1404 W. Vacation Rd. (off Ingraham St.), San Diego, CA 92109. © **800/344-2626** or 858/274-4630. Fax 858/581-5977. www.paradisepoint.com. 462 units. Memorial Day to Labor Day $220–$350 double; from $325 suite. Off-season $175–$325 double; from $300 suite. Extra person $20. Children 17 and under stay free in parents' room. Discounts and packages frequently available. AE, DC, DISC, MC, V. Free parking. Follow I-8 W to Mission Bay Dr. exit; take Ingraham St. N to Vacation Rd. **Amenities:** 3 restaurants; lounge; pool bar; 6 outdoor pools; 18-hole putting course; 6 lit tennis courts; croquet; sand volleyball; fitness center; full-service spa; Jacuzzi; bike rental; shuttle to area shopping; room service 7am–10pm; laundry service; dry cleaning. *In room:* A/C, TV w/pay movies, dataport, fridge, coffeemaker, hair dryer, iron.

MODERATE

Another beachfront choice in this price range is the **Best Western Blue Sea Lodge,** 707 Pacific Beach Dr. (© **800/BLUE-SEA** or 858/488-4700; www.bestwestern-bluesea.com).

The Beach Cottages *Kids*   This family-owned operation has a variety of guest quarters (most geared to the long-term visitor), but the cute little detached cottages steps from the sand give it real appeal. Most other units are perfectly adequate, especially for budget-minded families who want to log major hours on the beach, but stay away from the plain motel rooms—they're just dingy. All accommodations except the motel rooms have fully equipped kitchens. The Beach Cottages are within walking distance of shops and restaurants—look both ways for speeding cyclists before crossing the boardwalk—and enjoy shared barbecue grills, shuffleboard courts, and table tennis. The cottages themselves aren't pristine but have a rustic charm that makes them popular with young honeymooners and those nostalgic for the golden age of laid-back California beach culture. With one or two bedrooms, each cottage sleeps up to six; each has a patio with tables and chairs.

Kids **Family-Friendly Hotels**

The Beach Cottages (p. 648)   Kids enjoy the informal atmosphere and the location near the beach.

Catamaran Resort Hotel (p. 647)   Myriad sports facilities and a safe swimming beach make this resort an ideal place for families. Accommodations are comfortable, but not so posh that Mom and Dad need to worry.

Holiday Inn on the Bay (p. 640)   Kids under 18 stay free, so the hotel is well priced for strained family budgets, and even offers babysitting services for strained parents.

Loews Coronado Bay Resort (p. 655)   In the summer, the Commodore Kids Club, for children ages 4 to 12, provides supervised indoor and outdoor activities during the day and some evenings, too. Programs for older kids keep them out of harm's way without making them feel baby-sat.

Paradise Point Resort & Spa (p. 648)   This self-contained property in the middle of Mission Bay has plenty of space for kids to safely explore, and is just up the street from SeaWorld.

To make a reservation, call between 9am and 9pm, when the office is open. Reserve the most popular cottages well in advance.

4255 Ocean Blvd. (1 block S of Grand Ave.), San Diego, CA 92109-3995. (©) **858/483-7440.** Fax 858/273-9365. www.beachcottages.com. 61 units, 17 cottages. July 1–Labor Day $95–$115 double; $130 studio for up to 4; $150–$195 apt for up to 6; $150–$185 cottage for up to 6; $225–$245 2-bedroom suite for up to 6. Off-season discounts and off-season weekly rates available. AE, DC, DISC, MC, V. Free parking. Take I-5 to Grand/Garnet exit, go W on Grand Ave. and right on Mission Blvd. Bus: 34 or 34A. **Amenities:** Self-service laundry. *In room:* TV, fridge, coffeemaker.

Crystal Pier Hotel ★★ (finds)   When historic charm is higher on your wish list than hotel-style service, head to this utterly unique cluster of cottages sitting literally over the surf on the vintage Crystal Pier. Like renting your own self-contained hideaway, you'll get a separate living room and bedroom, fully equipped kitchen, and private patio with breathtaking ocean views—all within the white-washed walls of blue-shuttered cottages that date from 1936 but have been meticulously renovated. The sound of waves is soothing, but the boardwalk action is only a few steps (and worlds) away, and the pier is a great place for watching sunsets and surfers. Guests drive right out and park beside their cottages, a real boon on crowded weekends. There are vending machines and movie rentals; boogie boards, fishing poles, beach chairs, and umbrellas are also available, but it's strictly BYOBT (beach towels!). The office is open daily from 8am to 8pm. These accommodations book up fast, especially with long-term repeat guests, so reserve for summer at least 4 months in advance.

4500 Ocean Blvd. (at Garnet Ave.), San Diego, CA 92109. (©) **800/748-5894** or 858/483-6983. Fax 858/483-6811. www.crystalpier.com. 26 units. Cottages for 2–6 people $135–$335 mid-June to mid-Sept; $105–$275 mid-Sept to mid-June. 3-night minimum in summer. DISC, MC, V. Free parking. Take I-5 to Grand/Garnet exit; follow Garnet to the pier. Bus: 34 or 34A. **Amenities:** Beach equipment rental. *In room:* TV, kitchen.

Ocean Park Inn ★ This modern oceanfront motor hotel offers attractive, spacious rooms with well-coordinated contemporary furnishings. Although the inn has a level of sophistication uncommon in this casual, surfer-populated area, you won't find solitude and quiet. The cool marble lobby and plushly carpeted hallways will help you feel a little insulated from the raucous scene outside, though. You can't beat the location (directly on the beach) and the view (ditto). Rates vary according to view, but most rooms have at least a partial ocean view; each has a private balcony or patio. Units in front are most desirable, but it can get noisy directly above the boardwalk; try for the second or third floor. The Ocean Park Inn doesn't have its own restaurant, but the casual High Tide Café (p. 663) is outside the front door.

710 Grand Ave., San Diego, CA 92109. ℂ 800/231-7735 or 858/483-5858. Fax 858/274-0823. www.ocean parkinn.com. 73 units. Mid-May to mid-Sept $104–$239 double; $169–$304 suite. Winter $89–$214 double; $124–$274 suite. Rates include continental breakfast. AE, DC, DISC, MC, V. Free indoor parking. Take Grand/ Garnet exit off I-5; follow Grand Ave. to ocean. Bus: 34 or 34A/B. **Amenities:** Outdoor pool; Jacuzzi; laundry service; dry cleaning. *In room:* A/C, TV, dataport, fridge, coffeemaker, hair dryer.

INEXPENSIVE

Beach Haven Inn ★ A great spot for beach lovers, this motel is about half a block from the sand. Rooms face an inner courtyard, where guests enjoy a secluded ambience for relaxing by the pool. On the street side it looks kind of marginal, but once on the property I found all quarters well-maintained and sporting clean, modern furnishings—nearly all units have eat-in kitchens. The friendly staff provides free coffee in the lobby and rents out VCRs and movies.

4740 Mission Blvd. (at Missouri St.), San Diego (Pacific Beach), CA 92109. ℂ 800/831-6323 or 858/272-3812. Fax 858/272-3532. www.beachhaveninn.com. 23 units. Summer (June to mid-Sept) $110–$165 double; off-season $69–$145 double. Rates include continental breakfast. Children 11 and under stay free in parents' room. Extra person $5. AE, DC, DISC, MC, V. Free parking. Bus: 30 or 34. **Amenities:** Outdoor pool; Jacuzzi. *In room:* A/C, TV, kitchenette in most units.

Dana Inn and Marina Advertising itself as the closest lodging to SeaWorld (with a complimentary shuttle to and from the park), this friendly, low-tech hotel features several low-rise buildings with vaguely nautical blue-and-white exteriors. Some overlook bobbing sailboats in the recreational marina, others face onto the sunny kidney-shaped pool whose surrounding tiki torch-lit gardens offer shuffleboard and Ping-Pong. You'll pay a premium for bay and marina views; if view doesn't matter, save your money—every room is the same size, with rather plain but well-maintained furnishings. Convenient meals and room service (including poolside food and cocktail service) are available at the casual Red Hen Country Kitchen next door.

1710 W. Mission Bay Dr., San Diego, CA 92109. ℂ 800/345-9995 or 619/222-6440. Fax 619/222-5916. 196 units. Memorial Day weekend–Oct $131–$177 room for up to 5. Winter $116–$154 room for up to 5. AE, DC, DISC, MC, V. Free parking. Follow I-8 W to Mission Bay Dr. exit. **Amenities:** Outdoor heated pool and Jacuzzi; tennis court; bike and watersports rentals; room service 7am to 9pm; coin-op laundry; laundry service; dry cleaning. *In room:* A/C, TV, dataport, fridge, coffeemaker, iron, hair dryer.

LA JOLLA

While you'll have a hard time finding bargain accommodations in this upscale, conservative community, it's not to be missed for the sheer physical beauty of its coastline, as well as a compact downtown village that makes for delightful strolling. An additional choice worth checking out is the **Bed & Breakfast Inn at La Jolla,** 7753 Draper Ave., near Prospect (ℂ **800/582-2466** or 858/456-2066; www.InnLaJolla.com), set in an Irving Gill–designed house near the museum; rates range from inexpensive to expensive.

La Jolla

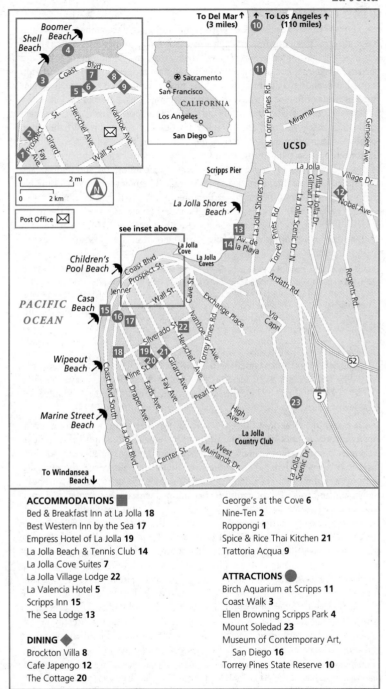

Boomer Beach

Shell Beach

Coast Blvd.

Girard St.

Prospect St.

Fay Ave.

Herschel Ave.

Ivanhoe Ave.

Wall St.

CALIFORNIA

Sacramento

San Francisco

Los Angeles

San Diego

To Del Mar↑ (3 miles)

To Los Angeles↑ (110 miles)

N. Torrey Pines Rd.

Miramar

Genesee Ave.

UCSD

La Jolla

Villa La Jolla Dr.

Gilman Dr.

Village Dr.

Nobel Ave.

Scripps Pier

La Jolla Shores Beach

La Jolla Shores Dr.

Torrey Pines Rd.

La Jolla Scenic Dr. N.

La Jolla Cove

La Jolla Caves

Av. de la Playa

Ardath Rd.

Regents Rd.

0   2 mi
0   2 km

Post Office ✉

see inset above

Children's Pool Beach

Coast Blvd.

Prospect St.

Jenner

Wall St.

Cave St.

Exchange Place

Via Capri

PACIFIC OCEAN

Casa Beach

Silverado St.

Ivanhoe Ave.

Torrey Pines Rd.

Herschel Ave.

Girard Ave.

52

Wipeout Beach

Coast Blvd. South

Kline St.

Draper Ave.

Eads Ave.

Fay Ave.

Pearl St.

High Ave.

5

Marine Street Beach

La Jolla Blvd.

Center St.

West Muirlands Dr.

La Jolla Country Club

La Jolla Scenic Dr. S.

To Windansea Beach ↓

ACCOMMODATIONS ■

Bed & Breakfast Inn at La Jolla **18**
Best Western Inn by the Sea **17**
Empress Hotel of La Jolla **19**
La Jolla Beach & Tennis Club **14**
La Jolla Cove Suites **7**
La Jolla Village Lodge **22**
La Valencia Hotel **5**
Scripps Inn **15**
The Sea Lodge **13**

DINING ◆

Brockton Villa **8**
Cafe Japengo **12**
The Cottage **20**

George's at the Cove **6**
Nine-Ten **2**
Roppongi **1**
Spice & Rice Thai Kitchen **21**
Trattoria Acqua **9**

ATTRACTIONS ●

Birch Aquarium at Scripps **11**
Coast Walk **3**
Ellen Browning Scripps Park **4**
Mount Soledad **23**
Museum of Contemporary Art, San Diego **16**
Torrey Pines State Reserve **10**

VERY EXPENSIVE

La Valencia Hotel ★★★ Within its bougainvillea-draped walls and wrought-iron garden gates, this gracious bastion of gentility does a fine job of resurrecting its golden-age elegance, when celebrities like Greta Garbo and Charlie Chaplin vacationed alongside the world's moneyed elite. The cliff-top hotel has been the centerpiece of La Jolla since opening in 1926. Today, brides pose in front of the lobby's picture window (against a backdrop of La Jolla Cove and the Pacific), well-coifed ladies lunch in the dappled shade of the garden patio, and neighborhood cronies quaff libations in the clubby Whaling Bar, once a western Algonquin for literary inebriates. One chooses La Valencia for its history and unbeatably scenic location, but you won't be disappointed by the old-world standards of service and style. Rooms are comfortably and traditionally furnished, each boasting an individual decor, lavish appointments, and all-marble bathrooms with signature toiletries. Because rates vary wildly according to view, my advice is to get a cheaper room and enjoy the view from one of the many cozy lounges or serene garden terraces. Room decor and layouts vary wildly, too—a few extra minutes spent with the reservationist will ensure a custom match for you.

1132 Prospect St. (at Herschel Ave.), La Jolla, CA 92037. ℂ 800/451-0772 or 858/454-0771. Fax 858/456-3921. www.lavalencia.com. 132 units. $250–$500 double; from $550 suite. Extra person $15. AE, DC, DISC, MC, V. Valet parking $14. Take Torrey Pines Rd. to Prospect Place and turn right. Prospect Place becomes Prospect St. **Amenities:** 3 restaurants; bar; outdoor pool; exercise room w/spa treatments; Jacuzzi; sauna; concierge; secretarial services; 24-hr. room service; babysitting; laundry service; dry cleaning. *In room:* A/C, TV/VCR, dataport, minibar, coffeemaker, hair dryer.

EXPENSIVE

You may also want to consider the La Jolla Beach & Tennis Club's sister property **The Sea Lodge,** 8110 Camino del Oro, at Avenida de la Playa (ℂ **800/237-5211** or 858/459-8271), also located on the beach. Or, for B&B ambience, try **Scripps Inn,** 555 Coast Blvd. S., at Cuvier (ℂ **858/454-3391**).

La Jolla Beach & Tennis Club ★★ Pack your best tennis whites for a stay at La Jolla's private "B&T" (as it's locally known), where CEOs and MDs come to relax and recreate. Surprisingly, rates for the club's overnight accommodations aren't that much higher than at the sister hotel next door, but the exclusive atmosphere and extensive amenities are far superior. Guest rooms are unexpectedly plain and frill-free, though they are equipped with the basic amenities you'll need. Most have well-stocked full kitchens that are ideal for families or longer stays. This historic property was founded in the 1920s, when original plans included constructing a private yacht harbor. Today it's known primarily for tennis. The beach is popular here; the staff sets up comfy sand chairs and umbrellas, and races to supply club members and guests with fluffy towels, beverages, and snacks. Kayaks and watersports equipment can be rented; there's even a sand croquet court. Surprisingly, there's no room service. Besides the on-site dining options, several cozy neighborhood trattorias are 2 blocks away. Take a peek into the hotel's distinctive Marine Room restaurant, where waves literally smash against the windows inches away from well-coifed diners. The menu is pricey, but for the price of a cocktail you can enjoy the same astounding view.

2000 Spindrift Dr., La Jolla, CA 92037. ℂ 800/624-CLUB or 858/454-7126. Fax 858/456-3805. www.ljbtc.com. 90 units. June–Sept $170–$349 double; from $275 suite. Off-season $139–$239 double; from $215 suite. Children 11 and under stay free in parents' room. Extra person $20. AE, DC, MC, V. Take La Jolla Shores Dr., turn left on Paseo Dorado, and follow to Spindrift Dr. **Amenities:** 2 restaurants; elegant Olympic-size pool; 9-hole pitch-and-putt course; 12 championship tennis courts and a tennis shop; fitness room;

watersports equipment rental; playground; massage; babysitting; laundry service; dry cleaning; coin-op laundry. *In room:* TV w/pay movies, dataport, coffeemaker, hair dryer, iron.

MODERATE

Best Western Inn by the Sea ⭐   Occupying an enviable location at the heart of La Jolla's charming village, this independently managed property puts guests just a short walk from the cliffs and beach. The low-rise tops out at five stories, with the upper floors enjoying ocean views (and the highest room rates). The Best Western (and the more formal Empress, a block away), offer a terrific alternative to pricier digs nearby. Rooms here are Best Western standard issue—freshly maintained but nothing special. All rooms do have balconies, though, and refrigerators are available at no extra charge; the hotel offers plenty of welcome amenities. Room service is from the adjacent International House of Pancakes.

7830 Fay Ave. (between Prospect and Silverado sts.), La Jolla, CA 92037. © **800/462-9732**, 800/526-4545 in Calif. and Canada, or 858/459-4461. Fax 858/456-2578. 132 units. $129–$229 double; $350–$475 suite. Rates include continental breakfast. Off-season discounts available. AE, DC, DISC, MC, V. Parking $7. Take Torrey Pines Rd. to Prospect Place and turn right. Prospect Place becomes Prospect St.; proceed to Fay Ave. and turn left. **Amenities:** Outdoor heated pool; car-rental desk; room service 7am–9pm; laundry service; dry cleaning. *In room:* A/C, TV w/pay movies, dataport, coffeemaker, hair dryer, iron.

Empress Hotel of La Jolla ⭐⭐   The Empress Hotel offers spacious quarters with traditional furnishings a block or two from La Jolla's main drag and the ocean. It's quieter here than at the premium clifftop properties, and you'll sacrifice little other than direct ocean views. (Many rooms on the top floors afford partial views.) If you're planning to explore La Jolla on foot, the Empress is a good base, and it exudes a classiness many comparably priced chains lack. Rooms are tastefully decorated (and frequently renovated), and well equipped. Bathrooms are of average size but exceptionally well appointed, and four "Empress" rooms have sitting areas with full-size sleeper sofas. On nice days, breakfast is set up on a serene sun deck.

7766 Fay Ave. (at Silverado), La Jolla, CA 92037. © **888/369-9900** or 858/454-3001. Fax 858/454-6387. www.empress-hotel.com. 73 units. $149–$229 double; $349 suite. Rates include continental breakfast. Children 17 and under stay free in parents' room. Off-season and long-stay discounts available. Extra person $10. AE, DC, DISC, MC, V. Valet parking $8. Take Torrey Pines Rd. to Girard Ave., turn right, then left on Silverado St. **Amenities:** Fitness room; spa; room service 11:30am–9pm. *In room:* A/C, TV, dataport, fridge, coffeemaker, hair dryer, iron.

La Jolla Cove Suites *(Value*   Tucked in beside prime oceanview condos across from Ellen Browning Scripps Park, this family-run 1950s-era complex actually sits closer to the ocean than pricey uphill neighbors La Valencia and the Grande Colonial. The to-die-for ocean view is completely unobstructed, and La Jolla Cove—one of California's prettiest swimming spots—is steps away from the hotel. The property is peaceful at night, but village dining and shopping are only a short walk away. You'll pay more depending on the quality of your view; about 80% of guest quarters have ocean views. On the plus side, rooms are wonderfully spacious, each featuring a fully equipped kitchen, plus private balcony or patio. On the minus side, their functional but almost institutional furnishings could use a touch of Martha Stewart. An oceanview rooftop deck offers lounge chairs and cafe tables; breakfast is served up here each morning, indoors or outdoors depending on the weather.

1155 Coast Blvd. (across from the cove), La Jolla, CA 92037. © **888/LA-JOLLA** or 858/459-2621. Fax 858/551-3405. www.lajollacove.com. 90 units. Summer (Memorial Day to Labor Day) $135–$175 double; $190–$280 suite. Winter $110–$135 double; $145–$225 suite. Rates include continental breakfast.

Midweek, AAA, and weekly discounts available. Extra person $15. AE, DC, DISC, MC, V. Free parking. Take Torrey Pines Rd. to Prospect Place and turn right. When the road forks, veer right (downhill) onto Coast Blvd. **Amenities:** Outdoor pool; Jacuzzi; car-rental desk; coin-op laundry. *In room:* TV, kitchen, safe.

INEXPENSIVE

Wealthy, image-conscious La Jolla is *really* not the best place for deep bargains, but if you're determined to stay here as cheaply as possible, you won't do better than the **La Jolla Village Lodge,** 1141 Silverado St., at Herschel Avenue (℃ **858/ 551-2001;** www.lajollavillagelodge.com). This 30-room motel is standard Americana, arranged around a small parking lot with cinder-block construction and small, basic rooms. The surrounding La Jolla glamour—and bargain rates as low as $80 including breakfast—make it an acceptable option.

CORONADO

The "island" (really a peninsula) of Coronado offers a great escape with its quiet, architecturally rich streets; a small-town, Navy-oriented atmosphere; and laid-back vacationing on one of the state's most beautiful and welcoming beaches. Choose a hotel on the ocean side for a view of Point Loma and the Pacific, or stay facing the city for a spectacular skyline vista (especially at night). You may feel pleasantly isolated here, so it isn't your best choice if you're planning to spend lots of time in more central parts of the city.

   A note on driving directions: To reach the places listed here, take I-5 to the Coronado Bridge, and then follow individual directions. If you're two or more in a car, stay in the far right lanes to avoid paying the bridge toll.

EXPENSIVE

Another upscale destination is **Coronado Island Marriott Resort,** 2000 Second St., at Glorietta Boulevard (℃ **800/228-9290** or 619/435-3000; http://marriott hotels.com/SANCI). Boasting a spa and vast recreational facilities, the Marriott has a low-key elegance and excellent service. Or consider the charming **Glorietta Bay Inn,** 1630 Glorietta Blvd., near Orange Avenue (℃ **800/283-9383** or 619/435-3101; www.gloriettabayinn.com), across the street from the "Del" in a 1908 mansion.

Hotel del Coronado ★★★   Opened in 1888 and designated a National Historic Landmark in 1977, the "Hotel Del," as it's affectionately known, is the last of California's grand old seaside hotels. Legend has it that the Duke of Windsor met his American duchess here, and Marilyn Monroe frolicked around the hotel in *Some Like It Hot.* This monument to Victorian grandeur boasts tall cupolas, red turrets, and gingerbread trim, all spread out over 26 acres. Rooms run the gamut from compact to extravagant, and all are packed with antique charm; most have custom-made furnishings. The best rooms have balconies fronting the ocean and large windows that take in one of the city's finest white-sand beaches. If you're a stickler for detail, ask to stay in the original building rather than in the contemporary tower additions.

   In 2000, the hotel completed a painstaking, multimillion-dollar, 3-year restoration. Purists will rejoice to hear that historical accuracy was paramount, resulting in this priceless grande dame being returned to its 19th-century splendor. Even if you don't stay here, don't miss a stroll through the grand, wood-paneled lobby or along the pristine wide beach. Accolades have been awarded to the **Prince of Wales Grill** (℃ **619/522-8496**), recently remodeled from a dark, clubby room to an airy, elegant salon with oceanfront dining. Cocktails and afternoon tea are served in the wood-paneled lobby and adjoining conservatory lounge.

1500 Orange Ave., Coronado, CA 92118. © **800/468-3533** or 619/435-8000. Fax 619/522-8238. www. hoteldel.com. 700 units. $215–$340 double (garden or city view), $360–$640 double (oceanview); suites from $700. Children 17 and under stay free in parents' room. Sport, spa, and romance packages available. AE, DC, DISC, MC, V. Valet parking $16; self-parking $12. From Coronado Bridge, turn left onto Orange Ave. Bus: 901. Ferry: From Broadway Pier. **Amenities:** 9 restaurants/lounges; 2 outdoor pools; 3 tennis courts; health club and spa; 2 Jacuzzis; bike rental; children's activities; concierge; car-rental desk; shopping arcade; 24-hr. room service; babysitting; laundry service; dry cleaning. *In room:* A/C, TV w/pay movies, dataport, mini-bar, hair dryer, iron, safe.

MODERATE

El Cordova Hotel ⭑ This Spanish hacienda across the street from the Hotel del Coronado began life as a private mansion in 1902. By the 1930s it had become a hotel, the original building augmented by a series of attachments housing retail shops along the ground-floor arcade. Shaped like a baseball diamond and surrounding a courtyard with meandering tiled pathways, flowering shrubs, a swimming pool, and patio seating for Miguel's Cocina Mexican restaurant, El Cordova hums pleasantly with activity.

Each room is a little different from the next—some sport a Mexican colonial ambience, while others evoke a comfy beach cottage. All feature ceiling fans and brightly tiled bathrooms, but lack the frills that would command exorbitant rates. El Cordova has a particularly inviting aura, and its prime location makes it a popular option; I advise reserving several months in advance, especially for the summer. Facilities include a barbecue area with picnic table.

1351 Orange Ave. (at Adella Ave.), Coronado, CA 92118. © **800/229-2032** or 619/435-4131. Fax 619/435-0632. www.elcordovahotel.com. 40 units. Mid-Apr to Sept $119–$167 double; $203–$306 suite. Winter $114–$155 double; $179–$246 suite. Children 11 and under stay free in parents' room. Weekly and monthly rates available in winter. AE, DC, DISC, MC, V. From Coronado Bridge, turn left onto Orange Ave. Street parking available. **Amenities:** Restaurant; outdoor pool; shopping arcade; coin-op laundry. *In room:* A/C, TV.

Loews Coronado Bay Resort ⭑⭑ *Kids* This luxury resort opened in 1991 on a secluded 15-acre peninsula, slightly removed from downtown Coronado and San Diego. It's perfect for those who prefer a self-contained resort in a getaway-from-it-all location, and is surprisingly successful in appealing to business travelers, convention groups, vacationing families, and romance-minded couples. All units offer terraces that look onto the hotel's private 80-slip marina, the Coronado Bay Bridge, or San Diego Bay. A private pedestrian underpass leads to nearby Silver Strand Beach. Rooms boast finely appointed marble bathrooms; VCRs come standard in suites, and are available free upon request to any room. Video rentals are available. A highlight here is the **Gondola Company** (© **619/429-6317**), which offers romantic and fun gondola cruises through the canals of tony Coronado Cays. The seasonal Commodore Kids Club, for children ages 4 to 12, offers supervised half-day, full-day, and evening programs with meals.

4000 Coronado Bay Rd., Coronado, CA 92118. © **800/81-LOEWS** or 619/424-4000. Fax 619/424-4400. 438 units. $145–$265 double; from $450 suite. Children 17 and under stay free in parents' room. Packages available. AE, DC, DISC, MC, V. Valet parking $16; covered self-parking $13. From Coronado Bridge, go left onto Orange Ave, continue 8 miles down Silver Strand Hwy. Turn left at Coronado Bay Rd., entrance to the resort. Pets under 25 lb. accepted. **Amenities:** 3 restaurants; lounge; 3 outdoor pools; tennis courts; fitness center; spa; Jacuzzi; watersports equipment rental; bike/skate rental; children's programs; concierge; car-rental desk; business center; salon; 24-hr. room service; in-room massage; babysitting; laundry service; dry cleaning. *In room:* A/C, TV, dataport, minibar, coffeemaker, hair dryer, iron, safe.

INEXPENSIVE

Also in this price range is the ideally located **Village Inn**, 1017 Park Place, at Orange Avenue (© **619/435-9318**), a modest, breakfast-included, European-style small hotel with charming rooms but teensy bathrooms.

Coronado Inn ⭐ Well-located and terrifically priced, this renovated 1940s courtyard motel has such an amiable ambience, it's like staying with old friends. Iced tea, lemonade, and fresh fruit are even provided poolside on summer days. It's still a motel, though—albeit with brand-new paint and fresh tropical floral decor—so rooms are pretty basic. The six rooms with bathtubs also have small kitchens; microwaves are available for the rest. Rooms close to the street are noisiest, so ask for one toward the back. The Coronado shuttle stops a block away; it serves the shopping areas and Hotel Del.

266 Orange Ave. (corner of 3rd St.), Coronado, CA 92118. © 800/598-6624 or 619/435-4121. www. coronadoinn.com. 30 units (most with shower only). Memorial Day to Labor Day $110–$175 up to 4 people; winter $90–$120. Rates include continental breakfast. Discounts available. AE, DISC, MC, V. Free parking. From Coronado Bridge, stay on 3rd St. Pets accepted for $10 nightly fee. **Amenities:** Outdoor pool; coin-op laundry. *In room:* A/C, TV, dataport, fridge, hair dryer and iron upon request.

4 Where to Dine

What follows is only a sampling of San Diego's dining scene. For a greater selection of reviews, see *Frommer's San Diego 2003*. To locate these restaurants, see the "San Diego Accommodations & Dining" map on p. 642, and the "La Jolla" map on p. 651.

DOWNTOWN
EXPENSIVE

Another well-regarded bay-front seafooder is **Star of the Sea,** 1380 N. Harbor Dr., at Ash Street (© **619/232-7408;** www.starofthesea.com), a venerable oldie with a new look, new chef, and sophisticated menu.

Croce's Restaurant & Bars ⭐ AMERICAN/ECLECTIC Ingrid Croce, widow of singer-songwriter Jim, was instrumental in the resurgence of the once-decayed Gaslamp Quarter, and her establishment has expanded to fill every corner of this 1890 Romanesque building. Croce's features a menu that fuses Southern soul food and Southwestern spice with Asian flavors and Continental standards. Add the raucous Top Hat Bar & Grille and the intimate Jazz Bar, and the complex is the hottest ticket in town, with crowds lining up for dinner tables and nightclub shows.

An evening in the Gaslamp Quarter isn't complete without at least strolling by the Croce's corner; expect a festive good time any night of the week. Those who dine in either of the restaurant's side-by-side seating areas can enter the two nightspots without paying the cover charge.

802 5th Ave. (at F St.). © 619/233-4355. www.croces.com. Reservations not accepted; call for same-day "priority seating" (before walk-ins). Main courses $14–$23. AE, DC, DISC, MC, V. Daily 5pm–midnight. Valet parking $7 with validation. Bus: 3, 5, 16, or 25. Trolley: Gaslamp Quarter.

Fio's ⭐⭐⭐ NORTHERN ITALIAN Fio's has been *the* spot to see and be seen in the Gaslamp Quarter since it opened, and it's the granddaddy of the new wave of trendy Italian restaurants. Set in an 1881 Italianate Victorian that once housed chic Marston's department store, Fio's has a sophisticated ambience and is *always* crowded. Once cutting-edge, the upscale trattoria menu is now practiced and consistently superior. It features jet-black linguini tossed with the freshest seafood, delicate angel-hair pasta perfectly balanced with basil and pine nuts, and gourmet pizzas served at regular tables and the special pizza bar. The menu pleases both light eaters (with antipasti and pastas) and heartier palates—the impressive list of meat entrees includes mustard-rosemary rack of lamb, veal shank on saffron risotto, and delicately sweet hazelnut-crusted pork loin with

Frangelico and peaches. If you stop by without a reservation, you can sit at the elegant cocktail bar and order from the complete menu.

801 5th Ave. (at F St.). ⓒ 619/234-3467. www.fioscucina.com. Reservations recommended. Main courses $11–$25. AE, DC, DISC, MC, V. Mon–Thurs 5–10:30pm, Fri–Sat 5–11pm, Sun 5–10pm. Valet parking $6 with validation. Bus: 3, 5, 16, or 25. Trolley: Gaslamp Quarter.

The Fish Market 🕯🕯 SEAFOOD   Ask any San Diegan where to go for the biggest selection of the freshest fish and they'll send you to the bustling Fish Market on the end of the G Street Pier on the Embarcadero. Chalkboards announce the day's catches—be it Mississippi catfish, Maine lobster, Canadian salmon, or Mexican yellowtail—sold by the pound or available in a number of classic, simple preparations in the casual restaurant. Upstairs, the related Top of the Market offers similar fare at jacked-up prices; I recommend having a cocktail in Top's posh clubby atmosphere with stupendous panoramic bay views, then head downstairs for affordable fare and/or treats from the sushi and oyster bars.

There is another Fish Market Restaurant in Del Mar at 640 Via de la Valle (ⓒ **858/755-2277**).

750 N. Harbor Dr. ⓒ **619/232-FISH.** www.thefishmarket.com. Reservations not accepted. Main courses $9–$25. AE, DC, DISC, MC, V. Daily 11am–10pm. Valet parking $4. Bus: 7/7B. Trolley: Seaport Village.

MODERATE

Other recommended choices in this price range include **Osteria Panevino,** 722 Fifth Ave., between F and G streets (ⓒ **619/595-7959**), a cozy New York–style trattoria with a richly sophisticated menu and prime people-watching Gaslamp location; and **Panda Inn,** Horton Plaza (ⓒ **619/233-7800**), a surprisingly upscale Chinese restaurant tucked away on the top floor of the Gaslamp Quarter's premier shopping mall.

Dakota Grill and Spirits 🕯🕯 AMERICAN/SOUTHWESTERN   This downtown business-lunch favorite is always busy and noisy; the Southwestern cowboy kitsch matches the cuisine but can be a little too theme-y for some. Little pistols on the menu indicate the most popular items, which include shrimp tasso (sautéed with Cajun ham and sweet peas in ancho-chile cream), spit-roasted chicken with orange chipotle glaze or Dakota barbecue sauce, and mixed grill served with roasted garlic and grilled red potatoes. When the kitchen is on, Dakota's innovation makes it one of San Diego's best, but an occasional dud results from the overzealous combination of too many disparate ingredients. Still, it's not losing any ground as one of the Gaslamp Quarter's star eateries, and the raucous, casual atmosphere fits the lively cuisine. A pianist plays weekend nights.

901 5th Ave. (at E St.). ⓒ 619/234-5554. Reservations recommended. Main courses $10–$20. AE, DC, DISC, MC, V. Mon–Fri 11:30am–2:30pm; Mon–Thurs 5–10pm, Fri–Sat 5–11pm, Sun 5–9pm. Valet parking (after 5pm) $5; self-parking nearby $7. Bus: 3, 5, 16, or 25. Trolley: Gaslamp Quarter.

INEXPENSIVE

Café Lulu 🕯 COFFEEHOUSE/VEGETARIAN   Smack-dab in the heart of the Gaslamp Quarter, Café Lulu aims for a hip, bohemian mood despite its location half a block from commercial Horton Plaza. Ostensibly a coffee bar, the cafe makes a terrific choice for casual dining; if the stylishly metallic interior is too harsh for you, watch the street action from a sidewalk table. The food is health-conscious, prepared with organic ingredients and no meat. Soups, salads, cheese melts, and veggie lasagna are on the menu; breads come from the incomparable Bread & Cie., 350 University Ave. (ⓒ **619/683-9322**). Eggs, granola, and waffles are served in the morning, but anytime is the right time to try one of the inventive coffee drinks, like cafe Bohème (mocha with almond syrup) or cafe L'amour (iced latte with a hazelnut tinge). Beer and wine are also served.

419 F St. (near 4th Ave.). ℂ **619/238-0114.** Main courses $3–$7. No credit cards. Sun–Thurs 10am–1am, Fri–Sat 9:30am–3am. Bus: 3, 5, 16, or 25. Trolley: Gaslamp Quarter.

Filippi's Pizza Grotto ★★ *Value* ITALIAN Think Little Italy and this is the picture that comes to mind. To get to the dining area, decorated with Chianti bottles and red-checked tablecloths, you walk through an Italian grocery store and deli strewn with cheeses, pastas, wines, bottles of olive oil, and salamis. You might even end up eating behind shelves of canned olives, but don't feel bad—this has been a tradition since 1950. The intoxicating smell of pizza wafts into the street; Filippi's has more than 15 varieties (including vegetarian), plus old-world spaghetti, lasagna, and other pasta. Children's portions are available, and kids will feel right at home.

The original of a dozen branches, this Filippi's has free parking. Other locations include 962 Garnet Ave., Pacific Beach (ℂ **858/483-6222**); Kearny Mesa; East Mission Valley; and Escondido.

1747 India St. (between Date and Fir sts.), Little Italy. ℂ **619/232-5095.** Main courses $5–$13. AE, DC, DISC, MC, V. Sun–Thurs 11am–10pm, Fri–Sat 11am–11pm. Free parking. Bus: 5. Trolley: County Center/Little Italy.

Kansas City Barbecue AMERICAN Kansas City Barbecue's honky-tonk mystique was fueled by its appearance as the fly-boy hangout in the movie *Top Gun.* Posters from the film share wall space with county-fair memorabilia, old Kansas car tags, and a photograph of official "bar wench" Carry Nation. This homey dive is right next to the railroad tracks and across from the tony Hyatt Regency. The spicy barbecue ribs, chicken, and hot links are slow-cooked over an open fire and served with sliced white bread and your choice of coleslaw, beans, fries, onion rings, potato salad, or corn on the cob. The food is okay, but the atmosphere is the real draw.

610 W. Market St. ℂ **619/231-9680.** Reservations accepted only for parties of 8 or more. Main courses $9–$12. MC, V. Daily 11am–1am. Trolley: Seaport Village.

HILLCREST/UPTOWN

Other choices in this fashionable neighborhood include **Cafe W,** 3680 Sixth Ave. (ℂ **619/291-0200**), the latest venture of former California-cuisine chef Chris Walsh, who does flavorful international tapas-style small plates in a revived Hillcrest cottage; **Hash House a Go Go,** 3628 Fifth Ave. (ℂ **619/298-4646**), another quirky old bungalow with an equally eclectic pun-filled menu, plus enormous portions and local-legend breakfasts; and **Hob Nob Hill,** 2271 First Ave., at Juniper (ℂ **619/239-8176**), a 1940s-era diner that's a favorite neighborhood hangout.

EXPENSIVE

California Cuisine ★★ CALIFORNIA While this excellent restaurant's name is no longer as cutting-edge as when it opened in the early 1980s, the always-creative menu keeps up with contemporary trends. A quiet, understated dining room and delightfully romantic patio set the stage as the smoothly professional and respectful staff proffers fine dining at reasonable prices to a casual crowd.

The menu changes daily and contains mouthwatering appetizers like sesame-seared ahi with hot-and-sour raspberry sauce, or caramelized onion and Gruyère tart on balsamic baby greens. Main courses are, more often than not, stacked in trendy towers, and their flavors are composed with equal care: Blackened beef tenderloin sits atop sun-dried mashed potatoes surrounded by bright tomato purée, and Chilean sea bass is poached in saffron broth with tangy capers and buttery Yukon gold potatoes. Parking can be scarce along this busy stretch of University. You'll spot the light-strewn bushes in front of the restaurant.

1027 University Ave. (E of 10th St.). *C* 619/543-0790. www.californiacuisine.com. Reservations recommended for dinner. Main courses $15–$23. AE, DISC, MC, V. Tues–Fri 11am–10pm, Sat–Sun 5–10pm. Bus: 8, 11, 16, or 25.

Laurel ★★★ FRENCH/MEDITERRANEAN   Given its sophisticated decor, pedigreed chefs, prime Balboa Park location, and well-composed menu of country-French dishes with a Mediterranean accent, it's no wonder this relatively new restaurant was an instant success. It's also popular with theatergoers, offering shuttle service to the Old Globe. Live piano music adds to the glamour of dining in this swank room on the ground floor of a new office building. Start by choosing from an extensive selection of tantalizing appetizers, including saffron-tinged red-pepper-and-shellfish soup, veal sweetbreads with portobello mushrooms and grainy mustard sauce, and warm caramelized onion and Roquefort tart. Main courses include crisp Muscovy duck confit, roasted salmon with tangy red-beet vinaigrette, and venison in a rich shallot–port wine sauce. One of the most stylish choices near often-funky Hillcrest, Laurel has an almost New York ambience coupled with reasonable prices.

505 Laurel St. (at 5th Ave.). *C* 619/239-2222. www.laurelrestaurant.com. Reservations recommended. Main courses $15–$26. AE, DC, DISC, MC, V. Sun–Thurs 5–10pm, Fri–Sat 5–11pm. Valet parking $6. Bus: 1, 3, or 25.

MODERATE

Mixx ★★ *Finds* CALIFORNIA/INTERNATIONAL   Aptly named for its subtle global fusion fare, Mixx embodies everything good about Hillcrest dining: an attractive, relaxing room; a sophisticated crowd; thoughtfully composed dinners; and polished, friendly service. It's easy to see why hip locals gravitate to Mixx's wood-paneled street-level cocktail lounge and the often-jovial dining room above. Menu standouts include a starter of pepper-seared ahi over ginger-jicama slaw, duck and wild-mushroom ravioli, and pepper filet mignon on truffle mashed potatoes with an armagnac, cream, and port-wine reduction. Even carnivores should check out chef Josh McGinnis's surprisingly inventive nightly vegetarian special. Prepared, plated, and presented with finesse, one meal here will quickly convince you that Mixx cares about style, substance, *and* value. Allow time to search for that elusive Hillcrest parking space!

3671 5th Ave. (at Pennsylvania Ave.). *C* 619/299-6499. Reservations recommended, especially on weekends. Main courses $14–$24. AE, DC, DISC, MC, V. Sun–Thurs 5–10pm, Fri–Sat 5–11pm. Bus: 1, 3, or 25.

Parallel 33 ★★ INTERNATIONAL FUSION   Inspired by a theory that all locales along the 33rd parallel of the globe might share the rich culinary traditions of the Tigris-Euphrates Valley (birthplace of civilization), chef Amiko Gubbins presents a cuisine that beautifully combines flavors from Morocco, Lebanon, India, China, and Japan. Even if you find the concept befuddling, you're sure to savor the creativity displayed in a menu that leaps happily from fragrant Moroccan chicken *b'stilla* to soft-shell crab crusted with *panko* (wispy Japanese bread crumbs) and black sesame seeds, then enthusiastically back to grilled duck with fiery Chinese five-spice sauce alongside crisp spring rolls. The ahi poke appetizer fuses a Hawaiian mainstay with sweet mango and Japanese wasabi—it's a winner! The restaurant is nice but not fancy, just an upscale neighborhood joint (in the most stylish section of town). A multiethnic

Indian-African-Asian decor throws soft shadows throughout, inviting conversation and leisurely dining. This place was instantly popular after opening in 1999, and devout fans show no signs of waning—so reserve a table in advance.

741 W. Washington St. (at Falcon), Mission Hills. (© 619/260-0033. Reservations recommended. Main courses $17–$28. AE, DISC, MC, V. Mon–Thurs 5:30–10pm, Fri–Sat 5:30–11pm. Bus: 3, 8 or 16.

INEXPENSIVE

Also consider Hillcrest's nostalgic crowd-pleaser, the 1950s flashback **Corvette Diner,** located at 3946 Fifth Ave., between Washington Street and University Avenue (© **619/542-1001**).

San Diego Chicken Pie Shop ★ (Value AMERICAN   Visitors might think this throwback diner is hidden away in a nondescript neighborhood northeast of Balboa Park, but residents and regulars know it well. Whether you're looking for a quick-but-hearty lunch, need a square meal on a Skid Row budget, desire a freezer-full of easy-bake dinners, or simply want to experience a genuine 1940s moment, this humble institution fits the bill. Decorated with 60-plus years' worth of chicken (and turkey) tchotchkes sent by grateful patrons, the dining room is welcoming enough for solo diners, and casual enough for the kids' soccer team. The eponymous pies (fresh-from-the-oven), are so good, I've never even wanted to try the baked ham, roast sirloin, chicken-fried steak, or sautéed chicken livers on the dinner menu. But they're there for dissenters, and a full dinner—including soup, potatoes, vegetable, coleslaw, bread, and dessert—clocks in at under $6! Order a $2 pie a la carte and you can still get a slice of apple pie for just 85¢. Ridiculous, huh? At lunchtime, sandwiches round out the menu.

2633 El Cajon Blvd. (at Oregon), North Park. (© 619/295-0156. Most menu items under $5. No credit cards. Sun–Thurs 10am–8pm, Fri–Sat 10am–8:30pm. Bus: 1.

The Vegetarian Zone ★★ VEGETARIAN   San Diego's only strictly vegetarian restaurant is a real treat, and word has gotten around—it's nearly always crowded, and everyone knows about it. Even if you're wary of tempeh, tofu, and meat substitutes, there are plenty of veggie ethnic selections on the menu. Greek spinach-and-feta pie has crispy edges and buttery phyllo layers; Indian turnovers are sweet and savory, flavored with pumpkin and curry; and the Mediterranean roasted-vegetable sandwich is accented with smoky mozzarella cheese. If you're ordering salad, don't miss the tangy miso-ginger dressing. In business since 1975, the Vegetarian Zone has opened a deli next door. There's seating indoors and on a casual patio; soothing music creates a pleasant ambience enjoyed by trendy Hillcrest types, business lunchers, and the health-conscious from all walks of life. Wine is served by the glass. In case you feel deserving of a treat after such a healthful meal, the heavenly Extraordinary Desserts is next door.

2949 5th Ave. (between Palm and Quince sts.). (© 619/298-7302, or 619/298-9232 for deli and takeout. Reservations accepted only for parties of 6 or more. Main courses $5–$10. AE, DC, DISC, MC, V. Mon–Thurs 11:30am–9pm, Fri 11:30am–10pm, Sat 10:30am–10pm, Sun 10:30am–9pm. Free parking. Bus: 1, 3, or 25.

OLD TOWN & MISSION VALLEY
EXPENSIVE

Cafe Pacifica ★★ CALIFORNIA   You can't judge a book by its cover: Inside this cozy Old Town casita, the decor is cleanly contemporary (but still romantic) and the food anything but Mexican. Established in 1980 by the now-revered duo of Kipp Downing and Deacon Brown, Cafe Pacifica serves upscale, imaginative seafood and produces kitchen alumni who go on to enjoy local fame.

Among the temptations on the menu are crab-stuffed portobello mushroom topped with grilled asparagus; anise-scented bouillabaisse; and daily fresh-fish selections served grilled with your choice of five sauces. Signature items include Hawaiian ahi with shiitake mushrooms and ginger butter, griddled mustard catfish, and the "Pomerita," a pomegranate margarita. Patrons tend to dress up, though it's not required. To avoid the crowds, arrive in the early evening.

2414 San Diego Ave. ℂ 619/291-6666. www.cafepacifica.com. Reservations recommended. Main courses $12–$22. AE, DC, DISC, MC, V. Mon–Sat 5:30–10pm, Sun 5–9:30pm. Valet parking $4. Bus: 5/5A. Trolley: Old Town.

El Agave Tequilaria ✿✿ REGIONAL MEXICAN   Don't be misled by this restaurant's less-than-impressive location above a liquor store on the outskirts of Old Town. This warm, bustling eatery continues to draw local gourmands for the regional Mexican cuisine and rustic elegance that leave the touristy fajitas-and-cerveza joints of Old Town far behind. El Agave is named for the agave plant from which tequilas are derived, and they boast over 600 boutique and artisan tequilas from throughout the Latin world—bottles of every size, shape, and jewel-like hue fill shelves and cases throughout the dining room. But even teetotalers will enjoy the restaurant's authentically flavored mole sauces (a peanut-rich version from Chiapas, tangy tomatillo from Oaxaca, and the more familiar dark mole flavored with chocolate and sesame), along with giant shrimp and sea bass prepared in a dozen variations, or El Agave's signature beef filet with goat cheese and dark tequila sauce.

2304 San Diego Ave. ℂ 619/220-0692. www.elagaverestaurant.com. Reservations recommended. Main courses $12–$22. AE, MC, V. Daily 11am–10pm. Street parking. Bus: 5/5A. Trolley: Old Town.

MODERATE

Berta's Latin American Restaurant ✿✿ *Finds* LATIN AMERICAN Berta's is a welcome change from the nacho-and-fajita joints that dominate Old Town dining, though it can attract as large a crowd on weekends. Housed in a charming, basic cottage tucked away on a side street, Berta's faithfully re-creates the sunny flavors of Central America, where slow cooking mellows the heat of chiles and other spices. Everyone starts with a basket of fresh flour tortillas and mild salsa verde, which usually vanishes before you're done contemplating such mouthwatering dishes as Guatemalan *chilimal,* a rich pork-and-vegetable casserole with chiles, tomatoes, cornmeal *masa,* cilantro, and cloves. Try the Salvadoran *pupusas* (at lunch only)—dense corn-mash turnovers with melted cheese and black beans, their texture perfectly offset with crunchy cabbage salad and one of Berta's special salsas. Or opt for a table full of Spanish-style tapas, grazing alternately on crispy empanadas (filled turnovers), strong Spanish olives, or *Pincho Moruno,* skewered lamb and onion redolent of spices and red saffron.

3928 Twiggs St. (at Congress St.). ℂ 619/295-2343. Main courses $5–$7 lunch, $11–$13 dinner. AE, MC, V. Tues–Sun 11am–10pm (lunch menu till 3pm). Bus: 5/5A. Trolley: Old Town.

INEXPENSIVE

Casa de Bandini ✿ *Kids* MEXICAN   As much an Old Town tradition as the mariachi music that's played here on weekends, Casa de Bandini is the most picturesque of several Mexican restaurants with predictable food and birdbath-size margaritas. It fills the nooks and crannies of an adobe hacienda built in 1823 for Juan Bandini, a local merchant and politician. The superbly renovated enclosed patio has iron gates, flowers blooming around a bubbling fountain, and umbrella-shaded tables for year-round alfresco dining. Some of the dishes are gourmet Mexican, others simple south-of-the-border fare. The crowd consists mainly of out-of-towners, but the ambience and towering tostada salads draw a lunchtime crowd. The setting makes this restaurant extra-special, and makes the less-than-remarkable meal worthwhile.

2754 Calhoun St. (opposite Old Town Plaza). © 619/297-8211. www.casadebandini.com. Reservations not accepted. Main courses $6–$16. AE, DC, DISC, MC, V. Daily 11am–9pm (till 10pm in summer). Free parking. Bus: 5/5A. Trolley: Old Town.

Old Town Mexican Café ℱ MEXICAN   This place is so popular that it's become an Old Town tourist attraction in its own right. It keeps expanding into additional colorful dining rooms and outdoor patios, but the wait for a table is still often 30 to 60 minutes. Pass the time gazing in from the sidewalk as tortillas are hand-patted the old-fashioned way, soon to be a hot-off-the-grill treat accompanying every meal. Once inside, order what some consider the best margarita in town, followed by one of the cafe's two specialties: *carnitas,* the traditional Mexican dish of deep-fried pork served with tortillas, guacamole, sour cream, beans, and rice; or rotisserie chicken with the same trimmings. It's loud and crowded and the cerveza flows like, well, beer . . . but this Old Town mainstay is the best in the city for traditional Mexican.

2489 San Diego Ave. © 619/297-4330. Reservations accepted only for parties of 10 or more. Main courses $7.50–$12. AE, DISC, MC, V. Sun–Thurs 7am–11pm, Fri–Sat 7am–midnight; bar service daily until 2am. Bus: 5/5A. Trolley: Old Town.

MISSION BAY & THE BEACHES

Another noteworthy beach spot is **Kono's Surf Club Cafe,** 704 Garnet Ave. (© **858/483-1669**), a Hawaiian-themed boardwalk breakfast shack that's cheap and delicious—a plump Kono's breakfast burrito provides enough fuel for an entire day of surfing or sightseeing, while a side order of savory "Kono Potatoes" is a meal in itself. And sushi lovers will want to head straight for **Sushi Ota,** 4529 Mission Bay Dr., at Bunker Hill (© **858/270-5670**), where the minimalist decor is a perfect backdrop for artful bundles of the best fresh seafood, plus a full menu of Japanese specialties.

EXPENSIVE

Baleen ℱℱℱ SEAFOOD/CALIFORNIA   Crowning the multimillion-dollar transformation of the former Vacation Village into the contemporary playground Paradise Point Resort, this fine waterfront eatery is exactly the touch-of-class planners hoped for when they lured celebrity restaurateur Robbin Haas (creator of Baleens in Coconut Grove and Naples, Fla.). With a spectacular bayfront view (and dining deck for pleasant weather), it's easy to miss the design details indoors—from a monkey motif that includes simians hanging off chandeliers to specialized serving platters for many of Baleen's artistically arranged dishes. Start with chilled lobster in a martini glass, a warm salad of roasted mushrooms and asparagus, or fresh oysters delivered in a small cart and shucked tableside. Then savor a selection of seafood simply grilled, wood-roasted, or sautéed, with hummus crust, honey wasabi glaze, or ginger sauce. Wood-roasted meats include Roquefort-crusted filet mignon and veal T-bone marinated in olive oil, rosemary, and roasted garlic. Should you have appetite—and credit—left over, indulge in an intricately rich dessert like chocolate fondue, or the quartet of fruit-infused custards.

In Paradise Point Resort, 1404 Vacation Rd., Mission Bay. © **858/490-6363**. www.paradisepoint.com. Reservations recommended. Main courses $10–$21 lunch, $18–$30 dinner. AE, DC, DISC, MC, V. Daily 7am–11pm. Follow I-8 W to Mission Bay Dr. exit; take Ingraham St. N to Vacation Rd.

MODERATE

Caffe Bella Italia ★★ NORTHERN ITALIAN You'd think passersby might flock to this excellent family-run Garnet Avenue newcomer, but most just look . . . and keep on walking or driving. They're discouraged by Bella Italia's—the kindest word I can think of is "underwhelming"—street presence, housed in a former plain-Jane stucco dry cleaner. Trust me on this one: It's lovely inside, and the food will knock your socks off. Romantic lighting, sheer draperies, and warmly earthy walls create an unexpected ambience, assisted by the lilting Milan accents of the staff. Each and every item on the menu bears the unmistakable flavor of freshness and homemade care—even the simplest curled-edge ravioli stuffed with ricotta, spinach, and pine nuts is elevated to culinary nirvana. Indulge in the traditional *tartufo* ice-cream dessert (bathed in a shot of espresso), and you'll leave wishing you could be adopted by this family.

1525 Garnet Ave. (between Ingraham and Haines), Pacific Beach. ⓒ **858/273-1224.** www.caffe bellaitalia.com. Reservations suggested for dinner. Main courses $7–$11 lunch, $9–$21 dinner. AE, MC, V. Tues–Sat 11am–2:30pm; Sun and Tues–Thurs 5–10pm, Fri–Sat 5–11pm. Free parking. Bus: 27.

The Green Flash ★ AMERICAN Known throughout Pacific Beach for its location and hip, local clientele, the Green Flash serves reasonably good (and typically beachy) food at decent prices. The menu includes plenty of grilled and deep-fried seafood, straightforward steaks, and giant main-course salads. You'll also find platters of shellfish (oysters, clams, shrimp) and ethnic appetizers. On the glassed-in patio, locals congregate every evening to catch a glimpse of the optical phenomenon for which this boardwalk hangout is named. It has something to do with the color spectrum at the moment the sun disappears below the horizon, but the scientific explanation becomes less important—and the decibel level rises—with every round of drinks.

701 Thomas Ave. (at Mission Blvd.), Pacific Beach. ⓒ **858/270-7715.** Reservations not accepted. Main courses $10–$20; sunset specials Sun–Thurs 4:30–7pm. AE, DC, DISC, MC, V. Daily 8am–10pm. Bus: 34/34A.

INEXPENSIVE

For all-day breakfast, light lunch, or a soup bowl–size caffe latte, follow the locals to **The Mission,** 3795 Mission Blvd., at San Jose (ⓒ **858/488-9060**), a funky and casual coffeehouse at the heart of the Mission Beach scene.

High Tide Café AMERICAN Ceiling fans stir the air in this cheerful, comfortably crowded place, and there's pleasant rooftop dining with an ocean view if you're lucky enough to snag a seat. Just off the Pacific Beach boardwalk, the cafe sees a lot of foot traffic and socializing locals. Those in the know go for great breakfasts—choices include Mexican-style eggs and breakfast burritos, French toast, and omelets. During happy hour (4–6pm), you'll find bargain prices on drinks and finger-lickin' appetizers. The rest of the menu is adequate, running the gamut from fish tacos to Tex-Mex fajitas to lasagna and all-American burgers.

722 Grand Ave., Pacific Beach. ⓒ **858/272-1999.** Reservations recommended on weekends. Main courses $6–$13. AE, DISC, MC, V. Sun–Thurs 7am–9pm, Fri–Sat 7am–10pm. Free parking. Bus: 34/34A.

LA JOLLA
EXPENSIVE

Other choices in this upscale neighborhood of many excellent restaurants include the stylish **Cafe Japengo,** 8960 University Center Lane, at the Hyatt Regency La Jolla (ⓒ **858/450-3355**), whose Pacific Rim fusion and unique take on sushi are often overshadowed by a chic, noisy scene; and **Roppongi,** 875 Prospect St., at Fay Avenue (ⓒ **858/551-5252**), where the cuisines of Japan,

Thailand, China, Vietnam, and India collide in a creative explosion of flavorful dishes designed for sharing.

George's at the Cove ★★★ CALIFORNIA   You'll find host and namesake George Hauer at his restaurant's door most nights; he greets loyal regulars by name, and his confidence assures newcomers that they'll leave impressed with this beloved La Jolla tradition. Voted most popular in the Zagat restaurant survey, George's wins consistent praise for impeccable service, gorgeous views of the cove, and outstanding California cuisine.

The menu, in typical San Diego fashion, presents many inventive seafood options, filtered through the myriad influences of chef Trey Foshee. Classical culinary training, Hawaiian ingenuity, and a stint at Robert Redford's Utah Sundance resort are among his many accomplishments. Dishes combine many flavors with practiced artistry, ranging from the Asian-tinged grilled swordfish atop gingered vegetables accented with Thai coconut sauce to a Provençal-inspired rack of lamb in aromatic spices with Foshee's version of ratatouille. George's signature smoked chicken, broccoli, and black-bean soup is still a mainstay; they'll even give out the recipe for this local legend. As an alternative to dinner's pricey main courses, try the tasting menu, which offers a seasonally composed five-course sampling for around $50 per person; or try the more reasonably priced lunch menu. The informal **Ocean Terrace Cafe** is upstairs.

1250 Prospect St. ⓒ **858/454-4244.** www.georgesatthecove.com. Reservations recommended. Main courses $13–$17 lunch, $25–$35 dinner. AE, DC, DISC, MC, V. Mon–Fri 11:30am–2:30pm, Sat–Sun 11:30am–3pm; Mon–Thurs 5:30–10pm, Fri–Sat 5–10:30pm, Sun 5–10pm. Valet parking $5–$6.

Nine-Ten ★★★ CALIFORNIA/MEDITERRANEAN   The anticipation was almost too much to bear as eager La Jollans awaited this overhaul of venerable Putnam's, and the arrival of pedigreed chef Michael Stebner. I'm happy to report, though, there are no signs of overhype or spotlight jitters here: Stebner delivers on a superbly crafted and executed menu in a warmly stylish and understated space. Window and sidewalk tables offer a street view of La Jolla's beautiful people, who in turn gaze in at mouthwatering seasonal presentations like chestnut *agnolotti* with fennel and sweet squash, rich veal tenderloin with rosemary and olives atop creamy polenta, and scallops braised in a rich mushroom broth. A favorite Stebner wouldn't dare take off the menu is the delicious porcini risotto topped with lobster and aromatic white truffle oil. I particularly appreciate the multitude of "tasting portions," a boon to smaller appetites or creative types who want to compose their own multi-course "sampling" meal. It also helps leave room for desserts like spicy carrot-parsnip cake, persimmon *panna cotta,* or refreshing honey-rosemary ice cream. When you're looking for a classy fine-dining experience—with none of the old-guard fancy attitude—this hotel eatery stands alone on the culinary scene.

910 Prospect St. (between Fay and Girard) ⓒ **858/964-5400.** www.thegrandecolonial.com. Reservations recommended. Main courses $8–$12 lunch, $18–$32 dinner. AE, DC, DISC, MC, V. Daily 6:30–11am, 11:30am–2:30pm, and 6–10:30pm.

Trattoria Acqua ★★ ITALIAN/MEDITERRANEAN   Nestled on tiled terraces close enough to catch ocean breezes, this excellent northern Italian spot has a more relaxed ambience than similarly sophisticated Gaslamp Quarter trattorias. Rustic walls and outdoor seating shaded by flowering vines evoke a romantic Tuscan villa. A mixed crowd of suits and well-heeled couples gather to enjoy expertly prepared seasonal dishes; every table starts with bread served with an indescribably pungent Mediterranean spread. Acqua's pastas (all available as appetizers or main courses) are as good as it gets—rich, heady flavor combinations like spinach, chard, and four-cheese gnocchi, or veal-and-mortadella tortellini in fennel cream sauce. Other specialties include *saltimbocca con funghi* (veal scaloppine with sage, prosciutto, and forest-mushroom sauce), cassoulet (traditional Toulouse-style duck confit, sausage, and braised lamb baked with white beans, tomato, and fresh thyme), and *salmone al pepe* (roasted peppercorn-crusted Atlantic salmon served over lentils with sherry-and-shallot vinaigrette). The well-chosen wine list has received *Wine Spectator* accolades several years in a row.

1298 Prospect St. (on Coast Walk). © 858/454-0709. www.trattoriaacqua.com. Reservations recommended. Main courses $13–$27. AE, MC, V. Daily 11:30am–2:30pm; Sun–Thurs 5–9:30pm, Fri–Sat 5–10:30pm. Validated self-parking.

MODERATE

Don't forget about the **Ocean Terrace** at George's at the Cove (see above), where many of the same dishes come with a fresh-air ocean view—and a slimmer bill than the downstairs dining room.

Brockton Villa ★★ *Finds* BREAKFAST/CALIFORNIA   In a restored 1894 beach bungalow, this charming cafe has a history as intriguing as its varied, eclectic menu. Named for an early resident's hometown (Brockton, Mass.), the cottage is imbued with the spirit of artistic souls drawn to this breathtaking perch overlooking La Jolla Cove. Rescued by the trailblazing Pannikin Coffee Company in the 1960s, the restaurant is now independently run by a Pannikin alum.

The biggest buzz is at breakfast, when you can enjoy inventive dishes such as soufflé-like "Coast Toast" (the house take on French toast) and Greek "steamers" (eggs scrambled with an espresso steamer, then mixed with feta cheese, tomato, and basil). The dozens of coffee drinks include the "Keith Richards"—four shots of espresso topped with Mexican hot chocolate (Mother's Little Helper indeed!). Lunch stars include homemade soups and salads, plus unusual sandwiches like turkey meatloaf on toasted sourdough bread with spicy tomato-mint chutney. The constantly expanding dinner menu includes salmon en croûte (wrapped in prosciutto, Gruyère, and sage, with a grainy mustard sauce), plus pastas, stews, and grilled meats. Steep stairs from the street limit access for wheelchair users.

1235 Coast Blvd. (across from La Jolla Cove). © 858/454-7393. Reservations recommended (call by Thurs for Sun brunch). Breakfast $4–$8; dinner main courses $12–$21. AE, DISC, MC, V. Mon 8am–5pm, Tues–Sun 8am–9pm.

Spice & Rice Thai Kitchen ★ THAI   This stylish Thai restaurant is a couple of blocks from the village's tourist crush—far enough to ensure effortless parking. The lunch crowd consists of shoppers and curious tourists, while dinner is quieter; all the local businesses have shut down and many diners are going to the old-fashioned Cove movie theater next door. The food is excellent, with polished presentations and expert renditions of the classics like pad Thai, satay, curry, and glazed duck. The starters often sound as good as the entrees—consider making a grazing meal of house specialties like "gold bags" (minced pork, vegetables, and herbs wrapped in crispy rice paper and served with earthy plum sauce) or minced roast duck spiced with chiles and lime juice; spicy calamari is flavored with ginger, cilantro, lime, and chili sauce. The romantically lit covered front patio has a secluded garden feel, and inside tables also have indirect lighting. Despite the passage of time, this all-around satisfier remains something of an insider's secret.

7734 Girard Ave. © **858/456-0466.** Reservations recommended. Main courses $8–$13. AE, MC, V. Mon–Sat 11am–3pm; Sun–Thurs 5–10pm, Fri–Sat 5–11pm.

INEXPENSIVE

The Cottage ⭐ BREAKFAST/CALIFORNIA   La Jolla's best—and friendliest—breakfast is served at this early-20th-century bungalow on a sunny village corner. Newly modernized, the cottage is light and airy, but most diners opt for tables outside, where a charming white picket fence encloses the trellis-shaded brick patio. Omelets and egg dishes feature Mediterranean, Asian, or classic American touches; my favorite has creamy mashed potatoes, bacon, and melted cheese folded inside. The Cottage bakes its own muffins, breakfast breads, and—you can quote me on this—the best brownies in San Diego. While breakfast dishes are served all day, toward lunch the kitchen begins turning out freshly made, healthful soups, light meals, and sandwiches. Summer dinners (never heavy, always tasty) are a delight, particularly when you're seated before dark on a balmy seaside night.

7702 Fay Ave. (at Kline St.). © **858/454-8409.** www.cottagelajolla.com. Reservations accepted for dinner only. Breakfast and lunch $5–$12; dinner main courses $8–$18. AE, DISC, MC, V. Daily year-round 7:30am–3pm; May 15–Sept 30 Tues–Sat 5–9:30pm.

CORONADO

If you're in the mood for a special-occasion meal that'll knock your socks off, consider **Azzura Point** (© **619/424-4000**), in Loews Coronado Bay Resort. With its plushly upholstered, gilded, and view-endowed setting, this stylish dining room wins continual raves from deep-pocketed San Diego foodies willing to cross the bay for inventive and artistic California-Mediterranean creations.

EXPENSIVE

Chez Loma ⭐⭐ FRENCH   You'd be hard-pressed to find a more romantic dining spot than this intimate Victorian cottage filled with antiques and subdued candlelight. The house dates from 1889, the French-Continental restaurant from 1975. Tables are scattered throughout the house and on the enclosed garden terrace; an upstairs wine salon, reminiscent of a Victorian parlor, is a cozy spot for coffee or conversation.

Among the creative entrees are salmon with smoked-tomato vinaigrette, and roast duckling with green-peppercorn sauce. All main courses are served with soup or salad, rice or potatoes, and fresh vegetables. California wines and American microbrews are available. Follow dinner with a creamy crème caramel or Kahlúa crème brûlée. Chez Loma's service is attentive, the herb rolls addictive, and early birds enjoy specially priced meals.

1132 Loma (off Orange Ave.). © **619/435-0661.** www.chezloma.com. Reservations recommended. Main courses $17–$25. AE, DC, MC, V. Daily 5–10pm; Sun 10am–2pm. Bus: 901.

Peohe's ⭐ PACIFIC RIM/SEAFOOD   With over-the-top Polynesian decor of which Disneyland would be proud, Peohe's is definitely touristy and definitely overpriced—but there's no denying the awesome view across the bay or the excellent Hawaiian-style seafood and Pacific Rim–accented cuisine. Every table in the giant, light- and plant-filled atrium has a view; there are even-better tables on the wooden deck at the water's edge. Dinner main courses include acclaimed crunchy coconut shrimp; island-style halibut sautéed with banana, macadamia nuts, and Frangelico liqueur; and rack of New Zealand lamb with Hunan barbecue sauce. Lunchtime options include more casual sandwiches and salads, and the tropical fantasy desserts are delectably rich. For those who love theme restaurants and Polynesian kitsch, Peohe's is a worthwhile splurge.

1201 1st St. (Ferry Landing Marketplace). ℂ 619/437-4474. www.peohes.com. Reservations recommended. Main courses $9–$16 lunch, $19–$30 dinner. AE, DC, DISC, MC, V. Daily 11:30am–2:30pm; Mon–Thurs 5:30–9pm, Fri 5:30–10pm, Sat 5–10pm, Sun 4:30–9pm. Bus: 901 or 904.

MODERATE

Bay Beach Cafe AMERICAN/SEAFOOD This loud, friendly gathering place isn't on the beach at all but enjoys a prime perch on San Diego Bay. Seated indoors or on a glassed-in patio, diners gaze endlessly at the city skyline, which is dramatic by day and breathtaking at night. The cafe is quite popular at happy hour, when the setting sun glimmers on downtown's mirrored high-rises. The ferry docks at a wooden pier a few steps away, discharging passengers into the complex of gift shops and restaurants with a New England fishing-village theme. At the Bay Beach Cafe, the food takes a back seat to the view, but the pub menu of burgers, sandwiches, salads, and appetizers is inexpensive and satisfying. Dinner entrees aren't quite good enough for the price.

1201 1st St. (Ferry Landing Marketplace). ℂ 619/435-4900. Reservations recommended for dinner on weekends. Main courses $9–$18; pub menu $6–$10. AE, DISC, MC, V. Mon–Fri 7–10:30am and 11am–4pm, Sat–Sun 7–11:30am and noon–4pm; daily 5–10:30pm. Free parking. Bus: 901 or 904.

INEXPENSIVE

Clayton's Coffee Shop AMERICAN The Hotel Del isn't the only relic of a bygone era in Coronado—just wait till you see this humble neighborhood favorite. Clayton's has occupied this corner spot seemingly forever, at least since a time when *everyone's* menus were full of plain American good eatin' in the $1-to-$5 range. Now their horseshoe counter, chrome barstools, and well-worn pleather-lined booths are "retro," but the burgers, fries, and chicken noodle soup are just as good—plus you can still play three oldies for a quarter on the tableside jukebox. Behind the restaurant, Clayton's Mexican takeout kitchen does a brisk business in homemade tamales.

959 Orange Ave. ℂ 619/437-8811. Menu items under $10. No credit cards. Mon–Sat 6am–8pm, Sun 6am–2pm. Bus: 901 or 904.

Primavera Pastry Caffé ★ (Value) SANDWICHES/LIGHT FARE If the name sounds familiar, it's because this fantastic little cafe—the best of its kind on the island—is part of the family that includes Primavera Ristorante, up the street. In addition to fresh-roasted coffee and espresso drinks, it serves omelets and other breakfast treats (till 1:30pm), burgers and deli sandwiches on the delicious house bread, and a daily fresh soup. It's the kind of spot where half the customers are greeted by name. Locals rave about the "Yacht Club" sandwich, a croissant filled with yellowfin tuna, and the breakfast croissant, topped with scrambled eggs and ham and cheddar cheese. I can't resist Primavera's fat, gooey cinnamon buns.

956 Orange Ave. ℂ 619/435-4191. Main courses $4–$6. MC, V. Daily 6:30am–5pm (till 6pm in summer). Bus: 901.

5 The Main Attractions: The Zoo, SeaWorld & the Wild Animal Park

San Diego Zoo ★★★ (Kids) More than 4,000 animals reside at this world-famous zoo, which was founded in 1916 with a handful of animals originally

San Diego Attractions

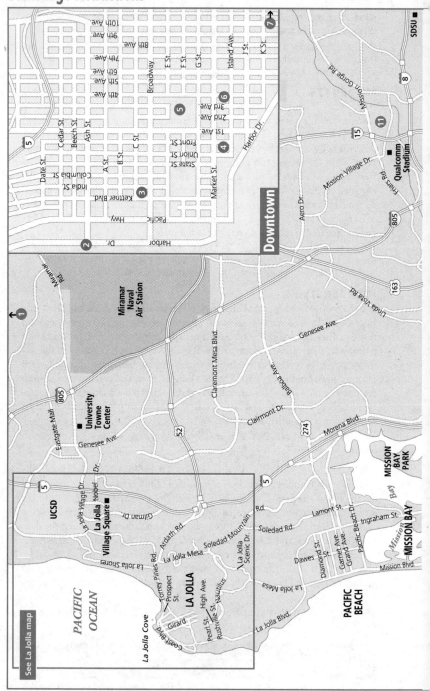

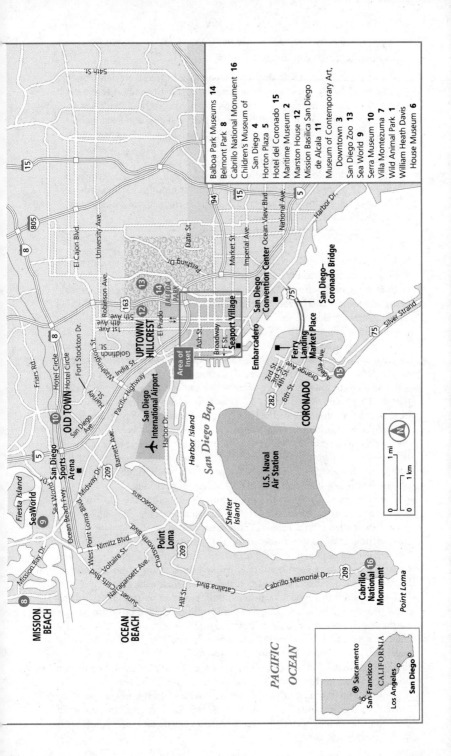

Balboa Park Museums **14**
Belmont Park **8**
Cabrillo National Monument **16**
Children's Museum of
 San Diego **4**
Horton Plaza **5**
Hotel del Coronado **15**
Maritime Museum **2**
Marston House **12**
Mission Basilica San Diego
 de Alcala **11**
Museum of Contemporary Art,
 Downtown **3**
San Diego Zoo **13**
Sea World **9**
Serra Museum **10**
Villa Montezuma **7**
Wild Animal Park **1**
William Heath Davis
 House Museum **6**

> ## Value Now That's What I Call a Deal!
>
> Always aware of what side their tourism bread is buttered on, San Diego's three main family attractions have joined forces with combo ticket deals that reward you with big savings for visitors with recreational stamina. Here's how it works: If you plan to visit both the zoo and Wild Animal Park, a two-park ticket (deluxe zoo package, Wild Animal Park admission) is $47 for adults and $28 for children ages 3 to 11. You get one visit to each attraction, to be used within 5 days of purchase.
>
> If SeaWorld is foremost in your plans, how about an almost "twofer"? For just $4 more than the regular 1-day admission price ($43 for adults, $33 for kids 3–11, free for kids under 3), you can trade up for a 2-day ticket in order to see it all without missing a beat.

brought here for the 1915–16 Panama–California International Exposition. The zoo is also an accredited botanical garden, representing more than 6,000 species of flora from many climate zones, all installed to help simulate the animals' native environments. The zoo's founder, Dr. Harry Wegeforth, a local physician and lifelong animal lover, once braved the fury of an injured tiger to toss medicine into its roaring mouth.

In the early days of the zoo, "Dr. Harry" traveled around the world and bartered native Southwestern animals such as rattlesnakes and sea lions for more exotic species. The loan of two giant pandas from the People's Republic of China was a twist on the long-standing tradition—instead of exchanging exotic species, the San Diego Zoo agreed to pay $1 million for each year that the pandas are here, to aid the conservation effort in China. The lovable pandas, which arrived in 1996, were an instant hit with zoo-goers, but their keepers' behind-the-scenes mission was to scientifically encourage the breeding of this near-extinct animal. In August 1999, their efforts were rewarded with the birth of Hua Mei, a healthy and perfect female cub. To ensure a glimpse of the panda family, call the zoo's panda-viewing hot line at ✆ **888/MY-PANDA** before visiting.

The giant pandas may be the big attention-getters, but the zoo has many other rare and exotic species: cuddly koalas from Australia, long-billed kiwis from New Zealand, wild Przewalski's horses from Mongolia, lowland gorillas from Africa, and giant tortoises from the Galapagos. Of course, the zoo's regulars—lions, elephants, giraffes, tigers, and bears—prowl around as well, and the zoo is home to a great number of tropical birds. Most of the animals are housed in barless, moated enclosures that resemble their natural habitats.

The zoo offers two types of bus tours. Both provide a narrated overview and allow you to see 75% of the park. On the **35-minute guided bus tour,** you get on the bus and complete a circuit around the zoo. It costs $4 for adults, $3 for children ages 3 to 11 (free for children under 3), and is included in the deluxe package. The **Kangaroo Bus Tour** allows you to get on and off the bus as many times as you want at any of the eight stops—you can even go around more than once. It costs $8 for adults and $5 for children. In general, it's better to take the tour early in the morning or later in the afternoon, when the animals are more active. Call the **Bus Tour Hot Line** (✆ **619/685-3264**) for information about these tours, as well as Spanish-language tours, a comedy tour, and signed tours for the hearing impaired.

You can also get an aerial perspective from the **Skyfari,** which costs $1 per person each way. The ride lasts about 5 minutes—but, because it doesn't get particularly close to the animals, it's better for a bird's-eye view of Balboa Park and a survey of the zoo.

The **Children's Zoo** is scaled to a youngster's viewpoint. There's a nursery with baby animals and a petting area where kids can cuddle up to sheep, goats, and the like. The resident wombat is a special favorite here.

2920 Zoo Dr., Balboa Park. ✆ 619/234-3153. www.sandiegozoo.org. Admission $20 adults, $12 children ages 3–11, military in uniform free. Deluxe package (admission, guided bus tour, round-trip Skyfari aerial tram) $32 adults, $20 children. Combination Zoo and Wild Animal Park package (deluxe zoo package, Wild Animal Park admission) $47 adults, $28 children; valid for 5 days from date of purchase. DISC, MC, V. Summer daily 9am–9pm (grounds close at 10pm); rest of year daily 9am–4pm (grounds close at 5pm). Bus: 7 or 7A/B.

San Diego Wild Animal Park ★★★ *Kids*   Just 30 miles north of San Diego, outside of Escondido, the Wild Animal Park transports you to the African plains and other landscapes. Originally begun as a breeding facility for the San Diego Zoo, the WAP now holds around 3,200 animals—many endangered species—roaming freely over the park's 1,800 acres. Approximately 650 baby animals are born every year in the park.

The simplest way to see the animals is by riding the 5-mile **monorail** (included in the price of admission); for the best views, sit on the right-hand side. During the 50-minute ride, you'll pass through areas resembling Africa and Asia, past waterholes and swaying grasses. Trains leave every 20 minutes from the station in Nairobi Village, the commercial hub of the park with more traditional animal exhibits, souvenir stores, and refreshment vendors. (It may sound persnickety, but the food inside the park is mediocre and overpriced . . . think about smuggling in your own snacks!)

Nairobi Village isn't much more than a small zoo whose best feature is the nursery area, where irresistible young 'uns can be seen, frolicking, being bottle-fed, and sleeping. If you want to experience the vast landscape and large animals that make the Wild Animal Park unique, you can take one of two self-guided walking trails: the 1¾-mile **Kilimanjaro safari walk,** which visits the Australian rain forest and East Africa, or the **Heart of Africa,** a ¾-mile trail that winds through dense forest, flourishing wetlands, sprawling savannas, and open plains.

The surest way to get up-close-and-personal, though, is to take a **photo caravan tour** ($65–$95 per person, park admission included). In my experience, the photos are secondary to the enjoyment. (How many of us point-and-shoot shutterbugs can really hope to top the professional shots gracing the official souvenir postcards, anyway?) What matters is crossing the fence to meet the rhinos, ostriches, zebras, deer, and giraffes on their home turf, even feeding giraffes along the way.

15500 San Pasqual Valley Rd., Escondido. ✆ 760/747-8702. www.wildanimalpark.org. Admission $27 adults, $24 seniors 60 and over, $20 children ages 3–11, free for children under 3 and military in uniform. Combination Zoo and Wild Animal Park package (includes deluxe zoo package) $47 adults, $28 children; valid for 5 days from date of purchase. DISC, MC, V. Daily 9am–4pm (grounds close at 5pm); extended hr. during summer and Festival of Lights in Dec. Parking $6 per car. Take I-15 to Via Rancho Pkwy.; follow signs for about 3 miles.

SeaWorld ★★★ *Kids*   One of the best-promoted attractions in California, SeaWorld may be your main reason for coming to San Diego. The 165-acre, multimillion-dollar aquatic playground is a showplace for marine life, made politically correct with a nominally educational atmosphere. Several successive

4-ton black-and-white killer whales have functioned as the park's mascot, Shamu. At its heart, SeaWorld is a family entertainment center where the performers are dolphins, otters, sea lions, walruses, and seals. Shows run continuously throughout the day, while visitors can rotate through the various theaters.

The 2-acre hands-on area called **Shamu's Happy Harbor** encourages kids to handle things—and features everything from a pretend pirate ship, with plenty of netted towers, to tube crawls, slides, and chances to get wet. The newest attraction is **Shipwreck Rapids,** a wet adventure ride on raft-like inner tubes through caverns, waterfalls, and wild rivers. Other draws include **Wild Arctic,** a virtual-reality trip to the frozen North, complete with polar bears, beluga whales, walruses, and harbor seals; and the 4-D interactive movie *Pirates,* a comic adventure written by *Monty Python's* Eric Idle and starring the deadpan Leslie Nielsen.

The **Dolphin Interaction Program** creates an opportunity for people to meet bottlenose dolphins. Although the program stops short of allowing you to swim with the dolphins, it does offer the opportunity to wade waist-deep, and plenty of time to stroke the mammals and give commands like the trainers. This 1-hour program includes some classroom time before you wriggle into a wetsuit and climb into the water; it costs $125 per person, not including admission to the rest of the adventure park. Space is limited, so advance reservations are required (© 877/4-DOLPHIN). Participants must be 6 or older.

Although SeaWorld is best known as Shamu's home, the facility also plays an important role in rescuing and rehabilitating beached animals found along the West Coast—including more than 300 seals, sea lions, marine birds, and dolphins in an average year. Following the successful rescue and 1998 release of a young California gray whale, SeaWorld turned its attention to the manatee, an unusual aquatic mammal rarely seen outside Florida's tropical waters—several permanent residents are on display in the **Manatee Rescue** exhibit area.

500 Sea World Dr., Mission Bay. © 619/226-3901. www.seaworld.com. Admission $39 adults, $35 seniors 55 and over, $30 children ages 3–11, free for children under 3. AE, DISC, MC, V. Parking $7. Guided 90-min. walking tours $8 adults, $7 children. Memorial Day to Labor Day daily 9am–11pm or midnight; Sept–May daily 10am–5pm. Bus: 9. By car from I-5, take Sea World Dr. exit; from I-8, take W. Mission Bay Dr. exit to Sea World Dr.

6 Beaches

San Diego County is blessed with more than 30 beaches that attract surfers, snorkelers, swimmers, and sunbathers. In summer, the beaches teem with locals and visitors alike. The rest of the year, they are popular places to walk and jog, and surfers don wet suits to pursue their passion. The following are some of my favorite San Diego beaches, arranged geographically from south to north.

IMPERIAL BEACH   Half an hour south of San Diego by car or trolley, and only a few minutes from the Mexican border, lies Imperial Beach. It's popular with surfers and local youths, who can be somewhat territorial about "their" sands in summer. The beach boasts 3 miles of surf breaks plus a guarded "swimmers only" stretch; check with lifeguards before getting wet, though, since sewage from nearby Mexico can sometimes foul the water. Imperial also plays host to the annual U.S. Open Sandcastle Competition each August, with world-class sand creations ranging from sea scenes to dragons to dinosaurs.

CORONADO BEACH   Lovely, wide, and sparkling white, this beach is conducive to strolling and lingering, especially in the late afternoon. The southeastern end fronts Ocean Boulevard and is especially pretty in front of the Hotel del

Coronado. Toward the north, you can watch fighter jets in formation flying from the Naval Air Station. Waves are gentle here, so the beach draws many Coronado families—and their dogs, who are allowed off-leash at the most northwesterly end. The islands visible from here, "Los Coronados," are 18 miles away and belong to Mexico.

OCEAN BEACH   The northern end of Ocean Beach Park is officially known as "Dog Beach," and is one of only two in San Diego where your pooch can roam freely on the sand (and frolic with several dozen other people's pets). Surfers generally congregate around the Ocean Beach Pier, mostly in the water but often at the snack shack on the end. Rip currents are strong here and discourage most swimmers from venturing beyond waist depth. Facilities at the beach include restrooms, showers, picnic tables, volleyball courts, and plenty of metered parking lots. To reach the beach, take West Point Loma Boulevard all the way to the end.

MISSION BAY PARK   In this 4,600-acre aquatic playground, you'll find 27 miles of bay front, picnic areas, children's playgrounds, and paths for biking, in-line skating, and jogging. The bay lends itself to windsurfing, sailing, riding personal watercraft, water-skiing, and fishing. There are dozens of access points; one of the most popular is off I-5 at Clairemont Drive, where there's a visitor information center.

MISSION BEACH   While Mission Bay Park is a body of salt water surrounded by land and bridges, Mission Beach is actually a beach on the Pacific Ocean. Surfing is popular year-round here, but the sands and wide cement "boardwalk" sizzle with activity and great people-watching in summer. The long beach and boardwalk extend from Pacific Beach Drive south to Belmont Park and beyond to the jetty. Parking is often tough, with your best bets being the public lots at Belmont Park or at the foot of West Mission Bay Drive.

PACIFIC BEACH   There's always some action at Pacific Beach, particularly along **Ocean Front Walk,** a paved promenade featuring a human parade akin to that at LA's Venice Beach boardwalk. It runs along Ocean Boulevard (just west of Mission Blvd.), north of Pacific Beach Drive. The beach is well staffed with lifeguards, but you're on your own to find street parking. Pacific Beach is also the home of **Tourmaline Surfing Park,** where the sport's old guard gathers to surf waters where swimmers are prohibited.

WINDANSEA   The fabled locale of Tom Wolfe's *Pump House Gang,* Windansea is legendary to this day among California's surf elite. Reached by way of Bonair Street (at Neptune Place), Windansea has no facilities, and street parking is first-come, first-served. Come to surf, watch surfers, or soak in the camaraderie and party atmosphere.

CHILDREN'S POOL BEACH   A man-made seawall protects this crescent of sand, originally intended as a safe swimming spot for children. Today, much of the beach is cordoned off for the resident sea lion population; the rest is inhabited by curious shutterbugs and families taking advantage of the same calm conditions that keep the sea lions around. The beach is at Coast Boulevard and Jenner Street; there's limited free street parking. *Tip:* Come here to admire the regal sea lions, but do your swimming elsewhere.

LA JOLLA COVE   The protected, calm waters—praised as the clearest along the California coast—attract swimmers, snorkelers, scuba divers, and families. There's a small sandy beach, and on the cliffs above, the **Ellen Browning**

Scripps Park. The cove's "look but don't touch" policy protects the colorful Garibaldi, California's state fish, plus other marine life, including abalone, octopus, and lobster. The unique Underwater Park stretches from here to the northern end of Torrey Pines State Reserve and incorporates kelp forests, artificial reefs, two deep submarine canyons, and tidal pools. La Jolla Cove is accessible from Coast Boulevard.

LA JOLLA SHORES BEACH The wide, flat mile of sand at La Jolla Shores is popular with joggers, swimmers, and beginning body- and board surfers, as well as families. It looks like a picture postcard, with powdery sand under blue skies, kissed by gentle waves. Weekend crowds can be enormous, though, quickly occupying both the sand and the metered parking spaces in the lot. There are rest rooms, showers, and picnic areas here, as well the grassy, palm-lined Kellogg Park across the street.

7 Exploring the Area

BALBOA PARK

Balboa Park is one of the nation's largest, loveliest, and most important municipal greenbelts. This is no simple city park; it boasts walkways, gardens, historical buildings, a restaurant, an ornate pavilion with one of the world's largest outdoor organs, and the world-famous San Diego Zoo (p. 667). Stroll along El Prado, the park's main street, and admire the distinctive Spanish-Mediterranean buildings, which house an amazing array of museums. Filled on weekends with locals, El Prado is also popular with musicians and other performers who provide an entertaining backdrop.

Entry to the park is free, but most of its museums have admission charges and varying open hours. A free tram will transport you around the park. Get details from the **Balboa Park Visitor Center,** located in the House of Hospitality (✆ **619/239-0512;** www.balboapark.org). Below are the highlights:

San Diego Aerospace Museum ★★, 2001 Pan American Plaza (✆ **619/234-8291;** www.aerospacemuseum.org). Great achievers and achievements in the history of aviation and aerospace are celebrated by this superb collection of historical aircraft and related artifacts, including art, models, dioramas, and films.

San Diego Museum of Art ★, 1450 El Prado (✆ **619/232-7931;** www.sdmart.com). With one of the grandest entrances along El Prado, the museum is known in the art world for outstanding collections of Italian Renaissance and Dutch and Spanish baroque art, along with an impressive collection of

---

Tips **Balboa Park Money-Savers**

Many Balboa Park attractions are open free-of-charge one Tuesday each month; there's a rotating schedule, so three or more participate each Tuesday. (Call ✆ **619/239-0512** or log on to www.balboapark.org for a complete schedule.) If you plan to visit more than three of the park's museums, buy the **Passport to Balboa Park,** a coupon booklet that allows one entrance to each of 13 museums (the rest are always free) and is valid for 1 week. The $30 passport can be purchased at any participating museum or the visitor center.

Balboa Park

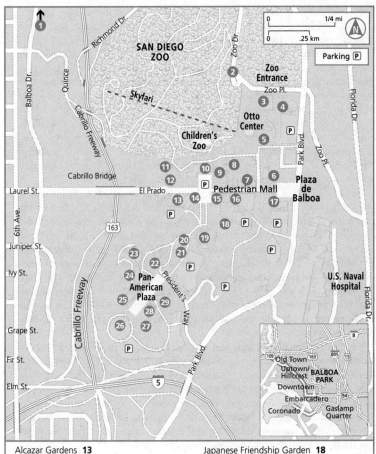

Alcazar Gardens **13**
Balboa Park Club **23**
Botanical Building **8**
Carousel **4**
Casa de Balboa **16**
    Hall of Champions Sports Museum
    Model Railroad Museum
    Museum of Photographic Arts
    San Diego Historical Society Museum
Casa del Prado **7**
Federal Building **29**
The Globe Theatres **11**
Hall of Nations **20**
House of Charm **14**
    Mingei International Museum
    San Diego Art Institute
House of Hospitality **15**
    Balboa Park Visitors Center
    Prado Restaurant
House of Pacific Relations
    International Cottages **22**

Japanese Friendship Garden **18**
Marston House Museum **1**
Municipal Museum **28**
Museum of Art **10**
Museum of Man **12**
Natural History Museum **6**
Palisades Building **24**
    Marie Hitchcock Puppet Theater
    Recital Hall
Reuben H. Fleet Science Center **17**
San Diego Aerospace Museum **26**
San Diego Automotive Museum **25**
San Diego Miniature Railroad **3**
San Diego Zoo **2**
Spanish Village Art Center **5**
Spreckels Organ Pavilion **19**
Starlight Bowl **27**
Timken Museum of Art **9**
United Nations Building **21**

Toulouse-Lautrec. Prestigious traveling exhibits are often shown here, and the museum's high-tech touch is an interactive computer-image system that allows visitors to locate museum highlights and custom-design a tour.

Museum of Photographic Arts, 1649 El Prado (© **619/238-7559;** www.mopa.org). If the names of Ansel Adams, Margaret Bourke-White, Imogen Cunningham, Edward Weston, and Henri Cartier-Bresson stimulate your interest, then don't miss the 3,600-plus-image collection of this museum—one of few in the United States devoted exclusively to the photographic arts.

San Diego Natural History Museum, 1788 El Prado (© **619/232-3821;** www.sdnhm.org). The museum focuses on the flora, fauna, and mineralogy of the Southwest. Kids marvel at the animals they find here and enjoy exploring the Desert Lab, home to live snakes and tarantulas. Call or check the museum's website for a current schedule of special visiting exhibits.

Reuben H. Fleet Science Center ✹✹, 1875 El Prado (© **619/238-1233;** www.rhfleet.org). Easily the park's busiest museum, the Science Center features five galleries with hands-on exhibits as intriguing for grown-ups as for kids, including SciTours, a simulator ride that voyages into space and the worlds of science and biology. Equally popular is the OMNIMAX movie theater, surrounding viewers with breathtaking adventure travelogues. You can avoid waiting in line by buying tickets in advance.

Museum of Man, 1350 El Prado (© **619/239-2001;** www.museumofman. org). This museum is devoted to the sociology and anthropology of the peoples of North and South America, and includes life-size replicas of a dozen varieties of Homo sapiens.

San Diego Automotive Museum ✹, 2080 Pan American Plaza (© **619/231-2886;** www.sdautomuseum.org). Even if you don't know a distributor from a dipstick, you're bound to ooh and aah over the classic, antique, and exotic cars here. Every one is so pristine you'd swear it just rolled off the line; some days you can take a peek at the ongoing restoration program.

Botanical Building, El Prado. More than a thousand varieties of tropical and flowering plants are sheltered within this graceful structure, and the lily pond out front attracts the occasional street performer.

Hall of Champions, 2131 Pan American Plaza (© **619/234-2544;** www. sandiegosports.org). Sports fans will want to check out this museum, which highlights dozens of different professional and amateur sports and athletes.

Japanese Friendship Garden ✹, 2125 Park Blvd. (© **619/232-2721;** www.niwa.org). Although parts of the garden are still being developed, visitors can sample the tranquillity of traditional elements like a koi-filled stream, pastoral meadow, and ancient *sekitei* (sand-and-stone garden). Visit the Japanese tearoom and snack bar for udon soup, sushi, or Pokémon candies.

Marston House Museum, 3525 Seventh Ave. at Upas Street, in the northwest corner of the park (© **619/298-3142**). Designed by local architect Irving Gill, this fine example of Craftsman-style architecture exhibits antique and reproduction period furniture.

Model Railroad Museum ✹, 1649 El Prado (© **619/696-0199;** www. sdmodelrailroadm.com). Four scale-model railroads depict Southern California's transportation history and terrain. There's a terrific gift shop, plus multimedia exhibits and hands-on Lionel trains for kids.

San Diego Historical Society Museum, 1649 El Prado (© **619/232-6203;** www.sandiegohistory.org). Photographs and other changing exhibits tell the city's story.

Spreckels Organ Pavilion (℃ 619/226-0819). The ornate pavilion houses a fantastic organ with more than 4,000 individual pipes. Free concerts are given Sundays at 2pm year-round and on summer evenings.

Mingei International Museum ⚐, 1439 El Prado (℃ 619/239-0003; www. mingei.org). Its name means "art of the people" in Japanese, and it offers changing exhibitions celebrating human creativity with textiles, costumes, jewelry, toys, pottery, paintings, and sculpture, all employing natural materials. This is one of only two major museums in the United States devoted to crafts on a worldwide scale (the other is in Santa Fe).

Christmas on the Prado takes place in Balboa Park from 5 to 9pm on the first Friday and Saturday nights in December. This popular event features free entry to all museums, carol singing in the Spreckels Organ Pavilion, holiday decorations, and various food booths.

MORE ATTRACTIONS IN & AROUND SAN DIEGO
DOWNTOWN

Cabrillo National Monument ⚐   Enjoy stunning views while you learn about California history at this monument commemorating Juan Rodríguez Cabrillo, the European discoverer of America's West Coast. At the restored Old Point Loma Lighthouse, you'll be treated to a sweeping vista of the ocean, bays, islands, mountains, valleys, and plains that make up San Diego. Visit between mid-December and mid-March and you can see the annual California gray-whale migration from a glassed-in observatory; films and other educational exhibits on the whales are offered as well. A road leads to tide pools that beg for exploration.

1800 Cabrillo Memorial Dr., Point Loma. ℃ 619/557-5450. www.nps.gov/cabr. Admission $5 per vehicle, $2 for walk-ins, free for children under 17 and seniors age 62 and over (with a National Parks Service Golden Age Passport). Daily 9am–5:15pm. Take I-5 or I-8 to Hwy. 209/Rosecrans St. and follow signs. Bus: 26.

Children's Museum of San Diego *(Kids*   This interactive attraction, which encourages participation, is a home away from home for kids. It provides ongoing supervised activities, as well as a monthly special celebration, recognizing important issues such as earth awareness or African-American history. The indoor-outdoor art studio is a big draw for kids ages 2 to 10. There is also a theater with costumes for budding actors to don, plus an observation walk above the exhibits that kids climb on and exit by way of a spiral slide. The museum shop is filled with toys, games, crafts, and books. School groups come in the morning, so you might want to schedule your visit for the afternoon.

200 W. Island Ave. ℃ 619/233-KIDS. www.sdchildrensmuseum.org. Admission $6 adults and children, $3 seniors, free for children under 2. Tues–Sat 10am–4pm. Trolley: Convention Center; museum is a block away. All-day parking (across the street) about $3.

Maritime Museum ⚐⚐ *(Kids*   This unique museum consists of a trio of fine ships: the full-rigged merchant vessel *Star of India* (1863), whose impressive masts are an integral part of the San Diego cityscape; the gleaming white San Francisco–Oakland steam-powered ferry *Berkeley* (1898), which worked round-the-clock to carry people to safety following the 1906 San Francisco earthquake; and the sleek *Medea* (1904), one of the world's few remaining large steam yachts. You can board and explore each vessel, and April through October you can watch movies on-deck (see "San Diego After Dark," later in this chapter).

1306 N. Harbor Dr. ℃ 619/234-9153. www.sdmaritime.com. Admission $6 adults, $4 seniors over 62 and youths 13–17, $2 children 6–12, free for children under 6. Daily 9am–8pm. Bus: 2. Trolley: America Plaza.

Museum of Contemporary Art, Downtown (MCA)   MCA Downtown is the second location of the Museum of Contemporary Art—the first is in La Jolla. Two large galleries and two smaller ones present changing exhibitions of distinguished contemporary artists. Lectures and tours for adults and children are offered.

1001 Kettner Blvd. (at Broadway). © 619/234-1001. www.mcasandiego.org. Free admission. Thurs–Tues 11am–5pm. Parking $2 with validation at America Plaza Complex. Trolley: America Plaza.

Villa Montezuma ★ *Finds*   Just east of downtown, this stunning mansion was built in 1887 for then internationally acclaimed musician and author Jesse Shepard. Lush with Victoriana, it features stained-glass windows depicting Mozart, Beethoven, Sappho, Rubens, St. Cecilia (patron saint of musicians), and other notables. The San Diego Historical Society painstakingly restored the house, which is on the National Register of Historic Places, and furnished it with period pieces. If you love Victorian houses, don't miss this one for its quirkiness.

1925 K St. (at 20th Ave.). © 619/239-2211. Admission $5 adults, $4 seniors and students, $2 kids 6–17, free for children under 6. Fri–Sun 10am–4:30pm. Bus: 3, 3A, 4, 5, 16, or 105 to Market and Imperial sts. By car, follow K St.

William Heath Davis House Museum   Shipped by boat to San Diego in 1850 from Portland, Maine, this is the oldest structure in the Gaslamp Quarter. It is a well-preserved example of a prefabricated "saltbox" family home and has remained structurally unchanged for more than 120 years. A museum on the first and second floors is open to the public, as is the small park adjacent to the house. The house is also home to the Gaslamp Quarter Historical Foundation, which sponsors walking tours of the quarter for about $8 (the fee includes museum admission). At least one tour is conducted each day; call ahead for specific schedule.

410 Island Ave. (at 4th Ave.). © 619/233-4692. www.gaslampquarter.org. Suggested donation $3. Tues–Sun 11am–3pm. Call ahead to verify hr. Bus: 1, 3, or 3A. Trolley: Gaslamp Quarter/Convention Center W.

OLD TOWN & BEYOND: A LOOK AT CALIFORNIA'S BEGINNINGS

The birthplace of San Diego is Old Town, the hillside where the Spanish Presidio and Father Junípero Serra's mission (the first in California) were built. By protecting the remaining adobes and historic buildings, **Old Town State Historic Park** brings to life Mexican California, which existed here until the mid-1800s. Much of the surrounding area, however, has become a mini–Mexican theme park. You can get to Old Town on the trolley or Coaster (see "Getting Around," earlier in this chapter), and free walking tours leave daily at 10:30am and 2pm from **Seeley Stables Visitor Center** (© **619/220-5422**). Other nearby sites of interest are listed below.

Heritage Park   This 7.8-acre county park contains seven original 19th-century houses moved here from other places and given new uses. Among them are a bed-and-breakfast, a doll shop, and a gift shop. The most recent addition is the small synagogue, placed near the park's entrance in 1989. A glorious coral tree crowns the top of the hill.

2450 Heritage Park Row (corner of Juan and Harney sts.), Old Town. For information, call the Parks Department at © 619/694-3049. Free admission. Daily 9:30am–3pm. Bus: 4, 5, or 105.

Mission Basilica San Diego de Alcala ★   Established in 1769, this was the first link in a chain of 21 missions founded by Spanish missionary Junípero

Serra. In 1774, the mission was moved to its present site for agricultural reasons, and to separate Native American converts from the fortress that included the original building. A few bricks belonging to the original mission can be seen in Presidio Park in Old Town. Mass is said daily in this active Catholic parish. Other missions in the San Diego area include Mission San Luis Rey de Francia in Oceanside, Mission San Antonia de Pala near Mount Palomar, and Mission Santa Ysabel near Julian.

10818 San Diego Mission Rd., Mission Valley. ℂ **619/281-8449**. Admission $3 adults, $2 seniors and students, $1 children under 13. Free Sun and for daily masses. Daily 9am–5pm; mass daily 7am and 5:30pm. Take I-8 to Mission Gorge Rd. to Twain Ave. Bus: 6, 16, 25, 43, or 81.

Serra Museum   Perched on a hill above Old Town, the stately mission-style building overlooks the hillside where, in 1769, the first mission and first non-native settlement on the west coast of the United States and Canada were founded. The museum's exhibits introduce visitors to the Native American, Spanish, and Mexican people who first called this place home. On display are their belongings, from cannons to cookware; a Spanish furniture collection; and one of the first paintings brought to California, which survived being damaged in an Indian attack. The mission remained San Diego's only settlement until the 1820s, when families began to move down the hill into what is now Old Town. You can also watch an ongoing archaeological dig uncovering more of the items used by early settlers. From the 70-foot tower, visitors can compare the spectacular view with historic photos to see how this land has changed over time.

2727 Presidio Dr., Presidio Park. ℂ **619/297-3258**. www.sandiegohistory.org. Admission $5 adults, $4 seniors and students, $2 children 6–17, free for children under 6. Fri–Sun 10am–4:30pm. Take I-8 to the Taylor St. exit. Turn right on Taylor, then left on Presidio Dr.

Whaley House Museum   In 1856, this striking two-story house (the first one in these parts) just outside Old Town State Historic Park was built for Thomas Whaley and his family. Whaley was a New Yorker who arrived here via San Francisco, where he had been lured by the gold rush. The house is one of only two authenticated haunted houses in California, and 10,000 schoolchildren come here each year to see for themselves. Exhibits include a life mask of Abraham Lincoln, one of only six made; the spinet piano used in the movie *Gone With the Wind;* and the concert piano that accompanied Swedish soprano Jenny Lind on her final U.S. tour in 1852.

2482 San Diego Ave. ℂ **619/297-7511**. Admission $5 adults, $4 seniors over 60, $3 children 3–12, free for children under 3. Wed–Mon 10am–4:30pm. Closed Dec 25 and Jan 1.

MISSION BAY & THE BEACHES

This area is great for walking, jogging, in-line skating, biking, and boating; for details, see "Outdoor Pursuits," below.

Giant Dipper Roller Coaster   A local landmark for 70 years, the Giant Dipper is one of two surviving fixtures from the original Belmont Amusement Park (the other is the Plunge swimming pool). After sitting dormant for 15 years, the vintage wooden roller coaster, with more than 2,600 feet of track and 13 hills, underwent extensive restoration and reopened in 1991. If you're in the neighborhood (especially with older kids), it's worth a stop. You must be 50 inches tall to ride the roller coaster. You can also ride on the Giant Dipper's neighbor, the Liberty Carousel ($1).

3190 Mission Blvd. ℂ **858/488-1549**. www.giantdipper.com. $3.50 per ride. MC, V. Sun–Thurs 11am–10pm, Fri–Sat 11am–11pm. Take I-5 to the SeaWorld exit, and follow W. Mission Bay Dr. to Belmont Park.

Finds **Hidden La Jolla**

While droves of folks stroll the sidewalks adjacent to the San Diego–La Jolla Underwater Park and La Jolla Cove, only a few know about **Coast Walk**. Starting behind the **Cave Store**, 1325 Coast Blvd. (© **858/459-0746**), it meanders along the wooded cliffs and affords a wonderful view of the beach and beyond. The shop also serves as entry for **Sunny Jim Cave,** a large and naturally occurring sea cave reached by a steep and narrow staircase through the rock. The tunnel was hand-carved in 1903—it lets out on a wood-plank observation deck from which you can gaze out at the sea. It's a cool treat, particularly on a hot summer day, and costs only $2 per person ($1 for kids). Hold the handrail and your little ones' hands tightly.

LA JOLLA

Some folks just enjoy driving around La Jolla, taking in the sea views and the 360° vista from the top of **Mount Soledad.** However, La Jolla also offers other attractions, including **Torrey Pines State Reserve** (© **858/755-2063**), which has an interpretive center, hiking trails with wonderful ocean views, and a chance to see the rare Torrey pine. Admission is free, as are the guided walks on Saturdays and Sundays. Access is via North Torrey Pines Road; parking costs $4 per car, $3 for seniors.

To locate these attractions, see the "La Jolla" map on p. 651.

Birch Aquarium at Scripps ★★   The aquarium offers close-up views of the Pacific Ocean in 33 marine-life tanks. The giant kelp forest is particularly impressive. World-renowned for its oceanic research, Scripps offers visitors a chance to view its marine aquarium and artificial outdoor tide pools. The museum has interpretive exhibits on the current and historical research done at the institution, which has been in existence since 1903.

2300 Expedition Way. © 858/534-FISH. www.aquarium.ucsd.edu. Admission $8.50 adults, $7.50 seniors, $5 children 3–17, free for children under 3. Parking $3. AE, MC, V. Daily 9am–5pm. Take I-5 to La Jolla Village Dr. exit, go W 1 mile, and turn left at Expedition Way. Bus: 34.

Museum of Contemporary Art, San Diego (MCA) ★★   Museum holdings include works from every major art movement of the past half century, with a strong representation of California artists and particularly noteworthy examples of minimalism, light and space work, conceptualism, installation, and site-specific art (including outdoor sculptures). The museum's facade incorporates the original Irving Gill architecture, and the rear galleries feature outstanding ocean views.

700 Prospect St. © 858/454-3541. www.mcasandiego.org. Admission $4 adults, $2 students and seniors, free for children under 12; free to all 3rd Tues and 1st Sun of each month. Summer (Memorial Day to Labor Day) Mon–Tues and Thurs–Fri 11am–8pm, Sat–Sun 11am–5pm; rest of year Thurs 11am–8pm, Fri–Tues 11am–5pm. Take the Ardath Rd. exit off I-5 N or the La Jolla Village Dr. W exit off I-5 S. Take Torrey Pines Rd. to Prospect Place and turn right. Prospect Place becomes Prospect St.

8 Outdoor Pursuits

For coverage of San Diego's best beaches, see section 6, earlier in this chapter.

BICYCLING & MOUNTAIN BIKING   Mission Bay and Coronado are especially good for leisurely bike rides. The boardwalks in Pacific Beach and

Mission Beach can get very crowded, especially on weekends. Most major thoroughfares offer bike lanes. Just remember to wear a helmet; it's the law. For information on bike rentals, see "Getting Around," earlier in this chapter.

Adventure Bike Tours, in the San Diego Marriott (© **619/234-1500,** ext. 6514), offers guided bicycle tours, bike rentals, and in-line-skate rentals. The "Bay to Breakers" ride starts in downtown San Diego and includes Coronado; $40 covers bike, helmet, and the ferry.

BOATING   Club Nautico, at the San Diego Marriott Marina, 333 W. Harbor Dr. (© **619/233-9311**), provides an exhilarating way to see the bay by the hour, half day, or full day in 20- to 27-foot offshore powerboats. Rentals start at $89 per hour. It also rents WaveRunners and allows its boats to be taken into the ocean, and provides diving, water-skiing, and fishing packages as well.

Seaforth Boat Rental, 1641 Quivira Rd., Mission Bay (© **888/834-2628;** www.seaforth-boat-rental.com), has a wide variety of fishing boats for the bay and ocean, powerboats for $55 to $95 per hour, and 14- to 30-foot sailboats for $20 to $45 per hour; inquire about half- and full-day rates. Canoes, pedal boats, kayaks, and rowboats are available for those who prefer a slower pace, as are bicycles and equipment with which you can fish off the Municipal Pier (see "Fishing," below).

Mission Bay Sportcenter, 1010 Santa Clara Place (© **858/488-1004;** www.mbsc.homestead.com), rents sailboats, catamarans, sailboards, kayaks, personal watercraft, and motorboats. Prices range from $12 to $72 an hour, with discounts for 4-hour and full-day rentals. Instruction is available.

Coronado Boat Rental, 1715 Strand Way, Coronado (© **619/437-1514**), has powerboats renting from $65 to $90 per hour, with half- and full-day rates available; 14- to 30-foot sailboats from $25 to $40 per hour; plus jet skis, ski boats, canoes, pedal boats, kayaks, fishing skiffs, and charter boats.

FISHING   Public fishing piers are at Shelter Island (where there's a statue dedicated to anglers), Ocean Beach, and Imperial Beach. Anglers of any age can fish free of charge without a license off any municipal pier in California. Call the **City Fish Line** (© **619/465-3474**) for information on fishing.

For **sport fishing,** you can go out on a large boat for about $25 for a half day, or $40 to $100 for three-quarters to a full day. To charter a boat for up to six people, the rates run about $550 for a half day and $1,000 for an entire day, more in summer; call around and compare prices. Summer and fall are excellent times for excursions. Locally, the waters around Point Loma are filled with bass, bonita, and barracuda; the Coronado Islands, which belong to Mexico but are only about 18 miles from San Diego, are popular for abalone, yellowtail, yellowfin, and big-eyed tuna. Some outfitters will take you farther into Baja California waters.

Fishing charters depart from Harbor and Shelter Islands, Point Loma, the Imperial Beach Pier, and Quivira Basin in Mission Bay (near the Hyatt Islandia Hotel). The following outfitters offer short or extended outings with daily departures: **H&M Landing** (© 619/222-1144), **Islandia Sportfishing** (© 619/222-1164), **Lee Palm Sportfishers** (© 619/224-3857), **Point Loma Sportfishing** (© 619/223-1627), and **Seaforth Boat Rentals** (© 888/834-2628). Participants over the age of 16 need a California fishing license.

GOLF   With nearly 80 courses, 50 of them open to the public, San Diego County has much to offer the golf enthusiast. Courses are diverse, some with vistas of the Pacific, others with views of country hillsides or of desert. **San**

Diego Golf Reservations (© 800/905-0230; www.sandiegogolfreservations. com) can arrange tee times for you at most golf courses.

Balboa Park Municipal Golf Course ★, 2600 Golf Course Dr., San Diego (© 619/239-1660), is a wooded 18-hole course with skyline views nestled in the southeast corner of Balboa Park. Convenient and affordable, it might remind you of your muni course back home, down to the bare-bones 1940s clubhouse where old guys hold down lunch-counter stools for hours after the game. Non-resident greens fees are $32 Monday through Friday and $37 Saturday and Sunday; cart rentals cost $20, pull carts $5. Reservations are suggested at least a week in advance.

Coronado Municipal Golf Course, 2000 Visalia Row, Coronado (© 619/435-3121), is the first sight that welcomes you as you cross the Coronado Bay Bridge (the course is off to the left). It's an 18-hole, par-72 course overlooking Glorietta Bay, and there's a coffee shop, pro shop, and driving range. Two-day prior reservations are strongly recommended; call any time after 7am. Greens fees are $20 to walk and $34 to ride for 18 holes; $10 to walk and $18 to ride after 4pm. Club rental costs $15, and pull-cart rental is $4.

Riverwalk Golf Club, 1150 Fashion Valley Rd., Mission Valley (© 619/296-4653; http://riverwalk.americangolf.com), is a Ted Robinson/Ted Robinson Jr.–designed course meandering along the Mission Valley floor. It features four lakes with waterfalls (in play on 13 of the 27 holes); open, undulating fairways; and the red San Diego Trolley speeding through the middle now and then. Non-resident greens fees—including cart—are $75 Monday through Thursday, $85 Friday and Sunday, and $95 Saturday (fees for residents are $30 less).

Torrey Pines Golf Course, 11480 Torrey Pines Rd., La Jolla (© 800/985-4653 or 858/452-3226; www.torreypinesgolfcourse.com), is actually two gorgeous 18-hole championship clifftop courses overlooking the ocean; the north course is more picturesque, the south course more challenging. Tee times are taken by telephone only, starting at 5am, up to 7 days in advance. *Insider tip:* Single golfers stand a good chance of getting on the course if they just turn up and wait for a threesome. Greens fees for out-of-towners are $55 during the week and $60 on Saturday, Sunday, and holidays for 18 holes; $30 for nine holes. Cart rental costs $30.

San Diego hosts some of the country's most important golf tournaments, including the **Buick Invitational of California,** held every February at Torrey Pines Golf Course in La Jolla (© 800/888-BUICK or 619/281-4653).

HIKING & WALKING   The **Sierra Club** sponsors regular hikes in the San Diego area, and non-members are welcome to participate; there are both day and evening hikes, most free. For a recorded schedule, call © 619/299-1744, or call the office at © 619/299-1743 Monday through Friday from noon to 5pm and Saturday from 10am to 4pm.

The Bayside Trail near **Cabrillo National Monument** is popular because it affords great views. Drive to the monument and follow signs to the trail. Parking costs $4 per car. **Mission Trails Regional Park,** 8 miles northeast of downtown, offers a glimpse of what San Diego looked like before development. Located between Calif. 52 and I-8 and east of I-15, its rugged hills, valleys, and open areas provide a quick escape from urban hustle-bustle. A visitor and interpretive center (© 619/668-3275) is open daily from 9am to 5pm. Access is via Mission Gorge Road from either Calif. 52 or I-8.

The best beaches for walking are La Jolla Shores, Mission Beach, and Coronado. You can also walk around **Mission Bay** on a series of connected footpaths.

If a four-legged friend is your walking companion, head for **Dog Beach** in Ocean Beach or **Fiesta Island** in Mission Bay, two of the few areas where dogs can legally go unleashed.

SKATING   Gliding around San Diego, especially the Mission Bay area, on in-line skates is as much a Southern California experience as sailing or surfing. Skate rentals along with necessary protective gear are available at **Skates Plus,** 3830 Mission Blvd. (© 858/488-PLUS) or **Hamel's Action Sports Center,** 704 Ventura Place, off Mission Boulevard at Ocean Front Walk (© 858/488-8889). In Pacific Beach, try **Pacific Beach Sun and Sea,** 4539 Ocean Blvd. (© 858/483-6613). In Coronado, go to **Mike's Bikes,** 1343 Orange Ave. (© 619/435-7744), or **Bikes and Beyond,** 1201 First St. and at the Ferry Landing (© 619/435-7180). Be sure to ask for protective gear.

SURFING   Get where-to-go info from section 6 above, and rent a board (if you didn't BYO) from **La Jolla Surf Systems,** 2132 Avenida de la Playa, La Jolla Shores (© **858/456-2777**), or **Emerald Surf & Sport,** 1118 Orange Ave., Coronado (© **619/435-6677**).

For surfing lessons, with all equipment provided, check with **Kahuna Bob's Surf School** (© **800/KAHUNAS** or 760/721-7700; www.kahunabob.com) or **San Diego Surfing Academy** (© **800/447-SURF** or 858/565-6892; www.surfsdsa.com).

TENNIS   There are 1,200 public and private tennis courts in San Diego. Public courts are located throughout the city, including the **La Jolla Recreation Center** (© **858/459-9950**), **Morley Field** (© **619/295-9278**) in Balboa Park, and the brand-new **Barnes Tennis Center,** 4490 W. Point Loma Blvd., near Ocean Beach and SeaWorld (© **619/221-9000;** www.tennissandiego.com).

9 Shopping

All-American San Diego has embraced the suburban shopping mall with vigor—several massive complexes in Mission Valley are where many residents do the bulk of their shopping, and every possible need can be met here. Local neighborhoods also offer individualized specialty shopping that meets the needs—and mirrors the personality—of those parts of town. For example, hip and trendy Hillcrest is the place to go for cutting-edge boutiques, while conservative La Jolla offers many upscale traditional shops, especially jewelers.

Sales tax in San Diego is 7.5%, and savvy out-of-state shoppers know to have larger items shipped directly home at the point of purchase, thereby avoiding the tax.

DOWNTOWN & GASLAMP QUARTER
Horton Plaza, 324 Horton Plaza (© **619/238-1596;** www.hortonplaza.shoppingtown.com), the Disneyland of shopping malls, is at the heart of the revitalized city center, bounded by Broadway, First and Fourth avenues, and G Street. This multi-level shopping center has 140 specialty shops, including art galleries, clothing and shoe stores, several fun shops for kids, bookstores, a 14-screen cinema, three major department stores, and a variety of restaurants and short-order eateries. With a rambling and confusing series of paths and bridges, the complex was supposedly inspired by European shopping districts. Parking is free the first 3 hours with validation (4 hr. at the movie theater and the Lyceum Theatre), $1 per half-hour thereafter; parking levels are confusing, and

temporarily losing your car is part of the Horton Plaza experience. Take bus no. 2, 7, 9, 29, 34, or 35, or the trolley to City Center.

Other downtown shopping opportunities include **Seaport Village,** on Harbor Drive at Kettner Boulevard (© **619/235-4014**), a Cape Cod–style "village" of cutesy shops snuggled alongside San Diego Bay; it's worth a visit for the 1890 carousel imported from Coney Island, New York.

Seekers of serious art might want to head to Little Italy's burgeoning **Studio Arts Complex,** north of downtown. Among the galleries housed at 2400 Kettner Blvd. is **David Zapf Gallery,** no. 104 (© **619/232-5004**), which features painting, sculpture, drawings, or furniture; they also distribute the *Arts Down Town* guide. Photographer **Steve McClelland,** no. 213 (© **619/582-9812**), divides his time between traveling (his images bring the colors, textures, and emotions of the world vividly to life) and commissioned architectural photography in color and black and white. Artist **Charlotte Bird,** no. 224 (© **619/239-9353**), works in fiber arts, producing fine quilts, dolls, and one-of-a-kind women's clothing. The **Pratt Gallery** (© **619/236-0211**) has a changing display space, often featuring innovative paintings, photography, or other highly individual work.

HILLCREST/UPTOWN

Compact Hillcrest is an ideal shopping destination for browsing unique and often wacky shops, but also for buying things at the area's vintage-clothing stores, memorabilia shops, recognizable chains, and snack-friendly bakeries and cafes. Start at the neighborhood's hub, the intersection of University and Fifth avenues. Street parking is available; most meters allow 2-hour parking and devour quarters at a rate of one per 15 minutes, so arm yourself with plenty of change. You can also park in an area parking lot—rates vary, but you'll come out ahead if you're planning to stroll for several hours.

San Diego's self-proclaimed **Antique Row** is located north of Balboa Park, along Park Boulevard (beginning at University Ave. in Hillcrest) and Adams Avenue (extending to around 40th St. in Normal Heights). For more information and an area brochure with map, contact the **Adams Avenue Business Association** (© **619/282-7329;** www.gothere.com/adamsave).

OLD TOWN & MISSION VALLEY

Old Town Historic Park is a restoration of some of San Diego's historic sites and adobe structures, a number of which now house shops that cater to tourists. Many have a "general-store" theme, and carry gourmet treats and inexpensive Mexican crafts alongside the obligatory T-shirts, baseball caps, and other San Diego–emblazoned souvenirs. More shops are concentrated in colorful **Bazaar del Mundo,** 2754 Calhoun St. (© **619/296-3161;** www.bazaardelmundo. com), arranged around a fountain courtyard.

Mission Valley is home to two giant malls (**Fashion Valley** and **Mission Valley**), with more than enough stores to satisfy any shopper. Here book lovers will find the local outposts of **Barnes & Noble,** 7610 Hazard Center Dr. (© **619/220-0175**), and **Borders,** 1072 Camino del Rio N. (© **619/295-2201**).

MISSION BAY & THE BEACHES

The beach communities all offer laid-back shopping in typical California fashion: plenty of surf shops, recreational gear, casual garb, and youth-oriented music stores. If you're in need of a new bikini, the best selection is at **Pilar's,** 3745 Mission Blvd., Pacific Beach (© **858/488-3056**), where dozens of racks are meticulously organized and choices range from chic designer suits to hot trends inspired by surf- and skate-wear. Some of San Diego's best **antiquing** can be found in Ocean Beach, along a single block of Newport Avenue, the town's main drag.

LA JOLLA
It's clear from the look of La Jolla's village that shopping is a major pastime in this upscale community of moneyed professionals and retirees. Women's-clothing boutiques tend toward conservative and costly, like those lining Girard and Prospect streets (Ann Taylor, Armani Exchange, Polo/Ralph Lauren, Talbots, and Sigi's Boutique).

Even if you're not in the market for furnishings and accessories, the many home-decor boutiques make for great window shopping, as do La Jolla's ubiquitous jewelers: Swiss watches, tennis bracelets, precious gems, and pearl necklaces sparkle at you from windows along every street. No visit to La Jolla is complete without seeing **John Cole's Book Shop,** 780 Prospect St. (© **858/ 454-4766**), an eclectic, family-run local favorite set in a charming old cottage.

CORONADO
This rather insular, conservative Navy community doesn't have a great many shopping opportunities; what there is lines Orange Avenue at the western end of the island. In addition to some scattered housewares and home-decor boutiques, as well as several small women's boutiques, there are gift shops at Coronado's major resorts. The **Ferry Landing Marketplace,** 1201 First St., at B Avenue (© **619/435-8895**), is a faux-seaport with shops, restaurants, and a sweeping view of the bay and the downtown skyline.

FARMERS MARKETS
Throughout San Diego County, there are no fewer than two dozen regularly occurring street markets featuring fresh fruits and vegetables from Southern California farms and augmented by crafts, ethnic-food vendors, flower stands, and other surprises. Below is a sampling.

In **Hillcrest,** the market sets up Sundays from 9am to noon at the corner of Normal Street and Lincoln Avenue, several blocks north of Balboa Park. The atmosphere is festive, and exotic culinary delights reflect Hillcrest's eclectic ambience. For more information, call the **Hillcrest Association** (© **619/299-3330**).

In **Ocean Beach,** there's a fun-filled market Wednesday evenings between 4 and 8pm (until 7pm in fall and winter) in the 4900 block of Newport Avenue. In addition to fresh-cut flowers, produce, and exotic fruits and foods laid out for sampling, the market features llama rides and other entertainment. For more information, call the **Ocean Beach Business Improvement District** (© **619/ 224-4906**).

Or head to **Pacific Beach** on Saturday from 8am to noon, when Mission Boulevard between Reed Avenue and Pacific Beach Drive is transformed into a bustling morning marketplace, as locals stock up for the week and visitors begin to enjoy the beach communities on vacation.

And on **Coronado** on Tuesday afternoons, the Ferry Landing Marketplace (corner of First and B sts.) hosts a produce-and-crafts market from 2:30 to 6pm.

10 San Diego After Dark

San Diego is hardly the wild 'n' crazy nightlife capital of America, but pockets of lively after-dark entertainment do exist around the city. On the more sedate side of things, the city offers wonderful and varied live theater experiences— both the Old Globe and La Jolla Playhouse have won Tony Awards for best regional theater.

For a rundown of the latest performances, gallery openings, and other events in the city, check the listings in "Night and Day," the Thursday entertainment section of the *San Diego Union-Tribune,* or the *Reader,* San Diego's free alternative newspaper, published every Thursday. For what's happening in the gay scene, get the weekly *San Diego Gay & Lesbian Times.* The *San Diego Performing Arts Guide,* produced every 2 months by the San Diego Theatre Foundation, is also very helpful; you can pick one up at the Arts Tix booth (see below).

THE PERFORMING ARTS

Half-price tickets to theater, music, and dance events are available at the **Arts Tix** booth, in Horton Plaza Park, at Broadway and Third Avenue (park in the Horton Plaza parking garage and have your parking validated, or pause at the curb nearby). The kiosk is open Tuesday through Saturday from 10am to 7pm. Half-price tickets are available only the day of the show except for Sunday and Monday performances, sold on Saturday. Only cash payments are accepted. For a daily listing of half-price offerings, call ℂ **619/497-5000.** Full-price advance tickets are also sold; the kiosk doubles as a Ticketmaster outlet, selling tickets to concerts throughout California.

THEATER & OPERA

The **San Diego Repertory Theatre** offers professional, culturally diverse productions of contemporary and classic dramas, comedies, and musicals at the Lyceum Theatre, 79 Broadway Circle, in Horton Plaza (ℂ **619/544-1000;** www.sandiegorep.com). Ticket prices are $21 to $32.

In Coronado, **Lamb's Players Theatre,** at 1142 Orange Ave. (ℂ **619/437-0600;** www.lambsplayers.org), is a professional repertory company whose season runs February through December. Shows are staged in its 340-seat theater in Coronado's historic Spreckels Building, where no seat is more than seven rows from the stage. Tickets range from $18 to $40.

The **San Diego Opera** performs at the Civic Theater, 202 C St. (ℂ **619/232-7636;** www.sdopera.com), and often showcases international stars. The season runs January through May; call for schedule. The box office is located across the plaza from the theater and is open Monday through Friday from 9am to 5pm. Tickets range from $31 to $112. Ask about standing room or student and senior discounts.

The Globe Theatres   This complex of three performance venues sits just inside Balboa Park, behind the Museum of Man. Though best known for the 581-seat Old Globe (fashioned after Shakespeare's), it also includes the 245-seat Cassius Carter Centre Stage and the 620-seat open-air Lowell Davies Festival Theatre. Between them, they mount 14 plays a year between January and October, from world premieres of such Broadway hits as *Into the Woods* or the live production of *The Full Monty* to the excellent Shakespeare San Diegans have come to expect from "their" Globe. Leading performers regularly grace the stage, including Marsha Mason, John Goodman, Hal Holbrook, Jon Voight, and Christopher Walken. Tours are offered year-round Saturday and Sunday at

11am and cost $3 for adults, $1 for students, seniors, and military. The box office is open Tuesday through Sunday from noon to 8:30pm. Balboa Park. ℭ 619/ 239-2255, or 619/23-GLOBE (24-hr. hot line). Fax 619/231-5879. www.theglobetheatres.org. Tickets $23–$39. Senior and student discounts available. Bus: 7 or 25. Free parking.

La Jolla Playhouse   Boasting a Hollywood pedigree (founded in 1947 by Gregory Peck, Dorothy McGuire, and Mel Ferrer), and a 1993 Tony Award for outstanding American regional theater, the Playhouse stages six productions each year (Apr or May–Nov) at two fine theaters on the UCSD campus. It seems like each one has something outstanding to recommend it; a nationally acclaimed director, for example, or highly touted revival (such as when Matthew Broderick starred in *How to Succeed in Business Without Really Trying* before it went on to Broadway). The box office is open daily from noon to 6pm. For each show, one Saturday matinee is a "pay-what-you-can" performance. Each night, any unsold tickets are available for $10 each in a "public rush" sale 10 minutes before curtain. 2910 La Jolla Village Dr. (at Torrey Pines Rd.). ℭ **858/550-1010.** Fax 858/ 550-1025. www.lajollaplayhouse.com. Tickets $21–$52. Bus: 30, 34, or 34A.

MOVIES, SAN DIEGO STYLE

Many multi-screen complexes around the city show first-run films. More avant-garde and artistic current releases play at **Hillcrest Cinema,** 3965 Fifth Ave., Hillcrest (ℭ **619/299-2100**), which offers 3 hours' free parking; the **Ken Cinema,** 4061 Adams Ave., Kensington near Hillcrest (ℭ **619/283-5909**); and the **Cove,** 7730 Girard Ave., La Jolla (ℭ **858/459-5404**). The irrepressible *Rocky Horror Picture Show* is resurrected every Friday and Saturday at midnight at the Ken. The **OMNIMAX** theater at the Reuben H. Fleet Science Center (ℭ **619/ 238-1233**), in Balboa Park, features movies and three-dimensional laser shows projected onto the 76-foot tilted dome screen. A truly unique movie venue is **Movies Before the Mast** (ℭ **619/234-9153**), aboard the *Star of India* at the Maritime Museum. Movies of the nautical genre (such as *Captain Blood, Hook,* or *The Muppets' Treasure Island*) are shown on a special "screensail" approximately March through October.

THE CLUB & MUSIC SCENE

A note on smoking: In January 1998, California enacted controversial legislation banning smoking in all restaurants and bars. While opponents immediately began lobbying to repeal the law, it's a good idea to check before you light up in nightclubs, lounges, and so on.

ROCK, POP, FOLK, JAZZ & BLUES

The Casbah, 2501 Kettner Blvd., near the airport (ℭ **619/232-4355;** www. casbahmusic.com), is a divey joint with a rep for breakthrough alternative and rock bands. **Croce's Bars,** 802 Fifth Ave., at F St. (ℭ **619/233-4355;** www. croces.com), are attached to one of the Gaslamp Quarter's most popular restaurants, and feature jazz and rhythm and blues. **4th & B,** 345 B St., downtown (ℭ **619/231-4343;** www.4thandb.com), is a quality venue with performances ranging from rock 'n' roll to chamber music. **Humphrey's,** 2241 Shelter Island Dr. (ℭ **619/523-1010;** www.humphreysconcerts.com), is a 900-seat outdoor venue set on the water, and has a seasonal (May–Oct) lineup that ranges from rock to folk to international. **Belly Up Tavern,** 143 Cedros Ave., Solana Beach (ℭ **760/481-9022;** www.bellyup.com), is a recycled Quonset hut worth the 20-minute drive from downtown for an eclectic mix of acclaimed artists.

DANCE CLUBS & DISCOS

The Gaslamp Quarter is the epicenter of the city's hottest dance clubs—the most popular at the moment are **Olé Madrid,** 751 Fifth Ave. (© 619/557-0146), a loud, energetic club with tapas and sangria from the adjoining Spanish restaurant; **Sevilla,** 555 Fourth Ave. (© 619/233-5979), where you can salsa and merengue to Brazilian dance music; and **Harmony on Fifth,** 322 Fifth Ave. (© 619/235-4646), where postmodern hipsters swing to 1940s tunes or recline with a martini.

GAY & LESBIAN CLUBS & BARS

Bourbon Street, 4612 Park Blvd., University Heights (© 619/291-0173), is a jazzy and elegant piano bar with a New Orleans–esque patio. **The Brass Rail,** 3796 Fifth Ave., Hillcrest (© 619/298-2233), is loud and proud, with energetic dancing, bright lights, and go-go boys. **The Flame,** 3780 Park Blvd. (© 619/295-4163), is the city's top lesbian dance club. **Kickers,** 308 University Ave., at Third Avenue, Hillcrest (© 619/491-0400), is a country-western dance hall that attracts both sexes for two-stepping, line-dancing, and the adjacent Hamburger Mary's restaurant. Finally, **Rich's,** 1051 University Ave., between 10th and 11th avenues (© 619/295-2195, or 619/497-4588 for upcoming events; www.richs-sandiego.com), is a high-energy, high-image dance club, with house music and a video bar.

BARS & COCKTAIL LOUNGES

Cannibal Bar, inside the Catamaran Hotel at 3999 Mission Blvd., Mission Beach (© 858/539-8650), features a tropical theme, Polynesian cocktails, DJ dancing, and occasional live bands. **The Bitter End,** 770 Fifth Ave., Gaslamp Quarter (© 619/338-9300; www.thebitterend.com), has three levels for its martini bar, late-night dance club, and relaxing cocktail lounge. **Martini Ranch,** 528 F St., Gaslamp Quarter (© 619/235-6100), is a split-level bar boasting 30 kinds of martinis and microrooms from video bars to conversation pits. **Top O' The Cove,** 1216 Prospect Ave., La Jolla (© 858/454-7779), offers an intimate setting for mellow piano music.

11 North County Beach Towns

Picturesque beach towns, each poised over their own stretch of sand, dot the coast of San Diego County from Del Mar to Oceanside. These make great day-trip destinations for sun worshippers and surfers.

ESSENTIALS

Getting there is easy: Del Mar is only 18 miles north of downtown San Diego; Carlsbad, about 33 miles; and Oceanside, 36 miles. If you're driving, follow I-5 north: You'll find freeway exits for Del Mar, Solana Beach, Cardiff by the Sea, Encinitas, Leucadia, Carlsbad, and Oceanside.

Check with **Amtrak** (© 800/USA-RAIL; www.amtrak.com) or the **Coaster** (© 800/COASTER) for transit information. The **San Diego North Convention and Visitors Bureau** (© 800/848-3336; www.sandiegonorth.com) is also a good information source.

DEL MAR

Less than 20 miles up the coast lies Del Mar, a small community with just over 5,000 inhabitants in a 2-square-mile municipality. The town has adamantly maintained its independence, eschewing incorporation into the city of San

Diego. Sometimes known as "the people's republic of Del Mar," this community was one of the nation's first to ban smoking. Come summer, the town explodes as visitors flock in for the thoroughbred horseracing season and the county's Del Mar Fair. The history and current popularity of Del Mar is, in fact, inextricably linked to the **Del Mar Race Track & Fairgrounds,** 2260 Jimmy Durante Blvd. (© **858/753-5555;** www.delmarfair.com), which, in turn, still glows with the aura of Hollywood celebrity. Established in the 1930s by crooner and actor Bing Crosby, the track still begins each season by playing "Where the Surf Meets the Turf."

Del Mar City Beach is a wide, well-patrolled beach popular for sunbathing, swimming, and bodysurfing. Get there by taking 15th Street west to Seagrove Park, where college kids can always be found playing volleyball and other lawn games while older folks snooze in the shade. There are **free concerts** in the park during July and August; for information, contact the City of Del Mar (© **858/ 755-9313**).

For more information about Del Mar, contact or visit the **Del Mar Chamber of Commerce Visitor Information Center,** 1104 Camino del Mar #101, Del Mar, CA 92014 (© **858/755-4844;** www.delmar.ca.us), which also provides a folding, detailed map of the area. Open hours vary according to volunteer staffing, but usually mimic weekday business hours.

WHERE TO STAY

Del Mar Motel on the Beach   The only property in Del Mar right on the beach, this simply furnished little white-stucco motel has been here since 1946. Upstairs rooms have one king-size bed; downstairs units have two double beds. Half are reserved for nonsmokers, and only oceanview rooms have bathtubs. This is a good choice for beach lovers, because you can walk along the shore for miles, and the popular seaside restaurants Poseidon and Jake's are right next door. The motel has a barbecue and picnic table for guests' use.

1702 Coast Blvd. (at 17th St.), Del Mar, CA 92014. © **800/223-8449** for reservations, or 858/755-1534. www.delmarmotelonthebeach.com. 45 units (some with shower only). $139–$199 double. Substantial off-season discounts available. AE, DC, DISC, MC, V. Take I-5 to Via de la Valle exit. Go W, then S on Hwy. 101 (Pacific Coast Hwy.); veer W onto Coast Blvd. *In room:* A/C, TV, fridge, coffeemaker.

L'Auberge Del Mar Resort and Spa ✸✸✸   Because Del Mar strives to keep a low profile, most lodgings here feel like an afterthought . . . except for prominent L'Auberge, the town's centerpiece. Sitting on the site of the historic Hotel Del Mar (1909–69), this luxurious yet intimate inn manages to attract casual weekenders as easily as the rich-and-famous horsey set, who flock here during summer racing season. Always improving itself, the resort has recently enhanced the lower-level full-service spa, polished up the poolside ambience, and completely revamped the dining room. The result is an atmosphere of complete relaxation and welcome. Guest rooms exude the elegance of a European country house, complete with marble bathrooms, architectural accents, well-placed casual seating, and the finest bed linens and appointments. Many boast romantic fireplaces; each has a private balcony or terrace (several with an unadvertised view to the ocean). The hotel is across the street from Del Mar's main shopping and dining scene, and a short jog from the sand. Redesigned in 2000, the hotel's Mediterranean dining room easily stands alone as one of Del Mar's fine restaurants; at the very least, don't miss its legendary breakfast huevos rancheros.

1540 Camino del Mar (at 15th St.), Del Mar, CA 92014. © **800/553-1336** or 858/259-1515. Fax 858/ 755-4940. www.laubergedelmar.com. 120 units. $225–$380 double; from $650 suite. Ask about off-season and midweek discounts. Spa, romance, and other packages available. AE, DC, MC, V. Valet parking $12. Take I-5 to Del Mar Heights Rd. W, then turn right onto Camino del Mar Rd. **Amenities:** Restaurant; lounge; 2 pools; 2 lit tennis courts; indoor/outdoor fitness center; full-service spa; Jacuzzi; concierge; courtesy van; room service 6:30am–10pm; laundry service; dry cleaning. *In room:* A/C, TV w/pay movies, dataport, minibar, coffeemaker, hair dryer, iron.

Wave Crest 🏠🏠 On a bluff overlooking the Pacific, these gray-shingled bungalow condominiums are beautifully maintained and wonderfully private. From the street it looks nothing like a hotel, because a good portion of these condos are owner-occupied year-round. The studios and suites surround a landscaped courtyard; each has a queen-size bed, sofa bed, artwork by local artists, a stereo, a full bathroom, and a fully equipped kitchen with dishwasher. The studios sleep one or two people; the one-bedroom accommodates up to four. It's a 5-minute walk to the beach, and shopping and dining spots are a few blocks away. There is an extra fee for maid service. Amenities include a common lounge with a fireplace, TV, and newspapers.

1400 Ocean Ave., Del Mar, CA 92014. © 858/755-0100. 31 units. $216–$246 studio summer (mid-June to mid-Sept), $174–$198 winter; $280–$396 suite summer, $204–$270 winter. Weekly rates available. MC, V. Take I-5 to Del Mar Heights Rd. W, turn right onto Camino del Mar, and drive to 15th St. Turn left and drive to Ocean Ave., and turn left. **Amenities:** Outdoor pool; Jacuzzi; self-service laundry. *In room:* TV/VCR, kitchen.

WHERE TO DINE

Head to the upper level of the centrally located Del Mar Plaza, at Camino del Mar and 15th Street. You'll find **Il Fornaio Cucina Italiana** (© 858/755-8876) for excellent Italian cuisine; **Epazote** (© 858/259-9966) for Mexican, Tex-Mex, and Southwestern fare; and **Pacifica Del Mar** (© 858/792-0476), which serves outstanding seafood. Kids like **Johnny Rockets** (© 858/755-1954), an old-fashioned diner on the lower level. On the beach, **Jake's Del Mar,** 1660 Coast Blvd. (© 858/755-2002), and **Poseidon Restaurant on the Beach,** 1670 Coast Blvd. (© 858/755-9345), are both good for California cuisine and sunset views. If you want to eat at either of these popular spots, reserve early. The racetrack crowd congregates at **Bully's Restaurant,** 1404 Camino del Mar (© 858/755-1660), for burgers, prime rib, and crab legs; the gold-card crowd heads for special-occasion meals at acclaimed **Pamplemousse Grill,** 514 Via de la Valle (© 858/792-9090). And if you're looking for fresh seafood—and lots of it—head to the Del Mar branch of San Diego's popular **Fish Market,** 640 Via de la Valle (© 858/755-2277), near the racetrack.

CARLSBAD & ENCINITAS

Fifteen miles north of Del Mar and a 45-minute drive from downtown San Diego, the pretty communities of Carlsbad and Encinitas provide many reasons to linger on the California coast: good swimming and surfing beaches, small-town atmosphere, an abundance of antiques and gift shops, and a seasonal display of the region's most beautiful flowers.

Carlsbad was named for Karlsbad, Czechoslovakia, because of the similar mineral (some say curative) waters they both produced, but the town's once-famous artesian well has long been plugged up. Carlsbad is also a noted commercial flower–growing region, along with its neighbor **Encinitas.** A colorful display can be seen at **Carlsbad Ranch** (© 760/431-0352) each spring, when 45 acres of solid ranunculus fields bloom into a breathtaking rainbow visible even from the freeway. In December, the nurseries are alive with holiday poinsettias. You can also stroll through 30 acres of California native plants, exotic tropicals, palms, cacti, and more at **Quail Botanical Gardens** in Encinitas

(© 760/436-3036). The **Carlsbad Visitor Information Center,** 400 Carlsbad Village Dr. (in the old Santa Fe Depot), Carlsbad, CA 92008 (© **800/ 227-5722** or 760/434-6093; www.carlsbadca.org), has lots of additional information on flower fields and nursery touring.

Carlsbad State Beach runs alongside downtown. It's a great place to stroll along a wide concrete walkway, surrounded by like-minded outdoors types walking, jogging, and in-line skating, even at night (thanks to good lighting). Enter on Ocean Boulevard at Tamarack Avenue; there's a $4 fee per vehicle.

Several miles south of town is **South Carlsbad State Beach,** almost 3 miles of cobblestone-strewn sand. A state-run campground at the north end is immensely popular year-round, and the southern portion is favored by area surfers. There's a $4 fee at the beach's entrance, along Carlsbad Boulevard at Poinsettia Lane.

Down in Encinitas, everyone flocks to **Moonlight Beach,** the city's sandy playground with plenty of facilities, including free parking, volleyball nets, restrooms, showers, picnic tables and fire grates, and the company of fellow sunbathers. The beach is accessed at the end of B Street (Encinitas Blvd.).

LEGOLAND ★★ *Kids* The ultimate monument to the world's most famous plastic building blocks, LEGOLAND (opened in 1999) is the third such theme park; the branches in Denmark and Britain have proven enormously successful. Attractions include hands-on interactive displays; a life-size menagerie of tigers, giraffes, and other animals; scale models of international landmarks (the Eiffel Tower, Sydney Opera House, and so on)—all constructed of real LEGO bricks! "MiniLand" is a 1:20 scale representation of American achievement, from a New England Pilgrim village to Mount Rushmore. There's a gravity coaster ride (don't worry, it's built from steel) through a LEGO castle, a DUPLO building area to keep smaller children occupied, and a high-tech ride where older kids can compete in LEGO TECHNIC car races.

While the park's official guidelines imply its attraction is geared toward children of all ages, I think the average MTV- and PlayStation-seasoned kid over 10 will find it kind of a snooze. Don't be afraid your toddler is too young, though—there'll be plenty for them to do. One last note on age: It may be "a country just for kids," but the sheer artistry of construction (especially MiniLand) can be enthralling for adults, too.

1 Legoland Dr. © 877/534-6526 or 760/918-LEGO. www.legoland.com. $40 adults, $34 seniors and kids 3–16, free for children under 3. AE, DISC, MC, V. Summer (Memorial Day to Labor Day) daily 10am–8pm; off-season Thurs–Mon 10am–5 or 6pm; open daily during Christmas and Easter vacation periods. Parking $7. From I-5 take the Cannon Rd. exit E, following signs for Legoland Dr.

WHERE TO STAY

For the ultimate pampering golf, tennis, or spa vacation in Carlsbad, head to the **Four Seasons Resort Aviara,** 7100 Four Seasons Point (© **800/332-3442** or 760/603-6800; www.fourseasons.com/aviara), or **La Costa Resort and Spa,** Costa del Mar Rd. (© **800/854-5000** or 760/438-9111; www.lacosta.com).

Beach Terrace Inn At Carlsbad's only beachside hostelry (others are across the road or a little farther away), the rooms and the swimming pool/Jacuzzi all have ocean views. This downtown Best Western property is tucked between rows of high-rent beach cottages and proffers its scenic location as its best quality. The rooms are extra large, and although they suffer from generic furnished-bachelor-pad-style interiors, some have balconies, fireplaces, and kitchenettes. Suites are affordable and have separate living rooms and bedrooms, making this a good choice for families. VCRs and films are available at the front desk. You can walk everywhere from here—except LEGOLAND, which is a 5-minute drive away.

2775 Ocean St., Carlsbad, CA 92003. ℂ 800/433-5415 outside Calif., 800/622-3224 in Calif., or 760/729-5951. Fax 760/729-1078. www.beachterraceinn.com. 49 units. Summer $140–$215 double; from $189 suite. Off-season $134–$174 double; from $154 suite. Extra person $20. Rates include continental breakfast. AE, DC, DISC, MC, V. Free parking. **Amenities:** Outdoor pool; Jacuzzi; self-service laundry; dry cleaning. *In room:* A/C, TV w/pay movies, dataport, fridge, coffeemaker, hair dryer, iron, safe.

Pelican Cove Inn ⍟   Located 2 blocks from the beach, this Cape Cod–style hideaway combines romance with luxury. Hosts Kris and Nancy Nayudu see to your every need, from furnishing guest rooms with soft feather beds and down comforters to providing beach chairs and towels or preparing a picnic basket (with 24 hours' notice). Each room features a fireplace and private entrance; some have private spa tubs. The airy, spacious La Jolla room is loveliest, with bay windows and a cupola ceiling. Breakfast can be enjoyed in the garden if weather permits. Courtesy transportation from the Oceanside train station is available.

320 Walnut Ave., Carlsbad, CA 92008. ℂ 888/PEL-COVE or 760/434-5995. www.pelican-cove.com. 8 units. $90–$180 double. Rates include full breakfast. Extra person $15. Midweek and seasonal discounts available. AE, MC, V. Free parking. From downtown Carlsbad, follow Carlsbad Blvd. S to Walnut Ave.; turn left and drive 2½ blocks. *In room:* TV, no phone.

Tamarack Beach Resort ⍟   This resort property's rooms, in the village across the street from the beach, are restfully decorated with beachy wicker furniture. Fully equipped suites—similar to Maui-style vacation condos—have stereos, full kitchens, washers, and dryers. The pretty Tamarack has a pleasant lobby and a sunny pool courtyard with barbecue grills. Dini's by the Sea is a good restaurant that is popular with locals.

3200 Carlsbad Blvd., Carlsbad, CA 92008. ℂ 800/334-2199 or 760/729-3500. Fax 760/434-5942. www.tamarackresort.com. 77 units. $140–$215 double; $210–$340 suite. Children 12 and under stay free in parents' room. Off-season discounts and weekly rates available. Rates include continental breakfast. AE, MC, V. Free underground parking. **Amenities:** Restaurant; outdoor pool; 2 Jacuzzis; exercise room. *In room:* A/C, TV/VCR, fridge, coffeemaker, hair dryer, iron.

WHERE TO DINE

The architectural centerpiece of Carlsbad is **Neiman's,** 2978 Carlsbad Blvd. (ℂ 760/729-4131), a restored Victorian mansion complete with turrets, cupolas, and waving flags. The menu includes rack of lamb, chicken Dijon, and smoked chicken with cheese quesadillas. There are also burgers, pastas, and salads. Sunday brunch is a tremendous buffet of breakfast and lunch items. An always-crowded local favorite is **Fidel's Norte,** 3003 Carlsbad Blvd. (ℂ 760/729-0903), a branch of the Solana Beach mainstay, known for reliably delicious Mexican food and kickin' margaritas.

Some of my favorites in Encinitas include **Vigilucci's,** 505 S. Hwy. 101 at D Street (ℂ 760/942-7332), where the wafting fragrance of garlic always draws a crowd in for authentic southern Italy trattoria fare served in a lively atmosphere accented with old-world touches like stained glass and a grand mahogany bar; and the nearby **Siamese Basil,** 527 S. Coast Hwy. 101 (ℂ 760/753-3940), whose innocuous facade and bland interior belie a well-deserved reputation for fresh zesty Thai food and a friendly attitude.

Bellefleur Winery & Restaurant ⍟⍟ CALIFORNIA/MEDITERRANEAN This popular restaurant boasts the "complete wine country experience" although there's no wine country evident among the surrounding outlet mall and car dealerships. But their cavernous semi-industrial dining room, coupled with the wood-fired and wine-enhanced aromas emanating from Bellefleur's clanging open kitchen, do somehow evoke the casual yet sophisticated ambience of California wine-producing regions like Santa Barbara and Napa. This multi-functional space includes a stylish tasting bar and open-air dining patio in addition to the main seating area and a glassed-in barrel-aging room. The place can be noisy and spirited, drawing both exhausted shoppers and savvy San Diegans for a cuisine that incorporates North County's abundant produce with fresh fish and meats. Lunchtime sandwiches and salads surpass the shopping-mall standard, while dinner choices feature oak-grilled beef tenderloin or Colorado rack of lamb, mashed potatoes enhanced with garlic, horseradish, or olive tapenade, and rich reduction sauces of premium balsamic vinegar, wild-mushroom demi-glace, or sweet-tart tamarind.

5610 Paseo del Norte, Carlsbad. ⓒ 760/603-1919. www.bellefleur.com. Reservations recommended for Fri–Sat dinner. Main courses $7–$15 lunch, $14–$23 dinner. AE, DISC, MC, V. Daily 11am–3pm; Sun–Thurs 5–9pm, Fri–Sat 5–10pm.

OCEANSIDE

The most northerly town in San Diego County (36 miles north of San Diego), Oceanside claims almost 4 miles of beaches and one of the West Coast's longest over-the-water wooden piers, where a tram does nothing but transport people from the street to the end of the 1,954-foot-long pier and back for 25¢ each way. The wide, sandy beach, pier, and well-tended recreational area with playground equipment and an outdoor amphitheater are within easy walking distance of the train station.

One of the nicest things to do in Oceanside is to take a stroll around the city's upscale **harbor;** it's bustling with pleasure craft, lined with condominiums, and boasts a Cape Cod–themed shopping village. A launch ramp, visitor boat slips, charter fishing, boat rentals, and the village of shops are found here; several restaurants, including **Chart House** at 314 Harbor Dr. S. (ⓒ **760/722-1345**), offer harbor-side dining. The **Harbor Days Festival** in mid-September typically attracts 100,000 visitors to its crafts fair, entertainment, and food booths. The **Marina Inn,** at 2008 Harbor Dr. N., Oceanside, CA 92054 (ⓒ **800/252-2033** or 760/722-1561; www.omihotel.com), has comfortable rooms and suites with ocean views.

Oceanside is home to the **California Surf Museum,** 223 North Coast Hwy. (ⓒ **760/721-6876;** www.surfmuseum.org). Founded in 1985, the museum has an unbelievably extensive collection. Boards and other relics chronicle the development of the sport—many belonged to the names revered by local surfers, including Hawaiian Duke Kahanamoku and local daredevil Bob Simmons. Vintage photographs, beach attire, 1960s beach graffiti, and surf music all lovingly bring surfing to life—there's even a photo display of the real-life Gidget.

The area's biggest attraction is **Mission San Luis Rey** (ⓒ **760/757-3651**), a few miles inland. Founded in 1798, it's the largest of California's 21 missions. There is a small charge to tour the mission, its impressive church, exhibits, grounds, and cemetery. You might recognize it as the backdrop for one of the Zorro movies.

The **Oceanside Beach** runs all the way from just outside Oceanside Harbor, where routine harbor dredging makes for a pretty substantial amount of clean white sand, continuing almost 4 miles south at the Carlsbad border. Along the way you can enjoy the **Strand,** a grassy park stretching alongside the beach between Fifth Street and Wisconsin Avenue. Around the pier are restrooms, showers, picnic areas, and volleyball nets.

Oceanside's world-famous surfing spots attract numerous competitions, including the **Longboard Surf Contest** and **World Bodysurfing Championships,** both in August.

For an information packet about Oceanside and its attractions, contact the **Oceanside Visitor & Tourism Center,** 928 North Coast Hwy., Oceanside, CA 92054 (© **800/350-7873** or 760/721-1101; www.oceansidechamber.com).

12 Julian: Apples, Pies & a Slice of Small-Town California

60 miles NE of San Diego; 35 miles W of Anza-Borrego Desert State Park

A trip to Julian (pop. 1,500) is a trip back in time. The old gold-mining town, now best known for its apples, has some good eateries and a handful of cute B&Bs, but its popularity is based on the fact that it provides a chance for city-weary folks to get away from it all.

ESSENTIALS

GETTING THERE   The 90-minute drive can be made via Calif. 78 or I-8 to Calif. 79. I suggest taking one route going and the other coming back. Calif. 79 winds through scenic Cuyamaca Rancho State Park, while Calif. 78 traverses open country and farmland.

VISITOR INFORMATION   Town maps and fliers for accommodations are available from the Town Hall, on Main Street at Washington Street. The town has a 24-hour hot line (© 760/765-0707) that provides information on lodging, dining, shopping, activities, upcoming events, weather, and road conditions. For a brochure on what to see and do, contact the **Julian Chamber of Commerce** (© 760/765-1857; www.julianca.com).

SPECIAL EVENTS   Julian's popular fall apple harvest starts in mid-September and continues for an entire month. The annual **Wildflower Show** lasts for a week in early May; there's also a **Spring Fine Arts Show** in May. And the annual **Julian Weed Show,** a tradition since 1961, is usually held the last few weeks in August or the beginning of September. Contact the Julian Chamber of Commerce (see above) for details on all of these events.

EXPLORING THE TOWN

This 1880s gold-mining town has managed to retain a rustic, woodsy sense of its historic origins. Radiating the dusty aura of the Old West, Julian offers an abundance of early California history, quaint Victorian streets filled with apple-pie shops and antiques stores, crisp fresh air, and friendly people. Be forewarned, however: Julian's charming downtown can become exceedingly crowded during the fall harvest season, so consider making your trip during another time in order to enjoy this unspoiled relic with a little privacy. (Rest assured, apple pies are being baked year-round.) At around 4,500 feet elevation, the autumn air is crisp and bracing, and Julian sees a dusting (and often more) of snow during the winter months.

The best way to experience tiny Julian is on foot. After stopping in at the **Chamber of Commerce** in the old Town Hall—check out the vintage photos of Julian's yesteryear—cross the street to the **Julian Drug Store & Miner's Diner,** 2134 Main St. (© 760/765-3753), an old-style soda fountain serving sparkling sarsaparilla, conjuring images of boys in buckskin and girls in bonnets. The **Eagle and High Peak Mines** (ca. 1870) at the end of C Street (© 760/765-0036), although seemingly a tourist trap, offers an interesting and educational look at the town's one-time economic mainstay.

The town's **Pioneer Cemetery** is a must-see for graveyard buffs; contemporary graves belie the haphazard, overgrown look of this hilly burial ground, and eroded older tombstones tell the intriguing story of Julian's rough pioneer history. You can drive in via the A Street entrance, or climb the steep stairway leading up from Main Street; until 1924 this ascent was the only point of entry, even for processionals.

Apple pie is the town's mainstay, and the **Julian Pie Company,** 2225 Main St. (© 760/765-2449), is the most charming pie shop of them all. It serves original, Dutch, apple–mountain berry, and no-sugar-added pies, as well as other baked goodies. Another great bakery is the aptly named **Mom's Pies,** 2119 Main St. (© 760/765-2472), whose special attraction is a sidewalk plate-glass window through which you can observe the Mom-on-duty rolling crust, filling pies, and crimping edges. Nearby is the **Julian Cider Mill,** 2103 Main St. (© 760/765-1430), where you can see cider presses at work October through March; it offers free tastes of the fresh nectar and sells jugs to take home.

There are dozens of **roadside fruit stands and orchards** in the Julian hills; during autumn they're open all day, every day, but in the off-season some might open only on weekends or close entirely. Most stands sell (depending on the season) apples, pears, peaches, cider, jams, jellies, and other homemade foodstuffs. Many are along Highway 78 between Julian and Wynola (3 miles away); there are also stands along Farmers Road, a scenic country lane leading north from downtown Julian. Happy hunting!

Ask any of the San Diegans who regularly make excursions to Julian: No trip would be complete without a stop at **Dudley's Bakery,** Calif. 78, Santa Ysabel (© 800/225-3348 or 760/765-0488), for a loaf or three of its popular bread. Loaves are stacked high, and folks are often three deep at the counter, clamoring for the 20 (!) varieties of bread baked fresh daily—varieties range from raisin-date-nut to jalapeño, with some garden-variety sourdough and multi-grain in between. Dudley's is a local tradition, built in 1963, and has expanded several times to accommodate an ever-growing business. It's open Wednesday through Sunday from 8am to 5pm (subject to early closure on Sun).

OUTDOOR PURSUITS

Within 10 miles of Julian are numerous hiking trails traversing rolling meadows, high chaparral, and thick pine forests. The most spectacular hike is at **Volcan Mountain Preserve,** north of town along Farmers Road. The trail to the top is a moderately challenging hike of around 3½ miles round-trip with a 1,400-foot elevation gain. From the top, hikers have a panoramic view of the desert, mountains, and sea. Docent-led hikes are offered year-round at no charge (usually on one Sat per month). For a hike schedule, call © 760/765-0650.

In **William Heise County Park,** off Frisius Drive outside of Pine Hills, the whole family can enjoy hikes ranging from a self-guided nature trail to a cedar-scented forest trail, plus moderate to vigorous trails into the mountains. A ranger kiosk at the entrance can provide trail maps.

Cuyamaca Rancho State Park covers 30,000 acres along Calif. 79 southeast of Julian, the centerpiece of which is **Cuyamaca Lake.** In addition to lake recreation (© 760/765-0515 or 760/447-8123; www.lakecuyamaca.org), there are several wooded picnic areas, three campgrounds, and 110 miles of hiking trails through the Cleveland National Forest. Activities at the lake include fishing (trout, bass, catfish, bluegill, and crappie) and boating; there's a general store and restaurant at lake's edge. The fishing fee (license required) is $4.75 per day for adults and $2.50 per day for kids ages 8 to 15; rowboats are $12 per day, and outboard motors an additional $13. Canoes and paddleboats can be rented by the hour for $4 to $7. For a trail map and further information about park recreation, stop in at **park headquarters,** on Calif. 79 (© **760/765-0755**), Monday through Friday between the hours of 8am and 5pm. An adjacent park museum is open Monday through Friday from 10am to 5pm and Saturday and Sunday from 10am to 4pm.

For a different way to tour, try **Llama Trek,** P.O. Box 2363, Julian, CA 92036 (© **800/LAMAPAK** or 760/765-1890; www.wikiupbnb.com). Trips include rural neighborhoods, a historic gold mine, mountain and lake views, and apple orchards. Rates run from $75 to $85 per person and include lunch; overnight wilderness treks are also available.

WHERE TO STAY

For a list and description of more than 20 B&Bs, contact the **Julian Bed & Breakfast Guild** (© **760/765-1555;** www.julianbnbguild.com). Noteworthy member inns are the **Artists' Loft** (© **760/765-0765**), a peaceful hilltop retreat offering two artistically decorated rooms and a cozy cabin with a wood-burning stove; the **Julian White House** (© **800/WHT-HOUS** or 760/765-1764), a lovely faux-antebellum mansion, several miles from Julian in Pine Hills, with four frilly Victorian-style guest rooms; and the romantic **Random Oaks Ranch** (© **800/BNB-4344** or 760/765-1094), which features two themed cottages, each with its own wood-burning fireplace and outdoor Jacuzzi.

A word of caution: Reservations for the fall harvest season must be made several months in advance.

Julian Hotel ✦   Built in 1897 by freed slave Albert Robinson, this frontier-style hotel is a living monument to the area's gold-boom days. Centrally located at the crossroads of downtown, the Julian Hotel isn't as secluded or plush as the many B&Bs in town, but if you seek historically accurate lodgings to complete your weekend time warp, this is the place. The 13 rooms and 2 cottages have been authentically restored (with nicely designed private bathrooms added where necessary) and boast antique furnishings; some rooms are also authentically tiny, so claustrophobes should inquire when reserving! An inviting private lobby is stocked with books, games, literature on local activities, and a wood-burning stove.

Main St. and B St., P.O. Box 1856, Julian, CA 92036. © **800/734-5854** or 760/765-0201. Fax 760/765-0327. www.julianhotel.com. 15 units. $82–$130 double; $120–$190 cottage. Rates include full breakfast and afternoon tea. AE, MC, V. *In room:* No phone.

Orchard Hill Country Inn ✦✦   Hosts Darrell and Pat Straube offer the most upscale lodging in Julian, a two-story lodge and four Craftsman cottages on a hill overlooking the town. Ten guest rooms, a guests-only dining room, and a great room with a massive stone fireplace are in the lodge. Twelve suites are in cottages spread over 3 acres of grounds. All units feature contemporary, unfrilly country furnishings and snacks. While rooms in the main lodge feel somewhat hotel-ish, the cottage suites are secluded and luxurious, with private porches, fireplaces, Jacuzzis, and robes. Several hiking trails lead from the lodge into adjacent woods.

2502 Washington St. (at 2nd St.), P.O. Box 2410, Julian, CA 92036. © **800/71-ORCHARD** or 760/765-1700. Fax 760/765-0290. www.orchardhill.com. 22 units. $185–$285 double. Rates include breakfast and hors d'oeuvres. Extra person $25. 2-night minimum stay if including Sat. AE, MC, V. From Calif. 79, turn left on Main St., then right on Washington St. *In room:* A/C, TV/VCR.

WHERE TO DINE

Julian Grille ☆ AMERICAN   Set in a cozy cottage festooned with lacy draperies, flickering candles, and a warm hearth, the Grille is the nicest eatery in town. Lunch here is an anything-goes affair, ranging from soups, sandwiches, and large salads to charbroiled burgers and hearty omelets. Dinner features grilled and broiled meats, seafood, and prime rib. I'm partial to delectable appetizers like baked brie with apples and mustard sauce, Baja-style shrimp cocktail, and "Prime tickler" (chunks of prime rib served cocktail-style *au jus* with horseradish sauce). Dinners include soup or salad, hot rolls, potatoes, and a vegetable.

2224 Main St. (at A St.). © 760/765-0173. Reservations required Fri–Sun. Main courses $13–$21. AE, MC, V. Daily 11am–3pm; Tues–Sun 5–9pm.

Romano's Dodge House ☆ ITALIAN   Occupying a historic home just off Main Street (vintage photos illustrate the little farmhouse's past), Romano's is proudly the only restaurant in town not serving apple pie. It's a home-style Italian spot, with red-checked tablecloths and straw-clad Chianti bottles. Romano's offers individual lunch pizzas, pastas bathed in rich marinara sauce, veal parmigiana, chicken cacciatore, and the signature dish, pork Juliana (loin chops in a whisky–apple cider sauce). There's seating on a narrow shaded porch, in the wood-plank dining room, and in a little saloon in back.

2718 B St. (just off Main). © 760/765-1003. www.romanosjulian.com. Reservations required for dinner Fri–Sat, recommended other nights. Main courses $8–$16. No credit cards. Wed–Mon 11am–8:30pm.

13 Anza-Borrego Desert State Park

35 miles E of Julian; 90 miles NE of San Diego

The sweeping 600,000-acre Anza-Borrego Desert State Park is home to fossils and rocks dating from 540 million years ago; human beings arrived only 10,000 years ago. The terrain ranges in elevation from 15 feet to more than 6,000 feet above sea level, and incorporates dry lake beds, sandstone canyons, granite mountains, palm groves fed by year-round springs, and more than 600 kinds of desert plants. After the spring rains, thousands of wildflowers burst into bloom, transforming the desert into a brilliant palette of pink, lavender, red, orange, and yellow. The rare bighorn sheep can often be spotted navigating rocky hillsides, and an occasional migratory bird stops off on the way to the Salton Sea. A sense of timelessness pervades this landscape; travelers tend to slow down and take a long look around.

When planning a trip here, keep in mind that temperatures rise to as high as 115°F (46°C) in summer.

ESSENTIALS

VISITOR INFORMATION   The **Anza-Borrego Desert State Park Visitor Center** lies just west of the town of Borrego Springs. You can contact park headquarters at © 760/767-4205 (www.anzaborrego.statepark.org); the visitor center is open October through May daily from 9am to 5pm, and June through September on weekends from 10am to 5pm.

For other local information, contact the **Borrego Springs Chamber of Commerce,** 786 Palm Canyon Dr., Borrego Springs, CA 92004 (© **800/ 559-5524** or 760/767-5555; www.borregosprings.org).

SPECIAL EVENT   From mid-March to the beginning of April, the desert wildflowers and cacti are usually in bloom, a hands-down, all-out natural special event that's not to be missed. The wildflower hot line is © **760/767-4684.**

EXPLORING THE DESERT

When you're touring in this area, remember that hydration is of paramount importance. Whether you're walking, cycling, or driving, always have a bottle of water at your side.

You can explore the desert's stark terrain via one of its trails or a self-guided driving tour; the visitor center can supply maps. For starters, the **Borrego Palm Canyon** self-guided hike (1½ miles each way), which starts at the campgrounds near the visitor center, is beautiful, easy to get to, and easy to do. Within about half an hour you'll come to a waterfall and massive fan palms.

You can also take a guided off-road tour of the desert with **Desert Jeep Tours** (© **888/BY-JEEPS;** www.desertjeeptours.com). View spectacular canyons, fossil beds, ancient Native American sites, caves, and more in excursions by desert denizen Paul Ford ("Borrego Paul"). Tours go to the awesome viewpoint at Font's Point, where you can look out on the Badlands—named by the early settlers because it was an impossible area for moving or grazing cattle. Along the way, you'll learn about the history and geology of the area. Tours include drinks, snacks, and pickup at any of Borrego Springs lodgings; prices range from $59 to $99 per person.

Call **Carrizo Bikes** (© **760/767-3872**) and talk with Dan Cain (a true desert rat) about bike rentals and tours in the area. For a thrilling 12-mile bicycle ride down Montezuma Valley Grade, try the Desert Descent offered by **Gravity Activated Sports** (© **800/985-4427** or 760/742-2294).

WHERE TO STAY

Borrego Springs is small, but there are enough accommodations to suit all travel styles and budgets. Other decent options include **Palm Canyon Resort,** 221 Palm Canyon Dr. (© **800/242-0044** or 760/767-5341), a large complex that includes a moderately priced hotel, RV park, restaurant, and recreational facilities; and **Borrego Valley Inn,** 405 Palm Canyon Dr. (© **800/333-5810** or 760/767-0311; www.borregovalleyinn.com), a newly built Southwestern complex featuring sand-colored pueblo-style rooms and upscale bed-and-breakfast amenities. Camping in the desert is a meditative experience, to be sure; but if you truly want to splurge, you can do that, too.

La Casa del Zorro Desert Resort 🌟🌟   This pocket of heaven on earth was built in 1937, and the tamarisk trees that were planted then have grown up around it. So have the many charming tile-roofed casitas, originally neighboring homes bought by the resort's longtime owners, San Diego's Copley newspaper family. Over time the property has grown into a cohesive blend of discreetly private cottages and luxurious two-story hotel buildings—each blessed with personalized service and unwavering standards—that make La Casa del Zorro unequaled in Borrego Springs. Courtesy carts ferry you around the lushly planted grounds, and to the resort's stunning new pool area by the resurfaced tennis courts. It's easy to understand why repeat guests book their favorite casitas year after year; some have a fireplace or pool, every bedroom has a separate bathroom, and they all have minifridges and microwaves (though a lack of dishes and utensils is calculated to get you into the Spanish-style main lodge's fine dining room). Outdoor diversions include horseshoes, Ping-Pong, volleyball, jogging trails, basketball, shuffleboard, and a life-size chess set.

3845 Yaqui Pass Rd., Borrego Springs, CA 92004. © **800/824-1884** or 760/767-5323. Fax 760/767-5963. www.lacasadelzorro.com. 77 units. Peak season (mid-Jan to mid-May) $225–380 double; casitas from $250. Off-peak $175–$300 double; casitas from $200. Extra person $10. Off-season and midweek discounts based on occupancy. Tennis, jazz, holiday, and other packages available. AE, DC, DISC, MC, V. **Amenities:**

Restaurant (men are required to wear a jacket and a collared shirt at dinner Oct–May); lounge; 5 outdoor pools; 9-hole putting green; 6 tennis courts; health club and spa; 2 Jacuzzis; bike rental; activities desk; courtesy car to golf; business center; salon; room service 7am–11pm; in-room massage; babysitting. *In room:* A/C, TV/VCR w/pay movies, dataport, minibar, fridge, coffeemaker, hair dryer, iron.

The Palms at Indian Head ★★ *Finds*   It takes a sense of nostalgia and an active imagination for most visitors to truly appreciate Borrego Springs's only bed-and-breakfast. The once-chic resort is slowly being renovated by its fervent owners, David and Cynthia Leibert. Originally opened in 1947, then rebuilt after a fire in 1958, the Art Deco–style hilltop lodge was a favorite hideaway for San Diego's and Hollywood's elite. It played host to movie stars like Bing Crosby, Clark Gable, and Marilyn Monroe. The Leiberts rescued it from extreme disrepair in 1993, clearing away some dilapidated guest bungalows and uncovering original wallpaper, light fixtures, and priceless memorabilia. As soon as they'd restored several rooms in luxurious Southwestern style, they began taking in guests to help finance the ongoing restoration.

Now up to 10 rooms, the inn also boasts a restaurant, the Krazy Coyote (p. 700), that's a culinary breath of fresh air in town. Also completely restored is the 42-by-109-foot pool, soon to be joined by the original subterranean grotto bar behind viewing windows at the deep end. The inn occupies the most envied site in the valley—shaded by palms and adjacent to the state park with a panoramic view across the entire Anza-Borrego region. A hiking trail begins just steps from the hotel. If you don't mind getting an insider's view of this work-in-progress, the Palms at Indian Head rewards you with charm, comfort, and convenience.

2220 Hoberg Rd., P.O. Box 525, Borrego Springs, CA 92004. (℃ **800/519-2624** or 760/767-7788. Fax 760/767-9717. www.thepalmsatindianhead.com. 10 units. Nov–May $105–$159 double; June–Oct $95 double. Midweek discounts available. Extra person $20. DC, DISC, MC, V. Take S22 into Borrego Springs; at Palm Canyon Dr., S22 becomes Hoberg Rd. Continue N ½ mile. **Amenities:** Restaurant; bar; fantastic outdoor pool; room service 8am–8pm; in-room massage; laundry service. *In room:* A/C, TV, fridge, coffeemaker.

CAMPING

The park has two developed campgrounds. **Borrego Palm Canyon,** with 117 sites, is 2½ miles west of Borrego Springs and near the visitor center. Full hookups are available, and there's an easy hiking trail. **Tamarisk Grove,** at Calif. 78 and county road S3, has 27 sites. Both have campfire programs and restrooms with showers; reservations are a good idea. The park allows open camping along all the trail routes. For more information, check with the visitor center ((℃ **760/767-4205**).

WHERE TO DINE

Your best bet—if you're not willing to break the bank at La Casa del Zorro's classy but pricey dining room—is the surprisingly good **Krazy Coyote,** which presents trendy ingredients and gourmet preparations previously unheard of in this small town; see below for a full review. One welcome newcomer is the **Badlands Market & Cafe,** 561 Palm Canyon Dr., in the Mall ((℃ **760/767-4058**), which offers a daily board of gourmet light meals, plus a prepared-foods deli and store that features imported mustards, marinated sun-dried tomatoes, delicate desserts, and other sophisticated treats. Or, you could follow legions of locals into the downtown mainstay **Carlee's Place,** 670 Palm Canyon Dr. ((℃ **760/767-3262**), a casual bar and grill with plenty of neon beer signs, well-worn pool table, and fuzzy-sounding jukebox. It's easy to understand why Carlee's is the watering hole of choice for motorcycle brigades that pass through town on recreational rides—and the food is tasty, hearty, and priced just right.

Kendall's Cafe COFFEE SHOP   Here's an economical little spot to grab a quick bite. Emu burgers from the local emu-and-ostrich farm are the specialty of the house. Buffalo burgers and Mexican dishes are also popular. Dinner choices include pork chops and chicken-fried steak. The cafe claims its apple pies are better than Julian's. Anything can be packed to go if you'd rather dine overlooking the desert.

In the Mall, Borrego Springs. ℂ **760/767-3491.** Lunch $3.50–$7.95; dinner $5.95–$11. MC, V. Sept–May daily 6am–8pm; June–Aug Thurs–Mon 6am–8pm.

Krazy Coyote Saloon & Grille ✦ ECLECTIC MENU   The same style and perfectionism that pervades David and Cynthia Leibert's bed-and-breakfast is evident in this casual restaurant, which overlooks the inn's swimming pool and the vast desert beyond. An eclectic menu encompasses quesadillas, club sandwiches, burgers, grilled meats and fish, and individual gourmet pizzas. The Krazy Coyote also offers breakfast (rich and hearty for an active day, or light and healthy for diet-watchers). The evening ambience is welcoming and romantic, as the sparse lights of tiny Borrego Springs twinkle on the desert floor below.

In the Palms at Indian Head, 2220 Hoberg Rd. ℂ **760/767-7788.** Main courses $7.50–$12 lunch, $10–$22 dinner. AE, MC, V. Open daily; call for seasonal hours.

Appendix: California in Depth

by Matthew Richard Poole

The more you know about California, the more you're likely to enjoy and appreciate everything the state has to offer. The pages that follow include a brief yet enlightening tale of how California came to be the most plentiful and powerful state in the nation.

1 California Today

A recent survey of the most popular name given to California's newborns says a lot about the direction in which the Golden State is headed. You probably didn't guess José, but then again, you may not have known that California is the most racially diverse state in the nation, playing host to every race, ethnic heritage, language group, and religion in the *world*. So if you're prone to xenophobia, you might want to spend your vacation elsewhere, because California will soon be the mother of all melting pots, where no single race or ethnic group will constitute a majority of the state's population.

The numbers are already bewildering: 35 million people, a whopping one-third of whom live in the Los Angeles basin. California already receives the highest numbers of immigrants in America each year—more than 200,000 annually. Whether this is a potential boon or time bomb for California's future is impossible to predict, but in the meantime it makes for a very interesting place to live and visit. Why bother traveling all the way to Europe or Asia when you can visit immigrant communities in Los Angeles and San Francisco that are uncanny replicas of the societies they've left behind?

2 History 101

EUROPEAN DISCOVERY & COLONIZATION

Although very little remains to mark the existence of West Coast Native Americans, anthropologists estimate that as many as half a million aborigines flourished on this naturally abundant land for thousands of years before the arrival of Europeans in the mid–16th century. Sailing from a small colony, established 10 years before, on the southern tip of Baja (lower) California, Portuguese explorer Juan Rodrígues Cabrillo is credited with being the first European to "discover" California, in 1542. Over the next 200 years, dozens of

Dateline

- 1542 Juan Cabrillo enters San Diego Bay and sails up California's coast in first documented European visit.
- 1579 Sir Francis Drake drops anchor in the San Francisco Bay area and claims the land for England's Queen Elizabeth I.
- 1602 Spanish explorer and merchant Sebastian Vizcano sails up the coast, naming many regions along the way.
- 1769 Mission San Diego de Alcala is founded by Franciscan monk Father Junípero Serra.
- 1775 Juan Manuel de Ayala maps San Francisco Bay.

continues

sailors mapped the coast, including British explorer Sir Francis Drake, who sailed his *Golden Hind* into what is now called Drake's Bay in 1579, and Spanish explorer Sebastian Vizcano, who, in 1602, bestowed most of the place-names that survive today, including San Diego, Santa Barbara, and Carmel.

European colonial competition and Catholic missionary zeal prompted Spain to establish settlements along the Alta (upper) California coast and claim the lands as its own. In 1769, Father Junípero Serra, accompanied by 300 soldiers and clergy, began forging a path from Mexico to Monterey. A small mission and presidio (fort) were established that year at San Diego, and by 1804, a chain of 21 missions, each a day's walk from the next along a dirt road called *Camino Real* (Royal Road), stretched all the way to Sonoma. Most of the solidly built missions still remain—Mission Delores, Mission San Juan Bautista, Mission San Diego de Alcala, to name just a few—and offer public tours.

During that time, thousands of Native Americans were converted to Christianity and coerced into labor. Many others died from imported diseases. Because not all the natives welcomed their conquerors with open arms, many missions and pueblos (small towns) suffered repeated attacks, leading to the construction of California's now ubiquitous—and fireproof—red-tile roofs.

No settlement had more than 100 inhabitants when Spain's sovereignty was compromised by an 1812 Russian outpost called Fort Ross, 60 miles north of San Francisco (which, remarkably enough, still stands and is open to the public). But the biggest threat came from the British—who had strengthened their own claims to America with the Hudson's Bay Company trading firm—and their short-lived, last-ditch effort to win

- 1777 Monterey is made capital of Spain's California territory.
- 1781 Los Angeles is founded.
- 1804 Spain divides its California territory into Baja (Lower) California and Alta (Upper) California; Jose Joaquin de Arrillaga becomes the first governor of Alta California.
- 1808 Connecticut sea captain William Shaler publishes his *Journal,* the first extensive account of California.
- 1821 Mexico wins independence from Spain and annexes California.
- 1836 Governor Juan Batista Alvarado declares California a "free and sovereign state."
- 1846 John C. Fremont leads the Bear Flag Revolt; California is drawn into the Mexican-American War; the U.S flag is raised in Yerba Buena (San Francisco) and Los Angeles.
- 1847 Yerba Buena is renamed San Francisco; the Donner Party is trapped by heavy Sierra Nevada snows.
- 1848 James Wilson Marshall discovers gold in Coloma; California is officially made a U.S. Territory.
- 1849 The gold rush is in full swing, bringing more than 300,000 men and women; a constitutional convention meets in Monterey; San Jose becomes the state capital.
- 1850 California becomes the 31st state.
- 1853 Levi Strauss sells his first pair of canvas trousers.
- 1854 Sacramento becomes the permanent state capital.
- 1857 Hungarian Agoston Haraszthy establishes the state's first winery, Buena Vista.
- 1859 Prospector James Finney discovers silver ore, the Comstock Load.
- 1861 California swears allegiance to the Union.
- 1862 The first telegraph line is established between San Francisco and New York.
- 1867 Anti-Chinese demonstrations take place in San Francisco in the wake of rising immigration.
- 1869 The transcontinental railroad is completed.
- 1873 The University of California opens its campus at Berkeley; the first cable car appears in San Francisco.

back their territories in the War of 1812.

Embattled at home as well as abroad, the Spanish finally relinquished their claim to Mexico and California in 1821. Under Mexican rule, Alta California's Spanish missionaries fell out of favor and lost much of their land to the increasingly wealthy *Californios*—Mexican immigrants who had been granted vast tracts of land.

AMERICAN EXPANSION

Beginning in the late 1820s, Americans from the East began to make their way to California via a 3-month sail around Cape Horn. Most of them settled in the territorial capital of Monterey and in Northern California.

From the 1830s on, inspired by the doctrine of Manifest Destiny—an almost religious belief that the United States was destined to cover the continent from coast to coast—more and more settlers headed west. Along with them came daring explorers. In 1843, Marcus Whitman, a missionary seeking to prove that settlers could travel overland through the Oregon Territory's Blue Mountains, helped blaze the Oregon Trail; the first covered-wagon train made the 4-month crossing in 1844. Over the next few years, several hundred Americans made the trek to California over the Sierra Nevada range via Truckee Pass, just north of Lake Tahoe. A memorial to the Donner Party—the most famous tragedy in the history of westward migration—marks the site of the ill-fated travelers.

As the drive to the west increased, the U.S. government sought to extend its control over Mexican territory north of the Rio Grande, the river that now divides the United States and Mexico. In 1846, President James Polk offered Mexico $40 million for California and New Mexico. The offer might have been accepted, but America's simultaneous annexation of Texas,

1879 The University of Southern California is founded.

1881 The *Los Angeles Times* begins publication.

1888 Lick Observatory is established.

1890 Yosemite gains National Park status.

1906 San Francisco is decimated by an earthquake and fire, leaving 300,000 people homeless.

1911 Hollywood's first film studio is established.

1915 The first transcontinental telephone call is made from San Francisco to New York.

1919 William Randolph Hearst begins construction of his castle at San Simeon.

1922 The Hollywood Bowl and amphitheater opens.

1924 The first transcontinental airmail flight is made from San Francisco to New York.

1928 Walt Disney creates Mickey Mouse.

1929 Hollywood hosts the first Academy Awards presentation.

1934 Alcatraz Island is converted to a maximum security penitentiary.

1935 Statewide irrigation system begins.

1936 The San Francisco–Oakland Bay Bridge opens.

1937 The Golden Gate Bridge opens.

1945 The United Nations is founded in San Francisco.

1955 Disneyland opens in Anaheim; actor James Dean dies in a car accident near Paso Robles at age 24.

1958 California acquires its first major-league baseball team, the San Francisco Giants.

1960 San Francisco's Candlestick Park opens.

1962 California becomes the most populous state in the Union.

1964 Mario Savio speaks before Free Speech Movement demonstrators at UC Berkeley.

1967 San Francisco's Haight-Ashbury experiences the "Summer of Love."

1968 Robert Kennedy is assassinated at LA's Ambassador Hotel.

1972 The BART system opens in San Francisco.

continues

to which Mexico still laid claim, resulted in a war between the two countries. Within months, the United States overcame Mexico and took possession of the entire West Coast.

GOLD & STATEHOOD
In 1848, California's non–Native American population was around 7,000. That same year, flakes of gold were discovered by workers building a sawmill along the American River. Word of the find spread quickly, bringing more than 300,000 men and women into California between 1849 and 1851, one of the largest mass migrations in American history. Of course, very few prospectors unearthed a gold mine, and within 15 years the gold had dissipated, though many of the new residents remained. In fact, much of the mining equipment and gold rush–era buildings remain today and are on display throughout the Gold Country.

In 1850, California was admitted to the Union as the 31st state. The state constitution on which California applied for admission included several noteworthy features. To protect the miners, slavery was prohibited. To attract women from the East Coast, legal recognition was given to the separate property of a married woman (California was the first state to offer such recognition). By 1870, almost 90% of the state's Native American population had been wiped out, and the bulk of the rest were removed to undesirable inland reservations.

- 1978 Steve Wozniak and Steve Jobs revolutionize personal computing with the launch of Apple Computers; San Francisco Mayor George Moscone and Supervisor Harvey Milk are assassinated at City Hall.
- 1984 Los Angeles hosts the Summer Olympic Games.
- 1989 An earthquake registering 7.1 on the Richter scale hits San Francisco, causing 63 deaths and $10 billion in damage.
- 1991 AIDS becomes San Francisco's number-one killer of men.
- 1992 Fire rages through the Berkeley/Oakland hills, destroying 2,800 homes.
- 1992 Los Angeles experiences the worst race riots in American history: 50 dead, hundreds injured; California becomes the first state in the Union to send two female senators to Washington.
- 1993 Firestorms sweep through Los Angeles area; an earthquake registering 6.2 on the Richter scale strikes.
- 1994 An earthquake measuring 6.8 on the Richter scale hits LA, killing more than 60 people and injuring thousands.
- 1996 Former Assembly Speaker Willie Brown is elected mayor of San Francisco.
- 1997 El Niño floods cause billions in damage throughout California.
- 1998 Gray Davis is elected governor, the first Democrat to hold the office since 1986.
- 2000 The sale of the *Los Angeles Times* to the Chicago-based *Tribune* is announced.
- 2001 Dot-coms falter; energy crisis results in rolling blackouts.
- 2002 Energy woes are fixed and Enron is blamed, but California's economy reels in the aftermath of the September 11, 2001, disaster.

Mexican and Chinese laborers were brought in to help local farmers and to work on the transcontinental railroad, which was completed in 1869. The new rail line transported Easterners to California in just 5 days, marking a turning point in the settlement of the West. Many of those same steam engines are on display at the California State Railroad Museum in Sacramento.

GROWTH & INDUSTRY
In 1875, when the Santa Fe Railroad reached Los Angeles, Southern California's population of just 10,000 was divided equally between Los Angeles and San Diego. Los Angeles, however, began to grow rapidly in 1911, when the film industry moved here from the East Coast to take advantage of cheap land and a

warm climate that enabled movies to be shot outdoors year-round. The movies' glamorous, idyllic portrayal of California boosted the region's popularity and population, especially during the Great Depression of the 1930s, when thousands of families (like the Joads in John Steinbeck's novel *The Grapes of Wrath*) packed up their belongings and headed west in search of a better life.

World War II brought heavy industry to California, in the form of munitions factories, shipyards, and airplane manufacturing. Freeways were built, military bases were opened, and suburbs were developed. In the 1950s, California in general, and San Francisco in particular, became popular with artists and intellectuals. The so-called Beat Generation appeared, later to inspire alternative-culture groups, most notably the "flower children" of the 1960s, in San Francisco's Haight-Ashbury district. During the "Summer of Love" in 1967, as the war in Vietnam escalated, student protests increased at Berkeley and elsewhere in California, as they did across the country. A year later, amid rising racial tensions, Martin Luther King Jr. was killed, setting off riots in the Watts section of Los Angeles and in other cities. Soon thereafter, Robert F. Kennedy was fatally shot in Los Angeles after winning the California Democratic Party presidential primary. Antiwar protests continued into the 1970s.

Perhaps in response to an increasingly violent society, the 1970s also gave rise to several exotic religions and cults, which found eager adherents in California. The spiritual "New Age" continued into the 1980s, along with a growing population, environmental pollution, and escalating social ills, especially in Los Angeles. California also became very rich. Real-estate values soared, the computer industry—centered in "Silicon Valley" south of San Francisco—boomed, and banks and businesses prospered.

RECESSION, REDEMPTION & TERRORISM

The late 1980s and early 1990s, however, brought a devastating recession to the state. Californians, like many other Americans, became increasingly more conservative. Though they remained concerned about the nation's problems—economic competition from abroad, the environment, drugs, and the blight of homelessness afflicting cities large and small—their fascination with alternative lifestyles ebbed as the former campus rebels among them settled into comfortable positions in industry and politics. In short, the baby boomers were growing up and settling down.

The plight of AIDS also became a major issue of the 1990s, particularly in San Francisco, where it quickly became the number-one killer of young men. Los Angeles had its problems as well, most notably the race riots spurred by a videotaping and subsequent acquittal of four white police officers beating a black motorist, Rodney King. Two years later, a major earthquake would cause billions of dollars in damage to LA's buildings and freeways, and leave thousands injured and homeless, while Oakland's hills became a raging inferno, killing 26 people and destroying 3,000 homes.

Midway through the 1990s, America's economy slowly yet surely began to improve, a welcome relief to recession-battered Californians. Crime and unemployment began to drop, while public schools received millions for much-needed improvements. Computer- and Internet-related industries flourished in the Bay Area, with entrepreneurialism fueling much of the explosive growth. As the stock market continued its record-setting pace through the end of the decade, no state reaped more benefits than California, which was gaining new millionaires by the day. At the millennium, optimism in the state's economy and quality of life was at an all-time high.

At the turn of the century the economy was still strong, the unemployment rate still low, and property rates still rising. Then came three out-of-the-blue sucker punches to California's rosy economy: 1) the rapid demise of many, if not most, of the dot-coms in the stock market slump (new websites gleefully chronicling the death throes of the fledgling enterprises popped up to amuse the formerly envious); 2) an energy deregulation scheme gone awry, leaving irate residents with periodic rolling blackouts and escalating energy bills (never have so many taken such a sudden, intense interest in ways to save and create energy); and 3) the terrorist attacks on September 11, 2001, which, along with the rest of the country, left us stunned and added a near–death blow to an already reeling economy.

But even the darkest clouds have a silver lining. The dot-com bomb has led to a massive rise in vacancies and declines in rent (though it's still outrageous) as the thousands of itinerant gold diggers hitched up and moved out. We solved our energy crisis by outing those greedy Enron execs living in the empire of Texas. And since 9/11 we've even surprised ourselves at how patriotic we still are as a nation. Every Californian was knocked senseless by the evil deeds of religious fanatics, but we quickly fought back—both literally and economically—to regain our national pride and peerless lifestyle.

Oh, California—if life hands us a lemon, we'll slice it into our imported water.

Index

America Online Keyword: Travel

Booked seat 6A, open return.

Rented red 4-wheel drive.

Reserved cabin, no running water.

Discovered space.

With over 700 airlines, 50,000 hotels, 50 rental car companies and 5,000 cruise and vacation packages, you can create the perfect getaway for you. Choose the car, the room, even the ground you walk on.

Travelocity.com
A Sabre Company
Go Virtually Anywhere.

Travelocity,® Travelocity.com® and the Travelocity skyline logo are trademarks and/or servicemarks of Travelocity.com L.P., and Sabre® is a trademark of an affiliate of Sabre Inc. © 2002 Travelocity.com L.P. All rights reserved.

America Online Keyword: Travel

You Need A Vacation.

700 Airlines, 50,000 Hotels, 50 Rental Car Companies, And A Million Ways To Save Money.

Travelocity.com
A Sabre Company
Go Virtually Anywhere.

Travelocity.® Travelocity.com® and the Travelocity skyline logo are trademarks and/or servicemarks of Travelocity.com L.P. and Sabre® is a trademark of an affiliate of Sabre Inc. © 2002 Travelocity.com L.P. All rights reserved.

 **the Unofficial Guide**

All the up-to-date, practical information and candid insider advice you need for the perfect trip

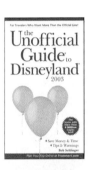
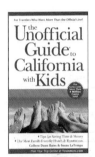
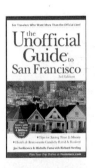

Available at bookstores everywhere.

You can't get any closer to the real Hollywood.

Universal Studios Hollywood™ puts you so close, you can hear the cameras rolling. Take a revealing inside look at the sets and uncover the secrets of today's biggest films. Then, ride into the thrilling worlds of your favorite movies as you take the monster plunge of Jurassic Park®—The Ride. Venture into The Mummy Returns: Chamber of Doom, and more. Plus, visit Universal CityWalk®, featuring L.A.'s hottest entertainment, dining and shopping. It can only happen in Hollywood—Universal Studios Hollywood.

WORLD'S LARGEST MOVIE STUDIO AND THEME PARK™

Save up to $24

This offer cannot be combined with any other offer or with per-capita sightseeing tours. Take $4 off admission per person when you present this coupon at the USH ticket booth. Good for up to 6 people. Offer valid through 12/31/02. Not valid for separately ticketed events or Universal Studios Florida. ©2002 Universal City Studios. LLLP. All Rights Reserved. Frommer's 02-ADV-189

SPEED CODE: ADULT 438 CHILD 439

WORLD'S LARGEST MOVIE STUDIO AND THEME PARK™

Jurassic Park TM and ©2002 Universal Studios, Inc. and Amblin' Entertainment, Inc. The Mummy ©2002 Universal Studios, Inc. ©2002 Universal City Studios LLLP. All Rights Reserved. 02-ADV-189